2848399

D0516156

2848399

HANDBOOK OF
U.S. LABOR
STATISTICS

HANDBOOK OF U.S. LABOR STATISTICS

Employment, Earnings, Prices, Productivity, and Other Labor Data

16th Edition
2013

Edited by Mary Meghan Ryan

 Bernan Press

Lanham, MD

Published in the United States of America
by Bernan Press, a wholly owned subsidiary of
The Rowman & Littlefield Publishing Group, Inc.
4501 Forbes Boulevard, Suite 200
Lanham, Maryland 20706

Bernan Press
800-865-3457
www.bernan.com

ISBN-13: 978-1-59888-610-8
eISBN-13: 978-1-59888-611-5

ISSN: 1526-2553

∞™ The paper used in this publication meets the minimum requirements of
American National Standard for Information Sciences—Permanence of
Paper for Printed Library Materials, ANSI/NISO Z39.48-1992.
Manufactured in the United States of America.

CONTENTS

LIST OF TABLES

CHAPTER 1: POPULATION, LABOR FORCE, AND EMPLOYMENT STATUS

POPULATION, LABOR FORCE, AND EMPLOYMENT STATUS

PERSONS WITH A DISABILITY: LABOR FORCE CHARACTERISTICS

EMPLOYMENT SITUATION OF VETERANS

CHAPTER 2: EMPLOYMENT, HOURS, AND EARNINGS

EMPLOYMENT AND HOURS

EARNINGS

CHAPTER 6: COMPENSATION OF EMPLOYEES

EMPLOYMENT COST INDEX (ECI)

EMPLOYER COSTS FOR EMPLOYEE COMPENSATION (ECEC)

EMPLOYEE BENEFITS SURVEY

CHAPTER 7: RECENT TRENDS IN THE LABOR MARKET

MASS LAYOFFS

JOB OPENINGS AND LABOR TURNOVER SURVEY

CHAPTER 11: CONSUMER EXPENDITURES

CHAPTER 12: AMERICAN TIME USE SURVEY

CHAPTER 13: INCOME DATA IN THE UNITED STATES (CENSUS BUREAU)

CHAPTER 14: OCCUPATIONAL SAFETY AND HEALTH

CHAPTER 15: GREEN JOBS, TECHNOLOGIES, AND PRACTICES

LIST OF FIGURES

PREFACE

Bernan Press is pleased to present a compilation of Bureau of Labor Statistics (BLS) data in this 16th edition of its award-winning *Handbook of U.S. Labor Statistics: Employment, Earnings, Prices, Productivity, and Other Labor Data.* BLS and the U.S. Census Bureau provide a treasure trove of historical information about all aspects of labor and employment in the United States. The current edition maintains the content of previous editions and updates the text with additional data and new features. The data in this *Handbook* are excellent sources of information for analysts in both government and the private sector.

The *Handbook* addresses many of the issues that are being discussed across the United States, such as high unemployment, employment projections for the future, the decline in income, the rapidly increasing costs of health care services, and the dramatic aging of the labor force. In addition, this publication provides an abundance of data on topics such as prices, productivity, consumer expenditures, occupational safety and health, international labor comparisons, and much more. For the first time, the *Handbook* includes a chapter on green jobs, technologies, and practices.

The comprehensive and historical data presented in the *Handbook* allow the user to understand the background of current events and compare today's economy with previous years. Select data in this publication go back to 1913 and several tables have data going back to the 1940s.

FEATURES OF THIS PUBLICATION

Over 225 tables that present authoritative data on labor market statistics, including employment and unemployment, mass layoffs, prices, productivity, and data from the American Time Use Survey (ATUS).

Each chapter is preceded by a figure that calls attention to noteworthy trends in the data.

In addition to the figures, the introductory material for to each chapter also contains highlights of other salient data.

The tables in each section are also preceded by notes and definitions, which contain concise descriptions of the data sources, concepts, definitions, and methodology from which the data are derived.

The introductory notes also include references to more comprehensive reports. These reports provide additional data and more extensive descriptions of estimation methods, sampling, and reliability measures.

NEW IN THIS EDITION

Several additions have been made in this edition. Most notably, Chapter 15, "Green Jobs, Technologies, and Prac-

tices," has been added. This chapter includes data from the Green Technologies and Practices and the Green Goods and Services surveys. In addition, numerous tables have been added in other chapters. Chapter 1 includes a new section on the employment status of veterans for the first time since 2009; Chapter 6 includes a table on workplaces that provide "quality of life" benefits including childcare, subsidized commuting, and flexible workplaces; and tables on eldercare have been added to Chapter 12.

SOURCES OF ADDITIONAL INFORMATION

BLS data are primarily derived from surveys conducted by the federal government or through federal-state cooperative arrangements. The comparability of data over time can be affected by changes in the surveys, which are essential for keeping pace with the current structure of economic institutions and for taking advantage of improved survey techniques. Revisions of current data are also periodically made as a result of the availability of new information. In addition, some tables in this *Handbook* were dropped due to the data being from a one-time survey that is now outdated or due to the survey being entirely restructured. Introductory notes to each chapter summarize specific factors that may affect the data. In the tables, the ellipsis character ("...") indicates that data are not available.

More extensive methodological information, including further discussion of the sampling and estimation procedures used for each BLS program, is contained in the *BLS Handbook of Methods.* This publication is in the process of being updated, and completed chapters are available on the BLS Web site at <http://www.bls.gov>. Other sources of current data and analytical include the *Monthly Labor Review* and a daily Internet publication, *The Editor's Desk* (TED). All of these publications can be found on the BLS Web site as well. Other relevant publications, including those from the Census Bureau, are noted in the notes and definitions in each chapter.

OTHER PUBLICATIONS BY BERNAN PRESS

The *Handbook of U.S. Labor Statistics: Employment, Earnings, Prices, Productivity, and Other Labor Data* is just one of a number of publications in Bernan Press's award-winning U.S. DataBook Series. Other titles include *The Almanac of American Education; Business Statistics of the United States: Patterns of Economic Change; Crime in the United States; Housing Statistics of the United States; State Profiles: The Population and Economy of Each U.S. State;* and *Vital Statistics of the United States: Births, Life Expectancy, Deaths, and Selected Health Data.* In addition, Bernan Press publishes *Employment, Hours, and Earnings: States and Areas* as a special edition of this *Handbook.* Each of these titles provides statistical information from official government sources.

Chapter One

POPULATION, LABOR FORCE, AND EMPLOYMENT STATUS

POPULATION, LABOR FORCE, AND EMPLOYMENT STATUS

HIGHLIGHTS

This chapter presents the detailed historical information collected in the Current Population Survey (CPS), a monthly survey of households that gathers data on the employment status of the population. Basic data on labor force, employment, and unemployment are shown for various characteristics of the population, including age, sex, race, Hispanic origin, and marital status.

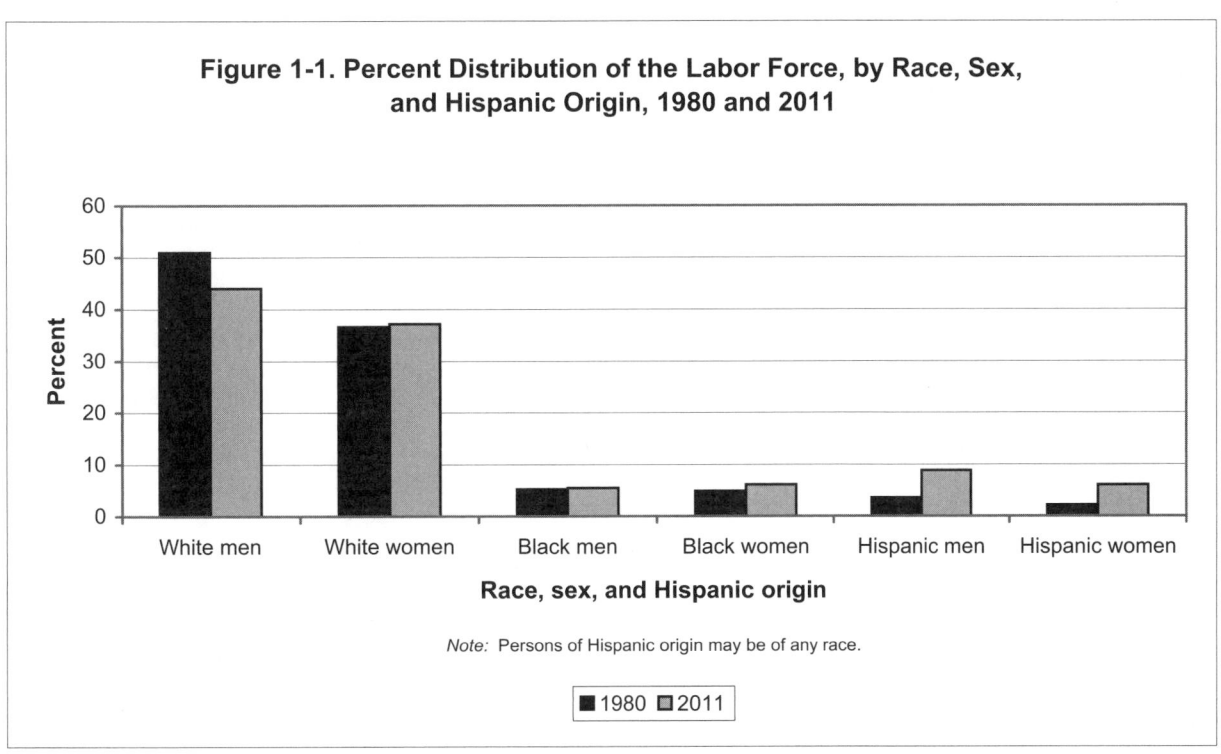

Figure 1-1. Percent Distribution of the Labor Force, by Race, Sex, and Hispanic Origin, 1980 and 2011

Note: Persons of Hispanic origin may be of any race.

While the proportion of the labor that is made up of White men declined from 1980 to 2011, the proportion of White women in the labor force increased slightly from 36.6 percent to 37.1 percent. Hispanic representation in the labor force rose significantly increasing from 5.7 percent in 1980 to nearly 15 percent in 2011. (See Table 1-7.)

OTHER HIGHLIGHTS

- In 2011, employment increased 0.6 percent after declining each year since 2008. Employment fell 3.8 percent from 2008 to 2009 and 0.6 percent between 2009 and 2010. (See Table 1-1.)

- While employment increased, the civilian labor force participation rate declined in 2011 for the third consecutive year to 64.1 percent—the lowest it has been since 1983. However, the labor force participation rate for those 65 years and over was 17.9 percent—the highest it has been since 1964. The labor force participation rate declined for every other age group. (See Table 1-8.)

- The number of part-time workers declined slightly in 2011 after increasing each year for the past five years. (See Table 1-9.)

NOTES AND DEFINITIONS

CURRENT POPULATION SURVEY OF HOUSEHOLDS

Collection and Coverage

The Current Population Survey (CPS) is a monthly survey that analyzes and publishes statistics on the labor force, employment, and unemployment, classified by a variety of demographic, social, and economic characteristics. This survey is conducted by the Census Bureau for the Bureau of Labor Statistics (BLS). The information is collected from a probability sample of approximately 60,000 households. Respondents are interviewed to obtain information about the employment status of each household member age 16 years and over. Persons under 16 years of age are excluded from the official estimates because child labor laws, compulsory school attendance, and general social custom in the United States severely limit the types and amount of work that these children can do.

The inquiry relates to the household member's employment status during the calendar week, Sunday through Saturday that includes the 12th day of the month. This is known as the "reference week." Actual field interviewing is conducted during the following week (the week that contains the 19th day of the month).

Concepts and Definitions

The concepts and definitions underlying the labor force data have been modified—but not substantially altered—since the inception of the survey in 1940 when it began as a Work Projects Administration program. Current definitions of some of the major concepts used in the CPS are described below.

The civilian noninstitutional population includes persons 16 years of age and over who reside in the 50 states and the District of Columbia who are not inmates of institutions (such as penal and mental facilities and homes for the aged) and who are not on active duty in the armed forces.

An *employed person* is any person who, during the reference week: (1) did any work at all (at least one hour) as a paid employees in their own business, profession, or on their own farm, or who worked 15 hours or more as an unpaid worker in an enterprise operated by a member of the family; and (2) any person who was not working but who had a job or business from which he or she was temporarily absent due to vacation, illness, bad weather, childcare problems, maternity or paternity leave, labor-management disputes, job training, or other family or personal reasons, despite whether the employee was being paid for the time off or was seeking other jobs.

Each employed person is counted only once, even if he or she holds more than one job. For purposes of occupation and industry classification, multiple jobholders are counted as being in the job at which they worked the greatest number of hours during the reference week.

Included in the total are employed citizens of foreign countries who were temporarily in the United States but not living on the premises of an embassy. Excluded are persons whose only activity during the reference week consisted of work around their own house (painting, repairing, or own home housework) or volunteer work for religious, charitable, and similar organizations.

Unemployed persons are all persons who had no employment during the reference week, but who were available for work (except for temporary illness) and had made specific efforts to find employment some time during the four-week period ending with the reference week. Persons who were waiting to be recalled to a job from which they had been laid off need not have been looking for work to be classified as unemployed.

Reasons for unemployment are divided into four major groups: (1) job losers, defined as (a) persons on temporary layoff, who have been given a date to return to work or who expect to return to work within six months; (b) permanent job losers, whose employment ended involuntarily and who began looking for work; and (c) persons who completed a temporary job and began looking for work after the job ended; (2) job leavers, defined as persons who quit or otherwise terminated their employment voluntarily and immediately began looking for work; (3) reentrants, defined as persons who previously worked but were out of the labor force prior to beginning their job search; and (4) new entrants, defined as persons who had never worked but were currently searching for work.

Duration of unemployment represents the length of time (through the current reference week) that persons classified as unemployed had been looking for work. For persons on layoff, duration of unemployment represents the number of full weeks they had been on layoff. Mean duration of unemployment is the arithmetic average computed from single weeks of unemployment; median duration of unemployment is the midpoint of a distribution of weeks of unemployment.

A *spell of unemployment* is a continuous period of unemployment of at least one week's duration and is terminated by either employment or withdrawal from the labor force.

Extent of unemployment refers to the number of workers and proportion of the labor force that were unemployed at some time during the year. The number of weeks unemployed is the total number of weeks accumulated during the entire calendar year.

The *unemployment rate* is the number of unemployed persons as a percentage of the civilian labor force.

The *civilian labor force* comprises all civilians classified as employed or unemployed.

The *participation rate* represents the proportion of the civilian noninstitutional population currently in the labor force.

The *employment-population ratio* represents the proportion of the population that is currently employed.

Persons not in the labor force are all persons in the civilian noninstitutional population who are neither employed nor unemployed. Information is collected about their desire for and availability to take a job at the time of the CPS interview, job search activity during the prior year, and reason for not looking for work during the four-week period ending with the reference week. Persons not in the labor force who want and are available for a job and who have looked for work within the past 12 months (or since the end of their last job, if they had held one within the past 12 months), but who are not currently looking, are designated as *marginally attached to the labor force*. The marginally attached are divided into those not currently looking because they believe their search would be futile—so-called *discouraged workers*—and those not currently looking for other reasons, such as family responsibilities, ill health, or lack of transportation.

Discouraged workers are defined as persons not in the labor force who want and are available for a job and who have looked for work sometime in the past 12 months (or since the end of their last job, if they held one within the past 12 months), but who are not currently looking because they believe that there are no jobs available or there are none for which they would qualify. The reasons for not currently looking for work include a person's belief that no work is available in his or her line of work or area; he or she could not find any work; he or she lacks necessary schooling, training, skills, or experience; employers would think he or she is too young or too old; or he or she would encounter hiring discrimination.

Usual full- or part-time status refers to hours usually worked per week. Full-time workers are those who usually work 35 hours or more (at all jobs). This group includes some individuals who worked less than 35 hours during the reference week for economic or noneconomic reasons. Part-time workers are those who usually work less than 35 hours per week (at all jobs), regardless of the number of hours worked during the reference week. These concepts are used to differentiate a person's normal schedule from his or her specific activity during the reference week. Unemployed persons who are looking for full-time work or who are on layoff from full-time jobs are counted as part of the full-time labor force; unemployed persons who are seeking part-time work or who are on layoff from part-time jobs are counted as part of the part-time labor force.

Year-round, full-time workers are workers who primarily worked at full-time jobs for 50 weeks or more during the preceding calendar year. Part-year workers worked either full- or part-time for 1 to 49 weeks.

At work part-time for economic reasons, sometimes called involuntary part-time, refers to individuals who gave an economic reason for working 1 to 34 hours during the reference week. Economic reasons include slack work or unfavorable business conditions, inability to find full-time work, and seasonal declines in demand. Those who usually work part-time must also indicate that they want and are available to work full-time to be classified as working part-time for economic reasons.

At work part-time for noneconomic reasons refers to persons who usually work part-time and were at work 1 to 34 hours during the reference week for a noneconomic reason. Noneconomic reasons include illness or other medical limitations, childcare problems or other family or personal obligations, school or training, retirement or Social Security limits on earnings, and being in a job where full-time work is less than 35 hours. This also includes workers who gave an economic reason for usually working 1 to 34 hours but said they do not want to work full-time or were unavailable for full-time work.

Absences are defined as instances in which persons who usually work 35 or more hours a week worked less than that during the reference period for reasons of illness or family obligations. Excluded are situations in which work was missed for vacation, holidays, or other reasons. The estimates are based on one-fourth of the sample only.

Earnings are all money income of $1 or more from wages and salaries and all net money income of $1 or more from farm and nonfarm self-employment.

Usual weekly earnings for wage and salary workers include any overtime pay, commissions, or tips usually received (at the main job in the case of multiple jobholders). Earnings reported on a basis other than weekly (such as annual, monthly, or hourly) are converted to weekly. The term "usual" is as perceived by the respondent. If the respondent asks for a definition of usual, interviewers are instructed to define the term as more than half the weeks worked during the past 4 or 5 months.

Minimum wage refers to the prevailing federal minimum wage which was $7.25 in 2011. It increased from $6.55 per hour to $7.25 per hour on July 24, 2009 and has remained at that level since. Data are for wage and salary workers who were paid hourly rates and refer to a person's earnings at the sole or principal job.

A *multiple jobholder* is an employed person who, during the reference week, had two or more jobs as a wage and salary worker, was self-employed and also held a wage and salary job, or worked as an unpaid family worker and also held a wage and salary job. Self-employed persons with multiple businesses and persons with multiple jobs as unpaid family workers are excluded.

Occupation, industry, and class of worker for members of the employed population are determined by the job held during the reference week. Persons with two or more jobs are classified as being in the job at which they worked the greatest number of hours. The unemployed are classified according to their last job. Beginning with data published in 2003, the systems used to classify occupational and industry data changed. They are currently based on the Standard Occupational Classification (SOC) system and the North American Industry Classification System (NAICS). (See the following section on historical comparability for a discussion of previous classification systems used in the CPS.) The class-of-worker breakdown assigns workers to one of the following categories: private and government wage and salary workers, self-employed workers, and unpaid family workers. Wage and salary workers receive wages, salaries, commissions, tips, or pay in kind from a private employer or from a government unit. Self-employed workers are those who work for profit or fees in their own businesses, professions, trades, or on their own farms. Only the unincorporated self-employed are included in the self-employed category in the class-of-worker typology. Self-employed workers who respond that their businesses are incorporated are included among wage and salary workers, because they are technically paid employees of a corporation. An unpaid family worker is a person working without pay for 15 hours or more per week on a farm or in a business operated by a member of the household to whom he or she is related by birth or marriage.

Educational attainment refers to years of school completed in regular schools, which include graded public, private, and parochial elementary, and high schools, whether day or night school. Colleges, universities, and professional schools are also included.

Tenure refers to length of time a worker has been continuously employed by his or her current employer. These data are collected through a supplement to the CPS. All employed persons were asked how long they had been working continuously for their present employer and, if the length of time was one or two years, a follow-up question was asked about the exact number of months. The follow-up question was included for the first time in the February 1996 supplement to the CPS. CPS supplements that obtained information on tenure in the January of 1983, 1987, and 1991 did not include the follow-up question. Prior to 1983, the question on tenure was asked differently. Data prior to 1983 are thus not strictly comparable to data for subsequent years.

White, Black, and Asian are terms used to describe the race of persons. Persons in these categories are those who selected that race only. Persons in the remaining race categories—American Indian or Alaskan Native, Native Hawaiian or Other Pacific Islander, and persons who selected more than one race category—are included in the estimates of total employment and unemployment but are not shown separately because the number of survey respondents is too small to develop estimates of sufficient quality for monthly publication.

Hispanic origin refers to persons who identified themselves in the enumeration process as being Spanish, Hispanic, or Latino. Persons of Hispanic or Latino origin may be of any race.

Single, never married; married, spouse present; and other marital status are the terms used to define the marital status of individuals at the time of the CPS interview. Married, spouse present, applies to a husband and wife if both were living in the same household, even though one may be temporarily absent on business, vacation, in a hospital, etc. Other marital status applies to persons who are married, spouse absent; widowed; or divorced. Married, spouse absent relates to persons who are separated due to marital problems, as well as husbands and wives living apart because one was employed elsewhere, on duty with the armed forces, or any other reason.

A *household* consists of all persons—related family members and all unrelated persons—who occupy a housing unit and have no other usual address. A house, an apartment, a group of rooms, or a single room is regarded as a housing unit when occupied or intended for occupancy as separate living quarters.

A *householder* is the person (or one of the persons) in whose name the housing unit is owned or rented. The term is not applied to either husbands or wives in married-couple families; it refers only to persons in families maintained by either men or women without a spouse.

A *family* is defined as a group of two or more persons residing together who are related by birth, marriage, or adoption. All such persons are considered as members of one family. Families are classified as either married-couple families or families maintained by women or men without spouses.

Children refer to "own" children of the husband, wife, or person maintaining the family, including sons and daughters, stepchildren, and adopted children. Excluded are other related children, such as grandchildren, nieces, nephews, cousins, and unrelated children.

Persons are referred to as *disabled* if they answer yes to the following questions: 1.) Are you deaf or do you have serious difficulty hearing? 2.) Are you blind or do you serious difficulty seeing even when wearing glasses? 3.) Because of a physical, mental, or emotional condition, do you have serious difficulty concentrating, remembering, or making decisions? 4.) Do you have serious difficulty walking or climbing stairs? 5.) Do you have difficulty dressing or bathing? 6.) Because of a physical, mental, or emotional condition, do you have difficulty doing errands alone such as visiting a doctor's office or shopping? Labor force measures are only tabulated for persons 16 years and over.

Veterans are men and women who previously served on active duty in the U.S. Armed Forces and who were civilians at the time they were surveyed.

Nonveterans are men and women who never served on active duty in the U.S. Armed Forces.

World War II, Korean War, Vietnam-era, and Gulf War-era veterans are men and women who served in the Armed

Forces during these periods, regardless of where they served.

Veterans of other service periods are men and women who served in the Armed Forces at any time other than World War II, the Korean War, the Vietnam era, or the Gulf War era.

Veteran status is obtained from responses to the question, "Did you ever serve on active duty in the U.S. Armed Forces?"

Period of service is obtained from answers to the question asked of veterans, "When did you serve on active duty in the U.S. Armed Forces?" The following service periods are identified:

Gulf War era II — September 2001–present
Gulf War era I — August 1990–August 2001
Vietnam era — August 1964–April 1975
Korean War — July 1950–January 1955
World War II — December 1941–December 1946
Other service periods — All other time periods

Veterans who served in Iraq, Afghanistan, or both are individuals who served in Iraq at any time since March 2003, in Afghanistan at any time since October 2001, or in both locations.

Presence of service-connected disability is determined by answers to the question, "Has the Department of Veterans Affairs (VA) or Department of Defense (DoD) determined that you have a service-connected disability, that is, a health condition or impairment caused or made worse by any of your military service?"

Service-connected disability rating is based on answers to the question, "What is your current service connected disability rating?" Answers can range from 0 to 100 percent, in increments of 10 percentage points.

Historical Comparability

While the concepts and methods are very similar to those used for the inaugural survey in 1940, a number of changes have been made over the years to improve the accuracy and usefulness of the data. Only recent major changes are described here.

Major changes to the CPS, such as the complete redesign of the questionnaire and the use of computer-assisted interviewing for the entire survey, were introduced in 1994. In addition, there were revisions to some of the labor force concepts and definitions, including the implementation of changes recommended in 1979 by the National Commission on Employment and Unemployment Statistics (NCEUS, also known as the Levitan Commission). Some of the major changes to the survey at this time were:

1) The introduction of a redesigned and automated questionnaire. The CPS questionnaire was totally redesigned in

order to obtain more accurate, comprehensive, and relevant information, and to take advantage of state-of-the-art computer interviewing techniques. Computer-assisted interviewing has important benefits most notably that it facilitates the use of a relatively complex questionnaire that incorporates complicated skip patterns and standardized follow-up questions. Additionally, certain questions are automatically tailored to the individual's situation to make them more understandable.

2) Official labor force measures were defined more precisely. While the labor force status of most people is straightforward, some persons are more difficult to classify correctly, especially if they are engaged in activities that are relatively informal or intermittent. Many of the changes to the questionnaire were made to deal with such cases. This was accomplished by rewording and adding questions to conform more precisely to the official definitions, making the questions easier to understand and answer, minimizing reliance on volunteered responses, revising response categories, and taking advantage of the benefits of an automated interview.

3) The amount of data available was expanded. The questionnaire redesign also made it possible to collect several types of data on topics such as multiple job holding and usual hours regularly for the first time.

4) Several labor definitions were modified. The most important definitional changes concerned discouraged workers. The Levitan Commission had criticized the former definition because it was based on a subjective desire for work and on somewhat arbitrary assumptions about an individual's availability to take a job. As a result of the redesign, two requirements were added: For persons to qualify as discouraged they must have engaged in some job search within the past year (or since they last worked, if they worked within the past year), and they must be currently available to take a job. (Formerly, availability was inferred from responses to other questions; now, there is a direct question.) Also, beginning in January 1994, questions on this subject are asked of the full CPS sample, permitting estimates of the number of discouraged workers to be published monthly (rather than quarterly).

Beginning in January 2003, several other changes were introduced into the CPS. These changes included the following:

1) Population controls that reflected the results of the 2000 census were introduced into the monthly CPS estimation process. The new controls increased the size of the civilian noninstitutional population by about 3.5 million in May 2002. As a result, they also increased the estimated numbers of people unemployed and employed. Because the increases were roughly proportional, however, the overall unemployment rate did not change significantly. Data from January 2000 through December 2002 were revised to reflect these new controls. Over and above these revisions, the U.S. Census Bureau introduced another large upward

adjustment to the controls as part of its annual update of population estimates for 2003. These updated population estimates were not available in time to incorporate them into the revised population controls for January 2000 to December 2002. Thus, the data on employment and unemployment levels for January 2003 (and beyond) are not strictly comparable with those for earlier months. The unemployment rate and other ratios, however, were not substantially affected by the 2003 population control revisions.

2) Questions on race and Hispanic origin were modified to comply with the new standards for maintaining, collecting, and presenting federal data on race and ethnicity for federal statistical agencies. The questions were reworded to indicate that individuals could select more than once race category and to convey more clearly that individuals should report their own perception of what race is. These changes had no impact on the overall civilian noninstitutional population and civilian labor force. However, they did reduce the population and labor force levels of Whites, Blacks, and Asians beginning in January 2003.

3) Improvements were introduced to both the second stage and composite weighting procedures. These changes adapted the weighting procedures to the new race/ethnic classification system and enhanced the stability over time for demographic groups. The second-stage weighting procedure substantially reduced the variability of estimates and corrected, to some extent, for CPS underreporting.

Changes in the Occupational and Industrial Classification System

In January 2003, the CPS adopted the 2002 census industry and occupational classification systems, which were derived, respectively, from the 2002 North American Industry Classification System (NAICS) and the 2000 Standard Occupational Classification (SOC) system. The 1990 Census occupational and industry classifications were replaced. The introduction of the new industry and occupational classification systems in 2003 created a complete break in comparability at all levels of industry and occupation aggregation. The composition of detailed occupations and industries changed substantially in the 2002 systems compared with the 1990 systems, as did the structure for aggregating them into major groups. Therefore, any comparisons of data on the different classifications are not possible without major adjustments.

Historical employment series on the 2002 Census classifications are available at broad levels of occupational and industry aggregation back to 1983. However, historical employment series at the detailed occupational and industry levels on the 2002 classifications are available back to 2000 only.

In 2009, BLS began using the 2007 Census industry classification system, which was derived from the 2007 NAICS series, and still uses it currently. The 2010 Census occupational classification was introduced with data for January 2011 and replaced an earlier version that was based on the 2000 SOC. As a result of the classification change, occupational data beginning with January 2011 are not strictly comparable with earlier years. Although the names of the broad- and intermediate-level occupational groups in the 2010 Census occupational classification remained the same, some detailed occupations were re-classified between the broader groups, affecting comparability over time.

Sources of Additional Information

A complete description of sampling and estimation procedures and further information on the impact of historical changes in the surveys can be found in the updated version of Chapter 1 of the *BLS Handbook of Methods*. This can be found on the BLS Web site at <http://www.bls.gov/opub/hom/>.

Table 1-1. Employment Status of the Civilian Noninstitutional Population, 1947–2011

(Thousands of people, percent.)

Year	Civilian noninstitutional population	Civilian labor force								Not in labor force
		Total	Participation rate	Employed				Unemployed		
				Total	Percent of population	Agriculture	Nonagricultural industries	Number	Unemployment rate	
1947	101 827	59 350	58.3	57 038	56.0	7 890	49 148	2 311	3.9	42 477
1948	103 068	60 621	58.8	58 343	56.6	7 629	50 714	2 276	3.8	42 447
1949	103 994	61 286	58.9	57 651	55.4	7 658	49 993	3 637	5.9	42 708
1950	104 995	62 208	59.2	58 918	56.1	7 160	51 758	3 288	5.3	42 787
1951	104 621	62 017	59.2	59 961	57.3	6 726	53 235	2 055	3.3	42 604
1952	105 231	62 138	59.0	60 250	57.3	6 500	53 749	1 883	3.0	43 093
1953	107 056	63 015	58.9	61 179	57.1	6 260	54 919	1 834	2.9	44 041
1954	108 321	63 643	58.8	60 109	55.5	6 205	53 904	3 532	5.5	44 678
1955	109 683	65 023	59.3	62 170	56.7	6 450	55 722	2 852	4.4	44 660
1956	110 954	66 552	60.0	63 799	57.5	6 283	57 514	2 750	4.1	44 402
1957	112 265	66 929	59.6	64 071	57.1	5 947	58 123	2 859	4.3	45 336
1958	113 727	67 639	59.5	63 036	55.4	5 586	57 450	4 602	6.8	46 088
1959	115 329	68 369	59.3	64 630	56.0	5 565	59 065	3 740	5.5	46 960
1960	117 245	69 628	59.4	65 778	56.1	5 458	60 318	3 852	5.5	47 617
1961	118 771	70 459	59.3	65 746	55.4	5 200	60 546	4 714	6.7	48 312
1962	120 153	70 614	58.8	66 702	55.5	4 944	61 759	3 911	5.5	49 539
1963	122 416	71 833	58.7	67 762	55.4	4 687	63 076	4 070	5.7	50 583
1964	124 485	73 091	58.7	69 305	55.7	4 523	64 782	3 786	5.2	51 394
1965	126 513	74 455	58.9	71 088	56.2	4 361	66 726	3 366	4.5	52 058
1966	128 058	75 770	59.2	72 895	56.9	3 979	68 915	2 875	3.8	52 288
1967	129 874	77 347	59.6	74 372	57.3	3 844	70 527	2 975	3.8	52 527
1968	132 028	78 737	59.6	75 920	57.5	3 817	72 103	2 817	3.6	53 291
1969	134 335	80 734	60.1	77 902	58.0	3 606	74 296	2 832	3.5	53 602
1970	137 085	82 771	60.4	78 678	57.4	3 463	75 215	4 093	4.9	54 315
1971	140 216	84 382	60.2	79 367	56.6	3 394	75 972	5 016	5.9	55 834
1972	144 126	87 034	60.4	82 153	57.0	3 484	78 669	4 882	5.6	57 091
1973	147 096	89 429	60.8	85 064	57.8	3 470	81 594	4 365	4.9	57 667
1974	150 120	91 949	61.3	86 794	57.8	3 515	83 279	5 156	5.6	58 171
1975	153 153	93 775	61.2	85 846	56.1	3 408	82 438	7 929	8.5	59 377
1976	156 150	96 158	61.6	88 752	56.8	3 331	85 421	7 406	7.7	59 991
1977	159 033	99 009	62.3	92 017	57.9	3 283	88 734	6 991	7.1	60 025
1978	161 910	102 251	63.2	96 048	59.3	3 387	92 661	6 202	6.1	59 659
1979	164 863	104 962	63.7	98 824	59.9	3 347	95 477	6 137	5.8	59 900
1980	167 745	106 940	63.8	99 303	59.2	3 364	95 938	7 637	7.1	60 806
1981	170 130	108 670	63.9	100 397	59.0	3 368	97 030	8 273	7.6	61 460
1982	172 271	110 204	64.0	99 526	57.8	3 401	96 125	10 678	9.7	62 067
1983	174 215	111 550	64.0	100 834	57.9	3 383	97 450	10 717	9.6	62 665
1984	176 383	113 544	64.4	105 005	59.5	3 321	101 685	8 539	7.5	62 839
1985	178 206	115 461	64.8	107 150	60.1	3 179	103 971	8 312	7.2	62 744
1986	180 587	117 834	65.3	109 597	60.7	3 163	106 434	8 237	7.0	62 752
1987	182 753	119 865	65.6	112 440	61.5	3 208	109 232	7 425	6.2	62 888
1988	184 613	121 669	65.9	114 968	62.3	3 169	111 800	6 701	5.5	62 944
1989	186 393	123 869	66.5	117 342	63.0	3 199	114 142	6 528	5.3	62 523
1990	189 164	125 840	66.5	118 793	62.8	3 223	115 570	7 047	5.6	63 324
1991	190 925	126 346	66.2	117 718	61.7	3 269	114 449	8 628	6.8	64 578
1992	192 805	128 105	66.4	118 492	61.5	3 247	115 245	9 613	7.5	64 700
1993	194 838	129 200	66.3	120 259	61.7	3 115	117 144	8 940	6.9	65 638
1994	196 814	131 056	66.6	123 060	62.5	3 409	119 651	7 996	6.1	65 758
1995	198 584	132 304	66.6	124 900	62.9	3 440	121 460	7 404	5.6	66 280
1996	200 591	133 943	66.8	126 708	63.2	3 443	123 264	7 236	5.4	66 647
1997	203 133	136 297	67.1	129 558	63.8	3 399	126 159	6 739	4.9	66 837
1998	205 220	137 673	67.1	131 463	64.1	3 378	128 085	6 210	4.5	67 547
1999	207 753	139 368	67.1	133 488	64.3	3 281	130 207	5 880	4.2	68 385
2000	212 577	142 583	67.1	136 891	64.4	2 464	134 427	5 692	4.0	69 994
2001	215 092	143 734	66.8	136 933	63.7	2 299	134 635	6 801	4.7	71 359
2002	217 570	144 863	66.6	136 485	62.7	2 311	134 174	8 378	5.8	72 707
2003	221 168	146 510	66.2	137 736	62.3	2 275	135 461	8 774	6.0	74 658
2004	223 357	147 401	66.0	139 252	62.3	2 232	137 020	8 149	5.5	75 956
2005	226 082	149 320	66.0	141 730	62.7	2 197	139 532	7 591	5.1	76 762
2006	228 815	151 428	66.2	144 427	63.1	2 206	142 221	7 001	4.6	77 387
2007	231 867	153 124	66.0	146 047	63.0	2 095	143 952	7 078	4.6	78 743
2008	233 788	154 287	66.0	145 362	62.2	2 168	143 194	8 924	5.8	79 501
2009	235 801	154 142	65.4	139 877	59.3	2 103	137 775	14 265	9.3	81 659
2010	237 830	153 889	64.7	139 064	58.5	2 206	136 858	14 825	9.6	83 941
2011	239 618	153 617	64.1	139 869	58.4	2 254	137 615	13 747	8.9	86 001

Table 1-2. Employment Status of the Civilian Noninstitutional Population, by Sex, 1975–2011

(Thousands of people, percent.)

Sex and year	Civilian noninstitutional population	Civilian labor force								Not in labor force
		Total	Participation rate	Employed				Unemployed		
				Total	Percent of population	Agriculture	Non-agricultural industries	Number	Unemploy-ment rate	
Men										
1975	72 291	56 299	77.9	51 857	71.7	2 824	49 032	4 442	7.9	15 993
1976	73 759	57 174	77.5	53 138	72.0	2 744	50 394	4 036	7.1	16 585
1977	75 193	58 396	77.7	54 728	72.8	2 671	52 057	3 667	6.3	16 797
1978	76 576	59 620	77.9	56 479	73.8	2 718	53 761	3 142	5.3	16 956
1979	78 020	60 726	77.8	57 607	73.8	2 686	54 921	3 120	5.1	17 293
1980	79 398	61 453	77.4	57 186	72.0	2 709	54 477	4 267	6.9	17 945
1981	80 511	61 974	77.0	57 397	71.3	2 700	54 697	4 577	7.4	18 537
1982	81 523	62 450	76.6	56 271	69.0	2 736	53 534	6 179	9.9	19 073
1983	82 531	63 047	76.4	56 787	68.8	2 704	54 083	6 260	9.9	19 484
1984	83 605	63 835	76.4	59 091	70.7	2 668	56 423	4 744	7.4	19 771
1985	84 469	64 411	76.3	59 891	70.9	2 535	57 356	4 521	7.0	20 058
1986	85 798	65 422	76.3	60 892	71.0	2 511	58 381	4 530	6.9	20 376
1987	86 899	66 207	76.2	62 107	71.5	2 543	59 564	4 101	6.2	20 692
1988	87 857	66 927	76.2	63 273	72.0	2 493	60 780	3 655	5.5	20 930
1989	88 762	67 840	76.4	64 315	72.5	2 513	61 802	3 525	5.2	20 923
1990	90 377	69 011	76.4	65 104	72.0	2 546	62 559	3 906	5.7	21 367
1991	91 278	69 168	75.8	64 223	70.4	2 589	61 634	4 946	7.2	22 110
1992	92 270	69 964	75.8	64 440	69.8	2 575	61 866	5 523	7.9	22 306
1993	93 332	70 404	75.4	65 349	70.0	2 478	62 871	5 055	7.2	22 927
1994	94 355	70 817	75.1	66 450	·70.4	2 554	63 896	4 367	6.2	23 538
1995	95 178	71 360	75.0	67 377	70.8	2 559	64 818	3 983	5.6	23 818
1996	96 206	72 087	74.9	68 207	70.9	2 573	65 634	3 880	5.4	24 119
1997	97 715	73 261	75.0	69 685	71.3	2 552	67 133	3 577	4.9	24 454
1998	98 758	73 959	74.9	70 693	71.6	2 553	68 140	3 266	4.4	24 799
1999	99 722	74 512	74.7	71 446	71.6	2 432	69 014	3 066	4.1	25 210
2000	101 964	76 280	74.8	73 305	71.9	1 861	71 444	2 975	3.9	25 684
2001	103 282	76 886	74.4	73 196	70.9	1 708	71 488	3 690	4.8	26 396
2002	104 585	77 500	74.1	72 903	69.7	1 724	71 179	4 597	5.9	27 085
2003	106 435	78 238	73.5	73 332	68.9	1 695	71 636	4 906	6.3	28 197
2004	107 710	78 980	73.3	74 524	69.2	1 687	72 838	4 456	5.6	28 730
2005	109 151	80 033	73.3	75 973	69.6	1 654	74 319	4 059	5.1	29 119
2006	110 605	81 255	73.5	77 502	70.1	1 663	75 838	3 753	4.6	29 350
2007	112 173	82 136	73.2	78 254	69.8	1 604	76 650	3 882	4.7	30 036
2008	113 113	82 520	73.0	77 486	68.5	1 650	75 836	5 033	6.1	30 593
2009	114 136	82 123	72.0	73 670	64.5	1 607	72 062	8 453	10.3	32 013
2010	115 174	81 985	71.2	73 359	63.7	1 665	71 694	8 626	10.5	33 189
2011	116 317	81 975	70.5	74 290	63.9	1 698	72 592	7 684	9.4	34 343
Women										
1975	80 860	37 475	46.3	33 989	42.0	584	33 404	3 486	9.3	43 386
1976	82 390	38 983	47.3	35 615	43.2	588	35 027	3 369	8.6	43 406
1977	83 840	40 613	48.4	37 289	44.5	612	36 677	3 324	8.2	43 227
1978	85 334	42 631	50.0	39 569	46.4	669	38 900	3 061	7.2	42 703
1979	86 843	44 235	50.9	41 217	47.5	661	40 556	3 018	6.8	42 608
1980	88 348	45 487	51.5	42 117	47.7	656	41 461	3 370	7.4	42 861
1981	89 618	46 696	52.1	43 000	48.0	667	42 333	3 696	7.9	42 922
1982	90 748	47 755	52.6	43 256	47.7	665	42 591	4 499	9.4	42 993
1983	91 684	48 503	52.9	44 047	48.0	680	43 367	4 457	9.2	43 181
1984	92 778	49 709	53.6	45 915	49.5	653	45 262	3 794	7.6	43 068
1985	93 736	51 050	54.5	47 259	50.4	644	46 615	3 791	7.4	42 686
1986	94 789	52 413	55.3	48 706	51.4	652	48 054	3 707	7.1	42 376
1987	95 853	53 658	56.0	50 334	52.5	666	49 668	3 324	6.2	42 195
1988	96 756	54 742	56.6	51 696	53.4	676	51 020	3 046	5.6	42 014
1989	97 630	56 030	57.4	53 027	54.3	687	52 341	3 003	5.4	41 601
1990	98 787	56 829	57.5	53 689	54.3	678	53 011	3 140	5.5	41 957
1991	99 646	57 178	57.4	53 496	53.7	680	52 815	3 683	6.4	42 468
1992	100 535	58 141	57.8	54 052	53.8	672	53 380	4 090	7.0	42 394
1993	101 506	58 795	57.9	54 910	54.1	637	54 273	3 885	6.6	42 711
1994	102 460	60 239	58.8	56 610	55.3	855	55 755	3 629	6.0	42 221
1995	103 406	60 944	58.9	57 523	55.6	881	56 642	3 421	5.6	42 462
1996	104 385	61 857	59.3	58 501	56.0	871	57 630	3 356	5.4	42 528
1997	105 418	63 036	59.8	59 873	56.8	847	59 026	3 162	5.0	42 382
1998	106 462	63 714	59.8	60 771	57.1	825	59 945	2 944	4.6	42 748
1999	108 031	64 855	60.0	62 042	57.4	849	61 193	2 814	4.3	43 175
2000	110 613	66 303	59.9	63 586	57.5	602	62 983	2 717	4.1	44 310
2001	111 811	66 848	59.8	63 737	57.0	591	63 147	3 111	4.7	44 962
2002	112 985	67 363	59.6	63 582	56.3	587	62 995	3 781	5.6	45 621
2003	114 733	68 272	59.5	64 404	56.1	580	63 824	3 868	5.7	46 461
2004	115 647	68 421	59.2	64 728	56.0	546	64 182	3 694	5.4	47 225
2005	116 931	69 288	59.3	65 757	56.2	544	65 213	3 531	5.1	47 643
2006	118 210	70 173	59.4	66 925	56.6	543	66 382	3 247	4.6	48 037
2007	119 694	70 988	59.3	67 792	56.6	490	67 302	3 196	4.5	48 707
2008	120 675	71 767	59.5	67 876	56.2	518	67 358	3 891	5.4	48 908
2009	121 665	72 019	59.2	66 208	54.4	496	65 712	5 811	8.1	49 646
2010	122 656	71 904	58.6	65 705	53.6	541	65 164	6 199	8.6	50 752
2011	123 300	71 642	58.1	65 579	53.2	556	65 023	6 063	8.5	51 658

Table 1-3. Employment Status of the Civilian Noninstitutional Population, by Sex, Age, Race, and Hispanic Origin, 1990–2011

(Thousands of people.)

Characteristic	1990	1991	1992	1993	1994	1995	1996	1997	1998	1999	2000
ALL RACES											
Both Sexes											
Civilian noninstitutional population	189 164	190 925	192 805	194 838	196 814	198 584	200 591	203 133	205 220	207 753	212 577
Civilian labor force	125 840	126 346	128 105	129 200	131 056	132 304	133 943	136 297	137 673	139 368	142 583
Employed	118 793	117 718	118 492	120 259	123 060	124 900	126 708	129 558	131 463	133 488	136 891
Agriculture	3 223	3 269	3 247	3 115	3 409	3 440	3 443	3 399	3 378	3 281	2 464
Nonagricultural industries	115 570	114 449	115 245	117 144	119 651	121 460	123 264	126 159	128 085	130 207	134 427
Unemployed	7 047	8 628	9 613	8 940	7 996	7 404	7 236	6 739	6 210	5 880	5 692
Not in labor force	63 324	64 578	64 700	65 638	65 758	66 280	66 647	66 837	67 547	68 385	69 994
Men, 16 Years and Over											
Civilian noninstitutional population	90 377	91 278	92 270	93 332	94 355	95 178	96 206	97 715	98 758	99 722	101 964
Civilian labor force	69 011	69 168	69 964	70 404	70 817	71 360	72 087	73 261	73 959	74 512	76 280
Employed	65 104	64 223	64 440	65 349	66 450	67 377	68 207	69 685	70 693	71 446	73 305
Agriculture	2 546	2 589	2 575	2 478	2 554	2 559	2 573	2 552	2 553	2 432	1 861
Nonagricultural industries	62 559	61 634	61 866	62 871	63 896	64 818	65 634	67 133	68 140	69 014	71 444
Unemployed	3 906	4 946	5 523	5 055	4 367	3 983	3 880	3 577	3 266	3 066	2 975
Not in labor force	21 367	22 110	22 306	22 927	23 538	23 818	24 119	24 454	24 799	25 210	25 684
Men, 20 Years and Over											
Civilian noninstitutional population	83 030	84 144	85 247	86 256	87 151	87 811	88 606	89 879	90 790	91 555	93 875
Civilian labor force	64 916	65 374	66 213	66 642	66 921	67 324	68 044	69 166	69 715	70 194	72 010
Employed	61 678	61 178	61 496	62 355	63 294	64 085	64 897	66 284	67 135	67 761	69 634
Agriculture	2 329	2 383	2 385	2 293	2 351	2 335	2 356	2 356	2 350	2 244	1 756
Nonagricultural industries	59 349	58 795	59 111	60 063	60 943	61 750	62 541	63 927	64 785	65 517	67 878
Unemployed	3 239	4 195	4 717	4 287	3 627	3 239	3 146	2 882	2 580	2 433	2 376
Not in labor force	18 114	18 770	19 034	19 613	20 230	20 487	20 563	20 713	21 075	21 362	21 864
Women, 16 Years and Over											
Civilian noninstitutional population	98 787	99 646	100 535	101 506	102 460	103 406	104 385	105 418	106 462	108 031	110 613
Civilian labor force	56 829	57 178	58 141	58 795	60 239	60 944	61 857	63 036	63 714	64 855	66 303
Employed	53 689	53 496	54 052	54 910	56 610	57 523	58 501	59 873	60 771	62 042	63 586
Agriculture	678	680	672	637	855	881	871	847	825	849	602
Nonagricultural industries	53 011	52 815	53 380	54 273	55 755	56 642	57 630	59 026	59 945	61 193	62 983
Unemployed	3 140	3 683	4 090	3 885	3 629	3 421	3 356	3 162	2 944	2 814	2 717
Not in labor force	41 957	42 468	42 394	42 711	42 221	42 462	42 528	42 382	42 748	43 175	44 310
Women, 20 Years and Over											
Civilian noninstitutional population	91 614	92 708	93 718	94 647	95 467	96 262	97 050	97 889	98 786	100 158	102 790
Civilian labor force	53 131	53 708	54 796	55 388	56 655	57 215	58 094	59 198	59 702	60 840	62 301
Employed	50 535	50 634	51 328	52 099	53 606	54 396	55 311	56 613	57 278	58 555	60 067
Agriculture	631	639	625	598	809	830	827	798	768	803	567
Nonagricultural industries	49 904	49 995	50 702	51 501	52 796	53 566	54 484	55 815	56 510	57 752	59 500
Unemployed	2 596	3 074	3 469	3 288	3 049	2 819	2 783	2 585	2 424	2 285	2 235
Not in labor force	38 483	39 000	38 922	39 260	38 813	39 047	38 956	38 691	39 084	39 318	40 488
Both Sexes, 16 to 19 Years											
Civilian noninstitutional population	14 520	14 073	13 840	13 935	14 196	14 511	14 934	15 365	15 644	16 040	15 912
Civilian labor force	7 792	7 265	7 096	7 170	7 481	7 765	7 806	7 932	8 256	8 333	8 271
Employed	6 581	5 906	5 669	5 805	6 161	6 419	6 500	6 661	7 051	7 172	7 189
Agriculture	264	247	237	224	249	275	261	244	261	234	141
Nonagricultural industries	6 317	5 659	5 432	5 580	5 912	6 144	6 239	6 417	6 790	6 938	7 049
Unemployed	1 212	1 359	1 427	1 365	1 320	1 346	1 306	1 271	1 205	1 162	1 081
Not in labor force	6 727	6 808	6 745	6 765	6 715	6 746	7 128	7 433	7 388	7 706	7 642
WHITE[1]											
Both Sexes											
Civilian noninstitutional population	160 625	161 759	162 972	164 289	165 555	166 914	168 317	169 993	171 478	173 085	176 220
Civilian labor force	107 447	107 743	108 837	109 700	111 082	111 950	113 108	114 693	115 415	116 509	118 545
Employed	102 261	101 182	101 669	103 045	105 190	106 490	107 808	109 856	110 931	112 235	114 424
Agriculture	2 998	3 026	3 018	2 895	3 162	3 194	3 276	3 208	3 160	3 083	2 320
Nonagricultural industries	99 263	98 157	98 650	100 150	102 027	103 296	104 532	106 648	107 770	109 152	112 104
Unemployed	5 186	6 560	7 169	6 655	5 892	5 459	5 300	4 836	4 484	4 273	4 121
Not in labor force	53 178	54 061	54 135	54 589	54 473	54 965	55 209	55 301	56 064	56 577	57 675
Men, 16 Years and Over											
Civilian noninstitutional population	77 369	77 977	78 651	79 371	80 059	80 733	81 489	82 577	83 352	83 930	85 370
Civilian labor force	59 638	59 656	60 168	60 484	60 727	61 146	61 783	62 639	63 034	63 413	64 466
Employed	56 703	55 797	55 959	56 656	57 452	58 146	58 888	59 998	60 604	61 139	62 289
Agriculture	2 353	2 384	2 378	2 286	2 347	2 347	2 436	2 389	2 376	2 273	1 743
Nonagricultural industries	54 350	53 413	53 580	54 370	55 104	55 800	56 452	57 608	58 228	58 866	60 546
Unemployed	2 935	3 859	4 209	3 828	3 275	2 999	2 896	2 641	2 431	2 274	2 177
Not in labor force	17 731	18 321	18 484	18 887	19 332	19 587	19 706	19 938	20 317	20 517	20 905
Men, 20 Years and Over											
Civilian noninstitutional population	71 457	72 274	73 040	73 721	74 311	74 879	75 454	76 320	76 966	77 432	78 966
Civilian labor force	56 116	56 387	56 976	57 284	57 411	57 719	58 340	59 126	59 421	59 747	60 850
Employed	53 685	53 103	53 357	54 021	54 676	55 254	55 977	56 986	57 500	57 934	59 119
Agriculture	2 148	2 192	2 197	2 114	2 151	2 132	2 224	2 201	2 182	2 094	1 640
Nonagricultural industries	51 537	50 912	51 160	51 907	52 525	53 122	53 753	54 785	55 319	55 839	57 479
Unemployed	2 431	3 284	3 620	3 263	2 735	2 465	2 363	2 140	1 920	1 813	1 731
Not in labor force	15 340	15 887	16 064	16 436	16 900	17 161	17 114	17 194	17 545	17 685	18 116

[1]Beginning in 2003, persons who selected this race group only; persons who selected more than one race group are not included. Prior to 2003, persons who reported more than one race group were included in the group they identified as the main race.

Table 1-3. Employment Status of the Civilian Noninstitutional Population, by Sex, Age, Race, and Hispanic Origin, 1990–2011—*Continued*

(Thousands of people.)

Characteristic	2001	2002	2003	2004	2005	2006	2007	2008	2009	2010	2011
ALL RACES											
Both Sexes											
Civilian noninstitutional population	215 092	217 570	221 168	223 357	226 082	228 815	231 867	233 788	235 801	237 830	239 618
Civilian labor force	143 734	144 863	146 510	147 401	149 320	151 428	153 124	154 287	154 142	153 889	153 617
Employed	136 933	136 485	137 736	139 252	141 730	144 427	146 047	145 362	139 877	139 064	139 869
Agriculture	2 299	2 311	2 275	2 232	2 197	2 206	2 095	2 168	2 103	2 206	2 254
Nonagricultural industries	134 635	134 174	135 461	137 020	139 532	142 221	143 952	143 194	137 775	136 858	137 615
Unemployed	6 801	8 378	8 774	8 149	7 591	7 001	7 078	8 924	14 265	14 825	13 747
Not in labor force	71 359	72 707	74 658	75 956	76 762	77 387	78 743	79 501	81 659	83 941	86 001
Men, 16 Years and Over											
Civilian noninstitutional population	103 282	104 585	106 435	107 710	109 151	110 605	112 173	113 113	114 136	115 174	116 317
Civilian labor force	76 886	77 500	78 238	78 980	80 033	81 255	82 136	82 520	82 123	81 985	81 975
Employed	73 196	72 903	73 332	74 524	75 973	77 502	78 254	77 486	73 670	73 359	74 290
Agriculture	1 708	1 724	1 695	1 688	1 654	1 663	1 604	1 650	1 607	1 665	1 698
Nonagricultural industries	71 488	71 179	71 636	72 836	74 319	75 838	76 650	75 836	72 062	71 694	72 592
Unemployed	3 690	4 597	4 906	4 456	4 059	3 753	3 882	5 033	8 453	8 626	7 684
Not in labor force	26 396	27 085	28 197	28 730	29 119	29 350	30 036	30 593	32 013	33 189	34 343
Men, 20 Years and Over											
Civilian noninstitutional population	95 181	96 439	98 272	99 476	100 835	102 145	103 555	104 453	105 493	106 596	107 736
Civilian labor force	72 816	73 630	74 623	75 364	76 443	77 562	78 596	79 047	78 897	78 994	79 080
Employed	69 776	69 734	70 415	71 572	73 050	74 431	75 337	74 750	71 341	71 230	72 182
Agriculture	1 613	1 629	1 614	1 596	1 577	1 579	1 514	1 552	1 514	1 589	1 611
Nonagricultural industries	68 163	68 104	68 801	69 976	71 473	72 852	73 823	73 198	69 828	69 641	70 571
Unemployed	3 040	3 896	4 209	3 791	3 392	3 131	3 259	4 297	7 555	7 763	6 898
Not in labor force	22 365	22 809	23 649	24 113	24 392	24 584	24 959	25 406	26 596	27 603	28 656
Women, 16 Years and Over											
Civilian noninstitutional population	111 811	112 985	114 733	115 647	116 931	118 210	119 694	120 675	121 665	122 656	123 300
Civilian labor force	66 848	67 363	68 272	68 421	69 288	70 173	70 988	71 767	72 019	71 904	71 642
Employed	63 737	63 582	64 404	64 728	65 757	66 925	67 792	67 876	66 208	65 705	65 579
Agriculture	591	587	580	547	544	543	490	518	496	541	556
Nonagricultural industries	63 147	62 995	63 824	64 181	65 213	66 382	67 302	67 358	65 712	65 164	65 023
Unemployed	3 111	3 781	3 868	3 694	3 531	3 247	3 196	3 891	5 811	6 199	6 063
Not in labor force	44 962	45 621	46 461	47 225	47 643	48 037	48 707	48 908	49 646	50 752	51 658
Women, 20 Years and Over											
Civilian noninstitutional population	103 983	105 136	106 800	107 658	108 850	109 992	111 330	112 260	113 265	114 333	115 107
Civilian labor force	63 016	63 648	64 716	64 923	65 714	66 585	67 516	68 382	68 856	68 990	68 810
Employed	60 417	60 420	61 402	61 773	62 702	63 834	64 799	65 039	63 699	63 456	63 360
Agriculture	558	557	550	515	519	520	460	491	471	519	534
Nonagricultural industries	59 860	59 863	60 852	61 258	62 182	63 315	64 339	64 548	63 228	62 936	62 826
Unemployed	2 599	3 228	3 314	3 150	3 013	2 751	2 718	3 342	5 157	5 534	5 450
Not in labor force	40 967	41 488	42 083	42 735	43 136	43 407	43 814	43 878	44 409	45 343	46 297
Both Sexes, 16 to 19 Years											
Civilian noninstitutional population	15 929	15 994	16 096	16 222	16 398	16 678	16 982	17 075	17 043	16 901	16 774
Civilian labor force	7 902	7 585	7 170	7 114	7 164	7 281	7 012	6 858	6 390	5 906	5 727
Employed	6 740	6 332	5 919	5 907	5 978	6 162	5 911	5 573	4 837	4 378	4 327
Agriculture	128	124	111	121	100	108	121	125	119	98	109
Nonagricultural industries	6 611	6 207	5 808	5 786	5 877	6 054	5 790	5 448	4 719	4 281	4 218
Unemployed	1 162	1 253	1 251	1 208	1 186	1 119	1 101	1 285	1 552	1 528	1 400
Not in labor force	8 027	8 409	8 926	9 108	9 234	9 397	9 970	10 218	10 654	10 995	11 048
WHITE[1]											
Both Sexes											
Civilian noninstitutional population	178 111	179 783	181 292	182 643	184 446	186 264	188 253	189 540	190 902	192 075	193 077
Civilian labor force	119 399	120 150	120 546	121 086	122 299	123 834	124 935	125 635	125 644	125 084	124 579
Employed	114 430	114 013	114 235	115 239	116 949	118 833	119 792	119 126	114 996	114 168	114 690
Agriculture	2 174	2 171	2 148	2 103	2 077	2 063	1 953	2 021	1 968	2 071	2 134
Nonagricultural industries	112 256	111 841	112 087	113 136	114 872	116 769	117 839	117 104	113 028	112 098	112 556
Unemployed	4 969	6 137	6 311	5 847	5 350	5 002	5 143	6 509	10 648	10 916	9 889
Not in labor force	58 713	59 633	60 746	61 558	62 148	62 429	63 319	63 905	65 258	66 991	68 498
Men, 16 Years and Over											
Civilian noninstitutional population	86 452	87 361	88 249	89 044	90 027	91 021	92 073	92 725	93 433	94 082	94 801
Civilian labor force	64 966	65 308	65 509	65 994	66 694	67 613	68 158	68 351	68 051	67 728	67 551
Employed	62 212	61 849	61 866	62 712	63 763	64 883	65 289	64 624	61 630	61 252	61 920
Agriculture	1 606	1 611	1 597	1 583	1 562	1 554	1 501	1 539	1 499	1 557	1 602
Nonagricultural industries	60 606	60 238	60 269	61 129	62 201	63 330	63 788	63 085	60 131	59 695	60 318
Unemployed	2 754	3 459	3 643	3 282	2 931	2 730	2 869	3 727	6 421	6 476	5 631
Not in labor force	21 486	22 053	22 740	23 050	23 334	23 408	23 915	24 374	25 382	26 353	27 249
Men, 20 Years and Over											
Civilian noninstitutional population	80 029	80 922	81 860	82 615	83 556	84 466	85 420	86 056	86 789	87 502	88 191
Civilian labor force	61 519	62 067	62 473	62 944	63 705	64 540	65 214	65 483	65 372	65 265	65 165
Employed	59 245	59 124	59 348	60 159	61 255	62 259	62 806	62 304	59 626	59 438	60 118
Agriculture	1 512	1 519	1 517	1 495	1 488	1 473	1 417	1 447	1 410	1 483	1 518
Nonagricultural industries	57 733	57 605	57 831	58 664	59 767	60 785	61 389	60 857	58 216	57 955	58 600
Unemployed	2 275	2 943	3 125	2 785	2 450	2 281	2 408	3 179	5 746	5 828	5 046
Not in labor force	18 510	18 855	19 386	19 671	19 851	19 927	20 206	20 573	21 417	22 236	23 026

[1]Beginning in 2003, persons who selected this race group only; persons who selected more than one race group are not included. Prior to 2003, persons who reported more than one race group were included in the group they identified as the main race.

Table 1-3. Employment Status of the Civilian Noninstitutional Population, by Sex, Age, Race, and Hispanic Origin, 1990–2011—Continued

(Thousands of people.)

Characteristic	1990	1991	1992	1993	1994	1995	1996	1997	1998	1999	2000
WHITE[1]											
Women, 16 Years and Over											
Civilian noninstitutional population	83 256	83 781	84 321	84 918	85 496	86 181	86 828	87 417	88 126	89 156	90 850
Civilian labor force	47 809	48 087	48 669	49 216	50 356	50 804	51 325	52 054	52 380	53 096	54 079
Employed	45 558	45 385	45 710	46 390	47 738	48 344	48 920	49 859	50 327	51 096	52 136
Agriculture	645	641	640	609	815	847	840	819	784	810	578
Nonagricultural industries	44 913	44 744	45 070	45 780	46 923	47 497	48 080	49 040	49 543	50 286	51 558
Unemployed	2 251	2 701	2 959	2 827	2 617	2 460	2 404	2 195	2 053	1 999	1 944
Not in labor force	35 447	35 695	35 651	35 702	35 141	35 377	35 503	35 363	35 746	36 060	36 770
Women, 20 Years and Over											
Civilian noninstitutional population	77 539	78 285	78 928	79 490	79 980	80 567	81 041	81 492	82 073	82 953	84 718
Civilian labor force	44 648	45 111	45 839	46 311	47 314	47 686	48 162	48 847	49 029	49 714	50 740
Employed	42 796	42 862	43 327	43 910	45 116	45 643	46 164	47 063	47 342	48 098	49 145
Agriculture	598	601	594	572	772	799	798	771	729	765	546
Nonagricultural industries	42 198	42 261	42 733	43 339	44 344	44 844	45 366	46 292	46 612	47 333	48 599
Unemployed	1 852	2 248	2 512	2 400	2 197	2 042	1 998	1 784	1 688	1 616	1 595
Not in labor force	32 891	33 174	33 089	33 179	32 666	32 881	32 879	32 645	33 044	33 239	33 978
Both Sexes, 16 to 19 Years											
Civilian noninstitutional population	11 630	11 200	11 004	11 078	11 264	11 468	11 822	12 181	12 439	12 700	12 535
Civilian labor force	6 683	6 245	6 022	6 105	6 357	6 545	6 607	6 720	6 965	7 048	6 955
Employed	5 779	5 216	4 985	5 113	5 398	5 593	5 667	5 807	6 089	6 204	6 160
Agriculture	252	233	228	209	239	262	254	236	250	224	135
Nonagricultural industries	5 528	4 984	4 757	4 904	5 158	5 331	5 413	5 571	5 839	5 980	6 025
Unemployed	903	1 029	1 037	992	960	952	939	912	876	844	795
Not in labor force	4 947	4 955	4 982	4 973	4 907	4 923	5 215	5 462	5 475	5 652	5 581
BLACK[1]											
Both Sexes											
Civilian noninstitutional population	21 477	21 799	22 147	22 521	22 879	23 246	23 604	24 003	24 373	24 855	24 902
Civilian labor force	13 740	13 797	14 162	14 225	14 502	14 817	15 134	15 529	15 982	16 365	16 397
Employed	12 175	12 074	12 151	12 382	12 835	13 279	13 542	13 969	14 556	15 056	15 156
Agriculture	142	160	153	143	136	101	98	117	138	117	77
Nonagricultural industries	12 034	11 914	11 997	12 239	12 699	13 178	13 444	13 852	14 417	14 939	15 079
Unemployed	1 565	1 723	2 011	1 844	1 666	1 538	1 592	1 560	1 426	1 309	1 241
Not in labor force	7 737	8 002	7 985	8 296	8 377	8 429	8 470	8 474	8 391	8 490	8 505
Men, 16 Years and Over											
Civilian noninstitutional population	9 573	9 725	9 896	10 083	10 258	10 411	10 575	10 763	10 927	11 143	11 129
Civilian labor force	6 802	6 851	6 997	7 019	7 089	7 183	7 264	7 354	7 542	7 652	7 702
Employed	5 995	5 961	5 930	6 047	6 241	6 422	6 456	6 607	6 871	7 027	7 082
Agriculture	124	139	138	128	118	93	86	103	118	99	67
Nonagricultural industries	5 872	5 822	5 791	5 919	6 122	6 329	6 371	6 504	6 752	6 952	7 015
Unemployed	806	890	1 067	971	848	762	808	747	671	671	620
Not in labor force	2 772	2 874	2 899	3 064	3 169	3 228	3 311	3 409	3 386	3 386	3 427
Men, 20 Years and Over											
Civilian noninstitutional population	8 364	8 479	8 652	8 840	9 171	9 280	9 414	9 575	9 727	9 926	9 952
Civilian labor force	6 221	6 357	6 451	6 568	6 646	6 730	6 806	6 910	7 053	7 182	7 240
Employed	5 602	5 692	5 706	5 681	5 964	6 137	6 167	6 325	6 530	6 702	6 741
Agriculture	119	117	131	131	115	89	83	101	112	96	67
Nonagricultural industries	5 483	5 576	5 575	5 550	5 849	6 048	6 084	6 224	6 418	6 606	6 675
Unemployed	619	664	745	886	682	593	639	585	524	480	499
Not in labor force	2 143	2 122	2 202	801	2 525	2 550	2 608	2 665	2 673	2 743	2 711
Women, 16 Years and Over											
Civilian noninstitutional population	11 904	12 074	12 251	12 438	12 621	12 835	13 029	13 241	13 446	13 711	13 772
Civilian labor force	6 938	6 946	7 166	7 206	7 413	7 634	7 869	8 175	8 441	8 713	8 695
Employed	6 180	6 113	6 221	6 334	6 595	6 857	7 086	7 362	7 685	8 029	8 073
Agriculture	18	21	15	15	18	8	13	14	20	18	10
Nonagricultural industries	6 162	6 092	6 206	6 320	6 577	6 849	7 073	7 348	7 665	8 011	8 064
Unemployed	758	833	944	872	818	777	784	813	756	684	621
Not in labor force	4 965	5 129	5 086	5 231	5 208	5 201	5 159	5 066	5 005	4 999	5 078
Women, 20 Years and Over											
Civilian noninstitutional population	10 760	10 959	11 152	11 332	11 496	11 682	11 833	12 016	12 023	12 451	12 561
Civilian labor force	6 517	6 572	6 778	6 824	7 004	7 175	7 405	7 686	7 912	8 224	8 215
Employed	5 884	5 874	5 978	6 095	6 320	6 556	6 762	7 013	7 290	7 663	7 703
Agriculture	18	20	15	14	17	7	12	13	19	17	9
Nonagricultural industries	5 867	5 853	5 963	6 081	6 303	6 548	6 749	7 000	7 272	7 646	7 694
Unemployed	633	698	800	729	685	620	643	673	622	561	512
Not in labor force	4 243	4 388	4 374	4 508	4 492	4 507	4 428	4 330	4 291	4 226	4 346
Both Sexes, 16 to 19 Years											
Civilian noninstitutional population	2 238	2 187	2 155	2 181	2 211	2 284	2 356	2 412	2 443	2 479	2 389
Civilian labor force	866	774	816	807	852	911	923	933	1 017	959	941
Employed	598	494	492	494	552	586	613	631	736	691	711
Agriculture	7	8	7	9	1	5	3	3	8	4	1
Nonagricultural industries	591	486	485	485	547	581	611	611	728	687	710
Unemployed	268	280	324	313	300	325	310	310	281	268	230
Not in labor force	1 372	1 413	1 339	1 374	1 360	1 372	1 434	1 434	1 427	1 520	1 448

[1]Beginning in 2003, persons who selected this race group only; persons who selected more than one race group are not included. Prior to 2003, persons who reported more than one race group were included in the group they identified as the main race.

Table 1-3. Employment Status of the Civilian Noninstitutional Population, by Sex, Age, Race, and Hispanic Origin, 1990–2011—Continued

(Thousands of people.)

Characteristic	2001	2002	2003	2004	2005	2006	2007	2008	2009	2010	2011
WHITE[1]											
Women, 16 Years and Over											
Civilian noninstitutional population	91 660	92 422	93 043	93 599	94 419	95 242	96 180	96 814	97 469	97 993	98 276
Civilian labor force	54 433	54 842	55 037	55 092	55 605	56 221	56 777	57 284	57 593	57 356	57 028
Employed	52 218	52 164	52 369	52 527	53 186	53 950	54 503	54 501	53 366	52 916	52 770
Agriculture	568	560	551	520	515	510	452	482	469	513	532
Nonagricultural industries	51 650	51 604	51 818	52 007	52 672	53 440	54 050	54 019	52 897	52 402	52 238
Unemployed	2 215	2 678	2 668	2 565	2 419	2 271	2 274	2 782	4 227	4 440	4 257
Not in labor force	37 227	37 581	38 006	38 508	38 814	39 021	39 403	39 531	39 876	40 638	41 248
Women, 20 Years and Over											
Civilian noninstitutional population	85 526	86 266	86 905	87 430	88 200	88 942	89 790	90 400	91 078	91 683	92 068
Civilian labor force	51 218	51 717	52 099	52 212	52 643	53 286	53 925	54 508	54 976	54 957	54 700
Employed	49 369	49 448	49 823	50 040	50 589	51 359	51 996	52 124	51 231	50 997	50 881
Agriculture	537	532	522	488	492	488	423	457	444	492	511
Nonagricultural industries	48 831	48 916	49 301	49 552	50 097	50 871	51 572	51 667	50 787	50 505	50 371
Unemployed	1 849	2 269	2 276	2 172	2 054	1 927	1 930	2 384	3 745	3 960	3 818
Not in labor force	34 308	34 548	34 806	35 218	35 557	35 656	35 864	35 892	36 101	36 725	37 368
Both Sexes, 16 to 19 Years											
Civilian noninstitutional population	12 556	12 596	12 527	12 599	12 690	12 856	13 043	13 084	13 035	12 891	12 818
Civilian labor force	6 661	6 336	5 973	5 929	5 950	6 009	5 795	5 644	5 295	4 861	4 714
Employed	5 817	5 441	5 064	5 039	5 105	5 215	4 990	4 697	4 138	3 733	3 691
Agriculture	125	121	109	116	97	102	113	118	114	96	105
Nonagricultural industries	5 692	5 320	4 955	4 923	5 008	5 113	4 877	4 580	4 025	3 637	3 585
Unemployed	845	925	909	890	845	794	805	947	1 157	1 128	1 024
Not in labor force	5 894	6 230	6 554	6 669	6 739	6 847	7 248	7 440	7 740	8 030	8 103
BLACK[1]											
Both Sexes											
Civilian noninstitutional population	25 138	25 578	25 686	26 065	26 517	27 007	27 485	27 843	28 241	28 708	29 114
Civilian labor force	16 421	16 565	16 526	16 638	17 013	17 314	17 496	17 740	17 632	17 862	17 881
Employed	15 006	14 872	14 739	14 909	15 313	15 765	16 051	15 953	15 025	15 010	15 051
Agriculture	62	69	63	50	51	60	53	55	66	59	52
Nonagricultural industries	14 944	14 804	14 676	14 859	15 261	15 705	15 998	15 898	14 959	14 951	14 999
Unemployed	1 416	1 693	1 787	1 729	1 700	1 549	1 445	1 788	2 606	2 852	2 831
Not in labor force	8 717	9 013	9 161	9 428	9 504	9 693	9 989	10 103	10 609	10 846	11 233
Men, 16 Years and Over											
Civilian noninstitutional population	11 172	11 391	11 454	11 656	11 882	12 130	12 361	12 516	12 705	12 939	13 164
Civilian labor force	7 647	7 794	7 711	7 773	7 998	8 128	8 252	8 347	8 265	8 415	8 454
Employed	6 938	6 959	6 820	6 912	7 155	7 354	7 500	7 398	6 817	6 865	6 953
Agriculture	56	63	52	43	43	51	46	49	56	53	47
Nonagricultural industries	6 882	6 896	6 768	6 869	7 111	7 303	7 454	7 350	6 761	6 812	6 905
Unemployed	709	835	891	860	844	774	752	949	1 448	1 550	1 502
Not in labor force	3 525	3 597	3 743	3 884	3 884	4 002	4 110	4 169	4 441	4 524	4 710
Men, 20 Years and Over											
Civilian noninstitutional population	9 993	10 196	10 278	11 656	10 659	10 864	11 057	11 194	11 379	11 626	11 882
Civilian labor force	7 200	7 347	7 346	7 773	7 600	7 720	7 867	7 962	7 914	8 076	8 125
Employed	6 627	6 652	6 586	6 912	6 901	7 079	7 245	7 151	6 628	6 680	6 765
Agriculture	55	62	51	274	43	49	45	47	55	52	46
Nonagricultural industries	55	6 591	6 535	6 638	6 858	7 030	7 201	7 104	6 573	6 628	6 719
Unemployed	573	695	760	860	699	640	622	811	1 286	1 396	1 360
Not in labor force	2 792	2 848	2 932	3 884	3 060	3 144	3 189	3 232	3 465	3 550	3 757
Women, 16 Years and Over											
Civilian noninstitutional population	13 966	14 187	14 232	14 409	14 635	14 877	15 124	15 328	15 536	15 769	15 950
Civilian labor force	8 774	8 772	8 815	8 865	9 014	9 186	9 244	9 393	9 367	9 447	9 427
Employed	8 068	7 914	7 919	7 997	8 158	8 410	8 551	8 554	8 208	8 145	8 098
Agriculture	6	6	11	7	8	9	7	6	10	6	5
Nonagricultural industries	8 062	7 907	7 908	7 990	8 150	8 402	8 544	8 548	8 198	8 139	8 093
Unemployed	706	858	895	868	856	775	693	839	1 159	1 302	1 329
Not in labor force	5 192	5 415	5 418	5 544	5 621	5 691	5 879	5 934	6 169	6 322	6 523
Women, 20 Years and Over											
Civilian noninstitutional population	12 758	12 966	13 026	14 409	13 377	13 578	13 788	13 974	14 178	14 425	14 638
Civilian labor force	8 323	8 348	8 409	8 865	8 610	8 723	8 828	8 991	8 988	9 110	9 110
Employed	7 741	7 610	7 636	7 997	7 876	8 068	8 240	8 260	7 956	7 944	7 906
Agriculture	6	5	10	7	7	7	7	6	10	6	5
Nonagricultural industries	7 735	7 604	7 626	7 701	7 868	8 060	8 233	8 254	7 946	7 938	7 901
Unemployed	582	738	772	868	734	656	588	732	1 032	1 165	1 204
Not in labor force	4 434	4 618	4 618	5 544	4 768	4 854	4 960	4 982	5 190	5 315	5 529
Both Sexes, 16 to 19 Years											
Civilian noninstitutional population	2 388	2 416	2 382	2 423	2 481	2 565	2 640	2 676	2 684	2 657	2 594
Civilian labor force	898	870	771	762	803	871	801	787	729	677	647
Employed	637	611	516	520	536	618	566	541	442	386	380
Agriculture	1	2	1	0	1	3	1	1	1	1	1
Nonagricultural industries	637	609	515	520	535	614	564	540	440	385	379
Unemployed	260	260	255	241	267	253	235	246	288	291	267
Not in labor force	1 490	1 546	1 611	1 661	1 677	1 694	1 839	1 889	1 954	1 980	1 947

[1]Beginning in 2003, persons who selected this race group only; persons who selected more than one race group are not included. Prior to 2003, persons who reported more than one race group were included in the group they identified as the main race.

Table 1-3. Employment Status of the Civilian Noninstitutional Population, by Sex, Age, Race, and Hispanic Origin, 1990–2011—*Continued*

(Thousands of people.)

Characteristic	1990	1991	1992	1993	1994	1995	1996	1997	1998	1999	2000
HISPANIC[2]											
Both Sexes											
Civilian noninstitutional population	15 904	16 425	16 961	17 532	18 117	18 629	19 213	20 321	21 070	21 650	23 938
Civilian labor force	10 720	10 920	11 338	11 610	11 975	12 267	12 774	13 796	14 317	14 665	16 689
Employed	9 845	9 828	10 027	10 361	10 788	11 127	11 642	12 726	13 291	13 720	15 735
Agriculture	517	512	524	523	560	604	609	660	742	734	536
Nonagricultural industries	9 328	9 315	9 503	9 838	10 227	10 524	11 033	12 067	12 549	12 986	15 199
Unemployed	876	1 092	1 311	1 248	1 187	1 140	1 132	1 069	1 026	945	954
Not in labor force	5 184	5 506	5 623	5 922	6 142	6 362	6 439	6 526	6 753	6 985	7 249
Men, 16 Years and Over											
Civilian noninstitutional population	8 041	8 296	8 553	8 824	9 104	9 329	9 604	10 368	10 734	10 713	12 174
Civilian labor force	6 546	6 664	6 900	7 076	7 210	7 376	7 646	8 309	8 571	8 546	9 923
Employed	6 021	5 979	6 093	6 328	6 530	6 725	7 039	7 728	8 018	8 067	9 428
Agriculture	449	453	468	469	494	527	537	571	651	642	449
Nonagricultural industries	5 572	5 526	5 625	5 860	6 036	6 198	6 502	7 157	7 367	7 425	8 979
Unemployed	524	685	807	747	680	651	607	582	552	480	494
Not in labor force	1 495	1 632	1 654	1 749	1 894	1 952	1 957	2 059	2 164	2 167	2 252
Men, 20 Years and Over											
Civilian noninstitutional population	7 126	7 392	7 655	7 930	8 178	8 375	8 611	9 250	9 573	9 523	10 841
Civilian labor force	6 034	6 198	6 432	6 621	6 747	6 898	7 150	7 779	8 005	7 950	9 247
Employed	5 609	5 623	5 757	5 992	6 189	6 367	6 655	7 307	7 570	7 576	8 859
Agriculture	415	419	437	441	466	501	510	544	621	602	423
Nonagricultural industries	5 195	5 204	5 320	5 551	5 722	5 866	6 145	6 763	6 949	6 974	8 435
Unemployed	425	575	675	629	558	530	495	471	436	374	388
Not in labor force	1 092	1 194	1 223	1 309	1 431	1 477	1 461	1 471	1 568	1 573	1 595
Women, 16 Years and Over											
Civilian noninstitutional population	7 863	8 130	8 408	8 708	9 014	9 300	9 610	9 953	10 335	10 937	11 764
Civilian labor force	4 174	4 256	4 439	4 534	4 765	4 891	5 128	5 486	5 746	6 119	6 767
Employed	3 823	3 848	3 934	4 033	4 258	4 403	4 602	4 999	5 273	5 653	6 307
Agriculture	68	59	57	55	66	76	72	89	91	92	87
Nonagricultural industries	3 755	3 789	3 877	3 978	4 191	4 326	4 531	4 910	5 182	5 561	6 220
Unemployed	351	407	504	501	508	488	525	488	473	466	460
Not in labor force	3 689	3 874	3 969	4 174	4 248	4 409	4 482	4 466	4 589	4 819	4 997
Women, 20 Years and Over											
Civilian noninstitutional population	7 041	7 301	7 569	7 846	8 122	8 382	8 654	8 950	9 292	9 821	10 574
Civilian labor force	3 941	4 110	4 218	4 421	4 520	4 779	5 106	5 304	5 666	6 275	6 557
Employed	3 567	3 603	3 693	3 800	3 989	4 116	4 341	4 705	4 928	5 290	5 903
Agriculture	62	53	51	49	61	72	69	83	85	88	81
Nonagricultural industries	3 505	3 549	3 642	3 751	3 928	4 044	4 272	4 622	4 843	5 202	5 822
Unemployed	289	339	418	418	431	404	438	401	376	376	371
Not in labor force	3 184	3 360	3 459	3 628	3 701	3 863	3 875	3 845	3 988	4 155	4 299
Both Sexes, 16 to 19 Years											
Civilian noninstitutional population	1 737	1 732	1 737	1 756	1 818	1 872	1 948	2 121	2 204	2 307	2 523
Civilian labor force	829	781	796	771	807	850	845	911	1 007	1 049	1 168
Employed	668	602	577	570	609	645	646	714	793	854	973
Agriculture	40	41	36	33	32	31	29	33	36	45	31
Nonagricultural industries	628	562	541	537	577	614	617	682	757	809	942
Unemployed	161	179	219	201	198	205	199	197	214	196	194
Not in labor force	907	951	941	985	1 010	1 022	1 103	1 210	1 197	1 257	1 355

[2]May be of any race.

Table 1-3. Employment Status of the Civilian Noninstitutional Population, by Sex, Age, Race, and Hispanic Origin, 1990–2011—*Continued*

(Thousands of people.)

Characteristic	2001	2002	2003	2004	2005	2006	2007	2008	2009	2010	2011
HISPANIC[2]											
Both Sexes											
Civilian noninstitutional population	24 942	25 963	27 551	28 109	29 133	30 103	31 383	32 141	32 891	33 713	34 438
Civilian labor force	17 328	17 943	18 813	19 272	19 824	20 694	21 602	22 024	22 352	22 748	22 898
Employed	16 190	16 590	17 372	17 930	18 632	19 613	20 382	20 346	19 647	19 906	20 269
Agriculture	423	448	446	441	423	428	426	441	426	480	523
Nonagricultural industries	15 767	16 141	16 927	17 489	18 209	19 185	19 956	19 904	19 221	19 426	19 746
Unemployed	1 138	1 353	1 441	1 342	1 191	1 081	1 220	1 678	2 706	2 843	2 629
Not in labor force	7 614	8 020	8 738	8 837	9 310	9 409	9 781	10 116	10 539	10 964	11 540
Men, 16 Years and Over											
Civilian noninstitutional population	12 695	13 221	14 098	14 417	14 962	15 473	16 154	16 524	16 897	17 359	17 753
Civilian labor force	10 279	10 609	11 288	11 587	11 985	12 488	13 005	13 255	13 310	13 511	13 576
Employed	9 668	9 845	10 479	10 832	11 337	11 887	12 310	12 248	11 640	11 800	12 049
Agriculture	345	361	350	356	350	347	352	364	344	377	418
Nonagricultural industries	9 323	9 484	10 129	10 476	10 987	11 540	11 958	11 884	11 296	11 423	11 631
Unemployed	611	764	809	755	647	601	695	1 007	1 670	1 711	1 527
Not in labor force	2 416	2 613	2 810	2 831	2 977	2 985	3 149	3 270	3 588	3 849	4 177
Men, 20 Years and Over											
Civilian noninstitutional population	11 386	11 928	12 797	13 082	13 586	14 046	14 649	14 971	15 305	15 693	15 941
Civilian labor force	9 595	9 977	10 756	11 020	11 408	11 888	12 403	12 629	12 730	12 958	13 030
Employed	9 100	9 341	10 063	10 385	10 872	11 391	11 827	11 769	11 256	11 438	11 685
Agriculture	328	345	336	335	341	337	337	351	332	367	405
Nonagricultural industries	8 773	8 996	9 727	10 050	10 532	11 054	11 490	11 418	10 924	11 071	11 281
Unemployed	495	636	693	635	536	497	576	860	1 474	1 519	1 345
Not in labor force	1 791	1 951	2 041	2 061	2 177	2 157	2 246	2 342	2 575	2 735	2 911
Women, 16 Years and Over											
Civilian noninstitutional population	12 247	12 742	13 452	13 692	14 172	14 630	15 229	15 616	15 993	16 353	16 685
Civilian labor force	7 049	7 334	7 525	7 685	7 839	8 206	8 597	8 769	9 043	9 238	9 322
Employed	6 522	6 744	6 894	7 098	7 295	7 725	8 072	8 098	8 007	8 106	8 220
Agriculture	77	87	96	85	73	80	74	77	82	103	105
Nonagricultural industries	6 445	6 657	6 798	7 013	7 222	7 645	7 999	8 021	7 925	8 003	8 115
Unemployed	527	590	631	587	544	480	525	672	1 036	1 132	1 102
Not in labor force	5 198	5 408	5 928	6 007	6 333	6 424	6 632	6 847	6 951	7 116	7 363
Women, 20 Years and Over											
Civilian noninstitutional population	11 049	11 528	12 211	12 420	12 858	13 262	13 791	14 127	14 463	14 776	15 090
Civilian labor force	6 863	7 096	7 096	7 257	7 377	7 735	8 108	8 274	8 560	8 789	8 902
Employed	6 121	6 367	6 541	6 752	6 913	7 321	7 662	7 707	59	7 788	7 918
Agriculture	73	84	91	78	70	77	69	75	78	101	104
Nonagricultural industries	6 048	6 283	6 450	6 674	6 843	7 244	7 593	7 632	7 570	7 687	7 814
Unemployed	436	496	555	504	464	414	446	567	911	1 001	984
Not in labor force	4 492	4 666	5 114	5 163	5 481	5 527	5 682	5 853	5 903	5 987	6 187
Both Sexes, 16 to 19 Years											
Civilian noninstitutional population	2 508	2 507	2 543	2 608	2 689	2 796	2 944	3 042	3 123	3 243	3 407
Civilian labor force	1 176	1 103	960	995	1 038	1 071	1 091	1 121	1 063	1 002	965
Employed	969	882	768	792	847	900	894	870	742	680	665
Agriculture	22	19	19	25	13	14	20	15	16	12	14
Nonagricultural industries	947	863	749	767	834	887	874	855	726	668	651
Unemployed	208	221	192	203	191	170	197	251	321	322	300
Not in labor force	1 331	1 404	1 583	1 612	1 651	1 725	1 853	1 921	2 061	2 242	2 442

[2]May be of any race.

Table 1-4. Employment Status of the Civilian Noninstitutional Population, by Sex, Race, and Marital Status, 1990–2011

(Thousands of people.)

Race, marital status, and year	Men				Women			
	Civilian noninstitutional population	Civilian labor force			Civilian noninstitutional population	Civilian labor force		
		Total	Employed	Unemployed		Total	Employed	Unemployed
ALL RACES								
Single								
1990	25 870	19 357	17 405	1 952	21 901	14 612	13 336	1 276
1991	26 197	19 411	17 011	2 400	22 173	14 681	13 198	1 482
1992	26 436	19 709	17 098	2 611	22 475	14 872	13 263	1 609
1993	26 570	19 706	17 261	2 445	22 713	15 031	13 484	1 547
1994	26 786	19 786	17 604	2 181	23 000	15 333	13 847	1 486
1995	26 918	19 841	17 833	2 007	23 151	15 467	14 053	1 413
1996	27 387	20 071	18 055	2 016	23 623	15 842	14 403	1 439
1997	28 311	20 689	18 783	1 906	24 285	16 492	15 037	1 455
1998	28 693	21 037	19 240	1 798	24 941	17 087	15 755	1 332
1999	29 104	21 351	19 686	1 665	25 576	17 575	16 267	1 308
2000	29 887	22 002	20 339	1 663	25 920	17 849	16 628	1 221
2001	30 646	22 285	20 298	1 988	26 462	18 021	16 635	1 386
2002	31 072	22 289	19 983	2 306	26 999	18 203	16 583	1 621
2003	31 691	22 297	19 841	2 457	27 802	18 397	16 723	1 674
2004	32 422	22 776	20 395	2 381	28 228	18 616	16 995	1 621
2005	33 125	23 214	21 006	2 209	29 046	19 183	17 588	1 595
2006	33 931	23 974	21 907	2 067	29 624	19 474	17 978	1 496
2007	34 650	24 276	22 143	2 132	30 219	19 745	18 322	1 422
2008	35 274	24 643	21 938	2 705	30 980	20 231	18 513	1 717
2009	36 087	24 640	20 628	4 011	31 500	20 224	17 800	2 424
2010	37 137	24 985	20 850	4 135	32 548	20 592	17 950	2 642
2011	37 782	25 301	21 474	3 827	33 266	20 878	18 266	2 612
Married, Spouse Present								
1990	53 793	42 275	40 829	1 446	52 917	30 901	29 714	1 188
1991	54 158	42 303	40 429	1 875	53 169	31 112	29 698	1 415
1992	54 509	42 491	40 341	2 150	53 501	31 700	30 100	1 600
1993	55 178	42 834	40 935	1 899	53 838	31 980	30 499	1 482
1994	55 560	43 005	41 414	1 592	54 155	32 888	31 536	1 352
1995	56 100	43 472	42 048	1 424	54 716	33 359	32 063	1 296
1996	56 363	43 739	42 417	1 322	54 970	33 618	32 406	1 211
1997	56 396	43 808	42 642	1 167	54 915	33 802	32 755	1 047
1998	56 670	43 957	42 923	1 034	55 331	33 857	32 872	985
1999	57 089	44 244	43 254	990	56 178	34 372	33 450	921
2000	58 167	44 987	44 078	908	57 557	35 146	34 209	937
2001	58 448	45 233	44 007	1 226	57 610	35 236	34 153	1 083
2002	59 102	45 766	44 116	1 650	58 165	35 477	34 153	1 323
2003	60 063	46 404	44 653	1 751	59 069	36 046	34 695	1 352
2004	60 412	46 550	45 084	1 466	59 278	35 845	34 600	1 244
2005	60 545	46 771	45 483	1 287	59 205	35 941	34 773	1 168
2006	60 751	46 842	45 700	1 142	59 576	36 314	35 272	1 042
2007	61 760	47 520	46 314	1 206	60 474	36 881	35 832	1 049
2008	61 794	47 450	45 860	1 590	60 554	37 194	35 869	1 325
2009	61 773	47 114	43 998	3 115	60 675	37 264	35 207	2 057
2010	61 254	46 430	43 292	3 138	60 257	36 742	34 582	2 160
2011	61 358	45 954	43 283	2 671	60 061	36 141	34 110	2 031
Divorced, Widowed, or Separated								
1990	10 714	7 378	6 871	508	23 968	11 315	10 639	676
1991	10 924	7 454	6 783	671	24 304	11 385	10 600	786
1992	11 325	7 763	7 001	762	24 559	11 570	10 689	881
1993	11 584	7 864	7 153	711	24 955	11 784	10 927	856
1994	12 008	8 026	7 432	594	25 304	12 018	11 227	791
1995	12 160	8 048	7 496	551	25 539	12 118	11 407	712
1996	12 456	8 276	7 735	541	25 791	12 397	11 691	706
1997	13 009	8 764	8 260	504	26 218	12 742	12 082	660
1998	13 394	8 965	8 530	435	26 190	12 771	12 143	628
1999	13 528	8 918	8 507	411	26 276	12 909	12 324	585
2000	13 910	9 291	8 888	403	27 135	13 308	12 748	559
2001	14 188	9 367	8 892	476	27 738	13 592	12 949	642
2002	14 411	9 445	8 804	641	27 821	13 683	12 846	837
2003	14 680	9 537	8 838	699	27 862	13 828	12 986	842
2004	14 875	9 654	9 045	608	28 141	13 961	13 133	828
2005	15 481	10 048	9 484	563	28 680	14 163	13 396	768
2006	15 923	10 440	9 895	545	29 010	14 385	13 675	709
2007	15 763	10 341	9 797	544	29 001	14 362	13 638	724
2008	16 044	10 427	9 688	739	29 141	14 342	13 494	849
2009	16 275	10 370	9 043	1 326	29 490	14 531	13 201	1 330
2010	16 783	10 570	9 217	1 352	29 851	14 570	13 173	1 397
2011	17 177	10 719	9 533	1 186	29 974	14 623	13 203	1 420

Note: See notes and definitions for information on historical comparability.

Table 1-4. Employment Status of the Civilian Noninstitutional Population, by Sex, Race, and Marital Status, 1990–2011—Continued

(Thousands of people.)

Race, marital status, and year	Men Civilian noninstitutional population	Men Civilian labor force Total	Men Civilian labor force Employed	Men Civilian labor force Unemployed	Women Civilian noninstitutional population	Women Civilian labor force Total	Women Civilian labor force Employed	Women Civilian labor force Unemployed
WHITE[1]								
Single								
1990	20 746	15 993	14 617	1 376	16 555	11 522	10 729	794
1991	20 899	15 989	14 233	1 756	16 569	11 497	10 557	939
1992	21 025	16 129	14 285	1 844	16 684	11 502	10 526	976
1993	20 974	16 033	14 303	1 730	16 768	11 613	10 633	980
1994	21 071	16 074	14 539	1 535	16 936	11 805	10 885	920
1995	21 132	16 080	14 674	1 406	17 046	11 830	10 967	864
1996	21 454	16 285	14 891	1 394	17 282	11 977	11 099	878
1997	22 236	16 810	15 507	1 303	17 728	12 322	11 443	879
1998	22 513	17 007	15 746	1 261	18 247	12 742	11 945	797
1999	22 788	17 272	16 116	1 157	18 635	13 029	12 206	823
2000	23 266	17 659	16 504	1 154	18 808	13 215	12 449	766
2001	23 979	17 970	16 561	1 409	19 253	13 368	12 491	877
2002	24 289	17 924	16 289	1 635	19 625	13 556	12 550	1 006
2003	24 419	17 755	16 031	1 723	19 924	13 462	12 461	1 001
2004	24 929	18 090	16 435	1 655	20 210	13 597	12 628	969
2005	25 436	18 338	16 833	1 505	20 702	13 906	12 957	949
2006	26 012	18 928	17 500	1 428	21 085	14 109	13 199	909
2007	26 431	19 063	17 580	1 483	21 408	14 255	13 357	897
2008	27 023	19 395	17 474	1 920	22 064	14 648	13 578	1 070
2009	27 559	19 392	16 528	2 864	22 371	14 733	13 193	1 540
2010	28 250	19 582	16 653	2 929	23 000	14 803	13 171	1 632
2011	28 707	19 823	17 175	2 648	23 455	14 988	13 421	1 567
Married, Spouse Present								
1990	47 841	37 515	36 338	1 177	47 240	27 271	26 285	986
1991	48 137	37 507	35 923	1 585	47 456	27 479	26 290	1 189
1992	48 416	37 671	35 886	1 785	47 705	27 951	26 623	1 329
1993	48 937	37 953	36 396	1 557	47 944	28 221	26 993	1 228
1994	49 169	38 008	36 719	1 288	48 120	29 017	27 888	1 129
1995	49 597	38 376	37 211	1 165	48 497	29 360	28 290	1 070
1996	49 800	38 616	37 522	1 094	48 684	29 517	28 496	1 020
1997	49 719	38 593	37 636	957	48 542	29 664	28 809	855
1998	49 901	38 629	37 793	836	48 722	29 534	28 727	808
1999	50 091	38 765	37 968	797	49 296	29 806	29 056	749
2000	50 775	39 169	38 451	717	50 194	30 344	29 582	762
2001	50 850	39 246	38 265	981	50 077	30 336	29 472	864
2002	51 284	39 580	38 261	1 319	50 489	30 511	29 463	1 048
2003	51 859	39 908	38 529	1 379	50 957	30 805	29 740	1 065
2004	51 992	39 935	38 774	1 161	50 939	30 544	29 549	996
2005	52 034	40 141	39 130	1 011	50 865	30 599	29 676	922
2006	52 035	40 103	39 207	896	51 200	30 950	30 111	839
2007	52 775	40 559	39 594	965	51 868	31 363	30 533	830
2008	52 708	40 404	39 157	1 247	51 637	31 456	30 367	1 089
2009	52 693	40 142	37 644	2 498	51 786	31 584	29 891	1 694
2010	52 211	39 489	36 999	2 490	51 364	31 161	29 412	1 748
2011	52 142	38 951	36 870	2 081	51 074	30 555	28 925	1 630
Divorced, Widowed, or Separated								
1990	8 782	6 131	5 748	382	19 461	9 016	8 544	471
1991	8 941	6 159	5 641	518	19 757	9 111	8 538	573
1992	9 210	6 368	5 788	580	19 931	9 216	8 561	654
1993	9 459	6 498	5 957	541	20 206	9 382	8 764	618
1994	9 819	6 644	6 193	451	20 439	9 533	8 965	569
1995	10 005	6 689	6 261	428	20 638	9 613	9 087	526
1996	10 234	6 883	6 474	408	20 862	9 831	9 325	506
1997	10 622	7 236	6 855	382	21 147	10 068	9 607	461
1998	10 937	7 398	7 064	334	21 157	10 104	9 656	449
1999	11 050	7 375	7 056	320	21 225	10 261	9 834	427
2000	11 329	7 638	7 333	305	21 847	10 521	10 105	416
2001	11 623	7 750	7 386	364	22 330	10 729	10 255	474
2002	11 789	7 804	7 299	505	22 308	10 775	10 151	624
2003	11 971	7 846	7 305	541	22 162	10 769	10 168	602
2004	12 124	7 969	7 503	466	22 450	10 950	10 350	600
2005	12 558	8 215	7 800	415	22 853	11 101	10 552	548
2006	12 974	8 583	8 176	407	22 957	11 162	10 640	523
2007	12 867	8 536	8 115	421	22 904	11 159	10 613	547
2008	12 995	8 552	7 992	560	23 112	11 180	10 556	624
2009	13 181	8 517	7 459	1 058	23 312	11 275	10 282	993
2010	13 620	8 657	7 601	1 056	23 630	11 392	10 333	1 059
2011	13 952	8 777	7 875	903	23 747	11 484	10 424	1 060

Note: See notes and definitions for information on historical comparability.

[1]Beginning in 2003, persons who selected this race group only; persons who selected more than one race group are not included. Prior to 2003, persons who reported more than one race group were included in the group they identified as their main race.

Table 1-4. Employment Status of the Civilian Noninstitutional Population, by Sex, Race, and Marital Status, 1990–2011—*Continued*

(Thousands of people.)

Race, marital status, and year	Men				Women			
	Civilian noninstitutional population	Civilian labor force			Civilian noninstitutional population	Civilian labor force		
		Total	Employed	Unemployed		Total	Employed	Unemployed
ALL OTHER RACES								
Single								
1990	5 124	3 364	2 788	576	5 346	3 090	2 607	482
1991	5 298	3 422	2 778	644	5 604	3 184	2 641	543
1992	5 411	3 580	2 813	767	5 791	3 370	2 737	633
1993	5 596	3 673	2 958	715	5 945	3 418	2 851	567
1994	5 715	3 712	3 065	646	6 064	3 528	2 962	566
1995	5 786	3 761	3 159	601	6 105	3 637	3 086	549
1996	5 933	3 786	3 164	622	6 341	3 865	3 304	561
1997	6 075	3 879	3 276	603	6 557	4 170	3 594	576
1998	6 180	4 030	3 494	537	6 694	4 345	3 810	535
1999	6 316	4 079	3 570	508	6 941	4 546	4 061	485
2000	6 621	4 343	3 835	509	7 112	4 634	4 179	455
2001	6 667	4 315	3 737	579	7 209	4 653	4 144	509
2002	6 783	4 365	3 694	671	7 374	4 647	4 033	615
2003	7 272	4 542	3 810	734	7 878	4 935	4 262	673
2004	7 493	4 686	3 960	726	8 018	5 019	4 367	652
2005	7 689	4 876	4 173	704	8 344	5 277	4 631	646
2006	7 919	5 046	4 407	639	8 539	5 365	4 779	587
2007	8 219	5 213	4 563	649	8 811	5 490	4 965	525
2008	8 251	5 248	4 464	785	8 916	5 583	4 935	647
2009	8 528	5 248	4 100	1 147	9 129	5 491	4 607	884
2010	8 887	5 403	4 197	1 206	9 548	5 789	4 779	1 010
2011	9 075	5 478	4 299	1 179	9 811	5 890	4 845	1 045
Married, Spouse Present								
1990	5 952	4 760	4 491	269	5 677	3 630	3 429	202
1991	6 021	4 796	4 506	290	5 713	3 633	3 408	226
1992	6 093	4 820	4 455	365	5 796	3 749	3 477	271
1993	6 241	4 881	4 539	342	5 894	3 759	3 506	254
1994	6 391	4 997	4 695	304	6 035	3 871	3 648	223
1995	6 503	5 096	4 837	259	6 219	3 999	3 773	226
1996	6 563	5 123	4 895	228	6 286	4 101	3 910	191
1997	6 677	5 215	5 006	210	6 373	4 138	3 946	192
1998	6 769	5 328	5 130	198	6 609	4 323	4 145	177
1999	6 998	5 479	5 286	193	6 882	4 566	4 394	172
2000	7 392	5 818	5 627	191	7 363	4 802	4 627	175
2001	7 598	5 987	5 742	245	7 533	4 900	4 681	219
2002	7 818	6 186	5 855	331	7 676	4 966	4 690	275
2003	8 204	6 496	6 124	372	8 112	5 241	4 955	287
2004	8 420	6 615	6 310	305	8 339	5 301	5 051	248
2005	8 511	6 630	6 353	276	8 340	5 342	5 097	246
2006	8 716	6 739	6 493	246	8 376	5 364	5 161	203
2007	8 985	6 961	6 720	241	8 606	5 518	5 299	219
2008	9 086	7 046	6 703	343	8 917	5 738	5 502	236
2009	9 080	6 972	6 354	617	8 889	5 680	5 316	363
2010	9 043	6 941	6 293	648	8 893	5 581	5 170	412
2011	9 216	7 003	6 413	590	8 987	5 586	5 185	401
Divorced, Widowed, or Separated								
1990	1 932	1 247	1 123	126	4 507	2 299	2 095	205
1991	1 983	1 295	1 142	153	4 547	2 274	2 062	213
1992	2 115	1 395	1 213	182	4 628	2 354	2 128	227
1993	2 125	1 366	1 196	170	4 749	2 402	2 163	238
1994	2 189	1 382	1 239	143	4 865	2 485	2 262	222
1995	2 155	1 359	1 235	123	4 901	2 505	2 320	186
1996	2 222	1 393	1 261	133	4 929	2 566	2 366	200
1997	2 387	1 528	1 405	122	5 071	2 674	2 475	199
1998	2 457	1 567	1 466	101	5 033	2 667	2 487	179
1999	2 478	1 543	1 451	91	5 051	2 648	2 490	158
2000	2 581	1 653	1 555	98	5 288	2 787	2 643	143
2001	2 565	1 617	1 506	112	5 408	2 863	2 694	168
2002	2 622	1 641	1 505	136	5 513	2 908	2 695	213
2003	2 709	1 691	1 533	158	5 700	3 059	2 818	240
2004	2 751	1 685	1 542	142	5 691	3 011	2 783	228
2005	2 923	1 833	1 684	148	5 827	3 062	2 844	220
2006	2 949	1 857	1 719	138	6 053	3 223	3 035	186
2007	2 896	1 805	1 682	123	6 097	3 203	3 025	177
2008	3 049	1 875	1 696	179	6 029	3 162	2 938	225
2009	3 094	1 853	1 584	268	6 178	3 256	2 919	337
2010	3 163	1 913	1 616	296	6 221	3 178	2 840	338
2011	3 225	1 942	1 658	283	6 227	3 139	2 779	360

Note: See notes and definitions for information on historical comparability.

Table 1-5. Employment Status of the Civilian Noninstitutional Population, by Region, Division, State, and Selected Territory, 2010–2011

(Thousands of people, percent.)

Region, division, and state	2010						2011					
	Civilian noninstitutional population	Civilian labor force					Civilian noninstitutional population	Civilian labor force				
		Total	Participation rate	Employed	Unemployed	Unemployment rate		Total	Participation rate	Employed	Unemployed	Unemployment rate
UNITED STATES[1]	237 830	153 889	64.7	139 064	14 825	9.6	239 618	153 617	64.1	139 869	13 747	8.9
Northeast	43 812	28 287	64.6	25 824	2 462	8.7	44 082	28 186	63.9	25 880	2 305	8.2
New England	11 520	7 756	67.3	7 097	659	8.5	11 589	7 740	66.8	7 140	599	7.7
Connecticut	2 796	1 917	68.6	1 738	178	9.3	2 822	1 918	68.0	1 749	169	8.8
Maine	1 073	701	65.3	643	57	8.2	1 079	704	65.2	651	53	7.5
Massachusetts	5 245	3 469	66.1	3 181	289	8.3	5 275	3 456	65.5	3 202	254	7.4
New Hampshire	1 056	739	70.0	694	45	6.1	1 060	738	69.6	698	40	5.4
Rhode Island	842	570	67.7	504	67	11.7	843	563	66.8	500	63	11.3
Vermont	508	360	70.9	337	23	6.4	511	359	70.3	339	20	5.6
Middle Atlantic	32 292	20 531	63.6	18 728	1 803	8.8	32 492	20 446	62.9	18 740	1 706	8.3
New Jersey	6 860	4 554	66.4	4 117	437	9.6	6 915	4 556	65.9	4 132	424	9.3
New York	15 379	9 587	62.3	8 762	825	8.6	15 452	9 504	61.5	8 730	775	8.2
Pennsylvania	10 053	6 390	63.6	5 849	541	8.5	10 125	6 386	63.1	5 879	507	7.9
Midwest	51 801	34 467	66.5	31 210	3 257	9.5	52 080	34 308	65.9	31 442	2 866	8.4
East North Central	36 016	23 473	65.2	21 014	2 459	10.5	36 172	23 281	64.4	21 143	2 137	9.2
Illinois	9 905	6 603	66.7	5 911	692	10.5	9 950	6 566	66.0	5 925	640	9.8
Indiana	4 964	3 177	64.0	2 856	320	10.1	5 006	3 188	63.7	2 901	287	9.0
Michigan	7 739	4 747	61.3	4 147	601	12.7	7 753	4 658	60.1	4 178	480	10.3
Ohio	8 970	5 864	65.4	5 279	586	10.0	8 999	5 806	64.5	5 305	501	8.6
Wisconsin	4 438	3 083	69.5	2 822	261	8.5	4 465	3 062	68.6	2 833	229	7.5
West North Central	15 785	10 994	69.6	10 196	798	7.3	15 908	11 028	69.3	10 299	729	6.6
Iowa	2 359	1 670	70.8	1 565	105	6.3	2 377	1 664	70.0	1 566	98	5.9
Kansas	2 150	1 505	70.0	1 397	108	7.2	2 166	1 505	69.5	1 404	101	6.7
Minnesota	4 117	2 959	71.9	2 742	217	7.3	4 152	2 978	71.7	2 787	191	6.4
Missouri	4 630	3 053	65.9	2 767	286	9.4	4 651	3 046	65.5	2 786	261	8.6
Nebraska	1 387	989	71.3	942	46	4.7	1 403	1 005	71.6	961	45	4.4
North Dakota	521	376	72.2	361	14	3.8	533	383	71.9	370	13	3.5
South Dakota	620	443	71.5	421	22	5.0	625	446	71.4	425	21	4.7
South	87 697	55 598	63.4	50 421	5 176	9.3	88 998	56 134	63.1	51 192	4 942	8.8
South Atlantic	46 422	29 489	63.5	26 560	2 929	9.9	47 108	29 747	63.1	26 986	2 760	9.3
Delaware	701	437	62.3	402	35	8.0	711	439	61.7	407	32	7.3
District of Columbia	503	343	68.2	309	35	10.1	514	344	66.9	309	35	10.2
Florida	14 941	9 132	61.1	8 102	1 030	11.3	15 215	9 249	60.8	8 278	970	10.5
Georgia	7 320	4 695	64.1	4 214	481	10.2	7 379	4 725	64.0	4 262	463	9.8
Maryland	4 486	3 057	68.1	2 818	239	787.8	4 545	3 072	67.6	2 856	217	7.0
North Carolina	7 286	4 617	63.4	4 112	505	10.9	7 405	4 654	62.8	4 165	489	10.5
South Carolina	3 566	2 151	60.3	1 909	241	11.2	3 616	2 157	59.7	1 936	221	10.3
Virginia	6 143	4 255	69.3	3 960	295	6.9	6 237	4 306	69.0	4 037	269	6.2
West Virginia	1 477	802	54.3	734	68	8.5	1 487	800	53.8	736	64	8.0
East South Central	14 197	8 641	60.9	7 784	857	9.9	14 323	8 735	61.0	7 910	824	9.4
Alabama	3 692	2 179	59.0	1 972	207	9.5	3 731	2 191	58.7	1 994	197	9.0
Kentucky	3 350	2 060	61.5	1 849	211	10.2	3 371	2 068	61.3	1 871	197	9.5
Mississippi	2 227	1 317	59.1	1 179	138	10.5	2 244	1 344	59.9	1 201	143	10.7
Tennessee	4 928	3 084	62.6	2 783	301	9.8	4 977	3 133	62.9	2 845	288	9.2
West South Central	27 078	17 468	64.5	16 078	1 390	8.0	27 567	17 653	64.0	16 296	1 357	7.7
Arkansas	2 233	1 357	60.8	1 249	108	7.9	2 253	1 370	60.8	1 260	110	8.0
Louisiana	3 439	2 070	60.2	1 915	155	7.5	3 475	2 061	59.3	1 909	151	7.3
Oklahoma	2 834	1 771	62.5	1 649	122	6.9	2 870	1 771	61.7	1 662	109	6.2
Texas	18 573	12 270	66.1	11 265	1 005	8.2	18 969	12 452	65.6	11 465	987	7.9
West	55 097	35 902	65.2	31 938	3 965	11.0	55 856	35 878	64.2	32 160	3 718	10.4
Mountain	16 737	11 073	66.2	10 007	1 066	9.6	16 926	10 989	64.9	10 009	980	8.9
Arizona	4 898	3 100	63.3	2 775	325	10.5	4 926	3 034	61.6	2 747	288	9.5
Colorado	3 870	2 725	70.4	2 481	244	8.9	3 922	2 723	69.4	2 497	226	8.3
Idaho	1 166	763	65.4	697	67	8.8	1 181	771	65.3	704	67	8.7
Montana	778	500	64.3	466	34	6.9	787	504	64.0	470	35	6.8
Nevada	2 062	1 386	67.2	1 195	190	13.7	2 095	1 386	66.2	1 198	188	13.5
New Mexico	1 560	934	59.9	860	74	7.9	1 583	928	58.6	859	69	7.4
Utah	1 972	1 362	69.1	1 253	109	8.0	1 996	1 338	67.0	1 248	90	6.7
Wyoming	431	303	70.3	282	21	7.0	438	304	69.4	286	18	6.0
Pacific	38 359	24 830	64.7	21 931	2 899	11.7	38 930	24 889	63.9	22 151	2 738	11.0
Alaska	518	364	70.3	335	29	8.0	529	367	69.4	339	28	7.6
California	28 531	18 316	64.2	16 052	2 265	12.4	28 968	18 385	63.5	16 227	2 158	11.7
Hawaii	1 028	649	63.1	605	45	6.9	1 051	661	62.9	616	44	6.7
Oregon	3 035	1 984	65.4	1 772	211	10.7	3 067	1 992	64.9	1 804	188	9.5
Washington	5 247	3 516	67.0	3 167	349	9.9	5 315	3 485	65.6	3 165	319	9.2

Note: Data refer to place of residence. Region and division data are derived from summing the component states. Sub-national data reflect revised population controls and model reestimation.

[1]Due to separate processing and weighing procedures, totals for the United States differ from the results obtained by aggregating data for regions, divisions, or states.

Table 1-6. Civilian Noninstitutional Population, by Age, Race, Sex, and Hispanic Origin, 1948–2011

(Thousands of people.)

Race, Hispanic origin, sex, and year	16 years and over	16 to 19 years			20 years and over						
		Total	16 to 17 years	18 to 19 years	Total	20 to 24 years	25 to 34 years	35 to 44 years	45 to 54 years	55 to 64 years	65 years and over
ALL RACES											
Both Sexes											
1948	103 068	8 449	4 265	4 185	94 618	11 530	22 610	20 097	16 771	12 885	10 720
1949	103 994	8 215	4 139	4 079	95 778	11 312	22 822	20 401	17 002	13 201	11 035
1950	104 995	8 143	4 076	4 068	96 851	11 080	23 013	20 681	17 240	13 469	11 363
1951	104 621	7 865	4 096	3 771	96 755	10 167	22 843	20 863	17 464	13 692	11 724
1952	105 231	7 922	4 234	3 689	97 305	9 389	23 044	21 137	17 716	13 889	12 126
1953	107 056	8 014	4 241	3 773	99 041	8 960	23 266	21 922	17 991	13 830	13 075
1954	108 321	8 224	4 336	3 889	100 095	8 885	23 304	22 135	18 305	14 085	13 375
1955	109 683	8 364	4 440	3 925	101 318	9 036	23 249	22 348	18 643	14 309	13 728
1956	110 954	8 434	4 482	3 953	102 518	9 271	23 072	22 567	19 012	14 516	14 075
1957	112 265	8 612	4 587	4 026	103 653	9 486	22 849	22 786	19 424	14 727	14 376
1958	113 727	8 986	4 872	4 114	104 737	9 733	22 563	23 025	19 832	14 923	14 657
1959	115 329	9 618	5 337	4 282	105 711	9 975	22 201	23 207	20 203	15 134	14 985
1960	117 245	10 187	5 573	4 615	107 056	10 273	21 998	23 437	20 601	15 409	15 336
1961	118 771	10 513	5 462	5 052	108 255	10 583	21 829	23 585	20 893	15 675	15 685
1962	120 153	10 652	5 503	5 150	109 500	10 852	21 503	23 797	20 916	15 874	16 554
1963	122 416	11 370	6 301	5 070	111 045	11 464	21 400	23 948	21 144	16 138	16 945
1964	124 485	12 111	6 974	5 139	112 372	12 017	21 367	23 940	21 452	16 442	17 150
1965	126 513	12 930	6 936	5 995	113 582	12 442	21 417	23 832	21 728	16 727	17 432
1966	128 058	13 592	6 914	6 679	114 463	12 638	21 543	23 579	21 977	17 007	17 715
1967	129 874	13 480	7 003	6 480	116 391	13 421	22 057	23 313	22 256	17 310	18 029
1968	132 028	13 698	7 200	6 499	118 328	13 891	22 912	23 036	22 534	17 614	18 338
1969	134 335	14 095	7 422	6 673	120 238	14 488	23 645	22 709	22 806	17 930	18 657
1970	137 085	14 519	7 643	6 876	122 566	15 323	24 435	22 489	23 059	18 250	19 007
1971	140 216	15 022	7 849	7 173	125 193	16 345	25 337	22 274	23 244	18 581	19 406
1972	144 126	15 510	8 076	7 435	128 614	17 143	26 740	22 358	23 338	19 007	20 023
1973	147 096	15 840	8 227	7 613	131 253	17 692	28 172	22 287	23 431	19 281	20 389
1974	150 120	16 180	8 373	7 809	133 938	17 994	29 439	22 461	23 578	19 517	20 945
1975	153 153	16 418	8 419	7 999	136 733	18 595	30 710	22 526	23 535	19 844	21 525
1976	156 150	16 614	8 442	8 171	139 536	19 109	31 953	22 796	23 409	20 185	22 083
1977	159 033	16 688	8 482	8 206	142 345	19 582	33 117	23 296	23 197	20 557	22 597
1978	161 910	16 695	8 484	8 211	145 216	20 007	34 091	24 099	22 977	20 875	23 166
1979	164 863	16 657	8 389	8 268	148 205	20 353	35 261	24 861	22 752	21 210	23 767
1980	167 745	16 543	8 279	8 264	151 202	20 635	36 558	25 578	22 563	21 520	24 350
1981	170 130	16 214	8 068	8 145	153 916	20 820	37 777	26 291	22 422	21 756	24 850
1982	172 271	15 763	7 714	8 049	156 508	20 845	38 492	27 611	22 264	21 909	25 387
1983	174 215	15 274	7 385	7 889	158 941	20 799	39 147	28 932	22 167	22 003	25 892
1984	176 383	14 735	7 196	7 538	161 648	20 688	39 999	30 251	22 226	22 052	26 433
1985	178 206	14 506	7 232	7 274	163 700	20 097	40 670	31 379	22 418	22 140	26 997
1986	180 587	14 496	7 386	7 110	166 091	19 569	41 731	32 550	22 732	22 011	27 497
1987	182 753	14 606	7 501	7 104	168 147	18 970	42 297	33 755	23 183	21 835	28 108
1988	184 613	14 527	7 284	7 243	170 085	18 434	42 611	34 784	24 004	21 641	28 612
1989	186 393	14 223	6 886	7 338	172 169	18 025	42 845	35 977	24 744	21 406	29 173
1990	189 164	14 520	6 893	7 626	174 644	18 902	42 976	37 719	25 081	20 719	29 247
1991	190 925	14 073	6 901	7 173	176 852	18 963	42 688	39 116	25 709	20 675	29 700
1992	192 805	13 840	6 907	6 933	178 965	18 846	42 278	39 852	27 206	20 604	30 179
1993	194 838	13 935	7 010	6 925	180 903	18 642	41 771	40 733	28 549	20 574	30 634
1994	196 814	14 196	7 245	6 951	182 619	18 353	41 306	41 534	29 778	20 635	31 012
1995	198 584	14 511	7 407	7 104	184 073	17 864	40 798	42 254	30 974	20 735	31 448
1996	200 591	14 934	7 678	7 256	185 656	17 409	40 252	43 086	32 167	20 990	31 751
1997	203 133	15 365	7 861	7 504	187 769	17 442	39 559	43 883	33 391	21 505	31 989
1998	205 220	15 644	7 895	7 749	189 576	17 593	38 778	44 299	34 373	22 296	32 237
1999	207 753	16 040	8 060	7 979	191 713	17 968	37 976	44 635	35 587	23 064	32 484
2000	212 577	15 912	7 978	7 934	196 664	18 311	38 703	44 312	37 642	24 230	33 466
2001	215 092	15 929	8 020	7 909	199 164	18 877	38 505	44 195	38 904	25 011	33 672
2002	217 570	15 994	8 099	7 895	201 576	19 348	38 472	43 894	39 711	26 343	33 808
2003	221 168	16 096	8 561	7 535	205 072	19 801	39 021	43 746	40 522	27 728	34 253
2004	223 357	16 222	8 574	7 648	207 134	20 197	38 939	43 226	41 245	28 919	34 609
2005	226 082	16 398	8 778	7 619	209 685	20 276	39 064	43 005	42 107	30 165	35 068
2006	228 815	16 678	9 089	7 589	212 137	20 265	39 230	42 753	42 901	31 375	35 613
2007	231 867	16 982	9 222	7 760	214 885	20 427	39 751	42 401	43 544	32 533	36 228
2008	233 788	17 075	9 133	7 942	216 713	20 409	39 993	41 699	43 960	33 491	37 161
2009	235 801	17 043	8 944	8 100	218 757	20 524	40 280	40 919	44 365	34 671	37 998
2010	237 830	16 901	8 943	7 957	220 929	21 047	40 903	40 090	44 297	35 885	38 706
2011	239 618	16 774	8 727	8 048	222 843	21 423	41 364	39 499	43 842	36 987	39 729

Table 1-6. Civilian Noninstitutional Population, by Age, Race, Sex, and Hispanic Origin, 1948–2011 —Continued

(Thousands of people.)

Race, Hispanic origin, sex, and year	16 years and over	16 to 19 years			20 years and over						
		Total	16 to 17 years	18 to 19 years	Total	20 to 24 years	25 to 34 years	35 to 44 years	45 to 54 years	55 to 64 years	65 years and over
ALL RACES											
Men											
1948	49 996	4 078	2 128	1 951	45 918	5 527	10 767	9 798	8 290	6 441	5 093
1949	50 321	3 946	2 062	1 884	46 378	5 405	10 871	9 926	8 379	6 568	5 226
1950	50 725	3 962	2 043	1 920	46 763	5 270	10 963	10 034	8 472	6 664	5 357
1951	49 727	3 725	2 039	1 687	46 001	4 451	10 709	10 049	8 551	6 737	5 503
1952	49 700	3 767	2 121	1 647	45 932	3 788	10 855	10 164	8 655	6 798	5 670
1953	50 750	3 823	2 122	1 701	46 927	3 482	11 020	10 632	8 878	6 798	6 119
1954	51 395	3 953	2 174	1 780	47 441	3 509	11 067	10 718	9 018	6 885	6 241
1955	52 109	4 022	2 225	1 798	48 086	3 708	11 068	10 804	9 164	6 960	6 380
1956	52 723	4 020	2 238	1 783	48 704	3 970	10 983	10 889	9 322	7 032	6 505
1957	53 315	4 083	2 284	1 800	49 231	4 166	10 889	10 965	9 499	7 109	6 602
1958	54 033	4 293	2 435	1 858	49 740	4 339	10 787	11 076	9 675	7 179	6 683
1959	54 793	4 652	2 681	1 971	50 140	4 488	10 625	11 149	9 832	7 259	6 785
1960	55 662	4 963	2 805	2 159	50 698	4 679	10 514	11 230	10 000	7 373	6 901
1961	56 286	5 112	2 742	2 371	51 173	4 844	10 440	11 286	10 112	7 483	7 006
1962	56 831	5 150	2 764	2 386	51 681	4 925	10 207	11 389	10 162	7 610	7 386
1963	57 921	5 496	3 162	2 334	52 425	5 240	10 165	11 476	10 274	7 740	7 526
1964	58 847	5 866	3 503	2 364	52 981	5 520	10 144	11 466	10 402	7 873	7 574
1965	59 782	6 318	3 488	2 831	53 463	5 701	10 182	11 427	10 512	7 990	7 649
1966	60 262	6 658	3 478	3 180	53 603	5 663	10 224	11 294	10 598	8 099	7 723
1967	60 905	6 537	3 528	3 010	54 367	5 977	10 495	11 161	10 705	8 218	7 809
1968	61 847	6 683	3 634	3 049	55 165	6 127	10 944	11 040	10 819	8 336	7 897
1969	62 898	6 928	3 741	3 187	55 969	6 379	11 309	10 890	10 935	8 464	7 990
1970	64 304	7 145	3 848	3 299	57 157	6 861	11 750	10 810	11 052	8 590	8 093
1971	65 942	7 430	3 954	3 477	58 511	7 511	12 227	10 721	11 129	8 711	8 208
1972	67 835	7 705	4 081	3 624	60 130	8 061	12 911	10 762	11 167	8 895	8 330
1973	69 292	7 855	4 152	3 703	61 436	8 429	13 641	10 746	11 202	8 990	8 426
1974	70 808	8 012	4 231	3 781	62 796	8 600	14 262	10 834	11 315	9 140	8 641
1975	72 291	8 134	4 252	3 882	64 158	8 950	14 899	10 874	11 298	9 286	8 852
1976	73 759	8 244	4 266	3 978	65 515	9 237	15 528	11 010	11 243	9 444	9 053
1977	75 193	8 288	4 290	4 000	66 904	9 477	16 108	11 260	11 144	9 616	9 297
1978	76 576	8 309	4 295	4 014	68 268	9 693	16 598	11 665	11 045	9 758	9 509
1979	78 020	8 310	4 251	4 060	69 709	9 873	17 193	12 046	10 944	9 907	9 746
1980	79 398	8 260	4 195	4 064	71 138	10 023	17 833	12 400	10 861	10 042	9 979
1981	80 511	8 092	4 087	4 005	72 419	10 116	18 427	12 758	10 797	10 151	10 170
1982	81 523	7 879	3 911	3 968	73 644	10 136	18 787	13 410	10 726	10 215	10 371
1983	82 531	7 659	3 750	3 908	74 872	10 140	19 143	14 067	10 689	10 261	10 573
1984	83 605	7 386	3 655	3 731	76 219	10 108	19 596	14 719	10 724	10 285	10 788
1985	84 469	7 275	3 689	3 586	77 195	9 746	19 864	15 265	10 844	10 392	11 084
1986	85 798	7 275	3 768	3 507	78 523	9 498	20 498	15 858	10 986	10 336	11 347
1987	86 899	7 335	3 824	3 510	79 565	9 195	20 781	16 475	11 215	10 267	11 632
1988	87 857	7 304	3 715	3 588	80 553	8 931	20 937	17 008	11 625	10 193	11 859
1989	88 762	7 143	3 524	3 619	81 619	8 743	21 080	17 590	11 981	10 092	12 134
1990	90 377	7 347	3 534	3 813	83 030	9 320	21 117	18 529	12 238	9 778	12 049
1991	91 278	7 134	3 548	3 586	84 144	9 367	20 977	19 213	12 554	9 780	12 254
1992	92 270	7 023	3 542	3 481	85 247	9 326	20 792	19 585	13 271	9 776	12 496
1993	93 332	7 076	3 595	3 481	86 256	9 216	20 569	20 037	13 944	9 773	12 717
1994	94 355	7 203	3 718	3 486	87 151	9 074	20 361	20 443	14 545	9 810	12 918
1995	95 178	7 367	3 794	3 573	87 811	8 835	20 079	20 800	15 111	9 856	13 130
1996	96 206	7 600	3 955	3 645	88 606	8 611	19 775	21 222	15 674	9 997	13 327
1997	97 715	7 836	4 053	3 783	89 879	8 706	19 478	21 669	16 276	10 282	13 469
1998	98 758	7 968	4 059	3 909	90 790	8 804	19 094	21 857	16 773	10 649	13 613
1999	99 722	8 167	4 143	4 024	91 555	8 899	18 565	21 969	17 335	11 008	13 779
2000	101 964	8 089	4 096	3 993	93 875	9 101	19 106	21 683	18 365	11 583	14 037
2001	103 282	8 101	4 102	3 999	95 181	9 368	19 056	21 643	18 987	11 972	14 155
2002	104 585	8 146	4 140	4 006	96 439	9 627	19 037	21 523	19 379	12 641	14 233
2003	106 435	8 163	4 365	3 797	98 272	9 878	19 347	21 463	19 784	13 305	14 496
2004	107 710	8 234	4 318	3 916	99 476	10 125	19 358	21 255	20 160	13 894	14 684
2005	109 151	8 317	4 481	3 836	100 835	10 181	19 446	21 177	20 585	14 502	14 944
2006	110 605	8 459	4 613	3 846	102 145	10 191	19 568	21 082	20 991	15 095	15 219
2007	112 173	8 618	4 658	3 960	103 555	10 291	19 858	20 910	21 313	15 658	15 525
2008	113 113	8 660	4 625	4 035	104 453	10 249	19 999	20 567	21 512	16 123	16 002
2009	114 136	8 643	4 548	4 095	105 493	10 284	20 167	20 199	21 731	16 698	16 414
2010	115 174	8 578	4 540	4 038	106 596	10 550	20 465	19 807	21 713	17 291	16 769
2011	116 317	8 582	4 486	4 095	107 736	10 844	20 711	19 446	21 451	17 810	17 474

Table 1-6. Civilian Noninstitutional Population, by Age, Race, Sex, and Hispanic Origin, 1948–2011
—Continued

(Thousands of people.)

Race, Hispanic origin, sex, and year	16 years and over	16 to 19 years			20 years and over						
		Total	16 to 17 years	18 to 19 years	Total	20 to 24 years	25 to 34 years	35 to 44 years	45 to 54 years	55 to 64 years	65 years and over
ALL RACES											
Women											
1948	53 071	4 371	2 137	2 234	48 700	6 003	11 843	10 299	8 481	6 444	5 627
1949	53 670	4 269	2 077	2 195	49 400	5 907	11 951	10 475	8 623	6 633	5 809
1950	54 270	4 181	2 033	2 148	50 088	5 810	12 050	10 647	8 768	6 805	6 006
1951	54 895	4 140	2 057	2 084	50 754	5 716	12 134	10 814	8 913	6 955	6 221
1952	55 529	4 155	2 113	2 042	51 373	5 601	12 189	10 973	9 061	7 091	6 456
1953	56 305	4 191	2 119	2 072	52 114	5 478	12 246	11 290	9 113	7 032	6 956
1954	56 925	4 271	2 162	2 109	52 654	5 376	12 237	11 417	9 287	7 200	7 134
1955	57 574	4 342	2 215	2 127	53 232	5 328	12 181	11 544	9 479	7 349	7 348
1956	58 228	4 414	2 244	2 170	53 814	5 301	12 089	11 678	9 690	7 484	7 570
1957	58 951	4 529	2 303	2 226	54 421	5 320	11 960	11 821	9 925	7 618	7 774
1958	59 690	4 693	2 437	2 256	54 997	5 394	11 776	11 949	10 157	7 744	7 974
1959	60 534	4 966	2 656	2 311	55 570	5 487	11 576	12 058	10 371	7 875	8 200
1960	61 582	5 224	2 768	2 456	56 358	5 594	11 484	12 207	10 601	8 036	8 435
1961	62 484	5 401	2 720	2 681	57 082	5 739	11 389	12 299	10 781	8 192	8 679
1962	63 321	5 502	2 739	2 764	57 819	5 927	11 296	12 408	10 754	8 264	9 168
1963	64 494	5 874	3 139	2 736	58 620	6 224	11 235	12 472	10 870	8 398	9 419
1964	65 637	6 245	3 471	2 775	59 391	6 497	11 223	12 474	11 050	8 569	9 576
1965	66 731	6 612	3 448	3 164	60 119	6 741	11 235	12 405	11 216	8 737	9 783
1966	67 795	6 934	3 436	3 499	60 860	6 975	11 319	12 285	11 379	8 908	9 992
1967	68 968	6 943	3 475	3 470	62 026	7 445	11 562	12 152	11 551	9 092	10 220
1968	70 179	7 015	3 566	3 450	63 164	7 764	11 968	11 996	11 715	9 278	10 441
1969	71 436	7 167	3 681	3 486	64 269	8 109	12 336	11 819	11 871	9 466	10 667
1970	72 782	7 373	3 796	3 578	65 408	8 462	12 684	11 679	12 008	9 659	10 914
1971	74 274	7 591	3 895	3 697	66 682	8 834	13 110	11 553	12 115	9 870	11 198
1972	76 290	7 805	3 994	3 811	68 484	9 082	13 829	11 597	12 171	10 113	11 693
1973	77 804	7 985	4 076	3 909	69 819	9 263	14 531	11 541	12 229	10 290	11 963
1974	79 312	8 168	4 142	4 028	71 144	9 393	15 177	11 627	12 263	10 377	12 304
1975	80 860	8 285	4 168	4 117	72 576	9 645	15 811	11 652	12 237	10 558	12 673
1976	82 390	8 370	4 176	4 194	74 020	9 872	16 425	11 786	12 166	10 742	13 030
1977	83 840	8 400	4 193	4 206	75 441	10 103	17 008	12 036	12 053	10 940	13 300
1978	85 334	8 386	4 189	4 197	76 948	10 315	17 493	12 435	11 932	11 118	13 658
1979	86 843	8 347	4 139	4 208	78 496	10 480	18 070	12 815	11 808	11 303	14 021
1980	88 348	8 283	4 083	4 200	80 065	10 612	18 725	13 177	11 701	11 478	14 372
1981	89 618	8 121	3 981	4 140	81 497	10 705	19 350	13 533	11 625	11 605	14 680
1982	90 748	7 884	3 804	4 081	82 864	10 709	19 705	14 201	11 538	11 694	15 017
1983	91 684	7 616	3 635	3 981	84 069	10 660	20 004	14 865	11 478	11 742	15 319
1984	92 778	7 349	3 542	3 807	85 429	10 580	20 403	15 532	11 501	11 768	15 645
1985	93 736	7 231	3 543	3 688	86 506	10 351	20 805	16 114	11 574	11 748	15 913
1986	94 789	7 221	3 618	3 603	87 567	10 072	21 233	16 692	11 746	11 675	16 150
1987	95 853	7 271	3 677	3 594	88 583	9 776	21 516	17 279	11 968	11 567	16 476
1988	96 756	7 224	3 569	3 655	89 532	9 503	21 674	17 776	12 378	11 448	16 753
1989	97 630	7 080	3 361	3 719	90 550	9 282	21 765	18 387	12 763	11 314	17 039
1990	98 787	7 173	3 359	3 813	91 614	9 582	21 859	19 190	12 843	10 941	17 198
1991	99 646	6 939	3 353	3 586	92 708	9 597	21 711	19 903	13 155	10 895	17 446
1992	100 535	6 818	3 366	3 452	93 718	9 520	21 486	20 267	13 935	10 828	17 682
1993	101 506	6 859	3 415	3 444	94 647	9 426	21 202	20 696	14 605	10 801	17 917
1994	102 460	6 993	3 528	3 465	95 467	9 279	20 945	21 091	15 233	10 825	18 094
1995	103 406	7 144	3 613	3 531	96 262	9 029	20 719	21 454	15 862	10 879	18 318
1996	104 385	7 335	3 723	3 612	97 050	8 798	20 477	21 865	16 493	10 993	18 424
1997	105 418	7 528	3 808	3 721	97 889	8 736	20 081	22 214	17 115	11 224	18 520
1998	106 462	7 676	3 835	3 840	98 786	8 790	19 683	22 442	17 600	11 646	18 625
1999	108 031	7 873	3 917	3 955	100 158	9 069	19 411	22 666	18 251	12 056	18 705
2000	110 613	7 823	3 882	3 941	102 790	9 211	19 597	22 628	19 276	12 647	19 430
2001	111 811	7 828	3 917	3 910	103 983	9 509	19 449	22 552	19 917	13 039	19 517
2002	112 985	7 848	3 959	3 889	105 136	9 721	19 435	22 371	20 332	13 703	19 575
2003	114 733	7 934	4 195	3 738	106 800	9 924	19 674	22 283	20 738	14 423	19 758
2004	115 647	7 989	4 257	3 732	107 658	10 072	19 581	21 970	21 085	15 025	19 925
2005	116 931	8 081	4 297	3 784	108 850	10 095	19 618	21 828	21 521	15 663	20 125
2006	118 210	8 218	4 476	3 742	109 992	10 074	19 662	21 671	21 910	16 280	20 394
2007	119 694	8 364	4 564	3 800	111 330	10 137	19 893	21 491	22 231	16 876	20 703
2008	120 675	8 415	4 508	3 907	112 260	10 160	19 994	21 132	22 448	17 367	21 160
2009	121 665	8 401	4 396	4 004	113 265	10 240	20 113	20 721	22 633	17 973	21 584
2010	122 656	8 323	4 403	3 919	114 333	10 497	20 438	20 283	22 584	18 594	21 937
2011	123 300	8 193	4 241	3 952	115 107	10 579	20 653	20 053	22 391	19 177	22 255

Table 1-6. Civilian Noninstitutional Population, by Age, Race, Sex, and Hispanic Origin, 1948–2011
—Continued

(Thousands of people.)

Race, Hispanic origin, sex, and year	16 years and over	16 to 19 years			20 years and over						
		Total	16 to 17 years	18 to 19 years	Total	20 to 24 years	25 to 34 years	35 to 44 years	45 to 54 years	55 to 64 years	65 years and over
WHITE											
Both Sexes											
1954	97 705	7 180	3 786	3 394	90 524	7 794	20 818	19 915	16 569	12 993	12 438
1955	98 880	7 292	3 874	3 419	91 586	7 912	20 742	20 110	16 869	13 169	12 785
1956	99 976	7 346	3 908	3 438	92 629	8 106	20 564	20 314	17 198	13 341	13 105
1957	101 119	7 505	4 007	3 498	93 612	8 293	20 342	20 514	17 562	13 518	13 383
1958	102 392	7 843	4 271	3 573	94 547	8 498	20 063	20 734	17 924	13 681	13 645
1959	103 803	8 430	4 707	3 725	95 370	8 697	19 715	20 893	18 257	13 858	13 951
1960	105 282	8 924	4 909	4 016	96 355	8 927	19 470	21 049	18 578	14 070	14 260
1961	106 604	9 211	4 785	4 427	97 390	9 203	19 289	21 169	18 845	14 304	14 581
1962	107 715	9 343	4 818	4 526	98 371	9 484	18 974	21 293	18 872	14 450	15 297
1963	109 705	9 978	5 549	4 430	99 725	10 069	18 867	21 398	19 082	14 681	15 629
1964	111 534	10 616	6 137	4 481	100 916	10 568	18 838	21 375	19 360	14 957	15 816
1965	113 284	11 319	6 049	5 271	101 963	10 935	18 882	21 258	19 604	15 215	16 070
1966	114 566	11 862	5 993	5 870	102 702	11 094	18 989	21 005	19 822	15 469	16 322
1967	116 100	11 682	6 051	5 632	104 417	11 797	19 464	20 745	20 067	15 745	16 602
1968	117 948	11 840	6 225	5 616	106 107	12 184	20 245	20 474	20 310	16 018	16 875
1969	119 913	12 179	6 418	5 761	107 733	12 677	20 892	20 156	20 546	16 305	17 156
1970	122 174	12 521	6 591	5 931	109 652	13 359	21 546	19 929	20 760	16 591	17 469
1971	124 758	12 937	6 750	6 189	111 821	14 208	22 295	19 694	20 907	16 884	17 833
1972	127 906	13 301	6 910	6 392	114 603	14 897	23 555	19 673	20 950	17 250	18 278
1973	130 097	13 533	7 021	6 512	116 563	15 264	24 685	19 532	20 991	17 484	18 607
1974	132 417	13 784	7 114	6 671	118 632	15 502	25 711	19 628	21 061	17 645	19 085
1975	134 790	13 941	7 132	6 808	120 849	15 980	26 746	19 641	20 981	17 918	19 587
1976	137 106	14 055	7 125	6 930	123 050	16 368	27 757	19 827	20 816	18 220	20 064
1977	139 380	14 095	7 150	6 944	125 285	16 728	28 703	20 231	20 575	18 540	20 508
1978	141 612	14 060	7 132	6 928	127 552	17 038	29 453	20 932	20 322	18 799	21 007
1979	143 894	13 994	7 029	6 964	129 900	17 284	30 371	21 579	20 058	19 071	21 538
1980	146 122	13 854	6 912	6 943	132 268	17 484	31 407	22 174	19 837	19 316	22 050
1981	147 908	13 516	6 704	6 813	134 392	17 609	32 367	22 778	19 666	19 485	22 487
1982	149 441	13 076	6 383	6 693	136 366	17 579	32 863	23 910	19 478	19 591	22 945
1983	150 805	12 623	6 089	6 534	138 183	17 492	33 286	25 027	19 349	19 625	23 403
1984	152 347	12 147	5 918	6 228	140 200	17 304	33 889	26 124	19 348	19 629	23 906
1985	153 679	11 900	5 922	5 978	141 780	16 853	34 450	27 100	19 405	19 620	24 352
1986	155 432	11 879	6 036	5 843	143 553	16 353	35 293	28 062	19 587	19 477	24 780
1987	156 958	11 939	6 110	5 829	145 020	15 808	35 667	29 036	19 965	19 242	25 301
1988	158 194	11 838	5 893	5 945	146 357	15 276	35 876	29 818	20 652	18 996	25 739
1989	159 338	11 530	5 506	6 023	147 809	14 879	35 951	30 774	21 287	18 743	26 175
1990	160 625	11 630	5 464	6 166	148 996	15 538	35 661	31 739	21 535	18 204	26 319
1991	161 759	11 200	5 451	5 749	150 558	15 516	35 342	32 854	22 052	18 074	26 721
1992	162 972	11 004	5 478	5 526	151 968	15 354	34 885	33 305	23 364	17 951	27 108
1993	164 289	11 078	5 562	5 516	153 210	15 087	34 365	33 919	24 456	17 892	27 493
1994	165 555	11 264	5 710	5 554	154 291	14 708	33 865	34 582	25 435	17 924	27 776
1995	166 914	11 468	5 822	5 646	155 446	14 313	33 355	35 222	26 418	17 986	28 153
1996	168 317	11 822	6 026	5 796	156 495	13 907	32 852	35 810	27 403	18 136	28 387
1997	169 993	12 181	6 213	5 968	157 812	13 983	32 091	36 325	28 388	18 511	28 514
1998	171 478	12 439	6 264	6 176	159 039	14 138	31 286	36 610	29 132	19 231	28 642
1999	173 085	12 700	6 342	6 358	160 385	14 394	30 516	36 755	30 048	19 855	28 818
2000	176 220	12 535	6 264	6 271	163 685	14 552	30 948	36 261	31 550	20 757	29 617
2001	178 111	12 556	6 291	6 265	165 556	15 001	30 770	36 113	32 475	21 434	29 762
2002	179 783	12 596	6 346	6 250	167 187	15 360	30 676	35 750	33 012	22 540	29 849
2003	181 292	12 527	6 629	5 898	168 765	15 536	30 789	35 352	33 466	23 589	30 033
2004	182 643	12 599	6 561	6 038	170 045	15 817	30 585	34 845	34 005	24 549	30 245
2005	184 446	12 690	6 768	5 921	171 757	15 871	30 592	34 554	34 649	25 534	30 556
2006	186 264	12 856	6 981	5 875	173 408	15 848	30 661	34 217	35 228	26 486	30 968
2007	188 253	13 043	7 026	6 018	175 210	15 945	31 011	33 770	35 665	27 392	31 426
2008	189 540	13 084	6 962	6 122	176 456	15 914	31 234	33 093	35 941	28 109	32 165
2009	190 902	13 035	6 775	6 261	177 867	15 963	31 471	32 378	36 166	29 022	32 867
2010	192 075	12 891	6 799	6 091	179 184	16 280	31 813	31 647	36 064	29 983	33 396
2011	193 077	12 818	6 673	6 145	180 259	16 562	32 136	31 030	35 526	30 799	34 206

Table 1-6. Civilian Noninstitutional Population, by Age, Race, Sex, and Hispanic Origin, 1948–2011
—Continued

(Thousands of people.)

Race, Hispanic origin, sex, and year	16 years and over	16 to 19 years			20 years and over						
		Total	16 to 17 years	18 to 19 years	Total	20 to 24 years	25 to 34 years	35 to 44 years	45 to 54 years	55 to 64 years	65 years and over
WHITE											
Men											
1954	46 462	3 455	1 902	1 553	43 007	3 074	9 948	9 688	8 172	6 341	5 787
1955	47 076	3 507	1 945	1 563	43 569	3 241	9 936	9 768	8 303	6 398	5 923
1956	47 602	3 500	1 955	1 546	44 102	3 464	9 851	9 848	8 446	6 455	6 038
1957	48 119	3 556	2 000	1 557	44 563	3 638	9 758	9 917	8 605	6 518	6 127
1958	48 745	3 747	2 140	1 607	44 998	3 783	9 656	10 018	8 765	6 574	6 203
1959	49 408	4 079	2 370	1 710	45 329	3 903	9 499	10 081	8 909	6 639	6 298
1960	50 065	4 349	2 476	1 874	45 716	4 054	9 373	10 131	9 042	6 721	6 395
1961	50 608	4 479	2 407	2 073	46 129	4 204	9 290	10 178	9 148	6 819	6 490
1962	51 054	4 520	2 426	2 094	46 534	4 306	9 080	10 239	9 191	6 917	6 801
1963	52 031	4 827	2 792	2 036	47 204	4 610	9 039	10 309	9 297	7 031	6 919
1964	52 869	5 148	3 090	2 059	47 721	4 862	9 024	10 301	9 417	7 153	6 963
1965	53 681	5 541	3 050	2 492	48 140	5 017	9 056	10 262	9 516	7 261	7 028
1966	54 061	5 820	3 023	2 798	48 241	4 974	9 085	10 136	9 592	7 362	7 092
1967	54 608	5 671	3 058	2 613	48 937	5 257	9 339	10 013	9 688	7 474	7 167
1968	55 434	5 787	3 153	2 635	49 647	5 376	9 752	9 902	9 790	7 585	7 242
1969	56 348	6 005	3 246	2 759	50 343	5 589	10 074	9 760	9 895	7 705	7 320
1970	57 516	6 179	3 329	2 851	51 336	5 988	10 441	9 678	9 999	7 822	7 409
1971	58 900	6 420	3 412	3 008	52 481	6 546	10 841	9 578	10 066	7 933	7 517
1972	60 473	6 627	3 503	3 125	53 845	7 042	11 495	9 568	10 078	8 089	7 573
1973	61 577	6 737	3 555	3 182	54 842	7 312	12 075	9 514	10 099	8 178	7 664
1974	62 791	6 851	3 604	3 247	55 942	7 476	12 599	9 564	10 165	8 288	7 849
1975	63 981	6 929	3 609	3 320	57 052	7 766	13 131	9 578	10 134	8 413	8 031
1976	65 132	6 993	3 609	3 384	58 138	7 987	13 655	9 674	10 063	8 556	8 203
1977	66 301	7 024	3 625	3 399	59 278	8 175	14 139	9 880	9 957	8 708	8 420
1978	67 401	7 022	3 619	3 404	60 378	8 335	14 528	10 236	9 845	8 826	8 608
1979	68 547	7 007	3 568	3 439	61 540	8 470	15 008	10 563	9 730	8 949	8 820
1980	69 634	6 941	3 508	3 433	62 694	8 581	15 529	10 863	9 636	9 059	9 027
1981	70 480	6 764	3 401	3 363	63 715	8 644	16 005	11 171	9 560	9 139	9 195
1982	71 211	6 556	3 249	3 307	64 655	8 621	16 260	11 756	9 463	9 188	9 367
1983	71 922	6 340	3 098	3 242	65 581	8 597	16 499	12 314	9 408	9 208	9 556
1984	72 723	6 113	3 019	3 094	66 610	8 522	16 816	12 853	9 434	9 217	9 768
1985	73 373	5 987	3 026	2 961	67 386	8 246	17 042	13 337	9 488	9 262	10 010
1986	74 390	5 977	3 084	2 894	68 413	8 002	17 564	13 840	9 578	9 201	10 229
1987	75 189	6 015	3 125	2 890	69 175	7 729	17 754	14 338	9 771	9 101	10 481
1988	75 855	5 968	3 015	2 953	69 887	7 473	17 867	14 743	10 114	9 001	10 688
1989	76 468	5 813	2 817	2 996	70 654	7 279	17 908	15 237	10 434	8 900	10 897
1990	77 369	5 913	2 809	3 103	71 457	7 764	17 766	15 770	10 598	8 680	10 879
1991	77 977	5 704	2 805	2 899	72 274	7 748	17 615	16 340	10 856	8 640	11 074
1992	78 651	5 611	2 819	2 792	73 040	7 676	17 403	16 579	11 513	8 602	11 268
1993	79 371	5 650	2 862	2 788	73 721	7 545	17 158	16 900	12 058	8 590	11 470
1994	80 059	5 748	2 938	2 810	74 311	7 357	16 915	17 247	12 545	8 618	11 629
1995	80 733	5 854	2 995	2 859	74 879	7 163	16 653	17 567	13 028	8 653	11 815
1996	81 489	6 035	3 099	2 936	75 454	6 971	16 395	17 868	13 518	8 734	11 968
1997	82 577	6 257	3 209	3 048	76 320	7 087	16 043	18 163	14 030	8 929	12 067
1998	83 352	6 386	3 233	3 153	76 966	7 170	15 644	18 310	14 400	9 286	12 155
1999	83 930	6 498	3 266	3 232	77 432	7 244	15 150	18 340	14 834	9 581	12 283
2000	85 370	6 404	3 224	3 181	78 966	7 329	15 528	18 003	15 578	10 028	12 501
2001	86 452	6 422	3 229	3 194	80 029	7 564	15 486	17 960	16 047	10 369	12 604
2002	87 361	6 439	3 251	3 189	80 922	7 750	15 470	17 792	16 317	10 918	12 676
2003	88 249	6 390	3 378	3 012	81 860	7 856	15 569	17 620	16 555	11 442	12 818
2004	89 044	6 429	3 301	3 129	82 615	8 024	15 486	17 404	16 834	11 922	12 946
2005	90 027	6 471	3 464	3 006	83 556	8 057	15 507	17 286	17 169	12 415	13 123
2006	91 021	6 555	3 551	3 004	84 466	8 052	15 567	17 143	17 467	12 891	13 346
2007	92 073	6 653	3 567	3 086	85 420	8 113	15 762	16 927	17 686	13 341	13 591
2008	92 725	6 669	3 550	3 120	86 056	8 072	15 884	16 599	17 830	13 698	13 972
2009	93 433	6 644	3 469	3 175	86 789	8 076	16 011	16 260	17 956	14 154	14 332
2010	94 082	6 580	3 473	3 107	87 502	8 240	16 174	15 920	17 919	14 634	14 615
2011	94 801	6 610	3 496	3 114	88 191	8 485	16 332	15 540	17 602	15 018	15 213

Table 1-6. Civilian Noninstitutional Population, by Age, Race, Sex, and Hispanic Origin, 1948–2011 —Continued

(Thousands of people.)

Race, Hispanic origin, sex, and year	16 years and over	16 to 19 years			20 years and over						
		Total	16 to 17 years	18 to 19 years	Total	20 to 24 years	25 to 34 years	35 to 44 years	45 to 54 years	55 to 64 years	65 years and over
WHITE											
Women											
1954	51 242	3 725	1 884	1 841	47 517	4 720	10 870	10 227	8 397	6 652	6 651
1955	51 802	3 785	1 929	1 856	48 017	4 671	10 806	10 342	8 566	6 771	6 862
1956	52 373	3 846	1 953	1 892	48 527	4 642	10 713	10 466	8 752	6 886	7 067
1957	52 998	3 949	2 007	1 941	49 049	4 655	10 584	10 597	8 957	7 000	7 256
1958	53 645	4 096	2 131	1 966	49 549	4 715	10 407	10 716	9 159	7 107	7 442
1959	54 392	4 351	2 337	2 015	50 041	4 794	10 216	10 812	9 348	7 219	7 653
1960	55 214	4 575	2 433	2 142	50 639	4 873	10 097	10 918	9 536	7 349	7 865
1961	55 993	4 732	2 378	2 354	51 261	4 999	9 999	10 991	9 697	7 485	8 091
1962	56 660	4 823	2 392	2 432	51 837	5 178	9 894	11 054	9 681	7 533	8 496
1963	57 672	5 151	2 757	2 394	52 521	5 459	9 828	11 089	9 785	7 650	8 710
1964	58 663	5 468	3 047	2 422	53 195	5 706	9 814	11 074	9 943	7 804	8 853
1965	59 601	5 778	2 999	2 779	53 823	5 918	9 826	10 996	10 088	7 954	9 042
1966	60 503	6 042	2 970	3 072	54 461	6 120	9 904	10 869	10 230	8 107	9 230
1967	61 491	6 011	2 993	3 019	55 480	6 540	10 125	10 732	10 379	8 271	9 435
1968	62 512	6 053	3 072	2 981	56 460	6 809	10 493	10 572	10 520	8 433	9 633
1969	63 563	6 174	3 172	3 002	57 390	7 089	10 818	10 396	10 651	8 600	9 836
1970	64 656	6 342	3 262	3 080	58 315	7 370	11 105	10 251	10 761	8 769	10 060
1971	65 857	6 518	3 338	3 180	59 340	7 662	11 454	10 117	10 841	8 951	10 315
1972	67 431	6 673	3 407	3 267	60 758	7 855	12 060	10 105	10 872	9 161	10 705
1973	68 517	6 796	3 466	3 331	61 721	7 951	12 610	10 018	10 891	9 306	10 943
1974	69 623	6 933	3 510	3 424	62 690	8 026	13 112	10 064	10 896	9 356	11 236
1975	70 810	7 011	3 523	3 488	63 798	8 214	13 615	10 063	10 847	9 505	11 556
1976	71 974	7 062	3 516	3 546	64 912	8 381	14 102	10 153	10 752	9 664	11 860
1977	73 077	7 071	3 525	3 545	66 007	8 553	14 564	10 351	10 618	9 832	12 088
1978	74 213	7 038	3 513	3 524	67 174	8 704	14 926	10 696	10 476	9 974	12 399
1979	75 347	6 987	3 460	3 527	68 360	8 815	15 363	11 017	10 327	10 122	12 717
1980	76 489	6 914	3 403	3 511	69 575	8 904	15 878	11 313	10 201	10 256	13 022
1981	77 428	6 752	3 303	3 449	70 677	8 965	16 362	11 606	10 106	10 346	13 292
1982	78 230	6 519	3 134	3 385	71 711	8 959	16 603	12 154	10 015	10 402	13 579
1983	78 884	6 282	2 991	3 292	72 601	8 895	16 788	12 714	9 941	10 418	13 847
1984	79 624	6 034	2 899	3 135	73 590	8 782	17 073	13 271	9 914	10 412	14 138
1985	80 306	5 912	2 895	3 017	74 394	8 607	17 409	13 762	9 917	10 358	14 342
1986	81 042	5 902	2 953	2 949	75 140	8 351	17 728	14 223	10 009	10 277	14 551
1987	81 769	5 924	2 985	2 939	75 845	8 079	17 913	14 698	10 194	10 141	14 820
1988	82 340	5 869	2 878	2 991	76 470	7 804	18 009	15 074	10 537	9 994	15 052
1989	82 871	5 716	2 690	3 027	77 154	7 600	18 043	15 537	10 853	9 843	15 278
1990	83 256	5 717	2 654	3 063	77 539	7 774	17 895	15 969	10 937	9 524	15 440
1991	83 781	5 497	2 646	2 850	78 285	7 768	17 726	16 514	11 196	9 435	15 647
1992	84 321	5 393	2 659	2 734	78 928	7 678	17 482	16 727	11 851	9 350	15 841
1993	84 918	5 428	2 700	2 728	79 490	7 542	17 206	17 019	12 398	9 302	16 023
1994	85 496	5 516	2 772	2 744	79 980	7 351	16 950	17 335	12 890	9 306	16 148
1995	86 181	5 614	2 827	2 787	80 567	7 150	16 702	17 654	13 390	9 333	16 337
1996	86 828	5 787	2 927	2 860	81 041	6 936	16 457	17 943	13 884	9 402	16 419
1997	87 417	5 924	3 004	2 920	81 492	6 896	16 047	18 162	14 357	9 582	16 447
1998	88 126	6 053	3 031	3 023	82 073	6 969	15 642	18 300	14 732	9 944	16 486
1999	89 156	6 202	3 076	3 127	82 953	7 150	15 366	18 415	15 214	10 274	16 536
2000	90 850	6 131	3 041	3 090	84 718	7 223	15 420	18 258	15 972	10 729	17 116
2001	91 660	6 134	3 062	3 071	85 526	7 438	15 284	18 153	16 428	11 065	17 158
2002	92 422	6 157	3 096	3 061	86 266	7 611	15 207	17 958	16 695	11 622	17 173
2003	93 043	6 137	3 251	2 886	86 905	7 680	15 220	17 731	16 911	12 147	17 216
2004	93 599	6 169	3 260	2 909	87 430	7 794	15 099	17 441	17 170	12 627	17 299
2005	94 419	6 219	3 304	2 915	88 200	7 814	15 086	17 268	17 480	13 119	17 433
2006	95 242	6 301	3 429	2 871	88 942	7 796	15 094	17 074	17 760	13 596	17 623
2007	96 180	6 390	3 458	2 932	89 790	7 832	15 249	16 843	17 979	14 051	17 835
2008	96 814	6 414	3 412	3 003	90 400	7 842	15 349	16 493	18 111	14 411	18 193
2009	97 469	6 391	3 306	3 086	91 078	7 887	15 460	16 118	18 210	14 868	18 535
2010	97 993	6 311	3 327	2 984	91 683	8 040	15 640	15 727	18 146	15 349	18 781
2011	98 276	6 208	3 177	3 031	92 068	8 077	15 803	15 490	17 925	15 781	18 992

Table 1-6. Civilian Noninstitutional Population, by Age, Race, Sex, and Hispanic Origin, 1948–2011
—Continued

(Thousands of people.)

Race, Hispanic origin, sex, and year	16 years and over	16 to 19 years			20 years and over						
		Total	16 to 17 years	18 to 19 years	Total	20 to 24 years	25 to 34 years	35 to 44 years	45 to 54 years	55 to 64 years	65 years and over
BLACK											
Both Sexes											
1974	15 329	2 137	1 122	1 014	13 192	2 137	3 103	2 382	2 202	1 679	1 689
1975	15 751	2 191	1 146	1 046	13 560	2 228	3 258	2 395	2 211	1 717	1 755
1976	16 196	2 264	1 165	1 098	13 932	2 303	3 412	2 435	2 220	1 736	1 826
1977	16 605	2 273	1 175	1 097	14 332	2 400	3 566	2 493	2 225	1 765	1 883
1978	16 970	2 270	1 169	1 101	14 701	2 483	3 717	2 547	2 226	1 794	1 932
1979	17 397	2 276	1 167	1 109	15 121	2 556	3 899	2 615	2 240	1 831	1 980
1980	17 824	2 289	1 171	1 119	15 535	2 606	4 095	2 687	2 249	1 870	2 030
1981	18 219	2 288	1 161	1 127	15 931	2 642	4 290	2 758	2 260	1 913	2 069
1982	18 584	2 252	1 119	1 134	16 332	2 697	4 438	2 887	2 263	1 935	2 113
1983	18 925	2 225	1 092	1 133	16 700	2 734	4 607	2 999	2 260	1 964	2 135
1984	19 348	2 161	1 056	1 105	17 187	2 783	4 789	3 167	2 288	1 977	2 183
1985	19 664	2 160	1 083	1 077	17 504	2 649	4 873	3 290	2 372	2 060	2 259
1986	19 989	2 137	1 090	1 048	17 852	2 625	5 026	3 410	2 413	2 079	2 298
1987	20 352	2 163	1 123	1 040	18 189	2 578	5 139	3 563	2 460	2 097	2 352
1988	20 692	2 179	1 130	1 049	18 513	2 527	5 234	3 716	2 524	2 110	2 402
1989	21 021	2 176	1 116	1 060	18 846	2 479	5 308	3 900	2 587	2 118	2 454
1990	21 477	2 238	1 101	1 138	19 239	2 554	5 407	4 328	2 618	1 970	2 362
1991	21 799	2 187	1 085	1 102	19 612	2 585	5 419	4 538	2 682	1 985	2 403
1992	22 147	2 155	1 086	1 069	19 992	2 615	5 404	4 722	2 809	1 996	2 446
1993	22 521	2 181	1 113	1 069	20 339	2 600	5 409	4 886	2 941	2 016	2 487
1994	22 879	2 211	1 168	1 044	20 668	2 616	5 362	5 038	3 084	2 045	2 524
1995	23 246	2 284	1 198	1 086	20 962	2 554	5 337	5 178	3 244	2 079	2 571
1996	23 604	2 356	1 238	1 118	21 248	2 519	5 311	5 290	3 408	2 110	2 609
1997	24 003	2 412	1 255	1 158	21 591	2 515	5 279	5 410	3 571	2 164	2 653
1998	24 373	2 443	1 241	1 202	21 930	2 546	5 221	5 510	3 735	2 224	2 695
1999	24 855	2 479	1 250	1 229	22 376	2 615	5 197	5 609	3 919	2 295	2 741
2000	24 902	2 389	1 205	1 183	22 513	2 611	5 089	5 488	4 168	2 407	2 750
2001	25 138	2 388	1 212	1 176	22 750	2 686	5 003	5 467	4 343	2 478	2 775
2002	25 578	2 416	1 235	1 181	23 162	2 779	5 015	5 460	4 513	2 571	2 823
2003	25 686	2 382	1 309	1 074	23 304	2 773	4 978	5 387	4 628	2 692	2 846
2004	26 065	2 423	1 350	1 072	23 643	2 821	5 020	5 335	4 739	2 827	2 899
2005	26 517	2 481	1 341	1 140	24 036	2 835	5 075	5 311	4 869	2 980	2 967
2006	27 007	2 565	1 408	1 157	24 442	2 851	5 133	5 302	4 992	3 137	3 027
2007	27 485	2 640	1 497	1 143	24 845	2 891	5 210	5 271	5 110	3 284	3 080
2008	27 843	2 676	1 459	1 217	25 168	2 914	5 262	5 198	5 183	3 429	3 182
2009	28 241	2 684	1 462	1 221	25 557	2 973	5 349	5 109	5 290	3 596	3 239
2010	28 708	2 657	1 438	1 219	26 051	3 097	5 491	5 031	5 322	3 773	3 337
2011	29 114	2 594	1 353	1 240	26 520	3 168	5 606	4 995	5 357	3 955	3 440
BLACK											
Men											
1974	6 875	1 027	554	471	5 848	956	1 381	1 055	997	753	707
1975	7 060	1 051	565	486	6 009	1 002	1 452	1 060	997	769	730
1976	7 265	1 099	579	518	6 167	1 036	1 521	1 077	999	774	756
1977	7 431	1 102	586	516	6 329	1 080	1 589	1 102	998	786	774
1978	7 577	1 093	579	514	6 484	1 120	1 657	1 128	995	794	789
1979	7 761	1 100	581	519	6 661	1 151	1 738	1 159	998	809	804
1980	7 944	1 110	583	526	6 834	1 171	1 828	1 191	999	825	822
1981	8 117	1 110	577	534	7 007	1 189	1 914	1 224	1 003	844	835
1982	8 283	1 097	556	542	7 186	1 225	1 983	1 282	1 003	848	846
1983	8 447	1 087	542	545	7 360	1 254	2 068	1 333	1 000	857	847
1984	8 654	1 055	524	531	7 599	1 292	2 164	1 411	1 012	858	861
1985	8 790	1 059	543	517	7 731	1 202	2 180	1 462	1 060	924	902
1986	8 956	1 049	548	503	7 907	1 195	2 264	1 517	1 072	934	924
1987	9 128	1 065	566	499	8 063	1 173	2 320	1 587	1 092	944	947
1988	9 289	1 074	569	505	8 215	1 151	2 367	1 656	1 121	951	970
1989	9 439	1 075	575	501	8 364	1 128	2 403	1 741	1 145	956	989
1990	9 573	1 094	555	540	8 479	1 144	2 412	1 968	1 183	855	917
1991	9 725	1 072	546	526	8 652	1 168	2 417	2 060	1 211	864	933
1992	9 896	1 056	544	512	8 840	1 194	2 409	2 150	1 268	868	951
1993	10 083	1 075	559	516	9 008	1 181	2 425	2 228	1 330	874	969
1994	10 258	1 087	586	501	9 171	1 207	2 399	2 300	1 392	889	985
1995	10 411	1 131	601	530	9 280	1 161	2 388	2 362	1 462	901	1 006
1996	10 575	1 161	623	538	9 414	1 154	2 373	2 413	1 534	914	1 025
1997	10 763	1 188	634	553	9 575	1 153	2 363	2 471	1 607	936	1 045
1998	10 927	1 201	623	578	9 727	1 166	2 335	2 520	1 682	956	1 068
1999	11 143	1 218	628	589	9 926	1 197	2 321	2 566	1 765	986	1 091
2000	11 129	1 178	605	572	9 952	1 195	2 277	2 471	1 889	1 067	1 053
2001	11 172	1 179	606	573	9 993	1 224	2 212	2 440	1 960	1 096	1 060
2002	11 391	1 195	615	580	10 196	1 281	2 223	2 437	2 042	1 137	1 075
2003	11 454	1 176	661	515	10 278	1 291	2 210	2 401	2 094	1 189	1 093
2004	11 656	1 195	680	516	10 461	1 326	2 242	2 382	2 150	1 250	1 111
2005	11 882	1 223	682	541	10 659	1 341	2 277	2 372	2 202	1 319	1 148
2006	12 130	1 266	713	552	10 864	1 355	2 318	2 369	2 261	1 390	1 170
2007	12 361	1 305	742	563	11 057	1 380	2 366	2 352	2 318	1 454	1 186
2008	12 516	1 322	718	604	11 194	1 384	2 398	2 313	2 335	1 519	1 245
2009	12 705	1 326	736	590	11 379	1 410	2 454	2 271	2 392	1 592	1 260
2010	12 939	1 313	715	598	11 626	1 474	2 540	2 234	2 406	1 673	1 299
2011	13 164	1 282	642	640	11 882	1 510	2 612	2 222	2 435	1 759	1 344

Table 1-6. Civilian Noninstitutional Population, by Age, Race, Sex, and Hispanic Origin, 1948–2011
—Continued

(Thousands of people.)

Race, Hispanic origin, sex, and year	16 years and over	16 to 19 years			20 years and over						
		Total	16 to 17 years	18 to 19 years	Total	20 to 24 years	25 to 34 years	35 to 44 years	45 to 54 years	55 to 64 years	65 years and over
BLACK											
Women											
1974	8 454	1 110	567	542	7 344	1 181	1 723	1 327	1 206	926	981
1975	8 691	1 141	581	560	7 550	1 226	1 806	1 334	1 213	948	1 025
1976	8 931	1 165	585	580	7 765	1 266	1 890	1 357	1 220	962	1 070
1977	9 174	1 171	590	581	8 003	1 320	1 978	1 390	1 228	979	1 108
1978	9 394	1 177	589	588	8 217	1 363	2 061	1 419	1 231	999	1 143
1979	9 636	1 176	586	589	8 460	1 405	2 160	1 455	1 242	1 022	1 176
1980	9 880	1 180	587	593	8 700	1 435	2 267	1 496	1 250	1 045	1 208
1981	10 102	1 178	584	593	8 924	1 453	2 376	1 534	1 257	1 069	1 234
1982	10 300	1 155	563	592	9 146	1 472	2 455	1 605	1 260	1 087	1 267
1983	10 477	1 138	550	588	9 340	1 480	2 539	1 666	1 260	1 107	1 288
1984	10 694	1 106	532	574	9 588	1 491	2 625	1 756	1 276	1 119	1 322
1985	10 873	1 101	540	560	9 773	1 447	2 693	1 828	1 312	1 136	1 357
1986	11 033	1 088	542	545	9 945	1 430	2 762	1 893	1 341	1 145	1 374
1987	11 224	1 098	557	541	10 126	1 405	2 819	1 976	1 368	1 153	1 405
1988	11 402	1 105	561	544	10 298	1 376	2 867	2 060	1 403	1 159	1 432
1989	11 582	1 100	541	559	10 482	1 351	2 905	2 159	1 441	1 162	1 464
1990	11 904	1 144	546	598	10 760	1 410	2 995	2 360	1 435	1 114	1 446
1991	12 074	1 115	539	576	10 959	1 417	3 003	2 478	1 471	1 121	1 470
1992	12 251	1 099	542	557	11 152	1 421	2 995	2 573	1 542	1 127	1 495
1993	12 438	1 106	554	552	11 332	1 419	2 983	2 659	1 611	1 142	1 518
1994	12 621	1 125	582	543	11 496	1 410	2 963	2 738	1 692	1 156	1 538
1995	12 835	1 153	597	556	11 682	1 392	2 948	2 816	1 782	1 178	1 565
1996	13 029	1 195	615	580	11 833	1 364	2 938	2 877	1 874	1 196	1 584
1997	13 241	1 225	620	604	12 016	1 362	2 916	2 939	1 964	1 228	1 608
1998	13 446	1 243	618	624	12 203	1 380	2 886	2 991	2 053	1 268	1 626
1999	13 711	1 261	621	640	12 451	1 418	2 876	3 043	2 153	1 310	1 650
2000	13 772	1 211	600	611	12 561	1 416	2 812	3 017	2 279	1 340	1 697
2001	13 966	1 209	606	603	12 758	1 462	2 790	3 026	2 383	1 382	1 714
2002	14 187	1 221	620	601	12 966	1 498	2 792	3 023	2 471	1 434	1 747
2003	14 232	1 206	648	558	13 026	1 482	2 768	2 986	2 534	1 504	1 753
2004	14 409	1 227	670	557	13 182	1 495	2 778	2 954	2 590	1 577	1 789
2005	14 635	1 258	659	598	13 377	1 494	2 797	2 939	2 666	1 661	1 819
2006	14 877	1 299	694	605	13 578	1 495	2 815	2 933	2 731	1 747	1 857
2007	15 124	1 336	755	581	13 788	1 511	2 844	2 918	2 792	1 830	1 893
2008	15 328	1 354	741	613	13 974	1 530	2 864	2 885	2 848	1 910	1 937
2009	15 536	1 357	726	631	14 178	1 563	2 895	2 839	2 898	2 004	1 979
2010	15 769	1 344	723	621	14 425	1 623	2 951	2 796	2 916	2 101	2 038
2011	15 950	1 312	712	600	14 638	1 657	2 994	2 773	2 922	2 196	2 096
HISPANIC											
Both Sexes											
1975	6 862	962	. . .	. . .	5 900	. . .	. . .	. . .	. . .	. . .	. . .
1976	6 910	953	494	480	6 075	1 053	1 775	1 261	936	570	479
1977	7 362	1 024	513	508	6 376	1 163	1 869	1 283	989	587	485
1978	7 912	1 076	561	515	6 836	1 265	2 004	1 378	1 033	627	529
1979	8 207	1 095	544	551	7 113	1 296	2 117	1 458	1 015	659	566
1980	9 598	1 281	638	643	8 317	1 564	2 508	1 575	1 190	782	698
1981	10 120	1 301	641	660	8 819	1 650	2 698	1 680	1 231	832	728
1982	10 580	1 307	639	668	9 273	1 724	2 871	1 779	1 264	880	755
1983	11 029	1 304	635	670	9 725	1 790	3 045	1 883	1 298	928	781
1984	11 478	1 300	633	667	10 178	1 839	3 224	1 996	1 336	973	810
1985	11 915	1 298	638	661	10 617	1 864	3 401	2 117	1 377	1 015	843
1986	12 344	1 302	658	644	11 042	1 899	3 510	2 239	1 496	1 023	875
1987	12 867	1 332	651	681	11 536	1 910	3 714	2 464	1 492	1 061	895
1988	13 325	1 354	662	692	11 970	1 948	3 807	2 565	1 571	1 159	920
1989	13 791	1 399	672	727	12 392	1 950	3 953	2 658	1 649	1 182	1 001
1990	15 904	1 737	821	915	14 167	2 428	4 589	3 001	1 817	1 247	1 084
1991	16 425	1 732	819	913	14 693	2 481	4 674	3 243	1 879	1 283	1 134
1992	16 961	1 737	836	901	15 224	2 444	4 806	3 458	1 980	1 321	1 216
1993	17 532	1 756	855	901	15 776	2 487	4 887	3 632	2 094	1 324	1 353
1994	18 117	1 818	902	916	16 300	2 518	5 000	3 756	2 223	1 401	1 401
1995	18 629	1 872	903	969	16 757	2 528	5 050	3 965	2 294	1 483	1 437
1996	19 213	1 948	962	986	17 265	2 524	5 181	4 227	2 275	1 546	1 512
1997	20 321	2 121	1 088	1 033	18 200	2 623	5 405	4 453	2 581	1 580	1 558
1998	21 070	2 204	1 070	1 135	18 865	2 731	5 447	4 636	2 775	1 615	1 662
1999	21 650	2 307	1 113	1 194	19 344	2 700	5 512	4 833	2 868	1 713	1 718
2000	23 938	2 523	1 214	1 309	21 415	3 255	6 466	5 189	3 061	1 736	1 708
2001	24 942	2 508	1 173	1 334	22 435	3 417	6 726	5 346	3 339	1 816	1 792
2002	25 963	2 507	1 216	1 291	23 456	3 508	7 010	5 606	3 494	1 953	1 885
2003	27 551	2 543	1 346	1 197	25 008	3 533	7 506	6 003	3 845	2 093	2 027
2004	28 109	2 608	1 337	1 270	25 502	3 666	7 470	6 055	3 987	2 208	2 115
2005	29 133	2 689	1 415	1 274	26 444	3 647	7 684	6 293	4 217	2 361	2 242
2006	30 103	2 796	1 518	1 277	27 307	3 603	7 856	6 519	4 466	2 516	2 347
2007	31 383	2 944	1 559	1 385	28 440	3 648	8 129	6 785	4 720	2 685	2 473
2008	32 141	3 042	1 620	1 422	29 098	3 620	8 147	6 946	4 937	2 840	2 609
2009	32 891	3 123	1 602	1 522	29 768	3 623	8 099	7 078	5 192	3 017	2 759
2010	33 713	3 243	1 673	1 570	30 469	3 880	8 084	7 123	5 351	3 167	2 864
2011	34 438	3 407	1 808	1 598	31 031	4 193	8 107	7 103	5 414	3 311	2 903

. . . = Not available.

Table 1-6. Civilian Noninstitutional Population, by Age, Race, Sex, and Hispanic Origin, 1948–2011
—Continued

(Thousands of people.)

Race, Hispanic origin, sex, and year	16 years and over	16 to 19 years			20 years and over						
		Total	16 to 17 years	18 to 19 years	Total	20 to 24 years	25 to 34 years	35 to 44 years	45 to 54 years	55 to 64 years	65 years and over
HISPANIC											
Men											
1975	3 219	...	...	...	2 741	...	...	...	...	...	...
1976	3 241	...	...	...	2 764	...	...	...	...	...	...
1977	3 483	...	...	...	2 982	...	...	...	...	...	...
1978	3 750	...	...	...	3 228	...	...	...	...	...	...
1979	3 917	...	...	...	3 362	...	...	...	...	...	...
1980	4 689	...	...	...	4 036	...	...	...	...	...	...
1981	4 968	...	...	...	4 306	...	...	...	...	...	...
1982	5 203	...	...	...	4 539	...	...	...	...	...	...
1983	5 432	...	...	...	4 771	...	...	...	...	...	...
1984	5 661	...	...	...	5 005	...	...	...	...	...	...
1985	5 885	...	...	...	5 232	...	...	...	...	...	...
1986	6 106	...	...	...	5 451	...	...	...	...	...	...
1987	6 371	...	...	...	5 700	...	...	...	...	...	...
1988	6 604	...	...	...	5 921	...	...	...	...	...	...
1989	6 825	...	...	...	6 114	...	...	...	...	...	...
1990	8 041	...	...	...	7 126	...	...	...	...	...	...
1991	8 296	...	...	...	7 392	...	...	...	...	...	...
1992	8 553	...	...	...	7 655	...	...	...	...	...	...
1993	8 824	...	...	...	7 930	...	...	...	...	...	...
1994	9 104	926	472	454	8 178	1 346	2 627	1 871	1 076	644	614
1995	9 329	954	481	473	8 375	1 337	2 657	1 966	1 127	668	619
1996	9 604	992	485	507	8 611	1 321	2 692	2 144	1 111	712	630
1997	10 368	1 119	585	534	9 250	1 439	2 872	2 275	1 266	747	651
1998	10 734	1 161	586	575	9 573	1 462	2 907	2 377	1 342	771	714
1999	10 713	1 190	571	619	9 523	1 398	2 805	2 407	1 397	767	749
2000	12 174	1 333	640	693	10 841	1 784	3 380	2 626	1 527	799	725
2001	12 695	1 310	619	690	11 386	1 846	3 529	2 765	1 650	848	749
2002	13 221	1 293	615	678	11 928	1 890	3 727	2 875	1 716	902	817
2003	14 098	1 301	674	627	12 797	1 905	4 033	3 098	1 910	989	862
2004	14 417	1 336	664	672	13 082	1 981	4 024	3 147	1 990	1 046	894
2005	14 962	1 376	730	646	13 586	1 956	4 155	3 284	2 114	1 123	953
2006	15 473	1 428	763	664	14 046	1 916	4 266	3 414	2 251	1 204	996
2007	16 154	1 505	790	714	14 649	1 928	4 430	3 563	2 384	1 287	1 058
2008	16 524	1 553	838	716	14 971	1 890	4 438	3 655	2 502	1 365	1 121
2009	16 897	1 593	818	774	15 305	1 875	4 405	3 735	2 647	1 459	1 184
2010	17 359	1 666	847	819	15 693	2 016	4 381	3 783	2 741	1 538	1 234
2011	17 753	1 812	951	861	15 941	2 278	4 379	3 702	2 717	1 604	1 260
HISPANIC											
Women											
1975	3 644	...	...	...	3 161	...	...	...	...	...	...
1976	3 669	...	...	...	3 263	...	...	...	...	...	...
1977	3 879	...	...	...	3 377	...	...	...	...	...	...
1978	4 159	...	...	...	3 608	...	...	...	...	...	...
1979	4 291	...	...	...	3 751	...	...	...	...	...	...
1980	4 909	...	...	...	4 281	...	...	...	...	...	...
1981	5 151	...	...	...	4 513	...	...	...	...	...	...
1982	5 377	...	...	...	4 734	...	...	...	...	...	...
1983	5 597	...	...	...	4 954	...	...	...	...	...	...
1984	5 816	...	...	...	5 173	...	...	...	...	...	...
1985	6 029	...	...	...	5 385	...	...	...	...	...	...
1986	6 238	...	...	...	5 591	...	...	...	...	...	...
1987	6 496	...	...	...	5 835	...	...	...	...	...	...
1988	6 721	...	...	...	6 050	...	...	...	...	...	...
1989	6 965	...	...	...	6 278	...	...	...	...	...	...
1990	7 863	...	...	...	7 041	...	...	...	...	...	...
1991	8 130	...	...	...	7 301	...	...	...	...	...	...
1992	8 408	...	...	...	7 569	...	...	...	...	...	...
1993	8 708	...	...	...	7 846	...	...	...	...	...	...
1994	9 014	892	430	462	8 122	1 173	2 373	1 885	1 147	757	787
1995	9 300	918	422	496	8 382	1 191	2 393	1 999	1 167	815	818
1996	9 610	956	477	479	8 654	1 203	2 489	2 082	1 164	834	882
1997	9 953	1 003	503	500	8 950	1 184	2 533	2 178	1 315	833	907
1998	10 335	1 044	483	560	9 292	1 269	2 539	2 259	1 433	844	948
1999	10 937	1 116	542	575	9 821	1 302	2 707	2 425	1 470	947	969
2000	11 764	1 190	574	616	10 574	1 471	3 086	2 564	1 534	937	982
2001	12 247	1 198	554	644	11 049	1 571	3 198	2 581	1 689	968	1 043
2002	12 742	1 214	601	613	11 528	1 617	3 283	2 732	1 777	1 051	1 068
2003	13 452	1 242	672	570	12 211	1 628	3 473	2 905	1 935	1 105	1 166
2004	13 692	1 272	674	598	12 420	1 685	3 447	2 908	1 997	1 162	1 221
2005	14 172	1 313	685	628	12 858	1 692	3 529	3 009	2 103	1 237	1 289
2006	14 630	1 368	755	613	13 262	1 688	3 590	3 105	2 215	1 313	1 351
2007	15 229	1 439	769	670	13 791	1 720	3 698	3 222	2 336	1 398	1 416
2008	15 616	1 489	782	706	14 127	1 730	3 710	3 291	2 435	1 475	1 488
2009	15 993	1 531	783	748	14 463	1 748	3 694	3 343	2 545	1 558	1 576
2010	16 354	1 578	826	752	14 776	1 864	3 703	3 340	2 610	1 628	1 630
2011	16 685	1 595	857	738	15 090	1 915	3 727	3 401	2 696	1 707	1 643

. . . = Not available.

Table 1-7. Civilian Labor Force, by Age, Sex, Race, and Hispanic Origin, 1948–2011

(Thousands of people.)

Race, Hispanic origin, sex, and year	16 years and over	16 to 19 years			20 years and over						
		Total	16 to 17 years	18 to 19 years	Total	20 to 24 years	25 to 34 years	35 to 44 years	45 to 54 years	55 to 64 years	65 years and over
ALL RACES											
Both Sexes											
1948	60 621	4 435	1 780	2 654	56 187	7 392	14 258	13 397	10 914	7 329	2 897
1949	61 286	4 288	1 704	2 583	57 000	7 340	14 415	13 711	11 107	7 426	3 010
1950	62 208	4 216	1 659	2 557	57 994	7 307	14 619	13 954	11 444	7 633	3 036
1951	62 017	4 103	1 743	2 360	57 914	6 594	14 668	14 100	11 739	7 796	3 020
1952	62 138	4 064	1 806	2 257	58 075	5 840	14 904	14 383	11 961	7 980	3 005
1953	63 015	4 027	1 727	2 299	58 989	5 481	14 898	15 099	12 249	8 024	3 236
1954	63 643	3 976	1 643	2 300	59 666	5 475	14 983	15 221	12 524	8 269	3 192
1955	65 023	4 092	1 711	2 382	60 931	5 666	15 058	15 400	12 992	8 513	3 305
1956	66 552	4 296	1 878	2 418	62 257	5 940	14 961	15 694	13 407	8 830	3 423
1957	66 929	4 275	1 843	2 433	62 653	6 071	14 826	15 847	13 768	8 853	3 290
1958	67 639	4 260	1 818	2 442	63 377	6 272	14 668	16 028	14 179	9 031	3 199
1959	68 369	4 492	1 971	2 522	63 876	6 413	14 435	16 127	14 518	9 227	3 158
1960	69 628	4 841	2 095	2 747	64 788	6 702	14 382	16 269	14 852	9 385	3 195
1961	70 459	4 936	1 984	2 951	65 524	6 950	14 319	16 402	15 071	9 636	3 146
1962	70 614	4 916	1 919	2 997	65 699	7 082	14 023	16 589	15 096	9 757	3 154
1963	71 833	5 139	2 171	2 966	66 695	7 473	14 050	16 788	15 338	10 006	3 041
1964	73 091	5 388	2 449	2 940	67 702	7 963	14 056	16 771	15 637	10 182	3 090
1965	74 455	5 910	2 486	3 425	68 543	8 259	14 233	16 840	15 756	10 350	3 108
1966	75 770	6 558	2 664	3 893	69 219	8 410	14 458	16 738	15 984	10 575	3 053
1967	77 347	6 521	2 734	3 786	70 825	9 010	15 055	16 703	16 172	10 792	3 097
1968	78 737	6 619	2 817	3 803	72 118	9 305	15 708	16 591	16 397	10 964	3 153
1969	80 734	6 970	3 009	3 959	73 763	9 879	16 336	16 458	16 730	11 135	3 227
1970	82 771	7 249	3 135	4 115	75 521	10 597	17 036	16 437	16 949	11 283	3 222
1971	84 382	7 470	3 192	4 278	76 913	11 331	17 714	16 305	17 024	11 390	3 149
1972	87 034	8 054	3 420	4 636	78 980	12 130	18 960	16 398	16 967	11 412	3 114
1973	89 429	8 507	3 665	4 839	80 924	12 846	20 376	16 492	16 983	11 256	2 974
1974	91 949	8 871	3 810	5 059	83 080	13 314	21 654	16 763	17 131	11 284	2 934
1975	93 775	8 870	3 740	5 131	84 904	13 750	22 864	16 903	17 084	11 346	2 956
1976	96 158	9 056	3 767	5 288	87 103	14 284	24 203	17 317	16 982	11 422	2 895
1977	99 009	9 351	3 919	5 431	89 658	14 825	25 500	17 943	16 878	11 577	2 934
1978	102 251	9 652	4 127	5 526	92 598	15 370	26 703	18 821	16 891	11 744	3 070
1979	104 962	9 638	4 079	5 559	95 325	15 769	27 938	19 685	16 897	11 931	3 104
1980	106 940	9 378	3 883	5 496	97 561	15 922	29 227	20 463	16 910	11 985	3 054
1981	108 670	8 988	3 647	5 340	99 682	16 099	30 392	21 211	16 970	11 969	3 042
1982	110 204	8 526	3 336	5 189	101 679	16 082	31 186	22 431	16 889	12 062	3 030
1983	111 550	8 171	3 073	5 098	103 379	16 052	31 834	23 611	16 851	11 992	3 040
1984	113 544	7 943	3 050	4 894	105 601	16 046	32 723	24 933	17 006	11 961	2 933
1985	115 461	7 901	3 154	4 747	107 560	15 718	33 550	26 073	17 322	11 991	2 907
1986	117 834	7 926	3 287	4 639	109 908	15 441	34 591	27 232	17 739	11 894	3 010
1987	119 865	7 988	3 384	4 604	111 878	14 977	35 233	28 460	18 210	11 877	3 119
1988	121 669	8 031	3 286	4 745	113 638	14 505	35 503	29 435	19 104	11 808	3 284
1989	123 869	7 954	3 125	4 828	115 916	14 180	35 896	30 601	19 916	11 877	3 446
1990	125 840	7 792	2 937	4 856	118 047	14 700	35 929	32 145	20 248	11 575	3 451
1991	126 346	7 265	2 789	4 476	119 082	14 548	35 507	33 312	20 828	11 473	3 413
1992	128 105	7 096	2 769	4 327	121 009	14 521	35 369	33 899	22 160	11 587	3 473
1993	129 200	7 170	2 831	4 338	122 030	14 354	34 780	34 562	23 296	11 599	3 439
1994	131 056	7 481	3 134	4 347	123 576	14 131	34 353	35 226	24 318	11 713	3 834
1995	132 304	7 765	3 225	4 540	124 539	13 688	34 198	35 751	25 223	11 860	3 819
1996	133 943	7 806	3 263	4 543	126 137	13 377	33 833	36 556	26 397	12 146	3 828
1997	136 297	7 932	3 237	4 695	128 365	13 532	33 380	37 326	27 574	12 665	3 887
1998	137 673	8 256	3 335	4 921	129 417	13 638	32 813	37 536	28 368	13 215	3 847
1999	139 368	8 333	3 337	4 996	131 034	13 933	32 143	37 882	29 388	13 682	4 005
2000	142 583	8 271	3 261	5 010	134 312	14 250	32 755	37 567	31 071	14 356	4 312
2001	143 734	7 902	3 088	4 814	135 832	14 557	32 361	37 404	32 025	15 104	4 382
2002	144 863	7 585	2 870	4 715	137 278	14 781	32 196	36 926	32 597	16 309	4 469
2003	146 510	7 170	2 857	4 313	139 340	14 928	32 343	36 695	33 270	17 312	4 792
2004	147 401	7 114	2 747	4 367	140 287	15 154	32 207	36 158	33 758	18 013	4 998
2005	149 320	7 164	2 825	4 339	142 157	15 127	32 341	36 030	34 402	18 979	5 278
2006	151 428	7 281	2 952	4 329	144 147	15 113	32 573	35 848	35 146	19 984	5 484
2007	153 124	7 012	2 771	4 242	146 112	15 205	33 130	35 527	35 697	20 750	5 804
2008	154 287	6 858	2 552	4 306	147 429	15 174	33 332	35 061	36 003	21 615	6 243
2009	154 142	6 390	2 227	4 163	147 752	14 971	33 298	34 239	36 205	22 505	6 534
2010	153 889	5 906	2 000	3 905	147 983	15 028	33 614	33 366	35 960	23 297	6 718
2011	153 617	5 727	1 873	3 853	147 890	15 270	33 724	32 660	35 360	23 765	7 112

Table 1-7. Civilian Labor Force, by Age, Sex, Race, and Hispanic Origin, 1948–2011—*Continued*

(Thousands of people.)

Race, Hispanic origin, sex, and year	16 years and over	16 to 19 years			20 years and over						
		Total	16 to 17 years	18 to 19 years	Total	20 to 24 years	25 to 34 years	35 to 44 years	45 to 54 years	55 to 64 years	65 years and over
ALL RACES											
Men											
1948	43 286	2 600	1 109	1 490	40 687	4 673	10 327	9 596	7 943	5 764	2 384
1949	43 498	2 477	1 056	1 420	41 022	4 682	10 418	9 722	8 008	5 748	2 454
1950	43 819	2 504	1 048	1 456	41 316	4 632	10 527	9 793	8 117	5 794	2 453
1951	43 001	2 347	1 081	1 266	40 655	3 935	10 375	9 799	8 205	5 873	2 469
1952	42 869	2 312	1 101	1 210	40 558	3 338	10 585	9 945	8 326	5 949	2 416
1953	43 633	2 320	1 070	1 249	41 315	3 053	10 736	10 437	8 570	5 975	2 543
1954	43 965	2 295	1 023	1 272	41 669	3 051	10 771	10 513	8 702	6 105	2 526
1955	44 475	2 369	1 070	1 299	42 106	3 221	10 806	10 595	8 838	6 122	2 526
1956	45 091	2 433	1 142	1 291	42 658	3 485	10 685	10 663	9 002	6 220	2 602
1957	45 197	2 415	1 127	1 289	42 780	3 629	10 571	10 731	9 153	6 222	2 477
1958	45 521	2 428	1 133	1 295	43 092	3 771	10 475	10 843	9 320	6 304	2 378
1959	45 886	2 596	1 206	1 390	43 289	3 940	10 346	10 899	9 438	6 345	2 322
1960	46 388	2 787	1 290	1 496	43 603	4 123	10 251	10 967	9 574	6 399	2 287
1961	46 653	2 794	1 210	1 583	43 860	4 253	10 176	11 012	9 668	6 530	2 220
1962	46 600	2 770	1 178	1 592	43 831	4 279	9 920	11 115	9 715	6 560	2 241
1963	47 129	2 907	1 321	1 586	44 222	4 514	9 876	11 187	9 836	6 675	2 135
1964	47 679	3 074	1 499	1 575	44 604	4 754	9 876	11 156	9 956	6 741	2 124
1965	48 255	3 397	1 532	1 866	44 857	4 894	9 903	11 120	10 045	6 763	2 132
1966	48 471	3 685	1 609	2 075	44 788	4 820	9 948	10 983	10 100	6 847	2 089
1967	48 987	3 634	1 658	1 976	45 354	5 043	10 207	10 859	10 189	6 937	2 118
1968	49 533	3 681	1 687	1 995	45 852	5 070	10 610	10 725	10 267	7 025	2 154
1969	50 221	3 870	1 770	2 100	46 351	5 282	10 941	10 556	10 344	7 058	2 170
1970	51 228	4 008	1 810	2 199	47 220	5 717	11 327	10 469	10 417	7 126	2 165
1971	52 180	4 172	1 856	2 315	48 009	6 233	11 731	10 347	10 451	7 155	2 090
1972	53 555	4 476	1 955	2 522	49 079	6 766	12 350	10 372	10 412	7 155	2 026
1973	54 624	4 693	2 073	2 618	49 932	7 183	13 056	10 338	10 416	7 028	1 913
1974	55 739	4 861	2 138	2 721	50 879	7 387	13 665	10 401	10 431	7 063	1 932
1975	56 299	4 805	2 065	2 740	51 494	7 565	14 192	10 398	10 401	7 023	1 914
1976	57 174	4 886	2 069	2 817	52 288	7 866	14 784	10 500	10 293	7 020	1 826
1977	58 396	5 048	2 155	2 893	53 348	8 109	15 353	10 771	10 158	7 100	1 857
1978	59 620	5 149	2 227	2 923	54 471	8 327	15 814	11 159	10 083	7 151	1 936
1979	60 726	5 111	2 192	2 919	55 615	8 535	16 387	11 531	10 008	7 212	1 943
1980	61 453	4 999	2 102	2 897	56 455	8 607	16 971	11 836	9 905	7 242	1 893
1981	61 974	4 777	1 957	2 820	57 197	8 648	17 479	12 166	9 868	7 170	1 866
1982	62 450	4 470	1 776	2 694	57 980	8 604	17 793	12 781	9 784	7 174	1 845
1983	63 047	4 303	1 621	2 682	58 744	8 601	18 038	13 398	9 746	7 119	1 842
1984	63 835	4 134	1 591	2 542	59 701	8 594	18 488	14 037	9 776	7 050	1 755
1985	64 411	4 134	1 663	2 471	60 277	8 283	18 808	14 506	9 870	7 060	1 750
1986	65 422	4 102	1 707	2 395	61 320	8 148	19 383	15 029	9 994	6 954	1 811
1987	66 207	4 112	1 745	2 367	62 095	7 837	19 656	15 587	10 176	6 940	1 899
1988	66 927	4 159	1 714	2 445	62 768	7 594	19 742	16 074	10 566	6 831	1 960
1989	67 840	4 136	1 630	2 505	63 704	7 458	19 905	16 622	10 919	6 783	2 017
1990	69 011	4 094	1 537	2 557	64 916	7 866	19 872	17 481	11 103	6 627	1 967
1991	69 168	3 795	1 452	2 343	65 374	7 820	19 641	18 077	11 362	6 550	1 924
1992	69 964	3 751	1 453	2 297	66 213	7 770	19 495	18 347	12 040	6 551	2 010
1993	70 404	3 762	1 497	2 265	66 642	7 671	19 214	18 713	12 562	6 502	1 980
1994	70 817	3 896	1 630	2 266	66 921	7 540	18 854	18 966	12 962	6 423	2 176
1995	71 360	4 036	1 668	2 368	67 324	7 338	18 670	19 189	13 421	6 504	2 201
1996	72 087	4 043	1 665	2 378	68 044	7 104	18 430	19 602	13 967	6 693	2 247
1997	73 261	4 095	1 676	2 419	69 166	7 184	18 110	20 058	14 564	6 952	2 298
1998	73 959	4 244	1 728	2 516	69 715	7 221	17 796	20 242	14 963	7 253	2 240
1999	74 512	4 318	1 732	2 587	70 194	7 291	17 318	20 382	15 394	7 477	2 333
2000	76 280	4 269	1 676	2 594	72 010	7 521	17 844	20 093	16 269	7 795	2 488
2001	76 886	4 070	1 568	2 501	72 816	7 640	17 671	20 018	16 804	8 171	2 511
2002	77 500	3 870	1 431	2 439	73 630	7 769	17 596	19 828	17 143	8 751	2 542
2003	78 238	3 614	1 405	2 209	74 623	7 906	17 767	19 762	17 352	9 144	2 692
2004	78 980	3 616	1 329	2 288	75 364	8 057	17 798	19 539	17 635	9 547	2 787
2005	80 033	3 590	1 368	2 222	76 443	8 054	17 837	19 495	18 053	10 045	2 959
2006	81 255	3 693	1 453	2 240	77 562	8 116	17 944	19 407	18 489	10 509	3 096
2007	82 136	3 541	1 354	2 187	78 596	8 095	18 308	19 299	18 801	10 904	3 188
2008	82 520	3 472	1 238	2 235	79 047	8 065	18 302	18 972	18 928	11 345	3 436
2009	82 123	3 226	1 103	2 123	78 897	7 839	18 211	18 518	19 001	11 730	3 598
2010	81 985	2 991	990	2 002	78 994	7 864	18 352	18 119	18 856	12 103	3 701
2011	81 975	2 895	917	1 978	79 080	8 101	18 469	17 686	18 483	12 350	3 990

Table 1-7. Civilian Labor Force, by Age, Sex, Race, and Hispanic Origin, 1948–2011—*Continued*

(Thousands of people.)

Race, Hispanic origin, sex, and year	16 years and over	16 to 19 years			20 years and over						
		Total	16 to 17 years	18 to 19 years	Total	20 to 24 years	25 to 34 years	35 to 44 years	45 to 54 years	55 to 64 years	65 years and over
ALL RACES											
Women											
1948	17 335	1 835	671	1 164	15 500	2 719	3 931	3 801	2 971	1 565	513
1949	17 788	1 811	648	1 163	15 978	2 658	3 997	3 989	3 099	1 678	556
1950	18 389	1 712	611	1 101	16 678	2 675	4 092	4 161	3 327	1 839	583
1951	19 016	1 756	662	1 094	17 259	2 659	4 293	4 301	3 534	1 923	551
1952	19 269	1 752	705	1 047	17 517	2 502	4 319	4 438	3 635	2 031	589
1953	19 382	1 707	657	1 050	17 674	2 428	4 162	4 662	3 679	2 049	693
1954	19 678	1 681	620	1 028	17 997	2 424	4 212	4 708	3 822	2 164	666
1955	20 548	1 723	641	1 083	18 825	2 445	4 252	4 805	4 154	2 391	779
1956	21 461	1 863	736	1 127	19 599	2 455	4 276	5 031	4 405	2 610	821
1957	21 732	1 860	716	1 144	19 873	2 442	4 255	5 116	4 615	2 631	813
1958	22 118	1 832	685	1 147	20 285	2 501	4 193	5 185	4 859	2 727	821
1959	22 483	1 896	765	1 132	20 587	2 473	4 089	5 228	5 080	2 882	836
1960	23 240	2 054	805	1 251	21 185	2 579	4 131	5 302	5 278	2 986	908
1961	23 806	2 142	774	1 368	21 664	2 697	4 143	5 390	5 403	3 106	926
1962	24 014	2 146	741	1 405	21 868	2 803	4 103	5 474	5 381	3 197	913
1963	24 704	2 232	850	1 380	22 473	2 959	4 174	5 601	5 502	3 331	906
1964	25 412	2 314	950	1 365	23 098	3 209	4 180	5 615	5 681	3 441	966
1965	26 200	2 513	954	1 559	23 686	3 365	4 330	5 720	5 711	3 587	976
1966	27 299	2 873	1 055	1 818	24 431	3 590	4 510	5 755	5 884	3 728	964
1967	28 360	2 887	1 076	1 810	25 475	3 966	4 848	5 844	5 983	3 855	979
1968	29 204	2 938	1 130	1 808	26 266	4 235	5 098	5 866	6 130	3 939	999
1969	30 513	3 100	1 239	1 859	27 413	4 597	5 395	5 902	6 386	4 077	1 057
1970	31 241	3 241	1 325	1 916	28 301	4 880	5 708	5 968	6 532	4 157	1 056
1971	32 202	3 298	1 336	1 963	28 904	5 098	5 983	5 957	6 573	4 234	1 059
1972	33 479	3 578	1 464	2 114	29 901	5 364	6 610	6 027	6 555	4 257	1 089
1973	34 804	3 814	1 592	2 221	30 991	5 663	7 320	6 154	6 567	4 228	1 061
1974	36 211	4 010	1 672	2 338	32 201	5 926	7 989	6 362	6 699	4 221	1 002
1975	37 475	4 065	1 674	2 391	33 410	6 185	8 673	6 505	6 683	4 323	1 042
1976	38 983	4 170	1 698	2 470	34 814	6 418	9 419	6 817	6 689	4 402	1 069
1977	40 613	4 303	1 765	2 538	36 310	6 717	10 149	7 171	6 720	4 477	1 078
1978	42 631	4 503	1 900	2 603	38 128	7 043	10 888	7 662	6 807	4 593	1 134
1979	44 235	4 527	1 887	2 639	39 708	7 234	11 551	8 154	6 889	4 719	1 161
1980	45 487	4 381	1 781	2 599	41 106	7 315	12 257	8 627	7 004	4 742	1 161
1981	46 696	4 211	1 691	2 520	42 485	7 451	12 912	9 045	7 101	4 799	1 176
1982	47 755	4 056	1 561	2 495	43 699	7 477	13 393	9 651	7 105	4 888	1 185
1983	48 503	3 868	1 452	2 416	44 636	7 451	13 796	10 213	7 105	4 873	1 198
1984	49 709	3 810	1 458	2 351	45 900	7 451	14 234	10 896	7 230	4 911	1 177
1985	51 050	3 767	1 491	2 276	47 283	7 434	14 742	11 567	7 452	4 932	1 156
1986	52 413	3 824	1 580	2 244	48 589	7 293	15 208	12 204	7 746	4 940	1 199
1987	53 658	3 875	1 638	2 237	49 783	7 140	15 577	12 873	8 034	4 937	1 221
1988	54 742	3 872	1 572	2 300	50 870	6 910	15 761	13 361	8 537	4 977	1 324
1989	56 030	3 818	1 495	2 323	52 212	6 721	15 990	13 980	8 997	5 095	1 429
1990	56 829	3 698	1 400	2 298	53 131	6 834	16 058	14 663	9 145	4 948	1 483
1991	57 178	3 470	1 337	2 133	53 708	6 728	15 867	15 235	9 465	4 924	1 489
1992	58 141	3 345	1 316	2 030	54 796	6 750	15 875	15 552	10 120	5 035	1 464
1993	58 795	3 408	1 335	2 073	55 388	6 683	15 566	15 849	10 733	5 097	1 459
1994	60 239	3 585	1 504	2 081	56 655	6 592	15 499	16 259	11 357	5 289	1 658
1995	60 944	3 729	1 557	2 172	57 215	6 349	15 528	16 562	11 801	5 356	1 618
1996	61 857	3 763	1 599	2 164	58 094	6 273	15 403	16 954	12 430	5 452	1 581
1997	63 036	3 837	1 561	2 277	59 198	6 348	15 271	17 268	13 010	5 713	1 590
1998	63 714	4 012	1 607	2 405	59 702	6 418	15 017	17 294	13 405	5 962	1 607
1999	64 855	4 015	1 606	2 410	60 840	6 643	14 826	17 501	13 994	6 204	1 673
2000	66 303	4 002	1 585	2 416	62 301	6 730	14 912	17 473	14 802	6 561	1 823
2001	66 848	3 832	1 520	2 313	63 016	6 917	14 690	17 386	15 221	6 932	1 870
2002	67 363	3 715	1 439	2 277	63 648	7 012	14 600	17 098	15 454	7 559	1 926
2003	68 272	3 556	1 452	2 104	64 716	7 021	14 576	16 933	15 919	8 168	2 099
2004	68 421	3 498	1 418	2 080	64 923	7 097	14 409	16 619	16 123	8 466	2 211
2005	69 288	3 574	1 457	2 117	65 714	7 073	14 503	16 535	16 349	8 934	2 319
2006	70 173	3 588	1 499	2 089	66 585	6 997	14 628	16 441	16 656	9 475	2 388
2007	70 988	3 471	1 417	2 055	67 516	7 110	14 822	16 227	16 896	9 846	2 615
2008	71 767	3 385	1 314	2 071	68 382	7 109	15 030	16 089	17 075	10 270	2 808
2009	72 019	3 163	1 124	2 039	68 856	7 132	15 087	15 720	17 204	10 776	2 937
2010	71 904	2 914	1 011	1 904	68 990	7 164	15 263	15 247	17 104	11 194	3 017
2011	71 642	2 832	957	1 875	68 810	7 169	15 255	14 973	16 876	11 414	3 121

Table 1-7. Civilian Labor Force, by Age, Sex, Race, and Hispanic Origin, 1948–2011—*Continued*

(Thousands of people.)

Race, Hispanic origin, sex, and year	16 years and over	16 to 19 years			20 years and over						
		Total	16 to 17 years	18 to 19 years	Total	20 to 24 years	25 to 34 years	35 to 44 years	45 to 54 years	55 to 64 years	65 years and over
WHITE											
Both Sexes											
1954	56 816	3 501	1 448	2 054	53 315	4 752	13 226	13 540	11 258	7 591	2 946
1955	58 085	3 598	1 511	2 087	54 487	4 941	13 267	13 729	11 680	7 810	3 062
1956	59 428	3 771	1 656	2 113	55 657	5 194	13 154	14 000	12 061	8 080	3 166
1957	59 754	3 775	1 637	2 135	55 979	5 283	13 044	14 117	12 382	8 091	3 049
1958	60 293	3 757	1 615	2 144	56 536	5 449	12 884	14 257	12 727	8 254	2 964
1959	60 952	4 000	1 775	2 225	56 952	5 544	12 670	14 355	13 048	8 411	2 925
1960	61 915	4 275	1 871	2 405	57 640	5 787	12 594	14 450	13 322	8 522	2 964
1961	62 656	4 362	1 767	2 594	58 294	6 026	12 503	14 557	13 517	8 773	2 917
1962	62 750	4 354	1 709	2 645	58 396	6 164	12 218	14 695	13 551	8 856	2 912
1963	63 830	4 559	1 950	2 608	59 271	6 537	12 229	14 859	13 789	9 067	2 790
1964	64 921	4 784	2 211	2 572	60 137	6 952	12 235	14 852	14 043	9 239	2 817
1965	66 137	5 267	2 221	3 044	60 870	7 189	12 391	14 900	14 162	9 392	2 839
1966	67 276	5 827	2 367	3 460	61 449	7 324	12 591	14 785	14 370	9 583	2 793
1967	68 699	5 749	2 432	3 318	62 950	7 886	13 123	14 765	14 545	9 817	2 821
1968	69 976	5 839	2 519	3 320	64 137	8 109	13 740	14 683	14 756	9 968	2 884
1969	71 778	6 168	2 698	3 470	65 611	8 614	14 289	14 564	15 057	10 132	2 954
1970	73 556	6 442	2 824	3 617	67 113	9 238	14 896	14 525	15 269	10 255	2 930
1971	74 963	6 681	2 894	3 787	68 282	9 889	15 445	14 374	15 343	10 351	2 880
1972	77 275	7 193	3 096	4 098	70 082	10 605	16 584	14 399	15 283	10 402	2 809
1973	79 151	7 579	3 320	4 260	71 572	11 182	17 764	14 440	15 256	10 240	2 687
1974	81 281	7 899	3 441	4 459	73 381	11 600	18 862	14 644	15 375	10 241	2 656
1975	82 831	7 899	3 375	4 525	74 932	12 019	19 897	14 753	15 308	10 287	2 668
1976	84 767	8 088	3 410	4 679	76 678	12 444	20 990	15 088	15 187	10 371	2 599
1977	87 141	8 352	3 562	4 790	78 789	12 892	22 099	15 604	15 053	10 495	2 647
1978	89 634	8 555	3 715	4 839	81 079	13 309	23 067	16 353	15 004	10 602	2 745
1979	91 923	8 548	3 668	4 881	83 375	13 632	24 101	17 123	14 965	10 767	2 787
1980	93 600	8 312	3 485	4 827	85 286	13 769	25 181	17 811	14 956	10 812	2 759
1981	95 052	7 962	3 274	4 688	87 089	13 926	26 208	18 445	14 993	10 764	2 753
1982	96 143	7 518	3 001	4 518	88 625	13 866	26 814	19 491	14 879	10 832	2 742
1983	97 021	7 186	2 765	4 421	89 835	13 816	27 237	20 488	14 798	10 732	2 766
1984	98 492	6 952	2 720	4 232	91 540	13 733	27 958	21 588	14 899	10 701	2 660
1985	99 926	6 841	2 777	4 065	93 085	13 469	28 640	22 591	15 101	10 679	2 605
1986	101 801	6 862	2 895	3 967	94 939	13 176	29 497	23 571	15 379	10 583	2 732
1987	103 290	6 893	2 963	3 931	96 396	12 764	29 956	24 581	15 792	10 497	2 806
1988	104 756	6 940	2 861	4 079	97 815	12 311	30 167	25 358	16 573	10 462	2 943
1989	106 355	6 809	2 685	4 124	99 546	11 940	30 388	26 312	17 278	10 533	3 094
1990	107 447	6 683	2 543	4 140	100 764	12 397	30 174	27 265	17 515	10 290	3 123
1991	107 743	6 245	2 432	3 813	101 498	12 248	29 794	28 213	18 028	10 129	3 086
1992	108 837	6 022	2 388	3 633	102 815	12 187	29 518	28 580	19 200	10 196	3 135
1993	109 700	6 105	2 458	3 647	103 595	11 987	29 027	29 056	20 181	10 215	3 129
1994	111 082	6 357	2 681	3 677	104 725	11 688	28 580	29 626	21 026	10 319	3 486
1995	111 950	6 545	2 749	3 796	105 404	11 266	28 325	30 112	21 804	10 432	3 466
1996	113 108	6 607	2 780	3 826	106 502	11 003	27 901	30 683	22 781	10 648	3 485
1997	114 693	6 720	2 779	3 941	107 973	11 127	27 362	31 171	23 709	11 086	3 517
1998	115 415	6 965	2 860	4 105	108 450	11 244	26 707	31 221	24 282	11 548	3 448
1999	116 509	7 048	2 849	4 199	109 461	11 436	25 978	31 391	25 102	11 960	3 595
2000	118 545	6 955	2 768	4 186	111 590	11 626	26 336	30 968	26 353	12 463	3 846
2001	119 399	6 661	2 626	4 035	112 737	11 883	26 010	30 778	27 062	13 121	3 883
2002	120 150	6 366	2 445	3 921	113 784	12 073	25 908	30 286	27 405	14 148	3 965
2003	120 546	5 973	2 414	3 560	114 572	12 064	25 752	29 788	27 786	14 944	4 238
2004	121 086	5 929	2 309	3 620	115 156	12 192	25 548	29 305	28 181	15 522	4 408
2005	122 299	5 950	2 390	3 560	116 349	12 109	25 548	29 107	28 685	16 275	4 624
2006	123 834	6 009	2 473	3 536	117 825	12 128	25 681	28 849	29 231	17 132	4 805
2007	124 935	5 795	2 326	3 470	119 139	12 176	26 076	28 394	29 627	17 782	5 085
2008	125 635	5 644	2 126	3 518	119 990	12 142	26 210	27 932	29 780	18 464	5 463
2009	125 644	5 295	1 883	3 413	120 349	11 995	26 277	27 263	29 903	19 199	5 711
2010	125 084	4 861	1 693	3 168	120 223	11 948	26 455	26 510	29 632	19 808	5 869
2011	124 579	4 714	1 581	3 134	119 865	12 120	26 511	25 834	29 036	20 188	6 175

Table 1-7. Civilian Labor Force, by Age, Sex, Race, and Hispanic Origin, 1948–2011—*Continued*

(Thousands of people.)

Race, Hispanic origin, sex, and year	16 years and over	16 to 19 years			20 years and over						
		Total	16 to 17 years	18 to 19 years	Total	20 to 24 years	25 to 34 years	35 to 44 years	45 to 54 years	55 to 64 years	65 years and over
WHITE											
Men											
1954	39 759	1 989	896	1 095	37 770	2 654	9 695	9 516	7 913	5 653	2 339
1955	40 197	2 056	935	1 121	38 141	2 803	9 721	9 597	8 025	5 654	2 343
1956	40 734	2 114	1 002	1 110	38 620	3 036	9 595	9 661	8 175	5 736	2 417
1957	40 826	2 108	992	1 114	38 718	3 152	9 483	9 719	8 317	5 735	2 307
1958	41 080	2 116	1 001	1 116	38 964	3 278	9 386	9 822	8 465	5 800	2 213
1959	41 397	2 279	1 077	1 202	39 118	3 409	9 261	9 876	8 581	5 833	2 158
1960	41 743	2 433	1 140	1 293	39 310	3 559	9 153	9 919	8 689	5 861	2 129
1961	41 986	2 439	1 067	1 372	39 547	3 681	9 072	9 961	8 776	5 988	2 068
1962	41 931	2 432	1 041	1 391	39 499	3 726	8 846	10 029	8 820	5 995	2 082
1963	42 404	2 563	1 183	1 380	39 841	3 955	8 805	10 079	8 944	6 090	1 967
1964	42 894	2 716	1 345	1 371	40 178	4 166	8 800	10 055	9 053	6 161	1 942
1965	43 400	2 999	1 359	1 639	40 401	4 279	8 824	10 023	9 130	6 188	1 959
1966	43 572	3 253	1 423	1 830	40 319	4 200	8 859	9 892	9 189	6 250	1 928
1967	44 041	3 191	1 464	1 727	40 851	4 416	9 102	9 785	9 260	6 348	1 944
1968	44 553	3 236	1 504	1 732	41 318	4 432	9 477	9 662	9 340	6 427	1 981
1969	45 185	3 413	1 583	1 830	41 772	4 615	9 773	9 509	9 413	6 467	1 996
1970	46 035	3 551	1 629	1 922	42 483	4 988	10 099	9 414	9 487	6 517	1 978
1971	46 904	3 719	1 681	2 039	43 185	5 448	10 444	9 294	9 528	6 550	1 922
1972	48 118	3 980	1 758	2 223	44 138	5 937	11 039	9 278	9 473	6 562	1 846
1973	48 920	4 174	1 875	2 300	44 747	6 274	11 621	9 212	9 445	6 452	1 740
1974	49 843	4 312	1 922	2 391	45 532	6 470	12 135	9 246	9 455	6 464	1 759
1975	50 324	4 290	1 871	2 418	46 034	6 642	12 579	9 231	9 415	6 425	1 742
1976	51 033	4 357	1 869	2 489	46 675	6 890	13 092	9 289	9 310	6 437	1 657
1977	52 033	4 496	1 949	2 548	47 537	7 097	13 575	9 509	9 175	6 492	1 688
1978	52 955	4 565	2 002	2 563	48 390	7 274	13 939	9 858	9 068	6 508	1 744
1979	53 856	4 537	1 974	2 563	49 320	7 421	14 415	10 183	8 968	6 571	1 761
1980	54 473	4 424	1 881	2 543	50 049	7 479	14 893	10 455	8 877	6 618	1 727
1981	54 895	4 224	1 751	2 473	50 671	7 521	15 340	10 740	8 836	6 530	1 704
1982	55 133	3 933	1 602	2 331	51 200	7 438	15 549	11 289	8 727	6 520	1 677
1983	55 480	3 764	1 452	2 312	51 716	7 406	15 707	11 817	8 649	6 446	1 691
1984	56 062	3 609	1 420	2 189	52 453	7 370	16 037	12 348	8 683	6 410	1 606
1985	56 472	3 576	1 467	2 109	52 895	7 122	16 306	12 767	8 730	6 376	1 595
1986	57 217	3 542	1 502	2 040	53 675	6 986	16 769	13 207	8 791	6 260	1 663
1987	57 779	3 547	1 524	2 023	54 232	6 717	16 963	13 674	8 945	6 200	1 733
1988	58 317	3 583	1 487	2 095	54 734	6 468	17 018	14 068	9 285	6 108	1 787
1989	58 988	3 546	1 401	2 146	55 441	6 316	17 077	14 516	9 615	6 082	1 835
1990	59 638	3 522	1 333	2 189	56 116	6 688	16 920	15 026	9 713	5 957	1 811
1991	59 656	3 269	1 266	2 003	56 387	6 619	16 709	15 523	9 926	5 847	1 763
1992	60 168	3 192	1 260	1 932	56 976	6 542	16 512	15 701	10 570	5 821	1 830
1993	60 484	3 200	1 292	1 908	57 284	6 449	16 244	15 971	11 010	5 784	1 825
1994	60 727	3 315	1 403	1 912	57 411	6 294	15 879	16 188	11 327	5 726	1 998
1995	61 146	3 427	1 429	1 998	57 719	6 096	15 669	16 414	11 730	5 809	2 000
1996	61 783	3 444	1 421	2 023	58 340	5 922	15 475	16 728	12 217	5 943	2 054
1997	62 639	3 513	1 440	2 073	59 126	6 029	15 120	17 019	12 710	6 154	2 094
1998	63 034	3 614	1 487	2 127	59 421	6 063	14 770	17 157	13 003	6 415	2 013
1999	63 413	3 666	1 478	2 188	59 747	6 151	14 292	17 201	13 368	6 618	2 117
2000	64 466	3 615	1 422	2 193	60 850	6 244	14 666	16 880	13 977	6 840	2 243
2001	64 966	3 446	1 334	2 112	61 519	6 363	14 536	16 809	14 400	7 169	2 241
2002	65 308	3 241	1 215	2 026	62 067	6 444	14 499	16 583	14 615	7 665	2 261
2003	65 509	3 036	1 193	1 843	62 473	6 479	14 529	16 398	14 708	7 973	2 386
2004	65 994	3 050	1 127	1 923	62 944	6 586	14 429	16 192	14 934	8 326	2 478
2005	66 694	2 988	1 162	1 826	63 705	6 562	14 426	16 080	15 273	8 734	2 631
2006	67 613	3 074	1 222	1 852	64 540	6 597	14 469	15 962	15 606	9 152	2 753
2007	68 158	2 944	1 147	1 798	65 214	6 567	14 715	15 765	15 846	9 500	2 821
2008	68 351	2 868	1 040	1 829	65 483	6 526	14 715	15 436	15 905	9 855	3 046
2009	68 051	2 679	933	1 746	65 372	6 348	14 669	15 066	15 943	10 160	3 186
2010	67 728	2 463	844	1 619	65 265	6 342	14 734	14 713	15 791	10 422	3 263
2011	67 551	2 386	780	1 606	65 165	6 539	14 785	14 317	15 400	10 629	3 494

Table 1-7. Civilian Labor Force, by Age, Sex, Race, and Hispanic Origin, 1948–2011—*Continued*

(Thousands of people.)

Race, Hispanic origin, sex, and year	16 years and over	16 to 19 years			20 years and over						
		Total	16 to 17 years	18 to 19 years	Total	20 to 24 years	25 to 34 years	35 to 44 years	45 to 54 years	55 to 64 years	65 years and over
WHITE											
Women											
1954	17 057	1 512	552	959	15 545	2 098	3 531	4 024	3 345	1 938	607
1955	17 888	1 542	576	966	16 346	2 138	3 546	4 132	3 655	2 156	719
1956	18 694	1 657	654	1 003	17 037	2 158	3 559	4 339	3 886	2 344	749
1957	18 928	1 667	645	1 021	17 261	2 131	3 561	4 398	4 065	2 356	742
1958	19 213	1 641	614	1 028	17 572	2 171	3 498	4 435	4 262	2 454	751
1959	19 555	1 721	698	1 023	17 834	2 135	3 409	4 479	4 467	2 578	767
1960	20 172	1 842	731	1 112	18 330	2 228	3 441	4 531	4 633	2 661	835
1961	20 670	1 923	700	1 222	18 747	2 345	3 431	4 596	4 741	2 785	849
1962	20 819	1 922	668	1 254	18 897	2 438	3 372	4 666	4 731	2 861	830
1963	21 426	1 996	767	1 228	19 430	2 582	3 424	4 780	4 845	2 977	823
1964	22 027	2 068	866	1 201	19 959	2 786	3 435	4 797	4 990	3 078	875
1965	22 737	2 268	862	1 405	20 469	2 910	3 567	4 877	5 032	3 204	880
1966	23 704	2 574	944	1 630	21 130	3 124	3 732	4 893	5 181	3 333	865
1967	24 658	2 558	968	1 591	22 100	3 471	4 021	4 980	5 285	3 469	877
1968	25 423	2 603	1 015	1 588	22 821	3 677	4 263	5 021	5 416	3 541	903
1969	26 593	2 755	1 115	1 640	23 839	3 999	4 516	5 055	5 644	3 665	958
1970	27 521	2 891	1 195	1 695	24 630	4 250	4 797	5 111	5 781	3 738	952
1971	28 060	2 962	1 213	1 748	25 097	4 441	5 001	5 080	5 816	3 801	958
1972	29 157	3 213	1 338	1 875	25 945	4 668	5 544	5 121	5 810	3 839	963
1973	30 231	3 405	1 445	1 960	26 825	4 908	6 143	5 228	5 811	3 788	947
1974	31 437	3 588	1 520	2 068	27 850	5 131	6 727	5 399	5 920	3 777	897
1975	32 508	3 610	1 504	2 107	28 898	5 378	7 318	5 522	5 892	3 862	926
1976	33 735	3 731	1 541	2 189	30 004	5 554	7 898	5 799	5 877	3 935	940
1977	35 108	3 856	1 614	2 243	31 253	5 795	8 523	6 095	5 877	4 003	959
1978	36 679	3 990	1 713	2 276	32 689	6 035	9 128	6 495	5 936	4 094	1 001
1979	38 067	4 011	1 694	2 318	34 056	6 211	9 687	6 940	5 997	4 196	1 024
1980	39 127	3 888	1 605	2 284	35 239	6 290	10 289	7 356	6 079	4 194	1 032
1981	40 157	3 739	1 523	2 216	36 418	6 406	10 868	7 704	6 157	4 235	1 049
1982	41 010	3 585	1 399	2 186	37 425	6 428	11 264	8 202	6 152	4 313	1 065
1983	41 541	3 422	1 314	2 109	38 119	6 410	11 530	8 670	6 149	4 285	1 074
1984	42 431	3 343	1 300	2 043	39 087	6 363	11 922	9 240	6 217	4 292	1 054
1985	43 455	3 265	1 310	1 955	40 190	6 348	12 334	9 824	6 371	4 303	1 010
1986	44 584	3 320	1 393	1 927	41 264	6 191	12 729	10 364	6 588	4 323	1 069
1987	45 510	3 347	1 439	1 908	42 164	6 047	12 993	10 907	6 847	4 297	1 073
1988	46 439	3 358	1 374	1 984	43 081	5 844	13 149	11 291	7 288	4 354	1 156
1989	47 367	3 262	1 284	1 978	44 105	5 625	13 311	11 796	7 663	4 451	1 259
1990	47 809	3 161	1 210	1 951	44 648	5 709	13 254	12 239	7 802	4 333	1 312
1991	48 087	2 976	1 166	1 810	45 111	5 629	13 085	12 689	8 101	4 282	1 324
1992	48 669	2 830	1 128	1 702	45 839	5 645	13 006	12 879	8 630	4 375	1 305
1993	49 216	2 905	1 167	1 739	46 311	5 539	12 783	13 085	9 171	4 430	1 304
1994	50 356	3 042	1 278	1 764	47 314	5 394	12 702	13 439	9 699	4 593	1 487
1995	50 804	3 118	1 320	1 798	47 686	5 170	12 656	13 697	10 074	4 622	1 466
1996	51 325	3 163	1 360	1 803	48 162	5 081	12 426	13 955	10 563	4 706	1 431
1997	52 054	3 207	1 339	1 867	48 847	5 099	12 242	14 153	10 999	4 932	1 422
1998	52 380	3 351	1 373	1 977	49 029	5 180	11 937	14 064	11 279	5 133	1 435
1999	53 096	3 382	1 371	2 010	49 714	5 285	11 685	14 190	11 734	5 342	1 478
2000	54 079	3 339	1 346	1 993	50 740	5 381	11 669	14 088	12 376	5 623	1 602
2001	54 433	3 215	1 292	1 923	51 218	5 519	11 474	13 969	12 662	5 952	1 642
2002	54 842	3 125	1 229	1 895	51 717	5 628	11 409	13 703	12 790	6 482	1 704
2003	55 037	2 937	1 221	1 716	52 099	5 584	11 223	13 390	13 078	6 970	1 852
2004	55 092	2 879	1 182	1 697	52 212	5 606	11 119	13 114	13 247	7 197	1 930
2005	55 605	2 962	1 228	1 733	52 643	5 546	11 123	13 027	13 413	7 542	1 993
2006	56 221	2 935	1 251	1 684	53 286	5 530	11 212	12 886	13 625	7 980	2 052
2007	56 777	2 851	1 179	1 672	53 925	5 609	11 360	12 629	13 781	8 282	2 264
2008	57 284	2 776	1 086	1 690	54 508	5 616	11 495	12 495	13 875	8 609	2 417
2009	57 593	2 616	950	1 667	54 976	5 647	11 608	12 197	13 960	9 039	2 525
2010	57 356	2 398	849	1 549	54 957	5 607	11 721	11 796	13 841	9 386	2 607
2011	57 028	2 328	800	1 528	54 700	5 581	11 726	11 517	13 636	9 559	2 681

Table 1-7. Civilian Labor Force, by Age, Sex, Race, and Hispanic Origin, 1948–2011—*Continued*

(Thousands of people.)

Race, Hispanic origin, sex, and year	16 years and over	16 to 19 years			20 years and over						
		Total	16 to 17 years	18 to 19 years	Total	20 to 24 years	25 to 34 years	35 to 44 years	45 to 54 years	55 to 64 years	65 years and over
BLACK											
Both Sexes											
1974	9 167	851	317	534	8 317	1 492	2 358	1 777	1 517	917	253
1975	9 263	838	312	524	8 426	1 477	2 466	1 775	1 519	929	258
1976	9 561	837	304	532	8 724	1 544	2 646	1 824	1 518	925	268
1977	9 932	861	304	557	9 072	1 641	2 798	1 894	1 530	943	267
1978	10 432	930	341	589	9 501	1 739	2 961	1 975	1 560	978	289
1979	10 678	912	340	572	9 766	1 793	3 094	2 039	1 584	974	281
1980	10 865	891	326	565	9 975	1 802	3 259	2 081	1 596	978	257
1981	11 086	862	308	554	10 224	1 828	3 365	2 164	1 608	1 009	249
1982	11 331	824	268	556	10 507	1 849	3 492	2 303	1 610	1 012	243
1983	11 647	809	248	561	10 838	1 871	3 675	2 406	1 630	1 032	224
1984	12 033	827	268	558	11 206	1 926	3 800	2 565	1 671	1 020	224
1985	12 364	889	311	578	11 476	1 854	3 888	2 681	1 742	1 059	252
1986	12 654	883	322	562	11 770	1 881	4 028	2 793	1 793	1 051	224
1987	12 993	899	336	563	12 094	1 818	4 147	2 942	1 838	1 098	251
1988	13 205	889	344	545	12 316	1 782	4 226	3 069	1 894	1 069	276
1989	13 497	925	353	572	12 573	1 789	4 295	3 227	1 954	1 023	285
1990	13 740	866	306	560	12 874	1 758	4 307	3 566	2 003	977	262
1991	13 797	774	266	508	13 023	1 750	4 254	3 719	2 042	1 001	256
1992	14 162	816	285	532	13 346	1 763	4 309	3 843	2 142	1 029	259
1993	14 225	807	283	524	13 418	1 764	4 232	3 960	2 212	1 013	237
1994	14 502	852	351	501	13 650	1 800	4 199	4 068	2 308	1 007	267
1995	14 817	911	366	545	13 906	1 754	4 267	4 165	2 404	1 046	271
1996	15 134	923	366	556	14 211	1 738	4 305	4 287	2 553	1 073	255
1997	15 529	933	352	580	14 596	1 783	4 329	4 401	2 724	1 093	265
1998	15 982	1 017	370	646	14 966	1 797	4 332	4 531	2 863	1 163	278
1999	16 365	959	352	607	15 406	1 866	4 430	4 653	2 992	1 180	285
2000	16 397	941	356	585	15 456	1 873	4 281	4 515	3 203	1 264	320
2001	16 421	898	332	565	15 524	1 878	4 180	4 483	3 298	1 335	350
2002	16 565	870	297	574	15 695	1 908	4 134	4 458	3 435	1 407	353
2003	16 526	771	289	482	15 755	1 892	4 060	4 465	3 506	1 466	366
2004	16 638	762	272	489	15 876	1 926	4 076	4 380	3 578	1 538	380
2005	17 013	803	279	525	16 209	1 957	4 145	4 370	3 686	1 647	403
2006	17 314	871	318	553	16 443	1 960	4 197	4 348	3 785	1 739	414
2007	17 496	801	300	501	16 695	1 974	4 254	4 357	3 866	1 811	432
2008	17 740	787	270	517	16 953	1 981	4 328	4 316	3 945	1 908	476
2009	17 632	729	231	499	16 902	1 961	4 300	4 175	3 976	1 995	495
2010	17 862	677	203	473	17 186	2 072	4 418	4 095	3 991	2 104	506
2011	17 881	647	188	459	17 234	2 105	4 434	4 029	3 957	2 155	555
BLACK											
Men											
1974	5 020	480	189	291	4 540	798	1 279	953	838	519	152
1975	5 016	447	168	279	4 569	790	1 328	948	833	520	150
1976	5 101	454	168	285	4 648	820	1 383	969	824	504	149
1977	5 263	476	178	299	4 787	856	1 441	1 003	818	515	154
1978	5 435	491	186	306	4 943	883	1 504	1 022	829	540	166
1979	5 559	480	179	301	5 079	928	1 577	1 049	844	524	156
1980	5 612	479	181	298	5 134	935	1 659	1 061	830	509	138
1981	5 685	462	169	293	5 223	940	1 702	1 093	829	524	134
1982	5 804	436	137	300	5 368	964	1 769	1 152	824	525	135
1983	5 966	433	134	300	5 533	997	1 840	1 196	845	536	119
1984	6 126	440	141	299	5 686	1 022	1 924	1 270	847	505	118
1985	6 220	471	162	310	5 749	950	1 937	1 313	879	544	125
1986	6 373	458	164	294	5 915	957	2 029	1 359	901	552	116
1987	6 486	463	179	284	6 023	914	2 074	1 406	915	586	130
1988	6 596	469	186	283	6 127	913	2 114	1 459	936	565	139
1989	6 701	480	190	291	6 221	904	2 157	1 544	945	530	141
1990	6 802	445	161	284	6 357	879	2 142	1 733	988	496	119
1991	6 851	400	140	260	6 451	896	2 111	1 806	1 010	507	122
1992	6 997	429	149	280	6 568	900	2 121	1 859	1 037	521	130
1993	7 019	425	154	270	6 594	875	2 118	1 918	1 065	506	112
1994	7 089	443	176	266	6 646	891	2 068	1 975	1 102	484	125
1995	7 183	453	184	269	6 730	866	2 089	1 987	1 148	490	150
1996	7 264	458	182	276	6 806	848	2 077	2 036	1 204	509	132
1997	7 354	444	178	266	6 910	832	2 052	2 096	1 287	508	134
1998	7 542	488	181	307	7 053	837	2 034	2 142	1 343	548	150
1999	7 652	470	180	291	7 182	835	2 069	2 206	1 387	547	138
2000	7 702	462	181	281	7 240	875	1 999	2 105	1 497	612	151
2001	7 647	447	166	281	7 200	853	1 915	2 073	1 537	645	177
2002	7 794	446	149	297	7 347	906	1 909	2 064	1 623	664	181
2003	7 711	365	138	228	7 346	918	1 872	2 058	1 627	685	186
2004	7 773	359	128	231	7 414	927	1 931	2 000	1 654	714	188
2005	7 998	399	139	260	7 600	940	1 948	2 028	1 732	756	196
2006	8 128	409	152	256	7 720	971	1 986	1 999	1 792	777	195
2007	8 252	384	137	247	7 867	981	2 037	2 030	1 822	791	206
2008	8 347	385	124	261	7 962	984	2 047	2 008	1 846	852	225
2009	8 265	350	111	239	7 914	954	2 041	1 932	1 852	904	231
2010	8 415	339	96	244	8 076	986	2 118	1 924	1 862	950	236
2011	8 454	329	89	241	8 125	1 012	2 159	1 860	1 854	983	257

Table 1-7. Civilian Labor Force, by Age, Sex, Race, and Hispanic Origin, 1948–2011—*Continued*

(Thousands of people.)

Race, Hispanic origin, sex, and year	16 years and over	16 to 19 years			20 years and over						
		Total	16 to 17 years	18 to 19 years	Total	20 to 24 years	25 to 34 years	35 to 44 years	45 to 54 years	55 to 64 years	65 years and over
BLACK											
Women											
1974	4 148	371	128	243	3 777	694	1 079	824	679	398	100
1975	4 247	391	144	245	3 857	687	1 138	827	686	409	108
1976	4 460	384	136	247	4 076	723	1 264	855	694	421	119
1977	4 670	385	127	258	4 286	785	1 357	891	712	429	113
1978	4 997	439	155	283	4 558	856	1 456	953	731	439	124
1979	5 119	432	161	271	4 687	865	1 517	990	740	451	124
1980	5 253	412	144	267	4 841	867	1 600	1 020	767	469	119
1981	5 401	400	139	261	5 001	888	1 663	1 071	779	485	115
1982	5 527	387	131	256	5 140	885	1 723	1 151	786	487	108
1983	5 681	375	114	261	5 306	874	1 835	1 210	785	496	105
1984	5 907	387	127	260	5 520	904	1 876	1 294	823	515	106
1985	6 144	417	149	268	5 727	904	1 951	1 368	862	515	127
1986	6 281	425	157	268	5 855	924	1 999	1 434	892	499	107
1987	6 507	435	157	278	6 071	904	2 073	1 537	924	512	121
1988	6 609	419	158	262	6 190	869	2 112	1 610	958	504	137
1989	6 796	445	163	281	6 352	885	2 138	1 683	1 009	493	144
1990	6 938	421	145	276	6 517	879	2 165	1 833	1 015	481	143
1991	6 946	374	126	248	6 572	854	2 143	1 913	1 032	494	135
1992	7 166	387	135	252	6 778	863	2 188	1 985	1 105	508	129
1993	7 206	383	129	254	6 824	889	2 115	2 042	1 147	506	125
1994	7 413	409	174	235	7 004	909	2 131	2 093	1 206	523	142
1995	7 634	458	182	276	7 175	887	2 177	2 178	1 256	556	121
1996	7 869	464	184	280	7 405	890	2 228	2 251	1 349	565	122
1997	8 175	489	175	314	7 686	951	2 277	2 305	1 437	585	131
1998	8 441	528	189	339	7 912	960	2 298	2 390	1 520	615	128
1999	8 713	489	172	316	8 224	1 031	2 360	2 447	1 606	633	147
2000	8 695	479	175	305	8 215	998	2 282	2 409	1 706	652	168
2001	8 774	451	166	284	8 323	1 025	2 265	2 410	1 762	690	173
2002	8 772	424	148	276	8 348	1 002	2 225	2 394	1 812	743	171
2003	8 815	406	151	255	8 409	973	2 188	2 407	1 879	781	180
2004	8 865	403	144	259	8 462	999	2 144	2 380	1 924	824	192
2005	9 014	405	140	265	8 610	1 017	2 197	2 342	1 954	891	207
2006	9 186	462	166	297	8 723	989	2 211	2 349	1 993	963	218
2007	9 244	417	163	254	8 828	993	2 218	2 328	2 044	1 019	227
2008	9 393	402	146	256	8 991	997	2 281	2 308	2 099	1 056	251
2009	9 367	379	119	260	8 988	1 008	2 258	2 243	2 124	1 091	264
2010	9 447	337	108	230	9 110	1 086	2 299	2 171	2 129	1 153	270
2011	9 427	318	99	219	9 110	1 093	2 275	2 168	2 104	1 172	298
HISPANIC											
Both Sexes											
1975	4 171	444	. . .	. . .	. . .	. . .	. . .	. . .	. . .	. . .	. . .
1976	4 205	447	176	285	3 820	729	1 248	875	625	294	48
1977	4 536	493	184	305	4 059	813	1 325	916	656	293	55
1978	4 979	533	221	312	4 446	901	1 446	1 008	701	323	67
1979	5 219	551	207	343	4 668	960	1 532	1 062	704	339	72
1980	6 146	645	241	404	5 502	1 136	1 843	1 163	860	414	85
1981	6 492	603	215	388	5 888	1 231	2 015	1 239	886	430	87
1982	6 734	585	192	393	6 148	1 251	2 163	1 313	891	444	85
1983	7 033	590	189	401	6 442	1 282	2 267	1 380	931	495	86
1984	7 451	618	209	409	6 833	1 325	2 436	1 509	954	524	84
1985	7 698	579	199	379	7 119	1 358	2 571	1 595	985	527	82
1986	8 076	571	203	368	7 505	1 414	2 685	1 713	1 097	511	84
1987	8 541	610	206	404	7 931	1 425	2 890	1 904	1 086	545	81
1988	8 982	671	234	437	8 311	1 486	2 957	1 996	1 147	621	103
1989	9 323	680	224	456	8 643	1 483	3 118	2 092	1 205	625	120
1990	10 720	829	276	554	9 891	1 839	3 590	2 386	1 320	647	110
1991	10 920	781	249	532	10 139	1 835	3 596	2 539	1 376	681	111
1992	11 338	796	263	533	10 542	1 815	3 740	2 735	1 442	687	122
1993	11 610	771	246	525	10 839	1 811	3 800	2 865	1 534	684	145
1994	11 975	807	285	522	11 168	1 863	3 865	2 965	1 626	698	151
1995	12 267	850	291	559	11 417	1 818	3 943	3 113	1 671	720	152
1996	12 774	845	284	561	11 929	1 845	4 054	3 361	1 697	806	166
1997	13 796	911	315	596	12 884	2 004	4 298	3 601	1 945	850	186
1998	14 317	1 007	320	688	13 310	2 077	4 372	3 707	2 090	894	169
1999	14 665	1 049	333	717	13 616	2 052	4 330	3 929	2 178	927	199
2000	16 689	1 168	368	800	15 521	2 546	5 197	4 241	2 387	940	209
2001	17 328	1 176	352	824	16 152	2 616	5 380	4 377	2 583	1 000	195
2002	17 943	1 103	335	769	16 840	2 678	5 645	4 545	2 657	1 091	224
2003	18 813	960	322	638	17 853	2 672	5 960	4 867	2 894	1 201	259
2004	19 272	995	297	698	18 277	2 732	5 931	4 931	3 093	1 284	306
2005	19 824	1 038	331	708	18 785	2 651	6 080	5 110	3 256	1 378	311
2006	20 694	1 071	360	710	19 623	2 681	6 295	5 337	3 452	1 490	369
2007	21 602	1 091	347	744	20 511	2 728	6 559	5 552	3 707	1 569	395
2008	22 024	1 121	353	768	20 903	2 668	6 557	5 698	3 862	1 701	417
2009	22 352	1 063	301	762	21 290	2 647	6 435	5 752	4 116	1 866	472
2010	22 748	1 002	264	738	21 747	2 760	6 517	5 783	4 238	1 936	513
2011	22 898	965	251	713	21 933	3 017	6 416	5 702	4 272	2 015	511

. . . = Not available.

Table 1-7. Civilian Labor Force, by Age, Sex, Race, and Hispanic Origin, 1948–2011—*Continued*

(Thousands of people.)

Race, Hispanic origin, sex, and year	16 years and over	16 to 19 years			20 years and over						
		Total	16 to 17 years	18 to 19 years	Total	20 to 24 years	25 to 34 years	35 to 44 years	45 to 54 years	55 to 64 years	65 years and over
HISPANIC											
Men											
1975	2 597	. . .	. . .	. . .	2 343	. . .	. . .	. . .	. . .	. . .	. . .
1976	2 580	260	104	155	2 326	433	771	541	398	189	34
1977	2 817	285	105	179	2 530	485	828	567	416	197	42
1978	3 041	299	129	171	2 742	546	882	620	425	217	52
1979	3 184	315	121	194	2 869	562	941	648	445	216	56
1980	3 818	392	147	245	3 426	697	1 161	713	522	270	62
1981	4 005	359	130	229	3 647	747	1 269	756	535	278	61
1982	4 148	333	111	221	3 815	759	1 361	808	539	290	58
1983	4 362	348	109	239	4 014	789	1 447	852	557	311	58
1984	4 563	345	113	232	4 218	822	1 540	910	570	325	51
1985	4 729	334	116	218	4 395	835	1 629	957	591	331	53
1986	4 948	336	114	222	4 612	888	1 669	1 015	661	323	56
1987	5 163	345	112	233	4 818	865	1 801	1 121	652	325	55
1988	5 409	378	123	255	5 031	897	1 834	1 189	686	355	69
1989	5 595	400	129	271	5 195	909	1 899	1 221	719	375	71
1990	6 546	512	165	346	6 034	1 182	2 230	1 403	775	380	65
1991	6 664	466	141	325	6 198	1 202	2 260	1 487	780	401	67
1992	6 900	468	154	314	6 432	1 141	2 366	1 593	844	414	74
1993	7 076	455	145	310	6 621	1 147	2 417	1 675	900	394	88
1994	7 210	463	163	300	6 747	1 184	2 430	1 713	922	410	89
1995	7 376	479	168	311	6 898	1 153	2 469	1 795	965	417	98
1996	7 646	496	156	340	7 150	1 132	2 510	1 966	967	469	105
1997	8 309	531	177	354	7 779	1 267	2 684	2 091	1 112	511	113
1998	8 571	565	188	377	8 005	1 288	2 733	2 173	1 164	541	106
1999	8 546	596	181	415	7 950	1 231	2 633	2 219	1 205	526	136
2000	9 923	676	204	471	9 247	1 590	3 181	2 451	1 337	555	134
2001	10 279	684	200	484	9 595	1 602	3 294	2 562	1 430	582	125
2002	10 609	632	183	449	9 977	1 627	3 484	2 647	1 478	607	134
2003	11 288	532	164	368	10 756	1 642	3 776	2 877	1 630	680	150
2004	11 587	567	156	410	11 020	1 671	3 765	2 934	1 736	728	186
2005	11 985	577	179	398	11 408	1 645	3 879	3 058	1 855	779	192
2006	12 488	600	189	411	11 888	1 646	4 014	3 203	1 960	838	228
2007	13 005	602	189	412	12 403	1 645	4 170	3 346	2 104	904	233
2008	13 255	626	202	424	12 629	1 594	4 172	3 425	2 216	979	243
2009	13 310	580	160	420	12 730	1 542	4 046	3 472	2 350	1 046	273
2010	13 511	553	132	420	12 958	1 612	4 061	3 515	2 407	1 061	302
2011	13 576	545	129	416	13 030	1 811	4 011	3 421	2 372	1 122	293
HISPANIC											
Women											
1975	1 574	. . .	. . .	. . .	1 384	. . .	. . .	. . .	. . .	. . .	. . .
1976	1 625	201	71	130	1 454	295	479	334	227	105	13
1977	1 720	204	80	125	1 523	327	497	349	240	96	13
1978	1 938	233	93	142	1 704	354	564	388	275	106	16
1979	2 035	235	86	149	1 800	397	590	413	258	124	15
1980	2 328	252	93	159	2 076	439	682	450	337	144	22
1981	2 486	244	85	159	2 242	484	745	483	351	152	27
1982	2 586	252	81	172	2 333	492	802	504	352	155	28
1983	2 671	242	80	162	2 429	493	820	529	374	184	29
1984	2 888	273	96	177	2 615	503	896	599	384	199	34
1985	2 970	245	84	161	2 725	524	943	639	394	196	29
1986	3 128	236	89	147	2 893	526	1 016	698	436	189	28
1987	3 377	265	94	171	3 112	559	1 090	783	434	220	27
1988	3 573	293	111	182	3 281	589	1 123	806	461	267	34
1989	3 728	280	95	185	3 448	574	1 219	871	486	251	49
1990	4 174	318	110	207	3 857	657	1 360	983	545	268	45
1991	4 256	315	107	207	3 941	633	1 336	1 052	596	279	44
1992	4 439	328	110	219	4 110	674	1 374	1 142	599	273	48
1993	4 534	316	101	215	4 218	664	1 383	1 190	633	290	57
1994	4 765	345	122	222	4 421	679	1 435	1 252	704	288	62
1995	4 891	371	123	249	4 520	666	1 473	1 318	706	303	54
1996	5 128	349	128	221	4 779	713	1 544	1 395	729	338	61
1997	5 486	381	138	242	5 106	737	1 614	1 510	833	338	73
1998	5 746	442	132	310	5 304	789	1 639	1 533	927	353	62
1999	6 119	453	151	302	5 666	821	1 698	1 710	973	401	63
2000	6 767	492	164	328	6 275	956	2 016	1 791	1 051	386	75
2001	7 049	492	152	340	6 557	1 014	2 086	1 815	1 153	418	70
2002	7 334	471	152	320	6 863	1 051	2 161	1 897	1 179	484	90
2003	7 525	428	158	271	7 096	1 030	2 183	1 990	1 264	520	109
2004	7 685	429	141	288	7 257	1 060	2 166	1 998	1 357	556	119
2005	7 839	462	152	310	7 377	1 005	2 201	2 052	1 401	599	119
2006	8 206	471	171	300	7 735	1 035	2 280	2 134	1 492	652	141
2007	8 597	489	158	332	8 108	1 083	2 389	2 205	1 604	665	162
2008	8 769	495	151	344	8 274	1 074	2 384	2 274	1 646	722	174
2009	9 043	483	141	342	8 560	1 105	2 388	2 280	1 767	820	200
2010	9 238	449	132	317	8 789	1 147	2 456	2 268	1 831	875	211
2011	9 322	419	122	297	8 902	1 206	2 406	2 282	1 899	893	217

. . . = Not available.

Table 1-8. Civilian Labor Force Participation Rates, by Age, Sex, Race, and Hispanic Origin, 1948–2011

(Percent.)

Race, Hispanic origin, sex, and year	16 years and over	16 to 19 years	20 years and over						
			Total	20 to 24 years	25 to 34 years	35 to 44 years	45 to 54 years	55 to 64 years	65 years and over
ALL RACES									
Both Sexes									
1948	58.8	52.5	59.4	64.1	63.1	66.7	65.1	56.9	27.0
1949	58.9	52.2	59.5	64.9	63.2	67.2	65.3	56.2	27.3
1950	59.2	51.8	59.9	65.9	63.5	67.5	66.4	56.7	26.7
1951	59.2	52.2	59.8	64.8	64.2	67.6	67.2	56.9	25.8
1952	59.0	51.3	59.7	62.2	64.7	68.0	67.5	57.5	24.8
1953	58.9	50.2	59.6	61.2	64.0	68.9	68.1	58.0	24.8
1954	58.8	48.3	59.6	61.6	64.3	68.8	68.4	58.7	23.9
1955	59.3	48.9	60.1	62.7	64.8	68.9	69.7	59.5	24.1
1956	60.0	50.9	60.7	64.1	64.8	69.5	70.5	60.8	24.3
1957	59.6	49.6	60.4	64.0	64.9	69.5	70.9	60.1	22.9
1958	59.5	47.4	60.5	64.4	65.0	69.6	71.5	60.5	21.8
1959	59.3	46.7	60.4	64.3	65.0	69.5	71.9	61.0	21.1
1960	59.4	47.5	60.5	65.2	65.4	69.4	72.2	60.9	20.8
1961	59.3	46.9	60.5	65.7	65.6	69.5	72.1	61.5	20.1
1962	58.8	46.1	60.0	65.3	65.2	69.7	72.2	61.5	19.1
1963	58.7	45.2	60.1	65.1	65.6	70.1	72.5	62.0	17.9
1964	58.7	44.5	60.2	66.3	65.8	70.0	72.9	61.9	18.0
1965	58.9	45.7	60.3	66.4	66.4	70.7	72.5	61.9	17.8
1966	59.2	48.2	60.5	66.5	67.1	71.0	72.7	62.2	17.2
1967	59.6	48.4	60.9	67.1	68.2	71.6	72.7	62.3	17.2
1968	59.6	48.3	60.9	67.0	68.6	72.0	72.8	62.2	17.2
1969	60.1	49.4	61.3	68.2	69.1	72.5	73.4	62.1	17.3
1970	60.4	49.9	61.6	69.2	69.7	73.1	73.5	61.8	17.0
1971	60.2	49.7	61.4	69.3	69.9	73.2	73.2	61.3	16.2
1972	60.4	51.9	61.4	70.8	70.9	73.3	72.7	60.0	15.6
1973	60.8	53.7	61.7	72.6	72.3	74.0	72.5	58.4	14.6
1974	61.3	54.8	62.0	74.0	73.6	74.6	72.7	57.8	14.0
1975	61.2	54.0	62.1	73.9	74.4	75.0	72.6	57.2	13.7
1976	61.6	54.5	62.4	74.7	75.7	76.0	72.5	56.6	13.1
1977	62.3	56.0	63.0	75.7	77.0	77.0	72.8	56.3	13.0
1978	63.2	57.8	63.8	76.8	78.3	78.1	73.5	56.3	13.3
1979	63.7	57.9	64.3	77.5	79.2	79.2	74.3	56.2	13.1
1980	63.8	56.7	64.5	77.2	79.9	80.0	74.9	55.7	12.5
1981	63.9	55.4	64.8	77.3	80.5	80.7	75.7	55.0	12.2
1982	64.0	54.1	65.0	77.1	81.0	81.2	75.9	55.1	11.9
1983	64.0	53.5	65.0	77.2	81.3	81.6	76.0	54.5	11.7
1984	64.4	53.9	65.3	77.6	81.8	82.4	76.5	54.2	11.1
1985	64.8	54.5	65.7	78.2	82.5	83.1	77.3	54.2	10.8
1986	65.3	54.7	66.2	78.9	82.9	83.7	78.0	54.0	10.9
1987	65.6	54.7	66.5	78.9	83.3	84.3	78.6	54.4	11.1
1988	65.9	55.3	66.8	78.7	83.3	84.6	79.6	54.6	11.5
1989	66.5	55.9	67.3	78.7	83.8	85.1	80.5	55.5	11.8
1990	66.5	53.7	67.6	77.8	83.6	85.2	80.7	55.9	11.8
1991	66.2	51.6	67.3	76.7	83.2	85.2	81.0	55.5	11.5
1992	66.4	51.3	67.6	77.0	83.7	85.1	81.5	56.2	11.5
1993	66.3	51.5	67.5	77.0	83.3	84.9	81.6	56.4	11.2
1994	66.6	52.7	67.7	77.0	83.2	84.8	81.7	56.8	12.4
1995	66.6	53.5	67.7	76.6	83.8	84.6	81.4	57.2	12.1
1996	66.8	52.3	67.9	76.8	84.1	84.8	82.1	57.9	12.1
1997	67.1	51.6	68.4	77.6	84.4	85.1	82.6	58.9	12.2
1998	67.1	52.8	68.3	77.5	84.6	84.7	82.5	59.3	11.9
1999	67.1	52.0	68.3	77.5	84.6	84.9	82.6	59.3	12.3
2000	67.1	52.0	68.3	77.8	84.6	84.8	82.5	59.2	12.9
2001	66.8	49.6	68.2	77.1	84.0	84.6	82.3	60.4	13.0
2002	66.6	47.4	68.1	76.4	83.7	84.1	82.1	61.9	13.2
2003	66.2	44.5	67.9	75.4	82.9	83.9	82.1	62.4	14.0
2004	66.0	43.9	67.7	75.0	82.7	83.6	81.8	62.3	14.4
2005	66.0	43.7	67.8	74.6	82.8	83.8	81.7	62.9	15.1
2006	66.2	43.7	67.9	74.6	83.0	83.8	81.9	63.7	15.4
2007	66.0	41.3	68.0	74.4	83.3	83.8	82.0	63.8	16.0
2008	66.0	40.2	68.0	74.4	83.3	84.1	81.9	64.5	16.8
2009	65.4	37.5	67.5	72.9	82.7	83.7	81.6	64.9	17.2
2010	64.7	34.9	67.0	71.4	82.2	83.2	81.2	64.9	17.4
2011	64.1	34.1	66.4	71.3	81.5	82.7	80.7	64.3	17.9

Table 1-8. Civilian Labor Force Participation Rates, by Age, Sex, Race, and Hispanic Origin, 1948–2011
—*Continued*

(Percent.)

Race, Hispanic origin, sex, and year	16 years and over	16 to 19 years	20 years and over						
			Total	20 to 24 years	25 to 34 years	35 to 44 years	45 to 54 years	55 to 64 years	65 years and over
ALL RACES									
Men									
1948	86.6	63.7	88.6	84.6	95.9	97.9	95.8	89.5	46.8
1949	86.4	62.8	88.5	86.6	95.8	97.9	95.6	87.5	47.0
1950	86.4	63.2	88.4	87.9	96.0	97.6	95.8	86.9	45.8
1951	86.3	63.0	88.2	88.4	96.9	97.5	95.9	87.2	44.9
1952	86.3	61.3	88.3	88.1	97.5	97.8	96.2	87.5	42.6
1953	86.0	60.7	88.0	87.7	97.4	98.2	96.5	87.9	41.6
1954	85.5	58.0	87.8	86.9	97.3	98.1	96.5	88.7	40.5
1955	85.4	58.9	87.6	86.9	97.6	98.1	96.4	87.9	39.6
1956	85.5	60.5	87.6	87.8	97.3	97.9	96.6	88.5	40.0
1957	84.8	59.1	86.9	87.1	97.1	97.9	96.3	87.5	37.5
1958	84.2	56.6	86.6	86.9	97.1	97.9	96.3	87.8	35.6
1959	83.7	55.8	86.3	87.8	97.4	97.8	96.0	87.4	34.2
1960	83.3	56.1	86.0	88.1	97.5	97.7	95.7	86.8	33.1
1961	82.9	54.6	85.7	87.8	97.5	97.6	95.6	87.3	31.7
1962	82.0	53.8	84.8	86.9	97.2	97.6	95.6	86.2	30.3
1963	81.4	52.9	84.4	86.1	97.1	97.5	95.7	86.2	28.4
1964	81.0	52.4	84.2	86.1	97.3	97.3	95.7	85.6	28.0
1965	80.7	53.8	83.9	85.8	97.2	97.3	95.6	84.6	27.9
1966	80.4	55.3	83.6	85.1	97.3	97.2	95.3	84.5	27.1
1967	80.4	55.6	83.4	84.4	97.2	97.3	95.2	84.4	27.1
1968	80.1	55.1	83.1	82.8	96.9	97.1	94.9	84.3	27.3
1969	79.8	55.9	82.8	82.8	96.7	96.9	94.6	83.4	27.2
1970	79.7	56.1	82.6	83.3	96.4	96.9	94.3	83.0	26.8
1971	79.1	56.1	82.1	83.0	95.9	96.5	93.9	82.1	25.5
1972	78.9	58.1	81.6	83.9	95.7	96.4	93.2	80.4	24.3
1973	78.8	59.7	81.3	85.2	95.7	96.2	93.0	78.2	22.7
1974	78.7	60.7	81.0	85.9	95.8	96.0	92.2	77.3	22.4
1975	77.9	59.1	80.3	84.5	95.2	95.6	92.1	75.6	21.6
1976	77.5	59.3	79.8	85.2	95.2	95.4	91.6	74.3	20.2
1977	77.7	60.9	79.7	85.6	95.3	95.7	91.1	73.8	20.0
1978	77.9	62.0	79.8	85.9	95.3	95.7	91.3	73.3	20.4
1979	77.8	61.5	79.8	86.4	95.3	95.7	91.4	72.8	19.9
1980	77.4	60.5	79.4	85.9	95.2	95.5	91.2	72.1	19.0
1981	77.0	59.0	79.0	85.5	94.9	95.4	91.4	70.6	18.4
1982	76.6	56.7	78.7	84.9	94.7	95.3	91.2	70.2	17.8
1983	76.4	56.2	78.5	84.8	94.2	95.2	91.2	69.4	17.4
1984	76.4	56.0	78.3	85.0	94.4	95.4	91.2	68.5	16.3
1985	76.3	56.8	78.1	85.0	94.7	95.0	91.0	67.9	15.8
1986	76.3	56.4	78.1	85.8	94.6	94.8	91.0	67.3	16.0
1987	76.2	56.1	78.0	85.2	94.6	94.6	90.7	67.6	16.3
1988	76.2	56.9	77.9	85.0	94.3	94.5	90.9	67.0	16.5
1989	76.4	57.9	78.1	85.3	94.4	94.5	91.1	67.2	16.6
1990	76.4	55.7	78.2	84.4	94.1	94.3	90.7	67.8	16.3
1991	75.8	53.2	77.7	83.5	93.6	94.1	90.5	67.0	15.7
1992	75.8	53.4	77.7	83.3	93.8	93.7	90.7	67.0	16.1
1993	75.4	53.2	77.3	83.2	93.4	93.4	90.1	66.5	15.6
1994	75.1	54.1	76.8	83.1	92.6	92.8	89.1	65.5	16.8
1995	75.0	54.8	76.7	83.1	93.0	92.3	88.8	66.0	16.8
1996	74.9	53.2	76.8	82.5	93.2	92.4	89.1	67.0	16.9
1997	75.0	52.3	77.0	82.5	93.0	92.6	89.5	67.6	17.1
1998	74.9	53.3	76.8	82.0	93.2	92.6	89.2	68.1	16.5
1999	74.7	52.9	76.7	81.9	93.3	92.8	88.8	67.9	16.9
2000	74.8	52.8	76.7	82.6	93.4	92.7	88.6	67.3	17.7
2001	74.4	50.2	76.5	81.6	92.7	92.5	88.5	68.3	17.7
2002	74.1	47.5	76.3	80.7	92.4	92.1	88.5	69.2	17.9
2003	73.5	44.3	75.9	80.0	91.8	92.1	87.7	68.7	18.6
2004	73.3	43.9	75.8	79.6	91.9	91.9	87.5	68.7	19.0
2005	73.3	43.2	75.8	79.1	91.7	92.1	87.7	69.3	19.8
2006	73.5	43.7	75.9	79.6	91.7	92.1	88.1	69.6	20.3
2007	73.2	41.1	75.9	78.7	92.2	92.3	88.2	69.6	20.5
2008	73.0	40.1	75.7	78.7	91.5	92.2	88.0	70.4	21.5
2009	72.0	37.3	74.8	76.2	90.3	91.7	87.4	70.2	21.9
2010	71.2	34.9	74.1	74.5	89.7	91.5	86.8	70.0	22.1
2011	70.5	33.7	73.4	74.7	89.2	90.9	86.2	69.3	22.8

Table 1-8. Civilian Labor Force Participation Rates, by Age, Sex, Race, and Hispanic Origin, 1948–2011
—Continued

(Percent.)

Race, Hispanic origin, sex, and year	16 years and over	16 to 19 years	20 years and over						
			Total	20 to 24 years	25 to 34 years	35 to 44 years	45 to 54 years	55 to 64 years	65 years and over
ALL RACES									
Women									
1948	32.7	42.0	31.8	45.3	33.2	36.9	35.0	24.3	9.1
1949	33.1	42.4	32.3	45.0	33.4	38.1	35.9	25.3	9.6
1950	33.9	41.0	33.3	46.0	34.0	39.1	37.9	27.0	9.7
1951	34.6	42.4	34.0	46.5	35.4	39.8	39.7	27.6	8.9
1952	34.7	42.2	34.1	44.7	35.4	40.4	40.1	28.7	9.1
1953	34.4	40.7	33.9	44.3	34.0	41.3	40.4	29.1	10.0
1954	34.6	39.4	34.2	45.1	34.4	41.2	41.2	30.0	9.3
1955	35.7	39.7	35.4	45.9	34.9	41.6	43.8	32.5	10.6
1956	36.9	42.2	36.4	46.3	35.4	43.1	45.5	34.9	10.8
1957	36.9	41.1	36.5	45.9	35.6	43.3	46.5	34.5	10.5
1958	37.1	39.0	36.9	46.3	35.6	43.4	47.8	35.2	10.3
1959	37.1	38.2	37.1	45.1	35.3	43.4	49.0	36.6	10.2
1960	37.7	39.3	37.6	46.1	36.0	43.4	49.9	37.2	10.8
1961	38.1	39.7	38.0	47.0	36.4	43.8	50.1	37.9	10.7
1962	37.9	39.0	37.8	47.3	36.3	44.1	50.0	38.7	10.0
1963	38.3	38.0	38.3	47.5	37.2	44.9	50.6	39.7	9.6
1964	38.7	37.0	38.9	49.4	37.2	45.0	51.4	40.2	10.1
1965	39.3	38.0	39.4	49.9	38.5	46.1	50.9	41.1	10.0
1966	40.3	41.4	40.1	51.5	39.8	46.8	51.7	41.8	9.6
1967	41.1	41.6	41.1	53.3	41.9	48.1	51.8	42.4	9.6
1968	41.6	41.9	41.6	54.5	42.6	48.9	52.3	42.4	9.6
1969	42.7	43.2	42.7	56.7	43.7	49.9	53.8	43.1	9.9
1970	43.3	44.0	43.3	57.7	45.0	51.1	54.4	43.0	9.7
1971	43.4	43.4	43.3	57.7	45.6	51.6	54.3	42.9	9.5
1972	43.9	45.8	43.7	59.1	47.8	52.0	53.9	42.1	9.3
1973	44.7	47.8	44.4	61.1	50.4	53.3	53.7	41.1	8.9
1974	45.7	49.1	45.3	63.1	52.6	54.7	54.6	40.7	8.1
1975	46.3	49.1	46.0	64.1	54.9	55.8	54.6	40.9	8.2
1976	47.3	49.8	47.0	65.0	57.3	57.8	55.0	41.0	8.2
1977	48.4	51.2	48.1	66.5	59.7	59.6	55.8	40.9	8.1
1978	50.0	53.7	49.6	68.3	62.2	61.6	57.1	41.3	8.3
1979	50.9	54.2	50.6	69.0	63.9	63.6	58.3	41.7	8.3
1980	51.5	52.9	51.3	68.9	65.5	65.5	59.9	41.3	8.1
1981	52.1	51.8	52.1	69.6	66.7	66.8	61.1	41.4	8.0
1982	52.6	51.4	52.7	69.8	68.0	68.0	61.6	41.8	7.9
1983	52.9	50.8	53.1	69.9	69.0	68.7	61.9	41.5	7.8
1984	53.6	51.8	53.7	70.4	69.8	70.1	62.9	41.7	7.5
1985	54.5	52.1	54.7	71.8	70.9	71.8	64.4	42.0	7.3
1986	55.3	53.0	55.5	72.4	71.6	73.1	65.9	42.3	7.4
1987	56.0	53.3	56.2	73.0	72.4	74.5	67.1	42.7	7.4
1988	56.6	53.6	56.8	72.7	72.7	75.2	69.0	43.5	7.9
1989	57.4	53.9	57.7	72.4	73.5	76.0	70.5	45.0	8.4
1990	57.5	51.6	58.0	71.3	73.5	76.4	71.2	45.2	8.6
1991	57.4	50.0	57.9	70.1	73.1	76.5	72.0	45.2	8.5
1992	57.8	49.1	58.5	70.9	73.9	76.7	72.6	46.5	8.3
1993	57.9	49.7	58.5	70.9	73.4	76.6	73.5	47.2	8.1
1994	58.8	51.3	59.3	71.0	74.0	77.1	74.6	48.9	9.2
1995	58.9	52.2	59.4	70.3	74.9	77.2	74.4	49.2	8.8
1996	59.3	51.3	59.9	71.3	75.2	77.5	75.4	49.6	8.6
1997	59.8	51.0	60.5	72.7	76.0	77.7	76.0	50.9	8.6
1998	59.8	52.3	60.4	73.0	76.3	77.1	76.2	51.2	8.6
1999	60.0	51.0	60.7	73.2	76.4	77.2	76.7	51.5	8.9
2000	59.9	51.2	60.6	73.1	76.1	77.2	76.8	51.9	9.4
2001	59.8	49.0	60.6	72.7	75.5	77.1	76.4	53.2	9.6
2002	59.6	47.3	60.5	72.1	75.1	76.4	76.0	55.2	9.8
2003	59.5	44.8	60.6	70.8	74.1	76.0	76.8	56.6	10.6
2004	59.2	43.8	60.3	70.5	73.6	75.6	76.5	56.3	11.1
2005	59.3	44.2	60.4	70.1	73.9	75.8	76.0	57.0	11.5
2006	59.4	43.7	60.5	69.5	74.4	75.9	76.0	58.2	11.7
2007	59.3	41.5	60.6	70.1	74.5	75.5	76.0	58.3	12.6
2008	59.5	40.2	60.9	70.0	75.2	76.1	76.1	59.1	13.3
2009	59.2	37.7	60.8	69.6	75.0	75.9	76.0	60.0	13.6
2010	58.6	35.0	60.3	68.3	74.7	75.2	75.7	60.2	13.8
2011	58.1	34.6	59.8	67.8	73.9	74.7	75.4	59.5	14.0

Table 1-8. Civilian Labor Force Participation Rates, by Age, Sex, Race, and Hispanic Origin, 1948–2011
—Continued

(Percent.)

Race, Hispanic origin, sex, and year	16 years and over	16 to 19 years	20 years and over						
			Total	20 to 24 years	25 to 34 years	35 to 44 years	45 to 54 years	55 to 64 years	65 years and over
WHITE									
Both Sexes									
1954	58.2	48.8	58.9	61.0	63.5	68.0	67.9	58.4	23.7
1955	58.7	49.3	59.5	62.4	64.0	68.3	69.2	59.3	23.9
1956	59.4	51.3	60.1	64.1	64.0	68.9	70.1	60.6	24.2
1957	59.1	50.3	59.8	63.7	64.1	68.8	70.5	59.9	22.8
1958	58.9	47.9	59.8	64.1	64.2	68.8	71.0	60.3	21.7
1959	58.7	47.4	59.7	63.7	64.3	68.7	71.5	60.7	21.0
1960	58.8	47.9	59.8	64.8	64.7	68.6	71.7	60.6	20.8
1961	58.8	47.4	59.9	65.5	64.8	68.8	71.7	61.3	20.0
1962	58.3	46.6	59.4	65.0	64.4	69.0	71.8	61.3	19.0
1963	58.2	45.7	59.4	64.9	64.8	69.4	72.3	61.8	17.9
1964	58.2	45.1	59.6	65.8	64.9	69.5	72.5	61.8	17.8
1965	58.4	46.5	59.7	65.7	65.6	70.1	72.2	61.7	17.7
1966	58.7	49.1	59.8	66.0	66.3	70.4	72.5	61.9	17.1
1967	59.2	49.2	60.3	66.8	67.4	71.2	72.5	62.3	17.0
1968	59.3	49.3	60.4	66.6	67.9	71.7	72.7	62.2	17.1
1969	59.9	50.6	60.9	67.9	68.4	72.3	73.3	62.1	17.2
1970	60.2	51.4	61.2	69.2	69.1	72.9	73.5	61.8	16.8
1971	60.1	51.6	61.1	69.6	69.3	73.0	73.4	61.3	16.1
1972	60.4	54.1	61.2	71.2	70.4	73.2	72.9	60.3	15.4
1973	60.8	56.0	61.4	73.3	72.0	73.9	72.7	58.6	14.4
1974	61.4	57.3	61.9	74.8	73.4	74.6	73.0	58.0	13.9
1975	61.5	56.7	62.0	75.2	74.4	75.1	73.0	57.4	13.6
1976	61.8	57.5	62.3	76.0	75.6	76.1	73.0	56.9	13.0
1977	62.5	59.3	62.9	77.1	77.0	77.1	73.2	56.6	12.9
1978	63.3	60.8	63.6	78.1	78.3	78.1	73.8	56.4	13.1
1979	63.9	61.1	64.2	78.9	79.4	79.3	74.6	56.5	12.9
1980	64.1	60.0	64.5	78.7	80.2	80.3	75.4	56.0	12.5
1981	64.3	58.9	64.8	79.1	81.0	81.0	76.2	55.2	12.2
1982	64.3	57.5	65.0	78.9	81.6	81.5	76.4	55.3	12.0
1983	64.3	56.9	65.0	79.0	81.8	81.9	76.5	54.7	11.8
1984	64.6	57.2	65.3	79.4	82.5	82.6	77.0	54.5	11.1
1985	65.0	57.5	65.7	79.9	83.1	83.4	77.8	54.4	10.7
1986	65.5	57.8	66.1	80.6	83.6	84.0	78.5	54.3	11.0
1987	65.8	57.7	66.5	80.7	84.0	84.7	79.1	54.6	11.1
1988	66.2	58.6	66.8	80.6	84.1	85.0	80.3	55.1	11.4
1989	66.7	59.1	67.3	80.2	84.5	85.5	81.2	56.2	11.8
1990	66.9	57.5	67.6	79.8	84.6	85.9	81.3	56.5	11.9
1991	66.6	55.8	67.4	78.9	84.3	85.9	81.8	56.0	11.6
1992	66.8	54.7	67.7	79.4	84.6	85.8	82.2	56.8	11.6
1993	66.8	55.1	67.6	79.5	84.5	85.7	82.5	57.1	11.4
1994	67.1	56.4	67.9	79.5	84.4	85.7	82.7	57.6	12.5
1995	67.1	57.1	67.8	78.7	84.9	85.5	82.5	58.0	12.3
1996	67.2	55.9	68.1	79.1	84.9	85.7	83.1	58.7	12.3
1997	67.5	55.2	68.4	79.6	85.3	85.8	83.5	59.9	12.3
1998	67.3	56.0	68.2	79.5	85.4	85.3	83.4	60.1	12.0
1999	67.3	55.5	68.2	79.5	85.1	85.4	83.5	60.2	12.5
2000	67.3	55.5	68.2	79.9	85.1	85.4	83.5	60.0	13.0
2001	67.0	53.1	68.1	79.2	84.5	85.2	83.3	61.2	13.0
2002	66.8	50.5	68.1	78.6	84.5	84.7	83.0	62.8	13.3
2003	66.5	47.7	67.9	77.7	83.6	84.3	83.0	63.3	14.1
2004	66.3	47.1	67.7	77.1	83.5	84.1	82.9	63.2	14.6
2005	66.3	46.9	67.7	76.3	83.5	84.2	82.8	63.7	15.1
2006	66.5	46.7	67.9	76.5	83.8	84.3	83.0	64.7	15.5
2007	66.4	44.4	68.0	76.4	84.1	84.1	83.1	64.9	16.2
2008	66.3	43.1	68.0	76.3	83.9	84.4	82.9	65.7	17.0
2009	65.8	40.6	67.7	75.1	83.5	84.2	82.7	66.2	17.4
2010	65.1	37.7	67.1	73.4	83.2	83.8	82.2	66.1	17.6
2011	64.5	36.8	66.5	73.2	82.5	83.3	81.7	65.5	18.1

Table 1-8. Civilian Labor Force Participation Rates, by Age, Sex, Race, and Hispanic Origin, 1948–2011
—Continued

(Percent.)

Race, Hispanic origin, sex, and year	16 years and over	16 to 19 years	20 years and over						
			Total	20 to 24 years	25 to 34 years	35 to 44 years	45 to 54 years	55 to 64 years	65 years and over
WHITE									
Men									
1954	85.6	57.6	87.8	86.3	97.5	98.2	96.8	89.1	40.4
1955	85.4	58.6	87.5	86.5	97.8	98.2	96.7	88.4	39.6
1956	85.6	60.4	87.6	87.6	97.4	98.1	96.8	88.9	40.0
1957	84.8	59.2	86.9	86.6	97.2	98.0	96.7	88.0	37.7
1958	84.3	56.5	86.6	86.7	97.2	98.0	96.6	88.2	35.7
1959	83.8	55.9	86.3	87.3	97.5	98.0	96.3	87.9	34.3
1960	83.4	55.9	86.0	87.8	97.7	97.9	96.1	87.2	33.3
1961	83.0	54.5	85.7	87.6	97.7	97.9	95.9	87.8	31.9
1962	82.1	53.8	84.9	86.5	97.4	97.9	96.0	86.7	30.6
1963	81.5	53.1	84.4	85.8	97.4	97.8	96.2	86.6	28.4
1964	81.1	52.7	84.2	85.7	97.5	97.6	96.1	86.1	27.9
1965	80.8	54.1	83.9	85.3	97.4	97.7	95.9	85.2	27.9
1966	80.6	55.9	83.6	84.4	97.5	97.6	95.8	84.9	27.2
1967	80.6	56.3	83.5	84.0	97.5	97.7	95.6	84.9	27.1
1968	80.4	55.9	83.2	82.4	97.2	97.6	95.4	84.7	27.4
1969	80.2	56.8	83.0	82.6	97.0	97.4	95.1	83.9	27.3
1970	80.0	57.5	82.8	83.3	96.7	97.3	94.9	83.3	26.7
1971	79.6	57.9	82.3	83.2	96.3	97.0	94.7	82.6	25.6
1972	79.6	60.1	82.0	84.3	96.0	97.0	94.0	81.1	24.4
1973	79.4	62.0	81.6	85.8	96.2	96.8	93.5	78.9	22.7
1974	79.4	62.9	81.4	86.6	96.3	96.7	93.0	78.0	22.4
1975	78.7	61.9	80.7	85.5	95.8	96.4	92.9	76.4	21.7
1976	78.4	62.3	80.3	86.3	95.9	96.0	92.5	75.2	20.2
1977	78.5	64.0	80.2	86.8	96.0	96.2	92.1	74.6	20.0
1978	78.6	65.0	80.1	87.3	95.9	96.3	92.1	73.7	20.3
1979	78.6	64.8	80.1	87.6	96.0	96.4	92.2	73.4	20.0
1980	78.2	63.7	79.8	87.2	95.9	96.2	92.1	73.1	19.1
1981	77.9	62.4	79.5	87.0	95.8	96.1	92.4	71.5	18.5
1982	77.4	60.0	79.2	86.3	95.6	96.0	92.2	71.0	17.9
1983	77.1	59.4	78.9	86.1	95.2	96.0	91.9	70.0	17.7
1984	77.1	59.0	78.7	86.5	95.4	96.1	92.0	69.5	16.4
1985	77.0	59.7	78.5	86.4	95.7	95.7	92.0	68.8	15.9
1986	76.9	59.3	78.5	87.3	95.5	95.4	91.8	68.0	16.3
1987	76.8	59.0	78.4	86.9	95.5	95.4	91.6	68.1	16.5
1988	76.9	60.0	78.3	86.6	95.2	95.4	91.8	67.9	16.7
1989	77.1	61.0	78.5	86.8	95.4	95.3	92.2	68.3	16.8
1990	77.1	59.6	78.5	86.2	95.2	95.3	91.7	68.6	16.6
1991	76.5	57.3	78.0	85.4	94.9	95.0	91.4	67.7	15.9
1992	76.5	56.9	78.0	85.2	94.9	94.7	91.8	67.7	16.2
1993	76.2	56.6	77.7	85.5	94.7	94.5	91.3	67.3	15.9
1994	75.9	57.7	77.3	85.5	93.9	93.9	90.3	66.4	17.2
1995	75.7	58.5	77.1	85.1	94.1	93.4	90.0	67.1	16.9
1996	75.8	57.1	77.3	85.0	94.4	93.6	90.4	68.0	17.2
1997	75.9	56.1	77.5	85.1	94.2	93.7	90.6	68.9	17.4
1998	75.6	56.6	77.2	84.6	94.4	93.7	90.3	69.1	16.6
1999	75.6	56.4	77.2	84.9	94.3	93.8	90.1	69.1	17.2
2000	75.5	56.5	77.1	85.2	94.5	93.8	89.7	68.2	17.9
2001	75.1	53.7	76.9	84.1	93.9	93.6	89.7	69.1	17.8
2002	74.8	50.3	76.7	83.2	93.7	93.2	89.6	70.2	17.8
2003	74.2	47.5	76.3	82.5	93.3	93.1	88.8	69.7	18.6
2004	74.1	47.4	76.2	82.1	93.2	93.0	88.7	69.8	19.1
2005	74.1	46.2	76.2	81.4	93.0	93.0	89.0	70.4	20.0
2006	74.3	46.9	76.4	81.9	92.9	93.1	89.3	71.0	20.6
2007	74.0	44.3	76.3	80.9	93.4	93.1	89.6	71.2	20.8
2008	73.7	43.0	76.1	80.8	92.6	93.0	89.2	71.9	21.8
2009	72.8	40.3	75.3	78.6	91.6	92.7	88.8	71.8	22.2
2010	72.0	37.4	74.6	77.0	91.1	92.4	88.1	71.2	22.3
2011	71.3	36.1	73.9	77.1	90.5	92.1	87.5	70.8	23.0

Table 1-8. Civilian Labor Force Participation Rates, by Age, Sex, Race, and Hispanic Origin, 1948–2011
    —Continued

(Percent.)

Race, Hispanic origin, sex, and year	16 years and over	16 to 19 years	20 years and over						
			Total	20 to 24 years	25 to 34 years	35 to 44 years	45 to 54 years	55 to 64 years	65 years and over
WHITE									
Women									
1954	33.3	40.6	32.7	44.4	32.5	39.3	39.8	29.1	9.1
1955	34.5	40.7	34.0	45.8	32.8	40.0	42.7	31.8	10.5
1956	35.7	43.1	35.1	46.5	33.2	41.5	44.4	34.0	10.6
1957	35.7	42.2	35.2	45.8	33.6	41.5	45.4	33.7	10.2
1958	35.8	40.1	35.5	46.0	33.6	41.4	46.5	34.5	10.1
1959	36.0	39.6	35.6	44.5	33.4	41.4	47.8	35.7	10.0
1960	36.5	40.3	36.2	45.7	34.1	41.5	48.6	36.2	10.6
1961	36.9	40.6	36.6	46.9	34.3	41.8	48.9	37.2	10.5
1962	36.7	39.8	36.5	47.1	34.1	42.2	48.9	38.0	9.8
1963	37.2	38.7	37.0	47.3	34.8	43.1	49.5	38.9	9.4
1964	37.5	37.8	37.5	48.8	35.0	43.3	50.2	39.4	9.9
1965	38.1	39.2	38.0	49.2	36.3	44.4	49.9	40.3	9.7
1966	39.2	42.6	38.8	51.0	37.7	45.0	50.6	41.1	9.4
1967	40.1	42.5	39.8	53.1	39.7	46.4	50.9	41.9	9.3
1968	40.7	43.0	40.4	54.0	40.6	47.5	51.5	42.0	9.4
1969	41.8	44.6	41.5	56.4	41.7	48.6	53.0	42.6	9.7
1970	42.6	45.6	42.2	57.7	43.2	49.9	53.7	42.6	9.5
1971	42.6	45.4	42.3	58.0	43.7	50.2	53.6	42.5	9.3
1972	43.2	48.1	42.7	59.4	46.0	50.7	53.4	41.9	9.0
1973	44.1	50.1	43.5	61.7	48.7	52.2	53.4	40.7	8.7
1974	45.2	51.7	44.4	63.9	51.3	53.6	54.3	40.4	8.0
1975	45.9	51.5	45.3	65.5	53.8	54.9	54.3	40.6	8.0
1976	46.9	52.8	46.2	66.3	56.0	57.1	54.7	40.7	7.9
1977	48.0	54.5	47.3	67.8	58.5	58.9	55.3	40.7	7.9
1978	49.4	56.7	48.7	69.3	61.2	60.7	56.7	41.1	8.1
1979	50.5	57.4	49.8	70.5	63.1	63.0	58.1	41.5	8.1
1980	51.2	56.2	50.6	70.6	64.8	65.0	59.6	40.9	7.9
1981	51.9	55.4	51.5	71.5	66.4	66.4	60.9	40.9	7.9
1982	52.4	55.0	52.2	71.8	67.8	67.5	61.4	41.5	7.8
1983	52.7	54.5	52.5	72.1	68.7	68.2	61.9	41.1	7.8
1984	53.3	55.4	53.1	72.5	69.8	69.6	62.7	41.2	7.5
1985	54.1	55.2	54.0	73.8	70.9	71.4	64.2	41.5	7.0
1986	55.0	56.3	54.9	74.1	71.8	72.9	65.8	42.1	7.3
1987	55.7	56.5	55.6	74.8	72.5	74.2	67.2	42.4	7.2
1988	56.4	57.2	56.3	74.9	73.0	74.9	69.2	43.6	7.7
1989	57.2	57.1	57.2	74.0	73.8	75.9	70.6	45.2	8.2
1990	57.4	55.3	57.6	73.4	74.1	76.6	71.3	45.5	8.5
1991	57.4	54.1	57.6	72.5	73.8	76.8	72.4	45.4	8.5
1992	57.7	52.5	58.1	73.5	74.4	77.0	72.8	46.8	8.2
1993	58.0	53.5	58.3	73.4	74.3	76.9	74.0	47.6	8.1
1994	58.9	55.1	59.2	73.4	74.9	77.5	75.2	49.4	9.2
1995	59.0	55.5	59.2	72.3	75.8	77.6	75.2	49.5	9.0
1996	59.1	54.7	59.4	73.3	75.5	77.8	76.1	50.1	8.7
1997	59.5	54.1	59.9	73.9	76.3	77.9	76.6	51.5	8.6
1998	59.4	55.4	59.7	74.3	76.3	76.9	76.6	51.6	8.7
1999	59.6	54.5	59.9	73.9	76.0	77.1	77.1	52.0	8.9
2000	59.5	54.5	59.9	74.5	75.7	77.2	77.5	52.4	9.4
2001	59.4	52.4	59.9	74.2	75.1	77.0	77.1	53.8	9.6
2002	59.3	50.8	60.0	74.0	75.0	76.3	76.6	55.8	9.9
2003	59.2	47.9	59.9	72.7	73.7	75.5	77.3	57.4	10.8
2004	58.9	46.7	59.7	71.9	73.6	75.2	77.1	57.0	11.2
2005	58.9	47.6	59.7	71.0	73.7	75.4	76.7	57.5	11.4
2006	59.0	46.6	59.9	70.9	74.3	75.5	76.7	58.7	11.6
2007	59.0	44.6	60.1	71.6	74.5	75.0	76.6	58.9	12.7
2008	59.2	43.3	60.3	71.6	74.9	75.8	76.6	59.7	13.3
2009	59.1	40.9	60.4	71.6	75.1	75.7	76.7	60.8	13.6
2010	58.5	38.0	59.9	69.7	74.9	75.0	76.3	61.1	13.9
2011	58.0	37.5	59.4	69.1	74.2	74.4	76.1	60.6	14.1

Table 1-8. Civilian Labor Force Participation Rates, by Age, Sex, Race, and Hispanic Origin, 1948–2011
—*Continued*

(Percent.)

Race, Hispanic origin, sex, and year	16 years and over	16 to 19 years	20 years and over						
			Total	20 to 24 years	25 to 34 years	35 to 44 years	45 to 54 years	55 to 64 years	65 years and over
BLACK									
Both Sexes									
1974	59.8	39.8	63.0	69.8	75.8	74.6	69.1	54.7	15.1
1975	58.8	38.2	62.0	66.1	75.6	74.1	69.0	54.3	14.9
1976	59.0	37.0	62.5	66.8	77.4	74.9	68.6	53.4	14.9
1977	59.8	37.9	63.2	68.2	78.3	75.9	69.0	53.7	14.5
1978	61.5	41.0	64.5	69.9	79.6	77.4	70.4	54.8	15.3
1979	61.4	40.1	64.5	70.0	79.2	77.9	71.1	53.5	14.5
1980	61.0	38.9	64.1	69.0	79.5	77.4	71.4	52.6	13.0
1981	60.8	37.7	64.2	69.2	78.5	78.4	71.2	52.8	12.0
1982	61.0	36.6	64.3	68.6	78.7	79.8	71.1	52.3	11.5
1983	61.5	36.4	64.9	68.4	79.8	80.2	72.1	52.5	10.5
1984	62.2	38.3	65.2	69.2	79.3	81.0	73.0	51.6	10.3
1985	62.9	41.2	65.6	70.0	79.8	81.5	73.4	51.4	11.2
1986	63.3	41.3	65.9	71.7	80.1	81.9	74.3	50.6	9.7
1987	63.8	41.6	66.5	70.5	80.7	82.6	74.7	52.4	10.7
1988	63.8	40.8	66.5	70.5	80.8	82.6	75.0	50.6	11.5
1989	64.2	42.5	66.7	72.2	80.9	82.7	75.5	48.3	11.6
1990	64.0	38.7	66.9	68.8	79.7	82.4	76.5	49.6	11.1
1991	63.3	35.4	66.4	67.7	78.5	82.0	76.2	50.4	10.7
1992	63.9	37.9	66.8	67.4	79.7	81.4	76.2	51.6	10.6
1993	63.2	37.0	66.0	67.8	78.3	81.0	75.2	50.2	9.5
1994	63.4	38.5	66.0	68.8	78.3	80.8	74.8	49.3	10.6
1995	63.7	39.9	66.3	68.7	80.0	80.4	74.1	50.3	10.5
1996	64.1	39.2	66.9	69.0	81.1	81.0	74.9	50.9	9.8
1997	64.7	38.7	67.6	70.9	82.0	81.4	76.3	50.5	10.0
1998	65.6	41.6	68.2	70.6	83.0	82.2	76.7	52.3	10.3
1999	65.8	38.7	68.9	71.4	85.2	83.0	76.4	51.4	10.4
2000	65.8	39.4	68.7	71.8	84.1	82.3	76.9	52.5	11.6
2001	65.3	37.6	68.2	69.9	83.6	82.0	75.9	53.9	12.6
2002	64.8	36.0	67.8	68.6	82.4	81.6	76.1	54.7	12.5
2003	64.3	32.4	67.6	68.2	81.6	82.9	75.8	54.4	12.9
2004	63.8	31.4	67.2	68.3	81.2	82.1	75.5	54.4	13.1
2005	64.2	32.4	67.4	69.0	81.7	82.3	75.7	55.3	13.6
2006	64.1	34.0	67.3	68.8	81.8	82.0	75.8	55.4	13.7
2007	63.7	30.3	67.2	68.3	81.7	82.7	75.7	55.1	14.0
2008	63.7	29.4	67.4	68.0	82.2	83.0	76.1	55.6	15.0
2009	62.4	27.2	66.1	66.0	80.4	81.7	75.2	55.5	15.3
2010	62.2	25.5	66.0	66.9	80.5	81.4	75.0	55.7	15.2
2011	61.4	24.9	65.0	66.5	79.1	80.6	73.9	54.5	16.1
BLACK									
Men									
1974	72.9	46.7	77.6	83.6	92.8	90.4	84.0	68.9	21.6
1975	70.9	42.6	76.0	78.7	91.6	89.4	83.5	67.7	20.7
1976	70.0	41.3	75.4	79.0	90.9	89.9	82.4	65.1	19.8
1977	70.6	43.2	75.6	79.2	90.7	91.0	82.0	65.5	20.0
1978	71.5	44.9	76.2	78.8	90.9	90.5	83.2	67.9	21.1
1979	71.3	43.6	76.3	80.7	90.8	90.4	84.5	64.8	19.5
1980	70.3	43.2	75.1	79.9	90.9	89.1	83.0	61.9	16.9
1981	70.0	41.6	74.5	79.2	88.9	89.3	82.7	62.1	16.0
1982	70.1	39.8	74.7	78.7	89.2	89.8	82.2	61.9	15.9
1983	70.6	39.9	75.2	79.4	89.0	89.7	84.5	62.6	14.0
1984	70.8	41.7	74.8	79.1	88.9	90.0	83.7	58.9	13.7
1985	70.8	44.6	74.4	79.0	88.8	89.8	83.0	58.9	13.9
1986	71.2	43.7	74.8	80.1	89.6	89.6	84.1	59.1	12.6
1987	71.1	43.6	74.7	77.8	89.4	88.6	83.7	62.1	13.7
1988	71.0	43.8	74.6	79.3	89.3	88.2	83.5	59.4	14.3
1989	71.0	44.6	74.4	80.2	89.7	88.7	82.5	55.5	14.3
1990	71.0	40.7	75.0	76.8	88.8	88.1	83.5	58.0	13.0
1991	70.4	37.3	74.6	76.7	87.3	87.7	83.4	58.7	13.0
1992	70.7	40.6	74.3	75.4	88.0	86.5	81.8	60.0	13.7
1993	69.6	39.5	73.2	74.1	87.3	86.1	80.0	57.9	11.6
1994	69.1	40.8	72.5	73.9	86.2	85.9	79.1	54.5	12.7
1995	69.0	40.1	72.5	74.6	87.5	84.1	78.5	54.4	14.9
1996	68.7	39.5	72.3	73.4	87.5	84.4	78.5	55.6	12.9
1997	68.3	37.4	72.2	72.1	86.8	84.8	80.1	54.3	12.9
1998	69.0	40.7	72.5	71.8	87.1	85.0	79.9	57.3	14.0
1999	68.7	38.6	72.4	69.8	89.2	86.0	78.5	55.5	12.7
2000	69.2	39.2	72.8	73.3	87.8	85.2	79.2	57.4	14.4
2001	68.4	37.9	72.1	69.7	86.6	84.9	78.4	58.9	16.7
2002	68.4	37.3	72.1	70.7	85.9	84.7	79.5	58.4	16.9
2003	67.3	31.1	71.5	71.1	84.7	85.7	77.7	57.6	17.0
2004	66.7	30.0	70.9	69.9	86.1	84.0	76.9	57.1	17.0
2005	67.3	32.6	71.3	70.1	85.5	85.5	78.6	57.3	17.1
2006	67.0	32.3	71.1	71.6	85.7	84.4	79.2	55.9	16.7
2007	66.8	29.4	71.2	71.1	86.1	86.3	78.6	54.4	17.3
2008	66.7	29.1	71.1	71.1	85.3	86.8	79.1	56.1	18.1
2009	65.0	26.4	69.6	67.6	83.2	85.1	77.4	56.8	18.3
2010	65.0	25.8	69.5	66.9	83.4	86.1	77.4	56.8	18.1
2011	64.2	25.7	68.4	67.0	82.6	83.7	76.1	55.9	19.1

Table 1-8. Civilian Labor Force Participation Rates, by Age, Sex, Race, and Hispanic Origin, 1948–2011
—Continued

(Percent.)

Race, Hispanic origin, sex, and year	16 years and over	16 to 19 years	20 years and over						
			Total	20 to 24 years	25 to 34 years	35 to 44 years	45 to 54 years	55 to 64 years	65 years and over
BLACK									
Women									
1974	49.0	33.4	51.4	58.8	62.4	62.2	56.4	42.8	10.4
1975	48.8	34.2	51.1	55.9	62.8	62.0	56.6	43.1	10.7
1976	49.8	32.9	52.5	56.9	66.7	63.0	56.8	43.7	11.3
1977	50.8	32.9	53.6	59.3	68.5	64.1	57.9	43.7	10.5
1978	53.1	37.3	55.5	62.7	70.6	67.2	59.4	43.8	11.1
1979	53.1	36.8	55.4	61.5	70.1	68.0	59.6	44.0	10.9
1980	53.1	34.9	55.6	60.2	70.5	68.1	61.4	44.8	10.2
1981	53.5	34.0	56.0	61.1	70.0	69.8	62.0	45.4	9.3
1982	53.7	33.5	56.2	60.1	70.2	71.7	62.4	44.8	8.5
1983	54.2	33.0	56.8	59.1	72.3	72.6	62.3	44.8	8.2
1984	55.2	35.0	57.6	60.7	71.5	73.7	64.5	46.1	8.0
1985	56.5	37.9	58.6	62.5	72.4	74.8	65.7	45.3	9.4
1986	56.9	39.1	58.9	64.6	72.4	75.8	66.5	43.6	7.8
1987	58.0	39.6	60.0	64.4	73.5	77.8	67.5	44.4	8.6
1988	58.0	37.9	60.1	63.2	73.7	78.1	68.3	43.4	9.6
1989	58.7	40.4	60.6	65.5	73.6	78.0	70.0	42.4	9.8
1990	58.3	36.8	60.6	62.4	72.3	77.7	70.7	43.2	9.9
1991	57.5	33.5	60.0	60.3	71.4	77.2	70.2	44.1	9.2
1992	58.5	35.2	60.8	60.8	73.1	77.1	71.7	45.1	8.6
1993	57.9	34.6	60.2	62.6	70.9	76.8	71.2	44.4	8.3
1994	58.7	36.3	60.9	64.5	71.9	76.4	71.3	45.3	9.2
1995	59.5	39.8	61.4	63.7	73.9	77.3	70.5	47.2	7.7
1996	60.4	38.9	62.6	65.2	75.9	78.2	72.0	47.2	7.7
1997	61.7	39.9	64.0	69.9	78.1	78.4	73.2	47.6	8.2
1998	62.8	42.5	64.8	69.6	79.6	79.9	74.0	48.5	7.9
1999	63.5	38.8	66.1	72.7	82.1	80.4	74.6	48.4	8.9
2000	63.1	39.6	65.4	70.5	81.1	79.9	74.9	48.6	9.9
2001	62.8	37.3	65.2	70.1	81.2	79.6	73.9	49.9	10.1
2002	61.8	34.7	64.4	66.9	79.7	79.2	73.3	51.8	9.8
2003	61.9	33.7	64.6	65.7	79.1	80.6	74.2	51.9	10.3
2004	61.5	32.8	64.2	66.8	77.2	80.6	74.3	52.3	10.7
2005	61.6	32.2	64.4	68.1	78.5	79.7	73.3	53.7	11.4
2006	61.7	35.6	64.2	66.2	78.6	80.1	73.0	55.1	11.8
2007	61.1	31.2	64.0	65.7	78.0	79.8	73.2	55.7	12.0
2008	61.3	29.7	64.3	65.2	79.6	80.0	73.7	55.3	13.0
2009	60.3	27.9	63.4	64.5	78.0	79.0	73.3	54.4	13.3
2010	59.9	25.1	63.2	66.9	77.9	77.7	73.0	54.9	13.3
2011	59.1	24.2	62.2	65.9	76.0	78.2	72.0	53.4	14.2
HISPANIC									
Both Sexes									
1975	60.8	46.2	. . .	. . .	. . .	. . .	. . .	. . .	. . .
1976	60.8	46.9	62.9	. . .	. . .	. . .	. . .	. . .	. . .
1977	61.6	48.2	63.7	. . .	. . .	. . .	. . .	. . .	. . .
1978	62.9	49.6	65.0	. . .	. . .	. . .	. . .	. . .	. . .
1979	63.6	50.3	65.6	. . .	. . .	. . .	. . .	. . .	. . .
1980	64.0	50.3	66.2	. . .	. . .	. . .	. . .	. . .	. . .
1981	64.1	46.4	66.8	. . .	. . .	. . .	. . .	. . .	. . .
1982	63.6	44.8	66.3	. . .	. . .	. . .	. . .	. . .	. . .
1983	63.8	45.3	66.2	. . .	. . .	. . .	. . .	. . .	. . .
1984	64.9	47.5	67.1	. . .	. . .	. . .	. . .	. . .	. . .
1985	64.6	44.6	67.1	. . .	. . .	. . .	. . .	. . .	. . .
1986	65.4	43.9	68.0	. . .	. . .	. . .	. . .	. . .	. . .
1987	66.4	45.8	68.8	. . .	. . .	. . .	. . .	. . .	. . .
1988	67.4	49.6	69.4	. . .	. . .	. . .	. . .	. . .	. . .
1989	67.6	48.6	69.7	. . .	. . .	. . .	. . .	. . .	. . .
1990	67.4	47.8	69.8	. . .	. . .	. . .	. . .	. . .	. . .
1991	66.5	45.1	69.0	. . .	. . .	. . .	. . .	. . .	. . .
1992	66.8	45.8	69.2	. . .	. . .	. . .	. . .	. . .	. . .
1993	66.2	43.9	68.7	. . .	. . .	. . .	. . .	. . .	. . .
1994	66.1	44.4	68.5	74.0	77.3	78.9	73.1	49.8	10.7
1995	65.8	45.4	68.1	71.9	78.1	78.5	72.8	48.6	10.5
1996	66.5	43.4	69.1	73.1	78.2	79.5	74.6	52.2	11.0
1997	67.9	43.0	70.8	76.4	79.5	80.9	75.4	53.8	11.9
1998	67.9	45.7	70.6	76.1	80.3	80.0	75.3	55.4	10.1
1999	67.7	45.5	70.4	76.0	78.6	81.3	75.9	54.1	11.6
2000	69.7	46.3	72.5	78.2	80.4	81.7	78.0	54.2	12.3
2001	69.5	46.9	72.0	76.6	80.0	81.9	77.4	55.1	10.9
2002	69.1	44.0	71.8	76.3	80.5	81.1	76.1	55.8	11.9
2003	68.3	37.7	71.4	75.6	79.4	81.1	75.3	57.4	12.8
2004	68.6	38.2	71.7	74.5	79.4	81.4	77.6	58.1	14.5
2005	68.0	38.6	71.0	72.7	79.1	81.2	77.2	58.4	13.9
2006	68.7	38.3	71.9	74.4	80.1	81.9	77.3	59.2	15.7
2007	68.8	37.1	72.1	74.8	80.7	81.8	78.6	58.5	16.0
2008	68.5	36.9	71.8	73.7	80.5	82.0	78.2	59.9	16.0
2009	68.0	34.0	71.5	73.1	79.5	81.3	79.3	61.9	17.1
2010	67.5	30.9	71.4	71.1	80.6	81.2	79.2	61.1	17.9
2011	66.5	28.3	70.7	72.0	79.1	80.3	78.9	60.8	17.6

. . . = Not available.

Table 1-8. Civilian Labor Force Participation Rates, by Age, Sex, Race, and Hispanic Origin, 1948–2011
—*Continued*

(Percent.)

Race, Hispanic origin, sex, and year	16 years and over	16 to 19 years	20 years and over						
			Total	20 to 24 years	25 to 34 years	35 to 44 years	45 to 54 years	55 to 64 years	65 years and over
HISPANIC									
Men									
1975	80.7	...	85.5	...	...	...	...	...	...
1976	79.6	...	84.2	...	...	...	...	...	...
1977	80.9	...	84.8	...	...	...	...	...	...
1978	81.1	...	84.9	...	...	...	...	...	...
1979	81.3	...	85.3	...	...	...	...	...	...
1980	81.4	...	84.9	...	...	...	...	...	...
1981	80.6	...	84.7	...	...	...	...	...	...
1982	79.7	...	84.0	...	...	...	...	...	...
1983	80.3	...	84.1	...	...	...	...	...	...
1984	80.6	...	84.3	...	...	...	...	...	...
1985	80.3	...	84.0	...	...	...	...	...	...
1986	81.0	...	84.6	...	...	...	...	...	...
1987	81.0	...	84.5	...	...	...	...	...	...
1988	81.9	...	85.0	...	...	...	...	...	...
1989	82.0	...	85.0	...	...	...	...	...	...
1990	81.4	...	84.7	...	...	...	...	...	...
1991	80.3	...	83.8	...	...	...	...	...	...
1992	80.7	...	84.0	...	...	...	...	...	...
1993	80.2	...	83.5	...	...	...	...	...	...
1994	79.2	50.0	82.5	88.0	92.5	91.5	85.7	63.6	14.4
1995	79.1	50.2	82.4	86.2	92.9	91.3	85.6	62.4	15.8
1996	79.6	50.0	83.0	85.7	93.2	91.7	87.0	65.9	16.7
1997	80.1	47.4	84.1	88.1	93.5	91.9	87.8	68.4	17.3
1998	79.8	48.7	83.6	88.1	94.0	91.4	86.7	70.2	14.9
1999	79.8	50.1	83.5	88.1	93.9	92.2	86.2	68.6	18.2
2000	81.5	50.7	85.3	89.1	94.1	93.3	87.6	69.4	18.5
2001	81.0	52.2	84.3	86.8	93.4	92.7	86.7	68.6	16.8
2002	80.2	48.8	83.6	86.1	93.5	92.1	86.1	67.3	16.3
2003	80.1	40.9	84.1	86.2	93.6	92.9	85.4	68.8	17.4
2004	80.4	42.4	84.2	84.4	93.6	93.2	87.2	69.6	20.8
2005	80.1	41.9	84.0	84.1	93.3	93.1	87.7	69.3	20.1
2006	80.7	42.0	84.6	85.9	94.1	93.8	87.1	69.6	22.9
2007	80.5	40.0	84.7	85.3	94.1	93.9	88.3	70.3	22.0
2008	80.2	40.3	84.4	84.3	94.0	93.7	88.6	71.7	21.7
2009	78.8	36.4	83.2	82.3	91.9	93.0	88.8	71.7	23.0
2010	77.8	33.2	82.6	80.0	92.7	92.9	87.8	69.0	24.5
2011	76.5	30.1	81.7	79.5	91.6	92.4	87.3	69.9	23.3
HISPANIC									
Women									
1975	43.2	...	43.8	...	...	...	...	...	...
1976	44.3	...	44.6	...	...	...	...	...	...
1977	44.3	...	45.1	...	...	...	...	...	...
1978	46.6	...	47.2	...	...	...	...	...	...
1979	47.4	...	48.0	...	...	...	...	...	...
1980	47.4	...	48.5	...	...	...	...	...	...
1981	48.3	...	49.7	...	...	...	...	...	...
1982	48.1	...	49.3	...	...	...	...	...	...
1983	47.7	...	49.0	...	...	...	...	...	...
1984	49.6	...	50.5	...	...	...	...	...	...
1985	49.3	...	50.6	...	...	...	...	...	...
1986	50.1	...	51.7	...	...	...	...	...	...
1987	52.0	...	53.3	...	...	...	...	...	...
1988	53.2	...	54.2	...	...	...	...	...	...
1989	53.5	...	54.9	...	...	...	...	...	...
1990	53.1	...	54.8	...	...	...	...	...	...
1991	52.4	...	54.0	...	...	...	...	...	...
1992	52.8	...	54.3	...	...	...	...	...	...
1993	52.1	...	53.8	...	...	...	...	...	...
1994	52.9	38.7	54.4	57.9	60.5	66.4	61.4	38.1	7.9
1995	52.6	40.4	53.9	55.9	61.6	65.9	60.5	37.2	6.6
1996	53.4	36.5	55.2	59.2	62.0	67.0	62.7	40.5	6.9
1997	55.1	38.0	57.0	62.3	63.7	69.3	63.3	40.6	8.1
1998	55.6	42.4	57.1	62.2	64.5	67.9	64.7	41.9	6.6
1999	55.9	40.6	57.7	63.0	62.7	70.5	66.2	42.4	6.5
2000	57.5	41.4	59.3	65.0	65.3	69.9	68.5	41.2	7.7
2001	57.6	41.1	59.3	64.6	65.2	70.3	68.3	43.2	6.7
2002	57.6	38.8	59.5	65.0	65.8	69.5	66.3	46.1	8.5
2003	55.9	34.5	58.1	63.3	62.9	68.5	65.3	47.1	9.4
2004	56.1	33.7	58.4	62.9	62.9	68.7	67.9	47.8	9.8
2005	55.3	35.2	57.4	59.4	62.4	68.2	66.6	48.4	9.3
2006	56.1	34.4	58.3	61.3	63.5	68.7	67.4	49.7	10.4
2007	56.5	34.0	58.8	62.9	64.6	68.4	68.7	47.6	11.4
2008	56.2	33.3	58.6	62.1	64.3	69.1	67.6	48.9	11.7
2009	56.5	31.6	59.2	63.2	64.7	68.2	69.4	52.6	12.7
2010	56.5	28.5	59.5	61.6	66.3	67.9	70.2	53.7	13.0
2011	55.9	26.3	59.0	63.0	64.5	67.1	70.4	52.3	13.2

. . . = Not available.

Table 1-9. Employed and Unemployed Full- and Part-Time Workers, by Age, Sex, and Race, 2000–2011

(Thousands of people.)

Race, sex, age, and year	Employed[1]								Unemployed	
	Full-time workers				Part-time workers				Looking for full-time work	Looking for part-time work
	Total	At work		Not at work	Total	At work[2]		Not at work		
		35 hours or more	1 to 34 hours for economic or noneconomic reasons			For economic reasons	For noneconomic reasons			
ALL RACES										
Both Sexes, 16 Years and Over										
2000	113 846	100 533	9 125	4 188	23 044	2 003	19 548	1 493	4 538	1 154
2001	113 573	99 047	10 464	4 061	23 361	2 297	19 494	1 570	5 546	1 254
2002	112 700	99 042	9 746	3 912	23 785	2 755	19 549	1 481	7 063	1 314
2003	113 324	99 539	9 841	3 944	24 412	3 184	19 702	1 525	7 361	1 413
2004	114 518	100 496	10 053	3 969	24 734	3 113	20 109	1 513	6 762	1 388
2005	117 016	103 044	9 983	3 990	24 714	2 963	20 229	1 522	6 175	1 415
2006	119 688	105 328	10 223	4 137	24 739	2 774	20 356	1 609	5 675	1 326
2007	121 091	106 990	9 976	4 125	24 956	2 851	20 511	1 594	5 789	1 289
2008	120 030	105 575	10 426	4 030	25 332	3 814	20 009	1 509	7 446	1 478
2009	112 634	95 911	12 853	3 870	27 244	6 353	19 327	1 563	12 523	1 741
2010	111 714	97 946	10 217	3 551	27 350	6 965	18 876	1 509	12 970	1 854
2011	112 556	98 976	10 047	3 534	27 313	6 872	18 984	1 457	11 914	1 833
Both Sexes, 20 Years and Over										
2000	111 353	98 439	8 787	4 127	18 348	1 747	15 297	1 304	3 978	632
2001	111 323	97 161	10 156	4 006	18 870	2 013	15 486	1 371	4 956	682
2002	110 679	97 342	9 474	3 862	19 475	2 448	15 704	1 322	6 395	730
2003	111 578	98 087	9 587	3 904	20 239	2 875	16 001	1 363	6 705	818
2004	112 747	99 034	9 789	3 924	20 598	2 817	16 436	1 345	6 178	764
2005	115 206	101 534	9 729	3 942	20 546	2 698	16 489	1 359	5 619	786
2006	117 844	103 779	9 974	4 090	20 421	2 510	16 478	1 433	5 117	765
2007	119 317	105 499	9 738	4 080	20 819	2 587	16 819	1 413	5 234	742
2008	118 404	104 212	10 204	3 989	21 385	3 492	16 543	1 350	6 790	849
2009	111 414	94 928	12 647	3 839	23 626	5 934	16 286	1 406	11 651	1 061
2010	110 622	97 037	10 057	3 528	24 064	6 552	16 138	1 373	12 155	1 142
2011	111 500	98 103	9 888	3 508	24 043	6 457	16 259	1 327	11 180	1 167
Men, 16 Years and Over										
2000	65 930	59 345	4 555	2 030	7 375	856	6 105	414	2 486	488
2001	65 623	58 386	5 241	1 996	7 573	1 021	6 129	424	3 144	546
2002	65 205	58 318	4 971	1 916	7 697	1 246	6 050	401	4 029	568
2003	65 379	58 428	5 023	1 927	7 953	1 473	6 056	423	4 291	615
2004	66 444	59 363	5 148	1 933	8 080	1 405	6 258	417	3 843	613
2005	67 858	60 825	5 096	1 937	8 115	1 316	6 370	429	3 444	616
2006	69 307	62 087	5 237	1 984	8 194	1 232	6 510	452	3 192	561
2007	70 035	62 965	5 095	1 975	8 220	1 319	6 424	477	3 326	556
2008	68 853	61 436	5 443	1 974	8 634	1 842	6 349	442	4 396	637
2009	63 951	55 317	6 772	1 862	9 719	3 035	6 170	514	7 696	757
2010	63 501	56 425	5 352	1 723	9 858	3 316	6 066	476	7 827	799
2011	64 333	57 413	5 189	1 731	9 957	3 262	6 216	479	6 903	781
Men, 20 Years and Over										
2000	64 464	58 095	4 370	2 000	5 170	733	4 109	328	2 162	214
2001	64 311	57 273	5 072	1 966	5 465	881	4 253	331	2 801	239
2002	64 006	57 302	4 815	1 889	5 728	1 093	4 299	336	3 642	254
2003	64 364	57 580	4 879	1 905	6 051	1 314	4 388	348	3 906	302
2004	65 377	58 471	5 000	1 906	6 196	1 251	4 600	345	3 511	281
2005	66 803	59 934	4 955	1 914	6 247	1 182	4 705	360	3 118	274
2006	68 193	61 140	5 095	1 958	6 238	1 100	4 762	376	2 861	270
2007	68 968	62 057	4 959	1 952	6 369	1 190	4 782	397	2 990	268
2008	67 895	60 625	5 315	1 955	6 855	1 675	4 802	378	3 994	303
2009	63 242	54 738	6 659	1 845	8 099	2 827	4 828	445	7 151	404
2010	62 854	55 887	5 258	1 710	8 376	3 102	4 857	417	7 336	427
2011	63 690	56 870	5 104	1 715	8 492	3 059	5 010	423	6 461	437
Women, 16 Years and Over										
2000	47 916	41 188	4 570	2 158	15 670	1 147	13 443	1 080	2 052	666
2001	47 950	40 661	5 223	2 065	15 788	1 276	13 365	1 146	2 402	709
2002	47 494	40 723	4 775	1 996	16 088	1 509	13 498	1 080	3 034	747
2003	47 946	41 111	4 818	2 017	16 459	1 711	13 646	1 102	3 070	798
2004	48 073	41 133	4 905	2 036	16 654	1 708	13 851	1 096	2 919	775
2005	49 158	42 219	4 887	2 052	16 598	1 647	13 859	1 092	2 732	799
2006	50 380	43 241	4 986	2 153	16 545	1 542	13 846	1 157	2 483	764
2007	51 056	44 025	4 881	2 150	16 736	1 532	14 087	1 117	2 463	732
2008	51 178	44 139	4 983	2 056	16 698	1 972	13 660	1 067	3 050	841
2009	48 683	40 594	6 080	2 009	17 525	3 318	13 157	1 050	4 827	984
2010	48 214	41 521	4 865	1 828	17 491	3 648	12 810	1 033	5 144	1 055
2011	48 224	41 563	4 858	1 802	17 355	3 610	12 767	977	5 011	1 052

Note: Beginning in January 2004, data reflect revised population controls used in the household survey. See notes and definitions for information on historical comparability.

[1]Employed persons are classified as full- or part-time workers based on their usual weekly hours at all jobs, regardless of the number of hours they were at work during the reference week. Persons absent from work are also classified according to their usual status.
[2]Includes some persons at work 35 hours or more classified by their reason for working part time.

Table 1-9. Employed and Unemployed Full- and Part-Time Workers, by Age, Sex, and Race, 2000–2011
—Continued

(Thousands of people.)

Race, sex, age, and year	Employed[1]								Unemployed	
	Full-time workers				Part-time workers					
		At work				At work[2]				
	Total	35 hours or more	1 to 34 hours for economic or noneco-nomic reasons	Not at work	Total	For economic reasons	For noneco-nomic reasons	Not at work	Looking for full-time work	Looking for part-time work
ALL RACES										
Women, 20 Years and Over										
2000	46 889	40 344	4 417	2 128	13 178	1 013	11 188	976	1 816	419
2001	47 012	39 889	5 083	2 040	13 405	1 132	11 233	1 040	2 155	444
2002	46 673	40 040	4 660	1 973	13 747	1 355	11 406	986	2 752	476
2003	47 215	40 507	4 708	2 000	14 188	1 560	11 613	1 015	2 799	515
2004	47 371	40 563	4 790	2 017	14 402	1 567	11 836	1 000	2 667	483
2005	48 403	41 600	4 774	2 028	14 299	1 516	11 784	999	2 501	512
2006	49 651	42 639	4 880	2 132	14 183	1 410	11 716	1 057	2 256	495
2007	50 349	43 442	4 779	2 128	14 450	1 397	12 037	1 016	2 244	474
2008	50 509	43 587	4 888	2 034	14 530	1 817	11 740	973	2 796	546
2009	48 171	40 190	5 988	1 994	15 527	3 107	11 459	961	4 500	657
2010	47 767	41 150	4 799	1 818	15 688	3 450	11 282	956	4 819	715
2011	47 810	41 233	4 784	1 792	15 551	3 398	11 249	904	4 719	730
WHITE[3]										
Men, 16 Years and Over										
2000	56 068	50 434	3 896	1 738	6 221	656	5 213	351	1 798	379
2001	55 830	49 625	4 504	1 701	6 381	793	5 225	364	2 323	431
2002	55 369	49 459	4 267	1 644	6 480	980	5 150	350	3 017	443
2003	55 216	49 323	4 266	1 628	6 650	1 146	5 148	357	3 164	479
2004	55 926	49 891	4 396	1 638	6 786	1 092	5 331	363	2 805	477
2005	56 955	50 965	4 334	1 656	6 808	1 014	5 424	370	2 459	471
2006	58 063	51 894	4 484	1 685	6 820	947	5 481	393	2 299	432
2007	58 494	52 460	4 359	1 676	6 795	1 022	5 368	406	2 444	425
2008	57 432	51 104	4 653	1 675	7 192	1 433	5 379	379	3 235	492
2009	53 506	46 153	5 770	1 583	8 124	2 438	5 240	446	5 819	602
2010	53 086	47 055	4 554	1 477	8 166	2 662	5 102	402	5 832	644
2011	53 727	47 865	4 397	1 465	8 193	2 560	5 227	405	5 020	611
Men, 20 Years and Over										
2000	54 778	49 335	3 733	1 710	4 341	558	3 505	278	1 566	165
2001	54 666	48 636	4 354	1 676	4 579	677	3 616	285	2 080	195
2002	54 333	48 581	4 133	1 619	4 790	857	3 640	293	2 743	200
2003	54 339	48 585	4 145	1 609	5 010	1 016	3 703	291	2 893	231
2004	55 005	49 124	4 267	1 614	5 154	961	3 895	299	2 567	217
2005	56 050	50 203	4 213	1 634	5 205	905	3 990	310	2 242	209
2006	57 108	51 081	4 365	1 662	5 150	840	3 987	324	2 074	208
2007	57 591	51 691	4 243	1 656	5 216	915	3 967	334	2 204	204
2008	56 623	50 421	4 542	1 660	5 681	1 302	4 055	324	2 944	235
2009	52 899	45 654	5 676	1 569	6 728	2 269	4 075	384	5 421	325
2010	52 530	46 592	4 472	1 466	6 907	2 484	4 071	352	5 481	347
2011	53 186	47 406	4 328	1 451	6 933	2 392	4 184	357	4 702	344
Women, 16 Years and Over										
2000	38 438	32 942	3 729	1 767	13 698	867	11 870	961	1 422	521
2001	38 445	32 491	4 252	1 702	13 773	971	11 787	1 015	1 664	551
2002	38 152	32 623	3 896	1 633	14 011	1 152	11 903	956	2 084	595
2003	38 249	32 659	3 939	1 652	14 120	1 304	11 860	956	2 038	629
2004	38 240	32 555	4 018	1 667	14 287	1 280	12 038	969	1 968	597
2005	38 973	33 325	3 976	1 672	14 213	1 207	12 043	963	1 807	612
2006	39 813	33 980	4 082	1 751	14 137	1 157	11 967	1 013	1 670	601
2007	40 238	34 486	4 014	1 738	14 265	1 143	12 148	973	1 694	579
2008	40 292	34 569	4 076	1 647	14 209	1 518	11 761	931	2 119	664
2009	38 456	31 885	4 946	1 626	14 910	2 579	11 418	913	3 442	785
2010	38 158	32 710	3 958	1 490	14 758	2 846	11 029	883	3 612	828
2011	38 152	32 731	3 944	1 477	14 618	2 775	10 994	850	3 450	807

Note: Beginning in January 2004, data reflect revised population controls used in the household survey. See notes and definitions for information on historical comparability.

[1]Employed persons are classified as full- or part-time workers based on their usual weekly hours at all jobs, regardless of the number of hours they were at work during the reference week. Persons absent from work are also classified according to their usual status.
[2]Includes some persons at work 35 hours or more classified by their reason for working part time.
[3]Beginning in 2003, persons who selected this race group only; persons who selected more than one race group are not included. Prior to 2003, persons who reported more than one race group were included in the group they identified as their main race.

Table 1-9. Employed and Unemployed Full- and Part-Time Workers, by Age, Sex, and Race, 2000–2011 —Continued

(Thousands of people.)

Race, sex, age, and year	Employed[1]								Unemployed	
	Full-time workers				Part-time workers					
		At work				At work[2]				
	Total	35 hours or more	1 to 34 hours for economic or noneconomic reasons	Not at work	Total	For economic reasons	For noneconomic reasons	Not at work	Looking for full-time work	Looking for part-time work
WHITE—Continued										
Women, 20 Years and Over										
2000	37 585	32 242	3 600	1 743	11 560	754	9 935	872	1 256	339
2001	37 658	31 839	4 139	1 680	11 711	853	9 933	924	1 492	357
2002	37 467	32 049	3 803	1 615	11 981	1 029	10 079	873	1 888	381
2003	37 640	32 158	3 845	1 637	12 183	1 180	10 124	879	1 866	411
2004	37 663	32 085	3 927	1 652	12 377	1 166	10 326	885	1 795	377
2005	38 354	32 820	3 882	1 652	12 235	1 108	10 248	879	1 653	401
2006	39 232	33 500	3 998	1 733	12 128	1 050	10 151	927	1 524	402
2007	39 670	34 015	3 932	1 722	12 326	1 037	10 402	887	1 547	383
2008	39 765	34 128	4 005	1 632	12 359	1 392	10 116	851	1 949	435
2009	38 033	31 547	4 872	1 614	13 198	2 411	9 952	835	3 216	529
2010	37 789	32 404	3 904	1 481	13 208	2 684	9 705	818	3 389	571
2011	37 816	32 466	3 882	1 468	13 065	2 597	9 683	785	3 255	563
BLACK[3]										
Men, 16 Years and Over										
2000	6 350	5 704	445	202	732	144	548	41	542	78
2001	6 178	5 509	468	200	761	165	557	39	626	83
2002	6 194	5 541	480	173	765	188	546	30	749	86
2003	6 055	5 414	453	188	765	221	505	39	804	87
2004	6 177	5 538	460	179	736	205	499	32	763	98
2005	6 381	5 745	463	174	773	207	533	33	742	102
2006	6 529	5 907	446	176	825	201	590	34	681	93
2007	6 673	6 068	429	176	826	195	589	42	660	92
2008	6 548	5 935	440	173	850	276	542	32	849	100
2009	5 871	5 166	556	150	946	379	530	36	1 348	100
2010	5 856	5 279	446	130	1 009	419	550	41	1 448	102
2011	5 892	5 293	445	154	1 060	452	566	43	1 393	108
Men, 20 Years and Over										
2000	6 222	5 594	429	199	520	125	363	32	468	31
2001	6 069	5 417	455	197	558	145	382	31	542	31
2002	6 073	5 437	465	171	579	166	387	26	660	35
2003	5 980	5 355	439	185	607	201	372	34	717	43
2004	6 089	5 463	449	177	592	189	376	27	689	44
2005	6 287	5 662	452	174	614	189	397	28	655	44
2006	6 424	5 816	433	175	655	185	441	30	596	44
2007	6 574	5 983	417	174	671	181	452	37	580	43
2008	6 461	5 860	430	171	690	252	409	29	764	46
2009	5 811	5 119	544	148	817	355	428	34	1 238	49
2010	5 803	5 235	439	129	877	392	447	37	1 344	52
2011	5 830	5 242	435	153	935	428	470	38	1 299	61
Women, 16 Years and Over										
2000	6 780	5 862	632	287	1 293	211	1 005	77	515	106
2001	6 761	5 777	715	270	1 307	223	998	85	584	122
2002	6 588	5 685	640	263	1 326	259	991	76	744	114
2003	6 552	5 709	595	247	1 367	274	1 017	76	774	121
2004	6 597	5 740	611	246	1 399	306	1 022	71	744	124
2005	6 750	5 871	619	260	1 407	320	1 018	70	723	133
2006	7 001	6 131	605	265	1 410	274	1 054	82	655	120
2007	7 119	6 272	584	263	1 432	273	1 085	75	589	104
2008	7 105	6 238	596	272	1 449	302	1 070	77	717	122
2009	6 666	5 696	718	252	1 542	480	984	78	1 027	132
2010	6 525	5 727	582	215	1 621	528	1 010	82	1 142	160
2011	6 450	5 651	592	207	1 648	573	1 004	72	1 165	164
Women, 20 Years and Over										
2000	6 651	5 753	615	283	1 052	197	788	67	456	56
2001	6 647	5 684	695	268	1 094	203	816	75	521	61
2002	6 492	5 605	626	261	1 117	234	816	68	671	67
2003	6 468	5 639	583	246	1 168	257	842	69	698	75
2004	6 512	5 674	595	243	1 195	287	844	64	679	76
2005	6 653	5 789	606	258	1 222	298	861	63	660	74
2006	6 893	6 042	588	263	1 175	255	848	72	588	67
2007	7 024	6 194	570	260	1 216	254	897	65	527	61
2008	7 006	6 160	580	267	1 254	283	902	68	654	78
2009	6 600	5 644	705	250	1 356	449	837	71	951	82
2010	6 471	5 681	575	215	1 473	504	894	75	1 063	103
2011	6 402	5 610	586	207	1 504	549	888	67	1 095	108

Note: Beginning in January 2004, data reflect revised population controls used in the household survey. See notes and definitions for information on historical comparability.

[1]Employed persons are classified as full- or part-time workers based on their usual weekly hours at all jobs, regardless of the number of hours they were at work during the reference week. Persons absent from work are also classified according to their usual status.
[2]Includes some persons at work 35 hours or more classified by their reason for working part time.
[3]Beginning in 2003, persons who selected this race group only; persons who selected more than one race group are not included. Prior to 2003, persons who reported more than one race group were included in the group they identified as their main race.

Table 1-10. Persons Not in the Labor Force, by Age, Sex, and Desire and Availability for Work, 2008–2011

(Thousands of people.)

Category	Total		Age						Sex			
			16 to 24 years		25 to 54 years		55 years and over		Men		Women	
	2008	2009	2008	2009	2008	2009	2008	2009	2008	2009	2008	2009
TOTAL, NOT IN THE LABOR FORCE	79 501	81 659	15 452	16 207	21 255	21 823	42 794	43 629	30 593	32 013	48 908	49 646
Do Not Want a Job Now[1]	74 519	75 765	13 719	14 263	19 087	19 199	41 712	42 303	28 365	29 234	46 154	46 531
Want a Job[1]	4 983	5 894	1 733	1 944	2 168	2 624	1 082	1 325	2 228	2 779	2 755	3 115
Did not search for work in the previous year	2 826	3 075	913	960	1 145	1 241	768	874	1 187	1 344	1 639	1 731
Searched for work in the previous year[2]	2 157	2 818	819	983	1 023	1 383	314	452	1 041	1 435	1 115	1 384
Not available to work now	543	592	252	275	244	256	48	61	214	251	329	341
Available to work now	1 614	2 226	568	708	780	1 127	266	391	827	1 184	787	1 043
Reason not currently looking:												
Discouragement over job prospects[3]	462	778	145	200	226	427	90	151	282	485	180	293
Reasons other than discouragement	1 152	1 449	422	509	554	699	176	240	545	699	607	749
Family responsibilities	171	209	35	38	111	131	25	41	45	50	126	159
In school or training	218	306	173	234	42	65	3	7	108	163	109	144
Ill health or disability	124	136	16	19	68	68	40	49	55	70	69	66
Other[4]	640	798	199	219	332	435	108	144	337	417	303	381

Category	Total		Age						Sex			
			16 to 24 years		25 to 54 years		55 years and over		Men		Women	
	2010	2011	2010	2011	2010	2011	2010	2011	2010	2011	2010	2011
TOTAL, NOT IN THE LABOR FORCE	83 941	86 001	17 014	17 201	22 350	22 961	44 577	45 839	33 189	34 343	50 752	51 658
Do Not Want a Job Now[1]	77 882	79 564	14 990	15 177	19 659	20 107	43 233	44 280	30 309	31 298	47 573	48 266
Want a Job[1]	6 059	6 437	2 024	2 023	2 691	2 854	1 344	1 560	2 880	3 045	3 179	3 392
Did not search for work in the previous year	2 948	3 268	968	1 010	1 189	1 303	791	955	1 279	1 463	1 669	1 804
Searched for work in the previous year[2]	3 111	3 169	1 056	1 014	1 502	1 551	553	605	1 601	1 582	1 510	1 587
Not available to work now	623	597	274	262	284	262	65	73	264	236	359	361
Available to work now	2 487	2 573	782	752	1 218	1 289	487	532	1 337	1 346	1 151	1 227
Reason not currently looking:												
Discouragement over job prospects[3]	1 173	989	291	222	595	519	287	248	731	579	442	410
Reasons other than discouragement	1 315	1 584	491	530	623	770	200	284	606	767	709	817
Family responsibilities	286	215	49	30	171	139	66	45	83	48	203	166
In school or training	350	323	262	245	81	75	7	4	191	183	158	140
Ill health or disability	50	169	4	18	21	93	25	58	21	86	29	83
Other[4]	629	877	176	238	350	463	102	177	311	449	318	428

[1]Includes some persons who were not asked if they wanted a job.
[2]Persons who had a job during the prior 12 months must have searched since the end of that job.
[3]Includes believes no work available, could not find work, lacks necessary schooling or training, employer thinks too young or old, and other types of discrimination.
[4]Includes those who did not actively look for work in the prior four weeks for reasons such as childcare and transportation problems, as well as a small number for whom reason for nonparticipation was not ascertained.

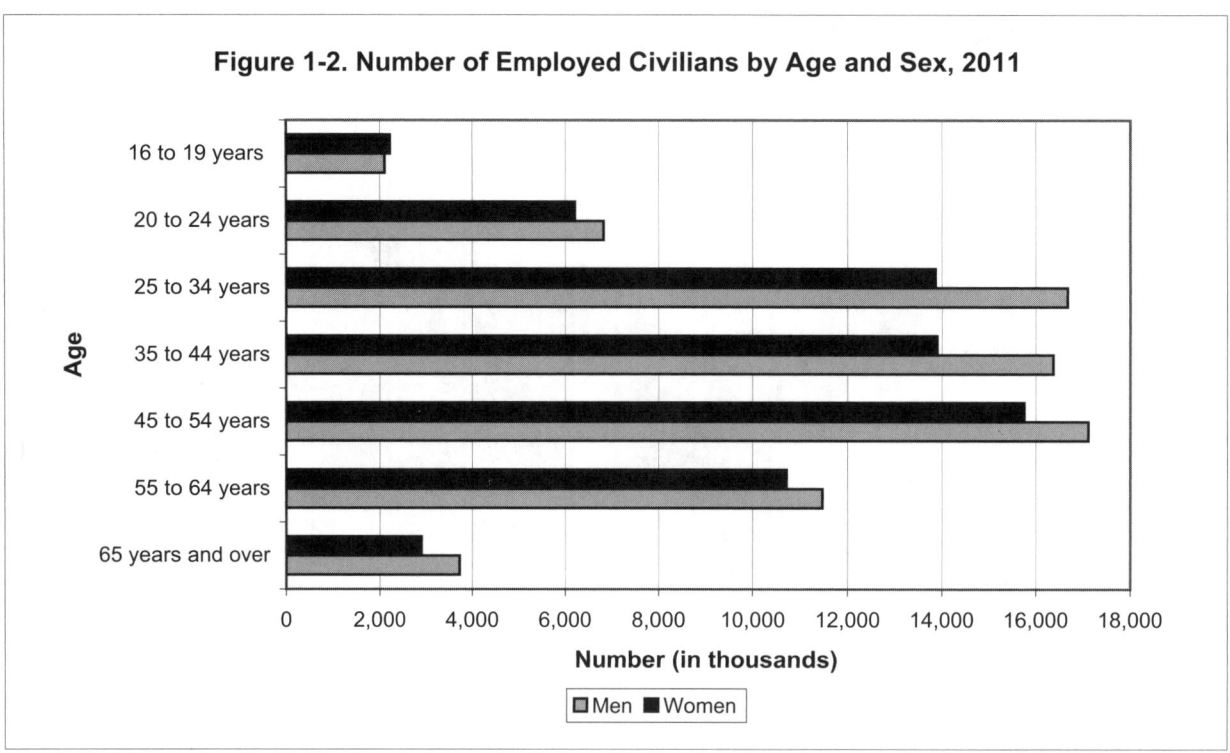

Figure 1-2. Number of Employed Civilians by Age and Sex, 2011

There were nearly 139.9 million employed civilians in the labor force in 2011, an increase of 0.6 percent from 2010 but a decline of 4.2 percent from 2007. Men outnumbered women in every age group except among the 16–19 year olds. In 2011, 53.1 percent of employed civilians were men. (See Table 1-11.)

OTHER HIGHLIGHTS

- While men made up 53.1 percent of employed civilians, they only made up 12.3 percent of employees in healthcare support occupations; 26.4 percent of employees in education, training, and library occupations; and 26.6 percent of employees in office and administrative support occupations. (See Table 1-13.)

- Among persons 25 years of age and over, employment increased for those with a least an associate's degree but declined for those without any type of degree. In 2011, employment increased 2.1 for those with an associates degree, 1.3 percent for those with only a bachelor's degree only, and 2.3 percent for those with a bachelor's degree or higher. (See Table 1-16.)

- The multiple jobholding rate continued to decline in May 2012 after remaining steady at 5.2 percent from 2008 through 2010. It was significantly higher for women (5.3 percent) than for men (4.8 percent). (See Table 1-17.)

- In 2011, slightly more than 9.0 million families had an unemployed member—a decline from nearly 9.7 million in 2010. (See Table 1-20.)

Table 1-11. Employed Civilians, by Age, Sex, Race, and Hispanic Origin, 1948–2011

(Thousands of people.)

Race, Hispanic origin, sex, and year	16 years and over	16 to 19 years			20 years and over						
		Total	16 to 17 years	18 to 19 years	Total	20 to 24 years	25 to 34 years	35 to 44 years	45 to 54 years	55 to 64 years	65 years and over
ALL RACES											
Both Sexes											
1948	58 343	4 026	1 600	2 426	54 318	6 937	13 801	13 050	10 624	7 103	2 804
1949	57 651	3 712	1 466	2 246	53 940	6 660	13 639	13 108	10 636	7 042	2 864
1950	58 918	3 703	1 433	2 270	55 218	6 746	13 917	13 424	10 966	7 265	2 899
1951	59 961	3 767	1 575	2 192	56 196	6 321	14 233	13 746	11 421	7 558	2 917
1952	60 250	3 719	1 626	2 092	56 536	5 572	14 515	14 058	11 687	7 785	2 919
1953	61 179	3 720	1 577	2 142	57 460	5 225	14 519	14 774	11 969	7 806	3 166
1954	60 109	3 475	1 422	2 053	56 634	4 971	14 190	14 541	11 976	7 895	3 060
1955	62 170	3 642	1 500	2 143	58 528	5 270	14 481	14 879	12 556	8 158	3 185
1956	63 799	3 818	1 647	2 171	59 983	5 545	14 407	15 218	12 978	8 519	3 314
1957	64 071	3 778	1 613	2 167	60 291	5 641	14 253	15 348	13 320	8 553	3 179
1958	63 036	3 582	1 519	2 063	59 454	5 571	13 675	15 157	13 448	8 559	3 045
1959	64 630	3 838	1 670	2 168	60 791	5 870	13 709	15 454	13 915	8 822	3 023
1960	65 778	4 129	1 770	2 360	61 648	6 119	13 630	15 598	14 238	8 989	3 073
1961	65 746	4 108	1 621	2 486	61 638	6 227	13 429	15 552	14 320	9 120	2 987
1962	66 702	4 195	1 607	2 588	62 508	6 446	13 311	15 901	14 491	9 346	3 013
1963	67 762	4 255	1 751	2 504	63 508	6 815	13 318	16 114	14 749	9 596	2 915
1964	69 305	4 516	2 013	2 503	64 789	7 303	13 449	16 166	15 094	9 804	2 973
1965	71 088	5 036	2 075	2 962	66 052	7 702	13 704	16 294	15 320	10 028	3 005
1966	72 895	5 721	2 269	3 452	67 178	7 964	14 017	16 312	15 615	10 310	2 961
1967	74 372	5 682	2 334	3 348	68 690	8 499	14 575	16 281	15 789	10 536	3 011
1968	75 920	5 781	2 403	3 377	70 141	8 762	15 265	16 220	16 083	10 745	3 065
1969	77 902	6 117	2 573	3 543	71 785	9 319	15 883	16 100	16 410	10 919	3 155
1970	78 678	6 144	2 598	3 546	72 534	9 731	16 318	15 922	16 473	10 974	3 118
1971	79 367	6 208	2 596	3 613	73 158	10 201	16 781	15 675	16 641	11 009	3 040
1972	82 153	6 746	2 787	3 959	75 407	10 999	18 082	15 822	16 457	11 044	3 003
1973	85 064	7 271	3 032	4 239	77 793	11 839	19 509	16 041	16 553	10 966	2 886
1974	86 794	7 448	3 111	4 338	79 347	12 101	20 610	16 203	16 633	10 964	2 835
1975	85 846	7 104	2 941	4 162	78 744	11 885	21 087	15 953	16 190	10 827	2 801
1976	88 752	7 336	2 972	4 363	81 416	12 570	22 493	16 468	16 224	10 912	2 747
1977	92 017	7 688	3 138	4 550	84 329	13 196	23 850	17 157	16 212	11 126	2 787
1978	96 048	8 070	3 330	4 739	87 979	13 887	25 281	18 128	16 338	11 400	2 946
1979	98 824	8 083	3 340	4 743	90 741	14 327	26 492	18 981	16 357	11 585	2 999
1980	99 303	7 710	3 106	4 605	91 593	14 087	27 204	19 523	16 234	11 586	2 960
1981	100 397	7 225	2 866	4 359	93 172	14 122	28 180	20 145	16 255	11 525	2 945
1982	99 526	6 549	2 505	4 044	92 978	13 690	28 149	20 879	15 923	11 414	2 923
1983	100 834	6 342	2 320	4 022	94 491	13 722	28 756	21 960	15 812	11 315	2 927
1984	105 005	6 444	2 404	4 040	98 562	14 207	30 348	23 598	16 178	11 395	2 835
1985	107 150	6 434	2 492	3 941	100 716	13 980	31 208	24 732	16 509	11 474	2 813
1986	109 597	6 472	2 622	3 850	103 125	13 790	32 201	25 861	16 949	11 405	2 919
1987	112 440	6 640	2 736	3 905	105 800	13 524	33 105	27 179	17 487	11 465	3 041
1988	114 968	6 805	2 713	4 092	108 164	13 244	33 574	28 269	18 447	11 433	3 197
1989	117 342	6 759	2 588	4 172	110 582	12 962	34 045	29 443	19 279	11 499	3 355
1990	118 793	6 581	2 410	4 171	112 213	13 401	33 935	30 817	19 525	11 189	3 346
1991	117 718	5 906	2 202	3 704	111 812	12 975	33 061	31 593	19 882	11 001	3 300
1992	118 492	5 669	2 128	3 540	112 824	12 872	32 667	31 923	21 022	10 998	3 341
1993	120 259	5 805	2 226	3 579	114 455	12 840	32 385	32 666	22 175	11 058	3 331
1994	123 060	6 161	2 510	3 651	116 899	12 758	32 286	33 599	23 348	11 228	3 681
1995	124 900	6 419	2 573	3 846	118 481	12 443	32 356	34 202	24 378	11 435	3 666
1996	126 708	6 500	2 646	3 853	120 208	12 138	32 077	35 051	25 514	11 739	3 690
1997	129 558	6 661	2 648	4 012	122 897	12 380	31 809	35 908	26 744	12 296	3 761
1998	131 463	7 051	2 762	4 289	124 413	12 557	31 394	36 278	27 587	12 872	3 725
1999	133 488	7 172	2 793	4 379	126 316	12 891	30 865	36 728	28 635	13 315	3 882
2000	136 891	7 189	2 759	4 431	129 701	13 229	31 549	36 433	30 310	14 002	4 179
2001	136 933	6 740	2 558	4 182	130 194	13 348	30 863	36 049	31 036	14 645	4 253
2002	136 485	6 332	2 330	4 002	130 154	13 351	30 306	35 235	31 281	15 674	4 306
2003	137 736	5 919	2 312	3 607	131 817	13 433	30 383	34 881	31 914	16 598	4 608
2004	139 252	5 907	2 193	3 714	133 345	13 723	30 423	34 580	32 469	17 331	4 819
2005	141 730	5 978	2 284	3 694	135 752	13 792	30 680	34 630	33 207	18 349	5 094
2006	144 427	6 162	2 444	3 719	138 265	13 878	31 051	34 569	34 052	19 389	5 325
2007	146 047	5 911	2 286	3 625	140 136	13 964	31 586	34 302	34 563	20 108	5 614
2008	145 362	5 573	1 989	3 584	139 790	13 629	31 383	33 457	34 529	20 812	5 979
2009	139 877	4 837	1 651	3 187	135 040	12 764	30 014	31 517	33 613	21 019	6 114
2010	139 064	4 378	1 418	2 960	134 686	12 699	30 229	30 663	33 191	21 636	6 268
2011	139 869	4 327	1 355	2 972	135 542	13 036	30 537	30 270	32 867	22 186	6 647

Table 1-11. Employed Civilians, by Age, Sex, Race, and Hispanic Origin, 1948–2011—*Continued*

(Thousands of people.)

Race, Hispanic origin, sex, and year	16 years and over	16 to 19 years			20 years and over						
		Total	16 to 17 years	18 to 19 years	Total	20 to 24 years	25 to 34 years	35 to 44 years	45 to 54 years	55 to 64 years	65 years and over
ALL RACES											
Men											
1948	41 725	2 344	996	1 348	39 382	4 349	10 038	9 363	7 742	5 587	2 303
1949	40 925	2 124	911	1 213	38 803	4 197	9 879	9 308	7 661	5 438	2 329
1950	41 578	2 186	909	1 277	39 394	4 255	10 060	9 445	7 790	5 508	2 336
1951	41 780	2 156	979	1 177	39 626	3 780	10 134	9 607	8 012	5 711	2 382
1952	41 682	2 107	985	1 121	39 578	3 183	10 352	9 753	8 144	5 804	2 343
1953	42 430	2 136	976	1 159	40 296	2 901	10 500	10 229	8 374	5 808	2 483
1954	41 619	1 985	881	1 104	39 634	2 724	10 254	10 082	8 330	5 830	2 414
1955	42 621	2 095	936	1 159	40 526	2 973	10 453	10 267	8 553	5 857	2 424
1956	43 379	2 164	1 008	1 156	41 216	3 245	10 337	10 385	8 732	6 004	2 512
1957	43 357	2 115	987	1 130	41 239	3 346	10 222	10 427	8 851	6 002	2 394
1958	42 423	2 012	948	1 064	40 411	3 293	9 790	10 291	8 828	5 955	2 254
1959	43 466	2 198	1 015	1 183	41 267	3 597	9 862	10 492	9 048	6 058	2 210
1960	43 904	2 361	1 090	1 271	41 543	3 754	9 759	10 552	9 182	6 105	2 191
1961	43 656	2 315	989	1 325	41 342	3 795	9 591	10 505	9 195	6 155	2 098
1962	44 177	2 362	990	1 372	41 815	3 898	9 475	10 711	9 333	6 260	2 138
1963	44 657	2 406	1 073	1 334	42 251	4 118	9 431	10 801	9 478	6 385	2 038
1964	45 474	2 587	1 242	1 345	42 886	4 370	9 531	10 832	9 637	6 478	2 039
1965	46 340	2 918	1 285	1 634	43 422	4 583	9 611	10 837	9 792	6 542	2 057
1966	46 919	3 253	1 389	1 863	43 668	4 599	9 709	10 764	9 904	6 668	2 024
1967	47 479	3 186	1 417	1 769	44 294	4 809	9 988	10 674	9 990	6 774	2 058
1968	48 114	3 255	1 453	1 802	44 859	4 812	10 405	10 554	10 102	6 893	2 093
1969	48 818	3 430	1 526	1 904	45 388	5 012	10 736	10 401	10 187	6 931	2 122
1970	48 990	3 409	1 504	1 905	45 581	5 237	10 936	10 216	10 170	6 928	2 094
1971	49 390	3 478	1 510	1 968	45 912	5 593	11 218	10 028	10 139	6 916	2 019
1972	50 896	3 765	1 598	2 167	47 130	6 138	11 884	10 088	10 139	6 929	1 953
1973	52 349	4 039	1 721	2 318	48 310	6 655	12 617	10 126	10 197	6 857	1 856
1974	53 024	4 103	1 744	2 359	48 922	6 739	13 119	10 135	10 181	6 880	1 869
1975	51 857	3 839	1 621	2 219	48 018	6 484	13 205	9 891	9 902	6 722	1 811
1976	53 138	3 947	1 626	2 321	49 190	6 915	13 869	10 069	9 881	6 724	1 732
1977	54 728	4 174	1 733	2 441	50 555	7 232	14 483	10 399	9 832	6 848	1 761
1978	56 479	4 336	1 800	2 535	52 143	7 559	15 124	10 845	9 806	6 954	1 855
1979	57 607	4 300	1 799	2 501	53 308	7 791	15 688	11 202	9 735	7 015	1 876
1980	57 186	4 085	1 672	2 412	53 101	7 532	15 832	11 355	9 548	6 999	1 835
1981	57 397	3 815	1 526	2 289	53 582	7 504	16 266	11 613	9 478	6 909	1 812
1982	56 271	3 379	1 307	2 072	52 891	7 197	16 002	11 902	9 234	6 781	1 776
1983	56 787	3 300	1 213	2 087	53 487	7 232	16 216	12 450	9 133	6 686	1 770
1984	59 091	3 322	1 244	2 078	55 769	7 571	17 166	13 309	9 326	6 694	1 703
1985	59 891	3 328	1 300	2 029	56 562	7 339	17 564	13 800	9 411	6 753	1 695
1986	60 892	3 323	1 352	1 971	57 569	7 250	18 092	14 266	9 554	6 654	1 753
1987	62 107	3 381	1 393	1 988	58 726	7 058	18 487	14 898	9 750	6 682	1 850
1988	63 273	3 492	1 403	2 089	59 781	6 918	18 702	15 457	10 201	6 591	1 911
1989	64 315	3 477	1 327	2 150	60 837	6 799	18 952	16 002	10 569	6 548	1 968
1990	65 104	3 427	1 254	2 173	61 678	7 151	18 779	16 771	10 690	6 378	1 909
1991	64 223	3 044	1 135	1 909	61 178	6 909	18 265	17 086	10 813	6 245	1 860
1992	64 440	2 944	1 096	1 848	61 496	6 819	17 966	17 230	11 365	6 173	1 943
1993	65 349	2 994	1 155	1 839	62 355	6 805	17 877	17 665	11 927	6 166	1 916
1994	66 450	3 156	1 288	1 868	63 294	6 771	17 741	18 111	12 439	6 142	2 089
1995	67 377	3 292	1 316	1 977	64 085	6 665	17 709	18 374	12 958	6 272	2 108
1996	68 207	3 310	1 318	1 992	64 897	6 429	17 527	18 816	13 483	6 470	2 172
1997	69 685	3 401	1 355	2 045	66 284	6 548	17 338	19 327	14 107	6 735	2 229
1998	70 693	3 558	1 398	2 161	67 135	6 638	17 097	19 634	14 544	7 052	2 171
1999	71 446	3 685	1 437	2 249	67 761	6 729	16 694	19 811	14 991	7 274	2 263
2000	73 305	3 671	1 394	2 276	69 634	6 974	17 241	19 537	15 871	7 606	2 406
2001	73 196	3 420	1 268	2 151	69 776	6 952	16 915	19 305	16 268	7 900	2 437
2002	72 903	3 169	1 130	2 040	69 734	6 978	16 573	18 932	16 419	8 378	2 455
2003	73 332	2 917	1 115	1 802	70 415	7 065	16 670	18 774	16 588	8 733	2 585
2004	74 524	2 952	1 037	1 915	71 572	7 246	16 818	18 700	16 951	9 174	2 683
2005	75 973	2 923	1 067	1 855	73 050	7 279	16 993	18 780	17 429	9 714	2 857
2006	77 502	3 071	1 182	1 888	74 431	7 412	17 134	18 765	17 920	10 192	3 008
2007	78 254	2 917	1 091	1 827	75 337	7 374	17 452	18 666	18 210	10 556	3 080
2008	77 486	2 736	926	1 810	74 750	7 145	17 183	18 097	18 124	10 919	3 282
2009	73 670	2 328	786	1 543	71 341	6 510	16 223	16 918	17 443	10 890	3 357
2010	73 359	2 129	675	1 454	71 230	6 466	16 358	16 585	17 242	11 140	3 439
2011	74 290	2 108	650	1 459	72 182	6 826	16 674	16 370	17 113	11 469	3 730

Table 1-11. Employed Civilians, by Age, Sex, Race, and Hispanic Origin, 1948–2011—*Continued*

(Thousands of people.)

Race, Hispanic origin, sex, and year	16 years and over	16 to 19 years			20 years and over						
		Total	16 to 17 years	18 to 19 years	Total	20 to 24 years	25 to 34 years	35 to 44 years	45 to 54 years	55 to 64 years	65 years and over
ALL RACES											
Women											
1948	16 617	1 682	604	1 078	14 936	2 588	3 763	3 687	2 882	1 516	501
1949	16 723	1 588	555	1 033	15 137	2 463	3 760	3 800	2 975	1 604	535
1950	17 340	1 517	524	993	15 824	2 491	3 857	3 979	3 176	1 757	563
1951	18 181	1 611	596	1 015	16 570	2 541	4 099	4 139	3 409	1 847	535
1952	18 568	1 612	641	971	16 958	2 389	4 163	4 305	3 543	1 981	576
1953	18 749	1 584	601	983	17 164	2 324	4 019	4 545	3 595	1 998	683
1954	18 490	1 490	541	949	17 000	2 247	3 936	4 459	3 646	2 065	646
1955	19 551	1 547	564	984	18 002	2 297	4 028	4 612	4 003	2 301	761
1956	20 419	1 654	639	1 015	18 767	2 300	4 070	4 833	4 246	2 515	802
1957	20 714	1 663	626	1 037	19 052	2 295	4 031	4 921	4 469	2 551	785
1958	20 613	1 570	571	999	19 043	2 278	3 885	4 866	4 620	2 604	791
1959	21 164	1 640	655	985	19 524	2 273	3 847	4 962	4 867	2 764	813
1960	21 874	1 768	680	1 089	20 105	2 365	3 871	5 046	5 056	2 884	882
1961	22 090	1 793	632	1 161	20 296	2 432	3 838	5 047	5 125	2 965	889
1962	22 525	1 833	617	1 216	20 693	2 548	3 836	5 190	5 158	3 086	875
1963	23 105	1 849	678	1 170	21 257	2 697	3 887	5 313	5 271	3 211	877
1964	23 831	1 929	771	1 158	21 903	2 933	3 918	5 334	5 457	3 326	934
1965	24 748	2 118	790	1 328	22 630	3 119	4 093	5 457	5 528	3 486	948
1966	25 976	2 468	880	1 589	23 510	3 365	4 308	5 548	5 711	3 642	937
1967	26 893	2 496	917	1 579	24 397	3 690	4 587	5 607	5 799	3 762	953
1968	27 807	2 526	950	1 575	25 281	3 950	4 860	5 666	5 981	3 852	972
1969	29 084	2 687	1 047	1 639	26 397	4 307	5 147	5 699	6 223	3 988	1 033
1970	29 688	2 735	1 094	1 641	26 952	4 494	5 382	5 706	6 303	4 046	1 023
1971	29 976	2 730	1 086	1 645	27 246	4 609	5 563	5 647	6 313	4 093	1 021
1972	31 257	2 980	1 188	1 792	28 276	4 861	6 197	5 734	6 318	4 115	1 051
1973	32 715	3 231	1 310	1 920	29 484	5 184	6 893	5 915	6 356	4 109	1 029
1974	33 769	3 345	1 367	1 978	30 424	5 363	7 492	6 068	6 451	4 084	966
1975	33 989	3 263	1 320	1 943	30 726	5 401	7 882	6 061	6 288	4 105	989
1976	35 615	3 389	1 346	2 043	32 226	5 655	8 624	6 400	6 343	4 188	1 017
1977	37 289	3 514	1 403	2 110	33 775	5 965	9 367	6 758	6 380	4 279	1 027
1978	39 569	3 734	1 530	2 204	35 836	6 328	10 157	7 282	6 532	4 446	1 091
1979	41 217	3 783	1 541	2 242	37 434	6 538	10 802	7 779	6 622	4 569	1 124
1980	42 117	3 625	1 433	2 192	38 492	6 555	11 370	8 168	6 686	4 587	1 125
1981	43 000	3 411	1 340	2 070	39 590	6 618	11 914	8 532	6 777	4 616	1 133
1982	43 256	3 170	1 198	1 972	40 086	6 492	12 147	8 977	6 689	4 634	1 147
1983	44 047	3 043	1 107	1 935	41 004	6 490	12 540	9 510	6 678	4 629	1 157
1984	45 915	3 122	1 161	1 962	42 793	6 636	13 182	10 289	6 852	4 700	1 133
1985	47 259	3 105	1 193	1 913	44 154	6 640	13 644	10 933	7 097	4 721	1 118
1986	48 706	3 149	1 270	1 879	45 556	6 540	14 109	11 595	7 395	4 751	1 165
1987	50 334	3 260	1 343	1 917	47 074	6 466	14 617	12 281	7 737	4 783	1 191
1988	51 696	3 313	1 310	2 003	48 383	6 326	14 872	12 811	8 246	4 841	1 286
1989	53 027	3 282	1 261	2 021	49 745	6 163	15 093	13 440	8 711	4 950	1 388
1990	53 689	3 154	1 156	1 998	50 535	6 250	15 155	14 046	8 835	4 811	1 437
1991	53 496	2 862	1 067	1 794	50 634	6 066	14 796	14 507	9 069	4 756	1 440
1992	54 052	2 724	1 032	1 692	51 328	6 053	14 701	14 693	9 657	4 825	1 398
1993	54 910	2 811	1 071	1 740	52 099	6 035	14 508	15 002	10 248	4 892	1 414
1994	56 610	3 005	1 222	1 783	53 606	5 987	14 545	15 488	10 908	5 085	1 592
1995	57 523	3 127	1 258	1 869	54 396	5 779	14 647	15 828	11 421	5 163	1 558
1996	58 501	3 190	1 328	1 862	55 311	5 709	14 549	16 235	12 031	5 269	1 518
1997	59 873	3 260	1 293	1 967	56 613	5 831	14 471	16 581	12 637	5 561	1 532
1998	60 771	3 493	1 364	2 128	57 278	5 919	14 298	16 644	13 043	5 820	1 554
1999	62 042	3 487	1 357	2 130	58 555	6 163	14 171	16 917	13 644	6 041	1 619
2000	63 586	3 519	1 364	2 154	60 067	6 255	14 308	16 897	14 438	6 396	1 773
2001	63 737	3 320	1 289	2 031	60 417	6 396	13 948	16 744	14 768	6 745	1 815
2002	63 582	3 162	1 200	1 962	60 420	6 374	13 733	16 303	14 863	7 296	1 851
2003	64 404	3 002	1 197	1 805	61 402	6 367	13 714	16 106	15 326	7 866	2 023
2004	64 728	2 955	1 156	1 799	61 773	6 477	13 605	15 880	15 518	8 157	2 135
2005	65 757	3 055	1 217	1 838	62 702	6 513	13 687	15 850	15 779	8 635	2 238
2006	66 925	3 091	1 261	1 830	63 834	6 467	13 917	15 804	16 132	9 198	2 316
2007	67 792	2 994	1 195	1 798	64 799	6 590	14 133	15 636	16 353	9 553	2 534
2008	67 876	2 837	1 063	1 774	65 039	6 484	14 200	15 360	16 406	9 893	2 697
2009	66 208	2 509	865	1 644	63 699	6 254	13 791	14 599	16 170	10 128	2 757
2010	65 705	2 249	743	1 506	63 456	6 233	13 870	14 078	15 949	10 496	2 830
2011	65 579	2 219	705	1 514	63 360	6 209	13 863	13 900	15 753	10 717	2 917

Table 1-11. Employed Civilians, by Age, Sex, Race, and Hispanic Origin, 1948–2011—*Continued*

(Thousands of people.)

Race, Hispanic origin, sex, and year	16 years and over	16 to 19 years			20 years and over						
		Total	16 to 17 years	18 to 19 years	Total	20 to 24 years	25 to 34 years	35 to 44 years	45 to 54 years	55 to 64 years	65 years and over
WHITE											
Both Sexes											
1954	53 957	3 078	1 257	1 822	50 879	4 358	12 616	13 000	10 811	7 262	2 831
1955	55 833	3 225	1 330	1 896	52 608	4 637	12 855	13 327	11 322	7 510	2 957
1956	57 269	3 389	1 465	1 922	53 880	4 897	12 748	13 637	11 706	7 822	3 068
1957	57 465	3 374	1 442	1 931	54 091	4 952	12 619	13 716	12 009	7 829	2 951
1958	56 613	3 216	1 370	1 847	53 397	4 908	12 128	13 571	12 113	7 849	2 828
1959	58 006	3 475	1 520	1 955	54 531	5 138	12 144	13 830	12 552	8 063	2 805
1960	58 850	3 700	1 598	2 103	55 150	5 331	12 021	13 930	12 820	8 192	2 855
1961	58 913	3 693	1 472	2 220	55 220	5 460	11 835	13 905	12 906	8 335	2 778
1962	59 698	3 774	1 447	2 327	55 924	5 676	11 703	14 173	13 066	8 511	2 795
1963	60 622	3 851	1 600	2 250	56 771	6 036	11 689	14 341	13 304	8 718	2 683
1964	61 922	4 076	1 846	2 230	57 846	6 444	11 794	14 380	13 596	8 916	2 717
1965	63 446	4 562	1 892	2 670	58 884	6 752	11 992	14 473	13 804	9 116	2 748
1966	65 021	5 176	2 052	3 124	59 845	6 986	12 268	14 449	14 072	9 356	2 713
1967	66 361	5 114	2 121	2 993	61 247	7 493	12 763	14 429	14 224	9 596	2 746
1968	67 750	5 195	2 193	3 002	62 555	7 687	13 410	14 386	14 487	9 781	2 804
1969	69 518	5 508	2 347	3 161	64 010	8 182	13 935	14 270	14 788	9 947	2 888
1970	70 217	5 571	2 386	3 185	64 645	8 559	14 326	14 092	14 854	9 979	2 835
1971	70 878	5 670	2 404	3 266	65 208	9 000	14 713	13 858	14 843	10 014	2 780
1972	73 370	6 173	2 581	3 592	67 197	9 718	15 904	13 940	14 845	10 077	2 714
1973	75 708	6 623	2 806	3 816	69 086	10 424	17 099	14 083	14 886	9 983	2 610
1974	77 184	6 796	2 881	3 916	70 388	10 676	18 040	14 196	14 948	9 958	2 568
1975	76 411	6 487	2 721	3 770	69 924	10 546	18 485	13 979	14 555	9 827	2 533
1976	78 853	6 724	2 762	3 962	72 129	11 119	19 662	14 407	14 549	9 923	2 470
1977	81 700	7 068	2 926	4 142	74 632	11 696	20 844	14 984	14 483	10 107	2 518
1978	84 936	7 367	3 085	4 282	77 569	12 251	22 008	15 809	14 550	10 311	2 642
1979	87 259	7 356	3 079	4 278	79 904	12 594	23 033	16 578	14 522	10 477	2 699
1980	87 715	7 021	2 861	4 161	80 694	12 405	23 653	17 071	14 405	10 475	2 684
1981	88 709	6 588	2 645	3 943	82 121	12 477	24 551	17 617	14 414	10 386	2 676
1982	87 903	5 984	2 317	3 667	81 918	12 097	24 531	18 268	14 083	10 283	2 656
1983	88 893	5 799	2 156	3 643	83 094	12 138	24 955	19 194	13 961	10 169	2 678
1984	92 120	5 836	2 209	3 627	86 284	12 451	26 235	20 552	14 239	10 227	2 580
1985	93 736	5 768	2 270	3 498	87 968	12 235	26 945	21 552	14 459	10 247	2 530
1986	95 660	5 792	2 386	3 406	89 869	12 027	27 746	22 515	14 750	10 176	2 654
1987	97 789	5 898	2 468	3 431	91 890	11 748	28 429	23 596	15 216	10 164	2 738
1988	99 812	6 030	2 424	3 606	93 782	11 438	28 796	24 468	16 054	10 153	2 874
1989	101 584	5 946	2 278	3 668	95 638	11 084	29 091	25 442	16 775	10 223	3 024
1990	102 261	5 779	2 141	3 638	96 481	11 498	28 773	26 282	16 933	9 960	3 035
1991	101 182	5 216	1 971	3 246	95 966	11 116	27 989	26 883	17 269	9 719	2 990
1992	101 669	4 985	1 904	3 081	96 684	11 031	27 552	27 097	18 285	9 701	3 019
1993	103 045	5 113	1 990	3 123	97 932	10 931	27 274	27 645	19 273	9 772	3 037
1994	105 190	5 398	2 210	3 188	99 792	10 736	27 101	28 442	20 247	9 912	3 354
1995	106 490	5 593	2 273	3 320	100 897	10 400	27 014	28 951	21 127	10 070	3 335
1996	107 808	5 667	2 325	3 343	102 141	10 149	26 678	29 566	22 071	10 313	3 364
1997	109 856	5 807	2 341	3 466	104 049	10 362	26 294	30 137	23 061	10 785	3 411
1998	110 931	6 089	2 436	3 653	104 842	10 512	25 729	30 320	23 662	11 272	3 347
1999	112 235	6 204	2 435	3 769	106 032	10 716	25 113	30 548	24 507	11 657	3 491
2000	114 424	6 160	2 383	3 777	108 264	10 944	25 500	30 151	25 762	12 169	3 738
2001	114 430	5 817	2 224	3 593	108 613	11 054	24 948	29 793	26 301	12 743	3 774
2002	114 013	5 441	2 037	3 404	108 572	11 096	24 568	29 049	26 401	13 630	3 828
2003	114 235	5 064	1 999	3 065	109 171	11 052	24 399	28 501	26 762	14 375	4 083
2004	115 239	5 039	1 895	3 145	110 199	11 233	24 337	28 176	27 228	14 965	4 260
2005	116 949	5 105	1 999	3 106	111 844	11 231	24 443	28 102	27 801	15 788	4 480
2006	118 833	5 215	2 099	3 117	113 618	11 296	24 652	27 929	28 419	16 652	4 670
2007	119 792	4 990	1 965	3 026	114 802	11 325	25 024	27 492	28 779	17 262	4 921
2008	119 126	4 697	1 703	2 994	114 428	11 055	24 875	26 736	28 686	17 829	5 247
2009	114 996	4 138	1 443	2 696	110 858	10 438	23 957	25 237	27 891	17 978	5 357
2010	114 168	3 733	1 248	2 485	110 435	10 334	24 097	24 540	27 502	18 464	5 496
2011	114 690	3 691	1 189	2 501	111 000	10 574	24 376	24 156	27 176	18 937	5 780

Table 1-11. Employed Civilians, by Age, Sex, Race, and Hispanic Origin, 1948–2011—*Continued*

(Thousands of people.)

Race, Hispanic origin, sex, and year	16 years and over	16 to 19 years			20 years and over						
		Total	16 to 17 years	18 to 19 years	Total	20 to 24 years	25 to 34 years	35 to 44 years	45 to 54 years	55 to 64 years	65 years and over
WHITE											
Men											
1954	37 846	1 723	771	953	36 123	2 394	9 287	9 175	7 614	5 412	2 241
1955	38 719	1 824	821	1 004	36 895	2 607	9 461	9 351	7 792	5 431	2 254
1956	39 368	1 893	890	1 002	37 475	2 850	9 330	9 449	7 950	5 559	2 336
1957	39 349	1 865	874	990	37 484	2 930	9 226	9 480	8 067	5 542	2 234
1958	38 591	1 783	852	932	36 808	2 896	8 861	9 386	8 061	5 501	2 103
1959	39 494	1 961	915	1 046	37 533	3 153	8 911	9 560	8 261	5 588	2 060
1960	39 755	2 092	973	1 119	37 663	3 264	8 777	9 589	8 372	5 618	2 043
1961	39 588	2 055	891	1 164	37 533	3 311	8 630	9 566	8 394	5 670	1 961
1962	40 016	2 098	883	1 215	37 918	3 426	8 514	9 718	8 512	5 749	1 998
1963	40 428	2 156	972	1 184	38 272	3 646	8 463	9 782	8 650	5 844	1 887
1964	41 115	2 316	1 128	1 188	38 799	3 856	8 538	9 800	8 787	5 945	1 872
1965	41 844	2 612	1 159	1 453	39 232	4 025	8 598	9 795	8 924	5 998	1 892
1966	42 331	2 913	1 245	1 668	39 418	4 028	8 674	9 719	9 029	6 096	1 871
1967	42 833	2 849	1 278	1 571	39 985	4 231	8 931	9 632	9 093	6 208	1 892
1968	43 411	2 908	1 319	1 589	40 503	4 226	9 315	9 522	9 198	6 316	1 926
1969	44 048	3 070	1 385	1 685	40 978	4 401	9 608	9 379	9 279	6 359	1 953
1970	44 178	3 066	1 374	1 692	41 112	4 601	9 784	9 202	9 271	6 340	1 914
1971	44 595	3 157	1 393	1 764	41 438	4 935	10 026	9 026	9 256	6 339	1 856
1972	45 944	3 416	1 470	1 947	42 528	5 431	10 664	9 047	9 236	6 363	1 786
1973	47 085	3 660	1 590	2 071	43 424	5 863	11 268	9 046	9 257	6 299	1 689
1974	47 674	3 728	1 611	2 117	43 946	5 965	11 701	9 027	9 242	6 304	1 706
1975	46 697	3 505	1 502	2 002	43 192	5 770	11 783	8 818	9 005	6 160	1 656
1976	47 775	3 604	1 501	2 103	44 171	6 140	12 362	8 944	8 968	6 176	1 579
1977	49 150	3 824	1 607	2 217	45 326	6 437	12 893	9 212	8 898	6 279	1 605
1978	50 544	3 950	1 664	2 286	46 594	6 717	13 413	9 608	8 840	6 339	1 677
1979	51 452	3 904	1 654	2 250	47 546	6 868	13 888	9 930	8 748	6 406	1 707
1980	51 127	3 708	1 534	2 174	47 419	6 652	14 009	10 077	8 586	6 412	1 684
1981	51 315	3 469	1 402	2 066	47 846	6 652	14 398	10 307	8 518	6 309	1 662
1982	50 287	3 079	1 214	1 865	47 209	6 372	14 164	10 593	8 267	6 188	1 624
1983	50 621	3 003	1 124	1 879	47 618	6 386	14 297	11 062	8 152	6 084	1 637
1984	52 462	3 001	1 140	1 861	49 461	6 647	15 045	11 776	8 320	6 108	1 564
1985	53 046	2 985	1 185	1 800	50 061	6 428	15 374	12 214	8 374	6 118	1 552
1986	53 785	2 966	1 225	1 741	50 818	6 340	15 790	12 620	8 442	6 012	1 612
1987	54 647	2 999	1 252	1 747	51 649	6 150	16 084	13 138	8 596	5 991	1 690
1988	55 550	3 084	1 248	1 836	52 466	5 987	16 241	13 590	8 992	5 909	1 748
1989	56 352	3 060	1 171	1 889	53 292	5 839	16 383	14 046	9 335	5 891	1 797
1990	56 703	3 018	1 119	1 899	53 685	6 179	16 124	14 496	9 383	5 744	1 760
1991	55 797	2 694	1 017	1 677	53 103	5 942	15 644	14 743	9 488	5 578	1 707
1992	55 959	2 602	990	1 612	53 357	5 855	15 357	14 842	10 027	5 503	1 772
1993	56 656	2 634	1 031	1 603	54 021	5 830	15 230	15 178	10 497	5 514	1 772
1994	57 452	2 776	1 144	1 632	54 676	5 738	15 052	15 562	10 910	5 490	1 925
1995	58 146	2 892	1 169	1 723	55 254	5 613	14 958	15 793	11 359	5 609	1 921
1996	58 888	2 911	1 161	1 750	55 977	5 444	14 820	16 136	11 834	5 755	1 987
1997	59 998	3 011	1 206	1 806	56 986	5 590	14 567	16 470	12 352	5 972	2 037
1998	60 604	3 103	1 233	1 870	57 500	5 659	14 259	16 715	12 661	6 251	1 955
1999	61 139	3 205	1 254	1 951	57 934	5 753	13 851	16 781	13 046	6 447	2 056
2000	62 289	3 169	1 205	1 965	59 119	5 876	14 238	16 477	13 675	6 678	2 175
2001	62 212	2 967	1 102	1 865	59 245	5 870	13 989	16 280	13 987	6 941	2 178
2002	61 849	2 725	987	1 738	59 124	5 882	13 727	15 910	14 060	7 360	2 184
2003	61 866	2 518	972	1 546	59 348	5 890	13 731	15 675	14 117	7 640	2 295
2004	62 712	2 553	903	1 650	60 159	6 026	13 735	15 572	14 418	8 018	2 390
2005	63 763	2 508	942	1 566	61 255	6 041	13 840	15 544	14 810	8 471	2 550
2006	64 883	2 625	1 020	1 605	62 259	6 114	13 903	15 480	15 189	8 893	2 680
2007	65 289	2 483	951	1 531	62 806	6 066	14 112	15 287	15 399	9 215	2 727
2008	64 624	2 320	808	1 512	62 304	5 858	13 931	14 775	15 300	9 518	2 922
2009	61 630	2 004	692	1 312	59 626	5 379	13 230	13 858	14 710	9 465	2 984
2010	61 252	1 815	598	1 217	59 438	5 347	13 282	13 583	14 542	9 637	3 047
2011	61 920	1 802	573	1 229	60 118	5 630	13 548	13 366	14 370	9 932	3 271

Table 1-11. Employed Civilians, by Age, Sex, Race, and Hispanic Origin, 1948–2011—*Continued*

(Thousands of people.)

Race, Hispanic origin, sex, and year	16 years and over	16 to 19 years			20 years and over						
		Total	16 to 17 years	18 to 19 years	Total	20 to 24 years	25 to 34 years	35 to 44 years	45 to 54 years	55 to 64 years	65 years and over
WHITE											
Women											
1954	16 111	1 355	486	869	14 756	1 964	3 329	3 825	3 197	1 850	590
1955	17 114	1 401	509	892	15 713	2 030	3 394	3 976	3 530	2 079	703
1956	17 901	1 496	575	920	16 405	2 047	3 418	4 188	3 756	2 263	732
1957	18 116	1 509	568	941	16 607	2 022	3 393	4 236	3 942	2 287	717
1958	18 022	1 433	518	915	16 589	2 012	3 267	4 185	4 052	2 348	725
1959	18 512	1 514	605	909	16 998	1 985	3 233	4 270	4 291	2 475	745
1960	19 095	1 608	625	984	17 487	2 067	3 244	4 341	4 448	2 574	812
1961	19 325	1 638	581	1 056	17 687	2 149	3 205	4 339	4 512	2 665	817
1962	19 682	1 676	564	1 112	18 006	2 250	3 189	4 455	4 554	2 762	797
1963	20 194	1 695	628	1 066	18 499	2 390	3 226	4 559	4 654	2 874	796
1964	20 807	1 760	718	1 042	19 047	2 588	3 256	4 580	4 809	2 971	845
1965	21 602	1 950	733	1 217	19 652	2 727	3 394	4 678	4 880	3 118	856
1966	22 690	2 263	807	1 456	20 427	2 958	3 594	4 730	5 043	3 260	842
1967	23 528	2 265	843	1 422	21 263	3 262	3 832	4 797	5 131	3 388	854
1968	24 339	2 287	874	1 413	22 052	3 461	4 095	4 864	5 289	3 465	878
1969	25 470	2 438	962	1 476	23 032	3 781	4 327	4 891	5 509	3 588	935
1970	26 039	2 505	1 012	1 493	23 534	3 959	4 542	4 890	5 582	3 640	921
1971	26 283	2 513	1 011	1 502	23 770	4 065	4 687	4 831	5 588	3 675	924
1972	27 426	2 755	1 111	1 645	24 669	4 286	5 240	4 893	5 608	3 714	928
1973	28 623	2 962	1 217	1 746	25 661	4 562	5 831	5 036	5 628	3 684	920
1974	29 511	3 069	1 269	1 799	26 442	4 711	6 340	5 169	5 706	3 654	862
1975	29 714	2 983	1 215	1 767	26 731	4 775	6 701	5 161	5 550	3 667	877
1976	31 078	3 120	1 260	1 860	27 958	4 978	7 300	5 462	5 580	3 746	891
1977	32 550	3 244	1 319	1 923	29 306	5 259	7 950	5 772	5 585	3 829	912
1978	34 392	3 416	1 420	1 996	30 975	5 535	8 595	6 201	5 710	3 972	964
1979	35 807	3 451	1 423	2 027	32 357	5 726	9 145	6 648	5 773	4 071	993
1980	36 587	3 314	1 327	1 986	33 275	5 753	9 644	6 994	5 818	4 064	1 001
1981	37 394	3 119	1 242	1 877	34 275	5 826	10 153	7 311	5 896	4 077	1 013
1982	37 615	2 905	1 103	1 802	34 710	5 724	10 367	7 675	5 816	4 095	1 032
1983	38 272	2 796	1 032	1 764	35 476	5 751	10 659	8 132	5 809	4 084	1 041
1984	39 659	2 835	1 069	1 766	36 823	5 804	11 190	8 776	5 920	4 118	1 015
1985	40 690	2 783	1 085	1 698	37 907	5 807	11 571	9 338	6 084	4 128	978
1986	41 876	2 825	1 160	1 665	39 050	5 687	11 956	9 895	6 307	4 164	1 042
1987	43 142	2 900	1 216	1 684	40 242	5 598	12 345	10 459	6 620	4 172	1 047
1988	44 262	2 946	1 176	1 770	41 316	5 450	12 555	10 878	7 062	4 244	1 126
1989	45 232	2 886	1 107	1 779	42 346	5 245	12 708	11 395	7 440	4 332	1 227
1990	45 558	2 762	1 023	1 739	42 796	5 319	12 649	11 785	7 551	4 217	1 275
1991	45 385	2 523	954	1 569	42 862	5 174	12 344	12 139	7 781	4 141	1 283
1992	45 710	2 383	915	1 468	43 327	5 176	12 195	12 254	8 258	4 198	1 246
1993	46 390	2 479	959	1 520	43 910	5 101	12 044	12 467	8 776	4 258	1 265
1994	47 738	2 622	1 066	1 556	45 116	4 997	12 049	12 880	9 338	4 423	1 429
1995	48 344	2 701	1 104	1 597	45 643	4 787	12 056	13 157	9 768	4 461	1 415
1996	48 920	2 756	1 164	1 592	46 164	4 705	11 858	13 430	10 237	4 558	1 376
1997	49 859	2 796	1 136	1 660	47 063	4 773	11 727	13 667	10 709	4 813	1 374
1998	50 327	2 986	1 203	1 783	47 342	4 853	11 470	13 604	11 001	5 021	1 392
1999	51 096	2 999	1 181	1 817	48 098	4 963	11 262	13 767	11 461	5 211	1 435
2000	52 136	2 991	1 178	1 813	49 145	5 068	11 262	13 674	12 087	5 490	1 564
2001	52 218	2 850	1 122	1 727	49 369	5 184	10 959	13 513	12 314	5 802	1 597
2002	52 164	2 716	1 050	1 665	49 448	5 214	10 842	13 138	12 341	6 269	1 644
2003	52 369	2 546	1 027	1 519	49 823	5 161	10 668	12 826	12 645	6 735	1 788
2004	52 527	2 486	991	1 495	50 040	5 207	10 602	12 604	12 810	6 947	1 870
2005	53 186	2 597	1 057	1 540	50 589	5 190	10 603	12 558	12 991	7 317	1 930
2006	53 950	2 590	1 079	1 512	51 359	5 182	10 750	12 449	13 230	7 758	1 991
2007	54 503	2 507	1 013	1 494	51 996	5 259	10 912	12 205	13 380	8 047	2 193
2008	54 501	2 377	895	1 482	52 124	5 197	10 943	11 961	13 386	8 312	2 325
2009	53 366	2 134	751	1 383	51 231	5 060	10 727	11 379	13 181	8 513	2 373
2010	52 916	1 918	650	1 268	50 997	4 988	10 815	10 958	12 960	8 827	2 450
2011	52 770	1 889	617	1 272	50 881	4 943	10 828	10 789	12 806	9 005	2 509

Table 1-11. Employed Civilians, by Age, Sex, Race, and Hispanic Origin, 1948–2011—*Continued*

(Thousands of people.)

Race, Hispanic origin, sex, and year	16 years and over	16 to 19 years			20 years and over						
		Total	16 to 17 years	18 to 19 years	Total	20 to 24 years	25 to 34 years	35 to 44 years	45 to 54 years	55 to 64 years	65 years and over
BLACK											
Both Sexes											
1974	8 203	554	190	364	7 649	1 231	2 157	1 682	1 452	884	243
1975	7 894	507	183	325	7 386	1 115	2 145	1 617	1 393	874	241
1976	8 227	508	170	338	7 719	1 193	2 309	1 679	1 416	870	252
1977	8 540	508	169	339	8 031	1 244	2 443	1 754	1 448	892	251
1978	9 102	571	191	380	8 531	1 359	2 641	1 848	1 479	932	273
1979	9 359	579	204	376	8 780	1 424	2 759	1 902	1 502	927	266
1980	9 313	547	192	356	8 765	1 376	2 827	1 910	1 487	925	239
1981	9 355	505	170	335	8 849	1 346	2 872	1 957	1 489	954	231
1982	9 189	428	138	290	8 761	1 283	2 830	2 025	1 469	928	225
1983	9 375	416	123	294	8 959	1 280	2 976	2 107	1 456	937	204
1984	10 119	474	146	328	9 645	1 423	3 223	2 311	1 533	945	209
1985	10 501	532	175	356	9 969	1 399	3 325	2 427	1 598	985	235
1986	10 814	536	183	353	10 278	1 429	3 464	2 524	1 666	982	214
1987	11 309	587	203	385	10 722	1 421	3 614	2 695	1 714	1 036	241
1988	11 658	601	223	378	11 057	1 433	3 725	2 839	1 783	1 018	261
1989	11 953	625	237	388	11 328	1 467	3 801	2 981	1 844	970	265
1990	12 175	598	194	404	11 577	1 409	3 803	3 287	1 897	933	248
1991	12 074	494	161	334	11 580	1 373	3 714	3 401	1 892	957	243
1992	12 151	492	157	335	11 659	1 343	3 699	3 441	1 964	965	246
1993	12 382	494	171	323	11 888	1 377	3 700	3 584	2 059	941	226
1994	12 835	552	224	328	12 284	1 449	3 732	3 722	2 178	953	251
1995	13 279	586	223	363	12 693	1 443	3 844	3 861	2 288	1 004	253
1996	13 542	613	233	380	12 929	1 411	3 851	3 974	2 426	1 025	241
1997	13 969	631	229	401	13 339	1 456	3 903	4 094	2 588	1 048	249
1998	14 556	736	246	490	13 820	1 496	3 967	4 238	2 739	1 118	262
1999	15 056	691	243	448	14 365	1 594	4 091	4 404	2 872	1 134	271
2000	15 156	711	260	451	14 444	1 593	3 993	4 261	3 073	1 226	300
2001	15 006	637	230	408	14 368	1 571	3 840	4 200	3 139	1 283	335
2002	14 872	611	193	417	14 262	1 543	3 726	4 109	3 220	1 332	332
2003	14 739	516	196	320	14 222	1 516	3 618	4 080	3 289	1 373	346
2004	14 909	520	169	351	14 389	1 572	3 635	4 039	3 332	1 452	359
2005	15 313	536	164	372	14 776	1 599	3 722	4 060	3 464	1 555	375
2006	15 765	618	215	402	15 147	1 643	3 809	4 072	3 570	1 659	394
2007	16 051	566	202	364	15 485	1 674	3 888	4 120	3 658	1 732	413
2008	15 953	541	172	369	15 411	1 625	3 870	4 015	3 670	1 791	440
2009	15 025	442	131	310	14 584	1 474	3 582	3 686	3 562	1 827	453
2010	15 010	386	106	280	14 624	1 532	3 641	3 561	3 531	1 899	460
2011	15 051	380	99	281	14 671	1 574	3 632	3 499	3 513	1 943	508
BLACK											
Men											
1974	4 527	322	114	209	4 204	668	1 176	912	803	500	145
1975	4 275	276	98	179	3 998	595	1 159	865	755	487	137
1976	4 404	283	100	184	4 120	635	1 217	897	763	472	137
1977	4 565	291	105	186	4 273	659	1 271	940	777	484	143
1978	4 796	312	106	206	4 483	697	1 357	969	788	516	155
1979	4 923	316	111	205	4 606	754	1 425	983	801	498	147
1980	4 798	299	109	191	4 498	713	1 438	975	770	478	126
1981	4 794	273	95	178	4 520	693	1 457	991	764	492	123
1982	4 637	223	65	158	4 414	660	1 414	997	750	471	122
1983	4 753	222	64	158	4 531	684	1 483	1 034	749	477	105
1984	5 124	252	79	173	4 871	750	1 635	1 138	780	460	108
1985	5 270	278	92	186	4 992	726	1 669	1 187	795	501	114
1986	5 428	278	96	182	5 150	732	1 756	1 211	831	507	112
1987	5 661	304	109	195	5 357	728	1 821	1 283	853	547	124
1988	5 824	316	122	193	5 509	736	1 881	1 348	878	536	131
1989	5 928	327	124	202	5 602	742	1 931	1 415	886	498	131
1990	5 995	303	99	204	5 692	702	1 895	1 586	926	469	114
1991	5 961	255	85	170	5 706	695	1 859	1 634	923	481	114
1992	5 930	249	78	170	5 681	679	1 819	1 650	930	478	124
1993	6 047	254	88	166	5 793	674	1 858	1 717	978	461	106
1994	6 241	276	107	169	5 964	718	1 850	1 795	1 030	455	115
1995	6 422	285	111	174	6 137	714	1 895	1 836	1 085	468	138
1996	6 456	289	109	180	6 167	685	1 867	1 878	1 129	482	126
1997	6 607	282	108	174	6 325	668	1 874	1 955	1 215	487	127
1998	6 871	341	120	221	6 530	686	1 886	2 008	1 284	524	142
1999	7 027	325	120	205	6 702	700	1 926	2 092	1 327	525	131
2000	7 082	341	129	211	6 741	730	1 865	1 984	1 425	596	142
2001	6 938	311	115	196	6 627	703	1 757	1 931	1 452	614	170
2002	6 959	306	95	212	6 652	725	1 729	1 899	1 503	624	172
2003	6 820	234	89	145	6 586	726	1 660	1 868	1 518	638	176
2004	6 912	231	76	155	6 681	739	1 720	1 840	1 534	668	180
2005	7 155	254	76	178	6 901	748	1 759	1 886	1 616	711	182
2006	7 354	275	99	175	7 079	804	1 797	1 882	1 680	734	184
2007	7 500	254	82	172	7 245	816	1 851	1 916	1 717	750	195
2008	7 398	247	70	177	7 151	794	1 805	1 854	1 703	792	204
2009	6 817	189	56	133	6 628	689	1 635	1 662	1 622	813	206
2010	6 865	185	48	137	6 680	692	1 710	1 638	1 594	834	211
2011	6 953	187	49	138	6 765	734	1 733	1 583	1 621	858	236

Table 1-11. Employed Civilians, by Age, Sex, Race, and Hispanic Origin, 1948–2011—*Continued*

(Thousands of people.)

Race, Hispanic origin, sex, and year	16 years and over	16 to 19 years			20 years and over						
		Total	16 to 17 years	18 to 19 years	Total	20 to 24 years	25 to 34 years	35 to 44 years	45 to 54 years	55 to 64 years	65 years and over
BLACK											
Women											
1974	3 677	232	77	155	3 445	562	981	770	649	383	98
1975	3 618	231	85	146	3 388	520	985	752	638	387	104
1976	3 823	224	70	154	3 599	558	1 092	782	653	398	115
1977	3 975	217	64	153	3 758	585	1 172	814	671	408	109
1978	4 307	260	85	175	4 047	662	1 283	879	691	416	118
1979	4 436	263	92	171	4 174	670	1 333	919	702	428	119
1980	4 515	248	82	165	4 267	663	1 389	936	717	448	113
1981	4 561	232	75	157	4 329	653	1 415	966	725	462	108
1982	4 552	205	73	132	4 347	623	1 416	1 028	719	457	103
1983	4 622	194	59	136	4 428	596	1 493	1 073	707	460	99
1984	4 995	222	67	155	4 773	673	1 588	1 173	753	485	101
1985	5 231	254	83	171	4 977	673	1 656	1 240	804	484	121
1986	5 386	259	87	171	5 128	696	1 708	1 313	835	475	102
1987	5 648	283	93	190	5 365	693	1 793	1 412	860	489	117
1988	5 834	285	101	184	5 548	697	1 844	1 491	905	482	129
1989	6 025	298	113	185	5 727	725	1 870	1 566	959	472	134
1990	6 180	296	96	200	5 884	707	1 907	1 701	971	464	135
1991	6 113	239	76	164	5 874	677	1 855	1 768	969	476	129
1992	6 221	243	79	164	5 978	664	1 880	1 791	1 034	487	123
1993	6 334	239	82	157	6 095	703	1 842	1 867	1 081	480	121
1994	6 595	275	117	158	6 320	731	1 882	1 926	1 147	497	136
1995	6 857	301	112	189	6 556	729	1 949	2 025	1 202	536	114
1996	7 086	324	124	200	6 762	726	1 984	2 096	1 297	543	115
1997	7 362	349	122	227	7 013	789	2 029	2 139	1 373	561	122
1998	7 685	395	126	268	7 290	810	2 081	2 230	1 455	594	120
1999	8 029	366	123	243	7 663	893	2 165	2 312	1 545	609	139
2000	8 073	370	131	240	7 703	862	2 128	2 277	1 647	630	158
2001	8 068	327	115	212	7 741	868	2 084	2 269	1 686	668	165
2002	7 914	304	99	205	7 610	819	1 997	2 209	1 717	708	160
2003	7 919	283	107	175	7 636	790	1 959	2 211	1 770	735	171
2004	7 997	289	93	196	7 707	833	1 914	2 199	1 798	784	179
2005	8 158	282	88	194	7 876	852	1 964	2 175	1 848	844	193
2006	8 410	343	116	227	8 068	839	2 012	2 191	1 890	925	210
2007	8 551	311	120	191	8 240	858	2 037	2 205	1 941	982	218
2008	8 554	294	102	192	8 260	831	2 065	2 161	1 967	1 000	236
2009	8 208	252	75	178	7 956	784	1 947	2 024	1 939	1 014	246
2010	8 145	201	58	143	7 944	841	1 931	1 923	1 936	1 065	248
2011	8 098	193	50	142	7 906	840	1 899	1 916	1 892	1 086	272
HISPANIC											
Both Sexes											
1975	3 663	322	. . .	. . .	. . .	. . .	. . .	. . .	. . .	. . .	. . .
1976	3 720	341	124	230	3 436	614	1 135	803	573	269	42
1977	4 079	381	135	245	3 715	715	1 212	860	608	269	50
1978	4 527	423	159	264	4 104	803	1 330	942	661	307	62
1979	4 785	445	152	292	4 340	860	1 430	996	666	319	69
1980	5 527	500	174	325	5 028	998	1 675	1 074	811	389	80
1981	5 813	459	155	304	5 354	1 060	1 837	1 147	829	399	82
1982	5 805	410	119	291	5 394	1 030	1 896	1 173	816	399	80
1983	6 072	423	125	297	5 649	1 068	1 997	1 224	837	441	81
1984	6 651	468	148	320	6 182	1 160	2 201	1 385	883	474	79
1985	6 888	438	144	294	6 449	1 187	2 316	1 473	913	486	75
1986	7 219	430	146	284	6 789	1 231	2 427	1 570	1 011	474	76
1987	7 790	474	149	325	7 316	1 273	2 668	1 775	1 010	512	76
1988	8 250	523	171	353	7 727	1 341	2 749	1 876	1 078	585	97
1989	8 573	548	165	383	8 025	1 325	2 900	1 968	1 129	589	114
1990	9 845	668	208	460	9 177	1 672	3 327	2 229	1 235	611	103
1991	9 828	602	169	433	9 225	1 622	3 264	2 333	1 266	637	103
1992	10 027	577	169	408	9 450	1 575	3 350	2 468	1 316	628	112
1993	10 361	570	160	410	9 792	1 574	3 446	2 605	1 402	630	135
1994	10 788	609	195	415	10 178	1 643	3 517	2 737	1 495	647	139
1995	11 127	645	194	450	10 483	1 609	3 618	2 889	1 565	666	135
1996	11 642	646	199	447	10 996	1 628	3 758	3 115	1 595	748	152
1997	12 726	714	228	487	12 012	1 798	4 029	3 371	1 846	794	173
1998	13 291	793	230	563	12 498	1 883	4 113	3 504	1 994	846	158
1999	13 720	854	254	600	12 866	1 881	4 097	3 738	2 074	886	190
2000	15 735	973	285	688	14 762	2 356	4 950	4 052	2 308	898	197
2001	16 190	969	268	701	15 221	2 404	5 065	4 149	2 472	944	187
2002	16 590	882	254	628	15 708	2 413	5 272	4 273	2 511	1 029	209
2003	17 372	768	242	525	16 604	2 399	5 541	4 573	2 711	1 132	249
2004	17 930	792	211	581	17 138	2 477	5 560	4 671	2 932	1 210	288
2005	18 632	847	253	595	17 785	2 423	5 756	4 879	3 114	1 317	296
2006	19 613	900	287	614	18 712	2 487	6 001	5 106	3 324	1 441	354
2007	20 382	894	269	625	19 488	2 516	6 237	5 314	3 547	1 499	376
2008	20 346	870	248	622	19 476	2 361	6 119	5 371	3 620	1 619	385
2009	19 647	742	192	550	18 905	2 218	5 704	5 168	3 700	1 680	435
2010	19 906	680	165	515	19 226	2 281	5 781	5 185	3 779	1 737	464
2011	20 269	665	155	510	19 604	2 544	5 747	5 179	3 848	1 820	465

. . . = Not available.

Table 1-11. Employed Civilians, by Age, Sex, Race, and Hispanic Origin, 1948–2011—*Continued*

(Thousands of people.)

Race, Hispanic origin, sex, and year	16 years and over	16 to 19 years			20 years and over						
		Total	16 to 17 years	18 to 19 years	Total	20 to 24 years	25 to 34 years	35 to 44 years	45 to 54 years	55 to 64 years	65 years and over
HISPANIC											
Men											
1975	2 301	. . .	. . .	. . .	2 117	. . .	. . .	. . .	. . .	. . .	. . .
1976	2 303	199	74	125	2 109	364	708	504	369	173	. . .
1977	2 564	225	78	147	2 335	427	763	540	394	184	. . .
1978	2 808	241	93	147	2 568	494	824	590	405	207	. . .
1979	2 962	260	93	168	2 701	511	891	615	427	205	. . .
1980	3 448	306	109	198	3 142	611	1 065	662	491	254	. . .
1981	3 597	272	90	182	3 325	642	1 157	707	504	259	. . .
1982	3 583	229	66	162	3 354	621	1 192	729	498	261	. . .
1983	3 771	248	71	177	3 523	655	1 280	760	499	275	. . .
1984	4 083	258	78	180	3 825	718	1 398	841	530	292	. . .
1985	4 245	251	82	169	3 994	727	1 473	888	550	308	. . .
1986	4 428	254	82	172	4 174	773	1 510	929	614	297	. . .
1987	4 713	268	81	188	4 444	777	1 664	1 044	606	303	. . .
1988	4 972	292	87	205	4 680	815	1 706	1 120	645	331	. . .
1989	5 172	319	94	225	4 853	821	1 787	1 152	676	350	. . .
1990	6 021	412	126	286	5 609	1 083	2 076	1 312	722	355	. . .
1991	5 979	356	94	263	5 623	1 063	2 050	1 360	719	369	. . .
1992	6 093	336	97	238	5 757	985	2 127	1 437	768	372	. . .
1993	6 328	337	95	242	5 992	1 003	2 200	1 527	822	360	. . .
1994	6 530	341	109	233	6 189	1 056	2 227	1 600	847	379	79
1995	6 725	358	110	248	6 367	1 030	2 284	1 675	908	384	85
1996	7 039	384	107	277	6 655	1 015	2 345	1 842	918	438	96
1997	7 728	420	130	290	7 307	1 142	2 547	1 978	1 059	477	105
1998	8 018	449	133	315	7 570	1 173	2 592	2 077	1 115	512	101
1999	8 067	491	139	352	7 576	1 135	2 524	2 135	1 151	502	130
2000	9 428	570	159	411	8 859	1 486	3 063	2 358	1 295	532	126
2001	9 668	568	149	419	9 100	1 473	3 142	2 446	1 375	545	119
2002	9 845	504	141	363	9 341	1 476	3 271	2 503	1 396	569	125
2003	10 479	415	121	294	10 063	1 485	3 537	2 724	1 533	639	144
2004	10 832	446	108	338	10 385	1 514	3 557	2 801	1 654	687	174
2005	11 337	465	137	328	10 872	1 511	3 711	2 939	1 781	748	183
2006	11 887	496	146	350	11 391	1 535	3 845	3 088	1 894	809	220
2007	12 310	483	145	338	11 827	1 524	3 982	3 220	2 012	869	220
2008	12 248	479	140	340	11 769	1 406	3 897	3 233	2 080	929	224
2009	11 640	383	94	289	11 256	1 287	3 576	3 108	2 104	930	251
2010	11 800	361	78	283	11 438	1 319	3 591	3 169	2 137	949	273
2011	12 049	364	76	287	11 685	1 535	3 615	3 124	2 141	1 006	266
HISPANIC											
Women											
1975	1 362	. . .	. . .	. . .	1 224	. . .	. . .	. . .	. . .	. . .	. . .
1976	1 417	155	50	106	1 288	249	427	300	204	96	. . .
1977	1 516	155	57	98	1 370	288	449	320	214	86	. . .
1978	1 719	182	65	117	1 537	308	506	352	256	99	. . .
1979	1 824	185	60	125	1 638	349	539	381	241	115	. . .
1980	2 079	193	65	128	1 886	387	610	412	320	136	. . .
1981	2 216	187	65	122	2 029	418	680	440	326	139	. . .
1982	2 222	181	52	129	2 040	409	704	444	318	139	. . .
1983	2 301	175	54	120	2 127	413	717	464	338	166	. . .
1984	2 568	211	71	140	2 357	442	804	544	354	181	. . .
1985	2 642	187	62	125	2 456	460	843	585	362	178	. . .
1986	2 791	176	64	112	2 615	458	917	641	397	177	. . .
1987	3 077	206	69	137	2 872	496	1 004	732	405	209	. . .
1988	3 278	231	84	147	3 047	526	1 042	756	434	254	. . .
1989	3 401	229	71	158	3 172	504	1 114	816	453	239	. . .
1990	3 823	256	82	174	3 567	588	1 251	917	513	256	. . .
1991	3 848	246	76	170	3 603	559	1 214	972	548	268	. . .
1992	3 934	242	72	170	3 693	591	1 223	1 031	548	256	. . .
1993	4 033	233	65	168	3 800	571	1 246	1 077	581	269	. . .
1994	4 258	268	86	182	3 989	587	1 290	1 137	648	268	59
1995	4 403	287	85	202	4 116	579	1 334	1 213	657	282	50
1996	4 602	261	92	169	4 341	612	1 412	1 273	677	310	56
1997	4 999	294	98	196	4 705	656	1 482	1 393	787	318	69
1998	5 273	345	97	247	4 928	710	1 521	1 428	879	334	57
1999	5 653	363	115	248	5 290	746	1 574	1 603	923	384	60
2000	6 307	404	127	277	5 903	870	1 887	1 695	1 013	366	72
2001	6 522	401	119	282	6 121	931	1 923	1 703	1 097	398	67
2002	6 744	378	113	265	6 367	937	2 001	1 770	1 114	460	84
2003	6 894	353	121	231	6 541	914	2 004	1 849	1 178	493	105
2004	7 098	346	103	243	6 752	964	2 003	1 870	1 279	523	114
2005	7 295	382	116	266	6 913	912	2 045	1 940	1 333	569	113
2006	7 725	404	140	264	7 321	951	2 155	2 018	1 430	632	135
2007	8 072	410	124	287	7 662	991	2 255	2 094	1 535	631	155
2008	8 098	391	108	282	7 707	955	2 222	2 138	1 541	690	161
2009	8 007	358	98	261	7 649	931	2 128	2 060	1 596	751	183
2010	8 106	318	87	231	7 788	962	2 189	2 016	1 642	788	191
2011	8 220	301	79	223	7 918	1 010	2 132	2 055	1 707	814	200

. . . = Not available.

Table 1-12. Civilian Employment-Population Ratios, by Sex, Age, Race, and Hispanic Origin, 1948–2011

(Percent.)

Race, Hispanic origin, and year	Both sexes			Men			Women		
	16 years and over	16 to 19 years	20 years and over	16 years and over	16 to 19 years	20 years and over	16 years and over	16 to 19 years	20 years and over
ALL RACES									
1948	56.6	47.7	57.4	83.5	57.5	85.8	31.3	38.5	30.7
1949	55.4	45.2	56.3	81.3	53.8	83.7	31.2	37.2	30.6
1950	56.1	45.5	57.0	82.0	55.2	84.2	32.0	36.3	31.6
1951	57.3	47.9	58.1	84.0	57.9	86.1	33.1	38.9	32.6
1952	57.3	46.9	58.1	83.9	55.9	86.2	33.4	38.8	33.0
1953	57.1	46.4	58.0	83.6	55.9	85.9	33.3	37.8	32.9
1954	55.5	42.3	56.6	81.0	50.2	83.5	32.5	34.9	32.3
1955	56.7	43.5	57.8	81.8	52.1	84.3	34.0	35.6	33.8
1956	57.5	45.3	58.5	82.3	53.8	84.6	35.1	37.5	34.9
1957	57.1	43.9	58.2	81.3	51.8	83.8	35.1	36.7	35.0
1958	55.4	39.9	56.8	78.5	46.9	81.2	34.5	33.5	34.6
1959	56.0	39.9	57.5	79.3	47.2	82.3	35.0	33.0	35.1
1960	56.1	40.5	57.6	78.9	47.6	81.9	35.5	33.8	35.7
1961	55.4	39.1	56.9	77.6	45.3	80.8	35.4	33.2	35.6
1962	55.5	39.4	57.1	77.7	45.9	80.9	35.6	33.3	35.8
1963	55.4	37.4	57.2	77.1	43.8	80.6	35.8	31.5	36.3
1964	55.7	37.3	57.7	77.3	44.1	80.9	36.3	30.9	36.9
1965	56.2	38.9	58.2	77.5	46.2	81.2	37.1	32.0	37.6
1966	56.9	42.1	58.7	77.9	48.9	81.5	38.3	35.6	38.6
1967	57.3	42.2	59.0	78.0	48.7	81.5	39.0	35.9	39.3
1968	57.5	42.2	59.3	77.8	48.7	81.3	39.6	36.0	40.0
1969	58.0	43.4	59.7	77.6	49.5	81.1	40.7	37.5	41.1
1970	57.4	42.3	59.2	76.2	47.7	79.7	40.8	37.1	41.2
1971	56.6	41.3	58.4	74.9	46.8	78.5	40.4	36.0	40.9
1972	57.0	43.5	58.6	75.0	48.9	78.4	41.0	38.2	41.3
1973	57.8	45.9	59.3	75.5	51.4	78.6	42.0	40.5	42.2
1974	57.8	46.0	59.2	74.9	51.2	77.9	42.6	41.0	42.8
1975	56.1	43.3	57.6	71.7	47.2	74.8	42.0	39.4	42.3
1976	56.8	44.2	58.3	72.0	47.9	75.1	43.2	40.5	43.5
1977	57.9	46.1	59.2	72.8	50.4	75.6	44.5	41.8	44.8
1978	59.3	48.3	60.6	73.8	52.2	76.4	46.4	44.5	46.6
1979	59.9	48.5	61.2	73.8	51.7	76.5	47.5	45.3	47.7
1980	59.2	46.6	60.6	72.0	49.5	74.6	47.7	43.8	48.1
1981	59.0	44.6	60.5	71.3	47.1	74.0	48.0	42.0	48.6
1982	57.8	41.5	59.4	69.0	42.9	71.8	47.7	40.2	48.4
1983	57.9	41.5	59.5	68.8	43.1	71.4	48.0	40.0	48.8
1984	59.5	43.7	61.0	70.7	45.0	73.2	49.5	42.5	50.1
1985	60.1	44.4	61.5	70.9	45.7	73.3	50.4	42.9	51.0
1986	60.7	44.6	62.1	71.0	45.7	73.3	51.4	43.6	52.0
1987	61.5	45.5	62.9	71.5	46.1	73.8	52.5	44.8	53.1
1988	62.3	46.8	63.6	72.0	47.8	74.2	53.4	45.9	54.0
1989	63.0	47.5	64.2	72.5	48.7	74.5	54.3	46.4	54.9
1990	62.8	45.3	64.3	72.0	46.6	74.3	54.3	44.0	55.2
1991	61.7	42.0	63.2	70.4	42.7	72.7	53.7	41.2	54.6
1992	61.5	41.0	63.0	69.8	41.9	72.1	53.8	40.0	54.8
1993	61.7	41.7	63.3	70.0	42.3	72.3	54.1	41.0	55.0
1994	62.5	43.4	64.0	70.4	43.8	72.6	55.3	43.0	56.2
1995	62.9	44.2	64.4	70.8	44.7	73.0	55.6	43.8	56.5
1996	63.2	43.5	64.7	70.9	43.6	73.2	56.0	43.5	57.0
1997	63.8	43.4	65.5	71.3	43.4	73.7	56.8	43.3	57.8
1998	64.1	45.1	65.6	71.6	44.7	73.9	57.1	45.5	58.0
1999	64.3	44.7	65.9	71.6	45.1	74.0	57.4	44.3	58.5
2000	64.4	45.2	66.0	71.9	45.4	74.2	57.5	45.0	58.4
2001	63.7	42.3	65.4	70.9	42.2	73.3	57.0	42.4	58.1
2002	62.7	39.6	64.6	69.7	38.9	72.3	56.3	40.3	57.5
2003	62.3	36.8	64.3	68.9	35.7	71.7	56.1	37.8	57.5
2004	62.3	36.4	64.4	69.2	35.9	71.9	56.0	37.0	57.4
2005	62.7	36.5	64.7	69.6	35.1	72.4	56.2	37.8	57.6
2006	63.1	36.9	65.2	70.1	36.3	72.9	56.6	37.6	58.0
2007	63.0	34.8	65.2	69.8	33.9	72.8	56.6	35.8	58.2
2008	62.2	32.6	64.5	68.5	31.6	71.6	56.2	33.7	57.9
2009	59.3	28.4	61.7	64.5	26.9	67.6	54.4	29.9	56.2
2010	58.5	25.9	61.0	63.7	24.8	66.8	53.6	27.0	55.5
2011	58.4	25.8	60.8	63.9	24.6	67.0	53.2	27.1	55.0

Table 1-12. Civilian Employment-Population Ratios, by Sex, Age, Race, and Hispanic Origin, 1948–2011
—Continued

(Percent.)

Race, Hispanic origin, and year	Both sexes			Men			Women		
	16 years and over	16 to 19 years	20 years and over	16 years and over	16 to 19 years	20 years and over	16 years and over	16 to 19 years	20 years and over
WHITE									
1954	55.2	42.9	56.2	81.5	49.9	84.0	31.4	31.4	31.1
1955	56.5	44.2	57.4	82.2	52.0	84.7	33.0	33.0	32.7
1956	57.3	46.1	58.2	82.7	54.1	85.0	34.2	34.2	33.8
1957	56.8	45.0	57.8	81.8	52.4	84.1	34.2	34.2	33.9
1958	55.3	41.0	56.5	79.2	47.6	81.8	33.6	33.6	33.5
1959	55.9	41.2	57.2	79.9	48.1	82.8	34.0	34.0	34.0
1960	55.9	41.5	57.2	79.4	48.1	82.4	34.6	34.6	34.5
1961	55.3	40.1	56.7	78.2	45.9	81.4	34.5	34.5	34.5
1962	55.4	40.4	56.9	78.4	46.4	81.5	34.7	34.7	34.7
1963	55.3	38.6	56.9	77.7	44.7	81.1	35.0	35.0	35.2
1964	55.5	38.4	57.3	77.8	45.0	81.3	35.5	35.5	35.8
1965	56.0	40.3	57.8	77.9	47.1	81.5	36.2	36.2	36.5
1966	56.8	43.6	58.3	78.3	50.1	81.7	37.5	37.5	37.5
1967	57.2	43.8	58.7	78.4	50.2	81.7	38.3	38.3	38.3
1968	57.4	43.9	59.0	78.3	50.3	81.6	38.9	38.9	39.1
1969	58.0	45.2	59.4	78.2	51.1	81.4	40.1	40.1	40.1
1970	57.5	44.5	59.0	76.8	49.6	80.1	40.3	40.3	40.4
1971	56.8	43.8	58.3	75.7	49.2	79.0	39.9	39.9	40.1
1972	57.4	46.4	58.6	76.0	51.5	79.0	40.7	40.7	40.6
1973	58.2	48.9	59.3	76.5	54.3	79.2	41.8	41.8	41.6
1974	58.3	49.3	59.3	75.9	54.4	78.6	42.4	42.4	42.2
1975	56.7	46.5	57.9	73.0	50.6	75.7	42.0	42.0	41.9
1976	57.5	47.8	58.6	73.4	51.5	76.0	43.2	43.2	43.1
1977	58.6	50.1	59.6	74.1	54.4	76.5	44.5	44.5	44.4
1978	60.0	52.4	60.8	75.0	56.3	77.2	46.3	46.3	46.1
1979	60.6	52.6	61.5	75.1	55.7	77.3	47.5	47.5	47.3
1980	60.0	50.7	61.0	73.4	53.4	75.6	47.8	47.8	47.8
1981	60.0	48.7	61.1	72.8	51.3	75.1	48.3	48.3	48.5
1982	58.8	45.8	60.1	70.6	47.0	73.0	48.1	48.1	48.4
1983	58.9	45.9	60.1	70.4	47.4	72.6	48.5	48.5	48.9
1984	60.5	48.0	61.5	72.1	49.1	74.3	49.8	49.8	50.0
1985	61.0	48.5	62.0	72.3	49.9	74.3	50.7	50.7	51.0
1986	61.5	48.8	62.6	72.3	49.6	74.3	51.7	51.7	52.0
1987	62.3	49.4	63.4	72.7	49.9	74.7	52.8	52.8	53.1
1988	63.1	50.9	64.1	73.2	51.7	75.1	53.8	53.8	54.0
1989	63.8	51.6	64.7	73.7	52.6	75.4	54.6	54.6	54.9
1990	63.7	49.7	64.8	73.3	51.0	75.1	54.7	54.7	55.2
1991	62.6	46.6	63.7	71.6	47.2	73.5	54.2	54.2	54.8
1992	62.4	45.3	63.6	71.1	46.4	73.1	54.2	54.2	54.9
1993	62.7	46.2	63.9	71.4	46.6	73.3	54.6	54.6	55.2
1994	63.5	47.9	64.7	71.8	48.3	73.6	55.8	55.8	56.4
1995	63.8	48.8	64.9	72.0	49.4	73.8	56.1	56.1	56.7
1996	64.1	47.9	65.3	72.3	48.2	74.2	56.3	56.3	57.0
1997	64.6	47.7	65.9	72.7	48.1	74.7	57.0	57.0	57.8
1998	64.7	48.9	65.9	72.7	48.6	74.7	57.1	57.1	57.7
1999	64.8	48.8	66.1	72.8	49.3	74.8	57.3	57.3	58.0
2000	64.9	49.1	66.1	73.0	49.5	74.9	57.4	57.4	58.0
2001	64.2	46.3	65.6	72.0	46.2	74.0	57.0	57.0	57.7
2002	63.4	43.2	64.9	70.8	42.3	73.1	56.4	56.4	57.3
2003	63.0	40.4	64.7	70.1	39.4	72.5	56.3	56.3	57.3
2004	63.1	40.0	64.8	70.4	39.7	72.8	56.1	56.1	57.2
2005	63.4	40.2	65.1	70.8	38.8	73.3	56.3	56.3	57.4
2006	63.8	40.6	65.5	71.3	40.0	73.7	56.6	56.6	57.7
2007	63.6	38.3	65.5	70.9	37.3	73.5	56.7	56.7	57.9
2008	62.8	35.9	64.8	69.7	34.8	72.4	56.3	56.3	57.7
2009	60.2	31.7	62.3	66.0	30.2	68.7	54.8	54.8	56.3
2010	59.4	29.0	61.6	65.1	27.6	67.9	54.0	54.0	55.6
2011	59.4	28.8	61.6	65.3	27.3	68.2	53.7	53.7	55.3

Table 1-12. Civilian Employment-Population Ratios, by Sex, Age, Race, and Hispanic Origin, 1948–2011
—Continued

(Percent.)

Race, Hispanic origin, and year	Both sexes			Men			Women		
	16 years and over	16 to 19 years	20 years and over	16 years and over	16 to 19 years	20 years and over	16 years and over	16 to 19 years	20 years and over
BLACK									
1975	50.1	23.1	54.5	60.6	26.3	66.5	41.6	20.2	44.9
1976	50.8	22.4	55.4	60.6	25.8	66.8	42.8	19.2	46.4
1977	51.4	22.3	56.0	61.4	26.4	67.5	43.3	18.5	47.0
1978	53.6	25.2	58.0	63.3	28.5	69.1	45.8	22.1	49.3
1979	53.8	25.4	58.1	63.4	28.7	69.1	46.0	22.4	49.3
1980	52.3	23.9	56.4	60.4	27.0	65.8	45.7	21.0	49.1
1981	51.3	22.1	55.5	59.1	24.6	64.5	45.1	19.7	48.5
1982	49.4	19.0	53.6	56.0	20.3	61.4	44.2	17.7	47.5
1983	49.5	18.7	53.6	56.3	20.4	61.6	44.1	17.0	47.4
1984	52.3	21.9	56.1	59.2	23.9	64.1	46.7	20.1	49.8
1985	53.4	24.6	57.0	60.0	26.3	64.6	48.1	23.1	50.9
1986	54.1	25.1	57.6	60.6	26.5	65.1	48.8	23.8	51.6
1987	55.6	27.1	58.9	62.0	28.5	66.4	50.3	25.8	53.0
1988	56.3	27.6	59.7	62.7	29.4	67.1	51.2	25.8	53.9
1989	56.9	28.7	60.1	62.8	30.4	67.0	52.0	27.1	54.6
1990	56.7	26.7	60.2	62.6	27.7	67.1	51.9	25.8	54.7
1991	55.4	22.6	59.0	61.3	23.8	65.9	50.6	21.5	53.6
1992	54.9	22.8	58.3	59.9	23.6	64.3	50.8	22.1	53.6
1993	55.0	22.6	58.4	60.0	23.6	64.3	50.9	21.6	53.8
1994	56.1	24.9	59.4	60.8	25.4	65.0	52.3	24.5	55.0
1995	57.1	25.7	60.5	61.7	25.2	66.1	53.4	26.1	56.1
1996	57.4	26.0	60.8	61.1	24.9	65.5	54.4	27.1	57.1
1997	58.2	26.1	61.8	61.4	23.7	66.1	55.6	28.5	58.4
1998	59.7	30.1	63.0	62.9	28.4	67.1	57.2	31.8	59.7
1999	60.6	27.9	64.2	63.1	26.7	67.5	58.6	29.0	61.5
2000	60.9	29.8	64.2	63.6	28.9	67.7	58.6	30.6	61.3
2001	59.7	26.7	63.2	62.1	26.4	66.3	57.8	27.0	60.7
2002	58.1	25.3	61.6	61.1	25.6	65.2	55.8	24.9	58.7
2003	57.4	21.7	61.0	59.5	19.9	64.1	55.6	23.4	58.6
2004	57.2	21.5	60.9	59.3	19.3	63.9	55.5	23.6	58.5
2005	57.7	21.6	61.5	60.2	20.8	64.7	55.7	22.4	58.9
2006	58.4	24.1	62.0	60.6	21.7	65.2	56.5	26.4	59.4
2007	58.4	21.4	62.3	60.7	19.5	65.5	56.5	23.3	59.8
2008	57.3	20.2	61.2	59.1	18.7	63.9	55.8	21.7	59.1
2009	53.2	16.5	57.1	53.7	14.3	58.2	52.8	18.6	56.1
2010	52.3	14.5	56.1	53.1	14.1	57.5	51.7	14.9	55.1
2011	51.7	14.7	55.3	52.8	14.6	56.9	50.8	14.7	54.0
HISPANIC									
1975	53.4	. . .	. . .	. . .	. . .	. . .	. . .	. . .	. . .
1976	53.8	. . .	56.6	. . .	. . .	. . .	. . .	. . .	. . .
1977	55.4	. . .	58.3	. . .	. . .	. . .	. . .	. . .	. . .
1978	57.2	. . .	60.0	. . .	. . .	. . .	. . .	. . .	. . .
1979	58.3	. . .	61.0	. . .	. . .	. . .	. . .	. . .	. . .
1980	57.6	. . .	60.5	. . .	. . .	. . .	. . .	. . .	. . .
1981	57.4	. . .	60.7	. . .	. . .	. . .	. . .	. . .	. . .
1982	54.9	. . .	58.2	. . .	. . .	. . .	. . .	. . .	. . .
1983	55.1	. . .	58.1	. . .	. . .	. . .	. . .	. . .	. . .
1984	57.9	. . .	60.7	. . .	. . .	. . .	. . .	. . .	. . .
1985	57.8	. . .	60.7	. . .	. . .	. . .	. . .	. . .	. . .
1986	58.5	. . .	61.5	. . .	. . .	. . .	. . .	. . .	. . .
1987	60.5	. . .	63.4	. . .	. . .	. . .	. . .	. . .	. . .
1988	61.9	. . .	64.6	. . .	. . .	. . .	. . .	. . .	. . .
1989	62.2	. . .	64.8	. . .	. . .	. . .	. . .	. . .	. . .
1990	61.9	. . .	64.8	. . .	. . .	. . .	. . .	. . .	. . .
1991	59.8	. . .	62.8	. . .	. . .	. . .	. . .	. . .	. . .
1992	59.1	. . .	62.1	. . .	. . .	. . .	. . .	. . .	. . .
1993	59.1	. . .	62.1	. . .	. . .	. . .	. . .	. . .	. . .
1994	59.5	33.5	62.4	71.7	36.8	. . .	47.2	30.1	. . .
1995	59.7	34.4	62.6	72.1	37.5	. . .	47.3	31.3	. . .
1996	60.6	33.1	63.7	73.3	38.8	. . .	47.9	27.3	. . .
1997	62.6	33.7	66.0	74.5	37.6	. . .	50.2	29.3	. . .
1998	63.1	36.0	66.2	74.7	38.6	. . .	51.0	33.0	. . .
1999	63.4	37.0	66.5	75.3	41.2	. . .	51.7	32.5	. . .
2000	65.7	38.6	68.9	77.4	42.8	81.7	53.6	33.9	55.8
2001	64.9	38.6	67.8	76.2	43.3	79.9	53.3	33.5	55.4
2002	63.9	35.2	67.0	74.5	39.0	78.3	52.9	31.1	55.2
2003	63.1	30.2	66.4	74.3	31.9	78.6	51.2	28.4	53.6
2004	63.8	30.4	67.2	75.1	33.4	79.4	51.8	27.2	54.4
2005	64.0	31.5	67.3	75.8	33.8	80.0	51.5	29.1	53.8
2006	65.2	32.2	68.5	76.8	34.8	81.1	52.8	29.5	55.2
2007	64.9	30.4	68.5	76.2	32.1	80.7	53.0	28.5	55.6
2008	63.3	28.6	66.9	74.1	30.9	78.6	51.9	26.2	54.6
2009	59.7	23.7	63.5	68.9	24.1	73.5	50.1	23.4	52.9
2010	59.0	21.0	63.1	68.0	21.7	72.9	49.6	20.2	52.7
2011	58.9	19.5	63.2	67.9	20.1	73.3	49.3	18.9	52.5

. . . = Not available.

Table 1-13. Employed Civilians, by Sex, Race, Hispanic Origin, and Occupation, 2009–2011

(Thousands of people.)

Year and occupation	Total	Men	Women	White	Black	Hispanic[1]
2009						
All Occupations	139 877	73 670	66 208	114 996	15 025	19 647
Management, professional, and related occupations	52 219	25 385	26 833	43 649	4 388	3 817
Management, business, and financial operations occupations	21 529	12 330	9 199	18 582	1 516	1 642
Computer and mathematical occupations	3 481	2 618	863	2 633	233	189
Architecture and engineering occupations	2 740	2 363	377	2 276	151	196
Life, physical and social science occupations	1 328	707	621	1 052	80	1 328
Community and social service occupations	2 341	868	1 474	1 764	463	2 341
Legal occupations	1 710	859	851	1 510	110	85
Education, training, and library occupations	8 627	2 221	6 407	7 343	797	671
Arts, design, entertainment, sports, and media occupations	2 724	1 453	1 271	2 387	183	239
Healthcare practitioner and technical occupations	7 738	1 968	5 770	6 101	855	488
Healthcare support occupations	3 309	350	2 959	2 258	836	456
Protective service occupations	3 164	2 457	707	2 411	594	389
Food preparation and serving related occupations	7 733	3 422	4 310	6 184	884	1 672
Building and grounds cleaning and maintenance occupations	5 349	3 186	2 163	4 304	737	1 823
Personal care and service occupations	5 043	1 106	3 937	3 804	733	721
Sales and related occupations	33 787	12 498	21 289	27 777	3 793	1 864
Office and administrative support occupations	18 146	4 618	13 527	14 715	2 298	2 313
Farming, fishing, and forestry occupations	926	736	190	834	46	377
Construction and extraction occupations	7 439	7 248	191	6 682	447	2 123
Installation, maintenance, and repair occupations	4 957	4 751	206	4 286	418	726
Production occupations	15 951	12 530	3 421	12 808	2 149	1 675
Transportation and material moving occupations	8 297	7 028	1 269	6 587	1 270	1 689
2010						
All Occupations	139 064	73 359	65 705	114 168	15 010	19 906
Management, professional, and related occupations	51 743	25 070	26 673	43 268	4 363	3 755
Management, business, and financial operations occupations	20 938	11 945	8 993	18 043	1 537	1 562
Computer and mathematical occupations	3 531	2 620	911	2 663	237	194
Architecture and engineering occupations	2 619	2 282	337	2 205	135	177
Life, physical and social science occupations	1 409	755	655	1 139	88	85
Community and social service occupations	2 337	836	1 500	1 750	451	229
Legal occupations	1 716	878	838	1 510	111	94
Education, training, and library occupations	8 628	2 261	6 367	7 325	810	686
Arts, design, entertainment, sports, and media occupations	2 759	1 484	1 276	2 430	152	244
Healthcare practitioner and technical occupations	7 805	2 009	5 796	6 204	842	484
Healthcare support occupations	3 332	370	2 962	2 252	849	506
Protective service occupations	3 289	2 587	703	2 530	585	437
Food preparation and serving related occupations	7 660	3 439	4 221	6 110	866	1 703
Building and grounds cleaning and maintenance occupations	5 328	3 164	2 164	4 290	722	1 877
Personal care and service occupations	5 024	1 092	3 932	3 756	741	734
Sales and related occupations	33 433	12 419	21 015	27 470	1 503	1 814
Office and administrative support occupations	18 047	4 716	13 331	14 685	2 259	2 413
Farming, fishing, and forestry occupations	987	755	231	889	51	412
Construction and extraction occupations	7 175	6 990	185	6 449	441	2 090
Installation, maintenance, and repair occupations	4 911	4 721	190	4 281	384	769
Production occupations	16 180	12 751	3 429	12 873	2 247	1 755
Transportation and material moving occupations	8 182	6 959	1 224	6 405	1 339	1 640
2011						
All Occupations	139 869	74 290	65 579	114 690	15 051	20 269
Management, professional, and related occupations	52 547	25 552	26 995	43 923	4 398	3 952
Management, business, and financial operations occupations	21 589	12 275	9 314	18 495	1 579	1 662
Computer and mathematical occupations	3 608	2 705	903	2 695	250	205
Architecture and engineering occupations	2 785	2 406	379	2 353	145	178
Life, physical and social science occupations	1 303	687	616	1 059	96	77
Community and social service occupations	2 352	835	1 518	1 794	427	251
Legal occupations	1 770	889	881	1 540	129	95
Education, training, and library occupations	8 619	2 274	6 345	7 319	834	713
Arts, design, entertainment, sports, and media occupations	2 779	1 499	1 281	2 442	166	252
Healthcare practitioner and technical occupations	7 740	1 982	5 758	6 227	773	518
Healthcare support occupations	3 359	413	2 945	2 290	826	466
Protective service occupations	3 210	2 546	664	2 478	560	404
Food preparation and serving related occupations	7 747	3 534	4 213	6 086	973	1 692
Building and grounds cleaning and maintenance occupations	5 492	3 359	2 133	4 423	755	1 909
Personal care and service occupations	4 979	1 077	3 902	3 750	702	730
Sales and related occupations	15 330	7 733	7 597	12 751	1 503	1 935
Office and administrative support occupations	17 736	4 717	13 019	14 328	2 239	2 435
Farming, fishing, and forestry occupations	1 001	785	216	919	43	430
Construction and extraction occupations	7 125	6 962	163	6 419	417	2 095
Installation, maintenance, and repair occupations	4 883	4 710	173	4 233	387	771
Production occupations	8 142	5 826	2 316	6 580	892	1 761
Transportation and material moving occupations	8 318	7 076	1 242	6 510	1 356	1 689

Note: Beginning with data for January 2011, the Current Population Survey (CPS) uses the 2010 Census Occupational Classification system derived from the 2010 Standard Occupational Classification (SOC) system. The 2010 classification system replaces an earlier version that was based on the 2000 SOC. As a result of the classification change, CPS occupational data beginning with January 2011 data are not strictly comparable with earlier years.

[1]May be of any race.

Table 1-14. Employed Civilians, by Selected Occupation and Industry, 2009–2011

(Thousands of people.)

Year and occupation	Total employed	Agriculture, forestry, fishing, and hunting	Mining	Construction	Manufacturing Total	Durable goods	Nondurable goods	Wholesale trade
2009								
All Occupations	139 877	2 103	707	9 702	14 202	8 927	5 275	3 808
Management, professional, and related occupations	52 219	1 008	187	1 987	4 406	3 044	1 362	677
Management, business, and financial operations occupations	21 529	977	108	1 746	2 433	1 604	829	528
Computer and mathematical occupations	3 481	3	11	21	455	368	87	149
Architecture and engineering occupations	2 740	3	38	171	1 017	866	151	33
Life, physical and social science occupations	1 328	20	23	8	216	42	174	11
Community and social service occupations	2 341	0	X	3	1	0	1	1
Legal occupations	1 710	0	4	6	24	16	8	5
Education, training, and library occupations	8 627	1	1	1	23	14	8	8
Arts, design, entertainment, sports, and media occupations	2 724	2	1	28	194	117	77	23
Healthcare practitioner and technical occupations	7 738	2	2	2	42	17	26	8
Healthcare support occupations	3 309	1	X	1	8	4	4	2
Protective service occupations	3 164	17	7	12	31	21	10	4
Food preparation and serving related occupations	7 733	6	2	5	47	11	36	9
Building and grounds cleaning and maintenance occupations	5 349	24	4	46	156	78	79	36
Personal care and service occupations	5 043	46	X	3	9	3	6	1
Sales and related occupations	15 641	15	7	101	643	358	285	1 424
Office and administrative support occupations	18 146	76	58	560	1 337	831	506	616
Farming, fishing, and forestry occupations	926	779	2	5	43	5	38	40
Construction and extraction occupations	7 439	8	236	6 114	299	230	69	30
Installation, maintenance, and repair occupations	4 957	25	64	499	760	495	265	131
Production occupations	15 951	98	142	368	6 463	3 847	2 616	838
Transportation and material moving occupations	8 297	77	93	240	1 108	556	552	701
2010								
All Occupations	139 064	2 206	731	9 077	14 081	8 789	5 293	3 805
Management, professional, and related occupations	51 743	1 022	195	1 825	4 274	2 942	1 332	698
Management, business, and financial operations occupations	20 938	982	121	1 610	2 317	1 515	802	538
Computer and mathematical occupations	3 531	6	6	18	434	349	85	61
Architecture and engineering occupations	2 619	3	44	140	995	850	144	27
Life, physical and social science occupations	1 409	24	21	6	215	41	175	21
Community and social service occupations	2 337	1	0	0	1	0	1	X
Legal occupations	1 716	1	0	6	29	16	13	5
Education, training, and library occupations	8 628	3	2	3	26	21	5	4
Arts, design, entertainment, sports, and media occupations	2 759	1	2	39	214	124	90	25
Healthcare practitioner and technical occupations	7 805	3	1	2	43	25	18	17
Healthcare support occupations	3 332	1	X	0	5	4	1	1
Protective service occupations	3 289	19	3	8	31	23	8	4
Food preparation and serving related occupations	7 660	6	1	6	38	8	29	11
Building and grounds cleaning and maintenance occupations	5 328	21	2	37	124	61	63	29
Personal care and service occupations	5 024	54	0	3	9	4	4	2
Sales and related occupations	15 386	20	7	86	630	320	311	1 368
Office and administrative support occupations	18 047	90	57	462	1 323	833	490	639
Farming, fishing, and forestry occupations	987	813	1	1	59	5	54	53
Construction and extraction occupations	7 175	14	269	5 786	296	232	64	31
Installation, maintenance, and repair occupations	4 911	29	61	510	662	431	231	136
Production occupations	7 998	24	40	131	5 539	3 410	2 130	133
Transportation and material moving occupations	8 182	94	93	222	1 092	516	575	700
2011								
All Occupations	139 869	2 254	817	9 039	14 336	9 007	5 329	3 798
Management, professional, and related occupations	52 547	1 066	202	1 780	4 390	3 002	1 388	699
Management, business, and financial operations occupations	21 589	1 017	115	1 552	2 435	1 563	872	541
Computer and mathematical occupations	3 608	5	6	16	412	335	77	69
Architecture and engineering occupations	2 785	5	49	168	1 059	898	161	22
Life, physical and social science occupations	1 303	31	26	7	209	23	186	9
Community and social service occupations	2 352	2	0	1	2	0	2	0
Legal occupations	1 770	X	0	7	24	15	8	6
Education, training, and library occupations	8 619	1	X	3	27	22	5	7
Arts, design, entertainment, sports, and media occupations	2 779	2	3	26	182	124	58	27
Healthcare practitioner and technical occupations	7 740	3	2	1	41	21	19	18
Healthcare support occupations	3 359	1	X	0	8	5	3	1
Protective service occupations	3 210	14	2	18	38	22	16	8
Food preparation and serving related occupations	7 747	2	1	4	40	8	32	10
Building and grounds cleaning and maintenance occupations	5 492	35	3	45	134	70	64	24
Personal care and service occupations	4 979	43	0	4	9	4	4	4
Sales and related occupations	15 330	19	14	111	627	342	285	1 301
Office and administrative support occupations	17 736	93	59	491	1 298	789	509	673
Farming, fishing, and forestry occupations	1 001	836	1	2	51	5	46	49
Construction and extraction occupations	7 125	9	334	5 733	285	232	53	31
Installation, maintenance, and repair occupations	4 883	22	60	465	676	435	242	142
Production occupations	8 142	28	53	124	5 684	3 538	2 147	133
Transportation and material moving occupations	8 318	87	89	262	1 094	555	540	723

Note: Beginning with data for January 2011, the Current Population Survey (CPS) uses the 2010 Census Occupational Classification system derived from the 2010 Standard Occupational Classification (SOC) system. The 2010 classification system replaces an earlier version that was based on the 2000 SOC. As a result of the classification change, CPS occupational data beginning with January 2011 data are not strictly comparable with earlier years.

X = Not applicable.

Table 1-14. Employed Civilians, by Selected Occupation and Industry, 2009–2011—*Continued*

(Thousands of people.)

Year and occupation	Retail trade	Transportation and warehousing	Utilities	Information	Finance and insurance	Real estate and rental and leasing	Professional and technical services
2009							
All Occupations	15 877	6 012	1 233	3 239	6 826	2 796	9 159
Management, professional, and related occupations	1 677	690	388	1 659	3 473	888	7 197
Management, business, and financial operations occupations	860	562	186	639	2 914	819	2 615
Computer and mathematical occupations	817	128	202	1 020	559	69	4 583
Architecture and engineering occupations	24	49	122	87	8	5	884
Life, physical and social science occupations	13	4	21	17	21	3	335
Community and social service occupations	2	0	0	1	19	5	10
Legal occupations	11	6	6	7	66	18	1 175
Education, training, and library occupations	23	12	5	109	24	3	10
Arts, design, entertainment, sports, and media occupations	181	4	7	540	24	9	629
Healthcare practitioner and technical occupations	444	2	5	2	28	7	189
Healthcare support occupations	30	2	X	1	3	6	41
Protective service occupations	66	31	7	11	36	25	24
Food preparation and serving related occupations	299	5	1	26	4	24	6
Building and grounds cleaning and maintenance occupations	149	54	18	19	22	183	23
Personal care and service occupations	46	171	0	32	6	24	33
Sales and related occupations	8 762	98	24	405	1 188	1 011	234
Office and administrative support occupations	2 417	1 478	200	604	2 037	330	1 291
Farming, fishing, and forestry occupations	13	7	1	X	0	X	1
Construction and extraction occupations	89	73	120	18	9	52	49
Installation, maintenance, and repair occupations	628	320	229	326	22	130	94
Production occupations	1 699	3 084	244	138	27	123	165
Transportation and material moving occupations	1 211	2 997	51	64	7	99	47
2010							
All Occupations	15 934	5 880	1 253	3 149	6 605	2 745	9 115
Management, professional, and related occupations	1 722	643	396	1 647	3 384	894	7 073
Management, business, and financial operations occupations	904	525	195	613	2 853	823	2 534
Computer and mathematical occupations	117	41	37	270	328	11	1 349
Architecture and engineering occupations	21	53	112	88	13	10	814
Life, physical and social science occupations	14	5	25	15	21	7	373
Community and social service occupations	2	X	0	1	11	2	9
Legal occupations	20	5	3	11	80	21	1 147
Education, training, and library occupations	22	7	2	122	22	6	50
Arts, design, entertainment, sports, and media occupations	186	5	12	526	28	12	620
Healthcare practitioner and technical occupations	436	2	8	1	28	3	178
Healthcare support occupations	36	1	0	1	7	4	53
Protective service occupations	66	43	15	5	39	22	29
Food preparation and serving related occupations	362	4	0	32	6	21	7
Building and grounds cleaning and maintenance occupations	177	51	16	18	21	201	30
Personal care and service occupations	42	157	0	44	7	28	24
Sales and related occupations	8 704	94	24	403	1 066	1 011	275
Office and administrative support occupations	2 430	1 418	217	562	2 003	298	1 282
Farming, fishing, and forestry occupations	14	8	0	1	0	0	2
Construction and extraction occupations	78	75	119	15	5	42	70
Installation, maintenance, and repair occupations	605	322	216	304	24	115	96
Production occupations	504	89	205	65	35	20	126
Transportation and material moving occupations	1 195	2 974	44	53	7	88	47
2011							
All Occupations	15 927	5 957	1 243	3 150	6 613	2 773	9 461
Management, professional, and related occupations	1 567	665	411	1 685	3 422	907	7 476
Management, business, and financial operations occupations	754	544	204	644	2 848	844	2 808
Computer and mathematical occupations	140	47	37	282	379	16	1 377
Architecture and engineering occupations	22	41	105	97	16	5	874
Life, physical and social science occupations	4	0	26	2	5	1	316
Community and social service occupations	2	0	0	1	18	4	10
Legal occupations	11	5	8	9	81	17	1 213
Education, training, and library occupations	29	16	10	117	22	4	45
Arts, design, entertainment, sports, and media occupations	173	8	15	530	25	12	643
Healthcare practitioner and technical occupations	432	4	5	4	29	4	190
Healthcare support occupations	46	5	X	0	7	6	41
Protective service occupations	62	39	20	11	27	22	21
Food preparation and serving related occupations	379	8	0	19	8	18	7
Building and grounds cleaning and maintenance occupations	165	61	18	20	24	233	32
Personal care and service occupations	51	44	1	34	5	37	33
Sales and related occupations	8 742	119	21	380	1 062	936	308
Office and administrative support occupations	2 518	1 380	208	536	2 009	335	1 223
Farming, fishing, and forestry occupations	11	4	4	0	0	X	4
Construction and extraction occupations	81	74	99	17	5	43	53
Installation, maintenance, and repair occupations	639	332	195	324	24	121	85
Production occupations	532	88	230	68	17	28	127
Transportation and material moving occupations	1 135	3 137	37	54	4	88	52

Note: Beginning with data for January 2011, the Current Population Survey (CPS) uses the 2010 Census Occupational Classification system derived from the 2010 Standard Occupational Classification (SOC) system. The 2010 classification system replaces an earlier version that was based on the 2000 SOC. As a result of the classification change, CPS occupational data beginning with January 2011 data are not strictly comparable with earlier years.

X = Not applicable.

Table 1-14. Employed Civilians, by Selected Occupation and Industry, 2009–2011—*Continued*

(Thousands of people.)

Year and occupation	Management, administrative, and waste services	Educational services	Health care and social assistance	Arts, entertainment, and recreation	Accommodation and food services	Other services (except public administration)	Public administration
2009							
All Occupations	5 849	13 188	18 632	3 018	9 717	6 935	6 875
Management, professional, and related occupations	1 125	10 011	9 980	994	1 464	1 558	2 850
Management, business, and financial operations occupations	796	1 203	1 547	276	1 387	689	1 244
Computer and mathematical occupations	329	8 808	8 433	718	77	869	1 606
Architecture and engineering occupations	32	42	24	11	7	10	175
Life, physical and social science occupations	17	203	191	10	2	11	202
Community and social service occupations	12	339	960	7	2	618	362
Legal occupations	33	11	37	3	0	14	285
Education, training, and library occupations	12	339	960	7	2	618	362
Arts, design, entertainment, sports, and media occupations	48	195	56	602	24	93	64
Healthcare practitioner and technical occupations	93	287	6 402	4	6	23	189
Healthcare support occupations	62	37	2 912	18	5	131	48
Protective service occupations	517	124	77	186	42	22	1 925
Food preparation and serving related occupations	21	419	376	278	6 121	52	32
Building and grounds cleaning and maintenance occupations	2 067	603	474	274	500	562	135
Personal care and service occupations	24	234	1 755	721	104	1 756	79
Sales and related occupations	285	65	81	143	721	403	30
Office and administrative support occupations	861	1 124	2 568	234	403	621	1 331
Farming, fishing, and forestry occupations	8	2	1	4	1	1	18
Construction and extraction occupations	91	49	38	19	12	29	106
Installation, maintenance, and repair occupations	195	139	101	71	49	1 023	151
Production occupations	593	381	268	76	297	777	170
Transportation and material moving occupations	415	340	131	61	211	349	94
2010							
All Occupations	6 138	13 155	18 907	2 966	9 564	6 769	6 983
Management, professional, and related occupations	1 086	10 049	10 150	1 007	1 384	1 502	2 790
Management, business, and financial operations occupations	765	1 283	1 522	289	1 305	606	1 153
Computer and mathematical occupations	86	204	192	20	8	45	299
Architecture and engineering occupations	34	36	24	9	2	16	179
Life, physical and social science occupations	22	189	230	13	2	17	188
Community and social service occupations	10	356	980	9	4	608	342
Legal occupations	26	16	30	2	1	20	293
Education, training, and library occupations	13	7 450	656	80	24	50	86
Arts, design, entertainment, sports, and media occupations	36	218	50	577	33	108	68
Healthcare practitioner and technical occupations	93	297	6 467	8	5	31	183
Healthcare support occupations	57	33	2 926	21	11	135	41
Protective service occupations	563	130	73	176	53	18	1 992
Food preparation and serving related occupations	17	402	374	246	6 045	44	39
Building and grounds cleaning and maintenance occupations	2 166	575	493	237	486	530	115
Personal care and service occupations	25	243	1 771	734	89	1 707	85
Sales and related occupations	280	75	69	146	745	351	32
Office and administrative support occupations	939	1 085	2 597	225	392	604	1 424
Farming, fishing, and forestry occupations	7	1	0	2	0	2	20
Construction and extraction occupations	93	61	43	20	13	27	117
Installation, maintenance, and repair occupations	186	149	113	80	49	1 100	152
Production occupations	237	52	158	16	94	445	82
Transportation and material moving occupations	480	300	140	56	201	303	95
2011							
All Occupations	6 358	12 965	18 902	2 922	9 775	6 724	6 853
Management, professional, and related occupations	1 173	10 050	10 185	1 043	1 471	1 498	2 856
Management, business, and financial operations occupations	862	1 303	1 585	293	1 393	632	1 216
Computer and mathematical occupations	84	209	176	18	14	37	286
Architecture and engineering occupations	36	48	17	13	6	17	185
Life, physical and social science occupations	21	207	217	10	2	12	200
Community and social service occupations	10	338	989	10	2	595	367
Legal occupations	42	16	34	2	1	14	279
Education, training, and library occupations	18	7 430	653	82	30	56	68
Arts, design, entertainment, sports, and media occupations	43	239	58	611	18	107	58
Healthcare practitioner and technical occupations	57	260	6 455	5	5	28	198
Healthcare support occupations	63	28	2 966	19	10	115	43
Protective service occupations	555	114	83	176	43	15	1 942
Food preparation and serving related occupations	28	396	408	233	6 106	47	32
Building and grounds cleaning and maintenance occupations	2 258	576	522	259	456	515	112
Personal care and service occupations	24	227	1 771	699	90	1 794	112
Sales and related occupations	268	68	55	146	796	318	40
Office and administrative support occupations	975	1 011	2 489	190	401	572	1 276
Farming, fishing, and forestry occupations	7	4	1	1	1	3	21
Construction and extraction occupations	106	59	43	24	13	25	92
Installation, maintenance, and repair occupations	194	123	104	62	49	1 107	159
Production occupations	240	37	141	21	95	427	68
Transportation and material moving occupations	465	273	136	50	243	290	101

Note: Beginning with data for January 2011, the Current Population Survey (CPS) uses the 2010 Census Occupational Classification system derived from the 2010 Standard Occupational Classification (SOC) system. The 2010 classification system replaces an earlier version that was based on the 2000 SOC. As a result of the classification change, CPS occupational data beginning with January 2011 data are not strictly comparable with earlier years.

Table 1-15. Employed Civilians in Agriculture and Nonagricultural Industries, by Class of Worker and Sex, 1990–2011

(Thousands of people.)

Sex and year	Total employed	Agriculture				Nonagricultural industries						
		Total	Wage and salary workers	Self-employed workers	Unpaid family workers	Total employed	Wage and salary workers				Self-employed workers	Unpaid family workers
							Total	Government	Private household	Other industries except private households		
Both Sexes												
1990	118 793	3 223	1 740	1 378	105	115 570	106 598	17 769	1 027	87 802	8 719	253
1991	117 718	3 269	1 729	1 423	118	114 449	105 373	17 934	1 010	86 429	8 851	226
1992	118 492	3 247	1 750	1 385	112	115 245	106 437	18 136	1 135	87 166	8 575	233
1993	120 259	3 115	1 689	1 320	106	117 144	107 966	18 579	1 126	88 261	8 959	218
1994	123 060	3 409	1 715	1 645	49	119 651	110 517	18 293	966	91 258	9 003	131
1995	124 900	3 440	1 814	1 580	45	121 460	112 448	18 362	963	93 123	8 902	110
1996	126 707	3 443	1 869	1 518	56	123 264	114 171	18 217	928	95 026	8 971	122
1997	129 558	3 399	1 890	1 457	51	126 159	116 983	18 131	915	97 937	9 056	120
1998	131 463	3 378	2 000	1 341	38	128 085	119 019	18 383	962	99 674	8 962	103
1999	133 488	3 281	1 944	1 297	40	130 207	121 323	18 903	933	101 487	8 790	95
2000	136 891	2 464	1 421	1 010	33	134 427	125 114	19 248	718	105 148	9 205	108
2001	136 933	2 299	1 283	988	28	134 635	125 407	19 335	694	105 378	9 121	107
2002	136 485	2 311	1 282	1 003	26	134 174	125 156	19 636	757	104 764	8 923	95
2003	137 736	2 275	1 299	951	25	135 461	126 015	19 634	764	105 616	9 344	101
2004	139 252	2 232	1 242	964	27	137 020	127 463	19 983	779	106 701	9 467	90
2005	141 730	2 197	1 212	955	30	139 532	129 931	20 357	812	108 761	9 509	93
2006	144 427	2 206	1 287	901	18	142 221	132 449	20 337	803	111 309	9 685	87
2007	146 047	2 095	1 220	856	19	143 952	134 283	21 003	813	112 467	9 557	112
2008	145 362	2 168	1 279	860	28	143 194	133 882	21 258	805	111 819	9 219	93
2009	139 877	2 103	1 242	836	25	137 775	128 713	21 178	783	106 752	836	25
2010	139 064	2 206	1 353	821	33	136 858	127 914	21 003	667	106 244	8 860	84
2011	139 869	2 254	1 380	846	28	137 615	128 934	20 536	722	107 676	8 603	78
Men												
1990	65 105	2 546	1 355	1 151	39	62 559	56 913	8 245	149	48 519	5 597	48
1991	64 223	2 589	1 359	1 185	45	61 634	55 899	8 300	143	47 456	5 700	35
1992	64 441	2 575	1 371	1 164	40	61 866	56 212	8 348	156	47 708	5 613	41
1993	65 349	2 478	1 323	1 117	39	62 871	56 926	8 435	146	48 345	5 894	50
1994	66 450	2 554	1 330	1 197	27	63 896	58 300	8 327	99	49 874	5 560	37
1995	67 377	2 559	1 395	1 138	26	64 818	59 332	8 267	96	50 969	5 461	25
1996	68 207	2 573	1 418	1 124	31	65 634	60 133	8 110	99	51 924	5 465	36
1997	69 685	2 552	1 439	1 084	29	67 133	61 595	8 015	81	53 499	5 506	31
1998	70 693	2 553	1 526	1 005	23	68 140	62 630	8 178	86	54 366	5 480	29
1999	71 446	2 432	1 450	962	20	69 014	63 624	8 278	74	55 272	5 366	25
2000	73 305	1 861	1 116	725	20	71 444	65 838	8 309	71	57 458	5 573	33
2001	73 196	1 708	990	703	15	71 488	65 930	8 342	63	57 524	5 527	31
2002	72 903	1 724	979	731	14	71 179	65 726	8 437	76	57 212	5 425	29
2003	73 332	1 695	991	694	11	71 636	65 871	8 368	59	57 444	5 736	30
2004	74 525	1 687	970	702	15	72 838	66 951	8 616	60	58 275	5 860	27
2005	75 973	1 654	949	688	17	74 319	68 345	8 760	67	59 518	5 944	30
2006	77 502	1 663	989	664	10	75 838	69 811	8 696	60	61 055	6 004	23
2007	78 254	1 604	973	623	8	76 650	70 697	9 022	76	61 599	5 920	32
2008	77 486	1 650	997	637	16	75 836	70 072	9 089	70	60 912	5 736	29
2009	73 670	1 607	977	613	17	72 062	66 517	9 013	74	57 430	5 527	19
2010	73 359	1 665	1 051	598	17	71 694	66 189	9 059	60	57 070	5 472	33
2011	74 290	1 698	1 050	632	16	72 592	67 306	8 922	78	58 307	5 262	24
Women												
1990	53 689	678	385	227	66	53 011	49 685	9 524	879	39 282	3 122	205
1991	53 495	680	369	237	73	52 815	49 474	9 635	867	38 972	3 150	191
1992	54 052	672	379	221	73	53 380	50 225	9 788	979	39 458	2 963	192
1993	54 910	637	367	204	67	54 273	51 040	10 144	980	39 916	3 065	168
1994	56 610	855	384	448	23	55 755	52 217	9 965	867	41 385	3 443	95
1995	57 523	881	419	442	20	56 642	53 115	10 095	867	42 153	3 440	86
1996	58 501	871	452	394	25	57 630	54 037	10 107	830	43 100	3 506	87
1997	59 873	847	451	373	23	59 026	55 388	10 116	834	44 438	3 550	89
1998	60 770	825	474	336	15	59 945	56 389	10 205	876	45 308	3 482	74
1999	62 042	849	494	335	20	61 193	57 699	10 625	859	46 215	3 424	70
2000	63 586	602	305	285	12	62 983	59 277	10 939	647	47 690	3 631	76
2001	63 737	591	293	284	13	63 147	59 477	10 993	630	47 853	3 594	75
2002	63 582	587	303	272	12	62 995	59 431	11 199	680	47 552	3 499	66
2003	64 404	580	309	257	14	63 824	60 144	11 267	705	48 172	3 609	72
2004	64 728	546	271	262	12	64 182	60 512	11 367	719	48 426	3 607	63
2005	65 757	544	263	267	13	65 213	61 586	11 598	745	49 243	3 565	63
2006	66 925	543	298	237	8	66 382	62 638	11 641	742	50 254	3 681	64
2007	67 792	490	247	233	11	67 302	63 586	11 981	737	50 868	3 637	80
2008	67 876	518	282	224	12	67 358	63 810	12 169	735	50 907	3 483	65
2009	66 208	496	265	223	8	65 712	62 197	12 165	709	49 322	3 468	47
2010	65 705	541	302	223	16	65 164	61 725	11 944	607	49 174	3 388	51
2011	65 579	556	330	214	12	65 023	61 628	11 614	644	49 370	3 341	54

Table 1-16. Number of Employed Persons Age 25 Years and Over, by Educational Attainment, Sex, Race, and Hispanic Origin, 2000–2011

(Thousands of people.)

Race, Hispanic origin, sex, and year	Total	Less than a high school diploma	High school graduate, no college	Some college, no degree	Associate's degree	College graduate or higher	
						Total	Bachelor's degree only
Both Sexes							
2000	116 473	11 692	36 452	21 601	10 707	36 020	23 706
2001	116 846	11 669	36 078	21 459	11 127	36 514	23 907
2002	116 802	11 535	35 779	20 928	11 166	37 395	24 570
2003	118 385	11 537	35 857	21 107	11 313	38 570	25 188
2004	119 622	11 408	35 944	21 284	11 693	39 293	25 484
2005	121 960	11 712	36 398	21 380	12 245	40 225	26 027
2006	124 386	11 892	36 702	21 630	12 514	41 649	26 960
2007	126 172	11 521	36 857	22 076	12 535	43 182	28 055
2008	126 161	11 073	36 097	22 092	12 948	43 951	28 460
2009	122 277	10 371	34 487	21 016	12 872	43 531	27 964
2010	121 987	10 115	34 293	20 838	12 910	43 832	27 977
2011	122 507	9 967	33 823	20 712	13 182	44 822	28 333
Men							
2000	62 661	7 199	19 388	11 260	5 013	19 800	12 742
2001	62 824	7 188	19 274	11 076	5 226	20 060	12 872
2002	62 756	7 220	19 154	10 811	5 221	20 350	13 076
2003	63 349	7 290	19 200	10 858	5 231	20 770	13 354
2004	64 326	7 276	19 535	10 896	5 426	21 192	13 575
2005	65 772	7 487	20 127	10 993	5 739	21 427	13 687
2006	67 019	7 614	20 345	11 110	5 835	22 114	14 138
2007	67 963	7 450	20 434	11 382	5 862	22 835	14 680
2008	67 605	7 108	20 093	11 356	6 021	23 027	14 845
2009	64 831	6 569	19 085	10 772	5 864	22 541	14 368
2010	64 765	6 434	19 159	10 737	5 829	22 606	14 359
2011	65 356	6 388	19 059	10 741	6 029	23 138	14 637
Women							
2000	53 812	4 493	17 064	10 341	5 694	16 220	10 964
2001	54 021	4 480	16 804	10 383	5 901	16 453	11 035
2002	54 046	4 315	16 624	10 117	5 945	17 045	11 493
2003	55 035	4 248	16 657	10 249	6 081	17 800	11 834
2004	55 296	4 132	16 409	10 387	6 267	18 101	11 908
2005	56 188	4 226	16 271	10 388	6 506	18 798	12 340
2006	57 367	4 278	16 357	10 520	6 678	19 535	12 822
2007	58 209	4 071	16 423	10 695	6 674	20 346	13 375
2008	58 555	3 965	16 004	10 737	6 926	20 924	13 614
2009	57 445	3 802	15 402	10 244	7 008	20 990	13 597
2010	57 222	3 681	15 134	10 101	7 080	21 226	13 618
2011	57 151	3 579	14 764	9 971	7 153	21 684	13 697
White[1]							
2000	97 320	9 544	30 438	17 770	9 075	30 493	20 078
2001	97 560	9 550	30 126	17 671	9 393	30 821	20 136
2002	97 476	9 394	29 836	17 209	9 440	31 597	20 670
2003	98 120	9 437	29 645	17 227	9 476	32 335	21 103
2004	98 967	9 335	29 571	17 445	9 817	32 799	21 299
2005	100 613	9 579	29 911	17 515	10 256	33 352	21 550
2006	102 322	9 720	30 188	17 632	10 424	34 357	22 272
2007	103 477	9 446	30 140	17 936	10 419	35 535	23 138
2008	103 373	9 036	29 495	17 873	10 742	36 228	23 511
2009	100 419	8 497	28 372	16 983	10 714	35 854	23 109
2010	100 100	8 290	28 128	16 800	10 707	36 176	23 179
2011	100 426	8 248	27 568	16 713	10 922	36 975	23 533
Black[1]							
2000	12 852	1 499	4 571	2 910	1 160	2 713	1 866
2001	12 797	1 492	4 492	2 871	1 216	2 727	1 921
2002	12 719	1 498	4 453	2 843	1 210	2 715	1 955
2003	12 706	1 376	4 465	2 780	1 199	2 887	2 056
2004	12 817	1 326	4 606	2 717	1 195	2 973	2 097
2005	13 177	1 369	4 742	2 720	1 288	3 057	2 106
2006	13 504	1 389	4 697	2 816	1 338	3 263	2 243
2007	13 811	1 293	4 783	2 912	1 389	3 435	2 362
2008	13 786	1 234	4 719	2 972	1 439	3 423	2 354
2009	13 110	1 096	4 375	2 855	1 422	3 363	2 253
2010	13 092	1 103	4 234	2 864	1 482	3 409	2 260
2011	13 097	1 013	4 298	2 792	1 519	3 474	2 257
Hispanic[2]							
2000	12 406	4 468	3 658	1 828	756	1 696	1 198
2001	12 817	4 601	3 796	1 916	781	1 723	1 223
2002	13 294	4 744	3 921	1 900	823	1 906	1 370
2003	14 205	5 073	4 169	2 037	889	2 039	1 468
2004	14 661	5 135	4 330	2 137	931	2 127	1 538
2005	15 362	5 367	4 535	2 230	997	2 232	1 595
2006	16 225	5 620	4 801	2 282	1 095	2 428	1 698
2007	16 973	5 677	5 110	2 382	1 160	2 644	1 898
2008	17 115	5 426	5 232	2 484	1 236	2 736	1 930
2009	18 642	6 064	5 658	2 670	1 357	2 894	2 063
2010	16 946	5 183	5 175	2 474	1 252	2 862	2 025
2011	17 059	5 156	5 216	2 513	1 317	2 857	1 982

[1]Beginning in 2003, persons who selected this race group only; persons who selected more than one race group are not included. Prior to 2003, persons who reported more than one race group were included in the group they identified as their main race.
[2]May be of any race.

Table 1-16. Number of Employed Persons Age 25 Years and Over, by Educational Attainment, Sex, Race, and Hispanic Origin, 2000–2011—*Continued*

(Thousands of people.)

Race, Hispanic origin, sex, and year	Total	Less than a high school diploma	High school graduate, no college	Some college, no degree	Associate's degree	College graduate or higher	
						Total	Bachelor's degree only
White Men[1]							
2000	53 243	6 085	16 373	9 435	4 320	17 030	11 029
2001	53 375	6 080	16 292	9 344	4 501	17 158	11 060
2002	53 242	6 072	16 148	9 102	4 497	17 423	11 217
2003	53 458	6 192	16 068	9 042	4 431	17 725	11 461
2004	54 133	6 188	16 297	9 125	4 613	17 910	11 555
2005	55 214	6 368	16 750	9 225	4 851	18 021	11 551
2006	56 145	6 448	17 018	9 244	4 952	18 483	11 881
2007	56 740	6 364	17 039	9 409	4 964	18 964	12 260
2008	56 446	6 066	16 741	9 397	5 070	19 171	12 482
2009	54 248	5 583	15 966	8 937	4 948	18 813	12 112
2010	54 091	5 461	15 952	8 846	4 922	18 910	12 128
2011	54 488	5 450	15 776	8 878	5 082	19 303	12 344
White Women[1]							
2000	44 077	3 459	14 065	8 335	4 755	13 463	9 049
2001	44 184	3 469	13 834	8 327	4 891	13 663	9 075
2002	44 234	3 322	13 688	8 107	4 944	14 173	9 453
2003	44 662	3 245	13 576	8 185	5 045	14 610	9 643
2004	44 834	3 146	13 275	8 320	5 203	14 888	9 744
2005	45 399	3 211	13 162	8 290	5 405	15 331	9 999
2006	46 177	3 272	13 171	8 388	5 473	15 874	10 391
2007	46 737	3 082	13 102	8 527	5 455	16 571	10 878
2008	46 928	2 970	12 753	8 477	5 672	17 056	11 029
2009	46 172	2 913	12 406	8 046	5 766	17 040	10 997
2010	46 010	2 829	12 176	7 953	5 785	17 266	11 051
2011	45 938	2 798	11 792	7 835	5 840	17 672	11 189
Black Men[1]							
2000	6 011	755	2 253	1 326	466	1 210	828
2001	5 924	762	2 232	1 258	486	1 186	834
2002	5 928	785	2 212	1 264	482	1 185	855
2003	5 860	693	2 190	1 256	492	1 230	890
2004	5 942	676	2 287	1 172	503	1 305	931
2005	6 153	697	2 417	1 171	558	1 310	938
2006	6 276	720	2 338	1 249	535	1 433	1 002
2007	6 429	653	2 340	1 320	570	1 547	1 076
2008	6 357	616	2 358	1 296	579	1 508	1 036
2009	5 939	551	2 199	1 225	544	1 419	958
2010	5 988	561	2 164	1 270	567	1 426	960
2011	6 031	532	2 225	1 235	591	1 449	968
Black Women[1]							
2000	6 841	743	2 318	1 583	694	1 503	1 038
2001	6 873	730	2 260	1 612	729	1 541	1 087
2002	6 791	713	2 241	1 579	729	1 530	1 101
2003	6 846	683	2 275	1 524	707	1 657	1 166
2004	6 874	650	2 319	1 545	691	1 668	1 166
2005	7 024	672	2 325	1 549	730	1 748	1 169
2006	7 228	669	2 359	1 567	803	1 830	1 241
2007	7 382	641	2 443	1 592	819	1 888	1 286
2008	7 429	617	2 361	1 676	859	1 915	1 318
2009	7 171	544	2 176	1 631	877	1 943	1 295
2010	7 104	542	2 070	1 594	915	1 983	1 300
2011	7 066	481	2 073	1 558	928	2 026	1 289
Hispanic Men[2]							
2000	7 373	2 937	2 128	995	397	916	634
2001	7 628	3 041	2 174	1 082	386	945	669
2002	7 865	3 141	2 244	1 029	415	1 035	732
2003	8 578	3 424	2 461	1 105	451	1 137	806
2004	8 872	3 508	2 583	1 158	468	1 155	837
2005	9 361	3 639	2 775	1 251	503	1 193	847
2006	9 856	3 823	2 932	1 260	547	1 293	891
2007	10 303	3 947	3 100	1 285	567	1 403	1 000
2008	10 363	3 714	3 231	1 371	607	1 439	1 008
2009	9 969	3 508	3 114	1 321	595	1 431	992
2010	10 120	3 517	3 176	1 341	595	1 491	1 045
2011	10 151	3 487	3 158	1 377	636	1 492	1 044
Hispanic Women[2]							
2000	5 033	1 531	1 529	833	359	780	564
2001	5 190	1 560	1 622	834	395	778	553
2002	5 429	1 604	1 676	871	408	871	638
2003	5 627	1 649	1 708	932	438	901	661
2004	5 789	1 628	1 746	980	463	972	701
2005	6 000	1 728	1 759	979	495	1 039	748
2006	6 370	1 797	1 868	1 021	548	1 135	807
2007	6 670	1 730	2 010	1 097	593	1 241	898
2008	6 752	1 712	2 001	1 113	629	1 297	922
2009	6 718	1 724	1 955	1 093	647	1 298	941
2010	6 826	1 666	1 999	1 133	656	1 371	979
2011	6 908	1 669	2 058	1 136	681	1 365	938

[1]Beginning in 2003, persons who selected this race group only; persons who selected more than one race group are not included. Prior to 2003, persons who reported more than one race group were included in the group they identified as their main race.
[2]May be of any race.

Table 1-17. Multiple Jobholders and Multiple Jobholding Rates, by Selected Characteristics, May of Selected Years, 1970–2012

(Thousands of people, percent, not seasonally adjusted.)

Year	Total employed	Multiple jobholders Total	Men	Women Number	Women Percent of all multiple jobholders	Multiple jobholding rate[1] Total	Men	Women	White	Black[2]	Asian	Hispanic[3]
1970	78 358	4 048	3 412	636	15.7	5.2	7.0	2.2	5.3	4.4	...	...
1971	78 708	4 035	3 270	765	19.0	5.1	6.7	2.6	5.3	3.8	...	...
1972	81 224	3 770	3 035	735	19.5	4.6	6.0	2.4	4.8	3.7	...	...
1973	83 758	4 262	3 393	869	20.4	5.1	6.6	2.7	5.1	4.7	...	...
1974	85 786	3 889	3 022	867	22.3	4.5	5.8	2.6	4.6	3.8	...	...
1975	84 146	3 918	2 962	956	24.4	4.7	5.8	2.9	4.8	3.7	...	...
1976	87 278	3 948	3 037	911	23.1	4.5	5.8	2.6	4.7	2.8	...	...
1977	90 482	4 558	3 317	1 241	27.2	5.0	6.2	3.4	5.3	2.6	...	...
1978	93 904	4 493	3 212	1 281	28.5	4.8	5.8	3.3	5.0	3.1	...	...
1979	96 327	4 724	3 317	1 407	29.8	4.9	5.9	3.5	5.1	3.0	...	...
1980	96 809	4 759	3 210	1 549	32.5	4.9	5.8	3.8	5.1	3.2	...	...
1985	106 878	5 730	3 537	2 192	38.3	5.4	5.9	4.7	5.7	3.2	...	...
1989	117 084	7 225	4 115	3 109	43.0	6.2	6.4	5.9	6.5	4.3	...	...
1991	116 626	7 183	4 054	3 129	43.6	6.2	6.4	5.9	6.4	4.9	...	...
1994	122 946	7 316	3 973	3 343	45.7	6.0	6.0	5.9	6.1	4.9	...	3.8
1995	124 554	7 952	4 225	3 727	46.9	6.4	6.3	6.5	6.6	5.2	...	3.6
1996	126 391	7 846	4 352	3 494	44.5	6.2	6.4	6.0	6.4	5.1	...	4.0
1997	129 565	8 197	4 398	3 800	46.4	6.3	6.3	6.4	6.5	5.7	...	4.1
1998	131 476	8 126	4 438	3 688	45.4	6.2	6.3	6.1	6.3	5.5	...	4.4
1999	133 411	7 895	4 117	3 778	47.9	5.9	5.8	6.1	6.0	5.5	...	3.6
2000	136 685	7 751	4 084	3 667	47.3	5.7	5.6	5.8	5.9	4.9	3.4	3.2
2001	137 121	7 540	3 914	3 626	48.1	5.5	5.3	5.7	5.6	5.3	3.7	3.4
2002	136 559	7 247	3 736	3 511	48.4	5.3	5.1	5.5	5.5	4.7	4.0	3.8
2003	137 567	7 338	3 841	3 498	47.7	5.3	5.3	5.4	5.5	4.3	4.2	3.4
2004	138 867	7 258	3 653	3 605	49.7	5.2	4.9	5.6	5.3	5.1	3.7	3.4
2005	141 591	7 348	3 741	3 607	49.1	5.2	4.9	5.5	5.4	4.4	3.5	2.8
2006	144 641	7 641	3 863	3 778	49.4	5.3	5.0	5.7	5.3	5.4	3.7	3.1
2007	145 864	7 693	3 835	3 858	50.1	5.3	4.9	5.7	5.5	4.4	3.7	3.0
2008	145 927	7 653	3 842	3 812	49.8	5.2	4.9	5.6	5.4	4.9	3.8	2.9
2009	140 363	7 265	3 540	3 725	51.3	5.2	4.8	5.6	5.3	4.8	3.9	3.0
2010	139 497	7 261	3 559	3 702	51.0	5.2	4.8	5.6	5.4	4.6	3.1	3.1
2011	140 028	7 084	3 491	3 593	50.7	5.1	4.7	5.5	5.3	4.5	3.1	3.3
2012	142 727	7 174	3 605	3 569	49.7	5.0	4.8	5.3	5.2	4.9	3.3	3.1

Note: Data prior to 1985 reflect 1970 census–based population controls; years 1985–1991 reflect 1980 census–based controls; years 1994–1999 reflect 1990 census–based controls adjusted for the estimated undercount; and data for years 2000–2002 have been revised to incorporate population controls from the 2000 census. Prior to 1994, data on multiple jobholders were collected only through special periodic supplements to the Current Population Survey (CPS) in May of various years; these supplemental surveys were not conducted in 1981–1984, 1986–1988, 1990, or 1992–1993. Beginning in 1994, data reflect the introduction of a major redesign of the CPS, including the collection of monthly data on multiple jobholders.

[1]Multiple jobholders as a percent of all employed persons in specified group.
[2]Data for years prior to 1977 refer to the Black-and-Other population group.
[3]May be of any race.
. . . = Not available.

Table 1-18. Multiple Jobholders, by Sex, Age, Marital Status, Race, Hispanic Origin, and Job Status, 2008–2011

(Thousands of people, percent.)

Characteristic	Both sexes				Men				Women			
	Number		Rate[1]		Number		Rate[1]		Number		Rate[1]	
	2008	2009	2008	2009	2008	2009	2008	2009	2008	2009	2008	2009
Age												
Total, 16 years and over[2]	7 620	7 271	5.2	5.2	3 837	3 530	5.0	4.8	3 783	3 741	5.6	5.6
16 to 19 years	225	186	4.0	3.8	94	71	3.4	3.1	131	115	4.6	4.6
20 to 24 years	752	710	5.5	5.6	329	307	4.6	4.7	423	403	6.5	6.4
25 to 34 years	1 555	1 546	5.0	5.1	846	795	4.9	4.9	710	750	5.0	5.4
35 to 44 years	1 841	1 675	5.5	5.3	941	822	5.2	4.9	900	853	5.9	5.8
45 to 54 years	1 958	1 903	5.7	5.7	959	907	5.3	5.2	999	996	6.1	6.2
55 to 64 years	1 067	1 039	5.1	4.9	539	507	4.9	4.7	528	532	5.3	5.2
65 years and over	223	212	3.7	3.5	129	120	3.9	3.6	94	92	3.5	3.3
Marital Status												
Single	2 089	1 989	5.2	5.2	989	890	4.5	4.3	1 100	1 099	5.9	6.2
Married, spouse present	4 166	3 993	5.1	5.0	2 386	2 212	5.2	5.0	1 780	1 781	5.0	5.1
Widowed, divorced, or separated	1 365	1 289	5.9	5.8	462	429	4.8	4.7	903	861	6.7	6.5
Race and Hispanic Origin												
White	6 405	6 166	5.4	5.4	1 923	3 016	5.0	4.9	3 151	3 150	5.8	5.9
Black	756	714	4.7	4.8	240	319	5.0	4.7	385	395	4.5	4.8
Hispanic[3]	671	643	3.3	3.3	235	354	3.1	3.0	294	289	3.6	3.6
Full- or Part-Time Status												
Primary job full time, secondary job part time	4 165	3 868	...	...	2 289	2 042	...	...	1 876	1 825	...	...
Primary and secondary jobs, both part time	1 791	1 821	...	...	588	599	...	...	1 203	1 222	...	...
Primary and secondary jobs, both full time	284	249	...	...	192	157	...	...	92	92	...	...
Hours vary on primary or secondary job	1 338	1 287	...	...	747	704	...	...	591	583	...	...

Characteristic	Both sexes				Men				Women			
	Number		Rate[1]		Number		Rate[1]		Number		Rate[1]	
	2010	2011	2010	2011	2010	2011	2010	2011	2010	2011	2010	2011
Age												
Total, 16 years and over[2]	6 878	6 880	4.9	4.9	3 326	3 384	4.5	4.6	3 552	3 496	5.4	5.3
16 to 19 years	167	183	3.8	4.2	61	78	2.9	3.7	106	104	4.7	4.7
20 to 24 years	695	697	5.5	5.3	289	294	4.5	4.3	406	403	6.5	6.5
25 to 34 years	1 519	1 496	5.0	4.9	768	802	4.7	4.8	751	694	5.4	5.0
35 to 44 years	1 554	1 483	5.1	4.9	798	736	4.8	4.5	756	747	5.4	5.4
45 to 54 years	1 724	1 697	5.2	5.2	809	804	4.7	4.7	916	894	5.7	5.7
55 to 64 years	1 021	1 083	4.7	4.9	490	523	4.4	4.6	531	561	5.1	5.2
65 years and over	197	241	3.1	3.6	112	148	3.2	4.0	86	93	3.0	3.2
Marital Status												
Single	2 000	2 026	5.2	5.1	895	939	4.3	4.4	1 105	1 087	6.2	6.0
Married, spouse present	3 644	3 646	4.7	4.7	2 015	2 044	4.7	4.7	1 629	1 602	4.7	4.7
Widowed, divorced, or separated	1 233	1 209	5.2	5.3	416	402	4.5	4.2	817	806	6.2	6.1
Race and Hispanic Origin												
White	5 857	5 812	5.1	5.1	2 861	2 883	4.7	4.7	5 857	2 929	5.7	5.6
Black	653	679	4.3	4.5	298	328	4.3	4.7	653	351	4.3	4.3
Hispanic[3]	638	611	3.2	3.0	360	358	3.1	3.0	638	253	3.4	3.1
Full- or Part-Time Status												
Primary job full time, secondary job part time	3 591	3 620	...	...	211	1 979	...	...	352	1 640	...	...
Primary and secondary jobs, both part time	1 805	1 811	...	...	67	619	...	...	152	1 193	...	...
Primary and secondary jobs, both full time	263	234	...	...	33	147	...	...	47	88	...	...
Hours vary on primary or secondary job	1 182	1 172	...	...	48	619	...	...	83	552	...	...

Note: Estimates for the above race groups (White or Black) do not sum to totals because data are not presented for all races. Beginning in January 2003, data reflect the revised population controls used in the household survey.

[1]Multiple jobholders as a percent of all employed persons in specified group.
[2]Includes a small number of persons who work part time at their primary job and full time at their secondary job(s), not shown separately.
[3]May be of any race.
. . . = Not available.

Table 1-19. Multiple Jobholders, by Sex and Industry of Principal Secondary Job, Annual Averages, 2009–2011

(Thousands of people.)

Year and industry of secondary job	Both sexes	Men	Women
2009			
All Nonagricultural Industries, Wage and Salary Workers	5 245	2 325	2 920
Mining, quarrying, and oil and gas extraction	2	2	0
Construction	206	165	40
Manufacturing	159	98	60
Durable goods	96	63	33
Nondurable goods	63	35	28
Wholesale and retail trade	1 060	435	626
Wholesale trade	77	47	30
Retail trade	984	388	596
Transportation and utilities	173	124	50
Transportation and warehousing	151	107	44
Utilities	22	17	5
Information	148	97	51
Financial activities	340	208	132
Professional and business services	784	446	338
Education and health services	1 635	510	1 125
Leisure and hospitality	1 173	549	623
Other services	582	266	316
Other services, except private households	498	259	239
Other services, private households	84	7	77
Public administration	186	119	67
2010			
All Nonagricultural Industries, Wage and Salary Workers	4 885	2 210	2 675
Mining, quarrying, and oil and gas extraction	8	8	...
Construction	188	158	30
Manufacturing	160	95	65
Durable goods	89	60	29
Nondurable goods	71	35	36
Wholesale and retail trade	902	392	511
Wholesale trade	58	37	21
Retail trade	844	354	490
Transportation and utilities	178	129	50
Transportation and warehousing	156	115	41
Utilities	22	14	8
Information	129	80	49
Financial activities	287	163	125
Professional and business services	713	399	314
Education and health services	1 640	542	1 097
Leisure and hospitality	1 040	489	551
Other services	499	208	291
Other services, except private households	449	204	245
Other services, private households	50	4	46
Public administration	196	128	68
2011			
All Nonagricultural Industries, Wage and Salary Workers	4 940	2 291	2 648
Mining, quarrying, and oil and gas extraction	6	5	0
Construction	201	161	40
Manufacturing	148	93	55
Durable goods	80	60	19
Nondurable goods	69	33	36
Wholesale and retail trade	1 003	409	594
Wholesale trade	97	61	36
Retail trade	907	349	558
Transportation and utilities	162	122	39
Transportation and warehousing	156	119	37
Utilities	6	4	2
Information	113	68	45
Financial activities	314	179	134
Professional and business services	777	443	334
Education and health services	1 605	543	1 062
Leisure and hospitality	1 058	518	540
Other services	509	252	258
Other services, except private households	455	245	210
Other services, private households	55	7	48
Public administration	178	116	62

Table 1-20. Employment and Unemployment in Families, by Race and Hispanic Origin, Annual Averages, 2000–2011

(Thousands of people, percent.)

Characteristic	2000	2001	2002	2003	2004	2005	2006	2007	2008	2009	2010	2011
ALL RACES												
Total Families	71 680	73 306	74 169	75 301	75 872	76 443	77 017	77 894	77 943	78 361	78 246	78 362
With employed member(s)	59 626	60 707	61 121	61 761	62 424	62 933	63 492	64 330	64 058	63 010	62 560	62 529
As percent of total families	83.2	82.8	82.4	82.0	82.3	82.3	82.4	82.6	82.2	80.4	80.0	79.8
Some usually work full time[1]	55 683	56 519	56 742	57 229	57 813	58 276	58 918	59 616	59 116	57 037	56 471	56 498
With no employed member	12 054	12 600	13 048	13 540	13 447	13 509	13 525	13 564	13 884	15 351	15 686	15 833
As percent of total families	16.8	17.2	17.6	18.0	17.7	17.7	17.6	17.4	17.8	19.6	20.0	20.2
With unemployed member(s)	4 110	4 847	5 809	6 079	5 593	5 318	4 913	4 914	6 104	9 381	9 695	9 043
As percent of total families	5.7	6.6	7.8	8.1	7.4	7.0	6.4	6.3	7.8	12.0	12.4	11.5
Some member(s) employed	2 973	3 494	4 126	4 285	3 915	3 717	3 419	3 497	4 319	6 438	6 566	6 079
As percent of families with unemployed member(s)	72.3	72.1	71.0	70.5	70.0	69.9	69.6	71.2	70.8	68.6	67.7	67.2
Some usually work full time[1]	2 675	3 122	3 668	3 790	3 494	3 310	3 049	3 096	3 830	5 460	5 572	5 211
As percent of families with unemployed member(s)	65.1	64.4	63.1	62.3	62.5	62.2	62.1	63.0	62.7	58.2	57.5	57.6
WHITE[2]												
Total Families	59 918	60 921	61 494	61 995	62 250	62 567	62 977	63 667	63 490	63 774	63 551	63 635
With employed member(s)	49 877	50 505	50 785	51 002	51 350	51 645	52 054	52 669	52 273	51 494	51 048	51 030
As percent of total families	83.2	83.0	82.6	82.3	82.5	82.5	82.7	82.7	82.3	80.7	80.3	80.2
Some usually work full time[1]	46 639	47 060	47 193	47 356	47 620	47 883	48 395	48 879	48 271	46 629	46 150	46 203
With no employed member	10 042	10 416	10 709	10 993	10 900	10 922	10 923	10 997	11 217	12 280	12 502	12 605
As percent of total families	16.8	17.0	17.4	17.7	17.5	17.5	17.3	17.3	17.7	19.3	19.7	19.8
With unemployed member(s)	3 010	3 553	4 275	4 411	4 078	3 801	3 556	3 587	4 506	7 089	7 202	6 608
As percent of total families	5.0	5.8	7.0	7.1	6.6	6.1	5.6	5.6	7.1	11.1	11.3	10.4
Some member(s) employed	2 276	2 661	3 164	3 245	3 000	2 782	2 582	2 653	3 332	5 072	5 069	4 627
As percent of families with unemployed member(s)	75.6	74.9	74.0	73.6	73.6	73.2	72.6	73.9	74.0	71.5	70.4	70.0
Some usually work full time[1]	2 052	2 379	2 808	2 873	2 677	2 477	2 306	2 350	2 955	4 294	4 289	3 964
As percent of families with unemployed member(s)	68.2	67.0	65.7	65.1	65.7	65.2	64.8	65.5	65.6	60.6	59.6	60.0
BLACK[2]												
Total Families	8 600	8 674	8 845	8 869	8 860	8 952	9 058	9 184	9 297	9 318	9 404	9 370
With employed member(s)	6 964	6 933	6 987	6 906	6 920	6 986	7 078	7 249	7 290	7 022	7 030	6 954
As percent of total families	81.0	80.0	79.0	77.9	78.1	78.0	78.1	78.9	78.4	75.4	74.8	74.2
Some usually work full time[1]	6 401	6 373	6 390	6 270	6 292	6 353	6 437	6 608	6 622	6 265	6 222	6 105
With no employed member	1 636	1 742	1 858	1 963	1 940	1 966	1 980	1 935	2 006	2 296	2 374	2 416
As percent of total families	19.0	20.1	21.0	22.1	21.9	22.0	21.9	21.1	21.6	24.6	25.2	25.8
With unemployed member(s)	881	990	1 162	1 213	1 127	1 140	1 036	990	1 188	1 624	1 807	1 767
As percent of total families	10.2	11.4	13.1	13.7	12.7	12.7	11.4	10.8	12.8	17.4	19.2	18.9
Some member(s) employed	535	596	689	695	625	657	596	591	686	886	1 009	985
As percent of families with unemployed member(s)	60.8	60.2	59.3	57.3	55.5	57.7	57.6	59.7	57.8	54.5	55.8	55.7
Some usually work full time[1]	476	533	611	612	556	583	526	519	605	748	862	835
As percent of families with unemployed member(s)	54.1	53.8	52.6	50.5	49.3	51.1	50.8	52.4	50.9	46.0	47.7	47.3
HISPANIC[3]												
Total Families	7 581	8 140	8 650	9 185	9 305	9 603	9 905	10 332	10 500	10 489	10 561	10 902
With employed member(s)	6 633	7 100	7 485	7 907	8 071	8 312	8 641	9 048	9 135	8 852	8 897	9 178
As percent of total families	87.5	87.2	86.5	86.1	86.7	86.6	87.2	87.6	87.0	84.4	84.2	84.2
Some usually work full time[1]	6 255	6 692	6 989	7 383	7 566	7 786	8 129	8 492	8 466	7 923	7 934	8 201
With no employed member	947	1 040	1 165	1 277	1 235	1 291	1 264	1 285	1 365	1 637	1 664	1 724
As percent of total families	12.5	12.8	13.5	13.9	13.3	13.4	12.8	12.4	13.0	15.6	15.8	15.8
With unemployed member(s)	679	809	965	1 020	950	860	793	876	1 159	1 770	1 841	1 781
As percent of total families	9.0	9.9	11.2	11.1	10.2	9.0	8.0	8.5	11.0	16.9	17.4	16.3
Some member(s) employed	493	592	686	715	664	606	544	619	846	1 228	1 262	1 226
As percent of families with unemployed member(s)	72.7	73.2	71.1	70.1	69.9	70.5	68.6	70.6	73.0	69.3	68.6	68.8
Some usually work full time[1]	446	537	615	640	594	544	491	554	743	1 021	1 060	1 030
As percent of families with unemployed member(s)	65.8	66.4	63.7	62.7	62.5	63.2	61.9	63.2	64.1	57.7	57.6	57.8

Note: The race or ethnicity of the family is determined by the race of the householder. Estimates for the above race groups (White or Black) do not sum to totals because data are not presented for all races.

[1]Usually work 35 hours or more a week at all jobs.
[2]Beginning in 2003, families where the householder selected this race group only; families where the householder selected more than one race group are excluded. Prior to 2003, families where the householder selected more than one race group were included in the group that the householder identified as the main race.
[3]May be of any race.

Table 1-21. Families, by Presence and Relationship of Employed Members and Family Type, Annual Averages, 2000–2011

(Thousands of people, percent.)

Characteristic	Number of families											
	2000	2001	2002	2003	2004	2005	2006	2007	2008	2009	2010	2011
MARRIED-COUPLE FAMILIES												
Total	54 704	55 749	56 280	57 074	57 188	57 167	57 509	58 145	58 125	58 124	57 524	57 290
Member(s) employed, total	45 967	46 680	46 976	47 535	47 767	47 895	48 196	48 676	48 541	47 876	47 238	46 910
Husband only	10 500	10 833	11 174	11 403	11 712	11 562	11 399	11 509	11 351	11 371	11 311	11 426
Wife only	2 946	3 257	3 613	3 863	3 843	3 715	3 754	3 858	4 036	4 909	4 937	4 764
Husband and wife	29 128	29 241	28 873	29 077	28 991	29 330	29 799	30 055	29 854	28 211	27 501	27 229
Other employment combinations	3 394	3 350	3 317	3 193	3 222	3 288	3 244	3 254	3 300	3 384	3 489	3 491
No member(s) employed	8 737	9 068	9 303	9 539	9 420	9 272	9 313	9 469	9 585	10 248	10 286	10 379
FAMILIES MAINTAINED BY WOMEN[1]												
Total	12 775	13 037	13 215	13 450	13 614	14 035	14 208	14 423	14 383	14 610	14 913	15 147
Member(s) employed, total	10 026	10 131	10 169	10 187	10 358	10 609	10 796	11 087	10 929	10 642	10 715	10 867
Householder only	5 581	5 667	5 944	5 987	6 021	6 052	6 103	6 307	6 250	6 135	6 189	6 248
Householder and other member(s)	2 806	2 778	2 559	2 539	2 701	2 830	2 955	2 994	2 870	2 642	2 603	2 683
Other member(s), not householder	1 639	1 686	1 666	1 660	1 636	1 727	1 738	1 785	1 809	1 866	1 923	1 937
No member(s) employed	2 749	2 906	3 047	3 263	3 255	3 426	3 412	3 336	3 454	3 968	4 198	4 280
FAMILIES MAINTAINED BY MEN[1]												
Total	4 200	4 521	4 674	4 777	5 071	5 242	5 300	5 327	5 435	5 627	5 809	5 926
Member(s) employed, total	3 632	3 895	3 976	4 039	4 299	4 430	4 500	4 568	4 589	4 492	4 607	4 752
Householder only	1 761	1 875	1 939	1 954	2 060	2 093	2 089	2 170	2 178	2 104	2 215	2 399
Householder and other member(s)	1 358	1 450	1 440	1 427	1 557	1 639	1 715	1 696	1 659	1 557	1 525	1 506
Other member(s), not householder	514	570	598	658	682	698	696	701	752	831	867	847
No member(s) employed	567	625	698	739	772	812	800	759	845	1 135	1 202	1 174

Characteristic	Percent distribution											
	2000	2001	2002	2003	2004	2005	2006	2007	2008	2009	2010	2011
MARRIED-COUPLE FAMILIES												
Total	100.0	100.0	100.0	100.0	100.0	100.0	100.0	100.0	100.0	100.0	100.0	100.0
Member(s) employed, total	84.0	83.7	83.5	83.3	83.5	83.8	83.8	83.7	83.5	82.4	82.1	81.9
Husband only	19.2	19.4	19.9	20.0	20.5	20.2	19.8	19.8	19.5	19.6	19.7	19.9
Wife only	5.4	5.8	6.4	6.8	6.7	6.5	6.5	6.6	6.9	8.4	8.6	8.3
Husband and wife	53.2	52.5	51.3	50.9	50.7	51.3	51.8	51.7	51.4	48.5	47.8	47.5
Other employment combinations	6.2	6.0	5.9	5.6	5.6	5.8	5.6	5.6	5.7	5.8	6.1	6.1
No member(s) employed	16.0	16.3	16.5	16.7	16.5	16.2	16.2	16.3	16.5	17.6	17.9	18.1
FAMILIES MAINTAINED BY WOMEN[1]												
Total	100.0	100.0	100.0	100.0	100.0	100.0	100.0	100.0	100.0	100.0	100.0	100.0
Member(s) employed, total	78.5	77.7	77.0	75.7	76.1	75.6	76.0	76.9	76.0	72.8	71.9	71.7
Householder only	43.7	43.5	45.0	44.5	44.2	43.1	43.0	43.7	43.5	42.0	41.5	41.2
Householder and other member(s)	22.0	21.3	19.4	18.9	19.8	20.2	20.8	20.8	20.0	18.1	17.5	17.7
Other member(s), not householder	12.8	12.9	12.6	12.3	12.0	12.3	12.2	12.4	12.6	12.8	12.9	12.8
No member(s) employed	21.5	22.3	23.1	24.3	23.9	24.4	24.0	23.1	24.0	27.2	28.1	28.3
FAMILIES MAINTAINED BY MEN[1]												
Total	100.0	100.0	100.0	100.0	100.0	100.0	100.0	100.0	100.0	100.0	100.0	100.0
Member(s) employed, total	86.5	86.2	85.1	84.6	84.8	84.5	84.9	85.7	84.4	79.8	79.3	80.2
Householder only	41.9	41.5	41.5	40.9	40.6	39.9	39.4	40.7	40.1	37.4	38.1	40.5
Householder and other member(s)	32.3	32.1	30.8	29.9	30.7	31.3	32.4	31.8	30.5	27.7	26.2	25.4
Other member(s), not householder	12.2	12.6	12.8	13.8	13.5	13.3	13.1	13.2	13.8	14.8	14.9	14.3
No member(s) employed	13.5	13.8	14.9	15.5	15.2	15.5	15.1	14.3	15.6	20.2	20.7	19.8

Note: Detail may not sum to total due to rounding.

[1]No spouse present.

Table 1-22. Unemployment in Families, by Presence and Relationship of Employed Members and Family Type, Annual Averages, 2000–2011

(Thousands of people, percent.)

Characteristic	Number											
	2000	2001	2002	2003	2004	2005	2006	2007	2008	2009	2010	2011
MARRIED-COUPLE FAMILIES												
With Unemployed Member(s), Total	2 584	3 081	3 772	3 857	3 521	3 243	2 968	2 978	3 796	6 056	6 147	5 576
No member employed	411	531	676	713	615	580	526	512	663	1 218	4 884	4 413
Some member(s) employed	2 174	2 550	3 096	3 144	2 906	2 664	2 442	2 467	3 133	4 838	1 263	1 162
Husband unemployed	836	1 160	1 523	1 600	1 333	1 190	1 061	1 110	1 439	2 808	2 813	2 387
Wife employed	531	736	993	1 023	850	753	679	725	927	1 799	1 783	1 497
Wife unemployed	789	918	1 117	1 129	1 041	1 004	898	902	1 114	1 630	1 697	1 610
Husband employed	694	809	969	991	913	873	772	783	975	1 397	1 455	1 350
Other family member unemployed	959	1 003	1 133	1 129	1 147	1 049	1 010	966	1 243	1 618	1 637	1 579
FAMILIES MAINTAINED BY WOMEN[1]												
With Unemployed Member(s), Total	1 194	1 324	1 504	1 612	1 521	1 539	1 429	1 416	1 666	2 309	2 446	2 498
No member employed	587	643	787	842	829	797	753	701	849	1 244	1 094	1 146
Some member(s) employed	607	681	717	770	692	743	675	714	817	1 065	1 351	1 352
Householder unemployed	522	593	737	791	758	746	688	650	796	1 141	1 227	1 268
Other member(s) employed	102	129	147	162	146	161	132	144	181	225	254	275
Other member(s) unemployed	672	731	767	821	764	793	740	766	870	1 168	1 218	1 229
FAMILIES MAINTAINED BY MEN[1]												
With Unemployed Member(s), Total	331	442	533	610	551	536	516	520	642	1 016	1 102	970
No member employed	139	178	220	239	234	225	215	205	274	482	587	520
Some member(s) employed	192	264	313	371	316	310	301	316	368	535	515	450
Householder unemployed	173	234	303	340	296	301	284	294	385	626	680	575
Other member(s) employed	67	96	129	158	117	122	118	137	164	239	259	231
Other member(s) unemployed	158	208	230	270	255	235	232	226	257	391	422	394

Characteristic	Percent distribution											
	2000	2001	2002	2003	2004	2005	2006	2007	2008	2009	2010	2011
MARRIED-COUPLE FAMILIES												
With Unemployed Member(s), Total	100.0	100.0	100.0	100.0	100.0	100.0	100.0	100.0	100.0	100.0	100.0	100.0
No member employed	15.9	17.2	17.9	18.5	17.5	17.9	17.7	17.2	17.5	20.1	79.4	79.2
Some member(s) employed	84.0	82.8	82.1	81.5	82.5	82.1	82.3	82.8	82.5	79.9	20.6	20.8
Husband unemployed	32.0	37.7	40.4	41.5	37.9	36.7	35.7	37.3	37.9	46.4	45.8	42.8
Wife employed	20.5	23.9	26.3	26.5	24.2	23.2	22.9	24.3	24.4	29.7	29.0	26.9
Wife unemployed	31.0	29.8	29.6	29.3	29.6	31.0	30.3	30.3	29.3	26.9	27.6	28.9
Husband employed	26.8	26.3	25.7	25.7	25.9	26.9	26.0	26.3	25.7	23.1	23.7	24.2
Other family member unemployed	37.0	32.6	30.0	29.3	32.6	32.4	34.0	32.4	32.7	26.7	26.6	28.3
FAMILIES MAINTAINED BY WOMEN[1]												
With Unemployed Member(s), Total	100.0	100.0	100.0	100.0	100.0	100.0	100.0	100.0	100.0	100.0	100.0	100.0
No member employed	49.1	48.6	52.3	52.3	54.5	51.8	52.7	49.5	50.9	53.9	44.7	45.9
Some member(s) employed	50.9	51.4	47.7	47.8	45.5	48.2	47.3	50.5	49.1	46.1	55.3	54.1
Householder unemployed	43.7	44.8	49.0	49.1	49.8	48.5	48.2	45.9	47.8	49.4	50.2	50.8
Other member(s) employed	8.5	9.7	9.8	10.0	9.6	10.5	9.3	10.2	10.9	9.7	10.4	11.0
Other member(s) unemployed	56.3	55.2	51.0	50.9	50.2	51.5	51.8	54.1	52.2	50.6	49.8	49.2
FAMILIES MAINTAINED BY MEN[1]												
With Unemployed Member(s), Total	100.0	100.0	100.0	100.0	100.0	100.0	100.0	100.0	100.0	100.0	100.0	100.0
No member employed	42.0	40.3	41.3	39.2	42.5	42.1	41.7	39.3	42.7	47.4	53.3	53.6
Some member(s) employed	58.0	59.7	58.7	60.8	57.5	57.9	58.3	60.7	57.3	52.6	46.7	46.4
Householder unemployed	52.2	52.9	56.8	55.7	53.7	56.1	55.0	56.6	60.0	61.6	61.7	59.4
Other member(s) employed	20.4	21.7	24.2	25.9	21.3	22.8	22.8	26.3	25.6	23.5	23.5	23.8
Other member(s) unemployed	47.8	47.1	43.2	44.3	46.3	43.9	45.0	43.4	40.0	38.4	38.3	40.6

Note: Detail may not sum to total due to rounding.

[1]No spouse present.

Table 1-23. Employment Status of the Population, by Sex, Marital Status, and Presence and Age of Own Children Under 18 Years, Annual Averages, 2002–2011

(Thousands of people, percent.)

Characteristic	2002			2003			2004			2005			2006		
	Both sexes	Men	Women	Both sexes	Men	Women	Both sexes	Men	Women	Both sexes	Men	Women	Both sexes	Men	Women
With Own Children Under 18 Years, Total															
Civilian noninstitutional population	64 399	28 137	36 263	64 932	28 402	36 530	64 758	28 272	36 486	64 482	28 065	36 417	65 941	29 449	36 492
Civilian labor force	52 566	26 529	26 036	52 727	26 739	25 988	52 288	26 607	25 681	52 056	26 399	25 657	53 590	27 730	25 861
Participation rate	81.6	94.3	71.8	81.2	94.1	71.1	80.7	94.1	70.4	80.7	94.1	70.5	81.3	94.2	70.9
Employed	50 022	25 474	24 549	50 103	25 638	24 466	49 957	25 696	24 261	49 882	25 587	24 294	51 561	26 948	24 614
Employment-population ratio	77.7	90.5	67.7	77.2	90.3	67.0	77.1	90.9	66.5	77.4	91.2	66.7	78.2	91.5	67.4
Full-time workers[1]	42 884	24 644	18 240	42 880	24 762	18 118	42 758	24 794	17 964	42 852	24 713	18 139	44 634	26 033	18 601
Part-time workers[2]	7 138	829	6 308	7 223	876	6 347	7 200	902	6 298	7 029	875	6 155	6 927	914	6 013
Unemployed	2 543	1 056	1 488	2 624	1 101	1 523	2 331	911	1 420	2 174	811	1 363	2 029	782	1 247
Unemployment rate	4.8	4.0	5.7	5.0	4.1	5.9	4.5	3.4	5.5	4.2	3.1	5.3	3.8	2.8	4.8
Married, Spouse Present															
Civilian noninstitutional population	51 947	25 781	26 166	52 476	26 049	26 427	52 109	25 852	26 258	51 519	25 578	25 942	52 930	26 908	26 022
Civilian labor force	42 492	24 425	18 067	42 776	24 638	18 138	42 247	24 449	17 798	41 905	24 215	17 690	43 336	25 494	17 842
Participation rate	81.8	94.7	69.0	81.5	94.6	68.6	81.1	94.6	67.8	81.3	94.7	68.2	81.9	94.7	68.6
Employed	40 867	23 533	17 334	41 128	23 712	17 416	40 847	23 703	17 144	40 614	23 556	17 058	42 134	24 854	17 280
Employment-population ratio	78.7	91.3	66.2	78.4	91.0	65.9	78.4	91.7	65.3	78.8	92.1	65.8	79.6	92.4	66.4
Full-time workers[1]	35 180	22 825	12 356	35 315	22 954	12 360	35 141	22 935	12 206	35 086	22 808	12 278	36 649	24 074	12 575
Part-time workers[2]	5 687	708	4 979	5 813	757	5 056	5 706	768	4 938	5 528	748	4 780	5 485	780	4 705
Unemployed	1 625	893	733	1 648	926	722	1 400	747	653	1 291	659	632	1 202	640	562
Unemployment rate	3.8	3.7	4.1	3.9	3.8	4.0	3.3	3.1	3.7	3.1	2.7	3.6	2.8	2.5	3.1
Other Marital Status[3]															
Civilian noninstitutional population	12 452	2 355	10 096	12 455	2 354	10 102	12 649	2 420	10 229	12 963	2 487	10 475	13 010	2 541	10 470
Civilian labor force	10 073	2 103	7 970	9 950	2 100	7 850	10 042	2 158	7 883	10 151	2 184	7 967	10 255	2 236	8 019
Participation rate	80.9	89.3	78.9	79.9	89.2	77.7	79.4	89.2	77.1	78.3	87.8	76.1	78.8	88.0	76.6
Employed	9 155	1 941	7 215	8 975	1 926	7 050	9 110	1 993	7 117	9 268	2 032	7 236	9 427	2 094	7 333
Employment-population ratio	73.5	82.4	71.5	72.1	81.8	69.8	72.0	82.4	69.6	71.5	81.7	69.1	72.5	82.4	70.0
Full-time workers[1]	7 704	1 820	5 885	7 566	1 807	5 759	7 617	1 859	5 757	7 766	1 905	5 861	7 985	1 960	6 026
Part-time workers[2]	1 451	122	1 329	1 411	118	1 291	1 494	134	1 360	1 502	127	1 375	1 442	134	1 308
Unemployed	918	163	755	976	175	800	931	165	766	883	152	731	827	142	686
Unemployment rate	9.1	7.8	9.5	9.8	8.3	10.2	9.3	7.6	9.7	8.7	7.0	9.2	8.1	6.3	8.5
With Own Children 6 to 17 Years, None Younger															
Civilian noninstitutional population	35 829	15 580	20 250	35 943	15 653	20 290	35 874	15 597	20 277	35 937	15 590	20 348	36 530	16 212	20 318
Civilian labor force	30 371	14 541	15 830	30 362	14 572	15 790	30 182	14 516	15 666	30 068	14 496	15 572	30 675	15 091	15 585
Participation rate	84.8	93.3	78.2	84.5	93.1	77.8	84.1	93.1	77.3	83.7	93.0	76.5	84.0	93.1	76.7
Employed	29 122	14 023	15 099	29 040	14 008	15 032	29 013	14 056	14 957	28 953	14 066	14 887	29 643	14 690	14 952
Employment-population ratio	81.3	90.0	74.6	80.8	89.5	74.1	80.9	90.1	73.8	80.6	90.2	73.2	81.1	90.6	73.6
Full-time workers[1]	25 225	13 586	11 638	25 116	13 558	11 557	25 069	13 597	11 473	25 074	13 606	11 468	25 835	14 206	11 629
Part-time workers[2]	3 898	437	3 461	3 925	450	3 475	3 944	459	3 485	3 880	460	3 419	3 808	485	3 323
Unemployed	1 249	518	731	1 322	564	758	1 170	460	709	1 115	430	684	1 032	400	632
Unemployment rate	4.1	3.6	4.6	4.4	3.9	4.8	3.9	3.2	4.5	3.7	3.0	4.4	3.4	2.7	4.1
With Own Children Under 6 Years															
Civilian noninstitutional population	28 570	12 557	16 013	28 988	12 749	16 240	28 884	12 675	16 210	28 545	12 475	16 070	29 411	13 237	16 174
Civilian labor force	22 194	11 988	10 206	22 365	12 167	10 198	22 106	12 091	10 014	21 988	11 903	10 085	22 915	12 639	10 276
Participation rate	77.7	95.5	63.7	77.2	95.4	62.8	76.5	95.4	61.8	77.0	95.4	62.8	77.9	95.5	63.5
Employed	20 900	11 450	9 450	21 063	11 630	9 433	20 944	11 640	9 304	20 928	11 521	9 407	21 919	12 257	9 661
Employment-population ratio	73.2	91.2	59.0	72.7	91.2	58.1	72.5	91.8	57.4	73.3	92.4	58.5	74.5	92.6	59.7
Full-time workers[1]	17 660	11 058	6 602	17 764	11 203	6 561	17 689	11 197	6 491	17 778	11 107	6 671	18 800	11 828	6 972
Part-time workers[2]	3 240	392	2 848	3 299	426	2 872	3 256	443	2 813	3 150	414	2 736	3 119	430	2 689
Unemployed	1 294	538	757	1 302	538	765	1 162	451	710	1 060	381	678	997	382	615
Unemployment rate	5.8	4.5	7.4	5.8	4.4	7.5	5.3	3.7	7.1	4.8	3.2	6.7	4.3	3.0	6.0
With No Own Children Under 18 Years															
Civilian noninstitutional population	151 715	74 993	76 722	154714	76 510	78 204	156900	77 739	79 160	159751	79 237	80 514	162874	81 156	81 718
Civilian labor force	90 971	49 644	41 327	92 319	50 036	42 284	93 511	50 771	42 740	95 545	51 914	43 631	97 837	53 525	44 312
Participation rate	60.0	66.2	53.9	59.7	65.4	54.1	59.6	65.3	54.0	59.8	65.5	54.2	60.1	66.0	54.2
Employed	85 187	46 154	39 034	86 233	46 294	39 939	87 748	47 282	40 467	90 171	48 709	41 462	92 866	50 554	42 312
Employment-population ratio	56.1	61.5	50.9	55.7	60.5	51.1	55.9	60.8	51.1	56.4	61.5	51.5	57.0	62.3	51.8
Full-time workers[1]	68 574	39 319	29 254	69 073	39 245	29 827	70 244	40 134	30 110	72 515	41 496	31 019	75 054	43 274	31 780
Part-time workers[2]	16 614	6 834	9 779	17 160	7 049	10 111	17 505	7 148	10 357	17 657	7 213	10 444	17 812	7 280	10 532
Unemployed	5 784	3 491	2 293	6 087	3 741	2 345	5 763	3 489	2 274	5 374	3 205	2 169	4 971	2 971	2 000
Unemployment rate	6.4	7.0	5.5	6.6	7.5	5.5	6.2	6.9	5.3	5.6	6.2	5.0	5.1	5.6	4.5

Note: Own children include sons, daughters, stepchildren, and adopted children. Not included are nieces, nephews, grandchildren, and other related and unrelated children. Detail may not sum to total due to rounding.

[1] Usually work 35 hours or more a week at all jobs.
[2] Usually work less than 35 hours a week at all jobs.
[3] Includes never-married, divorced, separated, and widowed persons.

Table 1-23. Employment Status of the Population, by Sex, Marital Status, and Presence and Age of Own Children Under 18 Years, Annual Averages, 2002–2011—*Continued*

(Thousands of people, percent.)

Characteristic	2007 Both sexes	2007 Men	2007 Women	2008 Both sexes	2008 Men	2008 Women	2009 Both sexes	2009 Men	2009 Women	2010 Both sexes	2010 Men	2010 Women	2011 Both sexes	2011 Men	2011 Women
With Own Children Under 18 Years, Total															
Civilian noninstitutional population	66 801	29 684	37 117	65 655	29 142	36 513	64 854	28 778	36 076	64 488	28 463	36 025	63 885	28 143	35 743
Civilian labor force	54 370	28 002	26 368	53 506	27 422	26 085	52 748	26 985	25 763	52 159	26 661	25 499	51 521	26 302	25 219
Participation rate	81.4	94.3	71.0	81.5	94.1	71.4	81.3	93.8	71.4	80.9	93.7	70.8	80.6	93.5	70.6
Employed	52 373	27 216	25 157	51 017	26 380	24 637	48 621	24 989	23 632	47 863	24 653	23 210	47 578	24 619	22 959
Employment-population ratio	78.4	91.7	67.8	77.7	90.5	67.5	75.0	86.8	65.5	74.2	86.6	64.4	74.5	87.5	64.2
Full-time workers[1]	45 336	26 282	19 053	43 967	25 338	18 629	41 003	23 583	17 419	7 581	1 477	6 104	7 303	1 374	5 930
Part-time workers[2]	7 037	933	6 104	7 050	1 042	6 008	7 618	1 406	6 212	74	87	64	74	88	64
Unemployed	1 998	786	1 211	2 490	1 041	1 448	4 128	1 996	2 132	4 296	2 008	2 289	3 943	1 683	2 260
Unemployment rate	3.7	2.8	4.6	4.7	3.8	5.6	7.8	7.4	8.3	8.2	7.5	9.0	7.7	6.4	9.0
Married, Spouse Present															
Civilian noninstitutional population	53 432	27 205	26 227	52 433	26 647	25 786	51 634	26 249	25 385	50 868	25 820	25 049	49 999	25 392	24 607
Civilian labor force	43 824	25 784	18 041	43 137	25 205	17 933	42 424	24 763	17 661	41 600	24 332	17 268	40 783	23 873	16 911
Participation rate	82.0	94.8	68.8	82.3	94.6	69.5	82.2	94.3	69.6	81.8	94.2	68.9	81.6	94.0	68.7
Employed	42 625	25 134	17 492	41 611	24 353	17 258	39 732	23 100	16 632	38 870	22 689	16 181	38 379	22 480	15 900
Employment-population ratio	79.8	92.4	66.7	79.4	91.4	66.9	76.9	88.0	65.5	76.4	87.9	64.6	76.8	88.5	64.6
Full-time workers[1]	37 120	24 332	12 788	36 128	23 444	12 685	33 846	21 871	11 975	5 728	1 245	4 482	5 440	1 158	4 282
Part-time workers[2]	5 505	802	4 704	5 482	909	4 573	5 886	1 229	4 657	76	88	65	77	88	65
Unemployed	1 199	650	549	1 527	852	675	2 692	1 663	1 029	2 730	1 643	1 087	2 404	1 393	1 011
Unemployment rate	2.7	2.5	3.0	3.5	3.4	3.8	6.3	6.7	5.8	6.6	6.8	6.3	5.9	5.8	6.0
Other Marital Status[3]															
Civilian noninstitutional population	13 369	2 479	10 890	13 222	2 495	10 727	13 221	2 529	10 691	13 620	2 643	10 977	13 886	2 751	11 135
Civilian labor force	10 546	2 219	8 328	10 369	2 217	8 152	10 325	2 223	8 102	10 559	2 329	8 230	10 737	2 429	8 308
Participation rate	78.9	89.5	76.5	78.4	88.9	76.0	78.1	87.9	75.8	77.5	88.1	75.0	77.3	88.3	74.6
Employed	9 747	2 082	7 665	9 406	2 027	7 379	8 889	1 889	7 000	8 994	1 964	7 029	9 198	2 139	7 059
Employment-population ratio	72.9	84.0	70.4	71.1	81.3	68.8	67.2	74.7	65.5	66.0	74.3	64.0	66.2	77.8	63.4
Full-time workers[1]	8 216	1 950	6 266	7 838	1 894	5 944	7 157	1 712	5 445	1 853	232	1 621	1 864	216	1 647
Part-time workers[2]	1 531	132	1 400	1 568	133	1 435	1 732	177	1 555	66	74	64	66	78	63
Unemployed	799	137	662	963	190	773	1 436	334	1 103	1 566	365	1 201	1 539	290	1 249
Unemployment rate	7.6	6.2	8.0	9.3	8.6	9.5	13.9	15.0	13.6	14.8	15.7	14.6	14.3	11.9	15.0
With Own Children 6 to 17 Years, None Younger															
Civilian noninstitutional population	36 983	16 384	20 599	36 581	16 256	20 325	35 885	15 982	19 903	35 402	15 639	19 763	35 027	15 431	19 596
Civilian labor force	31 179	15 269	15 910	30 846	15 128	15 718	30 200	14 821	15 379	29 625	14 515	15 110	29 193	14 289	14 904
Participation rate	84.3	93.2	77.2	84.3	93.1	77.3	84.2	92.7	77.3	83.7	92.8	76.5	83.3	92.6	76.1
Employed	30 176	14 866	15 310	29 590	14 588	15 003	28 059	13 775	14 284	27 421	13 482	13 939	27 178	13 422	13 756
Employment-population ratio	81.6	90.7	74.3	80.9	89.7	73.8	78.2	86.2	71.8	77.5	86.2	70.5	77.6	87.0	70.2
Full-time workers[1]	26 288	14 378	11 910	25 733	14 054	11 679	23 864	13 067	10 798	4 182	757	3 425	3 992	686	3 306
Part-time workers[2]	3 888	488	3 400	3 858	534	3 324	4 194	708	3 486	78	86	70	78	87	70
Unemployed	1 003	403	600	1 255	541	715	2 141	1 046	1 095	2 204	1 032	1 172	2 015	867	1 148
Unemployment rate	3.2	2.6	3.8	4.1	3.6	4.5	7.1	7.1	7.1	7.4	7.1	7.8	6.9	6.1	7.7
With Own Children Under 6 Years															
Civilian noninstitutional population	29 818	13 299	16 518	29 074	12 886	16 188	28 969	12 796	16 173	29 086	12 824	16 262	28 858	12 712	16 146
Civilian labor force	23 192	12 733	10 458	22 661	12 293	10 367	22 549	12 164	10 384	22 534	12 146	10 388	22 328	12 013	10 315
Participation rate	77.8	95.7	63.3	77.9	95.4	64.0	77.8	95.1	64.2	77.5	94.7	63.9	77.4	94.5	63.9
Employed	22 197	12 350	9 847	21 426	11 792	9 634	20 562	11 214	9 348	20 442	11 171	9 271	20 400	11 197	9 203
Employment-population ratio	74.4	92.9	59.6	73.7	91.5	59.5	71.0	87.6	57.8	70.3	87.1	57.0	70.7	88.1	57.0
Full-time workers[1]	19 048	11 904	7 143	18 234	11 284	6 950	17 138	10 517	6 622	3 399	720	2 679	3 311	687	2 624
Part-time workers[2]	3 149	446	2 704	3 193	508	2 684	3 424	697	2 726	70	87	57	71	88	57
Unemployed	995	383	611	1 234	501	733	1 987	950	1 036	2 092	975	1 117	1 928	816	1 112
Unemployment rate	4.3	3.0	5.8	5.4	4.1	7.1	8.8	7.8	10.0	9.3	8.0	10.8	8.6	6.8	10.8
With No Own Children Under 18 Years															
Civilian noninstitutional population	165 066	82 489	82 577	168 133	83 971	84 162	170 947	85 358	85 589	173342	86 711	86 631	175 732	88 175	87 558
Civilian labor force	98 754	54 134	44 620	100 780	55 098	45 682	101 394	55 138	46 256	101729	55 324	46 405	102 096	55 673	46 423
Participation rate	59.8	65.6	54.0	59.9	65.6	54.3	59.3	64.6	54.0	58.7	63.8	53.6	58.1	63.1	53.0
Employed	93 674	51 039	42 635	94 346	51 106	43 239	91 257	48 681	42 576	91 201	48 706	42 495	92 291	49 671	42 620
Employment-population ratio	56.7	61.9	51.6	56.1	60.9	51.4	53.4	57.0	49.7	52.6	56.2	49.1	52.5	56.3	48.7
Full-time workers[1]	75 755	43 752	32 003	76 064	43 515	32 549	71 631	40 368	31 263	19 769	8 381	11 387	20 010	8 584	11 426
Part-time workers[2]	17 919	7 286	10 632	18 282	7 592	10 690	19 626	8 313	11 313	53	56	49	52	56	49
Unemployed	5 080	3 095	1 984	6 435	3 992	2 443	10 137	6 457	3 680	10 528	6 618	3 910	9 805	6 002	3 803
Unemployment rate	5.1	5.7	4.4	6.4	7.2	5.3	10.0	11.7	8.0	10.3	12.0	8.4	9.6	10.8	8.2

Note: Own children include sons, daughters, stepchildren, and adopted children. Not included are nieces, nephews, grandchildren, and other related and unrelated children. Detail may not sum to total due to rounding.

[1] Usually work 35 hours or more a week at all jobs.
[2] Usually work less than 35 hours a week at all jobs.
[3] Includes never-married, divorced, separated, and widowed persons.

Table 1-24. Employment Status of Mothers with Own Children Under 3 Years of Age, by Age of Youngest Child and Marital Status, Annual Averages, 2002–2011

(Thousands of people, percent.)

Year and characteristic	Civilian noninstitutional population	Civilian labor force		Employed				Unemployed	
		Total	Percent of population	Total	Percent of population	Full-time workers[1]	Part-time workers[2]	Number	Percent of labor force
2002									
Total Mothers with Own Children Under 3 Years	9 350	5 632	60.2	5 181	55.4	3 513	1 667	451	8.0
2 years	2 949	1 895	64.3	1 758	59.6	1 234	524	137	7.2
1 year	3 310	2 003	60.5	1 852	56.0	1 241	610	151	7.5
Under 1 year	3 091	1 734	56.1	1 571	50.8	1 038	533	163	9.4
Married, Spouse Present with Own Children Under 3 Years	7 073	4 071	57.6	3 869	54.7	2 572	1 297	203	5.0
2 years	2 201	1 333	60.6	1 274	57.9	870	404	59	4.4
1 year	2 509	1 446	57.6	1 379	55.0	902	477	67	4.6
Under 1 year	2 363	1 292	54.7	1 216	51.5	800	416	77	6.0
Other Marital Status with Own Children Under 3 Years[3]	2 278	1 562	68.6	1 313	57.6	941	372	248	15.9
2 years	748	562	75.1	484	64.7	364	120	77	13.7
1 year	802	557	69.5	473	59.0	340	134	84	15.1
Under 1 year	728	443	60.9	356	48.9	237	118	87	19.6
2003									
Total Mothers with Own Children Under 3 Years	9 450	5 563	58.9	5 115	54.1	3 430	1 685	446	8.0
2 years	2 987	1 896	63.5	1 752	58.7	1 205	547	143	7.5
1 year	3 353	1 997	59.6	1 842	54.9	1 223	619	154	7.7
Under 1 year	3 110	1 670	53.7	1 521	48.9	1 002	519	149	8.9
Married, Spouse Present with Own Children Under 3 Years	7 165	4 068	56.8	3 872	54.0	2 529	1 342	197	4.8
2 years	2 243	1 350	60.2	1 281	57.1	853	428	69	5.1
1 year	2 541	1 458	57.4	1 395	54.9	906	488	64	4.4
Under 1 year	2 381	1 260	52.9	1 196	50.2	770	426	64	5.1
Other Marital Status with Own Children Under 3 Years[3]	2 287	1 495	65.4	1 244	54.4	902	341	250	16.7
2 years	744	546	73.4	471	63.3	352	118	75	13.7
1 year	813	539	66.3	448	55.1	317	131	91	16.9
Under 1 year	730	410	56.2	325	44.5	233	92	84	20.5
2004									
Total Mothers with Own Children Under 3 Years	9 345	5 377	57.5	4 964	53.1	3 360	1 604	414	7.7
2 years	2 813	1 746	62.1	1 630	57.9	1 152	477	116	6.6
1 year	3 273	1 906	58.2	1 759	53.7	1 172	587	147	7.7
Under 1 year	3 259	1 725	52.9	1 575	48.3	1 035	540	151	8.7
Married, Spouse Present with Own Children Under 3 Years	7 071	3 910	55.3	3 740	52.9	2 513	1 227	170	4.4
2 years	2 111	1 246	59.0	1 200	56.8	839	361	46	3.7
1 year	2 519	1 401	55.6	1 337	53.1	877	459	65	4.6
Under 1 year	2 441	1 262	51.7	1 203	49.3	797	406	59	4.7
Other Marital Status with Own Children Under 3 Years[3]	2 274	1 467	64.5	1 224	53.8	847	377	243	16.6
2 years	702	499	71.1	430	61.2	314	116	70	13.9
1 year	754	505	66.9	422	56.0	295	127	82	16.3
Under 1 year	818	463	56.6	372	45.4	238	134	91	19.7
2005									
Total Mothers with Own Children Under 3 Years	9 365	5 470	58.4	5 077	54.2	3 501	1 576	393	7.2
2 years	2 845	1 773	62.3	1 654	58.1	1 162	492	119	6.7
1 year	3 287	1 958	59.6	1 823	55.5	1 247	576	135	6.9
Under 1 year	3 233	1 740	53.8	1 600	49.5	1 092	508	140	8.0
Married, Spouse Present with Own Children Under 3 Years	6 951	3 939	56.7	3 776	54.3	2 588	1 188	164	4.2
2 years	2 118	1 268	59.9	1 214	57.3	840	374	55	4.3
1 year	2 435	1 389	57.0	1 337	54.9	901	436	52	3.7
Under 1 year	2 398	1 282	53.5	1 225	51.1	847	378	58	4.5
Other Marital Status with Own Children Under 3 Years[3]	2 414	1 531	63.4	1 301	53.9	913	388	230	15.0
2 years	726	504	69.5	440	60.6	322	118	64	12.7
1 year	852	569	66.8	486	57.0	346	139	83	14.6
Under 1 year	836	457	54.7	375	44.9	245	130	82	18.0
2006									
Total Mothers with Own Children Under 3 Years	9 431	5 675	60.2	5 315	56.4	3 751	1 564	360	6.3
2 years	2 864	1 847	64.5	1 746	61.0	1 280	466	101	5.5
1 year	3 318	2 006	60.5	1 883	56.7	1 305	577	123	6.1
Under 1 year	3 248	1 822	56.1	1 686	51.9	1 166	520	136	7.4
Married, Spouse Present with Own Children Under 3 Years	6 998	4 076	58.2	3 933	56.2	2 756	1 177	143	3.5
2 years	2 114	1 305	61.7	1 265	59.8	910	354	40	3.1
1 year	2 494	1 456	58.4	1 404	56.3	962	442	52	3.6
Under 1 year	2 390	1 315	55.0	1 264	52.9	883	381	51	3.9
Other Marital Status with Own Children Under 3 Years[3]	2 433	1 600	65.7	1 382	56.8	996	386	217	13.6
2 years	750	543	72.3	481	64.2	369	112	61	11.3
1 year	824	550	66.7	479	58.1	344	135	71	13.0
Under 1 year	859	507	59.0	422	49.2	283	139	85	16.7

Note: Own children include sons, daughters, stepchildren, and adopted children. Not included are nieces, nephews, grandchildren, and other related and unrelated children. Detail may not sum to total due to rounding. Updated population controls are introduced annually with the release of January data.

[1]Usually work 35 hours or more a week at all jobs.
[2]Usually work less than 35 hours a week at all jobs.
[3]Includes never-married, divorced, separated, and widowed persons.

Table 1-24. Employment Status of Mothers with Own Children Under 3 Years of Age, by Age of Youngest Child and Marital Status, Annual Averages, 2002–2011—*Continued*

(Thousands of people, percent.)

Year and characteristic	Civilian noninsti-tutional population	Civilian labor force						Unemployed	
		Total	Percent of population	Employed				Number	Percent of labor force
				Total	Percent of population	Full-time workers[1]	Part-time workers[2]		
2007									
Total Mothers with Own Children Under 3 Years	9 659	5 721	59.2	5 354	55.4	3 783	1 571	367	6.4
2 years	2 812	1 808	64.3	1 694	60.2	1 225	469	114	6.3
1 year	3 501	2 068	59.1	1 938	55.4	1 350	589	130	6.3
Under 1 year	3 346	1 845	55.1	1 721	51.4	1 208	513	123	6.7
Married, Spouse Present with Own Children Under 3 Years	7 018	4 027	57.4	3 888	55.4	2 730	1 157	140	3.5
2 years	2 076	1 281	61.7	1 230	59.2	881	349	51	4.0
1 year	2 536	1 433	56.5	1 388	54.7	954	434	46	3.2
Under 1 year	2 406	1 313	54.6	1 270	52.8	896	374	43	3.3
Other Marital Status with Own Children Under 3 Years[3]	2 641	1 694	64.1	1 466	55.5	1 052	414	227	13.4
2 years	736	528	71.6	464	63.1	344	120	63	12.0
1 year	965	635	65.8	551	57.1	396	155	84	13.2
Under 1 year	940	531	56.5	451	48.0	312	139	80	15.1
2008									
Total Mothers with Own Children Under 3 Years	9 595	5 792	60.4	5 354	55.8	3 782	1 573	438	7.6
2 years	2 934	1 852	63.1	1 734	59.1	1 264	470	118	6.4
1 year	3 342	2 069	61.9	1 905	57.0	1 337	568	164	7.9
Under 1 year	3 319	1 871	56.4	1 715	51.7	1 180	535	156	8.4
Married, Spouse Present with Own Children Under 3 Years	6 868	4 035	58.7	3 848	56.0	2 717	1 132	186	4.6
2 years	2 088	1 255	60.1	1 206	57.8	871	335	49	3.9
1 year	2 414	1 450	60.1	1 380	57.2	970	410	70	4.8
Under 1 year	2 366	1 330	56.2	1 263	53.4	875	388	67	5.0
Other Marital Status with Own Children Under 3 Years[3]	2 727	1 758	64.4	1 506	55.2	1 065	441	252	14.3
2 years	847	597	70.5	528	62.4	393	135	69	11.5
1 year	928	619	66.7	525	56.6	367	159	94	15.1
Under 1 year	953	542	56.8	452	47.5	305	147	89	16.5
2009									
Total Mothers with Own Children Under 3 Years	9 476	5 787	61.1	5 191	54.8	3 626	1 565	595	10.3
2 years	2 848	1 855	65.1	1 693	59.4	1 195	498	162	8.7
1 year	3 398	2 104	61.9	1 880	55.3	1 314	566	224	10.6
Under 1 year	3 231	1 828	56.6	1 619	50.1	1 117	502	209	11.4
Married, Spouse Present with Own Children Under 3 Years	6 784	4 047	59.7	3 780	55.7	2 657	1 123	267	6.6
2 years	2 053	1 288	62.7	1 208	58.8	858	350	80	6.2
1 year	2 425	1 465	60.4	1 369	56.4	963	406	96	6.6
Under 1 year	2 306	1 293	56.1	1 204	52.2	836	368	90	7.0
Other Marital Status with Own Children Under 3 Years[3]	2 693	1 740	64.6	1 411	52.4	969	442	328	18.9
2 years	795	567	71.3	485	61.0	337	148	82	14.4
1 year	973	639	65.6	511	52.5	351	160	127	20.0
Under 1 year	925	534	57.8	415	44.9	281	134	119	22.3
2010									
Total Mothers with Own Children Under 3 Years	9 503	5 770	60.7	5 114	53.8	3 570	1 543	656	11.4
2 years	2 968	1 908	64.3	1 708	57.5	1 200	509	199	10.5
1 year	3 351	2 062	61.5	1 815	54.2	1 243	572	246	12.0
Under 1 year	3 184	1 800	56.5	1 590	49.9	1 128	462	210	11.7
Married, Spouse Present with Own Children Under 3 Years	6 642	3 941	59.3	3 670	55.3	2 596	1 074	271	6.9
2 years	2 055	1 275	62.1	1 195	58.2	841	354	80	6.3
1 year	2 344	1 403	59.8	1 301	55.5	896	405	101	7.2
Under 1 year	3 184	1 800	56.5	1 590	49.9	1 128	462	210	11.7
Other Marital Status with Own Children Under 3 Years[3]	2 862	1 828	63.9	1 444	50.5	974	470	385	21.0
2 years	914	633	69.2	514	56.2	359	155	119	18.8
1 year	1 007	659	65.5	514	51.0	346	168	145	22.0
Under 1 year	941	537	57.0	416	44.2	269	147	121	22.5
2011									
Total Mothers with Own Children Under 3 Years	9 259	5 613	60.6	4 977	53.8	3 486	1 492	635	11.3
2 years	2 893	1 848	63.9	1 645	56.9	1 169	476	202	11.0
1 year	3 353	2 083	62.1	1 844	55.0	1 296	548	239	11.5
Under 1 year	3 013	1 682	55.8	1 488	49.4	1 021	467	194	11.5
Married, Spouse Present with Own Children Under 3 Years	6 488	3 854	59.4	3 603	55.5	2 594	1 009	251	6.5
2 years	1 999	1 220	61.0	1 138	56.9	822	316	82	6.7
1 year	2 381	1 434	60.2	1 342	56.4	967	375	92	6.4
Under 1 year	2 109	1 200	56.9	1 123	53.2	805	318	77	6.4
Other Marital Status with Own Children Under 3 Years[3]	2 771	1 759	63.5	1 375	49.6	892	483	384	21.8
2 years	894	628	70.3	508	56.8	347	161	120	19.2
1 year	973	649	66.8	502	51.6	329	173	147	22.6
Under 1 year	905	482	53.2	365	40.3	216	149	117	24.2

Note: Own children include sons, daughters, stepchildren, and adopted children. Not included are nieces, nephews, grandchildren, and other related and unrelated children. Detail may not sum to total due to rounding. Updated population controls are introduced annually with the release of January data.

[1] Usually work 35 hours or more a week at all jobs.
[2] Usually work less than 35 hours a week at all jobs.
[3] Includes never-married, divorced, separated, and widowed persons.

UNEMPLOYMENT

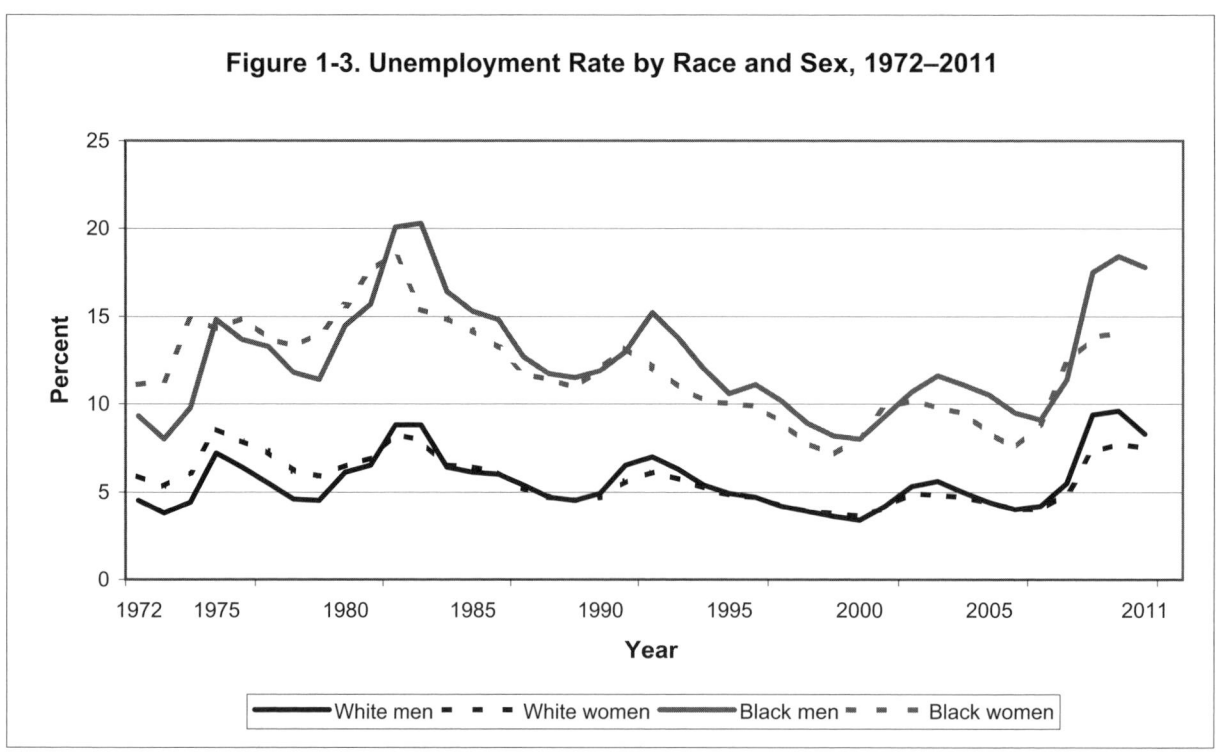

Figure 1-3. Unemployment Rate by Race and Sex, 1972–2011

The unemployment rate declined from 9.6 percent in 2010 to 8.9 percent in 2011. The unemployment rate continued to be substantially higher for men (9.4 percent) than for women (8.5 percent). All racial and ethnic groups experienced an decrease in unemployment in 2011. Black men had the highest unemployment rate at 17.8 percent followed by Black women with an unemployment rate of 14.1 percent. From 2010 to 2011, the unemployment rate decreased by 0.2 percent for Blacks and 0.8 percent for Whites. (See Table 1-27.)

OTHER HIGHLIGHTS

- While the unemployment rate decreased for every age group in 2011, the disparity in unemployment rates among age groups continued to be substantial as younger workers experienced much higher levels of unemployment. In 2011, the unemployment rate for those age 16 to 19 years was 24.4 percent, while it was only 6.6 percent for those age 55 to 64 years and 6.5 percent for those age 65 years and over. (See Table 1-27.)

- Among the major industries, construction had the highest unemployment rate at 16.4 percent, followed by agriculture and private wage salary workers (12.5 percent) and leisure and hospitality workers (11.6 percent). Government had the lowest unemployment rate at 4.7 percent. (See Table 1-29.)

- Although unemployment declined in 2011, the median duration of unemployment remained steady at 21.4 weeks. (See Table 1-30.)

- In 2011, unemployment rates ranged from a low of 3.5 percent in North Dakota to a high of 13.5 percent in Nevada. (See Table 1-5.)

Table 1-25. Unemployment Rate, by Selected Characteristics, 1948–2011

(Unemployment as a percent of civilian labor force.)

Year	All civilian workers	Both sexes, 16 to 19 years	Men, 20 years and over	Women, 20 years and over	White[1]	Black[1]	Asian[1]	Hispanic[2]	Men Single, never married	Men Married, spouse present	Men Widowed, divorced, or separated	Women Single, never married	Women Married, spouse present	Women Widowed, divorced, or separated
1948	3.8	9.2	3.2	3.6	...	...	...	...	...	...	...	...	...	...
1949	5.9	13.4	5.4	5.3	...	...	...	...	...	...	...	...	...	...
1950	5.3	12.2	4.7	5.1	...	...	...	...	...	...	...	...	...	...
1951	3.3	8.2	2.5	4.0	...	...	...	...	...	...	...	...	...	...
1952	3.0	8.5	2.4	3.2	...	...	...	...	...	...	...	...	...	...
1953	2.9	7.6	2.5	2.9	...	...	...	...	...	...	...	...	...	...
1954	5.5	12.6	4.9	5.5	5.0	...	...	...	...	...	...	...	...	...
1955	4.4	11.0	3.8	4.4	3.9	...	...	...	8.6	2.6	7.1	5.0	3.7	5.0
1956	4.1	11.1	3.4	4.2	3.6	...	...	...	7.7	2.3	6.2	5.3	3.6	5.0
1957	4.3	11.6	3.6	4.1	3.8	...	...	...	9.2	2.8	6.8	5.6	4.3	4.7
1958	6.8	15.9	6.2	6.1	6.1	...	...	...	13.3	5.1	11.2	7.4	6.5	6.7
1959	5.5	14.6	4.7	5.2	4.8	...	...	...	11.6	3.6	8.6	7.1	5.2	6.2
1960	5.5	14.7	4.7	5.1	5.0	...	...	...	11.7	3.7	8.4	7.5	5.2	5.9
1961	6.7	16.8	5.7	6.3	6.0	...	...	...	13.1	4.6	10.3	8.7	6.4	7.4
1962	5.5	14.7	4.6	5.4	4.9	...	...	...	11.2	3.6	9.9	7.9	5.4	6.4
1963	5.7	17.2	4.5	5.4	5.0	...	...	...	12.4	3.4	9.6	8.9	5.4	6.7
1964	5.2	16.2	3.9	5.2	4.6	...	...	...	11.5	2.8	8.9	8.7	5.1	6.4
1965	4.5	14.8	3.2	4.5	4.1	...	...	...	10.1	2.4	7.2	8.2	4.5	5.4
1966	3.8	12.8	2.5	3.8	3.4	...	...	...	8.6	1.9	5.5	7.9	3.7	4.7
1967	3.8	12.9	2.3	4.2	3.4	...	...	...	8.3	1.8	4.9	7.5	4.5	4.6
1968	3.6	12.7	2.2	3.8	3.2	...	...	...	8.0	1.6	4.2	7.6	3.9	4.2
1969	3.5	12.2	2.1	3.7	3.1	...	...	...	8.0	1.5	4.0	7.3	3.9	4.0
1970	4.9	15.3	3.5	4.8	4.5	...	...	...	11.2	2.6	6.4	9.0	4.9	5.2
1971	5.9	16.9	4.4	5.7	5.4	...	...	...	13.2	3.2	7.4	10.5	5.7	6.3
1972	5.6	16.2	4.0	5.4	5.1	10.4	...	...	12.4	2.8	7.0	10.1	5.4	6.1
1973	4.9	14.5	3.3	4.9	4.3	9.4	...	7.5	10.4	2.3	5.4	9.4	4.7	5.8
1974	5.6	16.0	3.8	5.5	5.0	10.5	...	8.1	11.8	2.7	6.2	10.5	5.3	6.3
1975	8.5	19.9	6.8	8.0	7.8	14.8	...	12.2	16.1	5.1	11.0	13.0	7.9	8.9
1976	7.7	19.0	5.9	7.4	7.0	14.0	...	11.5	14.9	4.2	9.8	12.1	7.1	8.7
1977	7.1	17.8	5.2	7.0	6.2	14.0	...	10.1	13.5	3.6	8.2	12.1	6.5	7.9
1978	6.1	16.4	4.3	6.0	5.2	12.8	...	9.1	11.7	2.8	6.6	10.9	5.5	6.9
1979	5.8	16.1	4.2	5.7	5.1	12.3	...	8.3	11.1	2.8	6.5	10.4	5.1	6.7
1980	7.1	17.8	5.9	6.4	6.3	14.3	...	10.1	13.6	4.2	8.6	10.9	5.8	7.2
1981	7.6	19.6	6.3	6.8	6.7	15.6	...	10.4	14.6	4.3	9.1	11.9	6.0	8.1
1982	9.7	23.2	8.8	8.3	8.6	18.9	...	13.8	17.7	6.5	12.4	13.6	7.4	9.5
1983	9.6	22.4	8.9	8.1	8.4	19.5	...	13.7	17.3	6.5	13.0	13.1	7.0	9.9
1984	7.5	18.9	6.6	6.8	6.5	15.9	...	10.7	13.5	4.6	9.4	11.1	5.7	8.4
1985	7.2	18.6	6.2	6.6	6.2	15.1	...	10.5	12.7	4.3	9.2	10.7	5.6	8.3
1986	7.0	18.3	6.1	6.2	6.0	14.5	...	10.6	12.2	4.4	8.8	10.7	5.2	7.7
1987	6.2	16.9	5.4	5.4	5.3	13.0	...	8.8	11.1	3.9	7.6	9.5	4.3	7.0
1988	5.5	15.3	4.8	4.9	4.7	11.7	...	8.2	9.9	3.3	7.0	8.6	3.9	6.3
1989	5.3	15.0	4.5	4.7	4.5	11.4	...	8.0	9.6	3.0	6.3	8.4	3.7	5.9
1990	5.6	15.5	5.0	4.9	4.8	11.4	...	8.2	10.1	3.4	6.9	8.7	3.8	6.0
1991	6.8	18.7	6.4	5.7	6.1	12.5	...	10.0	12.4	4.4	9.0	10.1	4.5	6.9
1992	7.5	20.1	7.1	6.3	6.6	14.2	...	11.6	13.2	5.1	9.8	10.8	5.0	7.6
1993	6.9	19.0	6.4	5.9	6.1	13.0	...	10.8	12.4	4.4	9.0	10.3	4.6	7.3
1994	6.1	17.6	5.4	5.4	5.3	11.5	...	9.9	11.0	3.7	7.4	9.7	4.1	6.6
1995	5.6	17.3	4.8	4.9	4.9	10.4	...	9.3	10.1	3.3	6.9	9.1	3.9	5.9
1996	5.4	16.7	4.6	4.8	4.7	10.5	...	8.9	10.0	3.0	6.5	9.1	3.6	5.7
1997	4.9	16.0	4.2	4.4	4.2	10.0	...	7.7	9.2	2.7	5.8	8.8	3.1	5.2
1998	4.5	14.6	3.7	4.1	3.9	8.9	...	7.2	8.5	2.4	4.8	7.8	2.9	4.9
1999	4.2	13.9	3.5	3.8	3.7	8.0	...	6.4	7.8	2.2	4.6	7.4	2.7	4.5
2000	4.0	13.1	3.3	3.6	3.5	7.6	3.6	5.7	7.6	2.0	4.3	6.8	2.7	4.2
2001	4.7	14.7	4.2	4.1	4.2	8.6	4.5	6.6	8.9	2.7	5.1	7.7	3.1	4.7
2002	5.8	16.5	5.3	5.1	5.1	10.2	5.9	7.5	10.3	3.6	6.8	8.9	3.7	6.1
2003	6.0	17.5	5.6	5.1	5.2	10.8	6.0	7.7	11.0	3.8	7.3	9.1	3.7	6.1
2004	5.5	17.0	5.0	4.9	4.8	10.4	4.4	7.0	10.5	3.1	6.3	8.7	3.5	5.9
2005	5.1	16.6	4.4	4.6	4.4	10.0	4.0	6.0	9.5	2.8	5.6	8.3	3.3	5.4
2006	4.6	15.4	4.0	4.1	4.0	8.9	3.0	5.2	8.6	2.4	5.2	7.7	2.9	4.9
2007	4.6	15.7	4.1	4.0	4.1	8.3	3.2	5.6	8.8	2.5	5.3	7.2	2.8	5.0
2008	5.8	18.7	5.4	4.9	5.2	10.1	4.0	7.6	11.0	3.4	7.1	8.5	3.6	5.9
2009	9.3	24.3	9.6	7.5	8.5	14.8	7.3	12.1	16.3	6.6	12.8	12.0	5.5	9.2
2010	9.6	25.9	9.8	8.0	8.7	16.0	7.5	12.5	16.5	6.8	12.8	12.8	5.9	9.6
2011	8.9	24.4	8.7	7.9	7.9	15.8	7.0	11.5	15.1	5.8	11.1	12.5	5.6	9.7

Note: See notes and definitions for information on historical comparability.

[1]Beginning in 2003, persons who selected this race group only; persons who selected more than one race group are not included. Prior to 2003, persons who reported more than one race group were included in the group they identified as their main race.
[2]May be of any race.
... = Not available.

Table 1-26. Unemployed Persons, by Age, Sex, Race, and Hispanic Origin, 1948–2011

(Thousands of people.)

Race, Hispanic origin, sex, and year	16 years and over	16 to 19 years			20 years and over						
		Total	16 to 17 years	18 to 19 years	Total	20 to 24 years	25 to 34 years	35 to 44 years	45 to 54 years	55 to 64 years	65 years and over
ALL RACES											
Both Sexes											
1948	2 276	409	180	228	1 869	455	457	347	290	226	93
1949	3 637	576	238	337	3 060	680	776	603	471	384	146
1950	3 288	513	226	287	2 776	561	702	530	478	368	137
1951	2 055	336	168	168	1 718	273	435	354	318	238	103
1952	1 883	345	180	165	1 539	268	389	325	274	195	86
1953	1 834	307	150	157	1 529	256	379	325	280	218	70
1954	3 532	501	221	247	3 032	504	793	680	548	374	132
1955	2 852	450	211	239	2 403	396	577	521	436	355	120
1956	2 750	478	231	247	2 274	395	554	476	429	311	109
1957	2 859	497	230	266	2 362	430	573	499	448	300	111
1958	4 602	678	299	379	3 923	701	993	871	731	472	154
1959	3 740	654	301	354	3 085	543	726	673	603	405	135
1960	3 852	712	325	387	3 140	583	752	671	614	396	122
1961	4 714	828	363	465	3 886	723	890	850	751	516	159
1962	3 911	721	312	409	3 191	636	712	688	605	411	141
1963	4 070	884	420	462	3 187	658	732	674	589	410	126
1964	3 786	872	436	437	2 913	660	607	605	543	378	117
1965	3 366	874	411	463	2 491	557	529	546	436	322	103
1966	2 875	837	395	441	2 041	446	441	426	369	265	92
1967	2 975	839	400	438	2 140	511	480	422	383	256	86
1968	2 817	838	414	426	1 978	543	443	371	314	219	88
1969	2 832	853	436	416	1 978	560	453	358	320	216	72
1970	4 093	1 106	537	569	2 987	866	718	515	476	309	104
1971	5 016	1 262	596	665	3 755	1 130	933	630	573	381	109
1972	4 882	1 308	633	676	3 573	1 132	878	576	510	368	111
1973	4 365	1 235	634	600	3 130	1 008	866	451	430	290	88
1974	5 156	1 422	699	722	3 733	1 212	1 044	559	498	321	99
1975	7 929	1 767	799	968	6 161	1 865	1 776	951	893	520	155
1976	7 406	1 719	796	924	5 687	1 714	1 710	849	758	510	147
1977	6 991	1 663	781	881	5 330	1 629	1 650	785	666	450	147
1978	6 202	1 583	796	787	4 620	1 483	1 422	694	552	345	123
1979	6 137	1 555	739	816	4 583	1 442	1 446	705	540	346	104
1980	7 637	1 669	778	890	5 969	1 835	2 024	940	676	399	94
1981	8 273	1 763	781	981	6 510	1 976	2 211	1 065	715	444	98
1982	10 678	1 977	831	1 145	8 701	2 392	3 037	1 552	966	647	107
1983	10 717	1 829	753	1 076	8 888	2 330	3 078	1 650	1 039	677	114
1984	8 539	1 499	646	854	7 039	1 838	2 374	1 335	828	566	97
1985	8 312	1 468	662	806	6 844	1 738	2 341	1 340	813	518	93
1986	8 237	1 454	665	789	6 783	1 651	2 390	1 371	790	489	91
1987	7 425	1 347	648	700	6 077	1 453	2 129	1 281	723	412	78
1988	6 701	1 226	573	653	5 475	1 261	1 929	1 166	657	375	87
1989	6 528	1 194	537	657	5 333	1 218	1 851	1 159	637	379	91
1990	7 047	1 212	527	685	5 835	1 299	1 995	1 328	723	386	105
1991	8 628	1 359	587	772	7 269	1 573	2 447	1 719	946	473	113
1992	9 613	1 427	641	787	8 186	1 649	2 702	1 976	1 138	589	132
1993	8 940	1 365	606	759	7 575	1 514	2 395	1 896	1 121	541	108
1994	7 996	1 320	624	696	6 676	1 373	2 067	1 627	971	485	153
1995	7 404	1 346	652	695	6 058	1 244	1 841	1 549	844	425	153
1996	7 236	1 306	617	689	5 929	1 239	1 757	1 505	883	406	139
1997	6 739	1 271	589	683	5 467	1 152	1 571	1 418	830	369	127
1998	6 210	1 205	573	632	5 005	1 081	1 419	1 258	782	343	122
1999	5 880	1 162	544	618	4 718	1 042	1 278	1 154	753	367	124
2000	5 692	1 081	502	579	4 611	1 022	1 207	1 133	762	355	132
2001	6 801	1 162	531	632	5 638	1 209	1 498	1 355	989	458	129
2002	8 378	1 253	540	714	7 124	1 430	1 890	1 691	1 315	635	163
2003	8 774	1 251	545	706	7 523	1 495	1 960	1 815	1 356	713	183
2004	8 149	1 208	554	653	6 942	1 431	1 784	1 578	1 288	682	179
2005	7 591	1 186	541	645	6 405	1 335	1 661	1 400	1 195	630	184
2006	7 001	1 119	509	610	5 882	1 234	1 521	1 279	1 094	595	159
2007	7 078	1 101	485	616	5 976	1 241	1 544	1 225	1 135	642	190
2008	8 924	1 285	563	722	7 639	1 545	1 949	1 604	1 473	803	264
2009	14 265	1 552	576	976	12 712	2 207	3 284	2 722	2 592	1 487	421
2010	14 825	1 528	582	945	13 297	2 329	3 386	2 703	2 769	1 660	449
2011	13 747	1 400	519	881	12 348	2 234	3 187	2 389	2 493	1 579	465

Table 1-26. Unemployed Persons, by Age, Sex, Race, and Hispanic Origin, 1948–2011—*Continued*

(Thousands of people.)

Race, Hispanic origin, sex, and year	16 years and over	16 to 19 years			20 years and over						
		Total	16 to 17 years	18 to 19 years	Total	20 to 24 years	25 to 34 years	35 to 44 years	45 to 54 years	55 to 64 years	65 years and over
ALL RACES											
Men											
1948	1 559	256	113	142	1 305	324	289	233	201	177	81
1949	2 572	353	145	207	2 219	485	539	414	347	310	125
1950	2 239	318	139	179	1 922	377	467	348	327	286	117
1951	1 221	191	102	89	1 029	155	241	192	193	162	87
1952	1 185	205	116	89	980	155	233	192	182	145	73
1953	1 202	184	94	90	1 019	152	236	208	196	167	60
1954	2 344	310	142	168	2 035	327	517	431	372	275	112
1955	1 854	274	134	140	1 580	248	353	328	285	265	102
1956	1 711	269	134	135	1 442	240	348	278	270	216	90
1957	1 841	300	140	159	1 541	283	349	304	302	220	83
1958	3 098	416	185	231	2 681	478	685	552	492	349	124
1959	2 420	398	191	207	2 022	343	484	407	390	287	112
1960	2 486	426	200	225	2 060	369	492	415	392	294	96
1961	2 997	479	221	258	2 518	458	585	507	473	375	122
1962	2 423	408	188	220	2 016	381	445	404	382	300	103
1963	2 472	501	248	252	1 971	396	445	386	358	290	97
1964	2 205	487	257	230	1 718	384	345	324	319	263	85
1965	1 914	479	247	232	1 435	311	292	283	253	221	75
1966	1 551	432	220	212	1 120	221	239	219	196	179	65
1967	1 508	448	241	207	1 060	235	219	185	199	163	60
1968	1 419	426	234	193	993	258	205	171	165	132	61
1969	1 403	440	244	196	963	270	205	155	157	127	48
1970	2 238	599	306	294	1 638	479	391	253	247	198	71
1971	2 789	693	346	347	2 097	640	513	320	313	239	71
1972	2 659	711	357	355	1 948	628	466	284	272	227	73
1973	2 275	653	352	300	1 624	528	439	211	219	171	57
1974	2 714	757	394	362	1 957	649	546	266	250	183	63
1975	4 442	966	445	521	3 476	1 081	986	507	499	302	103
1976	4 036	939	443	496	3 098	951	914	431	411	296	94
1977	3 667	874	421	453	2 794	877	869	373	326	252	97
1978	3 142	813	426	388	2 328	768	691	314	277	198	81
1979	3 120	811	393	418	2 308	744	699	329	272	196	67
1980	4 267	913	429	485	3 353	1 076	1 137	482	357	243	58
1981	4 577	962	431	531	3 615	1 144	1 213	552	390	261	55
1982	6 179	1 090	469	621	5 089	1 407	1 791	879	550	393	69
1983	6 260	1 003	408	595	5 257	1 369	1 822	947	613	433	73
1984	4 744	812	348	464	3 932	1 023	1 322	728	450	356	53
1985	4 521	806	363	443	3 715	944	1 244	706	459	307	55
1986	4 530	779	355	424	3 751	899	1 291	763	440	301	58
1987	4 101	732	353	379	3 369	779	1 169	689	426	258	49
1988	3 655	667	311	356	2 987	676	1 040	617	366	240	49
1989	3 525	658	303	355	2 867	660	953	619	351	234	49
1990	3 906	667	283	384	3 239	715	1 092	711	413	249	59
1991	4 946	751	317	433	4 195	911	1 375	990	550	305	64
1992	5 523	806	357	449	4 717	951	1 529	1 118	675	378	67
1993	5 055	768	342	426	4 287	865	1 338	1 049	636	336	64
1994	4 367	740	342	398	3 627	768	1 113	855	522	281	88
1995	3 983	744	352	391	3 239	673	961	815	464	233	94
1996	3 880	733	347	387	3 146	675	903	786	484	223	76
1997	3 577	694	321	373	2 882	636	772	732	457	217	69
1998	3 266	686	330	355	2 580	583	699	609	420	201	69
1999	3 066	633	295	338	2 433	562	624	571	403	203	70
2000	2 975	599	281	317	2 376	547	602	557	398	189	83
2001	3 690	650	300	350	3 040	688	756	714	536	272	74
2002	4 597	700	301	399	3 896	792	1 023	897	725	373	87
2003	4 906	697	291	407	4 209	841	1 097	988	764	412	107
2004	4 456	664	292	372	3 791	811	980	839	684	373	104
2005	4 059	667	300	367	3 392	775	844	715	624	331	102
2006	3 753	622	271	352	3 131	705	810	642	569	318	88
2007	3 882	623	263	360	3 259	721	856	634	591	349	108
2008	5 033	736	312	425	4 297	920	1 119	875	804	425	153
2009	8 453	898	317	581	7 555	1 329	1 988	1 600	1 558	840	241
2010	8 626	863	315	548	7 763	1 398	1 993	1 534	1 614	962	262
2011	7 684	786	267	520	6 898	1 275	1 795	1 316	1 370	882	261

Table 1-26. Unemployed Persons, by Age, Sex, Race, and Hispanic Origin, 1948–2011—*Continued*

(Thousands of people.)

Race, Hispanic origin, sex, and year	16 years and over	16 to 19 years			20 years and over						
		Total	16 to 17 years	18 to 19 years	Total	20 to 24 years	25 to 34 years	35 to 44 years	45 to 54 years	55 to 64 years	65 years and over
ALL RACES											
Women											
1948	717	153	67	86	564	131	168	114	89	49	12
1949	1 065	223	93	130	841	195	237	189	124	74	21
1950	1 049	195	87	108	854	184	235	182	151	82	20
1951	834	145	66	79	689	118	194	162	125	76	16
1952	698	140	64	76	559	113	156	133	92	50	13
1953	632	123	56	67	510	104	143	117	84	51	10
1954	1 188	191	79	79	997	177	276	249	176	99	20
1955	998	176	77	99	823	148	224	193	151	90	18
1956	1 039	209	97	112	832	155	206	198	159	95	19
1957	1 018	197	90	107	821	147	224	195	146	80	28
1958	1 504	262	114	148	1 242	223	308	319	239	123	30
1959	1 320	256	110	147	1 063	200	242	266	213	118	23
1960	1 366	286	125	162	1 080	214	260	256	222	102	26
1961	1 717	349	142	207	1 368	265	305	343	278	141	37
1962	1 488	313	124	189	1 175	255	267	284	223	111	38
1963	1 598	383	172	210	1 216	262	287	288	231	120	29
1964	1 581	385	179	207	1 195	276	262	281	224	115	32
1965	1 452	395	164	231	1 056	246	237	263	183	101	28
1966	1 324	405	175	229	921	225	202	207	173	86	27
1967	1 468	391	159	231	1 078	277	261	237	184	93	26
1968	1 397	412	180	233	985	285	238	200	149	87	27
1969	1 429	413	192	220	1 015	290	248	203	163	89	24
1970	1 855	506	231	275	1 349	387	327	262	229	111	33
1971	2 227	568	250	318	1 658	489	420	310	260	142	38
1972	2 222	598	276	322	1 625	503	413	293	237	141	38
1973	2 089	583	282	301	1 507	480	427	240	212	119	31
1974	2 441	665	305	360	1 777	564	497	294	248	137	36
1975	3 486	802	355	447	2 684	783	791	444	395	219	52
1976	3 369	780	352	429	2 588	763	795	417	346	214	53
1977	3 324	789	361	428	2 535	752	782	412	340	198	50
1978	3 061	769	370	399	2 292	714	731	381	275	148	43
1979	3 018	743	346	396	2 276	697	748	375	268	150	38
1980	3 370	755	349	407	2 615	760	886	459	318	155	36
1981	3 696	800	350	450	2 895	833	998	513	325	184	43
1982	4 499	886	362	524	3 613	985	1 246	673	416	254	38
1983	4 457	825	344	481	3 632	961	1 255	703	427	244	41
1984	3 794	687	298	390	3 107	815	1 052	607	378	211	45
1985	3 791	661	298	363	3 129	794	1 098	634	355	211	39
1986	3 707	675	310	365	3 032	752	1 099	609	350	189	33
1987	3 324	616	295	321	2 709	674	960	592	298	155	30
1988	3 046	558	262	297	2 487	585	889	550	291	136	38
1989	3 003	536	234	302	2 467	558	897	540	286	144	41
1990	3 140	544	243	301	2 596	584	902	617	310	137	46
1991	3 683	608	270	338	3 074	662	1 071	728	396	168	49
1992	4 090	621	283	338	3 469	698	1 173	858	463	210	66
1993	3 885	597	264	333	3 288	648	1 058	847	485	205	45
1994	3 629	580	282	298	3 049	605	954	772	449	204	66
1995	3 421	602	299	303	2 819	571	880	735	381	193	60
1996	3 356	573	270	303	2 783	564	854	720	399	183	63
1997	3 162	577	268	310	2 585	516	800	686	373	152	58
1998	2 944	519	242	277	2 424	498	720	650	362	141	53
1999	2 814	529	249	280	2 285	480	654	584	350	163	54
2000	2 717	483	221	262	2 235	475	604	577	364	165	50
2001	3 111	512	230	282	2 599	521	742	641	453	187	55
2002	3 781	553	238	315	3 228	638	866	795	591	263	76
2003	3 868	554	255	299	3 314	654	863	827	592	302	76
2004	3 694	543	262	281	3 150	619	804	739	605	309	75
2005	3 531	519	240	278	3 013	560	817	685	571	299	82
2006	3 247	496	238	258	2 751	530	711	637	524	277	71
2007	3 196	478	222	256	2 718	520	688	591	544	293	81
2008	3 891	549	251	297	3 342	625	830	730	669	377	111
2009	5 811	654	259	395	5 157	878	1 296	1 121	1 034	647	180
2010	6 199	665	268	397	5 534	931	1 392	1 169	1 156	698	187
2011	6 063	613	252	362	5 450	960	1 392	1 073	1 123	697	204

Table 1-26. Unemployed Persons, by Age, Sex, Race, and Hispanic Origin, 1948–2011—*Continued*

(Thousands of people.)

Race, Hispanic origin, sex, and year	16 years and over	16 to 19 years			20 years and over						
		Total	16 to 17 years	18 to 19 years	Total	20 to 24 years	25 to 34 years	35 to 44 years	45 to 54 years	55 to 64 years	65 years and over
WHITE											
Both Sexes											
1954	2 859	423	191	232	2 436	394	610	540	447	329	115
1955	2 252	373	181	191	1 879	304	412	402	358	300	105
1956	2 159	382	191	191	1 777	297	406	363	355	258	98
1957	2 289	401	195	204	1 888	331	425	401	373	262	98
1958	3 680	541	245	297	3 139	541	756	686	614	405	136
1959	2 946	525	255	270	2 421	406	526	525	496	348	120
1960	3 065	575	273	302	2 490	456	573	520	502	330	109
1961	3 743	669	295	374	3 074	566	668	652	611	438	139
1962	3 052	580	262	318	2 472	488	515	522	485	345	117
1963	3 208	708	350	358	2 500	501	540	518	485	349	107
1964	2 999	708	365	342	2 291	508	441	472	447	323	100
1965	2 691	705	329	374	1 986	437	399	427	358	276	91
1966	2 255	651	315	336	1 604	338	323	336	298	227	80
1967	2 338	635	311	325	1 703	393	360	336	321	221	75
1968	2 226	644	326	318	1 582	422	330	297	269	187	80
1969	2 260	660	351	309	1 601	432	354	294	269	185	66
1970	3 339	871	438	432	2 468	679	570	433	415	275	95
1971	4 085	1 011	491	521	3 074	887	732	517	500	338	100
1972	3 906	1 021	515	506	2 885	887	679	459	439	324	95
1973	3 442	955	513	443	2 486	758	664	358	371	257	77
1974	4 097	1 104	561	544	2 993	925	821	448	427	283	88
1975	6 421	1 413	657	755	5 007	1 474	1 413	774	753	460	136
1976	5 914	1 364	649	715	4 550	1 326	1 329	682	637	448	128
1977	5 441	1 284	636	648	4 157	1 195	1 255	621	569	388	129
1978	4 698	1 189	631	558	3 509	1 059	1 059	543	453	290	104
1979	4 664	1 193	589	603	3 472	1 038	1 068	545	443	290	87
1980	5 884	1 291	625	666	4 593	1 364	1 528	740	550	335	74
1981	6 343	1 374	629	745	4 968	1 449	1 658	827	578	379	77
1982	8 241	1 534	683	851	6 707	1 770	2 283	1 223	796	549	86
1983	8 128	1 387	609	778	6 741	1 678	2 282	1 294	837	563	88
1984	6 372	1 116	510	605	5 256	1 282	1 723	1 036	660	475	81
1985	6 191	1 074	507	567	5 117	1 235	1 695	1 039	642	432	75
1986	6 140	1 070	509	561	5 070	1 149	1 751	1 056	629	407	78
1987	5 501	995	495	500	4 506	1 017	1 527	984	576	333	68
1988	4 944	910	437	473	4 033	874	1 371	890	520	309	69
1989	4 770	863	407	456	3 908	856	1 297	871	503	311	70
1990	5 186	903	401	502	4 283	899	1 401	983	582	330	88
1991	6 560	1 029	461	568	5 532	1 132	1 805	1 330	759	410	96
1992	7 169	1 037	484	553	6 132	1 156	1 967	1 483	915	495	116
1993	6 655	992	468	523	5 663	1 057	1 754	1 411	907	442	92
1994	5 892	960	471	489	4 933	952	1 479	1 184	779	407	132
1995	5 459	952	476	476	4 507	866	1 311	1 161	676	362	131
1996	5 300	939	456	484	4 361	854	1 223	1 117	709	336	122
1997	4 836	912	438	475	3 924	765	1 068	1 035	648	302	106
1998	4 484	876	424	451	3 608	731	978	901	620	276	101
1999	4 273	844	414	430	3 429	720	865	843	595	303	104
2000	4 121	795	386	409	3 326	682	835	817	591	294	107
2001	4 969	845	402	443	4 124	829	1 062	985	761	378	109
2002	6 137	925	407	518	5 212	977	1 340	1 237	1 004	518	137
2003	6 311	909	414	495	5 401	1 012	1 354	1 287	1 025	569	155
2004	5 847	890	414	476	4 957	959	1 211	1 130	953	557	148
2005	5 350	845	391	454	4 505	878	1 106	1 006	884	488	144
2006	5 002	794	375	419	4 208	832	1 029	920	813	480	135
2007	5 143	805	361	444	4 338	851	1 052	902	848	520	164
2008	6 509	947	422	524	5 562	1 087	1 336	1 196	1 094	634	216
2009	10 648	1 157	440	717	9 491	1 556	2 320	2 026	2 012	1 221	355
2010	10 916	1 128	445	683	9 788	1 614	2 358	1 969	2 130	1 344	373
2011	9 889	1 024	391	633	8 865	1 546	2 135	1 678	1 859	1 251	395

Table 1-26. Unemployed Persons, by Age, Sex, Race, and Hispanic Origin, 1948–2011—*Continued*

(Thousands of people.)

Race, Hispanic origin, sex, and year	16 years and over	16 to 19 years			20 years and over						
		Total	16 to 17 years	18 to 19 years	Total	20 to 24 years	25 to 34 years	35 to 44 years	45 to 54 years	55 to 64 years	65 years and over
WHITE											
Men											
1954	1 913	266	125	142	1 647	260	408	341	299	241	98
1955	1 478	232	114	117	1 246	196	260	246	233	223	89
1956	1 366	221	112	108	1 145	186	265	212	225	177	81
1957	1 477	243	118	124	1 234	222	257	239	250	193	73
1958	2 489	333	149	184	2 156	382	525	436	404	299	110
1959	1 903	318	162	156	1 585	256	350	316	320	245	98
1960	1 988	341	167	174	1 647	295	376	330	317	243	86
1961	2 398	384	176	208	2 014	370	442	395	382	318	107
1962	1 915	334	158	176	1 581	300	332	311	308	246	84
1963	1 976	407	211	196	1 569	309	342	297	294	246	80
1964	1 779	400	217	183	1 379	310	262	255	266	216	70
1965	1 556	387	200	186	1 169	254	226	228	206	190	67
1966	1 241	340	178	162	901	172	185	173	160	154	57
1967	1 208	342	186	156	866	185	171	153	167	140	52
1968	1 142	328	185	143	814	206	162	140	142	111	55
1969	1 137	343	198	145	794	214	165	130	134	108	43
1970	1 857	485	255	230	1 372	388	316	212	216	177	64
1971	2 309	562	288	275	1 747	513	418	268	272	211	66
1972	2 173	564	288	276	1 610	506	375	231	237	199	60
1973	1 836	513	284	229	1 323	411	353	166	188	153	51
1974	2 169	584	311	274	1 585	505	434	218	213	161	53
1975	3 627	785	369	416	2 841	871	796	412	411	265	86
1976	3 258	754	368	385	2 504	750	730	346	341	259	78
1977	2 883	672	342	330	2 211	660	682	297	276	213	82
1978	2 411	615	338	277	1 797	558	525	250	227	169	68
1979	2 405	633	319	313	1 773	553	526	253	220	165	56
1980	3 345	716	347	369	2 629	827	884	378	291	206	44
1981	3 580	755	349	406	2 825	869	943	433	317	221	42
1982	4 846	854	387	467	3 991	1 066	1 385	696	460	331	53
1983	4 859	761	328	433	4 098	1 019	1 410	755	497	362	54
1984	3 600	608	280	328	2 992	722	991	572	363	302	42
1985	3 426	592	282	310	2 834	694	931	553	356	257	43
1986	3 433	576	276	299	2 857	645	978	586	349	248	51
1987	3 132	548	272	276	2 584	568	879	536	350	209	43
1988	2 766	499	239	260	2 268	480	777	477	293	200	40
1989	2 636	487	230	257	2 149	476	694	470	280	191	38
1990	2 935	504	214	290	2 431	510	796	530	330	214	51
1991	3 859	575	249	327	3 284	677	1 064	780	438	269	55
1992	4 209	590	270	319	3 620	686	1 155	858	543	318	58
1993	3 828	565	261	305	3 263	619	1 015	793	512	270	53
1994	3 275	540	259	280	2 735	555	827	626	417	236	74
1995	2 999	535	260	275	2 465	483	711	621	371	200	79
1996	2 896	532	260	273	2 363	478	655	592	383	188	67
1997	2 641	502	234	268	2 140	439	553	549	358	182	58
1998	2 431	510	254	257	1 920	405	512	441	342	164	58
1999	2 274	461	223	237	1 813	398	441	419	322	172	61
2000	2 177	446	217	229	1 731	368	428	403	302	162	68
2001	2 754	479	232	247	2 275	494	547	529	413	229	64
2002	3 459	516	228	288	2 943	562	772	672	554	305	77
2003	3 643	518	221	298	3 125	589	798	723	591	333	91
2004	3 282	497	224	274	2 785	560	694	620	516	307	88
2005	2 931	480	220	260	2 450	522	586	536	463	263	81
2006	2 730	449	202	247	2 281	483	567	482	417	259	73
2007	2 869	461	195	266	2 408	501	604	478	447	285	93
2008	3 727	548	231	317	3 179	668	784	662	604	337	124
2009	6 421	675	241	434	5 746	969	1 439	1 208	1 233	695	202
2010	6 476	648	246	402	5 828	995	1 452	1 131	1 249	785	216
2011	5 631	585	208	377	5 046	909	1 237	951	1 030	697	223

Table 1-26. Unemployed Persons, by Age, Sex, Race, and Hispanic Origin, 1948–2011—*Continued*

(Thousands of people.)

Race, Hispanic origin, sex, and year	16 years and over	16 to 19 years			20 years and over						
		Total	16 to 17 years	18 to 19 years	Total	20 to 24 years	25 to 34 years	35 to 44 years	45 to 54 years	55 to 64 years	65 years and over
WHITE											
Women											
1954	946	157	66	90	789	134	202	199	148	88	17
1955	774	141	67	74	633	108	152	156	125	77	16
1956	793	161	79	83	632	111	141	151	130	81	17
1957	812	158	77	80	654	109	168	162	123	69	25
1958	1 191	208	96	113	983	159	231	250	210	106	26
1959	1 043	207	93	114	836	150	176	209	176	103	22
1960	1 077	234	106	128	843	161	197	190	185	87	23
1961	1 345	285	119	166	1 060	196	226	257	229	120	32
1962	1 137	246	104	142	891	188	183	211	177	99	33
1963	1 232	301	139	162	931	192	198	221	191	103	27
1964	1 220	308	148	159	912	198	179	217	181	107	30
1965	1 135	318	129	188	817	183	173	199	152	86	24
1966	1 014	311	137	174	703	166	138	163	138	73	23
1967	1 130	293	125	169	837	209	189	183	154	81	23
1968	1 084	316	141	175	768	216	168	157	127	76	25
1969	1 123	317	153	164	806	218	189	164	135	77	23
1970	1 482	386	183	202	1 096	291	254	221	199	98	31
1971	1 777	449	203	246	1 328	376	314	249	228	126	34
1972	1 733	457	227	230	1 275	381	304	227	202	125	35
1973	1 606	442	228	214	1 164	347	311	192	183	104	26
1974	1 927	519	250	270	1 408	420	387	230	214	122	35
1975	2 794	628	288	340	2 166	602	617	362	342	195	49
1976	2 656	611	280	330	2 045	577	598	336	296	188	49
1977	2 558	612	294	318	1 946	536	573	323	293	175	47
1978	2 287	574	292	281	1 713	500	533	294	226	122	37
1979	2 260	560	270	290	1 699	485	542	293	223	125	32
1980	2 540	576	278	298	1 964	537	645	362	259	129	31
1981	2 762	620	281	339	2 143	580	715	394	261	158	36
1982	3 395	680	296	384	2 715	704	898	527	337	217	33
1983	3 270	626	282	345	2 643	659	872	539	340	201	33
1984	2 772	508	231	277	2 264	559	731	464	297	173	39
1985	2 765	482	225	257	2 283	541	763	486	286	175	32
1986	2 708	495	233	262	2 213	504	773	470	281	159	27
1987	2 369	447	223	224	1 922	449	648	448	227	124	25
1988	2 177	412	198	214	1 766	393	594	413	227	110	30
1989	2 135	376	177	199	1 758	380	603	401	223	120	32
1990	2 251	399	187	212	1 852	389	605	453	251	116	37
1991	2 701	453	212	241	2 248	455	741	550	320	141	41
1992	2 959	447	214	233	2 512	469	811	625	372	177	58
1993	2 827	426	208	219	2 400	438	739	618	395	172	39
1994	2 617	420	211	208	2 197	397	652	558	361	170	58
1995	2 460	418	216	201	2 042	384	600	540	306	162	52
1996	2 404	407	196	211	1 998	376	568	525	326	148	55
1997	2 195	411	204	207	1 784	326	515	486	290	119	49
1998	2 053	365	171	195	1 688	327	467	460	279	112	43
1999	1 999	383	190	193	1 616	322	423	423	273	131	43
2000	1 944	349	168	180	1 595	314	407	414	289	133	39
2001	2 215	366	170	196	1 849	335	515	456	348	150	45
2002	2 678	409	179	230	2 269	415	567	565	449	213	60
2003	2 668	391	194	197	2 276	423	555	564	434	235	64
2004	2 565	393	191	202	2 172	399	516	510	437	250	60
2005	2 419	365	172	193	2 054	356	520	469	421	225	63
2006	2 271	345	173	172	1 927	349	462	437	395	222	62
2007	2 274	344	166	178	1 930	350	448	425	401	235	71
2008	2 782	399	191	207	2 384	419	552	534	489	298	92
2009	4 227	482	199	283	3 745	587	881	818	780	526	153
2010	4 440	480	199	281	3 960	619	906	839	881	559	157
2011	4 257	439	184	255	3 818	637	899	728	829	554	171

Table 1-26. Unemployed Persons, by Age, Sex, Race, and Hispanic Origin, 1948–2011—*Continued*

(Thousands of people.)

Race, Hispanic origin, sex, and year	16 years and over	16 to 19 years			20 years and over						
		Total	16 to 17 years	18 to 19 years	Total	20 to 24 years	25 to 34 years	35 to 44 years	45 to 54 years	55 to 64 years	65 years and over
BLACK											
Both Sexes											
1974	965	297	127	170	666	261	201	95	65	33	10
1975	1 369	330	130	200	1 040	362	321	157	126	54	17
1976	1 334	330	134	195	1 005	350	338	145	101	54	16
1977	1 393	354	135	218	1 040	397	355	140	81	51	16
1978	1 330	360	150	210	972	379	320	127	82	47	17
1979	1 319	333	137	197	986	369	335	137	82	48	15
1980	1 553	343	134	210	1 209	426	433	171	109	53	18
1981	1 731	357	138	219	1 374	483	493	207	119	55	17
1982	2 142	396	130	266	1 747	565	662	278	141	84	17
1983	2 272	392	125	267	1 879	591	700	299	174	95	21
1984	1 914	353	122	230	1 561	504	577	253	138	75	15
1985	1 864	357	135	221	1 507	455	562	254	143	74	18
1986	1 840	347	138	209	1 493	453	564	269	127	69	10
1987	1 684	312	134	178	1 373	397	533	247	124	62	10
1988	1 547	288	121	167	1 259	349	502	230	111	51	15
1989	1 544	300	116	184	1 245	322	494	246	109	53	20
1990	1 565	268	112	156	1 297	349	505	278	106	44	14
1991	1 723	280	105	175	1 443	378	539	318	151	44	13
1992	2 011	324	127	197	1 687	421	610	402	178	64	13
1993	1 844	313	112	201	1 530	387	532	376	153	72	11
1994	1 666	300	127	173	1 366	351	468	346	130	55	16
1995	1 538	325	143	182	1 213	311	423	303	116	42	18
1996	1 592	310	133	177	1 282	327	454	313	127	48	13
1997	1 560	302	123	179	1 258	327	426	307	136	45	16
1998	1 426	281	124	156	1 146	301	366	294	125	45	16
1999	1 309	268	109	159	1 041	273	339	249	121	46	14
2000	1 241	230	96	134	1 011	281	289	254	131	38	20
2001	1 416	260	102	158	1 155	307	340	283	159	52	15
2002	1 693	260	103	156	1 433	365	407	349	215	76	21
2003	1 787	255	93	162	1 532	375	442	385	217	93	20
2004	1 729	241	103	138	1 487	353	441	341	245	86	21
2005	1 700	267	115	152	1 433	358	423	310	222	92	28
2006	1 549	253	102	151	1 296	318	388	276	214	81	19
2007	1 445	235	98	138	1 210	300	367	237	208	79	19
2008	1 788	246	98	148	1 542	355	458	301	275	117	36
2009	2 606	288	99	189	2 319	488	717	489	415	168	42
2010	2 852	291	97	194	2 562	539	776	534	461	204	47
2011	2 831	267	88	179	2 564	531	801	529	444	212	47
BLACK											
Men											
1974	494	159	75	82	336	129	103	41	35	19	8
1975	741	170	71	100	571	195	169	83	78	33	13
1976	698	170	69	103	528	185	166	73	60	32	13
1977	698	187	73	114	512	197	170	63	40	31	12
1978	641	180	80	101	462	185	148	53	40	24	11
1979	636	164	68	97	473	174	152	66	44	27	10
1980	815	179	72	108	636	222	222	88	60	32	12
1981	891	188	73	115	703	248	245	102	65	32	10
1982	1 167	213	72	141	954	304	355	154	74	54	12
1983	1 213	211	70	142	1 002	313	358	162	96	59	14
1984	1 003	188	62	126	815	272	289	132	67	45	9
1985	951	193	69	124	757	224	268	127	85	43	11
1986	946	180	68	112	765	225	273	148	70	44	5
1987	826	160	70	90	666	186	253	122	61	39	6
1988	771	154	64	90	617	177	233	111	58	30	8
1989	773	153	65	88	619	162	226	129	59	33	10
1990	806	142	62	80	664	177	247	146	62	27	6
1991	890	145	54	91	745	201	252	172	87	25	7
1992	1 067	180	71	109	886	221	301	208	107	42	6
1993	971	170	66	104	801	201	260	201	87	46	7
1994	848	167	69	97	682	173	218	180	72	29	10
1995	762	168	73	95	593	153	195	150	63	21	11
1996	808	169	73	96	639	163	210	158	75	26	7
1997	747	162	70	92	585	165	178	141	72	22	7
1998	671	147	61	86	524	151	148	133	60	24	8
1999	626	145	60	85	480	135	143	114	60	22	7
2000	620	121	52	70	499	145	134	121	72	17	9
2001	709	136	51	85	573	150	159	142	84	31	7
2002	835	140	54	85	695	181	180	165	120	40	9
2003	891	132	49	83	760	192	212	189	109	47	10
2004	860	128	52	75	733	188	211	160	120	46	8
2005	844	145	63	82	699	192	189	143	116	45	14
2006	774	134	53	81	640	167	189	118	112	43	11
2007	752	130	55	75	622	166	186	114	106	41	10
2008	949	138	54	84	811	190	242	154	143	61	21
2009	1 448	161	55	106	1 286	264	406	270	230	91	24
2010	1 550	154	47	107	1 396	294	408	286	268	116	24
2011	1 502	142	39	102	1 360	278	426	277	233	125	21

Table 1-26. Unemployed Persons, by Age, Sex, Race, and Hispanic Origin, 1948–2011—*Continued*

(Thousands of people.)

Race, Hispanic origin, sex, and year	16 years and over	16 to 19 years			20 years and over						
		Total	16 to 17 years	18 to 19 years	Total	20 to 24 years	25 to 34 years	35 to 44 years	45 to 54 years	55 to 64 years	65 years and over
BLACK											
Women											
1974	470	139	51	87	331	132	98	55	30	14	2
1975	629	160	60	100	469	167	153	75	48	22	4
1976	637	160	66	93	477	165	172	73	41	23	3
1977	695	167	63	104	528	200	185	77	41	21	4
1978	690	179	70	110	510	194	173	74	41	23	6
1979	683	169	69	100	513	195	183	71	38	21	5
1980	738	164	62	102	574	204	211	83	49	21	6
1981	840	169	65	104	671	235	248	105	54	23	7
1982	975	182	58	124	793	261	307	123	67	29	5
1983	1 059	181	56	125	878	278	342	137	77	36	7
1984	911	165	60	104	747	231	288	121	71	30	5
1985	913	164	66	98	750	231	295	127	58	31	7
1986	894	167	70	97	728	228	291	121	57	25	5
1987	858	152	64	88	706	211	280	125	63	23	4
1988	776	134	57	78	642	172	269	118	53	22	7
1989	772	147	51	96	625	160	267	118	50	21	9
1990	758	126	49	76	633	172	258	132	44	17	8
1991	833	135	51	84	698	177	288	145	64	19	6
1992	944	144	56	88	800	200	308	194	71	22	6
1993	872	143	46	97	729	186	272	175	66	26	5
1994	818	133	57	76	685	178	249	166	59	26	6
1995	777	157	. . .	87	620	158	228	153	53	20	7
1996	784	141	60	80	643	164	244	155	52	21	7
1997	813	140	53	87	673	163	248	166	64	24	9
1998	756	134	63	71	622	150	218	160	65	21	8
1999	684	123	49	74	561	138	196	135	61	25	7
2000	621	109	44	65	512	136	154	132	59	22	10
2001	706	124	52	72	582	157	181	141	75	21	8
2002	858	120	49	71	738	183	228	185	95	35	12
2003	895	123	44	79	772	183	230	195	109	46	10
2004	868	114	51	63	755	166	230	180	126	40	13
2005	856	123	52	70	734	166	233	168	106	47	14
2006	775	120	50	70	656	150	199	158	102	38	8
2007	693	106	43	63	588	135	181	123	103	38	9
2008	839	108	44	64	732	166	216	147	132	56	15
2009	1 159	127	44	82	1 032	223	311	219	185	77	17
2010	1 302	137	50	87	1 165	245	369	248	193	88	22
2011	1 329	125	49	76	1 204	253	376	252	211	86	25
HISPANIC[1]											
Both Sexes											
1975	508	123	. . .	. . .	. . .	. . .	. . .	. . .	. . .	. . .	. . .
1976	485	106	51	55	385	116	113	72	53	26	6
1977	456	113	50	60	344	98	114	56	48	24	5
1978	452	110	63	47	342	98	116	65	41	16	5
1979	434	106	54	51	329	100	102	65	37	20	4
1980	620	145	66	79	474	138	168	90	49	24	5
1981	678	144	60	84	533	171	178	92	57	31	5
1982	929	175	73	102	754	221	267	140	75	45	6
1983	961	167	64	104	793	214	270	156	93	54	5
1984	800	149	60	88	651	164	235	124	71	51	5
1985	811	141	55	85	670	171	256	123	73	41	7
1986	857	141	57	84	716	183	258	143	85	38	9
1987	751	136	57	79	615	152	222	128	75	33	5
1988	732	148	63	84	585	145	209	120	69	36	6
1989	750	132	59	73	618	158	218	124	76	36	6
1990	876	161	68	94	714	167	263	156	85	36	7
1991	1 092	179	79	99	913	214	332	206	110	44	8
1992	1 311	219	94	124	1 093	240	390	267	126	59	10
1993	1 248	201	86	115	1 047	237	354	261	132	54	10
1994	1 187	198	90	108	989	220	348	227	132	51	12
1995	1 140	205	96	109	934	209	325	224	106	54	16
1996	1 132	199	85	114	933	217	296	246	101	59	14
1997	1 069	197	87	110	872	206	269	229	99	56	13
1998	1 026	214	89	125	812	194	260	203	96	48	11
1999	945	196	79	117	750	171	233	190	104	42	10
2000	954	194	83	112	759	190	247	189	79	42	12
2001	1 138	208	84	123	931	212	315	228	111	56	9
2002	1 353	221	81	140	1 132	265	373	271	146	62	15
2003	1 441	192	79	113	1 249	273	419	294	183	69	10
2004	1 342	203	86	117	1 139	255	371	261	161	74	18
2005	1 191	191	78	113	1 000	227	324	231	142	61	15
2006	1 081	170	74	97	911	194	294	231	128	49	14
2007	1 220	197	78	119	1 023	213	322	238	161	70	19
2008	1 678	251	105	146	1 427	307	437	328	242	81	32
2009	2 706	321	109	212	2 385	429	731	584	416	186	38
2010	2 843	322	99	223	2 520	479	736	598	459	199	49
2011	2 629	300	96	203	2 329	473	669	524	424	195	45

[1]May be of any race.
. . . = Not available.

Table 1-26. Unemployed Persons, by Age, Sex, Race, and Hispanic Origin, 1948–2011—*Continued*

(Thousands of people.)

Race, Hispanic origin, sex, and year	16 years and over	16 to 19 years			20 years and over						
		Total	16 to 17 years	18 to 19 years	Total	20 to 24 years	25 to 34 years	35 to 44 years	45 to 54 years	55 to 64 years	65 years and over
HISPANIC[1]											
Men											
1975	296	...	...	...	225	...	...	...	...	...	...
1976	278	60	30	125	217	69	63	38	29	16	...
1977	253	60	27	147	195	57	65	28	22	15	...
1978	234	59	35	147	175	51	59	30	20	10	...
1979	223	55	29	168	168	52	50	33	19	11	...
1980	370	86	39	198	284	85	96	51	31	16	...
1981	408	87	40	182	321	105	113	49	31	19	...
1982	565	104	45	162	461	138	169	80	40	29	...
1983	591	100	38	177	491	134	168	92	57	36	...
1984	480	87	36	180	393	103	142	69	41	33	...
1985	483	82	34	169	401	108	156	69	40	23	...
1986	520	82	33	172	438	115	159	86	46	26	...
1987	451	77	32	188	374	88	137	77	46	22	...
1988	437	86	36	205	351	83	128	70	42	24	...
1989	423	81	36	225	342	88	113	69	43	25	...
1990	524	100	40	286	425	99	154	91	53	25	...
1991	685	110	47	263	575	139	210	126	62	33	...
1992	807	132	56	238	675	156	239	156	75	42	...
1993	747	118	50	242	629	144	217	148	79	33	...
1994	680	121	54	233	558	128	203	113	75	30	9
1995	651	121	59	248	530	123	185	120	57	33	13
1996	607	112	49	277	495	117	165	124	49	31	9
1997	582	110	47	290	471	125	137	113	54	35	8
1998	552	117	54	315	436	115	142	97	49	29	5
1999	480	106	42	352	374	96	109	83	54	24	7
2000	494	106	46	411	388	105	118	93	42	23	8
2001	611	117	52	419	495	129	152	116	55	36	6
2002	764	127	42	363	636	151	213	144	82	38	8
2003	809	116	42	294	693	157	239	153	98	41	5
2004	755	120	48	338	635	158	207	133	82	41	13
2005	647	112	42	328	536	134	168	119	74	31	9
2006	601	104	43	350	497	110	169	114	66	29	8
2007	695	119	44	338	576	121	189	126	92	35	13
2008	1 007	147	63	340	860	188	275	192	136	50	19
2009	1 670	196	66	289	1 474	255	470	364	246	117	21
2010	1 711	191	54	283	1 519	294	470	346	269	112	28
2011	1 527	182	53	287	1 345	277	395	297	231	116	28
HISPANIC[1]											
Women											
1975	212	...	...	...	160	...	...	...	...	...	...
1976	207	45	22	24	166	47	52	33	22	10	...
1977	204	50	23	27	153	40	49	28	25	11	...
1978	219	51	28	23	168	46	58	36	20	8	...
1979	211	50	26	24	160	48	52	32	18	10	...
1980	249	59	28	31	190	53	72	39	18	8	...
1981	269	57	20	37	212	65	65	43	25	13	...
1982	364	71	28	43	293	83	98	60	35	16	...
1983	369	68	26	42	302	80	102	65	36	18	...
1984	320	62	25	37	258	61	93	55	30	17	...
1985	327	58	22	37	269	63	100	54	32	18	...
1986	337	59	25	35	278	68	99	57	39	12	...
1987	300	59	25	34	241	64	85	51	29	11	...
1988	296	62	27	34	234	63	81	50	27	12	...
1989	327	51	23	28	276	70	105	55	33	11	...
1990	351	62	28	34	289	68	109	65	32	11	...
1991	407	69	32	37	339	74	122	80	48	12	...
1992	504	87	38	49	418	84	151	111	51	17	...
1993	501	83	36	47	418	93	136	113	53	21	...
1994	508	77	36	40	431	92	145	115	57	21	2
1995	488	84	38	46	404	86	140	104	50	21	3
1996	525	88	36	52	438	100	131	122	52	27	5
1997	488	87	40	46	401	81	132	117	46	21	4
1998	473	98	35	63	376	80	118	106	48	19	5
1999	466	90	36	54	376	75	124	107	50	17	3
2000	460	88	37	51	371	86	129	96	38	19	4
2001	527	91	33	58	436	83	163	112	56	20	3
2002	590	94	39	54	496	113	160	127	65	24	7
2003	631	76	37	39	555	116	180	141	86	28	5
2004	587	83	38	45	504	97	164	128	78	32	5
2005	544	80	36	43	464	93	156	112	68	30	6
2006	480	67	31	36	414	84	125	116	62	20	6
2007	525	79	34	45	446	92	134	111	69	35	6
2008	672	104	42	62	567	119	162	136	105	32	13
2009	1 036	125	44	81	911	174	260	220	170	70	17
2010	1 132	131	45	86	1 001	186	267	252	190	87	20
2011	1 102	118	44	74	984	196	274	227	192	78	17

[1]May be of any race.
. . . = Not available.

Table 1-27. Unemployment Rates of Civilian Workers, by Age, Sex, Race, and Hispanic Origin, 1948–2011

(Percent of labor force.)

Race, Hispanic origin, sex, and year	16 years and over	16 to 19 years			20 years and over						
		Total	16 to 17 years	18 to 19 years	Total	20 to 24 years	25 to 34 years	35 to 44 years	45 to 54 years	55 to 64 years	65 years and over
ALL RACES											
Both Sexes											
1948	3.8	9.2	10.1	8.6	3.3	6.2	3.2	2.6	2.7	3.1	3.2
1949	5.9	13.4	14.0	13.0	5.4	9.3	5.4	4.4	4.2	5.2	4.9
1950	5.3	12.2	13.6	11.2	4.8	7.7	4.8	3.8	4.2	4.8	4.5
1951	3.3	8.2	9.6	7.1	3.0	4.1	3.0	2.5	2.7	3.1	3.4
1952	3.0	8.5	10.0	7.3	2.7	4.6	2.6	2.3	2.3	2.4	2.9
1953	2.9	7.6	8.7	6.8	2.6	4.7	2.5	2.2	2.3	2.7	2.2
1954	5.5	12.6	13.5	10.7	5.1	9.2	5.3	4.5	4.4	4.5	4.1
1955	4.4	11.0	12.3	10.0	3.9	7.0	3.8	3.4	3.4	4.2	3.6
1956	4.1	11.1	12.3	10.2	3.7	6.6	3.7	3.0	3.2	3.5	3.2
1957	4.3	11.6	12.5	10.9	3.8	7.1	3.9	3.1	3.3	3.4	3.4
1958	6.8	15.9	16.4	15.5	6.2	11.2	6.8	5.4	5.2	5.2	4.8
1959	5.5	14.6	15.3	14.0	4.8	8.5	5.0	4.2	4.2	4.4	4.3
1960	5.5	14.7	15.5	14.1	4.8	8.7	5.2	4.1	4.1	4.2	3.8
1961	6.7	16.8	18.3	15.8	5.9	10.4	6.2	5.2	5.0	5.4	5.1
1962	5.5	14.7	16.3	13.6	4.9	9.0	5.1	4.1	4.0	4.2	4.5
1963	5.7	17.2	19.3	15.6	4.8	8.8	5.2	4.0	3.8	4.1	4.1
1964	5.2	16.2	17.8	14.9	4.3	8.3	4.3	3.6	3.5	3.7	3.8
1965	4.5	14.8	16.5	13.5	3.6	6.7	3.7	3.2	2.8	3.1	3.3
1966	3.8	12.8	14.8	11.3	2.9	5.3	3.1	2.5	2.3	2.5	3.0
1967	3.8	12.9	14.6	11.6	3.0	5.7	3.2	2.5	2.4	2.4	2.8
1968	3.6	12.7	14.7	11.2	2.7	5.8	2.8	2.2	1.9	2.0	2.8
1969	3.5	12.2	14.5	10.5	2.7	5.7	2.8	2.2	1.9	1.9	2.2
1970	4.9	15.3	17.1	13.8	4.0	8.2	4.2	3.1	2.8	2.7	3.2
1971	5.9	16.9	18.7	15.5	4.9	10.0	5.3	3.9	3.4	3.3	3.5
1972	5.6	16.2	18.5	14.6	4.5	9.3	4.6	3.5	3.0	3.2	3.6
1973	4.9	14.5	17.3	12.4	3.9	7.8	4.2	2.7	2.5	2.6	3.0
1974	5.6	16.0	18.3	14.3	4.5	9.1	4.8	3.3	2.9	2.8	3.4
1975	8.5	19.9	21.4	18.9	7.3	13.6	7.8	5.6	5.2	4.6	5.2
1976	7.7	19.0	21.1	17.5	6.5	12.0	7.1	4.9	4.5	4.5	5.1
1977	7.1	17.8	19.9	16.2	5.9	11.0	6.5	4.4	3.9	3.9	5.0
1978	6.1	16.4	19.3	14.2	5.0	9.6	5.3	3.7	3.3	2.9	4.0
1979	5.8	16.1	18.1	14.7	4.8	9.1	5.2	3.6	3.2	2.9	3.4
1980	7.1	17.8	20.0	16.2	6.1	11.5	6.9	4.6	4.0	3.3	3.1
1981	7.6	19.6	21.4	18.4	6.5	12.3	7.3	5.0	4.2	3.7	3.2
1982	9.7	23.2	24.9	22.1	8.6	14.9	9.7	6.9	5.7	5.4	3.5
1983	9.6	22.4	24.5	21.1	8.6	14.5	9.7	7.0	6.2	5.6	3.7
1984	7.5	18.9	21.2	17.4	6.7	11.5	7.3	5.4	4.9	4.7	3.3
1985	7.2	18.6	21.0	17.0	6.4	11.1	7.0	5.1	4.7	4.3	3.2
1986	7.0	18.3	20.2	17.0	6.2	10.7	6.9	5.0	4.5	4.1	3.0
1987	6.2	16.9	19.1	15.2	5.4	9.7	6.0	4.5	4.0	3.5	2.5
1988	5.5	15.3	17.4	13.8	4.8	8.7	5.4	4.0	3.4	3.2	2.7
1989	5.3	15.0	17.2	13.6	4.6	8.6	5.2	3.8	3.2	3.2	2.6
1990	5.6	15.5	17.9	14.1	4.9	8.8	5.6	4.1	3.6	3.3	3.0
1991	6.8	18.7	21.0	17.2	6.1	10.8	6.9	5.2	4.5	4.1	3.3
1992	7.5	20.1	23.1	18.2	6.8	11.4	7.6	5.8	5.1	5.1	3.8
1993	6.9	19.0	21.4	17.5	6.2	10.5	6.9	5.5	4.8	4.7	3.2
1994	6.1	17.6	19.9	16.0	5.4	9.7	6.0	4.6	4.0	4.1	4.0
1995	5.6	17.3	20.2	15.3	4.9	9.1	5.4	4.3	3.3	3.6	4.0
1996	5.4	16.7	18.9	15.2	4.7	9.3	5.2	4.1	3.3	3.3	3.6
1997	4.9	16.0	18.2	14.5	4.3	8.5	4.7	3.8	3.0	2.9	3.3
1998	4.5	14.6	17.2	12.8	3.9	7.9	4.3	3.4	2.8	2.6	3.2
1999	4.2	13.9	16.3	12.4	3.6	7.5	4.0	3.0	2.6	2.7	3.1
2000	4.0	13.1	15.4	11.6	3.4	7.2	3.7	3.0	2.5	2.5	3.1
2001	4.7	14.7	17.2	13.1	4.2	8.3	4.6	3.6	3.1	3.0	2.9
2002	5.8	16.5	18.8	15.1	5.2	9.7	5.9	4.6	4.0	3.9	3.6
2003	6.0	17.5	19.1	16.4	5.4	10.0	6.1	4.9	4.1	4.1	3.8
2004	5.5	17.0	20.2	15.0	4.9	9.4	5.5	4.4	3.8	3.8	3.6
2005	5.1	16.6	19.1	14.9	4.5	8.8	5.1	3.9	3.5	3.3	3.5
2006	4.6	15.4	17.2	14.1	4.1	8.2	4.7	3.6	3.1	3.0	2.9
2007	4.6	15.7	17.5	14.5	4.1	8.2	4.7	3.4	3.2	3.1	3.3
2008	5.8	18.7	22.1	16.8	5.2	10.2	5.8	4.6	4.1	3.7	4.2
2009	9.3	24.3	25.9	23.4	8.6	14.7	9.9	7.9	7.2	6.6	6.4
2010	9.6	25.9	29.1	24.2	9.0	15.5	10.1	8.1	7.7	7.1	6.7
2011	8.9	24.4	27.7	22.9	8.3	14.6	9.5	7.3	7.1	6.6	6.5

Table 1-27. Unemployment Rates of Civilian Workers, by Age, Sex, Race, and Hispanic Origin, 1948–2011
—Continued

(Percent of labor force.)

Race, Hispanic origin, sex, and year	16 years and over	16 to 19 years			20 years and over						
		Total	16 to 17 years	18 to 19 years	Total	20 to 24 years	25 to 34 years	35 to 44 years	45 to 54 years	55 to 64 years	65 years and over
ALL RACES											
Men											
1948	3.6	9.8	10.2	9.5	3.2	6.9	2.8	2.4	2.5	3.1	3.4
1949	5.9	14.3	13.7	14.6	5.4	10.4	5.2	4.3	4.3	5.4	5.1
1950	5.1	12.7	13.3	12.3	4.7	8.1	4.4	3.6	4.0	4.9	4.8
1951	2.8	8.1	9.4	7.0	2.5	3.9	2.3	2.0	2.4	2.8	3.5
1952	2.8	8.9	10.5	7.4	2.4	4.6	2.2	1.9	2.2	2.4	3.0
1953	2.8	7.9	8.8	7.2	2.5	5.0	2.2	2.0	2.3	2.8	2.4
1954	5.3	13.5	13.9	13.2	4.9	10.7	4.8	4.1	4.3	4.5	4.4
1955	4.2	11.6	12.5	10.8	3.8	7.7	3.3	3.1	3.2	4.3	4.0
1956	3.8	11.1	11.7	10.5	3.4	6.9	3.3	2.6	3.0	3.5	3.5
1957	4.1	12.4	12.4	12.3	3.6	7.8	3.3	2.8	3.3	3.5	3.4
1958	6.8	17.1	16.3	17.8	6.2	12.7	6.5	5.1	5.3	5.5	5.2
1959	5.2	15.3	15.8	14.9	4.7	8.7	4.7	3.7	4.1	4.5	4.8
1960	5.4	15.3	15.5	15.0	4.7	8.9	4.8	3.8	4.1	4.6	4.2
1961	6.4	17.1	18.3	16.3	5.7	10.8	5.7	4.6	4.9	5.7	5.5
1962	5.2	14.7	16.0	13.8	4.6	8.9	4.5	3.6	3.9	4.6	4.6
1963	5.2	17.2	18.8	15.9	4.5	8.8	4.5	3.5	3.6	4.3	4.5
1964	4.6	15.8	17.1	14.6	3.9	8.1	3.5	2.9	3.2	3.9	4.0
1965	4.0	14.1	16.1	12.4	3.2	6.4	2.9	2.5	2.5	3.3	3.5
1966	3.2	11.7	13.7	10.2	2.5	4.6	2.4	2.0	1.9	2.6	3.1
1967	3.1	12.3	14.5	10.5	2.3	4.7	2.1	1.7	2.0	2.3	2.8
1968	2.9	11.6	13.9	9.7	2.2	5.1	1.9	1.6	1.6	1.9	2.8
1969	2.8	11.4	13.8	9.3	2.1	5.1	1.9	1.5	1.5	1.8	2.2
1970	4.4	15.0	16.9	13.4	3.5	8.4	3.5	2.4	2.4	2.8	3.3
1971	5.3	16.6	18.7	15.0	4.4	10.3	4.4	3.1	3.0	3.3	3.4
1972	5.0	15.9	18.3	14.1	4.0	9.3	3.8	2.7	2.6	3.2	3.6
1973	4.2	13.9	17.0	11.4	3.3	7.3	3.4	2.0	2.1	2.4	3.0
1974	4.9	15.6	18.4	13.3	3.8	8.8	4.0	2.6	2.4	2.6	3.3
1975	7.9	20.1	21.6	19.0	6.8	14.3	6.9	4.9	4.8	4.3	5.4
1976	7.1	19.2	21.4	17.6	5.9	12.1	6.2	4.1	4.0	4.2	5.1
1977	6.3	17.3	19.5	15.6	5.2	10.8	5.7	3.5	3.2	3.6	5.2
1978	5.3	15.8	19.1	13.3	4.3	9.2	4.4	2.8	2.7	2.8	4.2
1979	5.1	15.9	17.9	14.3	4.2	8.7	4.3	2.9	2.7	2.7	3.4
1980	6.9	18.3	20.4	16.7	5.9	12.5	6.7	4.1	3.6	3.4	3.1
1981	7.4	20.1	22.0	18.8	6.3	13.2	6.9	4.5	4.0	3.6	2.9
1982	9.9	24.4	26.4	23.1	8.8	16.4	10.1	6.9	5.6	5.5	3.7
1983	9.9	23.3	25.2	22.2	8.9	15.9	10.1	7.1	6.3	6.1	3.9
1984	7.4	19.6	21.9	18.3	6.6	11.9	7.2	5.2	4.6	5.0	3.0
1985	7.0	19.5	21.9	17.9	6.2	11.4	6.6	4.9	4.6	4.3	3.1
1986	6.9	19.0	20.8	17.7	6.1	11.0	6.7	5.1	4.4	4.3	3.2
1987	6.2	17.8	20.2	16.0	5.4	9.9	5.9	4.4	4.2	3.7	2.6
1988	5.5	16.0	18.2	14.6	4.8	8.9	5.3	3.8	3.5	3.5	2.5
1989	5.2	15.9	18.6	14.2	4.5	8.8	4.8	3.7	3.2	3.5	2.4
1990	5.7	16.3	18.4	15.0	5.0	9.1	5.5	4.1	3.7	3.8	3.0
1991	7.2	19.8	21.8	18.5	6.4	11.6	7.0	5.5	4.8	4.6	3.3
1992	7.9	21.5	24.6	19.5	7.1	12.2	7.8	6.1	5.6	5.8	3.3
1993	7.2	20.4	22.9	18.8	6.4	11.3	7.0	5.6	5.1	5.2	3.2
1994	6.2	19.0	21.0	17.6	5.4	10.2	5.9	4.5	4.0	4.4	4.0
1995	5.6	18.4	21.1	16.5	4.8	9.2	5.1	4.2	3.5	3.6	4.3
1996	5.4	18.1	20.8	16.3	4.6	9.5	4.9	4.0	3.5	3.3	3.4
1997	4.9	16.9	19.1	15.4	4.2	8.9	4.3	3.6	3.1	3.1	3.0
1998	4.4	16.2	19.1	14.1	3.7	8.1	3.9	3.0	2.8	2.8	3.1
1999	4.1	14.7	17.0	13.1	3.5	7.7	3.6	2.8	2.6	2.7	3.0
2000	3.9	14.0	16.8	12.2	3.3	7.3	3.4	2.8	2.4	2.4	3.3
2001	4.8	16.0	19.1	14.0	4.2	9.0	4.3	3.6	3.2	3.3	3.0
2002	5.9	18.1	21.1	16.4	5.3	10.2	5.8	4.5	4.2	4.3	3.4
2003	6.3	19.3	20.7	18.4	5.6	10.6	6.2	5.0	4.4	4.5	4.0
2004	5.6	18.4	22.0	16.3	5.0	10.1	5.5	4.3	3.9	3.9	3.7
2005	5.1	18.6	22.0	16.5	4.4	9.6	4.7	3.7	3.5	3.3	3.4
2006	4.6	16.9	18.6	15.7	4.0	8.7	4.5	3.3	3.1	3.0	2.8
2007	4.7	17.6	19.4	16.5	4.1	8.9	4.7	3.3	3.1	3.2	3.4
2008	6.1	21.2	25.2	19.0	5.4	11.4	6.1	4.6	4.2	3.8	4.5
2009	10.3	27.8	28.7	27.4	9.6	17.0	10.9	8.6	8.2	7.2	6.7
2010	10.5	28.8	31.8	27.4	9.8	17.8	10.9	8.5	8.6	8.0	7.1
2011	9.4	27.2	29.1	26.3	8.7	15.7	9.7	7.4	7.4	7.1	6.5

Table 1-27. Unemployment Rates of Civilian Workers, by Age, Sex, Race, and Hispanic Origin, 1948–2011
—Continued

(Percent of labor force.)

Race, Hispanic origin, sex, and year	16 years and over	16 to 19 years			20 years and over						
		Total	16 to 17 years	18 to 19 years	Total	20 to 24 years	25 to 34 years	35 to 44 years	45 to 54 years	55 to 64 years	65 years and over
ALL RACES											
Women											
1948	4.1	8.3	10.0	7.4	3.6	4.8	4.3	3.0	3.0	3.1	2.3
1949	6.0	12.3	14.4	11.2	5.3	7.3	5.9	4.7	4.7	4.4	3.8
1950	5.7	11.4	14.2	9.8	5.1	6.9	5.7	4.4	4.4	4.5	3.4
1951	4.4	8.3	10.0	7.2	4.0	4.4	4.5	3.8	3.8	4.0	2.9
1952	3.6	8.0	9.1	7.3	3.2	4.5	3.6	3.0	3.0	2.5	2.2
1953	3.3	7.2	8.5	6.4	2.9	4.3	3.4	2.5	2.5	2.5	1.4
1954	6.0	11.4	12.7	7.7	5.5	7.3	6.6	5.3	5.3	4.6	3.0
1955	4.9	10.2	12.0	9.1	4.4	6.1	5.3	4.0	4.0	3.8	2.3
1956	4.8	11.2	13.2	9.9	4.2	6.3	4.8	3.9	3.9	3.6	2.3
1957	4.7	10.6	12.6	9.4	4.1	6.0	5.3	3.8	3.8	3.0	3.4
1958	6.8	14.3	16.6	12.9	6.1	8.9	7.3	6.2	6.2	4.5	3.7
1959	5.9	13.5	14.4	13.0	5.2	8.1	5.9	5.1	5.1	4.1	2.8
1960	5.9	13.9	15.5	12.9	5.1	8.3	6.3	4.8	4.8	3.4	2.9
1961	7.2	16.3	18.3	15.1	6.3	9.8	7.4	6.4	6.4	4.5	4.0
1962	6.2	14.6	16.7	13.5	5.4	9.1	6.5	5.2	5.2	3.5	4.2
1963	6.5	17.2	20.2	15.2	5.4	8.9	6.9	5.1	5.1	3.6	3.2
1964	6.2	16.6	18.8	15.2	5.2	8.6	6.3	5.0	5.0	3.3	3.3
1965	5.5	15.7	17.2	14.8	4.5	7.3	5.5	4.6	4.6	2.8	2.9
1966	4.8	14.1	16.6	12.6	3.8	6.3	4.5	3.6	3.6	2.3	2.8
1967	5.2	13.5	14.8	12.8	4.2	7.0	5.4	4.1	4.1	2.4	2.7
1968	4.8	14.0	15.9	12.9	3.8	6.7	4.7	3.4	3.4	2.2	2.7
1969	4.7	13.3	15.5	11.8	3.7	6.3	4.6	3.4	3.4	2.2	2.3
1970	5.9	15.6	17.4	14.4	4.8	7.9	5.7	4.4	4.4	2.7	3.1
1971	6.9	17.2	18.7	16.2	5.7	9.6	7.0	5.2	5.2	3.3	3.6
1972	6.6	16.7	18.8	15.2	5.4	9.4	6.2	4.9	4.9	3.3	3.5
1973	6.0	15.3	17.7	13.5	4.9	8.5	5.8	3.9	3.9	2.8	2.9
1974	6.7	16.6	18.2	15.4	5.5	9.5	6.2	4.6	4.6	3.2	3.6
1975	9.3	19.7	21.2	18.7	8.0	12.7	9.1	6.8	6.8	5.1	5.0
1976	8.6	18.7	20.8	17.4	7.4	11.9	8.4	6.1	6.1	4.9	5.0
1977	8.2	18.3	20.5	16.9	7.0	11.2	7.7	5.7	5.7	4.4	4.7
1978	7.2	17.1	19.5	15.3	6.0	10.1	6.7	5.0	5.0	3.2	3.8
1979	6.8	16.4	18.3	15.0	5.7	9.6	6.5	4.6	4.6	3.2	3.3
1980	7.4	17.2	19.6	15.6	6.4	10.4	7.2	5.3	5.3	3.3	3.1
1981	7.9	19.0	20.7	17.9	6.8	11.2	7.7	5.7	5.7	3.8	3.6
1982	9.4	21.9	23.2	21.0	8.3	13.2	9.3	7.0	7.0	5.2	3.2
1983	9.2	21.3	23.7	19.9	8.1	12.9	9.1	6.9	6.9	5.0	3.4
1984	7.6	18.0	20.4	16.6	6.8	10.9	7.4	5.6	5.6	4.3	3.8
1985	7.4	17.6	20.0	16.0	6.6	10.7	7.4	5.5	5.5	4.3	3.3
1986	7.1	17.6	19.6	16.3	6.2	10.3	7.2	5.0	5.0	3.8	2.8
1987	6.2	15.9	18.0	14.3	5.4	9.4	6.2	4.6	4.6	3.1	2.4
1988	5.6	14.4	16.6	12.9	4.9	8.5	5.6	4.1	4.1	2.7	2.9
1989	5.4	14.0	15.7	13.0	4.7	8.3	5.6	3.9	3.9	2.8	2.9
1990	5.5	14.7	17.4	13.1	4.9	8.5	5.6	4.2	4.2	2.8	3.1
1991	6.4	17.5	20.2	15.9	5.7	9.8	6.8	4.8	4.8	3.4	3.3
1992	7.0	18.6	21.5	16.6	6.3	10.3	7.4	5.5	5.5	4.2	4.5
1993	6.6	17.5	19.8	16.1	5.9	9.7	6.8	5.3	5.3	4.0	3.1
1994	6.0	16.2	18.7	14.3	5.4	9.2	6.2	4.7	4.7	3.9	4.0
1995	5.6	16.1	19.2	14.0	4.9	9.0	5.7	4.4	4.4	3.6	3.7
1996	5.4	15.2	16.9	14.0	4.8	9.0	5.5	4.2	4.2	3.4	4.0
1997	5.0	15.0	17.2	13.6	4.4	8.1	5.2	4.0	4.0	2.7	3.6
1998	4.6	12.9	15.1	11.5	4.1	7.8	4.8	3.8	3.8	2.4	3.3
1999	4.3	13.2	15.5	11.6	3.8	7.2	4.4	3.3	3.3	2.6	3.2
2000	4.1	12.1	13.9	10.8	3.6	7.1	4.1	3.3	3.3	2.5	2.7
2001	4.7	13.4	15.2	12.2	4.1	7.5	5.1	3.7	3.7	2.7	2.9
2002	5.6	14.9	16.6	13.8	5.1	9.1	5.9	4.6	4.6	3.5	3.9
2003	5.7	15.6	17.5	14.2	5.1	9.3	5.9	4.9	4.9	3.7	3.6
2004	5.4	15.5	18.5	13.5	4.9	8.7	5.6	4.4	4.4	3.6	3.4
2005	5.1	14.5	16.5	13.1	4.6	7.9	5.6	4.1	4.1	3.3	3.5
2006	4.6	13.8	15.9	12.4	4.1	7.6	4.9	3.9	3.9	2.9	3.0
2007	4.5	13.8	15.7	12.5	4.0	7.3	4.6	3.6	3.6	3.0	3.1
2008	5.4	16.2	19.1	14.3	4.9	8.8	5.5	4.5	4.5	3.7	3.9
2009	8.1	20.7	23.1	19.4	7.5	12.3	8.6	7.1	7.1	6.0	6.1
2010	8.6	22.8	26.5	20.9	8.0	13.0	9.1	7.7	7.7	6.2	6.2
2011	8.5	21.7	26.3	19.3	7.9	13.4	9.1	7.2	7.2	6.1	6.5

Table 1-27. Unemployment Rates of Civilian Workers, by Age, Sex, Race, and Hispanic Origin, 1948–2011
—Continued

(Percent of labor force.)

Race, Hispanic origin, sex, and year	16 years and over	16 to 19 years			20 years and over						
		Total	16 to 17 years	18 to 19 years	Total	20 to 24 years	25 to 34 years	35 to 44 years	45 to 54 years	55 to 64 years	65 years and over
WHITE											
Both Sexes											
1954	5.0	12.1	13.2	11.3	4.6	8.3	4.6	4.0	4.0	4.3	3.9
1955	3.9	10.4	12.0	9.2	3.4	6.2	3.1	2.9	3.1	3.8	3.4
1956	3.6	10.1	11.5	9.0	3.2	5.7	3.1	2.6	2.9	3.2	3.1
1957	3.8	10.6	11.9	9.6	3.4	6.3	3.3	2.8	3.0	3.2	3.2
1958	6.1	14.4	15.2	13.9	5.6	9.9	5.9	4.8	4.8	4.9	4.6
1959	4.8	13.1	14.4	12.1	4.3	7.3	4.2	3.7	3.8	4.1	4.1
1960	5.0	13.5	14.6	12.6	4.3	7.9	4.5	3.6	3.8	3.9	3.7
1961	6.0	15.3	16.7	14.4	5.3	9.4	5.3	4.5	4.5	5.0	4.8
1962	4.9	13.3	15.3	12.0	4.2	7.9	4.2	3.6	3.6	3.9	4.0
1963	5.0	15.5	17.9	13.7	4.2	7.7	4.4	3.5	3.5	3.8	3.8
1964	4.6	14.8	16.5	13.3	3.8	7.3	3.6	3.2	3.2	3.5	3.5
1965	4.1	13.4	14.8	12.3	3.3	6.1	3.2	2.9	2.5	2.9	3.2
1966	3.4	11.2	13.3	9.7	2.6	4.6	2.6	2.3	2.1	2.4	2.9
1967	3.4	11.0	12.8	9.8	2.7	5.0	2.7	2.3	2.2	2.3	2.7
1968	3.2	11.0	12.9	9.6	2.5	5.2	2.4	2.0	1.8	1.9	2.8
1969	3.1	10.7	13.0	8.9	2.4	5.0	2.5	2.0	1.8	1.8	2.2
1970	4.5	13.5	15.5	11.9	3.7	7.3	3.8	3.0	2.7	2.7	3.2
1971	5.4	15.1	17.0	13.8	4.5	9.0	4.7	3.6	3.3	3.3	3.5
1972	5.1	14.2	16.6	12.3	4.1	8.4	4.1	3.2	2.9	3.1	3.4
1973	4.3	12.6	15.4	10.4	3.5	6.8	3.7	2.5	2.4	2.5	2.9
1974	5.0	14.0	16.3	12.2	4.1	8.0	4.4	3.1	2.8	2.8	3.3
1975	7.8	17.9	19.5	16.7	6.7	12.3	7.1	5.2	4.9	4.5	5.1
1976	7.0	16.9	19.0	15.3	5.9	10.7	6.3	4.5	4.2	4.3	4.9
1977	6.2	15.4	17.9	13.5	5.3	9.3	5.7	4.0	3.8	3.7	4.9
1978	5.2	13.9	17.0	11.5	4.3	8.0	4.6	3.3	3.0	2.7	3.8
1979	5.1	14.0	16.1	12.4	4.2	7.6	4.4	3.2	3.0	2.7	3.1
1980	6.3	15.5	17.9	13.8	5.4	9.9	6.1	4.2	3.7	3.1	2.7
1981	6.7	17.3	19.2	15.9	5.7	10.4	6.3	4.5	3.9	3.5	2.8
1982	8.6	20.4	22.8	18.8	7.6	12.8	8.5	6.3	5.4	5.1	3.1
1983	8.4	19.3	22.0	17.6	7.5	12.1	8.4	6.3	5.7	5.2	3.2
1984	6.5	16.0	18.8	14.3	5.7	9.3	6.2	4.8	4.4	4.4	3.0
1985	6.2	15.7	18.3	13.9	5.5	9.2	5.9	4.6	4.3	4.0	2.9
1986	6.0	15.6	17.6	14.1	5.3	8.7	5.9	4.5	4.1	3.8	2.9
1987	5.3	14.4	16.7	12.7	4.7	8.0	5.1	4.0	3.7	3.2	2.4
1988	4.7	13.1	15.3	11.6	4.1	7.1	4.5	3.5	3.1	3.0	2.4
1989	4.5	12.7	15.2	11.1	3.9	7.2	4.3	3.3	2.9	3.0	2.3
1990	4.8	13.5	15.8	12.1	4.3	7.3	4.6	3.6	3.3	3.2	2.8
1991	6.1	16.5	19.0	14.9	5.5	9.2	6.1	4.7	4.2	4.0	3.1
1992	6.6	17.2	20.3	15.2	6.0	9.5	6.7	5.2	4.8	4.9	3.7
1993	6.1	16.2	19.0	14.4	5.5	8.8	6.0	4.9	4.5	4.3	3.0
1994	5.3	15.1	17.6	13.3	4.7	8.1	5.2	4.0	3.7	3.9	3.8
1995	4.9	14.5	17.3	12.5	4.3	7.7	4.6	3.9	3.1	3.5	3.8
1996	4.7	14.2	16.4	12.6	4.1	7.8	4.4	3.6	3.1	3.2	3.5
1997	4.2	13.6	15.8	12.0	3.6	6.9	3.9	3.3	2.7	2.7	3.0
1998	3.9	12.6	14.8	11.0	3.3	6.5	3.7	2.9	2.6	2.4	2.9
1999	3.7	12.0	14.5	10.2	3.1	6.3	3.3	2.7	2.4	2.5	2.9
2000	3.5	11.4	13.9	9.8	3.0	5.9	3.2	2.6	2.2	2.4	2.8
2001	4.2	12.7	15.3	11.0	3.7	7.0	4.1	3.2	2.8	2.9	2.8
2002	5.1	14.5	16.7	13.2	4.6	8.1	5.2	4.1	3.7	3.7	3.5
2003	5.2	15.2	17.2	13.9	4.7	8.4	5.3	4.3	3.7	3.8	3.7
2004	4.8	15.0	17.9	13.1	4.3	7.9	4.7	3.9	3.4	3.6	3.3
2005	4.4	14.2	16.4	12.7	3.9	7.2	4.3	3.5	3.1	3.0	3.1
2006	4.0	13.2	15.1	11.9	3.6	6.9	4.0	3.2	2.8	2.8	2.8
2007	4.1	13.9	15.5	12.8	3.6	7.0	4.0	3.2	2.9	2.9	3.2
2008	5.2	16.8	19.9	14.9	4.6	9.0	5.1	4.3	3.7	3.4	4.0
2009	8.5	21.8	23.4	21.0	7.9	13.0	8.8	7.4	6.7	6.4	6.2
2010	8.7	23.2	26.3	21.6	8.1	13.5	8.9	7.4	7.2	6.8	6.4
2011	7.9	21.7	24.7	20.2	7.4	12.8	8.1	6.5	6.4	6.2	6.4

Table 1-27. Unemployment Rates of Civilian Workers, by Age, Sex, Race, and Hispanic Origin, 1948–2011
—Continued

(Percent of labor force.)

Race, Hispanic origin, sex, and year	16 years and over	16 to 19 years			20 years and over						
		Total	16 to 17 years	18 to 19 years	Total	20 to 24 years	25 to 34 years	35 to 44 years	45 to 54 years	55 to 64 years	65 years and over
WHITE											
Men											
1954	4.8	13.4	14.0	13.0	4.4	9.8	4.2	3.6	3.8	4.3	4.2
1955	3.7	11.3	12.2	10.4	3.3	7.0	2.7	2.6	2.9	3.9	3.8
1956	3.4	10.5	11.2	9.7	3.0	6.1	2.8	2.2	2.8	3.1	3.4
1957	3.6	11.5	11.9	11.1	3.2	7.0	2.7	2.5	3.0	3.4	3.2
1958	6.1	15.7	14.9	16.5	5.5	11.7	5.6	4.4	4.8	5.2	5.0
1959	4.6	14.0	15.0	13.0	4.1	7.5	3.8	3.2	3.7	4.2	4.5
1960	4.8	14.0	14.6	13.5	4.2	8.3	4.1	3.3	3.6	4.1	4.0
1961	5.7	15.7	16.5	15.2	5.1	10.1	4.9	4.0	4.4	5.3	5.2
1962	4.6	13.7	15.2	12.7	4.0	8.1	3.8	3.1	3.5	4.1	4.0
1963	4.7	15.9	17.8	14.2	3.9	7.8	3.9	2.9	3.3	4.0	4.1
1964	4.1	14.7	16.1	13.3	3.4	7.4	3.0	2.5	2.9	3.5	3.6
1965	3.6	12.9	14.7	11.3	2.9	5.9	2.6	2.3	2.3	3.1	3.4
1966	2.8	10.5	12.5	8.9	2.2	4.1	2.1	1.7	1.7	2.5	3.0
1967	2.7	10.7	12.7	9.0	2.1	4.2	1.9	1.6	1.8	2.2	2.7
1968	2.6	10.1	12.3	8.3	2.0	4.6	1.7	1.4	1.5	1.7	2.8
1969	2.5	10.0	12.5	7.9	1.9	4.6	1.7	1.4	1.4	1.7	2.2
1970	4.0	13.7	15.7	12.0	3.2	7.8	3.1	2.3	2.3	2.7	3.2
1971	4.9	15.1	17.1	13.5	4.0	9.4	4.0	2.9	2.9	3.2	3.4
1972	4.5	14.2	16.4	12.4	3.6	8.5	3.4	2.5	2.5	3.0	3.3
1973	3.8	12.3	15.2	10.0	3.0	6.6	3.0	1.8	2.0	2.4	2.9
1974	4.4	13.5	16.2	11.5	3.5	7.8	3.6	2.4	2.2	2.5	3.0
1975	7.2	18.3	19.7	17.2	6.2	13.1	6.3	4.5	4.4	4.1	5.0
1976	6.4	17.3	19.7	15.5	5.4	10.9	5.6	3.7	3.7	4.0	4.7
1977	5.5	15.0	17.6	13.0	4.7	9.3	5.0	3.1	3.0	3.3	4.9
1978	4.6	13.5	16.9	10.8	3.7	7.7	3.8	2.5	2.5	2.6	3.9
1979	4.5	13.9	16.1	12.2	3.6	7.5	3.7	2.5	2.5	2.5	3.2
1980	6.1	16.2	18.5	14.5	5.3	11.1	5.9	3.6	3.3	3.1	2.5
1981	6.5	17.9	19.9	16.4	5.6	11.6	6.1	4.0	3.6	3.4	2.4
1982	8.8	21.7	24.2	20.0	7.8	14.3	8.9	6.2	5.3	5.1	3.2
1983	8.8	20.2	22.6	18.7	7.9	13.8	9.0	6.4	5.7	5.6	3.2
1984	6.4	16.8	19.7	15.0	5.7	9.8	6.2	4.6	4.2	4.7	2.6
1985	6.1	16.5	19.2	14.7	5.4	9.7	5.7	4.3	4.1	4.0	2.7
1986	6.0	16.3	18.4	14.7	5.3	9.2	5.8	4.4	4.0	4.0	3.0
1987	5.4	15.5	17.9	13.7	4.8	8.4	5.2	3.9	3.9	3.4	2.5
1988	4.7	13.9	16.1	12.4	4.1	7.4	4.6	3.4	3.2	3.3	2.2
1989	4.5	13.7	16.4	12.0	3.9	7.5	4.1	3.2	2.9	3.1	2.1
1990	4.9	14.3	16.1	13.2	4.3	7.6	4.7	3.5	3.4	3.6	2.8
1991	6.5	17.6	19.7	16.3	5.8	10.2	6.4	5.0	4.4	4.6	3.1
1992	7.0	18.5	21.5	16.5	6.4	10.5	7.0	5.5	5.1	5.5	3.2
1993	6.3	17.7	20.2	16.0	5.7	9.6	6.2	5.0	4.7	4.7	2.9
1994	5.4	16.3	18.5	14.7	4.8	8.8	5.2	3.9	3.7	4.1	3.7
1995	4.9	15.6	18.2	13.8	4.3	7.9	4.5	3.8	3.2	3.4	4.0
1996	4.7	15.5	18.3	13.5	4.1	8.1	4.2	3.5	3.1	3.2	3.2
1997	4.2	14.3	16.3	12.9	3.6	7.3	3.7	3.2	2.8	3.0	2.7
1998	3.9	14.1	17.1	12.1	3.2	6.7	3.5	2.6	2.6	2.6	2.9
1999	3.6	12.6	15.1	10.8	3.0	6.5	3.1	2.4	2.4	2.6	2.9
2000	3.4	12.3	15.3	10.4	2.8	5.9	2.9	2.4	2.2	2.4	3.0
2001	4.2	13.9	17.4	11.7	3.7	7.8	3.8	3.1	2.9	3.2	2.8
2002	5.3	15.9	18.8	14.2	4.7	8.7	5.3	4.1	3.8	4.0	3.4
2003	5.6	17.1	18.5	16.1	5.0	9.1	5.5	4.4	4.0	4.2	3.8
2004	5.0	16.3	19.8	14.2	4.4	8.5	4.8	3.8	3.5	3.7	3.5
2005	4.4	16.1	18.9	14.3	3.8	7.9	4.1	3.3	3.0	3.0	3.1
2006	4.0	14.6	16.5	13.4	3.5	7.3	3.9	3.0	2.7	2.8	2.7
2007	4.2	15.7	17.0	14.8	3.7	7.6	4.1	3.0	2.8	3.0	3.3
2008	5.5	19.1	22.2	17.3	4.9	10.2	5.3	4.3	3.8	3.4	4.1
2009	9.4	25.2	25.9	24.8	8.8	15.3	9.8	8.0	7.7	6.8	6.3
2010	9.6	26.3	29.2	24.8	8.9	15.7	9.9	7.7	7.9	7.5	6.6
2011	8.3	24.5	26.6	23.5	7.7	13.9	8.4	6.6	6.7	6.6	6.4

Table 1-27. Unemployment Rates of Civilian Workers, by Age, Sex, Race, and Hispanic Origin, 1948–2011
—Continued

(Percent of labor force.)

Race, Hispanic origin, sex, and year	16 years and over	16 to 19 years			20 years and over						
		Total	16 to 17 years	18 to 19 years	Total	20 to 24 years	25 to 34 years	35 to 44 years	45 to 54 years	55 to 64 years	65 years and over
WHITE											
Women											
1954	5.5	10.4	12.0	9.4	5.1	6.4	5.7	4.9	4.4	4.5	2.8
1955	4.3	9.1	11.6	7.7	3.9	5.1	4.3	3.8	3.4	3.6	2.2
1956	4.2	9.7	12.1	8.3	3.7	5.1	4.0	3.5	3.3	3.5	2.3
1957	4.3	9.5	11.9	7.8	3.8	5.1	4.7	3.7	3.0	2.9	3.4
1958	6.2	12.7	15.6	11.0	5.6	7.3	6.6	5.6	4.9	4.3	3.5
1959	5.3	12.0	13.3	11.1	4.7	7.0	5.2	4.7	3.9	4.0	2.9
1960	5.3	12.7	14.5	11.5	4.6	7.2	5.7	4.2	4.0	3.3	2.8
1961	6.5	14.8	17.0	13.6	5.7	8.4	6.6	5.6	4.8	4.3	3.8
1962	5.5	12.8	15.6	11.3	4.7	7.7	5.4	4.5	3.7	3.5	4.0
1963	5.8	15.1	18.1	13.2	4.8	7.4	5.8	4.6	3.9	3.5	3.3
1964	5.5	14.9	17.1	13.2	4.6	7.1	5.2	4.5	3.6	3.5	3.4
1965	5.0	14.0	15.0	13.4	4.0	6.3	4.9	4.1	3.0	2.7	2.7
1966	4.3	12.1	14.5	10.7	3.3	5.3	3.7	3.3	2.7	2.2	2.7
1967	4.6	11.5	12.9	10.6	3.8	6.0	4.7	3.7	2.9	2.3	2.6
1968	4.3	12.1	13.9	11.0	3.4	5.9	3.9	3.1	2.3	2.1	2.8
1969	4.2	11.5	13.7	10.0	3.4	5.5	4.2	3.2	2.4	2.1	2.4
1970	5.4	13.4	15.3	11.9	4.4	6.9	5.3	4.3	3.4	2.6	3.3
1971	6.3	15.1	16.7	14.1	5.3	8.5	6.3	4.9	3.9	3.3	3.6
1972	5.9	14.2	17.0	12.3	4.9	8.2	5.5	4.4	3.5	3.3	3.7
1973	5.3	13.0	15.8	10.9	4.3	7.1	5.1	3.7	3.2	2.7	2.8
1974	6.1	14.5	16.4	13.0	5.1	8.2	5.8	4.3	3.6	3.2	3.9
1975	8.6	17.4	19.2	16.1	7.5	11.2	8.4	6.5	5.8	5.0	5.3
1976	7.9	16.4	18.2	15.1	6.8	10.4	7.6	5.8	5.0	4.8	5.3
1977	7.3	15.9	18.2	14.2	6.2	9.3	6.7	5.3	5.0	4.4	4.9
1978	6.2	14.4	17.1	12.4	5.2	8.3	5.8	4.5	3.8	3.0	3.7
1979	5.9	14.0	15.9	12.5	5.0	7.8	5.6	4.2	3.7	3.0	3.1
1980	6.5	14.8	17.3	13.1	5.6	8.5	6.3	4.9	4.3	3.1	3.0
1981	6.9	16.6	18.4	15.3	5.9	9.1	6.6	5.1	4.2	3.7	3.4
1982	8.3	19.0	21.2	17.6	7.3	10.9	8.0	6.4	5.5	5.0	3.1
1983	7.9	18.3	21.4	16.4	6.9	10.3	7.6	6.2	5.5	4.7	3.1
1984	6.5	15.2	17.8	13.6	5.8	8.8	6.1	5.0	4.8	4.0	3.7
1985	6.4	14.8	17.2	13.1	5.7	8.5	6.2	4.9	4.5	4.1	3.1
1986	6.1	14.9	16.7	13.6	5.4	8.1	6.1	4.5	4.3	3.7	2.6
1987	5.2	13.4	15.5	11.7	4.6	7.4	5.0	4.1	3.3	2.9	2.4
1988	4.7	12.3	14.4	10.8	4.1	6.7	4.5	3.7	3.1	2.5	2.6
1989	4.5	11.5	13.8	10.1	4.0	6.8	4.5	3.4	2.9	2.7	2.5
1990	4.7	12.6	15.5	10.9	4.1	6.8	4.6	3.7	3.2	2.7	2.8
1991	5.6	15.2	18.2	13.3	5.0	8.1	5.7	4.3	4.0	3.3	3.1
1992	6.1	15.8	18.9	13.7	5.5	8.3	6.2	4.9	4.3	4.0	4.5
1993	5.7	14.7	17.8	12.6	5.2	7.9	5.8	4.7	4.3	3.9	3.0
1994	5.2	13.8	16.6	11.8	4.6	7.4	5.1	4.2	3.7	3.7	3.9
1995	4.8	13.4	16.4	11.2	4.3	7.4	4.7	3.9	3.0	3.5	3.5
1996	4.7	12.9	14.4	11.7	4.1	7.4	4.6	3.8	3.1	3.1	3.8
1997	4.2	12.8	15.2	11.1	3.7	6.4	4.2	3.4	2.6	2.4	3.4
1998	3.9	10.9	12.4	9.8	3.4	6.3	3.9	3.3	2.5	2.2	3.0
1999	3.8	11.3	13.9	9.6	3.3	6.1	3.6	3.0	2.3	2.5	2.9
2000	3.6	10.4	12.5	9.0	3.1	5.8	3.5	2.9	2.3	2.4	2.4
2001	4.1	11.4	13.1	10.2	3.6	6.1	4.5	3.3	2.7	2.5	2.7
2002	4.9	13.1	14.6	12.1	4.4	7.4	5.0	4.1	3.5	3.3	3.5
2003	4.8	13.3	15.9	11.5	4.4	7.6	4.9	4.2	3.3	3.4	3.5
2004	4.7	13.6	16.1	11.9	4.2	7.1	4.6	3.9	3.3	3.5	3.1
2005	4.4	12.3	14.0	11.1	3.9	6.4	4.7	3.6	3.1	3.0	3.2
2006	4.0	11.7	13.8	10.2	3.6	6.3	4.1	3.4	2.9	2.8	3.0
2007	4.0	12.1	14.1	10.6	3.6	6.2	3.9	3.4	2.9	2.8	3.1
2008	4.9	14.4	17.6	12.3	4.4	7.5	4.8	4.3	3.5	3.5	3.8
2009	7.3	18.4	20.9	17.0	6.8	10.4	7.6	6.7	5.6	5.8	6.0
2010	7.7	20.0	23.4	18.1	7.2	11.0	7.7	7.1	6.4	6.0	6.0
2011	7.5	18.9	22.9	16.7	7.0	11.4	7.7	6.3	6.1	5.8	6.4

Table 1-27. Unemployment Rates of Civilian Workers, by Age, Sex, Race, and Hispanic Origin, 1948–2011
—Continued

(Percent of labor force.)

Race, Hispanic origin, sex, and year	16 years and over	16 to 19 years			20 years and over						
		Total	16 to 17 years	18 to 19 years	Total	20 to 24 years	25 to 34 years	35 to 44 years	45 to 54 years	55 to 64 years	65 years and over
BLACK											
Both Sexes											
1974	10.5	35.0	40.0	31.8	8.0	17.5	8.5	5.4	4.3	3.6	3.9
1975	14.8	39.5	41.6	38.1	12.3	24.5	13.0	8.9	8.3	5.9	6.6
1976	14.0	39.3	44.2	36.7	11.5	22.7	12.8	8.0	6.7	5.9	5.9
1977	14.0	41.1	44.5	39.2	11.5	24.2	12.7	7.4	5.3	5.5	5.9
1978	12.8	38.7	43.9	35.7	10.2	21.8	10.8	6.4	5.2	4.8	5.8
1979	12.3	36.5	40.2	34.4	10.1	20.6	10.8	6.7	5.2	4.9	5.3
1980	14.3	38.5	41.1	37.1	12.1	23.6	13.3	8.2	6.8	5.4	6.9
1981	15.6	41.4	44.8	39.5	13.4	26.4	14.7	9.5	7.4	5.5	7.0
1982	18.9	48.0	48.6	47.8	16.6	30.6	19.0	12.1	8.7	8.3	7.1
1983	19.5	48.5	50.5	47.6	17.3	31.6	19.0	12.4	10.7	9.2	9.2
1984	15.9	42.7	45.7	41.2	13.9	26.1	15.2	9.9	8.2	7.4	6.5
1985	15.1	40.2	43.6	38.3	13.1	24.5	14.5	9.5	8.2	7.0	7.0
1986	14.5	39.3	43.0	37.2	12.7	24.1	14.0	9.6	7.1	6.6	4.5
1987	13.0	34.7	39.7	31.6	11.3	21.8	12.8	8.4	6.8	5.6	3.9
1988	11.7	32.4	35.1	30.7	10.2	19.6	11.9	7.5	5.9	4.8	5.5
1989	11.4	32.4	32.9	32.2	9.9	18.0	11.5	7.6	5.6	5.2	6.9
1990	11.4	30.9	36.5	27.8	10.1	19.9	11.7	7.8	5.3	4.6	5.3
1991	12.5	36.1	39.5	34.4	11.1	21.6	12.7	8.5	7.4	4.4	5.2
1992	14.2	39.7	44.7	37.1	12.6	23.8	14.2	10.5	8.3	6.2	4.9
1993	13.0	38.8	39.7	38.4	11.4	21.9	12.6	9.5	6.9	7.1	4.7
1994	11.5	35.2	36.1	34.6	10.0	19.5	11.1	8.5	5.6	5.4	6.2
1995	10.4	35.7	39.1	33.4	8.7	17.7	9.9	7.3	4.8	4.0	6.7
1996	10.5	33.6	36.3	31.7	9.0	18.8	10.5	7.3	5.0	4.4	5.3
1997	10.0	32.4	35.0	30.8	8.6	18.3	9.9	7.0	5.0	4.2	6.1
1998	8.9	27.6	33.6	24.2	7.7	16.8	8.4	6.5	4.4	3.9	5.6
1999	8.0	27.9	31.0	26.2	6.8	14.6	7.6	5.3	4.0	3.9	5.0
2000	7.6	24.5	26.9	22.9	6.5	15.0	6.7	5.6	4.1	3.0	6.1
2001	8.6	29.0	30.8	27.9	7.4	16.3	8.1	6.3	4.8	3.9	4.3
2002	10.2	29.8	34.9	27.2	9.1	19.1	9.9	7.8	6.3	5.4	5.9
2003	10.8	33.0	32.2	33.5	9.7	19.8	10.9	8.6	6.2	6.3	5.4
2004	10.4	31.7	37.8	28.3	9.4	18.4	10.8	7.8	6.9	5.6	5.5
2005	10.0	33.3	41.2	29.0	8.8	18.3	10.2	7.1	6.0	5.6	6.9
2006	8.9	29.1	32.2	27.3	7.9	16.2	9.3	6.3	5.7	4.6	4.7
2007	8.3	29.4	32.6	27.4	7.2	15.2	8.6	5.4	5.4	4.3	4.5
2008	10.1	31.2	36.3	28.5	9.1	17.9	10.6	7.0	7.0	6.1	7.5
2009	14.8	39.5	43.1	37.8	13.7	24.9	16.7	11.7	10.4	8.4	8.5
2010	16.0	43.0	47.8	40.9	14.9	26.0	17.6	13.0	11.5	9.7	9.2
2011	15.8	41.3	47.1	38.9	14.9	25.2	18.1	13.1	11.2	9.8	8.4
BLACK											
Men											
1974	9.8	33.1	39.9	28.3	7.4	16.2	8.1	4.3	4.2	3.6	5.3
1975	14.8	38.1	41.9	35.9	12.5	24.7	12.7	8.7	9.3	6.3	8.7
1976	13.7	37.5	40.8	36.0	11.4	22.6	12.0	7.5	7.3	6.3	8.7
1977	13.3	39.2	41.0	38.2	10.7	23.0	11.8	6.2	4.9	6.0	7.8
1978	11.8	36.7	43.0	32.9	9.3	21.0	9.8	5.1	4.9	4.4	6.6
1979	11.4	34.2	37.9	32.2	9.3	18.7	9.6	6.3	5.2	5.1	6.4
1980	14.5	37.5	39.7	36.2	12.4	23.7	13.4	8.2	7.2	6.2	8.7
1981	15.7	40.7	43.2	39.2	13.5	26.4	14.4	9.3	7.8	6.1	7.5
1982	20.1	48.9	52.7	47.1	17.8	31.5	20.1	13.4	9.0	10.3	9.3
1983	20.3	48.8	52.2	47.3	18.1	31.4	19.4	13.5	11.4	11.0	11.8
1984	16.4	42.7	44.0	42.2	14.3	26.6	15.0	10.4	7.9	8.9	7.9
1985	15.3	41.0	42.9	40.0	13.2	23.5	13.8	9.6	9.7	7.9	8.9
1986	14.8	39.3	41.4	38.2	12.9	23.5	13.5	10.9	7.8	8.0	4.3
1987	12.7	34.4	39.0	31.6	11.1	20.3	12.2	8.7	6.7	6.6	4.3
1988	11.7	32.7	34.4	31.7	10.1	19.4	11.0	7.6	6.2	5.2	5.6
1989	11.5	31.9	34.4	30.3	10.0	17.9	10.5	8.4	6.2	6.2	7.4
1990	11.9	31.9	38.8	28.0	10.4	20.1	11.5	8.4	6.3	5.4	4.6
1991	13.0	36.3	39.0	34.8	11.5	22.4	11.9	9.5	8.6	5.0	6.1
1992	15.2	42.0	47.5	39.1	13.5	24.6	14.2	11.2	10.3	8.1	4.9
1993	13.8	40.1	42.7	38.6	12.1	23.0	12.3	10.5	8.1	9.0	5.8
1994	12.0	37.6	39.3	36.5	10.3	19.4	10.6	9.1	6.5	6.0	8.2
1995	10.6	37.1	39.7	35.4	8.8	17.6	9.3	7.6	5.5	4.4	7.6
1996	11.1	36.9	39.9	34.9	9.4	19.2	10.1	7.8	6.3	5.2	5.0
1997	10.2	36.5	39.5	34.4	8.5	19.8	8.7	6.7	5.6	4.2	5.5
1998	8.9	30.1	33.9	27.9	7.4	18.0	7.3	6.2	4.4	4.5	5.2
1999	8.2	30.9	33.3	29.4	6.7	16.2	6.9	5.2	4.3	3.9	5.0
2000	8.0	26.2	28.5	24.7	6.9	16.6	6.7	5.8	4.8	2.7	6.3
2001	9.3	30.4	30.5	30.4	8.0	17.6	8.3	6.9	5.5	4.8	4.0
2002	10.7	31.3	36.6	28.7	9.5	20.0	9.4	8.0	7.4	6.1	5.0
2003	11.6	36.0	35.6	36.3	10.3	20.9	11.3	9.2	6.7	6.8	5.6
2004	11.1	35.6	40.8	32.7	9.9	20.3	10.9	8.0	7.2	6.4	4.2
2005	10.5	36.3	45.1	31.5	9.2	20.5	9.7	7.0	6.7	5.9	7.1
2006	9.5	32.7	34.8	31.5	8.3	17.2	9.5	5.9	6.3	5.5	5.8
2007	9.1	33.8	40.1	30.2	7.9	16.9	9.1	5.6	5.8	5.2	5.0
2008	11.4	35.9	43.9	32.0	10.2	19.3	11.8	7.7	7.7	7.1	9.5
2009	17.5	46.0	49.3	44.5	16.3	27.7	19.9	14.0	12.4	10.1	10.6
2010	18.4	45.4	49.4	43.9	17.3	29.8	19.3	14.9	14.4	12.2	10.4
2011	17.8	43.1	44.5	42.5	16.7	27.4	19.7	14.9	12.5	12.7	8.2

Table 1-27. Unemployment Rates of Civilian Workers, by Age, Sex, Race, and Hispanic Origin, 1948–2011
—Continued

(Percent of labor force.)

Race, Hispanic origin, sex, and year	16 years and over	16 to 19 years			20 years and over						
		Total	16 to 17 years	18 to 19 years	Total	20 to 24 years	25 to 34 years	35 to 44 years	45 to 54 years	55 to 64 years	65 years and over
BLACK											
Women											
1974	11.3	37.4	40.2	36.0	8.8	19.0	9.0	6.6	4.4	3.6	1.9
1975	14.8	41.0	41.2	40.6	12.2	24.3	13.4	9.0	7.0	5.3	3.6
1976	14.3	41.6	48.4	37.6	11.7	22.8	13.6	8.5	5.9	5.4	2.4
1977	14.9	43.4	49.5	40.4	12.3	25.5	13.6	8.7	5.8	4.8	3.4
1978	13.8	40.8	45.0	38.7	11.2	22.7	11.9	7.8	5.6	5.2	4.7
1979	13.3	39.1	42.7	36.9	10.9	22.6	12.1	7.2	5.2	4.7	3.9
1980	14.0	39.8	42.9	38.2	11.9	23.5	13.2	8.2	6.4	4.5	4.9
1981	15.6	42.2	46.5	39.8	13.4	26.4	14.9	9.8	6.9	4.7	6.0
1982	17.6	47.1	44.2	48.6	15.4	29.6	17.8	10.7	8.5	6.1	4.5
1983	18.6	48.2	48.6	48.0	16.5	31.8	18.6	11.4	9.9	7.3	6.3
1984	15.4	42.6	47.5	40.2	13.5	25.6	15.4	9.4	8.6	5.9	4.9
1985	14.9	39.2	44.3	36.4	13.1	25.6	15.1	9.3	6.8	6.0	5.2
1986	14.2	39.2	44.6	36.1	12.4	24.7	14.6	8.5	6.4	5.0	4.9
1987	13.2	34.9	40.5	31.7	11.6	23.3	13.5	8.1	6.9	4.5	3.4
1988	11.7	32.0	35.9	29.6	10.4	19.8	12.7	7.4	5.6	4.3	5.4
1989	11.4	33.0	31.1	34.0	9.8	18.1	12.5	7.0	5.0	4.2	6.4
1990	10.9	29.9	34.1	27.6	9.7	19.6	11.9	7.2	4.3	3.6	5.9
1991	12.0	36.0	40.1	33.9	10.6	20.7	13.4	7.6	6.2	3.8	4.4
1992	13.2	37.2	41.7	34.8	11.8	23.1	14.1	9.8	6.4	4.2	5.0
1993	12.1	37.4	36.1	38.1	10.7	20.9	12.9	8.6	5.8	5.1	3.6
1994	11.0	32.6	32.9	32.5	9.8	19.6	11.7	8.0	4.9	4.9	4.4
1995	10.2	34.3	38.5	31.5	8.6	17.8	10.5	7.0	4.2	3.6	. . .
1996	10.0	30.3	32.8	28.6	8.7	18.4	11.0	6.9	3.8	3.8	5.6
1997	9.9	28.7	30.3	27.8	8.8	17.1	10.9	7.2	4.4	4.1	6.6
1998	9.0	25.3	33.2	20.9	7.9	15.7	9.5	6.7	4.3	3.4	6.1
1999	7.8	25.1	28.5	23.3	6.8	13.4	8.3	5.5	3.8	3.9	5.0
2000	7.1	22.8	25.3	21.3	6.2	13.6	6.8	5.5	3.4	3.3	6.0
2001	8.1	27.5	31.2	25.4	7.0	15.3	8.0	5.8	4.3	3.1	4.6
2002	9.8	28.3	33.2	25.6	8.8	18.3	10.2	7.7	5.3	4.7	6.9
2003	10.2	30.3	29.1	31.1	9.2	18.8	10.5	8.1	5.8	5.9	5.3
2004	9.8	28.2	35.2	24.3	8.9	16.6	10.7	7.6	6.5	4.8	6.8
2005	9.5	30.3	37.3	26.6	8.5	16.3	10.6	7.2	5.4	5.3	6.6
2006	8.4	25.9	29.9	23.6	7.5	15.2	9.0	6.7	5.1	3.9	3.7
2007	7.5	25.3	26.4	24.7	6.7	13.6	8.1	5.3	5.0	3.7	4.0
2008	8.9	26.8	29.9	25.0	8.1	16.6	9.5	6.4	6.3	5.3	5.8
2009	12.4	33.4	37.2	31.7	11.5	22.2	13.8	9.7	8.7	7.1	6.6
2010	13.8	40.5	46.4	37.7	12.8	22.6	16.0	11.4	9.1	7.6	8.2
2011	14.1	39.4	49.5	34.8	13.2	23.1	16.5	11.6	10.0	7.4	8.5
HISPANIC[1]											
Both Sexes											
1975	12.2	27.7	30.0	26.5	10.3	16.7	9.9	8.6	8.1	7.7	9.9
1976	11.5	23.8	29.2	19.2	10.1	15.9	9.1	8.2	8.4	8.8	12.6
1977	10.1	22.9	27.0	19.6	8.5	12.0	8.6	6.1	7.3	8.2	9.2
1978	9.1	20.7	28.3	15.1	7.7	10.9	8.0	6.5	5.8	5.0	7.5
1979	8.3	19.2	26.0	14.9	7.0	10.4	6.7	6.2	5.2	6.0	5.7
1980	10.1	22.5	27.6	19.5	8.6	12.1	9.1	7.7	5.7	5.9	6.0
1981	10.4	23.9	28.0	21.7	9.1	13.9	8.8	7.4	6.4	7.3	5.4
1982	13.8	29.9	38.1	25.9	12.3	17.7	12.3	10.7	8.4	10.1	6.5
1983	13.7	28.4	33.8	25.8	12.3	16.7	11.9	11.3	10.0	10.9	5.8
1984	10.7	24.1	28.9	21.6	9.5	12.4	9.7	8.2	7.5	9.7	6.1
1985	10.5	24.3	27.8	22.5	9.4	12.6	9.9	7.7	7.4	7.8	8.1
1986	10.6	24.7	28.1	22.9	9.5	12.9	9.6	8.4	7.8	7.3	10.1
1987	8.8	22.3	27.7	19.5	7.8	10.6	7.7	6.7	6.9	6.0	6.5
1988	8.2	22.0	27.1	19.3	7.0	9.8	7.1	6.0	6.0	5.8	5.6
1989	8.0	19.4	26.4	16.0	7.2	10.7	7.0	5.9	6.3	5.8	5.3
1990	8.2	19.5	24.5	16.9	7.2	9.1	7.3	6.6	6.4	5.6	6.0
1991	10.0	22.9	31.9	18.7	9.0	11.6	9.2	8.1	8.0	6.5	7.0
1992	11.6	27.5	35.7	23.4	10.4	13.2	10.4	9.8	8.8	8.6	8.1
1993	10.8	26.1	35.1	21.8	9.7	13.1	9.3	9.1	8.6	8.0	6.6
1994	9.9	24.5	31.7	20.6	8.9	11.8	9.0	7.7	8.1	7.3	7.9
1995	9.3	24.1	33.1	19.5	8.2	11.5	8.2	7.2	6.4	7.5	10.6
1996	8.9	23.6	30.0	20.3	7.8	11.8	7.3	7.3	6.0	7.3	8.2
1997	7.7	21.6	27.7	18.4	6.8	10.3	6.3	6.4	5.1	6.5	6.8
1998	7.2	21.3	28.0	18.1	6.1	9.4	5.9	5.5	4.6	5.3	6.4
1999	6.4	18.6	23.7	16.3	5.5	8.3	5.4	4.8	4.8	4.5	5.0
2000	5.7	16.6	22.5	13.9	4.9	7.5	4.8	4.5	3.3	4.5	5.7
2001	6.6	17.7	24.0	15.0	5.8	8.1	5.9	5.2	4.3	5.6	4.5
2002	7.5	20.1	24.2	18.2	6.7	9.9	6.6	6.0	5.5	5.7	6.8
2003	7.7	20.0	24.6	17.7	7.0	10.2	7.0	6.0	6.3	5.7	3.9
2004	7.0	20.4	29.0	16.8	6.2	9.3	6.3	5.3	5.2	5.8	6.0
2005	6.0	18.4	23.6	16.0	5.3	8.6	5.3	4.5	4.4	4.4	4.9
2006	5.2	15.9	20.4	13.6	4.6	7.2	4.7	4.3	3.7	3.3	3.9
2007	5.6	18.1	22.5	16.0	5.0	7.8	4.9	4.3	4.5	4.5	4.9
2008	7.6	22.4	29.8	19.0	6.8	11.5	6.7	5.8	6.3	4.8	7.8
2009	12.1	30.2	36.3	27.8	11.2	16.2	11.4	10.2	10.1	10.0	8.0
2010	12.5	32.2	37.6	30.2	11.6	17.4	11.3	10.3	10.8	10.3	9.5
2011	11.5	31.1	38.3	28.5	10.6	15.7	10.4	9.2	9.9	9.7	8.8

[1]May be of any race.
. . . = Not available.

Table 1-27. Unemployment Rates of Civilian Workers, by Age, Sex, Race, and Hispanic Origin, 1948–2011
—Continued

(Percent of labor force.)

Race, Hispanic origin, sex, and year	16 years and over	16 to 19 years			20 years and over						
		Total	16 to 17 years	18 to 19 years	Total	20 to 24 years	25 to 34 years	35 to 44 years	45 to 54 years	55 to 64 years	65 years and over
HISPANIC[1]											
Men											
1975	11.4	27.6	29.3	26.5	9.6	16.3	9.6	7.9	7.0	6.8	. . .
1976	10.8	23.3	28.7	19.7	9.4	16.0	8.1	7.0	7.4	8.7	. . .
1977	9.0	20.9	25.9	18.2	7.7	11.7	7.9	4.9	5.4	7.4	. . .
1978	7.7	19.7	27.5	13.9	6.4	9.4	6.6	4.8	4.8	4.4	. . .
1979	7.0	17.5	23.5	13.8	5.8	9.2	5.3	5.1	4.4	5.0	. . .
1980	9.7	21.9	26.2	19.3	8.3	12.2	8.3	7.1	6.0	5.9	. . .
1981	10.2	24.3	30.9	20.3	8.8	14.1	8.9	6.5	5.9	6.7	. . .
1982	13.6	31.3	40.2	26.8	12.1	18.2	12.4	9.9	7.5	10.0	. . .
1983	13.6	28.7	34.7	25.9	12.2	17.0	11.6	10.8	10.3	11.7	. . .
1984	10.5	25.2	31.5	22.2	9.3	12.5	9.2	7.6	7.2	10.2	. . .
1985	10.2	24.7	29.1	22.4	9.1	12.9	9.6	7.2	6.8	7.0	. . .
1986	10.5	24.5	28.5	22.4	9.5	13.0	9.5	8.5	7.0	8.0	. . .
1987	8.7	22.2	28.2	19.3	7.8	10.2	7.6	6.9	7.1	6.7	. . .
1988	8.1	22.7	29.5	19.5	7.0	9.2	7.0	5.9	6.1	6.7	. . .
1989	7.6	20.2	27.6	16.8	6.6	9.7	5.9	5.7	6.0	6.6	. . .
1990	8.0	19.5	24.0	17.4	7.0	8.4	6.9	6.5	6.8	6.5	. . .
1991	10.3	23.5	33.6	19.2	9.3	11.6	9.3	8.5	7.9	8.1	. . .
1992	11.7	28.2	36.6	24.0	10.5	13.7	10.1	9.8	8.9	10.2	. . .
1993	10.6	25.9	34.5	21.9	9.5	12.6	9.0	8.8	8.8	8.5	. . .
1994	9.4	26.3	33.3	22.5	8.3	10.8	8.4	6.6	8.1	7.4	10.5
1995	8.8	25.3	34.8	20.2	7.7	10.6	7.5	6.7	5.9	7.9	12.9
1996	7.9	22.5	31.5	18.4	6.9	10.3	6.6	6.3	5.1	6.7	8.3
1997	7.0	20.8	26.5	17.9	6.1	9.8	5.1	5.4	4.8	6.8	7.2
1998	6.4	20.6	29.0	16.4	5.4	8.9	5.2	4.5	4.2	5.3	5.0
1999	5.6	17.8	23.4	15.3	4.7	7.8	4.1	3.8	4.5	4.6	5.0
2000	5.0	15.7	22.3	12.8	4.2	6.6	3.7	3.8	3.1	4.1	6.2
2001	5.9	17.1	25.8	13.4	5.2	8.1	4.6	4.5	3.8	6.3	4.8
2002	7.2	20.2	22.9	19.1	6.4	9.3	6.1	5.4	5.5	6.2	6.3
2003	7.2	21.9	25.9	20.1	6.4	9.6	6.3	5.3	6.0	6.0	3.6
2004	6.5	21.2	30.7	17.6	5.8	9.4	5.5	4.5	4.7	5.7	6.9
2005	5.4	19.3	23.4	17.5	4.7	8.2	4.3	3.9	4.0	4.0	4.8
2006	4.8	17.3	22.6	14.8	4.2	6.7	4.2	3.6	3.4	3.5	3.7
2007	5.3	19.7	23.4	18.0	4.6	7.4	4.5	3.8	4.4	3.9	5.5
2008	7.6	23.4	30.9	19.9	6.8	11.8	6.6	5.6	6.2	5.1	7.8
2009	12.5	33.8	41.1	31.1	11.6	16.6	11.6	10.5	10.5	11.2	7.8
2010	12.7	34.6	41.0	32.6	11.7	18.2	11.6	9.8	11.2	10.6	9.4
2011	11.2	33.3	40.7	31.0	10.3	15.3	9.9	8.7	9.8	10.4	9.5
HISPANIC[1]											
Women											
1975	13.5	27.9	31.0	26.4	11.5	17.2	10.5	9.9	10.0	9.3	. . .
1976	12.7	22.2	30.3	18.7	11.4	15.8	10.8	10.0	9.8	9.0	. . .
1977	11.9	24.4	28.5	21.9	10.1	12.1	9.8	8.2	10.6	11.0	. . .
1978	11.3	21.8	29.9	16.6	9.8	13.0	10.3	9.2	7.4	7.2	. . .
1979	10.3	21.2	30.0	15.8	8.9	12.1	8.9	7.7	7.1	7.9	. . .
1980	10.7	23.4	29.7	19.8	9.2	12.0	10.6	8.6	5.3	5.8	. . .
1981	10.8	23.4	23.5	23.4	9.5	13.5	8.7	8.9	7.2	8.4	. . .
1982	14.1	28.2	35.1	25.0	12.5	16.8	12.2	11.9	9.9	10.4	. . .
1983	13.8	28.0	32.5	25.7	12.4	16.2	12.5	12.2	9.7	9.6	. . .
1984	11.1	22.8	26.1	21.0	9.9	12.2	10.3	9.1	7.9	8.8	. . .
1985	11.0	23.8	26.2	22.6	9.9	12.1	10.6	8.5	8.1	9.2	. . .
1986	10.8	25.1	27.6	23.6	9.6	12.9	9.8	8.2	8.9	6.2	. . .
1987	8.9	22.4	27.1	19.9	7.7	11.4	7.8	6.5	6.7	5.0	. . .
1988	8.3	21.0	24.5	18.9	7.1	10.7	7.2	6.2	5.9	4.6	. . .
1989	8.8	18.2	24.7	14.9	8.0	12.2	8.6	6.3	6.7	4.5	. . .
1990	8.4	19.4	25.4	16.2	7.5	10.4	8.0	6.7	6.0	4.3	. . .
1991	9.6	21.9	29.6	17.9	8.6	11.7	9.1	7.6	8.1	4.1	. . .
1992	11.4	26.4	34.5	22.4	10.2	12.4	11.0	9.7	8.5	6.2	. . .
1993	11.0	26.3	36.0	21.7	9.9	14.0	9.9	9.5	8.3	7.2	. . .
1994	10.7	22.2	29.7	18.1	9.8	13.5	10.1	9.2	8.0	7.1	3.6
1995	10.0	22.6	30.7	18.7	8.9	13.0	9.5	7.9	7.0	6.8	6.4
1996	10.2	25.1	28.2	23.3	9.2	14.1	8.5	8.7	7.2	8.1	8.0
1997	8.9	22.7	29.2	19.1	7.9	11.0	8.2	7.7	5.5	6.1	6.0
1998	8.2	22.1	26.4	20.2	7.1	10.1	7.2	6.9	5.1	5.4	8.8
1999	7.6	19.8	24.0	17.7	6.6	9.1	7.3	6.3	5.1	4.3	4.8
2000	6.8	18.0	22.7	15.6	5.9	9.0	6.4	5.4	3.6	5.0	4.8
2001	7.5	18.5	21.6	17.1	6.6	8.2	7.8	6.2	4.8	4.8	4.0
2002	8.0	19.9	25.8	17.0	7.2	10.8	7.4	6.7	5.5	5.0	7.5
2003	8.4	17.7	23.2	14.4	7.8	11.3	8.2	7.1	6.8	5.3	4.4
2004	7.6	19.3	27.0	15.5	7.0	9.1	7.6	6.4	5.8	5.8	4.6
2005	6.9	17.2	23.8	14.0	6.3	9.2	7.1	5.5	4.8	5.0	5.1
2006	5.9	14.1	18.1	11.9	5.3	8.1	5.5	5.5	4.2	3.1	4.2
2007	6.1	16.1	21.3	13.6	5.5	8.5	5.6	5.1	4.3	5.2	4.0
2008	7.7	21.1	28.1	18.0	6.9	11.1	6.8	6.0	6.4	4.4	7.7
2009	11.5	25.8	30.8	23.8	10.6	15.7	10.9	9.7	9.6	8.5	8.3
2010	12.3	29.1	34.2	27.0	11.4	16.2	10.9	11.1	10.4	9.9	9.6
2011	11.8	28.1	35.7	25.0	11.1	16.3	11.4	9.9	10.1	8.8	8.0

[1]May be of any race.
. . . = Not available.

Table 1-28. Unemployed Persons and Unemployment Rates, by Selected Occupation, 2000–2011

(Thousands of people, percent of civilian labor force.)

Occupation	2000	2001	2002	2003	2004	2005	2006	2007	2008	2009	2010	2011
Total Unemployed Persons, 16 Years and Over[1]	5 692	6 801	8 378	8 774	8 149	7 591	7 001	7 078	8 924	14 265	14 825	13 747
Management, professional, and related	827	1 102	1 482	1 556	1 346	1 172	1 065	1 090	1 463	2 531	2 566	2 458
Management, business, and financial operations	320	455	622	627	544	464	427	429	619	1 105	1 117	1 067
Professional and related	507	647	859	929	801	708	638	662	844	1 427	1 449	1 392
Services	1 132	1 311	1 544	1 681	1 617	1 587	1 485	1 521	1 769	2 605	2 819	2 727
Sales and office	1 446	1 652	2 110	2 070	1 937	1 820	1 667	1 638	2 006	3 143	3 315	3 135
Sales and related	673	779	998	995	912	874	812	835	980	1 501	1 596	1 481
Office and administrative support	773	873	1 112	1 076	1 025	946	856	804	1 026	1 642	1 719	1 653
Natural resources, construction, and maintenance	758	943	1 155	1 244	1 140	1 069	1 007	1 052	1 421	2 464	2 504	2 000
Farming, fishing, and forestry	133	163	142	136	132	103	101	89	112	179	193	181
Construction and extraction	507	626	788	814	786	751	699	781	1 067	1 825	1 809	1 414
Installation, maintenance, and repair	119	154	225	295	222	214	207	182	243	459	503	406
Production, transportation, and material moving	1 081	1 318	1 530	1 555	1 393	1 245	1 127	1 128	1 474	2 453	2 365	2 099
Production	575	759	848	807	714	677	544	564	746	1 322	1 206	1 025
Transportation and material moving	505	559	682	748	679	568	583	564	727	1 131	1 159	1 073
Total Unemployment Rate, 16 Years and Over[1]	4.0	4.7	5.8	6.0	5.5	5.1	4.6	4.6	5.8	9.3	9.6	8.9
Management, professional, and related	1.8	2.3	3.0	3.1	2.7	2.3	2.1	2.1	2.7	4.6	4.7	4.5
Management, business, and financial operations	1.6	2.2	3.0	3.1	2.6	2.2	2.0	1.9	2.7	4.9	5.1	4.7
Professional and related	1.9	2.3	3.0	3.2	2.8	2.4	2.1	2.1	2.7	4.4	4.5	4.3
Services	5.2	5.8	6.6	7.1	6.6	6.4	5.9	5.9	6.7	9.6	10.3	9.9
Sales and office	3.8	4.4	5.6	5.5	5.2	4.8	4.4	4.3	5.3	8.5	9.0	8.7
Sales and related	4.1	4.7	5.9	5.9	5.4	5.0	4.7	4.8	5.7	8.8	9.4	8.8
Office and administrative support	3.6	4.2	5.4	5.2	5.0	4.6	4.2	4.0	5.1	8.3	8.7	8.5
Natural resources, construction, and maintenance	5.3	6.4	7.8	8.1	7.3	6.5	6.0	6.3	8.8	15.6	16.1	13.3
Farming, fishing, and forestry	10.2	13.4	12.0	11.4	11.8	9.6	9.5	8.5	10.2	16.2	16.3	15.3
Construction and extraction	6.2	7.3	9.1	9.1	8.4	7.6	6.8	7.6	11.0	19.7	20.1	16.6
Installation, maintenance, and repair	2.4	3.2	4.6	5.5	4.2	3.9	3.7	3.4	4.5	8.5	9.3	7.7
Production, transportation, and material moving	5.1	6.4	7.6	7.9	7.2	6.5	5.8	5.8	7.6	13.3	12.8	11.3
Production	4.8	6.6	7.8	7.7	7.0	6.7	5.5	5.7	7.7	14.7	13.1	11.2
Transportation and material moving	5.6	6.2	7.4	8.2	7.4	6.2	6.2	6.0	7.6	12.0	12.4	11.4

[1] Includes persons with no work experience and persons whose last job was in the armed forces.

Table 1-29. Unemployed Persons and Unemployment Rates, by Class of Worker and Industry, 2000–2011

(Thousands of people, percent.)

Class of worker and industry	2000	2001	2002	2003	2004	2005	2006	2007	2008	2009	2010	2011
Total Unemployed Persons, 16 Years and Over	5 692	6 801	8 378	8 774	8 149	7 591	7 001	7 078	8 924	14 265	14 825	13 747
Nonagricultural private wage and salary workers	4 483	5 540	6 926	7 131	6 484	5 989	5 523	5 559	7 118	11 654	11 808	10 655
Mining, quarrying, and oil and gas extraction	21	23	33	37	21	20	22	25	25	90	73	52
Construction	513	609	800	810	769	712	671	757	1 030	1 770	1 801	1 383
Manufacturing	691	992	1 205	1 166	966	812	699	706	945	1 890	1 622	1 373
Durable goods	400	630	789	762	590	485	410	436	597	1 279	1 074	887
Nondurable goods	290	362	416	404	375	326	289	270	348	611	548	485
Wholesale trade and retail trade	837	945	1 202	1 237	1 197	1 137	1 039	975	1 205	1 844	1 963	1 834
Transportation and utilities	193	236	274	283	236	232	229	233	312	525	492	484
Information	124	190	253	246	189	163	126	120	167	294	303	222
Financial activities	208	252	320	319	332	272	264	289	380	598	626	582
Professional and business services	573	768	1 009	1 042	861	792	746	740	921	1 522	1 561	1 430
Education and health services	383	463	570	640	617	627	568	575	698	1 100	1 243	1 217
Leisure and hospitality	720	833	961	1 006	972	921	865	896	1 102	1 543	1 592	1 527
Other services	219	229	301	347	324	301	293	241	332	477	533	551
Agriculture and related private wage and salary workers	134	153	139	140	129	104	95	78	123	200	211	190
Government workers	422	430	512	568	548	534	473	505	534	799	969	1 013
Self-employed and unpaid family workers	219	218	265	294	303	298	293	309	383	577	617	605
Total Unemployment Rate, 16 Years and Over[1]	4.0	4.7	5.8	6.0	5.5	5.1	4.6	4.6	5.8	9.3	9.6	8.9
Nonagricultural private wage and salary workers	4.1	5.0	6.2	6.3	5.7	5.2	4.7	4.7	5.9	9.8	9.9	9.0
Mining	4.4	4.2	6.3	6.7	3.9	3.1	3.2	3.4	3.1	11.6	9.4	6.1
Construction	6.2	7.1	9.2	9.3	8.4	7.4	6.7	7.4	10.6	19.0	20.6	16.4
Manufacturing	3.5	5.2	6.7	6.6	5.7	4.9	4.2	4.3	5.8	12.1	10.6	9.0
Durable goods	3.2	5.2	6.9	6.9	5.5	4.6	3.9	4.2	5.6	12.9	11.2	9.2
Nondurable goods	4.0	5.2	6.2	6.1	5.9	5.3	4.8	4.5	6.0	10.6	9.6	8.5
Wholesale trade and retail trade	4.3	4.9	6.1	6.0	5.8	5.4	4.9	4.7	5.9	9.0	9.5	8.9
Transportation and utilities	3.4	4.3	4.9	5.3	4.4	4.1	4.0	3.9	5.1	8.9	8.4	8.2
Information	3.2	4.9	6.9	6.8	5.7	5.0	3.7	3.6	5.0	9.2	9.7	7.3
Financial activities	2.4	2.9	3.5	3.5	3.6	2.9	2.7	3.0	3.9	6.4	6.9	6.4
Professional and business services	4.8	6.1	7.9	8.2	6.8	6.2	5.6	5.3	6.5	10.8	10.8	9.7
Education and health services	2.5	2.8	3.4	3.6	3.4	3.4	3.0	3.0	3.5	5.3	5.8	5.6
Leisure and hospitality	6.6	7.5	8.4	8.7	8.3	7.8	7.3	7.4	8.6	11.7	12.2	11.6
Other services	3.9	4.0	5.1	5.7	5.3	4.8	4.7	3.9	5.3	7.5	8.5	8.8
Agriculture and related private wage and salary workers	9.0	11.2	10.1	10.2	9.9	8.3	7.2	6.3	9.2	14.3	13.9	12.5
Government workers	2.1	2.2	2.5	2.8	2.7	2.6	2.3	2.3	2.4	3.6	4.4	4.7
Self-employed and unpaid family workers	2.1	2.1	2.6	2.7	2.8	2.7	2.7	2.8	3.6	5.5	5.9	6.0

Note: See notes and definitions for information on historical comparability.

[1]Includes persons with no work experience and persons whose last job was in the armed forces.

Table 1-30. Unemployed Persons, by Duration of Unemployment, 1948–2011

(Thousands of people, number of weeks.)

Year	Total unemployed	Duration of unemployment										Average duration, in weeks	Median duration, in weeks
		Less than 5 weeks		5 to 14 weeks		15 weeks and over							
								15 to 26 weeks		27 weeks and over			
		Number	Percent	Number	Percent	Number	Percent	Number	Percent	Number	Percent		
1948	2 276	1 300	57.1	669	29.4	309	13.6	193	8.5	116	5.1	8.6	. . .
1949	3 637	1 756	48.3	1 194	32.8	684	18.8	428	11.8	256	7.0	10.0	. . .
1950	3 288	1 450	44.1	1 055	32.1	782	23.8	425	12.9	357	10.9	12.1	. . .
1951	2 055	1 177	57.3	574	27.9	303	14.7	166	8.1	137	6.7	9.7	. . .
1952	1 883	1 135	60.3	516	27.4	232	12.3	148	7.9	84	4.5	8.4	. . .
1953	1 834	1 142	62.3	482	26.3	210	11.5	132	7.2	78	4.3	8.0	. . .
1954	3 532	1 605	45.4	1 116	31.6	812	23.0	495	14.0	317	9.0	11.8	. . .
1955	2 852	1 335	46.8	815	28.6	702	24.6	366	12.8	336	11.8	13.0	. . .
1956	2 750	1 412	51.3	805	29.3	533	19.4	301	10.9	232	8.4	11.3	. . .
1957	2 859	1 408	49.2	891	31.2	560	19.6	321	11.2	239	8.4	10.5	. . .
1958	4 602	1 753	38.1	1 396	30.3	1 452	31.6	785	17.1	667	14.5	13.9	. . .
1959	3 740	1 585	42.4	1 114	29.8	1 040	27.8	469	12.5	571	15.3	14.4	. . .
1960	3 852	1 719	44.6	1 176	30.5	957	24.8	503	13.1	454	11.8	12.8	. . .
1961	4 714	1 806	38.3	1 376	29.2	1 532	32.5	728	15.4	804	17.1	15.6	. . .
1962	3 911	1 663	42.5	1 134	29.0	1 119	28.6	534	13.7	585	15.0	14.7	. . .
1963	4 070	1 751	43.0	1 231	30.2	1 088	26.7	535	13.1	553	13.6	14.0	. . .
1964	3 786	1 697	44.8	1 117	29.5	973	25.7	491	13.0	482	12.7	13.3	. . .
1965	3 366	1 628	48.4	983	29.2	755	22.4	404	12.0	351	10.4	11.8	. . .
1966	2 875	1 573	54.7	779	27.1	526	18.3	287	10.0	239	8.3	10.4	. . .
1967	2 975	1 634	54.9	893	30.0	448	15.1	271	9.1	177	5.9	8.7	2.3
1968	2 817	1 594	56.6	810	28.8	412	14.6	256	9.1	156	5.5	8.4	4.5
1969	2 832	1 629	57.5	827	29.2	375	13.2	242	8.5	133	4.7	7.8	4.4
1970	4 093	2 139	52.3	1 290	31.5	663	16.2	428	10.4	235	5.8	8.6	4.9
1971	5 016	2 245	44.8	1 585	31.6	1 187	23.7	668	13.3	519	10.4	11.3	6.3
1972	4 882	2 242	45.9	1 472	30.2	1 167	23.9	601	12.3	566	11.6	12.0	6.2
1973	4 365	2 224	51.0	1 314	30.1	826	18.9	483	11.1	343	7.9	10.0	5.2
1974	5 156	2 604	50.5	1 597	31.0	955	18.5	574	11.1	381	7.4	9.8	5.2
1975	7 929	2 940	37.1	2 484	31.3	2 505	31.6	1 303	16.4	1 203	15.2	14.2	8.4
1976	7 406	2 844	38.4	2 196	29.6	2 366	32.0	1 018	13.8	1 348	18.2	15.8	8.2
1977	6 991	2 919	41.8	2 132	30.5	1 942	27.8	913	13.1	1 028	14.7	14.3	7.0
1978	6 202	2 865	46.2	1 923	31.0	1 414	22.8	766	12.3	648	10.5	11.9	5.9
1979	6 137	2 950	48.1	1 946	31.7	1 241	20.2	706	11.5	535	8.7	10.8	5.4
1980	7 637	3 295	43.2	2 470	32.3	1 871	24.5	1 052	13.8	820	10.7	11.9	6.5
1981	8 273	3 449	41.7	2 539	30.7	2 285	27.6	1 122	13.6	1 162	14.0	13.7	6.9
1982	10 678	3 883	36.4	3 311	31.0	3 485	32.6	1 708	16.0	1 776	16.6	15.6	8.7
1983	10 717	3 570	33.3	2 937	27.4	4 210	39.3	1 652	15.4	2 559	23.9	20.0	10.1
1984	8 539	3 350	39.2	2 451	28.7	2 737	32.1	1 104	12.9	1 634	19.1	18.2	7.9
1985	8 312	3 498	42.1	2 509	30.2	2 305	27.7	1 025	12.3	1 280	15.4	15.6	6.8
1986	8 237	3 448	41.9	2 557	31.0	2 232	27.1	1 045	12.7	1 187	14.4	15.0	6.9
1987	7 425	3 246	43.7	2 196	29.6	1 983	26.7	943	12.7	1 040	14.0	14.5	6.5
1988	6 701	3 084	46.0	2 007	30.0	1 610	24.0	801	12.0	809	12.1	13.5	5.9
1989	6 528	3 174	48.6	1 978	30.3	1 375	21.1	730	11.2	646	9.9	11.9	4.8
1990	7 047	3 265	46.3	2 257	32.0	1 525	21.6	822	11.7	703	10.0	12.0	5.3
1991	8 628	3 480	40.3	2 791	32.4	2 357	27.3	1 246	14.4	1 111	12.9	13.7	6.8
1992	9 613	3 376	35.1	2 830	29.4	3 408	35.4	1 453	15.1	1 954	20.3	17.7	8.7
1993	8 940	3 262	36.5	2 584	28.9	3 094	34.6	1 297	14.5	1 798	20.1	18.0	8.3
1994	7 996	2 728	34.1	2 408	30.1	2 860	35.8	1 237	15.5	1 623	20.3	18.8	9.2
1995	7 404	2 700	36.5	2 342	31.6	2 363	31.9	1 085	14.6	1 278	17.3	16.6	8.3
1996	7 236	2 633	36.4	2 287	31.6	2 316	32.0	1 053	14.6	1 262	17.4	16.7	8.3
1997	6 739	2 538	37.7	2 138	31.7	2 062	30.6	995	14.8	1 067	15.8	15.8	8.0
1998	6 210	2 622	42.2	1 950	31.4	1 637	26.4	763	12.3	875	14.1	14.5	6.7
1999	5 880	2 568	43.7	1 832	31.2	1 480	25.2	755	12.8	725	12.3	13.4	6.4
2000	5 692	2 558	44.9	1 815	31.9	1 318	23.2	669	11.8	649	11.4	12.6	5.9
2001	6 801	2 853	42.0	2 196	32.3	1 752	25.8	951	14.0	801	11.8	13.1	6.8
2002	8 378	2 893	34.5	2 580	30.8	2 904	34.7	1 369	16.3	1 535	18.3	16.6	9.1
2003	8 774	2 785	31.7	2 612	29.8	3 378	38.5	1 442	16.4	1 936	22.1	19.2	10.1
2004	8 149	2 696	33.1	2 382	29.2	3 072	37.7	1 293	15.9	1 779	21.8	19.6	9.8
2005	7 591	2 667	35.1	2 304	30.4	2 619	34.5	1 130	14.9	1 490	19.6	18.4	8.9
2006	7 001	2 614	37.3	2 121	30.3	2 266	32.4	1 031	14.7	1 235	17.6	16.8	8.3
2007	7 078	2 542	35.9	2 232	31.5	2 303	32.5	1 061	15.0	1 243	17.6	16.8	8.5
2008	8 924	2 932	32.8	2 804	31.4	3 188	35.7	1 427	16.0	1 761	19.7	17.9	9.4
2009	14 265	3 165	22.2	3 828	26.8	7 272	51.0	2 775	19.5	4 496	31.5	24.4	15.1
2010	14 825	2 771	18.7	3 267	22.0	8 786	59.3	2 371	16.0	6 415	43.3	33.0	21.4
2011	13 747	2 677	19.5	2 993	21.8	8 077	58.8	2 061	15.0	6 016	43.8	39.3	21.4

. . . = Not available.

Table 1-31. Long-Term Unemployment, by Industry and Selected Occupation, 2000–2011

(Thousands of people.)

Length of unemployment, industry, and occupation	2000	2001	2002	2003	2004	2005	2006	2007	2008	2009	2010	2011
UNEMPLOYED 15 WEEKS AND OVER												
Total	1 318	1 752	2 904	3 378	3 072	2 619	2 266	2 303	3 188	7 272	8 786	8 077
Wage and Salary Workers, by Industry												
Agriculture and related	32	44	39	44	38	29	30	28	42	96	100	99
Mining [1]	7	7	11	17	8	8	5	6	7	44	46	31
Construction	107	130	236	262	248	216	177	215	339	907	1 083	822
Manufacturing	184	303	528	575	467	326	257	259	385	1 059	1 122	922
Durable goods	99	183	348	389	293	199	140	162	246	702	773	611
Nondurable goods	86	120	180	186	174	127	116	97	139	357	350	311
Wholesale and retail trade	186	241	423	472	455	415	337	334	440	962	1 215	1 118
Transportation and utilities	57	71	124	132	114	91	87	95	142	290	343	343
Information	33	52	119	128	87	76	55	49	66	170	204	146
Financial activities	58	75	131	144	139	91	103	100	168	357	446	411
Professional and business services	143	217	377	440	345	299	266	247	346	810	985	878
Education and health services	124	149	232	300	304	271	263	253	320	691	898	910
Leisure and hospitality	146	196	279	328	321	277	259	274	356	755	898	830
Other services	54	58	95	132	126	117	97	80	132	245	310	336
Public administration	41	36	51	59	72	62	34	51	55	107	164	185
Experienced Workers, by Occupation												
Management, professional, and related	213	313	603	692	571	436	373	368	569	1 331	1 600	1 482
Services	246	323	447	564	565	511	464	482	595	1 243	1 557	1 500
Sales and office	331	419	759	810	750	641	561	560	741	1 675	2 048	1 949
Natural resources, construction, and maintenance	161	212	346	424	386	341	294	299	463	1 224	1 445	1 150
Production, transportation, and material moving	273	360	575	654	561	461	380	384	570	1 302	1 498	1 290
UNEMPLOYED 27 WEEKS AND OVER												
Total	649	801	1 535	1 936	1 779	1 490	1 235	1 243	1 761	4 496	6 415	6 016
Wage and Salary Workers, by Industry												
Agriculture and related	13	16	18	21	18	16	13	14	17	51	57	58
Mining [1]	4	3	5	10	6	4	3	3	4	23	37	22
Construction	44	60	111	132	133	108	92	107	168	530	773	617
Manufacturing	100	132	291	366	302	195	140	152	230	657	888	725
Durable goods	50	75	191	255	196	124	75	93	150	428	619	486
Nondurable goods	50	57	100	111	106	71	64	58	80	229	269	239
Wholesale and retail trade	80	114	226	261	261	230	183	171	237	607	904	833
Transportation and utilities	27	33	67	74	63	50	42	58	77	180	263	265
Information	18	21	62	80	58	41	30	29	38	115	159	116
Financial activities	32	34	131	88	79	56	56	50	97	232	332	315
Professional and business services	67	90	377	262	193	172	144	130	184	510	722	641
Education and health services	63	71	232	167	168	156	144	132	182	432	644	671
Leisure and hospitality	69	90	279	166	169	148	135	142	196	445	624	596
Other services	26	31	95	71	76	74	51	43	73	161	223	249
Public administration	23	18	51	33	44	38	21	29	29	66	121	140
Experienced Workers, by Occupation												
Management, professional, and related	101	135	340	429	356	269	206	207	569	840	6 415	1 121
Services	128	156	225	295	307	284	249	251	595	750	1 094	1 086
Sales and office	151	185	397	459	419	354	299	285	741	1 067	1 513	1 486
Natural resources, construction, and maintenance	74	96	164	229	221	186	158	157	463	724	1 042	855
Production, transportation, and material moving	140	162	313	388	336	261	206	219	570	814	1 142	973

Note: Beginning with data for January 2011, the Current Population Survey (CPS) uses the 2010 Census Occupational Classification system derived from the 2010 Standard Occupational Classification (SOC) system. The 2010 classification system replaces an earlier version that was based on the 2000 SOC. As a result of the classification change, CPS occupational data beginning with January 2011 data are not strictly comparable with earlier years.

[1]For 2009 through 2011, mining includes quarrying, and oil and gas extraction.

Table 1-32. Unemployed Persons and Unemployment Rates, by Reason for Unemployment, Sex, and Age, 1975–2011

(Thousands of people, percent.)

Sex, age, and year	Number of unemployed					Unemployed as a percent of the total civilian labor force			
	Total	Job losers and persons who completed temporary jobs	Job leavers	Entrants		Job losers and persons who completed temporary jobs	Job leavers	Entrants	
				Reentrants	New entrants			Reentrants	New entrants
Both Sexes, 16 Years and Over									
1975	7 929	4 386	827	1 892	823	4.7	0.9	2.0	0.9
1976	7 406	3 679	903	1 928	895	3.8	0.9	2.0	0.9
1977	6 991	3 166	909	1 963	953	3.2	0.9	2.0	1.0
1978	6 202	2 585	874	1 857	885	2.5	0.9	1.8	0.9
1979	6 137	2 635	880	1 806	817	2.5	0.8	1.7	0.8
1980	7 637	3 947	891	1 927	872	3.7	0.8	1.8	0.8
1981	8 273	4 267	923	2 102	981	3.9	0.8	1.9	0.9
1982	10 678	6 268	840	2 384	1 185	5.7	0.8	2.2	1.1
1983	10 717	6 258	830	2 412	1 216	5.6	0.7	2.2	1.1
1984	8 539	4 421	823	2 184	1 110	3.9	0.7	1.9	1.0
1985	8 312	4 139	877	2 256	1 039	3.6	0.8	2.0	0.9
1986	8 237	4 033	1 015	2 160	1 029	3.4	0.9	1.8	0.9
1987	7 425	3 566	965	1 974	920	3.0	0.8	1.6	0.8
1988	6 701	3 092	983	1 809	816	2.5	0.8	1.5	0.7
1989	6 528	2 983	1 024	1 843	677	2.4	0.8	1.5	0.5
1990	7 047	3 387	1 041	1 930	688	2.7	0.8	1.5	0.5
1991	8 628	4 694	1 004	2 139	792	3.7	0.8	1.7	0.6
1992	9 613	5 389	1 002	2 285	937	4.2	0.8	1.8	0.7
1993	8 940	4 848	976	2 198	919	3.8	0.8	1.7	0.7
1994	7 996	3 815	791	2 786	604	2.9	0.6	2.1	0.5
1995	7 404	3 476	824	2 525	579	2.6	0.6	1.9	0.4
1996	7 236	3 370	774	2 512	580	2.5	0.6	1.9	0.4
1997	6 739	3 037	795	2 338	569	2.2	0.6	1.7	0.4
1998	6 210	2 822	734	2 132	520	2.1	0.5	1.5	0.4
1999	5 880	2 622	783	2 005	469	1.9	0.6	1.4	0.3
2000	5 692	2 517	780	1 961	434	1.8	0.5	1.4	0.3
2001	6 801	3 476	835	2 031	459	2.4	0.6	1.4	0.3
2002	8 378	4 607	866	2 368	536	3.2	0.6	1.6	0.4
2003	8 774	4 838	818	2 477	641	3.3	0.6	1.7	0.4
2004	8 149	4 197	858	2 408	686	2.8	0.6	1.6	0.5
2005	7 591	3 667	872	2 386	666	2.5	0.6	1.6	0.4
2006	7 001	3 321	827	2 237	616	2.2	0.5	1.5	0.4
2007	7 078	3 515	793	2 142	627	2.3	0.5	1.4	0.4
2008	8 924	4 789	896	2 472	766	3.1	0.6	1.6	0.5
2009	14 265	9 160	882	3 187	1 035	5.9	0.6	2.1	0.7
2010	14 825	9 250	889	3 466	1 220	6.0	0.6	2.3	0.8
2011	13 747	8 106	956	3 401	1 284	5.3	0.6	2.2	0.8
Both Sexes, 16 to 19 Years									
1975	1 767	450	155	529	634	5.1	1.7	6.0	7.1
1976	1 719	387	153	496	683	4.3	1.7	5.5	7.5
1977	1 663	318	156	477	711	3.4	1.7	5.1	7.6
1978	1 583	300	167	455	660	3.1	1.7	4.7	6.8
1979	1 555	319	184	452	599	3.3	1.9	4.7	6.2
1980	1 669	388	156	481	643	4.1	1.7	5.1	6.9
1981	1 763	385	162	487	728	4.3	1.8	5.4	8.1
1982	1 977	460	134	509	874	5.4	1.6	6.0	10.2
1983	1 829	370	110	482	867	4.6	1.3	5.9	10.6
1984	1 499	271	114	370	745	3.4	1.4	4.7	9.4
1985	1 468	275	113	390	689	3.5	1.4	4.9	8.7
1986	1 454	240	145	374	695	3.0	1.8	4.7	8.8
1987	1 347	210	146	375	617	2.7	1.8	4.7	7.7
1988	1 226	207	159	310	550	2.6	2.0	3.9	6.8
1989	1 194	198	200	345	452	2.5	2.5	4.3	5.7
1990	1 212	233	181	338	460	3.0	2.3	4.3	5.9
1991	1 359	289	180	365	524	4.0	2.5	5.0	7.2
1992	1 427	259	149	377	643	3.6	2.1	5.3	9.1
1993	1 365	233	151	353	628	3.3	2.1	4.9	8.8
1994	1 320	185	84	634	416	2.5	1.1	8.5	5.6
1995	1 346	214	102	615	415	2.8	1.3	7.9	5.3
1996	1 306	182	91	625	409	2.3	1.2	8.0	5.2
1997	1 271	174	104	606	388	2.2	1.3	7.6	4.9
1998	1 205	181	86	577	361	2.2	1.0	7.0	4.4
1999	1 162	173	114	547	328	2.1	1.4	6.6	3.9
2000	1 081	157	109	516	299	1.9	1.3	6.2	3.6
2001	1 162	185	98	568	311	2.3	1.2	7.2	3.9
2002	1 253	197	91	597	368	2.6	1.2	7.9	4.9
2003	1 251	188	85	554	424	2.6	1.2	7.7	5.9
2004	1 208	165	76	510	456	2.3	1.1	7.2	6.4
2005	1 186	155	76	489	466	2.2	1.1	6.8	6.5
2006	1 119	145	78	461	435	2.0	1.1	6.3	6.0
2007	1 101	176	71	435	419	2.5	1.0	6.2	6.0
2008	1 285	203	80	490	511	3.0	1.2	7.1	7.5
2009	1 552	271	56	548	677	4.2	0.9	8.6	10.6
2010	1 528	220	42	487	778	3.7	0.7	8.2	13.2
2011	1 400	181	52	429	739	3.2	0.9	7.5	12.9

Note: See notes and definitions for information on historical comparability.

Table 1-32. Unemployed Persons and Unemployment Rates, by Reason for Unemployment, Sex, and Age, 1975–2011—*Continued*

(Thousands of people, percent.)

Sex, age, and year	Number of unemployed					Unemployed as a percent of the total civilian labor force			
	Total	Job losers and persons who completed temporary jobs	Job leavers	Entrants		Job losers and persons who completed temporary jobs	Job leavers	Entrants	
				Reentrants	New entrants			Reentrants	New entrants
Men, 20 Years and Over									
1975	3 476	2 598	298	506	76	5.0	0.6	1.0	0.1
1976	3 098	2 167	323	521	86	4.1	0.6	1.0	0.2
1977	2 794	1 816	335	540	103	3.4	0.6	1.0	0.2
1978	2 328	1 433	337	471	86	2.6	0.6	0.9	0.2
1979	2 308	1 464	325	446	73	2.6	0.6	0.8	0.1
1980	3 353	2 389	359	516	90	4.2	0.6	0.9	0.2
1981	3 615	2 565	356	592	102	4.5	0.6	1.0	0.2
1982	5 089	3 965	327	678	119	6.8	0.6	1.2	0.2
1983	5 257	4 088	336	695	138	6.9	0.6	1.2	0.2
1984	3 932	2 800	324	663	146	4.7	0.5	1.1	0.2
1985	3 715	2 568	352	671	124	4.3	0.6	1.1	0.2
1986	3 751	2 568	444	611	128	4.1	0.7	1.0	0.2
1987	3 369	2 289	413	558	108	3.7	0.7	0.9	0.2
1988	2 987	1 939	416	534	98	3.1	0.7	0.9	0.2
1989	2 867	1 843	394	541	88	2.9	0.6	0.8	0.1
1990	3 239	2 100	431	626	82	3.2	0.7	1.0	0.1
1991	4 195	2 982	411	698	105	4.6	0.6	1.1	0.2
1992	4 717	3 420	421	765	111	5.2	0.6	1.2	0.2
1993	4 287	2 996	429	747	114	4.5	0.6	1.1	0.2
1994	3 627	2 296	367	898	65	3.4	0.5	1.3	0.1
1995	3 239	2 051	356	775	57	3.0	0.5	1.2	0.1
1996	3 146	2 043	322	731	51	3.0	0.5	1.1	0.1
1997	2 882	1 795	358	675	55	2.6	0.5	1.0	0.1
1998	2 580	1 588	318	611	63	2.3	0.5	0.9	0.1
1999	2 433	1 459	336	592	46	2.1	0.5	0.8	0.1
2000	2 376	1 416	328	577	55	2.0	0.5	0.8	0.1
2001	3 040	1 999	372	612	56	2.7	0.5	0.8	0.1
2002	3 896	2 702	386	743	65	3.7	0.5	1.0	0.1
2003	4 209	2 899	376	846	88	3.9	0.5	1.1	0.1
2004	3 791	2 503	398	791	99	3.3	0.5	1.0	0.1
2005	4 059	2 188	445	1 067	359	2.7	0.5	1.0	0.1
2006	3 131	1 927	368	757	78	2.5	0.5	1.0	0.1
2007	3 259	2 064	371	723	101	2.6	0.5	0.9	0.1
2008	4 297	2 918	410	969	856	3.7	0.5	1.1	0.1
2009	7 555	5 796	407	1 190	162	7.3	0.5	1.5	0.2
2010	7 763	5 773	433	1 346	211	7.3	0.5	1.7	0.3
2011	6 898	4 856	464	1 312	267	6.1	0.6	1.7	0.3
Women, 20 Years and Over									
1975	2 684	1 339	375	858	114	4.0	1.1	2.6	0.3
1976	2 588	1 124	427	912	126	3.2	1.2	2.6	0.4
1977	2 535	1 031	419	945	140	2.8	1.2	2.6	0.4
1978	2 292	852	371	930	138	2.2	1.0	2.4	0.4
1979	2 276	851	370	908	145	2.1	0.9	2.3	0.4
1980	2 615	1 170	376	930	139	2.8	0.9	2.3	0.3
1981	2 895	1 317	404	1 023	151	3.1	1.0	2.4	0.4
1982	3 613	1 844	379	1 197	192	4.2	0.9	2.7	0.4
1983	3 632	1 801	384	1 235	212	4.0	0.9	2.8	0.5
1984	3 107	1 350	386	1 151	220	2.9	0.8	2.5	0.5
1985	3 129	1 296	412	1 195	227	2.7	0.9	2.5	0.5
1986	3 032	1 225	426	1 175	206	2.5	0.9	2.4	0.4
1987	2 709	1 067	406	1 041	194	2.2	0.8	2.1	0.4
1988	2 487	946	408	965	168	1.9	0.8	1.9	0.3
1989	2 467	942	430	958	137	1.8	0.8	1.8	0.3
1990	2 596	1 054	429	966	146	2.0	0.8	1.8	0.3
1991	3 074	1 423	413	1 075	163	2.6	0.8	2.0	0.3
1992	3 469	1 710	433	1 142	183	3.1	0.8	2.1	0.3
1993	3 288	1 619	395	1 098	176	2.9	0.7	2.0	0.3
1994	3 049	1 334	339	1 253	122	2.4	0.6	2.2	0.2
1995	2 819	1 211	366	1 135	107	2.1	0.6	2.0	0.2
1996	2 783	1 145	361	1 156	120	2.0	0.6	2.0	0.2
1997	2 585	1 069	333	1 057	126	1.8	0.6	1.8	0.2
1998	2 424	1 053	330	944	97	1.8	0.6	1.6	0.2
1999	2 285	990	333	866	96	1.6	0.5	1.4	0.2
2000	2 235	943	343	868	80	1.5	0.6	1.4	0.1
2001	2 599	1 291	365	850	92	2.0	0.6	1.3	0.1
2002	3 228	1 708	389	1 028	102	2.7	0.6	1.6	0.2
2003	3 314	1 751	357	1 076	130	2.7	0.6	1.7	0.2
2004	3 150	1 529	384	1 107	131	2.4	0.6	1.7	0.2
2005	3 013	1 417	391	1 103	101	2.2	0.6	1.7	0.2
2006	2 751	1 249	380	1 019	103	1.9	0.6	1.5	0.2
2007	2 718	1 276	351	984	107	1.9	0.5	1.7	0.4
2008	3 342	1 668	406	1 126	143	2.4	0.6	1.6	0.2
2009	5 157	3 093	419	1 449	196	4.5	0.6	2.1	0.3
2010	5 534	3 257	413	1 633	231	4.7	0.6	2.4	0.3
2011	5 450	3 070	441	1 661	279	4.5	0.6	2.4	0.4

Note: See notes and definitions for information on historical comparability.

Table 1-33. Percent of the Population with Work Experience During the Year, by Age and Sex, 1987–2011

(Percent.)

Sex and year	Total	16 to 17 years	18 to 19 years	20 to 24 years	25 to 34 years	35 to 44 years	45 to 54 years	55 to 59 years	60 to 64 years	65 to 69 years	70 years and over
Both Sexes											
1987	69.7	51.8	76.6	85.5	85.7	86.1	81.6	69.4	51.3	26.2	10.2
1988	70.2	50.6	75.5	85.7	86.0	86.8	82.2	70.5	52.2	27.9	10.3
1989	70.5	51.9	75.4	84.9	86.6	86.9	82.8	70.4	52.5	28.4	10.0
1990	70.2	48.6	74.2	84.1	86.2	87.0	82.8	70.9	53.4	28.3	10.2
1991	69.5	43.4	70.8	83.4	85.9	86.6	83.0	70.3	52.9	27.2	9.8
1992	69.1	43.8	69.9	82.7	85.2	85.9	82.8	70.8	53.5	25.5	9.8
1993	69.2	42.1	70.4	82.0	85.0	85.3	82.8	71.6	51.6	27.5	10.7
1994	69.6	44.1	71.5	82.5	85.5	85.6	83.8	72.2	52.8	27.5	10.0
1995	69.6	44.4	71.2	82.0	85.6	85.9	83.4	72.2	53.3	28.0	10.2
1996	69.9	43.3	70.5	83.1	86.1	85.7	84.3	73.3	54.3	27.8	10.4
1997	70.1	43.6	70.5	83.0	87.1	85.9	84.4	73.8	53.8	28.5	10.0
1998	70.1	42.1	69.9	82.9	86.7	86.3	84.2	73.7	54.5	29.2	10.6
1999	70.7	43.7	71.2	82.7	87.3	86.9	85.0	72.3	55.8	30.5	11.6
2000	70.5	42.2	69.6	82.6	87.1	87.0	84.6	72.9	55.1	30.8	11.4
2001	69.4	37.7	66.7	80.8	86.1	85.8	83.7	73.5	56.7	30.6	10.5
2002	68.5	34.5	62.8	78.5	84.4	85.0	83.7	74.7	56.8	33.1	10.4
2003	67.8	32.0	61.7	77.5	83.7	84.0	82.9	73.9	56.5	33.2	11.4
2004	67.7	32.6	59.8	76.9	83.3	84.2	82.6	73.9	57.0	32.7	12.2
2005	67.8	31.1	60.1	77.3	83.7	84.1	82.8	74.4	58.2	32.0	12.1
2006	67.9	30.9	58.3	76.9	84.4	84.3	82.8	74.5	58.2	33.6	12.6
2007	67.8	28.5	57.3	76.6	84.2	84.4	82.4	75.6	59.7	35.2	13.0
2008	67.1	24.6	55.3	76.0	84.1	83.9	81.8	74.6	60.3	34.9	13.5
2009	65.0	21.9	48.7	71.0	81.6	82.0	80.5	73.8	59.3	35.3	12.8
2010	63.8	17.8	43.9	69.1	80.2	81.3	79.2	73.8	58.4	37.1	13.0
2011	63.4	17.0	44.8	69.8	79.7	81.3	79.0	72.0	59.5	36.5	13.3
Men											
1987	78.9	52.4	77.4	90.4	94.3	94.1	91.9	83.3	63.2	34.2	15.4
1988	79.1	51.8	78.9	90.7	94.3	94.6	91.6	82.1	63.1	35.6	15.6
1989	79.4	53.2	77.7	89.9	94.7	94.7	91.9	82.0	64.2	35.4	15.1
1990	78.9	50.3	76.7	88.7	94.4	94.7	91.3	82.0	65.8	35.8	14.0
1991	77.9	45.4	72.2	87.9	93.5	93.6	91.3	81.5	63.6	35.0	14.4
1992	77.4	46.6	73.7	87.1	93.3	92.8	89.9	80.9	63.2	32.4	14.3
1993	76.8	43.9	71.4	86.6	92.5	92.0	89.3	79.8	59.1	34.3	15.3
1994	77.2	44.4	74.7	87.2	92.9	92.0	90.0	81.3	61.4	33.9	14.8
1995	77.0	43.7	73.6	86.4	92.6	92.2	89.7	81.5	62.1	34.5	14.9
1996	77.2	44.1	71.8	86.7	93.4	92.1	90.4	81.8	62.5	33.6	15.2
1997	77.1	43.4	70.3	86.6	94.1	92.3	90.7	81.4	62.9	33.8	13.9
1998	76.9	40.4	71.6	86.4	93.5	92.7	90.1	81.7	63.5	35.5	14.7
1999	77.3	44.7	72.3	85.5	93.9	93.2	89.9	79.2	65.1	37.4	16.5
2000	77.1	42.1	70.2	85.1	93.4	93.6	89.8	80.6	64.4	38.4	16.0
2001	76.3	37.4	67.7	84.8	93.2	92.2	89.1	80.4	64.3	37.8	14.5
2002	75.2	34.7	62.8	82.1	91.6	91.8	88.9	80.7	64.3	39.3	14.6
2003	74.3	32.8	61.7	80.2	90.8	90.9	87.7	80.9	63.1	37.3	15.8
2004	74.2	32.1	58.9	80.2	91.0	91.1	87.9	80.1	64.5	37.1	16.7
2005	74.6	31.1	60.7	80.8	91.3	91.6	88.2	80.1	64.3	37.6	17.0
2006	74.5	30.9	57.9	80.1	91.9	91.8	88.0	80.6	64.1	38.3	17.3
2007	74.3	28.5	59.0	80.5	90.5	91.5	88.2	80.3	66.2	39.3	17.9
2008	73.2	24.4	55.1	78.7	90.7	91.1	86.4	79.3	66.0	40.3	17.9
2009	70.8	22.2	48.0	73.3	87.7	89.1	85.0	78.3	64.8	39.8	17.2
2010	69.4	16.9	43.2	71.3	86.0	88.0	84.1	78.9	62.8	43.4	17.5
2011	69.0	16.1	43.2	71.6	86.2	88.1	84.3	76.7	64.0	42.6	18.2
Women											
1987	61.3	51.1	75.8	81.0	77.3	78.5	71.9	56.7	41.0	19.6	6.8
1988	62.1	49.3	72.2	81.0	78.1	79.4	73.5	60.0	42.5	21.4	6.8
1989	62.3	50.6	73.1	80.2	78.6	79.3	74.2	59.9	42.4	22.5	6.7
1990	62.2	46.8	71.7	79.6	78.0	79.6	74.9	60.4	42.5	22.1	7.7
1991	61.8	41.4	69.4	79.0	78.3	79.9	75.3	59.9	43.6	20.6	6.7
1992	61.5	40.9	66.1	78.4	77.2	79.1	76.1	61.5	44.4	20.0	6.7
1993	62.1	40.3	69.4	77.5	77.6	78.7	76.5	63.9	44.7	22.1	7.7
1994	62.5	43.7	68.4	77.8	78.1	79.4	78.0	63.9	45.0	22.2	6.8
1995	62.8	45.2	68.7	77.7	78.8	79.8	77.6	63.2	45.6	22.4	7.1
1996	63.2	42.5	69.2	79.5	78.9	79.5	78.4	65.4	46.9	23.0	7.1
1997	63.6	43.9	70.7	79.5	80.1	79.6	78.4	66.7	45.6	24.0	7.3
1998	63.7	44.1	68.2	79.4	80.1	80.0	78.6	66.3	46.2	23.8	7.8
1999	64.5	42.6	70.1	79.9	80.9	80.7	80.3	66.2	47.3	24.4	8.2
2000	64.3	42.3	69.0	80.2	80.9	80.5	79.5	65.7	47.0	23.9	8.2
2001	63.1	38.1	65.7	76.9	79.2	79.5	78.6	67.1	49.8	24.2	7.9
2002	62.3	34.3	62.8	74.9	77.2	78.4	78.7	69.1	50.0	27.8	7.4
2003	61.7	31.2	61.6	74.6	76.6	77.2	78.4	67.3	50.7	29.6	8.3
2004	61.5	33.1	60.7	73.7	75.6	77.4	77.5	68.2	50.3	28.7	9.0
2005	61.4	31.2	59.6	73.7	76.1	76.8	77.6	68.9	52.7	27.1	8.7
2006	61.6	30.9	58.7	73.7	76.9	76.9	77.9	68.8	53.0	29.5	9.3
2007	61.6	28.5	55.6	72.6	77.8	77.4	76.9	71.2	53.7	31.5	9.5
2008	61.3	24.8	55.4	73.2	77.3	76.7	77.3	70.1	55.0	30.1	10.3
2009	59.6	21.6	49.5	68.6	75.4	75.0	76.1	69.5	54.4	31.1	9.7
2010	58.5	18.7	44.5	66.9	74.3	74.7	74.4	69.1	54.2	31.6	9.6
2011	58.1	18.0	46.5	68.0	73.4	74.7	73.8	67.7	55.4	31.0	9.6

Note: See notes and definitions for information on historical comparability.

Table 1-34. Persons with Work Experience During the Year, by Industry and Class of Worker of Job Held the Longest, 2002–2011

(Thousands of people.)

Industry and class of worker	2002	2003	2004	2005	2006	2007	2008	2009	2010	2011
TOTAL	151 546	151 553	153 024	155 127	157 352	158 468	158 317	154 772	153 141	154 330
Agriculture	2 490	2 521	2 492	2 344	2 332	2 407	2 382	2 581	2 383	2 470
Wage and salary workers	1 583	1 605	1 549	1 501	1 495	1 525	1 522	1 733	1 578	1 679
Self-employed workers	875	894	918	829	812	846	824	813	788	750
Unpaid family workers	33	22	25	14	25	36	37	35	17	42
Nonagricultural Industries	149 055	149 032	150 532	152 783	155 021	156 061	155 934	152 191	150 759	151 859
Wage and salary workers	139 909	139 747	140 885	143 002	145 152	146 485	146 521	142 946	141 686	142 962
Mining	594	576	630	696	758	746	840	778	771	890
Construction	9 488	9 423	10 076	10 423	10 989	10 547	10 234	9 443	8 633	8 607
Manufacturing	17 660	17 349	17 196	17 243	17 112	16 641	16 332	14 956	14 865	15 139
Durable goods	11 013	10 622	10 814	10 930	10 995	10 687	10 477	9 342	9 288	9 586
Nondurable goods	6 647	6 727	6 382	6 313	6 116	5 954	5 855	5 613	5 577	5 552
Wholesale and retail trade	21 615	21 650	22 091	22 479	21 822	21 837	21 838	21 210	20 854	20 685
Wholesale trade	4 402	4 691	4 470	4 517	4 395	4 017	4 016	3 849	3 921	3 601
Retail trade	17 213	16 959	17 621	17 962	17 427	17 820	17 822	17 361	16 933	17 084
Transportation and utilities	7 039	6 934	7 040	7 248	7 413	8 023	7 675	7 309	6 993	7 173
Transportation and warehousing	5 745	5 736	5 827	6 095	6 197	6 750	6 365	6 025	5 701	5 944
Utilities	1 294	1 198	1 213	1 153	1 216	1 273	1 310	1 284	1 292	1 229
Information	3 989	3 755	3 359	3 495	3 710	3 687	3 455	3 375	3 380	3 137
Financial activities	9 591	9 822	9 956	9 748	10 101	10 013	9 671	9 409	9 239	9 443
Finance and insurance	6 986	7 135	7 192	7 011	7 190	7 347	6 994	6 792	6 726	6 909
Real estate and rental and leasing	2 605	2 687	2 764	2 737	2 912	2 666	2 677	2 617	2 512	2 534
Professional and business services	13 883	13 485	13 277	13 537	14 412	14 659	14 868	14 633	15 094	15 339
Professional, scientific, and technical services	7 989	7 855	7 793	7 768	8 294	8 676	8 742	8 475	8 841	9 054
Management, administration, and waste management services	5 894	5 629	5 484	5 769	6 118	5 982	6 127	6 159	6 253	6 285
Education and health services	29 343	29 571	29 814	30 552	31 314	31 921	32 828	33 465	33 596	33 424
Education services	12 765	13 026	13 169	13 282	13 659	13 989	14 396	14 457	14 157	13 917
Health care and social assistance services	16 578	16 544	16 645	17 270	17 655	17 932	18 432	19 008	19 439	19 507
Leisure and hospitality	13 260	13 110	13 345	13 405	13 455	13 959	14 242	13 917	13 718	14 293
Arts, entertainment, and recreation	2 852	2 789	2 888	2 877	2 797	3 124	3 047	3 284	2 993	3 116
Accommodation and food services	10 408	10 321	10 457	10 528	10 658	10 835	11 195	10 633	10 725	11 177
Other services and private household	6 416	6 529	6 473	6 490	6 341	6 603	6 590	6 233	6 111	6 717
Private households	873	897	907	866	912	888	912	757	816	773
Public administration	6 290	6 734	6 897	6 917	7 076	7 095	7 121	7 332	7 597	7 270
Self-employed workers	9 023	9 169	9 520	9 658	9 733	9 451	9 332	9 121	8 962	8 778
Unpaid family workers	124	116	128	123	135	126	82	124	111	120

Note: See notes and definitions for information on historical comparability.

Table 1-35. Number of Persons with Work Experience During the Year, by Extent of Employment and Sex, 1987–2011

(Thousands of people.)

Sex and year	Total	Full-time workers				Part-time workers			
		Total	50 to 52 weeks	27 to 49 weeks	1 to 26 weeks	Total	50 to 52 weeks	27 to 49 weeks	1 to 26 weeks
Both Sexes									
1987	128 315	100 288	77 015	13 361	9 912	28 027	10 973	6 594	10 460
1988	130 451	102 131	79 627	12 875	9 629	28 320	11 384	6 624	10 312
1989	132 817	104 876	81 117	14 271	9 488	27 941	11 275	6 987	9 679
1990	133 535	105 323	80 932	14 758	9 633	28 212	11 507	7 012	9 693
1991	133 410	104 472	80 385	14 491	9 596	28 938	11 946	7 003	9 989
1992	133 912	104 813	81 523	13 587	9 703	29 099	12 326	6 841	9 932
1993	136 354	106 299	83 384	13 054	9 861	30 055	12 818	6 777	10 460
1994	138 468	108 141	85 764	13 051	9 326	30 327	12 936	6 956	10 435
1995	139 724	110 063	88 173	12 970	8 920	29 661	12 725	6 831	10 105
1996	142 201	112 313	90 252	12 997	9 064	29 888	13 382	6 643	9 863
1997	143 968	113 879	92 631	12 508	8 740	30 089	13 810	6 565	9 714
1998	145 566	116 412	95 772	12 156	8 484	29 155	13 538	6 480	9 137
1999	148 295	119 096	97 941	12 294	8 861	29 199	13 680	6 317	9 202
2000	149 361	120 591	100 349	12 071	8 171	28 770	13 865	6 161	8 744
2001	151 042	121 921	100 357	13 172	8 392	29 121	14 038	6 139	8 944
2002	151 546	121 726	100 659	12 544	8 523	29 819	14 635	6 184	9 000
2003	151 553	121 158	100 700	11 972	8 486	30 395	15 333	6 027	9 035
2004	153 024	122 404	102 427	11 862	8 115	30 621	15 552	6 077	8 992
2005	155 127	124 683	104 876	11 816	7 991	30 444	15 374	6 161	8 909
2006	157 352	127 340	107 734	11 736	7 870	30 012	15 131	6 223	8 657
2007	158 468	128 332	108 617	11 901	7 814	30 136	15 477	6 194	8 466
2008	158 317	125 937	104 023	13 421	8 493	32 380	16 562	6 630	9 188
2009	154 772	121 355	99 306	12 350	9 698	33 418	17 417	6 674	9 327
2010	153 141	119 940	99 250	11 705	8 985	33 201	17 122	6 582	9 497
2011	154 330	121 400	101 700	11 040	8 661	32 929	17 261	6 288	9 380
Men									
1987	69 144	59 736	47 040	7 503	5 193	9 408	3 260	2 191	3 957
1988	70 021	60 504	48 299	7 329	4 876	9 517	3 468	2 199	3 850
1989	71 640	62 108	49 693	7 642	4 773	9 532	3 619	2 254	3 659
1990	71 953	62 319	49 175	8 188	4 956	9 634	3 650	2 322	3 662
1991	71 700	61 636	47 895	8 324	5 417	10 064	3 820	2 342	3 902
1992	72 007	61 722	48 300	7 965	5 457	10 285	3 864	2 354	4 067
1993	72 872	62 513	49 832	7 317	5 364	10 359	4 005	2 144	4 210
1994	73 958	63 634	51 582	7 094	4 958	10 324	3 948	2 358	4 018
1995	74 381	64 145	52 671	6 973	4 501	10 236	4 034	2 257	3 945
1996	75 760	65 356	53 795	6 891	4 670	10 404	4 321	2 136	3 947
1997	76 408	66 089	54 918	6 638	4 533	10 319	4 246	2 274	3 799
1998	76 918	67 250	56 953	6 208	4 089	9 669	4 197	2 090	3 382
1999	78 145	68 347	57 520	6 401	4 426	9 797	4 297	2 062	3 438
2000	78 804	68 925	58 756	6 094	4 075	9 879	4 485	1 957	3 437
2001	79 971	70 074	58 715	7 087	4 272	9 897	4 306	1 989	3 602
2002	80 282	70 132	58 765	6 804	4 563	10 151	4 519	2 042	3 590
2003	80 317	69 766	58 778	6 479	4 509	10 551	5 042	1 872	3 637
2004	81 261	70 780	60 096	6 428	4 256	10 482	4 987	1 992	3 503
2005	82 735	72 056	61 510	6 299	4 247	10 679	5 153	2 074	3 452
2006	83 767	73 578	63 058	6 373	4 147	10 189	4 747	2 046	3 396
2007	84 292	73 734	62 994	6 583	4 157	10 558	4 933	2 165	3 460
2008	83 889	72 204	59 869	7 645	4 690	11 685	5 425	2 457	3 803
2009	81 835	69 178	56 058	7 339	5 780	12 658	5 911	2 526	4 221
2010	81 076	68 402	56 416	6 760	5 225	12 674	5 883	2 523	4 267
2011	81 272	69 029	58 004	6 183	4 842	12 243	5 797	2 408	4 037
Women									
1987	59 171	40 552	29 975	5 858	4 719	18 619	7 713	4 403	6 503
1988	60 430	41 627	31 328	5 546	4 753	18 803	7 916	4 425	6 462
1989	61 178	42 768	31 424	6 629	4 715	18 410	7 656	4 733	6 021
1990	61 582	43 004	31 757	6 570	4 677	18 578	7 857	4 690	6 031
1991	61 712	42 837	32 491	6 167	4 179	18 875	8 126	4 662	6 087
1992	61 904	43 090	33 223	5 621	4 246	18 814	8 462	4 487	5 865
1993	63 481	43 785	33 552	5 736	4 497	19 696	8 813	4 633	6 250
1994	64 511	44 508	34 182	5 957	4 369	20 003	8 988	4 598	6 417
1995	65 342	45 917	35 502	5 997	4 418	19 425	8 691	4 574	6 160
1996	66 439	46 955	36 457	6 105	4 393	19 484	9 061	4 507	5 916
1997	67 559	47 790	37 713	5 870	4 207	19 769	9 564	4 291	5 914
1998	68 648	49 162	38 819	5 948	4 395	19 486	9 341	4 390	5 755
1999	70 150	50 748	40 421	5 892	4 435	19 402	9 383	4 255	5 764
2000	70 556	51 665	41 593	5 977	4 095	18 891	9 380	4 204	5 307
2001	71 071	51 848	41 642	6 085	4 120	19 223	9 731	4 150	5 342
2002	71 263	51 593	41 893	5 741	3 959	19 671	10 117	4 143	5 411
2003	71 236	51 391	41 921	5 493	3 977	19 844	10 291	4 155	5 398
2004	71 763	51 624	42 331	5 434	3 859	20 139	10 565	4 085	5 489
2005	72 392	52 627	43 366	5 517	3 744	19 765	10 222	4 087	5 456
2006	73 585	53 762	44 676	5 364	3 723	19 823	10 384	4 178	5 261
2007	74 176	54 598	45 622	5 318	3 657	19 579	10 543	4 029	5 006
2008	74 428	53 733	44 154	5 776	3 803	20 695	11 137	4 172	5 385
2009	72 937	52 177	43 248	5 012	3 918	20 760	11 506	4 147	5 107
2010	72 066	51 538	42 834	4 944	3 760	20 528	11 239	4 058	5 230
2011	73 058	52 371	43 696	4 857	3 818	20 687	11 464	3 880	5 343

Note: See notes and definitions for information on historical comparability.

Table 1-36. Percent Distribution of the Population with Work Experience During the Year, by Extent of Employment and Sex, 1987–2011

(Percent of total people with work experience.)

Sex and year	Total	Full-time workers				Part-time workers			
		Total	50 to 52 weeks	27 to 49 weeks	1 to 26 weeks	Total	50 to 52 weeks	27 to 49 weeks	1 to 26 weeks
Both Sexes									
1987	100.0	78.1	60.0	10.4	7.7	21.9	8.6	5.1	8.2
1988	100.0	78.3	61.0	9.9	7.4	21.7	8.7	5.1	7.9
1989	100.0	78.9	61.1	10.7	7.1	21.1	8.5	5.3	7.3
1990	100.0	78.9	60.6	11.1	7.2	21.2	8.6	5.3	7.3
1991	100.0	78.4	60.3	10.9	7.2	21.7	9.0	5.2	7.5
1992	100.0	78.2	60.9	10.1	7.2	21.7	9.2	5.1	7.4
1993	100.0	78.0	61.2	9.6	7.2	22.1	9.4	5.0	7.7
1994	100.0	78.0	61.9	9.4	6.7	21.8	9.3	5.0	7.5
1995	100.0	78.8	63.1	9.3	6.4	21.2	9.1	4.9	7.2
1996	100.0	79.0	63.5	9.1	6.4	21.0	9.4	4.7	6.9
1997	100.0	79.1	64.3	8.7	6.1	20.9	9.6	4.6	6.7
1998	100.0	80.0	65.8	8.4	5.8	20.1	9.3	4.5	6.3
1999	100.0	80.3	66.0	8.3	6.0	19.7	9.2	4.3	6.2
2000	100.0	80.8	67.2	8.1	5.5	19.3	9.3	4.1	5.9
2001	100.0	80.7	66.4	8.7	5.6	19.3	9.3	4.1	5.9
2002	100.0	80.3	66.4	8.3	5.6	19.7	9.7	4.1	5.9
2003	100.0	79.9	66.4	7.9	5.6	20.1	10.1	4.0	6.0
2004	100.0	80.0	66.9	7.8	5.3	20.1	10.2	4.0	5.9
2005	100.0	80.4	67.6	7.6	5.2	19.6	9.9	4.0	5.7
2006	100.0	80.9	68.5	7.5	5.0	19.1	9.6	4.0	5.5
2007	100.0	81.0	68.5	7.5	4.9	19.0	9.8	3.9	5.3
2008	100.0	79.5	65.7	8.5	5.4	20.5	10.5	4.2	5.8
2009	100.0	78.4	64.2	8.0	6.3	21.6	11.3	4.3	6.0
2010	100.0	78.3	64.8	7.6	5.9	21.7	11.2	4.3	6.2
2011	100.0	78.7	65.9	7.2	5.6	21.3	11.2	4.1	6.1
Men									
1987	100.0	86.4	68.0	10.9	7.5	13.6	4.7	3.2	5.7
1988	100.0	86.5	69.0	10.5	7.0	13.6	5.0	3.1	5.5
1989	100.0	86.8	69.4	10.7	6.7	13.3	5.1	3.1	5.1
1990	100.0	86.6	68.3	11.4	6.9	13.4	5.1	3.2	5.1
1991	100.0	86.0	66.8	11.6	7.6	14.0	5.3	3.3	5.4
1992	100.0	85.8	67.1	11.1	7.6	14.3	5.4	3.3	5.6
1993	100.0	85.8	68.4	10.0	7.4	14.2	5.5	2.9	5.8
1994	100.0	86.0	69.7	9.6	6.7	13.9	5.3	3.2	5.4
1995	100.0	86.3	70.8	9.4	6.1	13.7	5.4	3.0	5.3
1996	100.0	86.3	71.0	9.1	6.2	13.7	5.7	2.8	5.2
1997	100.0	86.5	71.9	8.7	5.9	13.6	5.6	3.0	5.0
1998	100.0	87.4	74.0	8.1	5.3	12.6	5.5	2.7	4.4
1999	100.0	87.5	73.6	8.2	5.7	12.5	5.5	2.6	4.4
2000	100.0	87.5	74.6	7.7	5.2	12.6	5.7	2.5	4.4
2001	100.0	87.6	73.4	8.9	5.3	12.4	5.4	2.5	4.5
2002	100.0	87.4	73.2	8.5	5.7	12.6	5.6	2.5	4.5
2003	100.0	86.9	73.2	8.1	5.6	13.1	6.3	2.3	4.5
2004	100.0	87.1	74.0	7.9	5.2	12.9	6.1	2.5	4.3
2005	100.0	87.0	74.3	7.6	5.1	12.9	6.2	2.5	4.2
2006	100.0	87.8	75.3	7.6	5.0	12.2	5.7	2.4	4.1
2007	100.0	87.5	74.7	7.8	4.9	12.5	5.9	2.6	4.1
2008	100.0	86.1	71.4	9.1	5.6	13.9	6.5	2.9	4.5
2009	100.0	84.5	68.5	9.0	7.1	15.5	7.2	3.1	5.2
2010	100.0	84.4	69.6	8.3	6.4	15.6	7.3	3.1	5.3
2011	100.0	84.9	71.4	7.6	6.0	15.1	7.1	3.0	5.0
Women									
1987	100.0	68.6	50.7	9.9	8.0	31.4	13.0	7.4	11.0
1988	100.0	68.9	51.8	9.2	7.9	31.1	13.1	7.3	10.7
1989	100.0	69.9	51.4	10.8	7.7	30.0	12.5	7.7	9.8
1990	100.0	69.9	51.6	10.7	7.6	30.2	12.8	7.6	9.8
1991	100.0	69.4	52.6	10.0	6.8	30.7	13.2	7.6	9.9
1992	100.0	69.7	53.7	9.1	6.9	30.4	13.7	7.2	9.5
1993	100.0	69.0	52.9	9.0	7.1	31.0	13.9	7.3	9.8
1994	100.0	69.0	53.0	9.2	6.8	30.9	13.9	7.1	9.9
1995	100.0	70.3	54.3	9.2	6.8	29.7	13.3	7.0	9.4
1996	100.0	70.7	54.9	9.2	6.6	29.3	13.6	6.8	8.9
1997	100.0	70.7	55.8	8.7	6.2	29.4	14.2	6.4	8.8
1998	100.0	71.6	56.5	8.7	6.4	28.4	13.6	6.4	8.4
1999	100.0	72.3	57.6	8.4	6.3	27.7	13.4	6.1	8.2
2000	100.0	73.2	58.9	8.5	5.8	26.8	13.3	6.0	7.5
2001	100.0	73.0	58.6	8.6	5.8	27.0	13.7	5.8	7.5
2002	100.0	72.5	58.8	8.1	5.6	27.6	14.2	5.8	7.6
2003	100.0	72.1	58.8	7.7	5.6	27.8	14.4	5.8	7.6
2004	100.0	72.0	59.0	7.6	5.4	28.0	14.7	5.7	7.6
2005	100.0	72.7	59.9	7.6	5.2	27.2	14.1	5.6	7.5
2006	100.0	73.1	60.7	7.3	5.1	26.9	14.1	5.7	7.1
2007	100.0	73.6	61.5	7.2	4.9	26.4	14.2	5.4	6.7
2008	100.0	72.2	59.3	7.8	5.1	27.8	15.0	5.6	7.2
2009	100.0	71.5	59.3	6.9	5.4	28.5	15.8	5.7	7.0
2010	100.0	71.5	59.4	6.9	5.2	28.5	15.6	5.6	7.3
2011	100.0	71.7	59.8	6.6	5.2	28.3	15.7	5.3	7.3

Note: See notes and definitions for information on historical comparability.

Table 1-37. Extent of Unemployment During the Year, by Sex, 1987–2011

(Thousands of people, percent.)

Sex and extent of unemployment	1987	1988	1989	1990	1991	1992	1993	1994	1995	1996	1997	1998
BOTH SEXES												
Total Who Worked or Looked for Work	130 353	132 185	134 394	135 408	135 826	136 654	139 786	141 325	142 413	144 528	146 096	147 295
Percent with unemployment	14.1	12.9	12.9	14.6	15.7	15.7	14.7	13.4	12.7	11.6	10.7	9.5
Total with Unemployment	18 399	17 096	17 273	19 809	21 276	21 455	20 527	18 966	18 067	16 789	15 637	14 044
Did not work but looked for work	2 037	1 735	1 577	1 874	2 415	2 742	3 432	2 857	2 690	2 329	2 129	1 729
Worked during the year	16 362	15 362	15 697	17 936	18 861	18 714	17 094	16 109	15 377	14 460	13 508	12 316
Year-round workers with 1 or 2 weeks of unemployment	792	830	833	1 056	966	871	688	746	715	589	611	630
Part-year workers with unemployment	15 570	14 532	14 864	16 880	17 895	17 843	16 406	15 363	14 662	13 871	12 897	11 686
1 to 4 weeks	3 363	3 256	3 489	3 645	3 224	2 944	2 626	2 788	2 812	2 550	2 582	2 323
5 to 10 weeks	3 191	3 148	3 359	3 669	3 655	3 496	2 898	2 983	2 725	2 671	2 601	2 495
11 to 14 weeks	2 258	2 128	2 235	2 501	2 587	2 574	2 300	2 265	2 147	2 020	1 822	1 701
15 to 26 weeks	3 904	3 479	3 600	4 316	4 927	4 877	4 549	4 158	4 013	3 662	3 378	3 019
27 weeks or more	2 854	2 521	2 181	2 749	3 502	3 952	4 033	3 169	2 965	2 968	2 514	2 148
With 2 or more spells of unemployment	5 149	5 136	5 073	5 811	5 864	5 734	5 338	4 783	4 468	4 237	4 044	3 628
2 spells	2 442	2 460	2 460	2 855	2 738	2 698	2 572	2 207	1 963	1 982	1 853	1 650
3 or more spells	2 707	2 676	2 613	2 956	3 126	3 036	2 766	2 576	2 505	2 255	2 191	1 978
MEN												
Total Who Worked or Looked for Work	69 995	70 738	72 362	72 844	72 909	73 387	74 516	75 244	75 698	76 786	77 385	77 704
Percent with unemployment	15.0	13.7	13.5	15.5	17.3	17.5	15.7	14.1	13.2	11.9	11.1	9.4
Total with Unemployment	10 504	9 696	9 792	11 307	12 642	12 844	11 723	10 582	9 996	9 157	8 604	7 284
Did not work but looked for work	852	717	723	891	1 210	1 379	1 641	1 286	1 317	1 026	978	787
Worked during the year	9 653	8 978	9 071	10 415	11 432	11 466	10 082	9 296	8 679	8 130	7 626	6 497
Year-round workers with 1 or 2 weeks of unemployment	536	585	568	711	612	567	449	527	462	395	382	386
Part-year workers with unemployment	9 117	8 393	8 503	9 704	10 820	10 899	9 633	8 769	8 217	7 735	7 244	6 111
1 to 4 weeks	1 561	1 633	1 742	1 819	1 591	1 563	1 343	1 365	1 398	1 272	1 275	1 085
5 to 10 weeks	1 824	1 808	1 890	2 041	2 111	2 039	1 647	1 666	1 434	1 478	1 474	1 363
11 to 14 weeks	1 415	1 279	1 365	1 462	1 659	1 615	1 354	1 370	1 253	1 258	1 068	980
15 to 26 weeks	2 514	2 124	2 188	2 645	3 206	3 165	2 862	2 449	2 439	2 076	1 949	1 585
27 weeks or more	1 803	1 549	1 318	1 737	2 253	2 517	2 427	1 919	1 693	1 651	1 478	1 098
With 2 or more spells of unemployment	3 300	3 366	3 178	3 689	3 886	3 889	3 451	2 940	2 793	2 554	2 437	2 014
2 spells	1 488	1 560	1 517	1 676	1 742	1 781	1 580	1 266	1 110	1 109	1 078	880
3 or more spells	1 812	1 806	1 661	2 013	2 144	2 108	1 871	1 674	1 683	1 445	1 359	1 134
WOMEN												
Total Who Worked or Looked for Work	60 357	61 447	62 032	62 564	62 917	63 267	65 270	66 081	66 716	67 742	68 710	69 591
Percent with unemployment	13.1	12.0	12.1	13.6	13.7	13.6	13.5	12.7	12.1	11.3	10.2	9.7
Total with Unemployment	7 895	7 400	7 481	8 502	8 634	8 611	8 804	8 383	8 070	7 632	7 033	6 760
Did not work but looked for work	1 185	1 017	854	982	1 205	1 363	1 791	1 570	1 373	1 303	1 151	942
Worked during the year	6 710	6 382	6 628	7 520	7 427	7 247	7 014	6 813	6 696	6 330	5 882	5 816
Year-round workers with 1 or 2 weeks of unemployment	255	244	265	344	354	304	239	219	253	194	229	243
Part-year workers with unemployment	6 455	6 138	6 363	7 176	7 073	6 943	6 775	6 594	6 443	6 136	5 653	5 573
1 to 4 weeks	1 802	1 623	1 747	1 827	1 633	1 380	1 284	1 422	1 413	1 279	1 307	1 237
5 to 10 weeks	1 368	1 340	1 469	1 627	1 544	1 457	1 252	1 317	1 291	1 192	1 127	1 131
11 to 14 weeks	844	849	870	1 038	927	959	946	896	893	762	754	721
15 to 26 weeks	1 391	1 354	1 413	1 671	1 720	1 712	1 687	1 708	1 574	1 586	1 429	1 434
27 weeks or more	1 050	972	864	1 013	1 249	1 435	1 606	1 251	1 272	1 317	1 036	1 050
With 2 or more spells of unemployment	1 849	1 769	1 895	2 122	1 979	1 844	1 887	1 843	1 675	1 682	1 607	1 614
2 spells	954	899	943	1 179	997	916	992	941	853	872	775	770
3 or more spells	895	870	952	943	982	928	895	902	822	810	832	844

Table 1-37. Extent of Unemployment During the Year, by Sex, 1987–2011—*Continued*

(Thousands of people, percent.)

Sex and extent of unemployment	1999	2000	2001	2002	2003	2004	2005	2006	2007	2008	2009	2010	2011
BOTH SEXES													
Total Who Worked or Looked for Work	149 798	150 786	153 056	154 205	154 315	155 576	157 549	159 259	160 565	161 506	160 624	159 706	160 545
Percent with unemployment	8.7	8.1	10.4	10.9	10.7	9.7	9.2	9.1	9.4	13.1	16.3	15.8	14.8
Total with Unemployment	13 068	12 269	15 843	16 824	16 462	15 074	14 558	14 447	15 130	21 231	26 151	25 262	23 752
Did not work but looked for work	1 503	1 425	2 014	2 660	2 762	2 551	2 422	1 907	2 097	3 189	5 851	6 564	6 216
Worked during the year	11 566	10 845	13 829	14 164	13 699	12 522	12 136	12 540	13 033	18 042	20 300	18 698	17 537
Year-round workers with 1 or 2 weeks of unemployment	562	573	602	584	534	465	431	450	500	763	693	591	417
Part-year workers with unemployment	11 004	10 272	13 227	13 580	13 165	12 057	11 705	12 090	12 533	17 279	19 607	18 107	17 119
1 to 4 weeks	2 361	2 233	2 368	2 002	1 839	1 985	1 941	2 601	2 593	2 794	2 528	2 267	2 211
5 to 10 weeks	2 218	2 014	2 557	2 373	2 264	2 100	2 170	2 107	2 090	2 944	2 562	2 397	2 276
11 to 14 weeks	1 594	1 505	2 038	1 970	1 749	1 773	1 698	1 615	1 888	2 438	2 414	2 302	2 064
15 to 26 weeks	2 803	2 641	3 683	3 848	3 778	3 448	3 349	3 176	3 373	4 859	5 698	5 116	4 949
27 weeks or more	2 028	1 879	2 582	3 387	3 535	2 751	2 547	2 592	2 589	4 244	6 405	6 025	5 619
With 2 or more spells of unemployment	3 225	3 079	3 421	3 226	3 093	2 896	3 095	3 076	3 108	3 991	4 152	3 875	3 527
2 spells	1 449	1 397	1 643	1 556	1 585	1 344	1 477	1 564	1 427	1 987	1 918	1 789	1 745
3 or more spells	1 776	1 682	1 779	1 670	1 508	1 552	1 618	1 513	1 681	2 004	2 234	2 086	1 782
MEN													
Total Who Worked or Looked for Work	78 905	79 546	80 975	81 651	81 804	82 478	83 951	84 736	85 368	85 563	85 161	84 738	84 486
Percent with unemployment	9.0	8.6	11.0	11.8	11.4	10.0	9.7	9.6	10.2	14.4	18.6	17.6	15.7
Total with Unemployment	7 091	6 806	8 928	9 621	9 339	8 256	8 116	8 115	8 698	12 331	15 877	14 900	13 273
Did not work but looked for work	760	742	1 004	1 369	1 487	1 217	1 216	969	1 076	1 674	3 325	3 662	3 214
Worked during the year	6 332	6 064	7 924	8 252	7 854	7 039	6 899	7 146	7 622	10 656	12 552	11 238	10 059
Year-round workers with 1 or 2 weeks of unemployment	373	379	421	365	359	289	296	295	365	484	458	379	271
Part-year workers with unemployment	5 959	5 685	7 502	7 887	7 495	6 750	6 603	6 850	7 257	10 172	12 093	10 859	9 788
1 to 4 weeks	1 166	1 070	1 247	1 075	958	1 028	1 052	1 283	1 367	1 523	1 466	1 186	1 170
5 to 10 weeks	1 168	1 135	1 446	1 342	1 314	1 170	1 209	1 267	1 214	1 701	1 594	1 423	1 240
11 to 14 weeks	937	880	1 207	1 186	1 039	1 021	1 024	961	1 163	1 467	1 558	1 441	1 277
15 to 26 weeks	1 655	1 595	2 191	2 282	2 178	2 065	1 923	1 868	2 058	3 035	3 564	3 233	2 941
27 weeks or more	1 033	1 005	1 412	2 002	2 006	1 466	1 395	1 472	1 455	2 445	3 911	3 577	3 159
With 2 or more spells of unemployment	1 845	1 809	2 100	1 920	1 882	1 828	1 975	1 936	1 992	2 623	2 865	2 623	2 450
2 spells	787	804	1 002	914	946	808	940	945	847	1 234	1 299	1 133	1 121
3 or more spells	1 058	1 005	1 099	1 006	936	1 020	1 035	991	1 145	1 389	1 566	1 491	1 329
WOMEN													
Total Who Worked or Looked for Work	70 893	71 240	72 081	72 554	72 511	73 097	73 598	74 523	75 197	75 943	75 463	74 968	76 060
Percent with unemployment	8.4	7.7	9.6	9.9	9.8	9.3	8.8	8.5	8.6	11.7	13.6	13.8	13.8
Total with Unemployment	5 976	5 463	6 915	7 203	7 123	6 818	6 442	6 332	6 432	8 900	10 274	10 362	10 479
Did not work but looked for work	743	683	1 010	1 291	1 275	1 334	1 206	938	1 021	1 514	2 526	2 903	3 002
Worked during the year	5 234	4 779	5 905	5 913	5 848	5 484	5 236	5 394	5 411	7 385	7 748	7 459	7 478
Year-round workers with 1 or 2 weeks of unemployment	189	193	180	220	176	177	136	154	135	279	235	211	147
Part-year workers with unemployment	5 045	4 586	5 725	5 693	5 672	5 307	5 100	5 240	5 276	7 106	7 513	7 248	7 331
1 to 4 weeks	1 194	1 164	1 121	927	882	957	888	1 317	1 226	1 270	1 061	1 081	1 041
5 to 10 weeks	1 050	878	1 111	1 031	950	929	961	840	876	1 243	968	974	1 036
11 to 14 weeks	657	625	831	784	710	752	674	655	725	971	857	861	787
15 to 26 weeks	1 148	1 045	1 492	1 566	1 600	1 384	1 426	1 307	1 316	1 823	2 134	1 883	2 008
27 weeks or more	996	874	1 170	1 385	1 530	1 285	1 151	1 120	1 134	1 800	2 494	2 448	2 459
With 2 or more spells of unemployment	1 379	1 270	1 321	1 306	1 211	1 069	1 120	1 140	1 116	1 368	1 287	1 252	1 077
2 spells	662	593	641	642	639	537	537	619	580	753	619	657	624
3 or more spells	717	677	680	664	572	532	583	521	536	616	668	595	453

Table 1-38. Percent Distribution of Persons with Unemployment During the Year, by Sex and Extent of Unemployment, 1987–2011

(Percent.)

Sex and extent of unemployment	1987	1988	1989	1990	1991	1992	1993	1994	1995	1996	1997	1998
BOTH SEXES												
Total with Unemployment Who Worked During the Year	100.0	100.0	100.0	100.0	100.0	100.0	100.0	100.0	100.0	100.0	100.0	100.0
Year-round workers with 1 or 2 weeks of unemployment	4.8	5.4	5.3	5.9	5.1	4.7	4.0	4.6	4.6	4.1	4.5	5.1
Part-year workers with unemployment	95.2	94.5	94.6	94.1	94.8	95.4	96.1	95.4	95.4	96.0	95.5	95.0
1 to 4 weeks	20.6	21.2	22.2	20.3	17.1	15.7	15.4	17.3	18.3	17.6	19.1	18.9
5 to 10 weeks	19.5	20.5	21.4	20.5	19.4	18.7	17.0	18.5	17.7	18.5	19.3	20.3
11 to 14 weeks	13.8	13.8	14.2	13.9	13.7	13.8	13.5	14.1	14.0	14.0	13.5	13.8
15 to 26 weeks	23.9	22.6	22.9	24.1	26.1	26.1	26.6	25.8	26.1	25.3	25.0	24.5
27 weeks or more	17.4	16.4	13.9	15.3	18.5	21.1	23.6	19.7	19.3	20.6	18.6	17.5
With 2 or more spells of unemployment	31.4	33.4	32.3	32.4	31.1	30.6	31.2	29.7	29.1	29.3	29.9	29.5
2 spells	14.9	16.0	15.7	15.9	14.5	14.4	15.0	13.7	12.8	13.7	13.7	13.4
3 or more spells	16.5	17.4	16.6	16.5	16.6	16.2	16.2	16.0	16.3	15.6	16.2	16.1
MEN												
Total with Unemployment Who Worked During the Year	100.0	100.0	100.0	100.0	100.0	100.0	100.0	100.0	100.0	100.0	100.0	100.0
Year-round workers with 1 or 2 weeks of unemployment	5.6	6.5	6.3	6.8	5.4	4.9	4.4	5.7	5.3	4.9	5.0	5.9
Part-year workers with unemployment	94.5	93.4	93.7	93.2	94.6	95.0	95.5	94.3	94.7	95.1	95.1	94.1
1 to 4 weeks	16.2	18.2	19.2	17.5	13.9	13.6	13.3	14.7	16.1	15.6	16.7	16.7
5 to 10 weeks	18.9	20.1	20.8	19.6	18.5	17.8	16.3	17.9	16.5	18.2	19.3	21.0
11 to 14 weeks	14.7	14.2	15.1	14.0	14.5	14.1	13.4	14.7	14.4	15.5	14.0	15.1
15 to 26 weeks	26.0	23.7	24.1	25.4	28.0	27.6	28.4	26.4	28.1	25.5	25.6	24.4
27 weeks or more	18.7	17.2	14.5	16.7	19.7	21.9	24.1	20.6	19.5	20.3	19.4	16.9
With 2 or more spells of unemployment	34.2	37.5	35.0	35.4	34.0	33.9	34.3	31.6	32.2	31.4	31.9	31.0
2 spells	15.4	17.4	16.7	16.1	15.2	15.5	15.7	13.6	12.8	13.6	14.1	13.5
3 or more spells	18.8	20.1	18.3	19.3	18.8	18.4	18.6	18.0	19.4	17.8	17.8	17.5
WOMEN												
Total With Unemployment Who Worked During the Year	100.0	100.0	100.0	100.0	100.0	100.0	100.0	100.0	100.0	100.0	100.0	100.0
Year-round workers with 1 or 2 weeks of unemployment	3.8	3.8	4.0	4.6	4.8	4.2	3.4	3.2	3.8	3.1	3.9	4.2
Part-year workers with unemployment	96.3	96.1	96.0	95.3	95.3	95.7	96.6	96.7	96.2	96.9	96.1	95.8
1 to 4 weeks	26.9	25.4	26.4	24.3	22.0	19.0	18.3	20.9	21.1	20.2	22.2	21.3
5 to 10 weeks	20.4	21.0	22.2	21.6	20.8	20.1	17.8	19.3	19.3	18.8	19.2	19.4
11 to 14 weeks	12.6	13.3	13.1	13.8	12.5	13.2	13.5	13.1	13.3	12.0	12.8	12.4
15 to 26 weeks	20.7	21.2	21.3	22.2	23.2	23.6	24.1	25.1	23.5	25.1	24.3	24.7
27 weeks or more	15.7	15.2	13.0	13.4	16.8	19.8	22.9	18.3	19.0	20.8	17.6	18.0
With 2 or more spells of unemployment	27.5	27.7	28.6	28.2	26.6	25.4	26.9	27.0	25.0	26.6	27.3	27.7
2 spells	14.2	14.1	14.2	15.7	13.4	12.6	14.1	13.8	12.7	13.8	13.2	13.2
3 or more spells	13.3	13.6	14.4	12.5	13.2	12.8	12.8	13.2	12.3	12.8	14.1	14.5

Table 1-38. Percent Distribution of Persons with Unemployment During the Year, by Sex and Extent of Unemployment, 1987–2011—_Continued_

(Percent.)

Sex and extent of unemployment	1999	2000	2001	2002	2003	2004	2005	2006	2007	2008	2009	2010	2011
BOTH SEXES													
Total with Unemployment Who Worked During the Year	100.0	100.0	100.0	100.0	100.0	100.0	100.0	100.0	100.0	100.0	100.0	100.0	100.0
Year-round workers with 1 or 2 weeks of unemployment	4.9	5.3	4.4	4.1	3.9	3.7	3.6	3.6	3.8	4.2	3.4	3.2	2.4
Part-year workers with unemployment	95.1	94.8	95.6	95.9	96.1	96.3	96.4	96.4	96.1	95.8	96.5	96.8	97.6
1 to 4 weeks	20.4	20.6	17.1	14.1	13.4	15.9	16.0	20.7	19.9	15.5	12.5	12.1	12.6
5 to 10 weeks	19.2	18.6	18.5	16.8	16.5	16.8	17.9	16.8	16.0	16.3	12.6	12.8	13.0
11 to 14 weeks	13.8	13.9	14.7	13.9	12.8	14.2	14.0	12.9	14.5	13.5	11.9	12.3	11.8
15 to 26 weeks	24.2	24.4	26.6	27.2	27.6	27.5	27.6	25.3	25.9	26.9	28.1	27.4	28.2
27 weeks or more	17.5	17.3	18.7	23.9	25.8	22.0	20.9	20.7	19.8	23.5	31.5	32.2	32.0
With 2 or more spells of unemployment	27.9	28.4	24.8	22.8	22.6	23.1	25.5	24.5	23.8	22.1	20.5	20.7	20.1
2 spells	12.5	12.9	11.9	11.0	11.6	10.7	12.2	12.5	10.9	11.0	9.4	9.6	10.0
3 or more spells	15.4	15.5	12.9	11.8	11.0	12.4	13.3	12.1	12.9	11.1	11.0	11.2	10.2
MEN													
Total with Unemployment Who Worked During the Year	100.0	100.0	100.0	100.0	100.0	100.0	100.0	100.0	100.0	100.0	100.0	100.0	100.0
Year-round workers with 1 or 2 weeks of unemployment	5.9	6.3	5.3	4.4	4.6	4.1	4.3	4.1	4.8	4.5	3.7	3.4	2.7
Part-year workers with unemployment	94.0	93.6	94.7	95.6	95.4	95.9	95.7	95.9	95.2	95.5	96.4	96.6	97.3
1 to 4 weeks	18.4	17.6	15.7	13.0	12.2	14.6	15.3	18.0	17.9	14.3	11.7	10.5	11.6
5 to 10 weeks	18.4	18.7	18.2	16.3	16.7	16.6	17.5	17.7	15.9	16.0	12.7	12.7	12.3
11 to 14 weeks	14.8	14.5	15.2	14.4	13.2	14.5	14.8	13.4	15.3	13.8	12.4	12.8	12.7
15 to 26 weeks	26.1	26.3	27.6	27.7	27.7	29.3	27.9	26.1	27.0	28.5	28.4	28.8	29.2
27 weeks or more	16.3	16.5	17.8	24.3	25.5	20.8	20.2	20.6	19.1	22.9	31.2	31.8	31.4
With 2 or more spells of unemployment	29.1	29.9	26.5	23.3	24.0	26.0	28.6	27.1	26.1	24.6	22.8	23.3	24.4
2 spells	12.4	13.3	12.6	11.1	12.1	11.5	13.6	13.2	11.1	11.6	10.3	10.1	11.1
3 or more spells	16.7	16.6	13.9	12.2	11.9	14.5	15.0	13.9	15.0	13.0	12.5	13.3	13.2
WOMEN													
Total With Unemployment Who Worked During the Year	100.0	100.0	100.0	100.0	100.0	100.0	100.0	100.0	100.0	100.0	100.0	100.0	100.0
Year-round workers with 1 or 2 weeks of unemployment	3.6	4.0	3.1	3.7	3.0	3.2	2.6	2.9	2.5	3.8	3.0	2.8	2.0
Part-year workers with unemployment	96.4	96.0	96.9	96.3	97.0	96.8	97.4	97.1	97.4	96.2	96.9	97.2	98.0
1 to 4 weeks	22.8	24.3	19.0	15.7	15.1	17.4	17.0	24.4	22.6	17.2	13.7	14.5	13.9
5 to 10 weeks	20.1	18.4	18.8	17.4	16.2	16.9	18.4	15.6	16.2	16.8	12.5	13.1	13.9
11 to 14 weeks	12.6	13.1	14.1	13.3	12.1	13.7	12.9	12.1	13.4	13.1	11.1	11.5	10.5
15 to 26 weeks	21.9	21.9	25.3	26.5	27.4	25.2	27.2	24.2	24.3	24.7	27.5	25.2	26.8
27 weeks or more	19.0	18.3	19.8	23.4	26.2	23.5	22.0	20.8	20.9	24.4	32.1	32.8	32.9
With 2 or more spells of unemployment	26.3	26.6	22.4	22.1	20.7	19.5	21.4	21.1	20.6	18.5	16.6	16.8	14.4
2 spells	12.6	12.4	10.9	10.9	10.9	9.8	10.3	11.5	10.7	10.2	8.0	8.8	8.3
3 or more spells	13.7	14.2	11.5	11.2	9.8	9.7	11.1	9.7	9.9	8.3	8.6	8.0	6.1

Table 1-39. Number and Median Annual Earnings of Year-Round, Full-Time Wage and Salary Workers, by Age, Sex, and Race, 1987–2011

(Thousands of people, dollars.)

Sex, age, and race	1987	1988	1989	1990	1991	1992	1993	1994	1995	1996	1997	1998
NUMBER												
Both Sexes, 16 Years and Over	71 069	73 598	74 898	74 728	74 449	75 517	77 427	79 875	83 407	85 611	86 905	89 748
16 to 24 years	7 563	7 400	7 471	6 978	6 571	6 224	6 685	6 684	6 892	6 809	7 063	7 618
25 to 44 years	42 211	44 036	45 082	45 086	44 811	45 022	45 951	47 150	48 695	49 225	49 513	50 264
25 to 34 years	22 884	23 727	23 721	23 201	22 541	22 469	22 637	23 193	23 310	23 071	23 186	23 048
35 to 44 years	19 327	20 309	21 361	21 885	22 270	22 553	23 314	23 957	25 385	26 154	26 327	27 216
45 to 54 years	12 764	13 506	13 848	14 070	14 718	15 652	16 424	17 366	18 436	19 714	20 109	21 274
55 to 64 years	7 406	7 529	7 321	7 458	7 219	7 590	7 208	7 500	8 122	8 455	8 901	9 273
65 years and over	1 125	1 127	1 177	1 137	1 130	1 029	1 159	1 174	1 263	1 408	1 318	1 318
Men, 16 Years and Over	42 490	43 785	45 107	44 574	43 523	43 894	45 494	47 255	49 334	50 407	50 772	52 509
16 to 24 years	4 145	4 165	4 223	3 982	3 596	3 457	3 853	3 918	4 094	3 942	4 021	4 479
25 to 44 years	25 293	26 246	27 321	27 069	26 353	26 335	27 161	28 000	28 940	29 282	29 453	29 763
25 to 34 years	13 659	14 163	14 439	13 941	13 303	13 146	13 400	13 749	13 844	13 817	13 735	13 612
35 to 44 years	11 634	12 083	12 882	13 128	13 050	13 189	13 761	14 251	15 096	15 465	15 718	16 151
45 to 54 years	7 726	8 086	8 276	8 168	8 479	8 908	9 522	10 120	10 589	11 372	11 388	12 030
55 to 64 years	4 654	4 616	4 562	4 650	4 403	4 588	4 238	4 460	4 884	4 908	5 133	5 438
65 years and over	672	672	725	705	694	606	719	757	827	903	775	801
Women, 16 Years and Over	28 579	29 812	29 791	30 155	30 925	31 622	31 933	32 619	34 073	35 203	36 133	37 239
16 to 24 years	3 418	3 235	3 249	2 995	2 976	2 767	2 832	2 767	2 798	2 867	3 041	3 140
25 to 44 years	16 918	17 790	17 760	18 017	18 458	18 688	18 790	19 150	19 755	19 942	20 060	20 503
25 to 34 years	9 225	9 564	9 282	9 260	9 238	9 323	9 237	9 444	9 467	9 254	9 451	9 437
35 to 44 years	7 693	8 226	8 478	8 757	9 220	9 365	9 553	9 706	10 288	10 688	10 609	11 066
45 to 54 years	5 037	5 420	5 572	5 902	6 239	6 744	6 902	7 246	7 847	8 343	8 721	9 244
55 to 64 years	2 752	2 913	2 758	2 808	2 816	3 002	2 970	3 040	3 238	3 547	3 767	3 836
65 years and over	453	455	451	433	436	423	439	417	436	505	543	517
White, 16 Years and Over	61 546	63 357	64 246	64 128	63 926	64 706	65 656	67 370	70 430	72 068	72 650	75 046
Men	37 461	38 449	39 430	38 915	38 018	38 267	39 347	40 589	42 608	43 554	43 429	44 901
Women	24 085	24 908	24 815	25 213	25 908	26 439	26 309	26 782	27 822	28 514	29 221	30 145
Black, 16 Years and Over	7 440	7 907	8 140	8 027	7 941	7 995	8 478	9 074	9 446	9 706	10 248	10 532
Men	3 838	3 976	4 219	4 162	4 001	4 011	4 259	4 598	4 686	4 682	5 026	5 202
Women	3 602	3 931	3 920	3 865	3 940	3 984	4 219	4 476	4 759	5 024	5 222	5 329
MEDIAN ANNUAL EARNINGS												
Both Sexes, 16 Years and Over	21 000	22 000	23 000	24 000	25 000	25 871	26 000	26 620	27 000	28 000	30 000	30 000
16 to 24 years	13 000	13 500	14 000	14 400	14 100	15 000	15 000	15 000	15 500	15 600	16 000	18 000
25 to 34 years	20 000	21 000	22 000	22 000	23 000	24 000	24 000	24 480	25 000	25 300	27 000	28 500
35 to 44 years	25 000	26 000	27 000	27 970	28 000	29 483	30 000	30 000	30 000	31 000	32 000	33 000
45 to 54 years	25 000	26 000	27 000	28 000	29 000	30 000	30 500	32 343	32 000	33 000	35 000	35 000
55 to 64 years	23 000	24 000	26 000	26 000	27 000	27 430	28 000	30 000	30 000	30 000	32 000	34 000
65 years and over	18 000	19 500	23 000	23 841	22 000	24 000	24 000	24 377	29 600	26 496	28 200	26 000
Men, 16 Years and Over	25 900	26 570	27 300	28 000	29 120	30 000	30 000	30 000	31 000	32 000	34 000	35 000
16 to 24 years	14 000	14 200	15 000	15 000	15 000	15 000	15 000	15 000	16 000	17 000	17 000	18 720
25 to 34 years	23 000	24 000	24 000	25 000	25 000	26 000	25 000	26 000	27 000	28 000	29 852	30 000
35 to 44 years	30 000	31 000	32 000	32 000	33 000	34 000	35 000	35 000	35 000	36 000	37 000	38 000
45 to 54 years	31 200	32 000	34 000	35 000	36 000	37 000	38 000	40 000	40 000	40 000	41 000	42 000
55 to 64 years	29 181	30 000	32 000	31 875	33 000	33 000	34 000	36 000	36 000	36 000	39 000	40 000
65 years and over	24 000	25 000	30 000	29 000	28 000	30 000	28 000	30 000	36 000	33 000	36 400	35 000
Women, 16 Years and Over	17 000	18 000	18 574	20 000	20 000	21 500	22 000	22 150	23 000	24 000	25 000	25 000
16 to 24 years	12 000	13 000	13 167	13 392	13 800	14 000	14 872	14 560	15 000	15 000	15 000	17 000
25 to 34 years	17 000	18 000	19 000	19 500	20 000	21 000	21 000	22 000	22 000	23 000	24 000	25 000
35 to 44 years	19 000	20 000	20 200	22 000	22 510	23 397	24 000	25 000	25 000	25 000	26 000	27 200
45 to 54 years	18 148	19 000	20 000	21 000	22 000	24 000	24 000	24 000	25 000	26 000	27 040	28 132
55 to 64 years	17 000	17 000	18 000	19 000	20 000	22 000	21 500	22 000	22 500	24 000	24 800	25 775
65 years and over	16 000	15 600	17 566	18 586	17 000	18 500	20 000	19 000	23 290	20 800	24 000	22 000
White, 16 Years and Over	22 000	23 000	24 000	25 000	25 000	26 200	27 000	28 000	28 000	29 000	30 000	31 000
Men	26 500	27 489	28 500	29 000	30 000	31 000	30 700	32 000	32 000	33 000	35 000	36 000
Women	17 000	18 000	19 000	20 000	20 500	22 000	22 000	23 000	23 000	24 000	25 000	26 000
Black, 16 Years and Over	17 000	18 000	19 000	19 350	20 000	21 000	20 800	21 000	22 000	23 784	24 000	25 000
Men	18 850	20 000	20 000	20 800	22 000	22 312	23 000	23 500	24 500	26 000	26 000	27 000
Women	15 500	16 200	17 115	18 000	18 500	20 000	19 843	20 000	20 000	21 000	22 000	23 000

Table 1-39. Number and Median Annual Earnings of Year-Round, Full-Time Wage and Salary Workers, by Age, Sex, and Race, 1987–2011—*Continued*

(Thousands of people, dollars.)

Sex, age, and race	1999	2000	2001	2002	2003	2004	2005	2006	2007	2008	2009	2010	2011
NUMBER													
Both Sexes, 16 Years and Over	91 722	94 359	94 531	94 526	94 731	96 098	98 632	101 353	102 441	98 493	94 012	94 110	96 562
16 to 24 years	7 631	8 384	7 989	7 903	7 631	7 702	7 956	8 113	8 064	7 242	6 302	6 073	6 411
25 to 44 years	50 532	51 159	49 939	49 120	48 343	48 421	49 149	50 056	49 725	47 364	44 579	44 441	45 166
25 to 34 years	22 952	23 044	22 744	22 657	22 512	22 405	22 808	23 613	23 646	22 786	21 572	21 894	21 989
35 to 44 years	27 580	28 115	27 195	26 463	25 831	26 016	26 341	26 443	26 080	24 578	23 007	22 546	23 177
45 to 54 years	22 375	23 307	23 855	23 999	24 507	25 074	25 661	26 338	26 566	25 722	24 877	24 388	24 782
55 to 64 years	9 594	9 870	10 948	11 584	12 207	12 812	13 605	14 340	15 248	15 286	15 274	16 073	16 622
65 years and over	1 590	1 639	1 800	1 921	2 042	2 090	2 262	2 507	2 837	2 879	2 980	3 135	3 582
Men, 16 Years and Over	53 132	54 477	54 630	54 420	54 575	55 610	57 020	58 533	58 673	55 973	52 362	52 793	54 542
16 to 24 years	4 347	4 602	4 605	4 570	4 421	4 493	4 663	4 812	4 719	4 112	3 494	3 462	3 649
25 to 44 years	29 738	30 080	29 271	28 855	28 499	28 763	29 151	29 589	29 004	27 546	25 324	25 449	25 959
25 to 34 years	13 471	13 497	13 386	13 400	13 288	13 430	13 629	13 933	13 706	13 208	12 085	12 475	12 616
35 to 44 years	16 267	16 583	15 885	15 455	15 211	15 333	15 522	15 655	15 298	14 337	13 239	12 974	13 343
45 to 54 years	12 546	13 045	13 363	13 330	13 616	13 975	14 382	14 758	14 810	14 199	13 521	13 373	13 723
55 to 64 years	5 498	5 693	6 253	6 502	6 872	7 165	7 489	7 905	8 449	8 397	8 289	8 727	9 066
65 years and over	1 003	1 057	1 138	1 163	1 165	1 213	1 334	1 469	1 692	1 720	1 733	1 782	2 146
Women, 16 Years and Over	38 591	39 887	39 901	40 106	40 156	40 488	41 613	42 820	43 768	42 520	41 650	41 318	42 020
16 to 24 years	3 285	3 782	3 384	3 333	3 210	3 209	3 293	3 301	3 345	3 130	2 808	2 611	2 762
25 to 44 years	20 794	21 081	20 668	20 264	19 844	19 656	19 997	20 467	20 721	19 819	19 255	18 992	19 207
25 to 34 years	9 481	9 548	9 358	9 257	9 224	8 974	9 179	9 679	9 940	9 578	9 487	9 420	9 373
35 to 44 years	11 313	11 533	11 310	11 007	10 620	10 682	10 818	10 788	10 782	10 240	9 768	9 572	9 834
45 to 54 years	9 829	10 263	10 493	10 669	10 891	11 099	11 279	11 580	11 757	11 524	11 356	11 016	11 059
55 to 64 years	4 096	4 178	4 695	5 082	5 335	5 647	6 116	6 434	6 799	6 889	6 984	7 346	7 556
65 years and over	586	583	662	758	877	877	927	1 038	1 146	1 158	1 247	1 354	1 436
White, 16 Years and Over	76 203	77 790	78 306	77 632	77 545	78 236	80 546	82 411	83 139	79 980	76 470	76 557	77 669
Men	45 211	46 105	46 373	45 823	45 816	46 317	47 790	48 897	48 825	46 608	43 622	44 018	45 037
Women	30 992	31 685	31 933	31 809	31 729	31 919	32 756	33 513	34 314	33 372	32 848	32 540	32 632
Black, 16 Years and Over	11 145	11 899	11 001	10 966	10 979	11 301	11 417	11 988	11 987	11 424	10 716	10 676	11 009
Men	5 411	5 636	5 281	5 150	5 196	5 470	5 402	5 679	5 689	5 377	4 952	4 957	5 111
Women	5 734	6 264	5 720	5 816	5 783	5 832	6 015	6 309	6 299	6 046	5 764	5 719	5 898
MEDIAN ANNUAL EARNINGS													
Both Sexes, 16 Years and Over	31 000	32 000	34 000	35 000	35 000	35 672	36 400	38 000	40 000	40 000	41 000	42 000	42 000
16 to 24 years	18 000	19 000	20 000	20 000	20 000	20 000	20 000	21 000	22 421	24 000	23 532	23 000	22 650
25 to 34 years	30 000	30 000	31 000	31 800	32 000	33 000	33 000	35 000	35 000	36 500	38 000	37 815	38 000
35 to 44 years	34 992	35 000	36 000	37 000	39 000	40 000	40 000	41 000	43 000	45 000	45 000	45 000	45 000
45 to 54 years	36 000	38 000	39 500	40 000	40 000	40 000	42 000	44 000	45 000	45 000	46 000	48 000	48 000
55 to 64 years	35 000	35 000	36 400	39 145	40 000	40 000	41 000	43 000	45 000	46 000	48 000	49 000	50 000
65 years and over	30 000	32 000	32 000	33 000	32 000	35 000	35 000	35 001	40 000	42 000	42 000	45 000	44 200
Men, 16 Years and Over	36 000	37 600	38 500	40 000	40 000	40 000	40 051	42 000	45 000	46 000	48 000	48 000	48 000
16 to 24 years	19 000	20 000	20 000	20 000	20 800	20 800	20 800	22 000	23 000	25 000	25 000	24 000	24 000
25 to 34 years	32 000	33 500	34 000	34 740	35 000	35 000	35 000	36 000	38 000	40 000	40 000	40 000	40 000
35 to 44 years	40 000	40 000	42 000	43 000	43 900	45 000	45 000	48 000	50 000	50 000	50 000	50 000	51 000
45 to 54 years	44 616	45 000	45 000	47 000	48 000	48 000	50 000	50 000	50 000	52 000	53 004	55 000	55 000
55 to 64 years	40 853	44 000	45 000	47 000	50 000	50 000	50 000	50 000	52 000	54 000	55 000	55 000	57 000
65 years and over	36 000	35 999	35 000	37 861	42 000	40 000	41 000	44 000	44 000	50 000	49 000	50 002	50 000
Women, 16 Years and Over	26 000	27 500	29 000	30 000	30 000	30 001	32 000	33 000	35 000	35 000	36 000	37 000	37 000
16 to 24 years	17 000	18 000	19 000	19 000	20 000	20 000	20 000	20 000	22 000	22 000	22 000	20 816	22 000
25 to 34 years	26 000	27 000	28 080	29 500	30 000	30 000	30 000	31 000	33 000	34 000	35 000	35 000	35 000
35 to 44 years	28 000	29 000	30 000	30 400	32 000	32 800	35 000	35 000	36 000	38 000	38 000	40 000	40 000
45 to 54 years	30 000	30 000	32 000	32 000	33 466	34 771	35 000	36 000	37 163	38 000	40 000	40 000	40 000
55 to 64 years	27 000	28 000	30 000	31 410	32 000	33 000	33 000	35 000	37 100	39 000	40 000	40 000	40 000
65 years and over	20 800	24 000	25 000	28 000	26 000	27 000	28 768	27 878	31 000	34 193	36 000	40 000	37 000
White, 16 Years and Over	32 000	34 000	35 000	35 000	36 000	37 000	38 000	40 000	40 000	41 600	42 000	43 502	44 000
Men	37 200	39 000	40 000	40 000	40 000	42 000	42 000	44 707	45 000	48 000	49 000	50 000	50 000
Women	27 000	28 000	30 000	30 000	31 000	31 800	32 000	34 000	35 000	35 500	36 002	38 000	38 000
Black, 16 Years and Over	25 760	26 000	28 500	29 000	30 000	30 000	30 000	31 000	33 000	34 000	35 000	35 000	35 000
Men	30 000	30 000	30 000	30 000	32 000	30 000	33 000	34 000	35 000	37 500	38 000	36 000	39 000
Women	24 000	25 000	26 000	26 000	27 000	28 000	29 141	30 000	30 000	30 002	32 000	32 000	34 000

Table 1-40. Number and Median Annual Earnings of Year-Round, Full-Time Wage and Salary Workers, by Sex and Occupation of Job Held the Longest, 2002–2011

(Thousands of people, dollars.)

Sex and occupation	2002	2003	2004	2005	2006	2007	2008	2009	2010	2011
Both Sexes, Number of Workers										
Management, business, and financial operations	15 707	15 552	15 575	16 299	16 806	17 115	17 259	16 491	16 889	17 396
Management	11 350	11 102	11 125	11 685	11 866	12 191	12 256	11 733	11 804	12 140
Business and financial operations	4 357	4 450	4 451	4 613	4 941	4 924	5 003	4 758	5 085	5 256
Professional and related	19 149	19 607	19 592	20 093	21 268	21 939	21 748	21 831	21 966	22 165
Computer and mathematical	2 644	2 598	2 680	2 779	2 888	3 180	3 089	3 100	2 993	3 171
Architecture and engineering	2 257	2 273	2 349	2 361	2 491	2 467	2 360	2 133	2 409	2 451
Life, physical, and social sciences	1 094	1 010	999	1 096	1 142	1 026	1 044	1 054	993	991
Community and social services	1 694	1 698	1 632	1 728	1 835	1 791	1 754	1 827	1 905	1 784
Legal	1 006	1 149	1 087	1 093	1 168	1 159	1 228	1 230	1 255	1 226
Education, training, and library	4 606	4 918	4 742	4 894	5 195	5 482	5 478	5 500	5 510	5 390
Arts, design, entertainment, sports, and media	1 453	1 374	1 416	1 362	1 633	1 554	1 415	1 404	1 380	1 449
Health care practitioner and technical	4 395	4 586	4 688	4 780	4 916	5 278	5 380	5 583	5 521	5 703
Services	12 011	11 990	12 457	13 117	13 236	13 553	13 034	12 944	12 855	13 676
Health care support	1 767	1 703	1 781	2 027	2 081	2 027	2 019	2 135	2 008	2 236
Protective services	2 042	2 385	2 406	2 429	2 506	2 511	2 472	2 593	2 589	2 571
Food preparation and serving related	3 592	3 223	3 383	3 586	3 646	3 769	3 504	3 307	3 408	3 797
Building and grounds cleaning and maintenance	2 843	2 942	3 116	3 285	3 120	3 198	3 027	2 870	2 942	3 098
Personal care and services	1 767	1 735	1 771	1 790	1 883	2 048	2 012	2 038	1 908	1 974
Sales and office	23 791	23 766	23 619	24 010	24 467	24 472	23 058	22 320	21 859	21 949
Sales and related	9 929	9 804	9 951	10 251	10 497	10 301	9 763	9 275	9 187	9 191
Office and administrative support	13 862	13 962	13 668	13 758	13 970	14 171	13 294	13 045	12 671	12 758
Natural resources, construction, and maintenance	9 823	9 709	10 574	10 864	11 295	10 745	10 002	8 599	8 298	8 584
Farming, fishing, and forestry	573	562	629	556	585	607	581	555	532	562
Construction and extraction	5 256	5 070	5 711	6 145	6 484	5 885	5 158	4 172	4 029	4 283
Installation, maintenance, and repair	3 994	4 077	4 234	4 163	4 226	4 252	4 264	3 872	3 737	3 739
Production, transportation, and material moving	13 386	13 391	13 648	13 586	13 704	13 907	12 649	11 062	11 518	12 041
Production	7 736	7 670	7 787	7 623	7 762	7 589	6 652	5 834	6 226	6 574
Transportation and material moving	5 650	5 721	5 861	5 963	5 942	6 318	5 997	5 228	5 292	5 467
Armed forces	658	717	632	664	576	709	744	765	727	749
Both Sexes, Median Annual Earnings										
Management, business, and financial operations	50 000	52 000	55 000	57 000	60 000	60 000	60 800	60 000	64 000	65 000
Management	55 000	58 000	60 000	60 000	62 500	65 000	65 000	65 000	68 000	70 000
Business and financial operations	44 000	45 000	45 000	49 000	50 000	50 000	52 000	55 000	56 000	57 000
Professional and related	46 000	46 000	48 000	50 000	50 000	51 000	54 000	55 000	55 000	56 000
Computer and mathematical	60 000	60 000	62 000	62 400	68 000	70 000	70 000	72 000	70 000	73 000
Architecture and engineering	59 400	62 000	60 000	65 000	69 000	70 000	70 000	70 000	75 000	75 000
Life, physical, and social sciences	50 000	50 000	50 000	53 500	57 000	60 000	57 532	60 000	60 000	61 599
Community and social services	34 000	34 349	36 000	36 000	36 780	39 000	40 000	40 000	40 000	40 000
Legal	61 860	75 000	70 000	72 000	70 000	70 000	75 000	80 000	75 000	85 000
Education, training, and library	38 000	39 000	40 000	40 000	40 282	44 984	45 000	46 000	45 000	46 200
Arts, design, entertainment, sports, and media	43 500	40 000	40 000	42 000	45 000	44 297	47 000	49 000	48 000	50 000
Health care practitioner and technical	46 000	46 000	50 000	50 000	52 000	52 800	55 000	55 000	57 638	58 000
Services	22 000	22 000	22 000	23 000	24 000	25 000	25 000	26 000	26 000	26 000
Health care support	22 100	22 000	22 000	22 000	23 000	24 500	26 000	26 000	26 270	26 000
Protective services	38 000	42 000	42 000	42 000	45 000	45 000	45 000	46 000	48 000	50 000
Food preparation and serving related	18 000	18 000	18 000	19 656	19 000	20 000	20 800	20 000	20 800	21 000
Building and grounds cleaning and maintenance	20 000	20 000	20 000	21 000	23 000	23 000	24 000	24 024	25 000	24 002
Personal care and services	21 840	20 678	22 537	23 000	23 000	25 000	25 000	25 000	25 000	25 000
Sales and office	30 000	30 000	30 000	31 200	32 002	34 000	35 000	35 000	35 000	35 002
Sales and related	35 000	35 000	35 000	35 000	37 000	38 000	38 500	38 000	40 000	40 000
Office and administrative support	28 000	29 000	30 000	30 000	30 000	32 000	32 500	34 000	34 000	35 000
Natural resources, construction, and maintenance	33 000	34 000	35 000	35 000	35 000	36 000	40 000	40 000	40 000	40 000
Farming, fishing, and forestry	20 000	20 000	20 000	21 000	20 000	24 000	24 000	24 000	23 000	24 000
Construction and extraction	31 200	32 000	33 000	32 000	35 000	35 000	39 000	40 000	40 000	39 500
Installation, maintenance, and repair	36 000	38 000	38 300	40 000	40 000	40 000	42 000	44 192	43 981	44 018
Production, transportation, and material moving	28 704	30 000	30 000	30 200	30 000	33 000	34 000	34 000	34 000	35 000
Production	28 000	30 000	30 000	30 000	30 000	33 000	34 000	32 006	34 000	35 000
Transportation and material moving	29 000	30 000	30 000	30 800	30 000	33 800	34 000	35 000	33 000	35 000
Armed forces	36 000	36 000	40 000	39 000	40 000	42 000	45 000	47 000	47 000	45 000

Table 1-40. Number and Median Annual Earnings of Year-Round, Full-Time Wage and Salary Workers, by Sex and Occupation of Job Held the Longest, 2002–2011—*Continued*

(Thousands of people, dollars.)

Sex and occupation	2002	2003	2004	2005	2006	2007	2008	2009	2010	2011
Men, Number of Workers										
Management, business, and financial operations	9 178	8 961	8 849	9 496	9 519	9 784	9 836	9 418	9 569	9 886
Management	7 145	6 991	6 911	7 477	7 361	7 619	7 714	7 300	7 249	7 497
Business and financial operations	2 033	1 970	1 938	2 019	2 157	2 165	2 122	2 117	2 320	2 389
Professional and related	9 299	9 535	9 497	9 561	10 387	10 274	10 074	10 036	10 126	10 228
Computer and mathematical	1 953	1 913	1 972	2 060	2 159	2 378	2 348	2 227	2 244	2 329
Architecture and engineering	1 984	2 004	2 049	2 041	2 174	2 172	2 068	1 859	2 110	2 144
Life, physical, and social sciences	667	668	626	668	748	611	581	575	562	605
Community and social services	726	730	705	713	756	744	675	707	701	679
Legal	490	610	537	490	546	515	595	645	605	616
Education, training, and library	1 407	1 476	1 386	1 421	1 587	1 651	1 535	1 650	1 601	1 522
Arts, design, entertainment, sports, and media	847	811	848	789	953	790	782	829	839	860
Health care practitioner and technical	1 225	1 323	1 374	1 378	1 464	1 413	1 490	1 544	1 464	1 473
Services	5 988	6 204	6 314	6 658	6 715	6 871	6 389	6 379	6 426	6 923
Health care support	181	178	208	240	252	261	204	247	242	268
Protective services	1 689	1 967	1 906	1 919	1 998	2 000	1 930	2 026	2 070	2 108
Food preparation and serving related	1 836	1 638	1 716	1 873	1 991	1 985	1 816	1 744	1 743	2 050
Building and grounds cleaning and maintenance	1 788	1 914	2 002	2 153	1 939	2 048	1 911	1 832	1 862	1 974
Personal care and services	494	508	482	473	535	576	527	530	508	523
Sales and office	9 453	9 398	9 380	9 464	9 747	9 694	9 128	8 680	8 872	8 971
Sales and related	5 933	5 891	5 892	5 896	6 125	6 019	5 690	5 231	5 363	5 425
Office and administrative support	3 520	3 507	3 488	3 568	3 622	3 675	3 438	3 449	3 509	3 545
Natural resources, construction, and maintenance	9 434	9 348	10 178	10 503	10 904	10 343	9 627	8 225	7 936	8 274
Farming, fishing, and forestry	463	470	536	469	482	516	489	425	430	474
Construction and extraction	5 156	4 972	5 576	6 026	6 344	5 753	5 056	4 068	3 909	4 192
Installation, maintenance, and repair	3 815	3 905	4 065	4 008	4 078	4 074	4 081	3 732	3 597	3 608
Production, transportation, and material moving	10 472	10 492	10 812	10 747	10 733	11 047	10 226	8 921	9 214	9 583
Production	5 517	5 513	5 637	5 503	5 525	5 461	4 983	4 370	4 612	4 813
Transportation and material moving	4 955	4 979	5 176	5 244	5 208	5 585	5 242	4 552	4 602	4 770
Armed forces	600	636	580	591	528	660	696	703	649	677
Men, Median Annual Earnings										
Management, business, and financial operations	60 000	60 200	65 000	69 000	68 000	70 000	72 000	72 000	75 000	75 000
Management	65 000	65 000	70 000	70 000	70 000	75 000	75 000	75 000	78 000	80 000
Business and financial operations	52 000	51 000	55 000	60 000	60 000	60 000	65 000	65 000	67 000	65 000
Professional and related	55 000	58 000	58 000	60 000	61 000	62 000	67 000	65 000	67 000	70 000
Computer and mathematical	60 000	65 000	65 000	65 000	70 000	70 000	74 000	75 000	75 000	79 000
Architecture and engineering	60 000	64 558	61 785	66 921	70 000	72 000	74 000	72 000	77 000	75 000
Life, physical, and social sciences	52 000	50 801	55 000	62 000	61 000	65 000	65 000	65 000	64 000	65 000
Community and social services	35 000	35 000	38 000	40 000	39 000	40 000	44 085	45 000	42 002	42 000
Legal	100 000	100 000	101 000	108 000	100 000	104 146	130 000	120 000	120 000	120 000
Education, training, and library	45 600	48 000	47 000	50 000	50 000	50 000	54 000	52 000	53 000	55 000
Arts, design, entertainment, sports, and media	46 000	45 000	45 000	50 000	50 000	50 000	52 000	50 000	50 000	55 000
Health care practitioner and technical	72 000	65 500	70 000	70 000	72 000	75 000	75 000	74 000	75 000	75 000
Services	25 000	26 000	25 000	26 000	29 000	29 000	30 000	30 000	30 002	30 000
Health care support	24 000	22 537	20 400	22 880	25 000	25 000	28 000	30 000	34 000	29 904
Protective services	40 000	44 000	44 000	45 000	46 886	49 000	49 000	49 500	50 000	50 000
Food preparation and serving related	20 000	18 720	18 720	20 000	20 000	21 000	21 500	21 000	23 000	23 400
Building and grounds cleaning and maintenance	24 500	22 156	24 000	24 000	25 000	25 000	27 012	26 000	28 600	27 000
Personal care and services	30 000	28 559	26 000	30 000	30 000	30 000	30 500	30 000	30 000	32 000
Sales and office	38 000	39 000	40 000	40 000	40 000	40 000	42 000	40 000	42 002	43 000
Sales and related	41 600	41 000	44 000	42 000	45 000	45 000	48 000	48 002	48 000	50 000
Office and administrative support	32 000	32 000	34 000	34 000	35 000	36 000	35 000	37 400	37 000	37 000
Natural resources, construction, and maintenance	33 592	34 283	35 000	35 000	35 674	36 000	40 000	40 000	40 000	40 000
Farming, fishing, and forestry	22 000	22 000	22 000	22 500	20 000	24 000	24 000	25 000	23 400	25 000
Construction and extraction	31 304	32 000	33 000	32 000	35 000	35 000	40 000	40 000	40 000	40 000
Installation, maintenance, and repair	36 000	38 000	38 870	40 000	40 000	40 000	42 685	45 000	44 000	45 000
Production, transportation, and material moving	30 000	32 000	33 000	34 000	33 358	35 000	35 360	35 198	36 000	38 500
Production	30 360	32 000	34 000	35 000	35 000	36 000	36 000	36 000	36 944	40 000
Transportation and material moving	30 000	30 000	32 000	32 760	32 000	35 000	35 000	35 000	35 000	37 440
Armed forces	36 000	36 000	40 000	40 000	40 000	42 000	45 000	47 000	47 000	45 000

Table 1-40. Number and Median Annual Earnings of Year-Round, Full-Time Wage and Salary Workers, by Sex and Occupation of Job Held the Longest, 2002–2011—*Continued*

(Thousands of people, dollars.)

Sex and occupation	2002	2003	2004	2005	2006	2007	2008	2009	2010	2011
Women, Number of Workers										
Management, business, and financial operations	6 529	6 591	6 726	6 803	7 287	7 332	7 423	7 073	7 320	7 511
Management	4 205	4 111	4 214	4 209	4 504	4 573	4 542	4 432	4 555	4 643
Business and financial operations	2 324	2 479	2 512	2 594	2 783	2 759	2 881	2 641	2 765	2 867
Professional and related	9 851	10 071	10 095	10 532	10 881	11 664	11 675	11 795	11 840	11 937
Computer and mathematical	691	685	708	718	729	802	741	873	748	842
Architecture and engineering	273	269	300	320	317	295	293	274	299	307
Life, physical, and social sciences	428	342	373	428	394	415	462	479	431	386
Community and social services	968	968	927	1 015	1 079	1 047	1 079	1 119	1 204	1 105
Legal	516	539	550	603	622	645	633	585	650	610
Education, training, and library	3 199	3 441	3 356	3 473	3 608	3 831	3 944	3 850	3 909	3 868
Arts, design, entertainment, sports, and media	606	563	568	573	681	764	633	575	541	589
Health care practitioner and technical	3 170	3 263	3 314	3 403	3 452	3 865	3 890	4 039	4 057	4 230
Services	6 026	5 786	6 144	6 459	6 522	6 682	6 645	6 565	6 429	6 753
Health care support	1 586	1 525	1 573	1 787	1 829	1 766	1 815	1 888	1 766	1 969
Protective services	354	419	500	510	509	511	541	567	519	463
Food preparation and serving related	1 757	1 585	1 668	1 713	1 655	1 784	1 688	1 563	1 665	1 747
Building and grounds cleaning and maintenance	1 055	1 029	1 115	1 132	1 181	1 150	1 116	1 038	1 079	1 125
Personal care and services	1 274	1 228	1 289	1 317	1 349	1 471	1 485	1 508	1 400	1 451
Sales and office	14 338	14 368	14 239	14 546	14 720	14 778	13 930	13 640	12 986	12 979
Sales and related	3 996	3 913	4 060	4 355	4 372	4 282	4 073	4 044	3 824	3 766
Office and administrative support	10 342	10 455	10 180	10 191	10 348	10 496	9 856	9 596	9 162	9 213
Natural resources, construction, and maintenance	391	361	396	360	391	402	376	374	361	310
Farming, fishing, and forestry	111	92	93	87	104	92	91	130	102	87
Construction and extraction	100	97	135	119	140	132	101	104	120	91
Installation, maintenance, and repair	180	172	169	155	148	178	183	140	140	131
Production, transportation, and material moving	2 914	2 899	2 835	2 839	2 971	2 861	2 423	2 141	2 304	2 458
Production	2 219	2 157	2 150	2 120	2 237	2 128	1 668	1 464	1 614	1 761
Transportation and material moving	695	742	685	719	734	733	755	676	690	697
Armed forces	58	81	52	73	48	49	49	62	78	72
Women, Median Annual Earnings										
Management, business, and financial operations	41 000	43 000	43 000	46 000	50 000	50 000	50 000	50 000	52 779	52 000
Management	44 000	47 000	46 000	50 000	52 000	52 000	55 000	52 999	55 000	55 000
Business and financial operations	38 500	40 000	40 000	41 000	46 000	45 000	48 000	48 000	50 000	50 000
Professional and related	40 000	40 000	40 000	42 000	43 000	45 000	46 000	48 002	49 000	50 000
Computer and mathematical	51 627	52 000	57 000	57 000	60 000	60 000	62 000	65 000	65 000	65 000
Architecture and engineering	50 000	48 000	47 500	55 000	52 000	55 000	50 000	61 000	60 000	62 400
Life, physical, and social sciences	44 000	45 000	45 995	50 000	48 000	48 000	49 000	54 651	56 000	55 000
Community and social services	33 000	33 000	35 000	35 000	36 000	37 000	37 700	39 000	39 000	40 000
Legal	45 000	45 000	46 000	47 500	50 000	47 500	52 001	60 000	57 257	51 875
Education, training, and library	35 000	35 000	37 000	38 000	38 632	41 000	42 000	43 000	42 000	45 000
Arts, design, entertainment, sports, and media	40 000	35 000	36 000	35 000	38 000	40 000	40 000	45 000	42 000	43 000
Health care practitioner and technical	41 000	43 000	45 000	46 000	48 000	50 000	50 000	52 000	53 000	53 000
Services	20 000	20 000	20 000	20 000	20 500	22 000	23 516	24 000	23 000	23 000
Health care support	22 000	22 000	22 000	21 000	23 000	24 500	26 000	25 000	25 000	26 000
Protective services	30 900	32 000	32 000	34 344	37 896	35 000	35 000	38 000	38 500	42 000
Food preparation and serving related	16 160	17 000	16 000	18 000	18 000	19 000	20 000	19 000	19 000	20 000
Building and grounds cleaning and maintenance	16 491	16 000	16 866	18 000	19 000	19 500	20 000	20 000	20 000	20 020
Personal care and services	20 000	20 000	21 000	20 800	20 000	24 000	24 000	24 700	23 000	23 000
Sales and office	26 989	28 000	28 000	29 000	30 000	30 000	30 600	31 400	32 000	33 000
Sales and related	25 000	26 000	26 000	26 000	26 000	28 000	29 000	30 000	30 000	30 000
Office and administrative support	27 000	28 000	28 000	29 800	30 000	30 002	32 000	32 100	33 000	34 000
Natural resources, construction, and maintenance	26 000	28 000	30 000	30 200	27 000	37 025	30 000	30 000	30 000	30 000
Farming, fishing, and forestry	17 000	16 000	15 700	18 000	18 808	24 117	24 685	21 000	20 000	20 000
Construction and extraction	26 000	29 500	40 000	31 200	24 980	40 000	34 500	31 000	33 670	28 323
Installation, maintenance, and repair	34 000	37 000	33 000	36 000	40 000	42 000	33 913	38 139	41 888	35 000
Production, transportation, and material moving	22 000	22 100	23 000	23 000	23 000	25 000	25 000	25 000	25 000	25 000
Production	21 632	22 000	23 000	23 400	23 000	25 000	25 000	25 000	25 000	25 000
Transportation and material moving	22 000	22 710	23 000	21 000	24 000	27 000	24 000	25 000	25 000	26 000
Armed forces	40 000	32 000	35 100	32 652	32 000	41 000	32 000	43 600	50 000	52 000

Table 1-41. Distribution of Employed Wage and Salary Workers by Tenure with Current Employer, Age, Sex, Race, and Hispanic Origin, January 2012

(Thousands of people, percent.)

Characteristic	Number employed/ (in thousands)	Percent distribution by tenure with current employer								
		Total	12 months or less	13 to 23 months	2 years	3 to 4 years	5 to 9 years	10 to 14 years	15 to 19 years	20 years or more
Both Sexes										
16 years and over	125 516	100.0	21.1	6.3	4.9	16.6	21.8	12.5	6.1	10.6
16 to 19 years	3 925	100.0	72.9	11.9	6.9	7.8	0.4	-	-	-
20 years and over	121 591	100.0	19.5	6.1	4.8	16.9	22.4	12.9	6.3	11.0
20 to 24 years	12 712	100.0	48.9	12.8	10.6	20.4	7.1	0.2	-	-
25 to 34 years	28 381	100.0	25.5	8.4	6.9	24.5	27.2	6.8	0.7	-
35 to 44 years	27 477	100.0	16.1	5.4	4.3	16.8	27.0	17.8	8.8	3.8
45 to 54 years	28 535	100.0	12.5	4.5	2.9	13.0	22.0	16.8	9.5	18.7
55 to 64 years	19 339	100.0	9.4	2.8	2.3	10.8	20.2	16.4	9.8	28.3
65 years and over	5 148	100.0	7.8	2.0	2.1	11.8	20.7	16.6	9.2	29.7
Men										
16 years and over	64 552	100.0	21.0	6.3	5.0	16.2	21.3	12.2	6.4	11.5
16 to 19 years	1 839	100.0	71.2	13.3	7.8	7.4	0.4	-	-	-
20 years and over	62 713	100.0	19.6	6.1	4.9	16.5	21.9	12.6	6.5	11.9
20 to 24 years	6 559	100.0	48.8	12.5	10.4	20.6	7.4	0.2	-	-
25 to 34 years	15 104	100.0	24.7	8.5	7.3	23.8	27.8	7.0	0.9	-
35 to 44 years	14 570	100.0	16.3	5.4	4.0	16.1	26.8	17.3	9.8	4.4
45 to 54 years	14 361	100.0	12.6	4.5	2.8	12.5	19.6	16.6	10.0	21.4
55 to 64 years	9 470	100.0	10.0	2.5	2.7	10.1	18.8	15.6	9.2	31.2
65 years and over	2 648	100.0	7.8	1.3	1.9	11.8	21.7	16.9	8.9	29.7
Women										
16 years and over	60 964	100.0	21.3	6.3	4.8	17.1	22.2	12.7	5.9	9.7
16 to 19 years	2 085	100.0	74.4	10.7	6.2	8.2	0.5	-	-	-
20 years and over	58 879	100.0	19.4	6.2	4.7	17.4	23.0	13.2	6.1	10.1
20 to 24 years	6 153	100.0	49.0	13.1	10.7	20.3	6.7	0.2	-	-
25 to 34 years	13 276	100.0	26.5	8.4	6.4	25.3	26.5	6.5	0.5	-
35 to 44 years	12 907	100.0	15.9	5.4	4.6	17.5	27.4	18.4	7.7	3.1
45 to 54 years	14 174	100.0	12.4	4.5	3.1	13.6	24.4	17.0	9.0	16.0
55 to 64 years	9 868	100.0	8.8	3.2	1.9	11.6	21.4	17.2	10.5	25.5
65 years and over	2 499	100.0	7.7	2.8	2.4	11.9	19.7	16.3	9.6	29.7
White										
16 years and over	100 679	100.0	20.7	6.4	4.8	16.1	21.7	12.6	6.6	11.3
Men	52 641	100.0	20.5	6.5	4.7	15.7	21.1	12.4	6.8	12.3
Women	48 039	100.0	20.9	6.3	4.8	16.4	22.2	12.9	6.3	10.2
Black										
16 years and over	14 204	100.0	22.2	5.6	5.2	18.5	22.1	12.4	4.5	9.5
Men	6 526	100.0	22.9	5.1	5.5	18.9	21.9	10.8	4.8	10.0
Women	7 678	100.0	21.6	6.0	5.0	18.2	22.2	13.8	4.2	9.1
Asian										
16 years and over	6 933	100.0	21.1	6.6	5.3	20.5	23.8	11.3	4.8	6.6
Men	3 502	100.0	21.2	5.8	6.6	19.0	23.8	12.8	4.3	6.5
Women	3 432	100.0	21.0	7.3	4.0	22.1	23.9	9.8	5.2	6.7
Hispanic[1]										
16 years and over	19 763	100.0	23.6	5.9	6.6	20.1	23.7	10.9	4.2	5.1
Men	11 262	100.0	24.5	6.0	6.8	20.8	22.4	10.0	4.3	5.2
Women	8 501	100.0	22.3	5.6	6.4	19.2	25.4	12.0	4.2	4.9

[1]May be of any race.
- = Data represents or rounds to zero.

Table 1-42. Median Years of Tenure with Current Employer for Employed Wage and Salary Workers, 25 Years and Over, by Educational Attainment, Sex, and Age, January 2012

(Percent.)

Year, sex, and age	Total employed	25 to 34 years	35 to 44 years	45 to 54 years	55 to 64 years	65 years and over
Both Sexes	5.4	3.2	5.3	7.8	10.3	10.3
Less than a high school diploma	4.8	3.2	4.6	5.3	8.0	9.8
High school graduates, no college	5.8	3.3	5.0	8.5	10.3	10.2
Some college, no degree	5.2	3.1	5.1	7.4	10.3	10.2
Associate degree	5.7	3.2	5.6	7.7	10.4	10.4
College graduates	5.5	3.1	5.7	8.2	10.5	11.0
Bachelor's degree	5.2	3.1	5.7	7.8	10.4	11.6
Master's degree	6.3	3.4	6.0	8.6	10.4	10.2
Doctoral or professional degree	5.6	2.3	5.0	9.6	11.9	14.8
Men	5.5	3.2	5.4	8.5	10.7	10.2
Less than a high school diploma	4.7	3.4	4.8	5.4	8.2	10.5
High school graduates, no college	5.7	3.3	5.1	9.6	10.6	9.7
Some college, no degree	5.3	3.1	5.2	8.6	10.2	9.8
Associate degree	6.2	3.4	6.3	8.4	11.2	10.0
College graduates	5.7	3.1	5.7	8.6	11.3	11.3
Bachelor's degree	5.5	3.2	5.9	8.3	11.3	10.4
Master's degree	6.4	3.3	5.8	8.9	10.5	9.9
Doctoral or professional degree	5.9	2.3	4.8	9.7	13.4	15.3
Women	5.4	3.1	5.2	7.3	10.0	10.5
Less than a high school diploma	4.8	2.9	4.2	5.2	7.8	7.8
High school graduates, no college	6.0	3.3	5.0	7.8	10.0	11.4
Some college, no degree	5.2	3.2	5.0	6.5	10.3	10.8
Associate degree	5.3	3.1	5.1	7.2	9.8	11.3
College graduates	5.3	3.1	5.7	7.9	10.2	10.7
Bachelor's degree	5.0	3.0	5.6	7.4	10.1	12.3
Master's degree	6.3	3.4	6.2	8.4	10.4	10.3
Doctoral or professional degree	5.2	2.4	5.4	9.4	10.3	10.0

Table 1-43. Median Years of Tenure with Current Employer for Employed Wage and Salary Workers, by Age and Sex, Selected Years, February 1996–January 2012

(Number of years.)

Sex and age	February 1996	February 1998	February 2000	January 2002	January 2004	January 2006	January 2008	January 2010	January 2012
Both Sexes									
16 years and over	3.8	3.6	3.5	3.7	4.0	4.0	4.1	4.4	4.6
16 to 17 years	0.7	0.6	0.6	0.7	0.7	0.6	0.7	0.7	0.7
18 to 19 years	0.7	0.7	0.7	0.8	0.8	0.7	0.8	1.0	0.8
20 to 24 years	1.2	1.1	1.1	1.2	1.3	1.3	1.3	1.5	1.3
25 years and over	5.0	4.7	4.7	4.7	4.9	4.9	5.1	5.2	5.4
25 to 34 years	2.8	2.7	2.6	2.7	2.9	2.9	2.7	3.1	3.2
35 to 44 years	5.3	5.0	4.8	4.6	4.9	4.9	4.9	5.1	5.3
45 to 54 years	8.3	8.1	8.2	7.6	7.7	7.3	7.6	7.8	7.8
55 to 64 years	10.2	10.1	10.0	9.9	9.6	9.3	9.9	10.0	10.3
65 years and over	8.4	7.8	9.4	8.6	9.0	8.8	10.2	9.9	10.3
Men									
16 years and over	4.0	3.8	3.8	3.9	4.1	4.1	4.2	4.6	4.7
16 to 17 years	0.6	0.6	0.6	0.8	0.7	0.7	0.7	0.7	0.6
18 to 19 years	0.7	0.7	0.7	0.8	0.8	0.7	0.8	1.0	0.8
20 to 24 years	1.2	1.2	1.2	1.4	1.3	1.4	1.4	1.6	1.4
25 years and over	5.3	4.9	4.9	4.9	5.1	5.0	5.2	5.3	5.5
25 to 34 years	3.0	2.8	2.7	2.8	3.0	2.9	2.8	3.2	3.2
35 to 44 years	6.1	5.5	5.3	5.0	5.2	5.1	5.2	5.3	5.4
45 to 54 years	10.1	9.4	9.5	9.1	9.6	8.1	8.2	8.5	8.5
55 to 64 years	10.5	11.2	10.2	10.2	9.8	9.5	10.1	10.4	10.7
65 years and over	8.3	7.1	9.0	8.1	8.2	8.3	10.4	9.7	10.2
Women									
16 years and over	3.5	3.4	3.3	3.4	3.8	3.9	3.9	4.2	4.6
16 to 17 years	0.7	0.6	0.6	0.7	0.6	0.6	0.6	0.7	0.7
18 to 19 years	0.7	0.7	0.7	0.8	0.8	0.7	0.8	1.0	0.8
20 to 24 years	1.2	1.1	1.0	1.1	1.3	1.2	1.3	1.5	1.3
25 years and over	4.7	4.4	4.4	4.4	4.7	4.8	4.9	5.1	5.4
25 to 34 years	2.7	2.5	2.5	2.5	2.8	2.8	2.6	3.0	3.1
35 to 44 years	4.8	4.5	4.3	4.2	4.5	4.6	4.7	4.9	5.2
45 to 54 years	7.0	7.2	7.3	6.5	6.4	6.7	7.0	7.1	7.3
55 to 64 years	10.0	9.6	9.9	9.6	9.2	9.2	9.8	9.7	10.0
65 years and over	8.4	8.7	9.7	9.4	9.6	9.5	9.9	10.1	10.5

Table 1-44. Median Years of Tenure with Current Employer for Employed Wage and Salary Workers, by Industry, Selected Years, February 2000–January 2012

(Number of years.)

Industry	February 2000	January 2002	January 2004	January 2006	January 2018	January 2010	January 2012
TOTAL, 16 YEARS AND OVER	3.5	3.7	4.0	4.0	4.1	4.4	4.6
Private Sector	3.2	3.3	3.5	3.6	3.6	4.0	4.2
Agriculture and related industries	3.7	4.2	3.7	3.8	4.3	4.8	4.1
Nonagricultural industries	3.2	3.3	3.5	3.6	3.6	4.0	4.2
Mining	4.8	4.5	5.2	3.8	4.1	4.8	3.5
Construction	2.7	3.0	3.0	3.0	3.5	4.2	4.3
Manufacturing	4.9	5.4	5.8	5.5	5.9	6.1	6.0
Durable goods manufacturing	4.8	5.5	6.0	5.6	6.1	6.6	6.1
Nonmetallic mineral product	5.5	5.3	4.8	5.0	4.8	7.7	7.0
Primary metals and fabricated metal product	5.0	6.3	6.4	6.2	5.2	7.2	5.6
Machinery manufacturing	5.3	6.8	6.4	6.6	6.0	8.3	5.4
Computers and electronic product	3.9	4.7	5.2	5.9	6.7	5.9	7.7
Electrical equipment and appliances	5.0	5.5	9.8	6.2	6.2	5.0	5.9
Transportation equipment	6.4	7.0	7.7	7.2	7.8	8.3	7.1
Wood product	3.7	4.3	5.0	4.7	6.2	4.7	5.3
Furniture and fixtures	4.4	4.7	4.7	4.2	5.2	5.0	6.5
Miscellaneous manufacturing	3.7	4.5	4.6	3.9	4.7	5.4	4.8
Nondurable goods manufacturing	5.0	5.3	5.5	5.4	5.4	5.5	5.8
Food manufacturing	4.6	5.0	4.9	5.2	4.3	4.7	4.9
Beverage and tobacco product	5.5	4.6	8.0	5.4	6.9	8.1	6.4
Textiles, apparel, and leather	4.7	5.0	5.0	4.4	4.6	4.7	4.3
Paper and printing	5.1	6.2	6.9	6.3	5.5	6.8	9.7
Petroleum and coal product	9.5	9.8	11.4	5.0	4.3	5.1	6.4
Chemicals	6.0	5.7	5.3	6.1	7.6	7.3	6.1
Plastics and rubber product	4.6	5.3	5.7	5.0	5.3	7.4	6.1
Wholesale and retail trade	2.7	2.8	3.1	3.1	3.2	3.6	3.7
Wholesale trade	3.9	3.9	4.3	4.6	5.0	5.2	5.5
Retail trade	2.5	2.6	2.8	2.8	2.9	3.3	3.3
Transportation and utilities	4.7	4.9	5.3	4.9	5.1	5.3	5.6
Transportation and warehousing	4.0	4.3	4.7	4.3	4.6	5.0	5.3
Utilities	11.5	13.4	13.3	10.4	10.1	9.1	9.5
Information[1]	3.4	3.3	4.3	4.8	4.7	5.0	5.4
Publishing, except Internet	4.2	4.8	4.7	5.3	4.7	5.6	6.6
Motion picture and sound recording industries	1.6	2.3	2.2	1.9	1.9	3.8	2.6
Broadcasting, except Internet	3.6	3.1	4.0	4.6	3.4	4.3	4.9
Telecommunications	4.3	3.4	4.6	5.3	6.9	6.6	7.4
Financial activities	3.5	3.6	3.9	4.0	4.5	4.6	4.9
Finance and insurance	3.6	3.9	4.1	4.1	4.7	4.8	5.0
Finance	3.3	3.6	4.0	3.9	4.4	4.5	4.7
Insurance	4.4	4.5	4.4	4.7	5.2	5.5	5.7
Real estate and rental and leasing	3.1	3.0	3.3	3.4	3.7	3.9	4.5
Real estate	3.1	3.2	3.5	3.5	3.9	4.1	4.5
Rental and leasing services	3.0	2.2	2.9	3.1	3.0	3.3	4.2
Professional and business services	2.4	2.7	3.2	3.2	3.1	3.4	3.8
Professional and technical services	2.6	3.1	3.6	3.8	3.3	4.0	4.4
Management, administrative, and waste services[1]	2.0	2.1	2.6	2.5	2.5	2.9	3.1
Administrative and support services	1.8	1.9	2.4	2.4	2.4	2.8	3.0
Waste management and remediation services	3.6	4.3	3.4	4.1	4.1	2.9	4.4
Education and health services	3.4	3.5	3.6	4.0	4.1	4.1	4.4
Education services	3.2	3.6	3.8	4.0	4.3	4.4	4.3
Health care and social assistance	3.5	3.5	3.6	4.1	4.1	4.1	4.4
Hospitals	5.1	4.9	4.7	5.2	5.4	5.3	6.0
Health services, except hospitals	3.2	3.1	3.3	3.6	3.6	3.6	3.8
Social assistance	2.4	2.5	2.8	3.1	3.0	3.1	3.1
Leisure and hospitality	1.7	1.8	2.0	1.9	2.1	2.5	2.4
Arts, entertainment, and recreation	2.6	2.3	2.8	3.1	2.8	3.3	3.1
Accommodation and food services	1.5	1.6	1.9	1.6	1.9	2.3	2.3
Accommodation	2.8	2.7	3.1	2.5	3.1	3.3	3.8
Food services and drinking places	1.4	1.4	1.6	1.4	1.6	2.2	2.1
Other services	3.1	3.3	3.3	3.2	3.3	4.0	3.8
Other services, except private households	3.2	3.3	3.5	3.3	3.4	4.1	3.8
Repair and maintenance	3.0	3.0	3.2	2.9	3.0	4.0	3.7
Personal and laundry services	2.7	2.8	3.4	2.8	3.2	3.5	3.5
Membership associations and organizations	4.0	4.1	3.9	4.2	4.4	4.5	4.3
Other services, private households	3.0	2.7	2.3	2.8	2.8	3.4	3.3
Public Sector	7.1	6.7	6.9	6.9	7.2	7.2	7.8
Federal government	11.5	11.3	10.4	9.9	9.9	7.9	9.5
State government	5.5	5.4	6.4	6.3	6.5	6.4	6.4
Local government	6.7	6.2	6.4	6.6	7.1	7.5	8.1

Note: Data beginning in 2000 reflect the introduction of Census 2000 population controls. Data for 2004 forward reflect updated population controls introduced annually with the release of January data. Beginning with data for January 2009, industries reflect the introduction of the 2007 census industry classification system into the Current Population Survey (CPS). This industry classification system is derived from the 2007 North American Industry Classification System.

[1] Includes other industries not shown separately.

Table 1-45. Employment Status of the Population, by Sex and Marital Status, March 1990–March 2012

(Thousands of people, percent.)

Marital status and year	Men						Women					
		Labor force						Labor force				
		Total		Employed	Unemployed			Total		Employed	Unemployed	
	Population	Number	Percent of population		Number	Percent of labor force	Population	Number	Percent of population		Number	Percent of labor force
Single												
1990	25 757	18 829	73.1	16 893	1 936	10.3	21 088	14 003	66.4	12 856	1 147	8.2
1991	26 220	19 014	72.5	16 418	2 596	13.7	21 688	14 125	65.1	12 887	1 238	8.8
1992	26 529	19 229	72.5	16 401	2 828	14.7	21 738	14 072	64.7	12 793	1 279	9.1
1993	26 951	19 625	72.8	16 858	2 767	14.1	21 848	14 091	64.5	12 711	1 380	9.8
1994	28 350	20 365	71.8	17 826	2 539	12.5	22 885	14 903	65.1	13 419	1 484	10.0
1995	28 318	20 449	72.2	18 286	2 163	10.6	22 853	14 974	65.5	13 673	1 301	8.7
1996	28 695	20 561	71.7	18 097	2 464	12.0	23 632	15 417	65.2	14 084	1 333	8.6
1997	29 294	20 942	71.5	18 683	2 259	10.8	24 215	16 178	66.8	14 747	1 431	8.8
1998	29 558	21 255	71.9	19 124	2 131	10.0	24 808	16 885	68.1	15 626	1 259	7.5
1999	29 883	21 329	71.4	19 465	1 864	8.7	25 674	17 486	68.1	16 185	1 301	7.4
2000	30 232	21 641	71.6	19 823	1 818	8.4	25 863	17 749	68.6	16 446	1 303	7.3
2001	30 968	22 232	71.8	20 239	1 993	9.0	26 180	17 900	68.4	16 631	1 269	7.1
2002	32 220	22 761	70.6	20 066	2 695	11.8	26 942	18 079	67.1	16 499	1 580	8.7
2003	32 852	22 821	69.5	20 194	2 627	11.5	27 527	17 901	65.0	16 219	1 682	9.4
2004	33 786	23 212	68.7	20 434	2 778	12.0	28 033	18 089	64.5	16 506	1 583	8.8
2005	34 069	23 335	68.5	20 831	2 504	10.7	28 508	18 554	65.1	16 902	1 652	8.9
2006	34 906	24 369	69.8	21 961	2 408	9.9	29 357	18 989	64.7	17 444	1 545	8.1
2007	35 359	24 506	69.3	22 224	2 281	9.3	29 695	19 218	64.7	17 935	1 284	6.7
2008	36 522	25 229	69.1	22 695	2 534	10.0	30 772	19 889	64.6	18 369	1 520	7.6
2009	36 907	24 930	67.5	20 645	4 284	17.2	31 038	19 785	63.7	17 714	2 071	10.5
2010	38 110	25 663	67.3	21 038	4 626	18.0	32 085	19 973	62.3	17 517	2 457	12.3
2011	38 766	25 646	66.2	21 389	4 256	16.6	33 041	20 581	62.3	18 117	2 463	12.0
2012	38 933	25 615	65.8	21 838	3 778	14.7	34 241	21 417	62.5	18 895	2 523	11.8
Married, Spouse Present												
1990	52 464	41 020	78.2	39 562	1 458	3.6	53 207	30 967	58.2	29 870	1 097	3.5
1991	52 460	40 883	77.9	38 843	2 040	5.0	53 176	31 103	58.5	29 668	1 435	4.6
1992	52 780	40 930	77.5	38 650	2 280	5.6	53 464	31 686	59.3	30 130	1 556	4.9
1993	53 488	41 255	77.1	39 069	2 186	5.3	54 198	32 158	59.4	30 757	1 401	4.4
1994	53 436	40 993	76.7	39 085	1 908	4.7	54 198	32 863	60.6	31 397	1 466	4.5
1995	54 166	41 806	77.2	40 262	1 544	3.7	54 902	33 563	61.1	32 267	1 296	3.9
1996	53 996	41 837	77.5	40 356	1 481	3.5	54 640	33 382	61.1	32 258	1 124	3.4
1997	53 981	41 967	77.7	40 628	1 339	3.2	54 611	33 907	62.1	32 836	1 071	3.2
1998	54 685	42 288	77.3	41 039	1 249	3.0	55 241	34 136	61.8	33 028	1 108	3.2
1999	55 256	42 557	77.0	41 476	1 081	2.5	55 801	34 349	61.6	33 403	946	2.8
2000	55 897	43 254	77.4	42 261	993	2.3	56 432	34 959	61.9	33 998	961	2.7
2001	56 152	43 463	77.4	42 245	1 218	2.8	56 740	35 234	62.1	34 273	961	2.7
2002	57 325	44 271	77.2	42 508	1 763	4.0	57 883	35 624	61.5	34 295	1 329	3.7
2003	57 940	44 700	77.1	42 797	1 903	4.3	58 545	36 185	61.8	34 806	1 379	3.8
2004	58 395	44 860	76.8	43 247	1 613	3.6	59 008	35 918	60.9	34 582	1 336	3.7
2005	58 854	45 263	76.9	43 763	1 500	3.3	59 449	35 809	60.2	34 738	1 071	3.0
2006	58 850	45 082	76.6	43 877	1 205	2.7	59 476	36 192	60.9	35 185	1 007	2.8
2007	60 126	46 129	76.7	44 813	1 317	2.9	60 656	37 335	61.6	36 370	965	2.6
2008	59 455	45 451	76.4	43 958	1 493	3.3	60 108	37 074	61.7	35 919	1 155	3.1
2009	60 132	45 741	76.1	42 667	3 074	6.7	60 818	37 536	61.7	35 540	1 996	5.3
2010	59 694	45 110	75.6	41 762	3 348	7.4	60 339	37 201	61.7	34 964	2 237	6.0
2011	59 477	44 553	74.9	41 667	2 886	6.5	60 095	36 383	60.5	34 340	2 043	5.6
2012	60 346	44 915	74.4	42 387	2 528	5.6	61 011	36 363	59.6	34 423	1 940	5.3
Widowed, Divorced, or Separated												
1990	11 152	7 513	67.4	6 959	554	7.4	23 857	11 168	46.8	10 530	638	5.7
1991	11 588	7 804	67.3	6 985	819	10.5	24 105	11 145	46.2	10 386	759	6.8
1992	11 927	8 049	67.5	7 140	909	11.3	24 582	11 486	46.7	10 610	876	7.6
1993	11 861	7 956	67.1	7 055	901	11.3	24 661	11 308	45.9	10 528	780	6.9
1994	12 239	8 156	66.6	7 382	774	9.5	25 098	11 879	47.3	10 995	884	7.4
1995	12 410	8 315	67.0	7 632	683	8.2	25 373	12 001	47.3	11 308	693	5.8
1996	13 176	8 697	66.0	7 976	721	8.3	25 786	12 430	48.2	11 742	688	5.5
1997	14 113	9 420	66.7	8 715	705	7.5	26 301	12 814	48.7	12 071	743	5.8
1998	14 166	9 482	66.9	8 954	528	5.6	26 092	12 880	49.4	12 235	645	5.0
1999	14 225	9 449	66.4	8 971	478	5.1	26 199	12 951	49.4	12 307	644	5.0
2000	14 289	9 623	67.3	9 152	471	4.9	26 354	13 228	50.2	12 657	571	4.3
2001	14 392	9 421	65.5	8 927	494	5.2	26 747	13 454	50.3	12 887	567	4.2
2002	14 617	9 650	66.0	8 931	719	7.5	27 802	13 716	49.3	12 855	861	6.3
2003	15 180	9 855	64.9	9 020	835	8.5	28 240	14 154	50.1	13 240	914	6.5
2004	15 059	9 789	65.0	9 059	730	7.5	28 228	14 194	50.3	13 324	870	6.1
2005	15 779	10 256	65.0	9 569	687	6.7	28 576	14 233	49.8	13 472	761	5.3
2006	16 405	10 815	65.9	10 141	674	6.2	28 981	14 220	49.1	13 539	681	4.8
2007	16 247	10 799	66.5	10 150	650	6.0	28 950	14 320	49.5	13 620	700	4.9
2008	16 718	10 896	65.2	10 083	812	7.5	29 419	14 553	49.5	13 765	787	5.4
2009	16 719	10 687	63.9	9 224	1 463	13.7	29 471	14 449	49.0	13 169	1 281	8.9
2010	17 016	10 863	63.8	9 188	1 675	15.4	29 915	14 707	49.2	13 285	1 422	9.7
2011	17 744	11 095	62.5	9 676	1 420	12.8	29 876	14 610	48.9	13 221	1 389	9.5
2012	17 704	11 076	62.6	9 884	1 192	10.8	30 367	14 825	48.8	13 543	1 283	8.7

Note: See notes and definitions for information on historical comparability.

Table 1-45. Employment Status of the Population, by Sex and Marital Status, March 1990–March 2012
—Continued

(Thousands of people, percent.)

Marital status and year	Men						Women					
	Population	Labor force		Employed	Unemployed		Population	Labor force		Employed	Unemployed	
		Total						Total				
		Number	Percent of population		Number	Percent of labor force		Number	Percent of population		Number	Percent of labor force
Widowed												
1990	2 331	519	22.3	490	29	5.6	11 477	2 243	19.5	2 149	94	4.2
1991	2 385	486	20.4	448	38	7.8	11 288	2 150	19.0	2 044	106	4.9
1992	2 529	566	22.4	501	65	11.5	11 325	2 131	18.8	2 029	102	4.8
1993	2 468	596	24.1	535	61	10.2	11 214	1 961	17.5	1 856	105	5.4
1994	2 220	474	21.4	440	34	7.2	11 073	1 945	17.6	1 825	120	6.2
1995	2 282	496	21.7	469	27	5.4	11 080	1 941	17.5	1 844	97	5.0
1996	2 476	487	19.7	466	21	4.3	11 070	1 916	17.3	1 820	96	5.0
1997	2 686	559	20.8	529	30	5.4	11 058	2 018	18.2	1 926	92	4.6
1998	2 567	563	21.9	551	12	2.1	11 027	2 157	19.6	2 071	86	4.0
1999	2 540	562	22.1	532	30	5.3	10 943	2 039	18.6	1 942	97	4.8
2000	2 601	583	22.4	547	36	6.2	11 061	2 011	18.2	1 911	100	5.0
2001	2 638	568	21.5	546	22	3.9	11 182	2 137	19.1	2 045	92	4.3
2002	2 635	629	23.9	581	48	7.6	11 411	2 001	17.5	1 887	114	5.7
2003	2 694	628	23.3	588	40	6.4	11 295	2 087	18.5	1 991	96	4.6
2004	2 651	581	21.9	558	23	4.0	11 159	2 157	19.3	2 048	109	5.1
2005	2 729	618	22.6	590	28	4.5	11 125	2 111	19.0	2 005	106	5.0
2006	2 626	610	23.2	563	47	7.7	11 305	2 164	19.1	2 094	70	3.2
2007	2 697	631	23.4	588	43	6.8	11 220	2 058	18.3	1 971	87	4.2
2008	2 911	656	22.5	611	44	6.8	11 399	2 218	19.5	2 101	117	5.3
2009	2 813	632	22.5	543	90	14.2	11 446	2 174	19.0	2 032	143	6.6
2010	2 969	776	26.1	684	92	11.8	11 379	2 214	19.5	2 036	178	8.0
2011	2 931	698	23.8	648	50	7.1	11 310	2 291	20.3	2 118	173	7.6
2012	2 864	639	22.3	595	43	6.8	11 197	2 179	19.5	2 044	135	6.2
Divorced												
1990	6 256	5 004	80.0	4 639	365	7.3	8 845	6 678	75.5	6 333	345	5.2
1991	6 586	5 262	79.9	4 722	540	10.3	9 152	6 779	74.1	6 365	414	6.1
1992	6 743	5 418	80.3	4 823	595	11.0	9 569	7 076	73.9	6 578	498	7.0
1993	6 770	5 330	78.7	4 736	594	11.1	9 879	7 183	72.7	6 736	447	6.2
1994	7 222	5 548	76.8	5 028	520	9.4	10 113	7 473	73.9	6 962	511	6.8
1995	7 343	5 739	78.2	5 266	473	8.2	10 262	7 559	73.7	7 206	353	4.7
1996	7 734	5 954	77.0	5 468	486	8.2	10 508	7 829	74.5	7 468	361	4.6
1997	8 191	6 298	76.9	5 851	447	7.1	11 102	8 092	72.9	7 666	426	5.3
1998	8 307	6 378	76.8	6 045	333	5.2	11 065	8 038	72.6	7 687	351	4.4
1999	8 529	6 481	76.0	6 151	330	5.1	11 130	8 171	73.4	7 841	330	4.0
2000	8 532	6 583	77.2	6 279	304	4.6	11 061	8 505	76.9	8 217	288	3.4
2001	8 580	6 403	74.6	6 074	329	5.1	11 719	8 662	73.9	8 335	327	3.8
2002	8 643	6 519	75.4	6 053	466	7.1	12 227	8 902	72.8	8 416	486	5.5
2003	8 938	6 621	74.1	6 052	569	8.6	12 653	9 191	72.6	8 673	518	5.6
2004	8 942	6 622	74.1	6 104	518	7.8	12 817	9 246	72.1	8 706	540	5.8
2005	9 196	6 754	73.4	6 281	473	7.0	12 950	9 253	71.5	8 836	417	4.5
2006	9 646	7 065	73.2	6 631	434	6.1	13 107	9 188	70.1	8 799	389	4.2
2007	9 608	7 110	74.0	6 679	431	6.1	13 214	9 334	70.6	8 896	439	4.7
2008	9 767	7 106	72.8	6 607	499	7.0	13 551	9 387	69.3	8 938	449	4.8
2009	9 938	7 052	71.0	6 064	988	14.0	13 301	9 176	69.0	8 402	774	8.4
2010	9 944	7 018	70.6	5 888	1 131	16.1	13 758	9 394	68.3	8 510	885	9.4
2011	10 635	7 394	69.5	6 430	965	13.0	13 757	9 230	67.1	8 407	823	8.9
2012	10 662	7 394	69.3	6 572	822	11.1	14 210	9 416	66.3	8 620	797	8.5
Separated												
1990	2 565	1 990	77.6	1 830	160	8.0	3 535	2 247	63.6	2 048	199	8.9
1991	2 616	2 057	78.6	1 816	241	11.7	3 665	2 216	60.5	1 977	239	10.8
1992	2 655	2 065	77.8	1 816	249	12.1	3 688	2 279	61.8	2 003	276	12.1
1993	2 623	2 030	77.4	1 784	246	12.1	3 568	2 165	60.7	1 937	228	10.5
1994	2 797	2 134	76.3	1 914	220	10.3	3 911	2 461	62.9	2 208	253	10.3
1995	2 784	2 081	74.7	1 898	183	8.8	4 031	2 501	62.0	2 258	243	9.7
1996	2 966	2 255	76.0	2 041	214	9.5	4 209	2 684	63.8	2 453	231	8.6
1997	3 236	2 563	79.2	2 335	228	8.9	4 141	2 705	65.3	2 480	225	8.3
1998	3 293	2 542	77.2	2 358	184	7.2	4 000	2 683	67.1	2 476	207	7.7
1999	3 156	2 405	76.2	2 287	118	4.9	4 126	2 740	66.4	2 523	217	7.9
2000	3 157	2 456	77.8	2 326	130	5.3	4 012	2 711	67.6	2 528	183	6.8
2001	3 174	2 450	77.2	2 307	143	5.8	3 846	2 654	69.0	2 507	147	5.5
2002	3 339	2 502	74.9	2 297	205	8.2	4 164	2 812	67.5	2 551	261	9.3
2003	3 548	2 606	73.4	2 380	226	8.7	4 293	2 877	67.0	2 576	301	10.5
2004	3 466	2 586	74.6	2 397	189	7.3	4 251	2 791	65.7	2 569	222	8.0
2005	3 855	2 884	74.8	2 698	186	6.4	4 501	2 870	63.8	2 632	238	8.3
2006	4 132	3 141	76.0	2 947	194	6.2	4 569	2 869	62.8	2 647	222	7.7
2007	3 943	3 058	77.6	2 883	176	5.7	4 516	2 927	64.8	2 753	174	6.0
2008	4 040	3 134	77.6	2 865	269	8.6	4 469	2 947	65.9	2 726	221	7.5
2009	3 968	3 002	75.7	2 617	386	12.8	4 725	3 099	65.6	2 734	364	11.8
2010	4 103	3 069	74.8	2 616	452	14.7	4 778	3 099	64.8	2 739	359	11.6
2011	4 178	3 004	71.9	2 598	406	13.5	4 809	3 089	64.2	2 696	393	12.7
2012	4 177	3 044	72.9	2 717	327	10.7	4 960	3 230	65.1	2 879	351	10.9

Note: See notes and definitions for information on historical comparability.

Table 1-46. Employment Status of All Women and Single Women, by Presence and Age of Children, March 1990–March 2012

(Thousands of women, percent.)

Presence and age of children and year	All women							Single women						
	Civilian labor force	Civilian labor force as percent of population	Employed			Unemployed		Civilian labor force	Civilian labor force as percent of population	Employed			Unemployed	
			Number	Percent full time	Percent part time	Number	Percent of labor force			Number	Percent full time	Percent part time	Number	Percent of labor force
Women with No Children Under 18 Years														
1990	33 942	52.3	32 391	74.4	25.6	1 551	4.6	12 478	68.1	11 611	65.9	34.1	866	6.9
1991	34 047	52.0	32 167	74.0	26.0	1 880	5.5	12 472	67.0	11 529	66.2	33.8	943	7.6
1992	34 487	52.3	32 481	74.3	25.7	2 006	5.8	12 355	66.9	11 374	66.6	33.4	982	7.9
1993	34 495	52.1	32 476	74.6	25.4	2 020	5.9	12 223	66.4	11 201	66.1	33.9	1 022	8.4
1994	35 454	53.1	33 343	72.7	27.3	2 110	6.0	12 737	66.8	11 674	64.5	35.5	1 063	8.3
1995	35 843	52.9	34 054	72.9	27.1	1 789	5.0	12 870	67.1	11 919	64.5	35.5	951	7.4
1996	36 509	53.0	34 698	73.3	26.7	1 811	5.0	13 172	66.1	12 255	64.6	35.4	918	7.0
1997	37 295	53.6	35 572	73.7	26.3	1 723	4.6	13 405	66.5	12 442	64.0	36.0	964	7.2
1998	38 253	54.1	36 680	74.1	25.9	1 573	4.1	13 888	67.2	13 082	64.8	35.2	806	5.8
1999	39 316	54.3	37 589	74.6	25.4	1 727	4.4	14 435	67.1	13 491	65.6	34.4	944	6.5
2000	40 142	54.8	38 408	75.4	24.6	1 733	4.3	14 677	67.6	13 713	66.6	33.4	964	6.6
2001	40 836	54.9	39 219	75.7	24.3	1 617	4.0	14 877	67.4	13 993	67.3	32.7	884	5.9
2002	41 278	54.0	39 038	75.1	24.9	2 241	5.4	14 855	65.6	13 682	65.9	34.1	1 173	7.9
2003	42 039	54.1	39 667	74.8	25.2	2 372	5.6	14 678	63.5	13 430	65.1	34.9	1 249	8.5
2004	42 289	53.8	40 000	74.6	25.4	2 289	5.4	14 828	63.0	13 670	65.5	34.5	1 157	7.8
2005	42 039	54.1	39 667	74.8	25.2	2 372	5.6	14 678	63.5	13 430	65.1	34.9	1 249	8.5
2006	43 392	53.6	41 440	75.3	24.7	1 952	4.5	15 673	63.4	14 547	66.5	33.5	1 125	7.2
2007	44 039	53.9	42 279	75.3	24.7	1 760	4.0	15 704	63.4	14 801	66.4	33.6	903	5.7
2008	45 585	54.3	43 417	75.7	24.3	2 168	4.8	16 378	63.4	15 261	67.4	32.6	1 116	6.8
2009	45 649	53.8	42 343	73.3	26.7	3 306	7.2	16 112	62.1	14 607	64.9	35.1	1 506	9.3
2010	46 098	53.5	42 256	73.5	26.5	3 842	8.3	16 331	60.7	14 533	65.6	34.4	1 798	11.0
2011	46 198	53.0	42 569	73.3	26.7	3 629	7.9	16 758	60.8	15 016	65.2	34.8	1 743	10.4
2012	47 222	52.6	43 494	74.0	26.0	3 728	7.9	17 310	60.7	15 473	66.3	33.7	1 837	10.6
Women with Children Under 18 Years														
1990	22 196	66.7	20 865	73.0	27.0	1 331	6.0	1 525	55.2	1 244	79.1	20.9	280	18.4
1991	22 327	66.6	20 774	73.0	27.0	1 552	7.0	1 654	53.6	1 358	76.4	23.6	296	17.9
1992	22 756	67.2	21 052	73.8	26.2	1 704	7.5	1 716	52.5	1 420	75.9	24.1	297	17.3
1993	23 063	66.9	21 521	73.9	26.1	1 541	6.7	1 869	54.4	1 510	74.8	25.2	359	19.2
1994	24 191	68.4	22 467	70.8	29.2	1 724	7.1	2 166	56.9	1 745	73.9	26.1	421	19.4
1995	24 695	69.7	23 195	71.7	28.3	1 500	6.1	2 104	57.5	1 754	73.6	26.4	350	16.6
1996	24 720	70.2	23 386	72.6	27.4	1 334	5.4	2 245	60.5	1 829	73.5	26.5	416	18.5
1997	25 604	72.1	24 082	74.1	25.9	1 522	5.9	2 772	68.1	2 305	76.6	23.4	467	16.8
1998	25 647	72.3	24 209	74.0	26.0	1 438	5.6	2 997	72.5	2 544	75.6	24.4	453	15.1
1999	25 469	72.1	24 305	74.1	25.9	1 165	4.6	3 051	73.4	2 694	75.8	24.2	357	11.7
2000	25 795	72.9	24 693	74.6	25.4	1 102	4.3	3 073	73.9	2 734	79.7	20.3	339	11.0
2001	25 751	73.1	24 572	75.6	24.4	1 179	4.6	3 022	73.8	2 638	81.8	18.2	385	12.7
2002	26 140	72.2	24 612	74.8	25.2	1 529	5.8	3 224	75.3	2 818	79.1	20.9	406	12.6
2003	26 202	71.7	24 598	74.3	25.7	1 603	6.1	3 222	73.1	2 789	79.5	20.5	433	13.4
2004	25 913	70.7	24 413	74.2	25.8	1 501	5.8	3 262	72.6	2 836	76.8	23.2	426	13.1
2005	26 202	71.7	24 598	74.3	25.7	1 603	6.1	3 222	73.1	2 789	79.5	20.5	433	13.4
2006	26 009	70.6	24 728	75.6	24.4	1 281	4.9	3 317	71.5	2 896	77.8	22.2	420	12.7
2007	26 834	71.3	25 646	75.2	24.8	1 188	4.4	3 514	71.4	3 133	76.4	23.6	381	10.8
2008	25 930	71.2	24 637	75.7	24.3	1 294	5.0	3 511	71.0	3 108	78.0	22.0	403	11.5
2009	26 122	71.6	24 079	74.6	25.4	2 043	7.8	3 673	72.0	3 108	75.8	24.2	566	18.2
2010	25 783	71.3	23 510	73.7	26.3	2 273	8.8	3 642	70.1	2 984	71.9	28.1	659	18.1
2011	25 376	70.9	23 109	74.2	25.8	2 266	8.9	3 822	70.0	3 102	71.9	28.1	721	18.9
2012	25 384	70.9	23 366	75.4	24.6	2 018	7.9	4 108	71.5	3 422	73.2	26.8	686	16.7
Women with Children Under 6 Years														
1990	9 397	58.2	8 732	69.6	30.4	664	7.1	929	48.7	736	75.0	25.0	194	20.9
1991	9 636	58.4	8 758	69.5	30.5	878	9.1	1 050	48.8	819	72.2	27.8	231	22.0
1992	9 573	58.0	8 662	70.2	29.8	911	9.5	1 029	45.8	829	73.2	26.8	200	19.4
1993	9 621	57.9	8 764	70.1	29.9	857	8.9	1 125	47.4	869	70.0	30.0	257	22.8
1994	10 328	60.3	9 394	67.1	32.9	935	9.1	1 379	52.2	1 062	70.0	30.0	317	23.0
1995	10 395	62.3	9 587	67.5	32.5	809	7.8	1 328	53.0	1 069	68.6	31.4	259	19.5
1996	10 293	62.3	9 592	68.4	31.6	701	6.8	1 378	55.1	1 099	67.3	32.7	279	20.2
1997	10 610	65.0	9 800	70.5	29.5	810	7.6	1 755	65.1	1 424	71.6	28.4	330	18.8
1998	10 619	65.2	9 839	69.8	30.2	780	7.3	1 755	67.3	1 448	71.7	28.3	307	17.5
1999	10 322	64.4	9 674	69.0	31.0	648	6.3	1 811	68.1	1 565	71.0	29.0	246	13.6
2000	10 316	65.3	9 763	70.5	29.5	553	5.4	1 835	70.5	1 603	75.3	24.7	232	12.6
2001	10 200	64.9	9 618	71.2	28.8	582	5.7	1 783	69.7	1 542	79.1	20.9	242	13.6
2002	10 193	64.1	9 441	70.4	29.6	752	7.4	1 819	71.0	1 568	74.5	25.5	251	13.8
2003	10 209	62.9	9 433	70.0	30.0	776	7.6	1 893	70.2	1 614	75.2	24.8	279	14.7
2004	10 131	62.2	9 407	69.4	30.6	724	7.1	1 885	68.4	1 605	70.1	29.9	279	14.8
2005	10 209	62.9	9 433	70.0	30.0	776	7.6	1 893	70.2	1 614	75.2	24.8	279	14.7
2006	10 430	63.0	9 779	72.0	28.0	651	6.2	1 934	68.6	1 659	72.8	27.2	276	14.3
2007	10 894	63.5	10 305	71.9	28.1	589	5.4	2 066	67.4	1 827	72.7	27.3	239	11.6
2008	10 452	63.6	9 794	72.1	27.9	657	6.3	1 982	66.0	1 705	72.2	27.8	277	14.0
2009	10 497	63.6	9 517	71.8	28.2	980	9.3	2 137	67.8	1 754	70.3	29.7	383	17.9
2010	10 536	64.2	9 452	70.9	29.1	1 085	10.3	2 076	65.6	1 643	67.0	33.0	433	20.9
2011	10 403	64.2	9 268	71.3	28.7	1 135	10.9	2 177	65.8	1 678	65.5	34.5	499	22.9
2012	10 462	64.7	9 458	72.6	27.4	1 004	9.6	2 408	68.1	1 958	69.0	31.0	450	18.7

Note: See notes and definitions for information on historical comparability.

Table 1-47. Employment Status of Ever-Married Women and Married Women, Spouse Present, by Presence and Age of Children, March 1990–March 2012

(Thousands of women, percent.)

Presence and age of children and year	Ever-married women[1]							Married women, spouse present						
	Civilian labor force	Civilian labor force as percent of population	Employed			Unemployed		Civilian labor force	Civilian labor force as percent of population	Employed			Unemployed	
			Number	Percent full time	Percent part time	Number	Percent of labor force			Number	Percent full time	Percent part time	Number	Percent of labor force
Women with No Children Under 18 Years														
1990	21 464	46.1	20 779	79.1	20.9	685	3.2	14 467	51.1	14 068	77.3	22.7	399	2.8
1991	21 575	46.1	20 637	78.4	21.6	937	4.3	14 529	51.2	13 976	77.6	22.4	552	3.8
1992	22 132	46.6	21 108	78.5	21.5	1 024	4.6	14 851	51.9	14 247	77.8	22.2	604	4.1
1993	22 273	46.6	21 275	79.0	21.0	998	4.5	15 211	52.4	14 630	77.6	22.4	581	3.8
1994	22 716	47.6	21 669	77.1	22.9	1 047	4.6	15 234	53.2	14 641	75.6	24.4	593	3.9
1995	22 973	47.3	22 134	77.4	22.6	839	3.7	15 594	53.2	15 072	76.3	23.7	522	3.3
1996	23 337	47.7	22 444	78.1	21.9	893	3.8	15 628	53.4	15 123	76.8	23.2	506	3.2
1997	23 890	48.3	23 130	78.9	21.1	760	3.2	15 750	54.2	15 315	77.7	22.3	435	2.8
1998	24 366	48.7	23 598	79.3	20.7	767	3.1	16 007	54.1	15 581	78.3	21.7	426	2.7
1999	24 881	48.9	24 098	79.7	20.3	783	3.1	16 484	54.4	16 061	78.2	21.8	423	2.6
2000	25 465	49.4	24 695	80.3	19.7	769	3.0	16 786	54.7	16 357	79.1	20.9	429	2.6
2001	25 959	49.6	25 226	80.4	19.6	733	2.8	16 909	54.8	16 528	78.7	21.3	381	2.3
2002	26 423	49.1	25 356	80.0	20.0	1 068	4.0	17 353	54.8	16 780	78.4	21.6	573	3.3
2003	27 361	50.1	26 238	79.7	20.3	1 123	4.1	17 901	55.7	17 273	78.6	21.4	628	3.5
2004	27 461	49.8	26 329	79.3	20.7	1 131	4.1	17 965	55.0	17 367	78.6	21.4	598	3.3
2005	27 361	50.1	26 238	79.7	20.3	1 123	4.1	17 901	55.7	17 273	78.6	21.4	628	3.5
2006	27 719	49.3	26 893	80.1	19.9	827	3.0	18 124	54.8	17 691	79.3	20.7	434	2.4
2007	28 335	49.8	27 477	80.1	19.9	858	3.0	18 766	55.4	18 326	79.6	20.4	441	2.3
2008	29 207	50.3	28 156	80.2	19.8	1 052	3.6	19 188	55.9	18 650	79.8	20.2	539	2.8
2009	29 536	50.2	27 737	77.8	22.2	1 800	6.1	19 541	55.8	18 521	77.3	22.7	1 019	5.2
2010	29 767	50.2	27 723	77.7	22.3	2 044	6.9	19 579	55.8	18 454	77.3	22.7	1 125	5.7
2011	29 440	49.4	27 553	77.7	22.3	1 886	6.4	19 316	54.6	18 285	77.4	22.6	1 031	5.3
2012	29 912	48.8	28 021	78.2	21.8	1 891	6.3	19 617	53.6	18 536	77.8	22.2	1 081	5.5
Women with Children Under 18 Years														
1990	20 671	67.8	19 621	72.6	27.4	1 051	5.1	16 500	66.3	15 803	69.8	30.2	698	4.2
1991	20 673	67.9	19 416	72.8	27.2	1 257	6.1	16 575	66.8	15 692	70.1	29.9	883	5.3
1992	21 040	68.8	19 633	73.6	26.4	1 407	6.7	16 835	67.8	15 884	71.3	28.7	952	5.7
1993	21 194	68.3	20 011	73.9	26.1	1 183	5.6	16 947	67.5	16 127	71.4	28.6	820	4.8
1994	22 025	69.8	20 722	70.5	29.5	1 303	5.9	17 628	69.0	16 755	68.0	32.0	873	5.0
1995	22 591	71.1	21 441	71.5	28.5	1 150	5.1	17 969	70.2	17 195	68.8	31.2	774	4.3
1996	22 475	71.4	21 556	72.5	27.5	919	4.1	17 754	70.0	17 136	69.6	30.4	618	3.5
1997	22 831	72.6	21 777	73.9	26.1	1 054	4.6	18 157	71.1	17 521	71.6	28.4	636	3.5
1998	22 650	72.3	21 665	73.8	26.2	985	4.3	18 129	70.6	17 447	71.5	28.5	682	3.8
1999	22 419	71.9	21 611	73.9	26.1	808	3.6	17 865	70.1	17 342	71.5	28.5	523	2.9
2000	22 722	72.7	21 960	74.0	26.0	763	3.4	18 174	70.6	17 641	71.7	28.3	533	2.9
2001	22 729	73.0	21 934	74.9	25.1	795	3.5	18 325	70.8	17 745	72.6	27.4	580	3.2
2002	22 917	71.8	21 794	74.3	25.7	1 122	4.9	18 271	69.6	17 515	71.7	28.3	756	4.1
2003	22 979	71.5	21 809	73.7	26.3	1 170	5.1	18 284	69.2	17 533	71.0	29.0	751	4.1
2004	22 651	70.5	21 576	73.8	26.2	1 075	4.7	17 953	68.2	17 215	71.3	28.7	738	4.1
2005	22 979	71.5	21 809	73.7	26.3	1 170	5.1	18 284	69.2	17 533	71.0	29.0	751	4.1
2006	22 692	70.5	21 831	75.3	24.7	861	3.8	18 067	68.4	17 494	73.0	27.0	574	3.2
2007	23 320	71.3	22 513	75.0	25.0	807	3.5	18 569	69.3	18 045	72.6	27.4	524	2.8
2008	22 419	71.2	21 529	75.4	24.6	890	4.0	17 886	69.4	17 269	73.6	26.4	616	3.4
2009	22 449	71.5	20 972	74.5	25.5	1 477	6.6	17 995	69.8	17 018	73.1	26.9	977	5.4
2010	22 141	71.5	20 526	74.0	26.0	1 615	7.3	17 622	69.7	16 510	72.6	27.4	1 112	6.3
2011	21 553	71.1	20 008	74.6	25.4	1 546	7.2	17 067	69.1	16 055	73.1	26.9	1 012	5.9
2012	21 276	70.7	19 944	75.8	24.2	1 332	6.3	16 746	68.5	15 887	74.1	25.9	859	5.1
Women with Children Under 6 Years														
1990	8 467	59.5	7 996	69.1	30.9	471	5.6	7 247	58.9	6 901	67.4	32.6	346	4.8
1991	8 585	59.9	7 938	69.2	30.8	647	7.5	7 434	59.9	6 933	67.5	32.5	501	6.7
1992	8 544	60.0	7 832	69.9	30.1	711	8.3	7 333	59.9	6 819	68.5	31.5	514	7.0
1993	8 496	59.6	7 895	70.2	29.8	600	7.1	7 289	59.6	6 840	68.8	31.2	450	6.2
1994	8 949	61.8	8 332	66.7	33.3	617	6.9	7 723	61.7	7 291	65.4	34.6	432	5.6
1995	9 067	63.9	8 517	67.4	32.6	550	6.1	7 759	63.5	7 349	66.1	33.9	409	5.3
1996	8 915	63.6	8 493	68.6	31.4	422	4.7	7 590	62.7	7 297	66.5	33.5	293	3.9
1997	8 856	64.9	8 376	70.3	29.7	480	5.4	7 582	63.6	7 252	69.1	30.9	330	4.4
1998	8 864	64.8	8 391	69.5	30.5	473	5.3	7 655	63.7	7 309	68.1	31.9	346	4.5
1999	8 511	63.7	8 109	68.6	31.4	402	4.7	7 246	61.8	6 979	67.1	32.9	267	3.7
2000	8 481	64.3	8 159	69.5	30.5	321	3.8	7 341	62.8	7 087	68.1	31.9	254	3.5
2001	8 417	64.0	8 077	69.7	30.3	340	4.0	7 319	62.5	7 062	68.5	31.5	257	3.5
2002	8 373	62.8	7 873	69.6	30.4	501	6.0	7 166	60.8	6 804	67.7	32.3	363	5.1
2003	8 315	61.4	7 818	68.9	31.1	497	6.0	7 175	59.8	6 826	67.1	32.9	349	4.9
2004	8 246	61.0	7 801	69.3	30.7	445	5.4	7 107	59.3	6 774	68.1	31.9	332	4.7
2005	8 315	61.4	7 818	68.9	31.1	497	6.0	7 175	59.8	6 826	67.1	32.9	349	4.9
2006	8 496	61.9	8 121	71.8	28.2	375	4.4	7 366	60.3	7 092	70.6	29.4	274	3.7
2007	8 829	62.7	8 479	71.7	28.3	350	4.0	7 664	61.5	7 407	70.8	29.2	257	3.4
2008	8 470	63.0	8 089	72.1	27.9	381	4.5	7 285	61.6	6 999	70.9	29.1	285	3.9
2009	8 360	62.6	7 763	72.1	27.9	597	7.1	7 231	61.6	6 805	71.4	28.6	426	5.9
2010	8 460	63.8	7 809	71.7	28.3	651	7.7	7 227	62.5	6 741	71.5	28.5	486	6.7
2011	8 226	63.7	7 590	72.5	27.5	636	7.7	7 061	62.3	6 608	71.9	28.1	453	6.4
2012	8 054	63.7	7 501	73.5	26.5	554	6.9	6 878	62.3	6 491	72.7	27.3	387	5.6

[1]Ever-married women are women who are, or have ever been, married.

Table 1-48. Employment Status of Women Who Maintain Families, by Marital Status and Presence and Age of Children, March 1995–March 2012

(Thousands of women, percent.)

Marital status, age of children, and year	Civilian noninstitutional population	Civilian labor force					Not in the labor force
		Number	Percent of the population	Employed	Unemployed		
					Number	Percent of the labor force	
Total, Women Who Maintain Families							
1995	12 762	8 192	64.2	7 527	665	8.1	4 570
1996	12 993	8 460	65.1	7 832	628	7.4	4 532
1997	13 258	8 998	67.9	8 192	806	9.0	4 260
1998	13 102	8 976	68.5	8 309	667	7.4	4 127
1999	13 191	9 213	69.8	8 596	617	6.7	3 978
2000	13 145	9 226	70.2	8 592	634	6.9	3 918
2001	12 930	9 034	69.9	8 453	581	6.4	3 897
2002	13 489	9 523	70.6	8 755	768	8.1	3 966
2003	14 000	9 759	69.7	8 898	861	8.8	4 241
2004	14 165	9 869	69.7	9 054	815	8.3	4 297
2005	14 391	9 941	69.1	9 140	801	8.1	4 450
2006	14 485	9 966	68.8	9 227	739	7.4	4 520
2007	14 833	10 172	68.6	9 510	661	6.5	4 662
2008	14 820	10 166	68.6	9 447	719	7.1	4 654
2009	14 813	10 140	68.5	9 034	1 106	10.9	4 673
2010	15 214	10 206	67.1	9 027	1 179	11.6	5 008
2011	15 461	10 462	67.7	9 141	1 321	12.6	5 000
2012	16 122	11 009	68.3	9 807	1 202	10.9	5 113
Women with No Children Under 18 Years							
1995	4 610	2 471	53.6	2 394	77	3.1	2 139
1996	4 847	2 552	52.7	2 462	90	3.5	2 295
1997	4 909	2 663	54.2	2 571	92	3.5	2 246
1998	4 952	2 649	53.5	2 578	71	2.7	2 303
1999	4 942	2 667	54.0	2 556	111	4.2	2 275
2000	5 097	2 707	53.1	2 546	161	5.9	2 390
2001	5 185	2 772	53.5	2 668	104	3.8	2 413
2002	5 119	2 764	54.0	2 628	136	4.9	2 355
2003	5 457	2 934	53.8	2 728	206	7.0	2 522
2004	5 551	3 052	55.0	2 855	197	6.5	2 499
2005	5 692	3 095	54.4	2 961	134	4.3	2 597
2006	5 693	3 088	54.2	2 945	143	4.6	2 604
2007	5 823	3 124	53.7	2 990	134	4.3	2 699
2008	6 022	3 352	55.7	3 167	185	5.5	2 670
2009	6 068	3 332	54.9	3 075	258	7.7	2 735
2010	6 414	3 417	53.3	3 131	286	8.4	2 997
2011	6 403	3 455	54.0	3 131	324	9.4	2 948
2012	6 773	3 779	55.8	3 464	316	8.4	2 994
Women with Children Under 18 Years							
1995	8 152	5 720	70.2	5 132	588	10.3	2 431
1996	8 146	5 908	72.5	5 370	538	9.1	2 237
1997	8 348	6 335	75.9	5 621	714	11.3	2 014
1998	8 151	6 327	77.6	5 731	596	9.4	1 823
1999	8 248	6 546	79.4	6 040	506	7.7	1 702
2000	8 048	6 520	81.0	6 046	474	7.3	1 528
2001	7 746	6 261	80.8	5 785	476	7.6	1 484
2002	8 370	6 759	80.8	6 127	632	9.4	1 611
2003	8 543	6 825	79.9	6 170	655	9.6	1 718
2004	8 614	6 817	79.1	6 199	618	9.1	1 798
2005	8 699	6 846	78.7	6 179	667	9.7	1 853
2006	8 793	6 878	78.2	6 282	596	8.7	1 915
2007	9 010	7 047	78.2	6 520	527	7.5	1 963
2008	8 798	6 814	77.4	6 280	535	7.8	1 984
2009	8 745	6 807	77.8	5 959	848	12.5	1 938
2010	8 800	6 789	77.1	5 896	893	13.2	2 011
2011	9 059	7 007	77.4	6 009	998	14.2	2 052
2012	9 349	7 230	77.3	6 343	887	12.3	2 119
Single Women with No Children Under 18 Years							
1995	779	534	68.5	508	26	4.9	245
1996	895	588	65.7	572	16	2.7	308
1997	860	585	68.0	563	22	3.8	275
1998	893	637	71.3	613	24	3.8	256
1999	969	674	69.6	638	36	5.3	295
2000	1 004	720	71.7	642	78	10.8	284
2001	1 096	787	71.8	756	31	3.9	309
2002	1 154	796	69.0	747	49	6.2	358
2003	1 254	814	64.9	713	101	12.4	440
2004	1 381	977	70.7	887	90	9.2	404
2005	1 388	926	66.7	855	71	7.7	463
2006	1 370	933	68.1	861	72	7.7	437
2007	1 413	986	69.8	930	57	5.7	427
2008	1 515	1 057	69.8	989	68	6.5	458
2009	1 531	1 069	69.8	967	102	9.6	462
2010	1 718	1 166	67.9	1 041	125	10.7	552
2011	1 729	1 178	68.2	1 047	132	11.2	551
2012	1 836	1 241	67.6	1 099	143	11.5	595

Note: See notes and definitions for information on historical comparability.

Table 1-48. Employment Status of Women Who Maintain Families, by Marital Status and Presence and Age of Children, March 1995–March 2012—*Continued*

(Thousands of women, percent.)

Marital status, age of children, and year	Civilian noninstitutional population	Civilian labor force					Not in the labor force
		Number	Percent of the population	Employed	Unemployed		
					Number	Percent of the labor force	
Single Women with Children Under 18 Years							
1995	2 613	1 510	57.8	1 261	249	16.5	1 102
1996	2 639	1 633	61.9	1 346	287	17.6	1 006
1997	3 012	2 087	69.3	1 749	338	16.2	925
1998	3 083	2 280	74.0	1 960	320	14.0	803
1999	3 163	2 415	76.4	2 146	269	11.1	748
2000	3 167	2 413	76.2	2 151	262	10.9	754
2001	3 097	2 351	75.9	2 055	296	12.6	745
2002	3 315	2 566	77.4	2 241	325	12.7	749
2003	3 421	2 584	75.5	2 272	312	12.1	837
2004	3 414	2 568	75.2	2 233	335	13.0	846
2005	3 591	2 708	75.4	2 325	383	14.1	882
2006	3 671	2 710	73.8	2 370	340	12.5	961
2007	3 748	2 782	74.2	2 491	291	10.4	966
2008	3 721	2 743	73.7	2 448	295	10.8	978
2009	3 872	2 877	74.3	2 448	429	14.9	995
2010	3 948	2 868	72.6	2 379	488	17.0	1 081
2011	4 193	3 072	73.3	2 522	550	17.9	1 120
2012	4 442	3 263	73.5	2 746	517	15.8	1 179
Widowed, Divorced, or Separated Women with No Children Under 18 Years							
1995	3 831	1 938	50.6	1 887	51	2.6	1 894
1996	3 952	1 964	49.7	1 890	74	3.8	1 988
1997	4 049	2 077	51.3	2 008	69	3.3	1 971
1998	4 058	2 011	49.6	1 965	46	2.3	2 047
1999	3 974	1 993	50.2	1 918	75	3.8	1 980
2000	4 093	1 987	48.5	1 904	83	4.2	2 106
2001	4 088	1 985	48.6	1 912	73	3.7	2 104
2002	3 964	1 968	49.6	1 882	86	4.4	1 997
2003	4 203	2 121	50.5	2 016	105	5.0	2 082
2004	4 170	2 075	49.8	1 968	107	5.2	2 095
2005	4 304	2 170	50.4	2 106	64	2.9	2 135
2006	4 323	2 156	49.9	2 084	72	3.3	2 168
2007	4 410	2 138	48.5	2 061	77	3.6	2 272
2008	4 507	2 295	50.9	2 178	117	5.1	2 213
2009	4 536	2 263	49.9	2 108	155	6.9	2 273
2010	4 696	2 251	47.9	2 090	161	7.1	2 445
2011	4 674	2 276	48.7	2 084	192	8.4	2 397
2012	4 937	2 538	51.4	2 365	173	6.8	2 399
Widowed, Divorced, or Separated Women with Children Under 18 Years							
1995	5 539	4 210	76.0	3 871	339	8.1	1 329
1996	5 507	4 275	77.6	4 024	251	5.9	1 231
1997	5 337	4 248	79.6	3 872	376	8.9	1 089
1998	5 068	4 047	79.9	3 771	276	6.8	1 020
1999	5 086	4 131	81.2	3 894	237	5.7	955
2000	4 881	4 107	84.1	3 895	212	5.2	774
2001	4 649	3 910	84.1	3 730	180	4.6	739
2002	5 056	4 193	82.9	3 886	307	7.3	862
2003	5 122	4 241	82.8	3 898	343	8.1	881
2004	5 201	4 249	81.7	3 966	283	6.7	952
2005	5 108	4 137	81.0	3 854	283	6.8	971
2006	5 121	4 167	81.4	3 912	255	6.1	955
2007	5 262	4 266	81.1	4 029	237	5.5	997
2008	5 077	4 071	80.2	3 832	239	5.9	1 006
2009	4 873	3 930	80.7	3 511	420	10.7	943
2010	4 852	3 922	80.8	3 517	405	10.3	931
2011	4 866	3 935	80.9	3 487	448	11.4	931
2012	4 907	3 966	80.8	3 597	370	9.3	940

Note: See notes and definitions for information on historical comparability.

Table 1-49. Number and Age of Children in Families, by Type of Family and Labor Force Status of Mother, March 1990–March 2012

(Thousands of children.)

Age of children and year	Total children	Mother in labor force	Mother not in labor force	Married-couple families			Families maintained by women			Families maintained by men
				Total	Mother in labor force	Mother not in labor force	Total	Mother in labor force	Mother not in labor force	
Children Under 18 Years										
1990	59 596	36 712	21 110	45 898	29 077	16 820	11 925	7 635	4 290	1 774
1991	60 330	36 968	21 526	45 912	29 056	16 856	12 582	7 912	4 670	1 836
1992	61 262	38 081	21 176	45 966	29 882	16 084	13 291	8 199	5 093	2 005
1993	62 020	38 542	21 444	46 499	30 054	16 445	13 487	8 488	4 999	2 034
1994	63 407	40 186	21 188	47 247	31 279	15 968	14 127	8 907	5 220	2 033
1995	63 989	41 365	20 421	47 675	32 190	15 486	14 111	9 176	4 935	2 202
1996	64 506	41 573	20 449	47 484	31 764	15 720	14 538	9 809	4 729	2 484
1997	64 710	42 747	19 223	47 529	32 263	15 265	14 441	10 483	3 958	2 740
1998	65 043	43 156	19 069	47 909	32 533	15 376	14 317	10 623	3 694	2 818
1999	65 191	43 419	19 074	47 945	32 193	15 752	14 547	11 226	3 322	2 699
2000	65 601	44 188	18 674	48 902	33 149	15 753	13 960	11 039	2 921	2 739
2001	65 777	44 051	18 864	49 352	33 436	15 916	13 563	10 615	2 948	2 862
2002	65 978	43 821	19 243	48 836	32 673	16 163	14 228	11 149	3 079	2 914
2003	66 521	43 769	19 782	49 004	32 411	16 593	14 547	11 359	3 189	2 970
2004	66 386	43 144	20 229	48 656	31 892	16 764	14 717	11 252	3 465	3 014
2005	66 526	43 239	20 179	48 688	31 886	16 802	14 729	11 352	3 377	3 108
2006	66 883	43 278	20 440	48 853	31 946	16 908	14 865	11 332	3 532	3 165
2007	67 228	44 116	20 073	48 927	32 496	16 431	15 263	11 620	3 643	3 038
2008	67 153	43 798	19 966	48 303	32 110	16 193	15 461	11 688	3 773	3 388
2009	66 913	43 509	20 074	48 384	32 065	16 315	15 204	11 444	3 759	3 326
2010	66 811	43 335	19 913	47 730	31 686	16 044	15 518	11 649	3 869	3 563
2011	66 804	42 882	20 260	47 051	30 902	16 149	16 091	11 980	4 111	3 662
2012	66 472	42 643	19 885	45 989	30 228	15 761	16 539	12 414	4 125	3 944
Children 6 to 17 Years Years										
1990	39 095	25 805	12 079	29 726	20 067	9 659	8 157	5 737	2 420	1 211
1991	39 470	25 806	12 392	29 598	19 907	9 691	8 599	5 899	2 701	1 272
1992	40 064	26 666	12 067	29 673	20 586	9 087	9 060	6 079	2 980	1 331
1993	40 622	27 046	12 291	30 233	20 796	9 437	9 104	6 249	2 854	1 285
1994	41 795	28 179	12 287	30 895	21 663	9 233	9 570	6 516	3 054	1 329
1995	42 423	28 931	12 000	31 298	22 239	9 059	9 633	6 692	2 941	1 492
1996	42 964	29 381	11 897	31 231	22 092	9 139	10 047	7 289	2 758	1 685
1997	43 488	30 308	11 400	31 509	22 602	8 906	10 199	7 705	2 493	1 781
1998	43 771	30 579	11 367	31 707	22 706	9 001	10 238	7 873	2 365	1 826
1999	44 110	30 885	11 370	31 975	22 706	9 269	10 281	8 179	2 101	1 855
2000	44 562	31 531	11 198	32 732	23 393	9 339	9 997	8 138	1 859	1 833
2001	44 458	31 411	11 153	32 957	23 599	9 358	9 608	7 813	1 795	1 894
2002	44 865	31 437	11 510	32 799	23 296	9 504	10 148	8 142	2 006	1 918
2003	45 273	31 559	11 635	32 782	23 160	9 622	10 412	8 399	2 013	2 080
2004	45 066	31 040	11 968	32 506	22 736	9 769	10 502	8 304	2 199	2 058
2005	45 027	30 930	11 995	32 412	22 565	9 847	10 514	8 366	2 148	2 102
2006	45 039	30 591	12 250	32 311	22 315	9 996	10 530	8 276	2 254	2 198
2007	45 155	31 252	11 855	32 417	22 788	9 629	10 690	8 464	2 226	2 048
2008	44 909	30 853	11 874	31 990	22 413	9 577	10 737	8 440	2 297	2 182
2009	44 595	30 600	11 811	31 966	22 425	9 537	10 449	8 175	2 274	2 180
2010	44 456	30 209	11 922	31 468	21 957	9 510	10 663	8 251	2 412	2 325
2011	44 471	29 904	12 244	31 072	21 365	9 707	11 076	8 539	2 537	2 323
2012	45 049	30 143	12 315	30 923	21 163	9 760	11 535	8 980	2 556	2 591
Children Under 6 Years										
1990	20 502	10 907	9 031	16 171	9 010	7 161	3 767	1 897	1 870	563
1991	20 860	11 162	9 134	16 313	9 148	7 165	3 983	2 013	1 969	563
1992	21 198	11 415	9 109	16 293	9 296	6 997	4 232	2 119	2 112	674
1993	21 398	11 496	9 153	16 266	9 258	7 008	4 383	2 239	2 145	749
1994	21 612	12 007	8 901	16 352	9 617	6 735	4 556	2 391	2 166	704
1995	21 566	12 435	8 421	16 377	9 951	6 427	4 478	2 484	1 995	710
1996	21 542	12 192	8 552	16 253	9 672	6 581	4 491	2 520	1 971	799
1997	21 222	12 439	7 823	16 020	9 661	6 359	4 243	2 778	1 464	959
1998	21 272	12 577	7 703	16 201	9 827	6 375	4 079	2 751	1 328	992
1999	21 081	12 533	7 704	15 971	9 487	6 484	4 267	3 046	1 220	844
2000	21 039	12 657	7 476	16 170	9 757	6 413	3 963	2 901	1 062	906
2001	21 318	12 640	7 711	16 395	9 837	6 558	3 956	2 802	1 153	968
2002	21 113	12 384	7 733	16 037	9 377	6 660	4 080	3 007	1 073	996
2003	21 248	12 210	8 147	16 222	9 251	6 971	4 136	2 960	1 176	890
2004	21 321	12 104	8 261	16 151	9 156	6 995	4 214	2 948	1 266	956
2005	21 498	12 308	8 184	16 276	9 321	6 955	4 216	2 987	1 229	1 006
2006	21 844	12 687	8 190	16 542	9 631	6 911	4 335	3 057	1 278	968
2007	22 073	12 864	8 218	16 509	9 708	6 802	4 572	3 156	1 416	991
2008	22 244	12 946	8 092	16 313	9 697	6 616	4 724	3 248	1 476	1 207
2009	22 318	12 909	8 263	16 418	9 640	6 778	4 755	3 270	1 485	1 146
2010	22 355	13 127	7 991	16 262	9 729	6 533	4 855	3 398	1 457	1 237
2011	22 333	12 978	8 015	15 979	9 537	6 442	5 015	3 441	1 573	1 340
2012	21 423	12 500	7 570	15 066	9 065	6 001	5 004	3 435	1 569	1 353

Note: See notes and definitions for information on historical comparability.

Table 1-50. Number of Families and Median Family Income, by Type of Family and Earner Status of Members, 1990–2011

(Thousands of families, dollars.)

Number and type of families and median family income	1990	1991	1992	1993	1994	1995	1996	1997	1998	1999
NUMBER OF FAMILIES										
Married-Couple Families,										
Total	52 241	52 549	53 254	53 248	53 929	53 621	53 654	54 362	54 829	55 352
No earners	6 765	7 101	7 250	7 281	7 225	7 276	7 145	7 286	7 257	7 160
One earner	11 630	11 553	12 053	11 806	11 715	11 708	11 493	11 700	12 246	12 290
Husband	9 110	8 907	9 182	8 715	8 673	8 792	8 611	8 770	9 173	9 062
Wife	1 816	1 987	2 145	2 405	2 364	2 251	2 207	2 298	2 411	2 585
Other family member	703	659	726	686	678	666	674	632	662	643
Two earners	25 896	26 037	26 344	26 742	27 263	27 180	27 260	27 712	27 593	28 010
Husband and wife	23 697	23 880	24 255	24 543	25 123	25 274	25 274	25 731	25 696	26 134
Husband and other family member	1 711	1 633	1 447	1 582	1 565	1 393	1 483	1 406	1 306	1 325
Husband not an earner	487	524	642	617	574	513	502	575	590	552
Three earners or more	7 950	7 858	7 606	7 419	7 727	7 456	7 756	7 664	7 733	7 892
Husband and wife	7 029	7 052	6 882	6 723	6 987	6 770	7 126	7 023	7 102	7 220
Husband, not wife	756	595	550	535	543	531	479	478	456	528
Husband not an earner	165	211	175	162	196	155	150	163	176	144
Families Maintained by Women, Total	11 771	12 214	12 504	12 982	12 771	13 007	13 277	13 115	13 206	13 164
No earners	2 623	2 925	2 968	3 100	2 848	2 664	2 574	2 332	2 143	1 883
One earner	5 672	5 926	6 184	6 407	6 506	6 815	7 027	7 091	7 351	7 441
Householder	4 585	4 812	5 042	5 278	5 415	5 590	5 817	5 841	6 167	6 127
Other family member	1 087	1 114	1 142	1 129	1 091	1 225	1 211	1 251	1 183	1 314
Two earners or more	3 476	3 363	3 352	3 476	3 417	3 527	3 675	3 692	3 712	3 840
Householder and other family member(s)	3 146	3 058	2 998	3 139	3 126	3 225	3 431	3 398	3 399	3 508
Householder not an earner	330	305	354	337	291	302	245	294	313	332
Families Maintained by Men, Total	2 948	3 079	3 094	2 992	3 287	3 557	3 924	3 982	4 041	4 086
No earners	296	310	345	329	383	357	359	344	381	376
One earner	1 396	1 541	1 544	1 593	1 705	1 800	1 972	2 104	2 027	2 044
Householder	1 133	1 289	1 305	1 352	1 428	1 548	1 667	1 791	1 725	1 721
Other family member	263	253	239	241	277	253	305	313	302	323
Two earners or more	1 257	1 228	1 204	1 070	1 198	1 400	1 593	1 534	1 634	1 666
Householder and other family member(s)	1 180	1 157	1 117	1 002	1 128	1 302	1 469	1 427	1 532	1 522
Householder not an earner	76	71	88	67	71	98	124	107	102	143
MEDIAN FAMILY INCOME										
Married-Couple Families,										
Total	39 802	40 746	42 000	43 000	44 893	47 000	49 614	51 475	54 043	56 792
No earners	19 221	20 415	20 023	19 983	20 604	21 888	22 622	23 782	24 525	25 262
One earner	31 020	31 671	32 500	32 084	33 393	35 100	36 468	39 140	40 519	41 261
Husband	32 422	33 208	34 714	34 401	35 000	36 052	38 150	40 300	42 000	44 200
Wife	25 228	26 500	27 343	27 502	28 661	32 098	30 301	34 050	35 625	35 546
Other family member	33 262	33 042	33 622	30 254	32 578	37 784	39 644	40 317	42 414	41 120
Two earners	44 000	45 359	47 737	49 650	51 190	53 500	56 000	58 020	61 300	64 007
Husband and wife	44 031	45 516	48 050	49 980	51 500	53 626	56 392	58 564	61 900	64 950
Husband and other family member	42 602	45 000	45 694	48 862	48 517	52 530	49 610	53 854	57 680	53 541
Husband not an earner	39 494	40 495	40 124	38 800	42 800	47 121	46 990	47 979	50 955	52 466
Three earners or more	59 336	61 120	61 640	63 535	66 172	68 996	70 400	75 593	78 973	81 940
Husband and wife	55 846	61 448	62 674	64 099	66 674	69 371	71 148	76 105	79 907	83 000
Husband, not wife	59 675	60 592	57 015	60 712	63 633	60 360	61 824	68 890	71 001	69 561
Husband not an earner	49 107	44 874	47 551	54 805	54 655	61 196	55 495	62 684	63 205	69 275
Families Maintained by Women, Total	16 351	16 054	16 431	16 800	17 600	19 306	19 416	20 470	21 875	23 100
No earners	5 880	6 060	5 964	6 492	6 805	7 440	7 092	7 476	7 737	8 010
One earner	15 987	16 284	16 468	16 745	17 226	18 824	18 500	19 000	20 000	20 092
Householder	15 001	15 542	15 905	15 700	16 603	17 890	18 000	18 000	18 800	19 000
Other family member	20 173	20 220	19 709	20 800	21 300	23 166	21 000	22 870	25 981	26 800
Two earners or more	30 500	31 508	32 705	33 300	33 820	35 000	36 400	39 275	40 000	41 144
Householder and other family member(s)	30 367	31 550	33 280	33 165	33 357	34 674	36 400	39 000	39 713	40 855
Householder not an earner	32 800	29 477	30 460	35 394	37 531	39 444	38 249	47 471	43 725	48 004
Families Maintained by Men, Total	28 493	28 000	27 400	25 856	27 486	30 000	31 500	32 984	35 000	37 000
No earners	11 386	11 196	9 416	10 900	11 293	12 240	12 030	14 252	15 468	13 752
One earner	25 000	23 715	23 020	22 300	24 011	25 337	26 100	26 897	29 125	31 038
Householder	24 150	23 309	23 000	22 079	24 000	25 069	25 874	27 000	29 125	30 483
Other family member	27 620	25 720	24 359	26 916	26 253	27 291	28 584	25 486	28 241	34 756
Two earners or more	40 000	37 700	39 000	38 000	41 439	43 100	44 275	49 900	51 288	51 040
Householder and other family member(s)	40 256	37 550	39 300	38 363	41 534	43 000	43 065	50 000	50 954	50 960
Householder not an earner	34 064	40 000	36 445	33 700	37 386	55 133	47 001	44 786	68 257	57 407

Note: See notes and definitions for information on historical comparability.

Table 1-50. Number of Families and Median Family Income, by Type of Family and Earner Status of Members, 1990–2011—*Continued*

(Thousands of families, dollars.)

Number and type of families and median family income	2000	2001	2002	2003	2004	2005	2006	2007	2008	2009	2010	2011
NUMBER OF FAMILIES												
Married-Couple Families, Total	55 650	56 798	57 362	57 767	58 180	58 225	59 050	58 490	59 181	58 521	58 135	59 071
No earners	7 297	7 662	7 803	8 043	7 998	8 017	8 091	7 914	8 083	8 467	8 626	9 152
One earner	12 450	12 852	13 503	14 061	14 385	14 301	14 562	14 272	14 625	15 046	15 421	15 981
Husband	9 319	9 573	10 121	10 478	10 853	10 611	10 706	10 396	10 567	10 570	10 895	11 308
Wife	2 545	2 689	2 821	3 027	2 993	3 097	3 264	3 267	3 437	3 854	3 935	4 016
Other family member	586	590	560	557	539	593	591	608	620	621	591	658
Two earners	28 329	28 779	28 891	28 693	28 806	28 802	29 216	29 256	29 466	28 371	27 821	27 661
Husband and wife	26 447	26 829	26 966	26 860	26 758	26 833	27 241	27 264	27 531	26 298	25 801	25 581
Husband and other family member	1 277	1 424	1 391	1 322	1 462	1 376	1 358	1 393	1 308	1 363	1 317	1 370
Husband not an earner	605	526	534	511	586	594	616	599	627	710	703	710
Three earners or more	7 575	7 504	7 165	6 970	6 991	7 104	7 181	7 048	7 008	6 638	6 267	6 277
Husband and wife	6 917	6 859	6 565	6 349	6 459	6 535	6 620	6 452	6 393	6 024	5 609	5 621
Husband, not wife	537	530	455	467	381	445	397	452	432	425	466	462
Husband not an earner	120	115	145	154	152	124	165	144	182	189	192	193
Families Maintained by Women, Total	12 950	13 517	14 033	14 196	14 404	14 505	14 852	14 846	14 842	15 236	15 491	16 154
No earners	1 786	2 076	2 228	2 451	2 610	2 616	2 627	2 502	2 678	3 076	3 297	3 373
One earner	7 462	7 693	8 153	8 012	8 074	8 052	8 303	8 418	8 381	8 475	8 638	8 790
Householder	6 132	6 436	6 832	6 725	6 788	6 724	6 904	7 020	6 978	6 941	7 158	7 303
Other family member	1 331	1 257	1 321	1 286	1 285	1 329	1 398	1 398	1 404	1 533	1 480	1 487
Two earners or more	3 702	3 748	3 652	3 733	3 720	3 836	3 923	3 925	3 783	3 685	3 555	3 991
Householder and other family member(s)	3 376	3 442	3 290	3 364	3 399	3 468	3 547	3 572	3 467	3 281	3 149	3 552
Householder not an earner	325	306	362	369	321	368	376	353	316	405	406	439
Families Maintained by Men, Total	4 316	4 499	4 747	4 778	4 953	5 193	5 119	5 181	5 301	5 630	5 649	5 975
No earners	380	461	466	530	492	537	555	532	611	539	775	838
One earner	2 223	2 319	2 434	2 466	2 573	2 661	2 584	2 703	2 636	2 801	2 911	3 106
Householder	1 879	1 911	2 026	2 053	2 152	2 196	2 155	2 297	2 199	2 261	2 389	2 535
Other family member	344	408	408	413	421	464	429	406	437	539	521	571
Two earners or more	1 713	1 719	1 847	1 782	1 888	1 995	1 979	1 947	2 054	2 030	1 963	2 031
Householder and other family member(s)	1 585	1 629	1 709	1 625	1 736	1 848	1 828	1 812	1 889	1 822	1 751	1 811
Householder not an earner	128	90	138	157	152	147	152	134	165	208	212	220
MEDIAN FAMILY INCOME												
Married-Couple Families, Total	59 200	60 100	61 000	62 388	63 627	65 586	69 300	72 802	72 805	71 464	72 224	73 678
No earners	25 356	25 900	25 954	26 312	26 798	28 376	30 000	30 134	31 164	32 093	32 350	33 756
One earner	44 424	44 400	45 000	46 546	47 749	50 000	50 400	52 686	53 865	53 087	55 000	56 609
Husband	47 010	47 500	48 004	48 948	50 000	52 000	53 360	55 350	56 000	55 333	56 533	59 842
Wife	36 458	36 140	39 072	41 180	41 000	43 505	45 000	47 000	47 015	47 550	50 150	52 007
Other family member	45 492	44 270	40 927	45 936	46 324	50 263	49 352	48 922	55 114	55 166	57 264	56 914
Two earners	67 500	69 543	71 282	73 309	75 100	76 960	81 500	85 012	85 500	86 361	88 500	90 001
Husband and wife	68 132	70 000	72 150	74 500	76 000	77 539	82 762	86 000	86 842	87 939	90 000	90 976
Husband and other family member	56 503	65 240	62 848	60 100	66 120	67 350	68 828	71 573	68 755	73 720	74 973	77 888
Husband not an earner	53 430	58 725	54 840	58 000	63 050	65 622	63 657	68 032	66 445	70 017	72 317	72 644
Three earners or more	83 990	86 090	88 632	93 000	94 212	98 000	103 803	106 747	105 618	107 000	107 542	111 000
Husband and wife	84 634	87 000	89 962	94 353	95 524	99 800	104 045	107 630	106 493	108 703	108 714	112 943
Husband, not wife	79 050	76 230	82 180	77 316	87 000	79 417	91 965	101 771	99 731	85 574	93 000	96 756
Husband not an earner	68 050	80 661	68 400	91 771	73 137	84 638	97 510	92 428	93 961	95 251	100 105	97 491
Families Maintained by Women, Total	25 000	25 064	26 000	26 000	26 400	27 000	28 218	30 000	29 698	29 025	28 774	29 848
No earners	8 988	8 160	8 808	8 344	8 400	8 228	8 657	8 873	9 404	10 037	9 600	9 600
One earner	22 306	23 008	24 597	24 752	25 040	25 308	26 393	27 795	28 060	29 000	29 009	28 912
Householder	21 400	22 001	23 760	23 832	24 801	24 505	25 381	26 644	27 000	27 928	27 924	27 488
Other family member	27 524	28 476	29 524	28 857	29 700	31 700	31 462	31 950	34 814	34 421	33 957	35 161
Two earners or more	43 035	45 244	46 580	47 576	48 549	50 000	52 400	55 749	54 369	54 500	55 047	56 000
Householder and other family member(s)	43 000	44 842	46 000	46 701	47 974	48 989	51 479	55 010	54 306	54 448	54 000	55 500
Householder not an earner	45 600	51 000	51 248	57 267	56 799	64 805	61 699	64 094	54 978	56 203	61 781	60 015
Families Maintained by Men, Total	37 040	36 000	37 440	37 914	40 000	40 293	41 130	44 001	43 050	41 000	42 500	43 000
No earners	14 946	12 840	15 200	15 408	14 167	13 950	15 462	12 921	15 557	15 653	16 176	17 945
One earner	30 160	30 800	30 139	32 097	35 000	35 001	35 100	37 716	36 806	35 116	37 707	38 000
Householder	30 816	30 500	30 014	31 355	35 000	35 075	35 011	37 720	37 569	35 117	37 990	38 069
Other family member	29 118	31 052	32 000	35 525	35 438	35 000	37 840	37 522	34 404	35 086	37 041	36 983
Two earners or more	55 010	55 024	55 000	57 840	57 600	60 024	61 000	63 600	64 077	64 747	66 000	67 301
Householder and other family member(s)	55 400	54 850	55 220	57 400	57 058	60 000	61 000	64 000	63 416	64 743	65 200	66 708
Householder not an earner	51 945	61 824	49 852	64 658	65 400	70 879	62 000	60 498	69 794	65 618	71 962	73 242

Note: See notes and definitions for information on historical comparability.

Table 1-51. Employment Status of the Foreign-Born and Native-Born Populations, by Selected Characteristics, 2010–2011

(Thousands of people, percent.)

Year and characteristic	Civilian noninstitutional population	Civilian labor force				
		Total	Participation rate	Employed	Unemployed	
					Number	Rate
2010						
TOTAL						
Both sexes, 16 years and over	237 830	153 889	64.7	139 064	14 825	9.6
Men	115 174	81 985	71.2	73 359	8 626	10.5
Women	122 656	71 904	58.6	65 705	6 199	8.6
FOREIGN BORN						
Both sexes, 16 years and over	35 869	24 356	67.9	21 969	2 387	9.8
Men	17 936	14 375	80.1	12 946	1 429	9.9
Women	17 934	9 981	55.7	9 023	958	9.6
Age						
16 to 24 years	3 533	1 975	55.9	1 661	314	15.9
25 to 34 years	7 714	5 936	77.0	5 387	550	9.3
35 to 44 years	8 470	6 884	81.3	6 265	619	9.0
45 to 54 years	6 949	5 719	82.3	5 172	547	9.6
55 to 64 years	4 528	3 011	66.5	2 727	284	9.4
65 years and over	4 674	831	17.8	757	74	8.9
Race and Hispanic Origin						
White, non-Hispanic	7 363	4 470	60.7	4 138	332	7.4
Black, non-Hispanic	2 898	2 162	74.6	1 893	269	12.4
Asian, non-Hispanic	8 073	5 315	65.8	4 928	386	7.3
Hispanic[1]	17 162	12 152	70.8	10 776	1 376	11.3
Educational Attainment						
Total, 25 years and over	32 336	22 381	69.2	20 308	2 073	9.3
Less than a high school diploma	9 620	5 930	61.6	5 219	712	12.0
High school graduate, no college[2]	8 284	5 663	68.4	5 087	576	10.2
Some college or associate's degree	5 200	3 818	73.4	3 463	355	9.3
Bachelor's degree or higher[3]	9 232	6 970	75.5	6 539	431	6.2
NATIVE BORN						
Both sexes, 16 years and over	201 960	129 533	64.1	117 095	12 438	9.6
Men	97 238	67 610	69.5	60 414	7 196	10.6
Women	104 722	61 923	59.1	56 682	5 242	8.5
Age						
16 to 24 years	34 415	18 960	55.1	15 417	3 543	18.7
25 to 34 years	33 189	27 678	83.4	24 842	2 836	10.2
35 to 44 years	31 620	26 482	83.8	24 398	2 084	7.9
45 to 54 years	37 348	30 242	81.0	28 019	2 223	7.4
55 to 64 years	31 357	20 286	64.7	18 909	1 377	6.8
65 years and over	34 032	5 886	17.3	5 511	375	6.4
Race and Hispanic Origin						
White, non-Hispanic	153 448	99 478	64.8	91 483	7 994	8.0
Black, non-Hispanic	24 691	14 996	60.7	12 529	2 467	16.5
Asian, non-Hispanic	2 900	1 782	61.5	1 641	141	7.9
Hispanic[1]	16 551	10 596	64.0	9 130	1 467	13.8
Educational Attainment						
Total, 25 years and over	167 546	110 573	66.0	101 679	8 895	8.0
Less than a high school diploma	16 046	5 949	37.1	4 896	1 053	17.7
High school graduates, no college[2]	53 753	32 573	60.6	29 206	3 367	10.3
Some college or associate's degree	47 022	33 022	70.2	30 284	2 738	8.3
Bachelor's degree or higher[3]	50 724	39 029	76.9	37 293	1 736	4.4

Note: Due to the introduction of revised population controls in January 2011, estimated levels for 2011 are not strictly comparable with those for 2010.

[1]May be of any race.
[2]Includes persons with a high school diploma or equivalent.
[3]Includes persons with bachelor's, master's, professional, and doctoral degrees.

Table 1-51. Employment Status of the Foreign-Born and Native-Born Populations, by Selected Characteristics, 2010–2011—*Continued*

(Thousands of people, percent.)

Year and characteristic	Civilian noninstitutional population	Civilian labor force				
		Total	Participation rate	Employed	Unemployed	
					Number	Rate
2011						
TOTAL						
Both sexes, 16 years and over	239 618	153 617	64.1	139 869	13 747	8.9
Men	116 317	81 975	70.5	74 290	7 684	9.4
Women	123 300	71 642	58.1	65 579	6 063	8.5
FOREIGN BORN						
Both sexes, 16 years and over	36 420	24 391	67.0	22 183	2 208	9.1
Men	18 090	14 379	79.5	13 120	1 260	8.8
Women	18 331	10 012	54.6	9 063	949	9.5
Age						
16 to 24 years	3 631	1 971	54.3	1 695	276	14.0
25 to 34 years	7 562	5 758	76.1	5 255	503	8.7
35 to 44 years	8 492	6 843	80.6	6 301	542	7.9
45 to 54 years	7 089	5 799	81.8	5 274	525	9.1
55 to 64 years	4 737	3 161	66.7	2 870	290	9.2
65 years and over	4 909	860	17.5	788	72	8.3
Race and Hispanic Origin						
White, non-Hispanic	7 617	4 583	60.2	4 237	346	7.6
Black, non-Hispanic	3 002	2 137	71.2	1 870	267	12.5
Asian, non-Hispanic	8 306	5 449	65.6	5 086	363	6.7
Hispanic[1]	17 132	11 963	69.8	10 751	1 212	10.1
Educational Attainment						
Total, 25 years and over	32 790	22 420	68.4	20 488	1 932	8.6
Less than a high school diploma	9 532	5 721	60.0	5 086	634	11.1
High school graduates, no college[2]	8 488	5 674	66.8	5 145	529	9.3
Some college or associate degree	5 389	3 927	72.9	3 584	343	8.7
Bachelor's degree and higher[3]	9 381	7 098	75.7	6 673	425	6.0
NATIVE BORN						
Both sexes, 16 years and over	203 197	129 226	63.6	117 686	11 539	8.9
Men	98 228	67 595	68.8	61 170	6 425	9.5
Women	104 970	61 630	58.7	56 516	5 115	8.3
Age						
16 to 24 years	34 567	19 026	55.0	15 668	3 358	17.7
25 to 34 years	33 801	27 967	82.7	25 282	2 685	9.6
35 to 44 years	31 006	25 817	83.3	23 970	1 847	7.2
45 to 54 years	36 753	29 560	80.4	27 593	1 967	6.7
55 to 64 years	32 250	20 604	63.9	19 315	1 289	6.3
65 years and over	34 819	6 252	18.0	5 858	393	6.3
Race and Hispanic Origin						
White, non-Hispanic	153 541	98 751	64.3	91 609	7 142	7.2
Black, non-Hispanic	24 911	14 973	60.1	12 526	2 447	16.3
Asian, non-Hispanic	2 917	1 793	61.5	1 647	147	8.2
Hispanic[1]	17 306	10 934	63.2	9 518	1 417	13.0
Educational Attainment						
Total, 25 years and over	168 630	110 200	65.4	102 019	8 181	7.4
Less than a high school diploma	15 590	5 878	37.7	4 881	998	17.0
High school graduates, no college[2]	53 444	31 670	59.3	28 679	2 992	9.4
Some college or associate degree	47 700	32 904	69.0	30 310	2 594	7.9
Bachelor's degree or higher[3]	51 896	39 747	76.6	38 149	1 598	4.0

Note: Due to the introduction of revised population controls in January 2011, estimated levels for 2011 are not strictly comparable with those for 2010.

[1]May be of any race.
[2]Includes persons with a high school diploma or equivalent.
[3]Includes persons with bachelor's, master's, professional, and doctoral degrees.

Table 1-52. Employment Status of the Foreign-Born and Native-Born Populations Age 16 Years and Over, by Sex and Presence and Age of Youngest Child, Annual Averages, 2010–2011

(Thousands of people, percent.)

Characteristic	2010			2011		
	Both sexes	Men	Women	Both sexes	Men	Women
FOREIGN BORN						
With Own Children Under 18 Years						
Civilian noninstitutional population	14 385	6 896	7 490	14 472	6 965	7 508
Civilian labor force	11 032	6 480	4 552	11 024	6 533	4 490
Participation rate	76.7	94.0	60.8	76.2	93.8	59.8
Employed	10 008	5 913	4 095	10 062	6 032	4 030
Employment-population ratio	69.6	85.7	54.7	69.5	86.6	53.7
Unemployed	1 025	568	457	961	501	460
Unemployment rate	9.3	8.8	10.0	8.7	7.7	10.2
With Own Children 6 to 17 Years, None Younger						
Civilian noninstitutional population	7 338	3 423	3 915	7 484	3 474	4 010
Civilian labor force	5 908	3 184	2 725	5 941	3 215	2 725
Participation rate	80.5	93.0	69.6	79.4	92.6	68.0
Employed	5 373	2 903	2 470	5 437	2 969	2 468
Employment-population ratio	73.2	84.8	63.1	72.6	85.5	61.5
Unemployed	536	281	255	504	247	257
Unemployment rate	9.1	8.8	9.4	8.5	7.7	9.4
With Own Children Under 6 Years						
Civilian noninstitutional population	7 047	3 473	3 574	6 989	3 491	3 497
Civilian labor force	5 124	3 296	1 827	5 083	3 318	1 765
Participation rate	72.7	94.9	51.1	72.7	95.0	50.5
Employed	4 635	3 010	1 625	4 625	3 063	1 562
Employment-population ratio	65.8	86.7	45.5	66.2	87.7	44.7
Unemployed	489	287	202	457	255	203
Unemployment rate	9.5	8.7	11.1	9.0	7.7	11.5
With Own Children Under 3 Years						
Civilian noninstitutional population	4 074	2 022	2 053	3 961	2 019	1 942
Civilian labor force	2 871	1 916	955	2 802	1 925	877
Participation rate	70.5	94.8	46.5	70.8	95.4	45.2
Employed	2 585	1 748	837	2 547	1 784	762
Employment-population ratio	63.4	86.4	40.8	64.3	88.4	39.3
Unemployed	286	168	118	256	141	115
Unemployment rate	10.0	8.8	12.3	9.1	7.3	13.1
With No Own Children Under 18 Years						
Civilian noninstitutional population	21 484	11 040	10 444	21 948	11 125	10 823
Civilian labor force	13 323	7 895	5 429	13 368	7 846	5 521
Participation rate	62.0	71.5	52.0	60.9	70.5	51.0
Employed	11 961	7 033	4 928	12 121	7 088	5 033
Employment-population ratio	55.7	63.7	47.2	55.2	63.7	46.5
Unemployed	1 362	862	501	1 247	758	489
Unemployment rate	10.2	10.9	9.2	9.3	9.7	8.9

Note: Due to the introduction of revised population controls in January 2011, estimated levels for 2011 are not strictly comparable with those for 2010.

Table 1-52. Employment Status of the Foreign-Born and Native-Born Populations Age 16 Years and Over, by Sex and Presence and Age of Youngest Child, Annual Averages, 2010–2011—*Continued*

(Thousands of people, percent.)

Characteristic	2010			2011		
	Both sexes	Men	Women	Both sexes	Men	Women
NATIVE BORN						
With Own Children Under 18 Years						
Civilian noninstitutional population	51 801	22 530	29 270	51 190	22 218	28 972
Civilian labor force	42 459	21 018	21 441	41 879	20 675	21 204
Participation rate	82.0	93.3	73.2	81.8	93.1	73.2
Employed	38 981	19 430	19 551	38 703	19 357	19 346
Employment-population ratio	75.3	86.2	66.8	75.6	87.1	66.8
Unemployed	3 478	1 588	1 890	3 176	1 318	1 858
Unemployment rate	8.2	7.6	8.8	7.6	6.4	8.8
With Own Children 6 to 17 Years, None Younger						
Civilian noninstitutional population	28 468	12 426	16 042	27 961	12 194	15 767
Civilian labor force	24 033	11 503	12 530	23 584	11 271	12 314
Participation rate	84.4	92.6	78.1	84.3	92.4	78.1
Employed	22 337	10 735	11 601	22 037	10 627	11 410
Employment-population ratio	78.5	86.4	72.3	78.8	87.1	72.4
Unemployed	1 697	768	929	1 548	644	903
Unemployment rate	7.1	6.7	7.4	6.6	5.7	7.3
With Own Children Under 6 Years						
Civilian noninstitutional population	23 333	10 104	13 229	23 229	10 024	13 205
Civilian labor force	18 426	9 515	8 911	18 295	9 404	8 891
Participation rate	79.0	94.2	67.4	78.8	93.8	67.3
Employed	16 644	8 695	7 949	16 666	8 730	7 936
Employment-population ratio	71.3	86.1	60.1	71.7	87.1	60.1
Unemployed	1 781	820	961	1 629	674	955
Unemployment rate	9.7	8.6	10.8	8.9	7.2	10.7
With Own Children Under 3 Years						
Civilian noninstitutional population	13 859	6 006	7 853	13 655	5 932	7 723
Civilian labor force	10 725	5 658	5 067	10 536	5 567	4 969
Participation rate	77.4	94.2	64.5	77.2	93.8	64.3
Employed	9 638	5 146	4 492	9 577	5 160	4 418
Employment-population ratio	69.5	85.7	57.2	70.1	87.0	57.2
Unemployed	1 087	511	575	958	407	551
Unemployment rate	10.1	9.0	11.4	9.1	7.3	11.1
With No Own Children Under 18 Years						
Civilian noninstitutional population	150 159	74 708	75 452	152 007	76 010	75 998
Civilian labor force	87 074	46 591	40 483	87 346	46 920	40 426
Participation rate	58.0	62.4	53.7	57.5	61.7	53.2
Employed	78 115	40 983	37 131	78 983	41 814	37 170
Employment-population ratio	52.0	54.9	49.2	52.0	55.0	48.9
Unemployed	8 960	5 608	3 352	8 363	5 107	3 256
Unemployment rate	10.3	12.0	8.3	9.6	10.9	8.1

Note: Due to the introduction of revised population controls in January 2011, estimated levels for 2011 are not strictly comparable with those for 2010.

Table 1-53. Employment Status of the Foreign-Born and Native-Born Populations Age 25 Years and Over, by Educational Attainment, Race, and Hispanic Origin, Annual Averages, 2010–2011

(Thousands of people, percent.)

Characteristic	2010				2011			
	Less than a high school diploma	High school graduate, no college[1]	Some college or associate's degree	Bachelor's degree or higher[2]	Less than a high school diploma	High school graduate, no college[1]	Some college or associate's degree	Bachelor's degree or higher[2]
FOREIGN BORN								
White, Non-Hispanic								
Civilian noninstitutional population	870	1 773	1 364	2 832	815	1 884	1 407	2 935
Civilian labor force	307	937	883	2 053	274	978	899	2 144
Participation rate	35.3	52.8	64.8	72.5	33.6	51.9	63.9	73.0
Employed	282	851	818	1 935	243	897	832	2 019
Employment-population ratio	32.4	48.0	60.0	68.3	29.9	47.6	59.1	68.8
Unemployed	25	85	66	118	30	81	67	125
Unemployment rate	8.0	9.1	7.4	5.7	11.1	8.3	7.4	5.8
Black, Non-Hispanic								
Civilian noninstitutional population	420	739	685	740	391	810	709	752
Civilian labor force	246	556	568	623	204	594	578	614
Participation rate	58.5	75.3	82.9	84.2	52.1	73.3	81.5	81.6
Employed	203	481	508	570	163	516	512	556
Employment-population ratio	48.3	65.1	74.2	77.1	41.7	63.7	72.2	74.0
Unemployed	43	75	60	53	41	78	66	57
Unemployment rate	17.4	13.6	10.6	8.5	19.9	13.2	11.4	9.3
Asian, Non-Hispanic								
Civilian noninstitutional population	931	1 536	1 088	3 877	955	1 628	1 149	3 892
Civilian labor force	414	977	767	2 889	404	1 014	807	2 936
Participation rate	44.5	63.6	70.6	74.5	42.3	62.3	70.3	75.4
Employed	368	901	703	2 724	366	935	749	2 785
Employment-population ratio	39.5	58.6	64.7	70.3	38.3	57.4	65.2	71.6
Unemployed	46	76	64	165	39	79	58	150
Unemployment rate	11.2	7.8	8.3	5.7	9.6	7.8	7.2	5.1
Hispanic[3]								
Civilian noninstitutional population	7 351	4 146	1 989	1 667	7 331	4 072	2 052	1 687
Civilian labor force	4 937	3 134	1 542	1 316	4 815	3 032	1 586	1 309
Participation rate	67.2	75.6	77.5	78.9	65.7	74.4	77.3	77.6
Employed	4 341	2 802	1 383	1 225	4 294	2 746	1 437	1 221
Employment-population ratio	59.1	67.6	69.5	73.5	58.6	67.4	70.0	72.4
Unemployed	595	332	159	91	521	286	149	88
Unemployment rate	12.1	10.6	10.3	6.9	10.8	9.4	9.4	6.7
NATIVE BORN								
White, Non-Hispanic								
Civilian noninstitutional population	10 172	41 667	36 307	43 147	9 841	41 003	36 755	44 100
Civilian labor force	3 654	24 684	25 135	32 916	3 609	23 710	24 997	33 543
Participation rate	35.9	59.2	69.2	76.3	36.7	57.8	68.0	76.1
Employed	3 086	22 458	23 275	31 582	3 103	21 813	23 315	32 316
Employment-population ratio	30.3	53.9	64.1	73.2	31.5	53.2	63.4	73.3
Unemployed	568	2 225	1 860	1 334	506	1 897	1 682	1 226
Unemployment rate	15.5	9.0	7.4	4.1	14.0	8.0	6.7	3.7
Black, Non-Hispanic								
Civilian noninstitutional population	3 036	6 895	5 826	3 798	2 924	7 075	5 924	3 866
Civilian labor force	1 057	4 304	4 214	2 986	1 015	4 297	4 188	3 013
Participation rate	34.8	62.4	72.3	78.6	34.7	60.7	70.7	77.9
Employed	798	3 605	3 682	2 752	745	3 613	3 635	2 810
Employment-population ratio	26.3	52.3	63.2	72.5	25.5	51.1	61.4	72.7
Unemployed	259	698	532	235	270	684	553	203
Unemployment rate	24.5	16.2	12.6	7.9	26.6	15.9	13.2	6.7
Asian, Non-Hispanic								
Civilian noninstitutional population	133	387	471	1 008	119	397	451	1 090
Civilian labor force	54	228	329	817	46	221	317	862
Participation rate	40.5	58.9	69.9	81.0	39.0	55.8	70.3	79.1
Employed	49	212	304	777	41	207	292	814
Employment-population ratio	37.1	54.7	64.6	77.1	34.9	52.1	64.8	74.7
Unemployed	4	16	25	40	5	15	25	48
Unemployment rate	8.3	7.1	7.5	4.9	10.4	6.7	7.8	5.6
Hispanic[3]								
Civilian noninstitutional population	2 295	3 769	3 314	2 059	2 281	3 927	3 414	2 074
Civilian labor force	1 033	2 714	2 583	1 728	1 043	2 781	2 628	1 722
Participation rate	45.0	72.0	77.9	83.9	45.7	70.8	77.0	83.0
Employed	842	2 373	2 343	1 637	862	2 470	2 393	1 636
Employment-population ratio	36.7	63.0	70.7	79.5	37.8	62.9	70.1	78.9
Unemployed	191	342	240	91	181	311	235	86
Unemployment rate	18.5	12.6	9.3	5.3	17.4	11.2	8.9	5.0

Note: Updated population controls are introduced annually with the release of January data.

[1]Includes persons with a high school diploma or equivalent.
[2]Includes persons with bachelor's, master's, professional, and doctoral degrees.
[3]May be of any race.

Table 1-54. Employed Foreign-Born and Native-Born Persons Age 16 Years and Over, by Occupation and Sex, 2010–2011 Annual Averages

(Thousands of people, percent.)

Occupation	2010					
	Foreign born			Native born		
	Both sexes	Male	Female	Both sexes	Male	Female
TOTAL EMPLOYED	21 969	12 946	9 023	117 095	60 414	56 682
Percent Employed	100.0	100.0	100.0	100.0	100.0	100.0
Management, professional, and related	28.0	25.3	31.7	38.9	36.1	42.0
Management, business, and financial operations	10.3	10.4	10.2	15.9	17.5	14.2
Management	7.5	8.2	6.5	11.4	13.6	9.1
Business and financial operations	2.8	2.2	3.7	4.5	4.0	5.2
Professional and related	17.6	14.9	21.5	23.0	18.5	27.8
Computer and mathematical	3.3	4.2	2.0	2.4	3.4	1.3
Architecture and engineering	1.8	2.6	0.7	1.9	3.2	0.5
Life, physical, and social sciences	1.1	1.0	1.3	1.0	1.0	1.0
Community and social services	1.0	0.6	1.5	1.8	1.2	2.4
Legal	0.5	0.4	0.6	1.4	1.4	1.4
Education, training, and library	3.6	2.1	5.7	6.7	3.3	10.3
Arts, design, entertainment, sports, and media	1.4	1.3	1.5	2.1	2.2	2.0
Health care practitioner and technical	5.0	2.6	8.4	5.7	2.8	8.9
Services	25.0	19.1	33.4	16.4	13.5	19.4
Health care support	2.8	0.7	6.0	2.3	0.5	4.3
Protective services	1.1	1.4	0.6	2.6	4.0	1.1
Food preparation and serving related	7.9	7.9	8.0	5.1	4.0	6.2
Building and grounds cleaning and maintenance	8.7	7.6	10.3	2.9	3.6	2.2
Personal care and services	4.4	1.6	8.5	3.5	1.5	5.6
Sales and office	17.3	12.8	23.8	25.3	17.8	33.3
Sales and related	8.9	7.8	10.5	11.5	11.1	11.9
Office and administrative support	8.4	5.0	13.4	13.8	6.7	21.4
Natural resources, construction, and maintenance	13.6	22.0	1.5	8.6	15.9	0.8
Farming, fishing, and forestry	1.8	2.4	1.0	0.5	0.7	0.2
Construction and extraction	8.6	14.4	0.3	4.5	8.5	0.3
Installation, maintenance, and repair	3.2	5.3	0.2	3.6	6.7	0.3
Production, transportation, and material moving	16.1	20.7	9.6	10.8	16.7	4.5
Production	8.7	10.0	6.9	5.2	7.5	2.8
Transportation and material moving	7.4	10.8	2.6	5.6	9.2	1.7

Occupation	2011					
	Foreign born			Native born		
	Both sexes	Male	Female	Both sexes	Male	Female
TOTAL EMPLOYED	22 183	13 120	9 063	117 686	61 170	56 516
Percent Employed	100.0	100.0	100.0	100.0	100.0	100.0
Management, professional, and related	28.6	26.5	31.6	39.3	36.1	42.7
Management, business, and financial operations	11.0	11.2	10.7	16.3	17.7	14.8
Management	7.6	8.5	6.3	11.5	13.6	9.3
Business and financial operations	3.4	2.6	4.5	4.7	4.1	5.5
Professional and related	17.6	15.4	20.9	23.0	18.4	27.9
Computer and mathematical	3.5	4.5	2.0	2.4	3.4	1.3
Architecture and engineering	2.0	2.8	0.7	2.0	3.3	0.6
Life, physical, and social sciences	1.0	0.9	1.2	0.9	0.9	0.9
Community and social services	0.9	0.7	1.2	1.8	1.2	2.5
Legal	0.4	0.2	0.7	1.4	1.4	1.4
Education, training, and library	3.7	2.1	5.9	6.6	3.3	10.3
Arts, design, entertainment, sports, and media	1.4	1.4	1.3	2.1	2.1	2.1
Health care practitioner and technical	4.8	2.6	7.9	5.7	2.7	8.9
Services	24.6	19.3	32.2	16.4	13.7	19.4
Health care support	2.6	0.7	5.4	2.4	0.5	4.3
Protective services	0.9	1.3	0.4	2.5	3.9	1.1
Food preparation and serving related	7.9	7.8	7.9	5.1	4.1	6.2
Building and grounds cleaning and maintenance	8.8	8.0	10.0	3.0	3.8	2.2
Personal care and services	4.3	1.5	8.4	3.4	1.4	5.6
Sales and office	17.5	12.6	24.5	24.8	17.6	32.6
Sales and related	8.7	7.4	10.7	11.4	11.1	11.7
Office and administrative support	8.7	5.2	13.8	13.4	6.6	20.8
Natural resources, construction, and maintenance	13.5	21.8	1.5	8.5	15.7	0.7
Farming, fishing, and forestry	1.9	2.4	1.0	0.5	0.8	0.2
Construction and extraction	8.5	14.1	0.3	4.5	8.3	0.2
Installation, maintenance, and repair	3.2	5.2	0.2	3.6	6.6	0.3
Production, transportation, and material moving	15.8	19.8	10.1	11.0	16.9	4.7
Production	8.7	9.3	7.7	5.3	7.5	2.9
Transportation and material moving	7.2	10.5	2.4	5.7	9.3	1.8

Note: Due to the introduction of revised population controls in January 2011, estimated levels for 2011 are not strictly comparable with those for 2010.

Table 1-55. Median Usual Weekly Earnings of Full-Time Wage and Salary Workers for the Foreign-Born and Native-Born Populations, by Selected Characteristics, 2010–2011 Annual Averages

(Thousands of people, dollars, percent.)

Year and characteristic	Foreign born		Native born		Earnings of foreign born as a percent of earnings of native born[1]
	Number	Median weekly earnings	Number	Median weekly earnings	
2010					
Both Sexes, 16 Years and Over	16 253	598	83 278	771	77.5
Men	10 056	610	45 003	873	69.9
Women	6 197	577	38 275	686	84.1
Age					
16 to 24 years	1 037	392	7 515	443	88.5
25 to 34 years	4 288	551	19 813	709	77.7
35 to 44 years	4 784	649	19 038	864	75.2
45 to 54 years	3 810	643	21 396	878	73.2
55 to 64 years	1 911	651	13 230	887	73.4
65 years and over	422	584	2 287	708	82.4
Race and Hispanic Origin					
White, non-Hispanic	2 809	850	64 060	824	103.2
Black, non-Hispanic	1 490	614	9 696	613	100.1
Asian, non-Hispanic	3 665	871	1 179	841	103.5
Hispanic[2]	8 092	480	6 745	629	76.4
Educational Attainment					
Total, 25 years and over	15 216	615	75 764	818	75.2
Less than a high school diploma	3 895	416	3 258	486	85.5
High school graduate, no college[3]	3 687	521	21 512	648	80.4
Some college	2 560	656	22 335	741	88.4
Bachelor's degree or higher[4]	5 073	1 119	28 658	1 147	97.6
2011					
Both Sexes, 16 Years and Over	16 441	609	84 015	780	78.0
Men	10 177	624	45 794	879	71.0
Women	6 264	585	38 222	701	83.5
Age					
16 to 24 years	1 081	405	7 643	448	90.3
25 to 34 years	4 120	569	20 177	718	79.3
35 to 44 years	4 812	671	18 970	875	76.7
45 to 54 years	3 962	680	21 172	899	75.6
55 to 64 years	2 039	662	13 602	910	72.8
65 years and over	429	621	2 452	760	81.8
Race and Hispanic Origin					
White, non-Hispanic	2 876	883	64 359	837	105.5
Black, non-Hispanic	1 467	614	9 638	617	99.5
Asian, non-Hispanic	3 876	868	1 226	878	98.8
Hispanic[2]	8 044	489	7 103	636	77.0
Educational Attainment					
Total, 25 years and over	15 361	628	76 373	831	75.6
Less than a high school diploma	3 822	417	3 197	497	83.9
High school graduates, no college[3]	3 828	530	21 328	661	80.2
Some college	2 580	665	22 625	746	89.2
Bachelor's degree and higher[4]	5 131	1 148	29 222	1 151	99.8

Note: Due to the introduction of revised population controls in January 2011, estimated levels for 2011 are not strictly comparable with those for 2010.

[1]These figures are computed using unrounded medians and may differ slightly from percentages computed using the rounded medians displayed in this table.
[2]May be of any race.
[3]Includes persons with a high school diploma or equivalent.
[4]Includes persons with bachelor's, master's, professional, and doctoral degrees.

Table 1-56. Percent Distribution of the Civilian Labor Force Age 25 to 64 Years, by Educational Attainment, Sex, and Race, March 1990–March 2012

(Thousands of people, percent.)

Sex, race, and year	Civilian labor force	Percent distribution				
		Total	Less than a high school diploma	4 years of high school only	1 to 3 years of college	4 or more years of college
Both Sexes						
1990	99 175	100.0	13.4	39.5	20.7	26.4
1991	100 480	100.0	13.0	39.4	21.1	26.5
1992	102 387	100.0	12.2	36.2	25.2	26.4
1993	103 504	100.0	11.5	35.2	26.3	27.0
1994	104 868	100.0	11.0	34.0	27.7	27.3
1995	106 519	100.0	10.8	33.1	27.8	28.3
1996	108 037	100.0	10.9	32.9	27.7	28.5
1997	110 514	100.0	10.9	33.0	27.4	28.6
1998	111 857	100.0	10.7	32.8	27.4	29.1
1999	112 542	100.0	10.3	32.3	27.4	30.0
2000	114 052	100.0	9.8	31.8	27.9	30.4
2001	115 073	100.0	9.8	31.4	28.1	30.7
2002	117 738	100.0	10.1	30.6	27.7	31.6
2003	119 261	100.0	10.1	30.1	27.8	31.9
2004	119 392	100.0	9.7	30.1	27.8	32.4
2005	120 461	100.0	9.8	30.1	27.8	32.3
2006	122 541	100.0	9.8	29.6	28.0	32.6
2007	124 581	100.0	9.8	29.3	27.3	33.6
2008	125 493	100.0	9.0	28.8	27.9	34.4
2009	125 655	100.0	9.0	28.7	27.9	34.3
2010	126 363	100.0	8.8	29.1	27.5	34.5
2011	125 385	100.0	8.5	28.2	28.0	35.4
2012	125 726	100.0	8.6	27.5	27.9	36.0
Men						
1990	54 476	100.0	15.1	37.2	19.7	28.0
1991	55 165	100.0	14.7	37.5	20.2	27.6
1992	55 917	100.0	13.9	34.7	23.8	27.5
1993	56 544	100.0	13.2	33.9	24.7	28.1
1994	56 633	100.0	12.7	32.9	25.8	28.6
1995	57 454	100.0	12.2	32.3	25.7	29.7
1996	58 121	100.0	12.7	32.2	26.0	29.1
1997	59 268	100.0	12.8	32.2	25.8	29.2
1998	59 905	100.0	12.3	32.3	25.8	29.6
1999	60 030	100.0	11.7	32.0	25.8	30.5
2000	60 510	100.0	11.1	31.8	26.1	30.9
2001	61 091	100.0	11.0	31.6	26.3	31.1
2002	62 794	100.0	11.8	30.6	25.9	31.7
2003	63 466	100.0	12.0	30.1	25.8	32.1
2004	63 699	100.0	11.5	30.5	25.8	32.2
2005	64 562	100.0	11.6	31.4	25.4	31.6
2006	65 708	100.0	11.8	30.7	25.7	31.8
2007	66 742	100.0	11.7	30.6	25.1	32.7
2008	66 957	100.0	11.0	30.3	25.8	33.0
2009	66 843	100.0	10.8	30.4	26.0	32.8
2010	67 261	100.0	10.6	31.2	25.3	32.9
2011	66 801	100.0	10.2	30.4	25.5	33.9
2012	66 539	100.0	10.1	29.7	25.9	34.3
Women						
1990	44 699	100.0	11.3	42.4	21.9	24.5
1991	45 315	100.0	10.9	41.6	22.2	25.2
1992	46 469	100.0	10.2	37.9	26.9	25.0
1993	46 961	100.0	9.3	36.7	28.2	25.8
1994	48 235	100.0	9.1	35.3	29.8	25.8
1995	49 065	100.0	9.1	34.1	30.2	26.6
1996	49 916	100.0	8.8	33.7	29.7	27.8
1997	51 246	100.0	8.7	34.0	29.3	28.0
1998	51 953	100.0	8.8	33.3	29.3	28.6
1999	52 512	100.0	8.7	32.7	29.2	29.5
2000	53 541	100.0	8.4	31.8	30.0	29.8
2001	53 982	100.0	8.5	31.1	30.1	30.2
2002	54 944	100.0	8.2	30.6	29.7	31.5
2003	55 795	100.0	8.0	30.1	30.1	31.8
2004	55 693	100.0	7.7	29.6	30.2	32.5
2005	55 899	100.0	7.8	28.6	30.5	33.1
2006	56 833	100.0	7.6	28.2	30.6	33.6
2007	57 839	100.0	7.5	27.9	29.9	34.6
2008	58 536	100.0	6.7	27.0	30.4	35.9
2009	58 811	100.0	7.0	26.9	30.2	35.9
2010	59 102	100.0	6.8	26.8	30.1	36.3
2011	58 584	100.0	6.5	25.7	30.7	37.1
2012	59 187	100.0	6.8	25.1	30.2	37.9

Table 1-56. Percent Distribution of the Civilian Labor Force Age 25 to 64 Years, by Educational Attainment, Sex, and Race, March 1990–March 2012—*Continued*

(Thousands of people, percent.)

Sex, race, and year	Civilian labor force	Percent distribution				
		Total	Less than a high school diploma	4 years of high school only	1 to 3 years of college	4 or more years of college
White[1]						
1990	85 238	100.0	12.6	39.6	20.6	27.1
1991	86 344	100.0	12.2	39.3	21.1	27.4
1992	87 656	100.0	11.3	36.1	25.5	27.1
1993	88 457	100.0	10.7	35.0	26.4	27.9
1994	89 009	100.0	10.5	33.7	27.7	28.1
1995	90 192	100.0	10.0	32.8	27.8	29.3
1996	91 506	100.0	10.4	32.8	27.5	29.3
1997	93 179	100.0	10.4	32.8	27.3	29.5
1998	93 527	100.0	10.2	32.7	27.4	29.8
1999	94 216	100.0	9.8	32.2	27.2	30.8
2000	95 073	100.0	9.5	31.8	27.7	31.0
2001	95 562	100.0	9.5	31.0	28.0	31.4
2002	97 699	100.0	9.8	30.6	27.6	32.0
2003	98 241	100.0	9.9	30.0	27.7	32.4
2004	98 030	100.0	9.5	29.8	27.8	32.9
2005	98 581	100.0	9.7	29.8	27.8	32.7
2006	100 205	100.0	9.7	29.3	28.1	32.9
2007	101 548	100.0	9.7	29.1	27.3	33.9
2008	102 077	100.0	8.9	28.7	27.8	34.6
2009	102 261	100.0	9.1	28.6	27.7	34.6
2010	102 634	100.0	8.8	29.0	27.4	34.8
2011	101 707	100.0	8.4	27.8	27.9	35.8
2012	100 382	100.0	8.6	27.4	27.7	36.4
Black[1]						
1990	10 537	100.0	19.9	42.5	22.1	15.5
1991	10 650	100.0	19.5	42.9	22.1	15.4
1992	10 936	100.0	19.2	40.3	24.9	15.6
1993	11 051	100.0	16.8	39.5	27.6	16.1
1994	11 368	100.0	14.5	39.3	29.2	17.0
1995	11 695	100.0	14.1	38.6	29.6	17.7
1996	11 891	100.0	14.2	37.2	31.2	17.4
1997	12 253	100.0	14.3	37.8	31.3	16.6
1998	12 893	100.0	14.3	37.3	30.1	18.2
1999	12 945	100.0	13.0	37.2	30.4	19.5
2000	13 383	100.0	11.8	36.1	31.5	20.7
2001	13 617	100.0	12.0	37.1	31.1	19.8
2002	13 319	100.0	12.4	34.5	32.0	21.0
2003	13 315	100.0	11.3	35.6	31.5	21.6
2004	13 372	100.0	11.0	36.6	30.5	21.9
2005	13 635	100.0	11.2	37.3	29.9	21.6
2006	13 855	100.0	10.9	35.6	30.4	23.0
2007	14 186	100.0	10.1	35.4	31.4	23.1
2008	14 356	100.0	9.5	34.3	32.1	24.1
2009	14 325	100.0	8.5	35.1	33.0	23.5
2010	14 483	100.0	8.9	34.5	32.4	24.2
2011	14 377	100.0	8.5	33.8	33.1	24.6
2012	14 721	100.0	8.5	32.0	33.4	26.0

[1]Beginning in 2003, persons who selected this race group only; persons who selected more than one race group are not included. Prior to 2003, persons who reported more than one race group were included in the group they identified as their main race.

Table 1-57. Labor Force Participation Rates of Persons Age 25 to 64 Years, by Educational Attainment, Sex, and Race, March 1990–March 2012

(Civilian labor force as a percent of the civilian noninstitutional population.)

Sex, race, and year	Participation rates				
	Total	Less than a high school diploma	4 years of high school only	1 to 3 years of college	4 or more years of college
Both Sexes					
1990	78.6	60.7	78.2	83.3	88.4
1991	78.6	60.7	78.1	83.2	88.4
1992	79.0	60.3	78.3	83.5	88.4
1993	78.9	59.6	77.7	82.9	88.3
1994	78.9	58.3	77.8	83.2	88.2
1995	79.3	59.8	77.3	83.2	88.7
1996	79.4	60.2	77.9	83.7	87.8
1997	80.1	61.7	78.5	83.7	88.5
1998	80.2	63.0	78.4	83.5	88.0
1999	80.0	62.7	78.1	83.0	87.6
2000	80.3	62.7	78.4	83.2	87.8
2001	80.2	63.5	78.4	83.0	87.0
2002	79.7	63.5	77.7	82.1	86.7
2003	79.4	64.1	76.9	81.9	86.2
2004	78.8	63.2	76.1	81.2	85.9
2005	78.5	62.9	75.7	81.1	85.7
2006	78.7	63.2	75.9	81.0	85.9
2007	79.0	63.7	76.3	81.1	85.9
2008	79.0	62.5	76.0	80.9	86.1
2009	78.6	62.3	75.7	80.3	85.9
2010	78.7	62.7	76.2	79.7	85.7
2011	77.6	61.0	74.3	78.6	85.3
2012	77.4	61.7	73.2	78.5	85.5
Men					
1990	88.8	75.1	89.9	91.5	94.5
1991	88.6	75.1	89.3	92.0	94.2
1992	88.6	75.1	89.0	91.8	93.7
1993	88.1	74.9	88.1	90.6	93.7
1994	87.0	71.5	86.8	90.3	93.2
1995	87.4	72.0	86.9	90.1	93.8
1996	87.5	74.3	86.9	90.0	92.9
1997	87.7	75.2	86.4	90.6	93.5
1998	87.8	75.3	86.7	90.0	93.4
1999	87.5	74.4	86.6	89.4	93.0
2000	87.5	74.9	86.2	88.9	93.3
2001	87.4	75.4	85.8	89.1	92.9
2002	87.0	75.5	85.3	88.8	92.4
2003	86.4	76.1	84.3	87.5	92.2
2004	85.9	75.2	83.8	87.0	91.9
2005	86.0	75.7	83.7	87.5	91.7
2006	86.0	76.3	83.4	87.8	91.7
2007	86.2	75.7	83.9	87.2	92.4
2008	85.8	74.8	83.6	86.5	91.9
2009	85.1	73.7	82.3	86.0	91.9
2010	85.3	74.5	83.2	85.3	91.5
2011	84.0	73.3	81.8	83.2	91.1
2012	84.1	72.9	80.7	84.3	91.4
Women					
1990	68.9	46.2	68.7	75.9	81.1
1991	69.1	46.2	68.6	75.2	81.8
1992	70.0	45.6	69.1	76.2	82.2
1993	70.0	44.2	68.8	76.1	82.2
1994	71.1	44.7	70.0	77.0	82.5
1995	71.5	47.2	68.9	77.3	82.8
1996	71.8	45.7	69.8	78.1	82.3
1997	72.8	47.1	71.4	77.6	83.2
1998	73.0	49.8	70.9	77.8	82.3
1999	72.8	50.5	70.4	77.4	81.9
2000	73.5	50.4	71.2	78.3	82.0
2001	73.4	51.7	71.3	77.7	80.9
2002	72.7	50.4	70.4	76.4	81.0
2003	72.6	50.5	69.8	77.1	80.1
2004	72.0	49.7	68.6	76.2	80.0
2005	71.4	48.7	67.4	75.8	79.8
2006	71.7	48.3	68.2	75.3	80.4
2007	72.1	49.6	68.4	76.0	79.7
2008	72.5	47.9	68.2	76.1	80.9
2009	72.4	49.0	68.7	75.4	80.5
2010	72.3	48.9	68.6	75.0	80.4
2011	71.3	46.8	66.1	74.7	80.0
2012	71.1	49.2	65.2	73.5	80.3

Table 1-57. Labor Force Participation Rates of Persons Age 25 to 64 Years, by Educational Attainment, Sex, and Race, March 1990–March 2012—*Continued*

(Civilian labor force as a percent of the civilian noninstitutional population.)

Sex, race, and year	Participation rates				
	Total	Less than a high school diploma	4 years of high school only	1 to 3 years of college	4 or more years of college
White[1]					
1990	79.2	62.5	78.4	83.3	88.3
1991	79.4	62.5	78.3	83.1	88.6
1992	79.8	61.5	78.7	83.8	88.7
1993	79.7	61.1	78.2	83.1	88.8
1994	79.8	60.3	78.3	83.5	88.5
1995	80.1	61.6	77.9	83.4	88.8
1996	80.4	62.5	78.6	83.9	88.2
1997	81.0	63.8	79.2	83.9	89.0
1998	80.6	63.8	78.6	83.5	88.3
1999	80.6	64.2	78.5	83.3	87.9
2000	80.8	64.2	78.7	83.1	87.9
2001	80.7	64.5	78.7	83.1	87.2
2002	80.3	65.0	78.2	82.4	87.0
2003	80.1	65.7	77.5	82.3	86.5
2004	79.5	64.6	76.7	81.6	86.2
2005	79.2	63.8	76.4	81.5	86.1
2006	79.5	65.1	76.5	81.4	86.2
2007	79.6	65.1	77.2	81.4	86.1
2008	79.6	63.8	76.8	81.2	86.3
2009	79.4	64.7	76.4	80.7	86.2
2010	79.5	64.5	77.1	80.4	86.0
2011	78.5	62.9	75.3	79.3	85.5
2012	78.3	63.8	74.2	78.8	86.0
Black[1]					
1990	74.6	54.5	78.2	84.2	92.0
1991	73.9	53.9	77.1	84.1	90.2
1992	74.4	55.4	76.9	83.4	89.1
1993	73.8	53.4	74.7	83.0	89.6
1994	73.5	49.4	75.2	82.4	89.5
1995	74.2	51.0	74.5	82.8	90.9
1996	73.7	50.1	74.3	83.0	87.9
1997	74.9	52.9	75.0	83.8	89.0
1998	77.7	59.3	77.0	85.0	88.8
1999	76.5	55.1	76.5	82.9	88.6
2000	77.9	55.5	77.0	84.2	90.3
2001	78.1	58.7	76.8	83.0	90.5
2002	76.4	56.6	75.0	81.7	88.9
2003	75.8	55.4	73.9	81.2	88.2
2004	75.0	55.2	73.4	79.0	87.9
2005	75.2	58.2	72.6	79.5	87.2
2006	75.0	54.0	73.3	79.6	87.7
2007	75.6	55.3	72.5	80.7	88.0
2008	75.6	54.3	72.8	80.0	87.5
2009	74.4	50.0	72.6	78.7	86.2
2010	74.2	52.2	71.7	77.5	87.0
2011	72.4	49.0	69.6	76.3	85.5
2012	72.9	50.8	68.6	77.2	85.7

[1]Beginning in 2003, persons who selected this race group only; persons who selected more than one race group are not included. Prior to 2003, persons who reported more than one race group were included in the group they identified as their main race.

Table 1-58. Unemployment Rates of Persons Age 25 to 64 Years, by Educational Attainment and Sex, March 1990–March 2012

(Unemployment as a percent of the civilian labor force.)

Sex, race, and year	Unemployment rates				
	Total	Less than a high school diploma	4 years of high school only	1 to 3 years of college	4 or more years of college
Both Sexes					
1990	4.5	9.6	4.9	3.7	1.9
1991	6.1	12.3	6.7	5.0	2.9
1992	6.7	13.5	7.7	5.9	2.9
1993	6.4	13.0	7.3	5.5	3.2
1994	5.8	12.6	6.7	5.0	2.9
1995	4.8	10.0	5.2	4.5	2.5
1996	4.8	10.9	5.5	4.1	2.2
1997	4.4	10.4	5.1	3.8	2.0
1998	4.0	8.5	4.8	3.6	1.8
1999	3.5	7.7	4.0	3.1	1.9
2000	3.3	7.9	3.8	3.0	1.5
2001	3.5	8.1	4.2	2.9	2.0
2002	5.0	10.2	6.1	4.5	2.8
2003	5.3	9.9	6.4	5.2	3.0
2004	5.1	10.5	5.9	4.9	2.9
2005	4.4	9.0	5.5	4.1	2.3
2006	4.1	8.3	4.7	3.9	2.3
2007	3.9	8.5	4.7	3.7	1.8
2008	4.4	10.1	5.8	4.2	2.1
2009	8.1	15.8	10.4	8.0	4.3
2010	9.1	16.8	12.1	8.8	4.7
2011	8.3	16.2	10.9	8.1	4.4
2012	7.4	14.3	9.2	7.9	4.1
Men					
1990	4.8	9.6	5.3	3.9	2.1
1991	6.8	13.4	7.7	5.2	3.2
1992	7.5	14.8	8.8	6.4	3.2
1993	7.3	14.1	8.7	6.3	3.4
1994	6.2	12.8	7.2	5.3	2.9
1995	5.1	10.9	5.7	4.4	2.6
1996	5.3	11.0	6.4	4.5	2.3
1997	4.7	9.9	5.6	4.0	2.1
1998	4.1	8.0	5.1	3.7	1.7
1999	3.5	7.0	4.1	3.2	1.9
2000	3.3	7.1	3.9	3.1	1.6
2001	3.7	7.5	4.6	3.2	1.9
2002	5.5	9.9	6.7	4.9	3.0
2003	5.8	9.5	6.9	6.0	3.2
2004	5.4	9.4	6.6	5.4	3.0
2005	4.7	7.9	6.0	4.3	2.5
2006	4.3	7.6	5.0	4.2	2.4
2007	4.3	8.4	5.5	3.9	1.9
2008	4.9	10.9	6.3	4.2	2.0
2009	9.5	16.5	12.4	9.3	4.7
2010	10.5	17.8	13.8	10.2	5.1
2011	9.2	16.7	12.2	8.7	4.6
2012	8.0	13.6	10.1	8.2	4.3
Women					
1990	4.2	9.5	4.6	3.5	1.7
1991	5.2	10.7	5.5	4.8	2.5
1992	5.7	11.4	6.5	5.3	2.5
1993	5.2	11.2	5.8	4.6	2.9
1994	5.4	12.4	6.2	4.7	2.9
1995	4.4	8.6	4.6	4.5	2.4
1996	4.1	10.7	4.4	3.8	2.1
1997	4.1	11.3	4.5	3.6	2.0
1998	3.9	9.3	4.4	3.5	1.9
1999	3.5	8.8	3.9	3.0	1.9
2000	3.2	9.1	3.6	2.9	1.4
2001	3.3	8.9	3.8	2.6	2.0
2002	4.6	10.6	5.4	4.1	2.6
2003	4.8	10.6	5.9	4.4	2.8
2004	4.7	12.2	5.2	4.3	2.9
2005	4.2	10.9	4.8	4.0	2.2
2006	3.8	9.4	4.4	3.7	2.1
2007	3.4	8.5	3.8	3.6	1.8
2008	4.0	8.5	5.1	4.2	2.1
2009	6.6	14.5	7.9	6.7	4.0
2010	7.5	15.0	9.8	7.5	4.3
2011	7.2	15.2	9.1	7.5	4.3
2012	6.8	15.4	8.1	7.7	3.8

Table 1-58. Unemployment Rates of Persons Age 25 to 64 Years, by Educational Attainment and Sex, March 1990–March 2012—*Continued*

(Unemployment as a percent of the civilian labor force.)

Sex, race, and year	Unemployment rates				
	Total	Less than a high school diploma	4 years of high school only	1 to 3 years of college	4 or more years of college
White[1]					
1990	4.0	8.3	4.4	3.3	1.8
1991	5.6	11.6	6.2	4.6	2.7
1992	6.0	12.9	6.8	5.3	2.7
1993	5.8	12.4	6.5	5.0	3.1
1994	5.2	11.7	5.8	4.5	2.6
1995	4.3	9.2	4.6	4.2	2.3
1996	4.2	10.2	4.6	3.7	2.1
1997	3.9	9.4	4.6	3.4	1.8
1998	3.5	7.5	4.2	3.2	1.7
1999	3.1	7.0	3.4	2.8	1.7
2000	3.0	7.5	3.3	2.7	1.4
2001	3.1	7.2	3.6	2.7	1.8
2002	4.6	9.1	5.5	4.1	2.6
2003	4.7	9.0	5.7	4.5	2.7
2004	4.6	9.6	5.4	4.4	2.8
2005	3.9	7.7	4.9	3.6	2.2
2006	3.5	7.1	4.0	3.5	2.1
2007	3.5	7.8	4.2	3.3	1.7
2008	4.0	9.2	5.1	3.7	1.9
2009	7.6	15.2	9.9	7.4	4.0
2010	8.4	16.3	11.3	8.1	4.3
2011	7.5	15.1	9.9	7.2	4.0
2012	6.7	13.5	8.3	6.9	3.7
Black[1]					
1990	8.6	15.9	8.6	6.5	1.9
1991	10.1	15.9	10.3	8.0	5.2
1992	12.4	17.2	14.1	10.7	4.8
1993	10.9	17.3	12.4	8.7	4.1
1994	10.6	17.4	12.2	8.3	4.9
1995	7.7	13.7	8.4	6.3	4.1
1996	8.9	15.3	10.8	6.9	3.3
1997	8.1	16.6	8.2	6.1	4.4
1998	7.3	13.4	8.4	6.4	2.1
1999	6.3	12.0	6.7	5.2	3.3
2000	5.4	10.4	6.3	4.3	2.5
2001	6.5	14.0	7.7	4.3	3.3
2002	8.1	15.4	9.7	6.0	4.1
2003	9.0	14.7	9.9	8.9	4.7
2004	8.4	15.8	9.3	7.9	3.7
2005	8.3	17.9	8.6	7.5	3.6
2006	7.8	16.4	9.0	6.5	3.6
2007	6.5	14.0	7.7	5.7	2.5
2008	7.6	16.7	9.3	6.5	3.3
2009	12.1	22.0	14.0	11.2	7.2
2010	14.1	22.4	17.5	12.9	7.9
2011	13.9	25.0	16.6	12.7	7.7
2012	12.3	21.4	14.2	12.7	6.3

[1]Beginning in 2003, persons who selected this race group only; persons who selected more than one race group are not included. Prior to 2003, persons who reported more than one race group were included in the group they identified as their main race.

Table 1-59. Workers Age 25 to 64 Years, by Educational Attainment, Occupation of Longest Job Held, and Sex, 2010–2011

(Thousands of people with work experience during the year.)

Year, sex, and occupation	Total	Less than a high school diploma	4 years of high school only	1 to 3 years of college	4 or more years of college
2010					
Both Sexes	125 135	10 202	34 760	35 442	44 731
Management, business, and financial operations	20 133	397	3 178	4 911	11 647
Management	14 113	361	2 537	3 547	7 668
Business and financial operations	6 020	36	641	1 363	3 980
Professional and related	28 996	149	2 075	6 380	20 391
Computer and mathematical	3 298	11	231	753	2 303
Architecture and engineering	2 687	8	231	612	1 836
Life, physical, and social sciences	1 241	3	62	127	1 049
Community and social services	2 264	15	185	398	1 665
Legal	1 554	4	70	255	1 225
Education, training, and library	8 176	49	598	1 075	6 455
Arts, design, entertainment, sports, and media	2 433	37	234	601	1 562
Health care practitioner and technical	7 342	23	464	2 559	4 296
Services	19 674	3 238	7 313	6 393	2 730
Health care support	2 888	259	926	1 312	390
Protective services	2 822	75	720	1 237	790
Food preparation and serving related	5 064	1 048	2 065	1 448	503
Building and grounds cleaning and maintenance	4 919	1 404	2 095	1 026	394
Personal care and services	3 982	451	1 508	1 370	653
Sales and office	28 106	1 262	9 060	10 275	7 509
Sales and related	12 206	670	3 733	3 838	3 965
Office and administrative support	15 901	593	5 327	6 437	3 543
Natural resources, construction, and maintenance	12 683	2 574	5 662	3 455	993
Farming, fishing, and forestry	838	412	278	100	48
Construction and extraction	7 407	1 753	3 406	1 717	531
Installation, maintenance, and repair	4 438	409	1 978	1 638	414
Production, transportation, and material moving	14 887	2 577	7 327	3 739	1 245
Production	7 618	1 391	3 663	1 923	641
Transportation and material moving	7 270	1 186	3 664	1 816	604
Armed forces	654	4	145	289	216
Men	66 276	6 488	19 756	17 286	22 746
Management, business, and financial operations	11 312	276	1 798	2 502	6 736
Management	8 625	261	1 592	2 047	4 724
Business and financial operations	2 687	14	206	455	2 012
Professional and related	12 128	62	746	2 287	9 033
Computer and mathematical	2 414	11	158	543	1 702
Architecture and engineering	2 320	8	194	548	1 570
Life, physical, and social sciences	679	. . .	40	83	555
Community and social services	767	2	64	127	574
Legal	742	2	10	29	701
Education, training, and library	2 120	14	79	192	1 834
Arts, design, entertainment, sports, and media	1 346	19	132	362	833
Health care practitioner and technical	1 740	6	69	402	1 263
Services	8 389	1 360	3 004	2 690	1 336
Health care support	297	28	82	124	61
Protective services	2 212	53	540	998	621
Food preparation and serving related	2 235	486	863	660	226
Building and grounds cleaning and maintenance	2 866	731	1 216	670	249
Personal care and services	779	62	302	237	178
Sales and office	10 309	481	3 012	3 271	3 544
Sales and related	6 276	259	1 737	1 857	2 424
Office and administrative support	4 032	223	1 275	1 414	1 120
Natural resources, construction, and maintenance	12 093	2 420	5 444	3 299	929
Farming, fishing, and forestry	629	296	220	78	35
Construction and extraction	7 216	1 734	3 316	1 670	496
Installation, maintenance, and repair	4 247	391	1 909	1 551	397
Production, transportation, and material moving	11 463	1 884	5 624	2 971	985
Production	5 370	880	2 557	1 460	472
Transportation and material moving	6 093	1 004	3 066	1 510	513
Armed forces	583	4	128	267	184
Women	58 859	3 714	15 004	18 155	21 985
Management, business, and financial operations	8 821	122	1 380	2 409	4 911
Management	5 489	100	944	1 501	2 944
Business and financial operations	3 333	22	435	908	1 968
Professional and related	16 869	87	1 329	4 093	11 359
Computer and mathematical	884	. . .	73	210	601
Architecture and engineering	368	. . .	37	64	266
Life, physical, and social sciences	563	3	21	44	494
Community and social services	1 496	13	122	271	1 091
Legal	812	2	60	226	524
Education, training, and library	6 056	35	518	882	4 621
Arts, design, entertainment, sports, and media	1 087	18	102	238	729
Health care practitioner and technical	5 602	17	395	2 157	3 033
Services	11 285	1 878	4 310	3 703	1 394
Health care support	2 591	231	843	1 188	329
Protective services	610	23	179	238	169
Food preparation and serving related	2 828	562	1 202	788	277
Building and grounds cleaning and maintenance	2 053	673	879	356	145
Personal care and services	3 202	389	1 206	1 132	475
Sales and office	17 798	781	6 048	7 004	3 965
Sales and related	5 929	411	1 996	1 981	1 541
Office and administrative support	11 868	370	4 052	5 023	2 423
Natural resources, construction, and maintenance	590	154	217	155	64
Farming, fishing, and forestry	209	116	58	22	13
Construction and extraction	191	19	90	47	35
Installation, maintenance, and repair	191	18	69	87	16
Production, transportation, and material moving	3 425	693	1 704	768	260
Production	2 248	510	1 106	463	169
Transportation and material moving	1 177	182	598	305	91
Armed forces	72	. . .	17	23	32

. . . = Not available.

Table 1-59. Workers Age 25 to 64 Years, by Educational Attainment, Occupation of Longest Job Held, and Sex, 2010–2011—*Continued*

(Thousands of people with work experience during the year.)

Year, sex, and occupation	Total	Less than a high school diploma	4 years of high school only	1 to 3 years of college	4 or more years of college
2011					
Both Sexes	125 188	10 391	34 165	35 113	45 520
Management, business, and financial operations	20 501	383	3 206	4 821	12 091
Management	14 294	342	2 531	3 513	7 909
Business and financial operations	6 207	41	675	1 308	4 182
Professional and related	28 610	164	2 078	6 071	20 297
Computer and mathematical	3 494	17	251	780	2 446
Architecture and engineering	2 648	. . .	227	602	1 819
Life, physical, and social sciences	1 164	1	53	114	995
Community and social services	2 174	30	192	380	1 572
Legal	1 494	6	78	231	1 178
Education, training, and library	7 858	24	532	1 028	6 274
Arts, design, entertainment, sports, and media	2 422	42	287	558	1 535
Health care practitioner and technical	7 357	44	458	2 377	4 478
Services	20 364	3 443	7 596	6 377	2 948
Health care support	3 059	251	1 034	1 414	361
Protective services	2 859	73	766	1 197	822
Food preparation and serving related	5 386	1 126	2 170	1 438	651
Building and grounds cleaning and maintenance	4 964	1 562	2 118	936	348
Personal care and services	4 096	431	1 507	1 391	767
Sales and office	27 659	1 245	8 576	10 276	7 563
Sales and related	11 914	690	3 500	3 744	3 980
Office and administrative support	15 745	555	5 076	6 531	3 584
Natural resources, construction, and maintenance	12 067	2 402	5 327	3 349	989
Farming, fishing, and forestry	883	435	293	96	59
Construction and extraction	6 959	1 542	3 222	1 674	522
Installation, maintenance, and repair	4 224	425	1 812	1 579	408
Production, transportation, and material moving	15 331	2 753	7 250	3 925	1 403
Production	7 816	1 393	3 716	1 965	741
Transportation and material moving	7 516	1 359	3 534	1 960	662
Armed forces	656	2	133	294	228
Men	65 963	6 473	19 405	17 214	22 870
Management, business, and financial operations	11 405	255	1 764	2 537	6 849
Management	8 684	231	1 549	2 103	4 801
Business and financial operations	2 722	25	215	434	2 048
Professional and related	11 812	60	731	2 127	8 894
Computer and mathematical	2 562	10	160	573	1 818
Architecture and engineering	2 289	. . .	190	550	1 549
Life, physical, and social sciences	648	1	42	79	526
Community and social services	750	14	55	113	569
Legal	723	. . .	7	19	696
Education, training, and library	1 930	2	50	158	1 720
Arts, design, entertainment, sports, and media	1 254	23	155	301	775
Health care practitioner and technical	1 655	9	71	334	1 241
Services	8 756	1 496	3 223	2 625	1 412
Health care support	321	15	101	144	62
Protective services	2 279	40	602	994	644
Food preparation and serving related	2 470	598	963	617	292
Building and grounds cleaning and maintenance	2 870	795	1 262	601	211
Personal care and services	816	48	296	269	203
Sales and office	10 220	433	2 855	3 362	3 570
Sales and related	6 326	222	1 669	1 934	2 501
Office and administrative support	3 895	211	1 186	1 428	1 069
Natural resources, construction, and maintenance	11 541	2 252	5 159	3 235	895
Farming, fishing, and forestry	679	321	243	71	44
Construction and extraction	6 803	1 517	3 166	1 642	478
Installation, maintenance, and repair	4 059	414	1 750	1 522	373
Production, transportation, and material moving	11 642	1 974	5 543	3 065	1 060
Production	5 439	843	2 622	1 474	501
Transportation and material moving	6 204	1 131	2 922	1 591	560
Armed forces	586	2	131	262	191
Women	59 226	3 917	14 760	17 899	22 650
Management, business, and financial operations	9 096	128	1 442	2 283	5 243
Management	5 610	111	982	1 410	3 108
Business and financial operations	3 486	17	460	874	2 135
Professional and related	16 798	103	1 347	3 944	11 403
Computer and mathematical	933	7	91	207	628
Architecture and engineering	359	. . .	36	52	270
Life, physical, and social sciences	516	. . .	11	36	469
Community and social services	1 424	15	137	268	1 003
Legal	771	6	71	212	482
Education, training, and library	5 927	21	482	870	4 554
Arts, design, entertainment, sports, and media	1 168	19	132	256	760
Health care practitioner and technical	5 701	34	387	2 043	3 237
Services	11 608	1 946	4 373	3 752	1 536
Health care support	2 738	235	933	1 271	299
Protective services	580	33	165	203	179
Food preparation and serving related	2 916	528	1 208	821	359
Building and grounds cleaning and maintenance	2 094	767	856	334	136
Personal care and services	3 280	383	1 211	1 122	564
Sales and office	17 439	811	5 721	6 914	3 993
Sales and related	5 588	468	1 831	1 810	1 479
Office and administrative support	11 851	343	3 889	5 104	2 514
Natural resources, construction, and maintenance	526	150	168	114	95
Farming, fishing, and forestry	204	114	50	25	15
Construction and extraction	157	26	56	31	44
Installation, maintenance, and repair	165	10	62	57	35
Production, transportation, and material moving	3 689	779	1 707	861	343
Production	2 377	551	1 094	492	240
Transportation and material moving	1 312	228	613	369	103
Armed forces	71	. . .	2	32	37

. . . = Not available.

Table 1-60. Percent Distribution of Workers Age 25 to 64 Years, by Educational Attainment, Occupation of Longest Job Held, and Sex, 2010–2011

(Percent of total workers in occupation.)

Year, sex, and occupation	Total	Less than a high school diploma	4 years of high school only	1 to 3 years of college	4 or more years of college
2010					
Both Sexes	100.0	8.2	27.8	28.3	35.7
Management, business, and financial operations	100.0	2.0	15.8	24.4	57.9
Management	100.0	2.6	18.0	25.1	54.3
Business and financial operations	100.0	0.6	10.6	22.6	66.1
Professional and related	100.0	0.5	7.2	22.0	70.3
Computer and mathematical	100.0	0.3	7.0	22.8	69.8
Architecture and engineering	100.0	0.3	8.6	22.8	68.3
Life, physical, and social sciences	100.0	0.2	5.0	10.3	84.5
Community and social services	100.0	0.7	8.2	17.6	73.6
Legal	100.0	0.3	4.5	16.4	78.8
Education, training, and library	100.0	0.6	7.3	13.1	79.0
Arts, design, entertainment, sports, and media	100.0	1.5	9.6	24.7	64.2
Health care practitioner and technical	100.0	0.3	6.3	34.9	58.5
Services	100.0	16.5	37.2	32.5	13.9
Health care support	100.0	9.0	32.1	45.4	13.5
Protective services	100.0	2.7	25.5	43.8	28.0
Food preparation and serving related	100.0	20.7	40.8	28.6	9.9
Building and grounds cleaning and maintenance	100.0	28.5	42.6	20.9	8.0
Personal care and services	100.0	11.3	37.9	34.4	16.4
Sales and office	100.0	4.5	32.2	36.6	26.7
Sales and related	100.0	5.5	30.6	31.4	32.5
Office and administrative support	100.0	3.7	33.5	40.5	22.3
Natural resources, construction, and maintenance	100.0	20.3	44.6	27.2	7.8
Farming, fishing, and forestry	100.0	49.2	33.1	11.9	5.7
Construction and extraction	100.0	23.7	46.0	23.2	7.2
Installation, maintenance, and repair	100.0	9.2	44.6	36.9	9.3
Production, transportation, and material moving	100.0	17.3	49.2	25.1	8.4
Production	100.0	18.3	48.1	25.2	8.4
Transportation and material moving	100.0	16.3	50.4	25.0	8.3
Armed forces	100.0	0.7	22.1	44.2	33.0
Men	100.0	9.8	29.8	26.1	34.3
Management, business, and financial operations	100.0	2.4	15.9	22.1	59.5
Management	100.0	3.0	18.5	23.7	54.8
Business and financial operations	100.0	0.5	7.7	16.9	74.9
Professional and related	100.0	0.5	6.1	18.9	74.5
Computer and mathematical	100.0	0.4	6.6	22.5	70.5
Architecture and engineering	100.0	0.3	8.4	23.6	67.7
Life, physical, and social sciences	100.0	. . .	6.0	12.2	81.8
Community and social services	100.0	0.3	8.3	16.6	74.8
Legal	100.0	0.3	1.3	3.9	94.5
Education, training, and library	100.0	0.7	3.8	9.1	86.5
Arts, design, entertainment, sports, and media	100.0	1.4	9.8	26.9	61.9
Health care practitioner and technical	100.0	0.3	3.9	23.1	72.6
Services	100.0	16.2	35.8	32.1	15.9
Health care support	100.0	9.6	27.8	41.9	20.7
Protective services	100.0	2.4	24.4	45.1	28.1
Food preparation and serving related	100.0	21.8	38.6	29.5	10.1
Building and grounds cleaning and maintenance	100.0	25.5	42.4	23.4	8.7
Personal care and services	100.0	7.9	38.8	30.5	22.8
Sales and office	100.0	4.7	29.2	31.7	34.4
Sales and related	100.0	4.1	27.7	29.6	38.6
Office and administrative support	100.0	5.5	31.6	35.1	27.8
Natural resources, construction, and maintenance	100.0	20.0	45.0	27.3	7.7
Farming, fishing, and forestry	100.0	47.0	35.0	12.4	5.6
Construction and extraction	100.0	24.0	45.9	23.1	6.9
Installation, maintenance, and repair	100.0	9.2	44.9	36.5	9.4
Production, transportation, and material moving	100.0	16.4	49.1	25.9	8.6
Production	100.0	16.4	47.6	27.2	8.8
Transportation and material moving	100.0	16.5	50.3	24.8	8.4
Armed forces	100.0	0.7	22.0	45.7	31.6
Women	100.0	6.3	25.5	30.8	37.4
Management, business, and financial operations	100.0	1.4	15.6	27.3	55.7
Management	100.0	1.8	17.2	27.3	53.6
Business and financial operations	100.0	0.6	13.1	27.3	59.0
Professional and related	100.0	0.5	7.9	24.3	67.3
Computer and mathematical	100.0	. . .	8.3	23.8	67.9
Architecture and engineering	100.0	. . .	10.2	17.5	72.3
Life, physical, and social sciences	100.0	0.5	3.8	7.8	87.8
Community and social services	100.0	0.9	8.1	18.1	72.9
Legal	100.0	0.2	7.4	27.9	64.5
Education, training, and library	100.0	0.6	8.6	14.6	76.3
Arts, design, entertainment, sports, and media	100.0	1.6	9.4	21.9	67.1
Health care practitioner and technical	100.0	0.3	7.1	38.5	54.1
Services	100.0	16.6	38.2	32.8	12.4
Health care support	100.0	8.9	32.5	45.8	12.7
Protective services	100.0	3.7	29.4	39.1	27.7
Food preparation and serving related	100.0	19.9	42.5	27.9	9.8
Building and grounds cleaning and maintenance	100.0	32.8	42.8	17.4	7.1
Personal care and services	100.0	12.2	37.7	35.4	14.8
Sales and office	100.0	4.4	34.0	39.4	22.3
Sales and related	100.0	6.9	33.7	33.4	26.0
Office and administrative support	100.0	3.1	34.1	42.3	20.4
Natural resources, construction, and maintenance	100.0	26.0	36.8	26.3	10.9
Farming, fishing, and forestry	100.0	55.6	27.7	10.4	6.3
Construction and extraction	100.0	10.0	47.4	24.4	18.2
Installation, maintenance, and repair	100.0	9.6	36.3	45.6	8.5
Production, transportation, and material moving	100.0	20.2	49.7	22.4	7.6
Production	100.0	22.7	49.2	20.6	7.5
Transportation and material moving	100.0	15.5	50.8	26.0	7.8
Armed forces	100.0	. . .	23.6	31.9	44.5

. . . = Not available.

Table 1-60. Percent Distribution of Workers Age 25 to 64 Years, by Educational Attainment, Occupation of Longest Job Held, and Sex, 2010–2011—*Continued*

(Percent of total workers in occupation.)

Year, sex, and occupation	Total	Less than a high school diploma	4 years of high school only	1 to 3 years of college	4 or more years of college
2011					
Both Sexes	100.0	8.3	27.3	28.0	36.4
Management, business, and financial operations	100.0	1.9	15.6	23.5	59.0
Management	100.0	2.4	17.7	24.6	55.3
Business and financial operations	100.0	0.7	10.9	21.1	67.4
Professional and related	100.0	0.6	7.3	21.2	70.9
Computer and mathematical	100.0	0.5	7.2	22.3	70.0
Architecture and engineering	100.0	. . .	8.6	22.7	68.7
Life, physical, and social sciences	100.0	0.1	4.6	9.8	85.5
Community and social services	100.0	1.4	8.8	17.5	72.3
Legal	100.0	0.4	5.2	15.5	78.9
Education, training, and library	100.0	0.3	6.8	13.1	79.8
Arts, design, entertainment, sports, and media	100.0	1.7	11.9	23.0	63.4
Health care practitioner and technical	100.0	0.6	6.2	32.3	60.9
Services	100.0	16.9	37.3	31.3	14.5
Health care support	100.0	8.2	33.8	46.2	11.8
Protective services	100.0	2.6	26.8	41.9	28.8
Food preparation and serving related	100.0	20.9	40.3	26.7	12.1
Building and grounds cleaning and maintenance	100.0	31.5	42.7	18.9	7.0
Personal care and services	100.0	10.5	36.8	34.0	18.7
Sales and office	100.0	4.5	31.0	37.2	27.3
Sales and related	100.0	5.8	29.4	31.4	33.4
Office and administrative support	100.0	3.5	32.2	41.5	22.8
Natural resources, construction, and maintenance	100.0	19.9	44.1	27.8	8.2
Farming, fishing, and forestry	100.0	49.2	33.2	10.9	6.7
Construction and extraction	100.0	22.2	46.3	24.0	7.5
Installation, maintenance, and repair	100.0	10.1	42.9	37.4	9.7
Production, transportation, and material moving	100.0	18.0	47.3	25.6	9.2
Production	100.0	17.8	47.5	25.1	9.5
Transportation and material moving	100.0	18.1	47.0	26.1	8.8
Armed forces	100.0	0.3	20.2	44.8	34.7
Men	100.0	9.8	29.4	26.1	34.7
Management, business, and financial operations	100.0	2.2	15.5	22.2	60.0
Management	100.0	2.7	17.8	24.2	55.3
Business and financial operations	100.0	0.9	7.9	16.0	75.2
Professional and related	100.0	0.5	6.2	18.0	75.3
Computer and mathematical	100.0	0.4	6.2	22.4	71.0
Architecture and engineering	100.0	. . .	8.3	24.0	67.7
Life, physical, and social sciences	100.0	0.2	6.5	12.1	81.1
Community and social services	100.0	1.9	7.3	15.0	75.8
Legal	100.0	. . .	1.0	2.7	96.3
Education, training, and library	100.0	0.1	2.6	8.2	89.1
Arts, design, entertainment, sports, and media	100.0	1.8	12.3	24.0	61.8
Health care practitioner and technical	100.0	0.6	4.3	20.2	75.0
Services	100.0	17.1	36.8	30.0	16.1
Health care support	100.0	4.8	31.3	44.7	19.2
Protective services	100.0	1.8	26.4	43.6	28.2
Food preparation and serving related	100.0	24.2	39.0	25.0	11.8
Building and grounds cleaning and maintenance	100.0	27.7	44.0	21.0	7.4
Personal care and services	100.0	5.9	36.2	33.0	24.9
Sales and office	100.0	4.2	27.9	32.9	34.9
Sales and related	100.0	3.5	26.4	30.6	39.5
Office and administrative support	100.0	5.4	30.5	36.7	27.5
Natural resources, construction, and maintenance	100.0	19.5	44.7	28.0	7.8
Farming, fishing, and forestry	100.0	47.3	35.8	10.5	6.5
Construction and extraction	100.0	22.3	46.5	24.1	7.0
Installation, maintenance, and repair	100.0	10.2	43.1	37.5	9.2
Production, transportation, and material moving	100.0	17.0	47.6	26.3	9.1
Production	100.0	15.5	48.2	27.1	9.2
Transportation and material moving	100.0	18.2	47.1	25.6	9.0
Armed forces	100.0	0.4	22.4	44.7	32.6
Women	100.0	6.6	24.9	30.2	38.2
Management, business, and financial operations	100.0	1.4	15.9	25.1	57.6
Management	100.0	2.0	17.5	25.1	55.4
Business and financial operations	100.0	0.5	13.2	25.1	61.2
Professional and related	100.0	0.6	8.0	23.5	67.9
Computer and mathematical	100.0	0.8	9.7	22.2	67.4
Architecture and engineering	100.0	. . .	10.2	14.6	75.3
Life, physical, and social sciences	100.0	. . .	2.1	7.0	90.9
Community and social services	100.0	1.1	9.7	18.8	70.5
Legal	100.0	0.8	9.2	27.5	62.5
Education, training, and library	100.0	0.4	8.1	14.7	76.8
Arts, design, entertainment, sports, and media	100.0	1.6	11.3	21.9	65.1
Health care practitioner and technical	100.0	0.6	6.8	35.8	56.8
Services	100.0	16.8	37.7	32.3	13.2
Health care support	100.0	8.6	34.1	46.4	10.9
Protective services	100.0	5.7	28.4	35.1	30.8
Food preparation and serving related	100.0	18.1	41.4	28.2	12.3
Building and grounds cleaning and maintenance	100.0	36.6	40.9	16.0	6.5
Personal care and services	100.0	11.7	36.9	34.2	17.2
Sales and office	100.0	4.7	32.8	39.6	22.9
Sales and related	100.0	8.4	32.8	32.4	26.5
Office and administrative support	100.0	2.9	32.8	43.1	21.2
Natural resources, construction, and maintenance	100.0	28.5	32.0	21.6	18.0
Farming, fishing, and forestry	100.0	55.8	24.4	12.3	7.6
Construction and extraction	100.0	16.4	35.8	19.9	27.9
Installation, maintenance, and repair	100.0	6.2	37.6	34.7	21.4
Production, transportation, and material moving	100.0	21.1	46.3	23.3	9.3
Production	100.0	23.2	46.0	20.7	10.1
Transportation and material moving	100.0	17.4	46.7	28.1	7.8
Armed forces	100.0	. . .	2.4	45.4	52.2

. . . = Not available.

Table 1-61. Median Annual Earnings of Year-Round, Full-Time Wage and Salary Workers Age 25 to 64 Years, by Educational Attainment and Sex, 2000–2011

(Thousands of workers, dollars.)

Year and sex	Total	Less than a high school diploma	4 years of high school only	1 to 3 years of college	4 or more years of college
2000					
Both Sexes					
Number of workers	84 337	7 354	26 144	24 064	26 775
Median annual earnings	35 000	20 000	28 600	34 000	50 000
Men					
Number of workers	48 816	4 738	15 057	13 242	15 780
Median annual earnings	40 000	22 500	33 000	40 000	60 000
Women					
Number of workers	35 521	2 616	11 087	10 822	10 995
Median annual earnings	29 000	16 000	24 000	28 000	40 000
2001					
Both Sexes					
Number of workers	84 743	7 623	25 522	23 719	27 879
Median annual earnings	35 000	20 800	29 000	35 000	50 000
Men					
Number of workers	48 887	5 049	14 655	12 968	16 215
Median annual earnings	40 000	24 000	33 800	40 000	60 000
Women					
Number of workers	35 856	2 574	10 867	10 751	11 664
Median annual earnings	30 000	17 000	24 000	30 000	42 000
2002					
Both Sexes					
Number of workers	84 702	7 578	25 078	23 604	28 443
Median annual earnings	36 000	21 000	30 000	35 100	52 000
Men					
Number of workers	48 687	5 102	14 306	12 677	16 602
Median annual earnings	41 000	23 400	34 000	41 500	61 000
Women					
Number of workers	36 015	2 476	10 772	10 927	11 841
Median annual earnings	30 000	18 000	25 000	30 000	43 500
2003					
Both Sexes					
Number of workers	85 058	7 245	25 352	23 702	28 759
Median annual earnings	37 752	21 000	30 000	36 000	53 000
Men					
Number of workers	48 988	4 879	14 657	12 766	16 686
Median annual earnings	42 000	24 000	35 000	42 000	62 000
Women					
Number of workers	36 070	2 366	10 695	10 936	12 073
Median annual earnings	32 000	18 000	25 111	31 000	45 000
2004					
Both Sexes					
Number of workers	86 306	7 648	25 786	23 897	28 976
Median annual earnings	38 000	21 840	30 000	37 000	55 000
Men					
Number of workers	49 904	5 178	15 263	12 822	16 642
Median annual earnings	42 900	24 000	35 000	43 000	65 000
Women					
Number of workers	36 402	2 470	10 523	11 074	12 334
Median annual earnings	32 000	18 000	25 280	31 200	45 000
2005					
Both Sexes					
Number of workers	88 415	7 758	26 023	24 623	30 012
Median annual earnings	39 768	22 880	31 000	38 000	55 000
Men					
Number of workers	51 022	5 376	15 451	13 199	16 996
Median annual earnings	44 000	25 000	35 360	45 000	65 000
Women					
Number of workers	37 393	2 381	10 571	11 424	13 016
Median annual earnings	33 644	18 200	26 000	32 000	46 700

Table 1-61. Median Annual Earnings of Year-Round, Full-Time Wage and Salary Workers Age 25 to 64 Years, by Educational Attainment and Sex, 2000–2011—*Continued*

(Thousands of workers, dollars.)

Year and sex	Total	Less than a high school diploma	4 years of high school only	1 to 3 years of college	4 or more years of college
2006					
Both Sexes					
Number of workers	90 733	7 951	26 233	24 737	31 812
Median annual earnings	40 000	23 000	32 000	39 482	57 588
Men					
Number of workers	52 252	5 485	15 525	13 204	18 038
Median annual earnings	45 000	25 000	36 665	45 000	68 000
Women					
Number of workers	38 481	2 466	10 708	11 533	13 774
Median annual earnings	35 000	19 000	26 800	33 000	49 000
2007					
Both Sexes					
Number of workers	91 540	7 123	25 925	25 574	32 918
Median annual earnings	41 000	24 000	33 000	40 000	60 000
Men					
Number of workers	52 262	4 902	15 390	13 655	18 316
Median annual earnings	47 000	25 000	38 000	45 188	70 000
Women					
Number of workers	39 277	2 221	10 535	11 919	14 603
Median annual earnings	35 000	19 200	27 120	35 000	50 000
2008					
Both Sexes					
Number of workers	88 373	6 600	24 531	24 887	32 355
Median annual earnings	42 000	24 000	34 000	40 000	60 000
Men					
Number of workers	50 141	4 503	14 480	13 283	17 876
Median annual earnings	49 564	27 000	39 040	47 000	72 000
Women					
Number of workers	38 231	2 097	10 051	11 604	14 479
Median annual earnings	36 000	19 567	28 000	35 000	50 000
2009					
Both Sexes					
Number of workers	84 730	5 847	23 277	23 515	32 091
Median annual earnings	43 000	24 000	34 320	40 000	60 000
Men					
Number of workers	47 135	3 809	13 620	12 283	17 424
Median annual earnings	50 000	26 000	40 000	49 000	71 000
Women					
Number of workers	37 595	2 037	9 657	11 233	14 667
Median annual earnings	38 000	20 000	29 000	35 000	52 000
2010					
Both Sexes					
Number of workers	84 902	5 548	22 768	23 725	32 861
Median annual earnings	44 217	24 000	35 000	40 000	60 000
Men					
Number of workers	47 549	3 653	13 526	12 405	17 965
Median annual earnings	50 000	26 500	40 000	48 000	72 000
Women					
Number of workers	37 353	1 895	9 241	11 321	14 896
Median annual earnings	38 000	20 000	30 000	35 000	51 000
2011					
Both Sexes					
Number of workers	86 570	5 858	22 921	23 947	33 843
Median annual earnings	45 000	25 000	35 000	41 000	62 000
Men					
Number of workers	48 748	3 971	13 750	12 705	18 322
Median annual earnings	50 000	27 819	40 000	50 000	75 000
Women					
Number of workers	37 822	1 887	9 171	11 243	15 521
Median annual earnings	39 000	20 000	30 000	35 000	52 000

Table 1-62.   Employment Status of the Civilian Noninstitutional Population by Disability Status and Selected Characteristics, 2011 Annual Averages

(Thousands of people, percent.)

Characteristic	Civilian noninstitutional population	Civilian labor force						Not in labor force
		Total	Participation rate	Employed		Unemployed		
				Total	Percent	Total	Rate	
TOTAL								
Total, 16 Years and Over	239 618	153 617	64.1	139 869	58.4	13 747	8.9	86 001
Men	116 317	81 975	70.5	74 290	63.9	7 684	9.4	34 343
Women	123 300	71 642	58.1	65 579	53.2	6 063	8.5	51 658
PERSONS WITH A DISABILITY	27 382	5 722	20.9	4 861	17.8	861	15.0	21 659
Sex								
Men	12 633	3 152	24.9	2 670	21.1	482	15.3	9 481
Women	14 749	2 571	17.4	2 192	14.9	379	14.7	12 178
Age								
16 to 64 years	15 047	4 854	32.3	4 067	27.0	787	16.2	10 192
16 to 19 years	589	124	21.0	71	12.1	53	42.4	465
20 to 24 years	726	302	41.6	220	30.3	82	27.1	424
25 to 34 years	1 697	740	43.6	579	34.1	161	21.7	958
35 to 44 years	2 167	793	36.6	661	30.5	133	16.7	1 374
45 to 54 years	4 212	1 359	32.3	1 167	27.7	193	14.2	2 853
55 to 64 years	5 656	1 536	27.2	1 370	24.2	167	10.8	4 119
65 years and over	12 335	868	7.0	794	6.4	74	8.5	11 467
Race and Hispanic Origin								
White	22 386	4 779	21.3	4 122	18.4	657	13.7	17 607
Black or African American	3 494	604	17.3	462	13.2	142	23.5	2 889
Asian	657	134	20.5	120	18.2	15	11.0	523
Hispanic[1]	2 527	517	20.5	412	16.3	105	20.3	2 010
Educational Attainment								
Total, 25 years and over	26 067	5 297	20.3	4 570	17.5	727	13.7	20 770
Less than a high school diploma	6 081	623	10.2	493	8.1	130	20.8	5 458
High school graduates, no college[2]	9 603	1 695	17.6	1 465	15.3	229	13.5	7 909
Some college or associate degree	6 312	1 656	26.2	1 408	22.3	248	15.0	4 656
Bachelor's degree and higher[3]	4 070	1 323	32.5	1 203	29.6	120	9.1	2 747

[1]May be of any race.
[2]Includes persons with a high school diploma or equivalent.
[3]Includes persons with bachelor's, master's, professional, and doctoral degrees.

Table 1-63.   Employed Full- and Part-Time Workers by Disability Status and Age, 2011 Annual Averages

(Thousands of people.)

Disability status and age	Employed			At work part-time for economic reasons[1]
	Total	Usually work full-time	Usually work part-time	
TOTAL				
Total, 16 Years and Over	139 869	112 556	27 313	8 560
16 to 64 years	133 222	108 671	24 551	8 302
65 years and over	6 647	3 885	2 762	258
Persons With a Disability				
16 years and over	4 861	3 259	1 602	370
16 to 64 years	4 067	2 887	1 180	335
65 years and over	794	372	422	35
Persons Without a Disability				
16 years and over	135 008	109 297	25 711	8 191
16 to 64 years	129 155	105 784	23 371	7 967
65 years and over	5 853	3 513	2 340	224

Note: Full time refers to persons who usually work 35 hours or more per week; part time refers to persons who usually work less than 35 hours per week.

[1]Refers to persons who, whether they usually work full or part time, worked 1 to 34 hours during the reference week for an economic reason such as slack work or unfavorable business conditions, inability to find full-time work, or seasonal declines in demand.

Table 1-64. Employed Persons by Disability Status, Occupation, and Sex, 2011 Annual Averages

(Number in thousands, percent.)

Occupation	Persons with a disability			Persons with no disability		
	Total	Men	Women	Total	Men	Women
TOTAL EMPLOYED	4 861	2 670	2 192	135 008	71 621	63 387
Occupation as a Percent of Total Employed						
Total	100.0	100.0	100.0	100.0	100.0	100.0
Management, professional, and related	31.7	30.2	33.4	37.8	34.5	41.4
Management, business, and financial operations	13.8	16.1	10.9	15.5	16.5	14.3
Management	9.9	12.5	6.8	10.9	12.7	8.9
Business and financial operations	3.9	3.7	4.1	4.6	3.8	5.4
Professional and related	17.9	14.1	22.4	22.3	18.0	27.1
Computer and mathematical	1.7	2.4	0.8	2.6	3.7	1.4
Architecture and engineering	1.5	2.3	0.4	2.0	3.3	0.6
Life, physical, and social science	0.9	0.7	1.0	0.9	0.9	0.9
Community and social services	1.8	1.2	2.5	1.7	1.1	2.3
Legal	1.3	1.3	1.2	1.3	1.2	1.3
Education, training, and library	5.3	2.8	8.3	6.2	3.1	9.7
Arts, design, entertainment, sports, and media	2.0	1.8	2.3	2.0	2.0	1.9
Healthcare practitioner and technical	3.5	1.6	5.9	5.6	2.7	8.9
Service	19.2	15.8	23.4	17.7	14.7	21.1
Healthcare support	2	1	4	2	1	4
Protective service	2.0	2.9	0.8	2.3	3.4	1.0
Food preparation and serving related	4.8	3.6	6.2	5.6	4.8	6.4
Building and grounds cleaning and maintenance	5.9	6.8	4.7	3.9	4.4	3.2
Personal care and service	4.4	1.9	7.4	3.5	1.4	5.9
Sales and office	24.6	16.3	34.7	23.6	16.8	31.3
Sales and related	10.8	9.6	12.2	11.0	10.4	11.6
Office and administrative support	13.8	6.7	22.5	12.6	6.3	19.8
Natural resources, construction, and maintenance	10.2	17.7	1.1	9.3	16.7	0.8
Farming, fishing, and forestry	0.8	1.2	0.4	0.7	1.1	0.3
Construction and extraction	5.2	9.3	0.3	5.1	9.4	0.2
Installation, maintenance, and repair	4.2	7.3	0.5	3.5	6.3	0.3
Production, transportation, and material moving	14.3	20.0	7.4	11.7	17.3	5.4
Production	7.1	9.1	4.6	5.8	7.8	3.5
Transportation and material moving	7.2	10.9	2.8	5.9	9.5	1.9

Table 1-65. Persons Not in the Labor Force by Disability Status, Age, and Sex, 2011 Annual Averages

(Thousands of people, percent distribution.)

Category	Total, 16 years and over	16 to 64 years			Total, 65 years and over
		Total	Men	Women	
Persons With a Disability					
Total not in the labor force	21 659	10 192	4 887	5 305	11 467
Persons who currently want a job	662	477	238	240	184
Marginally attached to the labor force[1]	235	198	106	92	37
Discouraged workers[2]	74	58	34	24	16
Other persons marginally attached to the labor force[3]	161	140	72	68	21
Persons Without a Disability					
Total not in the labor force	64 342	43 192	15 972	27 220	21 150
Persons who currently want a job	5 775	5 224	2 447	2 776	552
Marginally attached to the labor force[1]	2 338	2 178	1 135	1 043	160
Discouraged workers[2]	915	840	494	346	75
Other persons marginally attached to the labor force[3]	1 423	1 338	641	697	85

[1]Data refer to persons who want a job, have searched for work during the prior 12 months, and were available to take a job during the reference week, but had not looked for work in the past 4 weeks.
[2]Includes those who did not actively look for work in the prior 4 weeks for reasons such as thinks no work available, could not find work, lacks schooling or training, employer thinks too young or old, and other types of discrimination.
[3]Includes those who did not actively look for work in the prior 4 weeks for such reasons as school or family responsibilities, ill health, and transportation problems, as well as a number for whom reason for nonparticipation was not determined.

Table 1-66. Employment Status of Persons 18 Years and Over by Veteran Status, Period of Service, Sex, Race, and Hispanic or Latino Ethnicity, 2011 Annual Averages

(Thousands of people, percent.)

Characteristic	Civilian noninstitutional population	Civilian labor force							Not in labor force
		Total	Percent of population	Employed		Unemployed			
				Total	Percent of population	Total	Percent of labor force		

Characteristic	Civilian noninstitutional population	Total	Percent of population	Total	Percent of population	Total	Percent of labor force	Not in labor force
TOTAL								
Total, 18 Years and Over	230 891	151 743	65.7	138 515	60.0	13 229	8.7	79 147
Veterans	21 613	11 320	52.4	10 375	48.0	945	8.3	10 293
Gulf War era, total	5 323	4 397	82.6	3 992	75.0	405	9.2	925
Gulf War era II	2 387	1 937	81.2	1 704	71.4	234	12.1	450
Gulf War era I	2 936	2 460	83.8	2 289	78.0	172	7.0	476
WW II, Korean War, and Vietnam era	10 436	3 549	34.0	3 280	31.4	269	7.6	6 887
Other service periods	5 853	3 374	57.6	3 102	53.0	271	8.0	2 480
Nonveterans	209 278	140 424	67.1	128 140	61.2	12 284	8.7	68 854
MEN								
Total, 18 Years and Over	111 831	81 058	72.5	73 641	65.8	7 417	9.2	30 773
Veterans	19 812	10 204	51.5	9 360	47.2	844	8.3	9 608
Gulf War era, total	4 457	3 777	84.7	3 428	76.9	349	9.2	680
Gulf War era II	1 982	1 656	83.5	1 457	73.5	199	12.0	327
Gulf War era I	2 475	2 121	85.7	1 971	79.6	150	7.1	353
WW II, Korean War, and Vietnam era	10 106	3 441	34.0	3 181	31.5	260	7.6	6 665
Other service periods	5 248	2 986	56.9	2 751	52.4	235	7.9	2 262
Nonveterans	92 019	70 854	77.0	64 280	69.9	6 573	9.3	21 166
WOMEN								
Total, 18 Years and Over	119 060	70 685	59.4	64 874	54.5	5 811	8.2	48 374
Veterans	1 801	1 116	62.0	1 015	56.3	101	9.1	685
Gulf War era, total	865	620	71.7	564	65.2	56	9.1	245
Gulf War era II	405	281	69.5	246	60.9	35	12.4	123
Gulf War era I	461	339	73.5	318	68.9	21	6.3	122
WW II, Korean War, and Vietnam era	330	108	32.7	99	30.1	9	7.9	222
Other service periods	605	388	64.1	351	58.1	36	9.4	217
Nonveterans	117 259	69 570	59.3	63 859	54.5	5 710	8.2	47 689
WHITE								
Total, 18 Years and Over	186 403	122 998	66.0	113 501	60.9	9 497	7.7	63 405
Veterans	18 463	9 449	51.2	8 709	47.2	740	7.8	9 014
Gulf War era, total	4 176	3 498	83.8	3 199	76.6	299	8.5	678
Gulf War era II	1 865	1 531	82.1	1 357	72.7	174	11.4	335
Gulf War era I	2 310	1 967	85.1	1 842	79.7	125	6.3	343
WW II, Korean War, and Vietnam era	9 365	3 176	33.9	2 941	31.4	235	7.4	6 189
Other service periods	4 923	2 775	56.4	2 568	52.2	207	7.4	2 147
Nonveterans	167 941	113 550	67.6	104 792	62.4	8 757	7.7	54 391
BLACK								
Total, 18 Years and Over	27 799	17 732	63.8	14 988	53.9	2 743	15.5	10 068
Veterans	2 349	1 389	59.1	1 233	52.5	156	11.2	960
Gulf War era, total	855	676	79.0	595	69.6	81	11.9	180
Gulf War era II	394	316	80.1	271	68.7	45	14.3	78
Gulf War era I	462	360	78.0	325	70.3	35	9.8	101
WW II, Korean War, and Vietnam era	782	254	32.5	229	29.3	25	9.9	528
Other service periods	712	459	64.5	409	57.5	50	10.9	253
Nonveterans	25 450	16 343	64.2	13 755	54.0	2 588	15.8	9 107
ASIAN								
Total, 18 Years and Over	11 066	7 303	66.0	6 796	61.4	507	6.9	3 763
Veterans	262	154	58.9	147	56.1	7	4.8	108
Gulf War era, total	94	75	80.2	72	76.3	4	4.9	19
Gulf War era II	47	35	75.4	33	70.0	3	7.1	12
Gulf War era I	47	40	85.1	39	82.6	1	(¹)	7
WW II, Korean War, and Vietnam era	111	40	35.8	39	35.0	1	2.1	72
Other service periods	57	39	68.8	36	63.9	3	7.2	18
Nonveterans	10 804	7 149	66.2	6 650	61.5	499	7.0	3 656
HISPANIC¹								
Total, 18 Years and Over	32 570	22 572	69.3	20 048	61.6	2 524	11.2	9 999
Veterans	1 259	847	67.2	764	60.6	83	9.8	413
Gulf War era, total	547	464	84.7	406	74.2	57	12.4	84
Gulf War era II	287	239	83.4	199	69.3	41	17.0	48
Gulf War era I	260	224	86.2	207	79.7	17	7.5	36
WW II, Korean War, and Vietnam era	384	148	38.6	138	36.0	10	6.6	236
Other service periods	328	235	71.6	219	66.8	16	6.7	93
Nonveterans	31 311	21 725	69.4	19 284	61.6	2 441	11.2	9 586

Note: Veterans are men and women who served in the U.S. Armed Forces during World War II, the Korean War, the Vietnam era, the Gulf War era, and all other service periods. Nonveterans are men and women who never served in the U.S. Armed Forces. Other service periods include the periods between World War II and the Korean War, between the Korean War and the Vietnam era, and between the Vietnam era and the Gulf War era. Estimates for the above race groups (White, Black, and Asian) do not sum to totals because data are not presented for all races.

¹May be of any race.

Table 1-67. Employment Status of Persons 18 Years and Over by Veteran Status, Age, Period of Service, and Sex, 2011 Annual Averages

(Thousands of people, percent.)

Veteran status, age, period of service, and sex	Civilian noninstitutional population	Civilian labor force						Not in labor force
		Total	Percent of population	Employed		Unemployed		
				Total	Percent of population	Total	Percent of labor force	
TOTAL VETERANS								
Total, 18 years and over	21 613	11 320	52.4	10 375	48.0	945	8.3	10 293
18 to 24 years	299	213	71.4	149	49.8	64	30.2	85
25 to 34 years	1 590	1 318	82.9	1 160	73.0	158	12.0	272
35 to 44 years	2 364	2 090	88.4	1 940	82.1	150	7.2	274
45 to 54 years	3 636	2 989	82.2	2 761	75.9	228	7.6	647
55 to 64 years	5 084	2 976	58.5	2 747	54.0	229	7.7	2 108
65 years and over	8 640	1 733	20.1	1 618	18.7	115	6.7	6 907
Gulf War Era, Total								
Total, 18 years and over	5 323	4 397	82.6	3 992	75.0	405	9.2	925
18 to 24 years	299	213	71.4	149	49.8	64	30.2	85
25 to 34 years	1 590	1 318	82.9	1 160	73.0	158	12.0	272
35 to 44 years	1 874	1 665	88.8	1 546	82.5	119	7.1	209
45 to 54 years	1 025	871	85.0	826	80.5	45	5.2	154
55 to 64 years	436	298	68.3	281	64.4	17	5.7	138
65 years and over	99	33	33.1	30	30.7	2	. . .	66
Gulf War Era II								
Total, 18 years and over	2 387	1 937	81.2	1 704	71.4	234	12.1	450
18 to 24 years	299	213	71.4	149	49.8	64	30.2	85
25 to 34 years	1 218	1 000	82.1	870	71.4	130	13.0	218
35 to 44 years	412	358	86.9	337	81.7	22	6.0	54
45 to 54 years	339	287	84.6	275	81.2	12	4.1	52
55 to 64 years	103	71	69.3	66	63.9	6	7.8	32
65 years and over	16	7	. . .	7	. . .	0	. . .	8
Gulf War Era I								
Total, 25 years and over	2 936	2 460	83.8	2 289	78.0	172	7.0	476
25 to 34 years	372	318	85.6	290	78.1	28	8.7	54
35 to 44 years	1 462	1 306	89.4	1 209	82.7	97	7.4	155
45 to 54 years	686	584	85.1	551	80.2	33	5.7	102
55 to 64 years	333	226	68.0	215	64.6	11	5.0	106
65 years and over	83	25	30.5	24	28.3	2	. . .	58
World War II, Korean War, Vietnam War								
Total, 45 years and over	10 436	3 549	34.0	3 280	31.4	269	7.6	6 887
45 to 54 years	86	60	70.2	54	62.3	7	11.3	26
55 to 64 years	4 032	2 258	56.0	2 077	51.5	180	8.0	1 774
65 years and over	6 319	1 231	19.5	1 149	18.2	81	6.6	5 088
Other Service Periods								
Total, 35 years and over	5 853	3 374	57.6	3 102	53.0	271	8.0	2 480
35 to 44 years	490	426	86.9	395	80.5	31	7.3	64
45 to 54 years	2 525	2 058	81.5	1 882	74.5	176	8.6	467
55 to 64 years	616	420	68.2	388	63.0	32	7.6	196
65 years and over	2 222	470	21.1	438	19.7	32	6.7	1 753
Total Nonveterans								
Total, 18 years and over	209 278	140 424	67.1	128 140	61.2	12 284	8.7	68 854
18 to 24 years	29 172	18 910	64.8	15 859	54.4	3 051	16.1	10 262
25 to 34 years	39 774	32 406	81.5	29 377	73.9	3 030	9.3	7 367
35 to 44 years	37 135	30 569	82.3	28 330	76.3	2 239	7.3	6 565
45 to 54 years	40 209	32 373	80.5	30 106	74.9	2 267	7.0	7 836
55 to 64 years	31 905	20 791	65.2	19 439	60.9	1 352	6.5	11 114
65 years and over	31 084	5 374	17.3	5 029	16.2	345	6.4	25 710

Note: Veterans are men and women who served in the U.S. Armed Forces during World War II, the Korean War, the Vietnam era, the Gulf War era, and all other service periods. Nonveterans are men and women who never served in the U.S. Armed Forces. Other service periods include the periods between World War II and the Korean War, between the Korean War and the Vietnam era, and between the Vietnam era and the Gulf War era.

. . . = Not available.

Table 1-67. Employment Status of Persons 18 Years and Over by Veteran Status, Age, Period of Service, and Sex, 2011 Annual Averages—*Continued*

(Thousands of people, percent.)

Veteran status, age, period of service, and sex	Civilian noninstitutional population	Civilian labor force						Not in labor force
		Total	Percent of population	Employed		Unemployed		
				Total	Percent of population	Total	Percent of labor force	
Veterans, Men								
Total, 18 years and over	19 812	10 204	51.5	9 360	47.2	844	8.3	9 608
18 to 24 years	250	179	71.6	127	50.8	52	29.1	71
25 to 34 years	1 322	1 136	86.0	996	75.3	141	12.4	186
35 to 44 years	1 985	1 786	89.9	1 661	83.7	125	7.0	200
45 to 54 years	3 146	2 621	83.3	2 424	77.1	196	7.5	525
55 to 64 years	4 749	2 786	58.7	2 569	54.1	217	7.8	1 963
65 years and over	8 360	1 697	20.3	1 583	18.9	113	6.7	6 663
Gulf War Era, Total								
Total, 18 years and over	4 457	3 777	84.7	3 428	76.9	349	9.2	680
18 to 24 years	250	179	71.6	127	50.8	52	29.1	71
25 to 34 years	1 322	1 136	86.0	996	75.3	141	12.4	186
35 to 44 years	1 568	1 416	90.3	1 315	83.9	100	7.1	152
45 to 54 years	872	761	87.2	722	82.8	38	5.0	112
55 to 64 years	356	255	71.6	239	67.2	15	6.0	101
65 years and over	89	30	34.2	28	31.7	2	. . .	59
Gulf War Era II								
Total, 18 years and over	1 982	1 656	83.5	1 457	73.5	199	12.0	327
18 to 24 years	250	179	71.6	127	50.8	52	29.1	71
25 to 34 years	1 012	864	85.3	748	73.9	115	13.4	148
35 to 44 years	329	290	88.1	273	82.7	18	6.1	39
45 to 54 years	290	254	87.6	245	84.6	9	3.4	36
55 to 64 years	85	62	72.3	57	67.0	5	7.4	24
65 years and over	15	7	. . .	6	. . .	0	. . .	8
Gulf War Era I								
Total, 25 years and over	2 475	2 121	85.7	1 971	79.6	150	7.1	353
25 to 34 years	310	273	88.0	247	79.8	25	9.3	37
35 to 44 years	1 238	1 126	90.9	1 043	84.2	83	7.4	113
45 to 54 years	582	507	87.0	477	81.9	30	5.9	76
55 to 64 years	271	193	71.3	182	67.3	11	5.6	78
65 years and over	74	23	31.8	22	29.4	2	. . .	50
World War II, Korean War, and Vietnam War								
Total, 45 years and over	10 106	3 441	34.0	3 181	31.5	260	7.6	6 665
45 to 54 years	83	57	69.5	51	61.2	7	11.9	25
55 to 64 years	3 877	2 171	56.0	1 997	51.5	173	8.0	1 707
65 years and over	6 146	1 213	19.7	1 133	18.4	80	6.6	4 933
Other Service Periods								
Total, 35 years and over	5 248	2 986	56.9	2 751	52.4	235	7.9	2 262
35 to 44 years	417	370	88.6	346	82.8	24	6.5	48
45 to 54 years	2 191	1 802	82.3	1 651	75.4	151	8.4	388
55 to 64 years	515	360	70.0	332	64.5	29	7.9	155
65 years and over	2 125	453	21.3	422	19.9	31	6.9	1 672
Nonveterans, Men								
Total, 18 years and over	92 019	70 854	77.0	64 280	69.9	6 573	9.3	21 166
18 to 24 years	14 689	9 900	67.4	8 158	55.5	1 742	17.6	4 789
25 to 34 years	19 388	17 333	89.4	15 678	80.9	1 654	9.5	2 056
35 to 44 years	17 461	15 900	91.1	14 709	84.2	1 191	7.5	1 560
45 to 54 years	18 308	15 865	86.7	14 689	80.2	1 176	7.4	2 443
55 to 64 years	13 064	9 567	73.2	8 900	68.1	667	7.0	3 497
65 years and over	9 109	2 289	25.1	2 147	23.6	143	6.2	6 820

Note: Veterans are men and women who served in the U.S. Armed Forces during World War II, the Korean War, the Vietnam era, the Gulf War era, and all other service periods. Nonveterans are men and women who never served in the U.S. Armed Forces. Other service periods include the periods between World War II and the Korean War, between the Korean War and the Vietnam era, and between the Vietnam era and the Gulf War era.

. . . = Not available.

Table 1-67.   Employment Status of Persons 18 Years and Over by Veteran Status, Age, Period of Service, and Sex, 2011 Annual Averages—*Continued*

(Thousands of people, percent.)

Veteran status, age, period of service, and sex	Civilian noninstitutional population	Civilian labor force						Not in labor force
		Total	Percent of population	Employed		Unemployed		
				Total	Percent of population	Total	Percent of labor force	
Veterans, Women								
Total, 18 years and over	1 801	1 116	62.0	1 015	56.3	101	9.1	685
18 to 24 years	49	35	70.4	22	45.0	12	36.1	15
25 to 34 years	268	182	67.8	165	61.5	17	9.2	86
35 to 44 years	379	305	80.5	279	73.7	26	8.4	74
45 to 54 years	490	369	75.2	337	68.7	32	8.7	122
55 to 64 years	335	190	56.6	178	53.0	12	6.4	146
65 years and over	280	37	13.1	35	12.3	2	5.7	243
Gulf Era, Total								
Total, 18 years and over	865	620	71.7	564	65.2	56	9.1	245
18 to 24 years	49	35	70.4	22	45.0	12	36.1	15
25 to 34 years	268	182	67.8	165	61.5	17	9.2	86
35 to 44 years	306	249	81.2	230	75.2	18	7.4	57
45 to 54 years	153	110	72.1	103	67.6	7	6.2	43
55 to 64 years	80	43	53.9	41	51.9	2	3.6	37
65 years and over	10	2	. . .	2	. . .	0	. . .	8
Gulf Era II								
Total, 18 years and over	405	281	69.5	246	60.9	35	12.4	123
18 to 24 years	49	35	70.4	22	45.0	12	36.1	15
25 to 34 years	206	136	66.1	122	59.0	14	10.6	70
35 to 44 years	83	68	82.2	64	77.4	4	5.9	15
45 to 54 years	49	33	66.9	30	60.6	3	. . .	16
55 to 64 years	18	10	. . .	9	. . .	1	. . .	8
65 years and over	0	0	. . .	0	. . .	0	. . .	0
Gulf Era I								
Total, 25 Years and over	461	339	73.5	318	68.9	21	6.3	122
25 to 34 years	62	45	73.5	43	69.7	2	5.1	16
35 to 44 years	223	181	80.9	166	74.4	14	8.0	43
45 to 54 years	104	77	74.5	74	70.9	4	4.9	26
55 to 64 years	62	33	53.6	33	52.8	1	. . .	29
65 years and over	10	2	. . .	2	. . .	0	. . .	8
World War II, Korean War, and Vietnam Era								
Total, 45 years and over	330	108	32.7	99	30.1	9	7.9	222
45 to 54 years	3	3	. . .	3	. . .	0	. . .	0
55 to 64 years	154	87	56.3	80	51.8	7	8.0	67
65 years and over	173	18	10.5	17	9.6	2	. . .	155
Other Service Periods								
Total, 35 years and over	605	388	64.1	351	58.1	36	9.4	217
35 to 44 years	73	56	77.2	49	67.4	7	12.7	17
45 to 54 years	334	255	76.5	230	69.0	25	9.9	78
55 to 64 years	101	60	59.2	56	55.7	4	5.9	41
65 years and over	97	16	16.7	16	16.3	0	. . .	81
Nonveterans, Women								
Total, 18 years and over	117 259	69 570	59.3	63 859	54.5	5 710	8.2	47 689
18 to 24 years	14 483	9 010	62.2	7 701	53.2	1 309	14.5	5 473
25 to 34 years	20 385	15 074	73.9	13 699	67.2	1 375	9.1	5 311
35 to 44 years	19 674	14 669	74.6	13 621	69.2	1 047	7.1	5 005
45 to 54 years	21 901	16 508	75.4	15 417	70.4	1 091	6.6	5 393
55 to 64 years	18 841	11 224	59.6	10 539	55.9	685	6.1	7 617
65 years and over	21 975	3 085	14.0	2 883	13.1	202	6.6	18 890

Note: Veterans are men and women who served in the U.S. Armed Forces during World War II, the Korean War, the Vietnam era, the Gulf War era, and all other service periods. Nonveterans are men and women who never served in the U.S. Armed Forces. Other service periods include the periods between World War II and the Korean War, between the Korean War and the Vietnam era, and between the Vietnam era and the Gulf War era.

. . . = Not available.

Table 1-68. Employment Status of Gulf War Era Veterans by Reserve or National Guard Status, August 2011, Not Seasonally Adjusted

(Thousands of people, percent.)

Reserve or National Guard status	Civilian noninstitutional population	Civilian labor force							Not in labor force
		Total	Percent of population	Employed		Unemployed			
				Total	Percent of population	Total	Percent of labor force		
GULF WAR ERA									
Total	5 399	4 445	82.3	4 071	75.4	374	8.4		954
Current or past member of Reserve or National Guard	1 587	1 356	85.4	1 246	78.5	110	8.1		231
Never a member of Reserve or National Guard	2 842	2 313	81.4	2 113	74.4	200	8.6		529
Reserve or National Guard membership not reported	970	776	80.0	712	73.4	64	8.2		194
GULF WAR ERA II									
Total	2 394	1 951	81.5	1 759	73.5	192	9.8		443
Current or past member of Reserve or National Guard	724	630	87.1	573	79.2	57	9.1		93
Never a member of Reserve or National Guard	1 286	1 018	79.2	906	70.5	112	11.0		268
Reserve or National Guard membership not reported	383	302	78.8	279	72.9	22	7.5		81
GULF WAR ERA I									
Total	3 006	2 494	83.0	2 312	76.9	182	7.3		512
Current or past member of Reserve or National Guard	864	726	84.0	673	77.9	53	7.2		138
Never a member of Reserve or National Guard	1 555	1 294	83.2	1 206	77.6	88	6.8		261
Reserve or National Guard membership not reported	587	474	80.8	432	73.7	41	8.7		113

Note: Veterans are men and women who served in the U.S. Armed Forces during World War II, the Korean War, the Vietnam era, the Gulf War era, and all other service periods. The Gulf War era began in August 1990 and continues to the present day. It is divided into two periods of service: Gulf War era II (September 2001–present) and Gulf War era I (August 1990–August 2001).

Table 1-69. Employed Persons 18 Years and Over by Occupation, Sex, Veteran Status, and Period of Service, 2011 Annual Averages

(Number in thousands, percent distribution.)

| Occupation | Total veterans | Gulf War era | | | WWII, Korean War, and Vietnam War | Other services periods | Non-veteran |
		Total	Gulf War era II	Gulf War era I			
TOTAL							
Total, 18 Years and Over	10 375	3 992	1 704	2 289	3 280	3 102	128 140
Percent	100.0	100.0	100.0	100.0	100.0	100.0	100.0
Management, professional, and related occupations	37.6	37.6	35.1	39.4	40.3	34.6	37.9
Management, business, and financial operations occupations	18.1	16.6	14.8	17.9	21.6	16.4	15.4
Professional and related occupations	19.5	21.0	20.2	21.5	18.8	18.2	22.5
Service occupations	14.5	17.2	19.0	15.8	11.6	14.2	17.7
Sales and office occupations	16.9	16.7	16.9	16.5	17.2	17.0	24.1
Sales and related occupations	8.8	7.5	7.4	7.6	10.9	8.2	11.0
Office and administrative support occupations	8.2	9.2	9.5	8.9	6.3	8.9	13.1
Natural resources, construction, and maintenance occupations	14.0	14.3	16.1	13.0	12.8	15.0	9.0
Farming, fishing, and forestry occupations	0.4	0.3	0.3	0.3	0.5	0.3	0.7
Construction and extraction occupations	6.0	5.6	6.2	5.2	5.7	6.7	5.0
Installation, maintenance, and repair occupations	7.7	8.4	9.6	7.5	6.5	8.0	3.2
Production, transportation, and material moving occupations	16.9	14.2	13.0	15.2	18.1	19.2	11.4
Production occupations	7.3	7.0	6.2	7.6	6.8	8.2	5.8
Transportation and material moving occupations	9.7	7.2	6.8	7.6	11.4	11.0	5.6
MEN							
Total, 18 Years and Over	9 360	3 428	1 457	1 971	3 181	2 751	64 280
Percent	100.0	100.0	100.0	100.0	100.0	100.0	100.0
Management, professional, and related occupations	36.4	35.9	32.8	38.2	40.1	32.9	34.3
Management, business, and financial operations occupations	18.2	16.5	14.4	18.1	21.8	16.1	16.4
Professional and related occupations	18.2	19.4	18.4	20.1	18.3	16.8	17.9
Service occupations	14.5	17.3	19.7	15.5	11.7	14.1	14.5
Sales and office occupations	15.6	14.7	15.1	14.3	16.7	15.4	16.8
Sales and related occupations	9.0	7.6	7.5	7.7	11.0	8.3	10.5
Office and administrative support occupations	6.6	7.0	7.6	6.6	5.7	7.1	6.3
Natural resources, construction, and maintenance occupations	15.4	16.4	18.3	14.9	13.1	16.8	17.0
Farming, fishing, and forestry occupations	0.4	0.3	0.3	0.3	0.5	0.3	1.1
Construction and extraction occupations	6.6	6.4	7.0	6.1	5.9	7.5	9.8
Installation, maintenance, and repair occupations	8.4	9.6	11.0	8.6	6.6	8.9	6.1
Production, transportation, and material moving occupations	18.2	15.8	14.0	17.0	18.5	20.8	17.3
Production occupations	7.7	7.6	6.7	8.4	6.9	8.8	7.9
Transportation and material moving occupations	10.4	8.1	7.4	8.6	11.6	12.0	9.4
WOMEN							
Total, 18 Years and Over	1 015	564	246	318	99	351	63 859
Percent	100.0	100.0	100.0	100.0	100.0	100.0	100.0
Management, professional, and related occupations	48.0	47.8	48.5	47.3	49.7	48.0	41.4
Management, business, and financial operations occupations	17.4	17.1	17.5	16.8	15.0	18.6	14.3
Professional and related occupations	30.6	30.7	31.0	30.4	34.7	29.4	27.1
Service occupations	15.1	16.4	14.7	17.7	9.0	14.6	20.9
Sales and office occupations	29.7	28.9	27.3	30.1	32.4	30.2	31.4
Sales and related occupations	7.0	6.7	6.4	6.9	9.2	6.9	11.4
Office and administrative support occupations	22.7	22.2	20.9	23.2	23.2	23.2	19.9
Natural resources, construction, and maintenance occupations	1.6	1.9	2.8	1.1	1.9	1.0	0.8
Farming, fishing, and forestry occupations	0.3	0.3	0.4	0.3	0.5	0.0	0.3
Construction and extraction occupations	0.6	0.7	1.7	0.0	0.2	0.5	0.2
Installation, maintenance, and repair occupations	0.7	0.8	0.7	0.8	1.1	0.4	0.3
Production, transportation, and material moving occupations	5.7	5.1	6.8	3.8	7.1	6.3	5.4
Production occupations	3.1	3.0	3.4	2.8	2.5	3.4	3.6
Transportation and material moving occupations	2.6	2.1	3.4	1.0	4.6	2.9	1.9

Note: Veterans are men and women who served in the U.S. Armed Forces during World War II, the Korean War, the Vietnam era, the Gulf War era, and all other service periods. Nonveterans are men and women who never served in the U.S. Armed Forces. Other service periods include the periods between World War II and the Korean War, between the Korean War and the Vietnam era, and between the Vietnam era and the Gulf War era.

Table 1-70. Employed Persons 18 Years and Over by Industry, Class of Worker, Sex, Veteran Status, and Period of Service, 2011 Annual Averages

(Number in thousands, percent distribution.)

| Industry and class of worker | Total veterans | Gulf War era | | | WWII, Korean War, and Vietnam War | Other services periods | Non-veteran |
		Total	Gulf War era II	Gulf War era I			
TOTAL							
Total, 18 Years and Over	10 375	3 992	1 704	2 289	3 280	3 102	128 140
Percent	100.0	100.0	100.0	100.0	100.0	100.0	100.0
Agriculture and related industries	2.0	0.7	0.8	0.7	3.7	1.8	1.5
Wage and salary workers	0.7	0.4	0.5	0.4	1.1	0.7	1.0
Self-employed workers	1.3	0.3	0.3	0.3	2.6	1.1	0.6
Nonagricultural industries	98.0	99.3	99.2	99.3	96.3	98.2	98.5
Wage and salary workers	91.1	96.3	97.0	95.9	84.8	91.1	92.3
Private industries	69.5	69.9	69.8	69.9	67.7	70.8	78.0
Mining	0.9	1.1	1.2	1.1	0.9	0.6	0.5
Construction	5.2	4.9	4.8	4.9	4.4	6.4	5.0
Manufacturing	13.0	12.2	10.5	13.4	12.8	14.2	9.8
Wholesale trade	2.8	2.3	1.6	2.9	3.4	2.7	2.6
Retail trade	8.2	7.1	8.6	6.1	9.2	8.4	10.8
Transportation and utilities	7.1	6.1	5.7	6.4	7.0	8.4	3.7
Information	2.4	3.0	2.4	3.4	2.0	2.2	2.0
Financial activities	4.6	4.5	4.7	4.3	5.1	4.2	6.3
Professional and business services	10.1	12.0	12.2	11.8	8.9	8.9	9.6
Education and health services	8.2	9.1	8.5	9.6	7.4	7.9	15.2
Leisure and hospitality	4.0	4.5	5.6	3.7	3.3	4.0	8.3
Other services	3.1	3.1	3.9	2.5	3.3	3.0	4.2
Government	21.7	26.5	27.2	25.9	17.1	20.3	14.3
Federal	8.9	12.4	14.2	11.1	5.9	7.6	2.1
State	5.0	5.7	5.7	5.8	4.4	4.7	4.5
Local	7.8	8.4	7.3	9.1	6.8	7.9	7.7
Self-employed workers	6.8	2.9	2.2	3.4	11.4	7.1	6.1
MEN							
Total, 18 Years and Over	9 360	3 428	1 457	1 971	3 181	2 751	64 280
Percent	100	100	100	100	100	100	100
Agriculture and related industries	2.1	0.8	0.9	0.7	3.7	2.0	2.2
Wage and salary workers	0.8	0.4	0.5	0.4	1.1	0.8	1.5
Self-employed workers	1.4	0.3	0.4	0.3	2.7	1.2	0.8
Nonagricultural industries	97.9	99.2	99.1	99.3	96.3	98.0	97.8
Wage and salary workers	90.6	96.3	96.9	96.0	84.6	90.3	90.7
Private industries	69.8	70.1	69.4	70.7	68.0	71.4	79.7
Mining	1.0	1.3	1.4	1.2	0.9	0.6	0.9
Construction	5.6	5.5	5.3	5.7	4.5	6.9	9.0
Manufacturing	13.6	13.1	11.1	14.5	13.0	15.0	13.5
Wholesale trade	2.9	2.5	1.7	3.1	3.5	2.8	3.6
Retail trade	8.2	7.2	8.6	6.2	9.2	8.3	10.6
Transportation and utilities	7.6	6.7	6.4	7.0	7.2	9.1	5.6
Information	2.5	3.2	2.5	3.7	2.1	2.2	2.3
Financial activities	4.4	4.1	4.2	3.9	5.1	4.1	5.2
Professional and business services	10.2	12.2	12.8	11.9	9.1	8.9	10.7
Education and health services	6.6	6.9	6.1	7.5	6.8	6.1	6.6
Leisure and hospitality	3.9	4.4	5.6	3.5	3.3	4.1	7.9
Other services	3.2	3.0	3.7	2.5	3.4	3.2	3.8
Government	20.8	26.2	27.5	25.2	16.6	18.9	11.0
Federal	8.5	12.3	14.3	10.8	5.7	7.0	2.0
State	4.8	5.7	6.0	5.5	4.3	4.4	3.3
Local	7.5	8.2	7.2	8.9	6.7	7.6	5.6
Self-employed workers	7.2	2.9	2.3	3.3	11.6	7.6	7.0
WOMEN							
Total, 18 Years and Over	1 015	564	246	318	99	351	63 859
Percent	100.0	100.0	100.0	100.0	100.0	100.0	100.0
Agriculture and related industries	0.7	0.7	0.4	1.0	1.9	0.3	0.8
Wage and salary workers	0.4	0.5	0.4	0.6	0.5	0.2	0.5
Self-employed workers	0.3	0.2	0.0	0.4	1.4	0.1	0.3
Nonagricultural industries	99.3	99.3	99.6	99.0	98.1	99.7	99.2
Wage and salary workers	96.1	96.4	97.7	95.4	91.5	96.9	93.9
Private industries	66.7	68.2	72.2	65.1	59.1	66.3	76.2
Mining	0.2	0.2	0.2	0.1	0.0	0.3	0.1
Construction	1.3	0.9	1.6	0.3	1.5	2.0	1.1
Manufacturing	7.1	6.9	7.0	6.7	5.0	8.0	6.1
Wholesale trade	1.3	1.1	0.9	1.4	0.0	2.0	1.6
Retail trade	7.6	6.6	8.6	5.0	8.3	9.1	11.1
Transportation and utilities	2.4	2.1	1.6	2.4	3.2	2.9	1.8
Information	1.9	1.9	2.3	1.6	1.5	2.0	1.6
Financial activities	6.1	7.0	7.6	6.5	6.4	4.6	7.3
Professional and business services	8.9	10.3	9.0	11.3	3.2	8.2	8.5
Education and health services	22.6	22.6	22.7	22.4	25.3	22.0	23.8
Leisure and hospitality	4.4	5.2	5.3	5.1	2.8	3.5	8.7
Other services	2.8	3.6	5.3	2.3	2.1	1.6	4.5
Government	29.4	28.1	25.4	30.2	32.4	30.6	17.7
Federal	12.9	12.9	13.3	12.6	12.7	12.9	2.2
State	6.4	5.8	3.8	7.3	7.1	7.1	5.7
Local	10.1	9.4	8.3	10.3	12.6	10.5	9.8
Self-employed workers	3.2	2.9	1.9	3.7	6.6	2.6	5.2

Note: Veterans are men and women who served in the U.S. Armed Forces during World War II, the Korean War, the Vietnam era, the Gulf War era, and all other service periods. Nonveterans are men and women who never served in the U.S. Armed Forces. Other service periods include the periods between World War II and the Korean War, between the Korean War and the Vietnam era, and between the Vietnam era and the Gulf War era.

Table 1-71. Employed Persons 18 Years and Over by Veteran Status, Presence of Service-Connected Disability, Period of Service, and Class of Worker, August 2011, Not Seasonally Adjusted

(Numbers in thousands, percent distribution.)

Veteran status, presence of disability, and period of service	Total employed (number)	Total employed (percent)	Agriculture and related industries	Nonagricultural industries					Self-employed, unincorporated, and unpaid family workers
				Wage and salary workers					
				Total	Private sector	Government			
						Total	Federal	State and local	
Veterans, Total[1]	10 497	100.0	2.3	97.7	69.7	21.0	8.3	12.7	7.1
With service-connected disability	1 310	100.0	0.8	99.2	59.5	33.6	18.4	15.2	6.1
Without service-connected disability	7 246	100.0	2.8	97.2	71.3	19.0	6.3	12.7	6.9
Gulf War Era, Total[1]	4 071	100.0	0.7	99.3	70.7	25.5	11.0	14.5	3.1
With service-connected disability	824	100.0	-	100.0	59.3	36.6	20.9	15.6	4.1
Without service-connected disability	2 547	100.0	0.8	99.2	74.1	22.7	7.8	14.8	2.4
Gulf War Era II[1]	1 759	100.0	0.4	99.6	70.4	26.2	13.0	13.2	3.1
With service-connected disability	445	100.0	-	100.0	61.0	35.3	20.9	14.4	3.7
Without service-connected disability	1 036	100.0	0.6	99.4	74.1	22.9	9.8	13.1	2.4
Gulf War Era I[1]	2 312	100.0	1.0	99.0	70.9	25.0	9.5	15.5	3.2
With service-connected disability	379	100.0	-	100.0	57.3	38.1	21.0	17.1	4.6
Without service-connected disability	1 511	100.0	1.0	99.0	74.1	22.5	6.5	16.0	2.4
WW II, Korean War, and Vietnam Era[1]	3 332	100.0	4.5	95.5	68.9	16.0	5.7	10.3	10.7
With service-connected disability	253	100.0	4.1	95.9	59.8	26.6	14.3	12.3	9.5
Without service-connected disability	2 441	100.0	5.2	94.8	69.0	14.8	4.9	9.9	11.0
Other Service Periods[1]	3 094	100.0	1.9	98.1	69.4	20.4	7.5	12.9	8.3
With service-connected disability	233	100.0	-	100.0	60.1	30.5	13.7	16.8	9.4
Without service-connected disability	2 258	100.0	2.4	97.6	70.5	19.5	6.1	13.4	7.5
Nonveterans	128 265	100.0	1.7	98.3	78.4	13.7	2.1	11.6	6.2

Note: Veterans are men and women who served in the U.S. Armed Forces during World War II, the Korean War, the Vietnam era, the Gulf War era, and all other service periods. Nonveterans are men and women who never served in the U.S. Armed Forces. Other service periods include the periods between World War II and the Korean War, between the Korean War and the Vietnam era, and between the Vietnam era and the Gulf War era.

[1]Includes veterans who did not report presence of disability.
- = Quantity represents or rounds to zero.

Chapter Two

EMPLOYMENT, HOURS, AND EARNINGS

EMPLOYMENT, HOURS, AND EARNINGS

HIGHLIGHTS

The employment, hours, and earnings data in this section are presented by industry and state and are derived from the Current Employment Statistics (CES) survey, which covers approximately 557,000 individual worksites and 145,000 business and government agencies. The employment numbers differ from those presented in from the household survey in Chapter 1 because of dissimilarities in methodology, concepts, definitions, and coverage. As the CES survey data are obtained from payroll records, they are consistent for industry classifications.

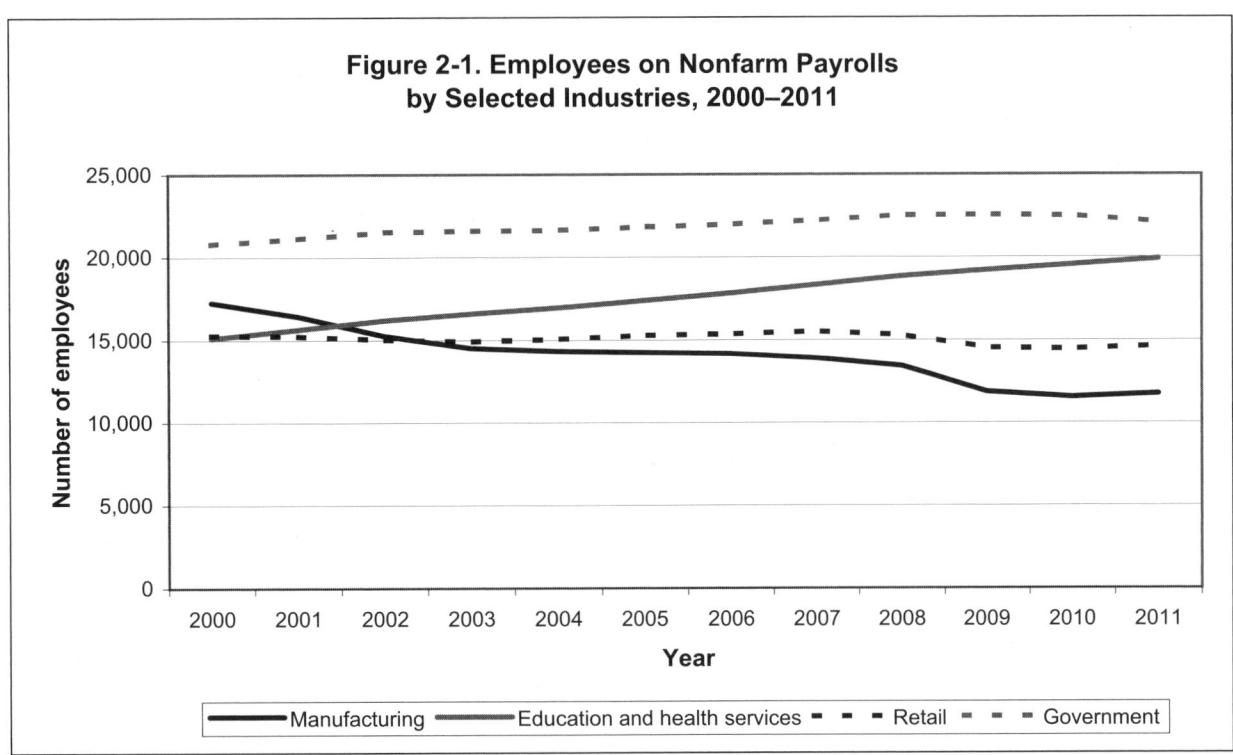

Figure 2-1. Employees on Nonfarm Payrolls by Selected Industries, 2000–2011

Although the number of employees on total nonfarm payrolls declined 0.3 percent from 2000 to 2011, nonfarm payroll employment increased 1.1 percent from 2010 to 2011. In 2011, employment increased in several sectors including manufacturing, education and health services, and retail trade but declined in government, construction, and information. (See Table 2-1.)

OTHER HIGHLIGHTS

- Nonfarm payroll employment increased 1.5 percent in the goods-producing sector and 1.8 percent in the private service-providing sector in 2011. Within the goods providing sector, mining and logging grew the fastest although it employees far less people than either manufacturing or construction. Professional and business services grew the fastest within the service-providing industry at 3.6 percent. (See Table 2-1.)

- Government employment declined 1.7 percent in 2011 after declining 0.3 percent in 2010. Employment in government increased each year from 2001 through 2009. (See Table 2-1.)

- Average weekly hours of all employees on private nonfarm payrolls increased slightly in 2011 to 34.4 hours. Employees in mining and logging worked the longest week (44.5 hours) while those in leisure and hospitality worked the shortest (25.9 hours). (See Table 2-6.)

NOTES AND DEFINITIONS

EMPLOYMENT, HOURS, AND EARNINGS

Collection and Coverage

The Bureau of Labor Statistics (BLS) works with State Employment Security Agencies (SESAs) to conduct the Current Employment Statistics (CES), or establishment, survey. This survey collects monthly data on employment, hours, and earnings from a sample of nonfarm establishments (including government). The CES sample includes about 145,000 businesses and government agencies and covers approximately 557,000 individual worksites. Each month the BLS publishes over 2,300 not seasonally adjusted employment series for all employees, production and nonsupervisory employees, and women employees. The series for all employees include over 900 industries at various levels of aggregation.

In addition, BLS also publishes approximately 3,100 all employees and production and nonsupervisory employees series for average hourly earnings, average weekly hours, and, in manufacturing, average weekly overtime hours each month on a non-seasonally adjusted basis which cover about 700 industries.

BLS collects data on employment, payroll, and paid hours from a sample of establishments. Establishments reporting information are classified into industries based on their principal product or activity. Data are submitted each month by the respondent and edited by the state agency. Data submitted are used in developing national, statewide, and major metropolitan area estimates All states' samples are combined to form a collective sample for developing national industry estimates. Statewide samples range from nearly 30,000 sample units in California to about 1,000 units in smaller states. It should be noted that state estimation procedures are designed to produce accurate data for each individual state. BLS independently develops the national employment series and does not force state estimates to sum to national totals nor vice versa.

Data are collected by telephone, touch-tone self response, computer-assisted interviews, fax technology, voice recognition, and mail. The use of electronic media has resulted in a more rapid response times and higher response rates.

Industry Classification

The CES survey completed a conversion from its original quota sample design to a probability-based sample survey design, and switched from the Standard Industrial Classification (SIC) system to the North American Industry Classification System (NAICS) in 2003. The industry-coding update included reconstruction of historical estimates in order to preserve time series for data users. The foundation of industrial classification with NAICS has changed how establishments are classified into industries and how

businesses, as they exist today, are recognized. With the release of January 2008 data on February 1, 2008, the CES National Nonfarm Payroll series was updated to the 2007 North American Industry Classification System (NAICS) from the 2002 NAICS basis. In February 2012, the CES National Nonfarm Payroll series was updated again from the 2007 version to the 2012 version of NAICS with the release of January data.

Industry Employment

Employment data refer to persons on establishment payrolls who received pay for any part of the pay period containing the 12th day of the month. The data exclude proprietors, the self-employed, unpaid volunteer or family workers, farm workers, and domestic workers. Salaried officers of corporations are included. Government employment covers only civilian employees; military personnel are excluded. Employees of the Central Intelligence Agency, the National Security Agency, the National Imagery and Mapping Agency, and the Defense Intelligence Agency are also excluded.

Persons on establishment payrolls who were on paid sick leave (for cases in which pay is received directly from the firm), paid holiday, or vacation leave, or who work during part of the pay period despite being unemployed or on strike during the rest of the period were counted as employed. Not counted as employed were persons on layoff, on leave without pay, on strike for the entire period, or who had been hired but had not yet reported during to their new jobs.

Beginning with the June 2003 publication of May 2003 data, the CES national federal government employment series has been estimated from a sample of federal establishments and benchmarked annually to counts from unemployment insurance tax records. It reflects employee counts as of the pay period containing the 12th day of the month, which is consistent with other CES industry series. Previously, the national series was an end-of-month count produced by the Office of Personnel Management.

The exclusion of farm employment, self-employment, and domestic service employment accounts from the payroll survey accounts for the differences in employment figures between the household and payroll surveys. The payroll survey also excludes workers on leave without pay. (These workers are counted as employed in the household survey.) Persons who worked in more than one establishment during the reporting period are counted each time their names appear on payrolls; these persons are only counted once in the household survey.

Concepts and Definitions

Production and related workers. This category includes working supervisors and all nonsupervisory workers (including group leaders and trainees) engaged in fabricating, processing, assembling, inspecting, receiving, storing, handling, packing, warehousing, shipping, trucking, hauling, maintenance, repair, janitorial, guard services, product development, auxiliary production for plant's own use (such as a power plant), record-keeping, and other services closely associated with production operations.

Construction workers. This group includes the following employees in the construction division: working supervisors, qualified craft workers, mechanics, apprentices, helpers, and laborers engaged in new work, alterations, demolition, repair, maintenance, and the like, whether working at the site of construction or at jobs in shops or yards at jobs (such as precutting and pre-assembling) ordinarily performed by members of the construction trades.

Nonsupervisory workers. This category consists of employees such as office and clerical workers, repairers, salespersons, operators, drivers, physicians, lawyers, accountants, nurses, social workers, research aides, teachers, drafters, photographers, beauticians, musicians, restaurant workers, custodial workers, attendants, line installers and repairers, laborers, janitors, guards, and other employees at similar occupational levels whose services are closely associated with those of the employees listed. It excludes persons in executive, managerial, and supervisory positions.

Payroll. This refers to payments made to full- and part-time production, construction, or nonsupervisory workers who received pay for any part of the pay period containing the 12th day of the month. The payroll is reported before deductions of any kind, such as those for old age and unemployment insurance, group insurance, withholding tax, bonds, or union dues. Also included is pay for overtime, holidays, and vacation, as well as for sick leave paid directly by the firm. Bonuses (unless earned and paid regularly each pay period), other pay not earned in the pay period reported (such as retroactive pay), tips, and the value of free rent, fuel, meals, or other payment-in-kind are excluded. Employee benefits (such as health and other types of insurance and contributions to retirement, as paid by the employer) are also excluded.

Total hours. During the pay period, total hours include all hours worked (including overtime hours), hours paid for standby or reporting time, and equivalent hours for which employees received pay directly from the employer for sick leave, holidays, vacations, and other leave. Overtime and other premium pay hours are not converted to straight-time equivalent hours. The concept of total hours differs from those of scheduled hours and hours worked. The average weekly hours derived from paid total hours reflect the effects of such factors as unpaid absenteeism, labor turnover, part-time work, and work stoppages, as well as fluctuations in work schedules.

Average weekly hours. The workweek information relates to the average hours for which pay was received and is different from standard or scheduled hours. Such factors as unpaid absenteeism, labor turnover, part-time work, and work stoppages cause average weekly hours to be lower than scheduled hours of work for an establishment. Group averages further reflect changes in the workweeks of component industries.

Overtime hours. These are hours worked by production or related workers for which overtime premiums were paid because the hours were in excess of the number of hours of either the straight-time workday or the total workweek. Weekend and holiday hours are included only if overtime premiums were paid. Hours for which only shift differential, hazard, incentive, or other similar types of premiums were paid are excluded.

Average overtime hours. Overtime hours represent the portion of average weekly hours that exceeded regular hours and for which overtime premiums were paid. If an employee worked during a paid holiday at regular rates, receiving as total compensation his or her holiday pay plus straight-time pay for hours worked that day, no overtime hours would be reported.

Since overtime hours are premium hours by definition, weekly hours and overtime hours do not necessarily move in the same direction from month to month. Factors such as work stoppages, absenteeism, and labor turnover may not have the same influence on overtime hours as on average hours. Diverse trends at the industry group level may also be caused by a marked change in hours for a component industry in which little or no overtime was worked in both the previous and current months.

Industry hours and earnings. Average hours and earnings data are derived from reports of payrolls and hours for production and related workers in manufacturing and natural resources and mining, construction workers in construction, and nonsupervisory employees in private service-providing industries.

Average hourly earnings. Average hourly earnings are on a "gross" basis. They reflect not only changes in basic hourly and incentive wage rates, but also such variable factors as premium pay for overtime and late-shift work and changes in output of workers paid on an incentive plan. They also reflect shifts in the number of employees between relatively high-paid and low-paid work and changes in workers' earnings in individual establishments. Averages for groups and divisions further reflect changes in average hourly earnings for individual industries.

Averages of hourly earnings differ from wage rates. Earnings are the actual return to the worker for a stated period; rates are the amount stipulated for a given unit of work or time. The earnings series do not measure the level of total labor costs on the part of the employer because the following items are excluded: irregular bonuses, retroactive items, payroll taxes paid by employers, and earnings for those employees not covered under the definitions of production workers, construction workers, or nonsupervisory employees.

Average hourly earnings, excluding overtime-premium pay, are computed by dividing the total production worker payroll for the industry group by the sum of total production worker hours and one-half of total overtime hours. No adjustments are made for other premium payment provisions, such as holiday pay, late-shift premiums, and overtime rates other than time and one-half.

Average weekly earnings. These estimates are derived by multiplying average weekly hours estimates by average hourly earnings estimates. Therefore, weekly earnings are affected not only by changes in average hourly earnings but also by changes in the length of the workweek. Monthly variations in factors, such as the proportion of part-time workers, work stoppages, labor turnover during the survey period, and absenteeism for which employees are not paid may cause the average workweek to fluctuate.

Long-term trends of average weekly earnings can be affected by structural changes in the makeup of the workforce. For example, persistent long-term increases in the proportion of part-time workers in retail trade and many of the services industries have reduced average workweeks in these industries and have affected the average weekly earnings series.

These earnings are in constant dollars and are calculated from the earnings averages for the current month using a deflator derived from the Consumer Price Index for Urban Wage Earnings and Clerical Workers (CPI-W). The reference year for these series is 1982.

Seasonally adjustment removes the change in employment that is due to normal seasonal hiring or layoffs, thus leaving an over-the-month change that reflects only employment changes due to trend and irregular movements. Seasonally adjusted estimates of employment and other series are generated using the X-12 ARIMA program developed by the United States Census Bureau.

Benchmarks

Employment estimates are adjusted annually to a complete count of jobs—called benchmarks—which are primarily derived from tax reports submitted by employers covered by state unemployment laws (which cover most establishments). A comprehensive account of employment is derived in March. In this re-anchoring of sample-based employment estimates to full population counts, the original sample-based estimates are replaced with the benchmark data from the previous year. The benchmark information is used to adjust monthly estimates between the new benchmark and the preceding benchmark, thereby preserving the continuity of the series and establishing the level of employment for the new benchmark month.

Sources of Additional Information

For further information on sampling and estimation methods for national data visit the Employment, Hours, and Earnings homepage on the BLS Web site at <http://www.bls.gov/ces>. For more information on state and area data, please visit the BLS Web site at <http://www.bls.gov/sae>.

Table 2-1. Employees on Nonfarm Payrolls, by Super Sector and Selected Component Groups, NAICS Basis, 2000–2011

(Thousands of people.)

Industry	2000	2001	2002	2003	2004	2005	2006	2007	2008	2009	2010	2011
TOTAL	131 785	131 826	130 341	129 999	131 435	133 703	136 086	137 598	136 790	130 807	129 874	131 359
Total Private	110 995	110 708	108 828	108 416	109 814	111 899	114 113	115 380	114 281	108 252	107 384	109 254
Goods-Producing	24 649	23 873	22 557	21 816	21 882	22 190	22 530	22 233	21 335	18 558	17 751	18 021
Mining and Logging	599	606	583	572	591	628	684	724	767	694	705	784
Mining	520	533	512	503	523	562	620	664	710	643	655	735
Logging	79	74	70	69	68	65	64	60	57	50	50	48
Construction	6 787	6 826	6 716	6 735	6 976	7 336	7 691	7 630	7 162	6 016	5 518	5 504
Construction of buildings	1 633	1 589	1 575	1 576	1 630	1 712	1 805	1 774	1 642	1 357	1 230	1 219
Heavy and civil engineering	937	953	931	903	907	951	985	1 005	965	851	825	829
Specialty trade contractors	4 217	4 284	4 210	4 256	4 439	4 673	4 901	4 850	4 556	3 808	3 463	3 455
Manufacturing	17 263	16 441	15 259	14 509	14 315	14 227	14 155	13 879	13 406	11 847	11 528	11 733
Durable goods	10 877	10 336	9 485	8 964	8 925	8 956	8 981	8 808	8 463	7 284	7 064	7 274
Wood product	615	576	557	540	552	561	561	517	458	360	342	335
Nonmetallic mineral product	554	545	516	494	506	505	510	501	465	394	371	367
Primary metals	622	571	509	477	467	466	464	456	442	362	362	390
Fabricated metal product	1 753	1 676	1 549	1 479	1 497	1 522	1 553	1 563	1 528	1 312	1 282	1 344
Machinery	1 457	1 371	1 232	1 152	1 145	1 166	1 183	1 187	1 188	1 029	996	1 057
Computer and electronic product	1 820	1 749	1 507	1 355	1 323	1 316	1 308	1 273	1 244	1 137	1 095	1 107
Electrical equipment and appliances	591	557	497	460	445	434	433	429	424	374	360	367
Transportation equipment	2 057	1 939	1 830	1 775	1 767	1 772	1 769	1 712	1 608	1 348	1 333	1 382
Furniture and related product	680	643	605	574	574	566	558	529	478	384	357	353
Miscellaneous manufacturing	728	710	683	658	651	647	644	642	629	584	567	573
Nondurable goods	6 386	6 105	5 774	5 546	5 390	5 271	5 174	5 071	4 943	4 564	4 464	4 460
Food manufacturing	1 553	1 551	1 526	1 518	1 494	1 478	1 479	1 484	1 481	1 456	1 451	1 456
Beverage and tobacco product	207	209	207	200	195	192	194	198	198	187	183	188
Textile mills	378	333	291	261	237	218	195	170	151	124	119	121
Textile product mills	230	217	204	188	183	176	167	158	147	126	119	117
Apparel	484	415	350	304	278	251	232	215	199	168	157	152
Paper and paper product	605	578	547	516	496	484	471	458	445	407	395	391
Printing and related support activities	807	768	707	680	663	646	634	622	594	522	488	469
Petroleum and coal product	123	121	118	114	112	112	113	115	117	115	114	112
Chemicals	980	959	928	906	887	872	866	861	847	804	787	788
Plastics and rubber product	951	896	847	814	805	802	786	757	729	625	625	636
Private Service-Providing	86 346	86 834	86 271	86 600	87 932	89 709	91 582	93 147	92 946	89 695	89 633	91 234
Trade, Transportation, and Utilities	26 225	25 983	25 497	25 287	25 533	25 959	26 276	26 630	26 293	24 906	24 636	25 019
Wholesale Trade	5 933	5 773	5 652	5 608	5 663	5 764	5 905	6 015	5 943	5 587	5 452	5 529
Durable goods	3 251	3 130	3 008	2 941	2 951	2 999	3 075	3 122	3 052	2 810	2 714	2 753
Nondurable goods	2 065	2 031	2 015	2 005	2 010	2 022	2 041	2 062	2 048	1 966	1 928	1 940
Electronic markets, agents, and brokers	618	611	629	662	702	743	789	832	843	811	811	836
Retail Trade	15 280	15 239	15 025	14 917	15 058	15 280	15 353	15 520	15 283	14 522	14 440	14 643
Motor vehicle and parts dealers	1 847	1 855	1 879	1 883	1 902	1 919	1 910	1 908	1 831	1 638	1 629	1 688
Furniture and home furnishing stores	544	541	539	547	563	576	587	575	531	449	438	442
Electronic and appliance stores	647	633	595	574	572	585	581	583	570	516	522	526
Building material and garden supply stores	1 142	1 152	1 177	1 185	1 227	1 276	1 324	1 309	1 248	1 156	1 132	1 141
Food and beverage stores	2 993	2 951	2 882	2 838	2 822	2 818	2 821	2 844	2 862	2 830	2 808	2 829
Health and personal care stores	928	952	939	938	941	954	961	993	1 003	986	981	981
Gasoline stations	936	925	896	882	876	871	864	862	842	826	819	828
Clothing and clothing accessories stores	1 322	1 321	1 313	1 305	1 364	1 415	1 451	1 500	1 468	1 364	1 353	1 356
Sporting goods, hobby, and music stores	603	601	592	585	586	598	606	623	622	589	579	574
General merchandise stores	2 820	2 842	2 812	2 822	2 863	2 934	2 935	3 021	3 026	2 966	2 998	3 080
Miscellaneous store retailers	1 007	993	960	931	914	900	881	865	843	782	762	767
Nonstore retailers	492	474	444	427	429	435	433	438	438	421	421	432
Transportation and Warehousing	4 410	4 372	4 224	4 185	4 249	4 361	4 470	4 541	4 508	4 236	4 191	4 292
Air transportation	614	615	564	528	515	501	487	492	491	463	458	456
Rail transportation	232	227	218	218	226	228	228	234	231	218	216	229
Water transportation	56	54	53	55	56	61	63	66	67	63	62	63
Truck transportation	1 406	1 387	1 339	1 326	1 352	1 398	1 436	1 439	1 389	1 268	1 250	1 299
Transit and ground passenger transportation	372	375	381	382	385	389	399	412	423	422	430	436
Pipeline transportation	46	45	42	40	38	38	39	40	42	43	42	43
Scenic and sightseeing transportation	28	29	26	27	27	29	28	29	28	28	27	29
Support activities for transportation	537	539	525	520	535	552	571	584	592	549	543	564
Couriers and messengers	605	587	561	562	557	571	582	581	573	546	528	529
Warehousing and storage	514	514	517	528	558	595	638	665	672	637	633	646
Utilities	601	599	596	577	564	554	549	553	559	560	553	555
Information	3 630	3 629	3 395	3 188	3 118	3 061	3 038	3 032	2 984	2 804	2 707	2 659
Publishing industries, except Internet	1 035	1 021	964	925	909	904	902	901	880	796	759	749
Motion picture and sound recording industry	383	377	388	376	385	378	376	381	371	358	370	361
Broadcasting, except Internet	344	345	334	324	325	328	328	325	319	301	290	282
Internet publishing and broadcasting and web search portals	111	100	76	67	66	67	69	73	81	83	92	108
Telecommunications	1 397	1 424	1 281	1 167	1 115	1 071	1 048	1 031	1 019	966	903	865
Other information services	157	147	124	116	117	118	121	126	134	135	142	159

Table 2-1. Employees on Nonfarm Payrolls, by Super Sector and Selected Component Groups, NAICS Basis, 2000–2011—*Continued*

(Thousands of people.)

Industry	2000	2001	2002	2003	2004	2005	2006	2007	2008	2009	2010	2011
Financial Activities	7 687	7 808	7 847	7 977	8 031	8 153	8 328	8 301	8 145	7 769	7 652	7 681
Finance and insurance	5 677	5 769	5 814	5 919	5 945	6 019	6 156	6 132	6 015	5 775	5 718	5 752
Monetary authorities, central bank	23	23	23	23	22	21	21	22	22	21	20	19
Credit intermediation	2 548	2 598	2 686	2 792	2 817	2 869	2 925	2 866	2 733	2 590	2 550	2 559
Securities, commodity contracts, and investments	805	831	789	758	766	786	818	849	864	811	801	807
Insurance carriers and related activities	2 221	2 234	2 233	2 266	2 259	2 259	2 304	2 307	2 305	2 264	2 261	2 282
Funds, trusts, and other financial vehicles	81	84	82	80	82	84	88	89	91	88	87	85
Real estate and rental and leasing	2 011	2 038	2 033	2 058	2 086	2 134	2 173	2 169	2 130	1 994	1 934	1 929
Real estate	1 316	1 343	1 357	1 387	1 419	1 461	1 499	1 500	1 485	1 420	1 396	1 402
Rental and leasing services	667	666	649	643	641	646	646	640	617	547	514	503
Lessors of nonfinancial intangible assets	28	29	28	27	26	27	28	28	28	27	25	24
Professional and Business Services	16 666	16 476	15 976	15 987	16 394	16 954	17 566	17 942	17 735	16 579	16 728	17 331
Professional and technical services	6 702	6 871	6 649	6 603	6 747	7 025	7 357	7 660	7 799	7 509	7 441	7 691
Management of companies and enterprises	1 796	1 779	1 705	1 687	1 724	1 759	1 811	1 866	1 905	1 867	1 872	1 915
Administrative and waste services	8 168	7 826	7 622	7 697	7 923	8 170	8 398	8 416	8 032	7 203	7 414	7 724
Administrative and support services	7 855	7 509	7 304	7 375	7 594	7 833	8 050	8 061	7 675	6 852	7 057	7 359
Waste management and remediation services	313	317	318	322	329	338	348	355	357	352	357	365
Education and Health Services	15 109	15 645	16 199	16 588	16 953	17 372	17 826	18 322	18 838	19 193	19 531	19 884
Education services	2 390	2 511	2 643	2 695	2 763	2 836	2 901	2 941	3 040	3 090	3 155	3 241
Health care and social assistance	12 718	13 134	13 556	13 893	14 190	14 536	14 925	15 380	15 798	16 103	16 375	16 643
Ambulatory health care services	4 320	4 462	4 633	4 786	4 952	5 114	5 286	5 474	5 647	5 793	5 975	6 146
Hospitals	3 954	4 051	4 160	4 245	4 285	4 345	4 423	4 515	4 627	4 667	4 679	4 731
Nursing and residential health facilities	2 583	2 676	2 743	2 786	2 818	2 855	2 893	2 958	3 016	3 082	3 124	3 169
Social assistance	1 860	1 946	2 020	2 075	2 135	2 222	2 324	2 433	2 508	2 560	2 599	2 597
Leisure and Hospitality	11 862	12 036	11 986	12 173	12 493	12 816	13 110	13 427	13 436	13 077	13 049	13 320
Arts, entertainment, and recreation	1 788	1 824	1 783	1 813	1 850	1 892	1 929	1 969	1 970	1 916	1 913	1 910
Performing arts and spectator sports	382	382	364	372	368	376	399	405	406	397	406	394
Museums, historical sites	110	115	114	115	118	121	124	130	132	129	128	132
Amusements, gambling, and recreation	1 296	1 327	1 305	1 327	1 364	1 395	1 406	1 434	1 433	1 389	1 379	1 383
Accommodation and food services	10 074	10 211	10 203	10 360	10 643	10 923	11 181	11 457	11 466	11 162	11 135	11 410
Accommodation	1 884	1 852	1 779	1 775	1 790	1 819	1 832	1 867	1 869	1 763	1 760	1 797
Food services and drinking places	8 189	8 359	8 425	8 584	8 854	9 104	9 349	9 590	9 598	9 399	9 376	9 613
Other Services	5 168	5 258	5 372	5 401	5 409	5 395	5 438	5 494	5 515	5 367	5 331	5 342
Repair and maintenance	1 242	1 257	1 247	1 234	1 229	1 236	1 249	1 253	1 227	1 150	1 139	1 160
Personal and laundry services	1 243	1 255	1 257	1 264	1 273	1 277	1 288	1 310	1 323	1 281	1 265	1 285
Membership associations and organizations	2 683	2 746	2 868	2 904	2 908	2 882	2 901	2 931	2 966	2 936	2 926	2 897
Government	20 790	21 118	21 513	21 583	21 621	21 804	21 974	22 218	22 509	22 555	22 490	22 104
Federal	2 865	2 764	2 766	2 761	2 730	2 732	2 732	2 734	2 762	2 832	2 977	2 858
Federal, excluding U.S. Postal Service	1 985	1 891	1 924	1 952	1 948	1 957	1 963	1 965	2 014	2 129	2 318	2 226
State	4 786	4 905	5 029	5 002	4 982	5 032	5 075	5 122	5 177	5 169	5 137	5 082
State, excluding education	2 756	2 792	2 786	2 748	2 744	2 772	2 782	2 804	2 823	2 809	2 764	2 698
Local	13 139	13 449	13 718	13 820	13 909	14 041	14 167	14 362	14 571	14 554	14 376	14 165
Local, excluding education	5 845	5 970	6 063	6 110	6 144	6 185	6 254	6 376	6 487	6 475	6 363	6 272

Table 2-2. Women Employees on Nonfarm Payrolls, by Super Sector and Selected Component Groups, NAICS Basis, 2000–2011

(Thousands of people.)

Industry	2000	2001	2002	2003	2004	2005	2006	2007	2008	2009	2010	2011
TOTAL NONFARM	63 282	63 741	63 427	63 299	63 783	64 744	65 549	66 834	67 121	65 250	64 719	65 084
Total Private	51 511	51 726	51 100	50 963	51 448	52 355	53 331	54 256	54 213	52 350	51 890	52 472
Goods-Producing	6 297	5 961	5 486	5 192	5 117	5 104	5 083	5 041	4 866	4 289	4 088	4 057
Mining and logging	92	90	85	80	80	79	82	93	101	98	98	105
Construction	846	832	827	822	841	890	944	947	916	801	723	711
Manufacturing	5 359	5 039	4 574	4 290	4 197	4 135	4 057	4 001	3 848	3 390	3 268	3 241
Private Service-Providing	45 214	45 765	45 613	45 771	46 331	47 252	48 248	49 215	49 347	48 061	47 801	48 416
Trade, transportation, and utilities	10 859	10 768	10 466	10 321	10 364	10 535	10 627	10 849	10 782	10 233	10 007	10 091
Wholesale trade	1 827	1 770	1 718	1 700	1 714	1 738	1 796	1 831	1 820	1 705	1 640	1 667
Retail trade	7 680	7 635	7 449	7 339	7 387	7 524	7 587	7 758	7 713	7 361	7 226	7 280
Transportation and warehousing	1 202	1 212	1 149	1 134	1 117	1 130	1 098	1 110	1 098	1 024	1 002	1 009
Utilities	151	151	150	147	146	143	146	150	151	143	139	135
Information	1 697	1 684	1 554	1 428	1 366	1 333	1 306	1 285	1 260	1 170	1 104	1 084
Financial activities	4 697	4 784	4 822	4 892	4 876	4 923	5 055	4 988	4 851	4 648	4 530	4 490
Professional and business services	7 680	7 591	7 314	7 248	7 360	7 574	7 779	8 007	7 946	7 472	7 454	7 686
Education and health services	11 586	12 037	12 474	12 786	13 073	13 408	13 764	14 178	14 574	14 851	15 067	15 277
Leisure and hospitality	6 082	6 224	6 215	6 319	6 516	6 708	6 903	7 054	7 056	6 861	6 819	6 964
Other services	2 614	2 677	2 769	2 779	2 776	2 772	2 814	2 854	2 880	2 824	2 820	2 823
Government	11 771	12 015	12 327	12 337	12 335	12 389	12 218	12 578	12 908	12 900	12 829	12 611
Federal	1 231	1 148	1 155	1 173	1 168	1 177	1 194	1 202	1 224	1 259	1 326	1 269
State	2 464	2 534	2 621	2 599	2 562	2 575	2 630	2 651	2 684	2 628	2 639	2 643
Local	8 076	8 333	8 551	8 565	8 606	8 637	8 395	8 725	9 000	9 014	8 864	8 700

Table 2-3. Production Workers on Private Nonfarm Payrolls, by Super Sector, NAICS Basis, 2000–2011

(Thousands of people.)

Industry	2000	2001	2002	2003	2004	2005	2006	2007	2008	2009	2010	2011
TOTAL PRIVATE	90 336	89 983	88 393	87 658	88 937	91 135	93 451	94 903	94 270	89 173	88 512	90 092
Goods-Producing	18 169	17 466	16 400	15 732	15 821	16 145	16 559	16 405	15 724	13 399	12 774	12 981
Mining and logging	446	457	436	420	440	473	519	547	574	510	525	590
Construction	5 295	5 332	5 196	5 123	5 309	5 611	5 903	5 883	5 521	4 567	4 172	4 161
Manufacturing	12 428	11 677	10 768	10 189	10 072	10 060	10 137	9 975	9 629	8 322	8 077	8 231
Private Service-Providing	72 167	72 517	71 993	71 926	73 116	74 990	76 893	78 498	78 547	75 774	75 738	77 111
Trade, transportation, and utilities	21 965	21 709	21 337	21 078	21 319	21 830	22 166	22 546	22 337	21 116	20 874	21 196
Wholesale trade	4 686	4 555	4 474	4 396	4 444	4 584	4 724	4 851	4 822	4 506	4 378	4 431
Retail trade	13 040	12 952	12 774	12 655	12 788	13 030	13 110	13 317	13 134	12 472	12 425	12 627
Transportation and warehousing	3 753	3 718	3 611	3 563	3 637	3 774	3 889	3 935	3 931	3 688	3 627	3 695
Utilities	485	483	478	464	450	443	443	444	450	451	444	443
Information	2 502	2 531	2 398	2 347	2 371	2 386	2 399	2 403	2 388	2 240	2 170	2 136
Financial activities	5 737	5 810	5 872	5 967	5 989	6 090	6 281	6 326	6 269	6 008	5 906	5 887
Professional and business services	13 790	13 588	13 049	12 911	13 287	13 854	14 446	14 784	14 585	13 520	13 699	14 253
Education and health services	13 362	13 846	14 311	14 532	14 771	15 129	15 539	15 999	16 488	16 841	17 125	17 420
Leisure and hospitality	10 516	10 662	10 576	10 666	10 955	11 263	11 568	11 861	11 873	11 560	11 507	11 743
Other services	4 296	4 373	4 449	4 426	4 425	4 438	4 494	4 578	4 606	4 488	4 458	4 475

Table 2-4. Production Workers on Manufacturing Payrolls, by Industry, NAICS Basis, 2000–2011

(Thousands of people.)

Industry	2000	2001	2002	2003	2004	2005	2006	2007	2008	2009	2010	2011
Total Manufacturing	12 428	11 677	10 768	10 189	10 072	10 060	10 137	9 975	9 629	8 322	8 077	8 231
Durable Goods	7 659	7 164	6 530	6 152	6 140	6 220	6 355	6 250	5 975	4 990	4 829	4 986
Wood products	507	470	450	434	445	454	451	407	358	278	269	267
Nometallic mineral products	440	427	399	375	388	387	391	384	363	303	284	278
Primary metals	490	447	396	370	364	363	363	358	348	272	275	302
Fabricated metal products	1 326	1 254	1 147	1 092	1 109	1 129	1 162	1 171	1 143	960	935	991
Machinery	961	891	787	732	730	749	770	774	772	641	616	663
Computer and electronic products	949	876	744	673	656	700	756	744	730	654	629	632
Electrical equipment and appliances	433	402	352	320	307	300	303	305	305	266	251	248
Transportation equipment	1 498	1 399	1 310	1 269	1 265	1 277	1 304	1 274	1 177	948	937	972
Furniture and related products	544	509	475	444	444	436	433	409	364	284	263	260
Miscellaneous manufacturing	510	490	469	442	432	424	423	425	416	382	370	373
Nondurable Goods	4 769	4 513	4 238	4 037	3 932	3 841	3 782	3 725	3 653	3 332	3 248	3 245
Food manufacturing	1 228	1 221	1 202	1 192	1 178	1 170	1 172	1 184	1 184	1 161	1 152	1 156
Beverage and tobacco products	117	116	120	106	106	112	115	118	112	112	106	108
Textile mills	315	276	242	217	194	174	158	137	122	99	96	99
Textile products mills	183	174	162	148	147	143	135	123	115	98	92	89
Apparel	404	341	286	242	219	193	182	173	163	132	120	112
Leather and allied products	55	47	40	35	33	31	29	27	28	24	22	23
Paper and paper products	468	446	421	393	374	365	357	350	344	313	302	298
Printing and related support	576	544	493	471	460	447	447	443	424	369	342	325
Petroleum and coal products	83	81	78	74	77	75	72	73	77	70	70	70
Chemicals	588	562	532	525	520	510	508	504	512	479	474	483
Plastics and rubber products	753	704	662	633	626	620	608	592	572	476	472	482

Table 2-5. Total Employees on Manufacturing Payrolls, by Industry, NAICS Basis, 2000–2011

(Thousands of people.)

Industry	2000	2001	2002	2003	2004	2005	2006	2007	2008	2009	2010	2011
Total Manufacturing	17 263	16 441	15 259	14 509	14 315	14 227	14 155	13 879	13 406	11 847	11 528	11 733
Durable Goods	10 877	10 336	9 485	8 964	8 925	8 956	8 981	8 808	8 463	7 284	7 064	7 274
Wood products	615	576	557	540	552	561	561	517	458	360	342	335
Nometallic mineral products	554	545	516	494	506	505	510	501	465	394	371	367
Primary metals	622	571	509	477	467	466	464	456	442	362	362	390
Fabricated metal products	1 753	1 676	1 549	1 479	1 497	1 522	1 553	1 563	1 528	1 312	1 282	1 344
Machinery	1 457	1 371	1 232	1 152	1 145	1 166	1 183	1 187	1 188	1 029	996	1 057
Computer and electronic products	1 820	1 749	1 507	1 355	1 323	1 316	1 308	1 273	1 244	1 137	1 095	1 107
Electrical equipment and appliances	591	557	497	460	445	434	433	429	424	374	360	367
Transportation equipment	2 057	1 939	1 830	1 775	1 767	1 772	1 769	1 712	1 608	1 348	1 333	1 382
Furniture and related products	680	643	605	574	574	566	558	529	478	384	357	353
Miscellaneous manufacturing	728	710	683	658	651	647	644	642	629	584	567	573
Nondurable Goods	6 386	6 105	5 774	5 546	5 390	5 271	5 174	5 071	4 943	4 564	4 464	4 460
Food manufacturing	1 553	1 551	1 526	1 518	1 494	1 478	1 479	1 484	1 481	1 456	1 451	1 456
Beverage and tobacco products	207	209	207	200	195	192	194	198	198	187	183	188
Textile mills	378	333	291	261	237	218	195	170	151	124	119	121
Textile products mills	230	217	204	188	183	176	167	158	147	126	119	117
Apparel	484	415	350	304	278	251	232	215	199	168	157	152
Leather and allied products	69	58	50	45	42	40	37	34	33	29	28	29
Paper and paper products	605	578	547	516	496	484	471	458	445	407	395	391
Printing and related support	807	768	707	680	663	646	634	622	594	522	488	469
Petroleum and coal products	123	121	118	114	112	112	113	115	117	115	114	112
Chemicals	980	959	928	906	887	872	866	861	847	804	787	788
Plastics and rubber products	951	896	847	814	805	802	786	757	729	625	625	636

Table 2-6. Average Weekly Hours of All Employees on Private Nonfarm Payrolls by NAICS Super Sector, 2007–2011

(Hours per week, seasonally adjusted.)

| Year and month | Total private | Mining and logging | Construction | Manufac-turing | Trade, transportation, and utilities | | | | Informa-tion | Financial activities | Profes-sional and business services | Education and health services | Leisure and hospitality | Other services |
					Total	Wholesale trade	Retail trade	Utilities						
2007	34.6	44.0	38.0	40.0	34.5	38.1	31.7	41.8	36.1	36.6	35.4	33.5	26.1	32.9
2008	34.5	43.7	37.8	39.8	34.4	38.4	31.4	42.0	36.5	36.5	35.2	33.7	25.9	32.9
2009	33.9	42.1	37.1	39.0	34.1	37.9	31.3	40.9	36.5	36.6	35.0	33.0	25.6	31.6
2010	34.1	43.4	37.8	40.2	34.2	38.1	31.3	41.1	36.5	36.9	35.4	32.8	25.7	31.6
2011	34.4	44.5	38.3	40.5	34.6	38.6	31.6	41.8	36.6	37.3	35.7	32.8	25.9	31.7
2007														
January	34.5	42.7	38.1	40.1	34.3	37.6	31.7	40.9	36.0	36.5	35.2	33.4	26.2	32.7
February	34.5	43.1	37.8	40.0	34.4	37.9	31.6	41.7	36.1	36.5	35.6	33.4	26.0	32.9
March	34.6	43.3	38.1	40.0	34.5	38.0	31.7	41.6	36.1	36.5	35.4	33.5	26.1	33.0
April	34.6	44.4	38.0	40.1	34.5	38.0	31.7	41.8	36.1	36.5	35.5	33.5	26.1	32.9
May	34.6	44.2	38.1	40.0	34.5	38.1	31.7	41.9	35.9	36.4	35.4	33.6	26.1	33.0
June	34.6	43.9	37.9	40.0	34.7	38.1	31.9	42.0	36.0	36.6	35.4	33.5	26.2	32.9
July	34.6	44.2	37.9	40.1	34.5	38.1	31.7	41.9	36.2	36.5	35.4	33.5	26.0	32.9
August	34.6	44.0	37.9	40.0	34.5	38.2	31.7	42.1	36.1	36.6	35.3	33.6	26.0	32.8
September	34.6	44.5	38.2	40.1	34.5	38.1	31.7	42.3	36.1	36.5	35.4	33.6	26.0	32.8
October	34.5	44.4	38.0	39.9	34.5	38.1	31.7	41.4	36.0	36.5	35.2	33.6	26.0	32.8
November	34.6	44.2	38.2	40.1	34.6	38.3	31.7	41.8	36.2	36.5	35.4	33.5	26.0	32.9
December	34.6	44.2	38.3	40.2	34.6	38.4	31.7	42.1	36.3	36.5	35.3	33.5	26.1	32.8
2008														
January	34.6	43.9	38.4	40.1	34.6	38.3	31.7	42.3	36.5	36.4	35.2	33.6	26.0	32.6
February	34.6	43.9	38.5	40.2	34.6	38.4	31.7	42.2	36.5	36.5	35.2	33.7	25.9	32.9
March	34.7	44.8	38.2	40.2	34.6	38.4	31.7	42.7	36.5	36.5	35.3	33.8	26.0	33.1
April	34.6	42.9	38.2	40.0	34.5	38.4	31.6	42.1	36.6	36.5	35.2	33.8	26.0	33.0
May	34.6	43.6	38.1	40.1	34.5	38.4	31.5	42.3	36.5	36.7	35.2	33.8	26.0	33.0
June	34.6	43.9	38.0	40.1	34.5	38.5	31.5	42.4	36.6	36.6	35.3	33.7	26.0	32.8
July	34.5	43.3	37.8	39.8	34.4	38.6	31.4	41.9	36.6	36.5	35.3	33.7	25.8	32.8
August	34.5	43.6	37.9	39.8	34.5	38.7	31.4	41.6	36.6	36.7	35.3	33.8	25.8	33.0
September	34.4	42.8	37.6	39.6	34.4	38.5	31.4	41.8	36.7	36.5	35.2	33.6	25.8	32.9
October	34.4	44.3	38.3	39.6	34.4	38.4	31.3	41.5	36.7	36.5	35.2	33.7	25.9	32.8
November	34.3	43.8	37.1	39.3	34.3	38.3	31.3	41.6	36.5	36.6	35.1	33.6	25.7	32.8
December	34.1	43.2	37.4	39.1	34.0	38.3	30.7	41.5	36.6	36.5	35.1	33.5	25.6	32.8
2009														
January	34.1	43.0	37.1	38.8	34.3	38.4	31.2	41.6	36.5	36.6	35.1	33.6	25.6	32.6
February	34.0	42.8	37.3	38.9	34.2	38.1	31.2	41.9	36.5	36.5	35.0	33.4	25.5	32.1
March	33.8	42.4	37.2	38.6	34.1	37.9	31.1	41.1	36.4	36.5	34.9	32.9	25.5	31.5
April	33.8	41.9	37.2	38.6	34.1	37.9	31.2	40.8	36.3	36.6	35.0	33.0	25.4	31.3
May	33.8	41.5	37.1	38.5	34.2	37.9	31.3	40.6	36.5	36.5	35.0	32.9	25.5	31.5
June	33.8	41.8	37.2	38.7	34.0	37.7	31.2	40.5	36.4	36.3	35.0	32.8	25.5	31.5
July	33.8	42.0	37.3	38.9	34.0	37.7	31.2	40.8	36.5	36.6	35.0	32.8	25.5	31.4
August	33.8	42.2	37.2	39.2	34.0	37.7	31.1	40.9	36.4	36.5	35.1	32.8	25.5	31.4
September	33.8	42.2	36.9	39.1	34.2	37.6	31.5	40.4	36.4	36.6	35.0	32.9	25.6	31.3
October	33.8	42.0	37.1	39.2	34.1	37.7	31.3	40.6	36.4	36.7	34.8	32.8	25.5	31.4
November	33.9	42.4	37.3	39.6	34.1	37.8	31.3	40.8	36.6	36.6	35.1	32.7	25.5	31.4
December	33.9	42.4	37.2	39.7	34.0	37.7	31.1	40.6	36.4	36.6	35.2	32.8	25.6	31.5
2010														
January	34.0	43.0	37.3	39.9	34.0	37.8	31.2	40.4	36.6	36.7	35.3	33.0	25.6	31.6
February	33.9	42.9	36.4	39.6	34.0	37.8	31.3	40.5	36.5	36.8	35.1	32.8	25.7	31.6
March	34.0	43.2	37.3	40.0	34.0	37.9	31.2	40.5	36.5	36.9	35.4	32.8	25.8	31.6
April	34.1	43.6	37.7	40.2	34.2	38.0	31.3	40.8	36.5	36.9	35.3	32.8	25.7	31.7
May	34.2	43.8	37.6	40.4	34.2	38.1	31.3	41.3	36.5	37.0	35.4	32.8	25.8	31.8
June	34.1	43.3	37.7	40.2	34.2	38.0	31.3	41.1	36.6	37.1	35.2	32.8	25.7	31.7
July	34.2	43.8	37.6	40.2	34.4	38.2	31.5	41.2	36.6	37.0	35.5	32.7	25.8	31.7
August	34.2	43.9	37.8	40.3	34.4	38.2	31.5	41.4	36.7	37.0	35.5	32.7	25.8	31.7
September	34.2	43.5	38.1	40.4	34.3	38.4	31.4	41.3	36.6	37.1	35.6	32.8	25.8	31.8
October	34.3	43.7	38.0	40.4	34.5	38.4	31.5	41.6	36.8	37.1	35.6	32.9	25.9	31.7
November	34.2	42.7	37.9	40.3	34.4	38.4	31.4	41.4	36.7	37.1	35.6	32.8	25.9	31.7
December	34.3	43.9	37.8	40.4	34.5	38.4	31.6	41.5	36.5	37.1	35.7	32.7	25.8	31.7
2011														
January	34.3	44.9	37.7	40.4	34.5	38.5	31.5	41.7	36.6	37.1	35.7	32.7	25.8	31.6
February	34.3	44.1	37.7	40.5	34.5	38.5	31.4	41.3	36.6	37.1	35.7	32.7	25.9	31.7
March	34.3	44.2	38.0	40.5	34.6	38.6	31.5	42.0	36.6	37.1	35.7	32.8	25.8	31.8
April	34.4	44.4	37.8	40.4	34.7	38.6	31.7	42.0	36.6	37.2	35.7	32.9	25.9	31.9
May	34.4	44.7	38.4	40.5	34.5	38.6	31.5	42.0	36.6	37.2	35.7	33.0	25.8	31.8
June	34.4	44.6	38.1	40.4	34.6	38.7	31.6	41.8	36.6	37.2	35.7	32.9	25.9	31.9
July	34.4	44.3	38.3	40.4	34.6	38.7	31.6	41.7	36.7	37.4	35.8	32.9	25.9	31.8
August	34.3	44.0	38.1	40.3	34.5	38.6	31.5	41.5	36.5	37.2	35.7	32.8	25.9	31.6
September	34.4	44.6	38.2	40.4	34.6	38.8	31.7	42.4	36.6	37.6	35.8	32.8	25.9	31.7
October	34.4	45.4	38.1	40.6	34.6	38.8	31.7	42.2	36.7	37.5	35.8	32.8	26.0	31.7
November	34.4	44.3	38.1	40.4	34.6	38.8	31.7	41.7	36.8	37.4	35.8	32.8	26.1	31.7
December	34.4	44.7	38.4	40.7	34.7	38.8	31.8	41.1	36.6	37.3	35.8	32.8	26.1	31.6

Table 2-7. Average Weekly Hours of Production Workers on Private Nonfarm Payrolls, by Super Sector, NAICS Basis, 2000–2011

(Hours.)

Industry	2000	2001	2002	2003	2004	2005	2006	2007	2008	2009	2010	2011
TOTAL PRIVATE	34.3	34.0	33.9	33.7	33.7	33.8	33.9	33.9	33.6	33.1	33.4	33.6
Goods-Producing	40.7	39.9	39.9	39.8	40.0	40.1	40.5	40.6	40.2	39.2	40.4	40.9
Mining and logging	44.4	44.6	43.2	43.6	44.5	45.6	45.6	45.9	45.1	43.2	44.6	46.7
Construction	39.2	38.7	38.4	38.4	38.3	38.6	39.0	39.0	38.5	37.6	38.4	39.0
Manufacturing	41.3	40.3	40.5	40.4	40.8	40.7	41.1	41.2	40.8	39.8	41.1	41.4
Private Service-Providing	32.7	32.5	32.5	32.3	32.3	32.4	32.4	32.4	32.3	32.1	32.2	32.4
Trade, transportation, and												
utilities	33.8	33.5	33.6	33.6	33.5	33.4	33.4	33.3	33.2	32.9	33.3	33.7
Wholesale trade	38.8	38.4	38.0	37.9	37.8	37.7	38.0	38.2	38.2	37.6	37.9	38.5
Retail trade	30.7	30.7	30.9	30.9	30.7	30.6	30.5	30.2	30.0	29.9	30.2	30.5
Transportation and												
warehousing	37.4	36.7	36.8	36.8	37.2	37.0	36.9	37.0	36.4	36.0	37.1	37.8
Utilities	42.0	41.4	40.9	41.1	40.9	41.1	41.4	42.4	42.7	42.0	42.0	42.1
Information	36.8	36.9	36.5	36.2	36.3	36.5	36.6	36.5	36.7	36.6	36.3	36.2
Financial activities	35.9	35.8	35.6	35.5	35.5	35.9	35.7	35.9	35.8	36.1	36.2	36.4
Professional and business services	34.5	34.2	34.2	34.1	34.2	34.2	34.6	34.8	34.8	34.7	35.1	35.2
Education and health services	32.2	32.3	32.4	32.3	32.4	32.6	32.5	32.6	32.5	32.2	32.1	32.3
Leisure and hospitality	26.1	25.8	25.8	25.6	25.7	25.7	25.7	25.5	25.2	24.8	24.8	24.8
Other services	32.5	32.3	32.1	31.4	31.0	30.9	30.9	30.9	30.8	30.5	30.7	30.7

Table 2-8. Employees on Total Nonfarm Payrolls, by State and Selected Territory, 1970–2011

(Thousands of people.)

State	1970	1971	1972	1973	1974	1975	1976	1977	1978	1979	1980	1981	1982	1983	1984
UNITED STATES	71 006	71 335	73 798	76 912	78 389	77 069	79 502	82 593	86 826	89 932	90 528	91 289	89 677	90 280	94 530
Alabama	1 010	1 022	1 072	1 136	1 170	1 155	1 207	1 269	1 337	1 362	1 356	1 348	1 313	1 329	1 388
Alaska	93	98	104	110	128	162	172	163	164	167	169	186	200	214	226
Arizona	547	581	646	714	746	729	759	809	895	980	1 014	1 041	1 030	1 078	1 182
Arkansas	536	551	582	615	641	624	660	696	733	750	742	740	720	741	780
California	6 946	6 917	7 210	7 622	7 834	7 847	8 154	8 600	9 200	9 665	9 849	9 985	9 810	9 918	10 390
Colorado	750	787	869	936	960	964	1 003	1 058	1 150	1 218	1 251	1 295	1 317	1 327	1 402
Connecticut	1 198	1 164	1 190	1 239	1 264	1 223	1 240	1 282	1 346	1 398	1 427	1 438	1 429	1 444	1 517
Delaware	217	225	232	239	233	230	237	239	248	257	259	259	259	266	280
District of Columbia	567	567	572	574	580	577	576	579	581	613	616	611	598	599	614
Florida	2 152	2 276	2 513	2 779	2 864	2 746	2 784	2 933	3 181	3 381	3 576	3 736	3 762	3 905	4 204
Georgia	1 558	1 603	1 695	1 803	1 828	1 756	1 839	1 927	2 050	2 128	2 159	2 199	2 202	2 280	2 449
Hawaii	294	302	313	328	336	343	349	359	377	394	404	405	399	406	413
Idaho	208	217	237	252	267	273	291	307	331	338	330	328	312	318	331
Illinois	4 346	4 296	4 315	4 467	4 546	4 419	4 565	4 656	4 789	4 880	4 850	4 732	4 593	4 531	4 672
Indiana	1 849	1 841	1 922	2 028	2 031	1 942	2 024	2 114	2 206	2 236	2 130	2 115	2 028	2 030	2 122
Iowa	877	883	912	961	999	999	1 037	1 079	1 119	1 132	1 110	1 089	1 042	1 040	1 075
Kansas	679	678	718	763	790	801	835	871	913	947	945	950	921	922	961
Kentucky	910	932	988	1 039	1 066	1 058	1 103	1 148	1 210	1 245	1 210	1 196	1 161	1 152	1 214
Louisiana	1 034	1 056	1 129	1 176	1 221	1 250	1 314	1 365	1 464	1 517	1 579	1 631	1 607	1 565	1 602
Maine	332	332	344	355	362	357	375	388	406	416	418	419	416	425	446
Maryland	1 349	1 372	1 415	1 472	1 494	1 479	1 498	1 546	1 626	1 691	1 712	1 716	1 676	1 724	1 814
Massachusetts	2 244	2 211	2 252	2 333	2 354	2 273	2 324	2 416	2 526	2 604	2 654	2 672	2 642	2 697	2 856
Michigan	2 999	2 995	3 119	3 284	3 278	3 137	3 283	3 442	3 609	3 637	3 443	3 364	3 193	3 223	3 381
Minnesota	1 315	1 310	1 357	1 436	1 481	1 474	1 521	1 597	1 689	1 767	1 770	1 761	1 707	1 718	1 820
Mississippi	584	602	649	693	711	692	728	766	814	838	829	819	791	793	821
Missouri	1 668	1 661	1 700	1 771	1 789	1 741	1 798	1 862	1 953	2 011	1 970	1 957	1 923	1 937	2 033
Montana	199	205	215	224	234	238	251	265	280	284	280	282	274	276	281
Nebraska	484	491	517	541	562	558	572	594	610	631	628	623	610	611	635
Nevada	203	211	224	245	256	263	280	308	350	384	400	411	401	403	426
New Hampshire	259	260	279	298	300	293	313	337	360	379	385	395	394	410	442
New Jersey	2 606	2 608	2 673	2 760	2 783	2 700	2 754	2 837	2 962	3 027	3 060	3 099	3 093	3 165	3 329
New Mexico	293	306	328	346	360	370	390	415	444	461	465	476	474	480	503
New York	7 157	7 011	7 039	7 132	7 077	6 830	6 790	6 858	7 045	7 179	7 207	7 287	7 255	7 313	7 570
North Carolina	1 783	1 814	1 912	2 018	2 048	1 980	2 083	2 171	2 278	2 373	2 380	2 392	2 347	2 419	2 565
North Dakota	164	167	176	184	194	204	215	221	234	244	245	249	250	251	253
Ohio	3 881	3 840	3 938	4 113	4 169	4 016	4 095	4 230	4 395	4 485	4 367	4 318	4 124	4 093	4 260
Oklahoma	763	774	812	852	887	900	931	972	1 036	1 088	1 138	1 201	1 217	1 171	1 180
Oregon	711	729	775	816	838	837	879	937	1 009	1 056	1 045	1 019	961	967	1 007
Pennsylvania	4 352	4 291	4 400	4 507	4 515	4 436	4 513	4 565	4 716	4 806	4 753	4 729	4 580	4 524	4 655
Rhode Island	344	343	358	366	367	349	367	382	396	400	398	401	391	396	416
South Carolina	842	863	920	984	1 016	983	1 038	1 082	1 138	1 176	1 189	1 197	1 162	1 189	1 263
South Dakota	175	179	190	199	207	209	219	227	237	241	238	236	230	235	247
Tennessee	1 328	1 357	1 450	1 531	1 558	1 506	1 575	1 648	1 737	1 777	1 747	1 755	1 703	1 719	1 812
Texas	3 625	3 684	3 884	4 142	4 360	4 463	4 684	4 907	5 272	5 602	5 851	6 180	6 263	6 194	6 492
Utah	357	369	393	415	434	440	463	489	525	548	551	558	561	567	601
Vermont	148	148	154	161	163	162	168	178	191	198	200	204	203	206	215
Virginia	1 519	1 567	1 656	1 753	1 805	1 779	1 848	1 930	2 034	2 115	2 157	2 161	2 146	2 207	2 333
Washington	1 079	1 064	1 100	1 152	1 199	1 226	1 283	1 367	1 485	1 581	1 608	1 612	1 569	1 586	1 660
West Virginia	517	520	541	562	572	575	596	612	633	659	646	629	608	582	597
Wisconsin	1 530	1 525	1 581	1 661	1 703	1 677	1 726	1 799	1 887	1 960	1 938	1 923	1 867	1 867	1 949
Wyoming	108	111	117	126	137	146	157	171	187	201	210	224	218	203	204
Puerto Rico	. . .	. . .	. . .	. . .	. . .	. . .	. . .	. . .	. . .	. . .	693	680	642	646	684
Virgin Islands	. . .	. . .	. . .	. . .	. . .	33	31	32	34	36	37	38	37	36	37

. . . = Not available.

Table 2-8. Employees on Total Nonfarm Payrolls, by State and Selected Territory, 1970–2011—*Continued*

(Thousands of people.)

State	1985	1986	1987	1988	1989	1990	1991	1992	1993	1994	1995	1996	1997
UNITED STATES	97 511	99 474	102 088	105 345	108 014	109 487	108 374	108 726	110 844	114 291	117 298	119 708	122 776
Alabama	1 427	1 463	1 508	1 559	1 601	1 636	1 642	1 674	1 717	1 758	1 804	1 829	1 866
Alaska	231	221	210	214	227	238	243	247	253	259	262	264	269
Arizona	1 279	1 338	1 386	1 419	1 454	1 483	1 491	1 517	1 584	1 692	1 793	1 892	1 985
Arkansas	797	814	837	865	893	924	937	963	994	1 034	1 070	1 087	1 105
California	10 770	11 086	11 473	11 912	12 238	12 500	12 359	12 154	12 046	12 160	12 422	12 744	13 130
Colorado	1 419	1 408	1 413	1 436	1 482	1 521	1 545	1 597	1 671	1 756	1 835	1 901	1 980
Connecticut	1 558	1 598	1 638	1 667	1 666	1 620	1 557	1 526	1 531	1 544	1 562	1 582	1 608
Delaware	293	303	321	334	344	348	342	341	349	356	366	376	388
District of Columbia	629	640	656	674	681	686	677	674	670	659	643	623	618
Florida	4 410	4 599	4 848	5 067	5 261	5 373	5 283	5 348	5 560	5 788	5 985	6 172	6 407
Georgia	2 570	2 672	2 782	2 876	2 941	2 992	2 938	2 987	3 109	3 266	3 402	3 527	3 614
Hawaii	426	439	460	478	506	528	539	543	539	536	533	531	532
Idaho	336	328	333	349	366	385	398	414	433	459	475	489	506
Illinois	4 755	4 791	4 928	5 098	5 214	5 288	5 233	5 235	5 330	5 463	5 593	5 685	5 771
Indiana	2 169	2 222	2 305	2 396	2 479	2 522	2 507	2 554	2 627	2 713	2 786	2 814	2 858
Iowa	1 074	1 074	1 109	1 156	1 200	1 226	1 238	1 253	1 278	1 320	1 358	1 383	1 407
Kansas	968	985	1 005	1 035	1 064	1 092	1 097	1 116	1 135	1 167	1 200	1 228	1 270
Kentucky	1 250	1 274	1 328	1 382	1 433	1 471	1 475	1 509	1 548	1 597	1 643	1 672	1 711
Louisiana	1 591	1 518	1 484	1 512	1 538	1 588	1 611	1 625	1 656	1 720	1 770	1 808	1 848
Maine	458	477	501	527	542	535	514	512	519	532	538	542	554
Maryland	1 888	1 952	2 028	2 102	2 155	2 173	2 102	2 084	2 104	2 148	2 184	2 213	2 269
Massachusetts	2 931	2 992	3 071	3 138	3 118	2 988	2 824	2 798	2 843	2 907	2 980	3 039	3 114
Michigan	3 562	3 657	3 736	3 819	3 922	3 946	3 884	3 919	3 999	4 141	4 268	4 352	4 439
Minnesota	1 866	1 892	1 962	2 028	2 087	2 136	2 146	2 194	2 252	2 320	2 388	2 442	2 500
Mississippi	839	848	864	896	919	936	938	960	1 002	1 056	1 074	1 089	1 107
Missouri	2 095	2 143	2 198	2 259	2 315	2 345	2 309	2 334	2 394	2 470	2 521	2 568	2 639
Montana	279	275	274	283	291	297	304	317	326	340	352	362	367
Nebraska	650	652	667	688	708	731	740	752	769	798	819	837	856
Nevada	446	468	500	538	581	621	629	639	672	738	786	843	891
New Hampshire	466	490	513	529	529	508	482	487	502	523	540	554	570
New Jersey	3 414	3 488	3 576	3 651	3 690	3 635	3 499	3 458	3 493	3 553	3 601	3 639	3 724
New Mexico	520	526	529	548	562	580	585	602	626	657	682	695	708
New York	7 751	7 908	8 059	8 187	8 247	8 214	7 888	7 732	7 762	7 833	7 894	7 941	8 070
North Carolina	2 651	2 744	2 863	2 987	3 074	3 125	3 080	3 144	3 247	3 355	3 455	3 540	3 657
North Dakota	252	250	252	257	260	266	271	277	285	295	302	309	314
Ohio	4 373	4 472	4 583	4 701	4 818	4 882	4 819	4 848	4 918	5 076	5 221	5 296	5 392
Oklahoma	1 165	1 124	1 108	1 132	1 164	1 184	1 199	1 210	1 235	1 268	1 304	1 342	1 381
Oregon	1 030	1 058	1 100	1 153	1 206	1 256	1 254	1 276	1 318	1 372	1 428	1 485	1 537
Pennsylvania	4 730	4 791	4 915	5 042	5 138	5 173	5 086	5 078	5 126	5 195	5 256	5 309	5 409
Rhode Island	429	443	452	459	462	454	424	424	430	434	439	441	450
South Carolina	1 296	1 338	1 392	1 449	1 500	1 542	1 512	1 527	1 570	1 607	1 646	1 678	1 723
South Dakota	249	252	257	266	276	288	296	308	318	331	342	347	353
Tennessee	1 868	1 930	2 012	2 092	2 167	2 196	2 186	2 248	2 331	2 426	2 503	2 537	2 588
Texas	6 663	6 564	6 517	6 678	6 840	7 101	7 181	7 275	7 488	7 758	8 029	8 263	8 614
Utah	624	634	640	660	691	724	745	769	810	860	908	954	994
Vermont	225	234	246	256	262	258	249	251	257	264	270	275	279
Virginia	2 455	2 558	2 680	2 772	2 862	2 894	2 829	2 848	2 919	3 004	3 070	3 136	3 232
Washington	1 710	1 770	1 852	1 941	2 047	2 143	2 177	2 222	2 257	2 304	2 347	2 416	2 515
West Virginia	597	598	599	610	615	630	629	640	652	674	688	699	708
Wisconsin	1 983	2 024	2 090	2 168	2 236	2 292	2 302	2 358	2 413	2 491	2 559	2 601	2 656
Wyoming	207	196	183	189	193	198	203	206	210	217	219	221	225
Puerto Rico	692	728	764	818	837	846	838	858	872	898	930	973	989
Virgin Islands	37	38	40	42	42	43	44	45	49	44	42	41	42

Table 2-8. Employees on Total Nonfarm Payrolls, by State and Selected Territory, 1970–2011—*Continued*

(Thousands of people.)

State	1998	1999	2000	2001	2002	2003	2004	2005	2006	2007	2008	2009	2010	2011
UNITED STATES	125 930	128 993	131 785	131 826	130 341	129 999	131 435	133 703	136 086	137 598	136 790	130 807	129 874	131 359
Alabama	1 898	1 920	1 931	1 909	1 883	1 876	1 902	1 945	1 980	2 006	1 992	1 886	1 871	1 866
Alaska	275	278	284	289	295	299	304	310	315	318	322	321	325	329
Arizona	2 075	2 163	2 243	2 265	2 267	2 298	2 383	2 511	2 637	2 677	2 620	2 429	2 382	2 406
Arkansas	1 122	1 142	1 159	1 154	1 146	1 145	1 158	1 178	1 199	1 204	1 202	1 165	1 161	1 160
California	13 597	13 992	14 489	14 603	14 458	14 394	14 533	14 802	15 065	15 184	14 995	14 092	13 937	14 060
Colorado	2 058	2 133	2 214	2 227	2 184	2 153	2 180	2 226	2 279	2 331	2 350	2 246	2 222	2 255
Connecticut	1 643	1 669	1 693	1 681	1 665	1 644	1 650	1 662	1 681	1 698	1 699	1 627	1 608	1 624
Delaware	400	413	420	420	415	416	425	433	438	439	437	417	414	417
District of Columbia	614	627	650	654	664	666	674	682	688	694	702	702	712	728
Florida	6 625	6 816	7 070	7 160	7 169	7 250	7 499	7 800	8 002	8 018	7 736	7 254	7 195	7 272
Georgia	3 741	3 855	3 949	3 943	3 870	3 845	3 898	4 001	4 089	4 146	4 102	3 881	3 843	3 880
Hawaii	531	535	551	555	557	568	583	602	617	625	619	592	587	592
Idaho	521	539	560	568	568	572	588	611	638	655	649	610	604	607
Illinois	5 899	5 958	6 045	5 995	5 884	5 811	5 816	5 862	5 933	5 980	5 949	5 657	5 613	5 663
Indiana	2 917	2 970	3 000	2 933	2 901	2 895	2 929	2 955	2 974	2 986	2 957	2 787	2 796	2 830
Iowa	1 443	1 469	1 478	1 466	1 447	1 440	1 457	1 480	1 504	1 519	1 524	1 479	1 469	1 478
Kansas	1 314	1 328	1 346	1 349	1 336	1 313	1 325	1 333	1 354	1 380	1 391	1 343	1 328	1 336
Kentucky	1 753	1 796	1 827	1 805	1 789	1 783	1 799	1 824	1 847	1 867	1 852	1 769	1 770	1 790
Louisiana	1 887	1 894	1 918	1 915	1 896	1 906	1 918	1 892	1 853	1 916	1 938	1 901	1 884	1 906
Maine	569	586	604	608	606	607	612	612	615	618	617	596	593	593
Maryland	2 326	2 392	2 455	2 472	2 480	2 487	2 518	2 556	2 589	2 608	2 600	2 524	2 518	2 548
Massachusetts	3 184	3 243	3 329	3 339	3 259	3 198	3 195	3 212	3 246	3 280	3 290	3 181	3 191	3 211
Michigan	4 514	4 585	4 676	4 564	4 487	4 416	4 399	4 390	4 326	4 268	4 162	3 871	3 863	3 936
Minnesota	2 564	2 622	2 685	2 690	2 664	2 660	2 681	2 723	2 758	2 771	2 763	2 655	2 641	2 676
Mississippi	1 134	1 153	1 154	1 130	1 124	1 115	1 125	1 130	1 141	1 153	1 148	1 096	1 091	1 090
Missouri	2 684	2 727	2 749	2 730	2 699	2 680	2 694	2 735	2 774	2 795	2 789	2 684	2 650	2 650
Montana	376	384	391	391	396	400	411	420	434	444	445	429	428	428
Nebraska	878	894	910	917	908	910	918	930	942	957	965	945	940	944
Nevada	926	983	1 027	1 051	1 052	1 088	1 153	1 223	1 280	1 292	1 264	1 148	1 117	1 125
New Hampshire	589	606	622	627	618	618	627	637	643	648	649	628	624	626
New Jersey	3 801	3 901	3 994	3 997	3 984	3 979	3 999	4 039	4 071	4 079	4 051	3 895	3 851	3 856
New Mexico	720	730	745	757	766	776	790	809	832	844	847	812	803	804
New York	8 239	8 459	8 638	8 595	8 462	8 410	8 465	8 537	8 618	8 734	8 793	8 556	8 567	8 683
North Carolina	3 762	3 853	3 919	3 898	3 840	3 792	3 840	3 919	4 044	4 149	4 139	3 913	3 879	3 922
North Dakota	320	324	328	330	330	333	338	345	352	358	367	367	376	394
Ohio	5 482	5 564	5 625	5 543	5 445	5 398	5 408	5 427	5 436	5 428	5 362	5 073	5 035	5 083
Oklahoma	1 428	1 449	1 477	1 494	1 474	1 445	1 461	1 500	1 540	1 569	1 593	1 542	1 530	1 550
Oregon	1 562	1 586	1 618	1 606	1 585	1 574	1 607	1 654	1 704	1 731	1 718	1 612	1 602	1 618
Pennsylvania	5 498	5 589	5 694	5 685	5 644	5 614	5 647	5 705	5 759	5 801	5 802	5 618	5 624	5 687
Rhode Island	458	466	477	478	479	484	488	491	493	493	482	460	459	460
South Carolina	1 786	1 833	1 862	1 825	1 806	1 810	1 835	1 869	1 909	1 948	1 929	1 816	1 812	1 832
South Dakota	360	370	378	379	378	378	384	390	399	406	411	404	403	406
Tennessee	2 642	2 689	2 733	2 688	2 664	2 663	2 706	2 743	2 783	2 797	2 775	2 620	2 615	2 656
Texas	8 943	9 160	9 432	9 514	9 416	9 370	9 497	9 740	10 065	10 393	10 604	10 304	10 341	10 557
Utah	1 023	1 048	1 075	1 081	1 073	1 074	1 104	1 148	1 204	1 253	1 252	1 189	1 182	1 208
Vermont	285	292	299	302	299	299	303	306	308	308	307	297	298	300
Virginia	3 320	3 412	3 516	3 517	3 494	3 498	3 584	3 664	3 726	3 761	3 763	3 642	3 638	3 680
Washington	2 595	2 649	2 711	2 697	2 654	2 658	2 701	2 777	2 859	2 934	2 959	2 822	2 786	2 820
West Virginia	719	726	736	735	733	728	737	746	756	758	762	746	747	754
Wisconsin	2 718	2 784	2 834	2 814	2 782	2 774	2 804	2 838	2 862	2 878	2 871	2 744	2 729	2 741
Wyoming	228	233	239	245	248	250	255	264	277	289	298	286	283	286
Puerto Rico	997	1 011	1 025	1 009	1 005	1 024	1 050	1 051	1 044	1 031	1 014	964	931	923
Virgin Islands	42	41	42	44	43	42	43	44	46	46	46	44	44	44

Table 2-9. Employees on Total Private Payrolls, by State and Selected Territory, 2000–2011

(Thousands of people.)

State	2000	2001	2002	2003	2004	2005	2006	2007	2008	2009	2010	2011
UNITED STATES	110 995	110 708	108 828	108 416	109 814	111 899	114 113	115 380	114 281	108 252	107 384	109 254
Alabama	1 580	1 557	1 529	1 517	1 542	1 582	1 609	1 629	1 608	1 503	1 484	1 486
Alaska	210	211	215	218	223	229	234	237	240	237	240	244
Arizona	1 876	1 888	1 876	1 905	1 984	2 108	2 229	2 256	2 187	2 006	1 966	1 995
Arkansas	968	960	951	947	958	974	991	994	989	948	943	941
California	12 171	12 221	12 011	11 967	12 136	12 382	12 612	12 690	12 476	11 612	11 488	11 662
Colorado	1 877	1 883	1 829	1 797	1 821	1 863	1 912	1 957	1 966	1 855	1 828	1 863
Connecticut	1 451	1 437	1 416	1 399	1 407	1 418	1 435	1 449	1 447	1 378	1 364	1 385
Delaware	364	363	358	358	367	373	377	377	374	353	350	353
District of Columbia	426	428	433	435	443	449	455	463	469	461	465	480
Florida	6 068	6 136	6 129	6 197	6 433	6 719	6 903	6 896	6 609	6 139	6 083	6 176
Georgia	3 352	3 334	3 246	3 214	3 264	3 355	3 430	3 473	3 412	3 193	3 164	3 211
Hawaii	437	441	439	449	463	482	496	503	494	466	462	467
Idaho	451	458	456	459	474	496	522	538	530	490	485	490
Illinois	5 205	5 145	5 023	4 958	4 971	5 016	5 087	5 131	5 094	4 800	4 759	4 826
Indiana	2 595	2 523	2 484	2 473	2 503	2 529	2 548	2 555	2 516	2 349	2 359	2 406
Iowa	1 235	1 220	1 203	1 196	1 213	1 235	1 257	1 269	1 272	1 224	1 216	1 228
Kansas	1 101	1 101	1 085	1 063	1 074	1 082	1 099	1 122	1 131	1 082	1 066	1 078
Kentucky	1 519	1 493	1 474	1 471	1 489	1 511	1 529	1 543	1 529	1 445	1 440	1 460
Louisiana	1 544	1 542	1 521	1 526	1 535	1 518	1 505	1 560	1 573	1 532	1 518	1 546
Maine	504	506	503	503	507	507	510	514	513	493	489	492
Maryland	2 005	2 015	2 016	2 025	2 055	2 090	2 118	2 130	2 112	2 030	2 016	2 041
Massachusetts	2 894	2 899	2 823	2 773	2 774	2 787	2 817	2 848	2 853	2 743	2 751	2 776
Michigan	3 995	3 879	3 800	3 731	3 719	3 716	3 661	3 612	3 512	3 224	3 228	3 317
Minnesota	2 277	2 280	2 251	2 248	2 269	2 308	2 342	2 357	2 344	2 238	2 225	2 268
Mississippi	920	893	884	874	883	890	902	909	900	847	842	844
Missouri	2 323	2 302	2 268	2 248	2 265	2 306	2 340	2 355	2 343	2 232	2 203	2 213
Montana	307	307	311	315	324	334	346	357	357	339	336	339
Nebraska	756	760	749	751	758	769	779	795	801	776	771	776
Nevada	905	925	922	955	1 015	1 080	1 130	1 137	1 102	991	964	976
New Hampshire	539	541	530	528	537	545	551	555	554	531	528	534
New Jersey	3 406	3 395	3 370	3 357	3 366	3 398	3 424	3 431	3 402	3 243	3 211	3 236
New Mexico	562	572	575	581	592	607	635	649	649	613	604	608
New York	7 171	7 127	6 970	6 923	6 981	7 048	7 133	7 233	7 277	7 032	7 056	7 195
North Carolina	3 304	3 269	3 206	3 158	3 195	3 263	3 372	3 461	3 433	3 204	3 173	3 223
North Dakota	255	257	256	257	263	270	277	283	291	289	297	315
Ohio	4 840	4 749	4 645	4 595	4 607	4 627	4 636	4 631	4 566	4 285	4 255	4 317
Oklahoma	1 189	1 197	1 173	1 150	1 160	1 187	1 219	1 244	1 264	1 202	1 190	1 214
Oregon	1 339	1 324	1 300	1 295	1 324	1 369	1 417	1 442	1 420	1 313	1 302	1 323
Pennsylvania	4 966	4 954	4 902	4 866	4 900	4 957	5 011	5 053	5 050	4 858	4 863	4 943
Rhode Island	412	413	413	418	423	426	428	428	418	398	397	400
South Carolina	1 538	1 501	1 480	1 482	1 509	1 540	1 577	1 609	1 581	1 468	1 465	1 492
South Dakota	307	305	303	304	309	315	323	331	335	326	325	328
Tennessee	2 334	2 285	2 254	2 252	2 291	2 330	2 366	2 376	2 347	2 191	2 182	2 224
Texas	7 870	7 928	7 790	7 724	7 841	8 056	8 359	8 660	8 828	8 487	8 484	8 743
Utah	890	891	879	878	905	946	999	1 046	1 041	974	965	988
Vermont	249	252	249	247	251	253	254	255	253	243	243	246
Virginia	2 892	2 888	2 859	2 860	2 933	3 003	3 052	3 078	3 069	2 942	2 933	2 970
Washington	2 228	2 192	2 138	2 137	2 177	2 250	2 329	2 400	2 413	2 273	2 236	2 279
West Virginia	593	594	590	585	594	603	611	613	615	596	594	602
Wisconsin	2 428	2 400	2 367	2 361	2 392	2 423	2 446	2 462	2 449	2 323	2 309	2 328
Wyoming	179	184	185	187	191	199	212	222	229	215	210	212
Puerto Rico	739	726	710	723	742	747	744	734	714	675	664	659
Virgin Islands	29	32	30	29	31	32	33	33	33	31	31	32

Table 2-10. Employees on Manufacturing Payrolls, by State and Selected Territory, NAICS Basis, 2000–2011

(Thousands of people.)

State	2000	2001	2002	2003	2004	2005	2006	2007	2008	2009	2010	2011
UNITED STATES	17 263	16 441	15 259	14 509	14 315	14 227	14 155	13 879	13 406	11 847	11 528	11 733
Alabama	351	326	307	294	292	299	303	296	284	247	236	237
Alaska	12	12	11	12	12	13	13	13	13	13	13	13
Arizona	210	202	184	175	177	182	186	182	173	154	149	150
Arkansas	240	227	214	206	204	202	200	191	184	164	160	158
California	1 856	1 781	1 634	1 545	1 523	1 505	1 490	1 464	1 425	1 282	1 241	1 246
Colorado	189	180	164	154	152	150	149	147	144	130	126	129
Connecticut	236	227	211	200	197	195	194	191	187	171	166	166
Delaware	42	39	37	36	35	33	34	33	32	28	26	26
District of Columbia	4	3	3	3	2	2	2	2	2	1	1	1
Florida	477	455	428	410	411	416	416	399	371	324	309	311
Georgia	538	505	471	452	448	450	448	431	409	358	345	350
Hawaii	16	16	15	15	15	15	15	15	15	14	13	13
Idaho	70	69	66	62	62	64	66	66	63	55	53	55
Illinois	871	815	754	714	697	688	683	675	657	577	561	574
Indiana	665	615	588	573	572	571	565	550	521	442	447	464
Iowa	252	240	227	220	223	229	231	230	227	203	201	207
Kansas	201	195	184	175	177	180	183	186	187	167	160	161
Kentucky	310	292	275	265	264	262	261	256	245	213	209	213
Louisiana	177	172	161	156	153	152	153	157	153	142	138	139
Maine	80	75	68	64	63	61	60	59	59	52	51	50
Maryland	172	166	155	145	141	139	135	132	128	119	114	113
Massachusetts	403	389	349	324	313	305	300	295	286	259	254	254
Michigan	897	822	762	718	699	679	650	619	574	465	476	506
Minnesota	397	379	356	343	343	347	346	342	336	300	293	301
Mississippi	223	201	188	179	180	178	176	170	160	141	136	134
Missouri	365	345	325	315	311	309	307	300	289	254	243	247
Montana	23	21	20	19	19	20	20	21	20	17	17	17
Nebraska	114	111	106	102	101	101	102	101	101	93	92	93
Nevada	43	44	43	44	46	48	50	50	48	40	38	38
New Hampshire	103	97	85	80	80	80	78	78	76	68	66	67
New Jersey	422	401	368	350	338	330	324	311	299	266	257	254
New Mexico	42	41	38	37	36	36	38	37	35	30	29	30
New York	749	707	651	612	596	579	566	552	532	476	457	458
North Carolina	758	704	644	599	577	565	553	539	516	448	432	434
North Dakota	24	24	24	24	25	26	26	26	26	24	23	24
Ohio	1 021	953	885	843	822	812	796	771	739	629	621	638
Oklahoma	177	170	152	143	142	145	149	151	150	129	123	129
Oregon	225	216	202	195	200	204	207	204	195	167	164	167
Pennsylvania	864	822	760	712	691	679	670	659	644	574	560	564
Rhode Island	71	68	62	59	57	55	53	51	48	42	40	41
South Carolina	336	313	289	275	267	260	252	249	241	213	207	216
South Dakota	44	41	38	38	39	40	42	42	43	38	37	39
Tennessee	497	454	429	413	412	409	399	380	361	309	299	304
Texas	1 067	1 026	948	899	890	897	924	934	925	839	812	836
Utah	126	122	114	112	115	118	123	128	126	113	111	114
Vermont	46	46	41	38	37	37	36	36	35	31	31	31
Virginia	364	341	320	305	299	296	288	278	265	239	231	229
Washington	332	316	285	267	264	273	286	293	291	266	258	269
West Virginia	76	72	69	65	63	62	61	59	57	51	49	50
Wisconsin	594	560	528	504	503	505	506	501	493	436	431	443
Wyoming	10	10	10	9	9	10	10	10	10	9	9	9
Puerto Rico	143	132	121	118	118	115	110	107	101	92	87	84
Virgin Islands	2	2	2	2	2	2	2	2	2	2	2	2

Table 2-11. Employees on Government Payrolls, by State and Selected Territory, NAICS Basis, 2000–2011

(Thousands of people.)

State	2000	2001	2002	2003	2004	2005	2006	2007	2008	2009	2010	2011
UNITED STATES	20 790	21 118	21 513	21 583	21 621	21 804	21 974	22 218	22 509	22 555	22 490	22 104
Alabama	352	352	355	358	359	363	370	377	384	384	387	380
Alaska	74	78	80	81	81	81	81	81	82	84	85	85
Arizona	367	378	390	394	399	403	408	421	432	423	416	410
Arkansas	191	194	195	198	200	204	208	211	214	217	218	219
California	2 318	2 382	2 447	2 426	2 398	2 420	2 452	2 495	2 519	2 480	2 448	2 399
Colorado	337	344	355	356	358	363	367	375	384	390	394	393
Connecticut	242	244	249	246	243	244	246	249	252	248	244	239
Delaware	57	57	57	57	58	60	61	62	63	63	64	64
District of Columbia	224	226	232	231	231	234	233	231	235	240	247	248
Florida	1 002	1 024	1 039	1 053	1 066	1 081	1 099	1 123	1 127	1 115	1 112	1 096
Georgia	597	610	624	631	635	647	660	672	691	688	679	669
Hawaii	115	114	118	119	120	120	121	122	125	126	125	125
Idaho	109	110	112	113	114	115	116	117	119	120	119	116
Illinois	840	850	861	853	845	846	846	849	856	858	854	837
Indiana	405	410	417	423	426	426	426	431	440	438	437	425
Iowa	243	245	244	245	245	245	247	250	253	255	253	250
Kansas	245	248	251	250	251	251	254	258	260	261	262	258
Kentucky	308	312	315	312	310	314	318	323	323	324	331	330
Louisiana	374	374	375	379	382	374	348	356	364	369	366	360
Maine	100	102	103	104	105	105	104	104	104	104	104	101
Maryland	450	457	465	462	462	466	471	478	488	494	502	507
Massachusetts	435	440	436	426	422	425	429	433	437	438	439	435
Michigan	681	685	687	685	680	674	665	656	650	647	636	618
Minnesota	408	409	414	412	412	415	416	415	419	417	416	408
Mississippi	234	238	240	241	242	241	239	244	248	250	249	246
Missouri	426	429	431	432	429	429	434	440	446	452	448	437
Montana	84	84	85	86	87	86	88	87	88	90	92	88
Nebraska	154	157	159	160	160	161	162	162	164	168	170	168
Nevada	122	127	130	134	138	143	149	156	161	157	154	150
New Hampshire	84	86	88	90	90	91	92	93	95	96	96	93
New Jersey	589	603	614	622	633	642	647	648	649	652	640	620
New Mexico	183	186	191	195	198	201	198	195	198	199	200	196
New York	1 467	1 467	1 492	1 487	1 484	1 489	1 485	1 501	1 516	1 524	1 511	1 488
North Carolina	615	629	634	634	645	656	672	688	706	709	706	699
North Dakota	72	73	74	75	75	75	76	76	76	78	80	79
Ohio	785	794	800	803	802	800	800	797	796	788	780	766
Oklahoma	288	296	301	296	302	312	321	325	329	340	340	336
Oregon	279	282	286	280	282	285	286	290	298	300	300	295
Pennsylvania	728	731	742	748	747	748	748	748	752	760	761	744
Rhode Island	64	65	66	66	66	65	65	64	64	62	62	61
South Carolina	324	324	327	328	326	329	332	339	348	348	347	340
South Dakota	71	73	74	75	75	75	75	76	76	78	79	78
Tennessee	399	403	410	411	415	413	417	421	428	428	433	432
Texas	1 562	1 586	1 626	1 646	1 655	1 683	1 705	1 733	1 776	1 818	1 856	1 814
Utah	185	190	195	197	199	202	204	207	212	215	218	220
Vermont	49	50	51	52	52	53	54	54	54	55	55	53
Virginia	625	629	635	638	651	662	675	683	694	700	705	710
Washington	483	505	516	521	524	527	530	534	546	550	550	542
West Virginia	143	141	143	142	143	144	145	145	147	150	153	152
Wisconsin	406	414	415	413	412	415	415	416	422	421	420	413
Wyoming	61	62	63	64	64	65	65	67	69	72	73	73
Puerto Rico	286	282	295	301	307	304	300	297	299	289	268	264
Virgin Islands	13	12	13	13	12	12	12	13	13	13	13	13

EARNINGS

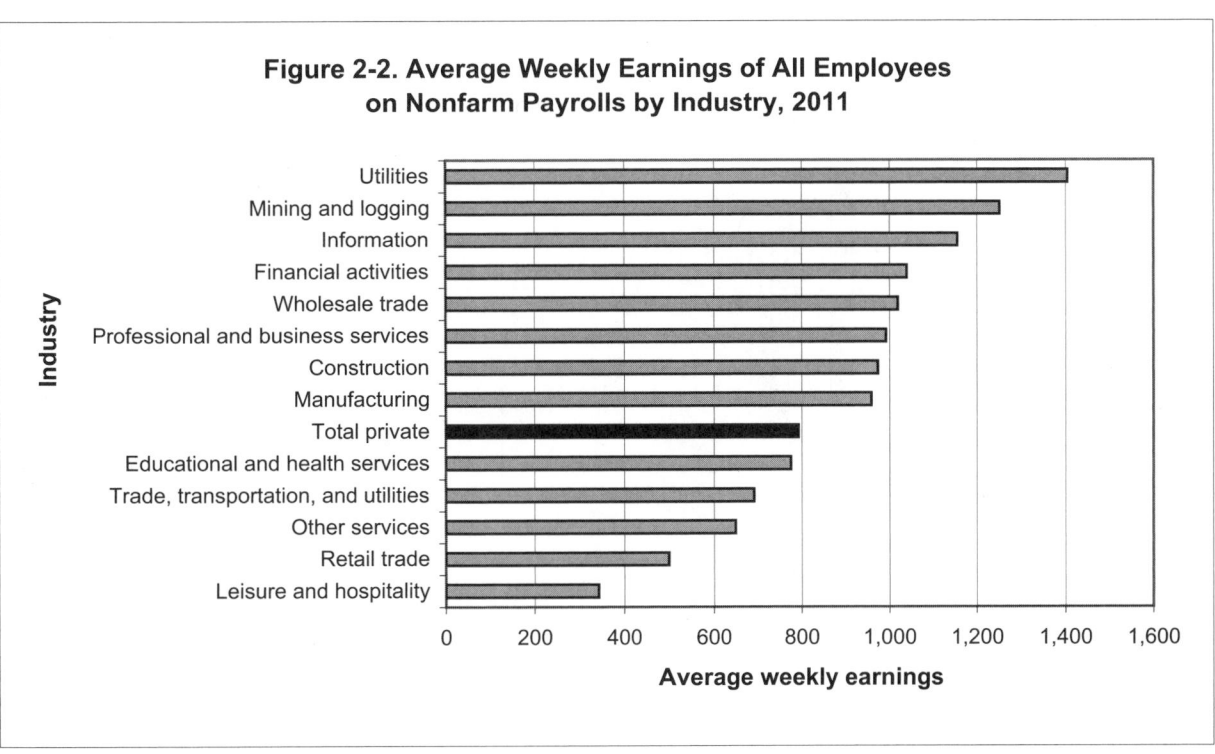

Figure 2-2. Average Weekly Earnings of All Employees on Nonfarm Payrolls by Industry, 2011

Utilities had the highest average weekly earnings ($1,404.27) followed by mining and logging ($1,251.83), and information ($1,156.06). The average weekly earnings for all employees was $793.10. All industries experienced an increase in average weekly earnings with mining and logging growing the fastest at 5.3 percent and leisure and hospitality growing the slowest at 1.7 percent. However, when adjusted for inflation, earnings declined 1.4 percent in leisure and hospitality but still increased 2.0 percent in mining and logging. (See Table 2-15.)

OTHER HIGHLIGHTS

- Average weekly earnings for all employees also varied significantly by state 2011. Earnings were highest in the District of Columbia ($1,257.15) followed by Connecticut ($957.43) and Washington ($941.53). Arkansas had the lowest average weekly earnings ($643.21) followed by South Dakota ($646.45) and Mississippi ($652.10). (See Table 2-17.)

- Average hourly earnings of production workers ranged from $11.45 in leisure and hospitality to $30.82 in utilities. (See Table 2-14.)

- From 2010 to 2011, average weekly earnings increased in all the states except for the following: Utah (-6.2 percent), Florida (-1.7 percent), Vermont (-1.3 percent), New Jersey (-1.0 percent), Maryland (-0.5 percent), and Nebraska (-0.1 percent). (See Table 2-17.)

Table 2-12. Average Hourly Earnings of All Employees on Total Private Payrolls by NAICS Super Sector, 2007–2011

(Dollars, seasonally adjusted.)

Year and month	Total private	Mining and logging	Construction	Manufacturing	Trade, transportation, and utilities				Information	Financial activities	Professional and business services	Education and health services	Leisure and hospitality	Other services
					Total	Whole-sale trade	Retail trade	Utilities						
2007	20.97	24.91	23.02	21.50	18.58	23.96	15.13	30.27	28.09	25.62	24.68	21.35	12.39	17.62
2008	21.62	26.20	23.96	22.16	18.93	24.37	15.21	32.22	28.66	26.16	25.82	22.12	12.77	18.17
2009	22.21	27.29	24.83	23.04	19.32	25.41	15.39	32.84	29.40	26.50	27.03	22.41	12.97	19.54
2010	22.59	27.39	25.19	23.31	19.65	26.13	15.56	32.55	30.53	27.20	27.24	22.96	13.08	20.16
2011	23.07	28.13	25.41	23.70	20.04	26.37	15.86	33.62	31.58	27.88	27.76	23.64	13.23	20.50
2007														
January	20.70	24.62	22.58	21.20	18.39	23.65	15.10	29.38	28.03	25.20	24.24	20.65	12.07	17.54
February	20.79	24.89	22.63	21.30	18.44	23.69	15.11	29.15	28.01	25.30	24.29	20.95	12.13	17.52
March	20.82	24.97	22.71	21.28	18.46	23.80	15.10	29.72	27.98	25.40	24.41	21.29	12.19	17.35
April	21.05	24.84	22.85	21.43	18.48	23.84	15.09	30.17	28.05	25.09	24.43	21.24	12.27	17.47
May	20.83	24.89	22.99	21.44	18.48	23.89	15.06	30.05	28.12	25.53	24.61	21.33	12.34	17.42
June	20.82	24.93	23.02	21.54	18.59	24.10	15.13	30.13	28.09	25.63	24.76	21.43	12.43	17.55
July	20.99	24.75	23.11	21.57	18.55	23.92	15.09	30.35	28.06	25.63	24.78	21.41	12.50	17.65
August	20.85	24.70	23.09	21.61	18.61	24.05	15.11	30.37	28.06	25.74	24.81	21.43	12.48	17.72
September	21.18	24.95	23.21	21.69	18.66	24.08	15.14	30.67	28.16	25.78	24.86	21.51	12.50	17.77
October	21.07	24.71	23.21	21.54	18.71	24.11	15.19	30.71	28.24	25.76	24.91	21.59	12.51	17.78
November	21.13	24.81	23.31	21.67	18.73	24.18	15.17	30.76	28.28	25.87	24.98	21.68	12.57	17.81
December	21.37	25.12	23.42	21.80	18.74	24.16	15.15	31.26	28.44	25.93	25.04	21.71	12.73	17.83
2008														
January	21.35	25.41	23.39	21.71	18.71	24.11	15.09	31.49	28.47	25.98	25.15	21.75	12.62	17.87
February	21.43	24.86	23.48	21.85	18.77	24.15	15.15	31.91	28.39	26.05	25.21	22.04	12.67	17.91
March	21.58	26.51	23.58	21.97	18.79	24.22	15.14	31.72	28.49	26.11	25.33	22.04	12.75	17.93
April	21.49	24.93	23.66	21.88	18.83	24.21	15.20	31.28	28.55	26.13	25.47	21.93	12.75	18.00
May	21.46	25.43	23.80	22.02	18.91	24.28	15.22	32.10	28.51	26.16	25.62	21.96	12.76	18.02
June	21.53	25.86	23.91	22.22	18.98	24.39	15.22	32.76	28.57	26.18	25.72	22.03	12.78	18.13
July	21.49	26.29	24.00	22.11	18.98	24.43	15.21	31.98	28.76	26.25	25.82	22.09	12.79	18.23
August	21.54	26.75	24.16	22.22	19.08	24.61	15.30	32.54	28.83	26.27	26.03	22.16	12.82	18.28
September	21.74	26.68	24.24	22.27	19.03	24.44	15.27	32.63	28.83	26.39	26.11	22.22	12.84	18.30
October	21.78	26.59	24.29	22.44	19.00	24.43	15.23	32.47	28.78	26.29	26.30	22.29	12.82	18.37
November	22.03	27.47	24.41	22.60	19.07	24.62	15.26	32.72	28.85	26.25	26.53	22.39	12.83	18.45
December	22.02	27.32	24.55	22.63	19.14	24.71	15.28	32.78	29.01	26.27	26.66	22.46	12.84	18.50
2009														
January	22.11	27.46	24.56	22.81	19.15	24.87	15.29	32.78	28.94	26.25	26.72	22.47	12.86	18.64
February	22.29	27.50	24.56	22.88	19.20	24.93	15.32	33.16	28.79	26.26	26.84	22.42	12.88	18.91
March	22.25	27.73	24.76	23.01	19.23	25.01	15.34	33.03	28.67	26.26	26.94	22.22	12.88	19.45
April	22.16	27.67	24.78	23.03	19.23	25.17	15.30	32.92	28.81	26.27	27.04	22.32	12.89	19.48
May	22.07	27.52	24.79	23.01	19.26	25.29	15.34	32.82	29.19	26.40	27.00	22.30	12.86	19.52
June	21.99	27.43	24.87	23.05	19.25	25.31	15.35	32.83	29.40	26.45	27.04	22.31	12.91	19.55
July	22.04	27.28	24.86	23.08	19.28	25.35	15.38	32.78	29.62	26.51	27.07	22.42	12.97	19.61
August	22.20	27.38	24.93	23.13	19.46	25.72	15.52	32.87	29.63	26.58	27.05	22.46	13.01	19.69
September	22.24	27.24	24.89	23.16	19.42	25.70	15.51	32.61	29.62	26.67	27.20	22.33	13.04	19.83
October	22.30	27.30	25.04	23.11	19.42	25.76	15.41	32.73	29.87	26.76	27.12	22.55	13.11	19.91
November	22.48	26.95	25.03	23.18	19.46	25.82	15.44	32.77	30.01	26.87	27.07	22.56	13.16	19.99
December	22.42	26.98	24.98	23.14	19.51	25.91	15.46	32.68	30.05	26.87	27.11	22.59	13.14	20.07
2010														
January	22.55	27.08	25.10	23.18	19.59	26.18	15.49	32.53	30.05	26.97	27.15	22.64	13.12	20.07
February	22.61	27.14	25.20	23.19	19.57	26.15	15.49	32.26	30.18	26.99	27.20	22.64	13.10	20.09
March	22.51	27.17	25.18	23.18	19.62	26.18	15.54	32.28	30.09	27.06	27.17	22.75	13.09	20.09
April	22.56	27.33	25.10	23.20	19.65	26.13	15.62	32.26	30.05	27.18	27.16	22.92	13.07	20.07
May	22.63	27.40	25.18	23.31	19.63	26.13	15.53	32.75	30.37	27.22	27.24	22.92	13.07	20.09
June	22.37	27.42	25.16	23.25	19.62	26.10	15.54	32.40	30.45	27.16	27.26	22.88	13.06	20.16
July	22.44	27.59	25.21	23.35	19.64	26.12	15.55	32.63	30.46	27.36	27.29	23.03	13.09	20.09
August	22.58	27.56	25.20	23.44	19.63	26.01	15.55	32.71	30.67	27.31	27.38	23.13	13.10	20.11
September	22.63	27.72	25.20	23.43	19.74	26.21	15.61	32.72	31.00	27.34	27.39	23.12	13.09	20.17
October	22.73	27.59	25.31	23.44	19.78	26.28	15.65	32.87	31.24	27.38	27.44	23.16	13.09	20.28
November	22.72	27.64	25.30	23.40	19.77	26.24	15.64	32.43	31.25	27.40	27.41	23.21	13.10	20.39
December	22.79	27.73	25.31	23.48	19.78	26.23	15.66	33.02	31.29	27.51	27.32	23.28	13.12	20.36
2011														
January	23.20	27.89	25.39	23.63	19.84	26.24	15.72	33.21	31.34	27.56	27.44	23.34	13.17	20.36
February	23.03	28.04	25.38	23.47	19.87	26.25	15.74	33.16	31.52	27.63	27.52	23.38	13.17	20.37
March	22.93	28.17	25.34	23.55	19.89	26.22	15.73	33.41	31.65	27.68	27.53	23.46	13.18	20.30
April	23.00	28.40	25.38	23.61	19.95	26.30	15.79	33.86	31.59	27.72	27.60	23.54	13.21	20.34
May	23.09	28.23	25.38	23.67	20.00	26.30	15.84	33.66	31.59	27.73	27.65	23.61	13.24	20.41
June	22.85	27.80	25.39	23.69	20.04	26.39	15.84	33.83	31.52	27.80	27.75	23.64	13.23	20.47
July	22.98	27.77	25.42	23.75	20.11	26.44	15.95	33.61	31.47	27.86	27.96	23.69	13.23	20.54
August	22.88	28.02	25.48	23.71	20.10	26.39	15.89	33.69	31.50	27.91	27.85	23.74	13.22	20.57
September	23.09	28.11	25.51	23.77	20.08	26.38	15.85	33.97	31.42	28.05	27.88	23.78	13.27	20.58
October	23.34	28.23	25.47	23.87	20.16	26.43	15.96	33.95	31.39	28.21	27.98	23.82	13.29	20.61
November	23.19	28.24	25.43	23.78	20.20	26.53	16.01	33.74	31.53	28.27	27.95	23.89	13.31	20.61
December	23.26	28.39	25.44	23.86	20.22	26.49	16.03	33.68	31.73	28.30	27.90	23.90	13.33	20.67

Table 2-13. Average Hourly Earnings of All Employees on Total Private Payrolls, by State, NAICS Basis, 2007–2011

(Dollars.)

State	2007	2008	2009	2010	2011
UNITED STATES	20.97	21.62	22.21	22.59	23.07
Alabama	19.37	19.56	19.68	19.86	20.14
Alaska	24.70	25.00	24.79	23.89	24.43
Arizona	19.84	20.69	22.03	22.16	22.56
Arkansas	16.27	17.21	17.97	18.07	18.36
California	24.68	24.69	25.47	26.38	26.92
Colorado	23.13	23.80	23.78	23.79	23.95
Connecticut	26.59	27.71	27.81	28.08	28.24
Delaware	21.98	22.73	22.30	22.72	22.32
District of Columbia	33.54	32.37	31.37	34.18	35.45
Florida	20.57	21.00	21.61	21.44	21.46
Georgia	20.44	20.77	21.08	21.57	21.83
Hawaii	20.68	20.80	21.11	21.65	22.15
Idaho	16.51	17.53	19.26	21.03	20.79
Illinois	22.94	22.67	23.05	23.15	23.58
Indiana	19.94	20.30	20.56	20.57	20.65
Iowa	18.01	18.35	20.01	20.38	20.22
Kansas	19.64	20.13	20.18	20.08	20.51
Kentucky	17.73	18.07	18.82	19.40	19.80
Louisiana	18.73	19.22	19.46	. . .	. . .
Maine	18.74	18.96	19.16	19.45	19.95
Maryland	24.04	24.56	25.42	26.18	25.80
Massachusetts	26.07	26.38	26.84	27.13	27.61
Michigan	21.55	21.62	21.89	22.26	22.35
Minnesota	23.13	23.23	23.41	23.85	24.54
Mississippi	16.46	16.89	17.87	18.05	18.13
Missouri	19.79	20.57	20.94	21.19	20.79
Montana	17.80	18.44	19.86	20.19	20.68
Nebraska	19.92	19.79	20.19	20.89	20.84
Nevada	19.64	19.75	19.56	19.13	19.36
New Hampshire	22.06	22.66	22.70	22.98	23.00
New Jersey	24.84	25.32	25.92	25.96	25.64
New Mexico	18.57	18.73	18.92	19.57	19.70
New York	25.26	25.48	25.70	26.06	26.48
North Carolina	19.25	19.91	20.59	20.61	20.89
North Dakota	18.34	18.75	19.21	20.19	21.44
Ohio	20.22	20.11	19.95	20.21	21.07
Oklahoma	17.34	17.43	18.07	19.20	20.36
Oregon	20.61	20.93	21.33	21.56	21.75
Pennsylvania	20.07	20.43	20.75	21.21	21.84
Rhode Island	22.17	22.50	22.52	22.67	23.73
South Carolina	18.76	18.80	19.17	19.89	20.58
South Dakota	16.47	16.53	17.94	18.55	19.05
Tennessee	19.01	19.40	19.52	19.94	20.20
Texas	21.07	21.30	21.39	21.36	21.97
Utah	21.41	21.10	22.48	24.31	23.10
Vermont	20.42	21.35	22.41	23.01	23.03
Virginia	22.46	22.31	22.58	23.54	24.66
Washington	24.19	25.23	26.32	26.95	27.25
West Virginia	17.04	17.70	18.09	18.65	18.94
Wisconsin	20.45	20.67	21.13	21.35	21.84
Wyoming	20.04	20.83	21.06	21.45	22.17

. . . = Not available.

Table 2-14. Average Hourly Earnings of Production Workers on Private Nonfarm Payrolls, by Super Sector, NAICS Basis, 2000–2011

(Dollars.)

Industry	2000	2001	2002	2003	2004	2005	2006	2007	2008	2009	2010	2011
TOTAL PRIVATE	14.02	14.54	14.97	15.37	15.69	16.13	16.76	17.43	18.08	18.63	19.07	19.47
Goods-Producing	15.27	15.78	16.33	16.80	17.19	17.60	18.02	18.67	19.33	19.90	20.28	20.66
Mining and logging	16.55	17.00	17.19	17.56	18.07	18.72	19.90	20.97	22.50	23.29	23.82	24.51
Construction	17.48	18.00	18.52	18.95	19.23	19.46	20.02	20.95	21.87	22.66	23.22	23.64
Manufacturing	14.32	14.76	15.29	15.74	16.14	16.56	16.81	17.26	17.75	18.24	18.61	18.94
Private Service-Providing	13.62	14.18	14.59	14.99	15.29	15.73	16.42	17.11	17.77	18.35	18.81	19.21
Trade, transportation, and utilities	13.31	13.70	14.02	14.34	14.58	14.92	15.39	15.78	16.16	16.48	16.82	17.15
Wholesale trade	16.28	16.77	16.98	17.36	17.65	18.16	18.91	19.59	20.13	20.84	21.54	21.97
Retail trade	10.87	11.29	11.67	11.90	12.08	12.36	12.57	12.75	12.87	13.01	13.24	13.51
Transportation and warehousing	15.05	15.33	15.76	16.25	16.52	16.70	17.27	17.72	18.41	18.81	19.16	19.50
Utilities	22.75	23.58	23.96	24.77	25.61	26.68	27.40	27.88	28.83	29.48	30.04	30.82
Information	19.07	19.80	20.20	21.01	21.40	22.06	23.23	23.96	24.78	25.45	25.87	26.61
Financial activities	14.98	15.59	16.17	17.14	17.52	17.94	18.80	19.64	20.28	20.85	21.52	21.91
Professional and business services	15.52	16.33	16.80	17.21	17.48	18.08	19.13	20.15	21.18	22.35	22.78	23.12
Education and health services	13.95	14.64	15.21	15.64	16.15	16.71	17.38	18.11	18.87	19.49	20.12	20.78
Leisure and hospitality	8.32	8.57	8.81	9.00	9.15	9.38	9.75	10.41	10.84	11.12	11.31	11.45
Other services	12.73	13.27	13.72	13.84	13.98	14.34	14.77	15.42	16.09	16.59	17.06	17.32

Table 2-15. Average Weekly Earnings of All Employees on Nonfarm Payrolls, by Industry, in Current and 1982–1984 Dollars, NAICS Basis, 2007–2011

(Dollars.)

Industry	2007	2008	2009	2010	2011
TOTAL PRIVATE					
Current dollars	725.22	744.97	753.18	770.71	793.10
1982–1984 dollars	349.77	346.01	351.07	353.45	352.58
Goods-Producing					
Current dollars	873.48	899.62	916.04	952.07	976.56
1982–1984 dollars	421.27	417.84	426.98	436.62	434.14
Mining and logging					
Current dollars	1 094.81	1 144.63	1 150.12	1 189.32	1 251.83
1982–1984 dollars	528.02	531.64	536.09	545.42	556.52
Construction					
Current dollars	875.06	905.68	922.54	952.78	973.51
1982–1984 dollars	422.04	420.65	430.01	436.94	432.79
Manufacturing					
Current dollars	861.19	882.19	898.64	937.34	959.39
1982–1984 dollars	415.35	409.74	418.87	429.86	426.51
Private Service-Providing					
Current dollars	689.95	709.65	719.10	734.84	756.49
1982–1984 dollars	332.76	329.61	335.19	337.00	336.31
Trade, transportation, and utilities					
Current dollars	641.51	651.96	659.78	672.58	692.54
1982–1984 dollars	309.40	302.81	307.54	308.44	307.88
Wholesale trade					
Current dollars	913.03	936.17	963.44	994.71	1 018.88
1982–1984 dollars	440.35	434.82	449.08	456.17	452.96
Retail trade					
Current dollars	479.81	478.00	481.18	487.66	500.74
1982–1984 dollars	231.41	222.01	224.29	223.64	222.61
Transportation and warehousing					
Current dollars	758.22	780.55	780.53	803.81	834.88
1982–1984 dollars	365.69	362.54	363.82	368.63	371.16
Utilities					
Current dollars	1 264.16	1 352.81	1 343.66	1 338.50	1 404.27
1982–1984 dollars	609.70	628.33	626.31	613.83	624.29
Information					
Current dollars	1 014.35	1 047.50	1 073.27	1 114.65	1 156.06
1982–1984 dollars	489.22	486.52	500.27	511.18	513.94
Financial activities					
Current dollars	936.56	954.82	970.00	1 003.31	1 038.87
1982–1984 dollars	451.70	443.48	452.14	460.12	461.85
Professional and business services					
Current dollars	874.68	909.23	947.10	963.79	991.93
1982–1984 dollars	421.85	422.30	441.46	441.99	440.98
Education and health services					
Current dollars	715.66	745.03	739.27	752.26	775.50
1982–1984 dollars	345.16	346.04	344.59	344.98	344.76
Leisure and hospitality					
Current dollars	323.54	330.32	331.64	336.83	342.67
1982–1984 dollars	156.04	153.42	154.58	154.47	152.34
Other services					
Current dollars	578.84	597.13	618.18	637.65	649.75
1982–1984 dollars	279.17	277.34	288.15	292.42	288.86

Table 2-16. Average Weekly Earnings of Production Workers on Nonfarm Payrolls, by Industry, in Current and 1982–1984 Dollars, NAICS Basis, 2000–2011

(Dollars.)

Industry	2000	2001	2002	2003	2004	2005	2006	2007	2008	2009	2010	2011
TOTAL PRIVATE												
Current dollars	481.13	493.79	506.75	518.06	529.09	544.33	567.87	590.04	607.95	617.18	636.92	654.87
1982–1984 dollars	284.86	284.61	288.09	288.13	286.77	284.99	288.11	290.99	288.06	294.41	297.67	295.55
Goods-Producing												
Current dollars	621.86	630.04	651.55	669.13	688.17	705.31	730.16	757.50	776.63	779.68	818.96	844.90
1982–1984 dollars	368.18	363.14	370.41	372.15	372.99	369.27	370.45	373.58	367.98	371.93	382.75	381.32
Mining and logging												
Current dollars	734.88	757.96	741.97	765.94	804.01	853.87	907.95	962.63	1 014.69	1 006.67	1 063.11	1 144.04
1982–1984 dollars	435.10	436.86	421.81	426.00	435.78	447.05	460.65	474.75	480.77	480.21	496.86	516.32
Construction												
Current dollars	685.78	695.86	711.82	727.00	735.55	750.37	781.59	816.23	842.61	851.76	891.83	921.66
1982–1984 dollars	406.03	401.07	404.67	404.34	398.67	392.86	396.54	402.55	399.24	406.32	416.81	415.96
Manufacturing												
Current dollars	590.77	595.15	618.62	635.99	658.52	673.34	691.05	711.53	724.46	726.12	765.15	784.68
1982–1984 dollars	349.78	343.03	351.69	353.72	356.92	352.53	350.61	350.91	343.26	346.38	357.60	354.14
Private Service-Providing												
Current dollars	445.74	461.08	473.80	484.71	494.22	509.56	532.60	554.89	574.20	588.20	606.12	622.42
1982–1984 dollars	263.91	265.75	269.36	269.58	267.87	266.79	270.22	273.66	272.06	280.59	283.28	280.91
Trade, transportation, and utilities												
Current dollars	449.96	459.53	471.27	481.14	488.51	498.46	514.37	525.91	536.11	541.88	559.63	577.84
1982–1984 dollars	266.41	264.86	267.92	267.60	264.78	260.97	260.97	259.37	254.02	258.49	261.55	260.79
Wholesale trade												
Current dollars	631.24	643.45	644.38	657.29	666.79	685.00	718.50	748.94	769.62	784.49	816.50	845.36
1982–1984 dollars	373.74	370.86	366.33	365.57	361.40	358.64	364.54	369.36	364.66	374.23	381.60	381.52
Retail trade												
Current dollars	333.41	346.16	360.84	367.18	371.16	377.58	383.12	385.00	386.21	388.57	400.05	412.10
1982–1984 dollars	197.40	199.52	205.14	204.22	201.17	197.69	194.38	189.87	182.99	185.36	186.97	185.99
Transportation and warehousing												
Current dollars	562.56	562.57	579.91	598.41	614.89	618.55	636.80	654.95	670.22	677.56	710.85	737.37
1982–1984 dollars	333.07	324.25	329.68	332.82	333.27	323.85	323.08	323.01	317.56	323.22	332.22	332.79
Utilities												
Current dollars	955.09	977.25	979.26	1 017.44	1 048.01	1 095.91	1 135.57	1 182.65	1 230.65	1 239.34	1 262.89	1 296.85
1982–1984 dollars	565.48	563.26	556.71	565.87	568.03	573.77	576.14	583.26	583.10	591.20	590.23	585.29
Information												
Current dollars	700.92	731.18	737.94	760.84	776.72	805.11	850.64	874.45	908.78	931.08	939.85	963.99
1982–1984 dollars	414.99	421.43	419.52	423.16	420.99	421.52	431.58	431.26	430.59	444.15	439.25	435.06
Financial activities												
Current dollars	537.37	558.05	575.54	609.08	622.87	645.10	672.21	705.13	727.07	752.03	778.43	797.76
1982–1984 dollars	318.16	321.64	327.20	338.75	337.60	337.75	341.05	347.75	344.50	358.74	363.81	360.04
Professional and business services												
Current dollars	535.07	557.84	574.60	587.02	597.39	618.66	662.27	700.64	737.70	775.81	798.54	813.71
1982–1984 dollars	316.80	321.52	326.66	326.48	323.79	323.91	336.01	345.54	349.53	370.09	373.21	367.24
Education and health services												
Current dollars	449.29	473.39	492.74	505.69	523.78	544.59	564.94	590.09	613.73	628.45	646.65	670.83
1982–1984 dollars	266.01	272.85	280.13	281.25	283.89	285.13	286.63	291.02	290.79	299.79	302.22	302.76
Leisure and hospitality												
Current dollars	217.20	220.73	227.31	230.49	234.86	241.36	250.34	265.54	273.39	275.95	280.87	283.77
1982–1984 dollars	128.60	127.22	129.23	128.19	127.30	126.37	127.01	130.96	129.54	131.64	131.27	128.07
Other services												
Current dollars	413.30	428.64	439.87	434.41	433.04	443.40	456.50	477.06	495.57	506.26	523.70	532.48
1982–1984 dollars	244.70	247.05	250.07	241.61	234.71	232.15	231.61	235.27	234.81	241.50	244.76	240.32

Table 2-17. Average Weekly Earnings of All Employees on Total Private Payrolls, by State, NAICS Basis, 2007–2011

(Dollars.)

State	2007	2008	2009	2010	2011
UNITED STATES	725.22	744.97	753.18	770.71	793.10
Alabama	709.45	704.70	685.64	697.58	710.08
Alaska	876.08	882.50	867.09	843.74	873.39
Arizona	698.92	720.48	766.66	780.54	790.24
Arkansas	570.46	604.90	621.81	630.17	643.21
California	851.88	844.71	861.05	896.82	925.86
Colorado	807.24	828.64	816.36	815.64	827.03
Connecticut	912.61	941.16	917.58	935.66	957.43
Delaware	753.48	768.72	728.90	736.75	738.50
District of Columbia	1 218.07	1 157.71	1 137.03	1 201.91	1 257.15
Florida	728.52	740.13	756.03	760.18	747.10
Georgia	727.20	732.70	729.62	749.47	757.45
Hawaii	674.38	678.14	686.33	709.93	738.31
Idaho	566.64	593.97	646.85	703.81	703.99
Illinois	788.70	777.78	793.55	795.37	815.01
Indiana	707.97	709.83	711.76	721.69	722.28
Iowa	616.33	620.68	667.25	694.75	687.10
Kansas	681.24	699.89	689.25	684.83	706.99
Kentucky	653.35	654.46	666.55	684.71	692.58
Louisiana	670.11	701.93	702.12	. . .	. . .
Maine	641.22	649.78	638.68	657.34	678.01
Maryland	837.14	851.61	875.84	891.99	887.11
Massachusetts	874.51	887.45	900.62	912.80	914.07
Michigan	752.68	739.92	729.65	750.94	763.91
Minnesota	780.56	776.97	763.37	785.94	816.88
Mississippi	587.88	602.04	632.95	647.54	652.10
Missouri	680.71	709.10	709.04	718.62	721.73
Montana	634.58	596.26	618.85	658.75	681.30
Nebraska	668.13	666.78	680.27	712.08	711.04
Nevada	731.88	730.92	701.22	660.77	665.86
New Hampshire	734.92	742.09	742.83	761.47	762.66
New Jersey	845.50	851.11	870.21	878.11	869.50
New Mexico	642.10	662.66	664.19	685.15	690.95
New York	861.67	869.91	867.35	884.28	903.30
North Carolina	669.49	682.39	696.52	701.81	716.12
North Dakota	605.54	607.86	614.76	659.34	730.13
Ohio	686.37	682.65	657.39	676.46	710.70
Oklahoma	607.21	619.08	634.58	682.84	721.67
Oregon	704.68	707.29	708.74	724.69	735.19
Pennsylvania	678.78	689.53	685.48	706.84	731.49
Rhode Island	743.45	766.54	762.52	768.25	784.17
South Carolina	676.26	669.28	665.74	691.69	715.49
South Dakota	542.83	543.30	598.13	627.92	646.45
Tennessee	670.09	682.78	686.92	703.65	710.39
Texas	768.26	771.90	754.09	767.41	807.68
Utah	747.80	730.03	804.82	862.42	808.54
Vermont	696.20	733.46	764.19	786.67	776.80
Virginia	791.55	779.94	781.60	832.99	873.33
Washington	852.90	873.47	904.13	920.28	941.53
West Virginia	599.84	623.37	622.91	651.68	654.16
Wisconsin	672.79	681.68	680.51	699.62	723.74
Wyoming	725.63	764.15	748.79	770.07	800.57

. . . = Not available.

NOTES AND DEFINITIONS

QUARTERLY CENSUS OF EMPLOYMENT AND WAGES

The Quarterly Census of Employment and Wages (QCEW), often referred to as the ES-202 program, is a cooperative endeavor of the Bureau of Labor Statistics (BLS) and the State Employment Security Agencies (SESAs). Using quarterly data submitted by the agencies, BLS summarizes the employment and wage data for workers covered by state unemployment insurance laws and civilian workers covered by the Unemployment Compensation for Federal Employees (UCFE) program.

Since the introduction of 2001 data, the QCEW data have been coded according to the North American Classification System, either NAICS 2002, which was used for the data up through 2006; NAICS 2007, which was used for data from 2007 through 2010; or NAICS 2012 which will be used from 2011 forward until the next revision. NAICS is the statistical classification standard underlying all establishment-based federal economic statistics classified by industry. Before 2001, QCEW data were coded according to the Standard Industrial Classification (SIC) system. Due to the differences in the classification systems, data coded according to NAICS are often not directly comparable to SIC coded data.

The QCEW data series is the most complete universe of employment and wage information by industry, county, and state. It includes 98 percent of all wage and salary civilian employment. These data serve as the basic source of benchmark information for employment by industry in the Current Employment Statistics (CES) survey, which is described in the first section of notes in this chapter. Therefore, the entire employment series is not presented here. The wage series is presented because the CES only provides earnings only for production and nonsupervisory employees. The QCEW is more comprehensive. BLS aggregates the data by industry and ownership; these aggregations are available at the national, state, county, and metropolitan statistical area (MSA) levels.

Collection and Coverage

Employment data under the QCEW program represent the number of covered workers who worked during, or received pay for, the pay period including the 12th of the month. Excluded are members of the armed forces, the self-employed, proprietors, domestic workers, unpaid family workers, and railroad workers covered by the railroad unemployment insurance system. Wages represent total compensation paid during the calendar quarter, regardless of when services were performed. Included in wages are pay for vacation and other paid leave, bonuses, stock options, tips, the cash value of meals and lodging, and in some states, contributions to deferred compensation plans (such as 401(k) plans). The QCEW program does provide partial information on agricultural industries and employees in private households.

Data from the QCEW program serve as an important input to many BLS programs. The QCEW data are used as the benchmark source for employment by the Current Employment Statistics program and the Occupational employment statistics program. The UI administrative records collected under the QCEW program serve as a sampling frame for BLS establishment surveys.

In addition, data from the QCEW program serve as an input to other federal and state programs. The Bureau of Economic Analysis (BEA) of the Department of Commerce uses QCEW data as the base for developing the wage and salary component of personal income. The Employment and Training Administration (ETA) of the Department of Labor and the SESAs use QCEW data to administer the employment security program. The QCEW data accurately reflect the extent of coverage of the state UI laws and are used to measure UI revenues; national, state and local area employment; and total and UI taxable wage trends.

Sources of Additional Information

Additional information is available on the BLS Web site at <http://www.bls.gov/cew>.

Table 2-18. Employment and Average Annual Pay for Covered Workers,[1] by Industry, NAICS Basis, 2006–2011

(Number, dollars.)

Industry	2006		2007		2008	
	Employment	Average annual pay	Employment	Average annual pay	Employment	Average annual pay
Total Private	112 718 858	42 414	114 012 221	44 362	113 188 643	45 371
Natural resources and mining	1 776 777	42 904	1 826 609	45 733	1 882 426	49 170
Agriculture, forestry, fishing, and hunting	1 160 179	24 132	1 166 333	25 191	1 169 029	25 986
Construction	7 602 148	44 496	7 562 732	46 784	7 124 886	49 013
Manufacturing	14 110 663	51 427	13 833 022	53 489	13 382 697	54 400
Wholesale trade	5 885 194	58 046	5 987 206	60 719	5 954 915	61 843
Retail trade	15 370 040	25 567	15 509 017	26 124	15 307 933	26 179
Transportation and warehousing	4 204 514	40 848	4 292 445	42 615	4 271 969	42 962
Utilities	546 521	78 341	549 539	82 275	557 983	84 153
Information	3 040 577	65 962	3 029 789	69 140	2 989 161	70 787
Financial activities	8 162 063	68 901	8 145 981	73 980	7 968 376	74 133
Professional and business services	17 469 679	51 974	17 859 796	55 139	17 705 280	57 476
Education and health services	16 916 228	39 115	17 433 162	40 528	17 954 103	41 984
Leisure and hospitality	13 024 615	17 781	13 327 559	18 495	13 395 477	18 946
Other services	4 364 889	26 923	4 438 439	27 970	4 484 907	28 773
Total Government	21 114 976	43 180	21 353 885	44 968	21 617 017	46 568
Federal	2 728 974	62 274	2 726 300	64 871	2 762 055	66 293
State	4 565 908	43 875	4 611 395	45 903	4 642 650	47 980
Local	13 820 093	39 179	14 016 190	40 790	14 212 311	42 274

Industry	2009		2010		2011	
	Employment	Average annual pay	Employment	Average annual pay	Employment	Average annual pay
Total Private	106 947 104	45 155	106 201 232	46 455	108 184 795	47 815
Natural resources and mining	1 783 558	47 425	1 798 592	49 820	1 890 359	53 691
Agriculture, forestry, fishing, and hunting	1 142 192	26 031	1 146 962	26 636	1 160 311	27 543
Construction	5 948 837	49 322	5 489 499	49 597	5 473 045	50 693
Manufacturing	11 810 371	54 873	11 487 496	57 526	11 701 497	59 210
Wholesale trade	5 561 787	61 595	5 466 463	63 629	5 545 802	66 142
Retail trade	14 544 111	26 162	14 481 324	26 652	14 666 625	27 118
Transportation and warehousing	3 985 037	42 823	3 943 659	44 197	4 055 639	45 336
Utilities	560 713	84 877	551 287	86 791	549 921	90 609
Information	2 807 721	71 191	2 703 886	74 395	2 674 852	78 331
Financial activities	7 589 821	70 045	7 401 812	73 977	7 416 409	77 366
Professional and business services	16 488 835	58 344	16 712 011	60 145	17 298 233	61 902
Education and health services	18 321 635	43 042	18 656 160	43 604	19 035 334	44 383
Leisure and hospitality	13 001 028	18 899	13 006 814	19 387	13 294 603	19 772
Other services	4 369 780	28 814	4 349 563	29 370	4 408 735	29 916
Total Government	21 660 738	47 552	21 619 210	48 202	21 226 299	49 205
Federal	2 826 713	67 756	2 980 813	69 198	2 863 132	73 001
State	4 639 715	48 742	4 606 001	48 960	4 553 697	50 252
Local	14 194 311	43 140	14 032 396	43 493	13 809 471	43 926

[1]Includes workers covered by unemployment insurance (UI) and Unemployment Compensation for Federal Employees (UCFE) programs.

Table 2-19. Employment and Average Annual Pay for Covered Workers,[1] **by State and Selected Territory, 2006–2011**

(Number, dollars.)

State	2006 Employment	2006 Average annual pay	2007 Employment	2007 Average annual pay	2008 Employment	2008 Average annual pay
UNITED STATES	133 833 834	42 535	135 366 106	44 458	134 805 659	45 563
Alabama	1 928 281	36 204	1 952 091	37 492	1 936 489	38 734
Alaska	307 637	41 750	310 810	43 972	315 285	45 805
Arizona	2 614 344	40 019	2 647 691	41 551	2 583 215	42 518
Arkansas	1 167 925	32 389	1 173 852	34 118	1 172 208	34 919
California	15 503 144	48 345	15 640 575	50 538	15 494 915	51 487
Colorado	2 242 012	43 506	2 292 630	45 396	2 310 865	46 614
Connecticut	1 672 109	54 814	1 686 043	58 029	1 687 902	58 395
Delaware	422 187	46 285	423 412	47 308	423 083	47 569
District of Columbia	671 143	70 151	678 119	73 450	685 069	76 518
Florida	7 952 023	38 485	7 945 162	39 746	7 666 374	40 568
Georgia	4 024 699	40 370	4 077 184	42 178	4 031 467	42 585
Hawaii	618 178	37 799	625 862	39 466	619 703	40 675
Idaho	643 671	32 580	660 683	33 544	653 108	33 897
Illinois	5 821 022	45 650	5 869 157	47 685	5 841 692	48 719
Indiana	2 892 419	36 553	2 905 725	37 528	2 872 442	38 403
Iowa	1 470 742	34 320	1 485 627	35 738	1 490 575	36 964
Kansas	1 327 677	35 696	1 356 966	37 044	1 366 878	38 178
Kentucky	1 779 202	35 201	1 801 907	36 480	1 791 017	37 434
Louisiana	1 807 563	36 604	1 868 986	38 229	1 890 007	40 381
Maine	598 525	33 794	602 321	35 129	602 074	36 317
Maryland	2 530 011	46 162	2 547 351	48 241	2 537 752	49 535
Massachusetts	3 194 914	52 435	3 234 357	55 244	3 245 983	56 746
Michigan	4 235 650	42 157	4 179 122	43 357	4 070 914	44 245
Minnesota	2 670 222	42 185	2 687 482	44 375	2 679 527	45 826
Mississippi	1 122 474	31 194	1 135 336	32 291	1 131 096	33 508
Missouri	2 699 860	37 143	2 719 380	38 603	2 715 183	40 361
Montana	426 182	30 596	436 656	32 224	437 591	33 305
Nebraska	902 383	33 814	916 580	35 238	922 929	36 243
Nevada	1 271 634	40 070	1 284 502	42 149	1 252 987	42 984
New Hampshire	627 371	42 447	630 204	43 863	628 763	44 912
New Jersey	3 951 210	51 645	3 961 341	53 853	3 934 789	55 280
New Mexico	807 063	34 567	821 484	36 379	825 736	37 910
New York	8 429 519	55 479	8 554 012	59 439	8 608 351	60 288
North Carolina	3 965 479	37 439	4 062 955	38 909	4 043 486	39 740
North Dakota	335 718	31 316	341 705	33 086	350 440	35 075
Ohio	5 314 572	38 568	5 306 812	39 917	5 235 972	40 784
Oklahoma	1 507 196	34 022	1 534 802	35 491	1 550 489	37 284
Oregon	1 699 932	38 077	1 727 886	39 569	1 713 764	40 500
Pennsylvania	5 607 139	41 349	5 652 547	43 239	5 658 771	44 381
Rhode Island	480 570	40 454	480 132	41 646	469 701	43 029
South Carolina	1 855 842	34 281	1 891 255	35 393	1 876 081	36 252
South Dakota	383 876	30 291	392 060	31 655	397 108	32 822
Tennessee	2 728 694	37 564	2 745 099	39 082	2 721 990	39 996
Texas	9 922 313	42 458	10 231 906	44 695	10 452 907	45 939
Utah	1 170 587	35 130	1 219 207	37 054	1 221 052	37 980
Vermont	303 205	35 542	303 448	36 956	302 627	38 328
Virginia	3 636 417	44 051	3 672 958	45 995	3 665 654	47 241
Washington	2 850 073	42 897	2 925 908	45 021	2 950 773	46 569
West Virginia	705 189	32 728	706 172	34 106	709 657	35 987
Wisconsin	2 767 141	36 821	2 780 924	38 050	2 772 889	39 119
Wyoming	266 894	36 662	277 721	39 254	286 333	41 487
Puerto Rico	1 036 802	23 707	1 016 362	24 741	1 001 120	25 554
Virgin Islands	45 114	35 357	45 922	36 521	45 796	37 005

[1] Includes workers covered by the unemployment insurance (UI) and Unemployment Compensation for Federal Employees (UCFE) programs.

Table 2-19. Employment and Average Annual Pay for Covered Workers,[1] by State and Selected Territory, 2006–2011—*Continued*

(Number, dollars.)

State	2009 Employment	2009 Average annual pay	2010 Employment	2010 Average annual pay	2011 Employment	2011 Average annual pay
UNITED STATES	128 607 842	45 559	127 820 442	46 751	129 411 095	48 043
Alabama	1 829 487	39 422	1 813 155	40 289	1 813 497	41 186
Alaska	313 802	47 103	316 691	48 230	322 084	49 383
Arizona	2 396 362	42 832	2 356 789	43 299	2 378 248	44 581
Arkansas	1 134 488	35 692	1 134 071	36 254	1 139 682	37 280
California	14 629 953	51 566	14 414 461	53 285	14 567 128	55 013
Colorado	2 201 427	46 861	2 176 986	47 868	2 213 059	49 082
Connecticut	1 615 356	57 771	1 595 713	59 465	1 612 292	61 145
Delaware	402 343	47 770	399 078	48 669	402 959	50 499
District of Columbia	681 875	77 483	693 274	80 200	707 359	81 529
Florida	7 182 815	40 970	7 109 630	41 581	7 195 232	42 313
Georgia	3 796 429	42 902	3 753 934	43 899	3 792 209	45 090
Hawaii	592 171	41 328	586 772	41 709	593 668	42 473
Idaho	613 814	34 124	605 571	34 900	607 504	35 626
Illinois	5 551 930	48 358	5 502 322	49 497	5 566 648	50 840
Indiana	2 705 331	38 270	2 709 831	39 256	2 755 826	40 248
Iowa	1 445 627	37 158	1 436 340	38 146	1 452 769	39 204
Kansas	1 317 029	38 154	1 297 779	38 936	1 303 799	39 989
Kentucky	1 710 677	37 996	1 712 178	38 720	1 734 503	39 646
Louisiana	1 849 303	40 579	1 832 357	41 461	1 848 399	42 375
Maine	581 796	36 617	577 790	37 338	579 838	38 020
Maryland	2 461 109	50 579	2 453 197	51 739	2 478 505	53 008
Massachusetts	3 135 497	56 267	3 149 169	57 770	3 189 753	59 671
Michigan	3 775 435	43 645	3 770 225	44 439	3 854 837	45 828
Minnesota	2 569 651	45 319	2 558 310	46 787	2 602 988	47 858
Mississippi	1 081 138	33 847	1 074 617	34 343	1 076 488	34 976
Missouri	2 607 595	40 022	2 573 703	40 679	2 585 009	41 461
Montana	421 566	33 762	419 231	34 595	422 726	35 791
Nebraska	901 470	36 644	896 936	37 324	901 584	38 269
Nevada	1 138 036	42 743	1 108 238	42 512	1 115 062	43 102
New Hampshire	605 004	44 932	600 697	45 957	605 853	47 281
New Jersey	3 771 296	55 168	3 735 703	56 382	3 734 660	57 546
New Mexico	791 509	38 529	781 694	39 264	781 226	40 032
New York	8 343 862	57 739	8 340 732	60 291	8 444 791	61 792
North Carolina	3 823 299	39 844	3 788 581	41 119	3 838 300	42 121
North Dakota	349 560	35 970	358 635	38 128	379 432	41 778
Ohio	4 943 970	40 900	4 908 571	41 788	4 968 724	42 972
Oklahoma	1 497 855	37 238	1 485 400	38 237	1 507 558	40 108
Oregon	1 607 915	40 757	1 598 173	41 675	1 616 634	43 090
Pennsylvania	5 468 176	44 829	5 472 171	45 733	5 535 283	47 035
Rhode Island	448 842	43 439	447 408	44 645	448 570	45 705
South Carolina	1 765 739	36 759	1 758 204	37 553	1 780 690	38 427
South Dakota	389 360	33 352	389 198	34 331	393 744	35 413
Tennessee	2 565 288	40 242	2 558 438	41 572	2 602 604	42 454
Texas	10 149 694	45 692	10 182 150	46 952	10 422 295	48 735
Utah	1 157 704	38 614	1 150 737	39 389	1 176 530	40 279
Vermont	292 406	38 778	293 058	39 434	295 512	40 293
Virginia	3 545 623	48 239	3 536 676	49 651	3 578 848	50 657
Washington	2 836 283	47 470	2 808 698	48 516	2 844 622	50 256
West Virginia	691 998	36 897	692 448	37 675	701 905	39 092
Wisconsin	2 644 190	39 131	2 633 572	39 966	2 664 920	41 003
Wyoming	274 758	40 709	271 151	41 963	274 743	43 394
Puerto Rico	954 555	26 359	930 319	26 617	923 451	26 678
Virgin Islands	43 799	37 299	44 267	38 936	43 799	38 597

[1]Includes workers covered by the unemployment insurance (UI) and Unemployment Compensation for Federal Employees (UCFE) programs.

BUSINESS EMPLOYMENT DYNAMICS

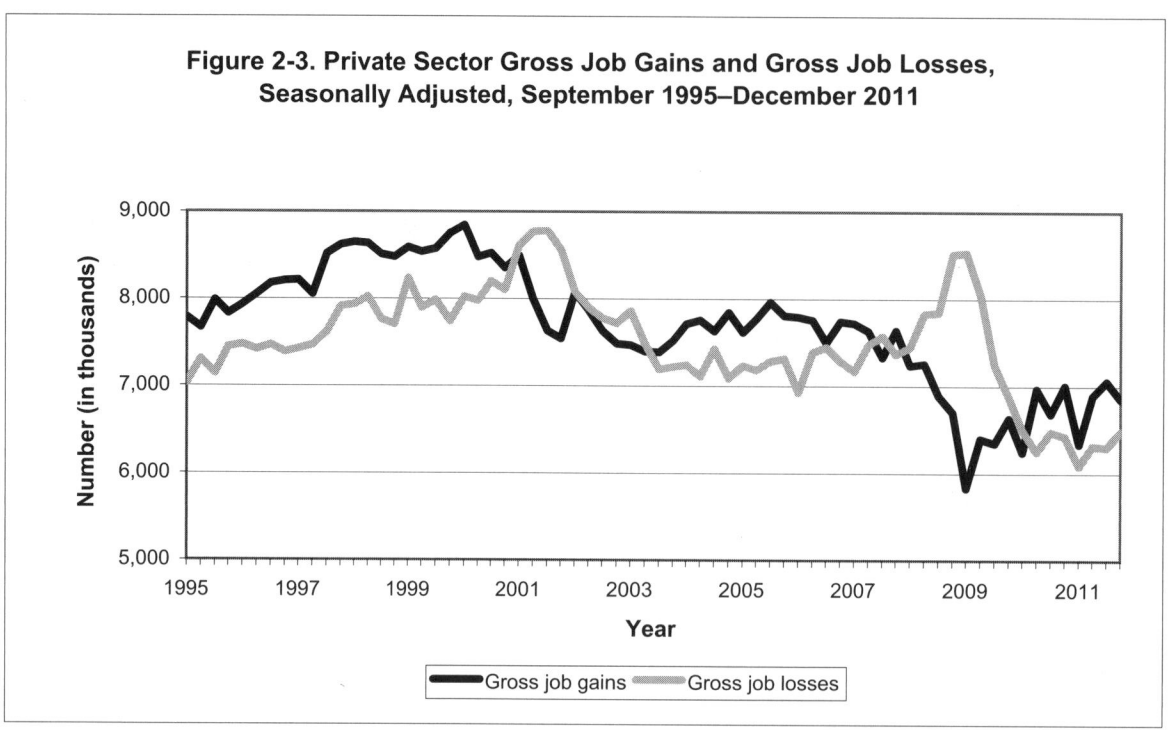

Figure 2-3. Private Sector Gross Job Gains and Gross Job Losses, Seasonally Adjusted, September 1995–December 2011

The change in the number of jobs is the net result of the gross increase in the number of jobs from expanding and opening establishments and the gross decrease in jobs from contracting and closing establishments. The net gain of 368,000 jobs in the fourth quarter of 2011 resulted from 6.854 million gross job gains and 6.486 million gross job losses. There was a net gain of jobs in seven consecutive quarters from June 2010 to December 2011. (See Table 2-20.)

OTHER HIGHLIGHTS

- Of the 6.484 million jobs that were lost in the fourth quarter of 2011, 80.4 percent resulted from contracting establishments while 19.6 percent were the result of establishments closing. (See Table 2-20.)

- The service-providing industries experienced a net job gain of 372,000 while the goods-producing industries suffered a net job loss of 4,000 in the fourth quarter of 2011. (See Table 2-22.)

- In professional and business services, gross job gains exceeded gross job losses by 91,000 in the fourth quarter of 2011—more than in any other sector. Meanwhile, there was a net loss of 33,000 jobs in construction. (See Table 2-22.)

- In nine states job losses exceeded job gains. These states included: Massachusetts (-6,199), Minnesota (-5,014), Wisconsin (-5,011), Alaska (-3,203), New Mexico (-3,126), Alabama (-1,909), Maine (-1,907), Rhode Island (-1,088), and Idaho (-662). (See Table 2-23.)

NOTES AND DEFINITIONS

BUSINESS EMPLOYMENT DYNAMICS (BED)

The Business Employment Dynamics (BED) data are a set of statistics generated from the federal-state cooperative program known as the Quarterly Census of Employment and Wages (QCEW), or the ES-202 program. These quarterly data series consist of gross job gains and gross job losses statistics from 1992 forward.

The Bureau of Labor Statistics (BLS) compiles the BED data from existing quarterly state unemployment insurance (UI) records. Most employers in the United States are required to file quarterly reports on the employment and wages of workers covered by UI laws and to pay quarterly UI taxes. The quarterly UI reports are sent by the State Workforce Agencies (SWAs) to BLS. These reports form the basis of the BLS establishment universe-sampling frame.

In the BED program, the quarterly UI records are linked across quarters to provide a longitudinal history for each establishment. The linkage process allows the tracking of net employment changes at the establishment level, which in turn allows estimations of jobs gained at opening and expanding establishments and of jobs lost at closing and contracting establishments. BLS publishes three different establishment-based employment measures for every given quarter. Each of these measures—the Current Employment Statistics (CES) survey, the QCEW program, and the BED data each make use of the quarterly UI employment reports. However, each measure has somewhat different types of universal coverage, estimation procedures, and publication products. (See the notes and corresponding tables for CES and QCEW in earlier sections of this chapter.)

Concepts and Definitions

The BED data measure the net change in employment at the establishment level. These changes can come about in four different ways. A net increase in employment can come from either opening establishments or expanding establishments. A net decrease in employment can come from either closing establishments or contracting establishments.

Gross job gains include the sum of all jobs added at either opening or expanding establishments.

Gross job losses include the sum of all jobs lost in either closing or contracting establishments. The net change in employment is the difference between gross job gains and gross job losses.

Openings consist of establishments with positive third-month employment for the first time in the current quarter, with no links to the prior quarter, or with positive third-month employment in the current quarter, following zero employment in the previous quarter.

Expansions include establishments with positive employment in the third month in both the previous and current quarters, with a net increase in employment over this period.

Closings consist of establishments with positive third-month employment in the previous quarter, with no employment or zero employment reported in the current quarter.

Contractions include establishments with positive employment in the third month in both the previous and current quarters, with a net decrease in employment over this period.

Sources of Additional Information

For additional information, see BLS news release 12-1530, "Business Employment Dynamics: Fourth Quarter 2011." An extensive article on the BED data appeared in the April 2004 edition of the *Monthly Labor Review*. These resources can be found on the BLS Web site at <http://www.bls.gov>.

Table 2-20. Private Sector Gross Job Gains and Job Losses, Seasonally Adjusted, March 1996– December 2011

(Thousands of jobs.)

Year and month	Net change[1]	Gross job gains			Gross job losses		
		Total	Expanding establishments	Opening establishments	Total	Contracting establishments	Closing establishments
1996							
March	457	7 933	6 179	1 754	7 476	5 967	1 509
June	631	8 051	6 282	1 769	7 420	5 903	1 517
September	704	8 177	6 373	1 804	7 473	5 942	1 531
December	816	8 206	6 396	1 810	7 390	5 875	1 515
1997							
March	784	8 214	6 407	1 807	7 430	5 886	1 544
June	584	8 055	6 330	1 725	7 471	5 931	1 540
September	901	8 515	6 718	1 797	7 614	5 927	1 687
December	708	8 617	6 697	1 920	7 909	6 024	1 885
1998							
March	711	8 648	6 599	2 049	7 937	6 077	1 860
June	610	8 629	6 552	2 077	8 019	6 224	1 795
September	742	8 508	6 607	1 901	7 766	6 093	1 673
December	768	8 475	6 737	1 738	7 707	6 025	1 682
1999							
March	353	8 585	6 626	1 959	8 232	6 395	1 837
June	644	8 539	6 661	1 878	7 895	6 210	1 685
September	588	8 571	6 734	1 837	7 983	6 250	1 733
December	1 005	8 749	6 956	1 793	7 744	6 076	1 668
2000							
March	827	8 849	6 960	1 889	8 022	6 342	1 680
June	503	8 479	6 794	1 685	7 976	6 373	1 603
September	324	8 525	6 756	1 769	8 201	6 479	1 722
December	251	8 351	6 673	1 678	8 100	6 444	1 656
2001							
March	-119	8 491	6 728	1 763	8 610	6 717	1 893
June	-780	7 991	6 302	1 689	8 771	7 036	1 735
September	-1 148	7 630	5 945	1 685	8 778	6 990	1 788
December	-1 009	7 547	5 912	1 635	8 556	6 870	1 686
2002							
March	-10	8 071	6 298	1 773	8 081	6 434	1 647
June	-30	7 868	6 145	1 723	7 898	6 274	1 624
September	-151	7 630	6 039	1 591	7 781	6 248	1 533
December	-241	7 483	5 938	1 545	7 724	6 185	1 539
2003							
March	-393	7 467	5 928	1 539	7 860	6 307	1 553
June	-90	7 398	5 929	1 469	7 488	6 030	1 458
September	204	7 392	5 923	1 469	7 188	5 828	1 360
December	297	7 521	6 005	1 516	7 224	5 800	1 424
2004							
March	470	7 715	6 204	1 511	7 245	5 795	1 450
June	644	7 754	6 235	1 519	7 110	5 639	1 471
September	206	7 633	6 060	1 573	7 427	5 888	1 539
December	757	7 844	6 243	1 601	7 087	5 663	1 424
2005							
March	384	7 620	6 131	1 489	7 236	5 801	1 435
June	593	7 774	6 231	1 543	7 181	5 776	1 405
September	677	7 965	6 387	1 578	7 288	5 844	1 444
December	494	7 807	6 252	1 555	7 313	5 948	1 365
2006							
March	874	7 797	6 354	1 443	6 923	5 636	1 287
June	371	7 758	6 246	1 512	7 387	6 015	1 372
September	52	7 499	6 061	1 438	7 447	6 097	1 350
December	455	7 740	6 223	1 517	7 285	5 941	1 344
2007							
March	555	7 723	6 303	1 420	7 168	5 871	1 297
June	155	7 630	6 222	1 408	7 475	6 073	1 402
September	-240	7 333	5 858	1 475	7 573	6 219	1 354
December	274	7 642	6 178	1 464	7 368	6 016	1 352
2008							
March	-215	7 234	5 831	1 403	7 449	6 086	1 363
June	-574	7 255	5 851	1 404	7 829	6 351	1 478
September	-955	6 893	5 526	1 367	7 848	6 467	1 381
December	-1 819	6 698	5 342	1 356	8 517	7 030	1 487
2009							
March	-2 696	5 830	4 651	1 179	8 526	7 109	1 417
June	-1 653	6 395	5 091	1 304	8 048	6 661	1 387
September	-893	6 345	5 127	1 218	7 238	5 881	1 357
December	-238	6 634	5 306	1 328	6 872	5 586	1 286
2010							
March	-254	6 246	5 084	1 162	6 500	5 299	1 201
June	721	6 969	5 687	1 282	6 248	5 086	1 162
September	205	6 685	5 427	1 258	6 480	5 255	1 225
December	582	7 009	5 631	1 378	6 427	5 199	1 228
2011							
March	252	6 338	5 230	1 108	6 086	4 969	1 117
June	578	6 892	5 627	1 265	6 314	5 083	1 231
September	753	7 058	5 745	1 313	6 305	5 160	1 145
December	368	6 854	5 542	1 312	6 486	5 212	1 274

[1]Net change is the difference between total gross job gains and total gross job losses.

Table 2-21. Private Sector Gross Job Gains and Job Losses, as a Percent of Employment,[1] Seasonally Adjusted, March 1996–December 2011

(Percent.)

Year and month	Net change[2]	Gross job gains			Gross job losses		
		Total	Expanding establishments	Opening establishments	Total	Contracting establishments	Closing establishments
1996							
March	0.5	8.1	6.3	1.8	7.6	6.1	1.5
June	0.7	8.2	6.4	1.8	7.5	6.0	1.5
September	0.7	8.2	6.4	1.8	7.5	6.0	1.5
December	0.8	8.2	6.4	1.8	7.4	5.9	1.5
1997							
March	0.9	8.2	6.4	1.8	7.3	5.8	1.5
June	0.6	7.9	6.2	1.7	7.3	5.8	1.5
September	1.0	8.4	6.6	1.8	7.4	5.8	1.6
December	0.8	8.4	6.5	1.9	7.6	5.8	1.8
1998							
March	0.7	8.4	6.4	2.0	7.7	5.9	1.8
June	0.6	8.3	6.3	2.0	7.7	6.0	1.7
September	0.7	8.1	6.3	1.8	7.4	5.8	1.6
December	0.7	8.0	6.4	1.6	7.3	5.7	1.6
1999							
March	0.3	8.0	6.2	1.8	7.7	6.0	1.7
June	0.6	8.0	6.2	1.8	7.4	5.8	1.6
September	0.6	8.0	6.3	1.7	7.4	5.8	1.6
December	1.0	8.1	6.4	1.7	7.1	5.6	1.5
2000							
March	0.8	8.1	6.4	1.7	7.3	5.8	1.5
June	0.4	7.7	6.2	1.5	7.3	5.8	1.5
September	0.2	7.7	6.1	1.6	7.5	5.9	1.6
December	0.2	7.5	6.0	1.5	7.3	5.8	1.5
2001							
March	-0.1	7.7	6.1	1.6	7.8	6.1	1.7
June	-0.8	7.2	5.7	1.5	8.0	6.4	1.6
September	-1.1	6.9	5.4	1.5	8.0	6.4	1.6
December	-1.0	7.0	5.5	1.5	8.0	6.4	1.6
2002							
March	0.0	7.5	5.9	1.6	7.5	6.0	1.5
June	0.0	7.3	5.7	1.6	7.3	5.8	1.5
September	-0.1	7.1	5.6	1.5	7.2	5.8	1.4
December	-0.3	6.9	5.5	1.4	7.2	5.8	1.4
2003							
March	-0.5	6.9	5.5	1.4	7.4	5.9	1.5
June	0.0	7.0	5.6	1.4	7.0	5.6	1.4
September	0.1	6.9	5.5	1.4	6.8	5.5	1.3
December	0.3	7.0	5.6	1.4	6.7	5.4	1.3
2004							
March	0.5	7.2	5.8	1.4	6.7	5.4	1.3
June	0.6	7.2	5.8	1.4	6.6	5.2	1.4
September	0.3	7.1	5.6	1.5	6.8	5.4	1.4
December	0.7	7.2	5.7	1.5	6.5	5.2	1.3
2005							
March	0.4	7.0	5.6	1.4	6.6	5.3	1.3
June	0.6	7.1	5.7	1.4	6.5	5.2	1.3
September	0.6	7.2	5.8	1.4	6.6	5.3	1.3
December	0.4	7.0	5.6	1.4	6.6	5.4	1.2
2006							
March	0.9	7.0	5.7	1.3	6.1	5.0	1.1
June	0.3	6.8	5.5	1.3	6.5	5.3	1.2
September	0.1	6.7	5.4	1.3	6.6	5.4	1.2
December	0.3	6.8	5.5	1.3	6.5	5.3	1.2
2007							
March	0.4	6.7	5.5	1.2	6.3	5.2	1.1
June	0.2	6.7	5.5	1.2	6.5	5.3	1.2
September	-0.3	6.4	5.1	1.3	6.7	5.5	1.2
December	0.2	6.7	5.4	1.3	6.5	5.3	1.2
2008							
March	-0.2	6.3	5.1	1.2	6.5	5.3	1.2
June	-0.6	6.3	5.1	1.2	6.9	5.6	1.3
September	-0.8	6.1	4.9	1.2	6.9	5.7	1.2
December	-1.6	6.0	4.8	1.2	7.6	6.3	1.3
2009							
March	-2.4	5.4	4.3	1.1	7.8	6.5	1.3
June	-1.5	6.0	4.8	1.2	7.5	6.2	1.3
September	-0.9	6.0	4.8	1.2	6.9	5.6	1.3
December	-0.2	6.3	5.0	1.3	6.5	5.3	1.2
2010							
March	-0.2	5.9	4.8	1.1	6.1	5.0	1.1
June	0.7	6.6	5.4	1.2	5.9	4.8	1.1
September	0.1	6.3	5.1	1.2	6.2	5.0	1.2
December	0.5	6.6	5.3	1.3	6.1	4.9	1.2
2011							
March	0.2	5.9	4.9	1.0	5.7	4.7	1.0
June	0.6	6.4	5.2	1.2	5.8	4.7	1.1
September	0.6	6.5	5.3	1.2	5.9	4.8	1.1
December	0.3	6.3	5.1	1.2	6.0	4.8	1.2

[1]The rates measure gross job gains and job losses as a percentage of the average of the previous and current employment.
[2]Net change is the difference between total gross job gains and total gross job losses.

Table 2-22. Three-Month Private Sector Job Gains and Losses, by Industry, Seasonally Adjusted, December 2010–December 2011

(Thousands of jobs.)

Industry	Gross job gains and job losses (3 months ended)					Gross job gains and losses as a percent of employment (3 months ended)				
	December 2010	March 2011	June 2011	September 2011	December 2011	December 2010	March 2011	June 2011	September 2011	December 2011
TOTAL PRIVATE[1]										
Gross job gains	7 009	6 338	6 892	7 058	6 854	6.6	5.9	6.4	6.5	6.3
Gross job losses	6 427	6 086	6 314	6 305	6 486	6.1	5.7	5.8	5.9	6.0
Net employment change	582	252	578	753	368	0.5	0.2	0.6	0.6	0.3
Goods-Producing										
Gross job gains	1 364	1 296	1 396	1 437	1 348	7.2	6.9	7.3	7.5	7.0
Gross job losses	1 406	1 268	1 264	1 259	1 352	7.5	6.8	6.6	6.6	7.0
Net employment change	-42	28	132	178	-4	-0.3	0.1	0.7	0.9	0.0
Natural Resources and Mining										
Gross job gains	284	261	276	301	293	15.6	14.2	15.0	16.0	15.1
Gross job losses	278	260	259	239	269	15.2	14.1	14.0	12.8	13.9
Net employment change	6	1	17	62	24	0.4	0.1	1.0	3.2	1.2
Construction										
Gross job gains	638	613	662	678	623	11.6	11.3	12.2	12.3	11.3
Gross job losses	697	638	626	613	656	12.8	11.8	11.5	11.2	11.8
Net employment change	-59	-25	36	65	-33	-1.2	-0.5	0.7	1.1	-0.5
Manufacturing										
Gross job gains	442	422	458	458	432	3.9	3.6	3.9	3.9	3.6
Gross job losses	431	370	379	407	427	3.8	3.2	3.2	3.4	3.7
Net employment change	11	52	79	51	5	0.1	0.4	0.7	0.5	-0.1
Service-Providing[1]										
Gross job gains	5 645	5 042	5 496	5 621	5 506	6.4	5.7	6.2	6.3	6.1
Gross job losses	5 021	4 818	5 050	5 046	5 134	5.7	5.5	5.7	5.7	5.8
Net employment change	624	224	446	575	372	0.7	0.2	0.5	0.6	0.3
Wholesale Trade										
Gross job gains	281	258	285	283	275	5.2	4.7	5.2	5.1	4.9
Gross job losses	253	246	243	256	251	4.6	4.4	4.3	4.6	4.5
Net employment change	28	12	42	27	24	0.6	0.3	0.9	0.5	0.4
Retail Trade										
Gross job gains	893	805	895	870	892	6.2	5.5	6.1	5.9	6.1
Gross job losses	812	814	768	864	813	5.6	5.6	5.2	5.8	5.6
Net employment change	81	-9	127	6	79	0.6	-0.1	0.9	0.1	0.5
Transportation and Warehousing										
Gross job gains	253	204	220	227	244	6.3	5.1	5.4	5.6	5.9
Gross job losses	193	223	200	196	202	4.8	5.5	4.9	4.8	4.9
Net employment change	60	-19	20	31	42	1.5	-0.4	0.5	0.8	1.0
Utilities										
Gross job gains	12	11	12	11	12	2.2	2.0	2.2	2.0	2.2
Gross job losses	11	9	13	12	12	2.0	1.7	2.4	2.2	2.2
Net employment change	1	2	-1	-1	0	0.2	0.3	-0.2	-0.2	0.0
Information										
Gross job gains	127	111	124	123	123	4.8	4.1	4.7	4.6	4.6
Gross job losses	138	130	129	122	135	5.1	4.8	4.8	4.5	5.1
Net employment change	-11	-19	-5	1	-12	-0.3	-0.7	-0.1	0.1	-0.5
Financial Activities										
Gross job gains	369	317	346	370	359	5.0	4.3	4.6	5.0	4.8
Gross job losses	346	334	352	336	352	4.7	4.5	4.8	4.6	4.7
Net employment change	23	-17	-6	34	7	0.3	-0.2	-0.2	0.4	0.1
Professional and Business Services										
Gross job gains	1 387	1 219	1 300	1 359	1 340	8.2	7.1	7.6	7.8	7.7
Gross job losses	1 176	1 134	1 212	1 152	1 249	6.9	6.6	7.0	6.7	7.2
Net employment change	211	85	88	207	91	1.3	0.5	0.6	1.1	0.5
Education and Health Services										
Gross job gains	842	733	777	841	800	4.5	3.8	4.1	4.4	4.2
Gross job losses	704	668	751	707	731	3.8	3.6	4.0	3.7	3.8
Net employment change	138	65	26	134	69	0.7	0.2	0.1	0.7	0.4
Leisure and Hospitality										
Gross job gains	1 131	1 037	1 166	1 170	1 099	8.6	7.9	8.8	8.8	8.1
Gross job losses	1 100	985	1 095	1 104	1 101	8.4	7.4	8.3	8.2	8.2
Net employment change	31	52	71	66	-2	0.2	0.5	0.5	0.6	-0.1
Other Services										
Gross job gains	272	258	280	277	259	7.3	6.9	7.4	7.3	6.9
Gross job losses	267	249	259	270	261	7.2	6.7	6.9	7.2	6.9
Net employment change	5	9	21	7	-2	0.1	0.2	0.5	0.1	0.0

[1]Includes unclassified sector, not shown separately.

Table 2-23. Private Sector Gross Job Gains and Losses, by State and Selected Territory, Seasonally Adjusted, December 2010–December 2011

(Number.)

State	Gross job gains (3 months ended)					Gross job losses (3 months ended)				
	December 2010	March 2011	June 2011	September 2011	December 2011	December 2010	March 2011	June 2011	September 2011	December 2011
UNITED STATES	7 009 000	6 338 000	6 892 000	7 058 000	6 854 000	6 427 000	6 086 000	6 314 000	6 305 000	6 486 000
Alabama	92 703	84 637	85 592	89 163	84 902	89 303	84 577	88 057	80 766	86 811
Alaska	23 714	23 704	26 682	24 543	22 945	25 098	21 076	23 216	23 016	26 148
Arizona	141 959	116 287	126 242	137 222	141 007	113 441	119 945	122 634	117 282	122 629
Arkansas	53 841	56 325	53 865	61 843	59 014	57 528	54 661	59 326	55 999	50 570
California	869 765	752 097	829 483	891 979	859 658	768 114	743 843	779 015	808 154	779 826
Colorado	130 478	122 766	131 469	131 059	128 595	121 381	115 795	114 903	116 008	122 675
Connecticut	73 952	68 916	77 071	73 048	72 755	71 930	69 652	66 307	68 789	70 840
Delaware	21 865	21 934	22 247	24 591	21 495	22 473	20 460	23 686	23 409	21 336
District of Columbia	27 326	32 551	28 237	25 787	25 702	24 844	21 185	25 721	24 632	24 711
Florida	449 196	379 849	425 637	434 967	435 381	410 096	363 736	394 012	388 491	412 001
Georgia	213 709	209 182	204 074	205 602	201 650	197 217	189 167	197 983	199 107	200 263
Hawaii	26 710	24 022	23 772	27 275	25 022	23 085	23 055	28 239	22 296	22 485
Idaho	40 396	35 101	37 182	41 201	37 046	38 004	37 154	37 510	33 989	37 708
Illinois	283 029	243 874	273 748	274 868	266 469	250 035	237 315	242 868	253 937	258 087
Indiana	147 601	134 570	134 642	147 420	141 985	130 056	116 631	127 648	128 058	133 390
Iowa	76 155	66 167	71 914	73 955	71 149	67 853	67 143	65 640	64 523	68 595
Kansas	71 306	59 023	63 561	66 004	65 001	59 548	60 921	62 431	61 473	61 692
Kentucky	92 394	81 058	86 726	88 635	87 176	80 264	83 398	80 396	78 431	81 718
Louisiana	104 538	101 107	96 036	105 596	99 191	101 157	91 929	103 403	88 932	96 098
Maine	35 285	31 923	36 874	36 194	33 038	35 153	33 587	34 606	32 251	34 945
Maryland	129 128	120 590	130 489	131 940	128 539	124 276	119 259	124 892	122 518	122 002
Massachusetts	157 256	140 586	159 052	167 845	144 205	149 093	140 876	142 030	146 737	150 404
Michigan	210 265	197 929	218 137	227 785	202 960	205 916	181 677	200 177	190 661	198 242
Minnesota	133 344	127 308	141 827	143 523	125 786	128 021	119 396	120 988	117 440	130 800
Mississippi	56 206	54 905	51 146	53 661	51 504	55 128	52 004	56 420	52 391	50 410
Missouri	125 381	124 161	128 455	128 195	135 130	118 878	121 614	122 957	127 272	122 259
Montana	27 412	24 773	27 613	28 498	28 859	27 464	24 600	25 488	24 128	26 620
Nebraska	42 503	40 626	42 236	42 691	43 312	41 662	39 873	40 384	39 740	39 971
Nevada	68 182	57 570	61 627	64 218	57 458	58 354	55 923	61 678	57 425	55 206
New Hampshire	36 320	32 184	35 249	35 229	35 786	33 028	32 166	33 877	33 518	33 721
New Jersey	204 445	187 187	220 220	204 955	209 431	192 833	196 954	191 595	195 289	195 955
New Mexico	40 203	35 792	39 688	40 942	37 164	38 293	36 000	38 632	37 790	40 290
New York	443 101	415 350	464 287	460 896	436 423	413 552	388 706	407 215	420 817	426 749
North Carolina	208 892	201 177	201 804	197 920	202 558	193 313	179 918	186 868	189 164	191 808
North Dakota	25 477	24 301	22 027	31 013	32 270	17 817	18 710	20 698	18 430	19 899
Ohio	263 829	232 634	255 425	258 434	252 833	248 000	225 754	224 156	224 984	238 467
Oklahoma	78 140	70 542	72 898	77 646	75 051	63 495	72 208	66 793	70 215	73 191
Oregon	93 768	90 387	87 393	100 035	92 624	91 329	85 528	84 050	78 502	92 328
Pennsylvania	287 353	256 356	276 634	264 527	276 936	255 340	245 437	249 470	265 920	245 749
Rhode Island	23 892	21 940	26 431	23 227	23 838	24 293	23 049	24 728	23 335	24 926
South Carolina	90 254	86 054	91 667	90 563	90 346	82 846	79 478	85 150	87 749	82 032
South Dakota	21 290	19 073	21 404	22 160	21 579	19 484	20 405	19 116	18 938	19 441
Tennessee	129 496	121 094	126 896	128 156	136 418	113 331	108 222	110 348	117 113	116 607
Texas	521 355	487 171	512 733	540 240	522 310	434 541	430 556	442 173	441 962	456 424
Utah	69 949	64 660	68 917	68 859	69 738	62 878	60 897	61 092	56 810	60 954
Vermont	19 007	15 834	18 615	18 533	20 184	16 786	17 121	18 265	18 741	16 318
Virginia	177 039	163 055	173 719	172 449	177 651	166 124	155 930	163 481	158 109	174 723
Washington	165 022	152 331	156 143	172 347	163 346	158 113	145 613	149 155	132 961	162 721
West Virginia	34 909	35 855	35 737	36 863	37 872	34 879	32 383	33 306	33 902	32 794
Wisconsin	138 480	126 622	133 862	131 978	125 731	128 104	123 857	122 475	123 201	130 742
Wyoming	19 363	16 627	17 857	19 903	19 756	18 449	17 712	18 183	15 437	17 401
Puerto Rico	45 464	36 260	38 389	41 592	45 676	37 113	41 528	41 232	36 646	37 845
Virgin Islands	2 417	2 134	1 848	1 772	1 845	1 774	2 192	2 836	2 213	1 920

Table 2-24. Private Sector Gross Job Gains and Losses as a Percent of Total Employment, by State and Selected Territory, Seasonally Adjusted, December 2010–December 2011

(Percent.)

State	Gross job gains (3 months ended)					Gross job losses (3 months ended)				
	December 2010	March 2011	June 2011	September 2011	December 2011	December 2010	March 2011	June 2011	September 2011	December 2011
UNITED STATES	6.6	5.9	6.4	6.5	6.3	6.1	5.7	5.8	5.9	6.0
Alabama	6.4	5.8	5.9	6.2	5.9	6.1	5.9	6.1	5.6	6.0
Alaska	10.0	9.8	11.0	10.0	9.4	10.5	8.8	9.5	9.4	10.7
Arizona	7.2	5.9	6.4	6.9	7.0	5.8	6.1	6.2	5.9	6.0
Arkansas	5.8	6.1	5.8	6.7	6.2	6.1	5.9	6.4	6.0	5.3
California	7.3	6.3	7.0	7.4	7.1	6.5	6.3	6.6	6.7	6.5
Colorado	7.2	6.8	7.2	7.1	7.0	6.7	6.4	6.2	6.3	6.6
Connecticut	5.4	5.1	5.7	5.3	5.3	5.3	5.2	4.8	5.0	5.2
Delaware	6.4	6.4	6.5	7.2	6.3	6.6	6.0	6.9	6.8	6.2
District of Columbia	6.2	7.2	6.2	5.7	5.6	5.6	4.7	5.6	5.4	5.4
Florida	7.4	6.3	7.0	7.0	7.0	6.7	6.0	6.4	6.3	6.7
Georgia	6.9	6.7	6.6	6.6	6.4	6.4	6.0	6.3	6.4	6.4
Hawaii	5.7	5.1	5.1	5.8	5.2	5.0	4.9	6.0	4.7	4.7
Idaho	8.2	7.1	7.5	8.3	7.4	7.7	7.5	7.6	6.8	7.5
Illinois	6.0	5.1	5.8	5.7	5.6	5.3	5.0	5.1	5.4	5.4
Indiana	6.4	5.8	5.8	6.2	6.0	5.6	5.0	5.4	5.4	5.6
Iowa	6.3	5.5	6.0	6.1	5.8	5.7	5.5	5.4	5.3	5.7
Kansas	6.8	5.6	6.1	6.2	6.1	5.7	5.7	5.9	5.9	5.8
Kentucky	6.5	5.8	6.1	6.2	6.1	5.7	5.9	5.7	5.5	5.7
Louisiana	7.0	6.7	6.3	7.0	6.5	6.8	6.1	6.9	5.9	6.4
Maine	7.4	6.7	7.7	7.5	6.8	7.4	7.0	7.2	6.7	7.3
Maryland	6.6	6.1	6.6	6.6	6.4	6.3	6.0	6.3	6.1	6.1
Massachusetts	5.8	5.2	5.9	6.1	5.2	5.5	5.2	5.2	5.3	5.5
Michigan	6.5	6.1	6.7	7.0	6.1	6.4	5.7	6.1	5.8	6.0
Minnesota	6.1	5.8	6.4	6.4	5.6	5.8	5.4	5.5	5.2	5.8
Mississippi	6.7	6.5	6.1	6.4	6.1	6.6	6.2	6.7	6.3	6.1
Missouri	5.9	5.8	6.0	6.0	6.3	5.6	5.7	5.7	5.9	5.7
Montana	8.1	7.4	8.2	8.4	8.4	8.1	7.3	7.5	7.1	7.8
Nebraska	5.7	5.5	5.7	5.7	5.8	5.7	5.4	5.5	5.4	5.3
Nevada	7.1	6.0	6.3	6.7	6.0	6.1	5.8	6.4	5.9	5.7
New Hampshire	7.0	6.2	6.8	6.7	6.9	6.4	6.2	6.6	6.4	6.5
New Jersey	6.5	5.9	7.0	6.4	6.5	6.2	6.2	6.0	6.2	6.2
New Mexico	6.8	6.0	6.6	6.9	6.3	6.5	6.1	6.5	6.4	6.7
New York	6.4	6.0	6.6	6.5	6.1	6.0	5.5	5.8	5.9	6.0
North Carolina	6.7	6.5	6.4	6.3	6.4	6.3	5.7	5.9	6.0	6.0
North Dakota	8.5	8.0	7.2	9.9	10.0	6.0	6.1	6.8	5.9	6.2
Ohio	6.3	5.5	6.1	6.1	5.9	5.9	5.4	5.3	5.3	5.6
Oklahoma	6.6	6.0	6.2	6.5	6.3	5.4	6.1	5.6	5.9	6.1
Oregon	7.1	6.8	6.6	7.5	6.9	6.9	6.5	6.3	5.9	6.8
Pennsylvania	6.0	5.4	5.8	5.5	5.7	5.4	5.1	5.2	5.5	5.1
Rhode Island	6.1	5.6	6.8	6.0	6.1	6.3	6.0	6.4	6.0	6.4
South Carolina	6.3	6.0	6.4	6.2	6.2	5.8	5.5	5.9	6.0	5.6
South Dakota	6.7	6.0	6.7	6.8	6.6	6.1	6.3	6.0	5.9	6.0
Tennessee	6.0	5.6	5.8	5.9	6.2	5.3	5.0	5.1	5.3	5.3
Texas	6.2	5.7	6.0	6.3	6.0	5.2	5.1	5.1	5.1	5.3
Utah	7.3	6.7	7.2	7.1	7.2	6.6	6.4	6.3	5.9	6.2
Vermont	7.9	6.5	7.7	7.7	8.3	7.0	7.1	7.6	7.7	6.7
Virginia	6.2	5.7	6.1	6.0	6.1	5.8	5.4	5.7	5.5	6.1
Washington	7.3	6.7	7.0	7.6	7.2	7.1	6.4	6.6	5.8	7.1
West Virginia	6.3	6.4	6.4	6.6	6.7	6.3	5.8	6.0	6.1	5.8
Wisconsin	6.1	5.6	5.9	5.8	5.5	5.7	5.5	5.4	5.4	5.7
Wyoming	9.3	8.0	8.6	9.6	9.3	8.9	8.5	8.7	7.4	8.2
Puerto Rico	6.8	5.4	5.8	6.2	6.8	5.5	6.2	6.2	5.4	5.6
Virgin Islands	7.7	6.7	5.8	5.6	6.0	5.6	6.9	9.0	7.1	6.2

Chapter Three

OCCUPATIONAL EMPLOYMENT AND WAGES

OCCUPATIONAL EMPLOYMENT AND WAGES

HIGHLIGHTS

This chapter presents employment and wage statistics from the Bureau of Labor Statistics Occupational Employment Statistics (OES) program.

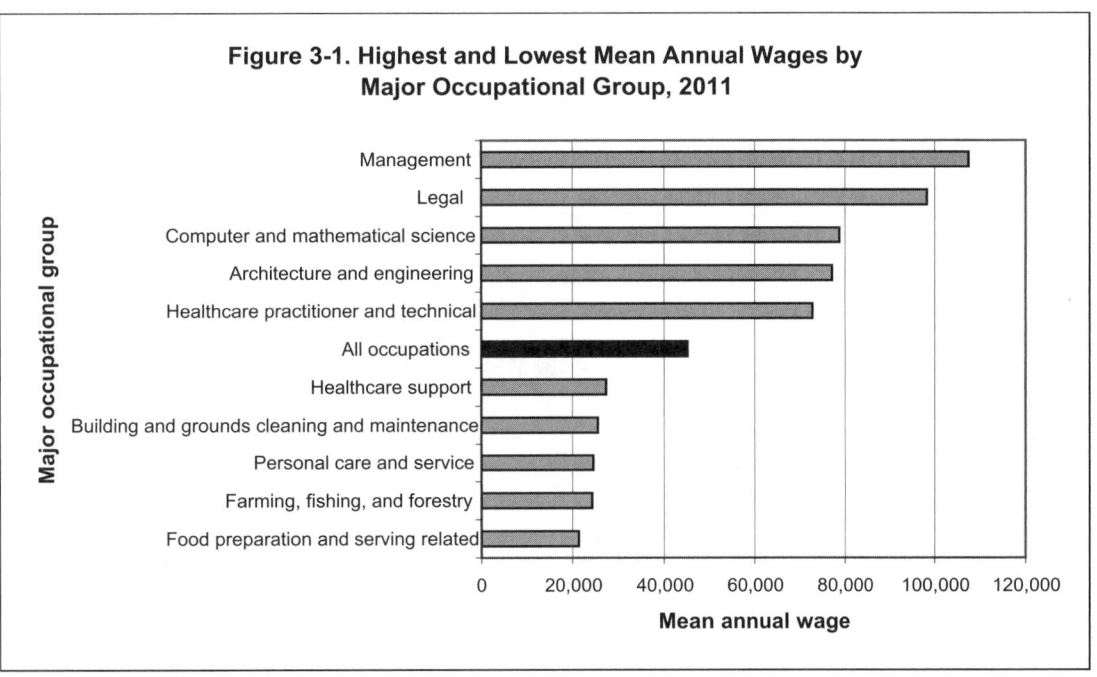

Figure 3-1. Highest and Lowest Mean Annual Wages by Major Occupational Group, 2011

In 2011, workers in management had the highest mean annual wage ($107,410) followed by those in legal occupations ($98,380), and computer and mathematical science occupations ($78,730). Meanwhile, workers in food preparation and serving related workers had the lowest mean annual wage at ($21,430). (See Table 3-1.)

OTHER HIGHLIGHTS

- Within management, chief executives had the highest salary at $176,550 while legislators had the lowest at $38,860. (See Table 3-3.)

- The mean annual wage increased for all the major occupational groups in 2011 except for farming, fishing, and forestry occupations. Wages grew the fastest in arts, design, entertainment, sports, and media at 3.0 percent. (See Table 3-1.)

- Nine of the top ten paying occupations were in the healthcare industry. Anesthesiologists earned a mean annual wage of $234,950—more than any other occupation. (See Table 3-3.)

- The mean average wages of those in the education, training, or library professions ranged from $25,270 for teacher assistants to $108,760 for postsecondary law teachers. (See Table 3-3.)

NOTES AND DEFINITIONS

Collection and Coverage

The Occupational Employment Statistics (OES) survey is a federal-state cooperative program conducted by the Bureau of Labor Statistics (BLS) and the State Workforce Agencies (SWAs). The OES program collects data on wage and salary workers in nonfarm establishments in order to produce employment and wage estimates for about 801 detailed occupations. Data from self-employed persons are not collected and are not included in the estimates. BLS funds the survey and provides procedural and technical support, while the SWAs collect the necessary data.

OES estimates are created from a sample of 1.2 million establishments. In March and November of each year, forms are mailed to two semiannual panels of around 200,000 sample establishments. May 2011 estimates are based on responses from six semiannual panels collected over a 3-year period: May 2011, November 2010, May 2010, November 2009, May 2009, and November 2008.

Scope of the Survey

Prior to 1996, the OES program collected only occupational employment data for selected industries in each year of the three-year survey cycle, and produced only industry-specific estimates of occupational employment. The 1996 survey round was the first year that the OES program began collecting occupational employment and wage data in every state. In addition, the program's three-year survey cycle was modified to collect data from all covered industries each year. In 1997, the OES program began producing estimates of cross-industry as well as industry-specific occupational employment and wages.

In 1999, the OES survey began using the Standard Occupational Classification (SOC) system. The SOC system is the first occupational classification system for federal agencies required by the Office of Management and Budget (OMB). The SOC system consists of 821 detailed occupations grouped into 449 broad occupations, 96 minor occupational groups, and 23 major occupational groups. The OES survey uses 22 of the 23 major occupational groups from the SOC to categorize workers into 801 detailed occupations. Military-specific occupations, which are not covered by the OES survey, are not included.

In 2002, the OES survey switched from the Standard Industrial Classification System (SIC) to the North American Industry Classification System (NAICS). In 2008, the OES survey switched to the 2007 NAICS from the 2002 NAICS. The most significant revisions were in the information sector, particularly within the telecommunications area. The May 2012 estimates will be based on the 2012

NAICS. More information about NAICS can be found on the BLS Web site at <http://www.bls.gov/bls/naics.htm>.

Concepts and Definitions

Employment is the estimate of total wage and salary employment in an occupation across the industries in which it was reported. The OES survey defines employment as the number of workers who can be classified as full-time or part-time employees, including workers on paid vacations or other types of leave; workers on unpaid short-term absences; employees who are salaried officers, executives, or staff members of incorporated firms; employees temporarily assigned to other units; and employees for whom the reporting unit is their permanent duty station regardless of whether that unit prepares their paycheck.

Occupations are classified based on work performed and required skills. Employees are assigned to an occupation based on the work they perform and not on their education or training. Employees who perform the duties of two or more occupations are reported as being in either the occupation that requires the highest level of skill or the occupation in which the most time is spent (if there is no measurable difference in skill requirements).

Wages are money that is paid or received for work or services performed in a specified period. Base rate, cost-of-living allowances, guaranteed pay, hazardous-duty pay, incentive pay (including commissions and production bonuses), tips, and on-call pay are included.

Mean wage refers to an average wage; an occupational mean wage estimate is calculated by summing the wages of all the employees in a given occupation and then dividing the total wages by the number of employees.

An *establishment* is defined as an economic unit that processes goods or provides services, such as a factory, store, or mine. The establishment is generally at a single physical location and is primarily engaged in one type of economic activity.

An *industry* is a group of establishments that produce similar products or provide similar services. A given industry, or even a particular establishment in that industry, might have employees in dozens of occupations. The North American Industry Classification System (NAICS) groups similar establishments into industries.

Additional Information

For additional data including area data, see BLS news release USDL 12-0548, "Occupational Employment and Wages, May 2011," and special reports on the BLS Web site at <http://www.bls.gov/OES/>.

Table 3-1. Employment and Wages, by Major Occupational Group, May 2008–May 2011

(Number, percent, dollars.)

Occupation	May 2008				May 2009			
	Employment		Mean hourly wage	Mean annual wage[1]	Employment		Mean hourly wage	Mean annual wage[1]
	Number	Percent			Number	Percent		
All Occupations	135 185 230	100.0	20.32	42 270	130 647 610	100.0	20.90	43 460
Management	6 152 650	4.6	48.23	100 310	6 116 380	4.7	49.47	102 900
Business and financial operations	6 135 520	4.5	31.12	64 720	6 063 670	4.6	31.68	65 900
Computer and mathematical sciences	3 308 260	2.4	35.82	74 500	3 303 690	2.5	36.68	76 290
Architecture and engineering	2 521 630	1.9	34.34	71 430	2 412 730	1.8	35.38	73 590
Life, physical, and social sciences	1 296 840	1.0	30.90	64 280	1 308 380	1.0	31.57	65 660
Community and social services	1 861 750	1.4	20.09	41 790	1 891 320	1.4	20.55	42 750
Legal	1 003 270	0.7	44.36	92 270	999 020	0.8	46.07	95 820
Education, training, and library	8 451 250	6.3	23.30	48 460	8 488 740	6.5	23.81	49 530
Arts, design, entertainment, sports, and media	1 804 940	1.3	24.36	50 670	1 745 670	1.3	24.87	51 720
Health care practitioner and technical	7 076 800	5.2	32.64	67 890	7 200 950	5.5	33.51	69 690
Health care support	3 779 280	2.8	12.66	26 340	3 886 690	3.0	12.84	26 710
Protective services	3 128 960	2.3	19.33	40 200	3 172 420	2.4	20.07	41 740
Food preparation and serving related	11 438 550	8.5	9.72	20 220	11 218 260	8.6	10.04	20 880
Building and grounds cleaning and maintenance	4 429 870	3.3	11.72	24 370	4 269 480	3.3	12.00	24 970
Personal care and services	3 437 520	2.5	11.59	24 120	3 461 910	2.6	11.87	24 680
Sales and related	14 336 430	10.6	17.35	36 080	13 715 050	10.5	17.32	36 020
Office and administrative support	23 231 750	17.2	15.49	32 220	22 336 450	17.1	15.86	32 990
Farming, fishing, and forestry	438 490	0.3	11.32	23 560	419 200	0.3	11.53	23 990
Construction and extraction	6 548 760	4.8	20.36	42 350	5 751 630	4.4	20.84	43 350
Installation, maintenance, and repair	5 374 850	4.0	19.82	41 230	5 114 150	3.9	20.30	42 210
Production	9 919 120	7.3	15.54	32 320	8 927 130	6.8	16.01	33 290
Transportation and material moving	9 508 750	7.0	15.12	31 450	8 844 700	6.8	15.47	32 180

Occupation	May 2010				May 2011			
	Employment		Mean hourly wage	Mean annual wage[1]	Employment		Mean hourly wage	Mean annual wage[1]
	Number	Percent			Number	Percent		
All Occupations	127 097 160	100.0	16.27	44 410	128 278 550	100.0	21.74	45 230
Management	6 022 860	4.7	43.96	105 440	6 183 820	4.8	51.64	107 410
Business and financial operations	6 090 910	4.8	29.17	67 690	6 178 070	4.8	33.05	68 740
Computer and mathematical sciences	3 283 950	2.6	35.44	77 230	3 406 720	2.7	37.85	78 730
Architecture and engineering	2 305 530	1.8	36.32	75 550	2 310 830	1.8	37.08	77 120
Life, physical, and social sciences	1 064 510	0.8	31.92	66 390	1 082 370	0.8	32.44	67 470
Community and social services	1 901 180	1.5	20.76	43 180	1 890 410	1.5	21.07	43 830
Legal	992 650	0.8	46.60	96 940	1 002 330	0.8	47.30	98 380
Education, training, and library	8 457 870	6.7	24.25	50 440	8 409 060	6.6	24.46	50 870
Arts, design, entertainment, sports, and media	1 716 640	1.4	25.14	52 290	1 725 670	1.3	25.89	53 850
Health care practitioner and technical	7 346 580	5.8	34.27	71 280	7 514 980	5.9	34.97	72 730
Health care support	3 962 930	3.1	12.94	26 920	3 954 070	3.1	13.16	27 370
Protective services	3 187 810	2.5	20.43	42 490	3 202 500	2.5	20.54	42 730
Food preparation and serving related	11 027 340	8.7	10.21	21 240	11 218 710	8.7	10.30	21 430
Building and grounds cleaning and maintenance	4 175 550	3.3	12.16	25 300	4 191 750	3.3	12.29	25 560
Personal care and services	3 425 220	2.7	11.82	24 590	3 619 250	2.8	11.84	24 620
Sales and related	13 437 980	10.6	17.69	36 790	13 646 450	10.6	18.04	37 520
Office and administrative support	21 503 800	16.9	16.09	33 470	21 384 330	16.7	16.40	34 120
Farming, fishing, and forestry	408 040	0.3	11.70	24 330	409 590	0.3	11.68	24 300
Construction and extraction	5 072 530	4.0	21.09	43 870	4 956 770	3.9	21.46	44 630
Installation, maintenance, and repair	4 928 960	3.9	20.58	42 810	4 988 980	3.9	20.86	43 390
Production	8 236 340	6.5	16.24	33 770	8 365 980	6.5	16.45	34 220
Transportation and material moving	8 547 980	6.7	15.70	32 660	8 635 940	6.7	15.96	33 200

[1]The annual wage has been calculated by multiplying the hourly mean wage by a "year-round, full-time" hours figure of 2,080 hours; for occupations with no published hourly mean wage, the annual wage has been directly calculated from the reported survey data.

Table 3-2. Distribution of Employment, by Wage Range and Occupational Group, May 2011

(Percent distribution.)

Occupation	Total	Under $11.50	$11.50 to $14.49	$14.50 to $18.24	$18.25 to $22.74	$22.75 to $28.74	$28.75 to $35.99	$36.00 to $45.24	$45.25 to $56.99	$57.00 to $71.49	Over $71.50
Management	100.0	1.2	1.2	3.0	5.5	9.4	13.8	17.0	16.9	13.3	18.8
Business and financial operations	100.0	2.2	3.3	8.0	14.0	19.8	20.0	16.2	9.4	4.0	3.3
Computer and mathematical sciences	100.0	1.0	2.2	5.0	9.0	13.8	18.7	21.4	17.0	8.3	3.5
Architecture and engineering	100.0	0.9	2.2	5.4	9.3	15.7	20.2	20.2	15.1	7.3	3.6
Life, physical, and social sciences	100.0	2.9	5.8	10.1	14.6	17.3	17.0	14.4	9.7	4.7	3.6
Community and social services	100.0	11.3	14.2	20.3	19.1	16.7	11.0	5.4	1.6	0.3	0.1
Legal	100.0	2.1	3.6	7.9	11.0	12.9	12.2	11.1	10.3	9.6	19.3
Education, training, and library	100.0	15.2	9.2	11.8	16.1	18.5	14.1	8.6	3.6	1.6	1.3
Arts, design, entertainment, sports, and media	100.0	17.2	10.3	13.5	14.7	14.1	11.8	8.2	4.6	2.2	3.3
Health care practitioner and technical	100.0	3.9	5.8	9.4	12.9	18.4	18.5	12.8	7.3	4.0	7.1
Health care support	100.0	44.4	25.8	17.6	7.8	3.1	1.0	0.2	-	-	-
Protective services	100.0	23.6	13.7	15.1	13.5	13.1	10.9	6.3	2.4	1.1	0.2
Food preparation and serving related	100.0	77.8	11.8	6.0	2.8	1.2	0.4	0.1	-	-	-
Building and grounds cleaning and maintenance	100.0	56.6	19.1	13.1	6.7	3.3	0.9	0.2	-	-	-
Personal care and services	100.0	66.6	15.0	8.4	4.8	2.8	1.5	0.6	0.2	0.1	-
Sales and related	100.0	47.5	12.6	10.2	8.5	6.7	5.1	3.7	2.4	1.4	1.8
Office and administrative support	100.0	25.5	21.1	21.5	15.8	10.8	3.7	1.2	0.3	0.1	-
Farming, fishing, and forestry	100.0	68.8	11.6	8.8	5.7	3.1	1.3	0.4	0.1	-	-
Construction and extraction	100.0	11.4	14.6	20.1	17.4	16.0	11.4	6.2	2.2	0.4	0.1
Installation, maintenance, and repair	100.0	12.3	13.0	19.0	19.5	18.4	12.0	4.6	1.0	0.2	-
Production	100.0	28.7	19.8	20.2	14.6	9.5	4.9	1.7	0.5	0.1	-
Transportation and material moving	100.0	35.7	18.5	17.6	13.0	8.3	4.4	1.4	0.6	0.3	0.3

- = Quantity represents or rounds to zero.

Table 3-3. Employment and Wages, by Occupation, May 2011

(Number of people, dollars.)

Occupation	May 2011			
	Employment	Median hourly wage	Mean hourly wage	Mean annual wage[1]
ALL OCCUPATIONS	128 278 550	16.57	21.74	45 230
Management				
Chief executives	267 370	80.25	84.88	176 550
General and operations managers	1 805 030	45.74	55.04	114 490
Legislators	62 180	([2])	([2])	38 860
Advertising and promotions managers	30 710	42.14	49.69	103 350
Marketing managers	168 410	55.78	60.67	126 190
Sales managers	328 230	48.87	56.18	116 860
Public relations and fundraising managers	53 200	44.86	50.81	105 690
Administrative services managers	249 600	38.24	41.69	86 720
Computer and information systems managers	300 830	56.74	60.41	125 660
Financial managers	477 690	51.52	57.91	120 450
Industrial production managers	151 850	42.40	46.33	96 370
Purchasing managers	66 990	46.70	49.57	103 110
Transportation, storage, and distribution managers	92 150	38.87	42.23	87 830
Compensation and benefits managers	24 580	44.37	48.62	101 130
Human resources managers	81 750	47.66	52.21	108 600
Training and development managers	27 150	44.10	47.73	99 280
Farmers, ranchers, and other agricultural managers	3 340	31.09	33.66	70 010
Construction managers	195 000	40.50	45.14	93 900
Education administrators, preschool and childcare center/program	49 320	21.07	24.66	51 290
Education administrators, elementary and secondary school	222 810	([2])	([2])	90 200
Education administrators, postsecondary	113 620	40.52	46.72	97 170
Education administrators, all other	28 090	36.89	39.46	82 070
Architectural and engineering managers	184 530	58.75	62.19	129 350
Food service managers	183 940	23.13	25.30	52 620
Gaming managers	3 570	32.32	35.95	74 780
Lodging managers	29 870	22.81	26.49	55 100
Medical and health services managers	287 560	41.54	46.17	96 030
Natural sciences managers	47 510	55.18	61.65	128 230
Postmasters and mail superintendents	24 410	30.25	29.85	62 080
Property, real estate, and community association managers	152 380	25.24	30.36	63 150
Social and community service managers	115 550	28.20	30.43	63 290
Emergency management directors	11 050	27.53	30.22	62 850
Managers, all other	343 560	47.85	50.44	104 910
Business and Financial Operations	6 178 070	29.67	33.05	68 740
Agents and business managers of artists, performers, and athletes	11 950	31.15	44.35	92 250
Buyers and purchasing agents, farm products	10 180	26.86	29.08	60 500
Wholesale and retail buyers, except farm products	105 610	24.27	27.31	56 810
Purchasing agents, except wholesale, retail, and farm products	274 540	27.68	29.46	61 280
Claims adjusters, examiners, and investigators	263 810	28.52	29.38	61 110
Insurance appraisers, auto damage	10 950	27.42	28.41	59 080
Compliance officers	210 510	29.20	30.66	63 760
Cost estimators	187 730	28.10	30.13	62 670
Farm labor contractors	960	14.02	17.17	35 720
Human resources, training, and labor relations specialists, all other	436 090	26.11	28.31	58 890
Logisticians	112 310	34.57	35.99	74 860
Management analysts	538 950	37.74	42.30	87 980
Meeting, convention, and event planners	64 020	22.13	23.96	49 840
Compensation, benefits, and job analysis specialists	94 710	27.86	29.34	61 030
Training and development specialists	205 680	26.51	28.14	58 540
Market research analysts and marketing specialists	318 190	28.97	32.27	67 130
Business operations specialists, all other	967 250	30.78	33.21	69 070
Accountants and auditors	1 085 150	30.22	33.72	70 130
Appraisers and assessors of real estate	60 930	23.49	26.18	54 460
Budget analysts	57 110	33.22	34.35	71 450
Credit analysts	59 140	29.20	33.48	69 640
Financial analysts	226 340	36.37	42.18	87 740
Personal financial advisors	161 790	32.01	43.70	90 900
Insurance underwriters	92 840	29.25	32.46	67 520
Financial examiners	28 050	36.18	40.20	83 620
Credit counselors	29 400	18.48	20.16	41 940
Loan officers	284 530	27.90	32.67	67 960
Tax examiners and collectors, and revenue agents	67 970	24.10	26.67	55 480
Tax preparers	59 180	15.54	18.95	39 410
Financial specialists, all other	152 200	28.76	31.59	65 700

[1]Annual wages have been calculated by multiplying the hourly mean wage by a "year-round, full-time" hours figure of 2,080 hours; for occupations with no published hourly mean wage, the annual wage has been directly calculated from the reported survey data.
[2]Wages for some occupations that do not generally entail year-round, full-time employment are reported as either hourly wages or annual salaries (depending on how employees are typically paid).

Table 3-3. Employment and Wages, by Occupation, May 2011—*Continued*

(Number of people, dollars.)

Occupation	May 2011			
	Employment	Median hourly wage	Mean hourly wage	Mean annual wage[1]
Computer and Mathematical				
Computer and information research scientists	25 160	48.59	49.59	103 160
Computer systems analysts	487 740	37.87	39.58	82 320
Computer programmers	320 100	34.92	36.54	76 010
Software developers, applications	539 880	42.92	44.27	92 080
Software developers, systems software	387 050	46.44	48.28	100 420
Database administrators	108 500	36.15	37.19	77 350
Network and computer systems administrators	341 800	34.12	35.71	74 270
Computer support specialists	632 490	22.91	24.91	51 820
Information security analysts, web developers, and computer network architects	272 670	37.49	39.27	81 670
Computer occupations, all other	177 630	38.43	38.70	80 500
Actuaries	19 590	43.78	49.52	103 000
Mathematicians	2 980	48.58	48.71	101 320
Operations research analysts	65 030	34.59	37.90	78 840
Statisticians	23 770	35.52	37.16	77 280
Mathematical technicians	1 060	22.32	24.47	50 910
Mathematical science occupations, all other	1 260	26.95	30.37	63 170
Architecture and Engineering				
Architects, except landscape and naval	83 590	35.26	38.13	79 300
Landscape architects	15 760	30.40	31.98	66 520
Cartographers and photogrammetrists	11 240	26.91	28.90	60 110
Surveyors	42 020	26.73	28.24	58 740
Aerospace engineers	79 400	49.24	49.94	103 870
Agricultural engineers	2 650	35.88	37.69	78 400
Biomedical engineers	16 590	40.71	42.48	88 360
Chemical engineers	27 860	44.68	47.81	99 440
Civil engineers	254 130	37.49	39.76	82 710
Computer hardware engineers	71 990	47.41	48.73	101 360
Electrical engineers	154 250	41.31	42.88	89 200
Electronics engineers, except computer	136 310	43.99	45.51	94 670
Environmental engineers	50 350	38.01	40.07	83 340
Health and safety engineers, except mining safety engineers and inspectors	23 170	36.28	37.76	78 540
Industrial engineers	211 490	37.13	38.39	79 840
Marine engineers and naval architects	5 470	40.80	44.10	91 730
Materials engineers	22 160	40.65	41.73	86 790
Mechanical engineers	238 260	38.09	40.17	83 550
Mining and geological engineers, including mining safety engineers	6 630	40.53	43.30	90 070
Nuclear engineers	18 430	49.01	50.56	105 160
Petroleum engineers	30 880	58.79	66.82	138 980
Engineers, all other	125 590	43.55	44.36	92 260
Architectural and civil drafters	85 740	22.72	24.11	50 160
Electrical and electronics drafters	28 010	26.19	27.52	57 240
Mechanical drafters	64 090	23.65	25.07	52 150
Drafters, all other	16 070	21.92	23.25	48 370
Aerospace engineering and operations technicians	9 290	29.55	29.93	62 260
Civil engineering technicians	71 890	22.55	23.31	48 480
Electrical and electronics engineering technicians	150 020	27.36	27.52	57 240
Electro-mechanical technicians	16 620	24.63	25.42	52 870
Environmental engineering technicians	19 490	21.56	23.51	48 910
Industrial engineering technicians	63 030	23.60	24.93	51 850
Mechanical engineering technicians	44 760	24.69	25.39	52 810
Engineering technicians, except drafters, all other	65 030	28.21	28.80	59 900
Surveying and mapping technicians	48 590	18.92	20.22	42 050
Life, Physical, and Social Science				
Animal scientists	2 190	29.44	35.66	74 170
Food scientists and technologists	12 040	28.05	30.85	64 170
Soil and plant scientists	11 860	28.34	30.72	63 890
Biochemists and biophysicists	25 160	38.09	42.13	87 640
Microbiologists	17 660	31.36	34.48	71 720
Zoologists and wildlife biologists	18 380	27.60	29.75	61 880
Biological scientists, all other	31 550	34.03	35.12	73 050
Conservation scientists	18 910	28.62	29.95	62 290
Foresters	9 000	26.53	26.99	56 130
Epidemiologists	4 610	30.87	33.49	69 660
Medical scientists, except epidemiologists	95 220	36.60	42.13	87 640
Life scientists, all other	10 020	30.95	35.68	74 220
Astronomers	2 080	45.91	48.86	101 630
Physicists	16 220	51.14	53.89	112 090
Atmospheric and space scientists	9 640	43.17	43.68	90 860
Chemists	80 040	33.54	35.95	74 780
Materials scientists	7 900	40.67	41.64	86 600
Environmental scientists and specialists, including health	83 090	30.25	33.08	68 810
Geoscientists, except hydrologists and geographers	32 490	40.61	46.97	97 700
Hydrologists	6 960	36.39	38.01	79 070

[1]Annual wages have been calculated by multiplying the hourly mean wage by a "year-round, full-time" hours figure of 2,080 hours; for occupations with no published hourly mean wage, the annual wage has been directly calculated from the reported survey data.

Table 3-3. Employment and Wages, by Occupation, May 2011—*Continued*

(Number of people, dollars.)

Occupation	May 2011			
	Employment	Median hourly wage	Mean hourly wage	Mean annual wage[1]
Life, Physical, and Social Science —*Continued*				
Physical scientists, all other	25 790	45.67	46.29	96 290
Economists	14 270	43.54	48.20	100 270
Survey researchers	17 060	19.30	22.95	47 740
Clinical, counseling, and school psychologists	100 850	32.64	35.14	73 090
Industrial-organizational psychologists	1 230	45.54	59.69	124 160
Psychologists, all other	10 580	43.27	41.27	85 830
Sociologists	2 830	35.42	38.20	79 460
Urban and regional planners	38 320	30.82	32.38	67 350
Anthropologists and archeologists	5 370	26.95	28.39	59 040
Geographers	1 430	35.94	35.66	74 170
Historians	3 190	25.18	27.70	57 610
Political scientists	5 340	49.93	50.50	105 040
Social scientists and related workers, all other	31 520	36.14	37.82	78 670
Agricultural and food science technicians	17 150	16.13	17.38	36 150
Biological technicians	72 140	18.98	20.33	42 290
Chemical technicians	59 650	20.23	21.42	44 560
Geological and petroleum technicians	14 680	23.89	27.81	57 840
Nuclear technicians	7 370	32.71	32.46	67 520
Social science research assistants	26 200	18.66	20.39	42 410
Environmental science and protection technicians, including health	30 320	20.32	21.76	45 270
Forensic science technicians	12 560	25.09	26.76	55 660
Forest and conservation technicians	30 620	16.78	18.01	37 460
Life, physical, and social science technicians, all other	58 890	20.73	22.00	45 770
Community and Social Service				
Substance abuse and behavioral disorder counselors	76 600	18.54	19.73	41 030
Educational, guidance, school, and vocational counselors	244 560	26.02	27.18	56 540
Marriage and family therapists	33 990	22.23	23.42	48 710
Mental health counselors	114 180	18.84	20.48	42 590
Rehabilitation counselors	110 690	16.22	17.82	37 070
Counselors, all other	27 140	20.21	21.56	44 850
Child, family, and school social workers	276 510	19.56	21.35	44 410
Healthcare social workers	133 890	23.37	24.28	50 500
Mental health and substance abuse social workers	115 390	18.86	20.50	42 650
Social workers, all other	63 110	25.91	26.07	54 220
Health educators	56 610	23.05	25.07	52 150
Probation officers and correctional treatment specialists	88 520	23.00	25.05	52 110
Social and human service assistants	359 860	13.82	14.77	30 710
Community and social service specialists, all other	121 580	18.19	19.83	41 250
Clergy	42 560	21.22	23.31	48 490
Directors, religious activities and education	17 560	17.54	20.04	41 690
Religious workers, all other	7 660	12.57	15.19	31 600
Legal				
Lawyers	570 950	54.48	62.74	130 490
Judicial law clerks	18 300	20.41	22.44	46 670
Administrative law judges, adjudicators, and hearing officers	14 460	40.96	42.47	88 340
Arbitrators, mediators, and conciliators	6 880	29.06	36.32	75 550
Judges, magistrate judges, and magistrates	26 570	57.75	53.34	110 940
Paralegals and legal assistants	252 250	22.47	24.02	49 960
Court reporters	18 440	23.33	25.82	53 710
Title examiners, abstractors, and searchers	49 760	19.60	21.56	44 850
Legal support workers, all other	44 720	25.19	28.88	60 070
Education, Training, and Library				
Business teachers, postsecondary	82 090	(²)	(²)	86 620
Computer science teachers, postsecondary	33 510	(²)	(²)	80 460
Mathematical science teachers, postsecondary	53 650	(²)	(²)	74 460
Architecture teachers, postsecondary	7 060	(²)	(²)	79 600
Engineering teachers, postsecondary	33 660	(²)	(²)	97 260
Agricultural sciences teachers, postsecondary	10 170	(²)	(²)	83 480
Biological science teachers, postsecondary	50 090	(²)	(²)	86 060
Forestry and conservation science teachers, postsecondary	2 520	(²)	(²)	82 640
Atmospheric, earth, marine, and space sciences teachers, postsecondary ...	10 660	(²)	(²)	91 350
Chemistry teachers, postsecondary	20 830	(²)	(²)	80 450
Environmental science teachers, postsecondary	4 990	(²)	(²)	84 140
Physics teachers, postsecondary	13 630	(²)	(²)	86 730
Anthropology and archeology teachers, postsecondary	5 790	(²)	(²)	81 860
Area, ethnic, and cultural studies teachers, postsecondary	9 250	(²)	(²)	79 840
Economics teachers, postsecondary	13 300	(²)	(²)	94 450
Geography teachers, postsecondary	4 280	(²)	(²)	72 300
Political science teachers, postsecondary	17 260	(²)	(²)	80 980
Psychology teachers, postsecondary	37 540	(²)	(²)	74 890
Sociology teachers, postsecondary	17 250	(²)	(²)	73 320
Social sciences teachers, postsecondary, all other	9 230	(²)	(²)	82 750

[1]Annual wages have been calculated by multiplying the hourly mean wage by a "year-round, full-time" hours figure of 2,080 hours; for occupations with no published hourly mean wage, the annual wage has been directly calculated from the reported survey data.
[2]Wages for some occupations that do not generally entail year-round, full-time employment are reported as either hourly wages or annual salaries (depending on how employees are typically paid).

Table 3-3. Employment and Wages, by Occupation, May 2011—*Continued*

(Number of people, dollars.)

Occupation	May 2011			
	Employment	Median hourly wage	Mean hourly wage	Mean annual wage[1]
Education, Training, and Library —*Continued*				
Health specialties teachers, postsecondary	153 430	(2)	(2)	99 210
Nursing instructors and teachers, postsecondary	55 930	(2)	(2)	67 810
Education teachers, postsecondary	63 330	(2)	(2)	65 050
Library science teachers, postsecondary	4 410	(2)	(2)	69 870
Criminal justice and law enforcement teachers, postsecondary	14 630	(2)	(2)	65 690
Law teachers, postsecondary	14 980	(2)	(2)	108 760
Social work teachers, postsecondary	9 970	(2)	(2)	71 030
Art, drama, and music teachers, postsecondary	90 030	(2)	(2)	72 660
Communications teachers, postsecondary	29 610	(2)	(2)	67 560
English language and literature teachers, postsecondary	72 700	(2)	(2)	68 760
Foreign language and literature teachers, postsecondary	29 010	(2)	(2)	66 720
History teachers, postsecondary	23 470	(2)	(2)	72 200
Philosophy and religion teachers, postsecondary	21 930	(2)	(2)	71 620
Graduate teaching assistants	110 130	(2)	(2)	33 180
Home economics teachers, postsecondary	5 490	(2)	(2)	68 080
Recreation and fitness studies teachers, postsecondary	18 660	(2)	(2)	63 820
Vocational education teachers, postsecondary	125 160	23.46	25.71	53 480
Postsecondary teachers, all other	182 130	(2)	(2)	74 360
Preschool teachers, except special education	349 430	12.80	14.50	30 150
Kindergarten teachers, except special education	164 910	(2)	(2)	52 350
Elementary school teachers, except special education	1 415 590	(2)	(2)	55 270
Middle school teachers, except special and career/technical education	642 820	(2)	(2)	55 780
Career/technical education teachers, middle school	16 870	(2)	(2)	56 100
Secondary school teachers, except special and career/technical education	1 004 850	(2)	(2)	56 760
Career/technical education teachers, secondary school	88 210	(2)	(2)	56 330
Special education teachers, preschool, kindergarten, and elementary school	220 220	(2)	(2)	56 460
Special education teachers, middle school	100 590	(2)	(2)	58 420
Special education teachers, secondary school	132 960	(2)	(2)	59 080
Adult basic and secondary education and literacy teachers and instructors	67 770	22.77	24.69	51 350
Self-enrichment education teachers	169 200	17.36	19.75	41 070
Teachers and instructors, all other	827 800	(2)	(2)	37 260
Archivists	5 460	22.48	24.11	50 140
Curators	10 340	23.46	25.74	53 540
Museum technicians and conservators	10 470	18.27	20.41	42 450
Librarians	145 710	26.59	27.41	57 020
Library technicians	106 560	14.63	15.42	32 070
Audio-visual and multimedia collections specialists	8 800	21.43	22.59	46 990
Farm and home management advisors	10 500	21.84	22.84	47 510
Instructional coordinators	130 230	28.50	29.67	61 720
Teacher assistants	1 214 090	(2)	(2)	25 270
Education, training, and library workers, all other	103 960	17.29	19.73	41 040
Arts, Design, Entertainment, Sports, and Media				
Art directors	30 680	39.07	45.92	95 500
Craft artists	4 810	12.82	15.51	32 270
Fine artists, including painters, sculptors, and illustrators	11 830	21.44	25.67	53 400
Multimedia artists and animators	28 400	29.25	32.72	68 060
Artists and related workers, all other	7 250	27.91	29.58	61 520
Commercial and industrial designers	28 710	29.21	30.56	63 570
Fashion designers	16 010	31.10	35.54	73 930
Floral designers	47 180	11.34	12.19	25 350
Graphic designers	191 550	21.16	23.41	48 690
Interior designers	40 950	22.90	25.39	52 810
Merchandise displayers and window trimmers	67 290	12.59	13.70	28 500
Set and exhibit designers	8 510	23.31	26.39	54 890
Designers, all other	8 070	21.92	24.83	51 640
Actors	60 830	19.14	33.82	(2)
Producers and directors	82 880	33.97	44.34	92 220
Athletes and sports competitors	12 630	(2)	(2)	79 830
Coaches and scouts	193 810	(2)	(2)	36 340
Umpires, referees, and other sports officials	15 630	(2)	(2)	29 640
Dancers	11 240	15.06	19.53	(2)
Choreographers	10 870	19.04	21.23	44 160
Music directors and composers	25 290	22.80	25.84	53 760
Musicians and singers	42 530	22.99	31.74	(2)
Entertainers and performers, sports and related workers, all other	17 920	15.23	23.34	(2)
Radio and television announcers	31 680	13.12	19.47	40 510
Public address system and other announcers	7 770	12.50	19.17	39 870
Broadcast news analysts	5 200	26.79	36.71	76 370
Reporters and correspondents	45 270	16.76	20.98	43 640
Public relations specialists	212 510	25.57	29.04	60 400
Editors	98 990	25.18	29.08	60 490
Technical writers	45 120	31.06	32.35	67 280

[1]Annual wages have been calculated by multiplying the hourly mean wage by a "year-round, full-time" hours figure of 2,080 hours; for occupations with no published hourly mean wage, the annual wage has been directly calculated from the reported survey data.
[2]Wages for some occupations that do not generally entail year-round, full-time employment are reported as either hourly wages or annual salaries (depending on how employees are typically paid).

Table 3-3. Employment and Wages, by Occupation, May 2011—*Continued*

(Number of people, dollars.)

Occupation	May 2011			
	Employment	Median hourly wage	Mean hourly wage	Mean annual wage[1]
Arts, Design, Entertainment, and Sports Media —*Continued*				
Writers and authors	40 930	26.86	32.72	68 060
Interpreters and translators	47 950	21.23	24.33	50 610
Media and communication workers, all other	23 610	20.95	25.34	52 700
Audio and video equipment technicians	49 180	20.01	22.12	46 010
Broadcast technicians	30 360	17.58	20.41	42 450
Radio operators	1 220	21.54	21.73	45 190
Sound engineering technicians	14 930	22.48	26.98	56 110
Photographers	54 410	13.88	17.59	36 580
Camera operators, television, video, and motion picture	16 270	19.31	23.77	49 430
Film and video editors	20 730	25.45	32.06	66 690
Media and communication equipment workers, all other	14 690	33.25	33.45	69 570
Healthcare Practitioners and Technical Workers				
Chiropractors	27 510	31.76	37.88	78 780
Dentists, general	90 950	68.62	77.76	161 750
Oral and maxillofacial surgeons	5 800	(3)	104.51	217 380
Orthodontists	5 040	(3)	98.40	204 670
Prosthodontists	560	52.55	62.89	130 820
Dentists, all other specialists	4 850	78.01	80.77	168 000
Dietitians and nutritionists	56 130	26.19	26.66	55 460
Optometrists	27 950	45.53	51.79	107 720
Pharmacists	272 320	54.51	53.92	112 160
Anesthesiologists	33 310	(3)	112.96	234 950
Family and general practitioners	101 800	80.29	85.26	177 330
Internists, general	46 740	88.06	90.97	189 210
Obstetricians and gynecologists	20 540	(3)	105.10	218 610
Pediatricians, general	29 640	76.04	81.08	168 650
Psychiatrists	23 140	81.90	83.73	174 170
Surgeons	42 340	(3)	111.32	231 550
Physicians and surgeons, all other	305 590	(3)	88.78	184 650
Physician assistants	83 540	42.62	43.01	89 470
Podiatrists	9 210	57.33	64.36	133 870
Registered nurses	2 724 570	31.71	33.23	69 110
Occupational therapists	103 570	35.49	36.05	74 970
Physical therapists	185 440	37.63	38.38	79 830
Radiation therapists	18 380	36.84	38.14	79 340
Recreational therapists	19 650	19.74	20.65	42 940
Respiratory therapists	113 980	26.56	27.05	56 260
Speech-language pathologists	117 210	33.22	34.61	72 000
Therapists, all other	15 720	23.61	25.43	52 890
Veterinarians	55 410	39.86	43.87	91 250
Audiologists	12 490	32.88	34.13	71 000
Health diagnosing and treating practitioners, all other	32 300	33.98	40.24	83 710
Medical and clinical laboratory technologists	165 220	27.41	27.94	58 120
Medical and clinical laboratory technicians	156 860	17.76	18.73	38 960
Dental hygienists	184 110	33.31	33.54	69 760
Cardiovascular technologists and technicians	50 410	24.53	25.08	52 160
Diagnostic medical sonographers	54 760	31.35	31.63	65 800
Nuclear medicine technologists	21 200	33.39	33.64	69 960
Radiologic technologists and technicians	220 540	26.50	27.29	56 760
Emergency medical technicians and paramedics	229 340	14.77	16.36	34 030
Dietetic technicians	23 490	12.85	14.04	29 200
Pharmacy technicians	343 550	13.91	14.43	30 020
Psychiatric technicians	69 840	13.69	15.08	31 370
Respiratory therapy technicians	13 940	22.28	22.76	47 330
Surgical technologists	94 490	19.69	20.41	42 460
Veterinary technologists and technicians	78 800	14.49	15.18	31 570
Licensed practical and licensed vocational nurses	729 140	19.79	20.21	42 040
Medical records and health information technicians	180 280	16.01	17.27	35 920
Opticians, dispensing	60 680	15.91	16.70	34 750
Orthotists and prosthetists	6 860	31.37	34.13	71 000
Health technologists and technicians, all other	103 120	18.31	20.11	41 830
Occupational health and safety specialists	57 950	31.86	32.37	67 340
Occupational health and safety technicians	11 090	22.13	23.19	48 240
Athletic trainers	18 240	(2)	(2)	44 640
Healthcare practitioners and technical workers, all other	55 450	21.61	25.64	53 330

[1]Annual wages have been calculated by multiplying the hourly mean wage by a "year-round, full-time" hours figure of 2,080 hours; for occupations with no published hourly mean wage, the annual wage has been directly calculated from the reported survey data.
[2]Wages for some occupations that do not generally entail year-round, full-time employment are reported as either hourly wages or annual salaries (depending on how employees are typically paid).
[3]Median hourly wage is equal to or greater than $80.00 per hour.

Table 3-3. Employment and Wages, by Occupation, May 2011—*Continued*

(Number of people, dollars.)

Occupation	May 2011			
	Employment	Median hourly wage	Mean hourly wage	Mean annual wage[1]
Healthcare Support				
Home health aides	924 650	9.91	10.49	21 820
Nursing aides, orderlies, and attendants	1 466 700	11.63	12.22	25 420
Psychiatric aides	71 570	12.10	13.11	27 270
Occupational therapy assistants	29 130	25.02	25.07	52 150
Occupational therapy aides	7 090	13.56	15.28	31 770
Physical therapist assistants	67 550	24.54	24.57	51 110
Physical therapist aides	47 640	11.39	12.11	25 190
Massage therapists	63 810	17.23	19.19	39 920
Dental assistants	296 810	16.42	16.70	34 740
Medical assistants	539 220	13.99	14.51	30 170
Medical equipment preparers	49 560	14.45	14.99	31 180
Medical transcriptionists	76 570	16.10	16.37	34 050
Pharmacy aides	45 130	10.56	11.23	23 350
Veterinary assistants and laboratory animal caretakers	72 530	10.98	11.75	24 430
Healthcare support workers, all other	196 100	14.80	15.50	32 240
Protective Service				
First-line supervisors of correctional officers	40 980	26.46	28.26	58 780
First-line supervisors of police and detectives	102 040	37.45	39.06	81 250
First-line supervisors of fire fighting and prevention workers	58 210	33.42	34.62	72 020
First-line supervisors of protective service workers, all other	55 910	22.32	23.37	48 620
Firefighters	304 080	21.84	22.94	47 720
Fire inspectors and investigators	12 560	25.64	27.45	57 100
Forest fire inspectors and prevention specialists	1 530	16.19	18.99	39 500
Bailiffs	16 730	18.72	19.79	41 160
Correctional officers and jailers	448 740	18.75	20.82	43 300
Detectives and criminal investigators	111 930	34.51	36.41	75 720
Fish and game wardens	7 180	24.07	26.77	55 670
Parking enforcement workers	9 310	16.99	17.35	36 090
Police and sheriff's patrol officers	636 410	26.07	27.05	56 260
Transit and railroad police	3 890	27.11	28.16	58 560
Animal control workers	14 960	15.61	16.54	34 390
Private detectives and investigators	26 080	21.01	23.37	48 610
Gaming surveillance officers and gaming investigators	7 580	14.62	15.97	33 210
Security guards	1 032 940	11.49	13.00	27 040
Crossing guards	68 520	11.27	12.44	25 880
Lifeguards, ski patrol, and other recreational protective service workers ...	123 140	9.09	10.02	20 850
Transportation security screeners (federal only)	45 320	17.74	17.98	37 400
Protective service workers, all other	74 470	15.05	16.69	34 720
Food Preparation and Serving Related				
Chefs and head cooks	90 300	20.36	22.40	46 600
First-line supervisors of food preparation and serving workers	787 540	14.21	15.39	32 020
Cooks, fast food	502 450	8.80	9.00	18 720
Cooks, institution and cafeteria	396 970	10.92	11.65	24 230
Cooks, private household	370	13.52	14.94	31 080
Cooks, restaurant	947 060	10.61	11.25	23 410
Cooks, short order	168 320	9.51	10.23	21 280
Cooks, all other	20 700	10.96	11.99	24 930
Food preparation workers	775 140	9.27	10.07	20 950
Bartenders	512 230	9.06	10.36	21 550
Combined food preparation and serving workers, including fast food	2 799 430	8.76	9.03	18 790
Counter attendants, cafeteria, food concession, and coffee shop	441 830	8.90	9.35	19 450
Waiters and waitresses	2 289 010	8.93	10.05	20 890
Food servers, nonrestaurant	221 000	9.40	10.52	21 890
Dining room and cafeteria attendants and bartender helpers	391 290	8.86	9.40	19 540
Dishwashers	504 280	8.83	9.06	18 840
Hosts and hostesses, restaurant, lounge, and coffee shop	329 070	8.92	9.45	19 660
Food preparation and serving related workers, all other	41 730	9.50	10.94	22 750
Building and Grounds Cleaning and Maintenance				
First-line supervisors of housekeeping and janitorial workers	171 960	16.94	18.16	37 760
First-line supervisors of landscaping, lawn service, and groundskeeping workers	100 460	20.22	21.71	45 160
Janitors and cleaners, except maids and housekeeping cleaners	2 068 460	10.75	11.94	24 840
Maids and housekeeping cleaners	877 980	9.32	10.31	21 440
Building cleaning workers, all other	12 370	13.14	13.89	28 890
Pest control workers	62 270	14.53	15.65	32 550
Landscaping and groundskeeping workers	821 750	11.26	12.33	25 650
Pesticide handlers, sprayers, and applicators, vegetation	23 540	14.42	15.24	31 690
Tree trimmers and pruners	38 530	15.06	15.85	32 970
Grounds maintenance workers, all other	14 430	12.07	14.07	29 270

[1]Annual wages have been calculated by multiplying the hourly mean wage by a "year-round, full-time" hours figure of 2,080 hours; for occupations with no published hourly mean wage, the annual wage has been directly calculated from the reported survey data.

Table 3-3. Employment and Wages, by Occupation, May 2011—Continued

(Number of people, dollars.)

Occupation	May 2011			
	Employment	Median hourly wage	Mean hourly wage	Mean annual wage[1]
Personal Care and Service				
Gaming supervisors	23 080	23.47	23.82	49 540
Slot supervisors	8 570	14.03	15.18	31 580
First-line supervisors of personal service workers	136 520	16.94	18.50	38 480
Animal trainers	10 530	12.49	14.67	30 510
Nonfarm animal caretakers	144 240	9.38	10.58	22 000
Gaming dealers	88 370	8.87	10.54	21 930
Gaming and sports book writers and runners	12 800	10.25	11.65	24 240
Gaming service workers, all other	10 270	10.61	12.24	25 450
Motion picture projectionists	8 890	9.78	10.67	22 200
Ushers, lobby attendants, and ticket takers	105 560	8.95	9.69	20 160
Amusement and recreation attendants	253 110	8.97	9.60	19 960
Costume attendants	5 460	15.77	19.52	40 600
Locker room, coatroom, and dressing room attendants	18 410	9.26	10.35	21 520
Entertainment attendants and related workers, all other	22 500	10.17	11.51	23 940
Embalmers	6 360	21.06	21.66	45 060
Funeral attendants	30 940	10.94	11.83	24 600
Funeral service managers, directors, morticians, and undertakers ...	29 760	25.38	29.55	61 460
Barbers	10 430	11.63	13.49	28 050
Hairdressers, hairstylists, and cosmetologists	357 030	10.85	12.72	26 460
Makeup artists, theatrical and performance	2 040	25.52	30.63	63 710
Manicurists and pedicurists	56 270	9.35	10.46	21 760
Shampooers	13 240	8.86	9.20	19 130
Skincare specialists	31 450	14.03	15.42	32 080
Baggage porters and bellhops	44 130	10.04	11.49	23 910
Concierges	22 650	13.15	13.96	29 030
Tour guides and escorts	30 730	11.36	12.82	26 660
Travel guides	4 110	14.74	15.91	33 090
Childcare workers	631 240	9.34	10.25	21 320
Personal care aides	820 600	9.49	9.88	20 560
Fitness trainers and aerobics instructors	231 500	14.92	17.38	36 150
Recreation workers	301 840	10.64	12.18	25 330
Residential advisors	76 450	11.80	12.72	26 460
Personal care and service workers, all other	70 170	9.84	11.10	23 100
Sales and Related				
First-line supervisors of retail sales workers	1 197 390	17.54	19.53	40 630
First-line supervisors of non-retail sales workers	235 630	33.91	39.62	82 400
Cashiers	3 314 870	9.05	9.73	20 230
Gaming change persons and booth cashiers	20 970	11.75	12.29	25 560
Counter and rental clerks	420 070	10.93	12.75	26 520
Parts salespersons	208 800	14.11	15.38	32 000
Retail salespersons	4 270 550	10.10	12.08	25 130
Advertising sales agents	144 760	21.76	26.65	55 430
Insurance sales agents	321 780	22.81	30.28	62 970
Securities, commodities, and financial services sales agents	307 020	34.64	47.50	98 810
Travel agents	67 490	16.31	17.18	35 740
Sales representatives, services, all other	596 480	24.34	29.01	60 340
Sales representatives, wholesale and manufacturing, technical and scientific products	375 500	35.94	41.23	85 750
Sales representatives, wholesale and manufacturing, except technical and scientific products	1 390 480	25.74	30.54	63 520
Demonstrators and product promoters	72 620	11.43	13.66	28 410
Models	2 760	8.97	13.38	27 830
Real estate brokers	38 200	28.53	40.31	83 830
Real estate sales agents	158 340	18.79	24.60	51 170
Sales engineers	65 580	42.95	46.79	97 320
Telemarketers	258 060	10.83	12.46	25 920
Door-to-door sales workers, news and street vendors, and related workers	6 910	10.66	13.27	27 600
Sales and related workers, all other	172 170	15.58	19.19	39 920
Office and Administrative Support				
First-line supervisors of office and administrative support workers	1 364 720	23.47	25.16	52 330
Switchboard operators, including answering service	132 680	12.18	12.84	26 710
Telephone operators	14 890	15.74	16.48	34 270
Communications equipment operators, all other	2 580	18.57	19.62	40 800
Bill and account collectors	390 800	15.35	16.24	33 770
Billing and posting clerks	485 820	15.81	16.31	33 920
Bookkeeping, accounting, and auditing clerks	1 643 470	16.70	17.37	36 120
Gaming cage workers	15 690	12.30	12.82	26 670
Payroll and timekeeping clerks	176 320	17.87	18.31	38 080
Procurement clerks	70 540	18.10	18.24	37 940
Tellers	544 150	11.82	12.27	25 510
Brokerage clerks	60 720	20.08	21.06	43 800
Correspondence clerks	8 680	16.51	17.04	35 450
Court, municipal, and license clerks	121 290	16.49	17.50	36 390
Credit authorizers, checkers, and clerks	51 240	16.13	17.21	35 790

[1]Annual wages have been calculated by multiplying the hourly mean wage by a "year-round, full-time" hours figure of 2,080 hours; for occupations with no published hourly mean wage, the annual wage has been directly calculated from the reported survey data.

Table 3-3. Employment and Wages, by Occupation, May 2011—*Continued*

(Number of people, dollars.)

Occupation	May 2011			
	Employment	Median hourly wage	Mean hourly wage	Mean annual wage[1]
Office and Administrative Support —*Continued*				
Customer service representatives	2 212 820	14.72	15.92	33 120
Eligibility interviewers, government programs	120 610	19.74	19.95	41 490
File clerks	165 250	12.32	13.20	27 460
Hotel, motel, and resort desk clerks	224 430	9.68	10.46	21 760
Interviewers, except eligibility and loan	200 150	14.21	14.91	31 010
Library assistants, clerical	109 440	11.27	12.30	25 570
Loan interviewers and clerks	186 240	16.74	17.21	35 810
New accounts clerks	60 830	14.92	15.56	32 360
Order clerks	215 390	13.91	14.76	30 690
Human resources assistants, except payroll and timekeeping	145 780	17.91	18.43	38 330
Receptionists and information clerks	973 800	12.35	12.85	26 730
Reservation and transportation ticket agents and travel clerks	126 790	16.01	16.19	33 670
Information and record clerks, all other	192 910	18.16	18.35	38 180
Cargo and freight agents	80 570	18.37	19.56	40 680
Couriers and messengers	83 250	11.90	12.79	26 600
Police, fire, and ambulance dispatchers	97 100	17.27	18.01	37 460
Dispatchers, except police, fire, and ambulance	182 310	16.92	18.23	37 910
Meter readers, utilities	40 630	17.02	18.17	37 800
Postal service clerks	65 040	25.53	25.41	52 860
Postal service mail carriers	315 330	26.52	24.71	51 390
Postal service mail sorters, processors, and processing machine operators	139 700	25.52	23.26	48 380
Production, planning, and expediting clerks	272 910	20.72	21.59	44 900
Shipping, receiving, and traffic clerks	687 940	13.84	14.65	30 480
Stock clerks and order fillers	1 782 800	10.52	11.66	24 250
Weighers, measurers, checkers, and samplers, recordkeeping	68 090	13.17	14.07	29 270
Executive secretaries and executive administrative assistants	952 030	21.91	23.13	48 120
Legal secretaries	220 680	20.41	21.30	44 310
Medical secretaries	502 850	14.93	15.59	32 430
Secretaries and administrative assistants, except legal, medical, and executive	1 955 570	15.32	15.87	33 020
Computer operators	77 280	18.26	18.89	39 280
Data entry keyers	211 200	13.32	13.95	29 010
Word processors and typists	96 330	16.47	16.94	35 240
Desktop publishers	18 620	17.69	18.77	39 030
Insurance claims and policy processing clerks	218 630	16.93	17.72	36 850
Mail clerks and mail machine operators, except postal service	115 010	12.79	13.47	28 010
Office clerks, general	2 828 140	13.07	13.90	28 920
Office machine operators, except computer	66 280	13.26	14.03	29 190
Proofreaders and copy markers	11 270	15.35	16.47	34 260
Statistical assistants	14 780	18.54	19.49	40 540
Office and administrative support workers, all other	261 990	14.96	16.07	33 420
Farming, Fishing, and Forestry				
First-line supervisors of farming, fishing, and forestry workers	18 920	20.48	21.97	45 690
Agricultural inspectors	13 780	19.90	20.25	42 120
Animal breeders	1 460	16.79	18.11	37 670
Graders and sorters, agricultural products	40 970	9.17	9.95	20 690
Agricultural equipment operators	22 680	12.13	12.90	26 830
Farmworkers and laborers, crop, nursery, and greenhouse	233 280	8.99	9.62	20 020
Farmworkers, farm, ranch, and aquacultural animals	29 790	10.62	11.60	24 130
Agricultural workers, all other	6 710	12.16	13.91	28 940
Fishers and related fishing workers	640	12.98	14.53	30 220
Forest and conservation workers	8 250	11.20	13.07	27 180
Fallers	5 020	17.77	20.49	42 620
Logging equipment operators	22 470	16.03	16.40	34 110
Log graders and scalers	2 810	15.60	16.11	33 500
Logging workers, all other	2 760	16.28	16.23	33 760
Construction and Extraction				
First-line supervisors of construction trades and extraction workers	459 830	28.44	30.25	62 910
Boilermakers	18 850	27.36	27.23	56 650
Brickmasons and blockmasons	62 560	22.50	24.40	50 760
Stonemasons	11 950	17.62	18.96	39 430
Carpenters	578 910	19.24	21.31	44 330
Carpet installers	24 670	17.67	19.55	40 650
Floor layers, except carpet, wood, and hard tiles	9 660	17.00	18.67	38 830
Floor sanders and finishers	4 970	16.04	16.82	34 990
Tile and marble setters	28 630	17.83	19.65	40 860
Cement masons and concrete finishers	135 330	17.11	18.93	39 370
Terrazzo workers and finishers	3 500	19.83	20.99	43 660
Construction laborers	779 370	14.30	16.43	34 170
Paving, surfacing, and tamping equipment operators	54 120	16.96	18.99	39 500
Pile-driver operators	3 830	21.88	25.07	52 140
Operating engineers and other construction equipment operators	335 410	19.96	21.98	45 720

[1]Annual wages have been calculated by multiplying the hourly mean wage by a "year-round, full-time" hours figure of 2,080 hours; for occupations with no published hourly mean wage, the annual wage has been directly calculated from the reported survey data.

Table 3-3. Employment and Wages, by Occupation, May 2011—*Continued*

(Number of people, dollars.)

Occupation	May 2011			
	Employment	Median hourly wage	Mean hourly wage	Mean annual wage[1]
Construction and Extraction—*Continued*				
Drywall and ceiling tile installers	75 520	17.78	20.01	41 620
Tapers	15 340	21.59	23.51	48 900
Electricians	512 290	23.71	25.44	52 910
Glaziers	41 960	17.96	20.01	41 620
Insulation workers, floor, ceiling, and wall	24 170	15.59	17.71	36 840
Insulation workers, mechanical	28 600	18.27	20.78	43 220
Painters, construction and maintenance	184 820	17.04	18.67	38 830
Paperhangers	4 230	18.16	20.10	41 810
Pipelayers	43 570	17.26	18.98	39 470
Plumbers, pipefitters, and steamfitters	349 320	22.96	24.92	51 830
Plasterers and stucco masons	22 810	17.71	20.07	41 750
Reinforcing iron and rebar workers	15 730	18.27	21.83	45 400
Roofers	95 840	16.96	18.54	38 570
Sheet metal workers	130 670	20.55	22.37	46 530
Structural iron and steel workers	56 920	21.97	24.11	50 160
Helpers–brickmasons, blockmasons, stonemasons, and tile and marble setters	26 750	13.38	14.65	30 470
Helpers–carpenters	40 160	12.69	13.20	27 470
Helpers–electricians	65 300	13.28	13.84	28 780
Helpers–painters, paperhangers, plasterers, and stucco masons	10 980	11.30	12.25	25 490
Helpers–pipelayers, plumbers, pipefitters, and steamfitters	51 420	12.99	13.66	28 420
Helpers–roofers	12 540	11.18	11.99	24 930
Helpers, construction trades, all other	19 020	12.17	13.14	27 340
Construction and building inspectors	89 620	25.57	26.43	54 970
Elevator installers and repairers	20 440	36.09	35.37	73 560
Fence erectors	21 000	14.22	15.31	31 850
Hazardous materials removal workers	36 270	18.33	20.07	41 750
Highway maintenance workers	143 760	16.93	17.47	36 340
Rail-track laying and maintenance equipment operators	15 590	21.64	21.78	45 300
Septic tank servicers and sewer pipe cleaners	24 940	16.22	17.13	35 630
Segmental pavers	1 330	15.55	16.27	33 850
Construction and related workers, all other	39 160	16.92	18.39	38 250
Derrick operators, oil and gas	19 480	21.74	22.66	47 120
Rotary drill operators, oil and gas	21 650	24.67	28.15	58 540
Service unit operators, oil, gas, and mining	46 880	19.59	21.48	44 670
Earth drillers, except oil and gas	17 020	19.33	20.62	42 900
Explosives workers, ordnance handling experts, and blasters	5 210	21.81	22.62	47 040
Continuous mining machine operators	12 280	24.33	23.88	49 680
Mine cutting and channeling machine operators	5 850	23.60	22.58	46 960
Mining machine operators, all other	2 980	21.94	22.01	45 790
Rock splitters, quarry	3 600	15.63	16.31	33 920
Roof bolters, mining	6 060	25.54	25.52	53 090
Roustabouts, oil and gas	51 540	15.86	16.67	34 680
Helpers–extraction workers	23 970	15.80	17.36	36 110
Extraction workers, all other	8 590	19.25	19.47	40 500
Installation, Maintenance, and Repair				
First-line supervisors of mechanics, installers, and repairers	418 530	28.77	29.90	62 190
Computer, automated teller, and office machine repairers	111 690	17.48	18.44	38 360
Radio, cellular, and tower equipment installers and repairs	12 920	20.27	21.27	44 250
Telecommunications equipment installers and repairers, except line installers	199 240	25.94	25.42	52 870
Avionics technicians	17 070	26.31	26.15	54 390
Electric motor, power tool, and related repairers	18 710	17.26	18.30	38 050
Electrical and electronics installers and repairers, transportation equipment	14 410	23.95	25.04	52 080
Electrical and electronics repairers, commercial and industrial equipment	67 220	25.16	25.20	52 420
Electrical and electronics repairers, powerhouse, substation, and relay	23 850	32.43	31.71	65 950
Electronic equipment installers and repairers, motor vehicles	13 610	14.52	15.81	32 890
Electronic home entertainment equipment installers and repairers	27 580	16.57	17.48	36 360
Security and fire alarm systems installers	56 330	19.01	20.24	42 110
Aircraft mechanics and service technicians	117 320	26.25	26.20	54 500
Automotive body and related repairers	131 040	18.36	19.99	41 570
Automotive glass installers and repairers	13 690	16.21	16.52	34 360
Automotive service technicians and mechanics	589 750	17.39	18.54	38 560
Bus and truck mechanics and diesel engine specialists	222 940	20.02	20.63	42 910
Farm equipment mechanics and service technicians	32 100	16.46	16.92	35 190
Mobile heavy equipment mechanics, except engines	109 810	21.92	22.48	46 770
Rail car repairers	19 480	22.95	22.50	46 800
Motorboat mechanics and service technicians	16 770	17.08	17.87	37 170
Motorcycle mechanics	15 010	15.58	16.44	34 190
Outdoor power equipment and other small engine mechanics	26 610	14.52	15.06	31 330
Bicycle repairers	9 950	11.16	11.76	24 460
Recreational vehicle service technicians	10 110	16.35	17.26	35 900

[1]Annual wages have been calculated by multiplying the hourly mean wage by a "year-round, full-time" hours figure of 2,080 hours; for occupations with no published hourly mean wage, the annual wage has been directly calculated from the reported survey data.

Table 3-3. Employment and Wages, by Occupation, May 2011—*Continued*

(Number of people, dollars.)

Occupation	May 2011			
	Employment	Median hourly wage	Mean hourly wage	Mean annual wage[1]
Installation, Maintenance, and Repair —*Continued*				
Tire repairers and changers	94 740	11.27	12.19	25 350
Mechanical door repairers	14 620	17.62	18.71	38 920
Control and valve installers and repairers, except mechanical door	42 450	23.85	24.40	50 740
Heating, air conditioning, and refrigeration mechanics and installers	231 160	20.86	21.89	45 540
Home appliance repairers	34 770	17.04	17.97	37 370
Industrial machinery mechanics	292 470	22.25	23.09	48 030
Maintenance workers, machinery	77 980	18.98	19.77	41 110
Millwrights	37 730	23.69	24.35	50 650
Refractory materials repairers, except brickmasons	2 040	20.53	21.57	44 860
Electrical power-line installers and repairers	105 570	28.94	28.58	59 450
Telecommunications line installers and repairers	148 930	24.87	24.68	51 330
Camera and photographic equipment repairers	2 650	17.86	20.07	41 750
Medical equipment repairers	34 710	21.57	22.60	47 010
Musical instrument repairers and tuners	6 850	14.95	16.27	33 850
Watch repairers	2 480	18.82	19.51	40 590
Precision instrument and equipment repairers, all other	12 230	24.87	24.99	51 970
Maintenance and repair workers, general	1 225 450	16.84	17.75	36 930
Coin, vending, and amusement machine servicers and repairers	36 940	14.82	15.58	32 400
Commercial divers	3 760	25.26	28.19	58 640
Fabric menders, except garment	760	13.45	14.22	29 580
Locksmiths and safe repairers	16 200	17.63	18.50	38 490
Manufactured building and mobile home installers	4 320	13.70	14.59	30 350
Riggers	13 750	20.68	21.39	44 480
Signal and track switch repairers	8 300	26.25	26.06	54 210
Helpers–installation, maintenance, and repair workers	122 820	11.57	12.78	26 580
Installation, maintenance, and repair workers, all other	119 580	17.65	19.07	39 670
Production				
First-line supervisors of production and operating workers	559 350	25.80	27.35	56 890
Aircraft structure, surfaces, rigging, and systems assemblers	36 570	22.22	23.23	48 310
Coil winders, tapers, and finishers	13 670	14.15	14.98	31 150
Electrical and electronic equipment assemblers	187 920	13.96	15.04	31 290
Electromechanical equipment assemblers	50 320	15.26	15.77	32 800
Engine and other machine assemblers	36 670	17.51	18.86	39 230
Structural metal fabricators and fitters	76 050	16.91	17.63	36 670
Fiberglass laminators and fabricators	19 070	13.72	14.16	29 440
Team assemblers	952 300	13.22	14.30	29 740
Timing device assemblers and adjusters	1 000	14.36	15.20	31 620
Assemblers and fabricators, all other	265 260	12.56	14.16	29 450
Bakers	149 910	11.18	12.10	25 160
Butchers and meat cutters	130 720	13.68	14.43	30 000
Meat, poultry, and fish cutters and trimmers	164 650	10.92	11.44	23 800
Slaughterers and meat packers	80 110	11.30	11.63	24 190
Food and tobacco roasting, baking, and drying machine operators and tenders	18 890	13.26	14.01	29 140
Food batchmakers	100 210	12.23	13.26	27 580
Food cooking machine operators and tenders	31 020	11.79	12.89	26 820
Computer-controlled machine tool operators, metal and plastic	128 870	16.93	17.56	36 520
Computer numerically controlled machine tool programmers, metal and plastic	20 370	22.06	23.30	48 460
Extruding and drawing machine setters, operators, and tenders, metal and plastic	75 170	15.53	16.40	34 120
Forging machine setters, operators, and tenders, metal and plastic	21 790	16.54	16.77	34 890
Rolling machine setters, operators, and tenders, metal and plastic	35 180	17.75	18.16	37 780
Cutting, punching, and press machine setters, operators, and tenders, metal and plastic	181 160	14.29	14.97	31 140
Drilling and boring machine tool setters, operators, and tenders, metal and plastic	21 560	16.11	17.02	35 410
Grinding, lapping, polishing, and buffing machine tool setters, operators, and tenders, metal and plastic	70 450	15.04	15.79	32 840
Lathe and turning machine tool setters, operators, and tenders, metal and plastic	39 930	17.34	17.89	37 210
Milling and planing machine setters, operators, and tenders, metal and plastic	21 700	17.37	18.03	37 510
Machinists	368 510	18.86	19.48	40 520
Metal-refining furnace operators and tenders	18 050	18.60	19.27	40 070
Pourers and casters, metal	11 070	16.41	17.08	35 520
Model makers, metal and plastic	5 780	21.56	22.34	46 460
Patternmakers, metal and plastic	4 290	19.21	19.94	41 470
Foundry mold and coremakers	11 680	14.81	15.28	31 790
Molding, coremaking, and casting machine setters, operators, and tenders, metal and plastic	118 300	13.69	14.61	30 380
Multiple machine tool setters, operators, and tenders, metal and plastic	77 290	15.97	16.61	34 550
Tool and die makers	70 320	22.43	23.16	48 170
Welders, cutters, solderers, and brazers	316 290	17.27	18.23	37 920
Welding, soldering, and brazing machine setters, operators, and tenders	40 350	16.72	17.36	36 120
Heat treating equipment setters, operators, and tenders, metal and plastic	20 770	16.15	16.89	35 130
Layout workers, metal and plastic	9 600	19.17	19.23	39 990
Plating and coating machine setters, operators, and tenders, metal and plastic	31 150	14.25	15.36	31 960
Tool grinders, filers, and sharpeners	11 860	16.62	17.15	35 670
Metal workers and plastic workers, all other	21 720	15.16	16.79	34 910
Prepress technicians and workers	43 430	17.82	18.69	38 870

[1]Annual wages have been calculated by multiplying the hourly mean wage by a "year-round, full-time" hours figure of 2,080 hours; for occupations with no published hourly mean wage, the annual wage has been directly calculated from the reported survey data.

Table 3-3. Employment and Wages, by Occupation, May 2011—*Continued*

(Number of people, dollars.)

Occupation	May 2011			
	Employment	Median hourly wage	Mean hourly wage	Mean annual wage[1]
Installation, Maintenance, and Repair—*Continued*				
Printing press operators	179 220	16.49	17.19	35 760
Print binding and finishing workers	53 980	14.15	14.98	31 150
Laundry and dry-cleaning workers	201 180	9.46	10.28	21 380
Pressers, textile, garment, and related materials	52 790	9.35	9.87	20 530
Sewing machine operators	142 860	10.15	11.10	23 080
Shoe and leather workers and repairers	5 360	11.26	12.35	25 680
Shoe machine operators and tenders	3 510	12.18	12.75	26 520
Sewers, hand	5 460	11.32	12.30	25 590
Tailors, dressmakers, and custom sewers	25 530	12.60	13.85	28 800
Textile bleaching and dyeing machine operators and tenders	11 870	11.22	12.01	24 980
Textile cutting machine setters, operators, and tenders	15 980	11.39	12.20	25 380
Textile knitting and weaving machine setters, operators, and tenders	21 160	12.55	12.86	26 760
Textile winding, twisting, and drawing out machine setters, operators, and tenders	27 400	12.66	12.72	26 460
Extruding and forming machine setters, operators, and tenders, synthetic and glass fibers	16 050	15.27	15.43	32 100
Fabric and apparel patternmakers	6 410	19.14	21.47	44 650
Upholsterers	28 260	14.31	15.21	31 640
Textile, apparel, and furnishings workers, all other	13 980	12.05	13.87	28 850
Cabinetmakers and bench carpenters	81 260	14.68	15.49	32 220
Furniture finishers	14 850	13.63	14.29	29 720
Model makers, wood	1 370	13.82	16.79	34 930
Patternmakers, wood	820	18.69	19.54	40 630
Sawing machine setters, operators, and tenders, wood	37 620	12.60	13.19	27 440
Woodworking machine setters, operators, and tenders, except sawing	58 730	13.02	13.54	28 160
Woodworkers, all other	7 600	12.05	13.84	28 790
Nuclear power reactor operators	6 240	36.82	37.28	77 550
Power distributors and dispatchers	11 600	33.99	34.79	72 360
Power plant operators	39 980	31.38	30.97	64 420
Stationary engineers and boiler operators	34 580	25.52	25.87	53 800
Water and wastewater treatment plant and system operators	109 190	20.09	20.93	43 530
Chemical plant and system operators	40 580	26.90	26.40	54 920
Gas plant operators	11 750	28.63	28.78	59 870
Petroleum pump system operators, refinery operators, and gaugers	41 570	29.45	28.99	60 290
Plant and system operators, all other	11 740	25.58	25.46	52 960
Chemical equipment operators and tenders	49 020	21.90	22.33	46 440
Separating, filtering, clarifying, precipitating, and still machine setters, opera and tenders	39 660	18.14	18.70	38 910
Crushing, grinding, and polishing machine setters, operators, and tenders	31 540	15.57	16.21	33 720
Grinding and polishing workers, hand	27 630	13.18	13.80	28 710
Mixing and blending machine setters, operators, and tenders	118 700	16.15	16.80	34 930
Cutters and trimmers, hand	14 670	11.83	12.75	26 510
Cutting and slicing machine setters, operators, and tenders	59 430	14.82	15.27	31 760
Extruding, forming, pressing, and compacting machine setters, operators, and tenders	66 330	14.99	15.85	32 960
Furnace, kiln, oven, drier, and kettle operators and tenders	18 940	16.96	17.63	36 680
Inspectors, testers, sorters, samplers, and weighers	434 170	16.36	17.64	36 690
Jewelers and precious stone and metal workers	21 640	16.36	18.37	38 200
Dental laboratory technicians	37 600	17.11	18.54	38 550
Medical appliance technicians	13 390	17.13	18.12	37 680
Ophthalmic laboratory technicians	27 630	13.82	14.38	29 920
Packaging and filling machine operators and tenders	354 810	12.32	13.44	27 950
Coating, painting, and spraying machine setters, operators, and tenders	77 090	14.43	15.10	31 410
Painters, transportation equipment	44 730	19.04	20.69	43 040
Painting, coating, and decorating workers	19 370	12.34	13.21	27 480
Semiconductor processors	22 070	15.64	16.45	34 220
Photographic process workers and processing machine operators	50 570	10.99	12.39	25 770
Adhesive bonding machine operators and tenders	16 040	14.22	14.90	30 990
Cleaning, washing, and metal pickling equipment operators and tenders	16 430	12.67	13.67	28 420
Cooling and freezing equipment operators and tenders	8 080	14.04	14.93	31 060
Etchers and engravers	8 260	13.71	14.48	30 120
Molders, shapers, and casters, except metal and plastic	30 600	13.92	14.70	30 570
Paper goods machine setters, operators, and tenders	93 290	16.48	16.89	35 140
Tire builders	16 690	19.59	18.92	39 360
Helpers–production workers	420 910	10.83	11.72	24 370
Production workers, all other	235 910	13.19	14.74	30 670

[1]Annual wages have been calculated by multiplying the hourly mean wage by a "year-round, full-time" hours figure of 2,080 hours; for occupations with no published hourly mean wage, the annual wage has been directly calculated from the reported survey data.

Table 3-3. Employment and Wages, by Occupation, May 2011—*Continued*

(Number of people, dollars.)

Occupation	May 2011			
	Employment	Median hourly wage	Mean hourly wage	Mean annual wage[1]
Transportation and Material Moving				
Aircraft cargo handling supervisors	6 710	22.52	24.28	50 500
First-line supervisors of helpers, laborers, and material movers, hand	166 560	21.43	22.52	46 840
First-line supervisors of transportation and material-moving machine and vehicle operators	198 690	25.45	26.54	55 210
Airline pilots, copilots, and flight engineers	68 350	([2])	([2])	118 070
Commercial pilots	31 630	([2])	([2])	76 050
Air traffic controllers	23 580	54.59	55.03	114 460
Airfield operations specialists	6 060	22.68	23.90	49 710
Flight attendants	87 190	([2])	([2])	41 720
Ambulance drivers and attendants, except emergency medical technicians	18 080	10.97	11.68	24 300
Bus drivers, transit and intercity	176 190	17.17	18.00	37 440
Bus drivers, school or special client	477 400	13.51	14.05	29 220
Driver/sales workers	387 950	10.95	13.22	27 490
Heavy and tractor-trailer truck drivers	1 508 620	18.24	19.15	39 830
Light truck or delivery services drivers	771 210	13.98	15.92	33 120
Taxi drivers and chauffeurs	166 890	10.94	12.03	25 020
Motor vehicle operators, all other	61 600	13.07	15.15	31 510
Locomotive engineers	38 790	23.74	25.45	52 940
Locomotive firers	1 670	21.50	23.47	48 820
Rail yard engineers, dinkey operators, and hostlers	5 060	19.71	20.93	43 540
Railroad brake, signal, and switch operators	23 830	24.24	23.61	49 110
Railroad conductors and yardmasters	44 280	25.90	27.03	56 230
Subway and streetcar operators	5 920	30.68	28.56	59 400
Rail transportation workers, all other	2 400	23.56	22.52	46 840
Sailors and marine oilers	31 280	17.69	18.59	38 670
Captains, mates, and pilots of water vessels	30 220	30.73	34.50	71 760
Motorboat operators	2 550	17.60	18.81	39 130
Ship engineers	10 010	34.06	35.84	74 540
Bridge and lock tenders	3 420	22.09	20.90	43 460
Parking lot attendants	126 160	9.53	10.38	21 600
Automotive and watercraft service attendants	102 090	9.58	10.33	21 480
Traffic technicians	6 280	20.34	21.54	44 810
Transportation inspectors	24 810	29.92	31.62	65 770
Transportation attendants, except flight attendants	27 040	10.41	11.64	24 210
Transportation workers, all other	30 180	16.38	17.42	36 230
Conveyor operators and tenders	37 200	14.09	14.90	30 990
Crane and tower operators	41 070	22.34	24.06	50 040
Dredge operators	1 590	16.12	18.32	38 100
Excavating and loading machine and dragline operators	47 530	17.97	19.48	40 520
Loading machine operators, underground mining	2 290	21.91	22.44	46 680
Hoist and winch operators	3 320	19.98	22.40	46 590
Industrial truck and tractor operators	503 290	14.43	15.31	31 840
Cleaners of vehicles and equipment	290 780	9.54	10.87	22 600
Laborers and freight, stock, and material movers, hand	2 063 580	11.42	12.62	26 240
Machine feeders and offbearers	110 950	12.99	13.67	28 430
Packers and packagers, hand	666 860	9.55	10.81	22 480
Gas compressor and gas pumping station operators	3 870	25.21	25.52	53 080
Pump operators, except wellhead pumpers	12 150	21.09	22.31	46 400
Wellhead pumpers	13 190	19.87	20.23	42 070
Refuse and recyclable material collectors	123 160	15.52	16.55	34 420
Mine shuttle car operators	3 080	24.43	24.50	50 970
Tank car, truck, and ship loaders	10 960	19.16	20.84	43 350
Material moving workers, all other	28 370	16.90	18.76	39 020

[1]Annual wages have been calculated by multiplying the hourly mean wage by a "year-round, full-time" hours figure of 2,080 hours; for occupations with no published hourly mean wage, the annual wage has been directly calculated from the reported survey data.
[2]Wages for some occupations that do not generally entail year-round, full-time employment are reported as either hourly wages or annual salaries (depending on how employees are typically paid).

Chapter Four

LABOR FORCE AND EMPLOYMENT PROJECTIONS BY INDUSTRY AND OCCUPATION

LABOR FORCE AND EMPLOYMENT PROJECTIONS
BY INDUSTRY AND OCCUPATION

HIGHLIGHTS

Every two years, the Bureau of Labor Statistics (BLS) develops decade-long projections for industry output, employment, and occupations. This chapter presents the employment outlook for the 2010–2020 period. The projections are based on a set of explicit assumptions and an application of a model of economic relationships.

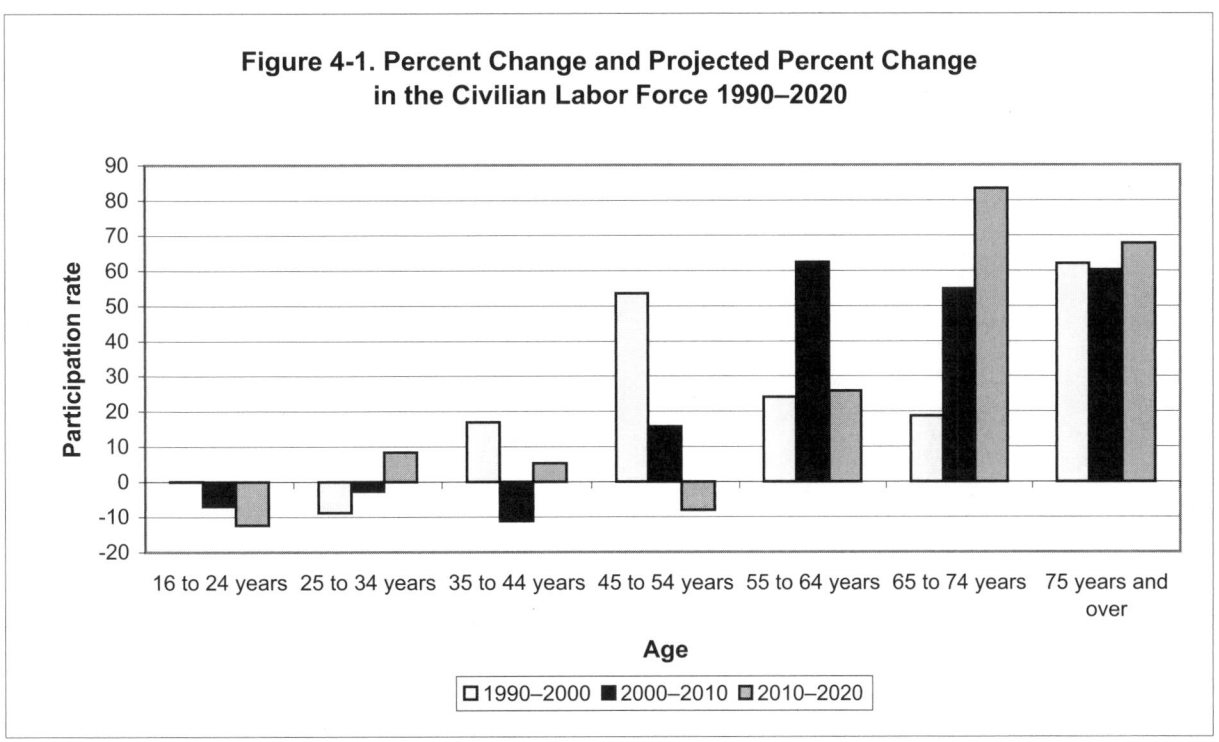

Figure 4-1. Percent Change and Projected Percent Change in the Civilian Labor Force 1990–2020

From 2010 to 2020, the civilian labor force is projected to grow by 6.8 percent, a much slower rate than the 7.9 percent increase from 2000 to 2010, or the 13.3 percent increase from 1990 to 2000. The aging of baby boomers has lead to a significant increase of older workers in the labor force. By 2020, persons 55 years of age and over are expected to make up 25.2 percent of the labor force, an increase from 19.5 percent of in 2010 and 13.1 percent in 2000. (See Table 4-1.)

OTHER HIGHLIGHTS

*   While the number of persons 55 years and over in the labor force is expected to increase, the number of 16- to 24-year olds in it is expected to decline. In 1990, 16- to 24-year-olds made up 17.9 percent of the labor force. It is projected that by 2020, this age group will only comprise 11.2 percent of the labor force. (See Table 4-1.)

*   The labor force in 2020 is expected to be more diverse. From 2010 to 2020, the number of Hispanics in the labor force is projected to increase by 34.0 percent, followed by the number of Asians at 30.1 percent and the number of Blacks at 10.2 percent. Meanwhile, the number of non-Hispanic Whites in the labor force is projected to decrease by 1.5 percent. (Hispanics may be of any race.) (See Table 4-1.)

*   The number of women in the labor force is expected to increase 7.4 percent from 2010 to 2020, significantly lower than the 8.4 percent increase from 2000 to 2010 or the 16.7 percent increase from 1990 to 2000. (See Table 4-1.)

NOTES AND DEFINITIONS

The Bureau of Labor Statistics (BLS) develops long-term projections of likely employment patterns in the U.S. economy. Since the early 1970s, projections have been prepared on a 2-year cycle. The last projections were released in February 2012. The projections cover the future size and composition of the labor force, aggregate economic growth, detailed estimates of industry production, and industry and occupational employment. The resulting data serve a variety of users who need information about expected patterns of economic growth and the effects these patterns are expected to have on employment. For example, information about future employment opportunities by occupation is used by counselors, educators, and others helping people choose a career and by officials who plan education and training programs.

The labor force projections are a function of two components—projections of the population and projections of labor force participation rates. Population projections are provided by the Census Bureau for detailed age, sex, race, and ethnicity groupings. BLS extrapolates participation rates for these same categories by applying well-specified smoothing and time series techniques to historical time series for the detailed participation rates.

Concepts and Definitions

Economic dependency ratio. This ratio is measured *by* measured by estimating the number of persons in the total population (including all Armed Forces personnel overseas and children) who are *not* in the labor force per hundred of those who are.

Employment. In the employment projections survey, employment is defined as a count of jobs, not a count of individual workers.

Employment change. The numerical change in employment measures the projected number of job gains or losses.

Employment change, percent. The percent change in employment measures the projected rate of change of employment in an occupation. A rapidly growing occupation usually indicates favorable prospects for employment. However, even modest employment growth in a large occupation can result in many more job openings due to growth than can rapid employment growth in a small occupation.

Job openings due to growth and replacement needs. Estimates of the projected number of net entrants into an occupation. For occupations that require training, the data may be used to assess the minimum number of workers who will need to be trained. The number of openings due to growth is the positive employment change from 2010 to 2020. If employment declines, then there are no job openings due to growth. The number of openings due to replacement needs is the net number of workers leaving an occupation who will need to be replaced.

On-the-Job Training Terms

Apprenticeship. An apprenticeship is a formal relationship between a worker and sponsor that combines technical instruction and on-the-job training. The typical programs provides at least 2,000 hours of on-the-job training per year over a 3-to-5 year period and 144 hours of technical instruction. Apprenticeship programs are sponsored by individual employers, joint employer-and-labor groups, and employer associations.

Internship/residency. An internship or residency typically involves supervised training in a professional setting such as a classroom or hospital. Internships and/or residency programs are often required for certification or to obtain a license in fields such as architecture, counseling, medicine, and teaching. This does not include internships that are recommended for advancement.

Moderate-term on-the-job training. Skills needed for a worker to become fully qualified can be acquired during 1 to 12 months of combined on-the-job experience and informal training. Examples include heavy and tractor-trailer truck drivers and medical secretaries.

Short-term on-the-job training. Skills needed for a worker to become fully qualified can be acquired during a short demonstration of job duties or during 1 month or less of on-the-job experience or instruction. Examples include retail salespersons and waiters and waitresses.

Long-term on-the-job training. More than 12 months of on-the-job training or, alternatively, combined work experience and formal classroom instruction are needed for workers to develop the skills to become fully qualified. This category includes formal or informal apprenticeships that may last up to 5 years. Long-term on-the-job training also includes intensive occupation-specific, employer-sponsored programs that workers must complete. Such programs include those offered by fire and police academies and schools for air traffic controllers and flight attendants. Individuals undergoing training usually are considered to be employed in the occupation. Also included in this category is the development of some natural ability.

Sources of Additional Information

A complete presentation of the projections, including analysis of results and additional tables and a comprehensive description of the methodology, can be found in the January 2012 edition of the *Monthly Labor Review* which is available on the BLS Web site at <www.bls.gov/opub/mlr/mlrhome.htm>. In addition, more information on employment projections can be found on the BLS Web site at <http://www.bls.gov/emp/>.

Table 4-1. Civilian Labor Force, by Age, Sex, Race, and Hispanic Origin, 1990, 2000, 2010, and Projected 2020

(Numbers in thousands, percent.)

Age, sex, race, and Hispanic origin	Labor force				Change			Percent change		
	1990	2000	2010	2020	1990–2000	2000–2010	1990–2020	1990–2000	2000–2010	2010–2020
Both Sexes, 16 Years and Over	125 840	142 583	153 889	164 360	16 743	11 306	10 471	13.3	7.9	6.8
16 to 24 years	22 492	22 520	20 934	18 330	28	-1 586	-2 604	0.1	-7.0	-12.4
16 to 19 years	7 792	8 270	5 906	4 548	478	-2 364	-1 358	6.1	-28.6	-23.0
20 to 24 years	14 700	14 250	15 028	13 783	-450	778	-1 245	-3.1	5.5	-8.3
25 to 54 years	88 322	101 394	102 940	104 619	13 072	1 546	1 679	14.8	1.5	1.6
25 to 34 years	35 929	32 756	33 614	36 421	-3 173	858	2 807	-8.8	2.6	8.4
35 to 44 years	32 145	37 566	33 366	35 147	5 421	-4 200	1 781	16.9	-11.2	5.3
45 to 54 years	20 248	31 072	35 960	33 051	10 824	4 888	-2 909	53.5	15.7	-8.1
55 years and over	15 026	18 669	30 014	41 411	3 643	11 345	11 397	24.2	60.8	38.0
55 to 64 years	11 575	14 357	23 297	29 298	2 782	8 940	6 001	24.0	62.3	25.8
65 to 74 years	2 952	3 505	5 424	9 945	553	1 919	4 521	18.7	54.8	83.4
75 years and over	498	807	1 293	2 168	309	486	875	62.0	60.2	67.7
Men, 16 Years and Over	69 011	76 280	81 985	87 128	7 269	5 705	5 143	10.5	7.5	6.3
16 to 24 years	11 960	11 789	10 855	9 690	-171	-934	-1 165	-1.4	-7.9	-10.7
16 to 19 years	4 094	4 268	2 991	2 413	174	-1 277	-578	4.3	-29.9	-19.3
20 to 24 years	7 866	7 521	7 864	7 276	-345	343	-588	-4.4	4.6	-7.5
25 to 54 years	48 456	54 206	55 326	56 386	5 750	1 120	1 060	11.9	2.1	1.9
25 to 34 years	19 872	17 844	18 352	19 667	-2 028	508	1 315	-10.2	2.8	7.2
35 to 44 years	17 481	20 093	18 119	19 303	2 612	-1 974	1 184	14.9	-9.8	6.5
45 to 54 years	11 103	16 269	18 856	17 415	5 166	2 587	-1 441	46.5	15.9	-7.6
55 years and over	8 594	10 285	15 803	21 052	1 691	5 518	5 249	19.7	53.7	33.2
55 to 64 years	6 627	7 796	12 103	14 662	1 169	4 307	2 559	17.6	55.2	21.1
65 to 74 years	1 664	2 018	2 971	5 236	354	953	2 265	21.3	47.2	76.2
75 years and over	303	471	729	1 155	168	258	426	55.4	54.8	58.4
Women, 16 Years and Over	56 829	66 303	71 904	77 232	9 474	5 601	5 328	16.7	8.4	7.4
16 to 24 years	10 532	10 731	10 079	8 641	199	-652	-1 438	1.9	-6.1	-14.3
16 to 19 years	3 698	4 002	2 914	2 134	304	-1 088	-780	8.2	-27.2	-26.8
20 to 24 years	6 834	6 729	7 164	6 506	-105	435	-658	-1.5	6.5	-9.2
25 to 54 years	39 866	47 188	47 614	48 233	7 322	426	619	18.4	0.9	1.3
25 to 34 years	16 058	14 912	15 263	16 754	-1 146	351	1 491	-7.1	2.4	9.8
35 to 44 years	14 663	17 473	15 247	15 844	2 810	-2 226	597	19.2	-12.7	3.9
45 to 54 years	9 145	14 803	17 104	15 635	5 658	2 301	-1 469	61.9	15.5	-8.6
55 years and over	6 431	8 384	14 211	20 358	1 953	5 827	6 147	30.4	69.5	43.3
55 to 64 years	4 948	6 561	11 194	14 637	1 613	4 633	3 443	32.6	70.6	30.8
65 to 74 years	1 288	1 487	2 453	4 709	199	966	2 256	15.5	65.0	92.0
75 years and over	195	336	564	1 012	141	228	448	72.3	67.9	79.4
White, 16 Years and Over	107 447	118 545	125 084	130 516	11 098	6 539	5 432	10.3	5.5	4.3
Men	59 638	64 466	67 728	70 379	4 828	3 262	2 651	8.1	5.1	3.9
Women	47 809	54 079	57 356	60 137	6 270	3 277	2 781	13.1	6.1	4.8
Black, 16 Years and Over	13 740	16 397	17 862	19 676	2 657	1 465	1 814	19.3	8.9	10.2
Men	6 802	7 702	8 415	9 393	900	713	978	13.2	9.3	11.6
Women	6 938	8 695	9 447	10 283	1 757	752	836	25.3	8.6	8.8
Asian, 16 Years and Over	4 653	6 270	7 248	9 430	1 617	978	2 182	34.8	15.6	30.1
Men	2 570	3 362	3 893	4 968	792	531	1 075	30.8	15.8	27.6
Women	2 083	2 908	3 355	4 462	825	447	1 107	39.6	15.4	33.0
All Other Groups,[1] 16 Years and Over	. . .	1 371	3 694	4 738	. . .	2 323	1 044	. . .	169.4	28.3
Men	. . .	750	1 949	2 388	. . .	1 199	439	. . .	159.9	22.5
Women	. . .	621	1 746	2 350	. . .	1 125	604	. . .	181.2	34.6
Hispanic,[2] 16 Years and Over	10 720	16 689	22 748	30 493	5 969	6 059	7 745	55.7	36.3	34.0
Men	6 546	9 923	13 511	17 859	3 377	3 588	4 348	51.6	36.2	32.2
Women	4 174	6 767	9 238	12 634	2 593	2 471	3 396	62.1	36.5	36.8
Non-Hispanic, 16 Years and Over	115 120	125 894	131 141	133 867	10 774	5 247	2 726	9.4	4.2	2.1
Men	62 465	66 357	68 474	69 269	3 892	2 117	795	6.2	3.2	1.2
Women	52 655	59 536	62 666	64 598	6 881	3 130	1 932	13.1	5.3	3.1
White Non-Hispanic, 16 Years and Over	97 818	102 729	103 947	102 371	4 911	1 218	-1 576	5.0	1.2	-1.5
Men	53 731	55 040	55 116	53 867	1 309	76	-1 249	2.4	0.1	-2.3
Women	44 087	47 689	48 831	48 504	3 602	1 142	-327	8.2	2.4	-0.7

[1]The "All other groups" category includes respondents who reported the racial categories of "American Indian and Alaska Native" or "Native Hawaiian and Other Pacific Islander," as well as those who reported two or more races. This category was not defined prior to 2003.
[2]May be of any race.
. . . = Not available.

Table 4-1. Civilian Labor Force, by Age, Sex, Race, and Hispanic Origin, 1990, 2000, 2010, and Projected 2020—*Continued*

(Numbers in thousands, percent.)

Age, sex, race, and Hispanic origin	Percent distribution				Annual growth rate (percent)		
	1990	2000	2010	2020	1990–2000	2000–2010	2010–2020
Both Sexes, 16 Years and Over	100.0	100.0	100.0	100.0	1.3	0.8	0.7
16 to 24 years	17.9	15.8	13.6	11.2	0.0	-0.7	-1.3
16 to 19 years	6.2	5.8	3.8	2.8	0.6	-3.3	-2.6
20 to 24 years	11.7	10.0	9.8	8.4	-0.3	0.5	-0.9
25 to 54 years	70.2	71.1	66.9	63.7	1.4	0.2	0.2
25 to 34 years	28.6	23.0	21.8	22.2	-0.9	0.3	0.8
35 to 44 years	25.5	26.3	21.7	21.4	1.6	-1.2	0.5
45 to 54 years	16.1	21.8	23.4	20.1	4.4	1.5	-0.8
55 years and over	11.9	13.1	19.5	25.2	2.2	4.9	3.3
55 to 64 years	9.2	10.1	15.1	17.8	2.2	5.0	2.3
65 to 74 years	2.3	2.5	3.5	6.1	1.7	4.5	6.2
75 years and over	0.4	0.6	0.8	1.3	4.9	4.8	5.3
Men, 16 Years and Over	54.8	53.5	53.3	53.0	1.0	0.7	0.6
16 to 24 years	9.5	8.3	7.1	5.9	-0.1	-0.8	-1.1
16 to 19 years	3.3	3.0	1.9	1.5	0.4	-3.5	-2.1
20 to 24 years	6.3	5.3	5.1	4.4	-0.4	0.4	-0.8
25 to 54 years	38.5	38.0	36.0	34.3	1.1	0.2	0.2
25 to 34 years	15.8	12.5	11.9	12.0	-1.1	0.3	0.7
35 to 44 years	13.9	14.1	11.8	11.7	1.4	-1.0	0.6
45 to 54 years	8.8	11.4	12.3	10.6	3.9	1.5	-0.8
55 years and over	6.8	7.2	10.3	12.8	1.8	4.4	2.9
55 to 64 years	5.3	5.5	7.9	8.9	1.6	4.5	1.9
65 to 74 years	1.3	1.4	1.9	3.2	1.9	3.9	5.8
75 years and over	0.2	0.3	0.5	0.7	4.5	4.5	4.7
Women, 16 Years and Over	45.2	46.5	46.7	47.0	1.6	0.8	0.7
16 to 24 years	8.4	7.5	6.5	5.3	0.2	-0.6	-1.5
16 to 19 years	2.9	2.8	1.9	1.3	0.8	-3.1	-3.1
20 to 24 years	5.4	4.7	4.7	4.0	-0.2	0.6	-1.0
25 to 54 years	31.7	33.1	30.9	29.3	1.7	0.1	0.1
25 to 34 years	12.8	10.5	9.9	10.2	-0.7	0.2	0.9
35 to 44 years	11.7	12.3	9.9	9.6	1.8	-1.4	0.4
45 to 54 years	7.3	10.4	11.1	9.5	4.9	1.5	-0.9
55 years and over	5.1	5.9	9.2	12.4	2.7	5.4	3.7
55 to 64 years	3.9	4.6	7.3	8.9	2.9	5.5	2.7
65 to 74 years	1.0	1.0	1.6	2.9	1.4	5.1	6.7
75 years and over	0.2	0.2	0.4	0.6	5.6	5.3	6.0
White, 16 Years and Over	85.4	83.1	81.3	79.4	1.0	0.5	0.4
Men	47.4	45.2	44.0	42.8	0.8	0.5	0.4
Women	38.0	37.9	37.3	36.6	1.2	0.6	0.5
Black, 16 Years and Over	10.9	11.5	11.6	12.0	1.8	0.9	1.0
Men	5.4	5.4	5.5	5.7	1.3	0.9	1.1
Women	5.5	6.1	6.1	6.3	2.3	0.8	0.9
Asian, 16 Years and Over	3.7	4.4	4.7	5.7	3.0	1.5	2.7
Men	2.0	2.4	2.5	3.0	2.7	1.5	2.5
Women	1.7	2.0	2.2	2.7	3.4	1.4	2.9
All Other Groups,[1] 16 Years and Over	. . .	1.0	2.4	2.9	. . .	10.4	2.5
Men	. . .	0.5	1.3	1.5	. . .	10.0	2.1
Women	. . .	0.4	1.1	1.4	. . .	10.9	3.0
Hispanic,[2] 16 Years and Over	8.5	11.7	14.8	18.6	4.5	3.1	3.0
Men	5.2	7.0	8.8	10.9	4.2	3.1	2.8
Women	3.3	4.7	6.0	7.7	5.0	3.2	3.2
Non-Hispanic, 16 Years and Over	91.5	88.3	85.2	81.4	0.9	0.4	0.2
Men	49.6	46.5	44.5	42.1	0.6	0.3	0.1
Women	41.8	41.8	40.7	39.3	1.2	0.5	0.3
White Non-Hispanic, 16 Years and Over	77.7	72.0	67.5	62.3	0.5	0.1	-0.2
Men	42.7	38.6	35.8	32.8	0.2	0.0	-0.2
Women	35.0	33.4	31.7	29.5	0.8	0.2	-0.1

[1]The "All other groups" category includes respondents who reported the racial categories of "American Indian and Alaska Native" or "Native Hawaiian and Other Pacific Islander," as well as those who reported two or more races. This category was not defined prior to 2003.
[2]May be of any race.
. . . = Not available.

PROJECTED EMPLOYMENT

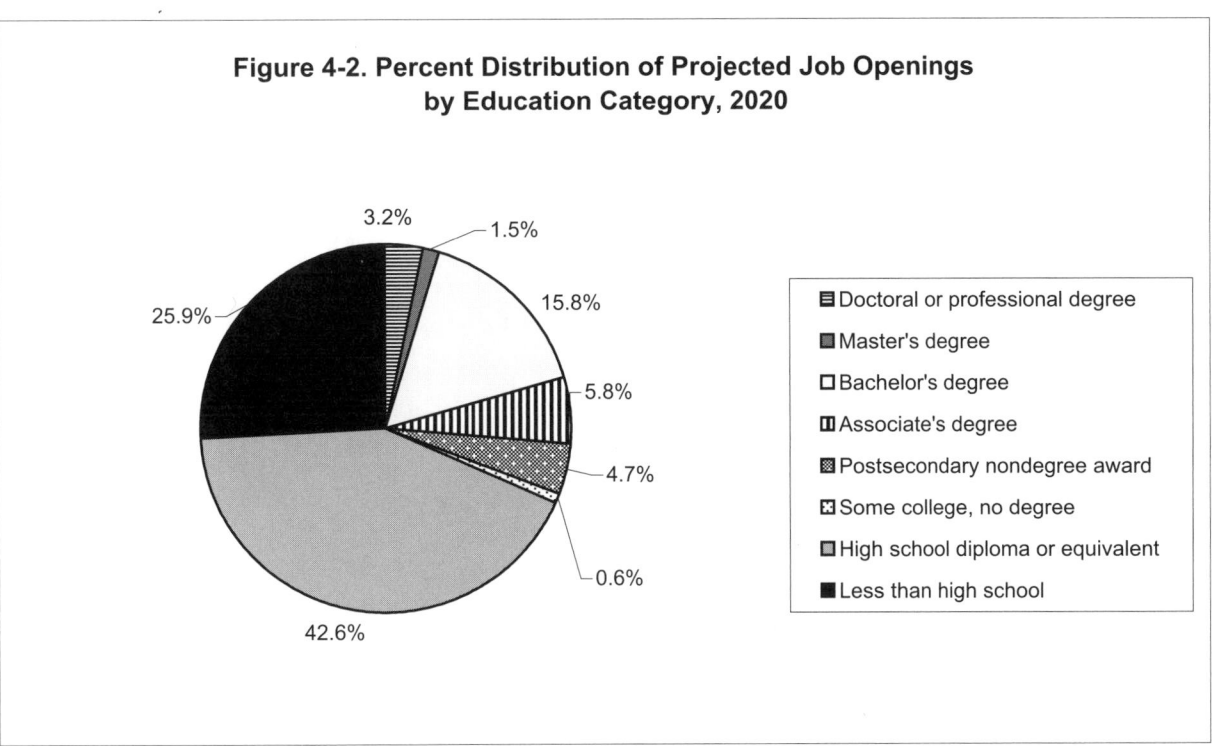

Figure 4-2. Percent Distribution of Projected Job Openings by Education Category, 2020

- Doctoral or professional degree
- Master's degree
- Bachelor's degree
- Associate's degree
- Postsecondary nondegree award
- Some college, no degree
- High school diploma or equivalent
- Less than high school

In 2020, only 1.5 percent of job openings will require a Master's degree. However, the number of job openings that require a Master's degree will grow by 21.7 percent—more than any other education category. Nearly 16 percent of jobs in 2020 will require a Bachelor's degree while 42.6 percent will require a high school diploma or equivalent. (See Table 4-9.)

OTHER HIGHLIGHTS

- Personal health care aides and home health care aids are projected to be the fastest-growing occupations between 2010 and 2020 at 70.5 percent and 69.4 percent, respectively.

- The occupations projected to add the highest number of jobs from 2008 to 2018 are registered nurses (711,900), retail salespersons (706,800), and home health aides (706,300). (See Table 4-3.)

- Of the ten occupations with the largest wage and salary growth in 2020, five of them are in health care and social assistance sector. Meanwhile, four of the top ten occupations with the largest declines are in the manufacturing sector while another three are in the federal government. (See Table 4-5.)

- The median age of the labor force has gradually increased each decade from 1980 (34.6 years) to 2010 (41.7 years). In 2020, the median age is expected to increase even further to 42.8 years. (See Table 4-6.)

Table 4-2. Fastest-Growing Occupations, 2010 and Projected 2020

(Numbers in thousands, percent.)

Occupation	Employment		Change, 2010–2020		Mean annual wage, 2010
	2010	2020	Number	Percent	
TOTAL, ALL OCCUPATIONS	143 068.1	163 537.1	20 468.9	14.3	33 840
Personal care aides	861.0	1 468.0	607.0	70.5	19 640
Home health aides	1 017.7	1 723.9	706.3	69.4	20 560
Biomedical engineers	15.7	25.4	9.7	61.7	81 540
Helpers–brickmasons, blockmasons, stonemasons, and tile and marble setters	29.4	47.0	17.6	60.1	27 780
Helpers–carpenters	46.5	72.4	25.9	55.7	25 760
Veterinary technologists and technicians	80.2	121.9	41.7	52.0	29 710
Reinforcing iron and rebar workers	19.1	28.4	9.3	48.6	38 430
Physical therapist assistants	67.4	98.2	30.8	45.7	49 690
Helpers–pipelayers, plumbers, pipefitters, and steamfitters	57.9	84.2	26.3	45.4	26 740
Meeting, convention, and event planners	71.6	102.9	31.3	43.7	45 260
Diagnostic medical sonographers	53.7	77.1	23.4	43.5	64 380
Occupational therapy assistants	28.5	40.8	12.3	43.3	51 010
Physical therapist aides	47.0	67.3	20.3	43.1	23 680
Glaziers	41.9	59.6	17.7	42.4	36 640
Interpreters and translators	58.4	83.1	24.6	42.2	43 300
Medical secretaries	508.7	718.9	210.2	41.3	30 530
Market research analysts and marketing specialists	282.7	399.3	116.6	41.2	60 570
Marriage and family therapists	36.0	50.8	14.8	41.2	45 720
Brickmasons and blockmasons	89.2	125.3	36.1	40.5	46 930
Physical therapists	198.6	276.0	77.4	39.0	76 310
Dental hygienists	181.8	250.3	68.5	37.7	68 250
Bicycle repairers	9.9	13.6	3.7	37.6	23 660
Audiologists	13.0	17.8	4.8	36.8	66 660
Health educators	63.4	86.6	23.2	36.5	45 830
Stonemasons	15.6	21.4	5.7	36.5	37 180
Cost estimators	185.4	252.9	67.5	36.4	57 860
Medical scientists, except epidemiologists	100.0	136.5	36.4	36.4	76 700
Mental health counselors	120.3	163.9	43.6	36.3	38 150
Pile-driver operators	4.1	5.6	1.5	36.0	47 860
Veterinarians	61.4	83.4	22.0	35.9	82 040

Table 4-3. Occupations with the Largest Job Growth, 2010–2020

(Numbers in thousands, percent.)

Occupation	Employment		Change, 2010–2020		Mean annual wage, 2010
	2010	2020	Number	Percent	
TOTAL, ALL OCCUPATIONS	143 068.2	163 537.1	20 468.9	14.3	33 840
Registered nurses	2 737.4	3 449.3	711.9	26.0	64 690
Retail salespersons	4 261.6	4 968.4	706.8	16.6	20 670
Home health aides	1 017.7	1 723.9	706.3	69.4	20 560
Personal care aides	861.0	1 468.0	607.0	70.5	19 640
Office clerks, general	2 950.7	3 440.2	489.5	16.6	26 610
Combined food preparation and serving workers, including fast food	2 682.1	3 080.1	398.0	14.8	17 950
Customer service representatives	2 187.3	2 525.6	338.4	15.5	30 460
Heavy and tractor-trailer truck drivers	1 604.8	1 934.9	330.1	20.6	37 770
Laborers and freight, stock, and material movers, hand	2 068.2	2 387.3	319.1	15.4	23 460
Postsecondary teachers	1 756.0	2 061.7	305.7	17.4	45 690
Nursing aides, orderlies, and attendants	1 505.3	1 807.2	302.0	20.1	24 010
Childcare workers	1 282.3	1 544.3	262.0	20.4	19 300
Bookkeeping, accounting, and auditing clerks	1 898.3	2 157.4	259.0	13.6	34 030
Cashiers	3 362.6	3 612.8	250.2	7.4	18 500
Elementary school teachers, except special education	1 476.5	1 725.3	248.8	16.8	51 660
Receptionists and information clerks	1 048.5	1 297.0	248.5	23.7	25 240
Janitors and cleaners, except maids and housekeeping cleaners	2 310.4	2 556.8	246.4	10.7	22 210
Landscaping and groundskeeping workers	1 151.5	1 392.3	240.8	20.9	23 400
Sales representatives, wholesale and manufacturing, except technical and scientific products	1 430.0	1 653.4	223.4	15.6	52 440
Construction laborers	998.8	1 211.2	212.4	21.3	29 280
Medical secretaries	508.7	718.9	210.2	41.3	30 530
First-line supervisors of office and administrative support workers	1 424.4	1 627.8	203.4	14.3	47 460
Carpenters	1 001.7	1 197.6	196.0	19.6	39 530
Waiters and waitresses	2 260.3	2 456.2	195.9	8.7	18 330
Security guards	1 035.7	1 230.7	195.0	18.8	23 920
Teacher assistants	1 288.3	1 479.3	191.1	14.8	23 220
Accountants and auditors	1 216.9	1 407.6	190.7	15.7	61 690
Licensed practical and licensed vocational nurses	752.3	920.8	168.5	22.4	40 380
Physicians and surgeons	691.0	859.3	168.3	24.4	111 570
Medical assistants	527.6	690.4	162.9	30.9	28 860

Table 4-4. Economic Dependency Ratio, 1980, 1990, 2000, 2010, and Projected 2020

(Number.)

Group	1980	1990	2000	2010	2020
TOTAL POPULATION	108.9	98.3	93.9	100.6	107.0
Under age 16	50.7	45.8	44.1	43.3	44.0
Ages 16 to 64	37.4	30.5	28.3	36.5	38.0
Ages 65 and older	20.8	22.1	21.6	21.8	26.0

Table 4-5. Industries with the Largest Wage and Salary Employment Growth and Declines, 2010–2020

(Number in thousands, percent.)

Industry	Sector	Employment		Change, 2010–2020	Annual rate of change, 2010–2020
		2010	2020		
Largest Growth					
Construction	Construction	5 525.6	7 365.1	1 839.5	2.9
Retail trade	Retail trade	14 413.7	16 182.2	1 768.5	1.2
Offices of health practitioners	Health care and social assistance	3 818.2	5 209.6	1 391.4	3.2
Hospitals	Health care and social assistance	4 685.3	5 563.6	878.3	1.7
Home health care services	Health care and social assistance	1 080.6	1 952.4	871.8	6.1
Food services and drinking places	Leisure and hospitality	9 351.8	10 212.2	860.4	0.9
Individual and family services	Health care and social assistance	1 215.0	2 066.4	851.4	5.5
Nursing and residential care facilities	Health care and social assistance	3 129.0	3 951.0	822.0	2.4
Wholesale trade	Wholesale trade	5 456.1	6 200.2	744.1	1.3
General local government educational services compensation	State and local government	8 010.4	8 751.4	741.0	0.9
Largest Declines					
Postal service	Federal government	656.4	474.6	-181.8	-3.2
General federal non-defense government compensation	Federal government	1 667.5	1 545.7	-121.8	-0.8
Apparel knitting mills	Manufacturing	157.7	66.1	-91.6	-8.3
Newspaper, periodical, book, and directory publishers	Information	501.3	439.7	-61.6	-1.3
Other miscellaneous manufacturing	Federal government	266.0	210.3	-55.7	-2.3
General federal defense government compensation	Manufacturing	545.5	496.0	-49.5	-0.9
Computer and peripheral equipment manufacturing	Manufacturing	161.6	117.5	-44.1	-3.1
Navigational, measuring, electromedical, and control instruments manufacturing	Manufacturing	406.0	363.2	-42.8	-1.1
Crop production	Agriculture, forestry, fishing and hunting	629.5	589.3	-40.2	-0.7
Drycleaning and laundry services	Other services	302.1	265.7	-36.4	-1.3

Table 4-6. Median Age of the Labor Force, by Sex, Race, and Ethnicity, 1980, 1990, 2000, 2010 and Projected 2020

(Number.)

	1980	1990	2000	2010	2020
TOTAL	34.6	36.4	39.3	41.7	42.8
Sex					
Men	35.1	36.5	39.2	41.5	42.4
Women	33.9	36.2	39.3	42.0	43.3
Race					
White	34.8	36.6	39.6	42.3	43.3
Black	33.3	34.8	37.4	39.3	40.4
Asian	34.1	35.8	37.9	41.2	44.0
Ethnicity					
Hispanic origin[1]	32.0	31.2	33.7	36.9	38.7
White non-Hispanic	35.2	37.1	40.5	43.6	44.8

[1]Persons of Hispanic origin may be of any race.

Table 4-7. Employment and Output, by Industry, 2000, 2010, and Projected 2020

(Number, percent, dollars.)

Industry	Employment							Output				
	Number of jobs (thousands)			Change		Average annual rate of change (percent)		Billions of chained (2005) dollars			Average annual rate of change (percent)	
	2000	2010	2020	2000–2020	2010–2020	2000–2010	2010–2020	2000	2010	2020	2000–2010	2010–2020
TOTAL	146 236	143 068	163 537	-3 168	20 469	-0.2	1.3	20 979	23 171	30 876	1.0	2.9
Nonagriculture Wage and Salary	132 425	130 436	150 177	-1 989	19 741	-0.2	1.4	20 694	22 870	30 507	1.0	2.9
Mining	520	656	681	136	25	2.3	0.4	393	388	441	-0.1	1.3
Oil and gas extraction	125	159	182	34	23	2.4	1.4	252	251	260	0.0	0.4
Mining, except oil and gas	225	203	203	-22	0	-1.0	0.0	72	52	69	-3.2	2.8
Coal mining	72	81	78	8	-3.0	1.1	-0.4	31	21	28	-3.9	2.9
Metal ore mining	38	36	28	-2	-8	-0.4	-2.5	19	7	9	-10.0	3.0
Nonmetallic mineral mining and quarrying	115	86	98	-29	12	-2.9	1.3	22	25	34	1.1	3.0
Support activities for mining	171	294	295	124	1	5.6	0.0	69	85	112	2.1	2.8
Utilities	601	552	516	-50	-36	-0.9	-0.7	478	354	432	-3.0	2.0
Electric power generation, transmission and distribution	434	397	361	-38	-36	-0.9	-0.9	321	237	300	-3.0	2.4
Natural gas distribution	121	108	96	-13	-12	-1.1	-1.2	147	109	122	-3.0	1.1
Water, sewage and other systems	46	47	59	1	12	0.2	2.3	10	9	12	-1.4	2.5
Construction	6 786	5 526	7 365	-1 261	1 840	-2.0	2.9	1 240	815	1 183	-4.1	3.8
Manufacturing	17 263	11 524	11 451	-5 739	-73	-4.0	-0.1	4 585	4 363	5 723	-0.5	2.8
Food manufacturing	1 553	1 447	1 470	-107	23	-0.7	0.2	498	531	610	0.6	1.4
Animal food manufacturing	55	50	47	-4	-4	-0.8	-0.8	30	26	32	-1.4	1.9
Grain and oilseed milling	65	58	56	-7	-2	-1.1	-0.4	63	53	63	-1.8	1.9
Sugar and confectionery product manufacturing	92	70	67	-23	-2	-2.8	-0.3	29	27	30	-0.4	0.9
Fruit and vegetable preserving and specialty food manufacturing	197	171	160	-26	-12	-1.4	-0.7	54	64	71	1.7	1.1
Dairy product manufacturing	136	128	122	-8	-6	-0.6	-0.5	71	75	89	0.6	1.6
Animal slaughtering and processing	507	490	537	-17	47	-0.3	0.9	138	150	175	0.8	1.6
Seafood product preparation and packaging	45	38	41	-7	3	-1.6	0.7	8	10	11	2.6	1.3
Bakeries and tortilla manufacturing	306	276	275	-30	-2	-1.0	-0.1	51	55	63	0.8	1.3
Other food manufacturing	150	165	166	14	2	0.9	0.1	55	71	78	2.6	1.0
Beverage and tobacco product	207	182	181	-25	-2	-1.3	-0.1	129	142	146	0.9	0.3
Beverage manufacturing	175	166	166	-9	0	-0.5	0.0	76	88	95	1.4	0.8
Tobacco manufacturing	32	17	15	-16	-2	-6.5	-1.0	53	54	52	0.3	-0.4
Textile mills and textile product mills	608	238	206	-370	-32	-9.0	-1.4	88	44	40	-6.7	-1.0
Apparel manufacturing	484	158	66	-326	-92	-10.6	-8.3	58	15	7	-12.7	-7.1
Leather and allied product manufacturing	69	28	13	-41	-15	-8.6	-7.6	9	4	3	-7.0	-3.3
Wood product manufacturing	613	341	424	-272	83	-5.7	2.2	104	89	118	-1.6	2.9
Sawmills and wood preservation	134	81	105	-53	24	-4.9	2.6	33	27	36	-2.0	3.1
Veneer, plywood, and engineered wood product manufacturing	122	65	95	-58	30	-6.2	3.9	24	23	31	-0.2	2.9
Other wood product manufacturing	357	195	224	-162	29	-5.9	1.4	48	39	51	-2.0	2.8
Paper manufacturing	605	397	366	-208	-31	-4.1	-0.8	170	140	167	-1.9	1.8
Pulp, paper, and paperboard mills	191	113	97	-79	-15	-5.2	-1.4	78	65	78	-1.8	1.8
Converted paper product manufacturing	413	284	269	-129	-15	-3.7	-0.5	92	75	89	-2.0	1.7
Printing and related support activities	807	487	455	-320	-32	-4.9	-0.7	111	85	112	-2.6	2.7
Petroleum and coal products manufacturing	123	114	100	-9	-14	-0.8	-1.3	419	441	543	0.5	2.1
Chemical manufacturing	980	784	728	-197	-56	-2.2	-0.7	519	548	725	0.5	2.9
Basic chemical manufacturing	188	142	122	-46	-21	-2.8	-1.6	139	126	172	-1.0	3.2
Resin, synthetic rubber, and artificial synthetic fibers and filaments manufacturing	136	90	84	-46	-5	-4.0	-0.6	86	71	95	-1.9	2.9
Pesticide, fertilizer, and other agricultural chemical manufacturing	48	35	28	-13	-8	-3.0	-2.5	26	23	28	-1.5	2.0
Pharmaceutical and medicine manufacturing	274	277	282	2	5	0.1	0.2	136	169	219	2.2	2.6
Paint, coating, and adhesive manufacturing	79	56	49	-23	-6	-3.4	-1.2	31	25	33	-1.8	2.7
Soap, cleaning compound, and toilet preparation manufacturing	129	101	95	-27	-6	-2.4	-0.6	61	86	111	3.6	2.5
Other chemical product and preparation manufacturing	127	83	69	-44	-14	-4.2	-1.9	40	47	68	1.6	3.8
Plastics and rubber products manufacturing	951	623	714	-328	91	-4.1	1.4	198	157	209	-2.3	2.9
Plastics product manufacturing	737	500	600	-237	100	-3.8	1.8	159	129	173	-2.1	3.0
Rubber product manufacturing	214	124	115	-90	-9	-5.3	-0.8	40	28	37	-3.3	2.7
Nonmetallic mineral product manufacturing	554	372	432	-182	60	-3.9	1.5	107	91	121	-1.6	2.9
Clay product and refractory manufacturing	82	40	44	-42	3	-6.8	0.8	10	8	10	-2.9	2.6
Glass and glass product manufacturing	141	81	69	-60	-12	-5.4	-1.6	25	22	28	-1.2	2.5
Cement and concrete product manufacturing	234	172	236	-62	64	-3.0	3.2	49	40	56	-2.0	3.4
Lime, gypsum and other nonmetallic mineral product manufacturing	97	79	83	-18	4	-2.0	0.5	23	21	28	-0.8	2.6
Primary metal manufacturing	622	361	366	-261	6	-5.3	0.2	198	175	231	-1.2	2.8
Iron and steel mills and ferroalloy manufacturing	135	85	74	-50	-11	-4.5	-1.4	75	74	98	-0.1	2.9
Steel product manufacturing from purchased steel	73	52	56	-21	4	-3.4	0.7	26	19	24	-2.8	2.1
Alumina and aluminum production and processing	101	55	52	-46	-3	-5.9	-0.5	33	31	43	-0.5	3.3
Nonferrous metal (except aluminum) production and processing	96	58	54	-38	-4	-5.0	-0.7	33	25	30	-3.0	2.0
Foundries	217	111	130	-106	20	-6.5	1.7	31	26	36	-2.0	3.5
Fabricated metal product manufacturing	1 753	1 285	1 436	-468	152	-3.1	1.1	294	285	381	-0.3	2.9
Forging and stamping	138	89	92	-49	3	-4.3	0.3	27	27	37	-0.3	3.4
Cutlery and handtool manufacturing	79	41	41	-38	1	-6.4	0.2	13	13	17	0.4	2.3
Architectural and structural metals manufacturing	428	320	403	-108	83	-2.9	2.3	67	71	98	0.5	3.3
Boiler, tank, and shipping container manufacturing	107	86	92	-20	6	-2.1	0.6	28	28	33	-0.1	1.8
Hardware manufacturing	50	23	22	-27	-2	-7.4	-0.8	13	13	16	-0.2	2.8
Spring and wire product manufacturing	81	42	39	-39	-3	-6.3	-0.8	13	9	12	-3.0	2.6
Machine shops; turned product; and screw, nut, and bolt manufacturing	365	312	330	-53	18	-1.6	0.5	51	49	66	-0.5	3.1
Coating, engraving, heat treating, and allied activities	175	122	144	-53	22	-3.5	1.7	22	20	28	-0.7	3.3
Other fabricated metal product manufacturing	330	249	275	-81	26	-2.8	1.0	60	56	74	-0.7	2.9
Machinery manufacturing	1 457	993	978	-464	-15	-3.8	-0.2	294	262	370	-1.1	3.5
Agriculture, construction, and mining machinery manufacturing	222	208	241	-14	32	-0.6	1.5	62	48	73	-2.6	4.3
Industrial machinery manufacturing	164	100	108	-65	9	-4.9	0.8	37	30	42	-1.9	3.4
Commercial and service industry machinery manufacturing	147	91	81	-56	-11	-4.7	-1.2	28	21	31	-2.8	4.0
Ventilation, heating, air-conditioning, and commercial refrigeration equipment manufacturing	194	123	118	-71	-5	-4.4	-0.4	38	30	42	-2.2	3.4
Metalworking machinery manufacturing	274	153	131	-120	-23	-5.6	-1.6	32	26	35	-1.9	3.0
Engine, turbine, and power transmission equipment manufacturing	111	91	81	-20	-11	-2.0	-1.2	40	34	45	-1.5	2.7
Other general purpose machinery manufacturing	344	226	220	-118	-6	-4.1	-0.3	58	73	103	2.3	3.5

Table 4-7. Employment and Output, by Industry, 2000, 2010, and Projected 2020—*Continued*

(Number, percent, dollars.)

Industry	Employment — Number of jobs (thousands) 2000	2010	2020	Change 2000–2020	2010–2020	Average annual rate of change (percent) 2000–2010	2010–2020	Output — Billions of chained (2005) dollars 2000	2010	2020	Average annual rate of change (percent) 2000–2010	2010–2020
Manufacturing—*Continued*												
Computer and electronic product manufacturing	1 820	1 100	943	-720	-157	-4.9	-1.5	417	466	896	1.1	6.8
Computer and peripheral equipment manufacturing	302	162	118	-140	-44	-6.1	-3.1	60	132	513	8.3	14.5
Communications equipment manufacturing	239	118	86	-121	-32	-6.8	-3.1	82	63	106	-2.6	5.3
Audio and video equipment manufacturing	52	20	18	-32	-2	-9.2	-0.9	10	12	16	2.1	3.1
Semiconductor and other electronic component manufacturing	676	370	337	-307	-33	-5.9	-0.9	133	144	290	0.8	7.3
Navigational, measuring, electromedical, and control instruments manufacturing	488	406	363	-82	-43	-1.8	-1.1	124	108	145	-1.4	3.0
Manufacturing and reproducing magnetic and optical media	63	25	22	-39	-3	-8.9	-1.3	10	7	11	-2.6	4.2
Electrical equipment, appliance, and component manufacturing	591	361	331	-230	-30	-4.8	-0.8	128	96	123	-2.8	2.5
Electric lighting equipment manufacturing	85	46	41	-39	-5	-6.0	-1.0	14	12	15	-1.6	1.8
Household appliance manufacturing	106	61	61	-45	0	-5.4	0.0	24	22	26	-0.8	1.9
Electrical equipment manufacturing	210	136	117	-73	-19	-4.2	-1.5	41	30	37	-3.1	2.2
Other electrical equipment and component manufacturing	191	118	112	-73	-6	-4.7	-0.5	49	32	45	-4.0	3.3
Transportation equipment manufacturing	2 057	1 330	1 333	-727	3	-4.3	0.0	640	586	801	-0.9	3.2
Motor vehicle manufacturing	291	151	166	-140	15	-6.3	0.9	233	186	267	-2.2	3.7
Motor vehicle body and trailer manufacturing	183	108	115	-75	7	-5.2	0.6	28	20	29	-3.2	3.6
Motor vehicle parts manufacturing	840	415	395	-424	-20	-6.8	-0.5	199	151	207	-2.7	3.2
Aerospace product and parts manufacturing	517	477	462	-40	-15	-0.8	-0.3	138	163	214	1.7	2.7
Railroad rolling stock manufacturing	33	20	25	-13	5	-4.8	2.1	10	11	16	1.1	4.0
Ship and boat building	154	126	128	-29	3	-2.0	0.2	21	30	35	3.4	1.6
Other transportation equipment manufacturing	40	33	42	-7	9	-1.8	2.4	11	25	32	8.5	2.4
Furniture and related product manufacturing	683	357	392	-325	34	-6.3	0.9	81	62	76	-2.6	2.1
Household and institutional furniture and kitchen cabinet manufacturing	443	223	234	-220	11	-6.6	0.5	46	35	41	-2.7	1.7
Office furniture (including fixtures) manufacturing	181	98	117	-84	19	-6.0	1.8	26	19	25	-3.2	2.9
Other furniture related product manufacturing	58	37	41	-22	5	-4.5	1.2	9	8	10	-0.5	2.2
Miscellaneous manufacturing	728	568	517	-160	-51	-2.5	-0.9	123	144	181	1.6	2.3
Medical equipment and supplies manufacturing	305	302	306	-3	5	-0.1	0.2	56	72	92	2.5	2.5
Other miscellaneous manufacturing	423	266	210	-157	-56	-4.5	-2.3	67	72	89	0.8	2.1
Wholesale Trade	5 934	5 456	6 200	-477	744	-0.8	1.3	897	1 176	1 649	2.8	3.4
Retail Trade	15 280	14 414	16 182	-866	1 769	-0.6	1.2	1 019	1 165	1 671	1.3	3.7
Transportation and Warehousing	4 410	4 183	5 036	-227	853	-0.5	1.9	640	709	978	1.0	3.3
Air transportation	614	464	480	-150	16	-2.8	0.3	146	130	166	-1.1	2.5
Rail transportation	232	215	214	-17	-1	-0.7	0.0	53	62	84	1.7	3.1
Water transportation	56	63	79	7	16	1.2	2.3	35	30	41	-1.6	3.0
Truck transportation	1 406	1 244	1 544	-162	300	-1.2	2.2	200	252	350	2.4	3.3
Transit and ground passenger transportation	372	432	536	60	103	1.5	2.2	28	33	44	1.6	2.9
Pipeline transportation	46	42	33	-4	-10	-0.8	-2.6	29	16	20	-5.9	2.7
Scenic and sightseeing transportation and support activities for transportation	565	567	689	2	121	0.0	2.0	58	63	93	0.8	4.0
Postal Service	880	656	475	-223	-182	-2.9	-3.2	74	62	58	-1.8	-0.8
Couriers and messengers	605	527	669	-78	142	-1.4	2.4	54	74	111	3.2	4.1
Warehousing and storage	514	628	794	114	165	2.0	2.4	38	49	71	2.6	3.6
Information	3 631	2 711	2 851	-920	140	-2.9	0.5	951	1 196	1 893	2.3	4.7
Publishing industries	1 035	761	791	-274	30	-3.0	0.4	265	321	556	1.9	5.7
Newspaper, periodical, book, and directory publishers	774	501	440	-273.0	-62	-4.3	-1.3	172	164	210	-0.5	2.5
Software publishers	261	260	352	-1	92	0.0	3.1	93	157	368	5.4	8.9
Motion picture, video, and sound recording industries	383	372	347	-11	-25	-0.3	-0.7	80	97	130	1.9	3.0
Broadcasting (except Internet)	344	295	325	-49	30	-1.5	1.0	88	99	137	1.2	3.2
Telecommunications	1 397	900	974	-497	74	-4.3	0.8	419	511	775	2.0	4.2
Data processing, hosting, related services, and other information services	473	384	415	-89	31	-2.1	0.8	99	168	303	5.4	6.1
Finance and Insurance	5 677	5 691	6 196	15	505	0.0	0.9	1 621	2 029	2 804	2.3	3.3
Monetary authorities, credit intermediation, and related activities	2 571	2 566	2 651	-5	85	0.0	0.3	597	917	1 303	4.4	3.6
Securities, commodity contracts, and other financial investments and related activities	805	801	1 002	-4	201	0.0	2.3	384	411	637	0.7	4.5
Insurance carriers and related activities	2 221	2 238	2 433	18	195	0.1	0.8	533	595	743	1.1	2.2
Insurance carriers	1 433	1 368	1 415	-65	47	-0.5	0.3	415	441	546	0.6	2.2
Agencies, brokerages, and other insurance related activities	788	871	1 018	83	148	1.0	1.6	118	155	198	2.7	2.5
Funds, trusts, and other financial vehicles	81	87	111	6	24	0.7	2.4	107	107	139	0.0	2.7
Real estate, rental, and leasing	2 011	1 939	2 214	-72	275	-0.4	1.3	1 066	1 300	1 765	2.0	3.1
Real estate	1 316	1 396	1 563	80	167	0.6	1.1	842	1 017	1 334	1.9	2.8
Rental and leasing services and lessors of intangible assets	695	543	651	-151	108	-2.4	1.8	224	283	434	2.4	4.3
Automotive equipment rental and leasing	208	163	177	-46	14	-2.4	0.8	43	50	72	1.5	3.8
Consumer goods rental and general rental centers	356	242	290	-114	48	-3.8	1.8	26	37	52	3.7	3.5
Commercial and industrial machinery and equipment rental and leasing	103	114	151	11	38	1.0	2.9	47	63	90	3.0	3.7
Lessors of nonfinancial intangible assets (except copyrighted works)	28	25	33	-3	8	-1.0	2.9	109	134	220	2.1	5.1
Professional, Scientific, and Technical Services	6 702	7 424	9 551	722	2 127	1.0	2.6	1 131	1 444	2 057	2.5	3.6
Legal services	1 066	1 114	1 178	48	64	0.4	0.6	229	244	293	0.6	1.9
Accounting, tax preparation, bookkeeping, and payroll services	866	888	975	22	87	0.2	0.9	119	129	178	0.8	3.3
Architectural, engineering, and related services	1 238	1 277	1 635	39	359	0.3	2.5	191	264	366	3.3	3.3
Specialized design services	132	111	140	-21	29	-1.7	2.4	24	31	43	2.5	3.4
Computer systems design and related services	1 254	1 442	2 113	187	671	1.4	3.9	165	259	467	4.6	6.1
Management, scientific, and technical consulting services	673	991	1 567	319	576	4.0	4.7	128	167	243	2.7	3.8
Scientific research and development services	515	620	694	105	74	1.9	1.1	103	141	194	3.2	3.3
Advertising and related services	497	408	490	-88	81	-1.9	1.8	84	120	171	3.6	3.7
Other professional, scientific, and technical services	462	573	760	112	187	2.2	2.9	88	92	125	0.5	3.1
Management of companies and enterprises	1 796	1 863	1 966	67	103	0.4	0.5	274	319	495	1.5	4.5
Administrative and support and waste management and remediation services	8 168	7 401	8 980	-767	1 579	-1.0	2.0	530	592	819	1.1	3.3
Administrative and support services	7 855	7 044	8 545	-811	1 501	-1.1	2.0	472	518	724	0.9	3.4
Office administrative services	264	412	504	148	93	4.6	2.1	45	44	63	-0.2	3.5
Facilities support services	97	134	178	37	44	3.3	2.9	15	17	20	1.1	1.8
Employment services	3 849	2 717	3 348	-1 133	631	-3.4	2.1	118	158	229	2.9	3.8
Business support services	787	807	973	20	166	0.2	1.9	63	66	91	0.4	3.3
Travel arrangement and reservation services	299	187	219	-112	33	-4.6	1.6	36	36	47	-0.2	2.8
Investigation and security services	689	777	969	88	192	1.2	2.2	39	44	62	1.3	3.5
Services to buildings and dwellings	1 571	1 743	2 045	172	302	1.0	1.6	110	118	164	0.7	3.4
Other support services	301	269	309	-32	40	-1.1	1.4	46	35	49	-2.5	3.3

Table 4-7. Employment and Output, by Industry, 2000, 2010, and Projected 2020—*Continued*

(Number, percent, dollars.)

Industry	Employment							Output				
	Number of jobs (thousands)			Change		Average annual rate of change (percent)		Billions of chained (2005) dollars			Average annual rate of change (percent)	
	2000	2010	2020	2000–2020	2010–2020	2000–2010	2010–2020	2000	2010	2020	2000–2010	2010–2020
Professional, Scientific, and Technical Services —*Continued*												
Waste management and remediation services	313	357	434	44	78	1.3	2.0	58	74	95	2.6	2.5
Education services	2 391	3 150	3 969	759	819	2.8	2.3	202	199	236	-0.2	1.7
Elementary and secondary schools	716	851	1 011	135	159	1.7	1.7	35	33	36	-0.6	0.8
Junior colleges, colleges, universities, and professional schools	1 275	1 694	2 171	419	477	2.9	2.5	123	123	146	0.0	1.7
Other educational services	399	604	787	205	183	4.2	2.7	43	43	53	-0.1	2.2
Health care and social assistance	12 718	16 415	22 054	3 696	5 639	2.6	3.0	1 142	1 526	2 026	2.9	2.9
Ambulatory health care services	4 320	5 976	8 633	1 656	2 657	3.3	3.7	508	708	982	3.4	3.3
Offices of health practitioners	2 966	3 818	5 210	853	1 391	2.6	3.2	369	513	693	3.4	3.0
Outpatient, laboratory, and other ambulatory care services	721	1 077	1 471	356	394	4.1	3.2	100	146	216	3.9	4.0
Home health care services	633	1 081	1 952	447	872	5.5	6.1	39	49	74	2.2	4.3
Hospitals, private	3 954	4 685	5 564	731	878	1.7	1.7	403	508	638	2.3	2.3
Nursing and residential care facilities	2 583	3 129	3 951	546	822	1.9	2.4	133	169	222	2.4	2.7
Social assistance	1 860	2 624	3 906	764	1 282	3.5	4.1	98	140	187	3.7	2.9
Individual and family services	678	1 215	2 066	537	851	6.0	5.5	41	65	89	4.8	3.2
Community, and vocational rehabilitation services	487	558	738	71	181	1.4	2.9	20	35	47	5.5	3.1
Child day care services	696	852	1 101	156	250	2.0	2.6	37	41	52	1.1	2.5
Arts, entertainment, and recreation	1 788	1 909	2 249	121	340	0.7	1.7	174	193	254	1.0	2.8
Performing arts, spectator sports, and related industries	382	410	487	28	77	0.7	1.7	80	99	136	2.2	3.2
Performing arts companies	132	111	124	-22	13	-1.8	1.1	13	14	18	0.1	2.8
Spectator sports	131	140	163	10	23	0.7	1.5	27	34	47	2.1	3.3
Promoters of events, and agents and managers	83	116	149	33	33	3.4	2.5	17	23	31	2.8	3.1
Independent artists, writers, and performers	36	44	51	8	8	1.9	1.7	22	29	40	2.9	3.3
Museums, historical sites, and similar institutions	110	127	151	17	23	1.4	1.7	9	14	19	4.9	3.2
Amusement, gambling, and recreation industries	1 296	1 371	1 612	76	240	0.6	1.6	86	80	99	-0.7	2.2
Accommodation and food services	10 074	11 111	12 113	1 037	1 002	1.0	0.9	580	677	869	1.6	2.5
Accommodation	1 884	1 759	1 901	-125	142	-0.7	0.8	164	197	254	1.8	2.6
Food services and drinking places	8 189	9 352	10 212	1 163	860	1.3	0.9	416	481	615	1.4	2.5
Other services	5 886	6 031	6 851	146	819	0.2	1.3	514	515	652	0.0	2.4
Repair and maintenance	1 242	1 137	1 400	-105	264	-0.9	2.1	184	175	235	-0.5	3.0
Automotive repair and maintenance	888	800	1 037	-88	238	-1.0	2.6	114	104	145	-0.9	3.4
Electronic and precision equipment repair and maintenance	107	98	101	-9	4	-0.9	0.4	21	27	35	2.5	2.7
Commercial and industrial machinery and equipment (except automotive and electronic) repair and maintenance	161	171	193	11	22	0.6	1.2	27	25	32	-0.7	2.5
Personal and household goods repair and maintenance	86	68	69	-18	1	-2.3	0.1	22	19	23	-1.6	2.1
Personal and laundry services	1 243	1 265	1 346	22	81	0.2	0.6	134	117	150	-1.3	2.5
Personal care services	490	600	699	111	98	2.1	1.5	43	42	54	-0.3	2.6
Death care services	136	132	141	-5	10	-0.3	0.7	19	14	17	-3.0	2.3
Drycleaning and laundry services	388	302	266	-86	-36	-2.5	-1.3	27	23	28	-1.5	2.2
Other personal services	229	231	240	1	10	0.1	0.4	46	39	50	-1.5	2.5
Religious, grantmaking, civic, professional, and similar organizations	2 683	2 962	3 406	279	443	1.0	1.4	180	207	250	1.4	1.9
Religious organizations	1 547	1 682	1 929	135	247	0.8	1.4	65	72	83	1.0	1.4
Grantmaking and giving services and social advocacy organizations	259	395	511	136	116	4.3	2.6	39	56	69	3.6	2.0
Civic, social, professional, and similar organizations	877	886	966	8	80	0.1	0.9	75	79	99	0.4	2.3
Private households	718	667	699	-51	32	-0.7	0.5	17	15	19	-0.8	2.2
Federal Government	2 865	2 968	2 596	103	-372	0.4	-1.3	732	1 012	939	3.3	-0.7
Postal Service	880	656	475	-223	-182	-2.9	-3.2	74	62	58	-1.8	-0.8
Federal electric utilities	30	22	19	-8	-3	-3.1	-1.2	11	13	16	1.6	2.4
Federal enterprises except the Postal Service and electric utilities	67	77	60	9	-16	1.3	-2.4	8	8	9	-0.1	1.1
Federal defense government compensation	510	546	496	36	-50	0.7	-0.9	197	242	225	2.1	-0.7
Federal defense government consumption of fixed capital	0	0	0	0	0	0.0	0.0	66	83	77	2.4	-0.7
Federal defense government except compensation and consumption of fixed capital	0	0	0	0	0	0.0	0.0	149	289	272	6.8	-0.6
Federal non-defense government compensation-except enterprises	1 379	1 668	1 546	289	-122	1.9	-0.8	125	147	129	1.7	-1.3
Federal non-defense government consumption of fixed capital	0	0	0	0	0	0.0	0.0	22	31	27	3.4	-1.3
Federal non-defense government except compensation and consumption of fixed capital	0	0	0	0	0	0.0	0.0	81	139	127	5.5	-0.8
Federal government except enterprises	1 888	2 213	2 042	325	-171	1.6	-0.8	640	930	857	3.8	-0.8
State and Local Government	17 925	19 513	21 155	1 588	1 642	0.9	0.8	1 574	1 759	2 120	1.1	1.9
Local government passenger transit	230	264	282	34	18	1.4	0.7	11	11	14	0.0	2.9
Local government enterprises except passenger transit	1 154	1 327	1 533	173	206	1.4	1.5	140	163	211	1.5	2.6
Local government hospitals-compensation	622	654	703	32	50.0	0.5	0.7	44	44	52	0.0	1.7
Local government educational services-compensation	7 294	8 010	8 751	717	741	0.9	0.9	358	373	442	0.4	1.7
Local government excluding enterprises, educational services, and hospitals-compensation	3 840	4 117	4 350	278	233	0.7	0.6	195	222	262	1.3	1.7
State government enterprises	528	518	485	-11	-33	-0.2	-0.7	20	24	31	1.9	2.6
State government hospitals-compensation	343	357	371	14	14	0.4	0.4	35	30	28	-1.5	-0.5
State government educational services-compensation	2 031	2 377	2 662	347	285	1.6	1.1	100	112	132	1.1	1.7
State government, other compensation	1 885	1 890	2 018	5	128	0.0	0.7	112	116	137	0.3	1.7
State and local government capital services	0	0	0	0	0	0.0	0.0	96	131	155	3.1	1.7
General state and local government except compensation and capital services	0	0	0	0	0	0.0	0.0	465	535	656	1.4	2.1
Owner-Occupied Dwellings	0	0	0	0	0	0.0	0.0	950	1 138	1 521	1.8	2.9
Agriculture, Forestry, Fishing, and Hunting	2 396	2 136	2 005	-261	-130	-1.1	-0.6	285	301	365	0.5	1.9
Crop production	1 036	982	913	-55	-69	-0.5	-0.7	124	123	143	-0.1	1.5
Animal production	1 036	833	785	-204	-47	-2.2	-0.6	119	139	175	1.5	2.4
Forestry	14	15	19	1	5	0.6	2.7	6	8	10	2.3	2.5
Logging	126	73	76	-53	4	-5.4	0.5	14	15	19	0.4	2.3
Fishing, hunting and trapping	55	47	39	-9	-8.0	-1.7	-1.8	6	6	6	0.1	-0.3
Support activities for agriculture and forestry	129	188	173	59	-15	3.8	-0.8	16	11	13	-3.7	2.0
Nonagriculture Self-Employed and Unpaid Family Worker	9 314	8 944	9 721	-370	777	-0.4	0.8	. . .	. . .	. . .	. . .	. . .
Secondary Wage and Salary Jobs in Agriculture and Private Household Industries	142	112	113	-30	1	-2.4	0.1	. . .	. . .	. . .	. . .	. . .
Secondary Jobs as a Self-Employed or Unpaid Family Worker	1 959	1 442	1 522	-518	81	-3.0	0.5	. . .	. . .	. . .	. . .	. . .

. . . = Not available.

Table 4-8. Employment, by Occupation, 2010 and Projected 2020

(Numbers in thousands, percent.)

Occupation	Employment				Change, 2010–2020		Total job openings due to growth and net replacements, 2010–2020[1]
	Number		Percent distribution		Number	Percent	
	2010	2020	2010	2020			
TOTAL, ALL OCCUPATIONS	143 068	163 537	100.0	100.0	20 469	14.3	54 787
Management, Business, and Financial	15 565	17 354	10.9	10.6	1 788	11.5	5 123
Management occupations	8 776	9 392	6.1	5.7	616	7.0	2 568
Top executives	2 205	2 302	1.5	1.4	97	4.4	537
Chief executives	370	385	0.3	0.2	15	4.2	112
General and operations managers	1 767	1 849	1.2	1.1	82	4.6	410
Legislators	68	68	0.0	0.0	0	0.3	16
Advertising, marketing, promotions, public relations, and sales managers	621	701	0.4	0.4	80	12.8	260
Advertising and promotions managers	39	44	0.0	0.0	5	13.3	16
Marketing and sales managers	520	585	0.4	0.4	64	12.4	216
Marketing managers	178	202	0.1	0.1	24	13.6	76
Sales managers	342	382	0.2	0.2	40	11.7	140
Public relations and fundraising managers	62	72	0.0	0.0	10	16.4	28
Operations specialties managers	1 540	1 722	1.1	1.1	182	11.8	501
Administrative services managers	254	291	0.2	0.2	37	14.5	100
Computer and information systems managers	308	364	0.2	0.2	56	18.1	103
Financial managers	527	573	0.4	0.4	46	8.8	143
Industrial production managers	150	164	0.1	0.1	14	9.1	49
Purchasing managers	68	73	0.0	0.0	5	7.2	26
Transportation, storage, and distribution managers	99	109	0.1	0.1	10	10.0	34
Compensation and benefits managers	32	33	0.0	0.0	1	2.8	9
Human resources managers	72	81	0.1	0.0	9	12.9	27
Training and development managers	30	34	0.0	0.0	4	14.6	12
Other Management occupations	4 411	4 668	3.1	2.9	257	5.8	1 270
Farmers, ranchers, and other agricultural managers	1 203	1 106	0.8	0.7	-96	-8.0	235
Construction managers	523	610	0.4	0.4	87	16.6	120
Education administrators	478	550	0.3	0.3	71	14.9	206
Education administrators, preschool and childcare center/program	64	80	0.0	0.0	16	24.9	34
Education administrators, elementary and secondary school	236	259	0.2	0.2	23	9.8	90
Education administrators, postsecondary	146	174	0.1	0.1	28	19.0	69
Education administrators, all other	33	37	0.0	0.0	4	13.6	14
Architectural and engineering managers	177	192	0.1	0.1	15	8.6	50
Food service managers	321	310	0.2	0.2	-11	-3.3	59
Gaming managers	3	4	0.0	0.0	0	11.5	1
Lodging managers	51	56	0.0	0.0	4	8.3	18
Medical and health services managers	303	371	0.2	0.2	68	22.4	142
Natural sciences managers	49	53	0.0	0.0	4	7.7	34
Postmasters and mail superintendents	25	18	0.0	0.0	-7	-27.8	5
Property, real estate, and community association managers	304	322	0.2	0.2	18	6.0	82
Social and community service managers	134	170	0.1	0.1	36	26.7	65
Emergency management directors	12	14	0.0	0.0	2	12.8	4
Managers, all other	828	894	0.6	0.5	65	7.9	249
Business and Financial Operations	6 789	7 962	4.7	4.9	1 173	17.3	2 555
Business operations specialists	4 152	4 903	2.9	3.0	751	18.1	1 563
Agents and business managers of artists, performers, and athletes	24	28	0.0	0.0	3	14.0	8
Buyers and purchasing agents	419	446	0.3	0.3	27	6.4	136
Buyers and purchasing agents, farm products	13	14	0.0	0.0	1	5.5	3
Wholesale and retail buyers, except farm products	122	133	0.1	0.1	11	9.0	42
Purchasing agents, except wholesale, retail, and farm products	284	299	0.2	0.2	15	5.3	91
Claims adjusters, appraisers, examiners, and investigators	291	298	0.2	0.2	8	2.6	83
Claims adjusters, examiners, and investigators	280	288	0.2	0.2	8	3.0	80
Insurance appraisers, auto damage	11	10	0.0	0.0	-1	-7.5	3
Compliance officers	217	249	0.2	0.2	32	15.0	59
Cost estimators	185	253	0.1	0.2	68	36.4	103
Human resources workers	443	533	0.3	0.3	91	20.5	165
Farm labor contractors	0	0	0.0	0.0	0	-0.7	0
Human resources, training, and labor relations specialists, all other	442	533	0.3	0.3	91	20.5	165
Logisticians	109	137	0.1	0.1	28	25.5	49
Management analysts	719	876	0.5	0.5	157	21.9	274
Meeting, convention, and event planners	72	103	0.1	0.1	31	43.7	45
Compensation, benefits, and job analysis specialists	110	115	0.1	0.1	6	5.0	24
Training and development specialists	218	279	0.2	0.2	62	28.3	98
Market research analysts and marketing specialists	283	399	0.2	0.2	117	41.2	192
Business operations specialists, all other	1 064	1 187	0.7	0.7	123	11.6	327
Financial specialists	2 637	3 058	1.8	1.9	421	16.0	992
Accountants and auditors	1 217	1 408	0.9	0.9	191	15.7	452
Appraisers and assessors of real estate	78	84	0.1	0.1	6	7.4	22
Budget analysts	62	69	0.0	0.0	7	10.4	20
Credit analysts	63	76	0.0	0.0	13	19.7	26
Financial analysts and advisors	545	671	0.4	0.4	127	23.2	234
Financial analysts	236	290	0.2	0.2	54	23.0	104
Personal financial advisors	207	273	0.1	0.2	66	32.1	90
Insurance underwriters	102	108	0.1	0.1	6	5.9	39
Financial examiners	29	37	0.0	0.0	8	27.0	14
Credit counselors and loan officers	323	370	0.2	0.2	48	14.8	130
Credit counselors	33	40	0.0	0.0	7	20.3	15
Loan officers	289	330	0.2	0.2	41	14.2	115
Tax examiners, collectors and preparers, and revenue agents	156	169	0.1	0.1	13	8.6	49
Tax examiners and collectors, and revenue agents	75	80	0.1	0.0	6	7.3	23
Tax preparers	82	90	0.1	0.1	8	9.8	26
Financial specialists, all other	165	175	0.1	0.1	10	6.1	45

Note: Data may not sum to totals or 100 percent due to rounding.

[1]Total job openings represent the sum of employment increases and net replacements. If employment change is negative, job openings due to growth are zero and total job openings equal net replacements.

Table 4-8. Employment, by Occupation, 2010 and Projected 2020—*Continued*

(Numbers in thousands, percent.)

Occupation	Employment				Change, 2010–2020		Total job openings due to growth and net replacements, 2010–2020[1]
	Number		Percent distribution		Number	Percent	
	2010	2020	2010	2020			
Computer, Engineering, and Science	7 205	8 427	5.0	5.2	1 222	17.0	2 782
Computer and mathematical occupations	3 543	4 321	2.5	2.6	778	22.0	1 438
Computer occupations	3 426	4 185	2.4	2.6	759	22.1	1 366
Computer and information research scientists	28	34	0.0	0.0	5	18.7	11
Computer systems analysts	544	665	0.4	0.4	120	22.1	223
Software developers and programmers	1 276	1 591	0.9	1.0	315	24.6	494
Computer programmers	363	407	0.3	0.2	44	12.0	128
Software developers, applications	521	665	0.4	0.4	144	27.6	198
Software developers, systems software	392	519	0.3	0.3	127	32.4	168
Database and systems administrators and network architects	458	589	0.3	0.4	131	28.5	208
Database administrators	111	145	0.1	0.1	34	30.6	53
Network and computer systems administrators	347	444	0.2	0.3	97	27.8	155
Computer support specialists	607	717	0.4	0.4	110	18.1	270
Information security analysts, web developers, and computer network architects	302	368	0.2	0.2	66	21.7	110
Computer occupations, all other	210	222	0.1	0.1	12	5.9	52
Mathematical science occupations	117	136	0.1	0.1	20	16.7	72
Actuaries	22	28	0.0	0.0	6	26.7	19
Mathematicians	3	4	0.0	0.0	1	15.7	2
Operations research analysts	65	74	0.0	0.0	9	14.6	30
Statisticians	25	29	0.0	0.0	4	14.1	19
Miscellaneous mathematical science occupations	2	3	0.0	0.0	0	11.0	2
Mathematical technicians	1	1	0.0	0.0	0	6.2	1
Mathematical science occupations, all other	1	2	0.0	0.0	0	14.7	1
Architecture and Engineering	2 433	2 686	1.7	1.6	253	10.4	798
Architects, surveyors, and cartographers	200	248	0.1	0.2	47	23.7	89
Architects, except naval	135	167	0.1	0.1	31	23.1	59
Architects, except landscape and naval	114	142	0.1	0.1	28	24.5	51
Landscape architects	22	25	0.0	0.0	4	16.0	8
Surveyors, cartographers, and photogrammetrists	65	81	0.0	0.0	16	24.8	30
Cartographers and photogrammetrists	14	17	0.0	0.0	3	22.2	6
Surveyors	51	64	0.0	0.0	13	25.4	24
Engineers	1 519	1 679	1.1	1.0	160	10.6	526
Aerospace engineers	81	85	0.1	0.1	4	4.9	22
Agricultural engineers	3	3	0.0	0.0	0	9.1	1
Biomedical engineers	16	25	0.0	0.0	10	61.7	13
Chemical engineers	30	32	0.0	0.0	2	5.9	11
Civil engineers	263	314	0.2	0.2	51	19.4	104
Computer hardware engineers	70	76	0.0	0.0	6	9.0	23
Electrical and electronics engineers	294	312	0.2	0.2	18	6.0	88
Electrical engineers	154	165	0.1	0.1	11	7.0	48
Electronics engineers, except computer	140	147	0.1	0.1	7	4.9	41
Environmental engineers	51	63	0.0	0.0	11	21.9	23
Industrial engineers, including health and safety	228	244	0.2	0.1	16	7.1	66
Health and safety engineers, except mining safety engineers and inspectors	24	27	0.0	0.0	3	13.0	8
Industrial engineers	204	217	0.1	0.1	13	6.4	58
Marine engineers and naval architects	6	7	0.0	0.0	1	17.5	2
Materials engineers	22	24	0.0	0.0	2	8.7	8
Mechanical engineers	243	265	0.2	0.2	21	8.8	100
Mining and geological engineers, including mining safety engineers	6	7	0.0	0.0	1	9.6	2
Nuclear engineers	19	21	0.0	0.0	2	10.2	6
Petroleum engineers	30	35	0.0	0.0	5	17.0	12
Engineers, all other	157	167	0.1	0.1	10	6.6	45
Drafters, engineering technicians, and mapping technicians	714	759	0.5	0.5	45	6.3	183
Drafters	205	217	0.1	0.1	11	5.6	52
Architectural and civil drafters	93	96	0.1	0.1	3	3.2	21
Electrical and electronics drafters	29	31	0.0	0.0	2	5.4	7
Mechanical drafters	67	75	0.0	0.0	8	11.1	21
Drafters, all other	16	15	0.0	0.0	-1	-4.0	3
Engineering technicians, except drafters	452	477	0.3	0.3	25	5.4	111
Aerospace engineering and operations technicians	9	9	0.0	0.0	0	-1.6	2
Civil engineering technicians	79	89	0.1	0.1	9	12.0	25
Electrical and electronics engineering technicians	151	154	0.1	0.1	3	1.9	32
Electro-mechanical technicians	16	17	0.0	0.0	0	0.5	3
Environmental engineering technicians	19	23	0.0	0.0	5	24.3	8
Industrial engineering technicians	63	65	0.0	0.0	3	4.2	15
Mechanical engineering technicians	45	47	0.0	0.0	2	3.9	10
Engineering technicians, except drafters, all other	71	74	0.0	0.0	3	4.7	17
Surveying and mapping technicians	57	66	0.0	0.0	9	15.9	20
Life, Physical, and Social Science	1 229	1 420	0.9	0.9	191	15.5	546
Life scientists	286	344	0.2	0.2	58	20.4	106
Agricultural and food scientists	34	37	0.0	0.0	4	10.4	17
Animal scientists	3	4	0.0	0.0	0	12.8	2
Food scientists and technologists	14	15	0.0	0.0	1	8.0	7
Soil and plant scientists	16	18	0.0	0.0	2	12.1	9
Biological scientists	101	115	0.1	0.1	14	14.0	37
Biochemists and biophysicists	25	33	0.0	0.0	8	30.8	13
Microbiologists	20	23	0.0	0.0	3	13.3	7
Zoologists and wildlife biologists	20	21	0.0	0.0	2	7.4	6
Biological scientists, all other	36	38	0.0	0.0	2	6.3	10
Conservation scientists and foresters	35	37	0.0	0.0	2	5.0	6
Conservation scientists	23	25	0.0	0.0	1	5.2	4
Foresters	12	12	0.0	0.0	1	4.7	2
Medical scientists	105	143	0.1	0.1	38	35.8	44
Epidemiologists	5	6	0.0	0.0	1	23.6	2
Medical scientists, except epidemiologists	100	137	0.1	0.1	36	36.4	43
Life scientists, all other	12	13	0.0	0.0	1	11.7	2

Note: Data may not sum to totals or 100 percent due to rounding.

[1]Total job openings represent the sum of employment increases and net replacements. If employment change is negative, job openings due to growth are zero and total job openings equal net replacements.

Table 4-8. Employment, by Occupation, 2010 and Projected 2020—*Continued*

(Numbers in thousands, percent.)

Occupation	Employment				Change, 2010–2020		Total job openings due to growth and net replacements, 2010–2020[1]
	Number		Percent distribution		Number	Percent	
	2010	2020	2010	2020			
Life, Physical, and Social Science—*Continued*							
Physical scientists	282	318	0.2	0.2	36	12.7	122
Astronomers and physicists	21	23	0.0	0.0	3	13.8	9
Astronomers	2	3	0.0	0.0	0	11.0	1
Physicists	18	21	0.0	0.0	3	14.2	8
Atmospheric and space scientists	10	10	0.0	0.0	1	10.6	2
Chemists and materials scientists	91	95	0.1	0.1	4	4.5	34
Chemists	82	85	0.1	0.1	3	3.8	30
Materials scientists	9	10	0.0	0.0	1	10.2	4
Environmental scientists and geoscientists	131	156	0.1	0.1	25	19.3	64
Environmental scientists and specialists, including health	89	106	0.1	0.1	17	18.7	43
Geoscientists, except hydrologists and geographers	34	41	0.0	0.0	7	21.2	17
Hydrologists	8	9	0.0	0.0	1	17.8	4
Physical scientists, all other	30	33	0.0	0.0	3	8.5	13
Social scientists and related workers	306	363	0.2	0.2	57	18.4	155
Economists	15	16	0.0	0.0	1	6.1	6
Survey researchers	20	24	0.0	0.0	5	24.1	10
Psychologists	174	212	0.1	0.1	38	21.6	93
Clinical, counseling, and school psychologists	154	188	0.1	0.1	34	21.9	82
Industrial-organizational psychologists	2	3	0.0	0.0	1	34.9	2
Psychologists, all other	18	21	0.0	0.0	3	18.2	9
Sociologists	4	5	0.0	0.0	1	18.1	2
Urban and regional planners	40	47	0.0	0.0	7	16.2	17
Miscellaneous social scientists and related workers	53	59	0.0	0.0	6	11.2	28
Anthropologists and archeologists	6	7	0.0	0.0	1	20.7	4
Geographers	2	2	0.0	0.0	1	35.4	1
Historians	4	5	0.0	0.0	1	17.9	2
Political scientists	6	6	0.0	0.0	0	7.9	3
Social scientists and related workers, all other	35	38	0.0	0.0	3	8.1	18
Life, physical, and social science technicians	355	395	0.2	0.2	40	11.4	163
Agricultural and food science technicians	21	23	0.0	0.0	2	7.0	9
Biological technicians	80	91	0.1	0.1	11	13.5	38
Chemical technicians	61	65	0.0	0.0	4	6.7	13
Geological and petroleum technicians	14	17	0.0	0.0	2	14.7	7
Nuclear technicians	7	8	0.0	0.0	1	13.5	3
Social science research assistants	30	34	0.0	0.0	4	15.0	17
Miscellaneous life, physical, and social science technicians	141	157	0.1	0.1	16	11.6	76
Environmental science and protection technicians, including health	30	37	0.0	0.0	7	23.6	20
Forensic science technicians	13	15	0.0	0.0	2	18.6	8
Forest and conservation technicians	37	36	0.0	0.0	0	-1.0	15
Life, physical, and social science technicians, all other	62	69	0.0	0.0	7	11.8	34
Education, Legal, Community Service, Arts, and Media	15 517	17 976	10.8	11.0	2 460	15.9	5 906
Community and social service occupations	2 403	2 985	1.7	1.8	582	24.2	1 098
Counselors, social workers, and other community and social service specialists	1 997	2 510	1.4	1.5	512	25.7	957
Counselors	685	863	0.5	0.5	179	26.1	325
Substance abuse and behavioral disorder counselors	86	109	0.1	0.1	23	27.3	42
Educational, guidance, school, and vocational counselors	281	335	0.2	0.2	53	19.0	114
Marriage and family therapists	36	51	0.0	0.0	15	41.2	23
Mental health counselors	120	164	0.1	0.1	44	36.3	69
Rehabilitation counselors	130	166	0.1	0.1	37	28.2	64
Counselors, all other	32	38	0.0	0.0	7	21.3	14
Social workers	651	812	0.5	0.5	161	24.8	315
Child, family, and school social workers	296	354	0.2	0.2	58	19.7	128
Healthcare social workers	153	204	0.1	0.1	51	33.5	87
Mental health and substance abuse social workers	126	166	0.1	0.1	40	31.3	69
Social workers, all other	76	88	0.1	0.1	12	16.2	30
Miscellaneous community and social service specialists	662	835	0.5	0.5	173	26.1	316
Health educators	63	87	0.0	0.1	23	36.5	37
Probation officers and correctional treatment specialists	93	110	0.1	0.1	17	18.4	37
Social and human service assistants	384	490	0.3	0.3	106	27.6	189
Community and social service specialists, all other	121	148	0.1	0.1	26	21.8	53
Religious workers	405	475	0.3	0.3	70	17.2	142
Clergy	231	271	0.2	0.2	41	17.5	80
Directors, religious activities and education	126	147	0.1	0.1	21	16.8	45
Religious workers, all other	49	57	0.0	0.0	8	17.0	17
Legal	1 212	1 343	0.8	0.8	131	10.8	344
Lawyers, judges, and related workers	821	901	0.6	0.6	80	9.8	235
Lawyers and judicial law clerks	758	834	0.5	0.5	76	10.0	219
Lawyers	728	802	0.5	0.5	74	10.1	212
Judicial law clerks	30	32	0.0	0.0	2	7.7	7
Judges, magistrates, and other judicial workers	63	67	0.0	0.0	5	7.3	17
Administrative law judges, adjudicators, and hearing officers	19	19	0.0	0.0	0	-0.1	4
Arbitrators, mediators, and conciliators	9	11	0.0	0.0	2	15.5	3
Judges, magistrate judges, and magistrates	34	37	0.0	0.0	3	9.2	10
Legal support workers	391	442	0.3	0.3	51	12.9	108
Paralegals and legal assistants	256	303	0.2	0.2	47	18.3	83
Miscellaneous legal support workers	135	139	0.1	0.1	4	2.7	25
Court reporters	22	25	0.0	0.0	3	14.1	6
Title examiners, abstractors, and searchers	59	58	0.0	0.0	-1	-1.4	9
Legal support workers, all other	54	56	0.0	0.0	1	2.6	10

Note: Data may not sum to totals or 100 percent due to rounding.

[1]Total job openings represent the sum of employment increases and net replacements. If employment change is negative, job openings due to growth are zero and total job openings equal net replacements.

Table 4-8. Employment, by Occupation, 2010 and Projected 2020—*Continued*

(Numbers in thousands, percent.)

Occupation	Employment				Change, 2010–2020		Total job openings due to growth and net replacements, 2010–2020[1]
	Number		Percent distribution		Number	Percent	
	2010	2020	2010	2020			
Education, Training, and Library	9 194	10 597	6.4	6.5	1 404	15.3	3 398
Postsecondary teachers	1 756	2 062	1.2	1.3	306	17.4	586
Preschool, primary, secondary, and special education school teachers	4 354	5 009	3.0	3.1	655	15.0	1 733
Preschool and kindergarten teachers	636	782	0.4	0.5	146	23.0	312
Preschool teachers, except special education	457	570	0.3	0.3	114	24.9	232
Kindergarten teachers, except special education	179	212	0.1	0.1	33	18.2	79
Elementary and middle school teachers	2 133	2 491	1.5	1.5	358	16.8	827
Elementary school teachers, except special education	1 477	1 725	1.0	1.1	249	16.8	573
Middle school teachers, except special and career/technical education	642	750	0.4	0.5	108	16.9	249
Career/technical education teachers, middle school	14	16	0.0	0.0	1	8.9	5
Secondary school teachers	1 126	1 199	0.8	0.7	73	6.5	381
Secondary school teachers, except special and career/technical education	1 038	1 110	0.7	0.7	72	6.9	356
Career/technical education teachers, secondary school	89	90	0.1	0.1	1	1.1	25
Special education teachers	460	537	0.3	0.3	77	16.8	213
Special education teachers, preschool, kindergarten, and elementary school	223	270	0.2	0.2	47	21.3	113
Special education teachers, middle school	98	118	0.1	0.1	20	20.2	49
Special education teachers, secondary school	139	149	0.1	0.1	10	7.3	51
Other teachers and instructors	1 220	1 402	0.9	0.9	182	14.9	368
Adult basic and secondary education and literacy teachers and instructors	87	100	0.1	0.1	13	14.6	26
Self-enrichment education teachers	253	306	0.2	0.2	53	20.9	92
Teachers and instructors, all other	881	997	0.6	0.6	116	13.2	251
Librarians, curators, and archivists	301	327	0.2	0.2	26	8.5	124
Archivists, curators, and museum technicians	30	34	0.0	0.0	5	15.0	13
Archivists	6	7	0.0	0.0	1	11.7	2
Curators	12	15	0.0	0.0	3	24.8	6
Museum technicians and conservators	12	13	0.0	0.0	1	6.8	4
Librarians	156	167	0.1	0.1	11	6.9	51
Library technicians	115	126	0.1	0.1	10	8.9	60
Other education, training, and library occupations	1 562	1 798	1.1	1.1	236	15.1	587
Audio-visual and multimedia collections specialists	8	10	0.0	0.0	1	12.7	3
Farm and home management advisors	13	15	0.0	0.0	2	16.6	5
Instructional coordinators	140	167	0.1	0.1	27	19.5	58
Teacher assistants	1 288	1 479	0.9	0.9	191	14.8	482
Education, training, and library workers, all other	112	127	0.1	0.1	14	12.8	39
Arts, Design, Entertainment, Sports, and Media	2 709	3 051	1.9	1.9	343	12.6	1 067
Art and design workers	777	853	0.5	0.5	76	9.8	309
Artists and related workers	197	213	0.1	0.1	15	7.7	62
Art directors	74	81	0.1	0.0	7	9.0	24
Craft artists	12	13	0.0	0.0	1	7.3	4
Fine artists, including painters, sculptors, and illustrators	26	28	0.0	0.0	2	7.8	8
Multimedia artists and animators	67	72	0.0	0.0	6	8.3	21
Artists and related workers, all other	19	20	0.0	0.0	0	1.0	5
Designers	580	640	0.4	0.4	61	10.5	247
Commercial and industrial designers	41	45	0.0	0.0	4	10.5	17
Fashion designers	22	22	0.0	0.0	0	0.2	7
Floral designers	67	60	0.0	0.0	-6	-9.3	21
Graphic designers	279	317	0.2	0.2	37	13.4	124
Interior designers	57	67	0.0	0.0	11	19.3	28
Merchandise displayers and window trimmers	91	103	0.1	0.1	12	12.8	40
Set and exhibit designers	12	13	0.0	0.0	1	9.9	5
Designers, all other	12	14	0.0	0.0	2	13.1	5
Entertainers and performers, sports and related workers	806	935	0.6	0.6	129	16.0	340
Actors, producers, and directors	189	205	0.1	0.1	16	8.5	70
Actors	67	69	0.0	0.0	3	3.9	20
Producers and directors	123	136	0.1	0.1	14	11.0	50
Athletes, coaches, umpires, and related workers	279	358	0.2	0.2	79	28.3	150
Athletes and sports competitors	17	20	0.0	0.0	4	21.6	8
Coaches and scouts	243	314	0.2	0.2	71	29.4	133
Umpires, referees, and other sports officials	20	23	0.0	0.0	4	19.9	9
Dancers and choreographers	26	30	0.0	0.0	5	18.0	15
Dancers	12	14	0.0	0.0	1	11.2	6
Choreographers	13	16	0.0	0.0	3	24.2	8
Musicians, singers, and related workers	269	297	0.2	0.2	27	10.2	93
Music directors and composers	93	103	0.1	0.1	10	10.2	32
Musicians and singers	176	194	0.1	0.1	18	10.1	61
Entertainers and performers, sports and related workers, all other	43	45	0.0	0.0	2	4.4	13
Media and communication workers	792	898	0.6	0.5	106	13.4	325
Announcers	62	66	0.0	0.0	4	6.6	21
Radio and television announcers	50	54	0.0	0.0	4	6.9	17
Public address system and other announcers	12	12	0.0	0.0	1	5.2	4
News analysts, reporters and correspondents	59	55	0.0	0.0	-3	-5.5	21
Broadcast news analysts	7	7	0.0	0.0	1	10.2	3
Reporters and correspondents	52	48	0.0	0.0	-4	-7.5	18
Public relations specialists	258	316	0.2	0.2	58	22.5	127
Writers and editors	323	341	0.2	0.2	19	5.8	103
Editors	127	128	0.1	0.1	1	0.6	37
Technical writers	50	58	0.0	0.0	9	17.2	18
Writers and authors	146	155	0.1	0.1	10	6.5	48
Miscellaneous media and communication workers	91	119	0.1	0.1	28	31.2	53
Interpreters and translators	58	83	0.0	0.1	25	42.2	40
Media and communication workers, all other	33	36	0.0	0.0	4	11.4	12

Note: Data may not sum to totals or 100 percent due to rounding.

[1]Total job openings represent the sum of employment increases and net replacements. If employment change is negative, job openings due to growth are zero and total job openings equal net replacements.

Table 4-8. Employment, by Occupation, 2010 and Projected 2020—*Continued*

(Numbers in thousands, percent.)

Occupation	Employment				Change, 2010–2020		Total job openings due to growth and net replacements, 2010–2020[1]
	Number		Percent distribution		Number	Percent	
	2010	2020	2010	2020			
Arts, Design, Entertainment, Sports, and Media—*Continued*							
Media and communication equipment workers	334	366	0.2	0.2	31	9.4	92
Broadcast and sound engineering technicians and radio operators	118	130	0.1	0.1	12	9.9	45
Audio and video equipment technicians	61	69	0.0	0.0	8	13.4	26
Broadcast technicians	37	40	0.0	0.0	3	9.0	14
Radio operators	1	1	0.0	0.0	0	7.0	0
Sound engineering technicians	19	19	0.0	0.0	0	0.6	6
Photographers	140	157	0.1	0.1	18	12.5	31
Television, video, and motion picture camera operators and editors	58	61	0.0	0.0	2	3.8	13
Camera operators, television, video, and motion picture	27	27	0.0	0.0	1	2.1	5
Film and video editors	32	33	0.0	0.0	2	5.2	7
Media and communication equipment workers, all other	18	18	0.0	0.0	0	0.3	3
Healthcare Practitioners and Technical	7 799	9 819	5.5	6.0	2 020	25.9	3 591
Health diagnosing and treating practitioners	4 852	6 128	3.4	3.7	1 276	26.3	2 219
Chiropractors	53	67	0.0	0.0	15	28.3	25
Dentists	156	188	0.1	0.1	32	20.7	78
Dentists, general	131	158	0.1	0.1	28	21.1	66
Oral and maxillofacial surgeons	8	10	0.0	0.0	2	21.3	4
Orthodontists	8	10	0.0	0.0	2	21.1	4
Prosthodontists	1	1	0.0	0.0	0	21.4	1
Dentists, all other specialists	8	9	0.0	0.0	1	11.7	3
Dietitians and nutritionists	64	77	0.0	0.0	13	19.7	35
Optometrists	34	46	0.0	0.0	11	33.1	23
Pharmacists	275	345	0.2	0.2	70	25.4	140
Physicians and surgeons	691	859	0.5	0.5	168	24.4	305
Physician assistants	84	108	0.1	0.1	25	29.5	41
Podiatrists	13	16	0.0	0.0	3	20.0	5
Registered nurses	2 737	3 449	1.9	2.1	712	26.0	1 207
Therapists	616	806	0.4	0.5	190	30.9	298
Occupational therapists	109	145	0.1	0.1	36	33.5	57
Physical therapists	199	276	0.1	0.2	77	39.0	101
Radiation therapists	17	20	0.0	0.0	3	20.3	7
Recreational therapists	22	26	0.0	0.0	4	17.1	12
Respiratory therapists	113	144	0.1	0.1	31	27.7	53
Speech-language pathologists	123	152	0.1	0.1	29	23.4	52
Therapists, all other	33	42	0.0	0.0	9	27.9	16
Veterinarians	61	83	0.0	0.1	22	35.9	34
Audiologists	13	18	0.0	0.0	5	36.8	6
Health diagnosing and treating practitioners, all other	56	66	0.0	0.0	11	19.0	21
Health technologists and technicians	2 799	3 519	2.0	2.2	720	25.7	1 297
Clinical laboratory technologists and technicians	331	374	0.2	0.2	43	13.0	107
Medical and clinical laboratory technologists	169	189	0.1	0.1	19	11.3	52
Medical and clinical laboratory technicians	161	185	0.1	0.1	24	14.7	55
Dental hygienists	182	250	0.1	0.2	69	37.7	105
Diagnostic related technologists and technicians	345	448	0.2	0.3	103	29.9	157
Cardiovascular technologists and technicians	49	64	0.0	0.0	15	29.3	22
Diagnostic medical sonographers	54	77	0.0	0.0	23	43.5	32
Nuclear medicine technologists	22	26	0.0	0.0	4	18.9	8
Radiologic technologists and technicians	220	281	0.2	0.2	61	27.8	95
Emergency medical technicians and paramedics	227	302	0.2	0.2	75	33.3	121
Health practitioner support technologists and technicians	621	805	0.4	0.5	184	29.6	292
Dietetic technicians	24	28	0.0	0.0	4	16.0	8
Pharmacy technicians	334	443	0.2	0.3	108	32.4	166
Psychiatric technicians	75	86	0.1	0.1	12	15.5	25
Respiratory therapy technicians	14	14	0.0	0.0	1	4.1	3
Surgical technologists	94	111	0.1	0.1	18	18.9	34
Veterinary technologists and technicians	80	122	0.1	0.1	42	52.0	56
Licensed practical and licensed vocational nurses	752	921	0.5	0.6	169	22.4	369
Medical records and health information technicians	180	217	0.1	0.1	38	21.0	74
Opticians, dispensing	63	81	0.0	0.0	18	28.9	31
Orthotists and prosthetists	6	7	0.0	0.0	1	12.1	2
Health technologists and technicians, all other	94	115	0.1	0.1	22	23.2	40
Other healthcare practitioners and technical occupations	148	171	0.1	0.1	23	15.8	75
Occupational health and safety specialists and technicians	69	76	0.0	0.0	6	9.2	31
Occupational health and safety specialists	59	64	0.0	0.0	5	8.5	26
Occupational health and safety technicians	11	12	0.0	0.0	1	12.9	5
Miscellaneous health practitioners and technical workers	79	96	0.1	0.1	17	21.6	45
Athletic trainers	18	24	0.0	0.0	6	30.0	12
Healthcare practitioners and technical workers, all other	60	72	0.0	0.0	12	19.0	33
Service	29 136	34 037	20.4	20.8	4 901	16.8	12 577
Healthcare support occupations	4 190	5 634	2.9	3.4	1 444	34.5	2 042
Nursing, psychiatric, and home health aides	2 591	3 609	1.8	2.2	1 019	39.3	1 353
Home health aides	1 018	1 724	0.7	1.1	706	69.4	838
Nursing aides, orderlies, and attendants	1 505	1 807	1.1	1.1	302	20.1	496
Psychiatric aides	68	78	0.0	0.0	10	15.1	19
Occupational therapy and physical therapist assistants and aides	150	216	0.1	0.1	66	43.8	89
Occupational therapy assistants and aides	36	51	0.0	0.0	15	41.2	20
Occupational therapy assistants	29	41	0.0	0.0	12	43.3	17
Occupational therapy aides	8	10	0.0	0.0	3	33.0	4
Physical therapist assistants and aides	114	166	0.1	0.1	51	44.6	69
Physical therapist assistants	67	98	0.0	0.1	31	45.7	41
Physical therapist aides	47	67	0.0	0.0	20	43.1	28

Note: Data may not sum to totals or 100 percent due to rounding.

[1]Total job openings represent the sum of employment increases and net replacements. If employment change is negative, job openings due to growth are zero and total job openings equal net replacements.

Table 4-8. Employment, by Occupation, 2010 and Projected 2020—*Continued*

(Numbers in thousands, percent.)

Occupation	Employment				Change, 2010–2020		Total job openings due to growth and net replacements, 2010–2020[1]
	Number		Percent distribution		Number	Percent	
	2010	2020	2010	2020			
Service—*Continued*							
Other healthcare support occupations	1 449	1 808	1.0	1.1	359	24.8	600
Massage therapists	154	185	0.1	0.1	31	20.1	56
Miscellaneous healthcare support occupations	1 295	1 624	0.9	1.0	329	25.4	544
Dental assistants	297	389	0.2	0.2	92	30.8	154
Medical assistants	528	690	0.4	0.4	163	30.9	244
Medical equipment preparers	49	58	0.0	0.0	9	17.5	16
Medical transcriptionists	95	101	0.1	0.1	6	5.9	20
Pharmacy aides	51	65	0.0	0.0	15	28.6	22
Veterinary assistants and laboratory animal caretakers	73	84	0.1	0.1	10	14.2	22
Healthcare support workers, all other	202	237	0.1	0.1	35	17.2	66
Protective service occupations	3 303	3 667	2.3	2.2	365	11.0	1 196
Supervisors of protective service workers	267	282	0.2	0.2	15	5.8	114
First-line supervisors of law enforcement workers	148	152	0.1	0.1	5	3.1	55
First-line supervisors of correctional officers	42	44	0.0	0.0	2	5.6	17
First-line supervisors of police and detectives	106	108	0.1	0.1	2	2.1	39
First-line supervisors of fire fighting and prevention workers	60	65	0.0	0.0	5	8.2	33
First-line supervisors of protective service workers, all other	59	65	0.0	0.0	6	9.9	26
Fire fighting and prevention workers	326	354	0.2	0.2	28	8.6	118
Firefighters	310	337	0.2	0.2	27	8.6	112
Fire inspectors	15	17	0.0	0.0	1	8.8	5
Fire inspectors and investigators	14	15	0.0	0.0	1	9.2	5
Forest fire inspectors and prevention specialists	2	2	0.0	0.0	0	5.8	1
Law enforcement workers	1 297	1 383	0.9	0.8	86	6.6	399
Bailiffs, correctional officers, and jailers	493	519	0.3	0.3	26	5.3	113
Bailiffs	18	19	0.0	0.0	1	8.0	5
Correctional officers and jailers	475	500	0.3	0.3	25	5.2	108
Detectives and criminal investigators	119	123	0.1	0.1	4	2.9	30
Fish and game wardens	8	8	0.0	0.0	0	4.7	2
Parking enforcement workers	10	11	0.0	0.0	1	9.6	3
Police officers	667	722	0.5	0.4	55	8.2	251
Police and sheriff's patrol officers	664	719	0.5	0.4	55	8.2	249
Transit and railroad police	4	4	0.0	0.0	0	6.5	1
Other protective service workers	1 413	1 649	1.0	1.0	236	16.7	565
Animal control workers	16	17	0.0	0.0	2	11.7	6
Private detectives and investigators	35	42	0.0	0.0	7	20.5	15
Security guards and gaming surveillance officers	1 043	1 238	0.7	0.8	196	18.8	361
Gaming surveillance officers and gaming investigators	7	7	0.0	0.0	1	9.1	2
Security guards	1 036	1 231	0.7	0.8	195	18.8	360
Miscellaneous protective service workers	321	352	0.2	0.2	31	9.7	183
Crossing guards	69	70	0.0	0.0	1	1.1	17
Lifeguards, ski patrol, and other recreational protective service workers	122	136	0.1	0.1	15	12.3	93
Transportation security screeners (federal only)	48	53	0.0	0.0	5	9.5	10
Protective service workers, all other	82	92	0.1	0.1	11	13.2	63
Food Preparation and Serving Related	11 150	12 243	7.8	7.5	1 093	9.8	5 103
Supervisors of food preparation and serving workers	902	979	0.6	0.6	78	8.6	266
Chefs and head cooks	101	100	0.1	0.1	-1	-0.8	18
First-line supervisors of food preparation and serving workers	801	880	0.6	0.5	79	9.8	248
cooks and food preparation workers	2 865	3 111	2.0	1.9	246	8.6	995
Cooks	2 051	2 213	1.4	1.4	162	7.9	618
Cooks, fast food	530	511	0.4	0.3	-19	-3.6	113
Cooks, institution and cafeteria	405	455	0.3	0.3	50	12.3	136
Cooks, private household	4	4	0.0	0.0	1	14.4	1
Cooks, restaurant	915	1 033	0.6	0.6	118	12.9	313
Cooks, short order	174	184	0.1	0.1	9	5.4	47
Cooks, all other	22	25	0.0	0.0	3	15.0	8
Food preparation workers	814	898	0.6	0.5	84	10.3	377
Food and beverage serving workers	6 100	6 804	4.3	4.2	704	11.5	3 139
Bartenders	503	549	0.4	0.3	46	9.0	221
Fast food and counter workers	3 128	3 553	2.2	2.2	425	13.6	1 497
Combined food preparation and serving workers, including fast food	2 682	3 080	1.9	1.9	398	14.8	1 147
Counter attendants, cafeteria, food concession, and coffee shop	446	473	0.3	0.3	27	6.2	350
Waiters and waitresses	2 260	2 456	1.6	1.5	196	8.7	1 324
Food servers, nonrestaurant	209	247	0.1	0.2	38	18.0	97
Other food preparation and serving related workers	1 284	1 349	0.9	0.8	65	5.0	703
Dining room and cafeteria attendants and bartender helpers	397	415	0.3	0.3	18	4.5	165
Dishwashers	510	546	0.4	0.3	36	7.0	269
Hosts and hostesses, restaurant, lounge, and coffee shop	331	344	0.2	0.2	14	4.1	246
Food preparation and serving related workers, all other	46	44	0.0	0.0	-3	-5.8	23
Building and Grounds Cleaning and Maintenance	5 499	6 163	3.8	3.8	664	12.1	1 655
Supervisors of building and grounds cleaning and maintenance workers	430	462	0.3	0.3	33	7.6	93
First-line supervisors of housekeeping and janitorial workers	227	229	0.2	0.1	2	0.8	33
First-line supervisors of landscaping, lawn service, and groundskeeping workers	203	234	0.1	0.1	31	15.1	60
Building cleaning and pest control workers	3 819	4 196	2.7	2.6	377	9.9	1 086
Building cleaning workers	3 751	4 110	2.6	2.5	359	9.6	1 037
Janitors and cleaners, except maids and housekeeping cleaners	2 310	2 557	1.6	1.6	246	10.7	682
Maids and housekeeping cleaners	1 427	1 539	1.0	0.9	112	7.8	352
Building cleaning workers, all other	13	14	0.0	0.0	1	7.3	3
Pest control workers	68	86	0.0	0.1	18	26.1	49
Grounds maintenance workers	1 250	1 504	0.9	0.9	255	20.4	476
Landscaping and groundskeeping workers	1 152	1 392	0.8	0.9	241	20.9	444
Pesticide handlers, sprayers, and applicators, vegetation	30	33	0.0	0.0	3	10.2	8
Tree trimmers and pruners	51	60	0.0	0.0	9	17.9	18
Grounds maintenance workers, all other	18	20	0.0	0.0	2	9.5	5

Note: Data may not sum to totals or 100 percent due to rounding.

[1]Total job openings represent the sum of employment increases and net replacements. If employment change is negative, job openings due to growth are zero and total job openings equal net replacements.

Table 4-8. Employment, by Occupation, 2010 and Projected 2020—*Continued*

(Numbers in thousands, percent.)

Occupation	Employment				Change, 2010–2020		Total job openings due to growth and net replacements, 2010–2020[1]
	Number		Percent distribution		Number	Percent	
	2010	2020	2010	2020			
Personal Care and Service	4 995	6 331	3.5	3.9	1 337	26.8	2 583
Supervisors of personal care and service workers	274	307	0.2	0.2	33	12.1	96
First-line supervisors of gaming workers	55	59	0.0	0.0	4	6.5	14
Gaming supervisors	36	39	0.0	0.0	3	6.9	9
Slot supervisors	19	20	0.0	0.0	1	5.7	5
First-line supervisors of personal service workers	219	249	0.2	0.2	30	13.5	83
Animal care and service workers	235	289	0.2	0.2	54	23.0	100
Animal trainers	46	47	0.0	0.0	2	3.2	6
Nonfarm animal caretakers	189	242	0.1	0.1	53	27.8	94
Entertainment attendants and related workers	560	637	0.4	0.4	78	13.9	382
Gaming services workers	119	138	0.1	0.1	19	16.0	70
Gaming dealers	91	107	0.1	0.1	16	17.1	55
Gaming and sports book writers and runners	15	17	0.0	0.0	2	12.1	8
Gaming service workers, all other	12	14	0.0	0.0	2	12.9	7
Motion picture projectionists	10	9	0.0	0.0	-1	-11.1	4
Ushers, lobby attendants, and ticket takers	109	120	0.1	0.1	11	10.2	75
Miscellaneous entertainment attendants and related workers	321	370	0.2	0.2	49	15.1	233
Amusement and recreation attendants	261	299	0.2	0.2	37	14.2	187
Costume attendants	6	6	0.0	0.0	1	9.9	4
Locker room, coatroom, and dressing room attendants	18	20	0.0	0.0	3	14.6	13
Entertainment attendants and related workers, all other	37	45	0.0	0.0	8	22.5	30
Funeral service workers	67	75	0.0	0.0	7	10.9	31
Embalmers	7	7	0.0	0.0	0	5.3	4
Funeral attendants	31	33	0.0	0.0	2	5.2	16
Funeral service managers, directors, morticians, and undertakers	29	35	0.0	0.0	5	18.2	11
Personal appearance workers	845	971	0.6	0.6	126	15.0	288
Barbers, hairdressers, hairstylists and cosmetologists	690	793	0.5	0.5	103	14.9	234
Barbers	62	67	0.0	0.0	5	7.2	16
Hairdressers, hairstylists, and cosmetologists	628	726	0.4	0.4	98	15.7	218
Miscellaneous personal appearance workers	155	179	0.1	0.1	23	15.1	54
Makeup artists, theatrical and performance	4	4	0.0	0.0	0	3.4	1
Manicurists and pedicurists	82	95	0.1	0.1	14	16.7	29
Shampooers	22	20	0.0	0.0	-2	-9.0	4
Skincare specialists	48	59	0.0	0.0	12	24.6	20
Baggage porters, bellhops, and concierges	66	74	0.0	0.0	8	12.2	25
Baggage porters and bellhops	46	52	0.0	0.0	6	12.4	17
Concierges	20	23	0.0	0.0	2	11.9	7
Tour and travel guides	39	46	0.0	0.0	7	18.5	22
Tour guides and escorts	35	41	0.0	0.0	6	17.9	20
Travel guides	4	5	0.0	0.0	1	23.6	3
Other personal care and service workers	2 909	3 932	2.0	2.4	1 023	35.2	1 639
Childcare workers	1 282	1 544	0.9	0.9	262	20.4	666
Personal care aides	861	1 468	0.6	0.9	607	70.5	675
Recreation and fitness workers	591	715	0.4	0.4	125	21.1	219
Fitness trainers and aerobics instructors	251	312	0.2	0.2	60	24.0	101
Recreation workers	339	403	0.2	0.2	64	19.0	119
Residential advisors	73	91	0.1	0.1	18	25.0	46
Personal care and service workers, all other	102	114	0.1	0.1	11	10.9	33
Sales and Related	14 916	16 785	10.4	10.3	1 869	12.5	6 454
Supervisors of sales workers	2 042	2 196	1.4	1.3	153	7.5	637
First-line supervisors of retail sales workers	1 620	1 756	1.1	1.1	136	8.4	514
First-line supervisors of non-retail sales workers	423	440	0.3	0.3	17	4.0	124
Retail sales workers	8 268	9 306	5.8	5.7	1 038	12.6	3 998
Cashiers	3 383	3 630	2.4	2.2	248	7.3	1 785
Cashiers	3 363	3 613	2.4	2.2	250	7.4	1 776
Gaming change persons and booth cashiers	20	18	0.0	0.0	-2	-12.1	9
Counter and rental clerks and parts salespersons	623	707	0.4	0.4	84	13.4	254
Counter and rental clerks	420	471	0.3	0.3	51	12.2	147
Parts salespersons	204	237	0.1	0.1	33	16.0	107
Retail salespersons	4 262	4 968	3.0	3.0	707	16.6	1 959
Sales representatives, services	1 528	1 800	1.1	1.1	272	17.8	675
Advertising sales agents	160	181	0.1	0.1	21	13.0	70
Insurance sales agents	412	502	0.3	0.3	90	21.9	184
Securities, commodities, and financial services sales agents	312	360	0.2	0.2	48	15.2	134
Travel agents	83	91	0.1	0.1	8	10.0	17
Sales representatives, services, all other	561	667	0.4	0.4	105	18.8	270
Sales representatives, wholesale and manufacturing	1 830	2 119	1.3	1.3	289	15.8	720
Sales representatives, wholesale and manufacturing, technical and scientific products	400	466	0.3	0.3	66	16.4	160
Sales representatives, wholesale and manufacturing, except technical and scientific products	1 430	1 653	1.0	1.0	223	15.6	560
Other sales and related workers	1 247	1 364	0.9	0.8	117	9.4	424
Models, demonstrators, and product promoters	91	107	0.1	0.1	16	17.5	43
Demonstrators and product promoters	90	106	0.1	0.1	16	17.5	42
Models	1	2	0.0	0.0	0	14.5	1
Real estate brokers and sales agents	466	519	0.3	0.3	53	11.3	157
Real estate brokers	99	106	0.1	0.1	8	7.6	30
Real estate sales agents	368	413	0.3	0.3	45	12.2	128
Sales engineers	66	76	0.0	0.0	10	14.4	32
Telemarketers	291	312	0.2	0.2	22	7.4	84
Door-to-door sales workers, news and street vendors, and related workers	154	142	0.1	0.1	-12	-7.5	34
Sales and related workers, all other	179	208	0.1	0.1	29	16.0	74

Note: Data may not sum to totals or 100 percent due to rounding.

[1]Total job openings represent the sum of employment increases and net replacements. If employment change is negative, job openings due to growth are zero and total job openings equal net replacements.

Table 4-8. Employment, by Occupation, 2010 and Projected 2020—*Continued*

(Numbers in thousands, percent.)

Occupation	Employment				Change, 2010–2020		Total job openings due to growth and net replacements, 2010–2020[1]
	Number		Percent distribution		Number	Percent	
	2010	2020	2010	2020			
Office and Administrative Support	22 603	24 938	15.8	15.2	2 336	10.3	7 450
Supervisors of office and administrative support workers	1 424	1 628	1.0	1.0	203	14.3	584
First-line supervisors of office and administrative support workers	1 424	1 628	1.0	1.0	203	14.3	584
Communications equipment operators	164	128	0.1	0.1	-36	-22.0	34
Switchboard operators, including answering service	143	109	0.1	0.1	-33	-23.3	28
Telephone operators	19	15	0.0	0.0	-3	-16.6	5
Communications equipment operators, all other	3	3	0.0	0.0	0	4.1	1
Financial clerks	3 645	4 097	2.5	2.5	453	12.4	1 133
Bill and account collectors	402	459	0.3	0.3	57	14.2	136
Billing and posting clerks	505	604	0.4	0.4	100	19.7	188
Bookkeeping, accounting, and auditing clerks	1 898	2 157	1.3	1.3	259	13.6	468
Gaming cage workers	16	14	0.0	0.0	-2	-12.7	3
Payroll and timekeeping clerks	187	214	0.1	0.1	27	14.6	66
Procurement clerks	77	81	0.1	0.0	4	5.7	36
Tellers	560	567	0.4	0.3	7	1.3	238
Information and record clerks	5 320	6 029	3.7	3.7	709	13.3	2 244
Brokerage clerks	58	61	0.0	0.0	3	5.9	20
Correspondence clerks	10	9	0.0	0.0	-1	-12.1	3
Court, municipal, and license clerks	130	140	0.1	0.1	10	8.0	47
Credit authorizers, checkers, and clerks	54	57	0.0	0.0	3	4.8	18
Customer service representatives	2 187	2 526	1.5	1.5	338	15.5	960
Eligibility interviewers, government programs	126	130	0.1	0.1	4	3.1	37
File clerks	185	176	0.1	0.1	-9	-4.8	49
Hotel, motel, and resort desk clerks	228	253	0.2	0.2	25	11.1	116
Interviewers, except eligibility and loan	214	250	0.1	0.2	37	17.3	80
Library assistants, clerical	116	128	0.1	0.1	12	10.3	64
Loan interviewers and clerks	183	177	0.1	0.1	-6	-3.1	34
New accounts clerks	68	69	0.0	0.0	1	2.0	20
Order clerks	212	228	0.1	0.1	16	7.4	75
Human resources assistants, except payroll and timekeeping	157	175	0.1	0.1	18	11.2	62
Receptionists and information clerks	1 049	1 297	0.7	0.8	249	23.7	566
Reservation and transportation ticket agents and travel clerks	124	132	0.1	0.1	7	5.8	31
Information and record clerks, all other	221	223	0.2	0.1	2	1.0	64
Material recording, scheduling, dispatching, and distributing workers	3 861	3 857	2.7	2.4	-5	-0.1	1 092
Cargo and freight agents	82	106	0.1	0.1	24	29.3	44
Couriers and messengers	116	131	0.1	0.1	15	12.6	43
Dispatchers	285	331	0.2	0.2	46	16.2	100
Police, fire, and ambulance dispatchers	100	112	0.1	0.1	12	11.7	31
Dispatchers, except police, fire, and ambulance	185	220	0.1	0.1	34	18.6	70
Meter readers, utilities	41	41	0.0	0.0	1	1.2	13
Postal service workers	524	386	0.4	0.2	-139	-26.4	126
Postal service clerks	66	34	0.0	0.0	-32	-48.2	16
Postal service mail carriers	317	279	0.2	0.2	-38	-12.0	103
Postal service mail sorters, processors, and processing machine operators	142	73	0.1	0.0	-69	-48.5	8
Production, planning, and expediting clerks	271	289	0.2	0.2	18	6.6	89
Shipping, receiving, and traffic clerks	688	690	0.5	0.4	2	0.3	177
Stock clerks and order fillers	1 787	1 808	1.2	1.1	21	1.2	465
Weighers, measurers, checkers, and samplers, recordkeeping	67	75	0.0	0.0	8	12.0	34
Secretaries and administrative assistants	4 010	4 503	2.8	2.8	493	12.3	1 031
Executive secretaries and executive administrative assistants	1 236	1 392	0.9	0.9	156	12.6	322
Legal secretaries	233	241	0.2	0.1	8	3.5	39
Medical secretaries	509	719	0.4	0.4	210	41.3	278
Secretaries and administrative assistants, except legal, medical, and executive	2 032	2 151	1.4	1.3	119	5.8	391
Other office and administrative support workers	4 178	4 696	2.9	2.9	518	12.4	1 333
Computer operators	86	79	0.1	0.0	-7	-8.6	8
Data entry and information processing workers	350	321	0.2	0.2	-29	-8.3	48
Data entry keyers	235	219	0.2	0.1	-16	-6.8	41
Word processors and typists	115	102	0.1	0.1	-13	-11.5	7
Desktop publishers	23	19	0.0	0.0	-3	-14.7	4
Insurance claims and policy processing clerks	248	270	0.2	0.2	22	8.7	96
Mail clerks and mail machine operators, except postal service	126	142	0.1	0.1	15	12.1	40
Office clerks, general	2 951	3 440	2.1	2.1	490	16.6	1 012
Office machine operators, except computer	70	63	0.0	0.0	-7	-9.7	20
Proofreaders and copy markers	14	15	0.0	0.0	1	4.8	3
Statistical assistants	17	18	0.0	0.0	1	6.0	4
Office and administrative support workers, all other	294	330	0.2	0.2	37	12.4	99
Farming, Fishing, and Forestry	972	953	0.7	0.6	-19	-2.0	291
Supervisors of farming, fishing, and forestry workers	47	46	0.0	0.0	-1	-1.5	14
First-line supervisors of farming, fishing, and forestry workers	47	46	0.0	0.0	-1	-1.5	14
Agricultural workers	826	806	0.6	0.5	-19	-2.3	249
Agricultural inspectors	19	20	0.0	0.0	0	1.5	6
Animal breeders	12	11	0.0	0.0	-1	-7.5	4
Graders and sorters, agricultural products	48	49	0.0	0.0	1	1.2	12
Miscellaneous agricultural workers	746	727	0.5	0.4	-19	-2.6	227
Fishing and hunting workers	33	31	0.0	0.0	-2	-6.2	9
Fishers and related fishing workers	32	30	0.0	0.0	-2	-6.3	9
Forest, conservation, and logging workers	67	69	0.0	0.0	2	3.6	19
Forest and conservation workers	14	14	0.0	0.0	0	1.0	4
Logging workers	53	56	0.0	0.0	2	4.3	15
Fallers	10	10	0.0	0.0	0	3.3	3
Logging equipment operators	35	36	0.0	0.0	1	3.7	10
Log graders and scalers	4	4	0.0	0.0	1	13.3	1
Logging workers, all other	5	5	0.0	0.0	0	3.0	1

Note: Data may not sum to totals or 100 percent due to rounding.

[1]Total job openings represent the sum of employment increases and net replacements. If employment change is negative, job openings due to growth are zero and total job openings equal net replacements.

Table 4-8. Employment, by Occupation, 2010 and Projected 2020—*Continued*

(Numbers in thousands, percent.)

Occupation	Employment				Change, 2010–2020		Total job openings due to growth and net replacements, 2010–2020[1]
	Number		Percent distribution		Number	Percent	
	2010	2020	2010	2020			
Construction and Extraction	6 328	7 735	4.4	4.7	1 407	22.2	2 760
Supervisors of construction and extraction workers	559	690	0.4	0.4	131	23.5	260
First-line supervisors of construction trades and extraction workers	559	690	0.4	0.4	131	23.5	260
Construction trades workers	4 865	5 961	3.4	3.6	1 096	22.5	2 085
Boilermakers	20	24	0.0	0.0	4	21.3	12
Brickmasons, blockmasons, and stonemasons	105	147	0.1	0.1	42	39.9	63
Brickmasons and blockmasons	89	125	0.1	0.1	36	40.5	55
Stonemasons	16	21	0.0	0.0	6	36.5	9
Carpenters	1 002	1 198	0.7	0.7	196	19.6	408
Carpet, floor, and tile installers and finishers	135	158	0.1	0.1	23	17.1	52
Carpet installers	48	52	0.0	0.0	5	10.4	15
Floor layers, except carpet, wood, and hard tiles	18	19	0.0	0.0	1	6.8	5
Floor sanders and finishers	11	13	0.0	0.0	2	18.2	4
Tile and marble setters	59	74	0.0	0.0	15	25.4	28
Cement masons, concrete finishers, and terrazzo workers	148	199	0.1	0.1	51	34.1	74
Cement masons and concrete finishers	145	195	0.1	0.1	50	34.6	73
Terrazzo workers and finishers	4	4	0.0	0.0	1	15.0	1
Construction laborers	999	1 211	0.7	0.7	212	21.3	292
Construction equipment operators	405	500	0.3	0.3	95	23.4	187
Paving, surfacing, and tamping equipment operators	52	63	0.0	0.0	11	22.1	22
Pile-driver operators	4	6	0.0	0.0	2	36.0	2
Operating engineers and other construction equipment operators	349	431	0.2	0.3	82	23.5	163
Drywall installers, ceiling tile installers, and tapers	130	167	0.1	0.1	37	28.8	73
Drywall and ceiling tile installers	107	136	0.1	0.1	29	27.5	59
Tapers	23	31	0.0	0.0	8	34.7	14
Electricians	577	711	0.4	0.4	134	23.2	289
Glaziers	42	60	0.0	0.0	18	42.4	33
Insulation workers	51	66	0.0	0.0	14	28.0	35
Insulation workers, floor, ceiling, and wall	23	29	0.0	0.0	5	23.4	15
Insulation workers, mechanical	28	37	0.0	0.0	9	31.8	20
Painters and paperhangers	400	473	0.3	0.3	73	18.3	159
Painters, construction and maintenance	391	463	0.3	0.3	72	18.5	157
Paperhangers	9	10	0.0	0.0	1	10.3	2
Pipelayers, plumbers, pipefitters, and steamfitters	473	594	0.3	0.4	121	25.6	258
Pipelayers	53	67	0.0	0.0	13	25.3	29
Plumbers, pipefitters, and steamfitters	420	528	0.3	0.3	108	25.6	229
Plasterers and stucco masons	28	33	0.0	0.0	5	17.1	11
Reinforcing iron and rebar workers	19	28	0.0	0.0	9	48.6	13
Roofers	137	161	0.1	0.1	24	17.8	53
Sheet metal workers	136	160	0.1	0.1	24	17.5	47
Structural iron and steel workers	60	73	0.0	0.0	13	21.9	25
Helpers, Construction trades	251	353	0.2	0.2	102	40.5	169
Helpers—brickmasons, blockmasons, stonemasons, and tile and marble setters	29	47	0.0	0.0	18	60.1	25
Helpers—carpenters	47	72	0.0	0.0	26	55.7	38
Helpers—electricians	74	96	0.1	0.1	23	30.6	42
Helpers—painters, paperhangers, plasterers, and stucco masons	12	15	0.0	0.0	3	22.0	6
Helpers—pipelayers, plumbers, pipefitters, and steamfitters	58	84	0.0	0.1	26	45.4	42
Helpers—roofers	13	14	0.0	0.0	1	9.6	5
Helpers, construction trades, all other	20	25	0.0	0.0	6	28.7	11
Other construction and related workers	428	491	0.3	0.3	63	14.8	184
Construction and building inspectors	102	121	0.1	0.1	18	17.9	49
Elevator installers and repairers	20	22	0.0	0.0	2	11.3	8
Fence erectors	32	40	0.0	0.0	8	23.8	16
Hazardous materials removal workers	38	47	0.0	0.0	9	23.1	19
Highway maintenance workers	149	161	0.1	0.1	12	8.2	51
Rail-track laying and maintenance equipment operators	15	15	0.0	0.0	0	1.9	4
Septic tank servicers and sewer pipe cleaners	25	31	0.0	0.0	5	20.7	12
Miscellaneous construction and related workers	1	2	0.0	0.0	0	33.1	1
Segmental pavers	1	2	0.0	0.0	0	33.1	1
Construction and related workers, all other	45	53	0.0	0.0	8	17.9	23
Extraction workers	225	241	0.2	0.1	16	6.9	63
Derrick, rotary drill, and service unit operators, oil, gas, and mining	82	89	0.1	0.1	7	8.4	24
Derrick operators, oil and gas	19	21	0.0	0.0	2	9.3	6
Rotary drill operators, oil and gas	23	24	0.0	0.0	2	7.2	6
Service unit operators, oil, gas, and mining	41	44	0.0	0.0	4	8.6	12
Earth drillers, except oil and gas	18	20	0.0	0.0	3	13.8	6
Explosives workers, ordnance handling experts, and blasters	7	7	0.0	0.0	0	0.2	1
Mining machine operators	24	25	0.0	0.0	0	0.7	5
Continuous mining machine operators	14	14	0.0	0.0	0	0.4	3
Mine cutting and channeling machine operators	7	7	0.0	0.0	0	2.1	2
Mining machine operators, all other	3	3	0.0	0.0	0	-1.1	1
Rock splitters, quarry	4	4	0.0	0.0	0	11.7	1
Roof bolters, mining	6	6	0.0	0.0	0	2.0	1
Roustabouts, oil and gas	53	57	0.0	0.0	4	8.3	16
Helpers—extraction workers	25	26	0.0	0.0	1	5.5	7
Extraction workers, all other	8	7	0.0	0.0	0	-2.9	2
Installation, Maintenance, and Repair	5 429	6 229	3.8	3.8	800	14.7	2 026
Supervisors of installation, maintenance, and repair workers	431	483	0.3	0.3	51	11.9	165
First-line supervisors of mechanics, installers, and repairers	431	483	0.3	0.3	51	11.9	165
Electrical and electronic equipment mechanics, installers, and repairers	611	683	0.4	0.4	72	11.8	201
Computer, automated teller, and office machine repairers	146	156	0.1	0.1	10	6.5	45
Radio and telecommunications equipment installers and repairers	205	236	0.1	0.1	31	15.3	64
Radio, cellular, and tower equipment installers and repairs	10	13	0.0	0.0	3	29.4	5
Telecommunications equipment installers and repairers, except line installers	195	223	0.1	0.1	28	14.6	59

Note: Data may not sum to totals or 100 percent due to rounding.

[1]Total job openings represent the sum of employment increases and net replacements. If employment change is negative, job openings due to growth are zero and total job openings equal net replacements.

Table 4-8. Employment, by Occupation, 2010 and Projected 2020—*Continued*

(Numbers in thousands, percent.)

Occupation	Employment				Change, 2010–2020		Total job openings due to growth and net replacements, 2010–2020[1]
	Number		Percent distribution		Number	Percent	
	2010	2020	2010	2020			
Installation, Maintenance, and Repair—*Continued*							
Miscellaneous electrical and electronic equipment mechanics, installers, and repairers	260	291	0.2	0.2	31	11.9	92
Avionics technicians	19	20	0.0	0.0	1	6.9	6
Electric motor, power tool, and related repairers	20	21	0.0	0.0	1	4.9	3
Electrical and electronics installers and repairers, transportation equipment	13	13	0.0	0.0	0	2.1	3
Electrical and electronics repairers, commercial and industrial equipment	69	70	0.0	0.0	1	1.1	18
Electrical and electronics repairers, powerhouse, substation, and relay	23	25	0.0	0.0	1	4.9	7
Electronic equipment installers and repairers, motor vehicles	16	16	0.0	0.0	0	2.8	4
Electronic home entertainment equipment installers and repairers	37	42	0.0	0.0	5	13.9	14
Security and fire alarm systems installers	64	85	0.0	0.1	21	33.0	37
Vehicle and mobile equipment mechanics, installers, and repairers	1 627	1 894	1.1	1.2	267	16.4	681
Aircraft mechanics and service technicians	124	132	0.1	0.1	8	6.3	45
Automotive technicians and repairers	894	1 052	0.6	0.6	158	17.6	386
Automotive body and related repairers	153	181	0.1	0.1	28	18.4	65
Automotive glass installers and repairers	18	23	0.0	0.0	5	25.0	9
Automotive service technicians and mechanics	723	848	0.5	0.5	125	17.2	312
Bus and truck mechanics and diesel engine specialists	242	277	0.2	0.2	35	14.5	88
Heavy vehicle and mobile equipment service technicians and mechanics	179	208	0.1	0.1	28	15.8	75
Farm equipment mechanics and service technicians	33	37	0.0	0.0	4	13.4	13
Mobile heavy equipment mechanics, except engines	125	145	0.1	0.1	20	16.2	53
Rail car repairers	22	25	0.0	0.0	4	16.9	9
Small engine mechanics	69	83	0.0	0.1	14	20.7	32
Motorboat mechanics and service technicians	21	25	0.0	0.0	4	20.6	10
Motorcycle mechanics	18	22	0.0	0.0	4	23.6	9
Outdoor power equipment and other small engine mechanics	30	36	0.0	0.0	6	19.1	14
Miscellaneous vehicle and mobile equipment mechanics, installers, and repairers	119	143	0.1	0.1	24	20.4	55
Bicycle repairers	10	14	0.0	0.0	4	37.6	6
Recreational vehicle service technicians	10	12	0.0	0.0	2	22.3	5
Tire repairers and changers	99	117	0.1	0.1	18	18.5	44
Other installation, maintenance, and repair occupations	2 759	3 169	1.9	1.9	410	14.8	979
Control and valve installers and repairers	57	60	0.0	0.0	3	5.5	14
Mechanical door repairers	13	16	0.0	0.0	3	24.6	6
Control and valve installers and repairers, except mechanical door	44	44	0.0	0.0	0	-0.1	8
Heating, air conditioning, and refrigeration mechanics and installers	268	358	0.2	0.2	90	33.7	138
Home appliance repairers	48	51	0.0	0.0	3	6.5	12
Industrial machinery installation, repair, and maintenance workers	396	461	0.3	0.3	65	16.4	143
Industrial machinery mechanics	287	349	0.2	0.2	62	21.6	117
Maintenance workers, machinery	70	74	0.0	0.0	5	6.5	17
Millwrights	37	35	0.0	0.0	-2	-4.8	8
Refractory materials repairers, except brickmasons	2	2	0.0	0.0	0	8.6	1
Line installers and repairers	269	305	0.2	0.2	36	13.5	104
Electrical power-line installers and repairers	108	123	0.1	0.1	14	13.2	53
Telecommunications line installers and repairers	161	183	0.1	0.1	22	13.6	51
Precision instrument and equipment repairers	65	79	0.0	0.0	14	21.4	32
Camera and photographic equipment repairers	3	4	0.0	0.0	0	10.3	1
Medical equipment repairers	38	50	0.0	0.0	12	31.5	22
Musical instrument repairers and tuners	6	6	0.0	0.0	0	1.9	2
Watch repairers	3	3	0.0	0.0	0	5.9	1
Precision instrument and equipment repairers, all other	15	16	0.0	0.0	1	9.3	6
Maintenance and repair workers, general	1 289	1 431	0.9	0.9	142	11.0	379
Miscellaneous installation, maintenance, and repair workers	225	264	0.2	0.2	39	17.5	115
Coin, vending, and amusement machine servicers and repairers	39	48	0.0	0.0	9	22.1	16
Commercial divers	4	4	0.0	0.0	1	16.2	1
Fabric menders, except garment	1	1	0.0	0.0	0	-6.3	0
Locksmiths and safe repairers	26	30	0.0	0.0	5	17.7	9
Manufactured building and mobile home installers	8	9	0.0	0.0	1	13.9	2
Riggers	15	17	0.0	0.0	2	10.6	4
Signal and track switch repairers	7	7	0.0	0.0	0	-2.0	1
Helpers–installation, maintenance, and repair workers	125	148	0.1	0.1	23	18.4	80
Installation, maintenance, and repair workers, all other	144	160	0.1	0.1	17	11.7	43
Production	8 594	8 951	6.0	5.5	357	4.2	2 231
Supervisors of production workers	589	599	0.4	0.4	11	1.9	88
First-line supervisors of production and operating workers	589	599	0.4	0.4	11	1.9	88
Assemblers and fabricators	1 627	1 715	1.1	1.0	88	5.4	409
Aircraft structure, surfaces, rigging, and systems assemblers	36	42	0.0	0.0	5	14.3	12
Electrical, electronics, and electromechanical assemblers	247	235	0.2	0.1	-12	-5.0	36
Coil winders, tapers, and finishers	15	13	0.0	0.0	-2	-15.9	2
Electrical and electronic equipment assemblers	183	172	0.1	0.1	-10	-5.7	26
Electromechanical equipment assemblers	49	50	0.0	0.0	0	0.8	8
Engine and other machine assemblers	34	36	0.0	0.0	2	5.3	8
Structural metal fabricators and fitters	81	94	0.1	0.1	13	15.7	28
Miscellaneous assemblers and fabricators	1 228	1 309	0.9	0.8	81	6.6	324
Fiberglass laminators and fabricators	19	19	0.0	0.0	0	-1.8	4
Team assemblers	953	1 005	0.7	0.6	52	5.5	241
Timing device assemblers and adjusters	2	2	0.0	0.0	0	1.2	0
Assemblers and fabricators, all other	255	283	0.2	0.2	29	11.3	79
Food processing workers	681	732	0.5	0.4	51	7.4	247
Bakers	150	153	0.1	0.1	4	2.3	47
Butchers and other meat, poultry, and fish processing workers	382	425	0.3	0.3	43	11.3	154
Butchers and meat cutters	127	137	0.1	0.1	10	7.9	47
Meat, poultry, and fish cutters and trimmers	166	192	0.1	0.1	26	15.5	74
Slaughterers and meat packers	89	97	0.1	0.1	7	8.3	33
Miscellaneous food processing workers	149	153	0.1	0.1	4	2.6	46
Food and tobacco roasting, baking, and drying machine operators and tenders	18	20	0.0	0.0	2	8.1	7
Food batchmakers	99	99	0.1	0.1	1	0.7	28
Food cooking machine operators and tenders	32	34	0.0	0.0	2	5.1	11
Metal workers and plastic workers	1 764	1 903	1.2	1.2	139	7.9	482

Note: Data may not sum to totals or 100 percent due to rounding.

[1]Total job openings represent the sum of employment increases and net replacements. If employment change is negative, job openings due to growth are zero and total job openings equal net replacements.

Table 4-8. Employment, by Occupation, 2010 and Projected 2020—*Continued*

(Numbers in thousands, percent.)

Occupation	Employment				Change, 2010–2020		Total job openings due to growth and net replacements, 2010–2020[1]
	Number		Percent distribution		Number	Percent	
	2010	2020	2010	2020			
Production—*Continued*							
Computer control programmers and operators	142	167	0.1	0.1	26	18.2	53
Computer-controlled machine tool operators, metal and plastic	125	149	0.1	0.1	24	19.2	48
Computer numerically controlled machine tool programmers, metal and plastic	17	18	0.0	0.0	2	10.8	5
Forming machine setters, operators, and tenders, metal and plastic	131	141	0.1	0.1	10	7.4	35
Extruding and drawing machine setters, operators, and tenders, metal and plastic	77	83	0.1	0.1	6	8.3	21
Forging machine setters, operators, and tenders, metal and plastic	23	23	0.0	0.0	1	3.0	5
Rolling machine setters, operators, and tenders, metal and plastic	32	35	0.0	0.0	3	8.2	9
Machine tool cutting setters, operators, and tenders, metal and plastic	342	345	0.2	0.2	3	0.8	52
Cutting, punching, and press machine setters, operators, and tenders, metal and plastic	184	189	0.1	0.1	5	2.5	18
Drilling and boring machine tool setters, operators, and tenders, metal and plastic	23	21	0.0	0.0	-2	-7.0	1
Grinding, lapping, polishing, and buffing machine tool setters, operators, and tenders, metal and plastic	73	74	0.1	0.0	1	1.4	12
Lathe and turning machine tool setters, operators, and tenders, metal and plastic	42	40	0.0	0.0	-2	-4.7	15
Milling and planing machine setters, operators, and tenders, metal and plastic	21	22	0.0	0.0	1	3.6	5
Machinists	370	402	0.3	0.2	32	8.5	100
Metal furnace operators, tenders, pourers, and casters	27	30	0.0	0.0	3	11.3	8
Metal-refining furnace operators and tenders	16	18	0.0	0.0	3	16.3	6
Pourers and casters, metal	12	12	0.0	0.0	1	4.5	3
Model makers and patternmakers, metal and plastic	11	10	0.0	0.0	-1	-5.5	1
Model makers, metal and plastic	6	6	0.0	0.0	-1	-8.2	0
Patternmakers, metal and plastic	5	4	0.0	0.0	0	-1.9	0
Molders and molding machine setters, operators, and tenders, metal and plastic	125	132	0.1	0.1	7	5.6	28
Foundry mold and coremakers	10	11	0.0	0.0	1	11.5	3
Molding, coremaking, and casting machine setters, operators, and tenders, metal and plastic	115	121	0.1	0.1	6	5.1	25
Multiple machine tool setters, operators, and tenders, metal and plastic	70	73	0.0	0.0	3	3.8	16
Tool and die makers	68	66	0.0	0.0	-2	-2.3	4
Welding, soldering, and brazing workers	379	432	0.3	0.3	53	14.1	155
Welders, cutters, solderers, and brazers	337	388	0.2	0.2	51	15.0	141
Welding, soldering, and brazing machine setters, operators, and tenders	42	44	0.0	0.0	3	6.6	14
Miscellaneous metal workers and plastic workers	99	104	0.1	0.1	6	5.7	33
Heat treating equipment setters, operators, and tenders, metal and plastic	19	19	0.0	0.0	0	0.8	15
Layout workers, metal and plastic	9	10	0.0	0.0	1	13.7	3
Plating and coating machine setters, operators, and tenders, metal and plastic	31	34	0.0	0.0	3	9.3	10
Tool grinders, filers, and sharpeners	13	14	0.0	0.0	1	7.0	2
Metal workers and plastic workers, all other	27	27	0.0	0.0	0	1.6	3
Printing workers	305	292	0.2	0.2	-13	-4.2	69
Prepress technicians and workers	51	43	0.0	0.0	-8	-15.9	12
Printing press operators	200	197	0.1	0.1	-3	-1.5	39
Print binding and finishing workers	54	52	0.0	0.0	-2	-3.1	18
Textile, apparel, and furnishings workers	682	616	0.5	0.4	-66	-9.6	98
Laundry and dry-cleaning workers	225	227	0.2	0.1	2	0.7	44
Pressers, textile, garment, and related materials	58	51	0.0	0.0	-7	-11.8	4
Sewing machine operators	163	121	0.1	0.1	-42	-25.8	9
Shoe and leather workers	13	10	0.0	0.0	-3	-23.1	4
Shoe and leather workers and repairers	10	9	0.0	0.0	-1	-13.6	3
Shoe machine operators and tenders	3	2	0.0	0.0	-2	-53.4	0
Tailors, dressmakers, and sewers	58	58	0.0	0.0	0	0.6	9
Sewers, hand	10	10	0.0	0.0	-1	-5.4	1
Tailors, dressmakers, and custom sewers	47	48	0.0	0.0	1	2.0	7
Textile machine setters, operators, and tenders	80	67	0.1	0.0	-13	-16.2	10
Textile bleaching and dyeing machine operators and tenders	14	12	0.0	0.0	-2	-15.2	2
Textile cutting machine setters, operators, and tenders	15	12	0.0	0.0	-3	-21.8	4
Textile knitting and weaving machine setters, operators, and tenders	23	18	0.0	0.0	-4	-18.2	1
Textile winding, twisting, and drawing out machine setters, operators, and tenders	29	25	0.0	0.0	-4	-12.4	3
Miscellaneous textile, apparel, and furnishings workers	84	82	0.1	0.1	-2	-2.9	18
Extruding and forming machine setters, operators, and tenders, synthetic and glass fibers	15	14	0.0	0.0	0	-1.6	2
Fabric and apparel patternmakers	6	4	0.0	0.0	-2	-35.6	1
Upholsterers	47	49	0.0	0.0	2	4.2	14
Textile, apparel, and furnishings workers, all other	17	15	0.0	0.0	-2	-12.1	1
Woodworkers	235	275	0.2	0.2	40	17.1	87
Cabinetmakers and bench carpenters	97	113	0.1	0.1	16	16.8	40
Furniture finishers	21	22	0.0	0.0	1	5.5	6
Model makers and patternmakers, wood	3	3	0.0	0.0	0	8.3	1
Model makers, wood	2	2	0.0	0.0	0	11.3	1
Patternmakers, wood	1	1	0.0	0.0	0	4.3	0
Woodworking machine setters, operators, and tenders	100	122	0.1	0.1	22	21.9	36
Sawing machine setters, operators, and tenders, wood	39	49	0.0	0.0	10	24.7	18
Woodworking machine setters, operators, and tenders, except sawing	61	73	0.0	0.0	12	20.2	17
Woodworkers, all other	15	16	0.0	0.0	1	4.4	4
Plant and system operators	317	318	0.2	0.2	2	0.5	109
Power plant operators, distributors, and dispatchers	56	55	0.0	0.0	-1	-2.0	20
Nuclear power reactor operators	5	5	0.0	0.0	0	3.6	2
Power distributors and dispatchers	10	10	0.0	0.0	0	-3.0	4
Power plant operators	41	40	0.0	0.0	-1	-2.5	14
Stationary engineers and boiler operators	38	40	0.0	0.0	2	6.2	11
Water and wastewater treatment plant and system operators	111	124	0.1	0.1	13	11.6	42
Miscellaneous plant and system operators	113	100	0.1	0.1	-12	-11.0	37
Chemical plant and system operators	43	38	0.0	0.0	-5	-12.2	14
Gas plant operators	14	13	0.0	0.0	-1	-6.5	5
Petroleum pump system operators, refinery operators, and gaugers	44	38	0.0	0.0	-6	-14.0	14
Plant and system operators, all other	11	11	0.0	0.0	0	-0.1	4

Note: Data may not sum to totals or 100 percent due to rounding.

[1]Total job openings represent the sum of employment increases and net replacements. If employment change is negative, job openings due to growth are zero and total job openings equal net replacements.

Table 4-8. Employment, by Occupation, 2010 and Projected 2020—*Continued*

(Numbers in thousands, percent.)

Occupation	Employment Number 2010	Employment Number 2020	Percent distribution 2010	Percent distribution 2020	Change, 2010–2020 Number	Change, 2010–2020 Percent	Total job openings due to growth and net replacements, 2010–2020[1]
Production—*Continued*							
Other production occupations	2 396	2 500	1.7	1.5	104	4.3	642
Chemical processing machine setters, operators, and tenders	86	84	0.1	0.1	-2	-1.9	16
Chemical equipment operators and tenders	47	44	0.0	0.0	-4	-7.5	8
Separating, filtering, clarifying, precipitating, and still machine setters, operators, and tenders	38	40	0.0	0.0	2	5.1	8
Crushing, grinding, polishing, mixing, and blending workers	186	187	0.1	0.1	1	0.6	59
Crushing, grinding, and polishing machine setters, operators, and tenders	33	35	0.0	0.0	2	5.1	12
Grinding and polishing workers, hand	28	30	0.0	0.0	2	7.7	11
Mixing and blending machine setters, operators, and tenders	125	122	0.1	0.1	-3	-2.2	37
Cutting workers	79	78	0.1	0.0	-1	-1.4	17
Cutters and trimmers, hand	17	16	0.0	0.0	-1	-5.7	4
Cutting and slicing machine setters, operators, and tenders	61	61	0.0	0.0	0	-0.1	14
Extruding, forming, pressing, and compacting machine setters, operators, and tenders	65	67	0.0	0.0	1	1.9	17
Furnace, kiln, oven, drier, and kettle operators and tenders	20	21	0.0	0.0	0	1.1	6
Inspectors, testers, sorters, samplers, and weighers	416	449	0.3	0.3	33	8.0	124
Jewelers and precious stone and metal workers	39	37	0.0	0.0	-2	-5.2	9
Medical, dental, and ophthalmic laboratory technicians	85	90	0.1	0.1	5	5.5	31
Dental laboratory technicians	41	41	0.0	0.0	0	0.8	13
Medical appliance technicians	14	15	0.0	0.0	1	3.7	5
Ophthalmic laboratory technicians	30	34	0.0	0.0	4	12.8	13
Packaging and filling machine operators and tenders	337	350	0.2	0.2	13	3.8	68
Painting workers	155	169	0.1	0.1	14	8.9	47
Coating, painting, and spraying machine setters, operators, and tenders	84	89	0.1	0.1	5	6.1	23
Painters, transportation equipment	46	51	0.0	0.0	4	9.4	14
Painting, coating, and decorating workers	25	30	0.0	0.0	4	17.2	10
Semiconductor processors	21	17	0.0	0.0	-4	-17.9	5
Photographic process workers and processing machine operators	59	54	0.0	0.0	-5	-7.7	15
Miscellaneous production workers	597	630	0.4	0.4	32	5.4	145
Adhesive bonding machine operators and tenders	15	16	0.0	0.0	1	4.5	3
Cleaning, washing, and metal pickling equipment operators and tenders	18	18	0.0	0.0	0	1.1	4
Cooling and freezing equipment operators and tenders	9	9	0.0	0.0	0	1.0	2
Etchers and engravers	11	11	0.0	0.0	0	-2.7	1
Molders, shapers, and casters, except metal and plastic	43	47	0.0	0.0	4	8.0	19
Paper goods machine setters, operators, and tenders	91	85	0.1	0.1	-6	-6.1	9
Tire builders	16	15	0.0	0.0	-1	-5.7	7
Helpers–production workers	395	430	0.3	0.3	34	8.7	100
Production workers, all other	250	268	0.2	0.2	18	7.1	83
Transportation and Material Moving	9 005	10 333	6.3	6.3	1 329	14.8	3 597
Supervisors of transportation and material moving workers	372	448	0.3	0.3	75	20.2	152
Aircraft cargo handling supervisors	6	8	0.0	0.0	1	20.3	3
First-line supervisors of helpers, laborers, and material movers, hand	167	213	0.1	0.1	46	27.2	80
First-line supervisors of transportation and material-moving machine and vehicle operators	199	227	0.1	0.1	28	14.3	69
Air transportation workers	228	239	0.2	0.1	11	4.9	81
Aircraft pilots and flight engineers	104	115	0.1	0.1	12	11.1	51
Airline pilots, copilots, and flight engineers	71	75	0.0	0.0	5	6.4	31
Commercial pilots	33	40	0.0	0.0	7	21.2	19
Air traffic controllers and airfield operations specialists	34	34	0.0	0.0	0	-0.6	13
Air traffic controllers	27	26	0.0	0.0	-1	-2.9	10
Airfield operations specialists	7	8	0.0	0.0	1	8.4	3
Flight attendants	91	90	0.1	0.1	0	-0.2	17
Motor vehicle operators	3 839	4 480	2.7	2.7	641	16.7	1 383
Ambulance drivers and attendants, except emergency medical technicians	20	26	0.0	0.0	6	32.1	10
Bus drivers	647	730	0.5	0.4	83	12.8	208
Bus drivers, transit and intercity	186	214	0.1	0.1	28	14.8	64
Bus drivers, school or special client	461	516	0.3	0.3	56	12.0	145
Driver/sales workers and truck drivers	2 867	3 365	2.0	2.1	498	17.4	1 068
Driver/sales workers	407	449	0.3	0.3	42	10.3	123
Heavy and tractor-trailer truck drivers	1 605	1 935	1.1	1.2	330	20.6	649
Light truck or delivery services drivers	856	982	0.6	0.6	126	14.7	296
Taxi drivers and chauffeurs	240	287	0.2	0.2	47	19.6	77
Motor vehicle operators, all other	65	72	0.0	0.0	7	11.1	20
Rail transportation workers	118	121	0.1	0.1	3	2.7	43
Locomotive engineers and operators	45	47	0.0	0.0	1	3.2	18
Locomotive engineers	39	40	0.0	0.0	2	4.4	16
Locomotive firers	1	1	0.0	0.0	0	-5.1	0
Rail yard engineers, dinkey operators, and hostlers	6	5	0.0	0.0	0	-3.6	2
Railroad brake, signal, and switch operators	22	21	0.0	0.0	-1	-4.2	7
Railroad conductors and yardmasters	41	43	0.0	0.0	2	4.7	14
Subway and streetcar operators	7	7	0.0	0.0	1	9.8	3
Rail transportation workers, all other	3	3	0.0	0.0	0	1.3	1
Water transportation workers	83	99	0.1	0.1	17	20.3	50
Sailors and marine oilers	33	41	0.0	0.0	7	21.3	22
Ship and boat captains and operators	39	47	0.0	0.0	8	19.9	22
Captains, mates, and pilots of water vessels	36	43	0.0	0.0	7	20.4	21
Motorboat operators	3	4	0.0	0.0	1	14.9	2
Ship engineers	10	12	0.0	0.0	2	18.0	6
Other transportation workers	308	336	0.2	0.2	29	9.4	121
Bridge and lock tenders	4	3	0.0	0.0	0	-1.1	1
Parking lot attendants	125	123	0.1	0.1	-2	-1.7	37
Automotive and watercraft service attendants	86	106	0.1	0.1	19	22.2	48
Traffic technicians	7	8	0.0	0.0	1	11.2	3
Transportation inspectors	27	31	0.0	0.0	4	14.4	11
Transportation attendants, except flight attendants	25	28	0.0	0.0	3	11.1	8
Transportation workers, all other	33	38	0.0	0.0	4	13.2	14

Note: Data may not sum to totals or 100 percent due to rounding.

[1] Total job openings represent the sum of employment increases and net replacements. If employment change is negative, job openings due to growth are zero and total job openings equal net replacements.

Table 4-8. Employment, by Occupation, 2010 and Projected 2020—*Continued*

(Numbers in thousands, percent.)

Occupation	Employment				Change, 2010–2020		Total job openings due to growth and net replacements, 2010–2020[1]
	Number		Percent distribution		Number	Percent	
	2010	2020	2010	2020			
Transportation and Material Moving—*Continued*							
Material moving workers	4 058	4 611	2.8	2.8	553	13.6	1 767
Conveyor operators and tenders	36	41	0.0	0.0	4	11.5	15
Crane and tower operators	40	46	0.0	0.0	6	15.7	17
Dredge, excavating, and loading machine operators	68	78	0.0	0.0	11	16.1	31
Dredge operators	2	2	0.0	0.0	0	14.8	1
Excavating and loading machine and dragline operators	62	72	0.0	0.0	11	17.3	29
Loading machine operators, underground mining	4	4	0.0	0.0	0	-2.4	1
Hoist and winch operators	3	3	0.0	0.0	0	6.5	1
Industrial truck and tractor operators	522	584	0.4	0.4	62	11.8	210
Laborers and material movers, hand	3 176	3 613	2.2	2.2	437	13.8	1 403
Cleaners of vehicles and equipment	311	371	0.2	0.2	60	19.4	152
Laborers and freight, stock, and material movers, hand	2 068	2 387	1.4	1.5	319	15.4	980
Machine feeders and offbearers	119	120	0.1	0.1	0	0.1	19
Packers and packagers, hand	677	735	0.5	0.4	58	8.6	252
Pumping station operators	30	31	0.0	0.0	1	2.1	10
Gas compressor and gas pumping station operators	5	4	0.0	0.0	-1	-10.1	1
Pump operators, except wellhead pumpers	11	11	0.0	0.0	0	3.7	4
Wellhead pumpers	15	16	0.0	0.0	1	4.6	5
Refuse and recyclable material collectors	140	168	0.1	0.1	28	20.2	70
Mine shuttle car operators	3	3	0.0	0.0	0	-6.2	1
Tank car, truck, and ship loaders	10	11	0.0	0.0	0	2.1	3
Material moving workers, all other	30	33	0.0	0.0	3	11.4	6

Note: Data may not sum to totals or 100 percent due to rounding.

[1]Total job openings represent the sum of employment increases and net replacements. If employment change is negative, job openings due to growth are zero and total job openings equal net replacements.

Table 4-9. Employment and Total Job Openings by Education, Work Experience, and On-the-Job Training Category, 2010 and Projected 2020

(Numbers in thousands, percent.)

Education, work experience, and on-the-job training	Employment				Change, 2010–2020		Total job openings due to growth and replacement needs, 2010–2020[1]	
	Number		Percent distribution		Number	Percent	Number	Percent distribution
	2010	2020	2010	2020				
TOTAL, ALL OCCUPATIONS	143 068.2	163 537.1	100.0	100.0	20 468.9	14.3	54 787.4	100.0
Typical Education Needed for Entry								
Doctoral or professional degree	4 409.7	5 286.3	3.1	3.2	876.6	19.9	1 701.8	3.1
Master's degree	1 986.0	2 417.2	1.4	1.5	431.2	21.7	903.9	1.6
Bachelor's degree	22 171.1	25 827.2	15.5	15.8	3 656.1	16.5	8 562.4	15.6
Associate's degree	7 994.6	9 434.6	5.6	5.8	1 440.0	18.0	2 941.0	5.4
Postsecondary non-degree award	6 524.0	7 624.9	4.6	4.7	1 100.9	16.9	2 389.6	4.4
Some college, no degree	811.6	953.8	0.6	0.6	142.2	17.5	362.0	0.7
High school diploma or equivalent	62 089.6	69 665.7	43.4	42.6	7 576.1	12.2	21 745.9	39.7
Less than high school	37 081.7	42 327.4	25.9	25.9	5 245.7	14.1	16 180.8	29.5
Work Experience in a Related Occupation[2]								
More than 5 years	4 612.4	4 956.0	3.2	3.0	343.6	7.4	1 368.5	2.5
1 to 5 years	17 103.0	19 078.2	12.0	11.7	1 975.2	11.5	5 638.7	10.3
Less than 1 year	3 129.6	3 535.2	2.2	2.2	405.6	13.0	1 125.2	2.1
None	118 223.3	135 967.7	82.6	83.1	17 744.5	15.0	46 654.9	85.2
Typical On-the-Job Training								
Internship/residency	5 374.2	6 271.5	3.8	3.8	897.3	16.7	2 193.6	4.0
Apprenticeship	2 539.0	3 109.2	1.8	1.9	570.2	22.5	1 183.0	2.2
Long-term	7 039.0	7 920.5	4.9	4.8	881.5	12.5	2 545.5	4.6
Moderate-term	25 007.0	28 244.5	17.5	17.3	3 237.5	12.9	8 682.0	15.8
Short-term	58 171.0	66 040.0	40.7	40.4	7 869.0	13.5	23 767.8	43.4
None	44 937.9	51 951.3	31.4	31.8	7 013.4	15.6	16 415.5	30.0

[1]Total job openings represent the sum of employment increases and replacement needs. If employment change is negative, then job openings due to growth are zero and total job openings equals replacements.
[2]Indicates if work experience in a related occupation is commonly considered necessary by employers for entry, or is a commonly accepted subtitute for formal types of training.

Chapter Five

PRODUCTIVITY AND COSTS

PRODUCTIVITY AND COSTS

HIGHLIGHTS

This chapter covers two kinds of productivity measures produced by the Bureau of Labor Statistics (BLS): output per hour (or labor productivity) and multifactor productivity. Multifactor productivity is designed to combine the joint influence of technological change, efficiency improvements, returns to scale, and other factors on economic growth.

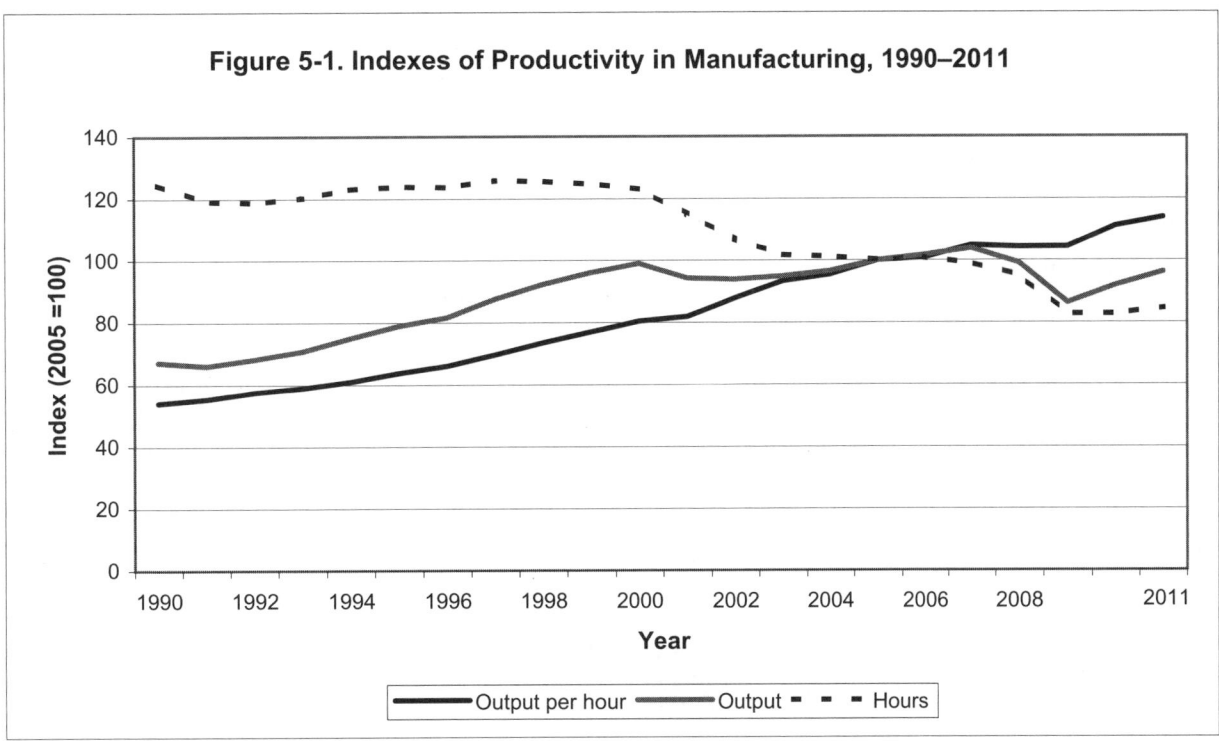

Figure 5-1. Indexes of Productivity in Manufacturing, 1990–2011

In 2011, labor productivity in manufacturing grew 2.4 percent as output grew 4.8 percent and hours grew 2.3 percent. Labor productivity also grew in business and nonfinancial corporations sectors. (See Table 5-1.)

OTHER HIGHLIGHTS:

- Employment and hours increased in 2011 in the manufacturing, business, and nonfinancial sectors after showing sharp declines just two years earlier in 2009. (See Table 5-1.)

- Labor productivity increased 2.2 percent in retail trade, 1.9 percent in labor productivity for wholesale trade, and remained unchanged in food services and drinking places from 2001 to 2011. Within retail trade, labor productivity for florists, nonstore retailers, and electronic shopping and mail-order increased by at least 14 percent. (See Table 5-3.)

- Between 1987 and 2011 productivity increased 3.1 percent in wholesale trade, 2.8 percent in retail trade, but only 0.6 percent in food services and drinking places. (See Table 5-3.)

NOTES AND DEFINITIONS

PRODUCTIVITY AND COSTS

The Bureau of Labor Statistics (BLS) publishes three sets of productivity measures for the major sectors and subsectors of the U.S. economy, each using a distinct methodology. One measure includes labor productivity for the major sectors of business, nonfarm business, and nonfinancial corporations and for the subsectors of total, durable, and nondurable manufacturing. The second set includes multifactor productivity for major sectors; and the third measures multifactor productivity for total industries. Each set of measures involves a comparison of output and input measures. Indexes of labor productivity show changes in the ratio of output to hours of labor input. These measures are used in economic analysis, public and private policymaking, and forecasting and analysis of prices, wages, and technological change.

Concepts and Definitions

Business sector output is constructed by excluding the following outputs from gross domestic product (GDP): general government, nonprofit institutions, paid employees of private households, and the rental value of owner-occupied dwellings. Corresponding exclusions are also made in labor inputs. These activities are excluded because theoretical or practical difficulties make it impossible to use them as a basis for the computation of meaningful productivity measures.

Hourly compensation costs are defined as the sum of wage and salary accruals and supplements to wages and salaries. Wage and salary accruals consist of the monetary remuneration of employees, including the compensation of corporate officers; commissions, tips, and bonuses; voluntary employee contributions to certain deferred compensation plans, such as 401(k) plans; employee gains from exercising nonqualified stock options; and receipts in kind that represent income. Supplements to wages and salaries consist of employer contributions for social insurance and employer payments (including payments in kind) to private pension and profit-sharing plans, group health and life insurance plans, privately administered workers' compensation plans. For employees (wage and salary workers), hourly compensation is measured relative to hours at work and includes payments made by employers for time not at work, such as vacation, holiday, and sick pay. Because compensation costs for the business and nonfarm business sectors would otherwise be severely understated, an estimate of the hourly compensation of proprietors of unincorporated businesses is made by assuming that their hourly compensation is equal to that of employees in the same sector.

Hours at work include paid time working, traveling between job sites, coffee breaks, and machine downtime. Hours at work, however, exclude hours for which employees are paid but not at work.

The *nonfarm business sector* is a subset of the domestic economy and excludes the economic activities of the following: general government, private households, nonprofit organizations serving individuals, and farms.

Nonfinancial corporations are a subset of the domestic economy and excludes the economic activities of the following: general government, private households, nonprofit organizations serving individuals, and those corporations classified as offices of bank holding companies, offices of other holding companies, or offices in the finance and insurance sector.

Nonlabor payments include profits, consumption of fixed capital, taxes on production and imports less subsidies, net interest and miscellaneous payments, business current transfer payments, rental income of persons, and the current surplus of government enterprises.

Output is measured as an annual-weighted index of the changes in the various products or services (in real terms) provided for sale outside the industry. Real industry output is usually derived by deflating nominal sales or values of production using BLS price indexes, but for some industries it is measured by physical quantities of output. Industry output measures are constructed primarily using data from the economic censuses and annual surveys of the U.S. Census Bureau, U.S. Department of Commerce, together with information on price changes primarily from BLS. Output measures for some mining and utilities industries are based on physical quantity data from the Energy Information Administration, U.S. Department of Energy, while output measures for some transportation industries are based on physical quantity data from the Bureau of Transportation Statistics, U.S. Department of Transportation. Other data sources for some industries include the U.S. Geological Survey, U.S. Department of the Interior; the U.S. Postal Service; the Federal Deposit Insurance Corporation; and the Postal Rate Commission.

Productivity measures describe the relationship between industry output and the labor time involved in its production. They show the changes from period to period in the amount of goods and services produced per hour. Although the labor productivity measures relate output to hours of employees or all persons in an industry, they do not measure the specific contribution of labor or any other factor of production. Rather, they reflect the joint effects of many influences, including changes in technology; capital investment; utilization of capacity, energy, and materials; the use of purchased services inputs, including contract employment services; the organization of production; managerial skill; and the characteristics and effort of the workforce.

Unit labor costs show the growth in compensation relative to that of real output. These costs are calculated by dividing total labor compensation by real output. Changes in unit labor costs can be approximated by subtracting the change in productivity from the change in hourly compensation.

Multifactor Productivity Concepts and Definitions

Multifactor productivity indexes for private business and private nonfarm business are derived by dividing an output index by an index of labor input and capital services. The output indexes are computed as chained superlative indexes of components of real output. BLS adjusts output measures from the Bureau of Economic Analysis (BEA) to remove the output of government enterprises.

Capital services measures the services derived from the stock of physical assets and software. The assets included are computers, software, communications and other information processing equipment, other fixed business equipment, structures, inventories, rental residences, and land. Investments, depreciation, capital income, and rental prices are estimated for each of these eight aggregates. Rental prices reflect the nominal rates of return and rates of economic depreciation and revaluation for the specific asset. Rental prices are adjusted for the effects of taxes. Data on investments in physical assets are obtained from BEA. Capital input measures constructed for the preliminary MFP measures are based on less detail than those for full MFP measure.

Combined inputs involve combining labor and capital inputs using a Tornqvist index. Growth rates of labor and capital input are combined with weights that represent each component's share of total costs. Total costs are defined as the value of output (Gross Product Originating) less a portion of taxes on production and imports. Most taxes on production and imports, such as excise taxes, are excluded from costs; however, property and motor vehicle taxes remain in total costs. The index uses changing weights: The share in each year is averaged with the preceding year's share.

Labor input is total hours worked multiplied by a labor composition index. Hours paid of employees are largely obtained from BLS's Current Employment Survey (CES). These hours of employees are then converted to an at-work basis by using information from the Employment Cost Index (ECI) of the National Compensation Survey (NCS) and the Hours at Work Survey. Hours at work for non-production and supervisory workers are derived using data from the CPS, the CES, and the NCS. The hours at work of proprietors, unpaid family workers, and farm employees are derived from the Current Population Survey.

Multifactor productivity measures describe the relationship between output in real terms and the inputs involved in its production. They do not measure the specific contributions of labor, capital, or any other factor of production. Rather, multifactor productivity is designed to measure the joint influences of output, capital, and labor on economic growth of technological change, efficiency improvements, returns to scale, reallocation of resources due to shifts in factor inputs across industries, and other factors. The multifactor productivity indexes for private business and private nonfarm business are derived by dividing an output index by an index of labor input and capital services. The output indexes are computed as chained superlative indexes (Fisher Ideal indexes) of components of real output. BLS adjusts BEA output measures to remove the output of government enterprises.

Sources of Additional Information

Productivity concepts and methodology are described in Chapters 10 and 11 of the *BLS Handbook of Methods*. More information on productivity can be found in BLS news releases on the BLS Web site at <http://www.bls.gov/lpc/>.

Table 5-1. Indexes of Productivity and Related Data, 1947–2011

(2005 = 100.)

Year	Business											
	Output per hour	Output	Hours	Hourly compen-sation	Real hourly compen-sation	Unit labor costs	Unit nonlabor payments	Implicit price deflator	Employment	Output per job	Compen-sation in current dollars	Nonlabor payments in current dollars
1947	23.5	12.6	53.6	4.3	34.3	18.2	14.1	16.6	46.3	27.3	2.3	1.8
1948	24.6	13.3	54.0	4.7	34.4	18.9	15.7	17.6	46.9	28.4	2.5	2.1
1949	25.2	13.2	52.3	4.7	35.3	18.7	15.5	17.5	45.8	28.8	2.5	2.0
1950	27.3	14.5	53.0	5.1	37.3	18.5	16.3	17.7	46.3	31.3	2.7	2.4
1951	28.1	15.4	54.7	5.5	37.9	19.7	18.0	19.0	47.5	32.4	3.0	2.8
1952	28.9	15.9	54.8	5.9	39.5	20.3	17.6	19.2	47.7	33.3	3.2	2.8
1953	30.0	16.7	55.5	6.3	41.7	20.9	17.2	19.4	48.4	34.4	3.5	2.9
1954	30.6	16.4	53.7	6.5	42.7	21.1	17.1	19.5	47.2	34.8	3.5	2.8
1955	31.9	17.8	55.7	6.6	44.0	20.7	18.2	19.7	48.6	36.6	3.7	3.2
1956	32.0	18.1	56.5	7.1	46.2	22.1	17.8	20.4	49.6	36.4	4.0	3.2
1957	33.0	18.4	55.7	7.5	47.6	22.8	18.3	21.0	49.5	37.1	4.2	3.4
1958	33.9	18.0	53.2	7.8	48.3	23.1	18.7	21.4	47.6	37.9	4.2	3.4
1959	35.2	19.5	55.4	8.2	50.0	23.2	19.1	21.6	49.1	39.8	4.5	3.7
1960	35.8	19.9	55.5	8.5	51.2	23.7	18.8	21.8	49.3	40.3	4.7	3.7
1961	37.1	20.3	54.7	8.8	52.6	23.8	19.1	22.0	48.8	41.6	4.8	3.9
1962	38.8	21.6	55.7	9.2	54.4	23.8	19.7	22.2	49.4	43.7	5.1	4.3
1963	40.3	22.6	56.1	9.6	55.6	23.7	20.2	22.3	49.7	45.5	5.4	4.6
1964	41.7	24.0	57.7	9.9	57.0	23.8	20.7	22.6	50.6	47.4	5.7	5.0
1965	43.1	25.7	59.6	10.3	58.2	23.9	21.5	22.9	52.1	49.4	6.1	5.5
1966	44.9	27.5	61.2	11.0	60.4	24.5	22.0	23.5	53.6	51.2	6.7	6.0
1967	45.9	28.0	61.0	11.6	61.9	25.3	22.3	24.1	54.4	51.5	7.1	6.3
1968	47.4	29.4	61.9	12.5	64.2	26.4	23.0	25.1	55.4	53.0	7.8	6.8
1969	47.7	30.3	63.5	13.4	65.1	28.1	23.3	26.2	57.2	53.0	8.5	7.1
1970	48.6	30.3	62.2	14.5	66.3	29.7	23.8	27.4	57.0	53.1	9.0	7.2
1971	50.6	31.4	62.1	15.4	67.5	30.3	25.8	28.5	57.1	55.0	9.5	8.1
1972	52.3	33.5	64.0	16.3	69.6	31.2	27.0	29.6	58.8	56.9	10.5	9.0
1973	53.9	35.8	66.5	17.7	71.0	32.9	28.4	31.1	61.3	58.4	11.8	10.2
1974	53.0	35.3	66.6	19.4	70.1	36.6	30.2	34.1	62.3	56.6	12.9	10.7
1975	54.8	34.9	63.7	21.4	70.8	39.0	35.0	37.4	60.4	57.8	13.6	12.2
1976	56.6	37.2	65.8	23.2	72.7	41.1	36.8	39.4	62.3	59.8	15.3	13.7
1977	57.5	39.3	68.3	25.1	73.7	43.6	39.0	41.8	65.0	60.5	17.1	15.3
1978	58.2	41.8	71.8	27.3	74.9	46.9	41.4	44.7	68.5	61.0	19.6	17.3
1979	58.1	43.2	74.3	29.9	74.9	51.4	44.1	48.5	71.2	60.6	22.2	19.1
1980	58.0	42.7	73.6	33.1	74.6	57.0	46.6	52.9	71.4	59.8	24.3	19.9
1981	59.2	43.9	74.1	36.2	74.5	61.1	52.6	57.8	72.1	60.9	26.8	23.1
1982	58.7	42.6	72.5	38.8	75.4	66.1	53.3	61.1	70.9	60.0	28.1	22.7
1983	60.8	44.8	73.7	40.4	75.3	66.4	58.1	63.1	71.5	62.7	29.8	26.1
1984	62.5	48.7	78.0	42.1	75.4	67.4	61.2	65.0	75.1	64.9	32.9	29.8
1985	63.9	51.0	79.8	44.1	76.3	69.0	62.7	66.5	77.0	66.2	35.2	32.0
1986	65.7	52.9	80.5	46.4	78.8	70.5	63.1	67.6	78.3	67.6	37.3	33.4
1987	65.9	54.6	82.9	48.0	79.0	72.9	63.7	69.2	80.4	68.0	39.8	34.8
1988	66.9	57.0	85.2	50.5	80.1	75.5	65.1	71.4	82.9	68.8	43.0	37.1
1989	67.6	59.1	87.4	51.9	78.9	76.7	69.9	74.0	84.7	69.8	45.4	41.3
1990	69.0	60.0	86.9	55.2	80.0	80.0	71.6	76.7	85.2	70.4	48.0	43.0
1991	70.1	59.5	84.9	58.0	81.1	82.8	73.6	79.2	83.9	70.9	49.3	43.8
1992	73.0	61.8	84.7	61.1	83.3	83.7	76.1	80.7	83.4	74.1	51.7	47.0
1993	73.4	63.8	86.9	62.5	83.1	85.1	77.9	82.3	85.2	74.9	54.3	49.7
1994	74.1	67.0	90.4	63.4	82.6	85.6	80.7	83.7	88.0	76.0	57.3	54.1
1995	74.1	68.8	92.9	64.7	82.4	87.4	81.9	85.2	90.5	76.0	60.1	56.4
1996	76.3	72.0	94.4	66.9	82.9	87.8	84.7	86.6	92.5	77.8	63.2	61.0
1997	77.6	75.7	97.5	69.1	83.8	89.1	86.2	87.9	95.0	79.7	67.4	65.3
1998	79.9	79.5	99.4	73.3	87.7	91.7	83.6	88.5	97.0	82.0	72.9	66.4
1999	82.7	83.9	101.4	76.6	89.8	92.6	84.0	89.2	98.5	85.2	77.7	70.5
2000	85.6	87.7	102.4	82.3	93.3	96.1	82.9	90.9	100.2	87.5	84.3	72.7
2001	88.2	88.4	100.3	86.1	95.0	97.7	84.5	92.5	99.4	89.0	86.4	74.7
2002	92.2	90.2	97.8	88.8	96.4	96.4	88.4	93.2	97.2	92.8	86.9	79.7
2003	95.7	93.0	97.2	93.0	98.7	97.2	90.3	94.5	97.0	95.9	90.4	83.9
2004	98.4	96.7	98.3	96.2	99.5	97.8	95.4	96.9	98.2	98.5	94.6	92.3
2005	100.0	100.0	100.0	100.0	100.0	100.0	100.0	100.0	100.0	100.0	100.0	100.0
2006	100.9	103.0	102.1	103.8	100.5	102.8	103.0	102.9	101.9	101.2	106.0	106.1
2007	102.4	105.1	102.6	108.1	101.8	105.5	105.6	105.6	102.6	102.4	110.9	111.0
2008	103.2	103.7	100.5	111.7	101.2	108.2	106.3	107.5	101.1	102.6	112.2	110.2
2009	106.3	99.2	93.3	113.2	103.0	106.5	110.2	107.9	95.3	104.1	105.6	109.3
2010	109.5	102.2	93.3	115.4	103.3	105.4	116.0	109.6	94.2	108.4	107.7	118.5
2011	110.0	104.6	95.1	118.4	102.8	107.7	118.7	112.0	95.6	109.4	112.6	124.1

Table 5-1. Indexes of Productivity and Related Data, 1947–2011—*Continued*

(2005 = 100.)

Year	Nonfarm business											
	Output per hour	Output	Hours	Hourly compensation	Real hourly compensation	Unit labor costs	Unit nonlabor payments	Implicit price deflator	Employment	Output per job	Compensation in current dollars	Nonlabor payments in current dollars
1947	27.2	12.4	45.5	4.6	36.7	16.9	13.4	15.5	38.9	31.9	2.1	1.7
1948	28.0	12.9	46.3	5.0	36.9	17.9	14.5	16.5	39.7	32.6	2.3	1.9
1949	28.9	12.9	44.5	5.1	38.5	17.8	15.0	16.7	38.6	33.3	2.3	1.9
1950	30.8	14.2	45.9	5.4	40.2	17.7	15.6	16.9	39.5	35.8	2.5	2.2
1951	31.7	15.2	48.1	5.9	40.5	18.7	16.8	18.0	41.3	36.9	2.8	2.6
1952	32.2	15.7	48.6	6.2	42.0	19.4	16.7	18.3	41.8	37.5	3.0	2.6
1953	33.0	16.4	49.8	6.6	44.0	20.0	16.6	18.7	43.1	38.2	3.3	2.7
1954	33.6	16.2	48.1	6.8	45.0	20.2	16.7	18.8	41.9	38.6	3.3	2.7
1955	35.0	17.5	50.1	7.1	46.9	20.1	17.7	19.2	43.2	40.6	3.5	3.1
1956	34.8	17.8	51.3	7.5	49.0	21.5	17.3	19.9	44.4	40.2	3.8	3.1
1957	35.7	18.2	51.0	7.9	50.2	22.2	17.9	20.5	44.6	40.8	4.0	3.2
1958	36.5	17.8	48.9	8.2	50.7	22.6	18.0	20.8	43.1	41.4	4.0	3.2
1959	37.9	19.4	51.1	8.6	52.3	22.6	18.7	21.0	44.6	43.4	4.4	3.6
1960	38.3	19.7	51.4	8.9	53.7	23.3	18.2	21.3	45.1	43.7	4.6	3.6
1961	39.5	20.1	50.9	9.2	54.9	23.3	18.6	21.5	44.8	44.9	4.7	3.7
1962	41.3	21.5	52.0	9.6	56.5	23.2	19.3	21.7	45.6	47.1	5.0	4.1
1963	42.7	22.5	52.6	9.9	57.7	23.2	19.7	21.8	46.1	48.8	5.2	4.4
1964	44.0	24.0	54.5	10.2	58.7	23.2	20.3	22.1	47.2	50.8	5.6	4.9
1965	45.4	25.7	56.6	10.6	59.7	23.3	21.0	22.4	48.9	52.5	6.0	5.4
1966	47.0	27.5	58.6	11.2	61.5	23.8	21.5	22.9	50.8	54.2	6.6	5.9
1967	47.8	28.0	58.6	11.8	63.1	24.8	21.9	23.6	51.7	54.2	6.9	6.1
1968	49.4	29.5	59.6	12.8	65.3	25.8	22.6	24.6	52.9	55.7	7.6	6.7
1969	49.5	30.4	61.3	13.6	66.2	27.5	22.8	25.7	54.8	55.4	8.4	6.9
1970	50.2	30.3	60.4	14.6	67.1	29.1	23.3	26.8	54.8	55.3	8.8	7.1
1971	52.3	31.5	60.2	15.5	68.4	29.8	25.2	28.0	55.0	57.2	9.4	7.9
1972	54.0	33.6	62.2	16.6	70.5	30.7	26.0	28.8	56.6	59.3	10.3	8.7
1973	55.7	36.0	64.7	17.9	71.8	32.2	26.3	29.9	59.2	60.9	11.6	9.5
1974	54.8	35.5	64.8	19.7	71.0	35.9	28.4	32.9	60.1	59.0	12.7	10.1
1975	56.3	34.9	62.0	21.6	71.6	38.4	33.5	36.5	58.4	59.8	13.4	11.7
1976	58.2	37.4	64.2	23.5	73.4	40.3	35.7	38.5	60.4	61.9	15.1	13.3
1977	59.1	39.5	66.8	25.4	74.5	42.9	37.8	40.9	63.1	62.5	16.9	14.9
1978	59.9	42.1	70.3	27.6	75.8	46.1	39.9	43.7	66.6	63.1	19.4	16.8
1979	59.6	43.4	72.8	30.2	75.7	50.7	42.3	47.4	69.5	62.4	22.0	18.4
1980	59.5	42.9	72.2	33.4	75.4	56.2	45.3	51.9	69.7	61.6	24.1	19.5
1981	60.3	43.8	72.7	36.7	75.5	60.8	50.9	56.9	70.5	62.2	26.6	22.3
1982	59.7	42.4	71.1	39.3	76.3	65.8	52.1	60.4	69.3	61.2	27.9	22.1
1983	62.3	45.1	72.5	40.9	76.2	65.7	57.2	62.4	70.0	64.5	29.6	25.8
1984	63.5	48.9	76.9	42.6	76.2	67.0	59.7	64.1	73.8	66.2	32.7	29.2
1985	64.6	51.0	78.9	44.5	76.9	68.9	61.5	66.0	75.9	67.1	35.1	31.3
1986	66.6	52.9	79.5	46.8	79.5	70.3	62.1	67.1	77.2	68.5	37.2	32.9
1987	66.8	54.7	81.9	48.5	79.7	72.7	62.7	68.7	79.4	68.9	39.7	34.3
1988	67.9	57.2	84.3	50.9	80.8	75.1	64.2	70.8	81.9	69.8	42.9	36.7
1989	68.4	59.2	86.6	52.2	79.4	76.4	68.7	73.4	83.8	70.7	45.2	40.7
1990	69.6	60.1	86.3	55.5	80.3	79.7	70.5	76.1	84.4	71.2	47.9	42.4
1991	70.7	59.5	84.2	58.4	81.6	82.6	72.8	78.7	83.0	71.7	49.1	43.3
1992	73.5	61.8	84.0	61.5	83.9	83.7	75.1	80.3	82.5	74.8	51.7	46.4
1993	73.9	63.9	86.4	62.7	83.5	84.9	77.3	81.9	84.5	75.6	54.2	49.4
1994	74.7	66.9	89.6	63.9	83.2	85.5	80.1	83.4	87.2	76.7	57.2	53.6
1995	75.0	69.0	92.0	65.2	82.9	86.9	81.6	84.8	89.7	76.9	60.0	56.3
1996	76.9	72.1	93.7	67.4	83.4	87.5	83.7	86.0	91.8	78.5	63.1	60.3
1997	78.1	75.7	96.9	69.4	84.2	88.9	85.6	87.6	94.4	80.2	67.3	64.8
1998	80.4	79.6	99.0	73.6	88.0	91.5	83.3	88.3	96.5	82.5	72.9	66.3
1999	83.1	84.1	101.2	76.8	89.9	92.4	84.1	89.1	98.2	85.6	77.7	70.7
2000	85.9	87.8	102.2	82.5	93.5	96.0	83.0	90.9	100.0	87.8	84.3	72.8
2001	88.4	88.6	100.2	86.2	95.0	97.5	84.6	92.4	99.3	89.2	86.3	74.9
2002	92.4	90.3	97.6	88.9	96.5	96.2	88.7	93.2	97.0	93.0	86.8	80.1
2003	95.8	93.0	97.1	93.1	98.8	97.1	90.1	94.4	96.9	96.0	90.4	83.9
2004	98.4	96.7	98.3	96.2	99.4	97.8	94.8	96.6	98.2	98.5	94.6	91.7
2005	100.0	100.0	100.0	100.0	100.0	100.0	100.0	100.0	100.0	100.0	100.0	100.0
2006	100.9	103.1	102.2	103.8	100.5	102.8	103.2	103.0	101.9	101.2	106.0	106.4
2007	102.5	105.3	102.7	107.9	101.6	105.3	105.4	105.4	102.7	102.5	110.9	111.0
2008	103.1	103.7	100.6	111.6	101.2	108.2	105.8	107.3	101.1	102.5	112.3	109.7
2009	106.1	99.0	93.3	113.2	103.0	106.7	110.4	108.1	95.3	103.9	105.6	109.3
2010	109.4	102.0	93.3	115.5	103.4	105.6	115.8	109.6	94.2	108.3	107.7	118.2
2011	110.2	104.7	95.1	118.6	102.9	107.6	117.9	111.7	95.5	109.6	112.7	123.5

Table 5-1. Indexes of Productivity and Related Data, 1947–2011—*Continued*

(2005 = 100.)

Year	Nonfinancial corporations												
	Output per hour	Output	Hours	Hourly compensation	Real hourly compensation	Unit labor costs	Unit nonlabor costs	Unit profits	Implicit price deflator	Employment	Output per job	Compensation in current dollars	Nonlabor payments in current dollars
1947	...	...	...	...	...	...	...	...	...	...	...	...	...
1948	...	...	...	...	...	...	...	...	...	...	...	...	...
1949	...	...	...	...	...	...	...	...	...	...	...	...	...
1950	...	...	...	...	...	...	...	...	...	...	...	...	...
1951	...	...	...	...	...	...	...	...	...	...	...	...	...
1952	...	...	...	...	...	...	...	...	...	...	...	...	...
1953	...	...	...	...	...	...	...	...	...	...	...	...	...
1954	...	...	...	...	...	...	...	...	...	...	...	...	...
1955	...	...	...	...	...	...	...	...	...	...	...	...	...
1956	...	...	...	...	...	...	...	...	...	...	...	...	...
1957	...	...	...	...	...	...	...	...	...	...	...	...	...
1958	36.5	15.0	41.0	9.5	58.7	26.1	21.0	28.3	25.1	36.5	41.0	3.9	3.5
1959	38.4	16.7	43.5	9.9	60.5	25.8	20.2	33.0	25.3	38.2	43.7	4.3	4.1
1960	39.0	17.2	44.2	10.3	61.8	26.3	20.6	30.4	25.4	39.0	44.2	4.5	4.1
1961	40.3	17.6	43.8	10.6	63.2	26.3	21.0	30.4	25.6	38.8	45.5	4.6	4.3
1962	42.1	19.1	45.5	11.0	65.0	26.2	20.7	32.8	25.7	40.1	47.7	5.0	4.8
1963	43.6	20.3	46.5	11.4	66.1	26.1	20.5	34.7	25.8	40.9	49.6	5.3	5.1
1964	44.3	21.7	49.0	11.6	66.5	26.1	20.5	36.0	26.0	42.4	51.2	5.7	5.6
1965	45.4	23.5	51.8	11.9	67.3	26.3	20.4	38.7	26.4	44.6	52.7	6.2	6.3
1966	46.2	25.2	54.6	12.6	69.1	27.2	20.4	38.6	27.0	47.2	53.4	6.9	6.7
1967	46.9	25.9	55.1	13.3	70.8	28.3	21.7	36.0	27.7	48.5	53.4	7.3	6.9
1968	48.6	27.6	56.7	14.3	73.1	29.4	23.0	35.9	28.7	50.2	54.9	8.1	7.6
1969	48.7	28.7	58.9	15.3	74.0	31.3	24.9	32.5	29.9	52.5	54.6	9.0	7.9
1970	49.0	28.4	58.0	16.3	74.9	33.3	28.0	26.5	31.1	52.6	54.1	9.5	7.8
1971	51.1	29.6	57.9	17.3	76.3	33.9	29.3	30.0	32.3	52.7	56.2	10.0	8.8
1972	52.2	31.9	61.1	18.3	77.9	35.0	29.3	32.6	33.3	55.4	57.6	11.2	9.7
1973	52.7	33.8	64.2	19.7	78.9	37.3	30.9	32.9	35.2	58.4	57.9	12.6	10.7
1974	51.7	33.3	64.5	21.5	77.8	41.7	35.4	29.2	38.6	59.5	55.9	13.9	11.1
1975	53.6	32.8	61.2	23.7	78.3	44.1	40.3	37.8	42.4	57.3	57.3	14.5	12.9
1976	55.5	35.5	64.0	25.6	80.1	46.2	40.1	42.7	44.2	59.8	59.3	16.4	14.5
1977	56.9	38.1	66.9	27.6	81.2	48.5	41.6	46.6	46.6	62.9	60.6	18.5	16.5
1978	57.7	40.6	70.4	30.2	82.9	52.3	43.6	48.4	49.7	66.4	61.2	21.3	18.4
1979	57.2	41.9	73.2	32.9	82.5	57.5	47.5	45.4	53.6	69.7	60.1	24.1	19.6
1980	57.0	41.5	72.7	36.2	81.7	63.5	55.6	40.7	58.7	70.0	59.2	26.3	20.9
1981	58.5	43.1	73.8	39.5	81.3	67.5	63.4	48.5	64.1	71.2	60.6	29.1	25.1
1982	58.6	42.1	71.8	42.1	81.7	71.7	70.2	44.7	67.9	69.6	60.5	30.2	25.9
1983	60.6	44.1	72.8	43.6	81.3	72.0	70.4	54.3	69.4	69.9	63.1	31.8	28.6
1984	62.0	48.0	77.5	45.4	81.3	73.3	69.7	65.2	71.4	74.0	64.9	35.2	32.7
1985	63.2	50.1	79.3	47.5	82.1	75.1	71.6	62.5	72.6	76.1	65.9	37.6	34.3
1986	64.6	51.3	79.5	49.8	84.7	77.2	75.0	53.6	73.7	77.2	66.5	39.6	34.7
1987	65.8	54.0	82.0	51.5	84.6	78.2	74.2	60.4	75.0	79.3	68.1	42.2	37.5
1988	67.5	57.1	84.6	53.7	85.1	79.5	75.2	66.8	76.8	82.0	69.7	45.4	41.3
1989	66.6	58.1	87.2	55.0	83.6	82.6	80.0	61.2	79.2	84.0	69.1	47.9	42.7
1990	67.3	58.9	87.5	57.6	83.4	85.6	83.6	58.9	81.7	85.5	68.9	50.4	44.3
1991	69.0	58.6	85.0	60.5	84.6	87.7	87.9	58.0	84.0	83.7	70.1	51.4	45.5
1992	70.7	60.4	85.4	63.4	86.5	89.7	85.8	61.5	85.2	83.7	72.1	54.1	46.8
1993	70.9	62.0	87.4	64.6	85.9	91.1	85.2	70.3	87.0	85.3	72.6	56.4	49.6
1994	72.3	65.9	91.1	65.7	85.6	90.9	85.5	82.4	88.5	88.5	74.5	59.9	55.7
1995	73.1	69.0	94.4	66.9	85.1	91.5	85.9	85.5	89.4	91.6	75.3	63.2	59.2
1996	75.7	72.8	96.1	68.9	85.3	90.9	85.4	92.5	89.8	94.0	77.5	66.2	64.0
1997	77.7	77.6	99.8	71.0	86.0	91.3	85.3	94.8	90.3	96.9	80.0	70.8	68.7
1998	80.4	82.0	102.0	75.2	90.0	93.5	85.8	83.1	90.3	99.3	82.6	76.7	69.6
1999	83.0	86.5	104.3	78.6	92.0	94.7	88.1	77.3	90.9	101.4	85.3	81.9	73.0
2000	86.4	91.2	105.6	84.4	95.6	97.7	91.1	64.3	91.9	103.4	88.2	89.1	74.7
2001	87.1	89.4	102.7	87.1	96.1	100.1	96.7	51.9	93.2	102.1	87.6	89.5	72.8
2002	90.4	90.0	99.6	89.5	97.1	99.0	97.1	59.5	93.5	99.1	90.8	89.1	75.8
2003	94.4	92.3	97.8	93.9	99.7	99.5	96.8	66.0	94.6	97.8	94.4	91.8	79.6
2004	97.8	96.5	98.7	96.5	99.7	98.6	95.7	88.0	96.6	98.5	98.0	95.2	89.9
2005	100.0	100.0	100.0	100.0	100.0	100.0	100.0	100.0	100.0	100.0	100.0	100.0	100.0
2006	101.9	103.8	101.9	103.3	100.0	101.3	103.0	111.6	103.0	101.5	102.3	105.2	110.0
2007	102.6	104.8	102.2	107.3	101.0	104.6	109.2	100.0	105.1	102.0	102.7	109.7	111.1
2008	102.9	103.4	100.5	111.2	100.8	108.0	113.6	91.6	107.3	100.6	102.8	111.7	109.6
2009	103.4	95.8	92.6	113.3	103.2	109.6	120.0	86.5	109.2	94.1	101.8	105.0	103.9
2010	109.4	101.5	92.8	115.3	103.2	105.3	114.9	113.3	108.7	93.1	109.1	106.9	116.1
2011	110.9	105.6	95.2	118.1	102.5	106.5	116.9	119.5	110.7	94.9	111.3	112.5	124.4

. . . = Not available.

Table 5-1. Indexes of Productivity and Related Data, 1947–2011—*Continued*

(2005 = 100.)

Year	Manufacturing											
	Output per hour	Output	Hours	Hourly compensation	Real hourly compensation	Unit labor costs	Unit nonlabor payments	Implicit price deflator	Employment	Output per job	Compensation in current dollars	Nonlabor payments in current dollars
1947	...	...	...	...	...	...	...	...	...	...	...	...
1948	...	...	...	...	...	...	...	...	...	...	...	...
1949	...	...	...	...	...	...	...	...	...	...	...	...
1950	...	...	...	...	...	...	...	...	...	...	...	...
1951	...	...	...	...	...	...	...	...	...	...	...	...
1952	...	...	...	...	...	...	...	...	...	...	...	...
1953	...	...	...	...	...	...	...	...	...	...	...	...
1954	...	...	...	...	...	...	...	...	...	...	...	...
1955	...	...	...	...	...	...	...	...	...	...	...	...
1956	...	...	...	...	...	...	...	...	...	...	...	...
1957	...	...	...	...	...	...	...	...	...	...	...	...
1958	...	...	...	...	...	...	...	...	...	...	...	...
1959	...	...	...	...	...	...	...	...	...	...	...	...
1960	...	...	...	...	...	...	...	...	...	...	...	...
1961	...	...	...	...	...	...	...	...	...	...	...	...
1962	...	...	...	...	...	...	...	...	...	...	...	...
1963	...	...	...	...	...	...	...	...	...	...	...	...
1964	...	...	...	...	...	...	...	...	...	...	...	...
1965	...	...	...	...	...	...	...	...	...	...	...	...
1966	...	...	...	...	...	...	...	...	...	...	...	...
1967	...	...	...	...	...	...	...	...	...	...	...	...
1968	...	...	...	...	...	...	...	...	...	...	...	...
1969	...	...	...	...	...	...	...	...	...	...	...	...
1970	...	...	...	...	...	...	...	...	...	...	...	...
1971	...	...	...	...	...	...	...	...	...	...	...	...
1972	...	...	...	...	...	...	...	...	...	...	...	...
1973	...	...	...	...	...	...	...	...	...	...	...	...
1974	...	...	...	...	...	...	...	...	...	...	...	...
1975	...	...	...	...	...	...	...	...	...	...	...	...
1976	...	...	...	...	...	...	...	...	...	...	...	...
1977	...	...	...	...	...	...	...	...	...	...	...	...
1978	...	...	...	...	...	...	...	...	...	...	...	...
1979	...	...	...	...	...	...	...	...	...	...	...	...
1980	...	...	...	...	...	...	...	...	...	...	...	...
1981	...	...	...	...	...	...	...	...	...	...	...	...
1982	...	...	...	...	...	...	...	...	...	...	...	...
1983	...	...	...	...	...	...	...	...	...	...	...	...
1984	...	...	...	...	...	...	...	...	...	...	...	...
1985	...	...	...	...	...	...	...	...	...	...	...	...
1986	...	...	...	...	...	...	...	...	...	...	...	...
1987	51.2	63.1	123.2	49.4	81.2	96.5	72.0	78.6	123.2	51.2	60.8	45.4
1988	52.3	66.3	126.9	51.2	81.1	97.9	74.7	81.0	125.4	52.9	64.9	49.5
1989	52.8	67.4	127.7	52.7	80.1	99.8	78.8	84.5	126.1	53.5	67.3	53.1
1990	54.0	67.2	124.5	55.2	80.0	102.4	81.7	87.3	124.2	54.1	68.8	54.9
1991	55.4	66.0	119.3	58.5	81.8	105.7	81.1	87.8	119.9	55.1	69.8	53.5
1992	57.5	68.2	118.7	61.3	83.5	106.6	82.2	88.9	117.9	57.9	72.7	56.1
1993	58.9	70.9	120.3	62.7	83.4	106.3	83.0	89.4	118.0	60.1	75.3	58.8
1994	61.0	75.1	123.1	64.2	83.7	105.3	84.3	90.0	119.5	62.8	79.0	63.3
1995	63.8	79.0	123.9	65.2	83.0	102.3	87.3	91.4	121.2	65.2	80.8	69.0
1996	66.1	81.7	123.6	66.4	82.2	100.4	88.7	91.9	121.0	67.5	82.0	72.5
1997	69.7	87.7	125.9	68.0	82.4	97.5	88.3	90.8	122.1	71.8	85.6	77.5
1998	73.5	92.3	125.5	72.2	86.3	98.2	84.2	88.0	123.1	75.0	90.6	77.7
1999	77.1	96.1	124.7	75.4	88.3	97.8	84.5	88.1	121.2	79.3	94.0	81.2
2000	80.5	99.0	123.1	81.2	92.0	100.9	85.5	89.7	120.9	81.9	99.9	84.7
2001	81.9	94.2	115.0	84.3	92.9	102.9	83.9	89.1	115.3	81.8	96.9	79.1
2002	87.8	93.9	106.9	88.9	96.5	101.2	83.3	88.2	107.0	87.8	95.0	78.2
2003	93.3	94.9	101.7	96.0	101.9	102.9	84.9	89.8	101.9	93.1	97.6	80.6
2004	95.4	96.5	101.1	96.8	100.0	101.4	91.3	94.1	100.5	96.0	97.9	88.2
2005	100.0	100.0	100.0	100.0	100.0	100.0	100.0	100.0	100.0	100.0	100.0	100.0
2006	100.9	101.7	100.7	102.0	98.8	101.1	104.3	103.5	99.4	102.2	102.8	106.1
2007	104.8	103.8	99.1	105.3	99.1	100.5	110.5	107.7	97.7	106.3	104.3	114.7
2008	104.2	99.1	95.1	109.8	99.6	105.3	118.6	115.0	94.2	105.2	104.4	117.5
2009	104.4	86.3	82.7	114.3	104.0	109.5	107.5	108.0	83.6	103.3	94.6	92.8
2010	111.1	91.9	82.7	115.6	103.5	104.1	114.7	111.8	81.3	113.0	95.6	105.4
2011	113.8	96.3	84.6	118.6	103.0	104.2	...	...	82.5	116.8	100.3	...

. . . = Not available.

Table 5-2. Average Annual Percent Change in Output Per Hour and Related Series, Selected Industries, 1987–2010 and 2009–2010

(Number, percent.)

Industry	NAICS code	2010 employment (thousands)	Average annual percent change, 1987–2010			Annual percent change, 2009–2010		
			Output per hour	Output	Hours	Output per hour	Output	Hours
Mining								
Mining	21	677	0.1	-0.1	-0.2	-2.0	2.5	4.6
Oil and gas extraction	211	163	1.1	-0.4	-1.4	8.7	2.8	-5.5
Mining, except oil and gas	212	208	1.8	0.3	-1.5	1.2	1.7	0.5
Coal mining	2121	81	1.9	-0.4	-2.2	-1.2	-1.3	-0.2
Metal ore mining	2122	37	2.5	2.1	-0.4	3.4	10.0	6.4
Nonmetallic mineral mining and quarrying	2123	90	0.6	-0.5	-1.1	0.1	-0.8	-0.9
Support activities for mining	213	306	2.1	4.1	1.9	12.7	27.3	12.9
Utilities								
Power generation and supply	2211	398	2.3	0.9	-1.3	3.3	1.5	-1.8
Natural gas distribution	2212	108	2.6	1.2	-1.4	5.7	2.9	-2.7
Transportation and Warehousing								
Air transportation	481	391	3.0	2.7	-0.2	6.6	4.4	-2.1
Line-haul railroads	482111	172	4.2	1.9	-2.2	8.1	12.8	4.4
Truck transportation	484	1 444	0.6	1.5	0.9	8.8	6.5	-2.1
General freight trucking	4841	1 044	1.3	2.1	0.8	11.0	7.9	-2.8
General freight trucking, local	48411	271	2.9	3.3	0.4	14.3	8.5	-5.1
General freight trucking, long-distance	48412	773	1.3	2.1	0.8	10.1	7.8	-2.1
Used household and office goods moving	48421	85	-0.7	-1.0	-0.3	-3.6	-1.2	2.5
Postal service	491	658	0.9	-0.2	-1.1	1.5	-5.7	-7.1
Couriers and messengers	492	562	-0.9	1.3	2.2	1.8	-5.5	-7.2
Warehousing and storage	493	642	2.9	5.6	2.7	8.7	9.5	0.7
General warehousing and storage	49311	540	5.1	7.9	2.7	7.9	9.4	1.3
Refrigerated warehousing and storage	49312	48	0.5	3.4	2.9	21.9	15.2	-5.5
Information								
Publishing	511	789	3.9	3.5	-0.3	7.2	1.6	-5.2
Newspaper, book, and directory publishers	5111	528	0.0	-1.8	-1.8	3.8	-5.2	-8.7
Software publishers	5112	261	13.5	20.3	6.0	5.9	7.9	1.9
Motion picture and video exhibition	51213	131	1.4	1.8	0.4	0.3	-0.2	-0.5
Broadcasting, except Internet	515	298	2.0	2.6	0.5	12.0	4.4	-6.7
Radio and television broadcasting	5151	216	1.0	0.7	-0.4	15.0	6.6	-7.2
Cable and other subscription programming	5152	82	3.7	7.6	3.8	8.5	2.4	-5.6
Wired telecommunications carriers	5171	611	4.1	3.3	-0.8	4.6	0.9	-3.5
Wireless telecommunications carriers	5172	175	10.5	21.3	9.7	16.0	10.1	-5.0
Finance and Insurance								
Commercial banking	52211	1 306	3.9	3.8	-0.1	-3.1	-4.0	-0.8
Real Estate and Rental and Leasing								
Passenger car rental	532111	100	2.0	2.2	0.2	8.5	4.4	-3.8
Truck, trailer and RV rental and leasing	53212	55	2.8	1.9	-0.8	-0.3	-2.9	-2.6
Video tape and disc rental	53223	67	5.1	2.6	-2.4	24.5	-11.2	-28.7
Professional and Technical Services								
Tax preparation services	541213	145	0.4	2.6	2.2	3.4	-1.9	-5.1
Architectural services	54131	177	1.1	1.9	0.8	-4.1	-10.9	-7.1
Engineering services	54133	902	1.0	2.7	1.7	-2.3	-3.3	-1.0
Advertising agencies	54181	183	2.3	2.4	0.1	9.4	8.2	-1.1
Photography studios, portrait	541921	68	0.3	1.8	1.4	12.5	-2.0	-12.9
Administrative and Waste Services								
Employment placement agencies	561311	230	6.2	6.7	0.5	-3.3	2.7	6.2
Travel arrangement and reservation services	5615	201	8.3	3.4	-4.5	11.8	7.5	-3.9
Travel agencies	56151	93	6.0	4.1	-1.8	13.7	10.8	-2.5
Janitorial services	56172	1 224	1.9	3.6	1.6	2.6	2.2	-0.4
Health Care and Social Assistance								
Medical and diagnostic laboratories	6215	237	3.2	6.3	3.0	-4.3	1.0	5.6
Medical laboratories	621511	163	2.8	5.6	2.8	-5.2	3.6	9.3
Diagnostic imaging centers	621512	74	3.8	7.4	3.5	-0.4	-2.8	-2.4
Arts, Entertainment, and Recreation								
Amusement and theme parks	71311	141	-0.5	2.2	2.7	-2.0	0.3	2.3
Bowling centers	71395	69	0.2	-1.9	-2.1	2.5	-1.7	-4.1
Accommodation and Food Services								
Accommodation and food services	72	11 379	0.9	2.0	1.2	2.2	1.7	-0.5
Accommodation	721	1 789	1.6	2.3	0.7	2.1	1.4	-0.7
Traveler accommodation	7211	1 716	1.6	2.3	0.7	2.1	1.4	-0.7
Food services and drinking places	722	9 590	0.7	2.0	1.3	2.3	1.8	-0.5
Full-service restaurants	7221	4 516	0.6	1.9	1.3	1.3	0.8	-0.5
Limited-service eating places	7222	4 050	0.8	2.3	1.4	4.3	3.1	-1.1
Special food services	7223	664	1.3	2.4	1.0	-0.7	1.3	2.0
Drinking places (alcoholic beverages)	7224	360	-0.4	-0.8	-0.3	-2.0	-0.9	1.1

Table 5-2. Average Annual Percent Change in Output Per Hour and Related Series, Selected Industries, 1987–2010 and 2009–2010—*Continued*

(Number, percent.)

Industry	NAICS code	2010 employment (thousands)	Average annual percent change, 1987–2010			Annual percent change, 2009–2010		
			Output per hour	Output	Hours	Output per hour	Output	Hours
Other Services								
Automotive repair and maintenance	8111	1 059	0.7	1.0	0.3	2.3	1.0	-1.3
Reupholstery and furniture repair	81142	21	-1.0	-3.4	-2.4	-4.8	-4.9	-0.1
Personal care services	8121	1 158	1.8	3.1	1.2	-2.2	1.3	3.7
Hair, nail and skin care services	81211	966	1.7	2.7	1.0	-1.0	1.9	2.9
Funeral homes and funeral services	81221	103	-0.5	-0.5	0.0	2.0	0.7	-1.2
Drycleaning and laundry services	8123	331	1.3	0.3	-1.0	3.0	0.7	-2.3
Coin-operated laundries and drycleaners	81231	45	2.0	0.5	-1.5	-0.2	3.9	4.1
Drycleaning and laundry services	81232	162	0.8	-1.1	-2.0	-0.3	-3.5	-3.3
Linen and uniform supply	81233	124	0.9	1.6	0.7	6.1	2.8	-3.1
Photofinishing	81292	15	2.3	-4.8	-7.0	22.3	-1.0	-19.0
Manufacturing								
Food	311	1 476	1.1	1.3	0.2	-1.2	-0.4	0.8
Animal food	3111	51	2.6	1.8	-0.7	-5.5	-5.8	-0.3
Grain and oilseed milling	3112	59	2.1	1.3	-0.8	-1.7	-1.6	0.1
Sugar and confectionery products	3113	70	1.0	-0.4	-1.4	7.6	1.8	-5.4
Fruit and vegetable preserving and specialty	3114	173	1.1	1.1	0.0	-4.9	-0.4	4.8
Dairy products	3115	133	1.8	1.1	-0.7	1.1	1.1	0.1
Animal slaughtering and processing	3116	492	1.0	2.1	1.1	0.0	-0.6	-0.6
Seafood product preparation and packaging	3117	38	1.1	0.2	-0.9	-9.3	-2.6	7.4
Bakeries and tortilla manufacturing	3118	295	0.5	0.2	-0.3	0.4	0.9	0.5
Other food products	3119	166	0.5	1.9	1.4	-2.0	1.8	3.8
Beverages and tobacco products	312	187	0.9	-0.3	-1.2	-2.4	0.0	2.5
Beverages	3121	171	2.1	1.4	-0.7	-3.5	-0.1	3.6
Tobacco and tobacco products	3122	16	1.4	-3.2	-4.6	7.7	0.4	-6.8
Textile mills	313	128	3.5	-2.8	-6.1	6.0	9.5	3.3
Fiber, yarn, and thread mills	3131	29	3.2	-2.4	-5.4	-1.1	7.4	8.6
Fabric mills	3132	60	4.6	-2.7	-6.9	-1.5	7.6	9.2
Textile and fabric finishing and coating mills	3133	39	1.4	-3.6	-5.0	23.7	13.7	-8.1
Textile product mills	314	128	0.9	-1.9	-2.8	10.0	3.9	-5.6
Textile furnishings mills	3141	61	0.5	-2.6	-3.0	8.1	0.8	-6.7
Other textile product mills	3149	67	2.1	-0.6	-2.6	13.6	8.5	-4.5
Apparel	315	179	-1.1	-8.1	-7.1	3.8	0.0	-3.7
Apparel knitting mills	3151	24	-0.1	-7.2	-7.1	0.5	7.4	6.8
Cut and sew apparel	3152	142	-1.3	-8.4	-7.2	3.3	-1.6	-4.7
Accessories and other apparel	3159	13	-2.0	-7.2	-5.2	11.4	1.0	-9.3
Leather and allied products	316	32	2.0	-4.6	-6.5	8.5	11.9	3.2
Leather and hide tanning and finishing	3161	4	1.5	-3.7	-5.1	37.9	52.2	10.4
Footwear	3162	12	2.7	-5.8	-8.3	15.5	5.1	-9.1
Other leather products	3169	15	0.3	-4.0	-4.3	-10.7	1.8	13.9
Wood products	321	365	1.5	-0.9	-2.3	9.2	6.3	-2.7
Sawmills and wood preservation	3211	85	2.7	-0.1	-2.7	3.2	10.7	7.3
Plywood and engineered wood products	3212	64	1.0	-1.3	-2.3	11.3	5.5	-5.2
Other wood products	3219	216	1.1	-1.1	-2.1	10.1	3.7	-5.8
Paper and paper products	322	397	1.9	-0.2	-2.0	2.7	2.5	-0.2
Pulp, paper, and paperboard mills	3221	112	3.0	-0.4	-3.3	6.7	2.9	-3.6
Converted paper products	3222	284	1.3	0.0	-1.3	0.8	2.1	1.3
Printing and related support activities	323	525	1.3	-0.6	-1.9	4.3	-0.3	-4.4
Petroleum and coal products	324	114	2.7	1.2	-1.5	5.2	4.0	-1.1
Chemicals	325	796	1.6	0.7	-0.9	6.1	6.4	0.3
Basic chemicals	3251	143	2.6	0.3	-2.2	19.4	19.3	-0.1
Resin, rubber, and artificial fibers	3252	90	2.5	0.5	-2.0	18.6	18.9	0.2
Agricultural chemicals	3253	37	2.7	0.5	-2.1	3.4	-1.2	-4.4
Pharmaceuticals and medicines	3254	278	0.0	2.0	2.1	-8.2	-8.3	-0.1
Paints, coatings, and adhesives	3255	57	1.0	-0.8	-1.8	9.4	9.2	-0.2
Soaps, cleaning compounds, and toiletries	3256	105	2.6	1.7	-0.9	-0.2	2.3	2.5
Other chemical products and preparations	3259	86	2.5	0.2	-2.3	13.0	15.5	2.2
Plastics and rubber products	326	627	2.0	1.1	-0.9	5.4	9.2	3.6
Plastics products	3261	504	1.9	1.4	-0.5	4.9	8.6	3.5
Rubber products	3262	123	2.4	0.1	-2.2	8.0	12.0	3.7
Nonmetallic mineral products	327	387	1.0	-0.4	-1.4	6.3	3.2	-2.9
Clay products and refractories	3271	51	0.7	-1.9	-2.6	5.6	14.1	8.1
Glass and glass products	3272	83	2.3	-0.1	-2.3	7.1	3.2	-3.6
Cement and concrete products	3273	172	0.1	-0.5	-0.5	3.9	-0.4	-4.2
Lime and gypsum products	3274	14	1.0	-1.1	-2.1	9.5	0.1	-8.6
Other nonmetallic mineral products	3279	67	1.8	0.7	-1.0	13.7	8.3	-4.8
Primary metals	331	366	2.5	-0.2	-2.6	15.5	23.2	6.6
Iron and steel mills and ferroalloy production	3311	87	4.5	1.5	-2.8	20.3	28.9	7.2
Steel products from purchased steel	3312	53	-0.6	-1.7	-1.1	29.3	42.6	10.3
Alumina and aluminum production	3313	55	2.5	-0.3	-2.8	7.5	16.3	8.2
Other nonferrous metal production	3314	59	1.0	-1.4	-2.4	9.2	17.2	7.3
Foundries	3315	112	2.4	-0.6	-2.9	13.1	16.9	3.4

Table 5-2. Average Annual Percent Change in Output Per Hour and Related Series, Selected Industries, 1987–2010 and 2009–2010—*Continued*

(Number, percent.)

Industry	NAICS code	2010 employment (thousands)	Average annual percent change, 1987–2010			Annual percent change, 2009–2010		
			Output per hour	Output	Hours	Output per hour	Output	Hours
Manufacturing—*Continued*								
Fabricated metal products	332	1 316	1.3	0.5	-0.9	5.1	6.6	1.4
Forging and stamping	3321	90	2.7	0.9	-1.8	9.1	15.1	5.5
Cutlery and hand tools	3322	42	2.2	-0.6	-2.7	15.4	10.6	-4.2
Architectural and structural metals	3323	327	0.7	0.3	-0.4	2.3	-3.8	-5.9
Boilers, tanks, and shipping containers	3324	86	0.9	-0.3	-1.2	8.2	5.0	-3.0
Hardware	3325	24	0.9	-3.3	-4.2	9.7	10.3	0.6
Spring and wire products	3326	42	2.7	-0.1	-2.7	8.2	9.3	1.0
Machine shops and threaded products	3327	329	2.0	2.3	0.3	7.5	14.7	6.7
Coating, engraving, and heat treating metals	3328	123	2.7	2.3	-0.4	7.8	15.1	6.7
Other fabricated metal products	3329	254	1.2	0.0	-1.2	1.1	5.1	4.0
Machinery	333	1 008	2.4	1.1	-1.3	9.3	11.8	2.3
Agriculture, construction, and mining machinery	3331	208	2.8	2.8	0.0	11.3	15.6	3.9
Industrial machinery	3332	102	2.5	0.9	-1.6	20.5	26.9	5.3
Commercial and service industry machinery	3333	92	1.4	-0.7	-2.1	4.4	1.9	-2.4
HVAC and commercial refrigeration equipment	3334	126	2.3	1.0	-1.3	5.6	5.4	-0.2
Metalworking machinery	3335	158	1.9	-0.4	-2.2	8.6	15.8	6.6
Turbine and power transmission equipment	3336	92	1.7	0.8	-0.9	11.4	10.0	-1.3
Other general purpose machinery	3339	230	2.6	1.1	-1.5	6.4	7.9	1.4
Computer and electronic products	334	1 104	11.2	8.3	-2.6	11.6	8.1	-3.1
Computer and peripheral equipment	3341	158	20.9	15.9	-4.2	-18.3	-22.5	-5.1
Communications equipment	3342	118	5.4	2.3	-2.9	8.8	2.3	-5.9
Audio and video equipment	3343	20	2.1	-2.7	-4.7	7.1	-7.7	-13.8
Semiconductors and electronic components	3344	374	16.5	14.2	-1.9	32.8	32.1	-0.5
Electronic instruments	3345	409	4.0	1.8	-2.1	9.4	6.4	-2.7
Magnetic media manufacturing and reproduction	3346	26	3.2	1.3	-1.8	10.7	-1.3	-10.8
Electrical equipment and appliances	335	362	2.4	-0.4	-2.7	5.6	5.3	-0.3
Electric lighting equipment	3351	46	1.9	-0.8	-2.6	1.6	-0.1	-1.7
Household appliances	3352	60	3.5	-0.1	-3.5	0.0	0.1	0.1
Electrical equipment	3353	137	2.0	-0.6	-2.5	-3.8	-2.7	1.2
Other electrical equipment and components	3359	119	2.2	-0.2	-2.4	17.8	15.6	-1.9
Transportation equipment	336	1 348	3.1	1.1	-2.0	15.7	17.8	1.8
Motor vehicles	3361	153	3.9	0.9	-2.9	26.1	39.9	11.0
Motor vehicle bodies and trailers	3362	109	1.0	0.2	-0.8	5.5	17.3	11.2
Motor vehicle parts	3363	425	3.4	1.7	-1.6	17.1	27.4	8.8
Aerospace products and parts	3364	481	2.0	-0.3	-2.3	7.5	2.6	-4.5
Railroad rolling stock	3365	19	5.3	3.7	-1.5	11.0	-7.1	-16.3
Ship and boat building	3366	127	2.5	0.6	-1.8	3.9	-0.6	-4.4
Other transportation equipment	3369	34	6.1	5.5	-0.5	2.6	-12.1	-14.3
Furniture and related products	337	385	1.5	-0.9	-2.4	6.7	-1.6	-7.9
Household and institutional furniture	3371	247	1.6	-1.2	-2.8	10.5	0.1	-9.4
Office furniture and fixtures	3372	102	1.1	-0.9	-1.9	0.9	-4.4	-5.3
Other furniture-related products	3379	37	2.0	1.0	-1.0	2.9	-1.9	-4.6
Miscellaneous manufacturing	339	620	3.1	2.5	-0.6	8.3	4.0	-4.0
Medical equipment and supplies	3391	313	3.6	4.6	1.0	6.5	2.6	-3.6
Other miscellaneous manufacturing	3399	308	2.4	0.6	-1.8	10.7	5.9	-4.4

Table 5-3.   Average Annual Percent Change in Output Per Hour and Related Series, Wholesale Trade, Retail Trade, Food Services and Drinking Places, 1987–2011 and 2010–2011

(Number, percent.)

Industry	NAICS code	2011 employment (thousands)	Average annual percent change, 1987–2011			Annual percent change, 2010–2011		
			Output per hour	Output	Hours	Output per hour	Output	Hours
Wholesale Trade								
Wholesale trade	42	5 704	3.1	3.4	0.3	1.9	4.8	2.9
Durable goods	423	2 846	5.0	4.9	0.0	6.3	9.1	2.6
Motor vehicles and parts	4231	320	3.6	3.1	-0.4	6.7	11.4	4.5
Furniture and furnishings	4232	95	1.7	0.8	-0.9	2.1	-4.2	-6.2
Lumber and construction supplies	4233	190	1.5	1.3	-0.1	5.5	4.5	-1.0
Commercial equipment	4234	631	14.2	14.5	0.3	4.1	7.5	3.3
Metals and minerals	4235	118	-1.0	-1.1	-0.1	-1.9	5.2	7.2
Electric goods	4236	313	8.2	7.5	-0.6	5.6	7.3	1.5
Hardware and plumbing	4237	227	1.5	1.8	0.3	2.9	4.3	1.4
Machinery and supplies	4238	629	2.4	2.2	-0.2	13.5	15.3	1.6
Miscellaneous durable goods	4239	325	1.1	2.1	1.0	3.2	10.3	6.9
Nondurable goods	424	2 013	1.4	1.5	0.1	-1.1	0.5	1.6
Paper and paper products	4241	123	1.6	0.6	-1.0	-3.1	-2.1	1.1
Druggists' goods	4242	191	4.1	5.4	1.3	6.6	6.7	0.0
Apparel and piece goods	4243	147	2.3	2.0	-0.4	-5.3	-3.4	2.1
Grocery and related products	4244	745	1.1	1.8	0.7	-0.1	3.2	3.4
Farm product raw materials	4245	79	0.7	-1.2	-2.0	-18.3	-16.0	2.8
Chemicals	4246	124	0.7	1.0	0.2	-0.4	2.4	2.8
Petroleum	4247	96	2.4	0.2	-2.1	-0.4	-0.2	0.2
Alcoholic beverages	4248	167	0.0	1.9	1.9	-2.6	1.7	4.4
Miscellaneous nondurable goods	4249	343	0.0	-0.5	-0.4	-1.8	-5.0	-3.2
Electronic markets and agents and brokers	425	845	1.4	3.9	2.4	-0.6	6.5	7.1
Retail Trade								
Retail trade	44-45	15 510	2.8	3.2	0.4	2.2	3.7	1.5
Motor vehicle and parts dealers	441	1 748	1.9	2.3	0.4	2.1	7.0	4.8
Automobile dealers	4411	1 095	2.0	2.3	0.4	1.0	8.2	7.1
Other motor vehicle dealers	4412	130	2.4	2.8	0.4	-0.2	0.7	0.8
Auto parts, accessories, and tire stores	4413	523	1.4	2.0	0.6	0.1	1.3	1.2
Furniture and home furnishings stores	442	481	3.8	3.3	-0.5	5.9	3.2	-2.5
Furniture stores	4421	229	3.1	2.8	-0.3	5.1	2.9	-2.1
Home furnishings stores	4422	251	4.7	3.9	-0.7	6.8	3.5	-3.1
Electronics and appliance stores	443	532	12.5	13.8	1.1	2.8	8.9	6.0
Building material and garden supply stores	444	1 194	2.6	3.2	0.6	3.3	3.1	-0.1
Building material and supplies dealers	4441	1 040	2.3	3.1	0.9	3.0	2.0	-1.0
Lawn and garden equipment and supplies stores	4442	154	4.3	3.7	-0.6	3.5	10.0	6.3
Food and beverage stores	445	2 925	0.4	0.2	-0.2	1.0	1.3	0.3
Grocery stores	4451	2 529	0.3	0.2	-0.1	0.6	1.3	0.7
Specialty food stores	4452	237	0.0	-0.6	-0.7	0.8	-3.3	-4.1
Beer, wine and liquor stores	4453	159	2.3	0.9	-1.4	2.4	4.1	1.6
Health and personal care stores	446	1 027	2.2	3.4	1.2	0.0	1.5	1.5
Gasoline stations	447	841	1.7	1.0	-0.8	-3.7	-3.1	0.7
Clothing and clothing accessories stores	448	1 469	4.4	4.0	-0.4	-0.3	3.7	4.1
Clothing stores	4481	1 098	4.7	4.6	-0.1	-0.7	4.1	4.8
Shoe stores	4482	188	3.4	2.2	-1.1	4.3	3.5	-0.8
Jewelry, luggage, and leather goods stores	4483	183	3.6	2.8	-0.8	-3.1	2.1	5.3
Sporting goods, hobby, book, and music stores	451	667	4.1	4.0	-0.1	6.5	5.5	-1.0
Sporting goods and musical instrument store	4511	531	4.7	5.1	0.4	4.7	7.4	2.5
Book, periodical, and music stores	4512	136	2.9	1.4	-1.4	13.4	-0.7	-12.5
General merchandise stores	452	3 088	3.0	4.9	1.8	-1.5	2.1	3.6
Department stores	4521	1 547	0.3	1.6	1.3	-5.4	-0.9	4.8
Other general merchandise stores	4529	1 541	6.0	8.5	2.3	0.8	3.4	2.6
Miscellaneous store retailers	453	921	4.0	3.5	-0.4	10.7	5.9	-4.4
Florists	4531	83	3.8	0.0	-3.7	20.6	7.6	-10.8
Office supplies, stationery and gift stores	4532	321	6.2	5.0	-1.1	9.3	3.9	-4.9
Used merchandise stores	4533	185	4.8	6.0	1.1	14.2	14.5	0.2
Other miscellaneous store retailers	4539	332	1.6	2.5	0.8	10.5	5.3	-4.7
Nonstore retailers	454	617	8.8	9.0	0.1	16.9	13.2	-3.2
Electronic shopping and mail-order houses	4541	313	11.2	15.0	3.4	14.6	15.9	1.1
Vending machine operators	4542	51	1.1	-1.9	-2.9	18.7	10.7	-6.8
Direct selling establishments	4543	254	3.3	1.4	-1.8	13.8	4.3	-8.4
Food Services and Drinking Places								
Food services and drinking places	722	9 853	0.6	2.0	1.4	0.0	3.4	3.4
Full-service restaurants	7221	4 635	0.6	2.1	1.4	1.9	5.4	3.4
Limited-service eating places	7222	4 163	0.5	2.1	1.6	-2.3	2.5	4.9
Special food services	7223	688	1.4	2.3	0.9	2.0	0.4	-1.5
Drinking places, alcoholic beverages	7224	368	-0.3	-0.8	-0.4	1.8	-0.7	-2.5

Table 5-4. Indexes of Multifactor Productivity and Related Measures, 1990–2011

(2005 = 100.)

Sector	1990	1991	1992	1993	1994	1995	1996	1997	1998	1999
PRIVATE BUSINESS										
Productivity										
Output per hour of all persons	68.6	69.7	72.6	73.1	73.8	73.8	76.0	77.3	79.6	82.4
Output per unit of capital services	108.1	104.4	106.3	106.5	108.0	106.5	106.6	106.5	105.3	104.3
Multifactor productivity	82.8	82.0	84.1	84.3	84.9	84.6	86.1	86.8	88.0	89.7
Real value-added output	59.5	59.1	61.4	63.4	66.6	68.5	71.7	75.4	79.2	83.6
Inputs										
Labor input	81.4	80.5	81.4	83.9	87.7	90.0	91.8	95.4	97.6	99.9
Capital services	55.1	56.6	57.8	59.6	61.7	64.3	67.2	70.8	75.2	80.2
Combined input quantity	71.9	72.0	73.0	75.3	78.4	80.9	83.2	86.9	89.9	93.3
Capital hours ratio	63.5	66.8	68.3	68.6	68.3	69.3	71.3	72.6	75.6	79.0
PRIVATE NONFARM BUSINESS										
Productivity										
Output per hour of all persons	69.2	70.3	73.1	73.6	74.4	74.7	76.7	77.8	80.1	82.7
Output per unit of capital services	110.0	106.0	107.6	108.0	109.2	107.9	107.6	107.2	105.9	104.7
Multifactor productivity	83.5	82.7	84.6	84.9	85.5	85.5	86.7	87.2	88.5	89.9
Real value-added output	59.6	59.1	61.3	63.5	66.5	68.7	71.7	75.4	79.3	83.8
Inputs										
Labor input	80.8	79.9	80.7	83.4	86.9	89.2	91.1	94.8	97.1	99.6
Capital services	54.2	55.7	57.0	58.8	60.9	63.6	66.7	70.4	74.9	80.0
Combined input quantity	71.4	71.4	72.5	74.9	77.8	80.3	82.8	86.5	89.6	93.1
Capital hours ratio	62.9	66.3	67.9	68.1	68.1	69.2	71.3	72.6	75.6	79.0
MANUFACTURING										
Productivity										
Output per hour	54.0	55.4	57.5	58.9	61.0	63.8	66.1	69.7	73.5	77.1
Output per unit of capital services	92.4	88.8	89.7	91.1	94.1	95.7	95.1	97.7	98.4	99.0
Sector output	67.2	66.0	68.2	70.9	75.1	79.0	81.7	87.7	92.3	96.1
Inputs										
Labor hours	124.5	119.3	118.7	120.3	123.1	123.9	123.6	125.8	125.5	124.7
Combined input quantity	87.0	85.8	89.2	90.4	93.3	96.5	99.6	104.0	108.1	111.2
Energy	88.1	87.9	87.0	89.9	93.2	95.8	93.3	91.4	94.9	117.0
Materials	66.9	66.6	72.4	72.9	76.1	80.2	87.4	94.4	102.4	108.7
Capital services	72.7	74.3	76.0	77.8	79.8	82.6	85.9	89.8	93.8	97.1
Purchased services	83.5	82.9	89.0	89.7	93.2	97.8	97.4	101.5	104.9	105.9

Sector	2000	2001	2002	2003	2004	2005	2006	2007	2008	2009	2010	2011
PRIVATE BUSINESS												
Productivity												
Output per hour of all persons	85.3	88.0	92.1	95.7	98.4	100.0	101.0	102.6	103.3	106.0	110.3	110.8
Output per unit of capital services	102.6	98.9	97.8	98.4	99.8	100.0	100.0	99.3	95.7	90.5	93.7	94.0
Multifactor productivity	91.2	91.9	94.1	96.7	99.0	100.0	100.5	100.8	99.6	98.8	102.2	102.5
Real value-added output	87.4	88.3	90.0	92.9	96.7	100.0	103.1	105.2	103.8	98.9	102.8	105.0
Inputs												
Labor input	101.1	99.3	97.4	97.0	98.1	100.0	102.4	103.6	102.1	95.5	96.0	97.9
Capital services	85.3	89.2	92.1	94.4	96.9	100.0	103.1	106.0	108.5	109.2	109.7	111.7
Combined input quantity	95.9	96.0	95.6	96.1	97.7	100.0	102.6	104.4	104.3	100.1	100.6	102.5
Capital hours ratio	83.2	89.0	94.2	97.3	98.6	100.0	101.0	103.2	108.0	117.1	117.8	117.8
PRIVATE NONFARM BUSINESS												
Productivity												
Output per hour of all persons	85.6	88.3	92.4	95.8	98.4	100.0	100.9	102.6	103.3	105.8	110.2	110.9
Output per unit of capital services	102.6	99.0	97.7	98.1	99.6	100.0	99.9	99.1	95.0	89.6	92.8	93.4
Multifactor productivity	91.4	92.1	94.2	96.6	98.9	100.0	100.4	100.7	99.3	98.3	101.7	102.3
Real value-added output	87.5	88.4	90.1	92.9	96.7	100.0	103.2	105.4	103.9	98.7	102.6	105.1
Inputs												
Labor input	100.8	99.2	97.2	96.9	98.1	100.0	102.5	103.8	102.2	95.6	96.1	98.0
Capital services	85.3	89.3	92.3	94.7	97.1	100.0	103.3	106.4	109.3	110.1	110.6	112.6
Combined input quantity	95.8	96.0	95.6	96.2	97.7	100.0	102.8	104.7	104.6	100.4	100.9	102.8
Capital hours ratio	83.4	89.2	94.6	97.7	98.8	100.0	101.0	103.6	108.7	118.1	118.8	118.8
MANUFACTURING												
Productivity												
Output per hour	80.5	81.9	87.9	93.3	95.5	100.0	101.0	104.9	104.3	104.3	111.1	. . .
Output per unit of capital services	99.5	93.8	93.3	94.5	96.9	100.0	100.9	101.7	94.8	82.5	88.0	. . .
Sector output	99.0	94.2	93.9	94.9	96.5	100.0	101.7	103.8	99.1	86.3	91.9	. . .
Inputs												
Labor hours	123.1	115.0	106.9	101.6	101.1	100.0	100.7	99.0	95.1	82.7	82.7	. . .
Combined input quantity	110.6	106.3	102.6	99.9	98.0	100.0	99.3	100.6	96.5	86.5	85.6	. . .
Energy	127.6	139.4	107.8	96.8	90.7	100.0	95.8	96.4	97.1	73.7	75.9	. . .
Materials	106.6	99.8	100.8	99.2	98.4	100.0	98.9	98.8	93.7	81.5	78.5	. . .
Capital services	99.5	100.5	100.7	100.4	99.6	100.0	100.7	102.1	104.6	104.7	104.4	. . .
Purchased services	104.4	102.6	99.3	98.5	92.4	100.0	97.3	105.7	95.6	86.8	87.2	. . .

. . . = Not available.

Chapter Six

COMPENSATION OF EMPLOYEES

COMPENSATION OF EMPLOYEES

HIGHLIGHTS

This chapter discusses the Employment Cost Index (ECI), which covers changes in wages and salaries and benefits; the Employer Costs for Employee Compensation (ECEC); and employee participation in various benefit plans.

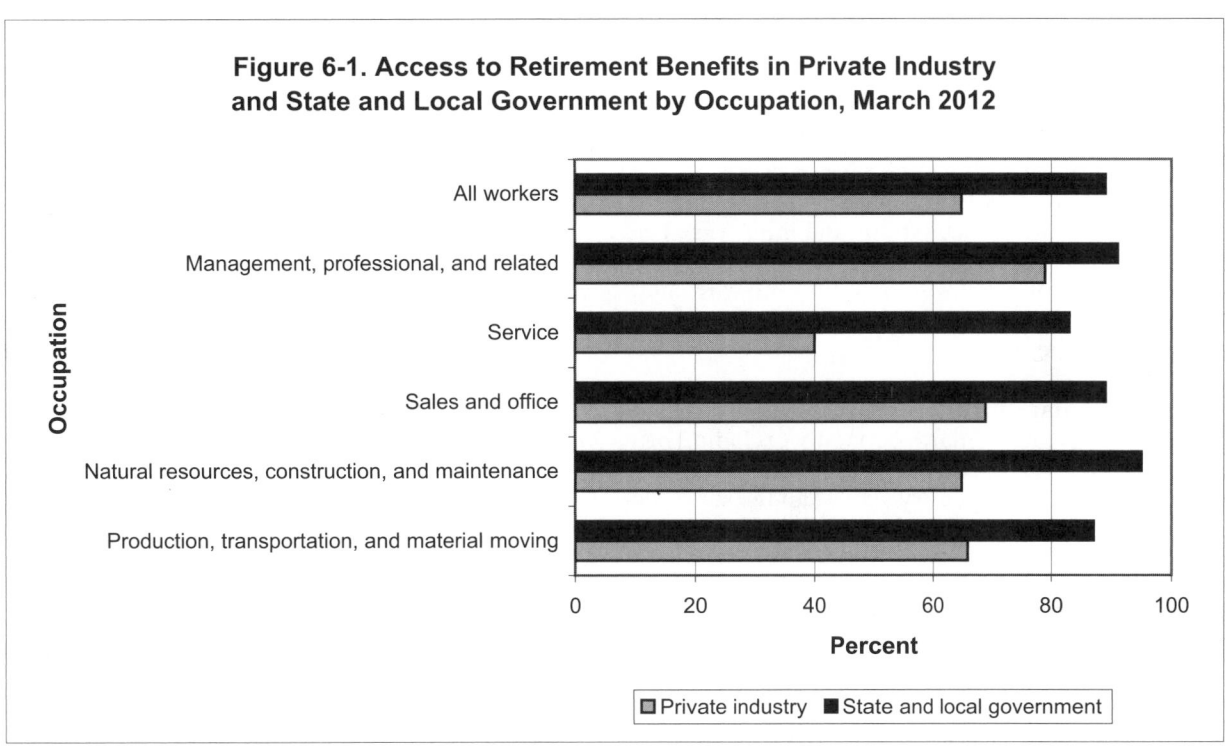

Figure 6-1. Access to Retirement Benefits in Private Industry and State and Local Government by Occupation, March 2012

Among all occupations, state and local government workers were far more likely to have access to retirement benefits than those in the private sector. Eighty-nine percent of state and local government workers had access to retirement benefits compared with 65 percent of private industry workers. (See Table 6-9.)

OTHER HIGHLIGHTS

- Wages and salaries made up 70.4 percent of employee compensation for private industry workers in June 2012. Legally required benefits, such as Social Security and Medicare, made up the second largest category of employee compensation at 8.2 percent followed by insurance at 8.1 percent. (See Table 6-5.)

- Total employer compensation costs per hour varied among the different Census divisions, ranging from $33.47 in the New England states (Connecticut, Maine, Massachusetts, New Hampshire, Rhode Island and Vermont) to $24.44 in the East South Central states (Alabama, Kentucky, Mississippi, and Tennessee). (See Table 6-6.)

- Union workers were far more likely to have access to retirement and medical benefits than those that were not in a union. In March 2012, 92 percent of union workers in private industry had access to retirement benefits compared with only 62 percent of nonunion workers. Similarly, 94 percent of union workers had access to medical care benefits compared with 67 percent of nonunion workers. (See Tables 6-9 and 6-10.)

NOTES AND DEFINITIONS

NATIONAL COMPENSATION SURVEY

The National Compensation Survey (NCS) is an establishment survey conducted by the Office of Compensation Levels and Trends (OCLT) at the Bureau of Labor Statistics (BLS). It provides data for the Employment Cost Index (ECI), the Employer Costs for Employee Compensation (ECEC), the occupational earnings series, and the employee benefits survey.

EMPLOYMENT COST INDEX

The Employment Cost Index (ECI) is a measure of the change in the cost of labor, free from the influence of employment shifts among occupations and industries. The compensation series includes changes in wages and salaries and employer costs for employee benefits. The wage and salary series and the benefit cost series are the two components of compensation.

The ECI provides data for the civilian economy, which includes the total private nonfarm economy excluding private households, and the public sector excluding the federal government. The private industry series and the state and local government series provide data for the two sectors separately.

To be included in the ECI, employees in occupations must receive cash payments from the establishment for services performed and the establishment must pay the employer's portion of Medicare taxes on that individual's wages. Major exclusions from the survey are the self-employed, individuals who set their own pay (for example, proprietors, owners, major stockholders, and partners in unincorporated firms), volunteers, unpaid workers, family members being paid token wages, individuals receiving long-term disability compensation, and U.S. citizens working overseas.

Data for the June 2012 reference period were collected from a probability sample of approximately 47,400 occupational observations selected from a sample of about 9,500 establishments in private industry and approximately 9,200 occupations from a sample of about 1,400 establishments in state and local governments. The state and local government sample, which is replaced less frequently than the private industry sample, was replaced in its entirety in September 2007. The private industry sample is rotated over approximately 5 years, which makes the sample more representative of the economy and reduces respondent burden. Data are collected for the pay period including the 12th day of the survey months of March, June, September, and December. The sample is replaced on a cross-area, cross-industry basis.

Beginning with the release of the March 2006 data, indexes were rebased to December 2005 = 100 from June 1989 = 100. The percentage changes shown in the current and constant-dollar historical tables were calculated from the rebased indexes. Thus, changes may differ from those published in previous edition of the handbook because of rounding.

Concepts and Definitions

Wages and salaries are defined as the hourly straight-time wage rate or, for workers not paid on an hourly basis, straight-time earnings divided by the corresponding hours. Straight-time wage and salary rates are total earnings before payroll deductions, excluding premium pay for overtime and for work on weekends and holidays, shift differentials, and nonproduction bonuses such as lump-sum payments provided in lieu of wage increases. Production bonuses, incentive earnings, commission payments, and cost-of-living adjustments are included in straight-time wage and salary rates.

Benefits covered by the ECI are: paid leave—vacations, holidays, sick leave, and personal leave; supplemental pay-premium pay for work in addition to the regular work schedule (such as overtime, weekends, and holidays), shift differentials, and nonproduction bonuses (such as referral bonuses and attendance bonuses); insurance benefits—life, health, short-term disability, and long-term disability; retirement and savings benefits—defined benefit and defined contribution plans; and legally required benefits—Social Security, Medicare, federal and state unemployment insurance, and workers' compensation.

Sources of Additional Information

Additional information on ECI methodology and more tables are available in Chapter 8 of the *BLS Handbook of Methods* and BLS new releases. The BLS publication *Compensation and Working Conditions* contains articles on all aspects of the NCS. All of these resources are on the BLS Web site at <http://www.bls.gov/ncs/ect/>.

Table 6-1. Employment Cost Index, Private Industry Workers, Total Compensation[1] and Wages and Salaries, by Selected Industry and Occupation, 2001–2012

(December 2005 = 100.)

Characteristic and year	Total compensation					Wages and salaries				
	Indexes				Percent change for 12 months (ended December)	Indexes				Percent change for 12 months (ended December)
	March	June	September	December		March	June	September	December	
WORKERS BY INDUSTRY										
Total Private										
2001	85.0	85.8	86.7	87.3	4.1	87.6	88.4	89.2	89.9	3.8
2002	88.2	89.2	89.7	90.0	3.1	90.7	91.6	92.0	92.2	2.6
2003	91.4	92.3	93.2	93.6	4.0	93.3	94.0	94.8	95.1	3.1
2004	94.9	95.9	96.7	97.2	3.8	95.7	96.5	97.3	97.6	2.6
2005	98.2	98.9	99.5	100.0	2.9	98.3	98.9	99.5	100.0	2.5
2006	100.8	101.7	102.5	103.2	3.2	100.7	101.7	102.5	103.2	3.2
2007	104.0	104.9	105.7	106.3	3.0	104.3	105.1	106.0	106.6	3.3
2008	107.3	108.0	108.7	108.9	2.4	107.6	108.4	109.1	109.4	2.6
2009	109.3	109.6	110.0	110.2	1.2	109.8	110.1	110.6	110.8	1.3
2010	111.1	111.7	112.2	112.5	2.1	111.4	111.9	112.4	112.8	1.8
2011	113.3	114.3	114.6	115.0	2.2	113.2	113.8	114.3	114.6	1.6
2012	115.7	116.4	116.9	. . .	. . .	115.3	115.9	116.4	. . .	. . .
Goods-Producing[2]										
2001	83.9	84.7	85.3	86.0	3.6	87.9	88.8	89.3	90.0	3.6
2002	87.0	87.7	88.2	89.0	3.5	90.7	91.4	91.9	92.6	2.9
2003	90.5	91.5	92.1	92.6	4.0	93.3	94.1	94.6	94.9	2.5
2004	94.5	95.4	96.5	96.9	4.6	95.6	96.2	97.2	97.2	2.4
2005	98.0	99.0	99.8	100.0	3.2	97.9	98.7	99.5	100.0	2.9
2006	100.3	101.3	102.0	102.5	2.5	100.7	101.8	102.3	102.9	2.9
2007	102.9	103.9	104.4	105.0	2.4	103.9	104.7	105.4	106.0	3.0
2008	106.1	106.8	107.2	107.5	2.4	107.1	108.0	108.6	109.0	2.8
2009	107.9	108.2	108.4	108.6	1.0	109.2	109.5	109.8	110.0	0.9
2010	109.7	110.3	111.0	111.1	2.3	110.5	110.9	111.5	111.6	1.5
2011	112.0	113.2	113.4	113.8	2.4	112.2	112.7	113.2	113.5	1.7
2012	114.1	114.7	115.3	. . .	. . .	114.0	114.5	115.1	. . .	. . .
Service-Providing[3]										
2001	85.4	86.2	87.1	87.8	4.4	87.4	88.3	89.2	89.8	3.8
2002	88.7	89.7	90.2	90.4	3.0	90.7	91.7	92.0	92.1	2.6
2003	91.7	92.5	93.6	94.0	4.0	93.3	93.9	94.9	95.2	3.4
2004	95.1	96.1	96.8	97.3	3.5	95.8	96.6	97.3	97.7	2.6
2005	98.3	98.9	99.5	100.0	2.8	98.4	99.0	99.5	100.0	2.4
2006	101.0	101.8	102.7	103.4	3.4	100.8	101.7	102.6	103.3	3.3
2007	104.3	105.2	106.1	106.7	3.2	104.4	105.3	106.1	106.8	3.4
2008	107.7	108.5	109.1	109.4	2.5	107.7	108.6	109.3	109.6	2.6
2009	109.8	110.1	110.5	110.8	1.3	110.0	110.3	110.8	111.1	1.4
2010	111.6	112.1	112.6	113.0	2.0	111.7	112.3	112.7	113.1	1.8
2011	113.8	114.6	115.0	115.3	2.0	113.5	114.1	114.6	114.9	1.6
2012	116.3	117.0	117.4	. . .	. . .	115.6	116.3	116.7	. . .	. . .
WORKERS BY OCCUPATION										
Management, Professional, and Related[4]										
2001	85.0	86.0	86.8	87.4	4.5	87.0	88.0	88.9	89.5	4.1
2002	88.3	89.2	89.5	89.7	2.6	90.4	91.3	91.6	91.7	2.5
2003	91.6	92.3	93.3	93.8	4.6	93.3	94.0	94.8	95.3	3.9
2004	94.9	95.7	96.5	97.1	3.5	96.0	96.5	97.3	97.8	2.6
2005	98.5	99.1	99.6	100.0	3.0	98.6	99.2	99.6	100.0	2.2
2006	101.1	101.9	102.9	103.5	3.5	101.1	102.0	103.0	103.6	3.6
2007	104.6	105.5	106.4	106.8	3.2	104.9	105.8	106.7	107.2	3.5
2008	108.1	108.9	109.6	109.9	2.9	108.5	109.3	110.1	110.5	3.1
2009	110.4	110.5	110.6	110.7	0.7	111.1	111.1	111.3	111.5	0.9
2010	111.8	112.2	112.7	113.0	2.1	112.5	112.9	113.4	113.7	2.0
2011	114.1	114.8	115.1	115.4	2.1	114.4	114.9	115.3	115.5	1.6
2012	116.4	117.1	117.4	. . .	. . .	116.3	117.0	117.3	. . .	. . .
Management, Business, and Financial										
2001	86.1	87.1	87.8	88.5	4.4	87.3	88.3	89.1	89.8	4.1
2002	89.5	90.7	90.7	90.6	2.4	90.8	92.2	92.4	92.1	2.6
2003	93.3	93.9	94.9	95.4	5.3	94.8	95.5	96.4	96.7	5.0
2004	95.9	96.8	97.3	97.9	2.6	96.8	97.5	98.1	98.5	1.9
2005	99.1	99.6	99.7	100.0	2.1	99.2	99.7	99.5	100.0	1.5
2006	101.3	102.0	102.7	103.1	3.1	101.3	102.2	102.8	103.1	3.1
2007	104.3	105.1	106.0	106.3	3.1	104.7	105.5	106.3	106.6	3.4
2008	108.0	108.7	109.3	109.5	3.0	108.2	109.0	109.7	110.0	3.2
2009	109.6	109.7	109.7	109.9	0.4	110.3	110.3	110.4	110.8	0.7
2010	111.3	111.7	112.0	112.3	2.2	112.0	112.6	112.8	113.2	2.2
2011	113.6	114.5	114.8	115.0	2.4	113.9	114.4	114.9	115.0	1.6
2012	116.0	116.9	116.9	. . .	. . .	115.7	116.7	116.7	. . .	. . .

[1]Includes wages, salaries, and employer costs for employee benefits.
[2]Includes mining, construction, and manufacturing.
[3]Includes the following industries: wholesale trade; retail trade; transportation and warehousing; utilities; information; finance and insurance; real estate and rental and leasing; professional, scientific, and technical services; management of companies and enterprises; administrative and support and waste management and remediation services; education services; health care and social assistance; arts, entertainment, and recreation; accommodation and food services; and other services, except public administration.
[4]Includes the following occupational groups: management, business, and financial; professional and related; sales and related; and office and administrative support.
. . . = Not available.

Table 6-1. Employment Cost Index, Private Industry Workers, Total Compensation[1] and Wages and Salaries, by Selected Industry and Occupation, 2001–2012—*Continued*

(December 2005 = 100.)

Characteristic and year	Total compensation					Wages and salaries				
	Indexes				Percent change for 12 months (ended December)	Indexes				Percent change for 12 months (ended December)
	March	June	September	December		March	June	September	December	
Professional and Related										
2001	84.1	85.0	86.0	86.5	4.7	86.9	87.8	88.7	89.3	4.1
2002	87.3	87.9	88.5	89.1	3.0	90.1	90.5	91.0	91.4	2.4
2003	90.3	91.0	92.0	92.6	3.9	92.1	92.7	93.6	94.2	3.1
2004	94.1	94.8	95.8	96.5	4.2	95.3	95.7	96.7	97.2	3.2
2005	98.0	98.8	99.5	100.0	3.6	98.2	98.8	99.6	100.0	2.9
2006	101.0	101.8	103.1	103.9	3.9	100.9	101.8	103.1	104.0	4.0
2007	104.9	105.9	106.7	107.3	3.3	105.1	106.0	107.0	107.6	3.5
2008	108.3	109.0	109.9	110.3	2.8	108.7	109.5	110.4	110.9	3.1
2009	111.0	111.1	111.4	111.4	1.0	111.6	111.8	112.1	112.1	1.1
2010	112.2	112.6	113.3	113.5	1.9	112.8	113.2	113.9	114.1	1.8
2011	114.6	115.1	115.4	115.7	1.9	114.8	115.2	115.6	115.9	1.6
2012	116.8	117.3	117.7	. . .	. . .	116.7	117.2	117.7	. . .	. . .
Sales and Related										
2001	84.9	86.0	86.3	87.2	3.3	86.8	88.0	87.9	88.6	2.4
2002	87.7	89.7	89.7	89.7	2.9	89.2	91.0	91.0	90.9	2.6
2003	90.6	91.7	93.2	92.9	3.6	91.5	92.5	94.3	93.8	3.2
2004	94.0	95.4	96.8	96.2	3.6	94.4	95.7	97.4	96.6	3.0
2005	97.2	97.9	99.2	100.0	4.0	97.3	97.8	99.2	100.0	3.5
2006	99.9	101.1	101.7	102.3	2.3	99.8	101.3	102.0	102.6	2.6
2007	102.4	103.6	104.2	105.2	2.8	102.8	104.0	104.4	105.5	2.8
2008	105.0	106.2	106.0	105.5	0.3	105.3	106.6	106.4	105.7	0.2
2009	104.3	104.5	105.3	105.8	0.3	104.3	104.7	105.7	106.2	0.5
2010	105.8	107.5	107.4	108.1	2.2	106.2	108.0	107.8	108.7	2.4
2011	107.8	109.8	110.3	110.7	2.4	107.8	109.8	110.4	110.9	2.0
2012	111.4	112.6	113.5	. . .	. . .	111.5	112.8	113.7	. . .	. . .
Office and Administrative Support										
2001	84.2	84.9	85.9	86.6	4.6	87.0	87.7	88.8	89.4	4.2
2002	87.9	88.6	89.3	89.9	3.8	90.7	91.3	91.8	92.4	3.4
2003	91.0	92.0	92.8	93.3	3.8	93.1	93.9	94.4	94.7	2.5
2004	94.7	95.8	96.5	97.2	4.2	95.6	96.4	97.1	97.6	3.1
2005	98.1	98.9	99.5	100.0	2.9	98.2	99.0	99.4	100.0	2.5
2006	100.9	101.9	102.7	103.4	3.4	100.9	101.9	102.6	103.3	3.3
2007	104.5	105.4	106.0	106.7	3.2	104.5	105.4	106.0	106.7	3.3
2008	107.8	108.5	109.2	109.6	2.7	107.7	108.5	109.2	109.7	2.8
2009	110.5	110.9	111.3	111.6	1.8	110.6	111.1	111.4	111.8	1.9
2010	112.6	113.1	113.7	114.0	2.2	112.2	112.6	113.3	113.6	1.6
2011	115.1	115.8	116.2	116.5	2.2	114.4	114.8	115.4	115.7	1.8
2012	117.5	118.1	118.5	. . .	. . .	116.4	117.0	117.4	. . .	. . .
Natural Resources, Construction, and Maintenance										
2001	84.3	85.0	86.4	86.6	4.0	87.6	88.4	89.9	90.0	3.8
2002	87.4	88.5	89.3	89.7	3.6	90.5	91.7	92.3	92.6	2.9
2003	90.8	92.0	92.8	93.3	4.0	93.2	94.1	94.8	95.2	2.8
2004	94.8	96.1	96.5	97.1	4.1	95.8	96.7	97.1	97.5	2.4
2005	97.9	98.9	99.5	100.0	3.0	97.8	98.7	99.4	100.0	2.6
2006	100.8	102.1	103.0	103.6	3.6	100.7	101.8	102.8	103.4	3.4
2007	104.0	105.0	105.9	106.7	3.0	104.2	105.1	106.2	107.1	3.6
2008	107.6	108.3	109.0	109.6	2.7	108.1	109.0	109.8	110.5	3.2
2009	109.9	110.3	110.8	111.2	1.5	110.6	111.0	111.6	112.0	1.4
2010	112.2	112.7	113.1	113.3	1.9	112.5	112.8	113.1	113.3	1.2
2011	113.8	114.9	115.5	115.8	2.2	113.7	114.4	115.2	115.4	1.9
2012	116.3	117.0	117.7	. . .	. . .	115.6	116.0	116.6	. . .	. . .
Construction, Extraction, Farming, Fishing, and Forestry										
2001	84.2	85.1	86.2	86.4	3.8	87.8	88.9	89.8	90.0	3.6
2002	87.3	88.1	88.8	89.5	3.6	90.6	91.3	91.9	92.4	2.7
2003	90.3	91.6	92.5	93.1	4.0	92.7	93.7	94.6	94.9	2.7
2004	94.7	95.8	96.4	97.2	4.4	95.8	96.6	96.9	97.5	2.7
2005	97.7	98.7	99.5	100.0	2.9	97.8	98.5	99.3	100.0	2.6
2006	100.7	102.2	103.1	103.7	3.7	100.7	102.0	103.0	103.7	3.7
2007	104.4	105.7	106.5	107.4	3.6	104.7	105.8	106.7	107.8	4.0
2008	108.6	109.7	110.3	110.8	3.2	109.2	110.1	110.8	111.5	3.4
2009	110.9	111.5	112.0	112.4	1.4	111.4	111.7	112.3	112.7	1.1
2010	113.1	113.6	114.3	114.4	1.8	112.9	113.3	113.9	114.0	1.2
2011	114.8	115.5	116.0	116.5	1.8	114.5	114.9	115.4	115.7	1.5
2012	116.6	117.1	117.8	. . .	. . .	115.7	116.0	116.8	. . .	. . .

[1] Includes wages, salaries, and employer costs for employee benefits.

. . . = Not available.

Table 6-1. Employment Cost Index, Private Industry Workers, Total Compensation[1] and Wages and Salaries, by Selected Industry and Occupation, 2001–2012—*Continued*

(December 2005 = 100.)

Characteristic and year	Total compensation					Wages and salaries				
	Indexes				Percent change for 12 months (ended December)	Indexes				Percent change for 12 months (ended December)
	March	June	September	December		March	June	September	December	
Installation, Maintenance, and Repair										
2001	84.4	84.9	86.8	86.8	4.1	87.4	87.9	90.1	90.1	4.3
2002	87.4	89.1	90.0	90.1	3.8	90.4	92.2	92.9	92.9	3.1
2003	91.4	92.5	93.1	93.6	3.9	93.8	94.6	95.1	95.5	2.8
2004	95.0	96.3	96.7	97.0	3.6	95.9	96.8	97.3	97.4	2.0
2005	98.1	99.3	99.6	100.0	3.1	97.8	99.1	99.5	100.0	2.7
2006	100.9	102.1	103.0	103.4	3.4	100.7	101.6	102.6	103.0	3.0
2007	103.5	104.1	105.2	105.8	2.3	103.7	104.2	105.6	106.1	3.0
2008	106.3	106.6	107.4	108.1	2.2	106.8	107.6	108.5	109.3	3.0
2009	108.6	108.9	109.4	109.8	1.6	109.7	110.2	110.7	111.2	1.7
2010	111.1	111.5	111.6	111.9	1.9	112.1	112.1	112.1	112.5	1.2
2011	112.6	114.2	114.9	115.0	2.8	112.7	113.9	115.0	115.0	2.2
2012	116.1	116.8	117.5	. . .	. . .	115.5	115.9	116.4	. . .	. . .
Production, Transportation, and Material Moving										
2001	85.3	85.8	86.7	87.4	3.6	88.7	89.4	90.2	91.0	3.9
2002	88.4	89.1	89.7	90.3	3.3	91.9	92.4	92.8	93.3	2.5
2003	91.5	92.4	93.2	93.6	3.7	94.0	94.6	95.1	95.4	2.3
2004	95.5	96.5	97.4	97.8	4.5	96.0	96.7	97.6	97.8	2.5
2005	98.5	99.0	99.7	100.0	2.2	98.3	98.9	99.6	100.0	2.2
2006	100.4	101.1	101.7	102.3	2.3	100.6	101.2	101.8	102.4	2.4
2007	102.5	103.3	103.9	104.5	2.2	103.1	103.8	104.5	105.0	2.5
2008	105.5	106.0	106.6	106.9	2.3	106.0	106.8	107.5	107.8	2.7
2009	107.7	108.1	108.6	108.9	1.9	108.3	108.8	109.4	109.6	1.7
2010	109.9	110.5	111.3	111.5	2.4	109.8	110.3	111.1	111.3	1.6
2011	112.2	113.5	113.8	114.2	2.4	111.6	112.0	112.5	112.8	1.3
2012	114.5	115.1	115.7	. . .	. . .	113.7	114.0	114.7	. . .	. . .
Production										
2001	84.9	85.2	86.0	86.7	3.2	88.4	89.1	89.7	90.5	3.7
2002	87.7	88.3	88.8	89.4	3.1	91.3	91.8	92.3	92.8	2.5
2003	91.0	91.7	92.5	93.0	4.0	93.6	94.1	94.8	95.1	2.5
2004	95.3	96.4	97.4	97.7	5.1	95.6	96.5	97.4	97.5	2.5
2005	98.6	99.1	99.6	100.0	2.4	98.3	98.9	99.5	100.0	2.6
2006	100.4	101.0	101.6	102.0	2.0	100.7	101.2	101.7	102.2	2.2
2007	102.1	102.8	103.2	104.0	2.0	103.1	103.6	104.2	104.6	2.3
2008	104.8	105.2	105.8	106.1	2.0	105.6	106.4	107.2	107.4	2.7
2009	107.1	107.6	108.0	108.2	2.0	108.1	108.5	109.0	109.3	1.8
2010	109.5	110.0	110.7	110.8	2.4	109.6	110.0	110.5	110.5	1.1
2011	111.7	113.2	113.4	113.8	2.7	111.1	111.5	112.0	112.3	1.6
2012	113.8	114.4	114.8	. . .	. . .	113.2	113.5	113.9	. . .	. . .
Transportation and Material Moving										
2001	85.8	86.7	87.7	88.5	4.2	89.0	89.9	90.8	91.6	4.1
2002	89.5	90.2	90.9	91.4	3.3	92.6	93.1	93.6	94.0	2.6
2003	92.4	93.4	94.0	94.4	3.3	94.7	95.3	95.6	95.8	1.9
2004	95.7	96.7	97.5	97.9	3.7	96.4	97.1	97.9	98.2	2.5
2005	98.3	99.0	99.8	100.0	2.1	98.5	98.9	99.7	100.0	1.8
2006	100.4	101.2	102.0	102.6	2.6	100.4	101.2	102.0	102.6	2.6
2007	103.1	104.1	104.9	105.3	2.6	103.2	104.1	105.0	105.4	2.7
2008	106.4	107.2	107.7	107.9	2.5	106.5	107.4	108.0	108.3	2.8
2009	108.4	108.9	109.6	109.7	1.7	108.5	109.2	109.9	110.1	1.7
2010	110.4	111.2	112.2	112.5	2.6	110.2	110.8	111.8	112.2	1.9
2011	113.0	114.0	114.4	114.9	2.1	112.2	112.8	113.2	113.6	1.2
2012	115.5	116.0	117.0	. . .	. . .	114.4	114.8	115.7	. . .	. . .
Service										
2001	87.1	87.7	88.2	89.4	3.8	89.7	90.2	90.6	91.7	3.4
2002	90.2	90.6	91.5	92.0	2.9	92.5	92.8	93.4	93.9	2.4
2003	93.0	93.4	94.4	95.0	3.3	94.5	94.8	95.6	96.1	2.3
2004	95.9	96.7	97.2	97.7	2.8	96.4	96.9	97.4	97.9	1.9
2005	98.5	99.0	99.5	100.0	2.4	98.6	99.0	99.6	100.0	2.1
2006	100.8	101.5	102.3	103.1	3.1	100.6	101.3	102.0	102.9	2.9
2007	104.5	105.2	106.4	107.0	3.8	104.6	105.3	106.5	107.1	4.1
2008	107.8	108.7	109.4	109.8	2.6	107.9	108.8	109.7	110.1	2.8
2009	110.7	110.9	111.7	111.8	1.8	111.0	111.2	112.1	112.3	2.0
2010	112.4	112.7	113.3	113.5	1.5	112.6	112.7	113.3	113.5	1.1
2011	114.5	114.7	115.0	115.4	1.7	114.2	114.2	114.6	115.1	1.4
2012	116.0	116.4	116.9	. . .	. . .	115.4	115.8	116.2	. . .	. . .

[1] Includes wages, salaries, and employer costs for employee benefits.
. . . = Not available.

Table 6-2. Employment Cost Index, Private Industry Workers, Total Compensation[1] and Wages and Salaries, by Bargaining Status and and Selected Industry, 2001–2012

(December 2005 = 100.)

Characteristic and year	Total compensation					Wages and salaries				
	Indexes				Percent change for 12 months (ended December)	Indexes				Percent change for 12 months (ended December)
	March	June	September	December		March	June	September	December	
WORKERS BY BARGAINING STATUS AND INDUSTRY										
Union Workers										
2001	82.0	82.9	83.7	84.8	4.2	86.5	87.4	88.3	89.6	4.3
2002	85.7	86.5	87.5	88.2	4.0	90.2	91.1	91.9	92.6	3.3
2003	89.5	90.7	91.6	92.3	4.6	93.0	93.8	94.4	94.9	2.5
2004	94.5	95.9	96.7	97.3	5.4	95.6	96.4	97.1	97.6	2.8
2005	97.9	98.8	99.6	100.0	2.8	97.9	98.7	99.5	100.0	2.5
2006	100.5	101.8	102.4	103.0	3.0	100.3	101.2	101.7	102.3	2.3
2007	102.7	103.9	104.4	105.1	2.0	102.8	103.7	104.4	104.7	2.3
2008	105.9	106.7	107.4	108.0	2.8	105.5	106.7	107.4	108.1	3.2
2009	109.1	109.8	110.5	111.1	2.9	108.8	109.6	110.2	110.9	2.6
2010	112.8	113.7	114.6	114.8	3.3	111.5	112.1	112.7	112.9	1.8
2011	115.6	117.1	117.4	117.9	2.7	113.6	114.0	114.6	114.9	1.8
2012	118.3	119.3	120.2	...	...	115.6	116.2	116.9	...	...
Union Workers, Goods-Producing[2]										
2001	81.9	82.7	83.4	84.0	2.9	87.2	88.2	88.9	89.5	3.5
2002	84.8	85.5	86.4	87.1	3.7	90.0	90.9	91.7	92.4	3.2
2003	88.9	90.2	90.9	91.7	5.3	92.9	94.0	94.5	95.0	2.8
2004	94.6	95.9	96.7	97.2	6.0	95.4	96.3	96.9	97.1	2.2
2005	97.7	98.8	99.6	100.0	2.9	97.5	98.5	99.2	100.0	3.0
2006	99.9	101.2	101.8	102.2	2.2	100.5	101.6	101.9	102.3	2.3
2007	101.5	102.8	103.1	104.0	1.8	102.7	103.6	104.3	104.3	2.0
2008	104.6	105.6	106.2	106.9	2.8	105.2	106.4	107.1	107.7	3.3
2009	108.0	108.9	109.5	110.0	2.9	108.2	108.8	109.5	109.8	1.9
2010	111.9	112.6	113.8	113.9	3.5	110.2	110.7	111.1	111.2	1.3
2011	114.3	116.4	116.3	116.9	2.6	111.7	112.1	112.8	112.9	1.5
2012	115.8	116.6	117.7	...	...	113.5	113.8	114.4	...	...
Union Workers, Manufacturing										
2001	81.1	81.4	82.0	83.0	2.7	87.3	88.1	88.8	89.7	3.7
2002	84.1	84.7	85.4	86.5	4.2	90.3	90.8	91.6	92.5	3.1
2003	88.6	89.5	90.1	91.0	5.2	93.3	94.2	94.5	95.0	2.7
2004	95.6	96.7	97.5	97.8	7.5	95.5	96.2	97.0	97.1	2.2
2005	98.3	99.1	99.7	100.0	2.2	97.6	98.3	99.0	100.0	3.0
2006	99.3	100.1	100.5	100.8	0.8	100.6	101.2	101.4	101.7	1.7
2007	99.2	100.0	100.0	101.0	0.2	102.0	102.5	102.9	102.6	0.9
2008	101.4	101.7	102.1	102.8	1.8	103.4	104.4	104.9	105.5	2.8
2009	104.4	104.8	105.3	105.8	2.9	106.0	106.4	107.0	107.3	1.7
2010	108.6	109.1	110.5	110.5	4.4	107.8	108.2	108.6	108.7	1.3
2011	110.9	113.8	113.2	113.8	3.0	109.4	109.8	110.6	110.7	1.8
2012	112.1	112.8	113.6	...	...	111.5	111.8	112.1	...	...
Union Workers, Service-Providing[3]										
2001	82.0	83.0	84.0	85.5	5.2	85.9	86.8	87.8	89.6	4.9
2002	86.4	87.3	88.4	89.1	4.2	90.3	91.2	92.0	92.7	3.5
2003	90.1	91.1	92.3	92.8	4.2	93.1	93.6	94.4	94.8	2.3
2004	94.4	95.8	96.6	97.3	4.8	95.7	96.5	97.3	98.0	3.4
2005	98.1	98.8	99.6	100.0	2.8	98.2	99.0	99.7	100.0	2.0
2006	101.0	102.2	102.9	103.6	3.6	100.1	100.9	101.6	102.2	2.2
2007	103.7	104.7	105.4	106.0	2.3	102.9	103.8	104.6	104.9	2.6
2008	107.0	107.5	108.3	108.8	2.6	105.8	106.9	107.7	108.3	3.2
2009	109.9	110.6	111.3	111.9	2.8	109.2	110.1	110.8	111.6	3.0
2010	113.4	114.5	115.2	115.5	3.2	112.4	113.1	113.8	114.2	2.3
2011	116.8	117.7	118.3	118.8	2.9	115.0	115.3	115.8	116.3	1.8
2012	120.4	121.5	122.2	...	...	117.0	117.9	118.7	...	...

[1]Includes wages, salaries, and employer costs for employee benefits.
[2]Includes mining, construction, and manufacturing.
[3]Includes the following industries: wholesale trade; retail trade; transportation and warehousing; utilities; information; finance and insurance; real estate and rental and leasing; professional, scientific, and technical services; management of companies and enterprises; administrative and support and waste management and remediation services; education services; health care and social assistance; arts, entertainment, and recreation; accommodation and food services; and other services, except public administration.
. . . = Not available.

Table 6-2. Employment Cost Index, Private Industry Workers, Total Compensation¹ and Wages and Salaries, by Bargaining Status and and Selected Industry, 2001–2012—Continued

(December 2005 = 100.)

Characteristic and year	Total compensation					Wages and salaries				
	Indexes				Percent change for 12 months (ended December)	Indexes				Percent change for 12 months (ended December)
	March	June	September	December		March	June	September	December	
Nonunion Workers										
2001	85.5	86.3	87.2	87.8	4.2	87.7	88.6	89.3	89.9	3.7
2002	88.7	89.6	90.0	90.3	2.8	90.8	91.7	92.0	92.2	2.6
2003	91.8	92.5	93.5	93.9	4.0	93.3	94.0	94.9	95.1	3.1
2004	95.0	95.9	96.7	97.2	3.5	95.8	96.5	97.3	97.6	2.6
2005	98.3	98.9	99.5	100.0	2.9	98.3	98.9	99.5	100.0	2.5
2006	100.9	101.7	102.6	103.2	3.2	100.8	101.8	102.7	103.3	3.3
2007	104.2	105.1	105.9	106.5	3.2	104.5	105.3	106.2	106.9	3.5
2008	107.5	108.3	108.9	109.1	2.4	107.9	108.7	109.4	109.6	2.5
2009	109.4	109.6	109.9	110.1	0.9	110.0	110.2	110.6	110.9	1.2
2010	110.9	111.4	111.8	112.1	1.8	111.4	111.9	112.4	112.7	1.6
2011	113.0	113.8	114.2	114.5	2.1	113.2	113.8	114.3	114.6	1.7
2012	115.3	116.0	116.4	...	...	115.2	115.9	116.3	...	...
Nonunion, Goods-Producing²										
2001	84.7	85.5	86.0	86.7	3.8	88.1	89.0	89.5	90.1	3.6
2002	87.8	88.5	88.8	89.7	3.5	91.0	91.6	91.9	92.7	2.9
2003	91.1	91.9	92.6	92.9	3.6	93.4	94.1	94.6	94.9	2.4
2004	94.5	95.2	96.4	96.8	4.2	95.6	96.2	97.3	97.3	2.5
2005	98.1	99.0	99.9	100.0	3.3	98.0	98.7	99.6	100.0	2.8
2006	100.5	101.4	102.0	102.5	2.5	100.7	101.9	102.4	103.0	3.0
2007	103.3	104.2	104.8	105.4	2.8	104.2	105.0	105.8	106.4	3.3
2008	106.5	107.1	107.6	107.7	2.2	107.7	108.4	109.0	109.3	2.7
2009	107.9	108.0	108.0	108.2	0.5	109.5	109.7	109.9	110.1	0.7
2010	109.1	109.5	110.1	110.2	1.8	110.6	111.0	111.6	111.7	1.5
2011	111.3	112.2	112.5	112.9	2.5	112.3	112.9	113.3	113.7	1.8
2012	113.5	114.1	114.6	...	...	114.2	114.7	115.3	...	...
Nonunion Workers, Manufacturing										
2001	84.5	85.3	85.8	86.3	3.6	88.5	89.4	89.8	90.3	3.4
2002	87.6	88.4	88.7	89.4	3.6	91.4	92.0	92.4	92.9	2.9
2003	91.2	91.9	92.6	92.8	3.8	93.9	94.5	94.9	95.2	2.5
2004	94.4	95.3	96.4	96.6	4.1	95.8	96.5	97.5	97.5	2.4
2005	98.2	99.1	99.8	100.0	3.5	98.4	99.0	99.8	100.0	2.6
2006	100.3	101.3	101.7	102.1	2.1	100.7	101.8	102.0	102.5	2.5
2007	102.8	103.7	104.1	104.6	2.4	103.6	104.2	104.9	105.5	2.9
2008	105.6	106.2	106.6	106.8	2.1	106.6	107.3	108.0	108.2	2.6
2009	107.1	107.3	107.3	107.5	0.7	108.6	108.9	109.1	109.3	1.0
2010	108.5	109.2	109.9	110.0	2.3	109.8	110.5	111.1	111.2	1.7
2011	111.6	112.5	112.8	113.0	2.7	112.1	112.6	113.0	113.3	1.9
2012	113.9	114.4	115.0	...	...	114.1	114.6	115.2	...	...
Nonunion, Service-Providing³										
2001	85.7	86.5	87.5	88.0	4.1	87.6	88.5	89.3	89.9	3.8
2002	88.9	89.9	90.4	90.5	2.8	90.8	91.7	92.0	92.1	2.4
2003	91.9	92.7	93.7	94.1	4.0	93.3	94.0	94.9	95.2	3.4
2004	95.2	96.1	96.9	97.3	3.4	95.8	96.6	97.3	97.7	2.6
2005	98.3	98.9	99.4	100.0	2.8	98.4	99.0	99.5	100.0	2.4
2006	101.0	101.8	102.7	103.4	3.4	100.8	101.7	102.7	103.4	3.4
2007	104.4	105.3	106.2	106.8	3.3	104.6	105.4	106.3	107.0	3.5
2008	107.7	108.6	109.2	109.4	2.4	107.9	108.8	109.4	109.7	2.5
2009	109.8	110.0	110.4	110.6	1.1	110.1	110.3	110.8	111.0	1.2
2010	111.3	111.9	112.3	112.7	1.9	111.6	112.2	112.6	113.0	1.8
2011	113.5	114.3	114.7	115.0	2.0	113.4	114.0	114.5	114.8	1.6
2012	115.8	116.5	116.9	...	...	115.5	116.2	116.5	...	...

¹Includes wages, salaries, and employer costs for employee benefits.
²Includes mining, construction, and manufacturing.
³Includes the following industries: wholesale trade; retail trade; transportation and warehousing; utilities; information; finance and insurance; real estate and rental and leasing; professional, scientific, and technical services; management of companies and enterprises; administrative and support and waste management and remediation services; education services; health care and social assistance; arts, entertainment, and recreation; accommodation and food services; and other services, except public administration.
... = Not available.

Table 6-3. Employment Cost Index, Private Industry Workers, Total Compensation[1] and Wages and Salaries, by Region, and Metropolitan Area Status, 2001–2012

(December 2005 = 100.)

Geography type and year	Total compensation					Wages and salaries				
	Indexes				Percent change for 12 months (ended December)	Indexes				Percent change for 12 months (ended December)
	March	June	September	December		March	June	September	December	
CENSUS REGIONS AND DIVISIONS[1]										
Northeast										
2001	84.3	85.3	86.2	86.7	3.8	86.8	87.8	88.6	89.2	3.8
2002	87.7	88.6	88.9	89.3	3.0	90.2	91.0	91.1	91.5	2.6
2003	90.6	91.4	92.4	92.9	4.0	92.4	93.2	94.1	94.5	3.3
2004	94.2	95.5	96.3	96.6	4.0	95.3	96.3	97.1	97.2	2.9
2005	97.6	98.5	99.2	100.0	3.5	97.8	98.6	99.2	100.0	2.9
2006	100.9	101.8	102.5	103.3	3.3	100.8	101.7	102.5	103.1	3.1
2007	104.0	105.1	106.2	106.8	3.4	104.0	105.0	106.1	106.6	3.4
2008	107.4	108.1	108.7	109.5	2.5	107.5	108.2	108.7	109.6	2.8
2009	109.8	110.2	110.7	111.0	1.4	109.9	110.3	110.8	111.1	1.4
2010	111.8	112.7	113.1	113.6	2.3	111.7	112.6	112.9	113.4	2.1
2011	114.4	115.3	115.7	116.1	2.2	113.7	114.6	114.9	115.3	1.7
2012	116.5	117.1	117.6	...	...	115.8	116.4	116.7	...	...
New England										
2006	100.7	101.4	102.1	103.1	3.1	100.7	101.5	102.3	103.1	3.1
2007	103.6	104.8	105.4	106.1	2.9	103.6	104.8	105.7	106.3	3.1
2008	106.7	107.1	107.8	109.5	3.2	107.1	107.6	108.3	110.3	3.8
2009	109.9	110.2	111.2	111.5	1.8	110.5	110.6	111.7	112.1	1.6
2010	112.3	113.1	113.4	114.1	2.3	112.6	113.4	113.5	114.3	2.0
2011	114.8	116.0	116.2	116.3	1.9	114.5	115.9	116.0	116.0	1.5
2012	116.9	117.4	118.1	...	...	116.6	117.2	117.8	...	...
Middle Atlantic										
2006	100.9	101.9	102.6	103.3	3.3	100.8	101.7	102.5	103.1	3.1
2007	104.2	105.3	106.5	107.1	3.7	104.2	105.1	106.4	106.7	3.5
2008	107.8	108.6	109.1	109.5	2.2	107.6	108.4	109.0	109.4	2.5
2009	109.8	110.2	110.6	110.8	1.2	109.7	110.1	110.4	110.7	1.2
2010	111.6	112.5	113.0	113.4	2.3	111.3	112.3	112.7	113.1	2.2
2011	114.3	115.1	115.5	116.0	2.3	113.4	114.0	114.5	115.0	1.7
2012	116.4	117.0	117.5	...	...	115.4	116.1	116.4	...	...
South										
2001	86.4	87.2	88.1	88.7	4.2	88.9	89.7	90.5	91.0	3.6
2002	89.5	90.5	91.2	91.2	2.8	91.8	92.7	93.3	93.2	2.4
2003	92.0	92.7	93.6	93.9	3.0	93.5	94.1	94.9	95.0	1.9
2004	95.2	96.2	97.1	97.7	4.0	95.8	96.7	97.5	98.0	3.2
2005	98.9	99.3	99.7	100.0	2.4	98.9	99.3	99.7	100.0	2.0
2006	101.0	101.6	102.8	103.5	3.5	101.0	101.6	102.9	103.6	3.6
2007	104.3	105.3	106.1	106.7	3.1	104.6	105.6	106.5	107.0	3.3
2008	107.8	108.5	109.1	109.3	2.4	108.1	109.1	109.8	110.0	2.8
2009	109.8	110.1	110.6	110.7	1.3	110.4	110.7	111.3	111.5	1.4
2010	111.5	112.0	112.5	112.8	1.9	111.9	112.4	112.9	113.4	1.7
2011	113.4	114.3	114.7	115.0	2.0	113.7	114.4	115.0	115.2	1.6
2012	116.0	116.8	117.3	...	...	116.0	116.7	117.3	...	...
South Atlantic										
2006	101.2	101.9	103.1	103.8	3.8	101.3	101.9	103.2	103.9	3.9
2007	104.9	106.0	106.8	107.3	3.4	105.0	106.1	106.9	107.5	3.5
2008	108.5	109.1	109.7	109.8	2.3	108.6	109.5	110.2	110.3	2.6
2009	110.3	110.7	111.3	111.5	1.5	110.8	111.3	111.9	112.2	1.7
2010	112.2	112.6	113.0	113.3	1.6	112.5	112.9	113.3	113.7	1.3
2011	113.8	114.6	115.1	115.4	1.9	114.0	114.6	115.4	115.6	1.7
2012	116.4	117.3	117.9	...	...	116.4	117.3	118.0	...	...
East South Central										
2006	100.7	100.9	101.5	102.3	2.3	100.7	101.5	102.1	103.1	3.1
2007	103.3	103.8	104.8	105.4	3.0	104.2	104.5	105.6	106.3	3.1
2008	106.5	107.2	108.0	108.0	2.5	107.2	107.9	109.0	109.0	2.5
2009	108.5	108.7	109.2	109.3	1.2	109.2	109.5	110.1	110.2	1.1
2010	110.0	110.8	111.0	110.9	1.5	110.8	111.4	111.6	111.5	1.2
2011	112.1	112.7	113.0	113.2	2.1	112.6	112.9	113.4	113.5	1.8
2012	114.0	115.1	115.4	...	...	114.1	114.8	114.9	...	...
West South Central										
2006	100.7	101.4	102.7	103.4	3.4	100.6	101.2	102.7	103.4	3.4
2007	103.7	104.8	105.6	106.1	2.6	104.1	105.3	106.1	106.6	3.1
2008	107.3	108.2	108.7	109.0	2.7	107.8	108.8	109.4	109.8	3.0
2009	109.4	109.5	109.9	109.9	0.8	110.1	110.2	110.8	110.9	1.0
2010	110.8	111.4	112.2	112.7	2.5	111.3	111.9	112.8	113.5	2.3
2011	113.2	114.4	114.7	115.0	2.0	113.7	114.5	115.0	115.2	1.5
2012	116.2	116.8	117.1	...	...	116.1	116.6	117.1	...	...

[1] Includes wages, salaries, and employer costs for employee benefits.
... = Not available.

Table 6-3. Employment Cost Index, Private Industry Workers, Total Compensation[1] and Wages and Salaries, by Region, and Metropolitan Area Status, 2001–2012—*Continued*

(December 2005 = 100.)

Geography type and year	Total compensation					Wages and salaries				
	Indexes				Percent change for 12 months (ended December)	Indexes				Percent change for 12 months (ended December)
	March	June	September	December		March	June	September	December	
Midwest										
2001	84.8	85.4	86.1	86.7	3.5	86.8	87.6	88.3	88.9	3.3
2002	88.0	88.7	89.0	89.5	3.2	90.3	91.0	91.3	91.7	3.1
2003	92.1	92.8	93.6	94.0	5.0	94.2	94.7	95.2	95.5	4.1
2004	95.0	95.9	96.6	96.9	3.1	95.6	96.1	96.9	97.1	1.7
2005	97.8	98.4	99.5	100.0	3.2	97.8	98.2	99.4	100.0	3.0
2006	100.7	101.7	102.3	102.8	2.8	100.4	101.4	102.0	102.6	2.6
2007	103.3	104.2	104.6	105.3	2.4	103.6	104.4	105.0	105.6	2.9
2008	106.0	107.0	107.4	107.6	2.2	106.3	107.5	107.9	108.0	2.3
2009	107.9	108.1	108.4	108.6	0.9	108.4	108.6	108.9	109.2	1.1
2010	109.9	110.4	111.0	111.3	2.5	109.9	110.4	110.9	111.2	1.8
2011	112.2	113.3	113.6	113.9	2.3	111.8	112.2	112.7	112.9	1.5
2012	114.7	115.3	115.7	. . .	. . .	113.8	114.3	114.7	. . .	. . .
East North Central										
2006	100.7	101.7	102.3	102.8	2.8	100.3	101.4	101.9	102.5	2.5
2007	103.2	104.1	104.4	105.0	2.1	103.6	104.4	104.7	105.3	2.7
2008	105.5	106.5	106.9	107.0	1.9	105.8	107.0	107.3	107.4	2.0
2009	107.0	107.3	107.5	107.8	0.7	107.5	107.7	108.0	108.3	0.8
2010	109.2	109.8	110.3	110.5	2.5	109.1	109.7	110.1	110.3	1.8
2011	111.6	112.7	113.1	113.2	2.4	110.9	111.3	111.8	111.9	1.5
2012	113.9	114.5	114.7	. . .	. . .	112.7	113.1	113.4	. . .	. . .
West North Central										
2006	100.6	101.5	102.4	102.7	2.7	100.6	101.5	102.4	102.7	2.7
2007	103.5	104.3	105.3	105.9	3.1	103.8	104.5	105.6	106.3	3.5
2008	107.3	108.4	108.8	109.0	2.9	107.9	108.9	109.5	109.7	3.2
2009	109.9	110.2	110.6	110.7	1.6	110.7	110.8	111.2	111.4	1.5
2010	111.6	112.0	112.8	113.2	2.3	111.9	112.4	113.1	113.5	1.9
2011	113.9	114.8	115.0	115.6	2.1	114.0	114.5	114.9	115.4	1.7
2012	116.9	117.5	118.3	. . .	. . .	116.5	117.1	118.0	. . .	. . .
West										
2001	84.1	85.0	85.9	86.9	5.2	87.4	88.3	89.2	90.2	4.8
2002	87.4	88.5	89.1	89.8	3.3	90.4	91.5	92.0	92.4	2.4
2003	90.9	92.0	92.3	93.8	4.5	93.0	93.9	95.1	95.5	3.4
2004	95.3	96.2	96.9	97.4	3.8	96.4	97.0	97.7	98.0	2.6
2005	98.4	99.3	99.7	100.0	2.7	98.4	99.3	99.6	100.0	2.0
2006	100.6	101.8	102.5	103.0	3.0	100.7	102.1	102.7	103.2	3.2
2007	104.2	104.9	105.7	106.5	3.4	104.8	105.4	106.2	107.0	3.7
2008	107.8	108.4	109.3	109.4	2.7	108.3	108.9	109.9	110.1	2.9
2009	109.9	110.0	110.3	110.6	1.1	110.5	110.8	111.2	111.6	1.4
2010	111.3	111.7	112.3	112.5	1.7	112.0	112.4	112.9	113.0	1.3
2011	113.5	114.3	114.6	115.1	2.3	113.6	114.1	114.5	114.9	1.7
2012	115.7	116.3	116.9	. . .	. . .	115.4	116.1	116.5	. . .	. . .
Mountain										
2006	101.0	101.8	102.7	103.1	3.1	100.6	101.7	102.8	103.2	3.2
2007	105.2	105.2	106.6	107.5	4.3	105.3	105.5	106.7	107.8	4.5
2008	108.4	109.4	110.3	110.4	2.7	108.9	109.9	110.8	111.0	3.0
2009	110.5	110.6	110.9	111.0	0.5	111.1	111.4	111.9	111.9	0.8
2010	111.3	112.3	113.0	112.8	1.6	112.3	113.2	114.1	113.7	1.6
2011	113.4	113.9	114.8	115.3	2.2	113.7	114.1	115.0	115.2	1.3
2012	115.4	116.0	116.5	. . .	. . .	115.2	115.7	116.3	. . .	. . .
Pacific										
2006	100.5	101.8	102.5	103.0	3.0	100.8	102.2	102.7	103.3	3.3
2007	103.9	104.8	105.4	106.1	3.0	104.6	105.3	106.0	106.8	3.4
2008	107.6	108.1	108.9	109.1	2.8	108.1	108.6	109.6	109.8	2.8
2009	109.7	109.9	110.1	110.5	1.3	110.3	110.6	110.9	111.5	1.5
2010	111.4	111.5	112.0	112.4	1.7	112.0	112.1	112.4	112.8	1.2
2011	113.6	114.5	114.6	115.1	2.4	113.6	114.1	114.4	114.9	1.9
2012	115.9	116.5	117.1	. . .	. . .	115.5	116.3	116.7	. . .	. . .

[1]Includes wages, salaries, and employer costs for employee benefits.
. . . = Not available.

Table 6-4. Employment Cost Index, Benefits, by Industry and Occupation, 2001–2012

(December 2005 = 100.)

Characteristic and year	Indexes				Percent change for 12 months (ended December)
	March	June	September	December	
Civilian Workers					
2001	78.0	78.8	79.9	80.8	1.1
2002	81.5	82.5	83.5	84.6	1.3
2003	86.3	87.5	88.9	90.0	1.2
2004	92.1	93.7	94.8	95.9	1.2
2005	97.5	98.4	99.4	100.2	0.8
2006	100.8	101.7	102.7	103.7	1.0
2007	104.0	105.2	106.0	107.0	0.9
2008	107.5	108.1	108.8	109.3	0.5
2009	109.6	109.9	110.4	110.9	0.5
2010	112.0	112.6	113.5	114.2	0.6
2011	115.4	116.7	117.1	117.9	0.7
2012	118.5	119.2	120.1	. . .	. . .
Total Private					
2001	78.8	79.5	80.6	81.5	1.1
2002	82.3	83.3	84.1	85.0	1.1
2003	87.0	88.1	89.4	90.5	1.2
2004	92.9	94.4	95.4	96.5	1.2
2005	98.0	98.8	99.7	100.3	0.6
2006	100.8	101.6	102.5	103.4	0.9
2007	103.1	104.2	105.0	105.9	0.9
2008	106.4	106.9	107.5	108.0	0.5
2009	108.0	108.2	108.7	109.1	0.4
2010	110.3	110.8	111.7	112.3	0.5
2011	113.5	115.1	115.4	116.3	0.8
2012	116.7	117.4	118.2	. . .	. . .
State and Local Government Workers					
2001	75.2	76.3	77.4	78.0	0.8
2002	78.8	79.9	81.4	82.9	1.8
2003	84.1	85.4	86.9	88.0	1.3
2004	89.5	91.1	92.5	93.9	1.5
2005	95.6	96.8	98.4	99.9	1.5
2006	100.8	102.0	103.5	105.1	1.5
2007	107.1	108.7	109.7	110.9	1.1
2008	111.5	112.4	113.3	114.1	0.7
2009	115.3	116.2	116.8	117.6	0.7
2010	118.2	119.1	120.2	121.0	0.7
2011	122.1	122.6	123.1	123.6	0.4
2012	124.9	126.0	127.0	. . .	. . .
WORKERS BY OCCUPATION					
Management, Professional, and Related					
2002	82.7	83.7	84.2	85.2	1.2
2003	87.1	88.0	89.5	90.7	1.3
2004	91.9	93.4	94.5	95.9	1.5
2005	97.9	98.8	99.8	100.4	0.6
2006	101.0	101.7	102.8	103.8	1.0
2007	103.5	104.8	105.5	106.4	0.9
2008	107.0	107.8	108.4	109.0	0.6
2009	108.5	108.7	108.9	109.4	0.5
2010	109.9	110.3	111.0	111.8	0.7
2011	113.0	114.5	114.8	115.9	1.0
2012	116.4	117.1	117.7	. . .	. . .
Sales and Office					
2002	81.8	83.2	84.2	85.1	1.1
2003	86.6	88.0	89.3	90.4	1.2
2004	92.5	94.2	95.2	96.1	0.9
2005	97.5	98.4	99.3	100.2	0.9
2006	100.7	101.5	102.1	103.0	0.9
2007	103.3	104.2	105.2	106.1	0.9
2008	106.5	107.0	107.6	108.0	0.4
2009	108.0	108.0	108.6	108.9	0.3
2010	110.1	110.9	111.6	112.1	0.4
2011	113.3	114.8	115.3	115.8	0.4
2012	116.6	117.4	118.1	. . .	. . .
Natural Resources, Construction, and Maintenance					
2002	81.2	82.1	83.3	84.6	1.6
2003	86.0	87.6	88.7	90.3	1.8
2004	92.9	94.5	95.4	96.9	1.6
2005	98.0	98.9	99.7	100.4	0.7
2006	101.1	102.4	103.4	104.4	1.0
2007	103.5	104.5	105.2	106.3	1.0
2008	106.6	106.7	107.4	108.0	0.6
2009	108.3	108.5	109.2	109.8	0.5
2010	111.6	112.0	112.9	113.5	0.5
2011	114.2	115.5	116.2	117.2	0.9
2012	117.9	118.7	120.0	. . .	. . .

. . . = Not available.

Table 6-4. Employment Cost Index, Benefits, by Industry and Occupation, 2001–2012—*Continued*

(December 2005 = 100.)

Characteristic and year	Indexes				Percent change for 12 months (ended December)
	March	June	September	December	
Production, Transportation, and Material Moving					
2002	81.8	82.7	83.7	84.8	1.3
2003	86.7	88.1	89.4	90.4	1.1
2004	94.4	96.0	97.1	98.0	0.9
2005	98.7	99.2	99.9	100.1	0.2
2006	100.0	100.8	101.6	102.3	0.7
2007	101.1	102.3	102.7	103.9	1.2
2008	104.3	104.4	104.8	105.4	0.6
2009	106.3	106.6	107.1	107.8	0.7
2010	109.8	110.5	111.7	112.5	0.7
2011	113.4	116.1	116.2	117.5	1.1
2012	116.0	116.7	117.6	. . .	. . .
Service					
2002	83.5	84.4	86.0	86.8	0.9
2003	88.5	89.4	90.8	92.0	1.3
2004	94.3	95.9	96.7	97.3	0.6
2005	98.0	98.8	99.5	100.3	0.8
2006	101.3	102.1	103.0	103.9	0.9
2007	104.0	105.0	106.0	107.0	0.9
2008	107.4	108.3	108.7	109.2	0.5
2009	109.5	109.8	110.4	110.9	0.5
2010	111.4	112.2	113.3	114.0	0.6
2011	115.1	115.8	116.1	117.0	0.8
2012	117.7	118.0	119.0	. . .	. . .
WORKERS BY INDUSTRY					
Goods-Producing					
2001	76.5	77.0	77.8	78.7	1.1
2002	79.9	80.6	81.2	82.5	1.6
2003	85.2	86.5	87.5	88.4	1.0
2004	92.4	93.8	95.0	96.5	1.6
2005	98.3	99.5	100.3	100.2	-0.1
2006	99.4	100.3	101.3	102.0	0.7
2007	100.9	102.1	102.4	103.4	1.0
2008	103.9	104.3	104.6	105.0	0.4
2009	105.3	105.4	105.7	106.3	0.6
2010	108.2	108.7	110.0	110.6	0.5
2011	111.6	113.7	113.8	115.1	1.1
2012	114.0	114.5	115.7	. . .	. . .
Manufacturing					
2001	75.4	75.8	76.4	77.4	1.2
2002	78.8	79.7	80.3	81.5	1.5
2003	84.7	85.7	86.8	87.5	0.8
2004	92.7	94.1	95.4	96.1	0.7
2005	98.2	99.4	100.1	100.1	0.0
2006	98.6	99.6	100.7	101.1	0.4
2007	99.4	100.8	100.9	101.9	1.0
2008	102.1	102.1	102.4	102.9	0.5
2009	103.2	103.3	103.4	104.2	0.8
2010	106.3	107.1	108.7	109.6	0.8
2011	110.8	113.4	113.4	114.7	1.1
2012	112.9	113.4	114.8	. . .	. . .
Service-Providing					
2001	79.7	80.5	81.7	82.6	1.1
2002	83.2	84.4	85.2	86.0	0.9
2003	87.7	88.8	90.2	91.4	1.3
2004	93.0	94.6	95.5	96.5	1.0
2005	97.9	98.6	99.4	100.3	0.9
2006	101.3	102.2	103.0	104.0	1.0
2007	104.0	105.1	106.0	106.9	0.8
2008	107.4	108.0	108.7	109.1	0.4
2009	109.2	109.3	109.9	110.2	0.3
2010	111.1	111.7	112.3	112.9	0.5
2011	114.3	115.7	116.0	116.8	0.7
2012	117.8	118.5	119.1	. . .	. . .

. . . = Not available.

NOTES AND DEFINITIONS

EMPLOYER COSTS FOR EMPLOYEE COMPENSATION

The Employer Costs for Employee Compensation (ECEC) measures the average cost per employee hour worked that employers pay for wages and salaries and benefits.

Survey Scope

The ECEC consists of data for the civilian economy, obtained from both private industry and state and local government. Excluded from private industry are the self-employed and farm and private household workers. Federal government workers are excluded from the public sector. The private industry series and the state and local government series provide separate data for the two sectors.

The cost levels for June 2012 were collected from a probability sample of 47,400 occupations selected from a sample of about 9,500 establishments in private industry and approximately 9,200 occupations from a sample of about 1,400 establishments in state and local governments. The private industry sample is rotated over approximately 5 years, which makes the sample more representative of the economy and reduces respondent burden. Data are collected for the pay period including the 12th day of the survey months of March, June, September, and December. The sample is replaced on a cross-area, cross-industry basis.

To be included in the ECEC, employees in occupations must receive cash payments from the establishment for services performed and the establishment must pay the employer's portion of Medicare taxes on that individual's wages. Major exclusions from the survey are the self-employed, individuals who set their own pay (for example, proprietors, owners, major stockholders, and partners in unincorporated firms), volunteers, unpaid workers, family members being paid token wages, individuals receiving long-term disability compensation, and U.S. citizens working overseas.

Current employment weights are used to calculate cost levels. These weights are derived from two BLS programs: the Quarterly Census of Employment and Wages (QCEW) and the Current Employment Statistics (CES). Combined, these programs provide the appropriate industry coverage and currency of data needed to match the ECEC.

Sources of Additional Information

Additional information may be obtained from BLS news release 12-1830 "Employer Costs for Employee Compensation—June 2012," and in various articles in the BLS e-publication, *Compensation and Working Conditions*. These resources are available on the BLS Web site at <http://www.bls.gov/ncs/ect/>.

Table 6-5. Employer Compensation Costs Per Hour Worked for Employee Compensation and Costs as a Percent of Total Compensation: Private Industry Workers, by Major Industry Group, June 2012

(Dollars, percent of total cost.)

Compensation component	All workers		Goods-producing[1]						Service-providing[2]			
			All goods-producing[1]		Construction		Manufacturing		All service-providing[2]		Trade, transportation, and utilities	
	Cost	Percent	Cost	Percent	Cost	Percent	Cost	Percent	Cost	Percent	Cost	Percent
TOTAL COMPENSATION	28.80	100.0	33.88	100.0	33.38	100.0	33.07	100.0	27.75	100.0	24.21	100.0
Wages and Salaries	20.27	70.4	22.60	66.7	23.17	69.4	21.74	65.7	19.79	71.3	17.12	70.7
Total Benefits	8.52	29.6	11.28	33.3	10.21	30.6	11.33	34.3	7.96	28.7	7.09	29.3
Paid leave	1.97	6.8	2.20	6.5	1.40	4.2	2.46	7.4	1.92	6.9	1.44	6.0
Vacation	1.02	3.5	1.16	3.4	0.73	2.2	1.29	3.9	0.99	3.6	0.75	3.1
Holiday	0.61	2.1	0.77	2.3	0.51	1.5	0.86	2.6	0.57	2.1	0.44	1.8
Sick	0.25	0.9	0.19	0.6	0.11	0.3	0.23	0.7	0.26	0.9	0.19	0.8
Personal	0.10	0.3	0.07	0.2	0.05	0.1	0.08	0.2	0.10	0.4	0.07	0.3
Supplemental pay	0.82	2.9	1.34	4.0	0.97	2.9	1.41	4.3	0.71	2.6	0.57	2.4
Overtime and premium pay[3]	0.25	0.9	0.55	1.6	0.59	1.8	0.52	1.6	0.19	0.7	0.25	1.1
Shift differentials	0.06	0.2	0.08	0.2	([4])	([5])	0.12	0.4	0.06	0.2	0.02	0.1
Nonproduction bonuses	0.51	1.8	0.71	2.1	0.38	1.1	0.77	2.3	0.47	1.7	0.30	1.2
Insurance	2.34	8.1	3.21	9.5	2.55	7.6	3.45	10.4	2.16	7.8	2.09	8.6
Life insurance	0.04	0.1	0.06	0.2	0.04	0.1	0.06	0.2	0.04	0.1	0.03	0.1
Health insurance	2.21	7.7	3.02	8.9	2.43	7.3	3.24	9.8	2.04	7.3	1.99	8.2
Short-term disability	0.05	0.2	0.08	0.2	0.05	0.2	0.09	0.3	0.04	0.2	0.03	0.1
Long-term disability	0.04	0.1	0.05	0.1	0.03	0.1	0.05	0.2	0.04	0.2	0.04	0.2
Retirement and savings	1.02	3.5	1.54	4.5	1.80	5.4	1.28	3.9	0.91	3.3	0.83	3.4
Defined benefit plans	0.43	1.5	0.83	2.4	1.14	3.4	0.60	1.8	0.35	1.3	0.40	1.7
Defined contribution plans	0.59	2.1	0.71	2.1	0.66	2.0	0.68	2.1	0.57	2.0	0.43	1.8
Legally required benefits	2.37	8.2	2.99	8.8	3.49	10.4	2.74	8.3	2.24	8.1	2.14	8.9
Social Security and Medicare	1.69	5.9	1.92	5.7	1.91	5.7	1.88	5.7	1.64	5.9	1.42	5.9
Social Security[6]	1.35	4.7	1.54	4.5	1.54	4.6	1.51	4.6	1.32	4.7	1.14	4.7
Medicare	0.33	1.2	0.37	1.1	0.37	1.1	0.37	1.1	0.33	1.2	0.28	1.1
Federal unemployment insurance	0.03	0.1	0.03	0.1	0.03	0.1	0.03	0.1	0.03	0.1	0.04	0.2
State unemployment insurance	0.23	0.8	0.30	0.9	0.37	1.1	0.28	0.9	0.21	0.8	0.21	0.9
Workers' compensation	0.42	1.5	0.74	2.2	1.18	3.5	0.54	1.6	0.35	1.3	0.48	2.0

Compensation component	Service-providing[2]											
	Information		Financial activities		Professional and business services		Education and health services		Leisure and hospitality		Other services	
	Cost	Percent	Cost	Percent	Cost	Percent	Cost	Percent	Cost	Percent	Cost	Percent
TOTAL COMPENSATION	45.08	100.0	40.14	100.0	34.80	100.0	30.88	100.0	12.20	100.0	25.42	100.0
Wages and Salaries	29.79	66.1	27.07	67.4	25.10	72.1	22.02	71.3	9.71	79.6	18.70	73.5
Total Benefits	15.29	33.9	13.07	32.6	9.70	27.9	8.86	28.7	2.49	20.4	6.73	26.5
Paid leave	3.98	8.8	3.30	8.2	2.57	7.4	2.37	7.7	0.37	3.0	1.56	6.1
Vacation	2.07	4.6	1.68	4.2	1.32	3.8	1.22	4.0	0.20	1.7	0.74	2.9
Holiday	1.05	2.3	0.98	2.4	0.82	2.4	0.66	2.1	0.12	1.0	0.52	2.0
Sick	0.48	1.1	0.47	1.2	0.32	0.9	0.34	1.1	0.03	0.3	0.23	0.9
Personal	0.39	0.9	0.18	0.4	0.11	0.3	0.15	0.5	0.02	0.1	0.07	0.3
Supplemental pay	1.35	3.0	2.09	5.2	0.96	2.8	0.57	1.9	0.13	1.0	0.31	1.2
Overtime and premium pay[3]	0.26	0.6	0.15	0.4	0.18	0.5	0.21	0.7	0.07	0.6	0.11	0.4
Shift differentials	0.05	0.1	0.02	([5])	0.03	0.1	0.20	0.7	([4])	([5])	([4])	([5])
Nonproduction bonuses	1.04	2.3	1.93	4.8	0.75	2.2	0.16	0.5	0.06	0.5	0.19	0.7
Insurance	4.23	9.4	3.37	8.4	2.40	6.9	2.57	8.3	0.55	4.5	1.75	6.9
Life insurance	0.06	0.1	0.06	0.1	0.05	0.2	0.03	0.1	([4])	([5])	0.03	0.1
Health insurance	3.93	8.7	3.15	7.8	2.23	6.4	2.45	7.9	0.53	4.4	1.67	6.6
Short-term disability	0.18	0.4	0.11	0.3	0.06	0.2	0.03	0.1	([4])	([5])	0.02	0.1
Long-term disability	0.07	0.2	0.07	0.2	0.06	0.2	0.05	0.2	([4])	([5])	0.02	0.1
Retirement and savings	2.64	5.9	1.60	4.0	1.07	3.1	0.98	3.2	0.12	1.0	0.89	3.5
Defined benefit plans	1.55	3.4	0.51	1.3	0.34	1.0	0.28	0.9	0.04	0.3	0.43	1.7
Defined contribution plans	1.09	2.4	1.09	2.7	0.73	2.1	0.70	2.3	0.09	0.7	0.47	1.8
Legally required benefits	3.09	6.9	2.70	6.7	2.69	7.7	2.37	7.7	1.32	10.8	2.21	8.7
Social Security and Medicare	2.52	5.6	2.23	5.6	2.06	5.9	1.82	5.9	0.85	7.0	1.55	6.1
Social Security[6]	2.02	4.5	1.77	4.4	1.64	4.7	1.46	4.7	0.69	5.6	1.25	4.9
Medicare	0.50	1.1	0.47	1.2	0.41	1.2	0.36	1.2	0.16	1.3	0.30	1.2
Federal unemployment insurance	0.03	0.1	0.03	0.1	0.03	0.1	0.03	0.1	0.04	0.3	0.03	0.1
State unemployment insurance	0.25	0.5	0.22	0.6	0.26	0.7	0.18	0.6	0.18	1.5	0.26	1.0
Workers' compensation	0.29	0.6	0.21	0.5	0.34	1.0	0.35	1.1	0.24	2.0	0.37	1.5

Note: Individual items may not sum to totals due to rounding.

[1]Includes mining, construction, and manufacturing. The agriculture, forestry, farming, and hunting sector is excluded.
[2]Includes utilities; wholesale trade; retail trade; transportation and warehousing; information; finance and insurance; real estate and rental and leasing; professional and technical services; management of companies and enterprises; administrative and waste services; education services; health care and social assistance; arts, entertainment, and recreation; accommodation and food services; and other services, except public administration.
[3]Includes premium pay for work in addition to the regular work schedule (such as overtime, weekends, and holidays).
[4]Cost per hour worked is $0.01 or less.
[5]Less than 0.05 percent.
[6]Comprises the Old Age, Survivors, and Disability Insurance (OASDI) program.

Table 6-6.   Employer Compensation Costs Per Hour Worked for Employee Compensation and Costs as a Percent of Total Compensation: Private Industry Workers, by Census Region and Area, June 2012

(Dollars, percent of total costs.)

Compensation component	Census region and division[1]					
	Northeast		Northeast divisions			
			New England		Middle Atlantic	
	Cost	Percent	Cost	Percent	Cost	Percent
TOTAL COMPENSATION	32.98	100.0	33.47	100.0	32.81	100.0
Wages and Salaries	22.80	69.1	23.41	70.0	22.58	68.8
Total Benefits	10.18	30.9	10.05	30.0	10.22	31.2
Paid leave	2.46	7.5	2.46	7.4	2.47	7.5
Vacation	1.24	3.7	1.27	3.8	1.22	3.7
Holiday	0.75	2.3	0.77	2.3	0.74	2.3
Sick	0.34	1.0	0.31	0.9	0.35	1.1
Personal	0.15	0.4	0.12	0.4	0.15	0.5
Supplemental pay	1.01	3.1	0.90	2.7	1.05	3.2
Overtime and premium pay[2]	0.24	0.7	0.24	0.7	0.24	0.7
Shift differentials	0.07	0.2	0.08	0.3	0.07	0.2
Nonproduction bonuses	0.70	2.1	0.57	1.7	0.74	2.3
Insurance	2.79	8.5	2.78	8.3	2.80	8.5
Life insurance	0.05	0.1	0.05	0.1	0.05	0.1
Health insurance	2.62	7.9	2.61	7.8	2.62	8.0
Short-term disability	0.08	0.2	0.06	0.2	0.08	0.3
Long-term disability	0.05	0.2	0.05	0.2	0.05	0.2
Retirement and savings	1.20	3.6	1.21	3.6	1.20	3.6
Defined benefit plans	0.49	1.5	0.48	1.4	0.50	1.5
Defined contribution plans	0.71	2.1	0.73	2.2	0.70	2.1
Legally required benefits	2.71	8.2	2.71	8.1	2.71	8.3
Social Security and Medicare	1.90	5.8	1.95	5.8	1.88	5.7
Social Security	1.52	4.6	1.56	4.7	1.50	4.6
Medicare	0.38	1.2	0.39	1.2	0.38	1.2
Federal unemployment insurance	0.03	0.1	0.03	0.1	0.04	0.1
State unemployment insurance	0.32	1.0	0.33	1.0	0.31	0.9
Workers' compensation	0.46	1.4	0.40	1.2	0.48	1.5

Compensation component	Census region and division[1]							
	South		South divisions					
			South Atlantic		East South Central		West South Central	
	Cost	Percent	Cost	Percent	Cost	Percent	Cost	Percent
TOTAL COMPENSATION	26.14	100.0	26.37	100.0	24.44	100.0	26.45	100.0
Wages and Salaries	18.71	71.6	19.04	72.2	17.22	70.5	18.78	71.0
Total Benefits	7.42	28.4	7.33	27.8	7.22	29.5	7.67	29.0
Paid leave	1.73	6.6	1.77	6.7	1.57	6.4	1.71	6.5
Vacation	0.87	3.3	0.90	3.4	0.79	3.2	0.86	3.2
Holiday	0.55	2.1	0.56	2.1	0.50	2.1	0.56	2.1
Sick	0.21	0.8	0.22	0.8	0.19	0.8	0.21	0.8
Personal	0.09	0.3	0.09	0.3	0.09	0.4	0.09	0.3
Supplemental pay	0.80	3.1	0.68	2.6	0.74	3.0	1.04	3.9
Overtime and premium pay[2]	0.27	1.0	0.23	0.9	0.29	1.2	0.32	1.2
Shift differentials	0.06	0.2	0.06	0.2	0.06	0.3	0.06	0.2
Nonproduction bonuses	0.48	1.8	0.39	1.5	0.38	1.6	0.66	2.5
Insurance	1.96	7.5	1.95	7.4	2.01	8.2	1.96	7.4
Life insurance	0.04	0.1	0.04	0.1	0.05	0.2	0.04	0.2
Health insurance	1.84	7.0	1.83	6.9	1.88	7.7	1.84	7.0
Short-term disability	0.04	0.2	0.04	0.2	0.04	0.2	0.04	0.1
Long-term disability	0.04	0.1	0.04	0.1	0.04	0.2	0.04	0.1
Retirement and savings	0.84	3.2	0.80	3.0	0.87	3.6	0.90	3.4
Defined benefit plans	0.33	1.3	0.29	1.1	0.42	1.7	0.37	1.4
Defined contribution plans	0.51	1.9	0.51	2.0	0.45	1.9	0.52	2.0
Legally required benefits	2.09	8.0	2.13	8.1	2.02	8.3	2.06	7.8
Social Security and Medicare	1.57	6.0	1.59	6.0	1.48	6.0	1.58	6.0
Social Security	1.26	4.8	1.27	4.8	1.20	4.9	1.26	4.8
Medicare	0.31	1.2	0.31	1.2	0.28	1.2	0.31	1.2
Federal unemployment insurance	0.03	0.1	0.03	0.1	0.03	0.1	0.02	0.1
State unemployment insurance	0.16	0.6	0.17	0.6	0.15	0.6	0.15	0.6
Workers' compensation	0.33	1.3	0.34	1.3	0.37	1.5	0.31	1.2

Note: Individual items may not sum to totals due to rounding.

[1]The states that comprise the Census divisions are: New England—Connecticut, Maine, Massachusetts, New Hampshire, Rhode Island, and Vermont; Middle Atlantic—New Jersey, New York, and Pennsylvania; South Atlantic—Delaware, District of Columbia, Florida, Georgia, Maryland, North Carolina, South Carolina, Virginia, and West Virginia; East South Central—Alabama, Kentucky, Mississippi, and Tennessee; West South Central—Arkansas, Louisiana, Oklahoma, and Texas; East North Central—Illinois, Indiana, Michigan, Ohio, and Wisconsin; West North Central—Iowa, Kansas, Minnesota, Missouri, Nebraska, North Dakota, and South Dakota; Mountain—Arizona, Colorado, Idaho, Montana, Nevada, New Mexico, Utah, and Wyoming; and Pacific—Alaska, California, Hawaii, Oregon, and Washington.
[2]Comprises the Old-Age, Survivors, and Disability Insurance (OASDI) program.

Table 6-6. Employer Compensation Costs Per Hour Worked for Employee Compensation and Costs as a Percent of Total Compensation: Private Industry Workers, by Census Region and Area, June 2012—*Continued*

(Dollars, percent of total costs.)

Compensation component	Census region and division[1]					
	Midwest		Midwest divisions			
			East North Central		West North Central	
	Cost	Percent	Cost	Percent	Cost	Percent
TOTAL COMPENSATION	28.06	100.0	28.00	100.0	28.18	100.0
Wages and Salaries	19.50	69.5	19.26	68.8	20.03	71.1
Total Benefits	8.56	30.5	8.74	31.2	8.15	28.9
Paid leave	1.86	6.6	1.84	6.6	1.89	6.7
Vacation	1.00	3.6	0.99	3.5	1.05	3.7
Holiday	0.57	2.0	0.57	2.1	0.56	2.0
Sick	0.20	0.7	0.19	0.7	0.21	0.8
Personal	0.09	0.3	0.09	0.3	0.07	0.2
Supplemental pay	0.77	2.7	0.84	3.0	0.60	2.1
Overtime and premium pay[2]	0.26	0.9	0.27	1.0	0.23	0.8
Shift differentials	0.07	0.3	0.08	0.3	0.05	0.2
Nonproduction bonuses	0.43	1.6	0.48	1.7	0.33	1.2
Insurance	2.55	9.1	2.63	9.4	2.37	8.4
Life insurance	0.04	0.1	0.04	0.1	0.04	0.2
Health insurance	2.41	8.6	2.49	8.9	2.23	7.9
Short-term disability	0.05	0.2	0.06	0.2	0.04	0.1
Long-term disability	0.05	0.2	0.04	0.2	0.05	0.2
Retirement and savings	1.09	3.9	1.11	3.9	1.05	3.7
Defined benefit plans	0.50	1.8	0.56	2.0	0.36	1.3
Defined contribution plans	0.59	2.1	0.55	1.9	0.69	2.4
Legally required benefits	2.29	8.2	2.32	8.3	2.24	8.0
Social Security and Medicare	1.63	5.8	1.63	5.8	1.63	5.8
Social Security	1.31	4.7	1.31	4.7	1.30	4.6
Medicare	0.32	1.1	0.32	1.1	0.33	1.2
Federal unemployment insurance	0.04	0.1	0.04	0.2	0.03	0.1
State unemployment insurance	0.24	0.9	0.25	0.9	0.22	0.8
Workers' compensation	0.39	1.4	0.40	1.4	0.36	1.3

Compensation component	Census region and division[1]					
	West		West divisions			
			Mountain		Pacific	
	Cost	Percent	Cost	Percent	Cost	Percent
TOTAL COMPENSATION	30.01	100.0	27.99	100.0	30.94	100.0
Wages and Salaries	21.28	70.9	20.18	72.1	21.78	70.4
Total Benefits	8.73	29.1	7.82	27.9	9.16	29.6
Paid leave	2.03	6.8	1.89	6.7	2.10	6.8
Vacation	1.07	3.6	1.03	3.7	1.09	3.5
Holiday	0.62	2.1	0.53	1.9	0.65	2.1
Sick	0.27	0.9	0.23	0.8	0.28	0.9
Personal	0.08	0.3	0.10	0.3	0.07	0.2
Supplemental pay	0.74	2.5	0.72	2.6	0.75	2.4
Overtime and premium pay[2]	0.22	0.7	0.21	0.8	0.22	0.7
Shift differentials	0.05	0.2	0.04	0.2	0.05	0.2
Nonproduction bonuses	0.48	1.6	0.46	1.7	0.49	1.6
Insurance	2.31	7.7	1.95	7.0	2.47	8.0
Life insurance	0.04	0.1	0.04	0.1	0.03	0.1
Health insurance	2.20	7.3	1.84	6.6	2.36	7.6
Short-term disability	0.04	0.1	0.03	0.1	0.04	0.1
Long-term disability	0.04	0.1	0.05	0.2	0.04	0.1
Retirement and savings	1.07	3.6	1.03	3.7	1.09	3.5
Defined benefit plans	0.45	1.5	0.32	1.1	0.51	1.6
Defined contribution plans	0.62	2.1	0.71	2.5	0.58	1.9
Legally required benefits	2.58	8.6	2.23	8.0	2.74	8.9
Social Security and Medicare	1.76	5.9	1.64	5.8	1.81	5.9
Social Security	1.41	4.7	1.30	4.7	1.46	4.7
Medicare	0.35	1.2	0.33	1.2	0.36	1.2
Federal unemployment insurance	0.03	0.1	0.03	0.1	0.04	0.1
State unemployment insurance	0.24	0.8	0.19	0.7	0.27	0.9
Workers' compensation	0.55	1.8	0.38	1.3	0.62	2.0

Note: Individual items may not sum to totals due to rounding.

[1]The states that comprise the Census divisions are: New England—Connecticut, Maine, Massachusetts, New Hampshire, Rhode Island, and Vermont; Middle Atlantic—New Jersey, New York, and Pennsylvania; South Atlantic—Delaware, District of Columbia, Florida, Georgia, Maryland, North Carolina, South Carolina, Virginia, and West Virginia; East South Central—Alabama, Kentucky, Mississippi, and Tennessee; West South Central—Arkansas, Louisiana, Oklahoma, and Texas; East North Central—Illinois, Indiana, Michigan, Ohio, and Wisconsin; West North Central—Iowa, Kansas, Minnesota, Missouri, Nebraska, North Dakota, and South Dakota; Mountain—Arizona, Colorado, Idaho, Montana, Nevada, New Mexico, Utah, and Wyoming; and Pacific—Alaska, California, Hawaii, Oregon, and Washington.
[2]Comprises the Old-Age, Survivors, and Disability Insurance (OASDI) program.

Table 6-7. Employer Compensation Costs Per Hour Worked for Employee Compensation and Costs as a Percent of Total Compensation: State and Local Government, by Major Occupational and Industry Group, June 2012

(Dollars, percent of total compensation.)

Characteristic	Total compensation	Wages and salaries	Benefit costs					
			Total	Paid leave	Supplemental pay	Insurance	Retirement and savings	Legally required benefits
COSTS PER HOUR WORKED								
State and Local Government Workers	41.10	26.70	14.41	3.04	0.34	4.97	3.51	2.53
Occupational Group								
Management, professional, and related	49.84	33.71	16.14	3.35	0.25	5.53	4.11	2.90
Professional and related	48.76	33.20	15.57	3.00	0.24	5.50	4.05	2.78
Teachers[1]	56.02	39.47	16.55	2.67	0.14	5.97	4.70	3.07
Primary, secondary, and special education school teachers	57.09	39.90	17.18	2.52	0.16	6.62	4.93	2.95
Sales and office	28.60	17.36	11.23	2.52	0.20	4.44	2.22	1.85
Office and administrative support	28.82	17.44	11.38	2.55	0.20	4.51	2.26	1.85
Service	31.23	18.52	12.72	2.76	0.59	4.06	3.21	2.10
Industry Group								
Education and health services	42.94	28.99	13.95	2.67	0.21	5.17	3.44	2.47
Education services	44.08	30.02	14.06	2.57	0.15	5.26	3.62	2.47
Elementary and secondary schools	43.65	29.76	13.89	2.26	0.16	5.45	3.63	2.39
Junior colleges, colleges, and universities	45.87	31.16	14.71	3.74	0.12	4.50	3.60	2.76
Health care and social assistance	35.88	22.59	13.29	3.28	0.57	4.61	2.36	2.47
Hospitals	38.79	24.37	14.42	3.63	0.74	4.99	2.54	2.52
Public administration	39.64	23.97	15.67	3.75	0.57	4.83	3.86	2.66
PERCENT OF TOTAL COMPENSATION								
State and Local Government Workers	100.0	65.0	35.0	7.4	0.8	12.1	8.5	6.2
Occupational Group								
Management, professional, and related	100.0	67.6	32.4	6.7	0.5	11.1	8.2	5.8
Professional and related	100.0	68.1	31.9	6.2	0.5	11.3	8.3	5.7
Teachers[1]	100.0	70.5	29.5	4.8	0.3	10.7	8.4	5.5
Primary, secondary, and special education school teachers	100.0	69.9	30.1	4.4	0.3	11.6	8.6	5.2
Sales and office	100.0	60.7	39.3	8.8	0.7	15.5	7.8	6.5
Office and administrative support	100.0	60.5	39.5	8.9	0.7	15.7	7.8	6.4
Service	100.0	59.3	40.7	8.8	1.9	13.0	10.3	6.7
Industry Group								
Education and health services	100.0	67.5	32.5	6.2	0.5	12.0	8.0	5.7
Education services	100.0	68.1	31.9	5.8	0.3	11.9	8.2	5.6
Elementary and secondary schools	100.0	68.2	31.8	5.2	0.4	12.5	8.3	5.5
Junior colleges, colleges, and universities	100.0	67.9	32.1	8.2	0.3	9.8	7.8	6.0
Health care and social assistance	100.0	63.0	37.0	9.1	1.6	12.8	6.6	6.9
Hospitals	100.0	62.8	37.2	9.3	1.9	12.9	6.5	6.5
Public administration	100.0	60.5	39.5	9.5	1.4	12.2	9.7	6.7

Note: Individual items may not sum to totals due to rounding.

[1] Includes postsecondary teachers; primary, secondary, and special education teachers; and other teachers and instructors.

Table 6-8. Employer Compensation Costs Per Hour Worked for Employee Compensation and Costs as a Percent of Total Compensation: Private Industry Workers, by Establishment Employment Size, June 2012

(Dollars, percent.)

Compensation component	1–99 workers						100 workers or more					
	1–99 workers		1–49 workers		50–99 workers		100 workers or more		100–499 workers		500 workers or more	
	Cost	Percent	Cost	Percent	Cost	Percent	Cost	Percent	Cost	Percent	Cost	Percent
TOTAL COMPENSATION	23.87	100.0	22.96	100.0	26.61	100.0	34.69	100.0	29.25	100.0	42.39	100.0
Wages and Salaries	17.62	73.8	17.14	74.6	19.07	71.7	23.45	67.6	20.38	69.7	27.79	65.6
Total Benefits	6.25	26.2	5.82	25.4	7.54	28.3	11.25	32.4	8.88	30.3	14.60	34.4
Paid leave	1.36	5.7	1.24	5.4	1.71	6.4	2.71	7.8	2.04	7.0	3.64	8.6
Vacation	0.68	2.9	0.62	2.7	0.87	3.3	1.42	4.1	1.06	3.6	1.93	4.5
Holiday	0.45	1.9	0.42	1.8	0.54	2.0	0.80	2.3	0.63	2.2	1.04	2.5
Sick	0.16	0.7	0.15	0.6	0.20	0.8	0.35	1.0	0.25	0.8	0.49	1.2
Personal	0.07	0.3	0.06	0.3	0.09	0.4	0.13	0.4	0.10	0.3	0.18	0.4
Supplemental pay	0.52	2.2	0.47	2.1	0.67	2.5	1.18	3.4	0.75	2.6	1.79	4.2
Overtime and premium pay[1]	0.18	0.7	0.16	0.7	0.24	0.9	0.33	1.0	0.30	1.0	0.38	0.9
Shift differentials	(²)	(³)	(²)	(³)	0.03	0.1	0.12	0.3	0.06	0.2	0.20	0.5
Nonproduction bonuses	0.33	1.4	0.31	1.3	0.40	1.5	0.73	2.1	0.39	1.3	1.20	2.8
Insurance	1.61	6.8	1.48	6.5	2.01	7.5	3.21	9.3	2.62	9.0	4.04	9.5
Life insurance	0.03	0.1	0.02	0.1	0.04	0.1	0.05	0.2	0.05	0.2	0.06	0.1
Health insurance	1.53	6.4	1.41	6.1	1.90	7.1	3.01	8.7	2.47	8.5	3.78	8.9
Short-term disability	0.03	0.1	0.02	0.1	0.04	0.2	0.08	0.2	0.06	0.2	0.10	0.2
Long-term disability	0.02	0.1	0.02	0.1	0.03	0.1	0.07	0.2	0.04	0.1	0.10	0.2
Retirement and savings	0.62	2.6	0.54	2.3	0.86	3.2	1.50	4.3	1.09	3.7	2.09	4.9
Defined benefit plans	0.23	1.0	0.21	0.9	0.29	1.1	0.67	1.9	0.44	1.5	1.00	2.3
Defined contribution plans	0.39	1.6	0.33	1.4	0.57	2.1	0.83	2.4	0.65	2.2	1.10	2.6
Legally required benefits	2.14	9.0	2.09	9.1	2.29	8.6	2.65	7.6	2.37	8.1	3.03	7.2
Social Security and Medicare	1.46	6.1	1.42	6.2	1.58	5.9	1.97	5.7	1.68	5.8	2.37	5.6
Social Security[4]	1.17	4.9	1.14	5.0	1.26	4.7	1.57	4.5	1.35	4.6	1.89	4.5
Medicare	0.28	1.2	0.28	1.2	0.31	1.2	0.39	1.1	0.33	1.1	0.48	1.1
Federal unemployment insurance	0.04	0.2	0.04	0.2	0.03	0.1	0.03	0.1	0.03	0.1	0.03	0.1
State unemployment insurance	0.23	1.0	0.23	1.0	0.23	0.9	0.23	0.7	0.23	0.8	0.22	0.5
Workers' compensation	0.42	1.8	0.41	1.8	0.45	1.7	0.42	1.2	0.42	1.4	0.41	1.0

[1]Includes premium pay for work in addition to the regular work schedule (such as overtime, weekends, and holidays).
²Cost per hour worked is $0.01 or less.
³Less than .05 percent.
⁴Comprises the Old-Age, Survivors, and Disability Insurance (OASDI) program.

NOTES AND DEFINITIONS

EMPLOYEE BENEFITS SURVEY

The Employee Benefits Survey provides data on the incidence and provisions of selected employee benefit plans.

Collection and Coverage

The March 2012 National Compensation Survey (NCS) benefits survey represented approximately 123 million civilian workers; of this number, about 104 million were private industry workers and 19 million were state and local government workers. It included a sample of 12,545 establishments.

Definitions

Access to a benefit is determined on an occupational basis within an establishment. An employee is considered to have access to a benefit if it is available for his or her use.

Participation refers to the proportion of employees covered by a benefit. There will be cases where employees with access to a plan will not participate. For example, some employees may decline to participate in a health insurance plan if there is an employee cost involved.

A *private establishment* is an economic unit that produces goods or services, a central administrative office, or an auxiliary unit providing support services to a company. For private industries, the establishment is usually at a single physical location. For state and local governments, an establishment is defined as an agency or entity such as a school district, college, university, hospital, nursing home, administrative body, court, police department, fire department, health or social service operation, highway maintenance operation, urban transit operation, or other governmental unit. It provides services under the authority of a specific state or local government organization within a defined geographic area or jurisdiction.

Take-up rates are the percentage of workers with access to a plan who participate in the plan. They are computed by using the number of workers participating in a plan divided by the number of workers with access to the plan, times 100 and rounded to the nearest one percent. Since the computation of take-up rates is based on the number of workers collected, rather the rounded percentage estimates, the take-up rates in the tables may not equal the ratio of participation to access estimates.

An employee is considered to be a *union worker* when all the following conditions are met: 1.) a labor organization is recognized as the bargaining agent for all workers in the occupation. 2.) wage and salary rates are determined through collective bargaining or negotiations. 3.) settlement terms, which must include earnings provisions and may include benefit provisions, are embodied in a signed, mutually binding collective bargaining agreement.

Sources of Additional Information

For more information, see Bureau of Labor Statistics (BLS) news release 12-1380 "Employee Benefits in the United States in the United States–March 2012". For a listing of selected benefit definitions, see the *Glossary of Compensation Terms*. These resources are available on the BLS Web site at <http://www.bls.gov/ncs/ebs/>.

Table 6-9. Retirement Benefits:[1] Access, Participation, and Take-Up Rates,[2] March 2012

(Percent.)

Characteristic	Civilian[3]			Private industry			State and local government		
	Access	Participation	Take-up rate	Access	Participation	Take-up rate	Access	Participation	Take-up rate
ALL WORKERS	68	54	79	65	48	75	89	84	95
Worker Characteristics									
Management, professional, and related	83	74	89	79	68	86	91	86	95
Management, business, and financial	84	76	91	83	74	90	-	-	-
Professional and related	82	72	88	78	65	84	91	86	95
Teachers	88	83	94	-	-	-	91	87	96
Primary, secondary, and special education school teachers	97	93	96	-	-	-	99	96	97
Registered nurses	82	69	84	-	-	-	-	-	-
Service	47	29	63	40	21	51	83	79	95
Protective service	76	60	78	56	22	40	91	87	96
Sales and office	71	54	76	69	51	74	89	85	95
Sales and related	67	42	63	67	41	62	-	-	-
Office and administrative support	73	61	83	70	57	81	90	86	96
Natural resources, construction, and maintenance	68	55	81	65	51	78	95	90	95
Construction, extraction, farming, fishing, and forestry	65	52	80	61	46	76	-	-	-
Installation, maintenance, and repair	71	58	81	69	55	80	-	-	-
Production, transportation, and material moving	67	52	77	66	50	76	87	82	95
Production	69	54	78	69	54	78	-	-	-
Transportation and material moving	65	49	75	64	47	73	-	-	-
Full-time workers	78	65	83	74	59	80	99	94	95
Part-time workers	38	21	54	38	19	50	39	35	90
Union workers	95	88	93	92	85	92	97	92	95
Nonunion workers	64	48	75	62	45	72	83	78	95
Average Wage Within the Following Percentiles[4]									
Lowest 25 percent	41	21	51	38	17	45	73	69	94
Lowest 10 percent	30	10	33	29	8	28	59	55	93
Second 25 percent	70	52	75	65	46	70	93	88	95
Third 25 percent	79	67	85	75	61	82	94	89	94
Highest 25 percent	88	80	91	85	75	89	98	94	96
Highest 10 percent	90	83	92	86	78	91	98	94	96
Establishment Characteristics									
Goods-producing industries	75	61	82	74	61	81	-	-	-
Service-providing industries	67	53	79	63	46	74	89	84	95
Education and health services	77	66	85	69	54	78	90	85	94
Educational services	86	80	93	71	60	84	91	86	95
Elementary and secondary schools	91	86	95	-	-	-	92	88	96
Junior colleges, colleges, and universities	87	78	90	90	77	87	86	78	91
Health care and social assistance	70	55	78	69	53	77	88	81	91
Hospitals	90	77	86	-	-	-	95	85	89
Public administration	90	86	95	-	-	-	90	86	95
Number of Workers									
1 to 99 workers	51	36	70	50	34	68	77	73	95
1 to 49 workers	47	33	70	46	32	69	69	66	96
50 to 99 workers	65	45	70	63	42	67	89	84	95
100 workers or more	84	71	84	82	65	80	91	86	95
100 to 499 workers	80	61	77	79	58	74	87	83	96
500 workers or more	89	80	91	86	76	88	92	87	94
Geographic Areas[5]									
New England	69	54	79	66	50	76	84	79	95
Middle Atlantic	69	56	82	65	51	79	91	84	92
East North Central	71	57	81	69	54	78	85	81	96
West North Central	72	57	79	68	52	76	91	83	91
South Atlantic	68	51	75	64	45	70	90	83	92
East South Central	72	57	79	66	47	72	92	90	97
West South Central	68	52	77	64	46	72	88	86	98
Mountain	66	50	76	63	45	71	88	85	97
Pacific	64	53	83	59	47	78	91	88	97

[1]Includes defined benefit pension plans and defined contribution retirement plans. Workers are considered as having access or as participating if they have access to or participate in at least one of these plan types.
[2]The take-up rate is an estimate of the percentage of workers with access to a plan who participate in the plan, rounded for presentation.
[3]Includes workers in the private nonfarm economy except those in private households, and workers in the public sector, except the federal government.
[4]The percentile groupings are based on the average wage for each occupation surveyed, which may include workers both above and below the threshold.
[5]The states that comprise the Census divisions are: New England—Connecticut, Maine, Massachusetts, New Hampshire, Rhode Island, and Vermont; Middle Atlantic—New Jersey, New York, and Pennsylvania; South Atlantic—Delaware, District of Columbia, Florida, Georgia, Maryland, North Carolina, South Carolina, Virginia, and West Virginia; East South Central—Alabama, Kentucky, Mississippi, and Tennessee; West South Central—Arkansas, Louisiana, Oklahoma, and Texas; East North Central—Illinois, Indiana, Michigan, Ohio, and Wisconsin; West North Central—Iowa, Kansas, Minnesota, Missouri, Nebraska, North Dakota, and South Dakota; Mountain—Arizona, Colorado, Idaho, Montana, Nevada, New Mexico, Utah, and Wyoming; and Pacific—Alaska, California, Hawaii, Oregon, and Washington.
- = No workers in this area or data does not meet standards of reliability or precision.

Table 6-10. Medical Care Benefits: Access, Participation, and Take-Up Rates,[1] March 2012

(Percent.)

Characteristic	Civilian[2]			Private industry			State and local government		
	Access	Participation	Take-up rate	Access	Participation	Take-up rate	Access	Participation	Take-up rate
ALL WORKERS	73	54	74	70	51	72	87	73	84
Worker Characteristics									
Management, professional, and related	88	69	78	87	67	76	89	74	83
Management, business, and financial	93	73	78	94	72	77	-	-	-
Professional and related	86	67	78	84	64	76	89	73	82
Teachers	86	70	81	-	-	-	88	72	82
Primary, secondary, and special education school teachers	97	79	81	-	-	-	98	80	82
Registered nurses	82	64	77	-	-	-	-	-	-
Service	47	32	68	41	25	62	81	69	85
Protective service	68	56	83	39	28	71	89	77	87
Sales and office	73	52	71	72	50	70	87	73	84
Sales and related	63	42	67	63	42	67	-	-	-
Office and administrative support	79	58	73	78	56	71	87	73	83
Natural resources, construction, and maintenance	78	60	76	77	57	75	95	83	87
Construction, extraction, farming, fishing, and forestry	72	57	78	70	53	76	-	-	-
Installation, maintenance, and repair	84	62	75	83	61	73	-	-	-
Production, transportation, and material moving	76	57	76	75	57	76	83	70	84
Production	82	64	78	82	64	77	-	-	-
Transportation and material moving	69	51	74	69	50	73	-	-	-
Full-time workers	88	67	76	86	64	74	99	83	84
Part-time workers	24	13	56	24	13	54	24	17	71
Union workers	95	79	83	94	78	83	95	79	83
Nonunion workers	69	50	72	67	48	71	80	68	84
Average Wage Within the Following Percentiles[3]									
Lowest 25 percent	38	22	59	34	19	57	68	55	81
Lowest 10 percent	21	11	51	19	9	50	54	43	79
Second 25 percent	77	55	72	74	51	69	91	78	86
Third 25 percent	87	68	78	86	65	76	93	79	85
Highest 25 percent	93	75	80	92	73	79	97	80	83
Highest 10 percent	95	76	80	93	74	79	97	82	84
Establishment Characteristics									
Goods-producing industries	86	67	78	86	67	78	-	-	-
Service-providing industries	70	52	74	67	47	71	87	73	84
Education and health services	80	60	75	76	53	70	88	72	82
Educational services	86	69	80	81	59	74	88	71	81
Elementary and secondary schools	88	70	79	-	-	-	89	71	80
Junior colleges, colleges, and universities	86	71	82	90	68	76	84	73	86
Health care and social assistance	76	54	71	75	52	69	88	73	84
Hospitals	89	68	77	-	-	-	94	79	84
Public administration	88	77	87	-	-	-	88	77	87
Number of Workers									
1 to 99 workers	58	41	72	57	41	71	73	63	87
1 to 49 workers	54	38	71	54	38	70	64	56	88
50 to 99 workers	70	51	72	69	49	71	87	74	85
100 workers or more	86	66	76	85	63	74	89	74	83
100 to 499 workers	82	60	73	82	59	72	85	72	84
500 workers or more	90	71	79	89	68	76	90	75	83
Geographic Areas[4]									
New England	74	54	72	72	51	71	87	68	78
Middle Atlantic	73	57	78	71	53	75	86	77	89
East North Central	73	54	73	72	52	72	80	62	78
West North Central	71	52	74	68	48	71	85	71	84
South Atlantic	72	52	72	69	47	69	90	75	84
East South Central	77	59	77	72	52	72	92	85	92
West South Central	72	53	74	69	50	72	90	73	80
Mountain	71	50	71	68	48	70	87	70	80
Pacific	72	56	78	69	53	76	88	75	85

[1]The take-up rate is an estimate of the percentage of workers with access to a plan who participate in the plan, rounded for presentation.
[2]Includes workers in the private nonfarm economy except those in private households, and workers in the public sector, except the federal government.
[3]The percentile groupings are based on the average wage for each occupation surveyed, which may include workers both above and below the threshold.
[4]The states that comprise the Census divisions are: New England—Connecticut, Maine, Massachusetts, New Hampshire, Rhode Island, and Vermont; Middle Atlantic—New Jersey, New York, and Pennsylvania; South Atlantic—Delaware, District of Columbia, Florida, Georgia, Maryland, North Carolina, South Carolina, Virginia, and West Virginia; East South Central—Alabama, Kentucky, Mississippi, and Tennessee; West South Central—Arkansas, Louisiana, Oklahoma, and Texas; East North Central—Illinois, Indiana, Michigan, Ohio, and Wisconsin; West North Central—Iowa, Kansas, Minnesota, Missouri, Nebraska, North Dakota, and South Dakota; Mountain—Arizona, Colorado, Idaho, Montana, Nevada, New Mexico, Utah, and Wyoming; and Pacific—Alaska, California, Hawaii, Oregon, and Washington.
- = No workers in this area or data does not meet standards of reliability or precision.

Table 6-11. Medical Plans: Share of Premiums Paid by Employer and Employee for Single Coverage, March 2012

(Percent.)

Characteristic	Civilian[1]		Private industry		State and local government	
	Employer share of premium	Employee share of premium	Employer share of premium	Employee share of premium	Employer share of premium	Employee share of premium
ALL WORKERS	81	19	79	21	87	13
Worker Characteristics						
Management, professional, and related	83	17	81	19	87	13
Management, business, and financial	81	19	80	20	-	-
Professional and related	83	17	81	19	87	13
Teachers	86	14	-	-	87	13
Primary, secondary, and special education school teachers	87	13	-	-	87	13
Registered nurses	80	20	-	-	-	-
Service	80	20	77	23	88	12
Protective service	85	15	77	23	88	12
Sales and office	79	21	78	22	88	12
Sales and related	74	26	74	26	-	-
Office and administrative support	81	19	79	21	88	12
Natural resources, construction, and maintenance	82	18	81	19	88	12
Construction, extraction, farming, fishing, and forestry	84	16	83	17	-	-
Installation, maintenance, and repair	81	19	80	20	-	-
Production, transportation, and material moving	81	19	80	20	87	13
Production	80	20	80	20	-	-
Transportation and material moving	81	19	80	20	-	-
Full-time workers	81	19	80	20	87	13
Part-time workers	75	25	74	26	83	17
Union workers	88	12	88	12	88	12
Nonunion workers	79	21	78	22	87	13
Average Wage Within the Following Percentiles[2]						
Lowest 25 percent	76	24	75	25	87	13
Lowest 10 percent	75	25	72	28	88	12
Second 25 percent	80	20	78	22	88	12
Third 25 percent	82	18	80	20	88	12
Highest 25 percent	83	17	81	19	86	14
Highest 10 percent	83	17	82	18	89	11
Establishment Characteristics						
Goods-producing industries	82	18	82	18	-	-
Service-providing industries	81	19	79	21	87	13
Education and health services	83	17	80	20	87	13
Educational services	85	15	79	21	87	13
Elementary and secondary schools	86	14	-	-	87	13
Junior colleges, colleges, and universities	85	15	79	21	88	12
Health care and social assistance	81	19	80	20	86	14
Hospitals	82	18	-	-	86	14
Public administration	88	12	-	-	88	12
Number of Workers						
1 to 99 workers	80	20	79	21	91	9
1 to 49 workers	80	20	79	21	91	9
50 to 99 workers	79	21	78	22	91	9
100 workers or more	82	18	80	20	87	13
100 to 499 workers	80	20	79	21	88	12
500 workers or more	83	17	81	19	87	13
Geographic Areas[3]						
New England	77	23	75	25	84	16
Middle Atlantic	83	17	81	19	89	11
East North Central	81	19	80	20	89	11
West North Central	82	18	79	21	91	9
South Atlantic	80	20	78	22	87	13
East South Central	81	19	78	22	87	13
West South Central	81	19	80	20	86	14
Mountain	81	19	79	21	88	12
Pacific	82	18	81	19	86	14

[1]Includes workers in the private nonfarm economy except those in private households, and workers in the public sector, except the federal government.
[2]The percentile groupings are based on the average wage for each occupation surveyed, which may include workers both above and below the threshold.
[3]The states that comprise the Census divisions are: New England—Connecticut, Maine, Massachusetts, New Hampshire, Rhode Island, and Vermont; Middle Atlantic—New Jersey, New York, and Pennsylvania; South Atlantic—Delaware, District of Columbia, Florida, Georgia, Maryland, North Carolina, South Carolina, Virginia, and West Virginia; East South Central—Alabama, Kentucky, Mississippi, and Tennessee; West South Central—Arkansas, Louisiana, Oklahoma, and Texas; East North Central—Illinois, Indiana, Michigan, Ohio, and Wisconsin; West North Central—Iowa, Kansas, Minnesota, Missouri, Nebraska, North Dakota, and South Dakota; Mountain—Arizona, Colorado, Idaho, Montana, Nevada, New Mexico, Utah, and Wyoming; and Pacific—Alaska, California, Hawaii, Oregon, and Washington.
- = No workers in this area or data does not meet standards of reliability or precision.

Table 6-12. Medical Plans: Share of Premiums Paid by Employer and Employee for Family Coverage, March 2012

(Percent.)

Characteristic	Civilian[1]		Private industry		State and local government	
	Employer share of premium	Employee share of premium	Employer share of premium	Employee share of premium	Employer share of premium	Employee share of premium
ALL WORKERS	69	31	68	32	71	29
Worker Characteristics						
Management, professional, and related	70	30	70	30	69	31
Management, business, and financial	70	30	69	31	-	-
Professional and related	70	30	71	29	68	32
Teachers	66	34	-	-	67	33
Primary, secondary, and special education school teachers	65	35	-	-	66	34
Registered nurses	71	29	-	-	-	-
Service	65	35	61	39	73	27
Protective service	75	25	63	37	77	23
Sales and office	67	33	67	33	73	27
Sales and related	64	36	64	36	-	-
Office and administrative support	69	31	68	32	72	28
Natural resources, construction, and maintenance	69	31	69	31	72	28
Construction, extraction, farming, fishing, and forestry	70	30	69	31	-	-
Installation, maintenance, and repair	69	31	69	31	-	-
Production, transportation, and material moving	73	27	73	27	70	30
Production	74	26	73	27	-	-
Transportation and material moving	71	29	72	28	-	-
Full-time workers	69	31	69	31	71	29
Part-time workers	66	34	66	34	69	31
Union workers	80	20	83	17	78	22
Nonunion workers	66	34	66	34	63	37
Average Wage Within the Following Percentiles[2]						
Lowest 25 percent	60	40	60	40	63	37
Lowest 10 percent	60	40	58	42	56	44
Second 25 percent	67	33	66	34	73	27
Third 25 percent	70	30	68	32	71	29
Highest 25 percent	72	28	72	28	73	27
Highest 10 percent	74	26	73	27	79	21
Establishment Characteristics						
Goods-producing industries	74	26	74	26	-	-
Service-providing industries	68	32	67	33	71	29
Education and health services	66	34	65	35	67	33
Educational services	66	34	64	36	66	34
Elementary and secondary schools	64	36	-	-	64	36
Junior colleges, colleges, and universities	71	29	69	31	72	28
Health care and social assistance	67	33	66	34	72	28
Hospitals	74	26	-	-	73	27
Public administration	77	23	-	-	77	23
Number of Workers						
1 to 99 workers	63	37	63	37	71	29
1 to 49 workers	63	37	63	37	73	27
50 to 99 workers	64	36	63	37	68	32
100 workers or more	72	28	73	27	71	29
100 to 499 workers	69	31	69	31	70	30
500 workers or more	74	26	77	23	71	29
Geographic Areas[3]						
New England	72	28	71	29	79	21
Middle Atlantic	75	25	72	28	87	13
East North Central	74	26	72	28	83	17
West North Central	70	30	70	30	69	31
South Atlantic	64	36	64	36	65	35
East South Central	62	38	66	34	55	45
West South Central	63	37	66	34	52	48
Mountain	67	33	67	33	63	37
Pacific	68	32	66	34	76	24

[1]Includes workers in the private nonfarm economy except those in private households, and workers in the public sector, except the federal government.
[2]The percentile groupings are based on the average wage for each occupation surveyed, which may include workers both above and below the threshold.
[3]The states that comprise the Census divisions are: New England—Connecticut, Maine, Massachusetts, New Hampshire, Rhode Island, and Vermont; Middle Atlantic—New Jersey, New York, and Pennsylvania; South Atlantic—Delaware, District of Columbia, Florida, Georgia, Maryland, North Carolina, South Carolina, Virginia, and West Virginia; East South Central—Alabama, Kentucky, Mississippi, and Tennessee; West South Central—Arkansas, Louisiana, Oklahoma, and Texas; East North Central—Illinois, Indiana, Michigan, Ohio, and Wisconsin; West North Central—Iowa, Kansas, Minnesota, Missouri, Nebraska, North Dakota, and South Dakota; Mountain—Arizona, Colorado, Idaho, Montana, Nevada, New Mexico, Utah, and Wyoming; and Pacific—Alaska, California, Hawaii, Oregon, and Washington.
- = No workers in this area or data does not meet standards of reliability or precision.

Table 6-13. Quality of Life Benefits:[1] Access for Civilian Workers, March 2012

(Percent.)

Characteristic	Childcare[2]	Flexible workplace	Subsidized commuting	Wellness programs	Employee assistance programs
ALL WORKERS	10	5	6	37	52
Worker Characteristics					
Management, professional, and related	17	11	11	52	68
Management, business, and financial	18	18	14	54	69
Professional and related	16	8	9	51	68
Teachers	13	3	5	49	67
Primary, secondary, and special education school teachers	10	1	3	46	66
Registered nurses	24	4	10	67	78
Service	8	1	4	23	36
Protective service	9	3	9	39	59
Sales and office	8	6	7	39	54
Sales and related	3	3	3	38	52
Office and administrative support	11	7	9	40	55
Natural resources, construction, and maintenance	5	2	4	27	40
Construction, extraction, farming, fishing, and forestry	2	1	4	20	32
Installation, maintenance, and repair	7	2	4	34	47
Production, transportation, and material moving	4	2	3	28	45
Production	6	2	3	33	47
Transportation and material moving	3	2	2	24	43
Full-time workers	11	7	8	41	57
Part-time workers	6	1	3	23	36
Union workers	14	2	9	49	77
Nonunion workers	9	6	6	35	48
Average Wage Within the Following Percentiles[3]					
Lowest 25 percent	5	1	2	20	31
Lowest 10 percent	5	-	1	14	23
Second 25 percent	8	3	5	36	50
Third 25 percent	11	7	9	41	58
Highest 25 percent	17	12	11	54	71
Highest 10 percent	18	15	13	56	74
Establishment Characteristics					
Goods-producing industries	7	5	3	35	49
Service-providing industries	10	6	7	37	52
Education and health services	15	3	7	47	62
Educational services	13	4	7	48	67
Elementary and secondary schools	9	1	2	44	67
Junior colleges, colleges, and universities	25	-	17	66	78
Health care and social assistance	16	2	7	46	58
Hospitals	27	3	14	80	91
Public administration	17	5	17	54	77
Number of Workers					
1 to 99 workers	5	4	3	18	29
1 to 49 workers	4	4	3	16	25
50 to 99 workers	6	4	4	25	42
100 workers or more	15	7	9	54	73
100 to 499 workers	8	4	5	43	61
500 workers or more	22	9	14	65	84
Geographic Areas[4]					
New England	12	5	8	39	54
Middle Atlantic	11	5	7	35	52
East North Central	11	6	6	40	51
West North Central	10	5	5	39	51
South Atlantic	9	6	5	37	53
East South Central	9	8	4	40	50
West South Central	9	5	3	37	53
Mountain	9	4	8	31	51
Pacific	9	5	11	36	51

[1]Includes workers in the private nonfarm economy except those in private households, and workers in the public sector, except the federal government.
[2]A workplace program that provides for either the full or partial cost of caring for an employee's children in a nursery, day care center, or a baby sitter in facilities either on or off the employer's premises.
[3]The categories are based on the average wage for each occupation surveyed, which may include workers with earnings both above and below the threshold.
[4]The states that comprise the Census divisions are: New England—Connecticut, Maine, Massachusetts, New Hampshire, Rhode Island, and Vermont; Middle Atlantic—New Jersey, New York, and Pennsylvania; South Atlantic—Delaware, District of Columbia, Florida, Georgia, Maryland, North Carolina, South Carolina, Virginia, and West Virginia; East South Central—Alabama, Kentucky, Mississippi, and Tennessee; West South Central—Arkansas, Louisiana, Oklahoma, and Texas; East North Central—Illinois, Indiana, Michigan, Ohio, and Wisconsin; West North Central—Iowa, Kansas, Minnesota, Missouri, Nebraska, North Dakota, and South Dakota; Mountain—Arizona, Colorado, Idaho, Montana, Nevada, New Mexico, Utah, and Wyoming; and Pacific—Alaska, California, Hawaii, Oregon, and Washington.
- = No workers in this area or data does not meet standards of reliability or precision.

Table 6-14. Access to Paid Sick Leave, Vacation, and Holidays, March 2012

(Percent.)

Characteristic	Civilian[1]			Private industry			State and local government		
	Paid sick leave	Paid vacation	Paid holidays	Paid sick leave	Paid vacation	Paid holidays	Paid sick leave	Paid vacation	Paid holidays
ALL WORKERS	66	74	76	61	77	77	89	59	67
Worker Characteristics									
Management, professional, and related	86	75	79	84	87	89	90	43	55
Management, business, and financial	90	94	95	90	96	97	-	-	-
Professional and related	84	67	73	81	83	85	90	36	49
Teachers	85	16	34	-	-	-	88	12	30
Primary, secondary, and special education school teachers	95	11	28	-	-	-	95	9	27
Registered nurses	81	82	84	-	-	-	-	-	-
Service	47	59	56	40	56	53	85	75	78
Protective service	69	78	80	40	64	70	90	88	87
Sales and office	67	79	81	65	-	81	89	84	85
Sales and related	52	67	70	52	67	69	-	-	-
Office and administrative support	75	86	88	73	86	89	90	84	86
Natural resources, construction, and maintenance	57	83	83	53	82	82	95	95	96
Construction, extraction, farming, fishing, and forestry	45	74	75	39	72	73	-	-	-
Installation, maintenance, and repair	68	91	91	65	90	90	-	-	-
Production, transportation, and material moving	54	82	83	52	83	84	87	63	73
Production	54	90	91	54	90	91	-	-	-
Transportation and material moving	53	73	76	51	75	77	-	-	-
Full-time workers	79	87	-	75	91	90	98	67	74
Part-time workers	25	34	39	23	35	40	40	20	29
Union workers	84	75	80	73	91	91	97	57	69
Nonunion workers	62	74	75	60	75	76	82	62	66
Average Wage Within the Following Percentiles[2]									
Lowest 25 percent	32	51	52	29	49	50	75	55	62
Lowest 10 percent	20	38	35	18	37	33	62	41	49
Second 25 percent	68	82	84	64	83	84	93	84	87
Third 25 percent	79	89	84	75	90	90	93	69	76
Highest 25 percent	87	79	82	84	90	91	96	36	49
Highest 10 percent	90	76	79	86	90	90	98	34	45
Establishment Characteristics									
Goods-producing industries	57	90	90	56	90	90	-	-	-
Service-providing industries	67	71	73	62	74	75	89	59	67
Education and health services	81	65	71	77	79	81	89	42	55
Educational services	87	41	53	79	59	65	89	36	50
Elementary and secondary schools	90	27	42	-	-	-	90	27	42
Junior colleges, colleges, and universities	85	68	78	82	73	80	87	66	77
Health care and social assistance	77	83	84	76	83	83	87	86	88
Hospitals	88	89	91	-	-	-	93	93	94
Public administration	89	89	88	-	-	-	89	89	88
Number of Workers									
1 to 99 workers	53	69	69	52	69	69	78	66	69
1 to 49 workers	51	67	67	50	67	67	70	65	66
50 to 99 workers	57	75	75	55	75	76	90	67	73
100 workers or more	77	79	82	73	86	87	90	58	67
100 to 499 workers	69	80	82	66	83	84	87	59	63
500 workers or more	86	78	82	82	90	91	91	58	68
Geographic Areas[3]									
New England	70	72	72	67	76	75	86	48	54
Middle Atlantic	69	73	77	65	76	79	89	58	62
East North Central	62	74	77	58	78	79	85	53	65
West North Central	64	72	74	59	75	75	90	58	69
South Atlantic	65	76	77	60	78	77	92	66	77
East South Central	65	76	77	57	78	79	90	66	71
West South Central	67	75	77	64	79	81	85	52	54
Mountain	61	74	73	58	77	75	83	54	59
Pacific	67	72	73	63	72	73	91	67	73

[1]Includes workers in the private nonfarm economy except those in private households, and workers in the public sector, except the federal government.
[2]The percentile groupings are based on the average wage for each occupation surveyed, which may include workers both above and below the threshold.
[3]The states that comprise the Census divisions are: New England—Connecticut, Maine, Massachusetts, New Hampshire, Rhode Island, and Vermont; Middle Atlantic—New Jersey, New York, and Pennsylvania; South Atlantic—Delaware, District of Columbia, Florida, Georgia, Maryland, North Carolina, South Carolina, Virginia, and West Virginia; East South Central—Alabama, Kentucky, Mississippi, and Tennessee; West South Central—Arkansas, Louisiana, Oklahoma, and Texas; East North Central—Illinois, Indiana, Michigan, Ohio, and Wisconsin; West North Central—Iowa, Kansas, Minnesota, Missouri, Nebraska, North Dakota, and South Dakota; Mountain—Arizona, Colorado, Idaho, Montana, Nevada, New Mexico, Utah, and Wyoming; and Pacific—Alaska, California, Hawaii, Oregon, and Washington.
- = No workers in this area or data does not meet standards of reliability or precision.

Chapter Seven

RECENT TRENDS IN THE LABOR MARKET

RECENT TRENDS IN THE LABOR MARKET

HIGHLIGHTS

This chapter contains information on mass layoff events, initial claimants for unemployment insurance, movement of work, job openings, hires, and separations.

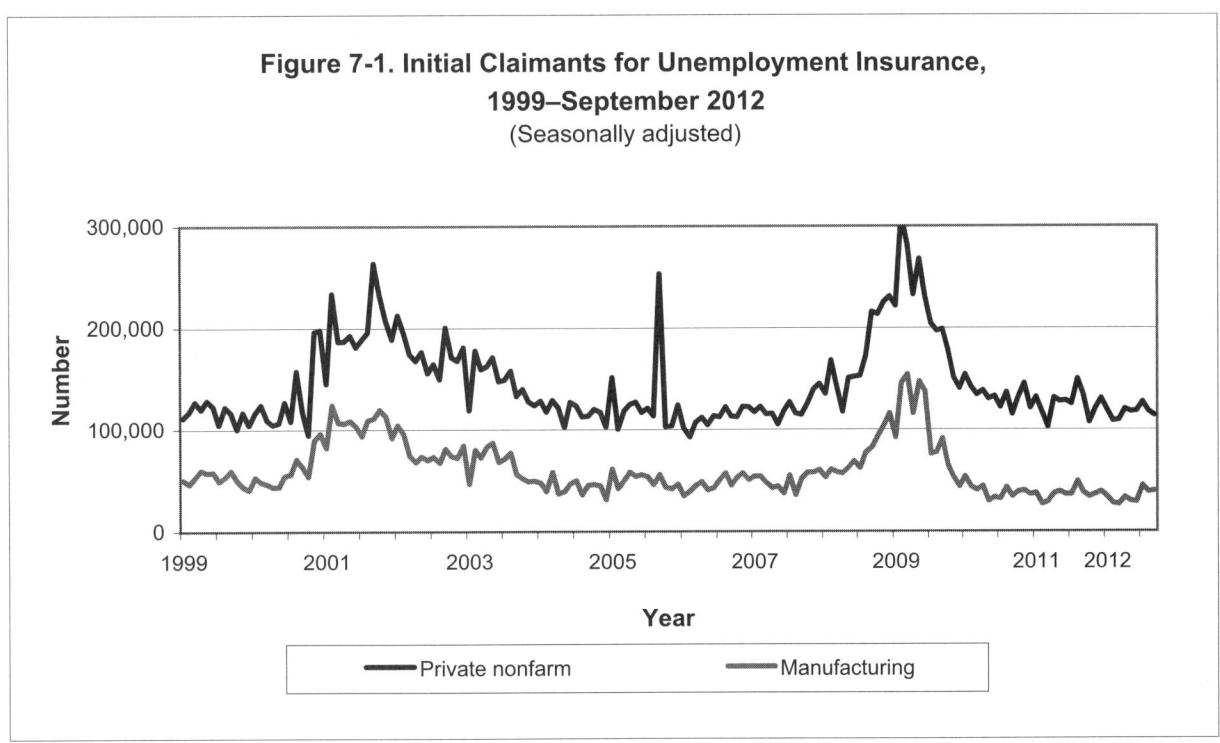

Figure 7-1. Initial Claimants for Unemployment Insurance, 1999–September 2012
(Seasonally adjusted)

In September 2012, 1,316 mass layoff events occurred compared to a high 3,059 mass layoff events in February 2009 (seasonally adjusted). A mass layoff event is when there are 50 or more initial claims from an employer during the five-week period, regardless of duration. (See Table 7-1.)

OTHER HIGHLIGHTS

- From January 2012 to September 2012, the number of mass layoff events (seasonally adjusted), reached 12,008 while the number of initial claims fell to 1,155,226. During the same time period in 2011, there 13,466 mass layoff events and 1,286,250 initial claims. (See Table 7-1.)

- The number of mass layoff events declined from 2010 to 2011 in most industries. However, they increased in transportation and warehousing, administrative and waste services, educational services, and health care and social assistance. (See Table 7-3.)

- Manufacturing accounted for the largest number of mass layoff events in 2011 at 4,397 even though the number of mass layoffs in manufacturing declined 2.8 percent from 2010 to 2011. (See Table 7-3.)

- According to preliminary data in September 2012, the number of job openings reached 3.56 million which down slightly from 3.66 million job openings one month earlier. The number of job openings were the highest in educational and heath services (697,000) and trade, transportation, and utilities (597,000) and lowest in manufacturing (238,000) and construction (77,000). (See Table 7-7.)

NOTES AND DEFINITIONS

MASS LAYOFFS

Collection and Coverage

The Mass Layoff Statistics (MLS) program is a federal-state program that identifies, describes, and tracks the effects of major job cutbacks, using data from each state's unemployment insurance database. Employers that have at least 50 initial claims filed against them during a consecutive 5-week period are contacted by the state agency to determine whether these separations are of at least 31 days duration, and, if so, information is obtained on the total number of persons separated, the reasons for these separations, and recall expectations. Employers are identified according to industry classification and location, and unemployment insurance claimants are identified by such demographic factors as age, race, gender, ethnic group, and place of residence. The program yields information on an individual's entire spell of unemployment, to the point when regular unemployment insurance benefits are exhausted.

A given month contains an aggregation of the weekly unemployment insurance claims filings for the Sunday through Saturday weeks in that month. All weeks are included for the particular month, except if the first day of the month falls on Saturday. In this case, the week is included in the prior month's tabulations. This means that some months will contain 4 weeks and others, 5 weeks, the number of weeks in a given month may be different from year to year, and the number of weeks in a year may vary. Therefore, analysis of over-the-month and over-the-year change in not seasonally adjusted series should take this calendar effect into consideration.

The latest quarterly data in these tables are considered preliminary. After the initial publication of quarterly information, more data are collected as remaining employer interviews for the quarter are completed and additional initial claimant information associated with extended layoff events is received.

The MLS program discontinued the collection of "domestic relocation" and "overseas relocation" as standard reasons for layoff beginning with data for the first quarter 2004. It was felt these reasons do not reflect an economic reason, and instead relate to the effect of the actual reason.

Concepts and Definitions

Employers in the MLS program include those covered by state unemployment insurance laws. Information on employers is obtained from the Quarterly Census of Employment and Wages (QCEW) program.

Extended layoff event is when there are fifty or more initial claims for unemployment insurance benefits from an employer during a 5-week period, with at least 50 workers separated for more than 30 days.

Initial claimant is a person who files any notice of unemployment to initiate a request either for a determination of entitlement to and eligibility for compensation, or for a subsequent period of unemployment within a benefit year or period of eligibility.

Layoff is the separation of persons from an employer as part of a mass layoff event. Such layoffs involve both persons subject to recall and those who are terminated by the establishment.

Mass layoff event is when there are fifty or more initial claims for unemployment insurance benefits from an employer during a five-week period, regardless of duration.

Movement-of-work action is relocation of work within the same company or to other companies, domestically or outside the United States. Because employers may cite more than one location to which work is moving, a layoff event may have more than one action associated with it.

Movement-of-work separations is the number of separations specifically associated with movement-of-work actions.

Outsourcing is the movement of work that was formerly conducted in-house by employees paid directly by a company to a different company under a contractual arrangement.

Seasonal adjustment is the process of estimating and removing the effect on time series data of regularly recurring seasonal events such as changes in the weather, holidays, and the beginning and ending of the school year. The use of seasonal adjustment makes it easier to observe fundamental changes in time series, particularly those associated with general economic expansions and contractions.

Separations is the total number of people laid-off in an extended mass layoff event for more than 30 days, according to the employer.

Worksite closure is the complete closure of either multi-unit or single-unit employers or the partial closure of a multi-unit employer where entire worksites affected by layoffs are closed or planned to be closed.

Sources of Additional Information

For more extensive information and the latest edition of the Mass Layoffs news release, please see <http://www.bls.gov/news.release/mmls.nr0.htm>.

Table 7-1. Mass Layoff Events and Initial Claimants for Unemployment Insurance, 1999–September 2012, Seasonally Adjusted

(Number.)

Year and month	Total		Private nonfarm		Manufacturing	
	Events	Initial claimants	Events	Initial claimants	Events	Initial claimants
1999						
January	1 399	129 104	1 122	111 713	429	50 593
February	1 321	136 296	1 074	117 827	404	46 526
March	1 354	148 022	1 112	127 562	460	53 087
April	1 251	134 118	1 058	120 142	457	60 125
May	1 278	146 682	1 063	128 874	438	57 589
June	1 217	138 397	1 053	123 191	446	58 202
July	1 136	117 941	951	104 930	358	49 567
August	1 188	140 981	1 000	122 361	408	53 579
September	1 355	134 430	1 152	116 756	374	59 783
October	995	115 894	797	100 478	344	50 194
November	1 258	138 992	1 025	117 116	337	44 140
December	1 174	119 033	973	104 519	298	40 825
2000						
January	1 100	126 440	968	116 846	371	53 270
February	1 280	151 107	1 018	124 497	379	48 372
March	1 159	126 309	965	109 445	393	46 564
April	1 030	115 068	913	104 865	407	43 829
May	1 196	126 525	976	106 893	376	44 019
June	1 220	145 766	1 020	127 239	406	54 672
July	1 065	118 649	922	108 499	417	56 465
August	1 282	178 789	1 060	157 762	423	71 141
September	1 260	134 153	1 045	117 266	407	63 394
October	938	107 676	798	94 783	385	54 006
November	1 643	215 381	1 447	196 166	599	89 869
December	1 691	214 601	1 514	197 944	575	96 295
2001						
January	1 288	158 580	1 144	145 584	529	82 504
February	1 912	253 943	1 684	233 524	828	124 430
March	1 761	202 344	1 569	186 565	800	107 481
April	1 622	200 683	1 484	186 898	776	106 255
May	1 676	206 062	1 523	192 500	750	108 773
June	1 608	195 802	1 432	181 264	740	103 468
July	1 710	201 363	1 574	189 030	721	93 949
August	1 732	207 416	1 568	195 777	791	109 611
September	2 407	277 955	2 236	263 773	841	111 520
October	2 177	242 507	2 051	232 371	923	119 873
November	2 104	218 378	1 940	206 999	948	113 776
December	1 824	200 677	1 673	188 836	746	92 019
2002						
January	1 841	224 765	1 711	212 461	764	104 909
February	1 823	207 788	1 663	194 840	701	95 406
March	1 697	187 212	1 525	174 281	604	74 492
April	1 666	183 005	1 494	167 848	584	68 282
May	1 730	190 129	1 561	176 744	613	73 612
June	1 632	171 213	1 436	155 960	547	70 137
July	1 632	179 407	1 461	164 741	557	73 479
August	1 468	161 431	1 324	149 847	563	67 831
September	1 918	217 299	1 737	200 635	615	81 292
October	1 749	187 851	1 573	171 346	611	73 940
November	1 651	178 739	1 507	167 723	590	72 329
December	1 834	194 852	1 646	180 976	676	84 247
2003						
January	1 336	132 819	1 160	119 199	382	46 839
February	1 831	191 434	1 650	178 003	650	80 285
March	1 784	175 384	1 589	159 467	609	72 679
April	1 702	172 252	1 555	162 323	637	83 268
May	1 744	185 159	1 556	171 221	646	87 077
June	1 726	164 597	1 518	147 553	640	68 197
July	1 661	165 130	1 450	149 233	567	71 319
August	1 546	171 996	1 383	157 968	563	77 405
September	1 571	149 250	1 370	133 276	479	56 454
October	1 525	157 759	1 319	140 086	422	51 872
November	1 370	139 572	1 225	127 963	379	49 219
December	1 395	136 166	1 226	124 009	428	49 789
2004						
January	1 414	145 593	1 221	128 305	396	47 882
February	1 257	130 205	1 111	117 788	365	39 214
March	1 362	138 397	1 222	129 094	396	58 213
April	1 349	136 837	1 175	121 841	347	37 115
May	1 240	116 392	1 077	102 443	340	39 208
June	1 397	139 975	1 231	127 229	370	46 998
July	1 315	135 186	1 165	123 768	371	49 945
August	1 417	127 814	1 226	112 867	344	36 298
September	1 275	124 279	1 149	113 689	337	45 732
October	1 265	129 312	1 153	120 337	366	46 319
November	1 306	129 014	1 161	117 300	374	44 939
December	1 163	114 258	1 009	102 732	285	31 445
2005						
January	1 509	161 805	1 367	151 530	413	61 483
February	1 075	111 437	948	100 564	344	42 035
March	1 193	129 288	1 045	118 827	361	50 086
April	1 238	135 353	1 107	124 881	384	58 255
May	1 266	139 915	1 124	127 071	395	54 052
June	1 185	125 919	1 072	117 229	359	55 621
July	1 257	133 036	1 116	121 311	392	53 945
August	1 118	124 738	996	113 784	340	46 067
September	2 241	299 151	2 028	253 431	423	55 855
October	1 113	111 868	994	102 840	323	43 326
November	1 176	115 215	1 040	103 701	328	41 868
December	1 272	135 737	1 142	124 459	356	46 211

Table 7-1. Mass Layoff Events and Initial Claimants for Unemployment Insurance, 1999–September 2012, Seasonally Adjusted—*Continued*

(Number.)

Year and month	Total		Private nonfarm		Manufacturing	
	Events	Initial claimants	Events	Initial claimants	Events	Initial claimants
2006						
January	1 086	111 484	955	101 462	290	35 030
February	935	100 482	837	92 542	299	39 328
March	1 044	115 705	942	107 238	308	45 044
April	1 162	122 174	1 028	112 014	351	48 735
May	1 106	114 200	995	104 870	302	40 491
June	1 128	122 783	1 021	113 724	352	42 960
July	1 181	122 246	1 058	112 645	367	50 719
August	1 231	131 837	1 095	122 479	370	57 150
September	1 140	121 613	1 031	113 304	365	45 207
October	1 184	121 126	1 071	112 667	404	53 017
November	1 223	132 407	1 107	122 718	412	57 192
December	1 196	132 153	1 094	122 556	367	50 644
2007						
January	1 236	129 105	1 079	117 477	399	54 155
February	1 272	131 822	1 150	122 921	377	54 021
March	1 203	124 120	1 091	115 440	380	47 707
April	1 239	126 856	1 102	115 752	361	42 682
May	1 144	112 391	1 050	105 525	344	44 415
June	1 198	127 343	1 086	118 633	339	37 556
July	1 299	135 184	1 197	127 315	400	54 934
August	1 208	123 551	1 121	116 211	314	35 737
September	1 224	121 211	1 131	114 929	430	51 677
October	1 331	134 995	1 205	126 002	439	58 056
November	1 395	149 871	1 266	139 924	407	57 837
December	1 546	154 450	1 430	145 008	467	60 484
2008						
January	1 439	146 850	1 300	135 422	421	53 254
February	1 724	179 955	1 567	168 003	485	60 752
March	1 515	151 628	1 400	141 316	441	58 254
April	1 290	128 643	1 157	117 639	453	57 044
May	1 567	160 475	1 432	150 893	470	62 776
June	1 612	163 425	1 471	152 133	491	68 862
July	1 589	163 572	1 452	153 060	465	62 210
August	1 763	181 853	1 632	172 147	578	77 464
September	2 159	229 180	1 990	215 749	629	82 011
October	2 201	226 853	2 043	213 454	698	93 252
November	2 406	239 239	2 247	225 404	907	103 836
December	2 437	244 889	2 261	230 621	935	116 181
2009						
January	2 254	235 371	2 083	221 653	726	92 293
February	3 059	326 392	2 901	310 378	1 251	145 839
March	2 999	299 322	2 800	282 414	1 230	154 168
April	2 566	249 129	2 349	232 632	1 007	116 051
May	2 710	284 468	2 516	267 869	1 181	147 184
June	2 466	247 597	2 257	230 502	1 048	137 649
July	2 186	222 941	1 979	203 911	636	75 728
August	2 340	216 047	2 115	197 172	751	77 894
September	2 261	214 018	2 048	198 761	786	91 125
October	1 969	195 752	1 772	178 172	571	65 217
November	1 757	164 454	1 588	151 172	472	52 855
December	1 719	155 056	1 543	140 835	424	44 096
2010						
January	1 707	168 044	1 529	154 187	471	53 817
February	1 631	156 292	1 465	141 831	374	43 620
March	1 676	149 816	1 469	134 518	356	40 705
April	1 637	154 558	1 452	138 503	368	44 506
May	1 608	150 996	1 357	130 273	302	29 932
June	1 695	151 435	1 475	132 742	325	33 298
July	1 519	138 091	1 316	122 162	304	32 253
August	1 588	159 329	1 399	136 697	390	43 154
September	1 510	133 576	1 295	115 349	328	34 333
October	1 654	149 589	1 446	132 146	354	38 937
November	1 592	161 145	1 410	145 494	360	39 977
December	1 477	135 849	1 271	121 171	322	36 267
2011						
January	1 536	148 952	1 348	131 869	337	37 477
February	1 434	131 569	1 242	116 745	297	26 696
March	1 275	115 391	1 118	102 722	251	28 988
April	1 548	145 836	1 383	131 317	341	37 053
May	1 600	144 412	1 404	127 793	374	39 180
June	1 513	143 384	1 334	128 410	344	36 265
July	1 562	145 078	1 348	125 285	346	36 312
August	1 551	164 275	1 347	149 874	382	49 194
September	1 447	147 353	1 306	134 038	364	38 026
October	1 335	118 924	1 205	107 330	341	33 926
November	1 332	131 627	1 192	120 760	324	36 563
December	1 384	145 648	1 238	130 583	351	39 081
2012						
January	1 434	129 920	1 298	119 102	341	33 597
February	1 293	119 463	1 153	108 577	282	27 388
March	1 273	121 310	1 125	109 421	261	26 348
April	1 388	135 600	1 222	120 213	287	33 243
May	1 380	130 191	1 222	117 654	264	29 675
June	1 317	131 406	1 171	118 451	267	29 093
July	1 340	137 420	1 208	127 092	364	44 920
August	1 267	127 454	1 148	117 952	314	38 667
September	1 316	122 462	1 198	113 824	366	39 748

Table 7-2. Mass Layoff Events and Initial Claimants for Unemployment Insurance, 1999–September 2012, Not Seasonally Adjusted

(Number.)

Year and month	Total		Private nonfarm		Manufacturing	
	Events	Initial claimants	Events	Initial claimants	Events	Initial claimants
1999						
January	2 421	226 995	2 142	206 615	861	94 887
February	1 067	89 800	810	73 846	289	28 322
March	880	91 890	737	80 063	302	31 317
April	1 270	136 885	1 100	123 987	450	56 668
May	1 032	102 738	895	93 006	303	32 958
June	1 140	130 951	925	109 848	268	32 610
July	1 741	221 334	1 496	201 412	808	137 688
August	698	75 691	638	70 285	246	26 606
September	717	75 288	592	64 942	212	28 968
October	1 098	118 938	814	97 984	373	55 222
November	1 336	139 508	977	110 200	347	45 431
December	1 509	162 381	1 353	150 171	446	60 349
2000						
January	1 934	223 322	1 807	212 805	741	100 397
February	1 045	103 898	780	81 103	268	30 358
March	986	106 748	827	92 565	329	38 434
April	924	101 359	838	93 631	323	34 061
May	984	92 193	841	81 125	262	25 838
June	1 597	192 025	1 269	160 685	404	60 258
July	1 333	164 978	1 159	152 243	664	100 874
August	751	97 215	679	90 877	256	35 687
September	936	106 842	767	93 327	319	46 865
October	874	103 755	684	84 922	321	48 877
November	1 697	216 514	1 397	190 626	617	93 966
December	2 677	326 743	2 477	311 623	1 074	166 928
2001						
January	1 522	200 343	1 405	188 504	632	107 028
February	1 501	172 908	1 285	156 183	576	79 784
March	1 527	171 466	1 371	158 108	659	86 874
April	1 450	176 265	1 353	166 167	608	78 845
May	1 434	159 365	1 331	151 186	528	64 887
June	2 107	253 826	1 784	226 022	737	116 005
July	2 117	273 807	1 952	259 128	1 144	168 877
August	1 490	166 148	1 386	158 307	603	79 515
September	1 327	160 402	1 214	151 161	485	58 544
October	1 831	215 483	1 676	202 053	742	107 030
November	2 721	295 956	2 373	270 268	1 122	151 969
December	2 440	268 893	2 319	259 497	1 103	136 820
2002						
January	2 146	263 777	2 028	252 245	892	128 825
February	1 382	138 808	1 253	129 849	481	58 784
March	1 460	161 316	1 335	151 305	500	59 613
April	1 506	165 814	1 378	153 216	461	50 897
May	1 723	179 799	1 571	166 801	488	52 720
June	1 584	162 189	1 266	136 424	336	42 130
July	2 042	245 294	1 819	226 892	907	135 271
August	1 248	128 103	1 151	119 874	427	48 668
September	1 062	124 522	957	114 736	352	43 755
October	1 497	171 100	1 270	149 327	493	64 655
November	2 153	240 171	1 860	216 237	719	92 712
December	2 474	264 158	2 324	252 807	984	126 826
2003						
January	2 315	225 430	2 130	210 918	822	90 244
February	1 363	124 965	1 222	116 264	435	48 161
March	1 207	113 026	1 099	104 468	390	41 063
April	1 581	161 412	1 470	152 937	499	62 349
May	1 703	174 204	1 538	160 729	499	61 278
June	1 691	157 552	1 336	127 743	389	40 845
July	2 087	226 435	1 815	206 901	946	136 410
August	1 258	133 839	1 163	124 131	405	52 620
September	868	82 647	756	73 914	271	31 428
October	1 523	158 240	1 265	137 706	438	53 741
November	1 438	138 543	1 234	123 524	408	48 419
December	1 929	192 633	1 793	182 750	648	77 915
2004						
January	2 428	239 454	2 226	220 687	848	89 551
February	941	84 201	832	76 577	240	23 043
March	920	92 554	847	87 782	258	34 686
April	1 458	157 314	1 316	142 657	343	36 172
May	988	87 501	878	78 786	219	22 141
June	1 379	134 588	1 077	110 804	222	27 307
July	2 094	253 929	1 860	234 877	885	145 895
August	809	69 033	745	63 876	194	17 698
September	708	68 972	637	63 102	189	25 808
October	1 242	127 918	1 101	117 375	372	48 265
November	1 399	130 423	1 201	115 549	412	44 243
December	1 614	161 271	1 487	152 092	436	50 726
2005						
January	2 564	263 952	2 421	253 409	823	108 985
February	810	74 644	722	68 372	230	24 931
March	806	88 937	733	83 793	246	33 030
April	1 373	158 582	1 263	148 133	395	59 129
May	986	101 358	891	93 332	249	30 424
June	1 157	120 463	941	103 307	216	32 783
July	1 981	244 216	1 745	222 377	856	136 210
August	645	67 582	598	63 484	188	22 531
September	1 662	213 281	1 505	179 042	318	47 497
October	905	91 941	757	80 694	249	37 276
November	1 254	116 127	1 079	102 182	363	41 442
December	2 323	254 258	2 168	242 753	706	96 382

Table 7-2. Mass Layoff Events and Initial Claimants for Unemployment Insurance, 1999–September 2012, Not Seasonally Adjusted—*Continued*

(Number.)

Year and month	Total		Private nonfarm		Manufacturing	
	Events	Initial claimants	Events	Initial claimants	Events	Initial claimants
2006						
January	1 245	117 946	1 123	108 701	331	35 097
February	719	66 555	658	62 208	210	24 892
March	921	111 838	856	106 177	285	44 688
April	1 140	121 589	1 038	112 964	296	39 538
May	872	84 809	794	78 663	192	23 570
June	1 489	164 761	1 224	140 687	319	41 095
July	1 511	166 857	1 335	154 342	648	96 152
August	708	72 844	656	69 054	203	28 494
September	865	87 699	785	81 274	296	39 076
October	964	98 804	820	88 133	311	46 737
November	1 315	136 186	1 172	125 009	455	58 473
December	2 249	254 503	2 126	244 783	735	105 462
2007						
January	1 407	134 984	1 263	124 475	456	53 615
February	935	86 696	861	82 097	273	36 170
March	1 082	123 974	1 015	118 431	367	49 886
April	1 219	127 444	1 115	118 040	309	35 229
May	923	85 816	856	81 153	224	26 527
June	1 599	172 810	1 318	148 669	313	36 571
July	1 599	175 419	1 450	164 939	684	101 390
August	963	93 458	908	88 345	220	23 361
September	717	67 385	667	64 026	246	29 381
October	1 083	108 455	929	97 716	338	50 918
November	1 799	198 220	1 593	181 184	514	75 413
December	2 167	224 214	2 071	216 898	699	91 754
2008						
January	1 647	154 503	1 520	144 191	488	54 418
February	1 269	119 508	1 178	113 587	361	42 527
March	1 089	114 541	1 039	110 147	333	43 740
April	1 272	130 810	1 172	121 625	394	48 188
May	1 552	159 471	1 438	150 462	388	51 698
June	1 622	166 742	1 315	140 916	309	42 097
July	1 891	200 382	1 687	186 018	760	108 733
August	1 427	139 999	1 343	133 146	414	51 912
September	1 292	129 586	1 202	122 505	361	46 391
October	2 125	221 784	1 917	205 553	689	100 457
November	2 574	241 589	2 389	226 657	997	107 620
December	3 377	351 305	3 232	340 220	1 378	172 529
2009						
January	3 806	388 813	3 633	375 293	1 461	172 757
February	2 262	218 438	2 173	210 755	945	103 588
March	2 191	228 387	2 107	221 397	940	114 747
April	2 547	256 930	2 385	243 321	887	100 872
May	2 738	289 628	2 572	274 047	1 005	123 683
June	2 519	256 357	2 051	216 063	674	85 726
July	3 054	336 654	2 659	296 589	1 133	154 208
August	1 428	125 024	1 334	117 193	436	41 151
September	1 371	123 177	1 258	115 141	448	51 126
October	1 934	193 904	1 678	172 883	566	69 655
November	1 870	164 496	1 679	150 751	517	55 053
December	2 310	214 648	2 166	203 655	615	64 540
2010						
January	2 860	278 679	2 682	265 074	962	104 846
February	1 183	102 818	1 091	96 022	282	30 728
March	1 197	111 727	1 111	105 514	273	29 745
April	1 840	199 690	1 697	184 654	424	55 178
May	1 354	123 333	1 170	109 203	216	19 334
June	1 861	171 190	1 355	125 872	212	21 083
July	2 124	206 254	1 732	172 248	532	64 200
August	976	92 435	897	83 021	230	23 088
September	920	77 654	806	67 987	187	19 403
October	1 642	148 638	1 373	127 865	351	40 861
November	1 676	158 048	1 477	142 591	389	41 383
December	1 931	184 130	1 763	172 881	465	52 816
2011						
January	2 558	246 463	2 372	229 765	693	75 006
February	1 024	85 585	919	78 718	222	18 471
March	908	85 095	844	80 014	191	20 869
April	1 750	189 919	1 625	176 478	397	47 104
May	1 367	119 911	1 221	108 531	270	25 199
June	1 661	159 930	1 238	122 821	226	22 986
July	2 176	216 774	1 759	174 078	602	71 814
August	961	99 213	875	93 159	228	26 916
September	1 189	117 232	1 095	107 300	296	32 058
October	1 101	96 914	950	83 748	265	28 447
November	1 393	127 750	1 245	117 474	349	37 799
December	2 433	263 665	2 258	247 916	658	75 033
2012						
January	1 705	141 703	1 587	132 754	415	38 021
February	895	73 974	820	69 076	196	16 555
March	1 125	117 817	1 040	110 954	242	24 241
April	1 421	146 358	1 293	132 697	256	32 518
May	1 201	109 259	1 081	100 434	186	18 800
June	1 890	198 537	1 485	158 334	255	28 570
July	1 515	157 753	1 321	144 340	559	74 963
August	1 063	104 045	992	97 694	251	31 193
September	811	70 570	749	66 214	221	22 748

Table 7-3. Industry Distribution: Mass Layoff Events and Initial Claimants for Unemployment Insurance, 2000–September 2012

(Number, not seasonally adjusted.)

Industry	2000	2001	2002	2003	2004	2005	2006	2007	2008	2009	2010	2011
	Mass layoff events											
ALL INDUSTRIES	15 738	21 467	20 277	18 963	15 980	16 466	13 998	15 493	21 137	28 030	19 564	18 521
Total, Private	15 028	20 763	19 376	17 846	15 018	15 534	13 238	14 714	20 130	26 437	17 887	17 046
Agriculture, forestry, fishing and hunting	1 503	1 314	1 164	1 025	811	711	651	668	698	742	733	645
Total, private nonfarm	13 525	19 449	18 212	16 821	14 207	14 823	12 587	14 046	19 432	25 695	17 154	16 401
Mining, quarrying, and oil and gas extraction	102	115	176	101	69	75	58	66	103	314	102	75
Utilities	37	33	44	40	25	25	20	20	28	39	30	30
Construction	1 638	1 688	1 939	2 013	1 821	1 975	1 546	1 952	2 393	2 833	2 262	1 994
Manufacturing	5 578	8 939	7 040	6 150	4 618	4 839	4 281	4 643	6 872	9 627	4 523	4 397
Food	826	879	826	850	797	751	648	595	678	771	745	810
Beverage and tobacco products	61	74	79	82	75	66	56	58	78	78	73	64
Textile mills	209	352	272	245	169	160	143	146	179	195	109	182
Textile product mills	83	91	113	111	93	86	66	63	69	76	59	61
Apparel	424	433	346	295	220	179	128	131	149	201	134	124
Leather and allied products	76	79	48	48	42	41	26	27	22	28	17	17
Wood products	381	359	383	350	226	273	341	418	557	553	309	279
Paper	148	212	167	156	82	98	86	78	146	241	93	95
Printing and related support activities	95	156	156	125	118	98	74	90	132	235	131	101
Petroleum and coal products	39	25	39	30	27	24	34	28	37	49	43	34
Chemicals	84	156	122	105	101	77	69	75	122	193	116	90
Plastics and rubber products	278	482	331	328	282	300	250	265	501	559	199	230
Nonmetallic mineral products	186	239	219	233	167	204	172	215	316	400	224	200
Primary metals	274	568	399	366	194	222	184	225	352	686	210	162
Fabricated metal products	327	675	482	397	322	311	288	293	574	949	292	246
Machinery	324	781	555	425	235	272	255	287	402	1 046	331	270
Computer and electronic products	231	1 050	817	481	230	217	173	190	285	626	198	184
Electrical equipment and appliance manufacturing	195	391	313	231	137	167	136	135	220	397	152	137
Transportation equipment	1 004	1 410	961	927	821	1 034	925	1 068	1 647	1 827	811	821
Furniture and related products	183	325	249	218	168	164	148	184	288	323	198	194
Miscellaneous manufacturing	150	202	163	147	112	95	79	72	118	194	79	96
Wholesale trade	236	334	336	318	222	251	184	220	363	653	328	262
Retail trade	906	1 249	1 351	1 327	1 165	1 196	991	1 048	1 457	1 965	1 574	1 448
Transportation and warehousing	717	908	947	965	853	1 011	934	982	1 267	1 491	1 160	1 180
Information	358	736	719	598	454	383	350	383	545	752	548	522
Finance and insurance	218	325	432	384	322	272	310	510	552	677	430	313
Real estate and rental and leasing	64	99	91	91	79	92	54	71	118	165	117	95
Professional and technical services	348	591	634	522	420	427	352	420	564	800	599	555
Management of companies and enterprises	40	47	40	35	38	27	28	42	61	104	60	49
Administrative and waste services	1 644	2 333	2 428	2 266	2 035	1 989	1 741	1 862	2 699	3 205	2 579	2 744
Educational services	34	51	69	82	60	70	63	67	100	149	161	167
Health care and social assistance	405	374	480	499	522	585	415	450	580	675	709	738
Arts, entertainment, and recreation	162	229	277	285	287	293	245	240	311	389	363	338
Accommodation and food services	729	1 032	916	886	980	1 083	844	905	1 238	1 606	1 386	1 294
Other services, except public administration	148	171	221	217	198	201	148	155	174	242	218	193
Unclassified	161	195	72	42	39	29	23	10	7	9	5	7
Government	710	704	901	1 117	962	932	760	779	1 007	1 593	1 677	1 475
Federal	172	143	125	134	142	154	119	134	118	166	204	149
State	152	165	171	205	177	196	130	136	184	305	292	331
Local	386	396	605	778	643	582	511	509	705	1 122	1 181	995

Table 7-3. Industry Distribution: Mass Layoff Events and Initial Claimants for Unemployment Insurance, 2000–September 2012—*Continued*

(Number, not seasonally adjusted.)

Industry	January 2012	February 2012	March 2012	April 2012	May 2012	June 2012	July 2012	August 2012	September 2012
	Mass layoff events								
ALL INDUSTRIES	1 705	895	1 125	1 421	1 201	1 890	1 515	1 063	811
Total, Private	1 634	865	1 083	1 378	1 099	1 539	1 385	1 016	768
Agriculture, forestry, fishing and hunting	47	45	43	85	18	54	64	24	19
Total, private nonfarm	1 587	820	1 040	1 293	1 081	1 485	1 321	992	749
Mining, quarrying, and oil and gas extraction	16	7	8	7	5	8	6	9	7
Utilities	4	...	(1)	(1)	(1)	(1)	3	(1)	(1)
Construction	194	81	121	138	129	91	86	96	65
Manufacturing	415	196	242	256	186	255	559	251	221
Food	56	45	69	86	48	63	77	47	41
Beverage and tobacco products	3	4	5	5	3	(1)	(1)	3	7
Textile mills	20	7	6	24	7	8	27	11	5
Textile product mills	5	4	4	3	4	10	9	(1)	4
Apparel	17	4	9	12	10	8	23	9	4
Leather and allied products	(1)	...	(1)	(1)	...	(1)	4	(1)	3
Wood products	35	13	14	10	4	5	24	15	8
Paper	8	6	8	3	6	5	10	4	(1)
Printing and related support activities	16	9	4	7	16	9	6	...	3
Petroleum and coal products	4	(1)	(1)	...	...	(1)	(1)	(1)	3
Chemicals	13	3	4	3	5	5	6	4	7
Plastics and rubber products	24	9	9	9	5	5	38	13	7
Nonmetallic mineral products	36	7	11	7	5	4	11	6	8
Primary metals	15	6	3	8	9	12	24	8	17
Fabricated metal products	23	10	18	7	6	12	33	13	12
Machinery	22	9	12	17	12	25	38	27	22
Computer and electronic products	15	15	14	14	12	17	16	20	12
Electrical equipment and appliance manufacturing	11	7	13	5	4	6	15	12	14
Transportation equipment	47	20	25	26	19	39	158	38	30
Furniture and related products	30	13	6	6	9	15	24	7	9
Miscellaneous manufacturing	13	4	5	(1)	(1)	(1)	13	7	3
Wholesale trade	29	17	20	29	16	20	20	21	20
Retail trade	181	135	100	105	117	132	92	115	86
Transportation and warehousing	137	32	72	171	38	191	65	94	29
Information	33	42	49	35	39	48	32	33	33
Finance and insurance	30	22	30	33	31	24	24	28	13
Real estate and rental and leasing	4	5	6	8	4	11	4	5	(1)
Professional and technical services	45	25	42	55	56	37	41	31	24
Management of companies and enterprises	6	5	5	6	4	5	(1)	8	6
Administrative and waste services	276	155	165	220	169	201	213	167	131
Educational services	17	6	9	18	11	41	25	15	5
Health care and social assistance	36	26	33	41	95	201	56	31	28
Arts, entertainment, and recreation	33	19	16	40	26	40	14	23	30
Accommodation and food services	114	37	112	110	120	131	66	52	43
Other services, except public administration	12	7	6	9	29	47	13	8	4
Unclassified	5	3	3	10	4	...	...	3	...
Government	71	30	42	43	102	351	130	47	43
Federal	13	5	4	5	7	6	8	6	1
State	25	10	17	13	24	36	25	8	11
Local	33	15	21	25	71	309	97	33	31

[1]Data do not meet BLS or state agency disclosure standards.
. . . = Not available.

Table 7-3. Industry Distribution: Mass Layoff Events and Initial Claimants for Unemployment Insurance, 2000–September 2012—Continued

(Number, not seasonally adjusted.)

Industry	2000	2001	2002	2003	2004	2005	2006	2007	2008	2009	2010	2011
	Initial claimants											
ALL INDUSTRIES	1 835 592	2 514 862	2 245 051	1 888 926	1 607 158	1 795 341	1 484 391	1 598 875	2 130 220	2 796 456	1 854 596	1 808 451
Total, Private	1 768 743	2 447 154	2 158 413	1 790 713	1 520 157	1 691 217	1 418 452	1 533 920	2 046 011	2 650 289	1 704 320	1 667 632
Agriculture, forestry, fishing and hunting	123 211	100 570	88 700	68 728	55 993	50 339	46 457	47 947	50 984	53 201	51 388	47 630
Total, private nonfarm	1 645 532	2 346 584	2 069 713	1 721 985	1 464 164	1 640 878	1 371 995	1 485 973	1 995 027	2 597 088	1 652 932	1 620 002
Mining, quarrying, and oil and gas extraction	9 271	14 887	16 672	9 852	5 985	6 483	5 582	5 327	9 273	27 872	8 192	6 056
Utilities	3 361	3 898	4 275	2 963	2 827	3 173	1 336	1 462	2 299	3 355	2 684	2 658
Construction	136 328	139 958	158 366	146 602	134 486	149 893	116 283	142 618	173 627	205 765	169 377	152 071
Manufacturing	782 543	1 236 178	904 856	744 473	565 535	670 620	583 274	610 215	870 310	1 137 106	502 665	481 702
Food	90 972	98 013	98 251	87 353	82 114	76 926	62 852	62 141	72 081	78 345	76 351	85 240
Beverage and tobacco products	5 955	6 242	6 564	6 775	6 594	4 714	4 404	4 679	6 466	7 205	5 952	5 806
Textile mills	33 064	57 009	43 511	37 734	19 669	22 213	19 070	19 527	21 620	23 439	13 872	22 948
Textile product mills	8 542	10 233	16 234	11 611	11 101	9 801	6 044	6 681	6 810	8 306	6 946	6 158
Apparel	40 474	50 423	41 320	29 887	24 729	21 889	14 170	11 508	13 970	18 545	11 663	12 940
Leather and allied products	8 204	7 867	3 903	5 170	4 733	4 960	2 757	3 077	2 862	2 280	2 187	2 037
Wood products	43 343	38 295	43 280	35 494	26 284	32 590	34 861	41 604	56 278	49 723	28 361	26 674
Paper	14 592	25 345	17 165	14 031	6 686	8 430	7 468	6 439	14 707	23 238	7 399	8 035
Printing and related support activities	9 030	13 799	15 019	9 976	10 534	8 005	6 131	7 414	12 000	22 793	11 396	8 859
Petroleum and coal products	3 609	2 518	3 611	2 292	2 343	2 262	2 874	2 333	3 114	3 689	3 405	2 801
Chemicals	8 960	15 659	11 161	10 811	8 707	7 713	6 164	6 665	10 227	15 692	9 880	7 230
Plastics and rubber products	35 828	59 024	38 596	35 054	28 409	30 714	26 098	24 611	49 196	58 926	17 354	20 740
Nonmetallic mineral products	19 272	25 246	21 712	22 031	15 389	18 956	15 980	19 204	27 834	32 179	18 013	17 202
Primary metals	38 835	81 601	48 671	40 641	23 193	27 469	21 866	27 016	37 765	76 288	20 467	16 238
Fabricated metal products	34 543	66 862	49 228	35 884	30 672	28 137	26 090	26 674	49 757	84 702	24 651	22 218
Machinery	57 793	121 724	87 710	60 370	28 407	33 713	40 069	45 831	53 673	164 176	44 916	38 655
Computer and electronic products	24 638	133 552	85 958	46 888	21 230	20 249	15 326	16 439	26 270	58 693	16 796	14 286
Electrical equipment and appliance manufacturing	39 205	60 387	48 413	36 496	24 443	30 804	24 503	23 274	37 732	48 250	20 199	21 154
Transportation equipment	228 380	303 139	176 505	178 282	163 026	253 681	221 257	228 213	323 622	304 693	133 554	114 874
Furniture and related products	23 252	39 362	33 640	24 551	16 315	18 168	17 366	19 510	33 617	39 554	22 467	19 271
Miscellaneous manufacturing	14 052	19 878	14 404	13 142	10 957	9 226	7 924	7 375	10 709	16 390	6 836	8 336
Wholesale trade	20 576	27 973	31 224	25 422	19 861	20 780	13 856	17 922	28 849	54 003	24 600	21 212
Retail trade	95 451	131 316	149 363	138 457	114 588	113 748	96 999	96 787	136 209	193 492	155 299	143 652
Transportation and warehousing	79 430	106 358	124 699	103 499	94 588	113 279	106 708	109 104	136 178	157 661	130 607	134 588
Information	80 618	103 122	100 982	80 715	72 820	72 100	64 365	64 404	70 066	96 127	75 518	88 998
Finance and insurance	17 532	27 881	36 099	27 870	24 954	20 884	22 213	40 917	42 152	55 876	33 122	23 889
Real estate and rental and leasing	4 564	7 611	7 324	6 412	6 329	7 615	4 082	5 139	8 754	11 567	7 861	7 279
Professional and technical services	57 135	77 862	82 223	52 700	49 547	49 719	40 739	49 223	57 144	72 962	56 713	56 890
Management of companies and enterprises	4 601	5 540	5 668	3 777	4 729	2 864	2 310	3 258	5 818	11 064	6 864	3 897
Administrative and waste services	191 073	258 542	257 530	206 765	184 369	187 156	153 655	168 460	246 670	294 709	221 024	242 692
Educational services	2 486	3 571	4 855	5 862	4 315	5 641	5 081	5 667	9 025	13 670	14 200	14 663
Health care and social assistance	36 759	32 255	40 364	38 108	40 118	51 371	33 972	38 848	44 139	52 058	55 205	58 964
Arts, entertainment, and recreation	14 399	20 542	23 517	21 387	21 191	27 564	16 531	16 874	21 550	29 853	28 366	28 501
Accommodation and food services	71 713	110 234	92 575	83 856	96 509	117 107	89 947	94 928	118 247	160 464	144 356	136 133
Other services, except public administration	13 287	15 742	20 049	18 617	18 226	18 753	13 478	13 936	14 310	18 889	15 849	15 659
Unclassified	24 405	23 114	9 072	4 648	3 187	2 128	1 584	884	407	595	430	498
Government	66 849	67 708	86 638	98 213	87 001	104 124	65 939	64 955	84 209	146 167	150 276	140 819
Federal	19 974	16 865	15 458	14 173	14 308	15 087	11 957	12 976	10 485	15 930	20 868	14 690
State	14 604	15 840	17 857	17 761	15 362	19 686	12 293	11 289	15 452	26 964	24 675	34 500
Local	32 271	35 003	53 323	66 279	57 331	69 351	41 689	40 690	58 272	103 273	104 733	91 629

Table 7-3. Industry Distribution: Mass Layoff Events and Initial Claimants for Unemployment Insurance, 2000–September 2012—*Continued*

(Number, not seasonally adjusted.)

Industry	January 2012	February 2012	March 2012	April 2012	May 2012	June 2012	July 2012	August 2012	September 2012
	Initial claimants								
ALL INDUSTRIES	141 703	73 974	117 817	146 358	109 259	198 537	157 753	104 045	70 570
Total, Private	135 663	71 884	113 790	140 376	101 354	162 321	148 561	99 596	67 323
Agriculture, forestry, fishing and hunting	2 909	2 808	2 836	7 679	920	3 987	4 221	1 902	1 109
Total, private nonfarm	132 754	69 076	110 954	132 697	100 434	158 334	144 340	97 694	66 214
Mining, quarrying, and oil and gas extraction	1 019	510	823	774	262	824	401	747	891
Utilities	350	. . .	(¹)	(¹)	(¹)	(¹)	7 490	(¹)	(¹)
Construction	13 743	5 395	9 148	9 720	9 617	7 909	6 583	6 554	4 765
Manufacturing	38 021	16 555	24 241	32 518	18 800	28 570	74 963	31 193	22 748
Food	4 964	4 208	7 701	8 735	4 487	6 158	8 647	4 958	3 143
Beverage and tobacco products	224	199	326	293	222	(¹)	(¹)	254	560
Textile mills	2 274	638	786	3 246	685	1 335	2 821	1 308	858
Textile product mills	444	512	335	260	266	1 028	813	(¹)	318
Apparel	1 899	379	651	(¹)	711	758	2 375	767	255
Leather and allied products	(¹)	. . .	(¹)	(¹)	. . .	(¹)	506	(¹)	183
Wood products	2 704	1 292	1 154	780	262	290	3 047	1 166	660
Paper	833	397	578	335	628	551	700	314	(¹)
Printing and related support activities	1 347	634	341	436	1 373	744	571	(¹)	203
Petroleum and coal products	273	(¹)	(¹)	. . .	. . .	(¹)	(¹)	(¹)	235
Chemicals	1 064	191	242	343	546	549	402	267	541
Plastics and rubber products	1 931	547	614	2 645	300	374	3 999	1 198	1 180
Nonmetallic mineral products	2 569	505	844	546	488	1 007	1 183	377	547
Primary metals	1 649	428	223	839	641	2 741	2 802	2 760	1 877
Fabricated metal products	1 643	699	1 084	788	384	1 139	2 991	1 087	1 007
Machinery	1 938	994	845	1 649	1 175	2 489	4 891	3 405	2 748
Computer and electronic products	876	1 008	1 432	1 366	913	1 240	1 210	1 432	711
Electrical equipment and appliance manufacturing	1 797	590	2 417	722	723	414	2 185	1 395	1 739
Transportation equipment	5 969	1 725	3 362	7 093	3 836	5 618	31 786	8 715	4 582
Furniture and related products	2 371	1 095	613	634	1 049	1 361	2 567	415	942
Miscellaneous manufacturing	1 113	467	396	(¹)	(¹)	(¹)	1 287	736	314
Wholesale trade	2 262	1 594	1 639	2 498	976	1 476	1 316	2 178	1 646
Retail trade	16 612	12 716	10 375	9 491	11 529	12 962	8 589	11 071	6 930
Transportation and warehousing	13 404	3 506	9 013	23 008	4 628	25 973	5 924	9 728	2 132
Information	2 925	4 456	9 195	4 024	5 349	8 612	4 303	4 653	4 673
Finance and insurance	2 076	1 891	2 168	2 095	2 478	2 099	1 656	2 359	1 085
Real estate and rental and leasing	207	305	359	601	428	821	255	657	(¹)
Professional and technical services	3 084	1 931	6 331	6 288	3 780	4 057	3 438	2 608	1 793
Management of companies and enterprises	432	344	517	485	516	731	(¹)	721	638
Administrative and waste services	21 596	11 920	16 911	17 166	12 483	18 652	17 369	14 043	10 087
Educational services	1 770	341	552	2 778	843	2 955	1 710	1 848	294
Health care and social assistance	2 053	1 686	2 752	3 133	9 725	17 167	4 113	2 010	1 962
Arts, entertainment, and recreation	3 107	1 442	1 110	3 344	1 920	2 812	774	1 884	2 173
Accommodation and food services	8 725	3 814	15 122	13 707	14 142	18 642	4 431	4 300	3 635
Other services, except public administration	1 019	526	405	521	2 595	3 718	850	874	451
Unclassified	349	144	228	452	222	. . .	. . .	145	. . .
Government	6 040	2 090	4 027	5 982	7 905	36 216	9 192	4 449	3 247
Federal	1 196	337	271	395	519	499	672	580	85
State	2 576	715	1 460	3 164	1 856	3 028	2 106	900	949
Local	2 268	1 038	2 296	2 423	5 530	32 689	6 414	2 969	2 213

¹Data do not meet BLS or state agency disclosure standards.
. . . = Not available.

Table 7-4. Mass Layoff Events and Initial Claimants for Unemployment Insurance, by Region and State, 2000–September 2012

(Number.)

Region and state	2000	2001	2002	2003	2004	2005	2006	2007	2008	2009	2010	2011
	Mass layoff events											
UNITED STATES[1]	15 738	21 467	20 277	18 963	15 980	16 466	13 998	15 493	21 137	28 030	19 564	18 521
Northeast	2 226	3 157	3 073	3 139	2 630	2 806	2 514	2 775	3 257	4 864	3 493	3 508
New England	427	691	615	493	359	426	352	358	427	745	504	495
Middle Atlantic	1 799	2 466	2 458	2 646	2 271	2 380	2 162	2 417	2 830	4 119	2 989	3 013
South	3 166	4 601	4 829	4 198	3 587	4 035	2 789	3 260	5 153	7 089	4 948	5 025
South Atlantic	1 538	2 249	2 275	2 068	1 802	1 585	1 475	1 727	2 561	3 782	2 753	2 813
East South Central	626	902	1 060	858	798	893	699	857	1 392	1 694	1 091	1 113
West South Central	1 002	1 450	1 494	1 272	987	1 557	615	676	1 200	1 613	1 104	1 099
Midwest	4 223	5 945	4 828	4 644	4 135	4 512	4 026	4 258	5 751	7 434	4 409	4 216
East North Central	3 309	4 682	3 679	3 622	3 292	3 585	3 183	3 381	4 551	5 734	3 286	3 129
West	6 123	7 764	7 547	6 982	5 628	5 113	4 669	5 200	6 976	8 643	6 714	5 772
Mountain	596	836	726	638	512	537	443	558	831	1 291	947	786
Pacific	5 527	6 928	6 821	6 344	5 116	4 576	4 226	4 642	6 145	7 352	5 767	4 986
Alabama	119	169	428	332	274	244	138	276	444	493	365	345
Alaska	30	31	36	36	35	24	30	19	27	72	70	54
Arizona	107	161	170	146	110	109	72	99	146	255	192	178
Arkansas	85	95	76	60	54	52	40	69	116	117	71	154
California	5 008	6 145	6 045	5 651	4 547	4 104	3 702	4 130	5 403	6 377	5 110	4 378
Colorado	62	143	126	104	74	72	65	80	93	188	153	114
Connecticut	45	73	73	80	49	55	60	51	65	125	101	88
Delaware	13	33	19	23	13	9	9	17	38	57	47	45
District of Columbia	14	24	14	14	8	7	5	6	11	17	16	22
Florida	525	870	936	866	876	700	593	795	1 333	1 748	1 231	1 091
Georgia	164	215	310	403	323	323	317	350	476	618	429	466
Hawaii	38	77	74	55	37	33	48	46	88	106	56	44
Idaho	117	144	126	122	90	82	65	92	145	137	113	110
Illinois	647	870	824	775	663	647	600	641	871	1 309	804	676
Indiana	333	497	460	506	434	443	403	375	680	730	353	327
Iowa	230	319	251	249	169	212	188	192	303	423	243	221
Kansas	92	110	129	119	102	103	88	92	136	211	119	112
Kentucky	261	409	363	277	289	328	330	346	540	719	373	390
Louisiana	185	225	241	204	206	956	134	107	311	282	240	214
Maine	48	50	45	44	48	43	33	40	33	68	46	63
Maryland	68	73	85	94	80	55	120	128	85	141	128	109
Massachusetts	188	356	325	262	152	178	123	128	162	275	170	170
Michigan	969	1 359	612	604	866	1 032	922	949	1 156	1 305	634	711
Minnesota	198	304	279	260	213	237	205	199	245	377	221	259
Mississippi	102	121	82	81	61	155	71	80	167	135	147	197
Missouri	352	432	374	292	256	276	289	329	433	551	420	375
Montana	25	35	32	46	36	48	40	49	54	93	76	63
Nebraska	24	50	80	65	71	72	48	32	47	66	83	87
Nevada	214	246	178	148	121	138	117	135	251	369	240	156
New Hampshire	37	79	61	31	29	40	29	31	42	90	66	47
New Jersey	405	427	509	481	449	485	452	503	518	690	569	585
New Mexico	31	37	40	44	42	44	49	55	73	123	84	83
New York	244	441	765	932	836	806	717	733	897	1 367	1 121	1 096
North Carolina	172	288	245	246	167	166	129	93	196	325	315	528
North Dakota	10	30	24	22	22	14	18	22	26	47	30	27
Ohio	653	963	901	913	699	761	608	716	1 027	1 205	712	668
Oklahoma	61	122	122	121	86	58	55	69	79	150	71	81
Oregon	277	410	368	342	282	202	246	258	367	472	301	281
Pennsylvania	1 150	1 598	1 184	1 233	986	1 089	993	1 181	1 415	2 062	1 299	1 332
Rhode Island	71	82	72	41	51	65	52	54	64	90	71	67
South Carolina	288	452	364	170	159	142	140	177	284	493	272	225
South Dakota	8	18	12	15	10	13	7	11	10	25	7	6
Tennessee	144	203	187	168	174	166	160	155	241	347	206	181
Texas	671	1 008	1 055	887	641	491	386	431	694	1 064	722	650
Utah	39	66	50	24	33	37	30	43	61	113	77	72
Vermont	38	51	39	35	30	45	55	54	61	97	50	60
Washington	174	265	298	260	215	213	200	189	260	325	230	229
West Virginia	23	19	39	23	20	13	19	19	22	53	25	24
Wisconsin	707	993	882	824	630	702	650	700	817	1 185	783	747
Wyoming	(²)	4	4	4	6	7	5	(²)	8	13	12	10

[1] Data for all states and the District of Columbia.
[2] Data do not meet BLS or state agency disclosure standards.

Table 7-4. Mass Layoff Events and Initial Claimants for Unemployment Insurance, by Region and State, 2000–September 2012—*Continued*

(Number.)

Region and state	January 2012	February 2012	March 2012	April 2012	May 2012	June 2012	July 2012	August 2012	September 2012
	Mass layoff events								
UNITED STATES[1]	1 705	895	1 125	1 421	1 201	1 890	1 515	1 063	811
Northeast	386	203	198	363	197	382	268	242	143
New England	49	25	31	55	31	63	46	28	10
Middle Atlantic	337	178	167	308	166	319	222	214	133
South	496	242	289	318	358	540	494	287	253
South Atlantic	287	145	149	186	189	325	286	152	140
East South Central	125	35	64	64	81	90	131	62	43
West South Central	84	62	76	68	88	125	77	73	70
Midwest	386	152	219	216	249	355	373	172	156
East North Central	293	119	164	156	181	269	294	134	116
West	437	298	419	524	397	613	380	362	259
Mountain	46	38	56	78	58	68	52	39	19
Pacific	391	260	363	446	339	545	328	323	240
Alabama	55	7	18	17	13	26	55	13	9
Alaska	8	(2)	3	9	7	(2)	(2)	8	(2)
Arizona	3	13	15	30	14	13	19	14	3
Arkansas	19	11	16	6	(2)	19	15	12	5
California	342	225	319	391	307	489	297	291	213
Colorado	5	6	9	12	10	12	10	3	4
Connecticut	8	5	(2)	6	11	15	15	7	3
Delaware	(2)	4	(2)	7	(2)	4	(2)	(2)	. . .
District of Columbia	4	(2)	. . .	. . .	3	3	(2)	(2)	. . .
Florida	87	65	55	70	75	127	78	60	57
Georgia	41	20	8	24	28	50	32	12	18
Hawaii	4	(2)	(2)	3	(2)	5	(2)	. . .	4
Idaho	6	6	7	7	3	5	3	9	(2)
Illinois	55	40	36	38	64	65	39	52	27
Indiana	40	4	18	17	23	32	23	13	15
Iowa	17	11	9	13	12	17	16	8	9
Kansas	8	4	11	9	11	14	14	3	6
Kentucky	33	18	26	25	20	26	51	28	19
Louisiana	8	13	7	13	21	26	16	5	27
Maine	8	3	5	7	3	6	10	3	. . .
Maryland	10	10	3	3	9	34	11	16	11
Massachusetts	18	5	11	17	9	19	13	10	4
Michigan	53	28	25	23	22	64	123	20	23
Minnesota	20	3	10	8	6	20	15	4	6
Mississippi	13	6	12	13	28	17	9	13	12
Missouri	42	7	20	27	28	26	27	18	13
Montana	5	. . .	(2)	6	3	7	. . .	(2)	(2)
Nebraska	4	8	4	3	9	5	6	3	4
Nevada	14	5	9	13	11	18	8	7	7
New Hampshire	7	3	3	6	(2)	6	(2)	5	. . .
New Jersey	51	26	21	65	22	90	35	25	26
New Mexico	5	5	8	4	11	8	7	(2)	(2)
New York	166	91	54	152	65	99	101	99	46
North Carolina	84	27	60	51	46	58	98	35	37
North Dakota	(2)	. . .	(2)	. . .	(2)	3	(2)	(2)	(2)
Ohio	67	25	48	34	37	50	65	21	30
Oklahoma	6	5	3	4	5	4	6	4	(2)
Oregon	19	19	20	17	15	30	21	13	9
Pennsylvania	120	61	92	91	79	130	86	90	61
Rhode Island	5	7	(2)	9	4	11	4	(2)	3
South Carolina	32	8	7	12	4	23	35	9	5
South Dakota	. . .	. . .	. . .	. . .	(2)	(2)	. . .	. . .	(2)
Tennessee	24	4	8	9	20	21	16	8	3
Texas	51	33	50	45	53	76	40	52	37
Utah	7	3	5	5	5	5	4	3	(2)
Vermont	3	(2)	8	10	3	6	(2)	(2)	. . .
Washington	18	13	19	26	8	20	8	11	13
West Virginia	3	. . .	(2)	5	(2)	. . .	. . .	4	. . .
Wisconsin	78	22	37	44	35	58	44	28	21
Wyoming	(2)	. . .	(2)	(2)	(2)	. . .	(2)	. . .	. . .

[1]Data for all states and the District of Columbia.
[2]Data do not meet BLS or state agency disclosure standards.
. . . = Not available.

Table 7-4. Mass Layoff Events and Initial Claimants for Unemployment Insurance, by Region and State, 2000–September 2012—Continued

(Number.)

Region and state	2000	2001	2002	2003	2004	2005	2006	2007	2008	2009	2010	2011
						Initial claimants						
UNITED STATES[1]	1 835 592	2 514 862	2 245 051	1 888 926	1 607 158	1 795 341	1 484 391	1 598 875	2 130 220	2 796 456	1 854 596	1 808 451
Northeast	235 083	340 246	338 965	306 462	270 788	280 628	254 684	273 079	316 191	465 208	350 507	367 033
New England	56 909	75 283	67 846	50 708	35 020	45 064	37 359	34 860	40 915	70 288	50 632	55 986
Middle Atlantic	178 174	264 963	271 119	255 754	235 768	235 564	217 325	238 219	275 276	394 920	299 875	311 047
South	360 330	546 222	545 907	435 387	355 561	485 505	312 892	356 812	533 687	691 460	469 957	487 823
South Atlantic	185 615	257 113	247 353	206 290	165 280	159 131	152 443	163 761	225 596	344 284	245 720	256 262
East South Central	69 619	107 661	127 477	98 450	91 565	131 138	95 861	115 114	180 702	183 287	113 934	119 348
West South Central	105 096	181 448	171 077	130 647	98 716	195 236	64 588	77 937	127 389	163 889	110 303	112 213
Midwest	583 290	841 597	614 121	552 140	485 255	571 950	508 798	509 431	676 591	892 202	466 753	444 743
East North Central	465 917	663 997	457 002	414 489	387 065	457 592	406 432	414 919	538 429	706 233	358 694	327 393
West North Central	117 373	177 600	157 119	137 651	98 190	114 358	102 366	94 512	138 162	185 969	108 059	117 350
West	656 889	786 797	746 058	594 937	495 554	457 258	408 017	459 553	603 751	747 586	567 379	508 852
Mountain	61 090	94 490	76 484	58 247	47 929	50 830	41 696	49 308	75 567	117 890	85 395	71 500
Pacific	595 799	692 307	669 574	536 690	447 625	406 428	366 321	410 245	528 184	629 696	481 984	437 352
Alabama	13 491	18 228	59 821	44 523	34 012	29 603	14 530	30 543	57 324	56 284	39 152	37 523
Alaska	2 706	2 814	2 846	2 973	2 930	2 326	2 770	1 798	2 888	7 056	6 796	5 631
Arizona	10 782	16 148	17 775	12 566	11 020	11 831	7 950	10 839	14 274	24 316	19 280	17 647
Arkansas	9 050	11 328	6 868	6 131	5 926	7 611	5 056	8 647	11 914	12 353	7 748	16 665
California	536 673	600 501	576 110	467 573	394 114	360 138	317 907	357 994	446 480	532 028	419 809	377 413
Colorado	5 967	14 127	12 601	9 422	6 856	6 759	5 905	6 567	8 200	16 424	13 915	11 036
Connecticut	4 393	6 122	7 360	7 054	4 203	4 972	6 595	4 975	5 505	10 559	8 835	7 679
Delaware	8 271	8 200	4 927	8 084	3 764	5 034	4 185	4 522	6 335	5 513	3 271	3 524
District of Columbia	1 572	2 301	1 688	1 160	807	565	346	418	1 195	1 504	1 352	2 022
Florida	39 407	70 889	71 635	61 863	63 087	51 535	42 593	55 696	94 656	131 190	88 776	79 766
Georgia	16 967	22 141	41 888	49 009	33 406	40 854	35 947	39 624	48 603	64 642	44 512	47 593
Hawaii	3 042	7 803	7 467	5 151	2 938	2 692	3 706	3 988	9 590	9 173	4 629	3 525
Idaho	13 121	17 144	15 579	13 690	8 148	7 233	5 665	8 245	13 591	12 405	9 267	9 158
Illinois	108 726	135 126	116 592	90 181	75 763	71 399	75 118	80 477	103 685	193 495	91 277	72 086
Indiana	50 892	71 521	67 134	70 393	58 853	62 574	56 395	47 923	80 027	84 555	42 895	39 956
Iowa	32 479	44 997	35 460	32 744	18 126	30 291	27 804	23 637	43 574	54 587	31 028	27 151
Kansas	13 145	21 657	18 186	16 102	10 782	9 740	9 785	10 654	17 243	27 741	13 212	16 111
Kentucky	33 975	60 327	42 094	34 709	37 809	55 078	61 246	59 399	89 953	87 321	46 854	47 950
Louisiana	14 799	28 373	22 113	17 329	16 519	120 600	12 915	13 042	31 664	26 098	20 739	18 042
Maine	7 407	4 713	4 377	3 828	4 293	3 445	2 622	3 035	2 536	5 922	4 058	5 383
Maryland	5 868	6 259	9 386	7 911	7 951	4 998	11 771	12 172	7 116	11 932	11 022	10 234
Massachusetts	27 907	36 693	33 705	25 352	13 960	18 114	11 188	10 785	14 911	25 608	15 749	21 084
Michigan	129 640	196 459	63 350	66 866	99 124	131 411	127 964	125 942	132 468	153 361	74 773	70 517
Minnesota	24 169	38 739	33 348	27 725	24 607	26 689	25 729	19 231	23 370	34 255	20 543	28 202
Mississippi	8 684	10 501	7 162	5 239	4 384	29 971	5 524	9 647	13 818	10 116	11 410	18 280
Missouri	43 765	60 026	57 373	50 379	35 034	37 005	29 324	33 557	43 451	54 046	32 586	32 823
Montana	3 489	4 048	3 570	4 379	3 600	4 567	3 726	3 873	4 731	8 260	6 094	5 407
Nebraska	2 102	6 363	8 371	6 761	6 764	8 332	5 907	3 440	5 204	7 371	7 061	9 381
Nevada	21 976	32 414	19 115	12 897	11 795	13 224	11 130	11 344	22 389	34 364	21 704	14 812
New Hampshire	4 615	10 903	8 080	3 030	2 726	4 666	2 996	3 053	3 873	8 548	7 214	5 488
New Jersey	45 173	52 530	63 369	49 815	51 252	48 732	51 128	52 738	51 623	68 149	61 398	66 811
New Mexico	2 243	3 045	2 894	3 129	3 071	3 469	4 226	4 619	6 253	9 680	6 509	6 063
New York	22 318	46 404	85 578	93 583	95 228	87 649	76 638	77 353	95 612	144 247	125 909	119 398
North Carolina	23 902	33 021	27 324	28 977	14 435	16 670	13 316	10 694	21 037	37 488	32 337	54 730
North Dakota	912	4 303	3 140	2 577	1 980	1 184	3 065	2 992	4 354	5 870	3 098	3 151
Ohio	94 419	139 218	103 577	102 864	86 850	113 165	80 291	83 429	131 813	147 712	71 382	71 334
Oklahoma	7 531	21 086	16 203	17 502	14 124	10 090	7 234	9 627	10 187	16 986	8 271	9 006
Oregon	32 159	55 449	44 944	35 508	28 401	22 231	24 386	29 391	42 780	52 900	31 404	29 795
Pennsylvania	110 683	166 029	122 172	112 356	89 288	99 183	89 559	108 128	128 041	182 524	112 568	124 838
Rhode Island	8 441	10 851	9 567	5 251	6 907	9 151	8 211	7 362	7 040	10 159	10 046	10 578
South Carolina	45 084	74 891	51 006	21 001	22 241	17 450	16 909	21 787	32 063	53 172	32 332	25 067
South Dakota	801	1 515	1 241	1 363	897	1 117	752	1 001	966	2 099	531	531
Tennessee	13 469	18 605	18 400	13 979	15 360	16 486	14 561	15 525	19 607	29 566	16 518	15 595
Texas	73 716	120 661	125 893	89 685	62 147	56 935	39 383	46 621	73 624	108 452	73 545	68 500
Utah	3 457	7 260	4 642	1 892	2 959	3 266	2 765	3 464	5 604	11 255	7 339	6 288
Vermont	4 146	6 001	4 757	6 193	2 931	4 716	5 747	5 650	7 050	9 492	4 730	5 774
Virginia	42 651	37 911	36 059	26 377	17 802	20 927	25 642	17 496	12 738	33 637	29 924	31 335
Washington	21 219	25 740	38 207	25 485	19 242	19 041	17 552	17 074	26 446	28 539	19 346	20 988
West Virginia	1 893	1 500	3 440	1 908	1 787	1 098	1 734	1 352	1 853	5 206	2 194	1 991
Wisconsin	82 240	121 673	106 349	84 185	66 475	79 043	66 664	77 148	90 436	127 110	78 367	73 500
Wyoming	. . .	304	308	272	480	481	329	. . .	525	1 186	1 287	1 089

[1]Data for all states and the District of Columbia.
. . . = Not available.

Table 7-4. Mass Layoff Events and Initial Claimants for Unemployment Insurance, by Region and State, 2000–September 2012—*Continued*

(Number.)

Region and state	January 2012	February 2012	March 2012	April 2012	May 2012	June 2012	July 2012	August 2012	September 2012
	Initial claimants								
UNITED STATES[1]	141 703	73 974	117 817	146 358	109 259	198 537	157 753	104 045	70 570
Northeast	34 860	18 074	18 520	48 882	18 817	46 039	30 266	25 277	12 110
New England	4 068	3 256	3 195	8 350	3 168	8 369	4 139	2 828	788
Middle Atlantic	30 792	14 818	15 325	40 532	15 649	37 670	26 127	22 449	11 322
South	43 925	19 704	31 925	30 733	33 270	53 862	52 296	30 553	23 427
South Atlantic	25 701	11 402	14 109	16 334	16 236	31 298	26 617	15 611	12 940
East South Central	11 893	2 816	6 899	7 239	8 628	8 221	19 210	5 496	4 135
West South Central	6 331	5 486	10 917	7 160	8 406	14 343	6 469	9 446	6 352
Midwest	31 060	13 591	24 470	26 205	26 349	37 944	46 431	18 179	14 914
East North Central	24 023	10 602	18 604	21 577	18 060	29 984	37 669	14 499	9 880
West North Central	7 037	2 989	5 866	4 628	8 289	7 960	8 762	3 680	5 034
West	31 858	22 605	42 902	40 538	30 823	60 692	28 760	30 036	20 119
Mountain	3 879	2 903	5 406	9 340	4 875	6 098	4 189	3 479	1 410
Pacific	27 979	19 702	37 496	31 198	25 948	54 594	24 571	26 557	18 709
Alabama	6 489	541	2 130	2 706	1 019	2 333	6 119	1 071	1 396
Alaska	731	(2)	178	1 008	619	(2)	(2)	792	(2)
Arizona	176	1 023	1 286	4 627	1 245	1 319	1 594	994	207
Arkansas	1 389	1 163	1 835	851	(2)	2 008	1 416	1 276	598
California	23 787	16 919	33 461	26 375	22 995	49 090	21 608	23 157	16 581
Colorado	556	478	1 165	1 401	902	1 138	765	224	307
Connecticut	547	505	(2)	530	864	2 233	1 137	540	200
Delaware	(2)	259	(2)	542	(2)	345	(2)	(2)	. . .
District of Columbia	263	(2)	. . .	. . .	187	335	(2)	(2)	. . .
Florida	6 044	3 742	4 836	4 913	4 621	11 476	5 203	4 677	3 549
Georgia	4 097	2 195	1 069	2 879	2 906	5 246	2 844	953	1 477
Hawaii	316	(2)	(2)	238	(2)	467	(2)	. . .	296
Idaho	445	399	694	771	201	315	181	1 129	. . .
Illinois	4 823	3 291	4 610	5 969	7 361	6 223	4 036	4 589	2 481
Indiana	3 594	314	1 830	4 867	2 078	2 965	2 307	3 425	1 317
Iowa	1 271	1 246	1 278	1 388	1 208	1 513	2 210	742	919
Kansas	815	447	1 588	726	1 092	1 607	1 596	216	798
Kentucky	2 847	1 338	2 601	2 946	1 886	2 452	10 614	2 933	1 556
Louisiana	518	1 294	423	1 067	1 884	2 192	1 189	318	2 039
Maine	658	163	415	696	295	399	1 263	353	. . .
Maryland	624	825	182	256	706	3 891	886	1 257	919
Massachusetts	1 821	358	1 073	3 291	1 142	1 850	1 026	896	418
Michigan	3 962	2 639	3 749	2 313	1 922	8 103	17 118	1 460	1 808
Minnesota	1 591	237	844	455	421	1 989	1 678	561	507
Mississippi	737	353	1 314	835	3 961	1 243	887	842	910
Missouri	2 860	449	1 614	1 770	4 491	1 927	2 433	1 625	1 908
Montana	503	. . .	(2)	526	223	514	. . .	(2)	(2)
Nebraska	324	610	378	289	924	360	629	377	352
Nevada	1 323	427	879	1 051	859	1 870	758	597	574
New Hampshire	504	209	339	928	(2)	1 154	(2)	578	. . .
New Jersey	4 273	2 246	2 065	10 222	1 967	15 028	2 667	1 960	2 156
New Mexico	299	348	765	327	999	520	492	(2)	(2)
New York	17 607	8 124	5 226	22 367	6 199	10 248	16 306	12 317	4 140
North Carolina	7 468	2 604	6 060	4 782	4 247	5 320	10 695	(2)	3 622
North Dakota	(2)	. . .	(2)	. . .	(2)	500	(2)	(2)	(2)
Ohio	5 630	2 381	4 638	3 651	3 401	5 491	9 720	2 576	(2)
Oklahoma	443	315	697	621	361	802	531	266	(2)
Oregon	1 699	1 497	2 153	1 276	1 416	2 865	2 118	1 347	632
Pennsylvania	8 912	4 448	8 034	7 943	7 483	12 394	7 154	8 172	5 026
Rhode Island	318	1 883	(2)	2 081	439	1 925	251	(2)	170
South Carolina	3 475	700	498	1 321	327	2 047	4 144	870	758
South Dakota	. . .	. . .	. . .	. . .	(2)	(2)	. . .	. . .	(2)
Tennessee	1 820	584	854	752	1 762	2 193	1 590	650	273
Texas	3 981	2 714	7 962	4 621	5 130	9 341	3 333	7 586	3 485
Utah	514	228	385	482	366	422	332	169	. . .
Vermont	220	(2)	1 123	824	334	808	(2)	(2)	. . .
Virginia	3 362	1 027	1 206	1 141	3 038	2 638	2 719	1 453	2 615
Washington	1 446	1 084	1 546	2 301	736	2 064	711	1 261	1 082
West Virginia	298	. . .	(2)	500	(2)	. . .	. . .	433	. . .
Wisconsin	6 014	1 977	3 777	4 777	3 298	7 202	4 488	2 449	1 742
Wyoming	(2)	. . .	(2)	(2)	(2)	. . .	(2)	. . .	. . .

[1]Data for all states and the District of Columbia.
[2]Data do not meet BLS or state agency disclosure standards.
. . . = Not available.

Table 7-5. Extended Mass Layoff Events by Reason for Layoff in Private Nonfarm Business, 2000–2012

(Number.)

Year and quarter	Business demand	Disaster/safety	Financial	Organizational	Production	Seasonal	Other miscellaneous
2000							
Quarter 1	315	45	104	147	21	325	97
Quarter 2	253	. . .	113	121	28	415	92
Quarter 3	292	. . .	89	118	26	174	91
Quarter 4	461	22	143	123	31	709	119
2001							
Quarter 1	635	19	212	230	44	232	138
Quarter 2	595	5	244	235	49	437	212
Quarter 3	717	10	242	238	32	191	153
Quarter 4	913	28	251	242	24	698	169
2002							
Quarter 1	687	14	177	310	25	240	109
Quarter 2	558	13	167	222	31	503	92
Quarter 3	483	3	164	214	26	167	85
Quarter 4	562	20	149	206	32	728	180
2003							
Quarter 1	564	15	148	218	31	283	196
Quarter 2	580	10	163	204	28	536	234
Quarter 3	460	3	96	175	25	182	207
Quarter 4	448	33	82	186	22	733	159
2004							
Quarter 1	416	17	116	206	20	359	205
Quarter 2	386	3	57	170	35	571	136
Quarter 3	322	15	63	160	21	191	114
Quarter 4	389	35	73	144	26	667	93
2005							
Quarter 1	378	31	64	175	22	373	99
Quarter 2	362	. . .	53	125	18	568	76
Quarter 3	315	346	48	133	31	183	80
Quarter 4	330	. . .	58	117	26	781	63
2006							
Quarter 1	361	38	60	147	22	248	87
Quarter 2	416	12	40	172	23	603	87
Quarter 3	446	4	57	135	21	177	89
Quarter 4	565	8	64	143	28	697	135
2007							
Quarter 1	437	20	99	127	24	261	142
Quarter 2	417	3	110	79	20	649	143
Quarter 3	421	3	122	99	15	218	140
Quarter 4	613	6	124	92	25	752	202
2008							
Quarter 1	600	8	122	114	29	246	221
Quarter 2	566	6	120	122	24	651	267
Quarter 3	642	32	192	122	30	216	347
Quarter 4	1 580	12	329	159	24	869	609
2009							
Quarter 1	2 160	6	428	201	17	340	827
Quarter 2	1 457	3	295	170	14	757	699
Quarter 3	941	4	172	113	15	286	503
Quarter 4	845	6	179	89	16	828	453
2010							
Quarter 1	738	7	165	117	15	418	410
Quarter 2	629	11	126	118	12	801	311
Quarter 3	487	. . .	110	83	17	372	300
Quarter 4	661	. . .	110	79	10	826	308
2011							
Quarter 1	564	7	120	94	24	391	290
Quarter 2	517	11	117	70	33	773	289
Quarter 3	629	9	102	76	17	303	257
Quarter 4	633	4	76	73	20	818	279
2012							
Quarter 1	519	4	115	75	16	325	240
Quarter 2[1]	637	. . .	103	94	18	825	280
Quarter 3[1]	393	3	63	62	18	179	167

[1]Preliminary.
. . . = Not available.

Table 7-6. Extended Mass Layoffs by Age and Sex in Private Nonfarm Business, 2000–2012

(Number.)

Year and quarter	Men	Women	Sex unknown	Total persons by age				
				Under 30 years	30–44 years	45–54 years	55 years and over	Age unknown
2000								
Quarter 1	57.7	42.0	0.3	21.4	41.7	23.2	12.9	0.8
Quarter 2	45.3	54.5	0.3	19.2	39.7	23.4	14.8	2.8
Quarter 3	57.3	42.2	0.5	18.7	39.8	25.3	13.9	2.2
Quarter 4	64.4	34.9	0.7	20.9	40.7	24.2	12.5	1.7
2001								
Quarter 1	58.5	40.6	1.0	22.2	40.1	23.6	11.9	2.2
Quarter 2	49.9	48.9	1.3	18.2	40.0	25.3	14.9	1.5
Quarter 3	54.0	45.1	0.9	19.8	40.9	24.2	12.9	2.2
Quarter 4	64.0	35.7	0.3	20.0	40.6	24.3	13.0	2.0
2002								
Quarter 1	56.4	43.1	0.5	19.4	39.8	24.7	14.5	1.6
Quarter 2	49.7	50.0	0.3	18.8	39.4	24.6	16.1	1.2
Quarter 3	56.9	42.8	0.2	17.8	38.9	25.8	15.2	2.2
Quarter 4	64.4	35.4	0.2	18.8	39.4	25.0	14.4	2.4
2003								
Quarter 1	58.8	40.9	0.3	20.0	39.1	25.1	14.5	1.3
Quarter 2	49.3	49.8	0.9	17.3	37.5	25.9	17.4	1.9
Quarter 3	56.1	43.7	0.2	19.1	38.7	25.8	15.1	1.4
Quarter 4	65.0	34.8	0.3	19.7	38.0	26.3	15.1	1.0
2004								
Quarter 1	58.9	40.7	0.4	21.8	36.6	25.0	15.2	1.4
Quarter 2	46.1	53.6	0.3	16.7	36.0	26.2	19.3	1.8
Quarter 3	51.0	48.6	0.4	18.9	36.4	25.9	16.7	2.0
Quarter 4	65.7	33.9	0.3	18.8	37.4	26.3	16.1	1.3
2005								
Quarter 1	60.6	38.9	0.5	19.1	37.2	26.1	16.1	1.5
Quarter 2	44.4	55.1	0.6	14.6	35.0	27.6	20.9	1.9
Quarter 3	52.4	47.4	0.3	19.7	35.1	25.8	16.6	2.8
Quarter 4	67.6	32.0	0.3	18.0	36.0	26.7	16.6	2.7
2006								
Quarter 1	60.4	39.3	0.3	17.1	34.6	28.2	18.2	2.0
Quarter 2	45.3	54.2	0.5	15.5	33.1	27.0	22.3	2.1
Quarter 3	58.9	40.4	0.7	19.0	34.6	26.6	17.5	2.3
Quarter 4	69.6	30.1	0.3	18.3	36.4	27.9	16.7	0.7
2007								
Quarter 1	63.5	36.2	0.3	20.2	35.7	27.1	16.6	0.3
Quarter 2	45.1	54.2	0.8	16.2	33.4	26.9	23.1	0.5
Quarter 3	57.0	42.5	0.5	19.9	35.9	25.6	18.2	0.5
Quarter 4	70.0	29.6	0.4	19.5	36.0	27.4	16.7	0.4
2008								
Quarter 1	63.2	36.3	0.5	20.2	34.5	26.8	18.1	0.4
Quarter 2	49.7	49.7	0.5	17.9	33.8	26.0	21.5	0.8
Quarter 3	59.5	39.9	0.6	20.9	34.5	25.8	17.8	1.0
Quarter 4	68.3	30.8	0.9	20.2	35.5	26.9	16.7	0.8
2009								
Quarter 1	65.3	33.4	1.2	19.8	34.5	26.8	18.2	0.8
Quarter 2	57.8	41.5	0.7	18.4	33.9	26.7	20.5	0.5
Quarter 3	63.3	36.1	0.6	21.1	34.0	26.0	18.4	0.5
Quarter 4	69.0	30.6	0.5	20.4	34.4	26.5	18.2	0.4
2010								
Quarter 1	61.2	38.2	0.6	23.9	32.8	24.2	18.5	0.6
Quarter 2	49.6	50.3	0.1	20.2	31.8	24.7	22.7	0.6
Quarter 3	57.7	42.2	0.2	22.4	32.6	24.4	20.3	0.3
Quarter 4	69.2	30.7	0.1	21.2	34.1	25.7	18.5	0.5
2011								
Quarter 1	62.1	37.8	0.2	22.3	33.2	24.6	19.6	0.2
Quarter 2	48.0	51.8	0.2	19.1	32.0	24.7	23.9	0.2
Quarter 3	60.1	39.8	0.2	22.2	34.4	24.5	18.7	0.2
Quarter 4	67.5	32.4	0.2	21.9	34.2	25.3	18.5	0.1
2012								
Quarter 1	61.4	38.5	0.1	23.3	33.8	23.8	18.9	0.1
Quarter 2[1]	49.4	50.5	0.1	20.0	32.6	24.3	23.0	0.1
Quarter 3[1]	58.2	41.6	0.1	21.9	33.2	24.5	20.2	0.1

[1]Preliminary.

NOTES AND DEFINITIONS

JOB OPENINGS AND LABOR TURNOVER SURVEY

Data from a sample of approximately 16,000 businesses for the Job Openings and Labor Turnover Survey (JOLTS) are collected and compiled monthly from a sample of business establishments by the Bureau of Labor Statistics (BLS). Each month, data are collected in a survey of business establishments for total employment, job openings, hires, quits, layoffs and discharges, and other separations. Data collection methods include computer-assisted telephone interviewing, touchtone data entry, fax, and mail.

Concepts and Definitions

The JOLTS program covers all private nonfarm establishments such as factories, offices, and stores, as well as federal, state, and local government entities in the 50 states and the District of Columbia.

Employment includes persons on the payroll who worked or received pay for the pay period that includes the 12th day of the reference month. Full-time, part-time, permanent, short-term, seasonal, salaried, and hourly employees are included, as are employees on paid vacations or other paid leave. Proprietors or partners of unincorporated businesses, unpaid family workers, or persons on leave without pay or on strike for the entire pay period, are not counted as employed. Employees of temporary help agencies, employee leasing companies, outside contractors, and consultants are counted by their employer of record, not by the establishment where they are working.

Job openings information is submitted by establishments for the last business day of the reference month. A job opening requires that: 1) a specific position exists and there is work available for that position, 2) work could start within 30 days regardless of whether a suitable candidate is found, and 3) the employer is actively recruiting from outside the establishment to fill the position. Included are full-time, part-time, permanent, short-term, and seasonal openings. Active recruiting means that the establishment is taking steps to fill a position by advertising in newspapers or on the Internet, posting help-wanted signs, accepting applications, or using other similar methods.

Jobs to be filled only by internal transfers, promotions, demotions, or recall from layoffs are excluded. Also excluded are jobs with start dates more than 30 days in the future, jobs for which employees have been hired but have not yet reported for work, and jobs to be filled by employees of temporary help agencies, employee leasing companies, outside contractors, or consultants. The job openings rate is computed by dividing the number of job openings by the sum of employment and job openings and multiplying that quotient by 100.

Hires are the total number of additions to the payroll occurring at any time during the reference month, including both new and rehired employees, full-time and part-time, permanent, short-term and seasonal employees, employees recalled to the location after a layoff lasting more than 7 days, on-call or intermittent employees who returned to work after having been formally separated, and transfers from other locations. The hires count does not include transfers or promotions within the reporting site, employees returning from strike, employees of temporary help agencies or employee leasing companies, outside contractors, or consultants. The hires rate is computed by dividing the number of hires by employment and multiplying that quotient by 100.

Separations are the total number of terminations of employment occurring at any time during the reference month, and are reported by type of separation—quits, layoffs and discharges, and other separations. Quits are voluntary separations by employees (except for retirements, which are reported as other separations). Layoffs and discharges are involuntary separations initiated by the employer and include layoffs with no intent to rehire, formal layoffs lasting or expected to last more than 7 days, discharges resulting from mergers, downsizing, or closings, firings or other discharges for cause, terminations of permanent or short-term employees, and terminations of seasonal employees. Other separations include retirements, transfers to other locations, deaths, and separations due to disability. Separations do not include transfers within the same location or employees on strike.

The separations rate is computed by dividing the number of separations by employment and multiplying that quotient by 100. The quits, layoffs and discharges, and other separations rates are computed similarly, dividing the number by employment and multiplying by 100.

The JOLTS annual level estimates for hires, quits, layoffs and discharges, other separations, and total separations are the sum of the 12 published monthly levels. The annual rate estimates are computed by dividing the annual level by the Current Employment Statistics (CES) annual average employment level, and multiplying that quotient by 100. This figure will be approximately equal to the sum of the 12 monthly rates.

Annual estimates are not calculated for job openings because job openings are a stock, or point-in-time, measurement for the last business day of each month. Only jobs still open on the last day of the month are counted. For the same reason job openings cannot be cumulated throughout each month, annual figures for job openings cannot be created by summing the monthly estimates. Hires and separations are flow measures and are cumulated over the month with a total reported for the month. Therefore, the annual figures can be created by summing the monthly estimates.

Sources of Additional Information

For more extensive information see the Job Openings and Labor Turnover Survey (JOLTS) page on the BLS Web site at <http://www.bls.gov/jlt/>.

Table 7-7. Job Openings Levels and Rates, by Industry, December 2000–September 2012

(Seasonally adjusted, levels in thousands, rates per 100.)

Year and month	Level											
	Total nonfarm[1]	Total private[1]	Construc-tion	Manufac-turing	Trade, transpor-tation, and utilities[2]	Retail trade	Profes-sional and business services	Education and health services	Leisure and hospitality[3]	Accommo-dation and food services	Govern-ment[4]	State and local govern-ment
2000												
December	5 191	4 695	231	450	798	489	841	879	595	560	497	434
2001												
January	5 186	4 714	184	421	893	494	760	813	694	626	472	410
February	4 702	4 277	242	397	864	514	714	797	644	592	426	369
March	4 774	4 336	211	394	691	447	893	759	697	570	438	385
April	4 653	4 192	230	310	817	493	842	723	598	548	460	403
May	4 452	3 993	216	298	703	459	825	744	559	492	459	399
June	4 337	3 832	189	312	689	440	739	757	462	403	505	451
July	4 231	3 771	160	294	663	397	633	786	582	502	461	419
August	4 139	3 671	131	268	597	373	602	860	575	507	468	425
September	4 006	3 604	142	303	586	365	635	729	600	532	402	358
October	3 583	3 151	112	260	549	339	539	736	460	405	432	384
November	3 538	3 117	135	230	548	343	562	680	470	405	422	376
December	3 559	3 140	127	214	572	378	502	727	469	403	419	374
2002												
January	3 572	3 204	103	248	571	382	586	751	385	334	369	330
February	3 370	2 935	111	248	490	312	494	749	397	355	434	392
March	3 560	3 137	130	225	596	358	545	728	450	345	422	374
April	3 373	2 986	91	238	545	325	530	698	409	352	387	345
May	3 482	3 067	108	245	551	327	629	641	426	362	415	369
June	3 251	2 880	127	240	525	333	531	708	320	275	371	345
July	3 403	2 987	95	249	522	352	591	668	410	371	416	373
August	3 415	2 998	117	240	513	317	600	688	415	361	417	373
September	3 290	2 891	127	229	511	328	564	703	380	343	399	353
October	3 560	3 165	126	228	589	397	692	652	401	356	395	351
November	3 513	3 091	112	226	499	303	667	705	415	367	422	370
December	3 056	2 696	96	215	430	235	566	629	370	336	360	320
2003												
January	3 618	3 211	115	212	516	315	894	608	407	373	408	356
February	3 378	3 003	94	196	526	332	787	585	357	304	375	328
March	3 056	2 710	89	189	489	311	634	570	354	322	346	304
April	3 107	2 762	143	192	440	307	496	615	424	335	345	317
May	3 108	2 799	97	195	498	322	605	623	392	355	309	269
June	3 196	2 810	107	194	504	324	601	591	421	356	385	321
July	3 106	2 783	127	184	506	300	676	520	365	315	323	263
August	3 182	2 881	105	209	542	339	765	543	345	303	301	251
September	3 051	2 756	54	200	536	350	657	539	373	330	295	252
October	3 140	2 814	79	202	575	377	573	579	407	359	327	285
November	3 286	2 992	104	251	581	376	648	577	391	353	294	254
December	3 255	2 949	108	220	567	319	622	533	504	447	306	260
2004												
January	3 322	3 003	126	231	521	321	586	620	429	363	319	269
February	3 415	3 085	118	215	547	382	679	586	437	377	331	284
March	3 394	3 046	124	252	612	381	547	592	430	384	348	299
April	3 524	3 170	131	268	607	388	691	596	412	371	354	291
May	3 620	3 271	135	299	627	409	666	603	425	360	349	318
June	3 423	3 089	114	268	633	396	710	514	445	399	334	282
July	3 807	3 463	113	272	687	429	754	589	450	406	344	303
August	3 623	3 299	131	277	643	434	685	594	460	417	324	284
September	3 754	3 403	113	263	695	471	706	601	468	408	352	301
October	3 836	3 445	144	284	623	415	732	645	469	410	391	343
November	3 383	3 013	149	246	547	314	607	602	393	341	370	323
December	3 808	3 415	148	271	633	389	705	637	463	390	393	331
2005												
January	3 638	3 313	140	284	602	406	646	587	540	480	325	285
February	3 757	3 401	154	276	679	421	686	607	502	435	356	316
March	3 916	3 572	148	273	706	472	739	683	516	450	344	299
April	4 057	3 695	143	278	710	480	796	642	551	481	362	324
May	3 877	3 519	142	271	706	428	790	661	477	419	358	307
June	4 064	3 698	142	278	691	424	883	640	497	417	366	323
July	4 155	3 760	147	313	682	426	851	692	506	418	395	350
August	4 102	3 733	149	299	685	431	871	649	505	438	369	324
September	4 275	3 860	161	340	707	418	831	668	493	452	415	364
October	4 221	3 854	171	270	753	448	842	657	500	439	367	321
November	4 437	4 067	232	387	817	535	849	650	545	477	371	323
December	4 278	3 854	161	346	711	465	831	651	566	498	424	367
2006												
January	4 296	3 916	140	317	696	455	875	698	554	490	380	331
February	4 282	3 887	141	360	685	407	847	729	586	538	395	340
March	4 472	4 037	183	380	725	415	746	723	554	495	434	389
April	4 438	4 014	186	363	739	426	713	722	553	484	424	373
May	4 487	4 066	182	317	791	450	868	683	562	502	421	376
June	4 333	3 903	187	345	701	417	754	703	492	437	430	381
July	4 076	3 585	208	313	679	362	618	630	566	502	491	432
August	4 498	4 049	202	337	750	435	749	773	547	488	449	397
September	4 563	4 075	185	342	866	464	692	778	546	449	489	446
October	4 434	4 023	164	349	791	427	714	777	585	497	411	366
November	4 705	4 273	160	352	791	449	803	781	708	623	432	394
December	4 583	4 167	128	363	872	519	701	773	633	566	416	382

[1]Includes natural resources and mining, information, financial activities, and other services, not shown separately.
[2]Includes wholesale trade and transportation, warehousing, and utilities, not shown separately.
[3]Includes arts, entertainment, and recreation, not shown separately.
[4]Includes federal government, not shown separately.

Table 7-7. Job Openings Levels and Rates, by Industry, December 2000–September 2012—*Continued*

(Seasonally adjusted, levels in thousands, rates per 100.)

Year and month	Rate											
	Total[1]	Total private[1]	Construc-tion	Manufac-turing	Trade, transpor-tation, and utilities[2]	Retail trade	Profes-sional and business services	Education and health services	Leisure and hospitality[3]	Accommo-dation and food services	Govern-ment[4]	State and local govern-ment
2000												
December	3.8	4.0	3.3	2.6	2.9	3.1	4.8	5.4	4.7	5.2	2.3	2.3
2001												
January	3.8	4.1	2.6	2.4	3.3	3.1	4.3	5.0	5.5	5.8	2.2	2.2
February	3.4	3.7	3.4	2.3	3.2	3.2	4.1	4.9	5.1	5.5	2.0	2.0
March	3.5	3.7	3.0	2.3	2.6	2.8	5.1	4.7	5.5	5.3	2.0	2.1
April	3.4	3.6	3.2	1.8	3.0	3.1	4.8	4.5	4.7	5.1	2.1	2.2
May	3.3	3.5	3.1	1.8	2.6	2.9	4.7	4.6	4.4	4.6	2.1	2.1
June	3.2	3.3	2.7	1.9	2.6	2.8	4.3	4.6	3.7	3.8	2.3	2.4
July	3.1	3.3	2.3	1.8	2.5	2.5	3.7	4.8	4.6	4.7	2.1	2.2
August	3.0	3.2	1.9	1.6	2.2	2.4	3.5	5.2	4.5	4.7	2.2	2.3
September	3.0	3.2	2.0	1.8	2.2	2.3	3.7	4.4	4.7	4.9	1.9	1.9
October	2.7	2.8	1.6	1.6	2.1	2.2	3.2	4.4	3.7	3.8	2.0	2.0
November	2.6	2.8	1.9	1.4	2.1	2.2	3.4	4.1	3.8	3.8	1.9	2.0
December	2.7	2.8	1.8	1.3	2.2	2.4	3.0	4.4	3.8	3.8	1.9	2.0
2002												
January	2.7	2.8	1.5	1.6	2.2	2.5	3.5	4.5	3.1	3.2	1.7	1.7
February	2.5	2.6	1.6	1.6	1.9	2.0	3.0	4.5	3.2	3.4	2.0	2.1
March	2.7	2.8	1.9	1.4	2.3	2.3	3.3	4.3	3.6	3.3	1.9	2.0
April	2.5	2.7	1.3	1.5	2.1	2.1	3.2	4.2	3.3	3.3	1.8	1.8
May	2.6	2.7	1.6	1.6	2.1	2.1	3.8	3.8	3.4	3.4	1.9	1.9
June	2.4	2.6	1.9	1.5	2.0	2.2	3.2	4.2	2.6	2.6	1.7	1.8
July	2.5	2.7	1.4	1.6	2.0	2.3	3.6	3.9	3.3	3.5	1.9	1.9
August	2.6	2.7	1.7	1.6	2.0	2.1	3.6	4.1	3.4	3.4	1.9	1.9
September	2.5	2.6	1.9	1.5	2.0	2.1	3.4	4.1	3.1	3.2	1.8	1.8
October	2.7	2.8	1.9	1.5	2.3	2.6	4.2	3.8	3.2	3.3	1.8	1.8
November	2.6	2.8	1.6	1.5	1.9	2.0	4.0	4.1	3.3	3.4	1.9	1.9
December	2.3	2.4	1.4	1.4	1.7	1.5	3.4	3.7	3.0	3.2	1.6	1.7
2003												
January	2.7	2.9	1.7	1.4	2.0	2.1	5.3	3.6	3.2	3.5	1.9	1.9
February	2.5	2.7	1.4	1.3	2.0	2.2	4.7	3.4	2.9	2.9	1.7	1.7
March	2.3	2.4	1.3	1.3	1.9	2.0	3.8	3.3	2.8	3.0	1.6	1.6
April	2.3	2.5	2.1	1.3	1.7	2.0	3.0	3.6	3.4	3.2	1.6	1.7
May	2.3	2.5	1.4	1.3	1.9	2.1	3.7	3.6	3.1	3.3	1.4	1.4
June	2.4	2.5	1.6	1.3	2.0	2.1	3.6	3.4	3.4	3.3	1.8	1.7
July	2.3	2.5	1.9	1.3	2.0	2.0	4.1	3.0	2.9	3.0	1.5	1.4
August	2.4	2.6	1.5	1.4	2.1	2.2	4.6	3.2	2.8	2.8	1.4	1.3
September	2.3	2.5	0.8	1.4	2.1	2.3	3.9	3.1	3.0	3.1	1.4	1.3
October	2.4	2.5	1.1	1.4	2.2	2.5	3.4	3.4	3.2	3.3	1.5	1.5
November	2.5	2.7	1.5	1.7	2.2	2.5	3.9	3.3	3.1	3.3	1.3	1.3
December	2.4	2.6	1.6	1.5	2.2	2.1	3.7	3.1	3.9	4.1	1.4	1.4
2004												
January	2.5	2.7	1.8	1.6	2.0	2.1	3.5	3.6	3.4	3.3	1.5	1.4
February	2.6	2.8	1.7	1.5	2.1	2.5	4.0	3.4	3.4	3.5	1.5	1.5
March	2.5	2.7	1.8	1.7	2.4	2.5	3.3	3.4	3.3	3.5	1.6	1.6
April	2.6	2.8	1.9	1.8	2.3	2.5	4.1	3.4	3.2	3.4	1.6	1.5
May	2.7	2.9	1.9	2.0	2.4	2.6	3.9	3.4	3.3	3.3	1.6	1.7
June	2.5	2.7	1.6	1.8	2.4	2.6	4.2	2.9	3.4	3.6	1.5	1.5
July	2.8	3.1	1.6	1.9	2.6	2.8	4.4	3.4	3.5	3.7	1.6	1.6
August	2.7	2.9	1.8	1.9	2.5	2.8	4.0	3.4	3.6	3.8	1.5	1.5
September	2.8	3.0	1.6	1.8	2.6	3.0	4.1	3.4	3.6	3.7	1.6	1.6
October	2.8	3.0	2.0	1.9	2.4	2.7	4.2	3.6	3.6	3.7	1.8	1.8
November	2.5	2.7	2.1	1.7	2.1	2.0	3.5	3.4	3.0	3.1	1.7	1.7
December	2.8	3.0	2.0	1.9	2.4	2.5	4.1	3.6	3.5	3.5	1.8	1.7
2005												
January	2.7	2.9	1.9	2.0	2.3	2.6	3.7	3.3	4.1	4.2	1.5	1.5
February	2.8	3.0	2.1	1.9	2.6	2.7	3.9	3.4	3.8	3.9	1.6	1.6
March	2.9	3.1	2.0	1.9	2.7	3.0	4.2	3.8	3.9	4.0	1.6	1.5
April	3.0	3.2	1.9	1.9	2.7	3.1	4.5	3.6	4.1	4.2	1.6	1.7
May	2.8	3.1	1.9	1.9	2.7	2.7	4.5	3.7	3.6	3.7	1.6	1.6
June	3.0	3.2	1.9	1.9	2.6	2.7	5.0	3.6	3.7	3.7	1.7	1.7
July	3.0	3.2	2.0	2.2	2.6	2.7	4.8	3.8	3.8	3.7	1.8	1.8
August	3.0	3.2	2.0	2.1	2.6	2.7	4.9	3.6	3.8	3.8	1.7	1.7
September	3.1	3.3	2.1	2.3	2.6	2.7	4.6	3.7	3.7	4.0	1.9	1.9
October	3.0	3.3	2.2	1.9	2.8	2.8	4.7	3.6	3.7	3.9	1.7	1.7
November	3.2	3.5	3.0	2.7	3.0	3.4	4.7	3.6	4.1	4.2	1.7	1.7
December	3.1	3.3	2.1	2.4	2.6	2.9	4.6	3.6	4.2	4.3	1.9	1.9
2006												
January	3.1	3.3	1.8	2.2	2.6	2.9	4.8	3.8	4.1	4.2	1.7	1.7
February	3.1	3.3	1.8	2.5	2.5	2.6	4.6	4.0	4.3	4.6	1.8	1.7
March	3.2	3.4	2.3	2.6	2.7	2.7	4.1	3.9	4.1	4.3	1.9	2.0
April	3.2	3.4	2.3	2.5	2.7	2.7	3.9	3.9	4.1	4.2	1.9	1.9
May	3.2	3.4	2.3	2.2	2.9	2.9	4.7	3.7	4.1	4.3	1.9	1.9
June	3.1	3.3	2.4	2.4	2.6	2.6	4.1	3.8	3.6	3.8	1.9	1.9
July	2.9	3.0	2.6	2.2	2.5	2.3	3.4	3.4	4.1	4.3	2.2	2.2
August	3.2	3.4	2.6	2.3	2.8	2.8	4.1	4.2	4.0	4.2	2.0	2.0
September	3.2	3.4	2.3	2.4	3.2	2.9	3.8	4.2	4.0	3.9	2.2	2.3
October	3.1	3.4	2.1	2.4	2.9	2.7	3.9	4.1	4.2	4.2	1.8	1.9
November	3.3	3.6	2.0	2.4	2.9	2.8	4.3	4.2	5.1	5.2	1.9	2.0
December	3.2	3.5	1.6	2.5	3.2	3.3	3.8	4.1	4.5	4.8	1.8	1.9

[1]Includes natural resources and mining, information, financial activities, and other services, not shown separately.
[2]Includes wholesale trade and transportation, warehousing, and utilities, not shown separately.
[3]Includes arts, entertainment, and recreation, not shown separately.
[4]Includes federal government, not shown separately.

Table 7-7. Job Openings Levels and Rates, by Industry, December 2000–September 2012—*Continued*

(Seasonally adjusted, levels in thousands, rates per 100.)

Year and month	Level											
	Total nonfarm[1]	Total private[1]	Construc-tion	Manufac-turing	Trade, transpor-tation, and utilities[2]	Retail trade	Profes-sional and business services	Education and health services	Leisure and hospitality[3]	Accommo-dation and food services	Govern-ment[4]	State and local govern-ment
2007												
January	4 602	4 148	251	357	845	463	782	720	581	483	454	408
February	4 483	4 045	267	356	759	467	710	660	578	504	438	388
March	4 707	4 267	211	384	859	437	811	719	580	502	440	390
April	4 498	4 046	178	351	825	402	790	758	541	457	452	394
May	4 479	4 037	166	357	704	373	795	773	591	528	442	390
June	4 690	4 257	157	354	798	458	805	801	596	530	433	392
July	4 404	3 946	158	359	786	416	699	718	606	547	459	416
August	4 491	4 041	159	323	807	404	766	765	611	543	450	403
September	4 536	4 088	124	313	769	388	776	840	642	575	448	401
October	4 275	3 851	143	294	707	360	749	738	611	542	424	378
November	4 396	3 945	132	338	753	387	750	731	683	583	452	399
December	4 256	3 827	127	303	730	386	783	738	585	539	430	373
2008												
January	4 229	3 819	127	287	669	346	767	716	601	541	410	372
February	4 035	3 612	124	271	645	342	778	749	558	489	423	379
March	4 016	3 601	100	255	602	378	788	780	565	501	415	368
April	3 942	3 549	89	281	602	364	777	728	526	464	393	364
May	3 931	3 506	155	284	626	383	654	730	542	476	425	371
June	3 773	3 339	107	252	541	309	737	732	478	433	433	377
July	3 786	3 354	108	250	622	370	661	748	432	377	433	369
August	3 647	3 232	86	253	555	347	690	697	412	349	416	342
September	3 209	2 803	128	215	523	320	605	580	369	331	406	349
October	3 383	2 995	71	233	623	440	610	628	405	347	388	326
November	3 149	2 791	71	163	557	379	590	618	300	266	358	327
December	2 988	2 697	87	157	495	339	548	608	320	283	291	262
2009												
January	2 842	2 410	32	115	530	417	505	615	237	209	432	315
February	2 794	2 425	67	136	414	306	532	567	289	261	369	305
March	2 590	2 224	52	117	390	255	458	525	282	256	365	255
April	2 315	1 960	21	99	331	204	417	495	308	283	355	281
May	2 409	2 129	35	93	464	325	388	529	261	237	280	237
June	2 391	2 077	57	100	420	272	367	519	260	244	314	256
July	2 186	1 899	41	94	304	190	426	524	239	225	287	230
August	2 268	1 988	61	125	430	254	363	527	202	181	280	253
September	2 487	2 177	67	124	378	263	436	535	295	269	311	238
October	2 400	2 013	64	127	334	218	425	507	230	214	387	263
November	2 392	2 061	72	143	323	210	427	523	242	217	331	239
December	2 432	2 113	68	171	339	211	428	539	215	197	319	253
2010												
January	2 728	2 297	58	137	368	243	434	573	250	232	432	238
February	2 571	2 216	68	163	395	279	401	523	238	216	355	233
March	2 669	2 254	82	162	481	345	398	522	237	210	415	253
April	3 167	2 543	78	178	436	281	505	519	280	253	625	248
May	2 843	2 472	72	186	419	263	562	507	298	254	371	241
June	2 666	2 353	72	202	416	252	483	478	298	250	313	218
July	2 919	2 594	88	227	427	268	528	512	321	280	325	246
August	2 924	2 630	57	181	427	251	629	465	345	308	294	223
September	2 772	2 456	75	180	408	230	551	513	307	273	315	230
October	3 030	2 690	78	203	446	256	596	585	309	275	339	276
November	3 057	2 758	93	219	440	262	709	534	270	243	299	219
December	2 902	2 529	48	197	459	283	573	531	292	248	374	289
2011												
January	2 860	2 536	67	212	502	282	478	506	294	257	325	258
February	3 012	2 697	48	214	479	253	601	542	376	328	315	259
March	3 189	2 865	70	239	515	281	609	590	367	325	323	269
April	3 014	2 688	119	223	500	296	557	536	305	268	326	279
May	3 077	2 774	100	227	513	303	626	575	301	268	303	257
June	3 241	2 911	58	212	540	355	672	596	352	302	330	280
July	3 366	3 044	77	246	589	337	667	606	362	291	322	268
August	3 152	2 818	103	238	491	321	622	606	362	321	334	287
September	3 501	3 100	78	249	599	359	692	600	392	336	400	345
October	3 408	3 062	80	240	594	334	644	622	404	342	345	279
November	3 274	2 925	83	240	581	316	561	616	434	376	349	299
December	3 540	3 188	78	252	574	323	785	605	441	397	352	301
2012												
January	3 477	3 119	86	261	584	315	695	630	432	360	358	305
February	3 565	3 163	73	271	584	365	710	655	408	402	402	338
March	3 741	3 362	92	308	598	368	787	670	431	375	378	310
April	3 447	3 093	69	259	562	338	660	665	419	358	354	282
May	3 657	3 285	69	297	591	348	718	687	432	381	372	302
June	3 722	3 346	68	296	588	348	693	713	460	413	376	304
July	3 593	3 211	67	273	585	334	641	689	469	419	382	329
August	3 661	3 257	81	257	592	350	761	661	405	355	404	327
September[5]	3 561	3 192	77	238	597	358	651	697	389	339	368	299

[1]Includes natural resources and mining, information, financial activities, and other services, not shown separately.
[2]Includes wholesale trade and transportation, warehousing, and utilities, not shown separately.
[3]Includes arts, entertainment, and recreation, not shown separately.
[4]Includes federal government, not shown separately.
[5]Preliminary data.

Table 7-7. Job Openings Levels and Rates, by Industry, December 2000–September 2012—*Continued*

(Seasonally adjusted, levels in thousands, rates per 100.)

Year and month	Total[1]	Total private[1]	Construction	Manufacturing	Trade, transportation, and utilities[2]	Retail trade	Professional and business services	Education and health services	Leisure and hospitality[3]	Accommodation and food services	Government[4]	State and local government
2007												
January	3.2	3.5	3.1	2.5	3.1	2.9	4.2	3.8	4.2	4.1	2.0	2.1
February	3.2	3.4	3.4	2.5	2.8	2.9	3.8	3.5	4.1	4.2	1.9	2.0
March	3.3	3.6	2.7	2.7	3.1	2.7	4.3	3.8	4.2	4.2	1.9	2.0
April	3.2	3.4	2.3	2.5	3.0	2.5	4.2	4.0	3.9	3.9	2.0	2.0
May	3.2	3.4	2.1	2.5	2.6	2.3	4.2	4.1	4.2	4.4	2.0	2.0
June	3.3	3.6	2.0	2.5	2.9	2.9	4.3	4.2	4.3	4.4	1.9	2.0
July	3.1	3.3	2.0	2.5	2.9	2.6	3.7	3.8	4.3	4.6	2.0	2.1
August	3.2	3.4	2.0	2.3	2.9	2.5	4.1	4.0	4.4	4.5	2.0	2.0
September	3.2	3.4	1.6	2.2	2.8	2.4	4.1	4.4	4.6	4.8	2.0	2.0
October	3.0	3.2	1.9	2.1	2.6	2.3	4.0	3.8	4.3	4.5	1.9	1.9
November	3.1	3.3	1.7	2.4	2.7	2.4	4.0	3.8	4.8	4.8	2.0	2.0
December	3.0	3.2	1.7	2.2	2.7	2.4	4.2	3.8	4.1	4.5	1.9	1.9
2008												
January	3.0	3.2	1.7	2.0	2.4	2.2	4.1	3.7	4.2	4.5	1.8	1.9
February	2.8	3.0	1.6	1.9	2.4	2.2	4.1	3.9	4.0	4.1	1.8	1.9
March	2.8	3.0	1.3	1.8	2.2	2.4	4.2	4.0	4.0	4.2	1.8	1.8
April	2.8	3.0	1.2	2.0	2.2	2.3	4.1	3.7	3.7	3.9	1.7	1.8
May	2.8	3.0	2.1	2.0	2.3	2.4	3.5	3.7	3.9	4.0	1.9	1.8
June	2.7	2.8	1.5	1.8	2.0	2.0	4.0	3.7	3.4	3.6	1.9	1.9
July	2.7	2.8	1.5	1.8	2.3	2.4	3.6	3.8	3.1	3.2	1.9	1.8
August	2.6	2.8	1.2	1.9	2.1	2.2	3.8	3.5	3.0	3.0	1.8	1.7
September	2.3	2.4	1.8	1.6	2.0	2.1	3.3	3.0	2.7	2.8	1.8	1.7
October	2.4	2.6	1.0	1.7	2.3	2.8	3.4	3.2	2.9	3.0	1.7	1.6
November	2.3	2.4	1.0	1.2	2.1	2.5	3.3	3.2	2.2	2.3	1.6	1.6
December	2.2	2.4	1.3	1.2	1.9	2.2	3.1	3.1	2.4	2.4	1.3	1.3
2009												
January	2.1	2.1	0.5	0.9	2.0	2.7	2.9	3.1	1.8	1.8	1.9	1.6
February	2.1	2.2	1.0	1.1	1.6	2.0	3.1	2.9	2.1	2.3	1.6	1.5
March	1.9	2.0	0.8	1.0	1.5	1.7	2.7	2.7	2.1	2.2	1.6	1.3
April	1.7	1.8	0.3	0.8	1.3	1.4	2.5	2.5	2.3	2.5	1.5	1.4
May	1.8	1.9	0.6	0.8	1.8	2.2	2.3	2.7	2.0	2.1	1.2	1.2
June	1.8	1.9	0.9	0.8	1.7	1.8	2.2	2.6	1.9	2.1	1.4	1.3
July	1.7	1.7	0.7	0.8	1.2	1.3	2.5	2.7	1.8	2.0	1.3	1.2
August	1.7	1.8	1.0	1.1	1.7	1.7	2.2	2.7	1.5	1.6	1.2	1.3
September	1.9	2.0	1.1	1.1	1.5	1.8	2.6	2.7	2.2	2.4	1.4	1.2
October	1.8	1.8	1.1	1.1	1.3	1.5	2.5	2.6	1.7	1.9	1.7	1.3
November	1.8	1.9	1.2	1.2	1.3	1.4	2.5	2.6	1.8	1.9	1.4	1.2
December	1.8	1.9	1.2	1.5	1.4	1.4	2.5	2.7	1.6	1.8	1.4	1.3
2010												
January	2.1	2.1	1.0	1.2	1.5	1.7	2.6	2.9	1.9	2.1	1.9	1.2
February	2.0	2.0	1.2	1.4	1.6	1.9	2.4	2.6	1.8	1.9	1.6	1.2
March	2.0	2.1	1.5	1.4	1.9	2.3	2.4	2.6	1.8	1.9	1.8	1.3
April	2.4	2.3	1.4	1.5	1.7	1.9	2.9	2.6	2.1	2.2	2.7	1.2
May	2.1	2.3	1.3	1.6	1.7	1.8	3.3	2.5	2.2	2.2	1.6	1.2
June	2.0	2.1	1.3	1.7	1.7	1.7	2.8	2.4	2.2	2.2	1.4	1.1
July	2.2	2.4	1.6	1.9	1.7	1.8	3.1	2.6	2.4	2.5	1.4	1.2
August	2.2	2.4	1.0	1.5	1.7	1.7	3.6	2.3	2.6	2.7	1.3	1.1
September	2.1	2.2	1.3	1.5	1.6	1.6	3.2	2.6	2.3	2.4	1.4	1.2
October	2.3	2.4	1.4	1.7	1.8	1.7	3.4	2.9	2.3	2.4	1.5	1.4
November	2.3	2.5	1.7	1.9	1.7	1.8	4.0	2.6	2.0	2.1	1.3	1.1
December	2.2	2.3	0.9	1.7	1.8	1.9	3.3	2.6	2.2	2.2	1.7	1.5
2011												
January	2.1	2.3	1.2	1.8	2.0	1.9	2.7	2.5	2.2	2.2	1.4	1.3
February	2.3	2.4	0.9	1.8	1.9	1.7	3.4	2.7	2.8	2.8	1.4	1.3
March	2.4	2.6	1.3	2.0	2.0	1.9	3.4	2.9	2.7	2.8	1.4	1.4
April	2.2	2.4	2.1	1.9	2.0	2.0	3.1	2.6	2.2	2.3	1.4	1.4
May	2.3	2.5	1.8	1.9	2.0	2.0	3.5	2.8	2.2	2.3	1.4	1.3
June	2.4	2.6	1.0	1.8	2.1	2.4	3.7	2.9	2.6	2.6	1.5	1.4
July	2.5	2.7	1.4	2.0	2.3	2.2	3.7	3.0	2.6	2.5	1.4	1.4
August	2.3	2.5	1.8	2.0	1.9	2.1	3.5	3.0	2.6	2.7	1.5	1.5
September	2.6	2.7	1.4	2.1	2.3	2.4	3.8	2.9	2.9	2.9	1.8	1.8
October	2.5	2.7	1.4	2.0	2.3	2.2	3.6	3.0	2.9	2.9	1.5	1.4
November	2.4	2.6	1.5	2.0	2.3	2.1	3.1	3.0	3.1	3.2	1.6	1.5
December	2.6	2.8	1.4	2.1	2.2	2.1	4.3	2.9	3.2	3.3	1.6	1.5
2012												
January	2.6	2.7	1.5	2.2	2.3	2.1	3.8	3.0	3.1	3.0	1.6	1.6
February	2.6	2.8	1.3	2.2	2.3	2.4	3.8	3.1	2.9	3.0	1.8	1.7
March	2.7	2.9	1.6	2.5	2.3	2.4	4.2	3.2	3.1	3.1	1.7	1.6
April	2.5	2.7	1.2	2.1	2.2	2.2	3.6	3.2	3.0	3.0	1.6	1.5
May	2.7	2.9	1.2	2.4	2.3	2.3	3.9	3.3	3.1	3.2	1.7	1.6
June	2.7	2.9	1.2	2.4	2.3	2.3	3.7	3.4	3.3	3.4	1.7	1.6
July	2.6	2.8	1.2	2.2	2.3	2.2	3.5	3.3	3.3	3.5	1.7	1.7
August	2.7	2.8	1.4	2.1	2.3	2.3	4.1	3.1	2.9	2.9	1.8	1.7
September[5]	2.6	2.8	1.4	2.0	2.3	2.4	3.5	3.3	2.8	2.8	1.6	1.5

[1]Includes natural resources and mining, information, financial activities, and other services, not shown separately.
[2]Includes wholesale trade and transportation, warehousing, and utilities, not shown separately.
[3]Includes arts, entertainment, and recreation, not shown separately.
[4]Includes federal government, not shown separately.
[5]Preliminary data.

Table 7-8. Hires Levels[1] and Rates,[2] by Industry, December 2000–September 2012

(Seasonally adjusted, levels in thousands, rates per 100.)

Year and month	Level[3]											
	Total[4]	Total private[4]	Construction	Manufacturing	Trade, transportation, and utilities[5]	Retail trade	Professional and business services	Education and health services	Leisure and hospitality[6]	Accommodation and food services	Government[7]	State and local government
2000												
December	5 438	5 114	410	484	1 189	886	974	522	962	832	324	283
2001												
January	5 790	5 433	483	522	1 169	856	1 169	493	946	825	357	316
February	5 396	5 031	469	447	1 062	732	927	528	960	810	365	335
March	5 614	5 261	531	466	1 113	818	1 037	524	960	825	353	317
April	5 386	5 032	450	442	1 128	799	850	497	1 074	914	354	320
May	5 507	5 140	442	406	1 220	869	1 117	496	948	778	367	327
June	5 116	4 766	441	389	1 101	819	921	489	943	766	350	308
July	5 173	4 843	459	346	1 095	775	922	518	955	774	330	288
August	5 090	4 723	404	349	1 043	752	930	521	895	741	367	331
September	4 937	4 662	402	345	1 057	780	904	519	904	758	276	252
October	5 030	4 697	439	380	1 068	765	890	512	840	706	334	300
November	4 957	4 612	457	363	1 002	694	881	498	833	714	345	310
December	4 771	4 435	429	372	972	676	835	457	828	702	335	294
2002												
January	4 858	4 549	426	351	984	694	916	512	804	687	309	271
February	4 903	4 580	426	388	1 001	670	942	474	848	731	324	280
March	4 637	4 320	406	354	915	621	941	455	769	633	318	277
April	4 984	4 651	420	407	1 037	716	945	486	828	700	332	284
May	4 997	4 646	409	406	1 021	720	1 006	466	811	688	350	300
June	4 840	4 517	417	394	1 016	707	869	496	793	670	323	285
July	5 047	4 720	448	401	1 043	739	936	483	874	708	327	290
August	4 845	4 510	412	370	984	676	915	453	834	699	335	287
September	4 862	4 581	429	386	1 027	710	937	457	817	682	281	228
October	4 811	4 480	426	355	969	687	983	453	788	681	331	281
November	4 893	4 530	415	376	999	716	974	440	814	674	362	313
December	4 965	4 661	430	369	1 006	716	1 031	474	826	676	305	267
2003												
January	5 000	4 671	457	389	958	677	963	496	869	710	329	285
February	4 676	4 393	351	357	960	704	935	447	798	679	284	245
March	4 402	4 115	411	334	918	635	730	431	773	640	287	248
April	4 583	4 299	432	316	892	638	911	435	798	663	285	260
May	4 589	4 326	444	318	908	650	834	469	836	675	263	231
June	4 725	4 424	449	338	953	670	903	471	807	688	301	260
July	4 616	4 285	429	340	930	633	908	437	729	618	331	296
August	4 637	4 395	476	343	971	682	885	450	801	674	242	207
September	4 744	4 487	460	334	988	671	875	501	798	686	257	223
October	4 896	4 571	411	345	1 080	761	897	492	829	702	325	284
November	4 666	4 388	451	363	956	673	834	472	826	694	279	240
December	4 980	4 671	445	360	1 053	728	876	452	926	797	310	268
2004												
January	4 819	4 527	438	365	1 092	751	858	470	821	691	292	255
February	4 712	4 401	439	361	1 032	719	722	470	861	706	310	268
March	5 157	4 815	512	393	1 098	740	908	476	877	744	342	306
April	5 131	4 827	444	419	1 111	773	995	466	857	725	304	253
May	4 943	4 655	435	391	1 042	714	886	459	886	742	288	264
June	4 991	4 697	460	375	1 046	698	935	438	865	727	294	261
July	4 891	4 586	414	383	1 072	756	900	459	835	696	305	271
August	5 094	4 795	430	409	1 106	747	932	488	868	735	299	269
September	5 057	4 733	444	388	1 072	726	920	462	897	729	324	293
October	5 155	4 824	494	376	1 119	781	897	502	887	748	331	295
November	5 199	4 855	437	370	1 130	807	993	490	859	753	344	304
December	5 190	4 866	452	358	1 135	802	992	501	853	733	324	278
2005												
January	5 193	4 857	451	352	1 105	756	966	483	908	769	336	297
February	5 224	4 908	494	363	1 121	768	1 029	486	855	731	316	281
March	5 210	4 899	442	364	1 135	811	989	524	890	757	311	273
April	5 308	4 988	512	370	1 144	799	993	517	878	740	320	285
May	5 320	5 002	497	384	1 154	784	1 028	509	849	728	318	279
June	5 303	5 005	476	349	1 138	794	1 070	500	945	777	298	260
July	5 310	4 961	432	370	1 137	809	1 051	497	922	784	349	317
August	5 443	5 133	512	373	1 142	808	1 089	502	910	774	310	272
September	5 455	5 153	521	397	1 127	780	1 083	535	942	778	302	258
October	5 026	4 720	498	396	1 076	742	847	486	885	765	306	271
November	5 232	4 894	497	380	1 108	712	901	501	916	796	338	297
December	5 143	4 814	479	361	1 127	742	897	498	917	792	328	285
2006												
January	5 194	4 889	490	375	1 114	777	953	485	933	827	305	261
February	5 377	5 033	471	367	1 166	817	954	497	983	870	344	293
March	5 363	4 988	475	415	1 127	790	937	480	962	834	375	319
April	5 096	4 740	457	361	1 117	784	848	501	868	748	355	294
May	5 532	5 179	470	392	1 174	812	1 168	570	877	734	353	291
June	5 357	4 999	409	409	1 192	842	1 014	491	905	764	358	301
July	5 419	5 049	462	383	1 159	791	973	546	938	787	370	305
August	5 222	4 851	410	371	1 166	775	936	518	893	765	371	306
September	5 237	4 840	405	348	1 113	766	977	536	868	766	397	323
October	5 187	4 871	396	341	1 113	771	966	525	924	789	316	282
November	5 540	5 190	472	362	1 144	796	1 100	522	1 024	881	350	302
December	5 261	4 938	450	365	1 092	767	963	523	979	842	323	282

[1]Hires are the number of hires during the entire month.
[2]The hires rate is the number of hires during the entire month as a percent of total employment.
[3]Detail will not necessarily add to totals because of the independent seasonal adjustment of the various series.
[4]Includes natural resources and mining, information, financial activities, and other services, not shown separately.
[5]Includes wholesale trade and transportation, warehousing, and utilities, not shown separately.
[6]Includes arts, entertainment, and recreation, not shown separately.
[7]Includes federal government, not shown separately.

Table 7-8. Hires Levels[1] and Rates,[2] by Industry, December 2000–September 2012—*Continued*

(Seasonally adjusted, levels in thousands, rates per 100.)

Year and month	Rate											
	Total[4]	Total private[4]	Construc-tion	Manufac-turing	Trade, transpor-tation, and utilities[5]	Retail trade	Profes-sional and business services	Education and health services	Leisure and hospitality[6]	Accommo-dation and food services	Govern-ment[7]	State and local govern-ment
2000												
December	4.1	4.6	6.0	2.8	4.5	5.8	5.8	3.4	8.0	8.2	1.6	1.6
2001												
January	4.4	4.9	7.1	3.1	4.5	5.6	6.9	3.2	7.9	8.1	1.7	1.7
February	4.1	4.5	6.9	2.6	4.0	4.8	5.5	3.4	8.0	7.9	1.7	1.8
March	4.2	4.7	7.7	2.7	4.2	5.3	6.2	3.4	8.0	8.1	1.7	1.7
April	4.1	4.5	6.6	2.6	4.3	5.2	5.1	3.2	8.9	9.0	1.7	1.8
May	4.2	4.6	6.5	2.4	4.7	5.7	6.7	3.2	7.9	7.6	1.7	1.8
June	3.9	4.3	6.4	2.4	4.2	5.4	5.6	3.1	7.8	7.5	1.7	1.7
July	3.9	4.4	6.7	2.1	4.2	5.1	5.6	3.3	7.9	7.5	1.6	1.6
August	3.9	4.3	5.9	2.2	4.0	4.9	5.7	3.3	7.4	7.2	1.7	1.8
September	3.8	4.2	5.9	2.1	4.1	5.1	5.5	3.3	7.5	7.4	1.3	1.4
October	3.8	4.3	6.5	2.4	4.1	5.0	5.5	3.2	7.0	6.9	1.6	1.6
November	3.8	4.2	6.7	2.3	3.9	4.6	5.5	3.1	6.9	7.0	1.6	1.7
December	3.6	4.1	6.3	2.4	3.8	4.5	5.2	2.9	6.9	6.9	1.6	1.6
2002												
January	3.7	4.2	6.3	2.3	3.8	4.6	5.7	3.2	6.7	6.7	1.4	1.5
February	3.8	4.2	6.3	2.5	3.9	4.4	5.9	3.0	7.1	7.2	1.5	1.5
March	3.6	4.0	6.0	2.3	3.6	4.1	5.9	2.8	6.4	6.2	1.5	1.5
April	3.8	4.3	6.3	2.6	4.1	4.8	5.9	3.0	6.9	6.9	1.5	1.6
May	3.8	4.3	6.1	2.6	4.0	4.8	6.3	2.9	6.8	6.8	1.6	1.6
June	3.7	4.2	6.2	2.6	4.0	4.7	5.4	3.1	6.7	6.6	1.5	1.5
July	3.9	4.3	6.7	2.6	4.1	4.9	5.9	3.0	7.3	7.0	1.5	1.5
August	3.7	4.2	6.2	2.4	3.9	4.5	5.7	2.8	7.0	6.9	1.6	1.5
September	3.7	4.2	6.4	2.6	4.0	4.7	5.9	2.8	6.8	6.7	1.3	1.2
October	3.7	4.1	6.4	2.4	3.8	4.6	6.2	2.8	6.5	6.6	1.5	1.5
November	3.8	4.2	6.2	2.5	3.9	4.8	6.1	2.7	6.7	6.5	1.7	1.7
December	3.8	4.3	6.4	2.5	4.0	4.8	6.5	2.9	6.8	6.6	1.4	1.4
2003												
January	3.8	4.3	6.8	2.6	3.8	4.5	6.0	3.0	7.1	6.9	1.5	1.5
February	3.6	4.0	5.3	2.4	3.8	4.7	5.9	2.7	6.6	6.6	1.3	1.3
March	3.4	3.8	6.2	2.3	3.6	4.3	4.6	2.6	6.4	6.2	1.3	1.3
April	3.5	4.0	6.5	2.2	3.5	4.3	5.7	2.6	6.6	6.4	1.3	1.4
May	3.5	4.0	6.6	2.2	3.6	4.4	5.2	2.8	6.9	6.6	1.2	1.2
June	3.6	4.1	6.7	2.3	3.8	4.5	5.7	2.8	6.7	6.7	1.4	1.4
July	3.6	4.0	6.4	2.4	3.7	4.3	5.7	2.6	6.0	6.0	1.5	1.6
August	3.6	4.1	7.0	2.4	3.8	4.6	5.5	2.7	6.6	6.5	1.1	1.1
September	3.7	4.1	6.8	2.3	3.9	4.5	5.5	3.0	6.5	6.6	1.2	1.2
October	3.8	4.2	6.1	2.4	4.3	5.1	5.6	3.0	6.8	6.7	1.5	1.5
November	3.6	4.0	6.6	2.5	3.8	4.5	5.2	2.8	6.7	6.6	1.3	1.3
December	3.8	4.3	6.5	2.5	4.2	4.9	5.4	2.7	7.5	7.6	1.4	1.4
2004												
January	3.7	4.2	6.4	2.6	4.3	5.0	5.3	2.8	6.7	6.6	1.4	1.4
February	3.6	4.0	6.4	2.5	4.1	4.8	4.5	2.8	7.0	6.7	1.4	1.4
March	3.9	4.4	7.4	2.7	4.3	4.9	5.6	2.8	7.1	7.0	1.6	1.6
April	3.9	4.4	6.4	2.9	4.4	5.1	6.1	2.8	6.9	6.8	1.4	1.3
May	3.8	4.2	6.3	2.7	4.1	4.7	5.4	2.7	7.1	7.0	1.3	1.4
June	3.8	4.3	6.6	2.6	4.1	4.6	5.7	2.6	6.9	6.8	1.4	1.4
July	3.7	4.2	5.9	2.7	4.2	5.0	5.5	2.7	6.7	6.5	1.4	1.4
August	3.9	4.4	6.1	2.9	4.3	5.0	5.7	2.9	7.0	6.9	1.4	1.4
September	3.8	4.3	6.3	2.7	4.2	4.8	5.6	2.7	7.1	6.8	1.5	1.6
October	3.9	4.4	7.0	2.6	4.4	5.2	5.4	2.9	7.0	7.0	1.5	1.6
November	3.9	4.4	6.2	2.6	4.4	5.3	6.0	2.9	6.8	7.0	1.6	1.6
December	3.9	4.4	6.4	2.5	4.4	5.3	6.0	2.9	6.8	6.8	1.5	1.5
2005												
January	3.9	4.4	6.4	2.5	4.3	5.0	5.8	2.8	7.2	7.1	1.5	1.6
February	3.9	4.4	6.9	2.5	4.3	5.1	6.2	2.8	6.7	6.7	1.5	1.5
March	3.9	4.4	6.2	2.6	4.4	5.3	5.9	3.0	7.0	7.0	1.4	1.4
April	4.0	4.5	7.0	2.6	4.4	5.2	5.9	3.0	6.9	6.8	1.5	1.5
May	4.0	4.5	6.8	2.7	4.4	5.1	6.1	2.9	6.6	6.7	1.5	1.5
June	4.0	4.5	6.5	2.5	4.4	5.2	6.3	2.9	7.4	7.1	1.4	1.4
July	4.0	4.4	5.9	2.6	4.4	5.3	6.2	2.9	7.2	7.2	1.6	1.7
August	4.1	4.6	6.9	2.6	4.4	5.3	6.4	2.9	7.1	7.0	1.4	1.4
September	4.1	4.6	7.0	2.8	4.3	5.1	6.3	3.1	7.3	7.1	1.4	1.3
October	3.7	4.2	6.7	2.8	4.1	4.8	4.9	2.8	6.9	7.0	1.4	1.4
November	3.9	4.3	6.6	2.7	4.2	4.6	5.2	2.9	7.1	7.3	1.5	1.6
December	3.8	4.3	6.4	2.5	4.3	4.8	5.2	2.8	7.1	7.2	1.5	1.5
2006												
January	3.8	4.3	6.4	2.6	4.3	5.1	5.5	2.8	7.2	7.5	1.4	1.4
February	4.0	4.4	6.2	2.6	4.4	5.3	5.5	2.8	7.6	7.9	1.6	1.5
March	4.0	4.4	6.2	2.9	4.3	5.1	5.4	2.7	7.4	7.5	1.7	1.7
April	3.8	4.2	5.9	2.5	4.3	5.1	4.9	2.8	6.6	6.7	1.6	1.5
May	4.1	4.5	6.1	2.8	4.5	5.3	6.7	3.2	6.7	6.6	1.6	1.5
June	3.9	4.4	5.3	2.9	4.5	5.5	5.8	2.8	6.9	6.9	1.6	1.6
July	4.0	4.4	6.0	2.7	4.4	5.2	5.5	3.1	7.1	7.0	1.7	1.6
August	3.8	4.2	5.3	2.6	4.4	5.1	5.3	2.9	6.8	6.8	1.7	1.6
September	3.8	4.2	5.2	2.5	4.2	5.0	5.5	3.0	6.6	6.8	1.8	1.7
October	3.8	4.3	5.2	2.4	4.2	5.0	5.5	2.9	7.0	7.0	1.4	1.5
November	4.1	4.5	6.2	2.6	4.3	5.2	6.2	2.9	7.7	7.8	1.6	1.6
December	3.8	4.3	5.9	2.6	4.1	5.0	5.4	2.9	7.4	7.4	1.5	1.5

[1]Hires are the number of hires during the entire month.
[2]The hires rate is the number of hires during the entire month as a percent of total employment.
[4]Includes natural resources and mining, information, financial activities, and other services, not shown separately.
[5]Includes wholesale trade and transportation, warehousing, and utilities, not shown separately.
[6]Includes arts, entertainment, and recreation, not shown separately.
[7]Includes federal government, not shown separately.

Table 7-8. Hires Levels[1] and Rates,[2] by Industry, December 2000–September 2012—*Continued*

(Seasonally adjusted, levels in thousands, rates per 100.)

Year and month	Level[3]											
	Total[4]	Total private[4]	Construc-tion	Manufac-turing	Trade, transpor-tation, and utilities[5]	Retail trade	Profes-sional and business services	Education and health services	Leisure and hospitality[6]	Accommo-dation and food services	Govern-ment[7]	State and local govern-ment
2007												
January	5 279	4 916	418	378	1 146	806	981	522	929	785	363	302
February	5 183	4 810	323	393	1 106	771	989	510	937	799	373	304
March	5 354	4 981	442	372	1 148	787	981	530	910	771	373	295
April	5 180	4 802	380	361	1 083	726	906	516	973	827	378	303
May	5 314	4 936	398	381	1 101	778	973	558	932	803	378	299
June	5 237	4 873	429	387	1 073	715	858	539	940	806	364	298
July	5 121	4 778	407	372	1 046	714	941	502	912	792	342	256
August	5 145	4 756	400	374	1 045	738	932	529	917	790	389	305
September	5 156	4 790	388	370	1 099	787	948	521	889	750	366	286
October	5 201	4 881	400	376	1 107	760	971	536	921	785	321	291
November	5 150	4 807	385	399	1 090	780	975	540	894	753	342	296
December	4 971	4 613	367	353	1 033	750	905	487	908	772	358	311
2008												
January	4 927	4 606	371	327	1 045	719	892	553	878	739	321	290
February	4 901	4 573	366	317	1 037	731	820	556	938	788	328	284
March	4 798	4 474	384	310	990	691	863	554	844	715	324	291
April	4 916	4 604	393	340	1 022	695	896	567	858	736	312	281
May	4 684	4 377	364	323	915	637	818	555	880	750	307	283
June	4 782	4 475	397	311	1 000	685	931	514	807	701	308	283
July	4 505	4 208	360	263	977	678	807	521	800	693	297	273
August	4 603	4 297	401	279	977	675	798	523	816	665	306	283
September	4 383	4 109	356	288	906	628	789	493	791	690	274	253
October	4 463	4 183	370	309	947	648	780	525	783	664	279	255
November	3 953	3 688	351	247	754	535	751	486	683	596	265	239
December	4 177	3 904	331	268	893	624	780	497	706	595	273	250
2009												
January	4 175	3 841	350	188	869	550	733	530	691	576	333	294
February	4 003	3 743	349	249	766	531	714	524	679	580	260	238
March	3 814	3 564	303	235	821	542	660	474	632	559	250	226
April	3 900	3 532	299	202	863	628	691	463	624	543	368	222
May	3 812	3 552	324	178	821	555	674	474	686	597	260	237
June	3 679	3 418	268	192	704	486	628	498	641	547	261	233
July	3 819	3 573	312	237	729	493	683	499	647	519	246	212
August	3 788	3 516	262	241	766	529	661	514	661	543	273	250
September	3 885	3 626	317	266	809	516	679	506	630	522	259	235
October	3 728	3 441	295	239	717	493	688	493	614	512	287	246
November	3 952	3 678	309	277	766	496	796	480	663	549	274	241
December	3 831	3 586	317	248	820	533	643	482	626	531	246	223
2010												
January	3 844	3 565	312	256	742	531	750	441	644	545	280	229
February	3 833	3 549	299	259	772	538	756	460	587	507	283	240
March	4 244	3 892	386	254	897	651	780	512	661	550	352	259
April	4 099	3 767	347	273	806	552	767	474	679	555	332	227
May	4 418	3 680	310	249	776	535	781	467	654	548	738	240
June	4 083	3 799	287	255	817	550	851	497	656	526	284	230
July	4 062	3 781	337	271	844	570	764	506	670	545	281	239
August	3 932	3 684	341	256	769	544	771	464	653	545	248	210
September	3 934	3 691	321	249	816	551	739	497	669	560	243	211
October	4 008	3 739	354	269	801	563	757	475	647	548	269	239
November	4 094	3 798	349	277	826	568	791	500	620	530	296	269
December	4 096	3 815	361	267	795	528	832	473	639	538	280	253
2011												
January	3 934	3 671	288	259	834	568	827	439	621	527	263	231
February	4 089	3 850	366	258	854	569	849	467	639	538	239	206
March	4 293	4 037	357	270	846	584	922	464	755	622	256	227
April	4 015	3 738	338	257	802	563	832	456	675	560	277	251
May	4 182	3 923	366	269	833	564	911	468	643	523	258	228
June	4 208	3 945	366	260	834	568	860	494	713	599	264	241
July	4 112	3 866	337	260	806	568	821	479	727	619	246	223
August	4 221	3 932	325	257	823	544	890	489	711	596	290	263
September	4 276	4 002	360	240	810	567	911	486	736	600	275	248
October	4 220	3 979	333	240	840	559	893	484	719	588	241	215
November	4 268	3 986	312	237	849	573	858	483	779	622	281	252
December	4 188	3 889	315	269	812	517	818	494	743	602	299	270
2012												
January	4 239	3 945	331	253	836	557	831	517	757	618	294	275
February	4 444	4 128	318	260	815	551	973	527	794	639	316	284
March	4 335	4 041	286	263	827	550	888	523	795	640	294	264
April	4 213	3 916	276	260	826	556	888	495	717	594	297	263
May	4 461	4 176	314	262	872	577	982	540	715	600	285	254
June	4 284	4 000	355	270	821	556	931	494	700	592	284	256
July	4 278	3 989	359	244	848	570	871	500	720	614	288	268
August	4 440	4 109	323	230	892	577	915	502	747	643	332	300
September[8]	4 185	3 908	346	226	824	548	863	497	695	594	277	243

[1]Hires are the number of hires during the entire month.
[2]The hires rate is the number of hires during the entire month as a percent of total employment.
[3]Detail will not necessarily add to totals because of the independent seasonal adjustment of the various series.
[4]Includes natural resources and mining, information, financial activities, and other services, not shown separately.
[5]Includes wholesale trade and transportation, warehousing, and utilities, not shown separately.
[6]Includes arts, entertainment, and recreation, not shown separately.
[7]Includes federal government, not shown separately.
[8]Preliminary data.

Table 7-8. Hires Levels[1] and Rates,[2] by Industry, December 2000–September 2012—*Continued*

(Seasonally adjusted, levels in thousands, rates per 100.)

Year and month	Rate											
	Total[4]	Total private[4]	Construction	Manufacturing	Trade, transportation, and utilities[5]	Retail trade	Professional and business services	Education and health services	Leisure and hospitality[6]	Accommodation and food services	Government[7]	State and local government
2007												
January	3.9	4.3	5.4	2.7	4.3	5.2	5.5	2.9	7.0	6.9	1.6	1.6
February	3.8	4.2	4.2	2.8	4.2	5.0	5.5	2.8	7.0	7.0	1.7	1.6
March	3.9	4.3	5.7	2.7	4.3	5.1	5.5	2.9	6.8	6.8	1.7	1.5
April	3.8	4.2	4.9	2.6	4.1	4.7	5.1	2.8	7.3	7.2	1.7	1.6
May	3.9	4.3	5.2	2.7	4.1	5.0	5.4	3.1	7.0	7.0	1.7	1.5
June	3.8	4.2	5.6	2.8	4.0	4.6	4.8	2.9	7.0	7.0	1.6	1.5
July	3.7	4.1	5.3	2.7	3.9	4.6	5.2	2.7	6.8	6.9	1.5	1.3
August	3.7	4.1	5.3	2.7	3.9	4.8	5.2	2.9	6.8	6.9	1.8	1.6
September	3.7	4.2	5.1	2.7	4.1	5.1	5.3	2.8	6.6	6.5	1.6	1.5
October	3.8	4.2	5.3	2.7	4.2	4.9	5.4	2.9	6.8	6.8	1.4	1.5
November	3.7	4.2	5.1	2.9	4.1	5.0	5.4	2.9	6.6	6.5	1.5	1.5
December	3.6	4.0	4.9	2.6	3.9	4.8	5.0	2.6	6.7	6.7	1.6	1.6
2008												
January	3.6	4.0	5.0	2.4	3.9	4.6	4.9	3.0	6.5	6.4	1.4	1.5
February	3.6	4.0	4.9	2.3	3.9	4.7	4.6	3.0	6.9	6.8	1.5	1.4
March	3.5	3.9	5.2	2.3	3.7	4.5	4.8	3.0	6.2	6.2	1.4	1.5
April	3.6	4.0	5.4	2.5	3.9	4.5	5.0	3.0	6.3	6.4	1.4	1.4
May	3.4	3.8	5.0	2.4	3.5	4.1	4.6	3.0	6.5	6.5	1.4	1.4
June	3.5	3.9	5.5	2.3	3.8	4.5	5.2	2.7	6.0	6.1	1.4	1.4
July	3.3	3.7	5.0	2.0	3.7	4.4	4.5	2.8	5.9	6.0	1.3	1.4
August	3.4	3.8	5.6	2.1	3.7	4.4	4.5	2.8	6.1	5.8	1.4	1.4
September	3.2	3.6	5.0	2.2	3.5	4.1	4.5	2.6	5.9	6.0	1.2	1.3
October	3.3	3.7	5.3	2.3	3.6	4.3	4.5	2.8	5.9	5.8	1.2	1.3
November	2.9	3.3	5.2	1.9	2.9	3.6	4.3	2.6	5.1	5.2	1.2	1.2
December	3.1	3.5	4.9	2.1	3.5	4.2	4.5	2.6	5.3	5.3	1.2	1.3
2009												
January	3.1	3.5	5.3	1.5	3.4	3.7	4.3	2.8	5.2	5.1	1.5	1.5
February	3.0	3.4	5.4	2.0	3.0	3.6	4.2	2.7	5.1	5.2	1.2	1.2
March	2.9	3.3	4.8	1.9	3.3	3.7	3.9	2.5	4.8	5.0	1.1	1.1
April	3.0	3.3	4.9	1.7	3.5	4.3	4.2	2.4	4.8	4.9	1.6	1.1
May	2.9	3.3	5.3	1.5	3.3	3.8	4.1	2.5	5.2	5.3	1.1	1.2
June	2.8	3.2	4.5	1.6	2.8	3.3	3.8	2.6	4.9	4.9	1.2	1.2
July	2.9	3.3	5.3	2.0	2.9	3.4	4.2	2.6	4.9	4.6	1.1	1.1
August	2.9	3.3	4.5	2.1	3.1	3.7	4.0	2.7	5.1	4.9	1.2	1.3
September	3.0	3.4	5.5	2.3	3.3	3.6	4.1	2.6	4.8	4.7	1.2	1.2
October	2.9	3.2	5.2	2.1	2.9	3.4	4.2	2.6	4.7	4.6	1.3	1.2
November	3.1	3.4	5.4	2.4	3.1	3.5	4.8	2.5	5.1	5.0	1.2	1.2
December	3.0	3.4	5.6	2.2	3.3	3.7	3.9	2.5	4.8	4.8	1.1	1.1
2010												
January	3.0	3.3	5.6	2.2	3.0	3.7	4.5	2.3	5.0	4.9	1.2	1.2
February	3.0	3.3	5.4	2.3	3.1	3.7	4.6	2.4	4.5	4.6	1.3	1.2
March	3.3	3.6	6.9	2.2	3.6	4.5	4.7	2.6	5.1	5.0	1.6	1.3
April	3.2	3.5	6.2	2.4	3.3	3.8	4.6	2.4	5.2	5.0	1.5	1.2
May	3.4	3.4	5.6	2.2	3.2	3.7	4.7	2.4	5.0	4.9	3.2	1.2
June	3.1	3.5	5.2	2.2	3.3	3.8	5.1	2.5	5.0	4.7	1.2	1.2
July	3.1	3.5	6.1	2.3	3.4	3.9	4.6	2.6	5.1	4.9	1.2	1.2
August	3.0	3.4	6.2	2.2	3.1	3.8	4.6	2.4	5.0	4.9	1.1	1.1
September	3.0	3.4	5.8	2.2	3.3	3.8	4.4	2.5	5.1	5.0	1.1	1.1
October	3.1	3.5	6.4	2.3	3.2	3.9	4.5	2.4	4.9	4.9	1.2	1.2
November	3.1	3.5	6.4	2.4	3.3	3.9	4.7	2.5	4.7	4.7	1.3	1.4
December	3.1	3.5	6.6	2.3	3.2	3.6	4.9	2.4	4.9	4.8	1.3	1.3
2011												
January	3.0	3.4	5.3	2.2	3.4	3.9	4.8	2.2	4.7	4.7	1.2	1.2
February	3.1	3.5	6.7	2.2	3.4	3.9	5.0	2.4	4.8	4.8	1.1	1.1
March	3.3	3.7	6.5	2.3	3.4	4.0	5.4	2.3	5.7	5.5	1.2	1.2
April	3.1	3.4	6.2	2.2	3.2	3.9	4.8	2.3	5.1	4.9	1.2	1.3
May	3.2	3.6	6.7	2.3	3.3	3.9	5.3	2.4	4.8	4.6	1.2	1.2
June	3.2	3.6	6.7	2.2	3.3	3.9	5.0	2.5	5.4	5.2	1.2	1.3
July	3.1	3.5	6.1	2.2	3.2	3.9	4.7	2.4	5.5	5.4	1.1	1.2
August	3.2	3.6	5.9	2.2	3.3	3.7	5.1	2.5	5.3	5.2	1.3	1.4
September	3.2	3.6	6.5	2.0	3.2	3.9	5.2	2.4	5.5	5.2	1.2	1.3
October	3.2	3.6	6.0	2.0	3.3	3.8	5.1	2.4	5.4	5.1	1.1	1.1
November	3.2	3.6	5.7	2.0	3.4	3.9	4.9	2.4	5.8	5.4	1.3	1.3
December	3.2	3.5	5.7	2.3	3.2	3.5	4.6	2.5	5.5	5.2	1.4	1.4
2012												
January	3.2	3.6	5.9	2.1	3.3	3.8	4.7	2.6	5.6	5.3	1.3	1.4
February	3.3	3.7	5.7	2.2	3.2	3.7	5.5	2.6	5.9	5.5	1.4	1.5
March	3.3	3.6	5.1	2.2	3.3	3.7	5.0	2.6	5.8	5.5	1.3	1.4
April	3.2	3.5	5.0	2.2	3.3	3.8	5.0	2.4	5.3	5.1	1.3	1.4
May	3.4	3.8	5.7	2.2	3.4	3.9	5.5	2.7	5.3	5.1	1.3	1.3
June	3.2	3.6	6.4	2.3	3.2	3.8	5.2	2.4	5.1	5.1	1.3	1.3
July	3.2	3.6	6.5	2.0	3.3	3.9	4.9	2.5	5.3	5.2	1.3	1.4
August	3.3	3.7	5.9	1.9	3.5	3.9	5.1	2.5	5.5	5.5	1.5	1.6
September[8]	3.1	3.5	6.3	1.9	3.2	3.7	4.8	2.4	5.1	5.1	1.3	1.3

[1] Hires are the number of hires during the entire month.
[2] The hires rate is the number of hires during the entire month as a percent of total employment.
[4] Includes natural resources and mining, information, financial activities, and other services, not shown separately.
[5] Includes wholesale trade and transportation, warehousing, and utilities, not shown separately.
[6] Includes arts, entertainment, and recreation, not shown separately.
[7] Includes federal government, not shown separately.
[8] Preliminary data.

Table 7-9. Separations Levels[1] and Rates,[2] by Industry, December 2000–September 2012

(Seasonally adjusted, levels in thousands, rates per 100.)

Year and month	Level[3]											
	Total[4]	Total private[4]	Construction	Manufacturing	Trade, transportation, and utilities[5]	Retail trade	Professional and business services	Education and health services	Leisure and hospitality[6]	Accommodation and food services	Government[7]	State and local government
2000												
December	5 335	5 055	446	562	1 125	834	1 022	481	894	764	281	247
2001												
January	5 838	5 509	429	594	1 266	877	1 193	442	960	836	329	288
February	5 344	5 037	461	524	1 144	779	963	474	889	746	308	276
March	5 787	5 484	501	564	1 218	901	1 151	467	974	852	303	269
April	5 557	5 242	415	559	1 225	873	944	462	1 042	911	315	285
May	5 474	5 144	444	552	1 191	838	1 133	427	903	757	330	296
June	5 320	5 061	459	544	1 169	841	968	469	913	739	258	233
July	5 343	5 076	451	494	1 151	807	981	468	956	769	266	231
August	5 163	4 832	427	495	1 020	719	991	446	890	736	331	296
September	5 213	4 948	430	467	1 096	770	997	452	965	793	265	234
October	5 434	5 133	446	544	1 139	789	996	500	914	769	301	260
November	5 128	4 847	473	483	1 049	696	958	447	871	726	280	239
December	4 857	4 547	435	454	1 046	734	888	410	801	674	309	256
2002												
January	5 051	4 761	422	470	1 080	750	982	460	789	654	290	250
February	5 032	4 709	447	454	1 040	686	976	425	850	735	324	278
March	4 749	4 483	408	429	977	659	981	415	770	644	266	223
April	5 030	4 702	432	447	1 045	721	907	459	867	714	328	285
May	4 949	4 668	440	458	1 030	732	979	430	790	678	281	248
June	4 840	4 544	416	440	1 030	725	862	407	788	676	297	251
July	5 221	4 904	466	451	1 028	723	1 024	460	905	702	317	274
August	4 821	4 527	406	445	1 040	724	877	420	801	668	294	255
September	4 923	4 612	437	439	1 032	711	962	431	789	671	310	267
October	4 757	4 435	438	430	965	679	965	435	735	638	322	284
November	4 794	4 466	383	438	1 002	715	957	391	784	664	328	276
December	5 069	4 766	451	428	978	695	1 109	460	795	657	303	259
2003												
January	4 880	4 586	435	430	998	698	914	443	805	658	294	256
February	4 823	4 522	397	433	1 003	746	913	416	804	676	300	260
March	4 694	4 396	412	398	1 007	698	837	415	810	664	297	259
April	4 641	4 329	401	425	891	621	904	384	819	673	311	269
May	4 632	4 335	431	370	932	651	781	445	870	700	297	253
June	4 752	4 482	431	400	1 000	692	884	465	751	645	270	231
July	4 654	4 358	429	438	971	637	876	436	707	609	296	261
August	4 688	4 369	472	368	968	668	911	435	762	638	320	279
September	4 633	4 335	447	367	918	623	820	459	787	660	298	264
October	4 720	4 455	407	367	1 048	736	855	454	805	676	265	219
November	4 612	4 312	434	382	973	689	773	429	816	673	299	238
December	4 809	4 502	422	388	1 020	701	820	415	860	738	307	272
2004												
January	4 653	4 354	420	377	999	712	851	434	786	668	299	258
February	4 639	4 336	457	373	1 018	707	715	452	806	659	304	259
March	4 923	4 622	448	391	1 081	726	909	429	834	713	301	265
April	4 873	4 593	419	382	1 086	763	900	439	847	701	280	255
May	4 653	4 367	385	358	1 008	683	787	440	848	714	286	244
June	4 884	4 581	430	372	997	673	928	423	845	699	303	264
July	4 866	4 570	407	383	1 087	771	882	433	846	698	296	263
August	4 957	4 678	424	407	1 084	728	898	445	878	744	279	250
September	4 877	4 572	420	401	992	680	882	480	837	687	306	274
October	4 796	4 486	443	374	1 062	738	802	402	852	713	310	268
November	5 152	4 843	414	396	1 131	818	975	465	860	740	309	268
December	5 036	4 704	409	394	1 099	792	958	455	821	694	332	284
2005												
January	5 053	4 770	487	379	1 059	723	929	448	878	749	283	251
February	4 966	4 653	445	355	1 045	721	963	472	810	687	314	277
March	5 152	4 839	410	377	1 140	830	979	503	864	746	314	279
April	4 988	4 681	422	379	1 083	762	973	485	789	674	306	267
May	5 155	4 859	470	373	1 117	746	949	470	863	743	295	268
June	5 020	4 711	421	367	1 087	756	992	454	902	742	308	263
July	4 934	4 677	402	374	1 075	767	1 002	442	870	759	257	221
August	5 223	4 922	489	394	1 100	784	1 022	470	870	750	301	267
September	5 317	4 987	497	400	1 121	796	988	490	951	785	330	286
October	4 963	4 649	453	392	1 043	727	846	463	941	800	314	280
November	4 923	4 613	428	394	1 079	725	805	454	892	774	310	270
December	5 061	4 748	472	368	1 168	787	859	473	896	764	313	260
2006												
January	4 938	4 618	463	362	1 038	748	914	430	914	800	320	282
February	5 095	4 770	423	382	1 112	793	893	440	943	832	325	278
March	5 096	4 752	444	415	1 109	779	869	444	910	791	345	289
April	4 945	4 609	394	343	1 130	830	865	489	820	718	336	279
May	5 503	5 157	473	418	1 212	851	1 067	551	898	749	346	289
June	5 203	4 849	390	379	1 160	830	951	499	891	762	354	292
July	5 165	4 836	434	405	1 114	775	922	517	872	729	329	270
August	4 977	4 641	405	384	1 135	761	844	472	861	736	337	267
September	5 024	4 696	413	375	1 071	744	972	446	851	736	329	251
October	5 143	4 817	433	373	1 056	733	986	487	896	772	325	287
November	5 374	5 037	470	403	1 132	807	1 016	473	979	834	338	284
December	5 246	4 918	435	421	1 095	795	973	500	945	811	328	279

[1]Total separations are the number of separations during the entire month.
[2]The total separations rate is the number of total separations during the entire month as a percent of total employment.
[3]Detail will not necessarily add to totals because of the independent seasonal adjustment of the various series.
[4]Includes natural resources and mining, information, financial activities, and other services, not shown separately.
[5]Includes wholesale trade and transportation, warehousing, and utilities, not shown separately.
[6]Includes arts, entertainment, and recreation, not shown separately.
[7]Includes federal government, not shown separately.

Table 7-9. Separations Levels[1] and Rates,[2] by Industry, December 2000–September 2012—*Continued*

(Seasonally adjusted, levels in thousands, rates per 100.)

Year and month	Rate											
	Total[4]	Total private[4]	Construction	Manufacturing	Trade, transportation, and utilities[5]	Retail trade	Professional and business services	Education and health services	Leisure and hospitality[6]	Accommodation and food services	Government[7]	State and local government
2000												
December	4.0	4.5	6.6	3.3	4.3	5.4	6.1	3.1	7.5	7.5	1.3	1.4
2001												
January	4.4	4.9	6.3	3.5	4.8	5.7	7.1	2.9	8.0	8.2	1.6	1.6
February	4.0	4.5	6.7	3.1	4.4	5.1	5.7	3.1	7.4	7.3	1.5	1.5
March	4.4	4.9	7.3	3.3	4.6	5.9	6.9	3.0	8.1	8.4	1.4	1.5
April	4.2	4.7	6.1	3.3	4.7	5.7	5.7	3.0	8.7	8.9	1.5	1.6
May	4.1	4.6	6.5	3.3	4.6	5.5	6.8	2.7	7.5	7.4	1.6	1.6
June	4.0	4.6	6.7	3.3	4.5	5.5	5.9	3.0	7.6	7.2	1.2	1.3
July	4.0	4.6	6.6	3.0	4.4	5.3	6.0	3.0	7.9	7.5	1.3	1.3
August	3.9	4.4	6.3	3.1	3.9	4.7	6.0	2.8	7.4	7.2	1.6	1.6
September	4.0	4.5	6.3	2.9	4.2	5.1	6.1	2.9	8.0	7.8	1.2	1.3
October	4.1	4.7	6.6	3.4	4.4	5.2	6.1	3.2	7.6	7.6	1.4	1.4
November	3.9	4.4	7.0	3.1	4.1	4.6	5.9	2.8	7.3	7.1	1.3	1.3
December	3.7	4.2	6.4	2.9	4.1	4.9	5.5	2.6	6.7	6.6	1.4	1.4
2002												
January	3.9	4.4	6.2	3.0	4.2	5.0	6.1	2.9	6.6	6.4	1.4	1.3
February	3.9	4.3	6.6	2.9	4.1	4.6	6.1	2.7	7.1	7.2	1.5	1.5
March	3.6	4.1	6.0	2.8	3.8	4.4	6.1	2.6	6.4	6.3	1.2	1.2
April	3.9	4.3	6.4	2.9	4.1	4.8	5.7	2.9	7.3	7.0	1.5	1.5
May	3.8	4.3	6.6	3.0	4.0	4.9	6.1	2.7	6.6	6.7	1.3	1.3
June	3.7	4.2	6.2	2.9	4.0	4.8	5.4	2.5	6.6	6.7	1.4	1.3
July	4.0	4.5	7.0	3.0	4.0	4.8	6.4	2.8	7.6	6.9	1.5	1.5
August	3.7	4.2	6.1	2.9	4.1	4.8	5.5	2.6	6.7	6.6	1.4	1.4
September	3.8	4.2	6.5	2.9	4.1	4.7	6.0	2.6	6.6	6.6	1.4	1.4
October	3.6	4.1	6.5	2.9	3.8	4.5	6.0	2.7	6.1	6.2	1.5	1.5
November	3.7	4.1	5.7	2.9	3.9	4.8	6.0	2.4	6.5	6.4	1.5	1.5
December	3.9	4.4	6.7	2.9	3.8	4.6	7.0	2.8	6.6	6.4	1.4	1.4
2003												
January	3.7	4.2	6.5	2.9	3.9	4.7	5.7	2.7	6.6	6.4	1.4	1.4
February	3.7	4.2	6.0	2.9	4.0	5.0	5.7	2.5	6.6	6.6	1.4	1.4
March	3.6	4.1	6.2	2.7	4.0	4.7	5.3	2.5	6.7	6.5	1.4	1.4
April	3.6	4.0	6.0	2.9	3.5	4.2	5.7	2.3	6.8	6.5	1.4	1.4
May	3.6	4.0	6.4	2.5	3.7	4.4	4.9	2.7	7.2	6.8	1.4	1.3
June	3.7	4.1	6.4	2.8	4.0	4.6	5.5	2.8	6.2	6.3	1.2	1.2
July	3.6	4.0	6.4	3.0	3.9	4.3	5.5	2.6	5.8	5.9	1.4	1.4
August	3.6	4.0	7.0	2.6	3.8	4.5	5.7	2.6	6.3	6.2	1.5	1.5
September	3.6	4.0	6.6	2.6	3.6	4.2	5.1	2.8	6.4	6.3	1.4	1.4
October	3.6	4.1	6.0	2.6	4.1	4.9	5.3	2.7	6.6	6.5	1.2	1.2
November	3.5	4.0	6.4	2.7	3.8	4.6	4.8	2.6	6.6	6.4	1.4	1.3
December	3.7	4.1	6.2	2.7	4.0	4.7	5.1	2.5	7.0	7.0	1.4	1.4
2004												
January	3.6	4.0	6.1	2.6	3.9	4.8	5.3	2.6	6.4	6.4	1.4	1.4
February	3.6	4.0	6.7	2.6	4.0	4.7	4.4	2.7	6.5	6.3	1.4	1.4
March	3.8	4.2	6.5	2.7	4.2	4.8	5.6	2.5	6.7	6.7	1.4	1.4
April	3.7	4.2	6.1	2.7	4.3	5.1	5.5	2.6	6.8	6.6	1.3	1.4
May	3.5	4.0	5.5	2.5	4.0	4.5	4.8	2.6	6.8	6.7	1.3	1.3
June	3.7	4.2	6.2	2.6	3.9	4.5	5.7	2.5	6.8	6.6	1.4	1.4
July	3.7	4.2	5.8	2.7	4.3	5.1	5.4	2.6	6.8	6.6	1.4	1.4
August	3.8	4.3	6.1	2.8	4.2	4.8	5.5	2.6	7.0	7.0	1.3	1.3
September	3.7	4.2	6.0	2.8	3.9	4.5	5.4	2.8	6.7	6.4	1.4	1.5
October	3.6	4.1	6.3	2.6	4.1	4.9	4.8	2.4	6.8	6.6	1.4	1.4
November	3.9	4.4	5.8	2.8	4.4	5.4	5.9	2.7	6.8	6.9	1.4	1.4
December	3.8	4.3	5.7	2.8	4.3	5.2	5.8	2.7	6.5	6.4	1.5	1.5
2005												
January	3.8	4.3	6.9	2.7	4.1	4.8	5.6	2.6	6.9	6.9	1.3	1.3
February	3.7	4.2	6.2	2.5	4.1	4.7	5.8	2.7	6.4	6.3	1.4	1.5
March	3.9	4.4	5.7	2.6	4.4	5.5	5.8	2.9	6.8	6.9	1.4	1.5
April	3.7	4.2	5.8	2.7	4.2	5.0	5.8	2.8	6.2	6.2	1.4	1.4
May	3.9	4.4	6.4	2.6	4.3	4.9	5.6	2.7	6.7	6.8	1.4	1.4
June	3.8	4.2	5.7	2.6	4.2	4.9	5.9	2.6	7.0	6.8	1.4	1.4
July	3.7	4.2	5.5	2.6	4.1	5.0	5.9	2.5	6.8	6.9	1.2	1.2
August	3.9	4.4	6.6	2.8	4.2	5.1	6.0	2.7	6.8	6.8	1.4	1.4
September	4.0	4.4	6.7	2.8	4.3	5.2	5.8	2.8	7.4	7.2	1.5	1.5
October	3.7	4.1	6.1	2.8	4.0	4.7	4.9	2.6	7.3	7.3	1.4	1.5
November	3.7	4.1	5.7	2.8	4.1	4.7	4.7	2.6	6.9	7.1	1.4	1.4
December	3.8	4.2	6.3	2.6	4.5	5.1	5.0	2.7	6.9	6.9	1.4	1.4
2006												
January	3.7	4.1	6.1	2.5	4.0	4.9	5.3	2.4	7.1	7.2	1.5	1.5
February	3.8	4.2	5.5	2.7	4.2	5.2	5.1	2.5	7.3	7.5	1.5	1.5
March	3.8	4.2	5.8	2.9	4.2	5.1	5.0	2.5	7.0	7.1	1.6	1.5
April	3.6	4.0	5.1	2.4	4.3	5.4	5.0	2.8	6.3	6.4	1.5	1.5
May	4.0	4.5	6.1	2.9	4.6	5.6	6.1	3.1	6.9	6.7	1.6	1.5
June	3.8	4.3	5.1	2.7	4.4	5.4	5.4	2.8	6.8	6.8	1.6	1.5
July	3.8	4.2	5.6	2.9	4.2	5.1	5.2	2.9	6.6	6.5	1.5	1.4
August	3.7	4.1	5.2	2.7	4.3	5.0	4.8	2.6	6.5	6.6	1.5	1.4
September	3.7	4.1	5.4	2.7	4.1	4.8	5.5	2.5	6.5	6.6	1.5	1.3
October	3.8	4.2	5.6	2.6	4.0	4.8	5.6	2.7	6.8	6.9	1.5	1.5
November	3.9	4.4	6.1	2.9	4.3	5.2	5.7	2.6	7.4	7.4	1.5	1.5
December	3.8	4.3	5.7	3.0	4.1	5.2	5.5	2.8	7.1	7.2	1.5	1.4

[1] Total separations are the number of separations during the entire month.
[2] The total separations rate is the number of total separations during the entire month as a percent of total employment.
[4] Includes natural resources and mining, information, financial activities, and other services, not shown separately.
[5] Includes wholesale trade and transportation, warehousing, and utilities, not shown separately.
[6] Includes arts, entertainment, and recreation, not shown separately.
[7] Includes federal government, not shown separately.

Table 7-9. Separations Levels[1] and Rates,[2] by Industry, December 2000–September 2012—*Continued*

(Seasonally adjusted, levels in thousands, rates per 100.)

Year and month	Level[3]											
	Total[4]	Total private[4]	Construc-tion	Manufac-turing	Trade, transpor-tation, and utilities[5]	Retail trade	Profes-sional and business services	Education and health services	Leisure and hospitality[6]	Accommo-dation and food services	Govern-ment[7]	State and local govern-ment
2007												
January	5 095	4 768	409	418	1 072	739	939	482	893	758	327	282
February	5 134	4 792	423	425	1 048	728	958	477	922	785	341	273
March	5 144	4 808	353	403	1 083	726	956	487	909	766	336	261
April	5 150	4 805	391	387	1 090	749	933	476	937	790	345	273
May	5 153	4 790	413	395	1 094	769	891	512	913	793	363	288
June	5 063	4 716	403	388	1 063	731	833	488	936	806	346	268
July	5 090	4 704	419	396	1 021	707	927	479	880	770	387	300
August	5 102	4 762	442	397	1 053	742	891	483	906	786	340	265
September	5 035	4 707	422	401	1 077	780	938	446	823	701	328	245
October	5 089	4 781	,414	396	1 078	749	954	489	888	763	308	271
November	5 101	4 793	425	409	1 052	738	948	514	897	757	308	269
December	5 009	4 696	423	384	1 084	787	893	456	902	767	313	276
2008												
January	4 963	4 669	405	370	1 058	728	912	505	873	735	295	255
February	5 029	4 753	414	370	1 070	744	865	514	963	809	276	245
March	4 849	4 556	402	360	993	688	904	509	856	724	293	266
April	5 132	4 834	454	389	1 116	776	938	529	863	737	298	272
May	4 854	4 569	410	353	1 007	695	845	498	917	777	285	262
June	4 948	4 676	451	376	1 085	748	941	471	829	719	272	250
July	4 680	4 423	415	334	1 032	721	868	479	794	688	256	236
August	4 891	4 605	433	331	1 087	747	871	488	859	698	286	266
September	4 786	4 499	430	370	1 032	696	864	463	816	697	287	268
October	4 926	4 614	448	404	1 040	703	910	504	795	687	311	287
November	4 696	4 425	476	364	988	666	903	448	740	653	271	247
December	4 776	4 506	438	417	1 021	699	909	475	733	626	270	244
2009												
January	4 941	4 654	487	495	1 009	635	878	483	726	611	288	265
February	4 730	4 450	443	430	896	573	881	508	733	630	281	264
March	4 624	4 370	443	424	990	624	779	463	702	613	254	235
April	4 675	4 410	457	381	1 051	733	857	477	689	584	265	244
May	4 252	3 936	385	369	889	573	741	405	650	574	316	234
June	4 178	3 858	355	350	799	524	720	464	673	559	320	245
July	4 207	3 919	427	305	827	547	726	481	661	530	287	265
August	4 089	3 809	347	284	815	547	698	487	708	585	280	254
September	4 063	3 792	388	304	904	577	689	474	605	535	271	254
October	3 933	3 653	348	279	788	533	688	458	645	528	279	249
November	3 906	3 631	325	286	796	497	717	437	670	557	274	236
December	3 931	3 641	366	251	797	536	647	459	665	557	290	253
2010												
January	3 870	3 605	382	274	749	491	695	430	652	545	265	249
February	3 902	3 609	355	267	774	513	716	438	599	525	293	259
March	4 006	3 714	346	252	850	618	758	441	641	527	292	256
April	3 876	3 582	351	242	792	562	702	471	625	518	293	251
May	3 936	3 628	357	219	745	511	767	427	648	541	308	244
June	4 251	3 703	299	241	838	576	760	471	645	517	548	272
July	4 164	3 733	362	251	814	565	767	488	667	529	431	248
August	3 985	3 548	327	263	761	540	715	439	634	524	438	290
September	3 945	3 562	338	242	789	536	726	480	607	505	383	276
October	3 771	3 505	338	262	747	522	694	410	654	536	266	228
November	3 908	3 597	334	262	789	549	696	456	620	521	311	283
December	3 993	3 695	393	248	754	503	795	466	606	510	298	276
2011												
January	3 816	3 560	309	223	784	533	772	423	624	520	256	227
February	3 877	3 610	320	230	813	545	785	440	590	497	267	242
March	3 988	3 730	341	246	793	561	796	437	699	574	258	233
April	3 799	3 496	358	233	714	509	803	408	623	509	304	272
May	4 177	3 867	369	258	793	548	894	438	688	538	310	281
June	4 112	3 819	370	239	825	560	846	464	668	563	293	260
July	4 023	3 723	339	231	788	551	790	437	702	600	300	270
August	4 112	3 835	338	247	805	544	845	460	716	600	276	245
September	4 089	3 808	324	236	811	567	857	409	716	576	281	250
October	4 065	3 781	325	227	813	539	831	450	663	549	285	253
November	4 057	3 750	300	236	770	520	807	462	715	573	307	268
December	4 023	3 695	303	239	773	509	792	468	695	562	328	292
2012												
January	4 017	3 729	308	217	837	579	745	501	700	575	288	262
February	4 124	3 823	317	235	780	543	850	458	747	594	301	269
March	4 167	3 869	281	234	832	566	835	473	753	625	299	267
April	4 142	3 838	290	239	817	560	855	470	710	577	304	271
May	4 463	4 163	359	248	835	586	1 035	479	712	577	300	270
June	4 249	3 943	342	263	827	558	921	493	679	578	306	276
July	4 088	3 789	358	228	815	556	807	463	685	579	299	271
August	4 355	4 062	316	250	883	587	911	474	730	642	292	262
September[8]	4 024	3 766	354	239	806	552	832	434	673	570	258	228

[1]Total separations are the number of separations during the entire month.
[2]The total separations rate is the number of total separations during the entire month as a percent of total employment.
[3]Detail will not necessarily add to totals because of the independent seasonal adjustment of the various series.
[4]Includes natural resources and mining, information, financial activities, and other services, not shown separately.
[5]Includes wholesale trade and transportation, warehousing, and utilities, not shown separately.
[6]Includes arts, entertainment, and recreation, not shown separately.
[7]Includes federal government, not shown separately.
[8]Preliminary data.

Table 7-9. Separations Levels[1] and Rates,[2] by Industry, December 2000–September 2012—*Continued*

(Seasonally adjusted, levels in thousands, rates per 100.)

Year and month	Rate											
	Total[4]	Total private[4]	Construction	Manufacturing	Trade, transportation, and utilities[5]	Retail trade	Professional and business services	Education and health services	Leisure and hospitality[6]	Accommodation and food services	Government[7]	State and local government
2007												
January	3.7	4.1	5.3	3.0	4.0	4.8	5.3	2.7	6.7	6.7	1.5	1.5
February	3.7	4.2	5.5	3.0	3.9	4.7	5.4	2.6	6.9	6.9	1.5	1.4
March	3.7	4.2	4.6	2.9	4.1	4.7	5.3	2.7	6.8	6.7	1.5	1.3
April	3.7	4.2	5.1	2.8	4.1	4.8	5.2	2.6	7.0	6.9	1.6	1.4
May	3.7	4.2	5.4	2.8	4.1	5.0	5.0	2.8	6.8	6.9	1.6	1.5
June	3.7	4.1	5.2	2.8	4.0	4.7	4.6	2.7	7.0	7.0	1.6	1.4
July	3.7	4.1	5.5	2.9	3.8	4.6	5.2	2.6	6.6	6.7	1.7	1.5
August	3.7	4.1	5.8	2.9	4.0	4.8	5.0	2.6	6.7	6.9	1.5	1.4
September	3.7	4.1	5.6	2.9	4.0	5.0	5.2	2.4	6.1	6.1	1.5	1.3
October	3.7	4.1	5.5	2.9	4.0	4.8	5.3	2.6	6.6	6.6	1.4	1.4
November	3.7	4.1	5.6	3.0	3.9	4.7	5.3	2.8	6.6	6.6	1.4	1.4
December	3.6	4.1	5.6	2.8	4.1	5.1	4.9	2.5	6.7	6.6	1.4	1.4
2008												
January	3.6	4.0	5.4	2.7	4.0	4.7	5.1	2.7	6.4	6.4	1.3	1.3
February	3.6	4.1	5.6	2.7	4.0	4.8	4.8	2.8	7.1	7.0	1.2	1.2
March	3.5	3.9	5.4	2.6	3.7	4.4	5.0	2.7	6.3	6.3	1.3	1.4
April	3.7	4.2	6.2	2.9	4.2	5.0	5.2	2.8	6.4	6.4	1.3	1.4
May	3.5	4.0	5.6	2.6	3.8	4.5	4.7	2.6	6.8	6.8	1.3	1.3
June	3.6	4.1	6.3	2.8	4.1	4.9	5.3	2.5	6.2	6.3	1.2	1.3
July	3.4	3.9	5.8	2.5	3.9	4.7	4.9	2.5	5.9	6.0	1.1	1.2
August	3.6	4.0	6.1	2.5	4.1	4.9	4.9	2.6	6.4	6.1	1.3	1.3
September	3.5	4.0	6.1	2.8	4.0	4.6	4.9	2.4	6.1	6.1	1.3	1.4
October	3.6	4.1	6.4	3.1	4.0	4.7	5.2	2.7	6.0	6.0	1.4	1.5
November	3.5	3.9	7.0	2.8	3.8	4.4	5.2	2.4	5.6	5.7	1.2	1.2
December	3.6	4.0	6.5	3.2	4.0	4.7	5.3	2.5	5.5	5.5	1.2	1.2
2009												
January	3.7	4.2	7.4	3.9	4.0	4.3	5.1	2.5	5.5	5.4	1.3	1.3
February	3.6	4.0	6.9	3.5	3.5	3.9	5.2	2.7	5.6	5.6	1.2	1.3
March	3.5	4.0	7.0	3.5	3.9	4.3	4.6	2.4	5.3	5.5	1.1	1.2
April	3.6	4.1	7.4	3.2	4.2	5.0	5.2	2.5	5.3	5.2	1.2	1.2
May	3.2	3.6	6.3	3.1	3.6	3.9	4.5	2.1	5.0	5.1	1.4	1.2
June	3.2	3.6	5.9	3.0	3.2	3.6	4.4	2.4	5.1	5.0	1.4	1.2
July	3.2	3.6	7.2	2.6	3.3	3.8	4.4	2.5	5.1	4.7	1.3	1.3
August	3.1	3.5	5.9	2.4	3.3	3.8	4.3	2.5	5.4	5.2	1.2	1.3
September	3.1	3.5	6.7	2.6	3.7	4.0	4.2	2.5	4.6	4.8	1.2	1.3
October	3.0	3.4	6.1	2.4	3.2	3.7	4.2	2.4	5.0	4.8	1.2	1.3
November	3.0	3.4	5.7	2.5	3.2	3.5	4.4	2.3	5.2	5.0	1.2	1.2
December	3.0	3.4	6.5	2.2	3.2	3.7	3.9	2.4	5.1	5.0	1.3	1.3
2010												
January	3.0	3.4	6.8	2.4	3.1	3.4	4.2	2.2	5.0	4.9	1.2	1.3
February	3.0	3.4	6.4	2.3	3.2	3.6	4.3	2.3	4.6	4.8	1.3	1.3
March	3.1	3.5	6.2	2.2	3.5	4.3	4.6	2.3	4.9	4.8	1.3	1.3
April	3.0	3.3	6.3	2.1	3.2	3.9	4.2	2.4	4.8	4.7	1.3	1.3
May	3.0	3.4	6.5	1.9	3.0	3.5	4.6	2.2	5.0	4.9	1.3	1.2
June	3.3	3.5	5.4	2.1	3.4	4.0	4.5	2.4	5.0	4.7	2.4	1.4
July	3.2	3.5	6.6	2.2	3.3	3.9	4.6	2.5	5.1	4.8	1.9	1.3
August	3.1	3.3	5.9	2.3	3.1	3.7	4.3	2.2	4.8	4.7	2.0	1.5
September	3.0	3.3	6.2	2.1	3.2	3.7	4.3	2.5	4.6	4.5	1.7	1.4
October	2.9	3.3	6.1	2.3	3.0	3.6	4.1	2.1	5.0	4.8	1.2	1.2
November	3.0	3.3	6.1	2.3	3.2	3.8	4.1	2.3	4.7	4.6	1.4	1.5
December	3.1	3.4	7.2	2.1	3.0	3.5	4.7	2.4	4.6	4.5	1.3	1.4
2011												
January	2.9	3.3	5.7	1.9	3.2	3.7	4.5	2.1	4.7	4.6	1.2	1.2
February	3.0	3.3	5.8	2.0	3.3	3.7	4.6	2.2	4.5	4.4	1.2	1.2
March	3.0	3.4	6.2	2.1	3.2	3.9	4.6	2.2	5.3	5.1	1.2	1.2
April	2.9	3.2	6.5	2.0	2.9	3.5	4.7	2.1	4.7	4.5	1.4	1.4
May	3.2	3.5	6.7	2.2	3.2	3.8	5.2	2.2	5.2	4.7	1.4	1.5
June	3.1	3.5	6.7	2.0	3.3	3.8	4.9	2.3	5.0	4.9	1.3	1.4
July	3.1	3.4	6.2	2.0	3.1	3.8	4.6	2.2	5.3	5.3	1.4	1.4
August	3.1	3.5	6.1	2.1	3.2	3.7	4.9	2.3	5.4	5.2	1.3	1.3
September	3.1	3.5	5.9	2.0	3.2	3.9	4.9	2.0	5.4	5.0	1.3	1.3
October	3.1	3.4	5.9	1.9	3.2	3.7	4.8	2.2	5.0	4.8	1.3	1.3
November	3.1	3.4	5.4	2.0	3.1	3.5	4.6	2.3	5.3	5.0	1.4	1.4
December	3.0	3.4	5.5	2.0	3.1	3.5	4.5	2.3	5.2	4.9	1.5	1.5
2012												
January	3.0	3.4	5.5	1.8	3.3	3.9	4.2	2.5	5.2	5.0	1.3	1.4
February	3.1	3.5	5.7	2.0	3.1	3.7	4.8	2.3	5.5	5.1	1.4	1.4
March	3.1	3.5	5.1	2.0	3.3	3.8	4.7	2.3	5.5	5.4	1.4	1.4
April	3.1	3.5	5.2	2.0	3.2	3.8	4.8	2.3	5.2	4.9	1.4	1.4
May	3.4	3.7	6.5	2.1	3.3	4.0	5.8	2.4	5.2	4.9	1.4	1.4
June	3.2	3.5	6.2	2.2	3.3	3.8	5.1	2.4	5.0	4.9	1.4	1.4
July	3.1	3.4	6.5	1.9	3.2	3.8	4.5	2.3	5.0	4.9	1.4	1.4
August	3.3	3.6	5.7	2.1	3.5	4.0	5.1	2.3	5.3	5.5	1.3	1.4
September[8]	3.0	3.4	6.4	2.0	3.2	3.7	4.6	2.1	4.9	4.9	1.2	1.2

[1]Total separations are the number of separations during the entire month.
[2]The total separations rate is the number of total separations during the entire month as a percent of total employment.
[4]Includes natural resources and mining, information, financial activities, and other services, not shown separately.
[5]Includes wholesale trade and transportation, warehousing, and utilities, not shown separately.
[6]Includes arts, entertainment, and recreation, not shown separately.
[7]Includes federal government, not shown separately.
[8]Preliminary data.

Table 7-10. Quits Levels[1] and Rates,[2] by Industry, December 2000–September 2012

(Seasonally adjusted, levels in thousands, rates per 100.)

Year and month	Total[4]	Total private[4]	Construction	Manufacturing	Trade, transportation, and utilities[5]	Retail trade	Professional and business services	Education and health services	Leisure and hospitality[6]	Accommodation and food services	Government[7]	State and local government
2000												
December	3 092	2 947	125	318	689	560	518	307	626	585	146	128
2001												
January	3 246	3 055	153	296	682	478	573	280	692	651	191	170
February	3 270	3 095	168	241	839	596	538	322	600	548	176	159
March	3 134	2 972	203	240	727	523	566	329	596	547	162	146
April	3 159	2 997	201	223	777	582	554	317	598	531	162	147
May	3 086	2 907	163	214	752	536	557	305	610	545	179	163
June	2 969	2 841	162	199	757	559	513	312	583	523	128	116
July	2 961	2 820	165	173	710	529	537	280	592	537	141	123
August	2 869	2 707	146	192	642	476	497	267	600	529	162	146
September	2 790	2 652	146	176	651	482	474	299	597	531	138	124
October	2 848	2 715	148	192	673	515	520	274	558	497	133	112
November	2 668	2 508	155	176	590	448	512	274	496	438	160	138
December	2 613	2 440	134	160	638	482	450	279	482	419	173	143
2002												
January	2 824	2 675	165	177	647	470	544	268	564	494	149	128
February	2 706	2 534	166	187	553	409	512	264	540	473	172	152
March	2 583	2 453	139	187	558	417	521	226	538	474	130	110
April	2 715	2 540	173	197	575	397	486	272	560	496	175	156
May	2 654	2 519	155	197	540	390	514	279	525	461	135	120
June	2 591	2 442	126	198	623	470	422	259	506	453	149	122
July	2 639	2 500	169	194	576	419	459	287	510	462	139	120
August	2 617	2 475	157	195	570	413	482	272	497	453	142	122
September	2 630	2 485	171	189	551	414	501	244	517	457	145	125
October	2 551	2 405	144	169	559	389	491	275	483	437	145	126
November	2 503	2 342	106	175	565	442	480	265	472	442	161	140
December	2 658	2 510	146	155	532	409	562	298	489	444	149	121
2003												
January	2 492	2 357	142	174	519	384	451	276	483	437	135	117
February	2 511	2 376	140	166	554	430	443	263	512	465	134	116
March	2 426	2 289	128	156	555	396	415	244	483	439	137	119
April	2 352	2 222	91	164	511	378	428	239	480	443	130	110
May	2 318	2 184	154	178	527	398	338	255	443	412	134	115
June	2 333	2 214	156	164	493	370	398	264	487	441	120	103
July	2 333	2 195	144	182	509	377	397	231	497	450	138	119
August	2 307	2 167	153	168	502	370	370	261	480	429	139	119
September	2 469	2 336	138	171	561	410	368	299	487	433	133	117
October	2 454	2 323	145	169	575	422	369	274	513	463	131	115
November	2 428	2 301	164	179	539	370	342	256	500	438	127	113
December	2 461	2 323	191	195	521	366	393	272	466	424	137	122
2004												
January	2 411	2 274	152	191	556	428	345	279	457	422	137	119
February	2 434	2 285	160	186	541	405	355	268	474	448	149	126
March	2 620	2 483	170	197	571	433	444	277	519	478	138	122
April	2 609	2 467	170	202	612	478	362	278	518	463	141	131
May	2 436	2 298	156	173	536	387	316	270	536	498	138	121
June	2 665	2 524	185	194	578	423	443	268	499	460	141	129
July	2 673	2 538	137	191	613	451	435	305	506	459	135	123
August	2 588	2 459	157	171	601	471	453	268	521	478	129	118
September	2 603	2 468	167	208	590	437	442	264	497	454	135	124
October	2 623	2 496	165	182	612	457	441	256	495	451	127	112
November	2 854	2 718	173	210	664	501	492	281	580	528	136	121
December	2 745	2 599	160	210	579	419	479	277	541	492	146	133
2005												
January	2 832	2 696	181	190	645	460	469	286	578	521	136	124
February	2 703	2 557	174	187	584	429	488	294	506	453	146	131
March	2 847	2 695	202	188	666	489	468	310	531	476	152	138
April	2 821	2 682	163	191	632	478	516	319	528	472	140	126
May	2 820	2 678	180	177	648	500	484	292	566	509	142	130
June	2 784	2 633	165	200	646	481	468	299	529	473	150	134
July	2 771	2 656	177	196	632	474	414	300	609	551	116	102
August	2 972	2 825	200	195	677	500	481	297	608	558	147	133
September	3 066	2 911	239	207	641	466	522	318	640	587	155	137
October	2 970	2 805	226	222	641	477	412	298	696	621	166	148
November	2 934	2 774	195	199	657	493	407	305	634	586	160	142
December	2 864	2 718	229	185	713	528	419	295	572	520	146	126
2006												
January	2 886	2 732	211	189	622	473	456	266	663	592	155	141
February	3 011	2 852	199	204	683	514	456	303	653	604	158	138
March	3 025	2 864	202	208	696	523	484	285	630	573	161	137
April	2 776	2 613	203	178	683	506	480	289	542	490	162	137
May	3 042	2 862	212	222	690	506	494	320	605	556	179	154
June	3 005	2 836	203	185	648	477	469	336	644	590	169	144
July	2 965	2 803	184	214	685	522	464	319	578	537	161	135
August	2 975	2 802	169	205	702	476	483	320	595	551	173	144
September	2 920	2 755	170	179	641	467	541	290	591	551	165	124
October	2 955	2 794	169	202	635	466	526	315	606	552	161	143
November	3 139	2 972	160	230	738	542	534	310	650	586	167	142
December	3 129	2 963	171	246	680	491	547	343	659	598	166	145

[1]Quits are the number of quits during the entire month.
[2]The quits rate is the number of quits during the entire month as a percent of total employment.
[3]Detail will not necessarily add to totals because of the independent seasonal adjustment of the various series.
[4]Includes natural resources and mining, information, financial activities, and other services, not shown separately.
[5]Includes wholesale trade and transportation, warehousing, and utilities, not shown separately.
[6]Includes arts, entertainment, and recreation, not shown separately.
[7]Includes federal government, not shown separately.

Table 7-10. Quits Levels[1] and Rates,[2] by Industry, December 2000–September 2012—*Continued*

(Seasonally adjusted, levels in thousands, rates per 100.)

Year and month	Rate											
	Total[4]	Total private[4]	Construction	Manufacturing	Trade, transportation, and utilities[5]	Retail trade	Professional and business services	Education and health services	Leisure and hospitality[6]	Accommodation and food services	Government[7]	State and local government
2000												
December	0.7	2.6	1.8	1.9	2.6	3.6	3.1	2.0	5.2	5.7	0.7	2.3
2001												
January	0.9	2.7	2.2	1.7	2.6	3.1	3.4	1.8	5.8	6.4	0.9	2.5
February	0.9	2.8	2.5	1.4	3.2	3.9	3.2	2.1	5.0	5.4	0.8	2.5
March	0.8	2.7	3.0	1.4	2.8	3.4	3.4	2.1	5.0	5.4	0.8	2.4
April	0.8	2.7	2.9	1.3	3.0	3.8	3.3	2.0	5.0	5.2	0.8	2.4
May	0.9	2.6	2.4	1.3	2.9	3.5	3.4	2.0	5.1	5.3	0.9	2.3
June	0.6	2.6	2.4	1.2	2.9	3.7	3.1	2.0	4.8	5.1	0.6	2.2
July	0.7	2.5	2.4	1.1	2.7	3.5	3.3	1.8	4.9	5.2	0.7	2.2
August	0.8	2.4	2.1	1.2	2.5	3.1	3.0	1.7	5.0	5.2	0.8	2.2
September	0.7	2.4	2.1	1.1	2.5	3.2	2.9	1.9	4.9	5.2	0.7	2.1
October	0.6	2.5	2.2	1.2	2.6	3.4	3.2	1.7	4.6	4.9	0.6	2.2
November	0.7	2.3	2.3	1.1	2.3	3.0	3.2	1.7	4.1	4.3	0.8	2.0
December	0.8	2.2	2.0	1.0	2.5	3.2	2.8	1.8	4.0	4.1	0.8	2.0
2002												
January	0.7	2.4	2.4	1.1	2.5	3.1	3.4	1.7	4.7	4.8	0.7	2.2
February	0.8	2.3	2.5	1.2	2.2	2.7	3.2	1.6	4.5	4.7	0.8	2.1
March	0.6	2.3	2.1	1.2	2.2	2.8	3.3	1.4	4.5	4.7	0.6	2.0
April	0.8	2.3	2.6	1.3	2.3	2.6	3.0	1.7	4.7	4.9	0.8	2.1
May	0.6	2.3	2.3	1.3	2.1	2.6	3.2	1.7	4.4	4.5	0.6	2.0
June	0.7	2.2	1.9	1.3	2.4	3.1	2.6	1.6	4.3	4.5	0.7	2.0
July	0.6	2.3	2.5	1.3	2.3	2.8	2.9	1.8	4.3	4.5	0.6	2.0
August	0.6	2.3	2.3	1.3	2.2	2.8	3.0	1.7	4.2	4.4	0.7	2.0
September	0.7	2.3	2.5	1.2	2.2	2.8	3.1	1.5	4.3	4.5	0.7	2.0
October	0.7	2.2	2.2	1.1	2.2	2.6	3.1	1.7	4.0	4.2	0.7	2.0
November	0.7	2.2	1.6	1.2	2.2	3.0	3.0	1.6	3.9	4.3	0.7	1.9
December	0.6	2.3	2.2	1.0	2.1	2.7	3.5	1.8	4.0	4.3	0.7	2.0
2003												
January	0.6	2.2	2.1	1.2	2.0	2.6	2.8	1.7	4.0	4.2	0.6	1.9
February	0.6	2.2	2.1	1.1	2.2	2.9	2.8	1.6	4.2	4.5	0.6	1.9
March	0.6	2.1	1.9	1.1	2.2	2.7	2.6	1.5	4.0	4.3	0.6	1.9
April	0.6	2.1	1.4	1.1	2.0	2.5	2.7	1.4	4.0	4.3	0.6	1.8
May	0.6	2.0	2.3	1.2	2.1	2.7	2.1	1.5	3.7	4.0	0.6	1.8
June	0.5	2.0	2.3	1.1	2.0	2.5	2.5	1.6	4.0	4.3	0.6	1.8
July	0.6	2.0	2.1	1.3	2.0	2.5	2.5	1.4	4.1	4.4	0.6	1.8
August	0.6	2.0	2.3	1.2	2.0	2.5	2.3	1.6	3.9	4.1	0.6	1.8
September	0.6	2.2	2.0	1.2	2.2	2.7	2.3	1.8	4.0	4.2	0.6	1.9
October	0.6	2.1	2.1	1.2	2.3	2.8	2.3	1.6	4.2	4.4	0.6	1.9
November	0.6	2.1	2.4	1.2	2.1	2.5	2.1	1.5	4.1	4.2	0.6	1.9
December	0.7	2.1	2.8	1.4	2.1	2.4	2.4	1.6	3.8	4.0	0.6	1.9
2004												
January	0.6	2.1	2.2	1.3	2.2	2.9	2.1	1.7	3.7	4.0	0.6	1.8
February	0.7	2.1	2.3	1.3	2.1	2.7	2.2	1.6	3.8	4.3	0.7	1.9
March	0.6	2.3	2.5	1.4	2.2	2.9	2.7	1.6	4.2	4.5	0.6	2.0
April	0.7	2.3	2.5	1.4	2.4	3.2	2.2	1.6	4.2	4.4	0.7	2.0
May	0.6	2.1	2.2	1.2	2.1	2.6	1.9	1.6	4.3	4.7	0.6	1.9
June	0.7	2.3	2.7	1.4	2.3	2.8	2.7	1.6	4.0	4.3	0.7	2.0
July	0.7	2.3	2.0	1.3	2.4	3.0	2.6	1.8	4.0	4.3	0.6	2.0
August	0.6	2.2	2.2	1.2	2.4	3.1	2.8	1.6	4.2	4.5	0.6	2.0
September	0.7	2.2	2.4	1.5	2.3	2.9	2.7	1.6	4.0	4.2	0.6	2.0
October	0.6	2.3	2.3	1.3	2.4	3.0	2.7	1.5	3.9	4.2	0.6	2.0
November	0.6	2.5	2.4	1.5	2.6	3.3	3.0	1.6	4.6	4.9	0.6	2.2
December	0.7	2.3	2.3	1.5	2.3	2.8	2.9	1.6	4.3	4.6	0.7	2.1
2005												
January	0.7	2.4	2.5	1.3	2.5	3.0	2.8	1.7	4.6	4.8	0.6	2.1
February	0.7	2.3	2.4	1.3	2.3	2.8	2.9	1.7	4.0	4.2	0.7	2.0
March	0.7	2.4	2.8	1.3	2.6	3.2	2.8	1.8	4.2	4.4	0.7	2.1
April	0.7	2.4	2.2	1.3	2.4	3.1	3.1	1.8	4.1	4.3	0.6	2.1
May	0.7	2.4	2.5	1.2	2.5	3.3	2.9	1.7	4.4	4.7	0.7	2.1
June	0.7	2.4	2.3	1.4	2.5	3.1	2.8	1.7	4.1	4.3	0.7	2.1
July	0.5	2.4	2.4	1.4	2.4	3.1	2.4	1.7	4.7	5.0	0.5	2.1
August	0.7	2.5	2.7	1.4	2.6	3.3	2.8	1.7	4.7	5.1	0.7	2.2
September	0.7	2.6	3.2	1.5	2.5	3.0	3.1	1.8	5.0	5.4	0.7	2.3
October	0.8	2.5	3.0	1.6	2.5	3.1	2.4	1.7	5.4	5.7	0.8	2.2
November	0.7	2.5	2.6	1.4	2.5	3.2	2.4	1.7	4.9	5.3	0.7	2.2
December	0.7	2.4	3.0	1.3	2.7	3.4	2.4	1.7	4.4	4.7	0.7	2.1
2006												
January	0.7	2.4	2.8	1.3	2.4	3.1	2.6	1.5	5.1	5.4	0.7	2.1
February	0.7	2.5	2.6	1.4	2.6	3.3	2.6	1.7	5.0	5.4	0.7	2.2
March	0.7	2.5	2.6	1.5	2.7	3.4	2.8	1.6	4.8	5.2	0.7	2.2
April	0.7	2.3	2.6	1.3	2.6	3.3	2.8	1.6	4.1	4.4	0.7	2.0
May	0.8	2.5	2.7	1.6	2.6	3.3	2.8	1.8	4.6	5.0	0.8	2.2
June	0.7	2.5	2.6	1.3	2.5	3.1	2.7	1.9	4.9	5.3	0.8	2.2
July	0.7	2.5	2.4	1.5	2.6	3.4	2.6	1.8	4.4	4.8	0.7	2.2
August	0.7	2.4	2.2	1.4	2.7	3.1	2.7	1.8	4.5	4.9	0.8	2.2
September	0.6	2.4	2.2	1.3	2.4	3.0	3.1	1.6	4.5	4.9	0.7	2.1
October	0.7	2.4	2.2	1.4	2.4	3.0	3.0	1.8	4.6	4.9	0.7	2.2
November	0.7	2.6	2.1	1.6	2.8	3.5	3.0	1.7	4.9	5.2	0.8	2.3
December	0.7	2.6	2.2	1.8	2.6	3.2	3.1	1.9	5.0	5.3	0.8	2.3

[1]Quits are the number of quits during the entire month.
[2]The quits rate is the number of quits during the entire month as a percent of total employment.
[4]Includes natural resources and mining, information, financial activities, and other services, not shown separately.
[5]Includes wholesale trade and transportation, warehousing, and utilities, not shown separately.
[6]Includes arts, entertainment, and recreation, not shown separately.
[7]Includes federal government, not shown separately.

Table 7-10. Quits Levels[1] and Rates,[2] by Industry, December 2000–September 2012—*Continued*

(Seasonally adjusted, levels in thousands, rates per 100.)

Year and month	Level[3]											
	Total[4]	Total private[4]	Construction	Manufacturing	Trade, transportation, and utilities[5]	Retail trade	Professional and business services	Education and health services	Leisure and hospitality[6]	Accommodation and food services	Government[7]	State and local government
2007												
January	2 990	2 826	163	241	651	465	533	301	618	573	164	148
February	2 993	2 839	143	211	686	489	513	316	635	580	154	133
March	3 008	2 833	143	225	654	467	514	304	618	559	176	147
April	2 903	2 736	153	205	662	477	468	308	635	586	168	144
May	3 006	2 827	160	212	681	487	465	336	615	571	180	153
June	2 836	2 673	135	198	658	467	458	289	627	575	163	136
July	2 880	2 715	182	189	584	433	483	318	639	585	165	135
August	2 892	2 741	166	209	604	447	464	311	632	569	151	127
September	2 597	2 440	138	188	606	450	457	262	471	421	158	126
October	2 845	2 692	162	198	625	457	462	290	625	574	153	138
November	2 793	2 642	160	189	541	404	475	312	663	608	151	138
December	2 876	2 741	160	212	677	513	437	291	638	574	135	125
2008												
January	2 843	2 702	148	198	658	483	440	314	596	530	141	129
February	2 844	2 705	168	193	624	441	483	304	601	552	139	128
March	2 624	2 493	111	189	574	412	410	317	594	551	131	122
April	2 888	2 738	165	176	623	448	529	333	598	550	150	140
May	2 670	2 531	132	157	592	415	473	266	632	580	138	131
June	2 658	2 526	145	161	582	417	478	284	576	533	131	124
July	2 454	2 330	147	141	538	391	437	293	545	492	124	117
August	2 462	2 318	158	141	561	417	357	282	516	474	143	135
September	2 453	2 318	110	150	558	415	404	277	534	488	136	128
October	2 404	2 277	110	141	536	370	437	286	518	481	126	119
November	2 107	1 990	89	121	482	350	363	250	461	432	117	112
December	2 070	1 947	82	100	508	365	360	235	445	420	123	116
2009												
January	1 988	1 883	86	111	455	346	356	239	423	395	105	99
February	1 921	1 820	87	101	384	290	289	266	423	388	101	98
March	1 839	1 741	85	86	435	319	280	237	399	369	98	95
April	1 749	1 650	66	81	365	263	299	227	394	357	99	96
May	1 745	1 647	79	87	367	269	304	237	380	341	98	87
June	1 750	1 652	79	90	379	288	275	254	386	341	99	92
July	1 690	1 589	69	86	385	280	260	237	365	326	101	98
August	1 689	1 585	62	79	388	293	252	241	383	345	104	93
September	1 605	1 514	72	95	373	267	254	257	297	286	91	86
October	1 653	1 551	57	76	367	268	266	255	348	317	102	98
November	1 766	1 662	83	71	393	263	271	249	388	349	104	95
December	1 689	1 581	80	69	370	280	265	255	359	328	108	98
2010												
January	1 700	1 598	100	81	345	250	272	237	398	342	102	99
February	1 780	1 664	76	100	412	317	291	235	371	339	116	104
March	1 815	1 705	81	87	390	291	307	241	376	345	109	97
April	1 874	1 772	64	93	443	339	305	284	375	338	102	93
May	1 783	1 688	59	85	403	304	305	239	383	347	95	82
June	1 914	1 783	66	99	414	312	362	258	352	324	131	105
July	1 822	1 714	73	93	423	325	325	240	365	335	108	88
August	1 827	1 711	85	104	392	287	334	231	371	336	116	100
September	1 893	1 768	80	98	429	332	332	246	366	329	124	112
October	1 842	1 738	76	97	401	312	351	242	384	333	104	95
November	1 811	1 703	53	99	419	319	307	253	365	324	108	100
December	1 929	1 824	89	99	397	289	362	242	391	348	105	98
2011												
January	1 803	1 693	65	96	377	275	355	231	370	334	110	102
February	1 918	1 809	69	91	456	321	390	236	358	318	109	101
March	1 979	1 877	74	110	439	333	377	259	409	364	102	94
April	1 874	1 769	98	107	411	314	360	236	389	347	105	96
May	1 996	1 874	91	109	473	351	366	247	383	344	122	113
June	1 930	1 819	78	109	453	342	344	241	408	366	110	101
July	2 002	1 880	74	104	425	321	392	241	406	362	122	113
August	2 048	1 932	69	99	439	327	387	270	439	394	116	106
September	2 015	1 902	80	99	456	336	395	244	403	358	114	104
October	1 983	1 869	80	105	461	330	368	242	374	334	114	102
November	1 976	1 860	91	121	413	294	380	247	370	335	116	106
December	2 008	1 867	76	113	447	331	363	265	388	340	141	131
2012												
January	2 002	1 876	70	97	449	342	352	282	398	355	125	116
February	2 072	1 947	75	102	461	345	371	287	425	368	125	113
March	2 159	2 025	74	112	472	343	380	284	471	425	134	122
April	2 114	1 969	70	114	455	332	396	266	445	398	145	132
May	2 176	2 041	79	117	440	318	439	269	448	396	136	124
June	2 133	1 998	86	108	465	330	400	269	440	391	135	126
July	2 163	2 033	87	107	482	340	386	279	432	385	130	119
August	2 151	2 025	75	113	471	337	386	277	430	386	125	115
September[8]	1 976	1 861	66	112	443	330	379	244	402	367	115	106

[1]Quits are the number of quits during the entire month.
[2]The quits rate is the number of quits during the entire month as a percent of total employment.
[3]Detail will not necessarily add to totals because of the independent seasonal adjustment of the various series.
[4]Includes natural resources and mining, information, financial activities, and other services, not shown separately.
[5]Includes wholesale trade and transportation, warehousing, and utilities, not shown separately.
[6]Includes arts, entertainment, and recreation, not shown separately.
[7]Includes federal government, not shown separately.
[8]Preliminary data.

Table 7-10. Quits Levels[1] and Rates,[2] by Industry, December 2000–September 2012—*Continued*

(Seasonally adjusted, levels in thousands, rates per 100.)

Year and month	Rate											
	Total[4]	Total private[4]	Construction	Manufacturing	Trade, transportation, and utilities[5]	Retail trade	Professional and business services	Education and health services	Leisure and hospitality[6]	Accommodation and food services	Government[7]	State and local government
2007												
January	0.8	2.5	2.1	1.7	2.5	3.0	3.0	1.7	4.6	5.0	0.7	2.2
February	0.7	2.5	1.9	1.5	2.6	3.2	2.9	1.7	4.8	5.1	0.7	2.2
March	0.8	2.5	1.9	1.6	2.5	3.0	2.9	1.7	4.6	4.9	0.8	2.2
April	0.7	2.4	2.0	1.5	2.5	3.1	2.6	1.7	4.7	5.1	0.8	2.1
May	0.8	2.4	2.1	1.5	2.6	3.1	2.6	1.8	4.6	5.0	0.8	2.2
June	0.7	2.3	1.8	1.4	2.5	3.0	2.6	1.6	4.7	5.0	0.7	2.1
July	0.7	2.4	2.4	1.4	2.2	2.8	2.7	1.7	4.8	5.1	0.7	2.1
August	0.7	2.4	2.2	1.5	2.3	2.9	2.6	1.7	4.7	5.0	0.7	2.1
September	0.6	2.1	1.8	1.4	2.3	2.9	2.5	1.4	3.5	3.7	0.7	1.9
October	0.7	2.3	2.1	1.4	2.3	2.9	2.6	1.6	4.6	5.0	0.7	2.1
November	0.7	2.3	2.1	1.4	2.0	2.6	2.6	1.7	4.9	5.3	0.7	2.0
December	0.6	2.4	2.1	1.5	2.5	3.3	2.4	1.6	4.7	5.0	0.6	2.1
2008												
January	0.7	2.3	2.0	1.4	2.5	3.1	2.4	1.7	4.4	4.6	0.6	2.1
February	0.6	2.3	2.3	1.4	2.3	2.8	2.7	1.6	4.4	4.8	0.6	2.1
March	0.6	2.2	1.5	1.4	2.2	2.7	2.3	1.7	4.4	4.8	0.6	1.9
April	0.7	2.4	2.3	1.3	2.3	2.9	2.9	1.8	4.4	4.8	0.7	2.1
May	0.7	2.2	1.8	1.2	2.2	2.7	2.6	1.4	4.7	5.0	0.6	1.9
June	0.6	2.2	2.0	1.2	2.2	2.7	2.7	1.5	4.3	4.6	0.6	1.9
July	0.6	2.0	2.1	1.0	2.0	2.6	2.5	1.6	4.1	4.3	0.6	1.8
August	0.7	2.0	2.2	1.1	2.1	2.7	2.0	1.5	3.8	4.1	0.6	1.8
September	0.6	2.0	1.6	1.1	2.1	2.7	2.3	1.5	4.0	4.3	0.6	1.8
October	0.6	2.0	1.6	1.1	2.1	2.4	2.5	1.5	3.9	4.2	0.6	1.8
November	0.6	1.8	1.3	0.9	1.9	2.3	2.1	1.3	3.5	3.8	0.5	1.6
December	0.6	1.7	1.2	0.8	2.0	2.5	2.1	1.2	3.4	3.7	0.5	1.5
2009												
January	0.5	1.7	1.3	0.9	1.8	2.3	2.1	1.3	3.2	3.5	0.5	1.5
February	0.5	1.7	1.4	0.8	1.5	2.0	1.7	1.4	3.2	3.5	0.4	1.4
March	0.5	1.6	1.3	0.7	1.7	2.2	1.7	1.2	3.0	3.3	0.4	1.4
April	0.5	1.5	1.1	0.7	1.5	1.8	1.8	1.2	3.0	3.2	0.4	1.3
May	0.4	1.5	1.3	0.7	1.5	1.8	1.8	1.2	2.9	3.0	0.4	1.3
June	0.5	1.5	1.3	0.8	1.5	2.0	1.7	1.3	3.0	3.0	0.4	1.3
July	0.5	1.5	1.2	0.7	1.6	1.9	1.6	1.2	2.8	2.9	0.4	1.3
August	0.5	1.5	1.1	0.7	1.6	2.0	1.5	1.3	2.9	3.1	0.5	1.3
September	0.4	1.4	1.2	0.8	1.5	1.9	1.6	1.3	2.3	2.6	0.4	1.2
October	0.5	1.4	1.0	0.7	1.5	1.9	1.6	1.3	2.7	2.9	0.5	1.3
November	0.5	1.6	1.5	0.6	1.6	1.8	1.6	1.3	3.0	3.1	0.5	1.4
December	0.5	1.5	1.4	0.6	1.5	1.9	1.6	1.3	2.8	3.0	0.5	1.3
2010												
January	0.5	1.5	1.8	0.7	1.4	1.7	1.6	1.2	3.1	3.1	0.5	1.3
February	0.5	1.6	1.4	0.9	1.7	2.2	1.8	1.2	2.9	3.1	0.5	1.4
March	0.5	1.6	1.5	0.8	1.6	2.0	1.9	1.2	2.9	3.1	0.5	1.4
April	0.5	1.7	1.2	0.8	1.8	2.4	1.8	1.5	2.9	3.0	0.5	1.4
May	0.4	1.6	1.1	0.7	1.6	2.1	1.8	1.2	2.9	3.1	0.4	1.4
June	0.5	1.7	1.2	0.9	1.7	2.2	2.2	1.3	2.7	2.9	0.6	1.5
July	0.4	1.6	1.3	0.8	1.7	2.2	1.9	1.2	2.8	3.0	0.5	1.4
August	0.5	1.6	1.5	0.9	1.6	2.0	2.0	1.2	2.8	3.0	0.5	1.4
September	0.6	1.6	1.5	0.9	1.7	2.3	2.0	1.3	2.8	2.9	0.6	1.5
October	0.5	1.6	1.4	0.8	1.6	2.1	2.1	1.2	2.9	3.0	0.5	1.4
November	0.5	1.6	1.0	0.9	1.7	2.2	1.8	1.3	2.8	2.9	0.5	1.4
December	0.5	1.7	1.6	0.9	1.6	2.0	2.1	1.2	3.0	3.1	0.5	1.5
2011												
January	0.5	1.6	1.2	0.8	1.5	1.9	2.1	1.2	2.8	3.0	0.5	1.4
February	0.5	1.7	1.2	0.8	1.8	2.2	2.3	1.2	2.7	2.8	0.5	1.5
March	0.5	1.7	1.4	0.9	1.8	2.3	2.2	1.3	3.1	3.2	0.5	1.5
April	0.5	1.6	1.8	0.9	1.6	2.1	2.1	1.2	2.9	3.1	0.5	1.4
May	0.6	1.7	1.7	0.9	1.9	2.4	2.1	1.2	2.9	3.0	0.6	1.5
June	0.5	1.7	1.4	0.9	1.8	2.3	2.0	1.2	3.1	3.2	0.5	1.5
July	0.6	1.7	1.3	0.9	1.7	2.2	2.3	1.2	3.0	3.2	0.6	1.5
August	0.6	1.8	1.3	0.8	1.8	2.2	2.2	1.4	3.3	3.4	0.5	1.6
September	0.5	1.7	1.4	0.8	1.8	2.3	2.3	1.2	3.0	3.1	0.5	1.5
October	0.5	1.7	1.5	0.9	1.8	2.2	2.1	1.2	2.8	2.9	0.5	1.5
November	0.6	1.7	1.7	1.0	1.6	2.0	2.2	1.2	2.8	2.9	0.5	1.5
December	0.7	1.7	1.4	1.0	1.8	2.2	2.1	1.3	2.9	2.9	0.6	1.5
2012												
January	0.6	1.7	1.3	0.8	1.8	2.3	2.0	1.4	2.9	3.1	0.6	0.6
February	0.6	1.8	1.3	0.9	1.8	2.3	2.1	1.4	3.1	3.2	0.6	0.6
March	0.6	1.8	1.3	0.9	1.9	2.3	2.1	1.4	3.5	3.6	0.6	0.6
April	0.7	1.8	1.3	1.0	1.8	2.3	2.2	1.3	3.3	3.4	0.7	0.7
May	0.6	1.8	1.4	1.0	1.7	2.2	2.5	1.3	3.3	3.4	0.6	0.6
June	0.7	1.8	1.6	0.9	1.8	2.2	2.2	1.3	3.2	3.3	0.6	0.7
July	0.6	1.8	1.6	0.9	1.9	2.3	2.2	1.4	3.2	3.3	0.6	0.6
August	0.6	1.8	1.4	0.9	1.9	2.3	2.2	1.4	3.2	3.3	0.6	0.6
September[8]	0.6	1.7	1.2	0.9	1.7	2.2	2.1	1.2	2.9	3.1	0.5	0.6

[1]Quits are the number of quits during the entire month.
[2]The quits rate is the number of quits during the entire month as a percent of total employment.
[4]Includes natural resources and mining, information, financial activities, and other services, not shown separately.
[5]Includes wholesale trade and transportation, warehousing, and utilities, not shown separately.
[6]Includes arts, entertainment, and recreation, not shown separately.
[7]Includes federal government, not shown separately.
[8]Preliminary data.

Table 7-11. Layoffs and Discharges Levels[1] and Rates,[2] by Industry, December 2000–September 2012

(Not seasonally adjusted, levels in thousands, rates per 100.)

Year and month	Level												
	Total	Total private	Mining and logging	Construc-tion	Manufac-turing	Durable goods	Non-durable goods	Trade, transpor-tation, and utilities	Whole-sale trade	Retail trade	Transpor-tation, ware-housing, and utilities	Infor-mation	Financial activities
2007	22 142	20 834	88	2 837	1 952	1 202	751	4 187	764	2 733	691	284	1 079
2008	24 166	23 015	120	3 420	2 252	1 441	809	4 718	898	3 027	796	364	1 030
2009	26 783	25 172	178	3 743	2 863	1 836	1 028	5 007	1 083	2 875	1 047	379	1 264
2010	21 784	19 729	98	3 105	1 655	954	701	3 720	741	2 315	669	292	776
2011	20 718	19 394	84	2 865	1 327	747	581	3 400	591	2 154	655	284	650
2000													
December	2 034	1 970	25	371	217	113	104	440	99	311	30	28	27
2001													
January	3 037	2 970	9	347	331	231	100	824	117	636	71	57	149
February	1 442	1 397	4	271	213	122	91	234	64	150	20	38	44
March	1 800	1 754	9	229	242	137	105	319	36	254	29	35	54
April	1 849	1 797	6	159	320	202	118	295	67	174	55	53	61
May	1 680	1 583	5	198	257	143	114	326	50	220	57	40	44
June	1 821	1 681	10	223	284	154	130	302	43	202	57	50	41
July	2 003	1 923	9	217	282	161	121	367	99	215	53	40	52
August	1 971	1 760	9	256	229	142	87	264	53	170	42	45	41
September	2 178	2 069	7	244	230	135	94	352	65	229	59	42	87
October	2 556	2 443	9	334	350	223	127	407	126	223	58	64	88
November	2 132	2 083	14	349	270	162	108	389	97	190	102	71	76
December	2 030	1 966	18	366	285	157	127	445	68	267	110	41	67
2002													
January	2 495	2 429	10	335	318	201	117	605	70	451	84	81	137
February	1 624	1 577	7	253	196	108	88	403	70	263	71	24	55
March	1 432	1 390	10	202	189	132	56	282	59	163	59	36	44
April	1 798	1 740	11	200	231	147	84	329	55	219	55	52	57
May	1 622	1 525	7	212	192	116	76	374	80	257	37	30	75
June	1 725	1 577	5	228	196	118	78	269	49	160	60	40	87
July	2 138	2 003	14	251	211	126	86	334	89	200	44	38	73
August	1 930	1 780	8	234	202	142	61	313	50	206	57	37	81
September	2 017	1 845	6	233	199	127	72	368	65	228	74	25	67
October	2 091	2 012	7	327	244	153	91	353	48	256	49	38	56
November	1 881	1 808	6	296	201	120	82	339	82	201	56	53	68
December	2 169	2 106	10	326	257	140	117	485	75	321	88	29	63
2003													
January	2 602	2 531	14	377	273	167	106	640	84	495	61	69	121
February	1 611	1 558	9	226	187	114	73	358	39	282	37	37	39
March	1 488	1 441	8	223	186	112	75	287	47	197	43	38	65
April	1 819	1 750	7	250	235	144	91	277	59	175	43	20	42
May	1 592	1 491	5	205	139	81	59	291	65	172	54	26	51
June	1 925	1 777	7	206	195	124	71	362	51	227	84	35	48
July	2 023	1 895	8	235	219	125	95	371	87	192	91	28	103
August	2 159	1 968	10	318	154	106	48	349	64	219	65	26	50
September	1 929	1 759	4	285	149	92	57	253	52	154	47	19	73
October	2 147	2 071	6	291	169	99	70	424	80	273	71	31	59
November	1 813	1 722	7	288	165	117	48	344	39	257	49	31	45
December	2 186	2 101	17	273	173	101	72	602	61	417	123	33	58
2004													
January	2 462	2 388	10	331	203	122	81	621	75	458	88	42	77
February	1 559	1 511	8	261	138	79	59	412	69	292	52	30	35
March	1 538	1 484	5	222	149	93	55	309	57	180	72	42	56
April	1 844	1 793	6	200	167	83	84	336	92	194	50	27	47
May	1 521	1 428	6	168	132	66	66	349	60	209	80	32	36
June	1 728	1 561	4	187	134	91	43	280	55	164	62	43	57
July	1 843	1 707	6	216	164	105	59	370	67	237	66	23	47
August	2 139	1 982	8	256	200	138	61	328	76	175	77	20	104
September	2 065	1 868	5	214	150	97	54	311	50	191	70	40	70
October	2 059	1 960	7	302	190	112	78	364	67	220	77	31	81
November	1 864	1 777	9	268	161	106	55	365	63	236	67	20	69
December	2 180	2 074	8	296	158	97	60	626	44	454	128	23	74
2005													
January	2 476	2 405	10	419	207	137	71	566	75	412	78	37	117
February	1 573	1 521	6	238	119	78	41	374	49	262	62	15	70
March	1 595	1 545	5	165	145	81	63	301	38	213	50	23	59
April	1 751	1 690	7	214	166	112	54	326	69	196	61	19	88
May	1 637	1 531	4	216	140	93	47	364	79	181	104	30	57
June	1 811	1 652	5	187	130	80	50	329	46	203	81	18	28
July	1 873	1 749	6	188	133	84	49	355	62	226	66	23	62
August	2 016	1 841	7	257	154	106	48	311	46	209	57	17	53
September	2 050	1 886	8	231	151	89	62	379	34	266	78	19	76
October	1 843	1 759	7	232	151	94	57	352	72	209	71	19	85
November	1 621	1 548	4	237	150	73	77	347	77	185	85	25	60
December	1 939	1 843	8	285	147	81	66	524	78	283	164	21	61
2006													
January	2 167	2 081	5	334	172	84	88	570	57	427	86	17	87
February	1 420	1 369	6	181	116	63	52	328	60	235	33	18	61
March	1 353	1 288	8	178	157	86	71	255	38	158	59	16	72
April	1 672	1 608	10	143	142	65	77	298	52	217	29	35	80
May	1 672	1 561	3	177	143	87	57	329	56	216	57	12	50
June	1 687	1 479	2	127	142	76	66	349	47	241	62	15	52
July	1 798	1 645	4	199	143	89	55	334	98	181	54	20	73
August	1 741	1 595	6	211	144	87	57	312	47	206	60	19	80
September	1 840	1 666	9	194	162	101	61	313	53	195	65	16	67
October	1 970	1 876	5	257	154	95	59	338	67	206	65	30	73
November	1 864	1 787	6	322	147	96	51	304	51	203	51	21	66
December	1 973	1 887	7	293	157	91	66	463	45	337	81	26	84

[1]Layoffs and discharges are the number of layoffs and discharges during the entire month.
[2]The layoffs and discharges rate is the number of layoffs and discharges during the entire month as a percent of total employment.

Table 7-11. Layoffs and Discharges Levels[1] and Rates,[2] by Industry, December 2000–September 2012 —Continued

(Not seasonally adjusted, levels in thousands, rates per 100.)

Year and month	Level												
	Finance and insurance	Real estate and rental and leasing	Professional and business services	Education and health services	Educational services	Health care and social assistance	Leisure and hospitality	Arts, entertainment, and recreation	Accommodation and food services	Other services	Government	Federal	State and local government
2007	592	488	4 679	1 711	369	1 341	3 078	864	2 213	936	1 308	219	1 090
2008	616	415	5 036	1 980	382	1 598	3 130	900	2 231	961	1 149	102	1 047
2009	693	571	5 010	2 183	453	1 728	3 316	833	2 483	1 231	1 610	224	1 387
2010	450	325	4 326	2 089	399	1 691	2 742	785	1 959	924	2 050	742	1 312
2011	344	307	4 720	1 814	369	1 445	3 145	953	2 197	1 101	1 324	133	1 194
2000													
December	22	5	514	119	40	79	194	57	137	35	64	6	58
2001													
January	133	16	737	155	25	129	265	77	188	97	67	14	53
February	22	23	327	91	9	82	149	51	98	25	46	5	41
March	23	30	457	87	9	78	245	39	206	76	46	6	41
April	45	15	330	99	25	74	399	62	337	75	51	5	46
May	31	13	419	99	17	82	169	38	131	25	97	6	91
June	21	19	337	152	22	130	237	53	184	46	141	5	136
July	42	10	364	212	35	177	322	90	231	56	80	7	74
August	26	14	376	177	58	119	261	101	160	102	211	8	203
September	32	55	432	111	14	98	505	223	282	59	108	10	98
October	53	36	498	173	27	146	460	106	355	59	113	12	101
November	34	42	366	99	12	87	404	113	291	43	49	6	44
December	30	37	395	83	9	74	240	43	197	26	64	9	55
2002													
January	108	30	436	180	32	148	233	59	174	93	66	16	50
February	40	15	312	104	8	96	185	26	159	38	47	7	40
March	24	19	330	123	18	105	142	32	109	33	42	10	32
April	39	18	373	129	20	109	271	91	180	86	58	10	49
May	56	19	313	123	22	101	159	24	135	40	97	6	91
June	61	26	304	156	27	130	215	25	190	77	149	9	140
July	41	32	460	169	28	140	346	109	236	107	135	12	124
August	43	38	324	149	26	122	303	131	171	130	150	8	142
September	28	40	372	141	34	108	360	131	229	73	172	15	158
October	29	27	494	115	10	105	330	65	265	49	78	11	67
November	35	33	401	71	3	68	328	118	209	45	73	13	60
December	36	27	543	112	23	89	228	63	165	52	63	7	56
2003													
January	64	56	476	143	15	128	325	91	234	93	71	13	57
February	29	9	355	101	13	88	178	48	130	68	53	8	45
March	34	31	288	105	9	96	199	56	143	43	47	6	41
April	24	17	438	108	20	88	303	111	192	71	69	8	62
May	31	20	313	160	35	125	264	77	187	37	101	11	90
June	23	25	383	218	66	151	210	27	183	113	148	10	137
July	48	56	418	227	70	157	184	33	151	102	128	10	117
August	27	23	442	191	55	136	271	104	167	156	191	12	180
September	40	33	376	119	19	100	397	158	239	85	170	13	157
October	37	22	511	131	22	109	370	102	268	79	76	20	57
November	25	21	379	104	16	89	305	99	206	53	91	25	65
December	25	34	464	84	17	67	311	56	255	86	85	5	80
2004													
January	39	38	577	132	20	112	340	74	266	55	74	12	62
February	24	11	262	108	13	95	207	72	134	49	48	9	40
March	28	28	342	110	18	92	210	45	166	40	55	7	48
April	25	22	526	129	14	115	287	93	195	69	51	5	46
May	23	13	324	135	30	106	192	55	136	54	92	9	83
June	27	31	371	166	49	118	271	51	220	46	168	20	147
July	28	19	391	125	24	101	293	61	233	72	136	9	128
August	66	38	381	171	33	138	344	129	215	171	157	11	147
September	34	36	362	172	37	135	454	236	219	90	197	12	185
October	44	37	356	104	8	96	485	131	354	40	98	12	86
November	39	29	413	115	18	97	254	80	174	103	86	7	80
December	31	43	504	127	18	108	209	56	153	50	106	24	82
2005													
January	70	47	507	141	17	124	302	57	245	98	70	10	60
February	26	44	327	116	12	104	196	42	154	59	53	9	44
March	34	25	398	153	22	131	235	36	200	60	50	7	42
April	59	29	444	141	17	125	231	58	173	53	61	10	51
May	33	24	283	159	45	114	196	41	155	83	106	7	99
June	20	9	446	157	30	127	304	54	250	49	159	19	140
July	35	27	562	133	30	103	227	29	198	61	123	14	109
August	41	11	459	166	24	143	250	92	158	169	175	16	159
September	29	47	357	130	34	96	454	250	204	81	165	16	149
October	36	48	419	116	17	99	323	96	226	56	84	8	76
November	20	40	335	94	12	82	260	88	172	35	73	10	63
December	26	35	408	120	35	86	215	59	156	54	96	28	68
2006													
January	50	38	409	145	23	122	270	33	237	72	85	12	74
February	39	21	342	89	8	82	176	34	142	52	51	8	43
March	34	38	283	109	18	91	183	36	147	27	65	12	53
April	43	36	368	141	24	117	230	46	185	161	64	13	51
May	27	23	376	225	52	172	195	67	128	51	111	12	99
June	28	24	358	174	54	121	193	40	153	64	208	24	183
July	31	42	389	178	42	137	227	55	172	77	153	22	131
August	45	35	306	147	28	119	267	98	169	105	146	28	118
September	38	29	351	121	27	94	346	157	189	86	174	25	149
October	33	39	434	114	23	91	379	105	274	93	93	10	84
November	25	41	419	93	13	80	348	99	249	61	77	9	68
December	54	30	463	106	26	80	226	53	173	62	86	15	70

[1]Layoffs and discharges are the number of layoffs and discharges during the entire month.
[2]The layoffs and discharges rate is the number of layoffs and discharges during the entire month as a percent of total employment.

Table 7-11. Layoffs and Discharges Levels[1] and Rates,[2] by Industry, December 2000–September 2012 —*Continued*

(Not seasonally adjusted, levels in thousands, rates per 100.)

Year and month	Rate												
	Total	Total private	Mining and logging	Construction	Manufacturing	Durable goods	Nondurable goods	Trade, transportation, and utilities	Wholesale trade	Retail trade	Transportation, warehousing, and utilities	Information	Financial activities
2007	16.1	18.1	12.2	37.2	14.1	13.6	14.8	15.7	12.7	17.6	13.6	9.4	13.0
2008	17.7	20.1	15.7	47.8	16.8	17.0	16.4	17.9	15.1	19.8	15.7	12.2	12.6
2009	20.5	23.3	25.6	62.2	24.2	25.2	22.5	20.1	19.4	19.8	21.8	13.5	16.3
2010	16.8	18.4	13.9	56.3	14.4	13.5	15.7	15.1	13.6	16.0	14.1	10.8	10.1
2011	15.8	17.8	10.7	52.1	11.3	10.3	13.0	13.6	10.7	14.7	13.5	10.7	8.5
2000													
December	1.5	1.8	4.2	5.5	1.3	1.0	1.6	1.6	1.7	1.9	0.6	0.7	0.4
2001													
January	2.3	2.7	1.6	5.4	1.9	2.1	1.6	3.2	2.0	4.2	1.4	1.6	1.9
February	1.1	1.3	0.7	4.2	1.3	1.1	1.5	0.9	1.1	1.0	0.4	1.0	0.6
March	1.4	1.6	1.6	3.5	1.4	1.3	1.7	1.2	0.6	1.7	0.6	0.9	0.7
April	1.4	1.6	1.1	2.4	1.9	1.9	1.9	1.1	1.2	1.2	1.1	1.4	0.8
May	1.3	1.4	0.9	2.9	1.5	1.4	1.9	1.3	0.9	1.5	1.1	1.1	0.6
June	1.4	1.5	1.6	3.1	1.7	1.5	2.1	1.2	0.7	1.3	1.1	1.4	0.5
July	1.5	1.7	1.5	3.0	1.7	1.6	2.0	1.4	1.7	1.4	1.1	1.1	0.7
August	1.5	1.6	1.4	3.6	1.4	1.4	1.4	1.0	0.9	1.1	0.8	1.2	0.5
September	1.7	1.9	1.1	3.5	1.4	1.3	1.6	1.4	1.1	1.5	1.2	1.2	1.1
October	1.9	2.2	1.4	4.8	2.2	2.2	2.1	1.6	2.2	1.5	1.2	1.8	1.1
November	1.6	1.9	2.4	5.1	1.7	1.6	1.8	1.5	1.7	1.2	2.1	2.0	1.0
December	1.5	1.8	3.0	5.5	1.8	1.6	2.2	1.7	1.2	1.7	2.3	1.2	0.9
2002													
January	1.9	2.3	1.7	5.3	2.1	2.1	2.0	2.4	1.2	3.0	1.8	2.3	1.8
February	1.3	1.5	1.2	4.0	1.3	1.1	1.5	1.6	1.2	1.8	1.5	0.7	0.7
March	1.1	1.3	1.8	3.1	1.2	1.4	1.0	1.1	1.1	1.1	1.2	1.0	0.6
April	1.4	1.6	2.0	3.1	1.5	1.5	1.5	1.3	1.0	1.5	1.2	1.5	0.7
May	1.2	1.4	1.2	3.1	1.3	1.2	1.3	1.5	1.4	1.7	0.8	0.9	1.0
June	1.3	1.4	0.8	3.3	1.3	1.2	1.3	1.1	0.9	1.1	1.2	1.2	1.1
July	1.6	1.8	2.4	3.6	1.4	1.4	1.5	1.3	1.6	1.3	0.9	1.1	0.9
August	1.5	1.6	1.4	3.3	1.3	1.5	1.0	1.2	0.9	1.4	1.2	1.1	1.0
September	1.5	1.7	1.0	3.4	1.3	1.4	1.2	1.4	1.1	1.5	1.5	0.8	0.9
October	1.6	1.8	1.2	4.7	1.6	1.6	1.6	1.4	0.8	1.7	1.0	1.1	0.7
November	1.4	1.7	1.1	4.3	1.3	1.3	1.4	1.3	1.4	1.3	1.2	1.6	0.9
December	1.7	1.9	1.8	4.9	1.7	1.5	2.1	1.9	1.3	2.1	1.8	0.9	0.8
2003													
January	2.0	2.4	2.5	6.0	1.8	1.8	1.9	2.5	1.5	3.3	1.3	2.1	1.5
February	1.3	1.5	1.5	3.6	1.3	1.3	1.3	1.4	0.7	1.9	0.8	1.2	0.5
March	1.2	1.3	1.4	3.5	1.3	1.2	1.3	1.1	0.8	1.3	0.9	1.2	0.8
April	1.4	1.6	1.3	3.8	1.6	1.6	1.6	1.1	1.0	1.2	0.9	0.6	0.5
May	1.2	1.4	0.9	3.0	1.0	0.9	1.1	1.2	1.2	1.2	1.1	0.8	0.6
June	1.5	1.6	1.2	3.0	1.3	1.4	1.3	1.4	0.9	1.5	1.8	1.1	0.6
July	1.6	1.7	1.5	3.3	1.5	1.4	1.7	1.5	1.6	1.3	1.9	0.9	1.3
August	1.7	1.8	1.8	4.5	1.1	1.2	0.9	1.4	1.1	1.5	1.4	0.8	0.6
September	1.5	1.6	0.7	4.1	1.0	1.0	1.0	1.0	0.9	1.0	1.0	0.6	0.9
October	1.6	1.9	1.1	4.2	1.2	1.1	1.3	1.7	1.4	1.8	1.5	1.0	0.7
November	1.4	1.6	1.2	4.2	1.2	1.3	0.9	1.3	0.7	1.7	1.0	1.0	0.6
December	1.7	1.9	3.0	4.1	1.2	1.1	1.3	2.3	1.1	2.7	2.6	1.0	0.7
2004													
January	1.9	2.2	1.8	5.1	1.4	1.4	1.5	2.5	1.3	3.1	1.8	1.3	1.0
February	1.2	1.4	1.5	4.1	1.0	0.9	1.1	1.6	1.2	2.0	1.1	1.0	0.4
March	1.2	1.4	0.9	3.4	1.0	1.1	1.0	1.2	1.0	1.2	1.5	1.3	0.7
April	1.4	1.6	1.0	2.9	1.2	0.9	1.6	1.3	1.6	1.3	1.0	0.8	0.6
May	1.2	1.3	0.9	2.4	0.9	0.7	1.2	1.4	1.1	1.4	1.7	1.0	0.4
June	1.3	1.4	0.7	2.6	0.9	1.0	0.8	1.1	1.0	1.1	1.3	1.4	0.7
July	1.4	1.5	1.0	3.0	1.1	1.2	1.1	1.4	1.2	1.6	1.4	0.7	0.6
August	1.6	1.8	1.3	3.5	1.4	1.5	1.1	1.3	1.3	1.2	1.6	0.6	1.3
September	1.6	1.7	0.8	2.9	1.0	1.1	1.0	1.2	0.9	1.3	1.4	1.3	0.9
October	1.5	1.8	1.1	4.1	1.3	1.2	1.4	1.4	1.2	1.5	1.6	1.0	1.0
November	1.4	1.6	1.5	3.7	1.1	1.2	1.0	1.4	1.1	1.5	1.4	0.6	0.9
December	1.6	1.9	1.4	4.2	1.1	1.1	1.1	2.4	0.8	2.9	2.6	0.7	0.9
2005													
January	1.9	2.2	1.8	6.3	1.5	1.5	1.3	2.2	1.3	2.7	1.6	1.2	1.5
February	1.2	1.4	1.0	3.6	0.8	0.9	0.8	1.5	0.9	1.8	1.3	0.5	0.9
March	1.2	1.4	0.9	2.4	1.0	0.9	1.2	1.2	0.7	1.4	1.0	0.8	0.7
April	1.3	1.5	1.1	3.0	1.2	1.2	1.0	1.3	1.2	1.3	1.2	0.6	1.1
May	1.2	1.4	0.6	2.9	1.0	1.0	0.9	1.4	1.4	1.2	2.1	1.0	0.7
June	1.3	1.5	0.7	2.5	0.9	0.9	0.9	1.3	0.8	1.3	1.6	0.6	0.3
July	1.4	1.5	0.9	2.5	0.9	0.9	0.9	1.4	1.1	1.5	1.4	0.7	0.8
August	1.5	1.6	1.0	3.3	1.1	1.2	0.9	1.2	0.8	1.4	1.2	0.5	0.6
September	1.5	1.7	1.3	3.0	1.1	1.0	1.2	1.5	0.6	1.7	1.6	0.6	0.9
October	1.4	1.6	1.1	3.0	1.1	1.0	1.1	1.3	1.2	1.4	1.4	0.6	1.0
November	1.2	1.4	0.6	3.1	1.1	0.8	1.5	1.3	1.3	1.2	1.7	0.8	0.7
December	1.4	1.6	1.2	3.8	1.0	0.9	1.3	2.0	1.3	1.8	3.3	0.7	0.7
2006													
January	1.6	1.9	0.8	4.6	1.2	0.9	1.7	2.2	1.0	2.8	1.7	0.6	1.1
February	1.1	1.2	0.9	2.5	0.8	0.7	1.0	1.3	1.0	1.6	0.7	0.6	0.7
March	1.0	1.1	1.2	2.4	1.1	1.0	1.4	1.0	0.6	1.0	1.2	0.5	0.9
April	1.2	1.4	1.4	1.9	1.0	0.7	1.5	1.1	0.9	1.4	0.6	1.2	1.0
May	1.2	1.4	0.4	2.3	1.0	1.0	1.1	1.3	0.9	1.4	1.1	0.4	0.6
June	1.2	1.3	0.4	1.6	1.0	0.8	1.3	1.3	0.8	1.6	1.2	0.5	0.6
July	1.3	1.4	0.6	2.5	1.0	1.0	1.1	1.3	1.7	1.2	1.1	0.7	0.9
August	1.3	1.4	0.8	2.6	1.0	1.0	1.1	1.2	0.8	1.3	1.2	0.6	0.9
September	1.3	1.5	1.3	2.4	1.1	1.1	1.2	1.2	0.9	1.3	1.3	0.5	0.8
October	1.4	1.6	0.8	3.2	1.1	1.1	1.1	1.3	1.1	1.3	1.3	1.0	0.9
November	1.4	1.5	0.8	4.1	1.0	1.1	1.0	1.1	0.9	1.3	1.0	0.7	0.8
December	1.4	1.6	1.0	3.9	1.1	1.1	1.3	1.7	0.8	2.1	1.6	0.9	1.0

[1] Layoffs and discharges are the number of layoffs and discharges during the entire month.
[2] The layoffs and discharges rate is the number of layoffs and discharges during the entire month as a percent of total employment.

Table 7-11. Layoffs and Discharges Levels[1] and Rates,[2] by Industry, December 2000–September 2012
—Continued

(Not seasonally adjusted, levels in thousands, rates per 100.)

Year and month	Rate												
	Finance and insurance	Real estate and rental and leasing	Profes-sional and business services	Education and health services	Educa-tional services	Health care and social assistance	Leisure and hospitality	Arts, enter-tainment, and recreation	Accommo-dation and food services	Other services	Govern-ment	Federal	State and local govern-ment
2007	9.7	22.5	26.1	9.3	12.5	8.7	22.9	43.9	19.3	17.0	5.9	8.0	5.6
2008	10.2	19.5	28.4	10.5	12.6	10.1	23.3	45.7	19.5	17.4	5.1	3.7	5.3
2009	12.0	28.6	30.2	11.4	14.7	10.7	25.4	43.5	22.2	22.9	7.1	7.9	7.0
2010	7.9	16.8	25.9	10.7	12.6	10.3	21.0	41.0	17.6	17.3	9.1	24.9	6.7
2011	6.0	15.9	27.2	9.1	11.4	8.7	23.6	49.9	19.3	20.6	6.0	4.7	6.2
2000													
December	0.4	0.2	3.1	0.8	1.6	0.6	1.7	3.5	1.4	0.7	0.3	0.2	0.3
2001													
January	2.3	0.8	4.5	1.0	1.1	1.0	2.3	4.9	1.9	1.9	0.3	0.5	0.3
February	0.4	1.1	2.0	0.6	0.3	0.6	1.3	3.2	1.0	0.5	0.2	0.2	0.2
March	0.4	1.5	2.8	0.6	0.4	0.6	2.1	2.4	2.1	1.5	0.2	0.2	0.2
April	0.8	0.8	2.0	0.6	0.9	0.6	3.3	3.5	3.3	1.4	0.2	0.2	0.2
May	0.5	0.6	2.5	0.6	0.7	0.6	1.4	2.0	1.3	0.5	0.5	0.2	0.5
June	0.4	0.9	2.0	1.0	0.9	1.0	1.9	2.5	1.7	0.9	0.7	0.2	0.7
July	0.7	0.5	2.2	1.4	1.6	1.3	2.5	4.2	2.2	1.1	0.4	0.2	0.4
August	0.5	0.7	2.3	1.2	2.6	0.9	2.1	4.8	1.5	1.9	1.1	0.3	1.2
September	0.6	2.7	2.6	0.7	0.5	0.7	4.1	11.8	2.7	1.1	0.5	0.4	0.5
October	0.9	1.8	3.0	1.1	1.0	1.1	3.9	5.9	3.5	1.1	0.5	0.4	0.5
November	0.6	2.1	2.3	0.6	0.4	0.7	3.5	6.8	2.9	0.8	0.2	0.2	0.2
December	0.5	1.8	2.5	0.5	0.3	0.6	2.1	2.6	2.0	0.5	0.3	0.3	0.3
2002													
January	1.9	1.5	2.8	1.1	1.3	1.1	2.0	3.7	1.8	1.8	0.3	0.6	0.3
February	0.7	0.8	2.0	0.6	0.3	0.7	1.6	1.6	1.6	0.7	0.2	0.3	0.2
March	0.4	1.0	2.1	0.8	0.6	0.8	1.2	1.9	1.1	0.6	0.2	0.4	0.2
April	0.7	0.9	2.3	0.8	0.7	0.8	2.3	5.3	1.8	1.6	0.3	0.3	0.3
May	1.0	0.9	2.0	0.8	0.8	0.7	1.3	1.3	1.3	0.7	0.4	0.2	0.5
June	1.1	1.3	1.9	1.0	1.1	1.0	1.7	1.2	1.8	1.4	0.7	0.3	0.7
July	0.7	1.5	2.9	1.1	1.2	1.0	2.8	5.4	2.3	2.0	0.7	0.4	0.7
August	0.7	1.9	2.0	0.9	1.1	0.9	2.4	6.5	1.6	2.4	0.7	0.3	0.8
September	0.5	1.9	2.3	0.9	1.3	0.8	3.0	7.1	2.2	1.4	0.8	0.5	0.8
October	0.5	1.3	3.1	0.7	0.3	0.8	2.7	3.7	2.6	0.9	0.4	0.4	0.4
November	0.6	1.6	2.5	0.4	0.1	0.5	2.8	7.1	2.1	0.8	0.3	0.5	0.3
December	0.6	1.3	3.4	0.7	0.8	0.6	1.9	3.8	1.6	1.0	0.3	0.2	0.3
2003													
January	1.1	2.8	3.1	0.9	0.6	0.9	2.8	5.6	2.4	1.7	0.3	0.5	0.3
February	0.5	0.5	2.3	0.6	0.4	0.6	1.5	2.9	1.3	1.3	0.2	0.3	0.2
March	0.6	1.5	1.8	0.6	0.3	0.7	1.7	3.3	1.4	0.8	0.2	0.2	0.2
April	0.4	0.9	2.8	0.6	0.7	0.6	2.5	6.3	1.9	1.3	0.3	0.3	0.3
May	0.5	1.0	2.0	1.0	1.3	0.9	2.1	4.1	1.8	0.7	0.5	0.4	0.5
June	0.4	1.2	2.4	1.3	2.7	1.1	1.7	1.3	1.7	2.1	0.7	0.4	0.7
July	0.8	2.6	2.6	1.4	2.9	1.1	1.4	1.6	1.4	1.9	0.6	0.4	0.7
August	0.5	1.1	2.7	1.2	2.3	1.0	2.1	5.0	1.6	2.9	0.9	0.4	1.0
September	0.7	1.6	2.3	0.7	0.7	0.7	3.2	8.4	2.3	1.6	0.8	0.5	0.8
October	0.6	1.0	3.1	0.8	0.8	0.8	3.0	5.8	2.6	1.5	0.3	0.7	0.3
November	0.4	1.0	2.3	0.6	0.5	0.6	2.5	5.9	2.0	1.0	0.4	0.9	0.3
December	0.4	1.6	2.9	0.5	0.6	0.5	2.6	3.3	2.5	1.6	0.4	0.2	0.4
2004													
January	0.7	1.9	3.7	0.8	0.7	0.8	2.9	4.5	2.6	1.0	0.3	0.4	0.3
February	0.4	0.6	1.7	0.6	0.5	0.7	1.7	4.4	1.3	0.9	0.2	0.3	0.2
March	0.5	1.4	2.1	0.6	0.6	0.7	1.7	2.6	1.6	0.7	0.2	0.2	0.2
April	0.4	1.1	3.2	0.8	0.5	0.8	2.3	5.1	1.8	1.3	0.2	0.2	0.2
May	0.4	0.6	2.0	0.8	1.1	0.7	1.5	2.9	1.3	1.0	0.4	0.3	0.4
June	0.5	1.4	2.2	1.0	1.9	0.8	2.1	2.5	2.0	0.8	0.8	0.7	0.8
July	0.5	0.9	2.4	0.8	1.0	0.7	2.2	2.8	2.1	1.3	0.7	0.3	0.7
August	1.1	1.8	2.3	1.0	1.4	1.0	2.6	6.1	2.0	3.1	0.8	0.4	0.8
September	0.6	1.7	2.2	1.0	1.4	0.9	3.6	12.2	2.0	1.7	0.9	0.4	1.0
October	0.7	1.8	2.1	0.6	0.3	0.7	3.9	7.2	3.3	0.7	0.4	0.4	0.4
November	0.7	1.4	2.5	0.7	0.6	0.7	2.1	4.7	1.6	1.9	0.4	0.2	0.4
December	0.5	2.1	3.0	0.7	0.6	0.8	1.7	3.3	1.4	0.9	0.5	0.9	0.4
2005													
January	1.2	2.3	3.1	0.8	0.6	0.9	2.5	3.5	2.4	1.8	0.3	0.4	0.3
February	0.4	2.1	2.0	0.7	0.4	0.7	1.6	2.5	1.5	1.1	0.2	0.3	0.2
March	0.6	1.2	2.4	0.9	0.8	0.9	1.9	2.1	1.9	1.1	0.2	0.3	0.2
April	1.0	1.4	2.6	0.8	0.6	0.9	1.8	3.1	1.6	1.0	0.3	0.4	0.3
May	0.5	1.1	1.7	0.9	1.6	0.8	1.5	2.1	1.4	1.5	0.5	0.3	0.5
June	0.3	0.4	2.6	0.9	1.2	0.9	2.3	2.5	2.2	0.9	0.7	0.7	0.7
July	0.6	1.3	3.3	0.8	1.2	0.7	1.7	1.3	1.7	1.1	0.6	0.5	0.6
August	0.7	0.5	2.7	1.0	0.9	1.0	1.9	4.2	1.4	3.1	0.8	0.6	0.9
September	0.5	2.2	2.1	0.7	1.2	0.7	3.5	12.6	1.8	1.5	0.8	0.6	0.8
October	0.6	2.2	2.4	0.7	0.6	0.7	2.5	5.2	2.1	1.0	0.4	0.3	0.4
November	0.3	1.9	1.9	0.5	0.4	0.6	2.1	5.0	1.6	0.7	0.3	0.4	0.3
December	0.4	1.6	2.4	0.7	1.2	0.6	1.7	3.4	1.4	1.0	0.4	1.0	0.3
2006													
January	0.8	1.8	2.4	0.8	0.8	0.8	2.2	2.0	2.2	1.3	0.4	0.4	0.4
February	0.6	1.0	2.0	0.5	0.3	0.6	1.4	2.0	1.3	1.0	0.2	0.3	0.2
March	0.5	1.8	1.6	0.6	0.6	0.6	1.4	2.0	1.3	0.5	0.3	0.4	0.3
April	0.7	1.7	2.1	0.8	0.8	0.8	1.8	2.4	1.7	3.0	0.3	0.5	0.3
May	0.4	1.1	2.1	1.3	1.8	1.2	1.5	3.3	1.1	0.9	0.5	0.4	0.5
June	0.5	1.1	2.0	1.0	2.0	0.8	1.4	1.8	1.3	1.2	1.0	0.9	1.0
July	0.5	1.9	2.2	1.0	1.6	0.9	1.6	2.5	1.5	1.4	0.7	0.8	0.7
August	0.7	1.6	1.7	0.8	1.1	0.8	1.9	4.4	1.5	1.9	0.7	1.0	0.7
September	0.6	1.3	2.0	0.7	0.9	0.6	2.6	7.8	1.7	1.6	0.8	0.9	0.8
October	0.5	1.8	2.4	0.6	0.7	0.6	2.9	5.5	2.4	1.7	0.4	0.4	0.4
November	0.4	1.9	2.3	0.5	0.4	0.5	2.7	5.5	2.2	1.1	0.3	0.3	0.3
December	0.9	1.4	2.6	0.6	0.8	0.5	1.7	2.9	1.5	1.1	0.4	0.6	0.4

[1]Layoffs and discharges are the number of layoffs and discharges during the entire month.
[2]The layoffs and discharges rate is the number of layoffs and discharges during the entire month as a percent of total employment.

Table 7-11. Layoffs and Discharges Levels[1] and Rates,[2] by Industry, December 2000–September 2012
—Continued

(Not seasonally adjusted, levels in thousands, rates per 100.)

Year and month	Total	Total private	Mining and logging	Construction	Manufacturing	Durable goods	Non-durable goods	Trade, transportation, and utilities	Wholesale trade	Retail trade	Transportation, warehousing, and utilities	Information	Financial activities
2007													
January	2 197	2 111	10	317	189	118	72	546	55	388	103	53	99
February	1 449	1 399	5	224	154	98	57	266	34	193	39	26	73
March	1 446	1 395	4	154	138	90	48	260	50	153	58	19	100
April	1 776	1 715	6	207	144	88	56	296	61	173	62	18	92
May	1 524	1 406	6	181	129	77	52	299	54	203	42	22	72
June	1 727	1 560	4	205	141	88	53	261	47	171	42	18	63
July	1 855	1 642	6	186	178	108	70	345	88	200	57	32	105
August	1 990	1 808	9	260	159	96	63	333	70	217	46	27	98
September	2 173	2 034	8	262	172	108	64	341	67	232	43	15	109
October	2 053	1 971	9	264	198	123	75	382	82	239	61	19	103
November	1 940	1 880	11	277	192	119	73	413	69	261	83	16	72
December	2 012	1 913	10	300	158	89	68	445	87	303	55	19	93
2008													
January	2 334	2 247	11	349	184	124	59	554	96	376	82	37	124
February	1 508	1 472	11	205	135	77	58	333	58	233	43	17	60
March	1 492	1 435	7	224	121	77	44	254	53	155	46	28	74
April	1 758	1 706	8	242	187	118	69	315	80	184	51	21	94
May	1 613	1 506	4	208	144	89	55	298	62	192	44	16	65
June	1 868	1 712	6	226	169	103	66	368	75	245	49	32	74
July	1 982	1 853	12	228	164	116	48	390	54	254	81	20	111
August	2 246	2 084	6	251	167	119	48	393	69	249	75	18	107
September	2 054	1 923	6	300	187	114	72	356	68	210	78	34	79
October	2 319	2 236	12	349	255	158	97	426	80	274	73	53	80
November	2 237	2 175	18	413	225	141	84	403	74	252	78	41	75
December	2 755	2 666	19	425	314	205	109	628	129	403	96	47	87
2009													
January	3 335	3 218	16	549	453	322	131	742	184	449	108	62	200
February	2 032	1 980	16	305	275	187	88	402	88	239	75	31	119
March	1 990	1 932	23	290	285	211	74	368	85	194	89	32	110
April	2 422	2 350	16	346	279	205	74	478	102	305	70	39	101
May	1 913	1 731	14	239	223	147	75	379	116	202	61	26	96
June	2 014	1 746	11	216	199	131	68	316	71	174	71	30	96
July	2 334	2 153	16	312	191	106	86	362	80	198	84	31	121
August	2 235	2 015	9	270	184	94	90	319	82	175	62	19	111
September	2 235	2 052	11	302	181	103	78	410	63	237	109	16	72
October	2 111	2 017	16	312	213	123	90	333	60	209	64	23	114
November	1 900	1 824	12	263	211	107	105	336	64	192	80	28	45
December	2 262	2 154	18	339	169	100	69	562	88	301	174	42	79
2010													
January	2 382	2 279	11	377	219	164	55	554	83	392	80	50	114
February	1 426	1 375	8	225	134	77	57	253	65	146	43	21	51
March	1 465	1 396	7	204	127	72	55	307	51	225	31	20	55
April	1 586	1 510	9	251	127	65	62	239	57	145	38	18	58
May	1 560	1 397	8	231	98	61	37	232	59	130	42	25	68
June	1 936	1 493	5	179	107	52	55	309	51	197	62	22	43
July	2 102	1 804	6	250	132	68	64	317	81	183	52	21	74
August	1 955	1 640	6	227	140	76	64	247	48	164	35	24	52
September	1 788	1 556	8	232	127	72	55	260	72	144	44	17	48
October	1 755	1 661	7	247	166	98	68	277	51	162	65	21	93
November	1 783	1 686	10	302	151	80	71	290	56	189	46	22	57
December	2 046	1 932	13	380	127	69	58	435	67	238	131	31	63
2011													
January	2 155	2 080	10	332	138	72	67	565	53	413	99	34	112
February	1 276	1 232	4	211	105	57	48	249	47	173	30	17	48
March	1 321	1 272	3	208	105	63	42	228	42	151	34	33	38
April	1 486	1 413	10	233	107	53	54	192	31	128	32	16	32
May	1 578	1 443	5	211	110	58	52	208	62	121	25	22	36
June	1 759	1 576	6	225	94	57	37	257	61	155	41	21	52
July	1 786	1 624	6	233	101	60	41	266	49	161	56	26	50
August	1 866	1 693	7	247	127	73	54	251	40	164	48	20	53
September	1 886	1 718	7	223	116	69	47	253	46	165	42	20	60
October	1 861	1 770	5	250	106	62	45	261	42	151	68	23	75
November	1 807	1 736	9	227	106	60	45	273	47	176	50	22	56
December	1 937	1 837	12	265	112	63	49	397	71	196	130	30	38
2012													
January	2 135	2 059	16	319	120	70	50	537	86	369	82	39	64
February	1 351	1 298	12	201	97	56	40	219	38	150	31	22	35
March	1 290	1 241	13	159	88	51	38	227	54	138	35	22	44
April	1 618	1 564	11	196	99	58	41	231	43	143	44	21	53
May	1 668	1 542	12	221	93	51	42	257	39	173	45	20	50
June	1 712	1 542	9	188	120	74	46	248	32	159	57	15	44
July	1 619	1 489	7	250	96	59	36	246	43	146	57	19	52
August	1 954	1 781	12	211	120	81	39	308	57	188	63	25	69
September[3]	1 789	1 658	7	280	103	72	31	257	53	136	68	14	33

[1]Layoffs and discharges are the number of layoffs and discharges during the entire month.
[2]The layoffs and discharges rate is the number of layoffs and discharges during the entire month as a percent of total employment.
[3]Preliminary data.

Table 7-11. Layoffs and Discharges Levels[1] and Rates,[2] by Industry, December 2000–September 2012
—Continued

(Not seasonally adjusted, levels in thousands, rates per 100.)

Year and month	Finance and insurance	Real estate and rental and leasing	Professional and business services	Education and health services	Educational services	Health care and social assistance	Leisure and hospitality	Arts, entertainment, and recreation	Accommodation and food services	Other services	Government	Federal	State and local government
2007													
January	51	48	422	139	34	105	275	76	199	61	86	15	71
February	40	33	340	100	22	78	182	48	134	27	50	13	37
March	50	50	349	134	18	116	188	49	139	49	51	15	37
April	43	49	455	133	23	109	254	89	165	109	61	14	47
May	28	44	286	155	38	117	222	52	169	37	118	16	102
June	45	19	292	216	71	146	255	44	211	104	167	24	143
July	65	40	372	139	21	117	176	28	148	102	213	28	185
August	70	29	341	184	61	123	266	57	209	130	182	26	156
September	61	48	382	156	19	137	455	143	312	135	139	27	112
October	60	42	470	130	15	115	344	114	230	53	82	11	71
November	21	51	461	117	23	94	246	109	137	74	60	9	51
December	58	35	509	108	24	84	215	55	160	55	99	21	78
2008													
January	78	46	500	170	25	145	248	63	185	70	86	17	69
February	37	24	299	128	15	113	230	59	171	53	36	7	29
March	52	22	367	130	12	118	174	59	116	55	57	6	51
April	64	30	443	133	35	98	208	68	141	54	52	8	44
May	32	33	262	204	39	165	207	62	145	97	107	5	102
June	53	20	382	210	56	155	195	39	156	51	155	9	147
July	67	44	392	212	50	163	198	29	169	125	129	7	122
August	69	38	423	206	51	155	375	143	232	137	162	7	155
September	43	37	376	150	21	128	357	121	236	79	131	7	123
October	37	43	438	139	26	112	383	115	267	101	83	9	74
November	32	43	531	110	22	88	302	76	226	57	62	5	57
December	52	35	623	188	30	158	253	66	187	82	89	15	74
2009													
January	114	86	568	190	22	168	302	74	228	137	117	10	107
February	70	49	447	146	18	128	183	36	147	55	52	5	47
March	61	49	397	140	13	127	205	38	167	82	57	6	52
April	63	38	576	185	31	154	248	63	185	82	72	11	61
May	72	24	315	150	52	98	207	25	181	83	182	63	119
June	57	39	339	214	59	154	227	40	187	99	268	61	207
July	72	49	427	304	96	207	234	52	182	155	182	9	173
August	47	64	357	252	72	179	342	102	241	152	220	9	211
September	29	43	354	173	31	142	371	106	265	163	182	7	175
October	46	68	363	145	25	120	407	136	271	91	94	12	82
November	23	22	411	132	12	120	328	99	229	57	76	17	59
December	39	40	456	152	22	131	262	62	200	75	108	14	94
2010													
January	43	71	443	160	21	139	253	45	209	97	102	6	97
February	28	23	323	138	11	126	128	19	109	94	50	8	42
March	33	22	334	122	13	109	172	57	115	47	69	13	56
April	36	22	420	139	17	122	195	66	129	54	76	18	58
May	43	25	321	160	39	121	189	46	143	65	163	39	124
June	26	16	298	233	72	161	231	58	173	67	442	239	203
July	37	37	413	294	69	226	218	60	158	79	298	153	145
August	37	15	305	223	64	159	257	91	167	158	316	129	187
September	40	8	301	202	40	162	302	119	183	60	231	91	141
October	58	35	305	113	12	101	343	101	242	89	93	26	68
November	28	29	358	138	18	120	282	81	201	74	97	11	86
December	41	22	505	167	23	145	172	42	130	40	113	9	105
2011													
January	49	63	424	136	22	114	245	58	188	83	75	10	65
February	27	21	291	110	19	92	126	23	104	69	44	5	39
March	27	11	312	102	14	87	197	54	143	45	50	6	44
April	13	19	455	107	15	92	178	66	112	85	73	9	64
May	26	10	402	150	38	112	220	73	148	77	135	7	128
June	27	25	401	237	69	168	211	36	175	72	182	10	173
July	29	21	375	215	62	153	222	34	188	131	162	10	153
August	28	25	378	202	38	163	284	89	195	125	173	21	152
September	39	22	371	133	29	104	411	182	230	123	168	20	149
October	25	49	401	134	20	114	387	114	273	128	91	14	77
November	32	25	403	149	20	129	407	156	251	84	71	11	60
December	22	16	507	139	23	117	257	68	190	79	100	10	90
2012													
January	32	32	405	182	40	142	307	70	237	70	76	8	68
February	19	16	372	97	11	86	181	43	138	62	52	6	46
March	20	24	343	116	11	105	183	57	125	47	49	6	43
April	34	18	497	153	20	133	201	81	120	101	54	7	47
May	31	20	451	173	40	133	177	55	123	88	125	7	119
June	24	20	418	267	80	188	177	26	151	56	169	9	161
July	27	25	356	208	59	149	192	30	162	64	131	6	124
August	41	28	453	184	34	150	299	48	251	101	173	20	153
September[3]	19	14	368	142	19	123	345	129	216	108	131	20	111

[1]Layoffs and discharges are the number of layoffs and discharges during the entire month.
[2]The layoffs and discharges rate is the number of layoffs and discharges during the entire month as a percent of total employment.
[3]Preliminary data.

Table 7-11. Layoffs and Discharges Levels[1] and Rates,[2] by Industry, December 2000–September 2012 —Continued

(Not seasonally adjusted, levels in thousands, rates per 100.)

Year and month	Rate												
	Total	Total private	Mining and logging	Construc-tion	Manufac-turing	Durable goods	Non-durable goods	Trade, transpor-tation, and utilities	Whole-sale trade	Retail trade	Transpor-tation, ware-housing, and utilities	Infor-mation	Financial activities
2007													
January	1.6	1.9	1.5	4.3	1.4	1.3	1.4	2.1	0.9	2.5	2.0	1.8	1.2
February	1.1	1.2	0.8	3.1	1.1	1.1	1.1	1.0	0.6	1.3	0.8	0.9	0.9
March	1.1	1.2	0.5	2.1	1.0	1.0	0.9	1.0	0.8	1.0	1.1	0.6	1.2
April	1.3	1.5	0.9	2.8	1.0	1.0	1.1	1.1	1.0	1.1	1.2	0.6	1.1
May	1.1	1.2	0.8	2.3	0.9	0.9	1.0	1.1	0.9	1.3	0.8	0.7	0.9
June	1.2	1.3	0.6	2.6	1.0	1.0	1.0	1.0	0.8	1.1	0.8	0.6	0.8
July	1.4	1.4	0.8	2.3	1.3	1.2	1.4	1.3	1.5	1.3	1.1	1.0	1.3
August	1.4	1.6	1.2	3.3	1.1	1.1	1.2	1.3	1.2	1.4	0.9	0.9	1.2
September	1.6	1.8	1.0	3.3	1.2	1.2	1.3	1.3	1.1	1.5	0.8	0.5	1.3
October	1.5	1.7	1.2	3.4	1.4	1.4	1.5	1.4	1.4	1.5	1.2	0.6	1.2
November	1.4	1.6	1.4	3.6	1.4	1.4	1.5	1.5	1.1	1.6	1.6	0.5	0.9
December	1.4	1.6	1.4	4.1	1.1	1.0	1.4	1.6	1.4	1.9	1.1	0.6	1.1
2008													
January	1.7	2.0	1.6	4.9	1.3	1.4	1.2	2.1	1.6	2.4	1.6	1.2	1.5
February	1.1	1.3	1.4	2.9	1.0	0.9	1.2	1.3	1.0	1.5	0.8	0.6	0.7
March	1.1	1.3	0.9	3.2	0.9	0.9	0.9	1.0	0.9	1.0	0.9	0.9	0.9
April	1.3	1.5	1.1	3.4	1.4	1.4	1.4	1.2	1.3	1.2	1.0	0.7	1.2
May	1.2	1.3	0.6	2.8	1.1	1.0	1.1	1.1	1.0	1.3	0.9	0.5	0.8
June	1.4	1.5	0.7	3.0	1.2	1.2	1.3	1.4	1.2	1.6	1.0	1.1	0.9
July	1.4	1.6	1.5	3.1	1.2	1.4	1.0	1.5	0.9	1.7	1.6	0.7	1.4
August	1.6	1.8	0.8	3.4	1.2	1.4	1.0	1.5	1.2	1.6	1.5	0.6	1.3
September	1.5	1.7	0.7	4.1	1.4	1.4	1.5	1.4	1.2	1.4	1.5	1.2	1.0
October	1.7	2.0	1.5	4.8	1.9	1.9	2.0	1.6	1.4	1.8	1.4	1.8	1.0
November	1.6	1.9	2.4	5.9	1.7	1.7	1.7	1.5	1.3	1.6	1.5	1.4	0.9
December	2.0	2.4	2.4	6.4	2.4	2.5	2.3	2.4	2.2	2.6	1.9	1.6	1.1
2009													
January	2.5	2.9	2.2	8.9	3.6	4.1	2.8	2.9	3.2	3.1	2.2	2.2	2.5
February	1.5	1.8	2.2	5.1	2.2	2.4	1.9	1.6	1.5	1.7	1.5	1.1	1.5
March	1.5	1.8	3.3	4.9	2.4	2.8	1.6	1.5	1.5	1.3	1.8	1.1	1.4
April	1.8	2.2	2.3	5.8	2.3	2.8	1.6	1.9	1.8	2.1	1.5	1.4	1.3
May	1.5	1.6	2.0	3.9	1.9	2.0	1.7	1.5	2.1	1.4	1.3	0.9	1.2
June	1.5	1.6	1.6	3.5	1.7	1.8	1.5	1.3	1.3	1.2	1.5	1.1	1.2
July	1.8	2.0	2.2	5.0	1.6	1.5	1.9	1.5	1.4	1.4	1.8	1.1	1.6
August	1.7	1.9	1.3	4.4	1.6	1.3	2.0	1.3	1.5	1.2	1.3	0.7	1.4
September	1.7	1.9	1.7	5.0	1.5	1.4	1.7	1.7	1.1	1.7	2.3	0.6	0.9
October	1.6	1.9	2.4	5.2	1.8	1.7	2.0	1.3	1.1	1.4	1.3	0.8	1.5
November	1.5	1.7	1.8	4.5	1.8	1.5	2.3	1.3	1.2	1.3	1.7	1.0	0.6
December	1.7	2.0	2.7	6.1	1.5	1.4	1.6	2.2	1.6	2.0	3.6	1.5	1.0
2010													
January	1.9	2.2	1.7	7.2	1.9	2.4	1.2	2.3	1.5	2.7	1.7	1.8	1.5
February	1.1	1.3	1.2	4.4	1.2	1.1	1.3	1.0	1.2	1.0	0.9	0.8	0.7
March	1.1	1.3	1.1	3.9	1.1	1.0	1.2	1.3	0.9	1.6	0.7	0.8	0.7
April	1.2	1.4	1.3	4.6	1.1	0.9	1.4	1.0	1.0	1.0	0.8	0.7	0.8
May	1.2	1.3	1.2	4.2	0.9	0.9	0.8	0.9	1.1	0.9	0.9	0.9	0.9
June	1.5	1.4	0.6	3.1	0.9	0.7	1.2	1.3	0.9	1.4	1.3	0.8	0.6
July	1.6	1.7	0.9	4.3	1.1	1.0	1.4	1.3	1.5	1.3	1.1	0.8	1.0
August	1.5	1.5	0.9	3.9	1.2	1.1	1.4	1.0	0.9	1.1	0.7	0.9	0.7
September	1.4	1.4	1.0	4.0	1.1	1.0	1.2	1.1	1.3	1.0	0.9	0.6	0.6
October	1.3	1.5	0.9	4.3	1.4	1.4	1.5	1.1	0.9	1.1	1.3	0.8	1.2
November	1.4	1.6	1.4	5.4	1.3	1.1	1.6	1.2	1.0	1.3	0.9	0.8	0.7
December	1.6	1.8	1.7	7.1	1.1	1.0	1.3	1.7	1.2	1.6	2.7	1.2	0.8
2011													
January	1.7	2.0	1.3	6.6	1.2	1.0	1.5	2.3	1.0	2.9	2.1	1.3	1.5
February	1.0	1.2	0.5	4.2	0.9	0.8	1.1	1.0	0.9	1.2	0.6	0.6	0.6
March	1.0	1.2	0.4	4.0	0.9	0.9	0.9	0.9	0.8	1.1	0.7	1.2	0.5
April	1.1	1.3	1.3	4.4	0.9	0.7	1.2	0.8	0.6	0.9	0.7	0.6	0.4
May	1.2	1.3	0.7	3.8	0.9	0.8	1.2	0.8	1.1	0.8	0.5	0.8	0.5
June	1.3	1.4	0.7	3.9	0.8	0.8	0.8	1.0	1.1	1.1	0.8	0.8	0.7
July	1.4	1.5	0.7	4.0	0.9	0.8	0.9	1.1	0.9	1.1	1.2	1.0	0.6
August	1.4	1.5	0.9	4.2	1.1	1.0	1.2	1.0	0.7	1.1	1.0	0.7	0.7
September	1.4	1.6	0.9	3.9	1.0	0.9	1.0	1.0	0.8	1.1	0.9	0.8	0.8
October	1.4	1.6	0.6	4.3	0.9	0.8	1.0	1.0	0.8	1.0	1.4	0.9	1.0
November	1.4	1.6	1.1	4.0	0.9	0.8	1.0	1.1	0.8	1.2	1.0	0.8	0.7
December	1.5	1.7	1.5	4.9	0.9	0.9	1.1	1.5	1.3	1.3	2.6	1.1	0.5
2012													
January	1.6	1.9	2.0	6.2	1.0	0.9	1.1	2.1	1.5	2.5	1.7	1.5	0.8
February	1.0	1.2	1.5	3.9	0.8	0.8	0.9	0.9	0.7	1.0	0.6	0.8	0.5
March	1.0	1.1	1.5	3.0	0.7	0.7	0.8	0.9	1.0	1.0	0.7	0.9	0.6
April	1.2	1.4	1.4	3.6	0.8	0.8	0.9	0.9	0.8	1.0	0.9	0.8	0.7
May	1.2	1.4	1.4	4.0	0.8	0.7	0.9	1.0	0.7	1.2	0.9	0.8	0.6
June	1.3	1.4	1.0	3.3	1.0	1.0	1.0	1.0	0.6	1.1	1.1	0.6	0.6
July	1.2	1.3	0.8	4.3	0.8	0.8	0.8	1.0	0.8	1.0	1.2	0.7	0.7
August	1.5	1.6	1.4	3.6	1.0	1.1	0.9	1.2	1.0	1.3	1.3	0.9	0.9
September[3]	1.3	1.5	0.9	4.9	0.9	1.0	0.7	1.0	0.9	0.9	1.4	0.5	0.4

[1]Layoffs and discharges are the number of layoffs and discharges during the entire month.
[2]The layoffs and discharges rate is the number of layoffs and discharges during the entire month as a percent of total employment.
[3]Preliminary data.

Table 7-11. Layoffs and Discharges Levels[1] and Rates,[2] by Industry, December 2000–September 2012 —Continued

(Not seasonally adjusted, levels in thousands, rates per 100.)

Year and month	Rate												
	Finance and insurance	Real estate and rental and leasing	Professional and business services	Education and health services	Educational services	Health care and social assistance	Leisure and hospitality	Arts, entertainment, and recreation	Accommodation and food services	Other services	Government	Federal	State and local government
2007													
January	0.8	2.2	2.4	0.8	1.2	0.7	2.2	4.4	1.8	1.1	0.4	0.6	0.4
February	0.6	1.5	1.9	0.5	0.7	0.5	1.4	2.7	1.2	0.5	0.2	0.5	0.2
March	0.8	2.3	2.0	0.7	0.6	0.8	1.5	2.7	1.2	0.9	0.2	0.5	0.2
April	0.7	2.3	2.5	0.7	0.8	0.7	1.9	4.7	1.5	2.0	0.3	0.5	0.2
May	0.4	2.0	1.6	0.8	1.3	0.8	1.6	2.6	1.5	0.7	0.5	0.6	0.5
June	0.7	0.8	1.6	1.2	2.6	0.9	1.8	2.0	1.8	1.9	0.8	0.9	0.7
July	1.1	1.8	2.1	0.8	0.8	0.8	1.3	1.3	1.3	1.8	1.0	1.0	1.0
August	1.1	1.3	1.9	1.0	2.3	0.8	1.9	2.6	1.8	2.3	0.9	0.9	0.9
September	1.0	2.2	2.1	0.8	0.7	0.9	3.3	7.0	2.7	2.5	0.6	1.0	0.6
October	1.0	1.9	2.6	0.7	0.5	0.7	2.6	5.9	2.0	1.0	0.4	0.4	0.4
November	0.3	2.4	2.5	0.6	0.7	0.6	1.9	5.9	1.2	1.3	0.3	0.3	0.3
December	1.0	1.6	2.8	0.6	0.8	0.5	1.6	3.0	1.4	1.0	0.4	0.8	0.4
2008													
January	1.3	2.2	2.8	0.9	0.9	0.9	1.9	3.5	1.7	1.3	0.4	0.6	0.4
February	0.6	1.1	1.7	0.7	0.5	0.7	1.8	3.3	1.5	1.0	0.2	0.3	0.1
March	0.9	1.0	2.1	0.7	0.4	0.8	1.3	3.2	1.0	1.0	0.3	0.2	0.3
April	1.1	1.4	2.5	0.7	1.1	0.6	1.6	3.5	1.2	1.0	0.2	0.3	0.2
May	0.5	1.5	1.5	1.1	1.3	1.0	1.5	3.0	1.2	1.8	0.5	0.2	0.5
June	0.9	0.9	2.1	1.1	2.0	1.0	1.4	1.7	1.3	0.9	0.7	0.3	0.7
July	1.1	2.0	2.2	1.1	1.8	1.0	1.4	1.3	1.4	2.2	0.6	0.3	0.7
August	1.2	1.7	2.4	1.1	1.8	1.0	2.7	6.4	2.0	2.5	0.8	0.2	0.8
September	0.7	1.7	2.1	0.8	0.7	0.8	2.6	6.0	2.0	1.4	0.6	0.3	0.6
October	0.6	2.0	2.5	0.7	0.8	0.7	2.9	6.0	2.3	1.8	0.4	0.3	0.4
November	0.5	2.1	3.0	0.6	0.7	0.6	2.3	4.2	2.0	1.0	0.3	0.2	0.3
December	0.9	1.7	3.6	1.0	0.9	1.0	1.9	3.7	1.7	1.5	0.4	0.5	0.4
2009													
January	1.9	4.3	3.4	1.0	0.7	1.1	2.4	4.3	2.1	2.6	0.5	0.4	0.5
February	1.2	2.4	2.7	0.8	0.6	0.8	1.5	2.1	1.4	1.0	0.2	0.2	0.2
March	1.1	2.5	2.4	0.7	0.4	0.8	1.6	2.1	1.5	1.5	0.3	0.2	0.3
April	1.1	1.9	3.5	1.0	1.0	1.0	1.9	3.4	1.7	1.5	0.3	0.4	0.3
May	1.3	1.2	1.9	0.8	1.7	0.6	1.5	1.3	1.6	1.5	0.8	2.2	0.6
June	1.0	1.9	2.1	1.1	2.0	1.0	1.7	1.9	1.6	1.8	1.2	2.2	1.0
July	1.3	2.4	2.6	1.6	3.5	1.3	1.7	2.4	1.6	2.8	0.9	0.3	0.9
August	0.8	3.2	2.2	1.3	2.6	1.1	2.5	4.7	2.1	2.8	1.0	0.3	1.1
September	0.5	2.1	2.1	0.9	1.0	0.9	2.8	5.3	2.4	3.0	0.8	0.3	0.9
October	0.8	3.5	2.2	0.7	0.8	0.7	3.1	7.3	2.4	1.7	0.4	0.4	0.4
November	0.4	1.1	2.5	0.7	0.4	0.7	2.6	5.6	2.1	1.1	0.3	0.6	0.3
December	0.7	2.0	2.8	0.8	0.7	0.8	2.1	3.6	1.8	1.4	0.5	0.5	0.5
2010													
January	0.8	3.7	2.7	0.8	0.7	0.9	2.1	2.7	2.0	1.9	0.5	0.2	0.5
February	0.5	1.2	2.0	0.7	0.3	0.8	1.0	1.1	1.0	1.8	0.2	0.3	0.2
March	0.6	1.2	2.0	0.6	0.4	0.7	1.4	3.3	1.1	0.9	0.3	0.4	0.3
April	0.6	1.2	2.5	0.7	0.5	0.7	1.5	3.5	1.2	1.0	0.3	0.6	0.3
May	0.8	1.3	1.9	0.8	1.2	0.7	1.4	2.3	1.3	1.2	0.7	1.1	0.6
June	0.5	0.8	1.8	1.2	2.4	1.0	1.7	2.7	1.5	1.2	1.9	7.5	1.0
July	0.6	1.9	2.5	1.5	2.4	1.4	1.6	2.7	1.4	1.5	1.4	5.0	0.8
August	0.6	0.8	1.8	1.2	2.2	1.0	1.9	4.1	1.4	3.0	1.5	4.3	1.0
September	0.7	0.4	1.8	1.0	1.3	1.0	2.3	5.9	1.6	1.1	1.0	3.1	0.7
October	1.0	1.8	1.8	0.6	0.4	0.6	2.6	5.4	2.2	1.7	0.4	0.9	0.3
November	0.5	1.5	2.1	0.7	0.5	0.7	2.2	4.6	1.8	1.4	0.4	0.4	0.4
December	0.7	1.1	2.9	0.8	0.7	0.9	1.3	2.4	1.2	0.7	0.5	0.3	0.5
2011													
January	0.9	3.4	2.5	0.7	0.7	0.7	2.0	3.5	1.7	1.6	0.3	0.4	0.3
February	0.5	1.1	1.7	0.6	0.6	0.6	1.0	1.3	0.9	1.3	0.2	0.2	0.2
March	0.5	0.6	1.8	0.5	0.4	0.5	1.5	3.1	1.3	0.8	0.2	0.2	0.2
April	0.2	1.0	2.6	0.5	0.4	0.6	1.3	3.5	1.0	1.6	0.3	0.3	0.3
May	0.5	0.5	2.3	0.8	1.2	0.7	1.6	3.7	1.3	1.4	0.6	0.3	0.7
June	0.5	1.3	2.3	1.2	2.3	1.0	1.5	1.7	1.5	1.3	0.8	0.3	0.9
July	0.5	1.1	2.2	1.1	2.1	0.9	1.6	1.5	1.6	2.4	0.8	0.3	0.9
August	0.5	1.2	2.2	1.0	1.3	1.0	2.0	4.1	1.7	2.3	0.8	0.7	0.8
September	0.7	1.1	2.1	0.7	0.9	0.6	3.0	9.1	2.0	2.3	0.8	0.7	0.8
October	0.4	2.5	2.3	0.7	0.6	0.7	2.9	6.1	2.4	2.4	0.4	0.5	0.4
November	0.5	1.3	2.3	0.7	0.6	0.8	3.1	8.9	2.2	1.6	0.3	0.4	0.3
December	0.4	0.8	2.9	0.7	0.7	0.7	2.0	3.9	1.7	1.5	0.4	0.4	0.5
2012													
January	0.6	1.7	2.3	0.9	1.2	0.8	2.4	4.1	2.1	1.3	0.3	0.3	0.4
February	0.3	0.8	2.1	0.5	0.3	0.5	1.4	2.5	1.2	1.2	0.2	0.2	0.2
March	0.3	1.2	1.9	0.6	0.3	0.6	1.4	3.2	1.1	0.9	0.2	0.2	0.2
April	0.6	0.9	2.8	0.7	0.6	0.8	1.5	4.3	1.0	1.9	0.2	0.3	0.2
May	0.5	1.0	2.5	0.8	1.2	0.8	1.3	2.8	1.0	1.6	0.6	0.2	0.6
June	0.4	1.0	2.3	1.3	2.6	1.1	1.2	1.2	1.3	1.0	0.8	0.3	0.8
July	0.5	1.2	2.0	1.0	2.0	0.9	1.3	1.4	1.3	1.2	0.6	0.2	0.7
August	0.7	1.4	2.5	0.9	1.1	0.9	2.1	2.2	2.1	1.9	0.8	0.7	0.8
September[3]	0.3	0.7	2.0	0.7	0.6	0.7	2.5	6.5	1.8	2.0	0.6	0.7	0.6

[1]Layoffs and discharges are the number of layoffs and discharges during the entire month.
[2]The layoffs and discharges rate is the number of layoffs and discharges during the entire month as a percent of total employment.
[3]Preliminary data.

Chapter Eight

LABOR-MANAGEMENT RELATIONS

LABOR-MANAGEMENT RELATIONS

HIGHLIGHTS

This chapter contains information on historical trends in union membership, earnings, and work stoppages.

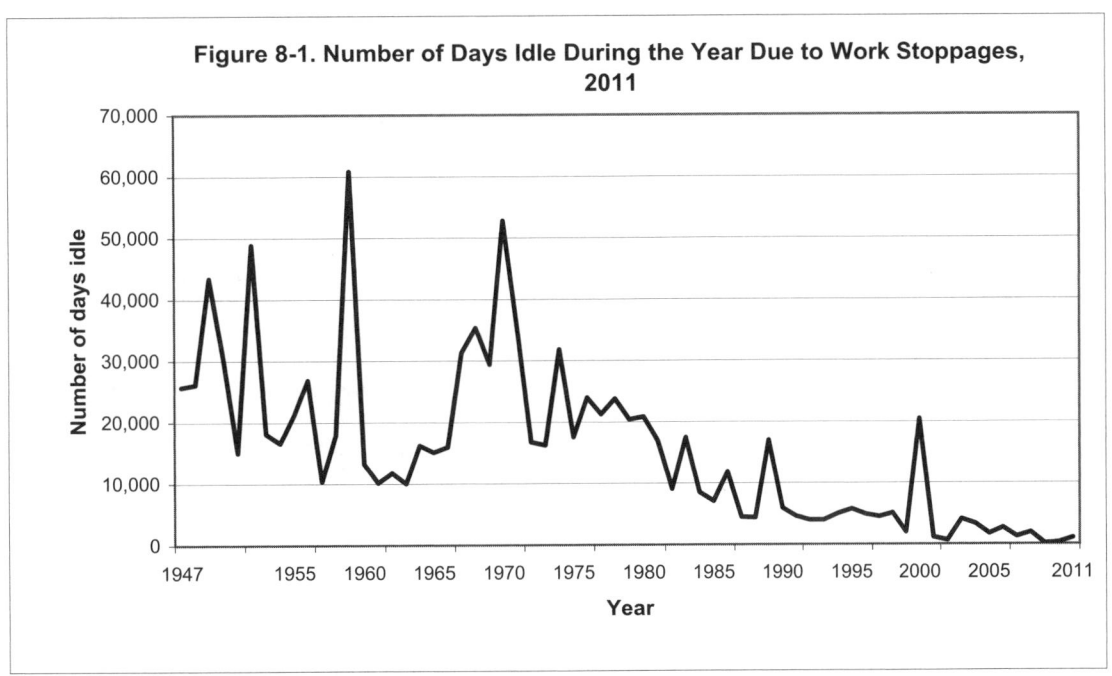

Figure 8-1. Number of Days Idle During the Year Due to Work Stoppages, 2011

While the number of work stoppages has declined dramatically since 1947, the number has been increasing the past two years. In 2009, only five work stoppages involving 1,000 or more workers took place compared with 11 work stoppages in 2010 and 19 in 2011. From 2010 to 2011, the number of days idle increased dramatically from 302 to 1,020. (See Table 8-1.)

OTHER HIGHLIGHTS

- Union membership was higher for men (12.4 percent) than for women (11.2 percent) in 2011. According to race, Black workers had the highest rate of union membership at 13.5 percent followed by Whites at 11.6 percent. Slightly more than 10 percent of Asian workers belonged to a union compared with 9.7 percent of Hispanic workers. Hispanics may be of any race. (See Table 8-2.)

- In 2011, the percentage of workers belonging to a union declined slightly to 11.8 percent. Approximately 14.7 million workers were union members in 2011 compared with 17.7 million in 1983. (See Tables 8-2 and 8-5.)

- Workers in the public sector were far more likely to be in a union than those in the private sector (37.0 percent compared with 6.9 percent). In the private sector, workers in utilities had the highest unionization rate (25.0 percent) while those in finance (1.0 percent) had the lowest. (See Table 8-3.)

- In 2011, 21 states had higher union membership rates than average. The states reporting the highest levels of union membership included: New York (24.1 percent), Alaska (22.1 percent), Hawaii (21.5 percent), Washington (19.0 percent), and Michigan (17.5 percent). (See Table 8-6.)

NOTES AND DEFINITIONS

WORK STOPPAGES

Collection and Coverage

Data on work stoppages measure the number and duration of major strikes or lockouts (involving 1,000 workers or more) during the year, the number of workers involved in these stoppages, and the amount of time lost due to these stoppages.

Information on work stoppages is obtained from reports issued by the Federal Mediation and Conciliation Service, state labor market information offices, Bureau of Labor Statistics (BLS) Strike Reports from the Office of Employment and Unemployment Statistics, and media sources such as the *Daily Labor Report* and the *Wall Street Journal*. One or both parties involved in the work stoppage (employer and/or union) is contacted to verify the duration of the stoppage and number of workers idled by the stoppage.

Concepts and Definitions

Days of idleness is calculated by taking the number of workers involved in the strike or lockout and multiplying it by the number of days workers are off the job. The number of working days lost for every major work stoppage is based on a 5-day workweek (Monday through Friday), excluding federal holidays.

Major work stoppage includes both worker-initiated strikes and employer-initiated lockouts involving 1,000 workers or more. BLS does not distinguish between lockouts and strikes in its statistics.

Workers involved consists of workers directly involved in the stoppage. This category does not measure the indirect or secondary effect of stoppages on other establishments whose employees are idle from material shortages or lack of service.

Sources of Additional Information

Additional information is available in BLS news release USDL 12-0215, "Major Work Stoppages in 2011" on the BLS Web site at <http://www.bls.gov/wsp/home.htm>.

UNION MEMBERSHIP

Collection and Coverage

The estimates of union membership are obtained from the Current Population Survey (CPS), which provides basic information on the labor force, employment, and unemployment. The survey is conducted monthly for the Bureau of Labor Statistics by the U.S. Census Bureau from a scientifically selected national sample of about 60,000 households. The union membership and earnings data are tabulated from one-quarter of the CPS monthly sample and are limited to wage and salary workers. All self-employed workers are excluded. The data in these tables are annual averages.

The Census Bureau introduces adjustments to the population controls for the CPS as part of its annual update of population estimates. The effect of the revised population controls on the union affiliation data is unknown. However, the effect of the new controls on the monthly CPS estimates was to decrease the December 2010 employment level by 347,000. The updated controls had little or no effect on unemployment rates and other ratios.

Concepts and Definitions

Full-time workers are workers who usually work 35 hours or more per week at their sole or principal job.

Part-time workers are workers who usually work fewer than 35 hours per week at their sole or principal job.

Wage and salary workers are workers who receive wages, salaries, commissions, tips, payment in kind, or piece rates. The group includes employees in both the private and public sectors, but, for the purposes of the union membership and earnings series, excludes all self-employed persons, regardless of whether or not their businesses are incorporated.

Hispanic or Latino ethnicity refers to persons who identified themselves in the enumeration process as being Spanish, Hispanic, or Latino. Persons whose ethnicity is identified as Hispanic or Latino may be of any race.

Union members are members of a labor union or an employee association similar to a union.

Represented by unions refers to union members, as well as to workers who have no union affiliation but whose jobs are covered by a union contract.

Median earnings is the amount which divides a given earnings distribution into two equal groups, one having earnings above the median and the other having earnings below the median. The estimating procedure places each reported or calculated weekly earnings value into $50-wide intervals which are centered around multiples of $50. The actual value is estimated through the linear interpolation of the interval in which the median lies.

Usual weekly earnings represent earnings before taxes and other deductions and include any overtime pay, commissions, or tips usually received (at the main job in the case of multiple jobholders). Prior to 1994, respondents were asked how much they usually earned per week. Since January 1994, respondents have been asked to identify the easiest way for them to report earnings (hourly, weekly, biweekly, twice monthly, monthly, annually, other) and how much they usually earn in the reported time period. Earnings reported on a basis other than weekly are converted to a weekly equivalent. The term "usual" is as perceived by the respondent. If the respondent asks for a definition of "usual," interviewers are instructed to define the term as more than half of the weeks worked during the past 4 or 5 months.

Sources of Additional Information

For additional information see BLS news release USDL 12-0094, "Union Members–2011."

Table 8-1. Work Stoppages Involving 1,000 Workers or More, 1947–2011

(Number, percent.)

Year	Stoppages beginning during the year		Days idle during the year[1]	
	Number	Workers involved (thousands)[2]	Number (thousands)	Percent of estimated total working time[3]
1947	270	1 629	25 720	. . .
1948	245	1 435	26 127	0.22
1949	262	2 537	43 420	0.38
1950	424	1 698	30 390	0.26
1951	415	1 462	15 070	0.12
1952	470	2 746	48 820	0.38
1953	437	1 623	18 130	0.14
1954	265	1 075	16 630	0.13
1955	363	2 055	21 180	0.16
1956	287	1 370	26 840	0.20
1957	279	887	10 340	0.07
1958	332	1 587	17 900	0.13
1959	245	1 381	60 850	0.43
1960	222	896	13 260	0.09
1961	195	1 031	10 140	0.07
1962	211	793	11 760	0.08
1963	181	512	10 020	0.07
1964	246	1 183	16 220	0.11
1965	268	999	15 140	0.10
1966	321	1 300	16 000	0.10
1967	381	2 192	31 320	0.18
1968	392	1 855	35 367	0.20
1969	412	1 576	29 397	0.16
1970	381	2 468	52 761	0.29
1971	298	2 516	35 538	0.19
1972	250	975	16 764	0.09
1973	317	1 400	16 260	0.08
1974	424	1 796	31 809	0.16
1975	235	965	17 563	0.09
1976	231	1 519	23 962	0.12
1977	298	1 212	21 258	0.10
1978	219	1 006	23 774	0.11
1979	235	1 021	20 409	0.09
1980	187	795	20 844	0.09
1981	145	729	16 908	0.07
1982	96	656	9 061	0.04
1983	81	909	17 461	0.08
1984	62	376	8 499	0.04
1985	54	324	7 079	0.03
1986	69	533	11 861	0.05
1987	46	174	4 481	0.02
1988	40	118	4 381	0.02
1989	51	452	16 996	0.07
1990	44	185	5 926	0.02
1991	40	392	4 584	0.02
1992	35	364	3 989	0.01
1993	35	182	3 981	0.01
1994	45	322	5 021	0.02
1995	31	192	5 771	0.02
1996	37	273	4 889	0.02
1997	29	339	4 497	0.01
1998	34	387	5 116	0.02
1999	17	73	1 996	0.01
2000	39	394	20 419	0.06
2001	29	99	1 151	([4])
2002	19	46	660	([4])
2003	14	129	4 091	0.01
2004	17	171	3 344	0.01
2005	22	100	1 736	0.01
2006	20	70	2 688	0.01
2007	21	189	1 265	([4])
2008	15	72	1 954	0.01
2009	5	13	124	([4])
2010	11	45	302	([4])
2011	19	113	1 020	([4])

[1]Days idle include all stoppages in effect during the reference period. For work stoppages that are still ongoing at the end of the calendar year, only those days of idleness during the calendar year are counted.
[2]Workers are counted more than once if involved in more than one stoppage during the reference period.
[3]Agricultural and government workers are included in the calculation of estimated working time; private household, forestry, and fishery workers are excluded.
[4]Less than 0.005 percent.
. . . = Not available.

Table 8-2. Union Affiliation of Employed Wage and Salary Workers, by Selected Characteristics, 2006–2011

(Numbers in thousands, percent.)

Characteristic	2006					2007					2008				
	Total employed	Member of union[1]		Represented by union[2]		Total employed	Member of union[1]		Represented by union[2]		Total employed	Member of union[1]		Represented by union[2]	
		Total	Percent of employed	Total	Percent of employed		Total	Percent of employed	Total	Percent of employed		Total	Percent of employed	Total	Percent of employed
SEX AND AGE															
Both Sexes, 16 Years and Over	128 237	15 359	12.0	16 860	13.1	129 767	15 670	12.1	17 243	13.3	129 377	16 098	12.4	17 761	13.7
16 to 24 years	19 538	857	4.4	978	5.0	19 395	939	4.8	1 068	5.5	18 705	930	5.0	1 062	5.7
25 years and over	108 699	14 502	13.3	15 883	14.6	110 372	14 731	13.3	16 176	14.7	110 672	15 168	13.7	16 699	15.1
25 to 34 years	28 805	2 899	10.1	3 195	11.1	29 409	3 050	10.4	3 358	11.4	29 276	3 120	10.7	3 443	11.8
35 to 44 years	30 526	3 997	13.1	4 356	14.3	30 296	3 972	13.1	4 362	14.4	29 708	3 993	13.4	4 365	14.7
45 to 54 years	29 401	4 710	16.0	5 131	17.5	29 731	4 664	15.7	5 087	17.1	29 787	4 767	16.0	5 228	17.6
55 to 64 years	16 095	2 568	16.0	2 832	17.6	16 752	2 691	16.1	2 967	17.7	17 430	2 887	16.6	3 209	18.4
65 years and over	3 872	328	8.5	370	9.5	4 183	355	8.5	402	9.6	4 471	401	9.0	454	10.2
Men, 16 Years and Over	66 811	8 657	13.0	9 360	14.0	67 468	8 767	13.0	9 494	14.1	66 846	8 938	13.4	9 724	14.5
16 to 24 years	10 130	543	5.4	608	6.0	9 959	551	5.5	627	6.3	9 537	555	5.8	617	6.5
25 years and over	56 682	8 114	14.3	8 752	15.4	57 509	8 217	14.3	8 867	15.4	57 309	8 383	14.6	9 107	15.9
25 to 34 years	15 677	1 650	10.5	1 793	11.4	15 994	1 736	10.9	1 884	11.8	15 780	1 750	11.1	1 909	12.1
35 to 44 years	16 159	2 309	14.3	2 488	15.4	16 070	2 318	14.4	2 501	15.6	15 653	2 307	14.7	2 491	15.9
45 to 54 years	14 867	2 617	17.6	2 807	18.9	15 040	2 578	17.1	2 745	18.3	14 988	2 608	17.4	2 812	18.8
55 to 64 years	7 990	1 370	17.1	1 474	18.4	8 286	1 403	16.9	1 532	18.5	8 657	1 525	17.6	1 682	19.4
65 years and over	1 989	167	8.4	190	9.6	2 119	181	8.5	205	9.7	2 230	193	8.7	213	9.6
Women, 16 Years and Over	61 426	6 702	10.9	7 501	12.2	62 299	6 903	11.1	7 749	12.4	62 532	7 160	11.4	8 036	12.9
16 to 24 years	9 408	315	3.3	370	3.9	9 436	388	4.1	441	4.7	9 168	374	4.1	445	4.8
25 years and over	52 018	6 388	12.3	7 131	13.7	52 863	6 514	12.3	7 308	13.8	53 364	6 785	12.7	7 592	14.2
25 to 34 years	13 127	1 249	9.5	1 401	10.7	13 416	1 313	9.8	1 474	11.0	13 496	1 370	10.1	1 534	11.4
35 to 44 years	14 368	1 687	11.7	1 867	13.0	14 226	1 653	11.6	1 861	13.1	14 055	1 685	12.0	1 874	13.3
45 to 54 years	14 534	2 093	14.4	2 325	16.0	14 691	2 086	14.2	2 341	15.9	14 799	2 159	14.6	2 416	16.3
55 to 64 years	8 106	1 198	14.8	1 358	16.8	8 466	1 288	15.2	1 435	17.0	8 773	1 363	15.5	1 527	17.4
65 years and over	1 883	160	8.5	180	9.5	2 065	174	8.4	197	9.5	2 241	208	9.3	241	10.7
RACE, HISPANIC ORIGIN, AND SEX															
White, 16 Years and Over[3]	104 668	12 259	11.7	13 424	12.8	105 515	12 487	11.8	13 715	13.0	105 052	12 863	12.2	14 222	13.5
Men	55 459	7 115	12.8	7 668	13.8	55 771	7 134	12.8	7 708	13.8	55 197	7 309	13.2	7 961	14.4
Women	49 209	5 144	10.5	5 756	11.7	49 743	5 352	10.8	6 007	12.1	49 855	5 555	11.1	6 261	12.6
Black, 16 Years and Over[3]	14 878	2 163	14.5	2 391	16.1	15 177	2 165	14.3	2 403	15.8	15 030	2 178	14.5	2 370	15.8
Men	6 788	1 056	15.6	1 158	17.1	6 945	1 097	15.8	1 205	17.3	6 809	1 081	15.9	1 159	17.0
Women	8 090	1 107	13.7	1 233	15.2	8 232	1 067	13.0	1 198	14.6	8 221	1 097	13.3	1 211	14.7
Asian, 16 Years and Over[3]	5 703	592	10.4	657	11.5	6 016	654	10.9	720	12.0	6 157	653	10.6	714	11.6
Men	3 015	286	9.5	316	10.5	3 168	324	10.2	348	11.0	3 216	310	9.6	339	10.6
Women	2 688	306	11.4	340	12.7	2 849	330	11.6	372	13.1	2 941	344	11.7	374	12.7
Hispanic, 16 Years and Over[4]	18 121	1 770	9.8	1 935	10.7	18 778	1 837	9.8	2 026	10.8	18 572	1 960	10.6	2 168	11.7
Men	10 842	1 064	9.8	1 144	10.6	11 163	1 108	9.9	1 208	10.8	10 998	1 204	11.0	1 317	12.0
Women	7 279	706	9.7	791	10.9	7 615	728	9.6	818	10.7	7 574	756	10.0	852	11.2
FULL- OR PART-TIME STATUS[5]															
Full-time workers	106 106	13 938	13.1	15 244	14.4	107 339	14 201	13.2	15 570	14.5	106 648	14 561	13.7	16 029	15.0
Part-time workers	21 863	1 382	6.3	1 573	7.2	22 172	1 437	6.5	1 635	7.4	22 497	1 505	6.7	1 697	7.5

[1]Data refer to members of a labor union or to an employee association similar to a union.
[2]Data refer to members of a labor union or to an employee association similar to a union, as well as to workers who report no union affiliation but whose jobs are covered by a union or an employee association contract.
[3]Beginning in 2003, persons who selected this race group only; persons who selected more than one race group are not included. Prior to 2003, persons who reported more than one race group were included in the group they identified as their main race. Additionally, estimates for the above race groups (White, Black, and Asian) do not sum to totals because data are not presented for all races.
[4]May be of any race.
[5]The distinction between full- and part-time workers is based on hours usually worked. Data will not sum to totals because full- or part-time status on the principal job is not identifiable for a small number of multiple job holders.

Table 8-2. Union Affiliation of Employed Wage and Salary Workers, by Selected Characteristics, 2006–2011
—Continued

(Numbers in thousands, percent.)

Characteristic	2009					2010					2011				
	Total employed	Member of union[1]		Represented by union[2]		Total employed	Member of union[1]		Represented by union[2]		Total employed	Member of union[1]		Represented by union[2]	
		Total	Percent of employed	Total	Percent of employed		Total	Percent of employed	Total	Percent of employed		Total	Percent of employed	Total	Percent of employed
SEX AND AGE															
Both Sexes, 16 Years and Over	124 490	15 327	12.3	16 904	13.6	124 073	14 715	11.9	16 290	13.1	125 187	14 764	11.8	16 290	13.0
16 to 24 years	17 173	813	4.7	941	5.5	16 638	722	4.3	836	5.0	16 910	737	4.4	845	5.0
25 years and over	107 317	14 514	13.5	15 962	14.9	107 435	13 993	13.0	15 453	14.4	108 278	14 027	13.0	15 444	14.3
25 to 34 years	28 067	2 942	10.5	3 262	11.6	28 363	2 860	10.1	3 179	11.2	28 682	2 829	9.9	3 155	11.0
35 to 44 years	28 066	3 669	13.1	4 035	14.4	27 356	3 512	12.8	3 888	14.2	27 231	3 470	12.7	3 804	14.0
45 to 54 years	29 054	4 551	15.7	4 994	17.2	28 860	4 340	15.0	4 774	16.5	28 693	4 286	14.9	4 707	16.4
55 to 64 years	17 599	2 926	16.6	3 186	18.1	18 199	2 849	15.7	3 126	17.2	18 751	2 949	15.7	3 219	17.2
65 years and over	4 530	425	9.4	485	10.7	4 657	432	9.3	486	10.4	4 920	494	10.0	559	11.4
Men, 16 Years and Over	63 539	8 441	13.3	9 176	14.4	63 531	7 994	12.6	8 761	13.8	64 686	8 006	12.4	8 731	13.5
16 to 24 years	8 555	493	5.8	560	6.5	8 291	419	5.0	476	5.7	8 636	435	5.0	486	5.6
25 years and over	54 984	7 947	14.5	8 616	15.7	55 240	7 575	13.7	8 286	15.0	56 050	7 571	13.5	8 246	14.7
25 to 34 years	14 952	1 633	10.9	1 786	11.9	15 148	1 603	10.6	1 759	11.6	15 465	1 541	10.0	1 706	11.0
35 to 44 years	14 679	2 077	14.1	2 250	15.3	14 430	1 966	13.6	2 151	14.9	14 412	1 946	13.5	2 114	14.7
45 to 54 years	14 421	2 492	17.3	2 693	18.7	14 423	2 349	16.3	2 554	17.7	14 415	2 327	16.1	2 513	17.4
55 to 64 years	8 647	1 536	17.8	1 654	19.1	8 895	1 430	16.1	1 566	17.6	9 212	1 497	16.2	1 623	17.6
65 years and over	2 285	211	9.2	233	10.2	2 343	227	9.7	256	10.9	2 547	260	10.2	290	11.4
Women, 16 Years and Over	60 951	6 887	11.3	7 727	12.7	60 542	6 722	11.1	7 528	12.4	60 502	6 758	11.2	7 558	12.5
16 to 24 years	8 619	320	3.7	381	4.4	8 347	303	3.6	361	4.3	8 274	302	3.6	360	4.3
25 years and over	52 333	6 567	12.5	7 346	14.0	52 195	6 418	12.3	7 167	13.7	52 228	6 456	12.4	7 199	13.8
25 to 34 years	13 116	1 309	10.0	1 476	11.3	13 215	1 257	9.5	1 420	10.7	13 218	1 288	9.7	1 449	11.0
35 to 44 years	13 387	1 593	11.9	1 785	13.3	12 926	1 546	12.0	1 737	13.4	12 819	1 524	11.9	1 690	13.2
45 to 54 years	14 633	2 060	14.1	2 302	15.7	14 437	1 991	13.8	2 219	15.4	14 278	1 959	13.7	2 195	15.4
55 to 64 years	8 952	1 390	15.5	1 532	17.1	9 303	1 419	15.3	1 560	16.8	9 540	1 452	15.2	1 596	16.7
65 years and over	2 245	215	9.6	252	11.2	2 314	205	8.8	230	10.0	2 373	233	9.8	269	11.3
RACE, HISPANIC ORIGIN, AND SEX															
White, 16 Years and Over[3]	101 581	12 330	12.1	13 595	13.4	101 042	11 865	11.7	13 111	13.0	101 768	11 853	11.6	13 061	12.8
Men	52 691	6 918	13.1	7 512	14.3	52 565	6 588	12.5	7 208	13.7	53 418	6 568	12.3	7 156	13.4
Women	48 889	5 412	11.1	6 083	12.4	48 477	5 277	10.9	5 903	12.2	48 351	5 285	10.9	5 905	12.2
Black, 16 Years and Over[3]	14 127	1 966	13.9	2 172	15.4	14 195	1 896	13.4	2 115	14.9	14 249	1 927	13.5	2 140	15.0
Men	6 257	964	15.4	1 046	16.7	6 347	938	14.8	1 031	16.2	6 440	940	14.6	1 020	15.8
Women	7 870	1 002	12.7	1 126	14.3	7 848	958	12.2	1 085	13.8	7 808	987	12.6	1 119	14.3
Asian, 16 Years and Over[3]	5 847	664	11.4	730	12.5	5 900	645	10.9	713	12.1	6 153	623	10.1	690	11.2
Men	3 075	332	10.8	370	12.0	3 112	292	9.4	325	10.4	3 269	296	9.1	331	10.1
Women	2 772	333	12.0	361	13.0	2 787	353	12.6	388	13.9	2 884	327	11.4	359	12.4
Hispanic, 16 Years and Over[4]	18 034	1 841	10.2	2 036	11.3	18 263	1 820	10.0	2 021	11.1	18 733	1 826	9.7	2 015	10.8
Men	10 518	1 108	10.5	1 199	11.4	10 646	1 090	10.2	1 196	11.2	10 980	1 078	9.8	1 186	10.8
Women	7 515	733	9.7	836	11.1	7 616	730	9.6	825	10.8	7 754	748	9.6	829	10.7
FULL- OR PART-TIME STATUS[5]															
Full-time workers	99 820	13 602	13.6	14 960	15.0	99 531	13 125	13.2	14 498	14.6	100 457	13 177	13.1	14 487	14.4
Part-time workers	24 431	1 698	7.0	1 913	7.8	24 351	1 560	6.4	1 760	7.2	24 502	1 557	6.4	1 769	7.2

[1]Data refer to members of a labor union or to an employee association similar to a union.
[2]Data refer to members of a labor union or to an employee association similar to a union, as well as to workers who report no union affiliation but whose jobs are covered by a union or an employee association contract.
[3]Beginning in 2003, persons who selected this race group only; persons who selected more than one race group are not included. Prior to 2003, persons who reported more than one race group were included in the group they identified as their main race. Additionally, estimates for the above race groups (White, Black, and Asian) do not sum to totals because data are not presented for all races.
[4]May be of any race.
[5]The distinction between full- and part-time workers is based on hours usually worked. Data will not sum to totals because full- or part-time status on the principal job is not identifiable for a small number of multiple job holders.

Table 8-3. Union Affiliation of Wage and Salary Workers, by Occupation and Industry, 2010–2011

(Thousands of people, percent.)

Occupation and industry	2010					2011				
	Total employed	Member of union[1]		Represented by union[2]		Total employed	Member of union[1]		Represented by union[2]	
		Total	Percent of employed	Total	Percent of employed		Total	Percent of employed	Total	Percent of employed
OCCUPATION										
Management, professional, and related	44 871	5 867	13.1	6 674	14.9	45 520	5 896	13.0	6 693	14.7
Management, business, and financial operations	16 684	782	4.7	973	5.8	17 196	851	4.9	1 039	6.0
Management	11 386	476	4.2	599	5.3	11 593	538	4.6	668	5.8
Business and financial operations	5 299	306	5.8	373	7.0	5 603	313	5.6	371	6.6
Professional and related	28 187	5 085	18.0	5 701	20.2	28 324	5 045	17.8	5 654	20.0
Computer and mathematical	3 350	136	4.0	180	5.4	3 438	136	4.0	167	4.9
Architecture and engineering	2 468	197	8.0	244	9.9	2 615	191	7.3	227	8.7
Life, physical, and social science	1 256	126	10.1	145	11.5	1 174	139	11.8	164	13.9
Community and social service	2 260	362	16.0	390	17.3	2 268	374	16.5	418	18.4
Legal	1 352	72	5.3	87	6.4	1 378	69	5.0	93	6.7
Education, training, and library	8 415	3 123	37.1	3 441	40.9	8 343	3 067	36.8	3 381	40.5
Arts, design, entertainment, sports, and media	1 899	112	5.9	139	7.3	1 904	132	6.9	146	7.7
Health care practitioner and technical	7 188	957	13.3	1 076	15.0	7 204	938	13.0	1 058	14.7
Services	22 463	2 467	11.0	2 683	11.9	22 508	2 429	10.8	2 653	11.8
Health care support	3 214	268	8.4	296	9.2	3 178	268	8.4	297	9.3
Protective service	3 287	1 122	34.1	1 202	36.6	3 207	1 107	34.5	1 180	36.8
Food preparation and serving related	7 555	297	3.9	328	4.3	7 677	305	4.0	351	4.6
Building and grounds cleaning and maintenance	4 549	469	10.3	518	11.4	4 603	489	10.6	532	11.6
Personal care and service	3 858	311	8.0	338	8.8	3 843	260	6.8	294	7.6
Sales and office	30 673	2 113	6.9	2 388	7.8	30 580	2 114	6.9	2 362	7.7
Sales and related	13 033	418	3.2	496	3.8	13 189	401	3.0	455	3.4
Office and administrative support	17 641	1 695	9.6	1 892	10.7	17 390	1 714	9.9	1 908	11.0
Natural resources, construction, and maintenance	10 879	1 808	16.6	1 912	17.6	10 955	1 838	16.8	1 959	17.9
Farming, fishing, and forestry	869	30	3.4	36	4.1	940	32	3.4	38	4.0
Construction and extraction	5 579	1 050	18.8	1 100	19.7	5 575	1 064	19.1	1 120	20.1
Installation, maintenance, and repair	4 431	728	16.4	776	17.5	4 440	742	16.7	801	18.0
Production, transportation, and material moving	15 186	2 460	16.2	2 633	17.3	15 625	2 487	15.9	2 622	16.8
Production	7 540	1 144	15.2	1 210	16.1	7 739	1 104	14.3	1 159	15.0
Transportation and material moving	7 647	1 316	17.2	1 423	18.6	7 886	1 383	17.5	1 463	18.6
INDUSTRY										
Private sector	103 040	7 092	6.9	7 884	7.7	104 737	7 202	6.9	7 969	7.6
Agriculture and related industries	1 131	18	1.6	23	2.0	1 183	16	1.4	21	1.8
Nonagricultural industries	101 909	7 074	6.9	7 861	7.7	103 554	7 186	6.9	7 948	7.7
Mining	695	55	8.0	61	8.8	780	56	7.2	61	7.8
Construction	6 103	801	13.1	838	13.7	6 244	874	14.0	928	14.9
Manufacturing	13 252	1 418	10.7	1 538	11.6	13 599	1 424	10.5	1 521	11.2
Durable goods	8 268	835	10.1	909	11.0	8 530	871	10.2	924	10.8
Nondurable goods	4 984	584	11.7	629	12.6	5 070	553	10.9	596	11.8
Wholesale and retail trade	17 800	860	4.8	949	5.3	18 002	859	4.8	959	5.3
Wholesale trade	3 321	173	5.2	186	5.6	3 419	150	4.4	165	4.8
Retail trade	14 479	687	4.7	763	5.3	14 582	709	4.9	794	5.4
Transportation and utilities	5 195	1 134	21.8	1 203	23.2	5 239	1 108	21.1	1 159	22.1
Transportation and warehousing	4 286	877	20.5	928	21.6	4 355	887	20.4	932	21.4
Utilities	909	257	28.3	275	30.3	884	221	25.0	228	25.7
Information[3]	2 743	265	9.6	299	10.9	2 756	279	10.1	298	10.8
Publishing, except Internet	577	29	5.0	38	6.5	554	25	4.5	26	4.7
Motion pictures and sound recording	341	32	9.3	36	10.6	337	47	13.8	48	14.1
Broadcasting, except Internet	561	29	5.1	38	6.8	576	34	5.9	40	7.0
Telecommunications	1 054	167	15.8	177	16.8	1 064	166	15.6	175	16.4
Financial activities	8 072	160	2.0	206	2.5	8 086	132	1.6	165	2.0
Finance and insurance	6 108	79	1.3	110	1.8	6 111	64	1.1	86	1.4
Finance	3 985	44	1.1	65	1.6	3 932	37	1.0	53	1.3
Insurance	2 123	35	1.6	45	2.1	2 179	27	1.2	33	1.5
Real estate and rental and leasing	1 964	81	4.1	95	4.9	1 976	67	3.4	79	4.0
Professional and business services	11 738	315	2.7	388	3.3	12 171	250	2.1	322	2.6
Professional and technical services	6 980	98	1.4	134	1.9	7 244	90	1.2	131	1.8
Management, administrative, and waste services	4 757	217	4.6	254	5.3	4 927	160	3.3	191	3.9
Education and health services	19 804	1 608	8.1	1 858	9.4	19 855	1 715	8.6	1 982	10.0
Education services	3 964	517	13.0	599	15.1	4 020	523	13.0	621	15.5
Health care and social assistance	15 840	1 091	6.9	1 259	7.9	15 835	1 192	7.5	1 361	8.6
Leisure and hospitality	11 111	301	2.7	337	3.0	11 355	305	2.7	344	3.0
Arts, entertainment, and recreation	2 111	113	5.3	126	5.9	2 107	111	5.3	121	5.7
Accommodation and food services	8 999	188	2.1	212	2.4	9 247	194	2.1	224	2.4
Accommodation	1 345	106	7.9	112	8.3	1 350	96	7.1	105	7.8
Food services and drinking places	7 654	82	1.1	100	1.3	7 898	98	1.2	119	1.5
Other services[3]	5 397	158	2.9	184	3.4	5 467	184	3.4	209	3.8
Other services, except private households	4 726	152	3.2	178	3.8	4 723	167	3.5	189	4.0
Public sector	21 033	7 623	36.2	8 406	40.0	20 450	7 562	37.0	8 321	40.7
Federal government	3 670	984	26.8	1 154	31.4	3 568	1 004	28.1	1 185	33.2
State government	6 328	1 969	31.1	2 191	34.6	6 261	1 973	31.5	2 189	35.0
Local government	11 035	4 670	42.3	5 061	45.9	10 621	4 586	43.2	4 947	46.6

Note: Updated population controls are introduced annually with the release of January data. Data refer to the sole or principal job of full- and part-time workers. Excluded are all self-employed workers, regardless of whether or not their businesses are incorporated.

[1] Data refer to members of a labor union or an employee association similar to a union.
[2] Data refer to members of a labor union or an employee association similar to a union, as well as to workers who report no union affiliation but whose jobs are covered by a union or an employee association contract.
[3] Includes other industries, not shown separately.

Table 8-4. Median Weekly Earnings of Full-Time Wage and Salary Workers, by Union Affiliation, Occupation, and Industry, 2010–2011

(Dollars.)

Occupation and industry	2010				2011			
	Total	Member of union[1]	Represented by union[2]	Non-union	Total	Member of union[1]	Represented by union[2]	Non-union
OCCUPATION								
Management, professional, and related	1 063	1 059	1 055	1 064	1 082	1 090	1 082	1 082
Management, business, and financial operations	1 155	1 138	1 145	1 156	1 160	1 169	1 171	1 159
Management	1 230	1 161	1 187	1 231	1 237	1 287	1 300	1 232
Business and financial operations	1 036	1 082	1 048	1 035	1 038	999	999	1 042
Professional and related	1 008	1 047	1 040	998	1 029	1 074	1 064	1 017
Computer and mathematical	1 289	1 062	1 074	1 311	1 305	1 156	1 169	1 324
Architecture and engineering	1 255	1 238	1 285	1 252	1 315	1 304	1 325	1 314
Life, physical, and social science	1 062	1 166	1 160	1 038	1 108	1 229	1 218	1 085
Community and social service	802	980	955	759	813	993	1 000	771
Legal	1 213	1 329	1 358	1 199	1 277	1 222	1 376	1 273
Education, training, and library	913	1 023	1 008	811	919	1 038	1 020	814
Arts, design, entertainment, sports, and media	920	999	1 015	915	929	1 179	1 152	910
Health care practitioner and technical	986	1 095	1 098	967	995	1 132	1 125	975
Services	479	723	707	447	486	742	732	455
Health care support	471	514	503	467	487	519	518	484
Protective service	747	995	980	629	757	1 008	1 004	627
Food preparation and serving related	406	508	503	402	409	504	500	405
Building and grounds cleaning and maintenance	446	595	590	421	465	635	626	431
Personal care and service	455	575	564	440	453	534	527	444
Sales and office	631	752	745	621	638	775	771	624
Sales and related	666	683	678	665	670	660	669	670
Office and administrative support	619	762	754	607	623	803	791	608
Natural resources, construction, and maintenance	719	1 013	1 006	664	732	1 016	1 008	676
Farming, fishing, and forestry	416	(3)	(3)	412	430	(3)	(3)	426
Construction and extraction	709	1 029	1 019	633	717	1 017	1 010	647
Installation, maintenance, and repair	794	1 005	1 001	745	806	1 036	1 021	767
Production, transportation, and material moving	599	817	809	564	609	798	794	582
Production	599	811	801	569	605	781	778	583
Transportation and material moving	599	824	816	557	614	813	808	580
INDUSTRY								
Private sector	717	864	855	703	729	878	875	716
Agriculture and related industries	465	(3)	(3)	463	483	(3)	(3)	481
Nonagricultural industries	721	865	856	707	732	879	875	721
Mining	1 032	1 076	1 053	1 026	1 064	1 030	1 005	1 069
Construction	735	1 051	1 046	692	746	1 059	1 037	698
Manufacturing	767	828	817	759	787	836	835	780
Durable goods	806	878	866	796	818	889	887	809
Nondurable goods	700	760	749	690	737	771	771	729
Wholesale and retail trade	612	669	657	610	613	622	622	612
Wholesale trade	777	770	774	777	759	798	773	758
Retail trade	575	613	608	572	578	591	592	577
Transportation and utilities	823	1 000	994	765	805	987	985	762
Transportation and warehousing	765	934	928	725	763	941	939	726
Utilities	1 102	1 199	1 193	1 014	1 081	1 132	1 132	1 027
Information[4]	912	1 018	998	895	940	1 122	1 117	916
Publishing, except Internet	876	(3)	(3)	871	910	(3)	(3)	902
Motion pictures and sound recording	917	(3)	(3)	893	965	(3)	(3)	926
Broadcasting, except Internet	821	(3)	(3)	814	834	(3)	(3)	834
Telecommunications	987	1 039	1 023	974	987	1 113	1 109	950
Financial activities	849	806	799	852	866	824	822	866
Finance and insurance	902	819	829	905	907	819	826	908
Finance	902	(3)	870	903	910	(3)	820	911
Insurance	902	(3)	(3)	908	899	(3)	(3)	900
Real estate and rental and leasing	702	786	713	701	736	836	815	734
Professional and business services	855	751	754	859	880	872	883	880
Professional and technical services	1 124	1 157	1 147	1 123	1 149	1 193	1 211	1 149
Management, administrative, and waste services	542	598	592	536	569	706	693	562
Education and health services	731	849	846	717	736	870	878	722
Education services	852	900	875	846	858	938	942	833
Health care and social assistance	698	817	823	686	706	801	809	697
Leisure and hospitality	469	580	575	461	479	607	605	473
Arts, entertainment, and recreation	616	636	632	614	612	632	625	611
Accommodation and food services	430	530	524	424	447	594	594	441
Accommodation	508	547	553	502	515	598	596	508
Food services and drinking places	417	517	509	416	427	585	592	424
Other services[4]	615	866	862	609	626	917	901	619
Other services, except private households	636	880	874	627	654	960	919	643
Public sector	878	961	956	801	895	981	977	810
Federal government	1 012	977	987	1 040	1 063	1 038	1 043	1 092
State government	829	922	917	769	852	956	946	785
Local government	854	971	962	743	861	973	967	743

Note: Updated population controls are introduced annually with the release of January data. Data refer to the sole or principal job of full- and part-time workers. Excluded are all self-employed workers, regardless of whether or not their businesses are incorporated.

[1] Data refer to members of a labor union or an employee association similar to a union.
[2] Data refer to members of a labor union or an employee association similar to a union, as well as to workers who report no union affiliation but whose jobs are covered by a union or an employee association contract.
[3] Data not shown where base is less than 50,000.
[4] Includes other industries, not shown separately.

Table 8-5. Union or Employee Association Members Among Wage and Salary Employees, 1977–2011

(Numbers in thousands, percent.)

Year	Total wage and salary employment	Union or employee association member	Union or association members as a percent of total wage and salary employment
1977	81 334	19 335	23.8
1978	84 968	19 548	23.0
1979	87 117	20 986	24.1
1980	87 480	20 095	23.0
1981	. . .	. . .	. . .
1982	. . .	. . .	. . .
1983[1]	88 290	17 717	20.1
1984	92 194	17 340	18.8
1985	94 521	16 996	18.0
1986	96 903	16 975	17.5
1987	99 303	16 913	17.0
1988	101 407	17 002	16.8
1989	103 480	16 980	16.4
1990	103 905	16 740	16.1
1991	102 786	16 568	16.1
1992	103 688	16 390	15.8
1993	105 087	16 598	15.8
1994[2]	107 989	16 748	15.5
1995	110 038	16 360	14.9
1996	111 960	16 269	14.5
1997	114 533	16 110	14.1
1998	116 730	16 211	13.9
1999	118 963	16 477	13.9
2000	120 786	16 258	13.5
2001	122 482	16 387	13.4
2002	121 826	16 145	13.3
2003	122 358	15 776	12.9
2004	123 554	15 472	12.5
2005	125 889	15 685	12.5
2006	128 237	15 359	12.0
2007	129 767	15 670	12.1
2008	129 377	16 098	12.4
2009	124 490	15 327	12.3
2010	124 073	14 715	11.9
2011	125 187	14 764	11.8

[1]Annual average data beginning in 1983 are not directly comparable with the data for 1977–1980.
[2]Data beginning in 1994 are not strictly comparable with data for 1993 and earlier years because of the introduction of a major redesign of the Current Population Survey questionnaire and collection methodology and the introduction of 1990 census–based population controls.
. . . = Not available.

Table 8-6. Union Affiliation of Employed Wage and Salary Workers, by State, 2010–2011

(Numbers in thousands, percent.)

State	2010					2011				
	Total employed	Member of union[1]		Represented by union[2]		Total employed	Member of union[1]		Represented by union[2]	
		Total	Percent of employed	Total	Percent of employed		Total	Percent of employed	Total	Percent of employed
UNITED STATES	124 073	14 715	11.9	16 290	13.1	125 187	14 764	11.8	16 290	13.0
Alabama	1 809	183	10.1	203	11.2	1 781	178	10.0	193	10.8
Alaska	295	68	22.9	73	24.8	306	68	22.1	73	23.7
Arizona	2 507	161	6.4	203	8.1	2 493	149	6.0	183	7.3
Arkansas	1 082	44	4.0	59	5.4	1 116	47	4.2	57	5.1
California	13 892	2 431	17.5	2 578	18.6	13 931	2 379	17.1	2 532	18.2
Colorado	2 130	140	6.6	171	8.0	2 186	179	8.2	203	9.3
Connecticut	1 549	258	16.7	270	17.4	1 542	259	16.8	272	17.7
Delaware	352	40	11.4	44	12.5	370	39	10.5	42	11.2
District of Columbia	287	26	9.0	30	10.5	281	23	8.3	28	9.9
Florida	7 033	392	5.6	488	6.9	7 283	460	6.3	557	7.6
Georgia	3 792	153	4.0	191	5.0	3 876	153	3.9	185	4.8
Hawaii	511	111	21.8	120	23.5	525	113	21.5	118	22.5
Idaho	584	42	7.1	50	8.6	594	31	5.1	36	6.1
Illinois	5 434	844	15.5	891	16.4	5 408	876	16.2	929	17.2
Indiana	2 554	279	10.9	313	12.2	2 681	302	11.3	333	12.4
Iowa	1 393	158	11.4	192	13.8	1 386	155	11.2	187	13.5
Kansas	1 222	84	6.8	111	9.1	1 268	97	7.6	128	10.1
Kentucky	1 642	147	8.9	166	10.1	1 678	150	8.9	173	10.3
Louisiana	1 742	76	4.3	96	5.5	1 717	77	4.5	91	5.3
Maine	543	63	11.6	71	13.0	554	63	11.3	74	13.4
Maryland	2 558	296	11.6	329	12.9	2 549	316	12.4	348	13.7
Massachusetts	2 866	415	14.5	446	15.6	2 882	422	14.6	445	15.4
Michigan	3 806	627	16.5	659	17.3	3 838	671	17.5	703	18.3
Minnesota	2 468	385	15.6	397	16.1	2 461	371	15.1	390	15.8
Mississippi	1 037	46	4.5	58	5.6	1 081	54	5.0	73	6.8
Missouri	2 469	244	9.9	274	11.1	2 531	275	10.9	316	12.5
Montana	364	46	12.7	52	14.4	377	49	13.0	55	14.6
Nebraska	813	75	9.3	96	11.8	828	65	7.9	83	10.0
Nevada	1 012	151	15.0	170	16.8	1 050	154	14.6	175	16.6
New Hampshire	622	63	10.2	73	11.7	617	68	11.1	77	12.5
New Jersey	3 734	637	17.1	660	17.7	3 816	615	16.1	641	16.8
New Mexico	750	55	7.3	72	9.7	726	49	6.8	65	9.0
New York	8 078	1 959	24.2	2 099	26.0	7 920	1 906	24.1	2 068	26.1
North Carolina	3 686	117	3.2	180	4.9	3 589	105	2.9	149	4.1
North Dakota	313	23	7.4	28	9.1	318	20	6.3	27	8.6
Ohio	4 787	655	13.7	702	14.7	4 813	647	13.4	706	14.7
Oklahoma	1 418	77	5.5	99	6.9	1 458	94	6.4	113	7.7
Oregon	1 515	245	16.2	268	17.7	1 574	270	17.1	286	18.1
Pennsylvania	5 224	770	14.7	831	15.9	5 348	779	14.6	846	15.8
Rhode Island	456	75	16.4	79	17.4	453	79	17.4	81	17.9
South Carolina	1 713	80	4.6	107	6.2	1 726	59	3.4	86	5.0
South Dakota	357	20	5.6	24	6.6	359	18	5.1	23	6.5
Tennessee	2 477	115	4.7	142	5.8	2 504	115	4.6	139	5.6
Texas	10 025	545	5.4	677	6.7	10 214	534	5.2	643	6.3
Utah	1 144	75	6.5	96	8.4	1 150	67	5.8	82	7.1
Vermont	289	34	11.8	40	13.6	290	35	12.0	39	13.5
Virginia	3 473	161	4.6	196	5.7	3 550	163	4.6	198	5.6
Washington	2 837	552	19.4	605	21.3	2 727	517	19.0	557	20.4
West Virginia	677	100	14.8	111	16.5	672	93	13.8	102	15.2
Wisconsin	2 508	355	14.2	380	15.1	2 538	339	13.3	358	14.1
Wyoming	246	18	7.4	21	8.4	250	18	7.2	21	8.4

Note: Updated population controls are introduced annually with the release of January data. Data refer to the sole or principal job of full- and part-time workers. Excluded are all self-employed workers, regardless of whether or not their businesses are incorporated.

[1]Data refer to members of a labor union or an employee association similar to a union.
[2]Data refer to members of a labor union or an employee association similar to a union, as well as to workers who report no union affiliation but whose jobs are covered by a union or an employee association contract.

Chapter Nine

PRICES

PRICES

HIGHLIGHTS

This chapter examines the movement of prices, which is one of the most important indicators of the state of the economy. Several indexes are covered: the Producer Price Index (PPI), which gives information about prices received by producers; the Consumer Price Index (CPI), which gives information about prices paid by consumers; and the Import Price Index (MPI) and the Export Price Index (XPI), which gives information about prices involved in various foreign trade, export, and import price indexes.

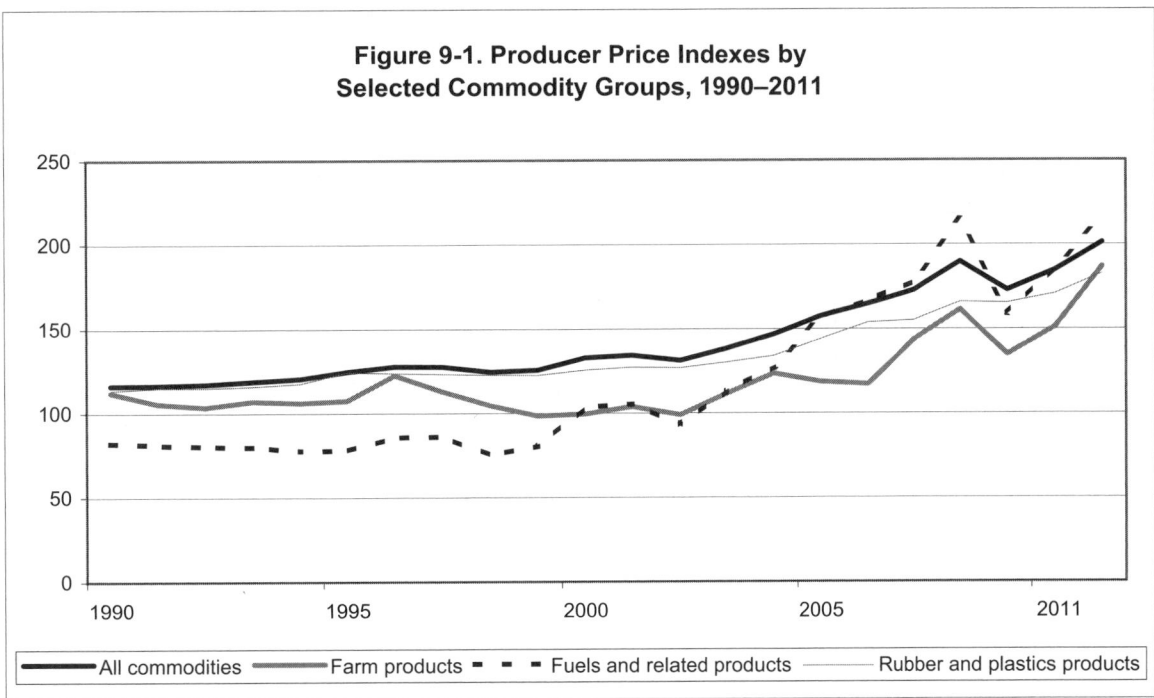

Figure 9-1. Producer Price Indexes by Selected Commodity Groups, 1990–2011

Legend: All commodities — Farm products — ▪ ▪ ▪ Fuels and related products — Rubber and plastics products

The PPI for all commodities increased for the second consecutive year in 2011, rising 8.8 percent, after declining sharply in 2009. The PPI for farm products increased 23.6 percent from 2010 to 2011 while the PPI for fuel and related products also grew quickly at 16.2 percent. (See Table 9-2.)

OTHER HIGHLIGHTS

- The PPI for crude materials for further processing also continued to rise quickly in 2011 after declining steeply in 2009. In 2011, it increased 17.5 percent after increasing 21.1 percent in 2010. (See Table 9-1.)

- In 2011, the PPI for finished consumer goods increased much faster than the PPI for capital equipment (7.5 percent compared with 1.5 percent). (See Table 9-1.)

- From 2000 through 2011, the producer price index increased 51.5 percent. Fuels and related products grew the fastest at 108.6 percent followed by farm products at 87.6 percent and chemicals and related products at 82.2 percent. (See Table 9-2.)

NOTES AND DEFINITIONS

PRODUCER PRICE INDEX

Coverage

The *Producer Price Index (PPI)* measures average changes in prices received by domestic producers of goods and services. PPIs measure price change from the perspective of the seller. This contrasts with other measures, such as the Consumer Price Index (CPI). CPIs measure price change from the purchaser's perspective. Sellers' and purchasers' prices can differ due to government subsidies, sales and excise taxes, and distribution costs.

The PPI is the oldest continuous series of the federal government. When first published in 1902, it covered the years from 1890 through 1901 and was named the Wholesale Price Index (WPI). It was renamed the Producer Price Index in 1978. Many major commodity-based indexes are available from the early 1900s. Indexes for the major stage-of-processing categories are available from 1947 to present. Most manufacturing and mining industry indexes, however, are available only since the early 1980s; most indexes for services began being introduced in the mid-2000s.

Over 25,000 establishments provide approximately 100,000 price quotations per month today. Establishments report selling prices on the Tuesday that includes the 13th of each month and they usually respond by mail or fax. Over 10,000 PPIs for individual products and groups of products are released each month.

PPIs are typically organized into one of three groups: (1) stage-of-processing indexes, (2) commodity indexes, and (3) indexes for the net output of industries. The stage-of-processing structure organizes products by class of buyer and degree of fabrication. The commodity structure organizes products by similarity of end use or material composition. The PPI publishes over 600 industry price indexes in combination with over 5,000 specific product line and product category sub-indexes.

The PPI is widely used in many aspects of business and government. It is commonly used as an economic indicator, a deflator of other economic series, and as a basis for contract escalation.

A PPI may go out of publication if there is not cooperation from a minimum number of establishments or if in any given month, the index does not have actual prices from a minimum number of reporting units.

Sources of Additional Information

For more information on the underlying concepts and methodology of the Producer Price Index, see Chapter 14 in the *BLS Handbook of Methods*, which is available on the BLS Web site at <http://www.bls.gov/opub/hom/>.

Table 9-1. Producer Price Indexes, by Stage of Processing, 1947–2011

(1982 = 100.)

Year	Crude materials for further processing				Intermediate materials, supplies, and components						Finished goods		
	Total	Foodstuffs and feedstuffs	Nonfood materials, except fuel	Fuel	Total	Materials and components for construction	Components for manufacturing	Processed fuels and lubricants	Containers	Supplies	Total	Consumer goods	Capital equipment
1947	31.7	45.1	24.0	7.5	23.3	22.5	21.3	14.4	23.4	28.5	26.4	28.6	19.8
1948	34.7	48.8	26.7	8.9	25.2	24.9	23.0	16.4	24.4	29.8	28.5	30.8	21.6
1949	30.1	40.5	24.3	8.8	24.2	24.9	23.4	14.9	24.5	28.0	27.7	29.4	22.7
1950	32.7	43.4	27.8	8.8	25.3	26.2	24.3	15.2	25.2	29.0	28.2	29.9	23.2
1951	37.6	50.2	32.0	9.0	28.4	28.7	27.6	15.9	29.6	32.6	30.8	32.7	25.5
1952	34.5	47.3	27.8	9.0	27.5	28.5	27.6	15.7	28.0	32.6	30.6	32.3	25.9
1953	31.9	42.3	26.6	9.3	27.7	29.0	28.1	15.8	28.0	31.0	30.3	31.7	26.3
1954	31.6	42.3	26.1	8.9	27.9	29.1	28.3	15.8	28.5	31.7	30.4	31.7	26.7
1955	30.4	38.4	27.5	8.9	28.4	30.3	29.5	15.8	28.9	31.2	30.5	31.5	27.4
1956	30.6	37.6	28.6	9.5	29.6	31.8	32.2	16.3	31.0	32.0	31.3	32.0	29.5
1957	31.2	39.2	28.2	10.1	30.3	32.0	33.5	17.2	32.4	32.3	32.5	32.9	31.3
1958	31.9	41.6	27.1	10.2	30.4	32.0	33.8	16.2	33.2	33.1	33.2	33.6	32.1
1959	31.1	38.8	28.1	10.4	30.8	32.9	34.2	16.2	33.0	33.5	33.1	33.3	32.7
1960	30.4	38.4	26.9	10.5	30.8	32.7	34.0	16.6	33.4	33.3	33.4	33.6	32.8
1961	30.2	37.9	27.2	10.5	30.6	32.2	33.7	16.8	33.2	33.7	33.4	33.6	32.9
1962	30.5	38.6	27.1	10.4	30.6	32.1	33.4	16.7	33.6	34.5	33.5	33.7	33.0
1963	29.9	37.5	26.7	10.5	30.7	32.2	33.4	16.6	33.2	35.0	33.4	33.5	33.1
1964	29.6	36.6	27.2	10.5	30.8	32.5	33.7	16.2	32.9	34.7	33.5	33.6	33.4
1965	31.1	39.2	27.7	10.6	31.2	32.8	34.2	16.5	33.5	35.0	34.1	34.2	33.8
1966	33.1	42.7	28.3	10.9	32.0	33.6	35.4	16.8	34.5	36.5	35.2	35.4	34.6
1967	31.3	40.3	26.5	11.3	32.2	34.0	36.5	16.9	35.0	36.8	35.6	35.6	35.8
1968	31.8	40.9	27.1	11.5	33.0	35.7	37.3	16.5	35.9	37.1	36.6	36.5	37.0
1969	33.9	44.1	28.4	12.0	34.1	37.7	38.5	16.6	37.2	37.8	38.0	37.9	38.3
1970	35.2	45.2	29.1	13.8	35.4	38.3	40.6	17.7	39.0	39.7	39.3	39.1	40.1
1971	36.0	46.1	29.4	15.7	36.8	40.8	41.9	19.5	40.8	40.8	40.5	40.2	41.7
1972	39.9	51.5	32.3	16.8	38.2	43.0	42.9	20.1	42.7	42.5	41.8	41.5	42.8
1973	54.5	72.6	42.9	18.6	42.4	46.5	44.3	22.2	45.2	51.7	45.6	46.0	44.2
1974	61.4	76.4	54.5	24.8	52.5	55.0	51.1	33.6	53.3	56.8	52.6	53.1	50.5
1975	61.6	77.4	50.0	30.6	58.0	60.1	57.8	39.4	60.0	61.8	58.2	58.2	58.2
1976	63.4	76.8	54.9	34.5	60.9	64.1	60.8	42.3	63.1	65.8	60.8	60.4	62.1
1977	65.5	77.5	56.3	42.0	64.9	69.3	64.5	47.7	65.9	69.3	64.7	64.3	66.1
1978	73.4	87.3	61.9	48.2	69.5	76.5	69.2	49.9	71.0	72.9	69.8	69.4	71.3
1979	85.9	100.0	75.5	57.3	78.4	84.2	75.8	61.6	79.4	80.2	77.6	77.5	77.5
1980	95.3	104.6	91.8	69.4	90.3	91.3	84.6	85.0	89.1	89.9	88.0	88.6	85.8
1981	103.0	103.9	109.8	84.8	98.6	97.9	94.7	100.6	96.7	96.9	96.1	96.6	94.6
1982	100.0	100.0	100.0	100.0	100.0	100.0	100.0	100.0	100.0	100.0	100.0	100.0	100.0
1983	101.3	101.8	98.8	105.1	100.6	102.8	102.4	95.4	100.4	101.8	101.6	101.3	102.8
1984	103.5	104.7	101.0	105.1	103.1	105.6	105.0	95.7	105.9	104.1	103.7	103.3	105.2
1985	95.8	94.8	94.3	102.7	102.7	107.3	106.4	92.8	109.0	104.4	104.7	103.8	107.5
1986	87.7	93.2	76.0	92.2	99.1	108.1	107.5	72.7	110.3	105.6	103.2	101.4	109.7
1987	93.7	96.2	88.5	84.1	101.5	109.8	108.8	73.3	114.5	107.7	105.4	103.6	111.7
1988	96.0	106.1	85.9	82.1	107.1	116.1	112.3	71.2	120.1	113.7	108.0	106.2	114.3
1989	103.1	111.2	95.8	85.3	112.0	121.3	116.4	76.4	125.4	118.1	113.6	112.1	118.8
1990	108.9	113.1	107.3	84.8	114.5	122.9	119.0	85.9	127.7	119.4	119.2	118.2	122.9
1991	101.2	105.5	97.5	82.9	114.4	124.5	121.0	85.3	128.1	121.4	121.7	120.5	126.7
1992	100.4	105.1	94.2	84.0	114.7	126.5	122.0	84.5	127.7	122.7	123.2	121.7	129.1
1993	102.4	108.4	94.1	87.1	116.2	132.0	123.0	84.7	126.4	125.0	124.7	123.0	131.4
1994	101.8	106.5	97.0	82.4	118.5	136.6	124.3	83.1	129.7	127.0	125.5	123.3	134.1
1995	102.7	105.8	105.8	72.1	124.9	142.1	126.5	84.2	148.8	132.1	127.9	125.6	136.7
1996	113.8	121.5	105.7	92.6	125.7	143.6	126.9	90.0	141.1	135.9	131.3	129.5	138.3
1997	111.1	112.2	103.5	101.3	125.6	146.5	126.4	89.3	136.0	135.9	131.8	130.2	138.2
1998	96.8	103.9	84.5	86.7	123.0	146.8	125.9	81.1	140.8	134.8	130.7	128.9	137.6
1999	98.2	98.7	91.1	91.2	123.2	148.9	125.7	84.6	142.5	134.2	133.0	132.0	137.6
2000	120.6	100.2	118.0	136.9	129.2	150.7	126.2	102.0	151.6	136.9	138.0	138.2	138.8
2001	121.0	106.1	101.5	151.4	129.7	150.6	126.4	104.5	153.1	138.7	140.7	141.5	139.7
2002	108.1	99.5	101.0	117.3	127.8	151.3	126.1	96.3	152.1	138.9	138.9	139.4	139.1
2003	135.3	113.5	116.9	185.7	133.7	153.6	125.9	112.6	153.7	141.5	143.3	145.3	139.5
2004	159.0	127.0	149.2	211.4	142.6	166.4	127.4	124.3	159.3	146.7	148.5	151.7	141.4
2005	182.2	122.7	176.7	279.7	154.0	176.6	129.9	150.0	167.1	151.9	155.7	160.4	144.6
2006	184.8	119.3	210.0	241.5	164.0	188.4	134.5	162.8	175.0	157.0	160.4	166.0	146.9
2007	207.1	146.7	238.7	236.8	170.7	192.5	136.3	173.9	180.3	161.7	166.6	173.5	149.5
2008	251.8	163.4	308.5	298.3	188.3	205.4	140.3	206.2	191.8	173.8	177.1	186.3	153.8
2009	175.2	134.5	211.1	166.3	172.5	202.9	141.0	161.9	195.8	172.2	172.5	179.1	156.7
2010	212.2	152.4	280.8	188.0	183.4	205.7	142.2	185.2	201.2	175.0	179.8	189.1	157.3
2011	249.4	188.4	342.0	181.5	199.8	212.8	145.8	215.0	205.4	184.2	190.5	203.3	159.7

Table 9-2. Producer Price Indexes, by Commodity Group, 1913–2011

(1982 = 100.)

Year	All commodities	Farm products	Processed foods and feeds	Industrial commodities													
				Total	Textile products and apparel	Hides, leather, and related products	Fuels and related products and power	Chemicals and allied products	Rubber and plastics products	Lumber and wood products	Pulp, paper, and allied products	Metals and metal products	Machinery and equipment	Furniture and household durables	Nonmetallic mineral products	Transportation equipment	Miscellaneous products
1913	12.0	18.0	...	11.9	...	...	...	...	...	...	...	...	...	...	...	...	...
1914	11.8	17.9	...	11.3	...	...	...	...	...	...	...	...	...	...	...	...	...
1915	12.0	18.0	...	11.6	...	...	...	...	...	...	...	...	...	...	...	...	...
1916	14.7	21.3	...	15.0	...	...	...	...	...	...	...	...	...	...	...	...	...
1917	20.2	32.6	...	19.5	...	...	...	...	...	...	...	...	...	...	...	...	...
1918	22.6	37.4	...	21.1	...	...	...	...	...	...	...	...	...	...	...	...	...
1919	23.9	39.8	...	22.0	...	...	...	...	...	...	...	...	...	...	...	...	...
1920	26.6	38.0	...	27.4	...	...	...	...	...	...	...	...	...	...	...	...	...
1921	16.8	22.3	...	17.8	...	...	...	...	...	...	...	...	...	...	...	...	...
1922	16.7	23.7	...	17.4	...	...	...	...	...	...	...	...	...	...	...	...	...
1923	17.3	24.9	...	17.8	...	...	...	...	...	...	...	...	...	...	...	...	...
1924	16.9	25.2	...	17.0	...	...	...	...	...	...	...	...	...	...	...	...	...
1925	17.8	27.7	...	17.5	...	...	...	...	...	...	...	...	...	...	...	...	...
1926	17.2	25.3	...	17.0	...	17.1	10.3	...	47.1	9.3	...	13.7	...	28.6	16.4	...	...
1927	16.5	25.1	...	16.0	...	18.4	9.1	...	35.7	8.8	...	12.9	...	27.9	15.7	...	...
1928	16.7	26.7	...	15.8	...	20.7	8.7	...	28.3	8.5	...	12.9	...	27.2	16.2	...	...
1929	16.4	26.4	...	15.6	...	18.6	8.6	...	24.6	8.8	...	13.3	...	27.0	16.0	...	...
1930	14.9	22.4	...	14.5	...	17.1	8.1	...	21.5	8.0	...	12.0	...	26.5	15.9	...	...
1931	12.6	16.4	...	12.8	...	14.7	7.0	...	18.3	6.5	...	10.8	...	24.4	14.9	...	...
1932	11.2	12.2	...	11.9	...	12.5	7.3	...	15.9	5.6	...	9.9	...	21.5	13.9	...	...
1933	11.4	13.0	...	12.1	...	13.8	6.9	16.2	16.7	6.7	...	10.2	...	21.6	14.7	...	...
1934	12.9	16.5	...	13.3	...	14.8	7.6	17.0	19.5	7.8	...	11.2	...	23.4	15.7	...	...
1935	13.8	19.8	...	13.3	...	15.3	7.6	17.7	19.6	7.5	...	11.2	...	23.2	15.7	...	...
1936	13.9	20.4	...	13.5	...	16.3	7.9	17.8	21.1	7.9	...	11.4	...	23.6	15.8	...	...
1937	14.9	21.8	...	14.5	...	17.9	8.0	18.6	24.9	9.3	...	13.1	...	26.1	16.1	...	...
1938	13.5	17.3	...	13.9	...	15.8	7.9	17.7	24.4	8.5	...	12.6	...	25.5	15.6	...	...
1939	13.3	16.5	...	13.9	...	16.3	7.5	17.6	25.4	8.7	...	12.5	14.8	25.4	15.3	...	...
1940	13.5	17.1	...	14.1	...	17.2	7.4	17.9	23.7	9.6	...	12.5	14.9	26.0	15.3	...	...
1941	15.1	20.8	...	15.1	...	18.4	7.9	19.5	25.5	11.5	...	12.8	15.1	27.6	15.7	...	...
1942	17.0	26.7	...	16.2	...	20.1	8.1	21.7	29.7	12.5	...	13.0	15.4	29.9	16.3	...	...
1943	17.8	30.9	...	16.5	...	20.1	8.3	21.9	30.5	13.2	...	12.9	15.2	29.7	16.4	...	...
1944	17.9	31.2	...	16.7	...	19.9	8.6	22.2	30.1	14.3	...	12.9	15.1	30.5	16.7	...	...
1945	18.2	32.4	...	17.0	...	20.1	8.7	22.3	29.2	14.5	...	13.1	15.1	30.5	17.4	...	...
1946	20.8	37.5	...	18.6	...	23.3	9.3	24.1	29.3	16.6	...	14.7	16.6	32.4	18.5	...	...
1947	25.6	45.1	33.0	22.7	50.6	31.7	11.1	32.1	29.2	25.8	25.1	18.2	19.3	37.2	20.7	...	26.6
1948	27.7	48.5	35.3	24.6	52.8	32.1	13.1	32.8	30.2	29.5	26.2	20.7	20.9	39.4	22.4	...	27.7
1949	26.3	41.9	32.1	24.1	48.3	30.4	12.4	30.0	29.2	27.3	25.1	20.9	21.9	40.1	23.0	...	28.2
1950	27.3	44.0	33.2	25.0	50.2	32.9	12.6	30.4	35.6	31.4	25.7	22.0	22.6	40.9	23.5	...	28.6
1951	30.4	51.2	36.9	27.6	56.0	37.7	13.0	34.8	43.7	34.1	30.5	24.5	25.3	44.4	25.0	...	30.3
1952	29.6	48.4	36.4	26.9	50.5	30.5	13.0	33.0	39.6	33.2	29.7	24.5	25.3	43.5	25.0	...	30.2
1953	29.2	43.8	34.8	27.2	49.3	31.0	13.4	33.4	36.9	33.1	29.6	25.3	25.9	44.4	26.0	...	31.0
1954	29.3	43.2	35.4	27.2	48.2	29.5	13.2	33.8	37.5	32.5	29.6	25.5	26.3	44.9	26.6	...	31.3
1955	29.3	40.5	33.8	27.8	48.2	29.4	13.2	33.7	42.4	34.1	30.4	27.2	27.2	45.1	27.3	...	31.3
1956	30.3	40.0	33.8	29.1	48.2	31.2	13.6	33.9	43.0	34.6	32.4	29.6	29.3	46.3	28.5	...	31.7
1957	31.2	41.1	34.8	29.9	48.3	31.2	14.3	34.6	42.8	32.8	33.0	30.2	31.4	47.5	29.6	...	32.6
1958	31.6	42.9	36.5	30.0	47.4	31.6	13.7	34.9	42.8	32.5	33.4	30.0	32.1	47.9	29.9	...	33.3
1959	31.7	40.2	35.6	30.5	48.1	35.9	13.7	34.8	42.6	34.7	33.7	30.6	32.8	48.0	30.3	...	33.4
1960	31.7	40.1	35.6	30.5	48.6	34.6	13.9	34.8	42.7	33.5	34.0	30.6	33.0	47.8	30.4	...	33.6
1961	31.6	39.7	36.2	30.4	47.8	34.9	14.0	34.5	41.1	32.0	33.0	30.5	33.0	47.5	30.5	...	33.7
1962	31.7	40.4	36.5	30.4	48.2	35.3	14.0	33.9	39.9	32.2	33.4	30.2	33.0	47.2	30.5	...	33.9
1963	31.6	39.6	36.8	30.3	48.2	34.3	13.9	33.5	40.1	32.8	33.1	30.3	33.1	46.9	30.3	...	34.2
1964	31.6	39.0	36.7	30.5	48.5	34.4	13.5	33.6	39.6	33.5	33.0	31.1	33.3	47.1	30.4	...	34.4

. . . = Not available.

Table 9-2. Producer Price Indexes, by Commodity Group, 1913–2011—*Continued*

(1982 = 100.)

Year	All com-modities	Farm products	Processed foods and feeds	Industrial commodities													
				Total	Textile products and apparel	Hides, leather, and related products	Fuels and related products and power	Chemi-cals and related products	Rubber and plastics products	Lumber and wood products	Pulp, paper, and allied products	Metals and metal products	Machin-ery and equip-ment	Furniture and house-hold durables	Non-metallic mineral products	Trans-porta-tion equip-ment	Miscel-laneous products
1965	32.3	40.7	38.0	30.9	48.8	35.9	13.8	33.9	39.7	33.7	33.3	32.0	33.7	46.8	30.4	. . .	34.7
1966	33.3	43.7	40.2	31.5	48.9	39.4	14.1	34.0	40.5	35.2	34.2	32.8	34.7	47.4	30.7	. . .	35.3
1967	33.4	41.3	39.8	32.0	48.9	38.1	14.4	34.2	41.4	35.1	34.6	33.2	35.9	48.3	31.2	. . .	36.2
1968	34.2	42.3	40.6	32.8	50.7	39.3	14.3	34.1	42.8	39.8	35.0	34.0	37.0	49.7	32.4	. . .	37.0
1969	35.6	45.0	42.7	33.9	51.8	41.5	14.6	34.2	43.6	44.0	36.0	36.0	38.2	50.7	33.6	40.4	38.1
1970	36.9	45.8	44.6	35.2	52.4	42.0	15.3	35.0	44.9	39.9	37.5	38.7	40.0	51.9	35.3	41.9	39.8
1971	38.1	46.6	45.5	36.5	53.3	43.4	16.6	35.6	45.2	44.7	38.1	39.4	41.4	53.1	38.2	44.2	40.8
1972	39.8	51.6	48.0	37.8	55.5	50.0	17.1	35.6	45.3	50.7	39.3	40.9	42.3	53.8	39.4	45.5	41.5
1973	45.0	72.7	58.9	40.3	60.5	54.5	19.4	37.6	46.6	62.2	42.3	44.0	43.7	55.7	40.7	46.1	43.3
1974	53.5	77.4	68.0	49.2	68.0	55.2	30.1	50.2	56.4	64.5	52.5	57.0	50.0	61.8	47.8	50.3	48.1
1975	58.4	77.0	72.6	54.9	67.4	56.5	35.4	62.0	62.2	62.1	59.0	61.5	57.9	67.5	54.4	56.7	53.4
1976	61.1	78.8	70.8	58.4	72.4	63.9	38.3	64.0	66.0	72.2	62.1	65.0	61.3	70.3	58.2	60.5	55.6
1977	64.9	79.4	74.0	62.5	75.3	68.3	43.6	65.9	69.4	83.0	64.6	69.3	65.2	73.2	62.6	64.6	59.4
1978	69.9	87.7	80.6	67.0	78.1	76.1	46.5	68.0	72.4	96.9	67.7	75.3	70.3	77.5	69.6	69.5	66.7
1979	78.7	99.6	88.5	75.7	82.5	96.1	58.9	76.0	80.5	105.5	75.9	86.0	76.7	82.8	77.6	75.3	75.5
1980	89.8	102.9	95.9	88.0	89.7	94.7	82.8	89.0	90.1	101.5	86.3	95.0	86.0	90.7	88.4	82.9	93.6
1981	98.0	105.2	98.9	97.4	97.6	99.3	100.2	98.4	96.4	102.8	94.8	99.6	94.4	95.9	96.7	94.3	96.1
1982	100.0	100.0	100.0	100.0	100.0	100.0	100.0	100.0	100.0	100.0	100.0	100.0	100.0	100.0	100.0	100.0	100.0
1983	101.3	102.4	101.8	101.1	100.3	103.2	95.9	100.3	100.8	107.9	103.3	101.8	102.7	103.4	101.6	102.8	104.8
1984	103.7	105.5	105.4	103.3	102.7	109.0	94.8	102.9	102.3	108.0	110.3	104.8	105.1	105.7	105.4	105.2	107.0
1985	103.2	95.1	103.5	103.7	102.9	108.9	91.4	103.7	101.9	106.6	113.3	104.4	107.2	107.1	108.6	107.9	109.4
1986	100.2	92.9	105.4	100.0	103.2	113.0	69.8	102.6	101.9	107.2	116.1	103.2	108.8	108.2	110.0	110.5	111.6
1987	102.8	95.5	107.9	102.6	105.1	120.4	70.2	106.4	103.0	112.8	121.8	107.1	110.4	109.9	110.0	112.5	114.9
1988	106.9	104.9	112.7	106.3	109.2	131.4	66.7	116.3	109.3	118.9	130.4	118.7	113.2	113.1	111.2	114.3	120.2
1989	112.2	110.9	117.8	111.6	112.3	136.3	72.9	123.0	112.6	126.7	137.8	124.1	117.4	116.9	112.6	117.7	126.5
1990	116.3	112.2	121.9	115.8	115.0	141.7	82.3	123.6	113.6	129.7	141.2	122.9	120.7	119.2	114.7	121.5	134.2
1991	116.5	105.7	121.9	116.5	116.3	138.9	81.2	125.6	115.1	132.1	142.9	120.2	123.0	121.2	117.2	126.4	140.8
1992	117.2	103.6	122.1	117.4	117.8	140.4	80.4	125.9	115.1	146.6	145.2	119.2	123.4	122.2	117.3	130.4	145.3
1993	118.9	107.1	124.0	119.0	118.0	143.7	80.0	128.2	116.0	174.0	147.3	119.2	124.0	123.7	120.0	133.7	145.4
1994	120.4	106.3	125.5	120.7	118.3	148.5	77.8	132.1	117.6	180.0	152.5	124.8	125.1	126.1	124.2	137.2	141.9
1995	124.7	107.4	127.0	125.5	120.8	153.7	78.0	142.5	124.3	178.1	172.2	134.5	126.6	128.2	129.0	139.7	145.4
1996	127.7	122.4	133.3	127.3	122.4	150.5	85.8	142.1	123.8	176.1	168.7	131.0	126.5	130.4	131.0	141.7	147.7
1997	127.6	112.9	134.0	127.7	122.6	154.2	86.1	143.6	123.2	183.8	167.9	131.8	125.9	130.8	133.2	141.6	150.9
1998	124.4	104.6	131.6	124.8	122.9	148.0	75.3	143.9	122.6	179.1	171.7	127.8	124.9	131.3	135.4	141.2	156.0
1999	125.5	98.4	131.1	126.5	121.1	146.0	80.5	144.2	122.5	183.6	174.1	124.6	124.3	131.7	138.9	141.8	166.6
2000	132.7	99.5	133.1	134.8	121.4	151.5	103.5	151.0	125.5	178.2	183.7	128.1	124.0	132.6	142.5	143.8	170.8
2001	134.2	103.8	137.3	135.7	121.3	158.4	105.3	151.8	127.2	174.4	184.8	125.4	123.7	133.2	144.3	145.2	181.3
2002	131.1	99.0	136.2	132.4	119.9	157.6	93.2	151.9	126.8	173.3	185.9	125.9	122.9	133.5	146.2	144.6	182.4
2003	138.1	111.5	143.4	139.1	119.8	162.3	112.9	161.8	130.1	177.4	190.0	129.2	121.9	133.9	148.2	145.7	179.6
2004	146.7	123.3	151.2	147.6	121.0	164.5	126.9	174.4	133.8	195.6	195.7	149.6	122.1	135.1	153.2	148.6	183.2
2005	157.4	118.5	153.1	160.2	122.8	165.4	156.4	192.0	143.8	196.5	202.6	160.8	123.7	139.4	164.2	151.0	195.1
2006	164.7	117.0	153.8	168.8	124.5	168.4	166.7	205.8	153.8	194.4	209.8	181.6	126.2	142.6	179.9	152.6	205.6
2007	172.6	143.4	165.1	175.1	125.8	173.6	177.6	214.8	155.0	192.4	216.9	193.5	127.3	144.7	186.2	155.0	210.3
2008	189.6	161.3	180.5	192.3	128.9	173.1	214.6	245.5	165.9	191.3	226.8	213.0	129.7	148.9	197.1	158.6	216.6
2009	172.9	134.6	176.2	174.8	129.5	157.0	158.7	229.4	165.2	182.8	225.6	186.8	131.3	153.1	202.4	162.2	217.5
2010	184.7	151.0	182.3	187.0	131.7	181.4	185.8	246.6	170.7	192.7	236.9	207.6	131.1	153.2	201.8	163.4	221.5
2011	201.0	186.7	197.5	202.0	141.7	199.9	215.9	275.1	182.7	194.7	245.1	225.9	132.7	156.4	205.0	166.1	229.2

. . . = Not available.

CONSUMER PRICE INDEX

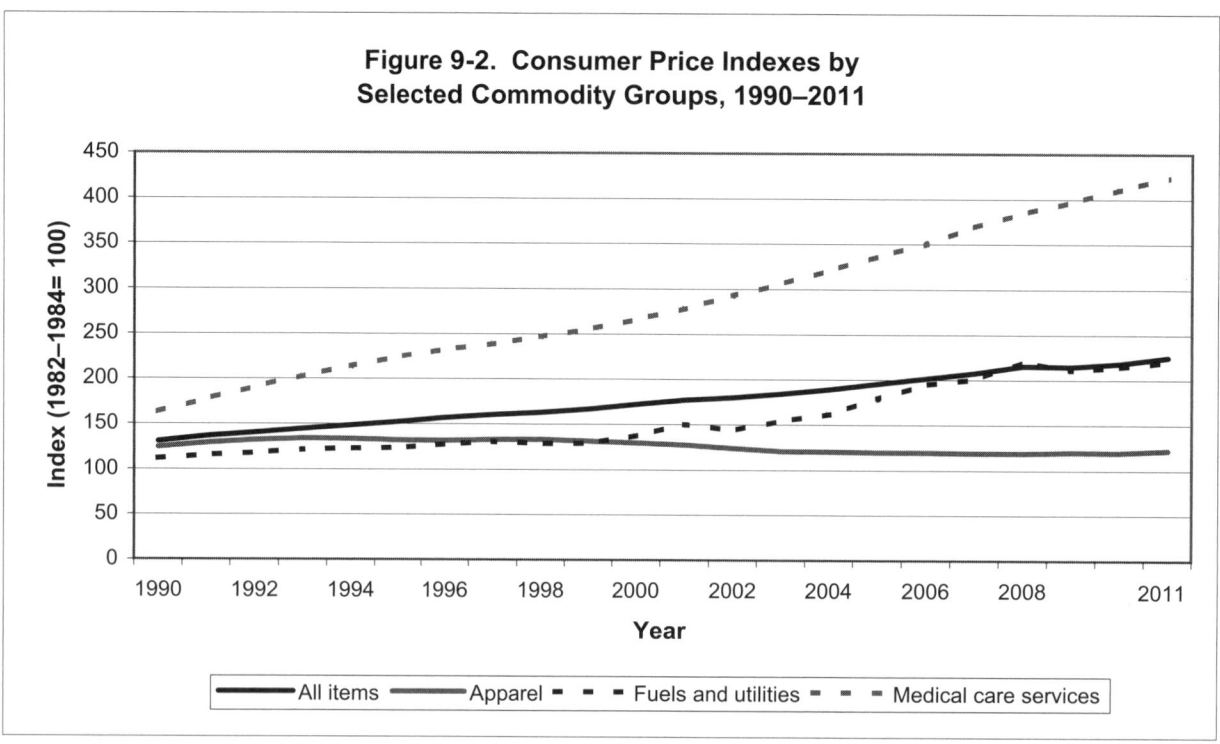

Figure 9-2. Consumer Price Indexes by
Selected Commodity Groups, 1990–2011

The CPI for medical care has grown at a much faster rate than average. From 1990 to 2011, the CPI for all urban consumers has grown 72.0 percent while the CPI for medical care has grown 145.9 percent. Within medical care, hospital and related services has grown the fastest at 260.4 percent from 1990 to 2011. (See Table 9-7.)

OTHER HIGHLIGHTS

- The CPI-U for energy commodities continued to increase rapidly in 2011 after sharply declining in 2009. In 2009, the CPI-U for energy commodities declined 27.8 percent but increased 26.3 percent in just one year from 2010 to 2011. (See Table 9-4.)

- After declining for the first time since 1955 in 2009, the CPI-W continued to increase, rising 3.6 percent from 2010 to 2011. (See Table 9-6)

- The CPI-U in Pittsburgh, PA increased 4.5 percent in 2011—faster than any other MSA listed in Table 9-9. The CPI-U grew the slowest in San Francisco-Oakland-San Jose, CA at 2.6 percent from 2010 to 2011. (See Table 9-9.)

NOTES AND DEFINITIONS

CONSUMER PRICE INDEX

The Consumer Price Index (CPI) is a measure of the average change over time in the prices of consumer items—goods and services that people buy for day-to-day living. The CPI is a complex construct that combines economic theory with sampling and other statistical techniques and uses data from several surveys to produce a timely and precise measure of average price change for the consumption sector of the American economy.

The Bureau of Labor Statistics (BLS) publishes CPIs for the following population groups: (1) the CPI for Urban Wage Earners and Clerical Workers (CPI-W), which covers households of wage earners and clerical workers that comprise approximately 32 percent of the total population and (2) the CPI for All Urban Consumers (CPI-U) and the Chained CPI for All Urban Consumers (C-CPI-U), which cover approximately 87 percent of the total population and include in addition to wage earners and clerical worker households, groups such as professional, managerial, and technical workers, the self-employed, short-term workers, the unemployed, and retirees and others not in the labor force. BLS began publishing the CPI-U in January 1978, but did not begin publishing the C-CPI-U until August 2002 with data beginning in January 2000. The CPI-W is much older than either the CPI-U or C-CPI-U.

The CPIs are based on prices of food, clothing, shelter, and fuels, transportation fares, charges for doctors' and dentists' services, drugs, and other goods and services that people buy for day-to-day living. Prices are collected each month in 87 urban areas across the country from about 23,000 retail and service establishments. Data on rents are collected from about 50,000 landlords or tenants. All taxes directly associated with the purchase and use of items are included in the index.

Various indexes have been devised to measure different aspects of inflation. The CPI measures inflation as experienced by consumers in their day-to-day living expenses; the Producer Price Index (PPI), as described earlier in this chapter, measures inflation at earlier stages of the production process; the Employment Cost Index (ECI), as described in Chapter 6, measures it in the labor market; the BLS International Price Program measures it for imports and exports; and the Gross Domestic Product Deflator (GDP Deflator) measures inflation experienced by both consumers themselves as well as governments and other institutions providing goods and services to consumers. Finally, there are specialized measures, such as measures of interest rates. The CPI is generally the best measure for adjusting payments to consumers when the intent is to allow consumers to purchase at today's prices, a market basket of goods and services equivalent to one that they could purchase in an earlier period.

The CPI does have some limitation, however. The CPI may not be applicable to all population groups. For example, the CPI-U is designed to measure inflation for the U.S. urban population and thus may not accurately reflect the experience of people living in rural areas. In addition, the CPI does not produce official estimates for the rate of inflation experienced by subgroups of the population, such as the elderly or the poor.

The Consumer Price Index Research Series Using Current Methods (CPI-U-RS), shown in Table 9-10 provides estimates for the period since 1977 of what the CPI would have been had the most current methods been in effect. Each time there are new methods introduced into the CPI, the CPI-U-RS is revised from 1978 forward.

The CPI-U-RS provides an annual inflation series that adjusts only for specified changes in BLS methodology. It does not incorporate all possible research results on past inflation.

Sources of Additional Information

An extensive description of the methodology is available in the updated version of Chapter 17 in the *BLS Handbook of Methods*. Additional detailed data can be found in the *Consumer Price Index Detailed Report* and in special reports. These resources can be found on the BLS Web site at <http://www.bls.gov>.

Table 9-3. Consumer Price Indexes, All Urban Consumers (CPI-U): U.S. City Average, Major Groups, 1957–2011

(1982–1984 = 100, unless otherwise specified.)

Year	All items	Food and beverages	Housing	Apparel	Transportation	Medical care	Recreation[1]	Education and communication[1]	Other goods and services
1957	28.1	. . .	. . .	44.5	27.7	19.7	. . .	. . .	. . .
1958	28.9	. . .	. . .	44.6	28.6	20.6	. . .	. . .	. . .
1959	29.1	. . .	. . .	45.0	29.8	21.5	. . .	. . .	. . .
1960	29.6	. . .	. . .	45.7	29.8	22.3	. . .	. . .	. . .
1961	29.9	. . .	. . .	46.1	30.1	22.9	. . .	. . .	. . .
1962	30.2	. . .	. . .	46.3	30.8	23.5	. . .	. . .	. . .
1963	30.6	. . .	. . .	46.9	30.9	24.1	. . .	. . .	. . .
1964	31.0	. . .	. . .	47.3	31.4	24.6	. . .	. . .	. . .
1965	31.5	. . .	. . .	47.8	31.9	25.2	. . .	. . .	. . .
1966	32.4	. . .	. . .	49.0	32.3	26.3	. . .	. . .	. . .
1967	33.4	35.0	30.8	51.0	33.3	28.2	. . .	. . .	35.1
1968	34.8	36.2	32.0	53.7	34.3	29.9	. . .	. . .	36.9
1969	36.7	38.1	34.0	56.8	35.7	31.9	. . .	. . .	38.7
1970	38.8	40.1	36.4	59.2	37.5	34.0	. . .	. . .	40.9
1971	40.5	41.4	38.0	61.1	39.5	36.1	. . .	. . .	42.9
1972	41.8	43.1	39.4	62.3	39.9	37.3	. . .	. . .	44.7
1973	44.4	48.8	41.2	64.6	41.2	38.8	. . .	. . .	46.4
1974	49.3	55.5	45.8	69.4	45.8	42.4	. . .	. . .	49.8
1975	53.8	60.2	50.7	72.5	50.1	47.5	. . .	. . .	53.9
1976	56.9	62.1	53.8	75.2	55.1	52.0	. . .	. . .	57.0
1977	60.6	65.8	57.4	78.6	59.0	57.0	. . .	. . .	60.4
1978	65.2	72.2	62.4	81.4	61.7	61.8	. . .	. . .	64.3
1979	72.6	79.9	70.1	84.9	70.5	67.5	. . .	. . .	68.9
1980	82.4	86.7	81.1	90.9	83.1	74.9	. . .	. . .	75.2
1981	90.9	93.5	90.4	95.3	93.2	82.9	. . .	. . .	82.6
1982	96.5	97.3	96.9	97.8	97.0	92.5	. . .	. . .	91.1
1983	99.6	99.5	99.5	100.2	99.3	100.6	. . .	. . .	101.1
1984	103.9	103.2	103.6	102.1	103.7	106.8	. . .	. . .	107.9
1985	107.6	105.6	107.7	105.0	106.4	113.5	. . .	. . .	114.5
1986	109.6	109.1	110.9	105.9	102.3	122.0	. . .	. . .	121.4
1987	113.6	113.5	114.2	110.6	105.4	130.1	. . .	. . .	128.5
1988	118.3	118.2	118.5	115.4	108.7	138.6	. . .	. . .	137.0
1989	124.0	124.9	123.0	118.6	114.1	149.3	. . .	. . .	147.7
1990	130.7	132.1	128.5	124.1	120.5	162.8	. . .	. . .	159.0
1991	136.2	136.8	133.6	128.7	123.8	177.0	. . .	. . .	171.6
1992	140.3	138.7	137.5	131.9	126.5	190.1	. . .	. . .	183.3
1993	144.5	141.6	141.2	133.7	130.4	201.4	90.7	85.5	192.9
1994	148.2	144.9	144.8	133.4	134.3	211.0	92.7	88.8	198.5
1995	152.4	148.9	148.5	132.0	139.1	220.5	94.5	92.2	206.9
1996	156.9	153.7	152.8	131.7	143.0	228.2	97.4	95.3	215.4
1997	160.5	157.7	156.8	132.9	144.3	234.6	99.6	98.4	224.8
1998	163.0	161.1	160.4	133.0	141.6	242.1	101.1	100.3	237.7
1999	166.6	164.6	163.9	131.3	144.4	250.6	102.0	101.2	258.3
2000	172.2	168.4	169.6	129.6	153.3	260.8	103.3	102.5	271.1
2001	177.1	173.6	176.4	127.3	154.3	272.8	104.9	105.2	282.6
2002	179.9	176.8	180.3	124.0	152.9	285.6	106.2	107.9	293.2
2003	184.0	180.5	184.8	120.9	157.6	297.1	107.5	109.8	298.7
2004	188.9	186.6	189.5	120.4	163.1	310.1	108.6	111.6	304.7
2005	195.3	191.2	195.7	119.5	173.9	323.2	109.4	113.7	313.4
2006	201.6	195.7	203.2	119.5	180.9	336.2	110.9	116.8	321.7
2007	207.3	203.3	209.6	119.0	184.7	351.1	111.4	119.6	333.3
2008	215.3	214.2	216.3	118.9	195.5	364.1	113.3	123.6	345.4
2009	214.5	218.2	217.1	120.1	179.3	375.6	114.3	127.4	368.6
2010	218.1	220.0	216.3	119.5	193.4	388.4	113.3	129.9	381.3
2011	224.9	227.9	219.1	122.1	212.4	400.3	113.4	131.5	387.2

[1]December 1997 = 100.
. . . = Not available.

Table 9-4. Consumer Price Indexes, All Urban Consumers (CPI-U): U.S. City Average, Commodity, Service, and Special Groups, 1957–2011

(1982–1984 = 100, unless otherwise specified.)

Year	All items less food	All items less shelter	All items less medical care	All items less energy	All items less food and energy	Commodities	Commodities less food and beverages	Commodities less food and energy	Energy commodities	Nondurables	Nondurables less food	Nondurables less food and apparel
1957	28.0	29.7	28.7	28.9	28.9	32.6	. . .	37.4	21.6	30.9	32.9	28.5
1958	28.6	30.6	29.5	29.7	29.6	33.3	. . .	37.9	21.3	31.7	33.1	28.8
1959	29.2	30.8	29.8	29.9	30.2	33.3	. . .	38.4	21.5	31.5	33.5	29.2
1960	29.7	31.3	30.2	30.4	30.6	33.6	. . .	38.5	21.9	32.0	34.1	29.7
1961	30.0	31.7	30.5	30.7	31.0	33.8	. . .	38.6	21.9	32.2	34.3	29.8
1962	30.3	32.0	30.8	31.1	31.4	34.1	. . .	38.9	22.0	32.5	34.5	30.1
1963	30.7	32.4	31.1	31.5	31.8	34.4	. . .	39.2	22.1	32.9	34.8	30.4
1964	31.1	32.8	31.5	32.0	32.3	34.8	. . .	39.6	21.9	33.2	35.1	30.6
1965	31.6	33.3	32.0	32.5	32.7	35.2	. . .	39.8	22.6	33.8	35.6	31.2
1966	32.3	34.3	33.0	33.5	33.5	36.1	. . .	40.3	23.2	35.1	36.4	31.8
1967	33.4	35.2	33.7	34.4	34.7	36.8	38.3	41.3	23.9	35.7	37.6	32.6
1968	34.9	36.7	35.1	35.9	36.3	38.1	39.7	42.9	24.4	37.1	39.1	33.7
1969	36.8	38.4	37.0	38.0	38.4	39.9	41.4	44.7	25.2	38.9	40.9	34.9
1970	39.0	40.3	39.2	40.3	40.8	41.7	43.1	46.7	25.6	40.8	42.5	36.3
1971	40.8	42.0	40.8	42.0	42.7	43.2	44.7	48.5	26.1	42.1	44.0	37.6
1972	42.0	43.3	42.1	43.4	44.0	44.5	45.8	49.7	26.4	43.5	45.0	38.6
1973	43.7	46.2	44.8	46.1	45.6	47.8	47.3	51.1	29.1	47.5	46.9	40.3
1974	48.0	51.4	49.8	50.6	49.4	53.5	52.4	55.0	40.4	54.0	52.9	46.9
1975	52.5	56.0	54.3	55.1	53.9	58.2	57.3	60.1	43.4	58.3	57.0	51.5
1976	56.0	59.3	57.2	58.2	57.4	60.7	60.2	63.2	45.4	60.5	59.5	54.1
1977	59.6	63.1	60.8	61.9	61.0	64.2	63.6	66.5	48.7	64.0	62.5	57.2
1978	63.9	67.4	65.4	66.7	65.5	68.8	67.3	70.5	51.0	68.6	65.5	60.4
1979	71.2	74.2	72.9	73.4	71.9	76.6	75.2	76.4	68.7	77.2	74.6	71.2
1980	81.5	82.9	82.8	81.9	80.8	86.0	85.7	83.5	95.2	87.6	88.4	87.1
1981	90.4	91.0	91.4	90.1	89.2	93.2	93.1	90.0	107.6	95.2	96.7	96.8
1982	96.3	96.2	96.8	96.1	95.8	97.0	96.9	95.3	102.9	97.8	98.3	98.2
1983	99.7	99.8	99.6	99.6	99.6	99.8	100.0	100.2	99.0	99.7	100.0	100.0
1984	104.0	103.9	103.7	104.3	104.6	103.2	103.1	104.4	98.1	102.5	101.7	101.8
1985	108.0	107.0	107.2	108.4	109.1	105.4	105.2	107.1	98.2	104.8	104.1	104.1
1986	109.8	108.0	108.8	112.6	113.5	104.4	101.4	108.6	77.2	103.5	98.5	96.9
1987	113.6	111.6	112.6	117.2	118.2	107.7	104.0	111.8	80.2	107.5	101.8	100.3
1988	118.3	115.9	117.0	122.3	123.4	111.5	107.3	115.8	80.8	111.8	105.8	104.0
1989	123.7	121.6	122.4	128.1	129.0	116.7	111.6	119.6	87.9	118.2	111.7	111.3
1990	130.3	128.2	128.8	134.7	135.5	122.8	117.0	123.6	101.2	126.0	119.9	120.9
1991	136.1	133.5	133.8	140.9	142.1	126.6	120.4	128.8	99.1	130.3	124.5	125.7
1992	140.8	137.3	137.5	145.4	147.3	129.1	123.2	132.5	98.3	132.8	127.6	128.9
1993	145.1	141.4	141.2	150.0	152.2	131.5	125.3	135.2	97.3	135.1	129.3	130.7
1994	149.0	144.8	144.7	154.1	156.5	133.8	126.9	137.1	97.6	136.8	129.7	131.6
1995	153.1	148.6	148.6	158.7	161.2	136.4	128.9	139.3	98.8	139.3	130.9	134.1
1996	157.5	152.8	152.8	163.1	165.6	139.9	131.5	141.3	105.7	143.5	134.5	139.5
1997	161.1	155.9	156.3	167.1	169.5	141.8	132.2	142.3	105.7	146.4	136.3	141.8
1998	163.4	157.2	158.6	170.9	173.4	141.9	130.5	143.2	92.1	146.9	134.6	139.2
1999	167.0	160.2	162.0	174.4	177.0	144.4	132.5	144.1	100.0	151.2	139.4	147.5
2000	173.0	165.7	167.3	178.6	181.3	149.2	137.7	144.9	129.5	158.2	149.1	162.9
2001	177.8	169.7	171.9	183.5	186.1	150.7	137.2	145.3	125.2	160.6	149.1	164.1
2002	180.5	170.8	174.3	187.7	190.5	149.7	134.2	143.7	117.1	161.1	147.4	163.3
2003	184.7	174.6	178.1	190.6	193.2	151.2	134.5	140.9	136.7	165.3	151.9	172.1
2004	189.4	179.3	182.7	194.4	196.6	154.7	136.7	139.6	161.2	172.2	159.3	183.8
2005	196.0	186.1	188.7	198.7	200.9	160.2	142.5	140.3	197.4	180.2	170.1	201.2
2006	202.7	191.9	194.7	203.7	205.9	164.0	145.9	140.6	223.0	186.7	178.2	213.9
2007	208.1	196.6	200.1	208.9	210.7	167.5	147.5	140.1	241.0	193.5	184.0	223.4
2008	215.5	205.5	207.8	214.8	215.6	174.8	153.0	140.2	284.4	205.9	197.3	244.4
2009	214.0	203.3	206.6	218.4	219.2	169.7	144.4	142.0	205.3	198.5	181.5	218.7
2010	217.8	208.6	209.7	220.5	221.3	174.6	150.4	143.6	242.6	205.3	191.9	235.6
2011	224.5	217.0	216.3	224.8	225.0	183.9	159.9	145.5	306.4	219.0	209.6	262.1

. . . = Not available.

Table 9-4. Consumer Price Indexes, All Urban Consumers (CPI-U): U.S. City Average, Commodity, Service, and Special Groups, 1957–2011—*Continued*

(1982–1984 = 100, unless otherwise specified.)

Year	Total services[1]	Rent of shelter[2]	Gasoline, all types	Transportation services	Medical care services	Other services	Services less medical care	Energy	Services less energy
1957	21.8	...	23.8	24.1	17.0	...	22.8	21.5	21.9
1958	22.6	...	23.5	25.6	17.9	...	23.6	21.5	22.7
1959	23.3	...	23.7	26.5	18.7	...	24.2	21.9	23.4
1960	24.1	...	24.4	27.2	19.5	...	25.0	22.4	24.2
1961	24.5	...	24.1	27.8	20.2	...	25.4	22.5	24.7
1962	25.0	...	24.3	28.3	20.9	...	25.9	22.6	25.2
1963	25.5	...	24.2	28.6	21.5	...	26.3	22.6	25.7
1964	26.0	...	24.1	29.2	22.0	...	26.8	22.5	26.2
1965	26.6	...	25.1	30.3	22.7	...	27.4	22.9	26.9
1966	27.6	...	25.6	31.6	23.9	...	28.3	23.3	28.0
1967	28.8	...	26.4	32.6	26.0	36.0	29.3	23.8	29.3
1968	30.3	...	26.8	33.9	27.9	38.1	30.8	24.2	30.9
1969	32.4	...	27.7	36.3	30.2	40.0	32.9	24.8	33.2
1970	35.0	...	27.9	40.2	32.3	42.2	35.6	25.5	36.0
1971	37.0	...	28.1	43.4	34.7	44.4	37.5	26.5	38.0
1972	38.4	...	28.4	44.4	35.9	45.6	38.9	27.2	39.4
1973	40.1	...	31.2	44.7	37.5	47.7	40.6	29.4	41.1
1974	43.8	...	42.2	46.3	41.4	51.3	44.3	38.1	44.8
1975	48.0	...	45.1	49.8	46.6	55.1	48.3	42.1	48.8
1976	52.0	...	47.0	56.9	51.3	58.4	52.2	45.1	52.7
1977	56.0	...	49.7	61.5	56.4	62.1	55.9	49.4	56.5
1978	60.8	...	51.8	64.4	61.2	66.4	60.7	52.5	61.3
1979	67.5	...	70.2	69.5	67.2	71.9	67.5	65.7	68.2
1980	77.9	...	97.5	79.2	74.8	78.7	78.2	86.0	78.5
1981	88.1	...	108.5	88.6	82.8	86.1	88.7	97.7	88.7
1982	96.0	...	102.8	96.1	92.6	93.5	96.4	99.2	96.3
1983	99.4	102.7	99.4	99.1	100.7	100.0	99.2	99.9	99.2
1984	104.6	107.7	97.8	104.8	106.7	106.5	104.4	100.9	104.5
1985	109.9	113.9	98.6	110.0	113.2	113.0	109.6	101.6	110.2
1986	115.4	120.2	77.0	116.3	121.9	119.4	114.6	88.2	116.5
1987	120.2	125.9	80.1	121.9	130.0	125.7	119.1	88.6	122.0
1988	125.7	132.0	80.8	128.0	138.3	132.6	124.3	89.3	127.9
1989	131.9	138.0	88.5	135.6	148.9	140.9	130.1	94.3	134.4
1990	139.2	145.5	101.0	144.2	162.7	150.2	136.8	102.1	142.3
1991	146.3	152.1	99.2	151.2	177.1	159.8	143.3	102.5	149.8
1992	152.0	157.3	99.0	155.7	190.5	168.5	148.4	103.0	155.9
1993	157.9	162.0	97.7	162.9	202.9	177.0	153.6	104.2	161.9
1994	163.1	167.0	98.2	168.6	213.4	185.4	158.4	104.6	167.6
1995	168.7	172.4	99.8	175.9	224.2	193.3	163.5	105.2	173.7
1996	174.1	178.0	105.9	180.5	232.4	201.4	168.7	110.1	179.4
1997	179.4	183.4	105.8	185.0	239.1	209.6	173.9	111.5	185.0
1998	184.2	189.6	91.6	187.9	246.8	216.9	178.4	102.9	190.6
1999	188.8	195.0	100.1	190.7	255.1	223.1	182.7	106.6	195.7
2000	195.3	201.3	128.6	196.1	266.0	229.9	188.9	124.6	202.1
2001	203.4	208.9	124.0	201.9	278.8	238.0	196.6	129.3	209.6
2002	209.8	216.7	116.0	209.1	292.9	246.4	202.5	121.7	217.5
2003	216.5	221.9	135.1	216.3	306.0	254.4	208.7	136.5	223.8
2004	222.8	227.9	159.7	220.6	321.3	261.3	214.5	151.4	230.2
2005	230.1	233.7	194.7	225.7	336.7	268.4	221.2	177.1	236.6
2006	238.9	241.9	219.9	230.8	350.6	277.5	229.6	196.9	244.7
2007	246.8	250.8	238.0	233.7	369.3	285.6	236.8	207.7	253.1
2008	255.5	257.2	277.5	244.1	384.9	295.8	245.0	236.7	261.0
2009	259.2	259.9	201.6	251.0	397.3	304.0	248.1	193.1	265.9
2010	261.3	258.8	238.6	259.8	411.2	309.6	249.6	211.4	268.3
2011	265.8	262.2	301.7	268.0	423.8	314.4	253.6	243.9	273.1

[1]Includes tenants, household insurance, water, sewer, trash, and household operations services, not shown separately.
[2]December 1982 = 100.
. . . = Not available.

Table 9-5. Consumer Price Indexes, All Urban Consumers (CPI-U): U.S. City Average, Selected Groups and Purchasing Power of the Consumer Dollar, 1913–2011

(1982–1984 = 100, unless otherwise specified.)

Year	All items	Food	Rent of primary residence	Owners' equivalent of primary residence[1]	Apparel	Purchasing power of the consumer dollar
1913	9.9	10.0	21.0	. . .	14.9	1 007.7
1914	10.0	10.2	21.0	. . .	15.0	994.2
1915	10.1	10.0	21.1	. . .	15.3	984.3
1916	10.9	11.3	21.3	. . .	16.8	915.2
1917	12.8	14.5	21.2	. . .	20.2	779.3
1918	15.1	16.7	21.5	. . .	27.3	663.5
1919	17.3	18.6	23.3	. . .	36.2	577.9
1920	20.0	21.0	27.4	. . .	43.1	498.9
1921	17.9	15.9	31.5	. . .	33.2	558.5
1922	16.8	14.9	32.4	. . .	27.0	596.2
1923	17.1	15.4	33.2	. . .	27.1	585.7
1924	17.1	15.2	34.4	. . .	26.8	584.5
1925	17.5	16.5	34.6	. . .	26.3	570.1
1926	17.7	17.0	34.2	. . .	25.9	564.7
1927	17.4	16.4	33.7	. . .	25.3	575.5
1928	17.1	16.3	32.9	. . .	25.0	583.3
1929	17.1	16.5	32.1	. . .	24.7	583.3
1930	16.7	15.6	31.2	. . .	24.2	598.6
1931	15.2	12.9	29.6	. . .	22.0	656.3
1932	13.7	10.7	26.5	. . .	19.5	731.7
1933	13.0	10.4	22.9	. . .	18.8	771.2
1934	13.4	11.6	21.4	. . .	20.6	746.4
1935	13.7	12.4	21.4	. . .	20.8	728.1
1936	13.9	12.6	21.9	. . .	21.0	721.3
1937	14.4	13.1	22.9	. . .	22.0	696.1
1938	14.1	12.1	23.7	. . .	21.9	709.3
1939	13.9	11.8	23.7	. . .	21.6	719.5
1940	14.0	12.0	23.7	. . .	21.8	712.6
1941	14.7	13.1	24.2	. . .	22.8	678.8
1942	16.3	15.4	24.7	. . .	26.7	613.2
1943	17.3	17.1	24.7	. . .	27.8	577.9
1944	17.6	16.9	24.8	. . .	29.8	568.0
1945	18.0	17.3	24.8	. . .	31.4	555.2
1946	19.5	19.8	25.0	. . .	34.4	511.5
1947	22.3	24.1	25.8	. . .	39.9	447.4
1948	24.1	26.1	27.5	. . .	42.5	415.1
1949	23.8	25.0	28.7	. . .	40.8	419.3
1950	24.1	25.4	29.7	. . .	40.3	415.1
1951	26.0	28.2	30.9	. . .	43.9	384.6
1952	26.5	28.7	32.2	. . .	43.5	376.5
1953	26.7	28.3	33.9	. . .	43.1	373.5
1954	26.9	28.2	35.1	. . .	43.1	371.7
1955	26.8	27.8	35.6	. . .	42.9	373.2
1956	27.2	28.0	36.3	. . .	43.7	367.8
1957	28.1	28.9	37.0	. . .	44.5	354.9
1958	28.9	30.2	37.6	. . .	44.6	345.7
1959	29.1	29.7	38.2	. . .	45.0	342.7
1960	29.6	30.0	38.7	. . .	45.7	337.3
1961	29.9	30.4	39.2	. . .	46.1	334.0
1962	30.2	30.6	39.7	. . .	46.3	330.4
1963	30.6	31.1	40.1	. . .	46.9	326.5
1964	31.0	31.5	40.5	. . .	47.3	322.0
1965	31.5	32.2	40.9	. . .	47.8	316.6
1966	32.4	33.8	41.5	. . .	49.0	308.0
1967	33.4	34.1	42.2	. . .	51.0	299.3
1968	34.8	35.3	43.3	. . .	53.7	287.3
1969	36.7	37.1	44.7	. . .	56.8	272.6
1970	38.8	39.2	46.5	. . .	59.2	257.4
1971	40.5	40.4	48.7	. . .	61.1	246.6
1972	41.8	42.1	50.4	. . .	62.3	239.1
1973	44.4	48.2	52.5	. . .	64.6	225.1
1974	49.3	55.1	55.2	. . .	69.4	202.9
1975	53.8	59.8	58.0	. . .	72.5	185.9
1976	56.9	61.6	61.1	. . .	75.2	175.7
1977	60.6	65.5	64.8	. . .	78.6	164.9
1978	65.2	72.0	69.3	. . .	81.4	153.2
1979	72.6	79.9	74.3	. . .	84.9	138.0

[1]December 1982 = 100.
. . . = Not available.

Table 9-5. Consumer Price Indexes, All Urban Consumers (CPI-U): U.S. City Average, Selected Groups and Purchasing Power of the Consumer Dollar, 1913–2011—*Continued*

(1982–1984 = 100, unless otherwise specified.)

Year	All items	Food	Rent of primary residence	Owners' equivalent of primary residence[1]	Apparel	Purchasing power of the consumer dollar
1980	82.4	86.8	80.9	. . .	90.9	121.5
1981	90.9	93.6	87.9	. . .	95.3	109.8
1982	96.5	97.4	94.6	. . .	97.8	103.5
1983	99.6	99.4	100.1	102.5	100.2	100.3
1984	103.9	103.2	105.3	107.3	102.1	96.1
1985	107.6	105.6	111.8	113.2	105.0	92.8
1986	109.6	109.0	118.3	119.4	105.9	91.3
1987	113.6	113.5	123.1	124.8	110.6	88.0
1988	118.3	118.2	127.8	131.1	115.4	84.6
1989	124.0	125.1	132.8	137.4	118.6	80.7
1990	130.7	132.4	138.4	144.8	124.1	76.6
1991	136.2	136.3	143.3	150.4	128.7	73.4
1992	140.3	137.9	146.9	155.5	131.9	71.3
1993	144.5	140.9	150.3	160.5	133.7	69.2
1994	148.2	144.3	154.0	165.8	133.4	67.5
1995	152.4	148.4	157.8	171.3	132.0	65.6
1996	156.9	153.3	162.0	176.8	131.7	63.8
1997	160.5	157.3	166.7	181.9	132.9	62.3
1998	163.0	160.7	172.1	187.8	133.0	61.4
1999	166.6	164.1	177.5	192.9	131.3	60.0
2000	172.2	167.8	183.9	198.7	129.6	58.1
2001	177.1	173.1	192.1	206.3	127.3	56.5
2002	179.9	176.2	199.7	214.7	124.0	55.6
2003	184.0	180.0	205.5	219.9	120.9	54.4
2004	188.9	186.2	211.0	224.9	120.4	53.0
2005	195.3	190.7	217.3	230.2	119.5	51.2
2006	201.6	195.2	225.1	238.2	119.5	49.6
2007	207.3	202.9	234.7	246.2	119.0	48.2
2008	215.3	214.1	243.3	252.4	118.9	46.5
2009	214.5	218.0	248.8	256.6	120.1	46.6
2010	218.1	219.6	249.4	256.6	119.5	45.9
2011	224.9	227.8	253.6	259.6	122.1	44.5

[1]December 1982 = 100.

. . . = Not available.

Table 9-6. Consumer Price Indexes, Urban Wage Earners and Clerical Workers (CPI-W): U.S. City Average, Major Groups, 1913–2011

(1982–1984 = 100, unless otherwise specified.)

Year	All items	Food and beverages	Housing	Apparel	Transportation	Medical care	Recreation[1]	Education and communication[1]	Other goods and services
1913	10.0	. . .	. . .	15.0	. . .	. . .	. . .	. . .	. . .
1914	10.1	. . .	. . .	15.1	. . .	. . .	. . .	. . .	. . .
1915	10.2	. . .	. . .	15.4	. . .	. . .	. . .	. . .	. . .
1916	11.0	. . .	. . .	16.9	. . .	. . .	. . .	. . .	. . .
1917	12.9	. . .	. . .	20.3	. . .	. . .	. . .	. . .	. . .
1918	15.1	. . .	. . .	27.5	. . .	. . .	. . .	. . .	. . .
1919	17.4	. . .	. . .	36.4	. . .	. . .	. . .	. . .	. . .
1920	20.1	. . .	. . .	43.3	. . .	. . .	. . .	. . .	. . .
1921	18.0	. . .	. . .	33.4	. . .	. . .	. . .	. . .	. . .
1922	16.9	. . .	. . .	27.2	. . .	. . .	. . .	. . .	. . .
1923	17.2	. . .	. . .	27.2	. . .	. . .	. . .	. . .	. . .
1924	17.2	. . .	. . .	26.9	. . .	. . .	. . .	. . .	. . .
1925	17.6	. . .	. . .	26.4	. . .	. . .	. . .	. . .	. . .
1926	17.8	. . .	. . .	26.0	. . .	. . .	. . .	. . .	. . .
1927	17.5	. . .	. . .	25.5	. . .	. . .	. . .	. . .	. . .
1928	17.2	. . .	. . .	25.1	. . .	. . .	. . .	. . .	. . .
1929	17.2	. . .	. . .	24.8	. . .	. . .	. . .	. . .	. . .
1930	16.8	. . .	. . .	24.3	. . .	. . .	. . .	. . .	. . .
1931	15.3	. . .	. . .	22.1	. . .	. . .	. . .	. . .	. . .
1932	13.7	. . .	. . .	19.6	. . .	. . .	. . .	. . .	. . .
1933	13.0	. . .	. . .	18.9	. . .	. . .	. . .	. . .	. . .
1934	13.5	. . .	. . .	20.7	. . .	. . .	. . .	. . .	. . .
1935	13.8	. . .	. . .	20.9	14.1	10.2	. . .	. . .	. . .
1936	13.9	. . .	. . .	21.1	14.2	10.3	. . .	. . .	. . .
1937	14.4	. . .	. . .	22.1	14.5	10.4	. . .	. . .	. . .
1938	14.2	. . .	. . .	22.0	14.6	10.4	. . .	. . .	. . .
1939	14.0	. . .	. . .	21.7	14.2	10.4	. . .	. . .	. . .
1940	14.1	. . .	. . .	21.9	14.1	10.4	. . .	. . .	. . .
1941	14.8	. . .	. . .	23.0	14.6	10.5	. . .	. . .	. . .
1942	16.4	. . .	. . .	26.8	15.9	10.8	. . .	. . .	. . .
1943	17.4	. . .	. . .	28.0	15.8	11.3	. . .	. . .	. . .
1944	17.7	. . .	. . .	30.0	15.8	11.6	. . .	. . .	. . .
1945	18.1	. . .	. . .	31.5	15.8	11.9	. . .	. . .	. . .
1946	19.6	. . .	. . .	34.6	16.6	12.6	. . .	. . .	. . .
1947	22.5	. . .	. . .	40.1	18.4	13.6	. . .	. . .	. . .
1948	24.2	. . .	. . .	42.7	20.4	14.5	. . .	. . .	. . .
1949	24.0	. . .	. . .	41.0	22.0	14.9	. . .	. . .	. . .
1950	24.2	. . .	. . .	40.5	22.6	15.2	. . .	. . .	. . .
1951	26.1	. . .	. . .	44.1	24.0	15.9	. . .	. . .	. . .
1952	26.7	. . .	. . .	43.7	25.6	16.8	. . .	. . .	. . .
1953	26.9	. . .	. . .	43.3	26.3	17.4	. . .	. . .	. . .
1954	27.0	. . .	. . .	43.3	25.9	17.9	. . .	. . .	. . .
1955	26.9	. . .	. . .	43.1	25.6	18.3	. . .	. . .	. . .
1956	27.3	. . .	. . .	44.0	26.1	19.0	. . .	. . .	. . .
1957	28.3	. . .	. . .	44.7	27.6	19.8	. . .	. . .	. . .
1958	29.1	. . .	. . .	44.8	28.4	20.7	. . .	. . .	. . .
1959	29.3	. . .	. . .	45.2	29.6	21.6	. . .	. . .	. . .
1960	29.8	. . .	. . .	45.9	29.6	22.4	. . .	. . .	. . .
1961	30.1	. . .	. . .	46.3	30.0	23.0	. . .	. . .	. . .
1962	30.4	. . .	. . .	46.6	30.6	23.6	. . .	. . .	. . .
1963	30.8	. . .	. . .	47.1	30.8	24.2	. . .	. . .	. . .
1964	31.2	. . .	. . .	47.5	31.2	24.7	. . .	. . .	. . .
1965	31.7	. . .	. . .	48.0	31.7	25.3	. . .	. . .	. . .
1966	32.6	. . .	. . .	49.2	32.2	26.4	. . .	. . .	. . .
1967	33.6	35.0	31.1	51.2	33.1	28.3	. . .	. . .	35.4
1968	35.0	36.2	32.3	54.0	34.1	30.0	. . .	. . .	37.2
1969	36.9	38.0	34.3	57.1	35.5	32.1	. . .	. . .	39.1
1970	39.0	40.1	36.7	59.5	37.3	34.1	. . .	. . .	41.3
1971	40.7	41.3	38.3	61.4	39.2	36.3	. . .	. . .	43.3
1972	42.1	43.1	39.8	62.7	39.7	37.5	. . .	. . .	45.1
1973	44.7	48.8	41.5	65.0	41.0	39.0	. . .	. . .	46.9
1974	49.6	55.5	46.2	69.8	45.5	42.6	. . .	. . .	50.2
1975	54.1	60.2	51.1	72.9	49.8	47.7	. . .	. . .	54.4
1976	57.2	62.0	54.2	75.6	54.7	52.3	. . .	. . .	57.6
1977	60.9	65.7	57.9	79.0	58.6	57.3	. . .	. . .	60.9
1978	65.6	72.1	62.9	81.7	61.5	62.1	. . .	. . .	64.8
1979	73.1	79.9	70.7	85.2	70.4	68.0	. . .	. . .	69.4

[1]December 1997 = 100.

. . . = Not available.

Table 9-6. Consumer Price Indexes, Urban Wage Earners and Clerical Workers (CPI-W): U.S. City Average, Major Groups, 1913–2011—*Continued*

(1982–1984 = 100, unless otherwise specified.)

Year	All items	Food and beverages	Housing	Apparel	Transportation	Medical care	Recreation[1]	Education and communication[1]	Other goods and services
1980	82.9	86.9	81.7	90.9	82.9	75.6	. . .	. . .	75.6
1981	91.4	93.6	91.1	95.6	93.0	83.5	. . .	. . .	82.5
1982	96.9	97.3	97.7	97.8	97.0	92.5	. . .	. . .	90.9
1983	99.8	99.5	100.0	100.2	99.2	100.5	. . .	. . .	101.3
1984	103.3	103.2	102.2	102.0	103.8	106.9	. . .	. . .	107.9
1985	106.9	105.5	106.6	105.0	106.4	113.6	. . .	. . .	114.2
1986	108.6	108.9	109.7	105.8	101.7	122.0	. . .	. . .	120.9
1987	112.5	113.3	112.8	110.4	105.1	130.2	. . .	. . .	127.8
1988	117.0	117.9	116.8	114.9	108.3	139.0	. . .	. . .	136.5
1989	122.6	124.6	121.2	117.9	113.9	149.6	. . .	. . .	147.4
1990	129.0	131.8	126.4	123.1	120.1	162.7	. . .	. . .	158.9
1991	134.3	136.5	131.2	127.4	123.1	176.5	. . .	. . .	171.7
1992	138.2	138.3	135.0	130.7	125.8	189.6	. . .	. . .	183.3
1993	142.1	141.2	138.5	132.4	129.4	200.9	91.2	86.0	192.2
1994	145.6	144.4	142.0	132.2	133.4	210.4	93.0	89.1	196.4
1995	149.8	148.3	145.4	130.9	138.8	219.8	94.7	92.3	204.2
1996	154.1	153.2	149.6	130.9	142.8	227.6	97.5	95.4	212.2
1997	157.6	157.2	153.4	132.1	143.6	234.0	99.7	98.5	221.6
1998	159.7	160.4	156.7	131.6	140.5	241.4	100.9	100.4	236.1
1999	163.2	163.8	160.0	130.1	143.4	249.7	101.3	101.5	261.9
2000	168.9	167.7	165.4	128.3	152.8	259.9	102.4	102.7	276.5
2001	173.5	173.0	172.1	126.1	153.6	271.8	103.6	105.3	289.5
2002	175.9	176.1	175.7	123.1	151.8	284.6	104.6	107.6	302.0
2003	179.8	179.9	180.4	120.0	156.3	296.3	105.5	109.0	307.0
2004	184.5	186.2	185.0	120.0	161.5	309.5	106.3	110.0	312.6
2005	191.0	190.5	191.2	119.1	173.0	322.8	106.8	111.4	322.2
2006	197.1	194.9	198.5	119.1	180.3	335.7	108.2	113.9	330.9
2007	202.8	202.5	204.8	118.5	184.3	350.9	108.6	116.3	344.0
2008	211.1	213.5	211.8	118.7	195.7	364.2	110.1	119.8	357.9
2009	209.6	217.5	213.1	119.8	176.7	376.1	111.0	123.0	391.6
2010	214.0	219.2	212.9	118.7	192.6	389.8	109.8	124.9	409.3
2011	221.6	227.3	215.8	121.3	213.3	402.2	109.9	125.5	416.9

[1]December 1997 = 100.
. . . = Not available.

Table 9-7. Consumer Price Indexes, All Urban Consumers (CPI-U): U.S. City Average, by Expenditure Category, 1990–2011

(1982–1984 = 100, unless otherwise specified.)

Expenditure category	1990	1991	1992	1993	1994	1995	1996	1997	1998	1999	2000
ALL ITEMS	130.7	136.2	140.3	144.5	148.2	152.4	156.9	160.5	163.0	166.6	172.2
Food and Beverages	132.1	136.8	138.7	141.6	144.9	148.9	153.7	157.7	161.1	164.6	168.4
Food	132.4	136.3	137.9	140.9	144.3	148.4	153.3	157.3	160.7	164.1	167.8
Food at home	132.3	135.8	136.8	140.1	144.1	148.8	154.3	158.1	161.1	164.2	167.9
Cereals and bakery product	140.0	145.8	151.5	156.6	163.0	167.5	174.0	177.6	181.1	185.0	188.3
Meats, poultry, fish, and eggs	130.0	132.6	130.9	135.5	137.2	138.8	144.8	148.5	147.3	147.9	154.5
Dairy and related product	126.5	125.1	128.5	129.4	131.7	132.8	142.1	145.5	150.8	159.6	160.7
Fruits and vegetables	149.0	155.8	155.4	159.0	165.0	177.7	183.9	187.5	198.2	203.1	204.6
Nonalcoholic beverages and beverage materials	113.5	114.1	114.3	114.6	123.2	131.7	128.6	133.4	133.0	134.3	137.8
Other food at home	123.4	127.3	128.8	130.5	135.6	140.8	142.9	147.3	150.8	153.5	155.6
Sugar and sweets	124.7	129.3	133.1	133.4	135.2	137.5	143.7	147.8	150.2	152.3	154.0
Fats and oils	126.3	131.7	129.8	130.0	133.5	137.3	140.5	141.7	146.9	148.3	147.4
Other food	131.2	137.1	140.1	143.7	147.5	151.1	156.2	161.2	165.5	168.9	172.2
Other miscellaneous food[1]	. . .	. . .	. . .	. . .	. . .	. . .	. . .	. . .	102.6	104.9	107.5
Food away from home	133.4	137.9	140.7	143.2	145.7	149.0	152.7	157.0	161.1	165.1	169.0
Other food away from home[1]	. . .	. . .	. . .	. . .	. . .	. . .	. . .	. . .	101.6	105.2	109.0
Alcoholic beverages	129.3	142.8	147.3	149.6	151.5	153.9	158.5	162.8	165.7	169.7	174.7
Housing	128.5	133.6	137.5	141.2	144.8	148.5	152.8	156.8	160.4	163.9	169.6
Shelter	140.0	146.3	151.2	155.7	160.5	165.7	171.0	176.3	182.1	187.3	193.4
Rent of primary residence	138.4	143.3	146.9	150.3	154.0	157.8	162.0	166.7	172.1	177.5	183.9
Lodging away from home[1]	. . .	. . .	. . .	. . .	. . .	. . .	. . .	. . .	109.0	112.3	117.5
Owners' equivalent rent of primary residence[2]	144.8	150.4	155.5	160.5	165.8	171.3	176.8	181.9	187.8	192.9	198.7
Tenants' and household insurance[1]	. . .	. . .	. . .	. . .	. . .	. . .	. . .	. . .	99.8	101.3	103.7
Fuels and utilities	111.6	115.3	117.8	121.3	122.8	123.7	127.5	130.8	128.5	128.8	137.9
Household energy	104.5	106.7	108.1	111.2	111.7	111.5	115.2	117.9	113.7	113.5	122.8
Fuel oil and other fuels	99.3	94.6	90.7	90.3	88.8	88.1	99.2	99.8	90.0	91.4	129.7
Energy services	109.3	112.6	114.8	118.5	119.2	119.2	122.1	125.1	121.2	120.9	128.0
Water, sewer, and trash collection services[1]	. . .	. . .	. . .	. . .	. . .	. . .	. . .	. . .	101.6	104.0	106.5
Household furnishings and operations	113.3	116.0	118.0	119.3	121.0	123.0	124.7	125.4	126.6	126.7	128.2
Household operations[1]	. . .	. . .	. . .	. . .	. . .	. . .	. . .	. . .	101.5	104.5	110.5
Apparel	124.1	128.7	131.9	133.7	133.4	132.0	131.7	132.9	133.0	131.3	129.6
Men's and boys' apparel	120.4	124.2	126.5	127.5	126.4	126.2	127.7	130.1	131.8	131.1	129.7
Women's and girls' apparel	122.6	127.6	130.4	132.6	130.9	126.9	124.7	126.1	126.0	123.3	121.5
Infants' and toddlers' apparel	125.8	128.9	129.3	127.1	128.1	127.2	129.7	129.0	126.1	129.0	130.6
Footwear	117.4	120.9	125.0	125.9	126.0	125.4	126.6	127.6	128.0	125.7	123.8
Transportation	120.5	123.8	126.5	130.4	134.3	139.1	143.0	144.3	141.6	144.4	153.3
Private transportation	118.8	121.9	124.6	127.5	131.4	136.3	140.0	141.0	137.9	140.5	149.1
New and used motor vehicles[1]	. . .	. . .	. . .	91.8	95.5	99.4	101.0	100.5	100.1	100.1	100.8
New vehicles	121.4	126.0	129.2	132.7	137.6	141.0	143.7	144.3	143.4	142.9	142.8
Used cars and trucks	117.6	118.1	123.2	133.9	141.7	156.5	157.0	151.1	150.6	152.0	155.8
Motor fuel	101.2	99.4	99.0	98.0	98.5	100.0	106.3	106.2	92.2	100.7	129.3
Gasoline (all types)	101.0	99.2	99.0	97.7	98.2	99.8	105.9	105.8	91.6	100.1	128.6
Motor vehicle parts and equipment	100.9	102.2	103.1	101.6	101.4	102.1	102.2	101.9	101.1	100.5	101.5
Motor vehicle maintenance and repair	130.1	136.0	141.3	145.9	150.2	154.0	158.4	162.7	167.1	171.9	177.3
Public transportation	142.6	148.9	151.4	167.0	172.0	175.9	181.9	186.7	190.3	197.7	209.6
Medical Care	162.8	177.0	190.1	201.4	211.0	220.5	228.2	234.6	242.1	250.6	260.8
Medical care commodities	163.4	176.8	188.1	195.0	200.7	204.5	210.4	215.3	221.8	230.7	238.1
Medical care services	162.7	177.1	190.5	202.9	213.4	224.2	232.4	239.1	246.8	255.1	266.0
Professional services	156.1	165.7	175.8	184.7	192.5	201.0	208.3	215.4	222.2	229.2	237.7
Hospital and related services	178.0	196.1	214.0	231.9	245.6	257.8	269.5	278.4	287.5	299.5	317.3
Recreation[1]	. . .	. . .	. . .	90.7	92.7	94.5	97.4	99.6	101.1	102.0	103.3
Video and audio[1]	. . .	. . .	. . .	96.5	95.4	95.1	96.6	99.4	101.1	100.7	101.0
Education and Communication[1]	. . .	. . .	. . .	85.5	88.8	92.2	95.3	98.4	100.3	101.2	102.5
Education[1]	. . .	. . .	. . .	78.4	83.3	88.0	92.7	97.3	102.1	107.0	112.5
Educational books and supplies	171.3	180.3	190.3	197.6	205.5	214.4	226.9	238.4	250.8	261.7	279.9
Tuition, other school fees, and childcare	175.7	191.4	208.5	225.3	239.8	253.8	267.1	280.4	294.2	308.4	324.0
Communication[1]	. . .	. . .	. . .	96.7	97.6	98.8	99.6	100.3	98.7	96.0	93.6
Information and information processing[1]	. . .	. . .	. . .	97.7	98.6	98.7	99.5	100.4	98.5	95.5	92.8
Telephone services[1]	. . .	. . .	. . .	. . .	. . .	. . .	. . .	100.7	100.1	98.5	99.3
Information technology, hardware, and services[3]	93.5	88.6	83.7	78.8	72.0	63.8	57.2	50.1	39.9	30.5	25.9
Personal computers and peripheral equipment[1]	. . .	. . .	. . .	. . .	. . .	. . .	. . .	. . .	875.1	598.7	459.9
Other Goods and Services	159.0	171.6	183.3	192.9	198.5	206.9	215.4	224.8	237.7	258.3	271.1
Tobacco and smoking product	181.5	202.7	219.8	228.4	220.0	225.7	232.8	243.7	274.8	355.8	394.9
Personal care	130.4	134.9	138.3	141.5	144.6	147.1	150.1	152.7	156.7	161.1	165.6
Personal care product	128.2	132.8	136.5	139.0	141.5	143.1	144.3	144.2	148.3	151.8	153.7
Personal care services	132.8	137.0	140.0	144.0	147.9	151.5	156.6	162.4	166.0	171.4	178.1
Miscellaneous personal services	158.4	168.8	177.5	186.1	195.9	205.9	215.6	226.1	234.7	243.0	252.3

[1]December 1997 = 100.
[2]December 1982 = 100.
[3]December 1988 = 100.
. . . = Not available.

Table 9-7. Consumer Price Indexes, All Urban Consumers (CPI-U): U.S. City Average, by Expenditure Category, 1990–2011—*Continued*

(1982–1984 = 100, unless otherwise specified.)

Expenditure category	2001	2002	2003	2004	2005	2006	2007	2008	2009	2010	2011
ALL ITEMS	177.1	179.9	184.0	188.9	195.3	201.6	207.3	215.3	214.5	218.1	224.9
Food and Beverages	173.6	176.8	180.5	186.6	191.2	195.7	203.3	214.2	218.2	220.0	227.9
Food	173.1	176.2	180.0	186.2	190.7	195.2	202.9	214.1	218.0	219.6	227.8
Food at home	173.4	175.6	179.4	186.2	189.8	193.1	201.2	214.1	215.1	215.8	226.2
Cereals and bakery product	193.8	198.0	202.8	206.0	209.0	212.8	222.1	244.9	252.6	250.4	260.3
Meats, poultry, fish, and eggs	161.3	162.1	169.3	181.7	184.7	186.6	195.6	204.7	203.8	207.7	223.2
Dairy and related product	167.1	168.1	167.9	180.2	182.4	181.4	194.8	210.4	197.0	199.2	212.7
Fruits and vegetables	212.2	220.9	225.9	232.7	241.4	252.9	262.6	278.9	272.9	273.5	284.7
Nonalcoholic beverages and beverage materials	139.2	139.2	139.8	140.4	144.4	147.4	153.4	160.0	163.0	161.6	166.8
Other food at home	159.6	160.8	162.6	164.9	167.0	169.6	173.3	184.2	191.2	191.1	197.4
Sugar and sweets	155.7	159.0	162.0	163.2	165.2	171.5	176.8	186.6	196.9	201.2	207.8
Fats and oils	155.7	155.4	157.4	167.8	167.7	168.0	172.9	196.8	201.2	200.6	219.2
Other food	176.0	177.1	178.8	179.7	182.5	185.0	188.2	198.1	205.5	204.6	209.3
Other miscellaneous food[1]	108.9	109.2	110.3	110.4	111.3	113.9	115.1	119.9	122.4	121.7	124.0
Food away from home	173.9	178.3	182.1	187.5	193.4	199.4	206.7	215.8	223.3	226.1	231.4
Other food away from home[1]	113.4	117.7	121.3	125.3	131.3	136.6	144.1	150.6	155.9	159.3	162.8
Alcoholic beverages	179.3	183.6	187.2	192.1	195.9	200.7	207.0	214.5	220.8	223.3	226.7
Housing	176.4	180.3	184.8	189.5	195.7	203.2	209.6	216.3	217.1	216.3	219.1
Shelter	200.6	208.1	213.1	218.8	224.4	232.1	240.6	246.7	249.4	248.4	251.6
Rent of primary residence	192.1	199.7	205.5	211.0	217.3	225.1	234.7	243.3	248.8	249.4	253.6
Lodging away from home[1]	118.6	118.3	119.3	125.9	130.3	136.0	142.8	143.7	134.2	133.7	137.4
Owners' equivalent rent of primary residence[2]	206.3	214.7	219.9	224.9	230.2	238.2	246.2	252.4	256.6	256.6	259.6
Tenants' and household insurance[1]	106.2	108.7	114.8	116.2	117.6	116.5	117.0	118.8	121.5	125.7	127.4
Fuels and utilities	150.2	143.6	154.5	161.9	179.0	194.7	200.6	220.0	210.7	214.2	220.4
Household energy	135.4	127.2	138.2	144.4	161.6	177.1	181.7	200.8	188.1	189.3	193.6
Fuel oil and other fuels	129.3	115.5	139.5	160.5	208.6	234.9	251.5	334.4	239.8	275.1	337.1
Energy services	142.4	134.4	145.0	150.6	166.5	182.1	186.3	202.2	193.6	192.9	194.4
Water, sewer, and trash collection services[1]	109.6	113.0	117.2	124.0	130.3	136.8	143.7	152.1	161.1	170.9	179.6
Household furnishings and operations	129.1	128.3	126.1	125.5	126.1	127.0	126.9	127.8	128.7	125.5	124.9
Household operations[1]	115.6	119.0	121.8	125.0	130.3	136.6	140.6	147.5	150.3	150.3	151.8
Apparel	127.3	124.0	120.9	120.4	119.5	119.5	119.0	118.9	120.1	119.5	122.1
Men's and boys' apparel	125.7	121.7	118.0	117.5	116.1	114.1	112.4	113.0	113.6	111.9	114.7
Women's and girls' apparel	119.3	115.8	113.1	113.0	110.8	110.7	110.3	107.5	108.1	107.1	109.2
Infants' and toddlers' apparel	129.2	126.4	122.1	118.5	116.7	116.5	113.9	113.8	114.5	114.2	113.6
Footwear	123.0	121.4	119.6	119.3	122.6	123.5	122.4	124.2	126.9	128.0	128.5
Transportation	154.3	152.9	157.6	163.1	173.9	180.9	184.7	195.5	179.3	193.4	212.4
Private transportation	150.0	148.8	153.6	159.4	170.2	177.0	180.8	191.0	174.8	188.7	207.6
New and used motor vehicles[1]	101.3	99.2	96.5	94.2	95.6	95.6	94.3	93.3	93.5	97.1	99.8
New vehicles	142.1	140.0	137.9	137.1	137.9	137.6	136.3	134.2	135.6	138.0	141.9
Used cars and trucks	158.7	152.0	142.9	133.3	139.4	140.0	135.7	134.0	127.0	143.1	149.0
Motor fuel	124.7	116.6	135.8	160.4	195.7	221.0	239.1	279.7	202.0	239.2	302.6
Gasoline (all types)	124.0	116.0	135.1	159.7	194.7	219.9	238.0	277.5	201.6	238.6	301.7
Motor vehicle parts and equipment	104.8	106.9	107.8	108.7	111.9	117.3	121.6	128.7	134.1	137.0	143.9
Motor vehicle maintenance and repair	183.5	190.2	195.6	200.2	206.9	215.6	223.0	233.9	243.3	248.0	253.1
Public transportation	210.6	207.4	209.3	209.1	217.3	226.6	230.0	250.5	236.3	251.4	269.4
Medical Care	272.8	285.6	297.1	310.1	323.2	336.2	351.1	364.1	375.6	388.4	400.3
Medical care commodities	247.6	256.4	262.8	269.3	276.0	285.9	290.0	296.0	305.1	314.7	324.1
Medical care services	278.8	292.9	306.0	321.3	336.7	350.6	369.3	384.9	397.3	411.2	423.8
Professional services	246.5	253.9	261.2	271.5	281.7	289.3	300.8	311.0	319.4	328.2	335.7
Hospital and related services	338.3	367.8	394.8	417.9	439.9	468.1	498.9	534.0	567.9	607.7	641.5
Recreation[1]	104.9	106.2	107.5	108.6	109.4	110.9	111.4	113.3	114.3	113.3	113.4
Video and audio[1]	101.5	102.8	103.6	104.2	104.2	104.6	102.9	102.6	101.3	99.1	98.4
Education and Communication[1]	105.2	107.9	109.8	111.6	113.7	116.8	119.6	123.6	127.4	129.9	131.5
Education[1]	118.5	126.0	134.4	143.7	152.7	162.1	171.4	181.3	190.9	199.3	207.8
Educational books and supplies	295.9	317.6	335.4	351.0	365.6	388.9	420.4	450.2	482.1	505.6	529.5
Tuition, other school fees, and childcare	341.1	362.1	386.7	414.3	440.9	468.1	494.1	522.1	549.0	573.2	597.2
Communication[1]	93.3	92.3	89.7	86.7	84.7	84.1	83.4	84.2	85.0	84.7	83.3
Information and information processing[1]	92.3	90.8	87.8	84.6	82.6	81.7	80.7	81.4	81.9	81.5	80.0
Telephone services[1]	99.7	98.3	95.8	94.9	95.8	98.2	100.5	102.4	102.4	101.2	. . .
Information technology, hardware, and services[3]	21.3	18.3	16.1	14.8	13.6	12.5	10.6	10.1	9.7	9.4	9.0
Personal computers and peripheral equipment[1]	330.1	248.4	196.9	171.2	143.2	120.9	108.4	94.9	82.3	76.4	68.9
Other Goods and Services	282.6	293.2	298.7	304.7	313.4	321.7	333.3	345.4	368.6	381.3	387.2
Tobacco and smoking product	425.2	461.5	469.0	478.0	502.8	519.9	554.2	588.7	730.3	807.3	834.8
Personal care	170.5	174.7	178.0	181.7	185.6	190.2	195.6	201.3	204.6	206.6	208.6
Personal care product	155.1	154.7	153.5	153.9	154.4	155.8	158.3	159.3	162.6	161.1	160.5
Personal care services	184.3	188.4	193.2	197.6	203.9	209.7	216.6	223.7	227.6	229.6	230.8
Miscellaneous personal services	263.1	274.4	283.5	293.9	303.0	313.6	325.0	338.9	344.5	354.1	362.9

[1]December 1997 = 100.
[2]December 1982 = 100.
[3]December 1988 = 100.
. . . = Not available.

Table 9-8. Relative Importance of Components in the Consumer Price Index: U.S. City Average, Selected Groups, December 1997–December 2011

(Percent distribution.)

Index and year	All items	Food and beverages	Housing	Apparel	Transportation	Medical care	Recreation	Education and communication	Other goods and services
ALL URBAN CONSUMERS (CPI-U)									
December 1997	100.0	16.3	39.6	4.9	17.6	5.6	6.1	5.5	4.3
December 1998	100.0	16.4	39.8	4.8	17.0	5.7	6.1	5.5	4.6
December 1999	100.0	16.3	39.6	4.7	17.5	5.8	6.0	5.4	4.7
December 2000	100.0	16.2	40.0	4.4	17.6	5.8	5.9	5.3	4.8
December 2001[1]	100.0	16.4	40.5	4.2	16.6	6.0	5.9	5.4	4.9
December 2001[2]	100.0	15.7	40.9	4.4	17.1	5.8	6.0	5.8	4.3
December 2002	100.0	15.6	40.9	4.2	17.3	6.0	5.9	5.8	4.4
December 2003	100.0	15.4	42.1	4.0	16.9	6.1	5.9	5.9	3.8
December 2004	100.0	15.3	42.0	3.8	17.4	6.1	5.7	5.8	3.8
December 2005	100.0	15.1	42.2	3.7	17.7	6.2	5.6	5.8	3.7
December 2006	100.0	15.0	42.7	3.7	17.2	6.3	5.6	6.0	3.5
December 2007	100.0	14.9	42.4	3.7	17.7	6.2	5.6	6.1	3.3
December 2008	100.0	15.8	43.4	3.7	15.3	6.4	5.7	6.3	3.4
December 2009	100.0	14.8	42.0	3.7	16.7	6.5	6.4	6.4	3.5
December 2010	100.0	14.8	42.0	3.7	16.7	6.5	6.4	3.0	3.5
December 2011	100.0	15.3	41.0	3.6	16.9	7.1	6.0	6.8	3.4
URBAN WAGE EARNERS AND WORKERS (CPI-W)									
December 1997	100.0	17.9	36.5	5.3	19.8	4.6	6.0	5.4	4.5
December 1998	100.0	18.0	36.7	5.2	19.2	4.7	5.9	5.4	5.0
December 1999	100.0	17.9	36.5	5.0	19.7	4.7	5.8	5.3	5.1
December 2000	100.0	17.8	36.8	4.8	19.9	4.7	5.7	5.2	5.2
December 2001[1]	100.0	18.0	37.3	4.6	18.8	4.9	5.7	5.3	5.4
December 2001[2]	100.0	17.2	38.1	4.8	19.4	4.6	5.6	5.6	4.5
December 2002	100.0	17.1	38.1	4.6	19.7	4.7	5.6	5.6	4.6
December 2003	100.0	17.2	39.1	4.4	19.1	5.0	5.7	5.6	3.9
December 2004	100.0	17.0	39.0	4.2	19.8	5.0	5.5	5.5	3.9
December 2005	100.0	16.8	39.2	4.0	20.1	5.1	5.4	5.4	3.9
December 2006	100.0	16.5	40.5	4.0	19.5	5.2	5.0	5.6	3.7
December 2007	100.0	15.9	40.0	4.0	20.1	5.2	5.3	6.0	3.5
December 2008	100.0	16.9	41.3	4.0	17.1	5.4	5.5	6.2	3.7
December 2009	100.0	16.4	39.8	3.8	18.6	5.3	6.0	6.2	3.9
December 2010	100.0	16.4	39.8	3.8	18.6	5.3	6.0	6.2	3.9
December 2011	100.0	15.9	39.8	3.6	19.0	5.7	5.6	6.8	3.5

[1]1993–1995 weights.
[2]1999–2000 weights.

Table 9-9. Consumer Price Indexes, All Urban Consumers (CPI-U), All Items: Selected Metropolitan Statistical Areas, Selected Years, 1975–2011

(1982–1984 = 100, unless otherwise specified.)

Area	1975	1980	1985	1986	1987	1988	1989	1990	1991	1992	1993	1994	1995	1996	1997
NORTHEAST															
Boston-Brockton-Nashua, MA-NH-ME-CT	55.8	82.6	109.4	112.2	117.1	124.2	131.3	138.9	145.0	148.6	152.9	154.9	158.6	163.3	167.9
New York-Northern New Jersey-Long Island, NY-NJ-CT-PA	57.6	82.1	108.7	112.3	118.0	123.7	130.6	138.5	144.8	150.0	154.5	158.2	162.2	166.9	170.8
Philadelphia-Wilmington-Atlantic City, PA-NJ-DE-MD	56.8	83.6	108.8	111.5	116.8	122.4	128.3	135.8	142.2	146.6	150.2	154.6	158.7	162.8	166.5
Pittsburgh, PA	52.4	81.0	106.9	108.2	111.4	114.9	120.1	126.2	131.3	136.0	139.9	144.6	149.2	153.2	157.0
NORTH CENTRAL															
Chicago-Gary-Kenosha, IL-IN-WI	52.8	82.2	107.7	110.0	114.5	119.0	125.0	131.7	137.0	141.1	145.4	148.6	153.3	157.4	161.7
Cincinnati-Hamilton, OH-KY-IN	51.8	82.1	106.6	107.6	111.9	116.1	120.9	126.5	131.4	134.1	137.8	142.4	146.2	149.6	152.1
Cleveland-Akron, OH	50.2	78.9	107.8	109.4	112.7	116.7	122.7	129.0	134.2	136.8	140.3	144.4	147.9	152.0	156.1
Detroit-Ann Arbor-Flint, MI	53.9	85.3	106.8	108.3	111.7	116.1	122.3	128.6	133.1	135.9	139.6	144.0	148.6	152.5	156.3
Kansas City, MO-KS	53.2	83.6	107.7	108.7	113.1	117.4	121.6	126.0	131.2	134.3	138.1	141.3	145.3	151.6	155.8
Milwaukee-Racine, WI	50.8	81.4	107.0	107.4	111.5	115.9	120.8	126.2	132.2	137.1	142.1	147.0	151.0	154.7	157.7
Minneapolis-St. Paul, MN-WI	51.2	78.9	107.0	108.4	111.6	117.2	122.0	127.0	130.4	135.0	139.2	143.6	147.0	151.9	155.4
St. Louis, MO-IL	52.6	82.5	107.1	108.6	112.2	115.7	121.8	128.1	132.1	134.7	137.5	141.3	145.2	149.6	152.9
SOUTH															
Atlanta, GA	53.6	80.3	108.9	112.2	116.5	120.4	126.1	131.7	135.9	138.5	143.4	146.7	150.9	156.0	158.9
Dallas-Fort Worth, TX	50.4	81.5	108.2	109.9	112.9	116.1	119.5	125.1	130.8	133.9	137.3	141.2	144.9	148.8	151.4
Houston-Galveston-Brazoria, TX	51.4	82.7	104.9	103.9	106.5	109.5	114.1	120.6	125.1	129.1	133.4	137.9	139.8	142.7	145.4
Miami-Fort Lauderdale, FL	. . .	81.1	106.5	107.9	111.8	116.8	121.5	128.0	132.3	134.5	139.1	143.6	148.9	153.7	158.4
Tampa-St. Petersburg-Clearwater, FL[1]	. . .	. . .	. . .	. . .	100.0	103.7	107.2	111.7	116.4	119.2	124.0	126.5	129.7	131.6	134.0
Washington-Baltimore, DC-MD-VA-WV[2]	. . .	. . .	. . .	. . .	. . .	. . .	. . .	. . .	. . .	. . .	. . .	. . .	. . .	. . .	100.8
WEST															
Anchorage, AK	57.1	85.5	105.8	107.8	108.2	108.6	111.7	118.6	124.0	128.2	132.2	135.0	138.9	142.7	144.8
Denver-Boulder-Greeley, CO	48.4	78.4	107.1	107.9	110.8	113.7	115.8	120.9	125.6	130.3	135.8	141.8	147.9	153.1	158.1
Honolulu, HI	56.3	83.0	106.8	109.4	114.9	121.7	128.7	138.1	148.0	155.1	160.1	164.5	168.1	170.7	171.9
Los Angeles-Riverside-Orange County, CA	53.3	83.7	108.4	111.9	116.7	122.1	128.3	135.9	141.4	146.5	150.3	152.3	154.6	157.5	160.0
Phoenix-Mesa, AZ	. . .	. . .	. . .	. . .	. . .	. . .	. . .	. . .	. . .	. . .	. . .	. . .	. . .	. . .	. . .
Portland-Salem, OR-WA	53.5	87.2	106.7	108.2	110.9	114.7	120.4	127.4	133.9	139.8	144.7	148.9	153.2	158.6	164.0
San Diego, CA	47.6	79.4	110.4	113.5	117.5	123.4	130.6	138.4	143.4	147.4	150.6	154.5	156.8	160.9	163.7
San Francisco-Oakland-San Jose, CA	51.8	80.4	108.4	111.6	115.4	120.5	126.4	132.1	137.9	142.5	146.3	148.7	151.6	155.1	160.4
Seattle-Tacoma-Bremerton, WA	51.1	82.7	105.6	106.7	109.2	112.8	118.1	126.8	134.1	139.0	142.9	147.8	152.3	157.5	163.0

Area	1998	1999	2000	2001	2002	2003	2004	2005	2006	2007	2008	2009	2010	2011
NORTHEAST														
Boston-Brockton-Nashua, MA-NH-ME-CT	171.7	176.0	183.6	191.5	196.5	203.9	209.5	216.4	223.1	227.4	235.4	233.8	237.4	243.9
New York-Northern New Jersey-Long Island, NY-NJ-CT-PA	173.6	177.0	182.5	187.1	191.9	197.8	204.8	212.7	220.7	226.9	235.8	236.8	240.9	247.7
Philadelphia-Wilmington-Atlantic City, PA-NJ-DE-MD	168.2	171.9	176.5	181.3	184.9	188.8	196.5	204.2	212.1	216.7	224.1	223.3	227.7	233.8
Pittsburgh, PA	159.2	162.5	168.0	172.5	174.0	177.5	183.0	189.8	195.7	201.5	211.3	212.1	215.4	225.1
NORTH CENTRAL														
Chicago-Gary-Kenosha, IL-IN-WI	165.0	168.4	173.8	178.3	181.2	184.5	188.6	194.3	198.3	204.8	212.5	210.0	212.9	218.7
Cincinnati-Hamilton, OH-KY-IN	155.1	159.2	164.8	167.9	170.0	173.4	176.5	181.6	188.6	193.9	201.5	200.6	204.7	211.1
Cleveland-Akron, OH	159.8	162.5	168.0	172.9	173.3	176.2	181.6	187.9	191.1	196.0	203.0	200.5	204.6	211.0
Detroit-Ann Arbor-Flint, MI	159.8	163.9	169.8	174.4	178.9	182.5	185.4	190.8	196.6	200.1	204.7	203.5	205.1	211.8
Kansas City, MO-KS	157.8	160.1	166.6	172.2	174.0	177.0	180.7	185.3	190.1	194.5	201.2	201.0	205.4	213.5
Milwaukee-Racine, WI	160.3	163.7	168.6	171.7	174.0	177.7	180.2	185.2	189.9	194.1	203.0	203.0	209.6	216.9
Minneapolis-St. Paul, MN-WI	158.3	163.3	170.1	176.5	179.6	182.7	187.9	193.1	196.2	201.2	209.0	207.9	211.7	219.3
St. Louis, MO-IL	154.5	157.6	163.1	167.3	169.1	173.4	180.3	186.2	189.5	193.2	198.7	198.5	203.2	209.8
SOUTH														
Atlanta, GA	161.2	164.8	170.6	176.2	178.2	180.8	183.2	188.9	193.8	200.0	206.5	201.0	203.5	209.1
Dallas-Fort Worth, TX	153.6	158.0	164.7	170.4	172.7	176.2	178.7	184.7	190.1	193.2	201.8	200.5	201.6	207.9
Houston-Galveston-Brazoria, TX	146.8	148.7	154.2	158.8	159.2	163.7	169.5	175.6	180.6	183.8	190.0	190.5	194.2	200.5
Miami-Fort Lauderdale, FL	160.5	162.4	167.8	173.0	175.5	180.6	186.5	194.3	203.9	212.4	222.1	221.4	223.1	230.9
Tampa-St. Petersburg-Clearwater, FL[1]	137.5	140.6	145.7	148.8	153.9	158.1	162.0	168.5	175.2	184.3	190.1	189.9	193.5	198.9
Washington-Baltimore, DC-MD-VA-WV[2]	102.1	104.2	107.6	110.4	113.0	116.2	119.5	124.3	128.8	133.5	139.5	139.8	142.2	147.0
WEST														
Anchorage, AK	146.9	148.4	150.9	155.2	158.2	162.5	166.7	171.8	177.3	181.2	189.5	191.7	195.1	201.4
Denver-Boulder-Greeley, CO	161.9	166.6	173.2	181.3	184.8	186.8	187.0	190.9	197.7	202.0	209.9	208.5	212.4	220.3
Honolulu, HI	171.5	173.3	176.3	178.4	180.3	184.3	190.6	197.8	209.4	219.5	228.9	230.0	234.9	243.6
Los Angeles-Riverside-Orange County, CA	162.3	166.1	171.6	177.3	182.2	187.0	193.2	201.8	210.4	217.3	225.0	223.2	225.9	231.9
Phoenix-Mesa, AZ	. . .	. . .	. . .	. . .	101.2	103.3	105.2	108.3	111.5	115.3	119.3	117.6	118.2	121.5
Portland-Salem, OR-WA	167.1	172.6	178.0	182.4	183.8	186.3	191.1	196.0	201.1	208.6	215.4	215.6	218.3	224.6
San Diego, CA	166.9	172.8	182.8	191.2	197.9	205.3	212.8	220.6	228.1	233.3	242.3	242.3	245.5	252.9
San Francisco-Oakland-San Jose, CA	165.5	172.5	180.2	189.9	193.0	196.4	198.8	202.7	209.2	216.0	222.8	224.4	227.5	233.4
Seattle-Tacoma-Bremerton, WA	167.7	172.8	179.2	185.7	189.3	192.3	194.7	200.2	207.6	215.7	224.7	226.0	226.7	232.8

[1]1987 = 100.
[2]November 1996 = 100.
. . . = Not available.

Table 9-10. Consumer Price Index Research Series, Using Current Methods (CPI-U-RS), by Month and Annual Average, 1977–2011

(December 1977 = 100.)

Year	January	February	March	April	May	June	July	August	September	October	November	December	Annual average
1977	100.0	. . .	. . .	. . .	. . .	. . .	. . .	. . .	. . .	. . .	. . .	. . .	. . .
1978	100.5	101.1	101.8	102.7	103.6	104.6	105.0	105.5	106.1	106.7	107.3	107.9	104.4
1979	108.7	109.7	110.7	111.8	113.0	114.1	115.2	116.0	117.1	117.9	118.5	119.5	114.4
1980	120.9	122.4	123.8	124.8	125.8	126.7	127.6	128.6	130.0	130.8	131.5	132.4	127.1
1981	133.6	135.3	136.4	137.1	137.9	138.7	139.7	140.7	141.8	142.4	142.9	143.4	139.2
1982	144.2	144.7	144.9	145.1	146.1	147.5	148.5	148.8	149.5	150.2	150.5	150.7	147.6
1983	151.1	151.2	151.3	152.4	153.2	153.8	154.4	154.8	155.6	156.0	156.2	156.4	153.9
1984	157.3	158.0	158.4	159.1	159.5	160.0	160.5	161.1	161.9	162.3	162.3	162.4	160.2
1985	162.6	163.3	164.0	164.7	165.3	165.8	166.1	166.4	167.0	167.4	167.9	168.3	165.7
1986	168.8	168.3	167.5	167.1	167.7	168.5	168.5	168.7	169.7	169.7	169.8	169.9	168.7
1987	170.9	171.6	172.3	173.2	173.7	174.3	174.6	175.6	176.4	176.8	176.9	176.8	174.4
1988	177.3	177.6	178.3	179.2	179.8	180.5	181.1	181.9	183.0	183.5	183.6	183.7	180.8
1989	184.6	185.2	186.2	187.5	188.4	188.8	189.3	189.5	190.2	190.9	191.2	191.5	188.6
1990	193.3	194.2	195.2	195.5	195.8	196.9	197.6	199.3	200.9	202.1	202.3	202.4	198.0
1991	203.3	203.5	203.6	203.9	204.4	204.9	205.0	205.6	206.4	206.6	207.1	207.2	205.1
1992	207.5	208.1	209.0	209.3	209.6	210.1	210.4	211.0	211.6	212.2	212.5	212.3	210.3
1993	212.9	213.7	214.3	214.9	215.3	215.5	215.6	216.1	216.4	217.1	217.3	217.1	215.5
1994	217.4	218.0	218.8	219.0	219.2	219.9	220.4	221.1	221.5	221.6	221.9	221.8	220.1
1995	222.6	223.3	224.0	224.7	225.1	225.6	225.7	226.1	226.5	227.1	226.9	226.8	225.4
1996	227.9	228.7	229.8	230.6	231.2	231.3	231.7	232.0	232.7	233.4	233.8	233.8	231.4
1997	234.5	235.2	235.6	235.9	235.8	236.2	236.3	236.7	237.5	237.9	237.8	237.4	236.4
1998	237.8	238.2	238.6	239.1	239.4	239.6	239.8	240.2	240.5	241.0	241.0	240.7	239.7
1999	241.4	241.7	242.4	244.1	244.1	244.2	244.9	245.6	246.7	247.2	247.3	247.3	244.7
2000	248.0	249.4	251.4	251.6	251.8	253.2	253.7	253.8	255.1	255.5	255.7	255.5	252.9
2001	257.1	258.2	258.8	259.8	260.9	261.4	260.6	260.7	261.8	260.9	260.4	259.4	260.0
2002	260.1	261.1	262.5	264.0	264.0	264.2	264.5	265.3	265.8	266.3	266.3	265.7	264.2
2003	266.8	268.9	270.5	269.9	269.5	269.8	270.1	271.1	271.9	271.7	270.9	270.6	270.1
2004	272.0	273.5	275.2	276.1	277.6	278.5	278.2	278.3	278.8	280.4	280.5	279.5	277.4
2005	280.0	281.6	283.8	285.7	285.5	285.6	286.9	288.3	291.9	292.5	290.2	288.9	286.7
2006	291.2	291.8	293.5	295.9	297.3	297.9	298.8	299.5	298.0	296.4	295.9	296.4	296.1
2007	297.2	298.8	301.6	303.5	305.4	306.0	305.9	305.3	306.2	306.8	308.6	308.4	304.5
2008	310.0	310.9	313.6	315.5	318.1	321.3	323.0	321.7	321.3	318.0	311.9	308.7	316.2
2009	310.1	311.6	312.4	313.1	314.0	316.7	316.2	316.9	317.1	317.5	317.7	317.1	315.0
2010	318.2	318.3	319.6	320.1	320.4	320.1	320.1	320.6	320.8	321.2	321.3	321.9	320.2
2011	323.4	325.0	328.2	330.3	331.8	331.5	331.8	332.7	333.2	332.5	332.2	331.4	330.3

. . . = Not available.

NOTES AND DEFINITIONS

IMPORT AND EXPORT PRICE INDEXES

Collection and Coverage

The International Price Program (IPP) at the Bureau of Labor Statistics (BLS) produces Import/Export Price Indexes (MXP) which contain data on changes in the prices of goods and services traded between the U.S. and the rest of the world. Price indexes are available for nearly all merchandise categories. Military goods, works of art, used items, charity donations, railroad equipment, items leased for less than a year, rebuilt and repaired items, and selected exports are not included in the IPP program.

The (IPP) selects sample establishments based upon their relative trade value in imports and exports during the course of a year. After an establishment is selected for inclusion, a BLS field economist visits the establishment to enlist cooperation and to select the exact items that will be priced on a monthly basis. All information provided by the establishment is protected under BLS confidentiality rules.

The MXP are primarily used to deflate foreign trade statistics produced by the U.S. government. The MXP are also a valuable input into the processes of measuring inflation, formulating fiscal and monetary policy, forecasting future prices, conducting elasticity studies, measuring U.S. industrial competitiveness, analyzing exchange rates, negotiating trade contracts, and analyzing import prices by locality of origin. The IPP collects prices as close as possible to the first day of each reference month.

The formula used to calculate the MXP is a modified form of the Laspeyres index. A Laspeyres index uses fixed base period quantities to aggregate prices. This means that the quality of goods and services is fixed; new goods do not appear, and the prices of goods that disappear must be observable. Because these implications are not consistent with the actually workings of the economy, adjustments must be made to the index. All MXP data are not seasonally adjusted.

Items are classified by end use for the Bureau of Economic Analysis System, by industry according to the North American Industry Classification System (NAICS), and product category according to the Harmonized System (HS). While classification by end use and product category are self-explanatory, a couple of notes are in order for classifying items by industry. In the NAICS tables, for both imports and exports, items are classified by output industry, not input industry. As an example, NAICS import index 326 (plastics and rubber products) includes outputs such as manufactured plastic rather than inputs such as petroleum. The NAICS classification structure also matches the classification system used by the PPI to produce the NAICS primary products indexes.

Although import and export transaction prices are used to calculate the MXP, the IPP does not publish price information. For this reason, the MXP cannot be used to measure differences in price levels among different products and services or among different localities of origin.

Sources of Additional Information

Concepts and methodology are described in Chapter 15 of the *BLS Handbook of Methods* and in monthly BLS press releases. These resources are available on the BLS Web site at <http://www.bls.gov>.

Table 9-11. U.S. Export Price Indexes for Selected Categories of Goods, by End Use, 2000–2011

(2000 = 100, unless otherwise indicated.)

Commodity	2000				2001				2002			
	March	June	September	December	March	June	September	December	March	June	September	December
ALL COMMODITIES	100.0	100.1	100.4	100.1	100.0	99.4	99.0	97.6	97.6	98.0	98.8	98.6
Foods, Feeds, and Beverages	100.8	100.8	98.7	101.2	101.0	100.4	102.6	100.7	99.7	101.5	109.8	108.7
Agricultural foods, feeds, and beverages excluding distilled beverages	100.9	100.9	98.6	101.5	101.2	101.2	103.6	101.6	100.0	101.7	110.7	109.5
Nonagricultural foods (fish, distilled beverages)	99.6	99.9	99.7	98.2	99.4	92.6	92.9	92.1	98.3	100.7	101.3	102.3
Industrial Supplies and Materials	100.1	100.2	101.7	100.0	98.9	97.2	95.2	91.4	91.9	94.6	95.9	96.0
Industrial supplies and materials, durable	100.7	99.9	100.4	99.5	98.6	97.6	95.9	93.8	94.4	96.0	96.4	96.6
Industrial supplies and materials, nondurable	99.8	100.4	102.4	100.2	99.0	96.9	94.8	90.0	90.4	93.9	95.8	95.8
Agricultural industrial supplies and materials	98.0	98.6	103.2	104.6	101.7	99.3	96.8	93.3	93.6	95.8	98.4	101.9
Fuels and lubricants	103.1	97.3	111.3	104.9	100.3	102.8	103.2	83.5	85.6	86.7	92.9	91.3
Nonagricultural supplies and materials excluding fuels and building materials	99.8	100.8	100.2	98.8	98.5	96.1	93.8	92.3	92.6	95.7	96.4	96.4
Selected building materials	100.5	100.2	99.7	99.2	97.5	97.0	95.5	94.2	94.2	94.2	96.2	96.2
Capital Goods	99.9	99.9	100.0	100.2	100.6	100.3	100.0	99.4	99.4	98.7	98.4	98.1
Electrical generating equipment	99.6	100.0	100.7	100.5	100.9	101.7	101.6	101.5	102.1	102.0	102.0	101.9
Nonelectrical machinery	100.2	100.0	99.8	99.7	99.7	99.1	98.6	97.7	97.5	96.6	96.0	95.4
Transportation equipment excluding motor vehicles[1]	. . .	. . .	. . .	. . .	. . .	. . .	. . .	100.0	100.9	100.8	101.7	102.5
Automotive Vehicles, Parts, and Engines	99.9	99.9	100.3	100.1	100.3	100.4	100.4	100.5	100.9	100.9	101.1	101.3
Consumer Goods, Excluding Automotives	100.0	99.9	99.9	99.7	99.6	99.4	99.7	99.9	99.1	99.1	99.3	99.3
Nondurables, manufactured	100.1	99.8	99.8	99.6	99.0	99.0	99.1	99.1	98.1	98.5	98.7	98.7
Durables, manufactured	99.8	100.1	100.1	99.9	100.2	100.0	100.4	100.5	99.7	99.4	99.6	99.6
Agricultural Commodities	100.4	100.5	99.4	102.0	101.3	100.9	102.5	100.2	98.9	100.7	108.6	108.2
Nonagricultural Commodities	100.0	100.0	100.5	99.9	99.9	99.3	98.6	97.4	97.5	97.8	98.0	97.8

Commodity	2003				2004				2005			
	March	June	September	December	March	June	September	December	March	June	September	December
ALL COMMODITIES	99.7	99.5	99.8	100.8	103.0	103.4	103.8	104.8	106.4	106.7	107.5	107.7
Foods, Feeds, and Beverages	108.2	111.3	115.3	122.4	130.5	129.1	118.7	116.9	120.9	125.2	122.8	121.9
Agricultural foods, feeds, and beverages excluding distilled beverages	108.1	111.2	116.3	123.8	132.4	131.1	119.3	116.6	120.7	125.6	122.6	121.7
Nonagricultural foods (fish, distilled beverages)	110.0	113.1	106.5	108.5	112.1	110.7	113.0	118.4	121.8	120.1	123.6	123.6
Industrial Supplies and Materials	100.6	100.1	100.2	102.5	108.1	109.9	114.0	118.0	122.3	122.3	127.4	127.9
Industrial supplies and materials, durable	99.2	99.7	100.4	103.3	110.3	111.8	116.0	120.2	122.6	122.7	123.4	129.1
Industrial supplies and materials, nondurable	101.7	100.6	100.4	102.2	107.0	108.9	112.9	116.9	122.2	122.1	129.8	127.4
Agricultural industrial supplies and materials	104.8	104.4	107.3	117.5	117.2	110.7	109.4	109.5	115.6	115.8	116.4	117.4
Fuels and lubricants	108.0	97.0	97.6	99.0	108.9	114.9	121.5	125.4	143.8	148.8	184.8	163.4
Nonagricultural supplies and materials excluding fuels and building materials	99.9	100.7	100.5	102.5	108.1	110.0	114.4	118.9	121.4	120.6	122.2	125.7
Selected building materials	96.4	96.3	98.4	99.5	102.3	103.4	104.0	104.4	105.3	106.2	105.7	106.5
Capital Goods	98.3	97.6	97.5	97.5	98.0	97.8	97.8	98.2	98.4	98.4	97.6	97.7
Electrical generating equipment	101.6	101.6	101.7	101.7	102.0	102.0	102.4	103.6	103.9	103.4	102.6	103.6
Nonelectrical machinery	95.6	94.5	94.3	94.1	94.5	94.1	93.9	93.9	93.9	93.7	92.7	92.5
Transportation equipment excluding motor vehicles[1]	103.5	104.0	105.1	105.7	106.6	107.2	108.3	109.5	111.1	111.8	112.6	113.8
Automotive Vehicles, Parts, and Engines	101.5	101.6	101.8	101.8	101.9	102.3	102.5	102.9	103.3	103.4	103.7	103.9
Consumer Goods, Excluding Automotives	99.4	99.6	99.4	99.9	100.2	100.4	101.0	101.2	101.6	101.5	101.9	101.9
Nondurables, manufactured	98.7	98.8	98.5	99.2	99.9	100.0	101.0	101.0	101.5	101.2	101.5	101.6
Durables, manufactured	99.7	100.1	100.1	100.3	100.1	100.7	100.9	101.1	101.5	101.5	101.8	101.5
Agricultural Commodities	107.5	110.0	114.7	122.7	129.7	127.4	117.6	115.4	119.9	123.9	121.5	121.0
Nonagricultural Commodities	99.1	98.7	98.6	99.1	100.9	101.5	102.8	104.1	105.4	105.4	106.5	106.8

[1]December 2001 = 100.
. . . = Not available.

Table 9-11. U.S. Export Price Indexes for Selected Categories of Goods, by End Use, 2000–2011—*Continued*

(2000 = 100, unless otherwise indicated.)

Commodity	2006				2007				2008			
	March	June	September	December	March	June	September	December	March	June	September	December
ALL COMMODITIES	108.8	111.2	111.7	112.5	114.7	116.0	116.7	119.3	123.8	126.1	124.9	115.8
Foods, Feeds, and Beverages	121.7	125.6	128.8	138.7	146.9	148.6	157.8	171.1	196.9	198.0	190.4	155.1
Agricultural foods, feeds, and beverages excluding distilled beverages	121.5	125.7	129.1	140.5	149.2	151.0	160.8	175.2	202.6	204.0	195.6	156.6
Nonagricultural foods (fish, distilled beverages)	123.2	125.0	126.0	123.5	128.0	128.5	133.0	136.1	148.3	146.1	145.5	143.5
Industrial Supplies and Materials	131.3	138.8	139.5	139.4	145.5	149.0	148.8	154.1	165.5	173.2	169.4	139.6
Industrial supplies and materials, durable	135.7	146.2	146.9	150.1	160.2	160.9	155.5	159.2	172.7	172.9	167.1	141.5
Industrial supplies and materials, nondurable	129.0	134.9	135.7	133.9	137.6	142.8	145.5	151.9	162.0	174.2	171.6	139.1
Agricultural industrial supplies and materials	116.8	117.3	118.1	123.9	127.3	128.7	140.0	144.7	159.3	158.0	157.4	126.1
Fuels and lubricants	173.5	196.3	191.1	183.5	188.8	201.1	200.9	222.8	249.5	297.2	267.2	166.8
Nonagricultural supplies and materials excluding fuels and building materials	128.5	134.7	136.3	136.8	143.5	146.1	145.0	148.5	158.2	161.6	160.8	138.8
Selected building materials	108.5	109.8	110.0	111.5	112.7	113.9	114.4	113.7	114.2	113.8	115.4	115.1
Capital Goods	98.2	98.4	98.5	98.8	99.2	99.6	99.9	100.6	101.2	102.0	101.8	101.5
Electrical generating equipment	104.4	104.8	105.1	106.2	106.0	106.5	106.7	107.5	108.6	108.9	109.5	109.0
Nonelectrical machinery	92.7	92.7	92.6	92.6	92.8	92.9	93.1	93.6	93.7	94.2	93.9	93.3
Transportation equipment excluding motor vehicles[1]	116.0	117.1	117.7	119.1	121.1	122.3	123.4	125.0	128.1	130.3	130.7	131.5
Automotive Vehicles, Parts, and Engines	104.4	104.9	105.2	105.5	105.9	106.1	106.3	106.7	107.1	107.4	107.9	108.0
Consumer Goods, Excluding Automotives	102.3	103.5	104.0	104.0	104.8	105.8	106.2	107.3	108.0	108.2	109.3	109.0
Nondurables, manufactured	102.4	103.3	103.8	104.0	105.0	106.7	107.0	108.2	109.3	110.1	109.0	107.2
Durables, manufactured	101.3	102.4	103.1	102.8	103.4	103.7	104.2	105.2	105.4	105.2	108.7	109.7
Agricultural Commodities	120.7	124.1	127.1	137.3	145.0	146.7	156.8	169.3	194.3	195.2	188.3	150.8
Nonagricultural Commodities	108.0	110.3	110.6	110.7	112.6	113.8	113.8	115.7	118.8	121.2	120.4	113.2

Commodity	2009				2010				2011			
	March	June	September	December	March	June	September	December	March	June	September	December
ALL COMMODITIES	115.5	117.8	117.9	119.7	121.2	122.2	123.7	127.5	132.7	134.5	135.3	132.1
Foods, Feeds, and Beverages	156.7	174.8	158.2	165.1	163.4	164.5	174.6	191.1	206.9	210.6	213.8	199.0
Agricultural foods, feeds, and beverages excluding distilled beverages	158.3	178.6	160.7	167.9	165.7	166.7	177.6	194.6	212.1	214.6	217.3	201.2
Nonagricultural foods (fish, distilled beverages)	144.4	141.5	137.3	140.9	145.9	147.2	149.4	161.1	157.9	174.6	184.6	183.8
Industrial Supplies and Materials	136.5	140.4	143.9	150.1	155.1	159.8	162.6	172.6	188.3	191.8	192.8	184.6
Industrial supplies and materials, durable	143.4	144.0	150.7	157.7	160.4	165.5	167.0	174.8	186.1	190.3	196.6	188.2
Industrial supplies and materials, nondurable	133.1	139.0	140.5	146.2	152.6	157.2	160.8	172.2	190.4	193.6	191.7	183.4
Agricultural industrial supplies and materials	122.9	131.0	142.2	152.5	155.7	162.5	173.2	223.0	258.9	234.8	212.5	200.7
Fuels and lubricants	146.9	175.2	171.9	189.6	197.0	208.0	213.1	233.9	276.4	284.0	284.6	270.6
Nonagricultural supplies and materials excluding fuels and building materials	138.2	138.5	142.7	147.3	152.2	155.8	158.0	164.4	173.8	178.5	181.2	173.8
Selected building materials	114.0	113.0	114.0	113.5	116.0	118.7	117.1	116.2	116.3	116.2	115.8	115.6
Capital Goods	102.3	103.1	103.5	103.3	103.8	103.5	103.5	103.9	104.0	104.6	104.6	104.6
Electrical generating equipment	106.8	107.2	107.4	109.3	109.8	109.3	108.7	109.8	111.1	113.6	114.1	112.8
Nonelectrical machinery	93.8	94.4	94.9	94.5	94.7	94.3	94.3	94.4	93.9	94.2	94.2	94.3
Transportation equipment excluding motor vehicles[1]	135.1	137.3	137.2	136.5	139.1	139.5	140.1	141.6	144.5	145.3	144.9	145.6
Automotive Vehicles, Parts, and Engines	108.2	108.0	108.0	108.2	108.6	108.5	108.7	109.1	109.7	110.3	111.4	111.9
Consumer Goods, Excluding Automotives	108.5	108.4	109.2	109.4	110.2	110.4	111.8	112.7	113.9	116.3	117.4	116.6
Nondurables, manufactured	107.1	108.5	109.4	110.0	111.9	111.5	112.9	114.0	113.4	114.1	114.7	113.9
Durables, manufactured	109.9	108.1	109.5	109.2	107.7	108.2	109.9	110.9	112.9	112.7	113.6	113.3
Agricultural Commodities	151.6	169.7	156.9	164.7	163.3	165.3	176.1	198.5	218.8	217.2	216.0	200.5
Nonagricultural Commodities	112.9	114.1	115.1	116.5	118.1	119.1	120.0	122.4	126.5	128.6	129.5	127.3

[1]December 2001 = 100.

Table 9-12. U.S. Import Price Indexes for Selected Categories of Goods, by End Use, 2000–2011

(2000 = 100, unless otherwise indicated.)

Commodity	2000				2001				2002			
	March	June	September	December	March	June	September	December	March	June	September	December
ALL COMMODITIES	99.9	100.2	101.6	100.5	98.3	97.6	95.9	91.4	92.8	94.1	95.5	95.2
Foods, Feeds, and Beverages	101.0	99.4	98.9	99.3	98.9	95.4	95.0	94.6	95.0	96.2	99.7	100.2
Agricultural foods, feeds, and beverages, excluding distilled beverages	102.1	99.2	97.3	99.3	101.0	97.0	97.8	98.3	99.5	101.3	105.4	106.0
Nonagricultural foods (fish and distilled beverages)	98.5	99.7	102.3	99.2	94.5	92.2	89.2	86.8	85.5	85.1	87.3	87.5
Industrial Supplies and Materials	99.0	100.7	105.5	102.9	96.0	95.5	91.0	77.6	84.9	89.8	95.2	94.6
Fuels and lubricants	97.2	101.3	111.3	106.1	91.1	90.9	86.1	61.6	76.4	85.8	96.2	94.7
Paper and paper base stocks	95.5	100.0	103.2	104.5	104.4	100.0	93.9	90.7	88.0	87.1	90.5	89.1
Materials associated with nondurable supplies and materials	98.5	99.9	101.1	101.5	102.8	100.3	97.9	96.2	95.9	97.1	99.4	100.1
Selected building materials	107.1	100.3	94.3	94.7	91.9	111.1	103.7	92.9	100.7	99.1	97.6	95.0
Unfinished metals related to durable goods	102.7	100.7	101.5	99.5	99.5	93.6	87.1	82.1	83.8	88.5	89.7	91.5
Finished metals related to durable goods	100.6	100.5	100.3	99.4	98.3	99.4	98.2	97.9	97.1	96.5	97.1	96.8
Nonmetals related to durable goods	100.2	99.5	99.7	99.7	101.6	100.6	100.4	99.0	97.2	96.7	96.9	97.1
Industrial Supplies and Materials, Durable	102.9	100.4	99.6	98.5	98.1	99.1	94.1	89.1	91.1	92.3	92.7	92.7
Industrial Supplies and Materials, Excluding Fuels[1]	. . .	. . .	. . .	. . .	. . .	. . .	. . .	100.0	101.0	102.1	103.4	103.6
Industrial Supplies and Materials, Excluding Petroleum	98.9	99.9	101.0	105.4	102.1	99.8	94.2	90.0	90.3	92.9	93.9	95.2
Industrial Supplies and Materials, Nondurable, Excluding Petroleum	94.6	99.3	102.6	112.9	106.4	100.7	94.2	90.9	89.3	93.4	95.2	98.1
Capital Goods	100.5	100.0	99.7	98.9	98.7	97.7	96.8	96.2	95.2	95.1	94.7	93.9
Electric generating equipment	98.7	101.1	100.3	99.8	102.1	101.8	101.4	100.6	95.5	95.1	95.7	94.9
Nonelectrical machinery	100.9	99.9	99.5	98.6	98.0	96.7	95.6	94.9	94.4	94.4	93.7	92.8
Transportation equipment, excluding motor vehicles[1]	. . .	. . .	. . .	. . .	. . .	. . .	. . .	100.0	100.5	100.4	101.0	101.0
Automotive Parts and Accessories	99.4	100.9	100.3	100.0	99.3	98.7	98.0	97.4	97.1	98.0	98.3	98.0
Consumer Goods, Excluding Automotive	100.3	99.6	99.8	99.5	99.8	99.3	99.1	98.7	98.2	98.1	98.1	98.0
Nondurables, manufactured	100.3	99.6	99.8	99.6	100.2	99.8	99.6	99.7	99.2	99.1	99.5	99.7
Nonmanufactured consumer goods	100.3	98.2	99.8	99.0	99.3	99.2	97.9	96.4	96.1	95.6	95.4	95.4
All Imports, Excluding Fuels	. . .	. . .	. . .	. . .	. . .	. . .	. . .	100.0	99.7	99.9	100.1	100.0
All Imports, Excluding Petroleum	100.0	99.9	100.0	100.7	100.0	98.9	97.3	96.2	95.8	96.2	96.4	96.5

Commodity	2003				2004				2005			
	March	June	September	December	March	June	September	December	March	June	September	December
ALL COMMODITIES	99.1	96.2	96.2	97.5	100.2	101.7	104.1	104.0	107.8	109.2	114.4	112.3
Foods, Feeds, and Beverages	102.6	100.7	101.8	103.2	105.9	106.9	108.7	111.5	115.9	114.1	114.2	117.5
Agricultural foods, feeds, and beverages, excluding distilled beverages	109.6	107.1	108.3	110.9	113.0	114.3	116.4	120.7	125.7	123.5	122.6	127.2
Nonagricultural foods (fish and distilled beverages)	86.9	86.6	87.6	86.0	90.1	90.3	91.4	91.0	94.0	93.1	95.6	95.9
Industrial Supplies and Materials	109.7	98.2	98.9	103.6	112.7	119.3	128.5	126.4	139.8	145.5	167.2	158.6
Fuels and lubricants	125.2	100.3	99.4	107.2	120.2	130.9	146.2	141.0	165.6	178.0	222.1	202.4
Paper and paper base stocks	91.0	94.1	94.0	93.9	95.6	99.0	101.1	101.3	103.8	103.8	104.3	106.1
Materials associated with nondurable supplies and materials	104.2	103.0	102.5	104.4	105.4	106.0	108.0	109.8	113.0	113.5	117.3	117.8
Selected building materials	96.3	96.7	110.3	108.0	118.4	120.5	125.6	115.6	122.7	118.1	117.6	116.9
Unfinished metals related to durable goods	92.8	92.2	93.4	99.2	114.9	124.4	133.1	138.5	140.4	139.9	138.2	145.8
Finished metals related to durable goods	96.1	97.4	99.0	101.0	104.8	108.1	112.4	114.7	115.9	116.6	117.3	117.6
Nonmetals related to durable goods	97.9	98.2	97.5	98.2	99.3	98.7	98.8	99.7	100.8	100.9	100.7	100.5
Industrial Supplies and Materials, Durable	93.6	93.7	97.3	99.5	108.5	112.8	117.8	118.0	120.8	119.7	119.1	121.4
Industrial Supplies and Materials, Excluding Fuels[1]	105.8	105.7	107.9	110.1	116.5	119.8	124.1	124.8	128.0	127.5	128.5	130.3
Industrial Supplies and Materials, Excluding Petroleum	104.3	99.9	100.3	102.1	107.9	112.5	114.4	118.8	119.9	120.2	126.8	132.2
Industrial Supplies and Materials, Nondurable, Excluding Petroleum	117.1	107.2	103.8	105.0	107.1	112.0	110.2	119.7	118.7	120.7	135.4	144.3
Capital Goods	93.7	93.8	93.5	92.9	93.1	92.2	92.0	92.2	92.3	92.3	91.5	91.0
Electric generating equipment	95.5	96.6	95.8	96.8	97.8	97.0	97.4	98.0	98.8	98.8	99.0	99.3
Nonelectrical machinery	92.5	92.3	92.1	91.1	91.2	90.1	89.8	89.9	89.8	89.8	88.7	88.1
Transportation equipment, excluding motor vehicles[1]	101.6	102.0	102.2	102.8	103.5	104.0	103.9	104.5	105.6	106.0	106.4	106.1
Automotive Parts and Accessories	98.0	98.3	97.8	98.8	99.6	100.1	100.2	101.5	101.8	102.0	102.1	101.8
Consumer Goods, Excluding Automotive	97.9	98.1	97.9	98.1	98.7	98.5	98.4	99.0	99.9	99.9	99.7	99.6
Nondurables, manufactured	99.7	99.8	99.7	100.1	101.3	100.9	100.8	101.4	102.8	102.8	103.1	102.7
Nonmanufactured consumer goods	95.7	96.2	95.7	96.2	96.4	96.8	97.9	98.2	100.3	101.8	100.6	101.2
All Imports, Excluding Fuels	100.3	100.3	100.6	101.0	102.4	102.7	103.4	104.0	105.0	104.9	104.8	105.1
All Imports, Excluding Petroleum	98.1	97.3	97.3	97.7	99.1	99.7	100.1	101.3	102.0	102.0	102.8	103.7

[1]December 2001 = 100.
. . . = Not available.

Table 9-12. U.S. Import Price Indexes for Selected Categories of Goods, by End Use, 2000–2011—*Continued*

(2000 = 100, unless otherwise indicated.)

Commodity	2006				2007				2008			
	March	June	September	December	March	June	September	December	March	June	September	December
ALL COMMODITIES	112.7	117.3	116.2	115.1	115.9	120.0	121.8	127.3	133.5	145.5	137.8	114.5
Foods, Feeds, and Beverages	117.0	118.0	120.9	122.6	124.6	127.8	131.8	134.4	141.8	147.7	147.9	142.3
Agricultural foods, feeds, and beverages, excluding distilled beverages	125.4	126.8	130.4	133.7	135.1	139.5	144.4	148.3	157.3	165.1	165.1	159.4
Nonagricultural foods (fish and distilled beverages)	98.3	98.5	99.8	97.9	101.3	101.5	103.5	103.0	106.8	108.4	109.1	103.8
Industrial Supplies and Materials	160.4	178.1	172.2	166.6	169.8	185.6	190.7	211.3	234.5	283.0	248.9	150.4
Fuels and lubricants	201.5	230.2	216.3	204.3	209.6	238.2	250.0	290.3	329.0	423.7	346.3	153.9
Paper and paper base stocks	107.7	111.3	113.1	112.8	111.5	110.8	111.2	109.2	114.1	117.3	119.9	113.2
Materials associated with nondurable supplies and materials	119.3	120.6	121.8	123.0	124.0	125.4	128.2	135.3	147.8	152.9	162.4	148.5
Selected building materials	118.0	117.2	115.8	110.6	111.4	113.1	116.9	116.0	114.1	119.2	122.7	118.1
Unfinished metals related to durable goods	161.1	193.2	194.4	195.9	202.9	219.7	209.1	217.2	241.5	273.2	255.4	185.7
Finished metals related to durable goods	119.2	125.3	128.4	128.9	125.4	133.7	134.8	135.0	145.8	158.7	159.9	140.8
Nonmetals related to durable goods	100.8	101.1	101.3	101.7	101.8	101.6	102.5	103.8	105.2	107.6	111.4	109.0
Industrial Supplies and Materials, Durable	127.2	139.1	139.8	139.2	141.0	148.4	146.3	149.1	158.9	173.5	169.7	141.8
Industrial Supplies and Materials, Excluding Fuels[1]	134.9	143.7	144.7	144.7	146.2	151.6	151.2	155.4	166.8	178.8	179.5	155.1
Industrial Supplies and Materials, Excluding Petroleum	128.1	133.9	135.1	138.3	139.3	144.6	141.0	147.5	159.4	173.7	167.4	146.0
Industrial Supplies and Materials, Nondurable, Excluding Petroleum	128.3	126.7	128.5	136.3	136.3	139.1	133.6	144.5	159.3	173.0	163.5	150.8
Capital Goods	91.1	91.2	91.3	91.5	91.1	91.3	91.9	92.2	92.2	93.2	93.3	92.7
Electric generating equipment	100.1	102.1	102.7	103.0	104.3	105.7	106.5	107.9	109.3	112.0	112.9	111.4
Nonelectrical machinery	88.0	87.8	87.8	87.9	87.2	87.2	87.7	87.7	87.5	88.2	88.2	87.5
Transportation equipment, excluding motor vehicles[1]	107.0	107.9	108.3	109.1	110.1	111.0	113.4	114.7	115.3	117.7	118.2	120.2
Automotive Parts and Accessories	101.6	102.7	103.2	103.0	103.5	103.3	103.6	104.8	106.2	106.7	107.4	108.8
Consumer Goods, Excluding Automotive	99.6	99.8	100.5	101.0	101.3	101.4	102.1	102.6	104.0	104.9	105.1	104.4
Nondurables, manufactured	102.8	102.6	103.0	103.4	104.1	104.3	105.0	105.5	107.5	107.9	108.2	108.2
Nonmanufactured consumer goods	98.2	98.6	100.5	101.8	102.2	102.6	103.4	103.8	104.3	106.6	106.6	103.6
All Imports, Excluding Fuels	105.7	107.2	107.8	108.1	108.4	109.5	110.1	111.4	113.9	116.5	116.8	112.7
All Imports, Excluding Petroleum	103.0	104.2	104.8	105.7	105.9	107.1	107.1	108.9	111.6	114.9	114.0	109.9

Commodity	2009				2010				2011			
	March	June	September	December	March	June	September	December	March	June	September	December
ALL COMMODITIES	113.6	120.0	121.3	124.4	126.3	125.2	125.7	131.0	139.3	142.2	141.7	142.2
Foods, Feeds, and Beverages	137.0	139.8	140.6	143.7	147.4	148.7	153.3	162.7	174.9	174.8	174.7	172.4
Agricultural foods, feeds, and beverages, excluding distilled beverages	151.3	155.5	156.8	160.8	165.8	166.1	171.1	182.6	198.9	197.0	196.5	194.0
Nonagricultural foods (fish and distilled beverages)	104.8	104.4	104.1	104.9	105.6	109.2	113.0	117.4	120.7	124.5	125.3	123.7
Industrial Supplies and Materials	149.3	177.3	183.0	196.2	205.0	199.5	200.1	222.6	256.3	266.1	262.5	263.6
Fuels and lubricants	162.3	222.1	228.5	249.7	262.4	245.8	247.1	285.2	343.7	359.0	348.2	356.3
Paper and paper base stocks	106.6	101.8	99.1	103.1	107.6	115.5	117.5	117.5	116.3	119.4	117.1	114.8
Materials associated with nondurable supplies and materials	136.7	137.5	134.8	140.6	144.6	146.2	147.7	157.0	165.8	173.0	175.9	175.1
Selected building materials	116.2	116.0	118.9	120.9	127.6	131.9	124.6	127.0	131.5	129.3	131.2	130.7
Unfinished metals related to durable goods	171.6	178.3	204.0	221.5	233.4	244.6	244.2	266.0	290.2	297.0	304.9	277.8
Finished metals related to durable goods	132.7	133.2	137.1	140.4	142.4	146.5	147.7	152.7	157.4	161.1	165.6	162.1
Nonmetals related to durable goods	105.2	103.0	104.3	105.4	107.1	107.2	107.7	108.7	112.1	114.3	116.3	115.2
Industrial Supplies and Materials, Durable	134.7	136.0	145.7	152.5	158.4	163.7	162.5	171.2	181.4	184.7	189.3	179.9
Industrial Supplies and Materials, Excluding Fuels[1]	145.5	146.5	151.7	158.6	164.3	168.9	168.9	178.0	187.8	192.8	196.6	190.0
Industrial Supplies and Materials, Excluding Petroleum	133.1	132.1	134.4	145.2	149.7	151.6	151.0	159.4	168.4	172.5	174.5	167.8
Industrial Supplies and Materials, Nondurable, Excluding Petroleum	131.0	127.4	121.0	136.3	139.4	137.5	137.5	145.5	153.1	158.2	157.4	153.5
Capital Goods	91.8	91.9	91.9	91.9	91.4	91.5	91.8	92.0	92.6	92.7	92.9	93.1
Electric generating equipment	109.4	110.0	110.3	111.3	111.0	111.4	112.7	113.7	115.6	117.1	118.4	118.4
Nonelectrical machinery	86.6	86.5	86.5	86.4	85.9	86.0	86.1	86.2	86.5	86.4	86.4	86.4
Transportation equipment, excluding motor vehicles[1]	120.6	122.4	123.2	122.6	121.5	121.3	121.6	121.9	124.8	126.1	126.4	130.0
Automotive Parts and Accessories	108.9	108.5	109.2	110.0	109.9	110.2	111.5	112.0	113.7	115.7	116.6	117.0
Consumer Goods, Excluding Automotive	103.9	104.3	104.1	104.3	104.5	104.4	104.2	104.2	104.7	105.8	106.6	107.7
Nondurables, manufactured	108.4	108.1	107.8	107.9	109.0	109.3	110.0	110.4	110.3	111.6	112.8	114.4
Nonmanufactured consumer goods	101.2	101.4	101.2	102.1	102.5	102.4	103.0	103.7	107.8	111.8	114.9	119.3
All Imports, Excluding Fuels	110.7	111.2	111.9	113.0	113.7	114.4	114.7	116.4	118.7	120.1	120.9	120.4
All Imports, Excluding Petroleum	107.3	107.4	107.9	109.7	110.3	110.7	111.0	112.6	115.0	116.4	117.0	116.4

[1] December 2001 = 100.

Table 9-13. U.S. Import Price Indexes for Selected Categories of Goods, by Locality of Origin, 1990–2011

(2000 = 100, unless otherwise indicated.)

Category and year	Relative importance[1]	Month			
		March	June	September	December
INDUSTRIALIZED COUNTRIES[2]					
Total Goods	100.0				
1990					89.8
1991		89.6	87.9	87.9	88.9
1992		89.2	89.6	90.9	90.1
1993		90.5	91.4	91.5	91.7
1994		92.3	93.4	94.8	96.1
1995		97.4	99.8	100.0	100.0
1996		99.7	98.8	99.3	99.4
1997		97.4	96.5	96.4	96.1
1998		94.6	94.0	93.3	93.8
1999		94.1	94.8	96.4	97.5
2000		99.5	100.1	100.9	101.4
2001		100.2	99.0	96.5	93.7
2002		94.3	95.7	96.9	96.7
2003		100.0	98.4	98.6	100.0
2004		103.4	104.7	106.3	107.5
2005		109.7	110.0	113.5	114.1
2006		113.5	117.4	117.0	116.4
2007		117.9	119.7	120.4	124.2
2008		130.9	139.6	135.1	119.1
2009		117.5	119.3	120.4	123.9
2010		125.7	124.0	124.5	128.1
2011		130.7	133.8	133.0	133.2
Nonmanufactured Articles	12.6				
1990					68.6
1991		64.2	62.2	62.3	62.7
1992		62.0	63.8	64.6	63.7
1993		64.5	63.8	61.8	58.7
1994		58.2	64.3	64.3	64.1
1995		66.3	67.6	65.2	66.0
1996		71.6	72.3	76.0	84.3
1997		73.3	68.9	69.4	68.5
1998		59.3	56.8	57.2	55.7
1999		56.9	65.1	78.7	83.2
2000		92.7	102.2	107.5	118.2
2001		103.9	97.2	85.2	69.9
2002		82.9	93.8	102.4	102.7
2003		134.3	113.7	108.9	112.4
2004		122.9	133.1	138.7	147.1
2005		156.7	158.0	203.0	199.2
2006		170.9	190.0	183.7	184.9
2007		185.6	197.9	195.4	228.2
2008		275.6	346.8	279.0	154.5
2009		143.9	170.6	169.1	198.8
2010		209.7	188.0	188.2	218.3
2011		236.7	251.9	233.1	246.4
Manufactured Articles	86.8				
1990					90.2
1991		91.6	90.1	90.1	91.3
1992		91.8	91.7	93.0	92.4
1993		92.8	93.8	94.1	94.6
1994		95.1	95.9	97.4	98.8
1995		100.0	102.6	102.9	102.9
1996		102.1	101.1	101.4	100.7
1997		99.5	98.9	98.8	98.6
1998		97.8	97.5	96.7	97.3
1999		97.6	97.7	98.1	98.9
2000		100.2	99.9	100.2	99.8
2001		99.9	99.2	97.6	96.0
2002		95.6	96.3	96.9	96.7
2003		97.8	97.7	98.2	99.4
2004		102.1	102.8	104.0	104.6
2005		106.3	106.6	106.7	107.7
2006		109.0	111.8	111.8	111.1
2007		112.5	113.5	114.5	116.3
2008		120.1	124.3	124.2	115.7
2009		114.9	114.9	116.1	117.9
2010		118.9	118.8	119.2	120.8
2011		122.0	124.1	124.9	123.9

[1]Based on 2010 trade values.
[2]Includes Western Europe, Canada, Japan, Australia, New Zealand and South Africa.

Table 9-13. U.S. Import Price Indexes for Selected Categories of Goods, by Locality of Origin, 1990–2011
—Continued

(2000 = 100, unless otherwise indicated.)

Category and year	Relative importance[1]	Month			
		March	June	September	December
OTHER COUNTRIES					
Total Goods	100.0				
1990					107.2
1991		94.1	93.5	93.8	93.6
1992		92.2	94.7	95.0	94.4
1993		94.2	93.5	92.3	89.6
1994		90.1	94.2	95.0	95.7
1995		97.5	98.7	97.4	97.6
1996		99.8	99.0	101.3	102.7
1997		100.6	99.4	98.7	96.6
1998		92.4	90.7	89.5	86.8
1999		87.7	90.3	94.5	96.9
2000		99.8	100.4	102.5	99.5
2001		97.0	96.6	95.0	88.6
2002		90.9	92.2	94.3	93.4
2003		96.7	93.1	93.3	94.1
2004		96.3	97.9	101.5	99.7
2005		105.0	107.0	112.1	109.5
2006		110.8	115.5	114.0	111.8
2007		113.1	118.0	121.1	127.5
2008		133.3	147.3	139.0	111.2
2009		110.3	118.7	120.0	122.1
2010		124.2	123.1	123.7	129.0
2011		138.9	141.2	141.1	142.0
Nonmanufactured Articles	25.3				
1990					88.2
1991		64.8	63.8	64.6	63.8
1992		61.0	65.5	66.0	63.7
1993		64.9	62.8	59.1	51.9
1994		52.0	63.8	64.8	65.5
1995		69.5	70.3	66.1	67.3
1996		73.7	72.1	80.9	84.5
1997		75.8	72.6	72.2	68.8
1998		57.1	54.9	54.5	46.8
1999		53.0	63.6	80.3	89.2
2000		99.9	102.4	109.2	97.4
2001		88.9	89.7	86.1	65.3
2002		81.3	88.2	99.6	96.4
2003		113.3	98.0	98.8	106.5
2004		118.1	123.2	141.5	130.3
2005		158.0	169.5	199.8	181.3
2006		191.7	215.4	204.6	191.1
2007		192.4	220.6	241.6	279.0
2008		314.6	402.3	336.0	160.2
2009		166.8	225.6	231.3	247.8
2010		260.8	248.9	254.0	288.8
2011		351.8	367.1	356.0	363.9
Manufactured Articles	74.3				
1990					105.3
1991		105.2	105.1	104.9	105.2
1992		105.5	105.7	105.7	105.4
1993		104.6	104.5	104.2	103.7
1994		104.2	105.1	105.8	106.5
1995		107.3	108.8	108.6	108.4
1996		108.9	108.4	107.9	108.6
1997		108.4	107.8	107.0	105.3
1998		103.5	102.2	100.6	99.6
1999		98.8	98.9	99.0	99.3
2000		99.8	99.7	100.3	100.2
2001		99.6	98.8	97.9	96.0
2002		95.6	95.9	96.2	95.8
2003		96.5	95.1	95.1	94.5
2004		95.2	96.2	97.2	97.1
2005		98.4	98.7	99.3	99.6
2006		99.4	101.2	101.2	100.7
2007		102.0	103.6	104.1	106.0
2008		107.8	111.8	111.3	103.4
2009		101.7	103.5	104.3	104.5
2010		105.0	105.3	105.3	106.8
2011		110.0	110.6	111.8	111.8

[1]Based on 2010 trade values.

Table 9-13. U.S. Import Price Indexes for Selected Categories of Goods, by Locality of Origin, 1990–2011
—Continued

(2000 = 100, unless otherwise indicated.)

Category and year	Relative importance[1]	Month			
		March	June	September	December
CANADA					
Total Goods	100.0				
1990					90.2
1991		87.2	87.3	86.9	87.2
1992		86.5	87.4	87.5	86.3
1993		86.5	85.9	85.2	85.1
1994		85.5	87.2	88.1	90.2
1995		92.1	93.8	94.8	94.7
1996		94.3	93.5	93.8	95.1
1997		93.2	92.6	93.2	92.0
1998		90.1	89.7	89.3	88.7
1999		88.8	90.6	93.5	94.7
2000		97.2	99.8	102.4	105.6
2001		102.6	101.8	97.0	93.2
2002		96.1	97.8	99.6	99.2
2003		106.6	103.1	103.9	104.4
2004		110.0	112.3	114.4	116.6
2005		120.1	119.6	128.2	129.6
2006		125.4	130.6	129.7	129.2
2007		130.2	135.0	135.0	142.3
2008		152.0	171.2	160.1	129.8
2009		124.4	129.0	131.1	137.7
2010		143.7	139.3	139.9	148.1
2011		155.7	159.7	155.0	155.4
Nonmanufactured Articles	29.1				
1990					66.8
1991		59.2	59.5	58.9	58.6
1992		58.1	60.7	61.2	60.0
1993		60.6	60.3	58.1	55.3
1994		54.7	61.1	60.1	60.3
1995		61.7	64.4	63.9	64.8
1996		70.3	70.7	74.4	84.3
1997		69.9	66.6	68.1	66.4
1998		58.4	56.6	56.5	56.3
1999		56.5	64.2	76.8	79.9
2000		89.3	103.6	107.6	124.4
2001		108.1	97.9	83.1	69.8
2002		83.8	96.8	104.1	104.9
2003		143.1	119.0	111.5	114.0
2004		126.1	138.0	138.9	150.5
2005		157.9	159.8	210.8	207.4
2006		171.3	189.2	183.1	187.1
2007		187.8	195.9	187.7	222.3
2008		273.7	345.1	273.0	150.8
2009		139.7	163.4	161.6	192.5
2010		204.6	181.3	182.0	211.4
2011		228.2	241.7	223.1	236.2
Manufactured Articles	69.9				
1990					92.8
1991		93.2	93.1	93.0	93.6
1992		92.9	92.5	92.4	91.4
1993		91.6	90.8	90.4	90.9
1994		91.4	92.3	93.6	95.9
1995		98.0	99.4	100.7	100.5
1996		99.0	98.0	97.7	97.4
1997		98.0	98.0	98.3	97.3
1998		96.7	96.6	96.3	95.5
1999		95.5	96.1	96.9	97.7
2000		98.8	98.9	101.3	101.8
2001		101.6	102.8	99.9	98.1
2002		99.1	98.7	99.5	98.9
2003		100.9	101.1	103.2	103.3
2004		107.4	108.2	110.3	110.7
2005		113.7	112.9	113.1	115.6
2006		117.2	120.0	119.9	118.7
2007		119.5	123.7	125.3	127.6
2008		128.8	137.5	138.7	126.8
2009		122.7	123.0	125.8	127.3
2010		131.7	132.0	132.5	135.5
2011		140.5	141.9	141.1	137.8

[1]Based on 2010 trade values.

Table 9-13. U.S. Import Price Indexes for Selected Categories of Goods, by Locality of Origin, 1990–2011
—Continued

(2000 = 100, unless otherwise indicated.)

Category and year	Relative importance[1]	Month			
		March	June	September	December
EUROPEAN UNION					
Total Goods	100.0				
1990					93.8
1991		95.2	91.6	91.7	94.0
1992		94.2	94.9	97.7	93.1
1993		92.2	92.9	92.0	91.8
1994		91.9	93.1	94.9	96.2
1995		97.7	99.5	99.7	100.4
1996		101.3	101.0	101.7	101.9
1997		100.5	100.0	99.1	100.1
1998		98.9	98.8	98.7	99.4
1999		98.8	99.1	99.9	100.3
2000		100.8	100.1	100.0	98.9
2001		99.0	98.8	98.2	97.4
2002		97.4	99.2	101.0	100.9
2003		103.2	102.8	102.8	104.3
2004		107.4	108.5	110.0	111.6
2005		113.8	114.1	115.7	114.5
2006		117.7	120.4	120.5	119.6
2007		121.3	121.6	122.3	124.1
2008		129.7	133.9	131.5	124.3
2009		123.6	124.4	125.4	127.4
2010		128.3	127.7	128.4	129.1
2011		132.8	135.9	136.5	136.3
Nonmanufactured Articles	2.4				
1990					74.8
1991		76.8	71.8	72.4	73.8
1992		73.0	73.9	74.9	74.1
1993		74.8	72.7	70.3	67.6
1994		67.6	73.5	71.9	72.0
1995		72.8	74.5	71.2	73.0
1996		78.8	80.6	85.7	91.7
1997		89.3	82.2	76.5	78.4
1998		65.6	58.7	58.8	53.4
1999		53.6	66.6	81.3	88.7
2000		100.4	102.9	107.9	106.2
2001		96.0	99.5	89.1	75.7
2002		86.6	88.7	99.6	104.1
2003		118.8	106.7	111.5	118.8
2004		128.4	135.1	157.9	163.1
2005		177.1	177.5	209.7	191.1
2006		211.4	231.9	219.9	198.7
2007		205.2	234.6	274.9	304.8
2008		323.4	400.2	332.3	230.8
2009		188.3	230.0	235.3	250.2
2010		252.4	250.4	251.9	274.1
2011		322.2	367.3	350.5	364.0
Manufactured Articles	97.4				
1990					93.8
1991		94.8	92.1	92.0	94.4
1992		95.1	95.7	98.9	93.9
1993		93.0	93.8	93.0	92.8
1994		92.9	93.9	95.8	97.1
1995		98.6	100.4	100.9	101.5
1996		102.3	101.8	102.4	102.3
1997		101.0	100.8	100.1	101.0
1998		100.4	100.6	100.5	101.5
1999		100.9	100.6	100.8	100.8
2000		100.8	99.9	99.6	98.6
2001		99.2	98.8	98.7	98.4
2002		98.1	99.9	101.5	101.4
2003		103.3	103.2	103.2	104.5
2004		107.4	108.4	109.3	110.9
2005		112.8	113.0	113.8	112.9
2006		116.0	118.0	118.4	118.0
2007		119.5	119.2	119.7	121.1
2008		126.5	130.1	128.2	121.8
2009		121.5	122.1	123.0	124.9
2010		125.8	125.2	125.9	126.4
2011		129.6	132.3	133.0	132.7

[1] Based on 2010 trade values.

Table 9-13. U.S. Import Price Indexes for Selected Categories of Goods, by Locality of Origin, 1990–2011
  —Continued

(2000 = 100, unless otherwise indicated.)

Category and year	Relative importance[1]	Month			
		March	June	September	December
LATIN AMERICA					
Total Goods	100.0				
1998		84.3	83.9	83.0	80.4
1999		81.7	85.3	90.7	94.2
2000		98.9	100.9	103.5	99.5
2001		99.5	98.9	97.2	90.6
2002		94.0	96.2	100.0	98.9
2003		104.8	99.6	99.8	102.6
2004		106.3	108.6	114.7	113.1
2005		122.1	126.3	133.8	131.0
2006		134.0	142.8	140.2	136.4
2007		138.1	146.3	152.3	161.5
2008		171.6	193.9	181.7	135.4
2009		132.1	146.7	148.5	154.0
2010		157.4	154.5	155.5	163.9
2011		179.7	181.4	179.8	181.5
Nonmanufactured Articles	35.7				
1998		60.8	59.7	59.4	51.9
1999		59.3	67.2	82.1	90.2
2000		100.2	103.5	107.8	93.6
2001		89.3	89.0	86.0	67.3
2002		83.5	90.7	103.0	99.3
2003		111.7	103.5	100.9	109.8
2004		121.1	125.9	144.6	130.1
2005		161.0	175.1	205.1	184.6
2006		195.5	217.2	205.7	197.1
2007		199.3	225.0	250.7	289.5
2008		320.9	409.2	348.3	181.5
2009		188.9	254.3	257.1	273.9
2010		286.4	269.3	278.8	314.4
2011		382.1	391.4	378.8	399.4
Manufactured Articles	63.8				
1998		94.8	95.0	93.8	93.5
1999		92.0	93.6	94.6	96.0
2000		98.3	99.6	101.6	102.3
2001		104.2	103.5	102.5	101.4
2002		101.5	102.4	104.2	103.8
2003		108.2	103.6	104.4	105.8
2004		107.5	109.1	112.0	113.9
2005		117.1	118.6	120.1	122.2
2006		123.2	128.9	128.4	125.8
2007		127.4	131.4	132.5	134.3
2008		139.3	146.0	145.4	127.7
2009		121.7	125.0	126.5	129.3
2010		130.3	130.5	129.5	131.9
2011		136.1	136.0	136.8	134.3
CHINA					
Total Goods	100.0				
2004		99.5	99.7	99.6	99.0
2005		98.8	98.8	98.4	98.5
2006		97.9	97.4	97.4	97.3
2007		97.4	98.1	99.1	99.6
2008		101.1	102.8	103.7	102.4
2009		100.9	100.4	100.5	100.6
2010		100.1	100.4	100.5	101.4
2011		102.7	103.7	104.4	105.1

[1]Based on 2010 trade values.

Table 9-13. U.S. Import Price Indexes for Selected Categories of Goods, by Locality of Origin, 1990–2011
—Continued

(2000 = 100, unless otherwise indicated.)

Category and year	Relative importance[1]	Month			
		March	June	September	December
JAPAN					
Total Goods	100.0				
1990					93.7
1991		94.5	93.4	93.9	95.2
1992		95.8	95.5	96.4	97.7
1993		98.5	100.9	103.5	104.4
1994		105.2	105.8	107.0	108.0
1995		108.6	112.5	112.0	111.0
1996		110.1	108.4	107.8	106.5
1997		104.6	103.2	102.7	101.0
1998		99.8	98.2	96.8	98.0
1999		98.2	98.2	98.6	99.6
2000		99.6	100.0	99.9	99.9
2001		99.4	98.6	97.8	97.0
2002		95.6	95.4	95.0	94.6
2003		94.4	94.2	93.8	94.7
2004		95.2	95.1	95.3	95.9
2005		95.9	95.8	95.8	95.2
2006		94.6	94.7	94.4	94.1
2007		93.9	94.0	93.9	94.2
2008		94.6	95.1	94.9	96.0
2009		96.3	96.9	97.2	97.8
2010		98.1	98.6	99.0	99.8
2011		101.1	101.5	101.7	102.1
ASIAN NEWLY INDUSTRIALIZED COUNTRIES[2]					
Total Goods	100.0				
1990					121.4
1991		120.4	120.3	120.4	121.0
1992		121.5	121.8	121.9	121.8
1993		121.5	121.2	121.2	120.8
1994		120.7	120.4	120.2	120.2
1995		120.9	121.3	121.5	120.8
1996		120.6	119.6	118.1	117.3
1997		116.6	115.3	113.8	111.3
1998		108.7	105.2	103.0	102.0
1999		101.3	100.8	100.7	100.8
2000		100.6	99.9	100.0	99.3
2001		97.3	96.4	95.2	93.8
2002		93.3	92.6	92.5	91.3
2003		91.2	91.5	91.7	90.9
2004		90.3	90.6	91.0	90.6
2005		90.9	90.0	89.7	88.5
2006		88.8	89.2	89.3	89.1
2007		88.7	88.5	88.8	88.9
2008		89.2	91.1	93.2	89.2
2009		85.4	85.7	86.1	86.5
2010		87.0	88.1	88.6	88.5
2011		91.0	92.4	91.8	90.6

[1]Based on 2010 trade values.
[2]Includes Western Europe, Canada, Japan, Australia, New Zealand and South Africa.

Table 9-14. U.S. International Price Indexes for Selected Transportation Services, 1990–2011

(2000 = 100.)

Category and year	March	June	September	December
AIR FREIGHT				
Import Air Freight				
1990	. . .	. . .	96.4	105.6
1991	104.5	100.4	99.8	101.8
1992	102.8	98.5	101.6	99.5
1993	97.5	104.2	104.5	103.8
1994	103.5	105.7	108.9	110.9
1995	115.8	118.7	112.9	115.1
1996	113.7	112.2	112.0	110.6
1997	104.1	104.5	102.5	100.1
1998	93.0	94.2	92.8	100.2
1999	101.5	98.7	100.6	102.8
2000	100.7	100.1	100.2	99.0
2001	98.9	96.0	95.9	95.6
2002	96.7	99.7	101.2	106.9
2003	110.2	111.5	116.8	114.9
2004	117.1	117.5	120.0	126.8
2005	128.6	128.4	129.7	128.9
2006	129.7	135.2	133.1	131.2
2007	130.7	132.3	134.2	141.8
2008	144.4	158.7	157.1	138.5
2009	132.9	132.8	134.8	163.9
2010	158.3	162.5	163.2	170.1
2011	172.8	184.3	185.5	177.1
Export Air Freight				
1996	. . .	. . .	. . .	112.9
1997	111.1	110.4	109.0	105.4
1998	107.1	106.6	108.0	109.2
1999	102.1	102.5	100.8	99.1
2000	99.1	100.8	100.8	99.4
2001	99.7	98.4	98.6	97.9
2002	95.5	97.9	98.3	95.2
2003	96.3	95.2	95.1	95.4
2004	97.1	99.1	100.3	106.1
2005	106.4	110.1	110.9	112.0
2006	113.6	115.9	117.9	116.7
2007	117.0	117.0	119.8	127.1
2008	132.0	140.8	144.3	135.0
2009	124.1	117.4	121.6	122.9
2010	124.0	126.3	125.7	128.1
2011	139.2	147.4	146.4	144.2
Inbound Air Freight				
1990	. . .	. . .	98.6	107.1
1991	105.3	103.4	103.3	105.8
1992	106.5	103.2	105.8	100.7
1993	98.7	104.9	105.1	104.6
1994	104.4	106.6	107.1	108.9
1995	113.6	116.5	111.0	111.7
1996	108.6	107.7	108.2	107.6
1997	101.3	101.8	100.3	97.9
1998	93.9	94.4	92.7	99.0
1999	99.6	97.6	99.5	102.8
2000	100.7	100.1	100.2	99.0
2001	97.9	95.1	94.9	95.1
2002	93.9	98.3	100.3	105.9
2003	108.8	109.4	112.5	112.9
2004	116.2	116.6	118.7	125.1
2005	126.3	125.6	127.5	124.6
2006	124.6	129.2	128.9	127.1
2007	126.6	127.3	129.6	138.1
2008	140.7	152.1	151.6	136.8
2009	127.5	125.1	127.4	147.3
2010	144.3	147.1	147.2	153.4
2011	157.0	164.4	164.2	160.7

. . . = Not available.

Table 9-14. U.S. International Price Indexes for Selected Transportation Services, 1990–2011—*Continued*

(2000 = 100.)

Category and year	March	June	September	December
Outbound Air Freight				
1992	. . .	. . .	109.9	108.6
1993	106.9	106.1	105.0	105.9
1994	106.0	105.7	105.6	106.9
1995	108.2	108.1	108.6	107.8
1996	107.3	107.6	107.0	107.3
1997	108.0	107.3	107.7	105.7
1998	105.2	103.8	103.7	103.0
1999	100.3	100.4	100.3	99.2
2000	99.2	100.3	100.2	100.2
2001	100.1	98.0	97.6	97.8
2002	95.9	98.4	97.3	95.4
2003	97.2	95.4	95.5	94.9
2004	96.1	99.0	100.7	104.7
2005	103.8	107.2	112.4	112.0
2006	113.5	117.2	116.9	113.8
2007	112.3	114.3	117.0	124.3
2008	128.9	143.7	147.0	130.4
2009	119.7	112.1	111.9	114.6
2010	118.1	122.4	122.8	126.2
2011	136.4	142.1	143.9	144.6
AIR PASSENGER FARES				
Import Air Passenger Fares				
1990	64.7	70.2	75.1	74.2
1991	77.7	79.2	80.5	77.1
1992	76.8	82.5	86.8	76.6
1993	76.5	82.4	83.0	76.0
1994	76.5	81.4	83.6	78.5
1995	80.2	88.1	86.4	82.6
1996	82.0	88.1	86.8	84.3
1997	84.7	95.5	94.0	88.0
1998	87.1	94.9	95.1	88.6
1999	87.5	98.9	99.5	89.7
2000	92.5	103.5	105.1	98.9
2001	101.1	112.8	116.4	105.7
2002	103.1	119.1	125.2	107.2
2003	108.6	122.3	125.9	107.0
2004	103.6	123.1	121.0	111.7
2005	110.0	128.1	124.0	116.3
2006	114.9	136.7	130.9	125.4
2007	122.9	144.6	140.2	135.3
2008	131.3	171.6	161.3	157.3
2009	134.9	147.3	137.9	152.3
2010	149.8	175.3	160.9	169.9
2011	161.2	184.0	174.6	179.5
Export Air Passenger Fares				
1990	71.5	74.7	79.0	80.5
1991	82.7	84.3	85.2	83.0
1992	83.5	87.3	90.5	83.2
1993	84.5	89.7	91.0	86.0
1994	87.3	90.2	92.9	89.6
1995	92.4	99.4	96.4	91.6
1996	93.0	94.4	97.7	94.7
1997	85.3	97.7	95.0	87.4
1998	89.5	90.2	90.6	93.1
1999	95.5	96.8	100.6	98.6
2000	98.1	101.5	102.6	97.7
2001	99.6	100.4	102.5	98.4
2002	97.5	103.2	108.1	103.2
2003	108.4	117.0	118.0	118.4
2004	123.2	123.8	130.1	134.0
2005	136.3	136.2	139.5	128.3
2006	130.8	139.3	142.4	137.3
2007	140.2	147.3	154.6	155.7
2008	156.4	171.4	171.9	164.6
2009	141.7	138.2	141.3	156.1
2010	157.7	176.3	172.2	169.0
2011	172.8	186.6	192.7	191.1

. . . = Not available.

Chapter Ten

INTERNATIONAL LABOR COMPARISONS

INTERNATIONAL LABOR COMPARISONS

HIGHLIGHTS

This chapter compares several summary statistics of labor force status, manufacturing productivity, and consumer prices for the United States with similar statistics for other countries. Different concepts and methodologies can make comparisons between countries difficult, but the Bureau of Labor Statistics (BLS) makes adjustments to reconcile as much of the data as possible.

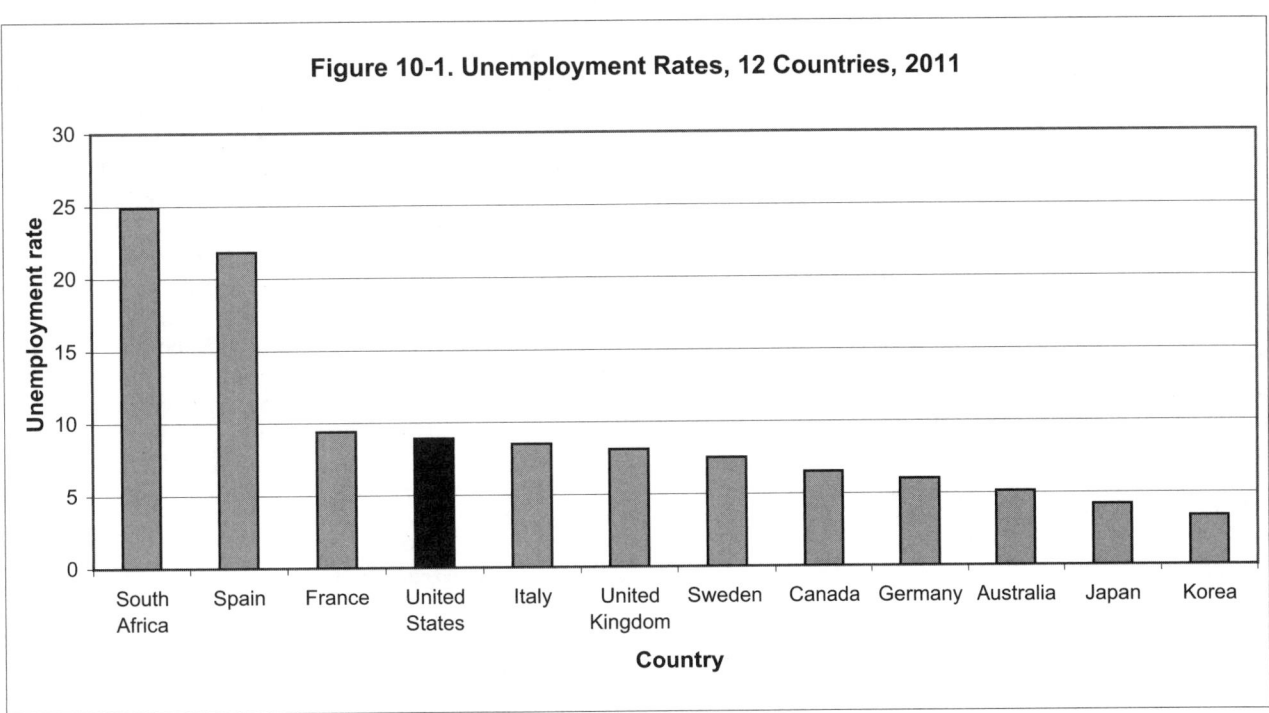

Figure 10-1. Unemployment Rates, 12 Countries, 2011

Only South Africa, Spain, and France had a higher unemployment rate than the United States in 2011 among the 12 countries being compared. While unemployment remained high in the United States and Western Europe it was relatively low in Asia. Korea had the lowest unemployment rate at 3.4 percent, followed by Japan at 4.2 percent. (See Table 10-1.)

OTHER HIGHLIGHTS

- From 1979 to 2011, employment increased at an average annual rate of 1.1 percent in the United States. In comparison, it increased 2.0 percent in Australia, 1.8 percent in the Republic of Korea, but only 0.5 percent in the United Kingdom. (See Table 10-1.)

- In 2011, the average employed person in the United States worked 1,758.4 hours, up from 1,742.0 hours in 2010. This ranked second highest among the countries being compared. Workers in Italy clocked in the most hours at 1,773.7 while those in Germany worked the least (1,411.2 hours). (See Table 10-10.)

- Real Gross Domestic Product (GDP) per capita, stated in U.S. dollars, increased in every country compared except the United Kingdom and Japan in 2011. Norway continued to have the highest real GDP per capita among all the countries at ($61,869) followed by the United States ($48,282) and the Netherlands ($42,824). (See Table 10-12.)

NOTES AND DEFINITIONS

Collection and Coverage

From its inception, the Bureau of Labor Statistics (BLS) has conducted a program of research and statistical analysis that compares labor conditions in the United States with those in selected foreign countries. The principal comparative measures of the International Labor Comparisons (ILC) program (formerly called the Foreign Labor Statistics program) cover the labor force, employment, and unemployment; trends in labor productivity and unit labor costs in manufacturing; hourly compensation costs for manufacturing production workers, and consumer prices. All of the measures are based upon statistical data and other source materials from (a) the statistical agencies of the foreign countries studied; (b) international and supranational bodies such as the United Nations, the International Labour Office (ILO), the Organisation for Economic Co-operation and Development (OECD), and the Statistical Office of the European Communities (EUROSTAT), which attempt to obtain comparable country data; and (c) private agencies such as banks, industry associations, and research institutions.

International statistical comparisons should be made with caution, as the statistical concepts and methods in each country are primarily fashioned to meet domestic (rather than international) needs. Whenever possible, BLS adjusts the data to improve comparability.

Labor Force, Employment, and Unemployment

To compare unemployment across countries, BLS publishes data for several countries that have been adjusted as closely as possible to U.S. concepts. BLS publishes additional annual labor force statistics on a civilian basis including: working-age population, labor force, employment by major economic sector (agriculture, industry, manufacturing, and services), unemployment, employment-population ratios by sex, unemployment rates by age and sex, and women's share of the labor force.

Foreign country data are adjusted as closely as possible to the U.S. definitions. Primary areas of adjustment address conceptual differences in upper age limits and definitions of employment and unemployment, provided that reliable data are available to make these adjustments. Adjustments are made where applicable to include employed and unemployed persons above upper age limits; some European countries do not include persons older than age 64 in their labor force measures, because a large portion of this population has retired. Adjustments are made to exclude active duty military from employment figures, although a small number of career military may be included in some European countries. Adjustments are made to exclude unpaid family workers who worked fewer than 15 hours per week from employment figures; U.S. concepts do not

include them in employment; most foreign countries include all unpaid family workers regardless of the number of hours worked. Adjustments are made to include full-time students seeking work and available for work as unemployed when they are classified as not in the labor force.

Where possible, lower age limits are based on the age at which compulsory schooling ends in each country, rather than based on the U.S. standard of 16 years of age and over.

Some adjustments for comparability are not made because data are unavailable for adjustment purposes. For example, no adjustments to unemployment are usually made for deviations from U.S. concepts in the treatment of persons waiting to start a new job or passive job seekers. These conceptual differences have little impact on the measures. Furthermore, BLS studies have concluded that no adjustments should be made for persons on layoff who are counted as employed in some countries because of their strong job attachment as evidenced by, for example, payment of salary or the existence of a recall date. In the United States, persons on layoff have weaker job attachment and are classified as unemployed. Finally, employment data by economic sector are not fully comparable with U.S. definitions for some countries because all data required to make adjustments at the sector level are not available. Therefore, the sum of employment by sector may not equal total adjusted employment

Hourly Compensation Costs

Measures of hourly compensation costs are prepared by BLS to assess international differences in manufacturing employer labor costs. For several reasons, comparisons based on the more readily available average earnings statistics published by many countries can be misleading. National definitions of average earnings differ considerably; average earnings do not include all items of labor compensation, and the omitted items of compensation frequently represent a large proportion of total compensation. For many years, data on hourly compensation costs covered production workers only; recently, the series has been extended to cover all employees as well.

Hourly compensation costs include (1) hourly direct pay and (2) employer social insurance expenditures and other labor taxes. Hourly direct pay includes all payments made directly to the worker, before payroll deductions of any kind, consisting of pay for time worked and other direct pay. Social insurance expenditures and other labor taxes include employer expenditures for legally required insurance programs, contractual and private benefit plans, and other labor taxes. Other labor taxes refer to taxes on payrolls or employment (or reductions to reflect subsidies), even if they do not finance programs that directly benefit workers, because such taxes are regarded as labor costs.

Productivity and Unit Labor Costs

Time series indexes of manufacturing labor productivity (output per hour) and unit labor costs are constructed from three basic aggregate measures: Total real output, hours worked, and nominal compensation. Indexes for unit labor costs are prepared on a national currency basis and, using currency exchange rates, a U.S. dollar basis. With the additional collection of annual employment in manufacturing and the use of consumer price indexes, a total of 15 time series indexes are constructed.

The employment, hours, and compensation measures refer to employees (wage and salary workers) in Belgium and Taiwan and to all employed persons (employees plus the self-employed and unpaid family workers) in all other economies.

In general, the measures relate to total manufacturing as defined by the International Standard Industrial Classification (ISIC). However, the measures for France include parts of mining. Data for the United States are in accordance with the North American Industry Classification System (NAICS), except compensation data before 1987, which are based on SIC 1987. Canadian data are in accordance with NAICS starting in 1961.

The data for the most recent years are based on the United Nations System of National Accounts 1993 (SNA 93). For earlier years, data were compiled according to previously used systems.

To obtain historical time series, BLS sometimes links together data series that were compiled according to different accounting systems by national statistical offices.

Real Gross Domestic Product per Capita and per Employed Person

Measures of gross domestic product (GDP), population, and employment are obtained from national statistical sources. While these data are generally comparable to one another, some differences remain in the countries' statistical methodologies, which may affect comparability. The GDP measures used for all countries come from their national accounts sources. For all countries, the most recent series use the 1993 United Nations System of National Accounts (SNA 93). However, some earlier series have been prepared using 1968 United Nations System of National Accounts (SNA 68). The U.S. GDP series is based on the system of national income and product accounts (NIPAs) estimated by the Bureau of Economic Analysis (BEA).

Sources of Additional Information

An extensive description of the methodology can be found in Chapter 12 in the *BLS Handbook of Methods*. For more information on international comparisons, see the BLS reports titled "International Comparisons of GDP per Capita and per Hour 1960–2011," "International Indexes of Consumer Prices," and "International Comparisons of Annual Labor Force Statistics, Adjusted to U.S. Concepts, 16 Countries, 1970–2011" on the BLS Web site at <http://www.bls.gov/fls/>.

Table 10-1. Employment Status of the Working-Age Population, Adjusted to U.S. Concepts, 12 Countries, 1975–2011

(Numbers in thousands, percent.)

Category and year	United States	Australia	Canada	France	Germany[1]	Italy	Japan	Korea	South Africa	Spain	Sweden	United Kingdom
Employed												
1975	85 846	5 866	9 284	20 869	25 536	19 395	51 532	11 691	...	...	4 056	24 758
1976	88 752	5 946	9 652	21 041	25 396	19 504	52 034	12 412	...	...	4 082	24 611
1977	92 017	6 000	9 825	21 235	25 428	19 668	52 720	12 812	...	12 322	4 093	24 638
1978	96 048	6 038	10 124	21 326	25 647	19 725	53 371	13 412	...	12 126	4 109	24 774
1979	98 824	6 111	10 561	21 392	26 074	19 932	54 040	13 602	...	11 955	4 174	25 031
1980	99 303	6 284	10 872	21 443	26 486	20 195	54 598	13 683	...	11 623	4 226	24 917
1981	100 397	6 416	11 192	21 345	26 453	20 279	55 057	14 023	...	11 316	4 219	24 256
1982	99 526	6 415	10 847	22 173	26 149	20 246	55 618	14 379	...	11 209	4 213	23 782
1983	100 834	6 300	10 936	22 134	25 765	20 320	56 545	14 505	...	11 150	4 218	23 607
1984	105 005	6 494	11 211	21 939	25 826	20 392	56 866	14 429	...	10 847	4 249	24 115
1985	107 150	6 697	11 557	21 966	26 018	20 492	57 255	14 970	...	10 732	4 293	24 422
1986	109 597	6 974	11 895	22 161	26 383	20 614	57 736	15 505	...	10 937	4 326	24 578
1987	112 440	7 129	12 221	22 161	26 584	20 591	58 315	16 354	...	11 477	4 340	25 073
1988	114 968	7 398	12 591	22 239	26 799	20 868	59 303	16 869	...	11 932	4 410	25 905
1989	117 342	7 720	12 876	22 556	27 201	20 773	60 493	17 560	...	12 379	4 480	26 588
1990	118 793	7 859	12 964	22 629	27 952	21 080	61 706	18 085	...	12 711	4 513	26 713
1991	117 718	7 676	12 754	22 535	36 871	21 364	62 920	18 649	...	12 828	4 447	26 007
1992	118 492	7 637	12 643	22 494	36 390	21 233	63 632	19 009	...	12 611	4 265	25 399
1993	120 259	7 680	12 705	22 323	35 989	21 091	63 826	19 234	...	12 097	4 027	25 173
1994	123 060	7 921	12 975	22 255	35 756	20 697	63 860	19 848	...	12 026	3 990	25 386
1995	124 900	8 236	13 210	22 535	35 780	20 555	63 897	20 414	...	12 328	4 053	25 684
1996	126 708	8 340	13 337	22 659	35 637	20 615	64 197	20 853	...	12 686	4 014	25 928
1997	129 558	8 429	13 639	22 591	35 508	20 643	64 897	21 214	...	13 175	3 974	26 407
1998	131 463	8 618	13 974	22 799	36 059	20 827	64 454	19 938	...	13 728	4 036	26 684
1999	133 488	8 762	14 326	23 100	36 042	21 045	63 924	20 291	...	14 522	4 116	27 049
2000	136 891	8 989	14 677	23 731	36 236	21 358	63 790	21 156	...	15 332	4 230	27 375
2001	136 933	9 088	14 860	24 063	36 350	21 720	63 460	21 572	...	15 970	4 303	27 618
2002	136 485	9 271	15 210	24 325	36 018	21 994	62 650	22 169	...	16 459	4 311	27 835
2003	137 736	9 485	15 576	24 380	35 615	22 020	62 511	22 139	...	17 130	4 301	28 096
2004	139 252	9 662	15 835	24 442	35 604	22 124	62 641	22 557	...	17 810	4 279	28 388
2005	141 730	9 998	16 032	24 601	36 123	22 290	62 908	22 856	...	18 796	4 334	28 681
2006	144 427	10 257	16 317	24 794	36 949	22 721	63 209	23 151	...	19 596	4 416	28 942
2007	146 047	10 576	16 704	25 218	37 763	22 953	63 509	23 433	...	20 202	4 530	29 148
2008	145 362	10 873	16 985	25 588	38 345	23 144	63 250	23 577	13 864	20 108	4 581	29 354
2009	139 877	10 953	16 732	25 356	38 279	22 760	62 241	23 506	13 453	18 735	4 487	28 878
2010	139 064	11 247	16 969	25 400	38 549	22 597	62 011	23 829	13 059	18 309	4 534	28 945
2011	139 869	11 435	17 238	25 474	39 544	22 712	62 307	24 244	13 263	17 972	4 631	29 086
Unemployed												
1975	7 929	303	690	773	890	690	1 000	501	...	...	67	1 174
1976	7 406	298	716	869	890	790	1 080	499	...	...	66	1 414
1977	6 991	358	836	991	900	840	1 100	504	...	689	75	1 470
1978	6 202	405	898	1 037	870	850	1 240	437	...	925	94	1 453
1979	6 137	408	831	1 184	780	920	1 170	540	...	1 156	88	1 432
1980	7 637	409	854	1 276	770	920	1 140	748	...	1 533	86	1 833
1981	8 273	394	887	1 511	1 090	1 040	1 260	660	...	1 892	108	2 609
1982	10 678	495	1 298	1 653	1 560	1 160	1 360	654	...	2 162	137	2 875
1983	10 717	697	1 437	1 730	1 900	1 270	1 560	613	...	2 394	151	3 081
1984	8 539	641	1 377	2 028	1 970	1 280	1 610	568	...	2 794	136	3 241
1985	8 312	603	1 293	2 164	2 010	1 310	1 470	622	...	3 005	124	3 151
1986	8 237	613	1 205	2 199	1 860	1 680	1 630	611	...	2 975	117	3 160
1987	7 425	629	1 123	2 243	1 800	1 760	1 570	519	...	2 977	100	2 940
1988	6 701	576	999	2 167	1 810	1 790	1 440	435	...	2 906	86	2 445
1989	6 528	508	982	2 034	1 640	1 760	1 340	463	...	2 632	74	2 082
1990	7 047	585	1 083	1 976	1 460	1 590	1 280	454	...	2 510	84	2 053
1991	8 628	814	1 386	2 021	2 204	1 580	1 270	461	...	2 545	147	2 530
1992	9 613	925	1 507	2 258	2 615	1 680	1 350	490	...	2 883	261	2 822
1993	8 940	939	1 533	2 526	3 113	2 296	1 600	571	...	3 599	416	2 929
1994	7 996	856	1 372	2 690	3 318	2 493	1 720	504	...	3 880	426	2 676
1995	7 404	764	1 246	2 550	3 200	2 616	1 920	430	...	3 716	404	2 436
1996	7 236	779	1 282	2 711	3 505	2 619	2 040	435	...	3 650	441	2 296
1997	6 739	778	1 247	2 746	3 907	2 641	2 110	568	...	3 464	445	1 988
1998	6 210	721	1 160	2 652	3 693	2 681	2 540	1 490	...	3 177	368	1 788
1999	5 880	652	1 072	2 594	3 333	2 593	2 810	1 374	...	2 722	313	1 727
2000	5 692	602	955	2 239	3 065	2 408	2 920	979	...	2 496	260	1 587
2001	6 801	658	1 026	2 046	3 110	2 173	3 020	899	...	1 904	227	1 489
2002	8 378	630	1 146	2 107	3 396	2 058	3 216	752	...	2 155	234	1 529
2003	8 774	599	1 146	2 294	3 661	2 050	2 985	818	...	2 242	264	1 490
2004	8 149	551	1 091	2 411	4 107	1 960	2 726	860	...	2 214	300	1 426
2005	7 591	531	1 024	2 432	4 573	1 889	2 476	887	...	1 913	361	1 467
2006	7 001	516	949	2 433	4 257	1 673	2 346	827	...	1 837	332	1 674
2007	7 078	484	922	2 223	3 601	1 506	2 400	783	...	1 834	293	1 654
2008	8 924	483	951	2 068	3 136	1 692	2 410	769	4 104	2 591	296	1 783
2009	14 265	649	1 326	2 581	3 228	1 945	3 120	889	4 215	4 150	404	2 394
2010	14 825	621	1 294	2 653	2 946	2 102	3 100	920	4 332	4 632	411	2 479
2011	13 747	614	1 196	2 628	2 502	2 108	2 733	855	4 397	4 999	373	2 560

[1]Unified Germany from 1991 onward; data for previous years relate to the former West Germany.
. . . = Not available.

Table 10-1. Employment Status of the Working-Age Population, Adjusted to U.S. Concepts, 12 Countries, 1975–2011—*Continued*

(Numbers in thousands, percent.)

Category and year	United States	Australia	Canada	France	Germany[1]	Italy	Japan	Korea	South Africa	Spain	Sweden	United Kingdom
Civilian Labor Force Participation Rate												
1975	61.2	63.2	61.1	56.9	55.0	47.7	62.4	58.3	...	...	65.9	63.1
1976	61.6	62.7	62.5	57.2	54.6	48.0	62.4	59.7	...	...	66.0	63.0
1977	62.3	62.7	62.8	57.5	54.4	48.2	62.5	59.4	...	51.3	66.0	62.7
1978	63.2	61.9	63.7	57.3	54.4	47.8	62.8	59.9	...	50.9	66.1	62.6
1979	63.7	61.6	64.5	57.3	54.5	48.0	62.7	59.5	...	50.4	66.6	62.7
1980	63.8	62.1	65.0	57.2	54.7	48.1	62.6	59.0	...	49.9	66.9	62.8
1981	63.9	61.9	65.7	57.0	54.7	48.3	62.6	58.5	...	49.4	66.8	62.7
1982	64.0	61.7	64.9	58.9	54.6	47.7	62.7	58.6	...	49.3	66.8	61.9
1983	64.0	61.4	65.2	58.5	54.3	47.5	63.1	57.7	...	49.3	66.7	61.6
1984	64.4	61.5	65.5	58.2	54.4	47.3	62.7	55.8	...	49.0	66.6	62.7
1985	64.8	61.7	66.0	58.1	54.7	47.2	62.2	56.6	...	48.6	66.9	62.9
1986	65.3	62.8	66.4	58.2	54.9	47.8	62.1	57.1	...	48.6	67.0	62.9
1987	65.6	63.0	66.8	57.8	55.0	47.6	61.8	58.3	...	49.8	66.5	63.2
1988	65.9	63.3	67.1	57.3	55.1	47.4	61.8	58.5	...	50.4	66.9	63.8
1989	66.5	64.2	67.5	57.2	55.2	47.3	62.1	59.6	...	50.2	67.3	64.3
1990	66.5	64.7	67.4	56.8	55.0	47.2	62.6	60.0	...	50.5	67.4	64.3
1991	66.2	64.2	66.8	56.3	58.8	47.8	63.1	60.6	...	50.5	67.0	63.7
1992	66.4	63.9	65.9	56.4	58.1	47.5	63.3	60.9	...	50.4	65.8	62.9
1993	66.3	63.6	65.5	56.3	57.8	49.4	63.2	60.9	...	50.5	64.5	62.6
1994	66.6	63.9	65.2	56.2	57.4	48.8	62.9	61.6	...	50.7	63.7	62.4
1995	66.6	64.6	64.9	56.2	57.1	48.6	62.8	61.9	...	50.7	64.0	62.4
1996	66.8	64.6	64.8	56.6	57.1	48.7	62.8	62.1	...	51.0	63.9	62.4
1997	67.1	64.3	65.1	56.1	57.3	48.7	63.0	62.5	...	51.4	63.3	62.5
1998	67.1	64.3	65.4	56.0	57.7	49.1	62.6	60.6	...	51.7	62.9	62.4
1999	67.1	64.0	65.8	56.1	56.9	49.3	62.0	60.6	...	52.2	62.7	62.8
2000	67.1	64.4	66.0	56.3	56.7	49.5	61.7	61.2	...	53.3	63.8	62.8
2001	66.8	64.4	66.1	56.1	56.7	49.7	61.2	61.4	...	52.7	63.7	62.7
2002	66.6	64.3	67.1	56.3	56.4	49.9	60.4	62.0	...	53.9	63.9	62.9
2003	66.2	64.6	67.7	56.4	56.0	49.6	59.9	61.5	...	55.1	63.9	62.9
2004	66.0	64.6	67.6	56.3	56.4	49.1	59.6	62.1	...	56.1	63.6	62.9
2005	66.0	65.4	67.3	56.2	57.5	48.7	59.5	62.0	...	57.0	64.8	63.1
2006	66.2	65.8	67.2	56.1	58.1	48.9	59.6	61.9	...	58.1	64.9	63.5
2007	66.0	66.2	67.5	56.2	58.3	48.6	59.8	61.8	...	58.6	65.3	63.4
2008	66.0	66.7	67.7	56.3	58.4	49.0	59.5	61.5	58.0	59.6	65.3	63.5
2009	65.4	66.7	67.2	56.6	58.5	48.4	59.3	60.8	56.1	59.7	64.8	63.4
2010	64.7	66.5	67.0	56.5	58.6	48.1	59.1	61.0	54.3	59.8	64.9	63.2
2011	64.1	66.5	66.8	56.3	59.2	48.1	58.7	61.1	54.3	59.8	65.1	63.2
Unemployment Rate												
1975	8.5	4.9	6.9	3.6	3.4	3.4	1.9	4.1	...	...	1.6	4.5
1976	7.7	4.8	6.9	4.0	3.4	3.9	2.0	3.9	...	...	1.6	5.4
1977	7.1	5.6	7.8	4.5	3.4	4.1	2.0	3.8	...	5.3	1.8	5.6
1978	6.1	6.3	8.1	4.6	3.3	4.1	2.3	3.2	...	7.1	2.2	5.5
1979	5.8	6.3	7.3	5.2	2.9	4.4	2.1	3.8	...	8.8	2.1	5.4
1980	7.1	6.1	7.3	5.6	2.8	4.4	2.0	5.2	...	11.7	2.0	6.9
1981	7.6	5.8	7.3	6.6	4.0	4.9	2.2	4.5	...	14.3	2.5	9.7
1982	9.7	7.2	10.7	6.9	5.6	5.4	2.4	4.4	...	16.2	3.1	10.8
1983	9.6	10.0	11.6	7.2	6.9	5.9	2.7	4.1	...	17.7	3.5	11.5
1984	7.5	9.0	10.9	8.5	7.1	5.9	2.8	3.8	...	20.5	3.1	11.8
1985	7.2	8.3	10.1	9.0	7.2	6.0	2.5	4.0	...	21.9	2.8	11.4
1986	7.0	8.1	9.2	9.0	6.6	7.5	2.7	3.8	...	21.4	2.6	11.4
1987	6.2	8.1	8.4	9.2	6.3	7.9	2.6	3.1	...	20.6	2.3	10.5
1988	5.5	7.2	7.4	8.9	6.3	7.9	2.4	2.5	...	19.6	1.9	8.6
1989	5.3	6.2	7.1	8.3	5.7	7.8	2.2	2.6	...	17.5	1.6	7.3
1990	5.6	6.9	7.7	8.0	5.0	7.0	2.0	2.4	...	16.5	1.8	7.1
1991	6.8	9.6	9.8	8.2	5.6	6.9	2.0	2.4	...	16.6	3.2	8.9
1992	7.5	10.8	10.7	9.1	6.7	7.3	2.1	2.5	...	18.6	5.8	10.0
1993	6.9	10.9	10.8	10.2	8.0	9.8	2.4	2.9	...	22.9	9.4	10.4
1994	6.1	9.8	9.6	10.8	8.5	10.8	2.6	2.5	...	24.4	9.6	9.5
1995	5.6	8.5	8.6	10.2	8.2	11.3	2.9	2.1	...	23.2	9.1	8.7
1996	5.4	8.5	8.8	10.7	9.0	11.3	3.1	2.0	...	22.3	9.9	8.1
1997	4.9	8.5	8.4	10.8	9.9	11.3	3.1	2.6	...	20.8	10.1	7.0
1998	4.5	7.7	7.7	10.4	9.3	11.4	3.8	7.0	...	18.8	8.4	6.3
1999	4.2	6.9	7.0	10.1	8.5	11.0	4.2	6.3	...	15.8	7.1	6.0
2000	4.0	6.3	6.1	8.6	7.8	10.1	4.4	4.4	...	14.0	5.8	5.5
2001	4.7	6.8	6.5	7.8	7.9	9.1	4.5	4.0	...	10.7	5.0	5.1
2002	5.8	6.4	7.0	8.0	8.6	8.6	4.9	3.3	...	11.6	5.1	5.2
2003	6.0	5.9	6.9	8.6	9.3	8.5	4.6	3.6	...	11.6	5.8	5.0
2004	5.5	5.4	6.4	9.0	10.3	8.1	4.2	3.7	...	11.1	6.6	4.8
2005	5.1	5.0	6.0	9.0	11.2	7.8	3.8	3.7	...	9.2	7.7	4.9
2006	4.6	4.8	5.5	8.9	10.3	6.9	3.6	3.4	...	8.6	7.0	5.5
2007	4.6	4.4	5.2	8.1	8.7	6.2	3.6	3.2	...	8.3	6.1	5.4
2008	5.8	4.3	5.3	7.5	7.6	6.8	3.7	3.2	22.8	11.4	6.1	5.7
2009	9.3	5.6	7.3	9.2	7.8	7.9	4.8	3.6	23.9	18.1	8.3	7.7
2010	9.6	5.2	7.1	9.5	7.1	8.5	4.8	3.7	24.9	20.2	8.3	7.9
2011	8.9	5.1	6.5	9.4	6.0	8.5	4.2	3.4	24.9	21.8	7.5	8.1

[1]Unified Germany from 1991 onward; data for previous years relate to the former West Germany.
. . . = Not available.

Table 10-2. Unemployment Rates by Sex and Country, Adjusted to U.S. Concepts, 12 Countries, 1975–2011

(Percent.)

Sex and year	United States	Australia	Canada	France	Germany¹	Italy	Japan	Korea	South Africa	Spain	Sweden	United Kingdom
Men												
1975	7.9	3.8	6.2	2.7	3.3	2.5	1.8	5.0	...	...	1.3	4.1
1976	7.1	3.9	6.3	2.8	3.0	2.7	2.2	5.0	...	...	1.3	5.2
1977	6.3	4.6	7.3	3.2	2.9	2.8	2.0	4.6	...	5.1	1.5	5.3
1978	5.3	5.4	7.5	3.4	2.7	2.8	2.2	3.7	...	6.6	2.1	5.1
1979	5.1	5.2	6.7	3.9	2.3	3.0	1.9	4.7	...	8.2	1.9	4.9
1980	6.9	5.1	6.9	3.9	2.3	2.9	1.7	6.2	...	10.9	1.7	6.7
1981	7.4	4.8	7.0	4.9	3.4	3.3	2.0	5.7	...	13.3	2.4	10.3
1982	9.9	6.3	11.1	5.4	5.0	3.8	2.1	5.5	...	14.8	3.0	11.6
1983	9.9	9.7	12.1	5.8	6.2	4.1	2.5	5.2	...	16.1	3.4	12.3
1984	7.4	8.7	11.1	7.0	6.2	4.2	2.5	4.8	...	19.0	3.0	12.0
1985	7.0	7.9	10.2	7.6	6.2	4.2	2.2	5.0	...	20.1	2.7	11.8
1986	6.9	7.7	9.3	7.7	5.6	5.2	2.4	4.9	...	19.3	2.6	11.8
1987	6.2	7.8	8.3	7.5	5.4	5.5	2.2	3.9	...	16.9	2.2	10.9
1988	5.5	6.8	7.2	7.1	5.3	5.5	2.0	3.0	...	15.0	2.2	10.9
1989	5.2	5.7	7.0	6.4	4.6	5.4	1.8	3.1	...	13.0	1.6	7.4
1990	5.7	6.7	7.9	6.3	4.2	4.8	1.7	2.9	...	12.0	1.9	7.4
1991	7.2	9.9	10.5	6.5	4.6	4.9	1.7	2.7	...	12.2	3.5	9.9
1992	7.9	11.4	11.6	7.4	5.5	5.3	1.8	2.8	...	14.3	6.8	11.8
1993	7.2	11.5	11.5	8.8	6.7	7.3	2.1	3.3	...	18.9	11.0	12.4
1994	6.2	10.0	10.2	9.5	7.3	8.3	2.3	2.8	...	19.8	11.0	11.3
1995	5.6	8.8	9.1	8.7	7.3	8.7	2.6	2.3	...	18.2	9.9	10.1
1996	5.4	8.8	9.2	9.4	8.4	8.7	2.8	2.4	...	17.6	10.4	9.5
1997	4.9	8.7	8.7	9.6	9.4	8.7	2.8	2.8	...	16.0	10.4	7.9
1998	4.4	8.0	8.0	9.1	8.9	8.8	3.5	7.8	...	13.7	8.7	7.0
1999	4.1	7.1	7.3	8.9	8.1	8.4	4.0	7.2	...	11.0	7.4	6.6
2000	3.9	6.5	6.3	7.4	7.6	7.8	4.1	5.0	...	9.6	6.2	6.0
2001	4.8	7.0	6.9	6.6	7.8	7.0	4.4	4.5	...	7.6	5.3	5.7
2002	5.9	6.5	7.6	7.2	8.8	6.6	4.7	3.7	...	8.3	5.6	5.8
2003	6.3	5.9	7.3	7.8	9.7	6.6	4.3	3.8	...	8.5	6.3	5.6
2004	5.6	5.3	6.8	8.1	10.6	6.5	3.9	3.9	...	8.2	6.9	5.2
2005	5.1	4.9	6.3	8.2	11.5	6.3	3.5	4.0	...	7.1	7.8	5.3
2006	4.6	4.7	5.8	8.2	10.4	5.5	3.3	3.8	...	6.4	6.9	5.9
2007	4.7	4.0	5.6	7.6	8.6	5.0	3.2	3.7	...	6.4	5.8	5.7
2008	6.1	4.0	5.8	7.0	7.5	5.6	3.2	3.6	19.8	10.1	5.8	6.2
2009	10.3	5.7	8.5	9.1	8.2	6.9	4.4	4.1	22.0	17.9	8.6	8.7
2010	10.5	5.1	7.8	9.2	7.6	7.7	4.6	4.0	22.8	19.9	8.5	8.7
2011	9.4	4.9	7.0	9.0	6.2	7.7	4.1	3.6	22.5	21.4	7.5	8.7
Women												
1975	9.3	7.0	8.1	5.0	3.5	5.7	3.9	2.5	...	...	2.0	5.2
1976	8.6	6.4	7.9	5.8	3.9	6.7	3.9	2.0	...	...	2.0	5.8
1977	8.2	7.5	8.8	6.4	4.3	6.8	4.3	2.4	...	5.8	2.2	6.2
1978	7.2	7.9	9.2	6.5	4.2	6.9	4.3	2.2	...	8.4	2.4	6.2
1979	6.8	8.2	8.3	7.3	3.9	7.4	4.1	2.4	...	10.3	2.3	6.2
1980	7.4	7.9	7.9	8.1	3.6	7.4	3.3	3.5	...	13.6	2.3	7.1
1981	7.9	7.4	7.8	9.1	4.8	8.1	3.5	2.4	...	16.9	2.7	8.8
1982	9.4	8.5	10.1	9.1	6.5	8.7	3.5	2.5	...	19.5	3.4	9.5
1983	9.2	10.4	10.9	9.3	7.9	9.4	3.7	2.2	...	21.4	3.5	10.5
1984	7.6	9.5	10.6	10.4	8.5	9.3	3.3	2.2	...	24.1	3.2	11.6
1985	7.4	8.8	9.9	10.8	8.6	9.4	3.0	2.4	...	26.1	2.9	11.0
1986	7.1	8.7	9.1	10.8	8.1	11.8	3.3	2.1	...	26.3	2.7	10.9
1987	6.2	8.6	8.6	11.4	7.8	12.2	3.2	1.8	...	28.3	2.3	10.0
1988	5.6	7.9	7.6	11.2	7.8	12.3	2.9	1.7	...	28.6	1.9	8.3
1989	5.4	6.9	7.1	10.7	7.2	12.1	2.7	1.8	...	26.4	1.7	7.1
1990	5.5	7.2	7.5	10.2	6.1	10.8	2.5	1.8	...	25.1	1.8	6.8
1991	6.4	9.2	9.0	10.4	7.0	10.4	2.5	2.0	...	24.7	2.9	7.5
1992	7.0	10.0	9.4	11.2	8.4	10.8	2.5	2.1	...	26.3	4.6	7.7
1993	6.6	10.1	9.9	11.8	9.6	14.0	3.0	2.3	...	30.0	7.6	7.9
1994	6.0	9.4	8.8	12.4	10.1	14.7	3.1	2.0	...	32.2	8.2	7.4
1995	5.6	8.1	8.0	11.9	9.4	15.5	3.4	1.7	...	31.3	8.1	6.9
1996	5.4	8.2	8.2	12.2	9.6	15.3	3.5	1.6	...	30.0	9.3	6.4
1997	5.0	8.2	8.0	12.3	10.6	15.4	3.7	2.3	...	28.5	9.7	5.9
1998	4.6	7.4	7.2	11.9	9.8	15.5	4.2	5.7	...	26.8	8.0	5.4
1999	4.3	6.7	6.6	11.5	8.9	14.8	4.5	5.1	...	23.2	6.7	5.2
2000	4.1	6.0	5.8	10.1	8.1	13.6	4.8	3.6	...	20.6	5.3	4.9
2001	4.7	6.4	6.0	9.2	7.9	12.1	4.8	3.3	...	15.4	4.7	4.5
2002	5.6	6.2	6.4	8.9	8.3	11.4	5.2	2.8	...	16.5	4.7	4.5
2003	5.7	6.0	6.3	9.5	8.8	11.4	4.9	3.3	...	16.1	5.2	4.4
2004	5.4	5.5	6.0	9.9	10.0	10.6	4.6	3.4	...	15.1	6.1	4.3
2005	5.1	5.2	5.6	9.9	10.9	10.1	4.1	3.4	...	12.3	7.5	4.4
2006	4.6	4.9	5.2	9.7	10.2	8.8	4.0	2.9	...	11.6	7.1	5.0
2007	4.5	4.8	4.8	8.6	8.8	7.9	4.2	2.6	...	10.9	6.4	5.0
2008	5.4	4.6	4.8	8.0	7.7	8.6	4.3	2.6	26.4	13.1	6.3	5.1
2009	8.1	5.4	6.1	9.4	7.3	9.3	5.2	3.0	26.2	18.5	7.9	6.5
2010	8.6	5.4	6.2	9.8	6.5	9.7	5.0	3.3	27.5	20.6	8.2	6.9
2011	8.5	5.3	5.9	9.8	5.6	9.6	4.4	3.1	27.8	22.2	7.4	7.3

¹Unified Germany from 1991 onward; data for previous years relate to the former West Germany.
. . . = Not available.

Table 10-3. Unemployment Rates Among Youth, Adjusted to U.S. Concepts, 12 Countries, 1970–2011

(Percent.)

Year	United States	Australia	Canada	France	Germany[1]	Italy	Japan	Korea	South Africa	Spain	Sweden	United Kingdom
1970	11.0	...	...	4.9	0.4	10.4	2.0	...	...	...	2.9	...
1971	12.7	...	...	5.5	0.6	10.3	2.1	...	...	...	5.1	...
1972	12.1	...	...	5.9	0.7	13.6	2.5	...	...	...	5.8	...
1973	10.5	...	...	5.8	0.8	13.2	2.3	...	...	...	5.4	...
1974	11.9	...	...	6.3	2.2	12.0	2.4	...	...	...	4.5	...
1975	16.1	...	...	7.9	4.7	13.2	3.1	...	...	...	3.8	...
1976	14.7	...	12.4	9.0	4.8	15.2	3.2	...	...	...	3.8	...
1977	13.6	...	13.8	10.6	5.0	14.9	3.6	...	...	12.6	4.5	...
1978	12.3	12.6	13.9	11.1	4.5	15.4	3.8	...	...	17.8	5.6	...
1979	11.8	13.0	12.6	12.7	3.6	16.0	3.7	...	...	21.8	5.1	...
1980	13.9	12.5	12.7	14.2	3.7	15.8	3.5	...	...	28.8	5.0	...
1981	14.9	11.4	12.6	16.8	5.7	17.3	4.0	...	...	35.1	6.5	...
1982	17.8	13.8	18.1	15.5	8.2	19.4	4.3	10.0	...	39.4	7.7	...
1983	17.2	18.3	19.1	16.5	9.6	20.9	4.6	9.2	...	42.8	8.2	...
1984	13.9	16.8	17.2	20.1	10.7	21.6	4.9	8.8	...	47.3	6.1	19.8
1985	13.6	15.2	15.6	20.2	10.0	22.2	4.7	10.0	...	49.0	5.8	18.0
1986	13.3	15.1	14.5	19.1	8.0	25.6	5.1	9.0	...	47.4	5.7	18.2
1987	12.2	14.9	13.0	18.2	7.4	25.8	5.0	7.6	...	44.2	5.4	15.4
1988	11.0	13.4	11.2	17.1	7.0	24.8	4.7	7.2	...	41.0	4.3	12.6
1989	10.9	11.2	10.5	15.4	5.5	23.9	4.4	6.8	...	35.3	3.9	10.1
1990	11.2	13.0	12.0	15.5	4.6	21.3	4.3	7.0	...	33.0	4.6	10.6
1991	13.4	17.5	15.4	16.1	5.6	21.1	4.2	7.3	...	31.7	7.9	14.3
1992	14.2	19.4	16.8	17.7	6.4	22.8	4.4	7.6	...	35.0	13.9	16.8
1993	13.4	18.7	16.7	20.7	7.8	27.3	5.1	9.0	...	43.9	23.5	18.0
1994	12.5	17.0	15.0	22.4	8.5	28.9	5.2	7.3	...	45.9	23.9	16.8
1995	12.1	15.4	13.9	20.5	8.4	30.1	5.9	6.3	...	43.3	20.2	15.7
1996	12.0	15.7	14.5	21.8	9.7	30.1	6.4	6.1	...	42.8	21.5	15.4
1997	11.3	16.1	15.5	22.3	10.6	29.9	6.4	7.6	...	39.6	21.2	14.1
1998	10.4	14.6	14.6	20.9	9.4	29.4	7.4	15.8	...	35.8	17.1	13.5
1999	9.9	13.3	13.4	20.6	8.8	28.2	8.7	14.1	...	29.8	14.7	12.9
2000	9.3	12.1	11.7	16.4	8.6	26.5	8.9	10.8	...	26.4	12.1	12.4
2001	10.6	13.5	11.9	15.7	8.4	23.4	9.1	10.2	...	21.5	12.0	12.0
2002	12.0	12.8	12.9	16.6	10.0	22.3	9.5	8.5	...	22.7	13.1	12.2
2003	12.4	12.0	12.8	18.7	10.8	24.0	9.6	10.1	...	23.2	14.0	12.4
2004	11.8	11.4	12.5	20.3	12.9	23.8	9.0	10.4	...	22.4	17.1	12.4
2005	11.3	10.7	11.4	20.9	15.5	24.2	8.1	10.2	...	20.0	22.3	13.1
2006	10.5	10.1	10.6	21.9	13.8	22.0	7.5	10.0	...	18.2	21.4	14.2
2007	10.5	9.4	10.1	19.4	11.9	20.6	7.5	8.8	...	18.5	18.9	14.4
2008	12.8	8.8	10.4	18.8	10.5	21.5	7.0	9.3	45.5	25.0	19.3	15.2
2009	17.6	11.5	13.9	23.5	11.2	25.7	8.9	9.8	48.1	38.5	24.9	19.3
2010	18.4	11.5	13.6	23.1	9.8	28.2	9.0	9.8	50.5	42.3	25.0	19.9
2011	17.3	11.3	12.8	22.3	8.5	29.4	8.1	9.6	49.8	47.1	22.7	21.2

Note: Youth are defined as 16- to 24-year-olds in the United States, Canada, France, Sweden, and the United Kingdom; otherwise, they are defined as 15- to 24-year-olds.

[1]Unified Germany from 1991 onward; data for previous years relate to the former West Germany.
. . . = Not available.

Table 10-4. Employment-Population Ratios by Sex, Adjusted to U.S. Concepts, 12 Countries, 1975–2011

(Ratio.)

Sex and year	United States	Australia	Canada	France	Germany¹	Italy	Japan	Korea	South Africa	Spain	Sweden	United Kingdom
Men												
1975	71.7	79.1	73.5	72.3	70.9	68.8	79.5	73.5	...	...	76.0	77.9
1976	72.0	78.3	74.2	71.9	70.3	68.5	79.2	73.6	...	...	75.5	76.7
1977	72.8	77.3	73.3	71.4	69.9	67.5	78.7	75.1	...	74.5	74.5	75.9
1978	73.8	75.5	73.4	70.6	69.7	66.8	78.2	75.0	...	72.4	73.5	75.3
1979	73.8	75.3	74.3	69.8	69.8	66.3	78.2	73.3	...	70.2	73.7	75.0
1980	72.0	75.1	74.1	69.1	69.6	66.0	77.9	71.7	...	67.3	73.6	73.3
1981	71.3	75.1	73.9	67.6	68.5	65.6	77.8	71.5	...	64.9	72.0	70.1
1982	69.0	73.4	69.3	68.7	67.0	64.4	77.4	70.9	...	63.1	71.3	68.0
1983	68.8	70.1	68.3	67.5	65.8	63.5	77.1	69.8	...	61.5	70.4	66.7
1984	70.7	70.5	68.9	65.8	65.7	62.9	76.4	68.7	...	58.8	70.2	67.2
1985	70.9	70.6	69.6	65.1	65.8	62.5	75.9	68.7	...	57.2	70.5	67.1
1986	71.0	70.8	70.4	64.6	66.3	61.8	75.4	68.6	...	57.3	70.6	66.6
1987	71.5	70.3	71.0	64.0	66.2	60.9	74.9	69.7	...	58.5	69.7	67.2
1988	72.0	70.9	71.6	63.5	65.9	60.4	75.0	70.7	...	59.3	70.3	69.0
1989	72.5	72.0	71.8	63.5	65.9	59.9	75.1	71.2	...	60.3	70.9	70.2
1990	72.0	71.3	70.6	62.8	65.6	60.0	75.4	71.8	...	60.8	70.6	70.0
1991	70.4	68.1	67.6	61.8	67.9	60.6	75.8	73.0	...	60.2	69.2	67.3
1992	69.8	66.5	65.7	61.0	66.3	59.8	76.1	73.6	...	57.7	65.7	64.8
1993	70.0	65.9	65.3	59.3	64.7	59.6	75.9	73.2	...	54.1	61.6	63.7
1994	70.4	67.0	65.9	58.6	63.8	58.1	75.4	74.2	...	53.0	60.9	64.2
1995	70.8	68.1	66.2	58.8	63.1	57.3	75.0	74.6	...	53.5	62.0	64.7
1996	70.9	67.9	65.8	58.7	62.1	57.1	74.9	74.4	...	53.9	61.5	64.8
1997	71.3	67.6	66.4	58.1	61.3	56.9	74.9	73.9	...	54.9	61.0	65.9
1998	71.6	67.9	66.8	57.9	61.9	56.9	73.9	69.2	...	56.6	62.1	66.2
1999	71.6	68.2	67.5	58.1	60.7	57.1	73.0	69.1	...	58.6	62.5	66.6
2000	71.9	68.4	68.2	59.1	60.6	57.4	72.5	70.7	...	60.1	64.2	66.9
2001	70.9	67.6	67.7	59.1	60.2	57.7	71.5	71.0	...	61.1	64.4	66.9
2002	69.7	67.8	67.9	58.9	58.9	58.1	70.4	72.2	...	61.2	64.3	66.7
2003	68.9	68.1	68.3	58.2	57.5	57.6	69.9	71.9	...	61.7	63.7	66.9
2004	69.2	68.8	68.5	57.6	57.3	56.9	69.6	72.0	...	62.3	63.0	66.9
2005	69.6	69.4	68.6	57.3	57.7	56.8	69.7	71.6	...	63.6	63.8	66.8
2006	70.1	69.8	68.4	57.1	58.6	57.3	69.8	71.3	...	64.5	64.5	66.7
2007	69.8	70.4	68.7	57.3	59.7	57.3	70.1	71.3	...	64.6	65.4	66.7
2008	68.5	70.7	68.8	57.6	60.5	56.9	69.6	70.9	52.7	62.2	65.4	66.4
2009	64.5	69.1	65.9	56.5	59.9	55.3	68.0	70.1	49.7	56.2	63.0	64.1
2010	63.7	69.5	66.2	56.3	60.2	54.4	67.5	70.1	47.7	54.3	63.5	63.8
2011	63.9	69.5	66.6	56.1	61.5	54.2	67.6	70.5	47.4	52.9	64.0	63.6
Women												
1975	42.0	41.4	40.7	39.2	37.9	25.3	44.0	39.4	...	...	54.1	44.2
1976	43.2	41.5	42.6	39.7	37.8	25.8	44.1	42.3	...	...	54.7	44.0
1977	44.5	41.5	42.9	40.1	37.7	26.9	44.9	40.7	...	25.4	55.5	44.0
1978	46.4	41.0	44.0	40.4	37.9	26.8	45.5	42.3	...	24.7	56.1	44.4
1979	47.5	40.7	45.7	40.5	38.4	27.3	45.6	42.3	...	24.1	57.2	45.0
1980	47.7	41.9	46.9	40.4	38.8	27.9	45.6	41.3	...	23.0	58.0	45.1
1981	48.0	42.1	48.2	40.3	38.7	28.0	45.6	41.2	...	21.9	58.5	44.3
1982	47.7	41.5	47.0	42.4	38.1	27.6	45.9	42.3	...	21.6	58.4	43.5
1983	48.0	40.8	47.3	42.3	37.3	27.6	46.7	41.9	...	21.6	58.6	43.5
1984	49.5	41.7	48.2	42.1	37.3	27.6	46.4	39.8	...	20.9	59.1	44.4
1985	50.4	43.0	49.6	42.0	37.6	27.8	46.3	40.9	...	20.5	59.7	45.2
1986	51.4	45.0	50.7	42.5	38.1	28.1	46.2	42.2	...	20.7	60.1	45.8
1987	52.5	45.6	51.6	42.2	38.5	28.2	46.2	44.1	...	22.2	60.5	46.9
1988	53.4	46.8	53.0	42.1	39.0	28.3	46.6	44.2	...	23.2	61.2	48.5
1989	54.3	48.7	53.9	42.5	39.7	28.6	47.4	45.7	...	24.1	61.7	49.9
1990	54.3	49.4	54.1	42.7	40.5	29.2	48.0	46.2	...	25.0	61.8	50.3
1991	53.7	48.2	53.2	42.6	44.3	29.7	48.6	46.2	...	25.5	60.6	49.6
1992	53.8	47.8	52.4	42.5	43.4	29.7	48.7	46.1	...	25.5	58.4	49.1
1993	54.1	47.5	51.9	42.7	42.7	30.7	48.2	46.0	...	24.8	55.5	49.1
1994	55.3	48.6	52.4	42.6	42.3	30.3	48.0	46.9	...	24.7	54.3	49.3
1995	55.6	50.3	52.7	43.1	42.7	30.2	47.7	47.6	...	25.5	54.7	49.8
1996	56.0	50.4	52.6	43.2	42.8	30.5	47.7	48.1	...	26.4	53.9	50.4
1997	56.8	50.4	53.2	42.8	42.7	30.7	47.9	48.6	...	27.4	53.0	51.0
1998	57.1	51.0	54.3	43.3	43.5	31.2	47.4	44.4	...	28.4	53.3	51.4
1999	57.4	51.3	55.2	43.7	44.1	31.9	46.6	45.2	...	30.4	54.2	52.0
2000	57.5	52.5	56.0	44.6	44.4	32.7	46.4	47.0	...	32.5	56.0	52.5
2001	57.0	52.6	56.2	45.1	44.8	33.8	46.2	47.7	...	33.9	56.7	52.7
2002	56.3	52.9	57.1	45.5	44.7	34.3	45.4	48.4	...	34.9	57.1	53.0
2003	56.1	53.6	58.0	45.6	44.5	34.2	45.3	47.4	...	36.5	56.8	53.1
2004	56.0	53.7	58.2	45.5	44.3	34.2	45.5	48.3	...	38.1	56.1	53.4
2005	56.2	55.0	58.1	45.6	44.9	34.1	45.7	48.4	...	40.4	56.0	53.7
2006	56.6	55.7	58.7	45.7	46.0	34.7	46.0	48.8	...	42.1	56.4	53.8
2007	56.6	56.4	59.5	46.6	47.1	34.9	46.1	48.9	...	43.4	57.4	53.6
2008	56.2	57.2	59.6	47.1	47.8	35.3	45.9	48.7	37.4	43.7	57.3	53.8
2009	54.4	56.9	58.7	46.7	48.3	34.7	45.7	47.7	36.2	41.9	55.9	53.2
2010	53.6	56.6	58.5	46.5	48.9	34.5	45.7	47.8	34.3	41.4	55.6	52.9
2011	53.2	56.8	58.5	46.4	50.2	34.7	45.6	48.1	34.6	41.0	56.6	52.8

¹Unified Germany from 1991 onward; data for previous years relate to the former West Germany.
. . . = Not available.

Table 10-5. Women's Share of the Labor Force, Adjusted to U.S. Concepts, 12 Countries, 1970–2011

(Percent.)

Year	United States	Australia	Canada	France	Germany[1]	Italy	Japan	Korea	South Africa	Spain	Sweden	United Kingdom
1970	38.1	32.8	33.6	36.6	36.5	28.3	39.4	35.9	...	...	39.6	...
1971	38.2	33.2	34.4	37.0	36.8	28.3	39.0	36.1	...	...	40.3	37.4
1972	38.5	33.4	34.9	37.4	37.3	28.1	38.7	35.9	...	...	40.8	37.6
1973	38.9	34.1	35.6	37.7	37.7	28.8	38.8	36.9	...	...	41.1	38.2
1974	39.4	34.8	36.1	38.0	38.0	29.1	38.1	36.4	...	...	41.9	38.7
1975	40.0	35.5	36.9	38.2	38.5	29.4	37.9	35.9	...	...	42.7	38.8
1976	40.5	35.6	37.4	38.8	38.8	30.2	37.9	37.5	...	...	43.1	38.9
1977	41.0	36.1	37.9	39.3	39.0	31.4	38.7	36.5	...	27.7	43.8	39.2
1978	41.7	36.3	38.6	39.8	39.2	31.5	39.0	37.6	...	27.8	44.4	39.7
1979	42.1	36.4	39.2	40.2	39.3	32.2	39.1	37.8	...	28.1	44.8	40.1
1980	42.5	37.1	39.8	40.6	39.5	32.7	38.9	37.5	...	28.1	45.3	40.4
1981	43.0	37.2	40.5	41.0	39.7	33.0	38.9	37.3	...	28.0	46.1	40.6
1982	43.3	37.3	40.9	41.8	39.8	33.2	39.1	38.4	...	28.5	46.4	40.7
1983	43.5	37.5	41.4	42.1	39.8	33.5	39.6	38.5	...	29.2	46.7	41.1
1984	43.8	38.0	41.8	42.6	39.9	33.7	39.4	37.7	...	29.4	47.0	41.8
1985	44.2	38.6	42.4	42.8	40.1	34.0	39.5	38.3	...	29.7	47.2	42.2
1986	44.5	39.6	42.7	43.2	40.2	34.9	39.6	39.1	...	30.1	47.3	42.7
1987	44.8	40.0	43.1	43.5	40.3	35.3	39.8	39.9	...	32.4	47.7	43.0
1988	45.0	40.5	43.6	43.7	40.7	35.6	40.0	39.8	...	33.6	47.8	43.2
1989	45.2	41.2	43.9	43.9	41.0	36.0	40.3	40.4	...	33.9	47.8	43.5
1990	45.2	41.6	44.2	44.2	41.5	36.3	40.5	40.5	...	34.4	47.8	43.7
1991	45.3	41.8	44.6	44.5	42.8	36.3	40.6	40.2	...	34.9	47.7	43.8
1992	45.4	41.9	44.7	44.8	42.8	36.6	40.6	40.0	...	35.7	47.7	44.0
1993	45.5	42.0	44.9	45.3	42.8	37.9	40.5	40.0	...	36.3	47.7	44.3
1994	46.0	42.4	44.9	45.6	42.9	38.1	40.5	40.2	...	37.2	47.6	44.5
1995	46.1	42.9	45.1	45.8	43.1	38.4	40.5	40.3	...	37.9	47.7	44.7
1996	46.2	43.0	45.2	45.8	43.3	38.8	40.5	40.6	...	38.2	47.7	44.9
1997	46.2	43.1	45.3	45.8	43.4	39.0	40.7	41.0	...	38.7	47.5	45.1
1998	46.3	43.3	45.5	46.2	43.5	39.4	40.7	40.0	...	38.8	47.2	45.3
1999	46.5	43.5	45.7	46.3	44.0	39.8	40.6	40.5	...	39.1	47.3	45.4
2000	46.5	44.0	45.9	46.4	44.3	40.1	40.8	41.1	...	39.7	47.5	45.6
2001	46.5	44.3	46.0	46.6	44.4	40.5	40.9	41.4	...	39.2	47.7	45.6
2002	46.5	44.4	46.2	46.7	44.7	40.6	40.9	41.4	...	39.9	47.8	45.7
2003	46.6	44.8	46.5	47.0	45.0	40.7	41.1	41.0	...	40.5	47.8	45.7
2004	46.4	44.6	46.5	47.3	45.1	40.7	41.3	41.4	...	41.0	47.8	45.8
2005	46.4	45.0	46.5	47.4	45.2	40.5	41.4	41.5	...	41.4	47.5	45.9
2006	46.3	45.2	46.8	47.5	45.5	40.6	41.6	41.7	...	42.0	47.5	45.9
2007	46.4	45.3	47.0	47.8	45.7	40.6	41.6	41.7	...	42.4	47.6	45.8
2008	46.5	45.4	47.0	47.8	45.7	41.0	41.7	41.6	45.4	43.1	47.5	45.8
2009	46.7	45.5	47.2	48.0	45.9	41.1	42.1	41.3	45.2	44.0	47.4	46.0
2010	46.7	45.4	47.2	48.0	46.0	41.3	42.2	41.4	44.9	44.6	47.2	46.1
2011	46.6	45.6	47.2	48.0	46.2	41.6	42.1	41.5	45.4	45.2	47.4	46.2

[1]Unified Germany from 1991 onward; data for previous years relate to the former West Germany.

Table 10-6. Percent of Employment in Agriculture, Adjusted to U.S. Concepts, 12 Countries, 1970–2011

(Percent.)

Year	United States	Australia	Canada	France	Germany[1]	Italy	Japan	Korea	South Africa	Spain	Sweden	United Kingdom[2]
1970	4.4	8.1	7.6	. . .	8.5	20.1	16.9	50.4	. . .	. . .	8.2	. . .
1971	4.3	7.7	7.5	16.0	8.0	20.1	15.5	48.2	. . .	. . .	7.8	3.2
1972	4.2	7.9	6.9	15.0	7.6	19.0	14.5	50.5	. . .	. . .	7.5	3.0
1973	4.1	7.4	6.5	14.1	7.2	18.2	13.1	49.8	. . .	. . .	7.2	3.0
1974	4.0	7.0	6.3	13.3	6.9	17.4	12.6	48.0	. . .	. . .	6.7	2.8
1975	4.0	6.9	6.1	12.9	6.7	16.7	12.4	45.7	. . .	. . .	6.5	2.8
1976	3.8	6.6	5.6	12.3	6.2	16.4	11.9	44.4	. . .	. . .	6.2	2.8
1977	3.6	6.7	5.4	11.8	5.9	15.8	11.6	41.7	. . .	. . .	6.1	2.8
1978	3.5	6.4	5.2	11.4	5.7	15.4	11.4	38.4	. . .	. . .	6.1	2.8
1979	3.4	6.5	5.1	11.1	5.3	14.9	10.8	35.8	. . .	. . .	5.8	2.7
1980	3.4	6.5	4.9	10.7	5.2	14.2	10.1	34.0	. . .	. . .	5.6	2.6
1981	3.4	6.5	4.8	10.3	5.0	13.3	9.7	34.2	. . .	. . .	5.6	2.7
1982	3.4	6.5	4.9	9.6	4.9	12.4	9.4	32.1	. . .	. . .	5.6	2.7
1983	3.4	6.6	5.0	9.3	4.8	12.3	8.9	29.7	. . .	. . .	5.5	2.7
1984	3.2	6.2	4.8	9.1	4.7	11.7	8.5	27.1	. . .	. . .	5.2	2.6
1985	3.0	6.1	4.7	8.7	4.5	11.0	8.4	24.9	. . .	. . .	4.9	2.3
1986	2.9	6.1	4.7	8.4	4.3	10.7	8.1	23.6	. . .	. . .	4.7	2.2
1987	2.9	5.8	4.5	8.0	4.1	10.4	8.0	21.9	. . .	. . .	4.5	2.3
1988	2.8	5.8	4.4	7.7	3.9	9.8	7.6	20.6	. . .	. . .	4.4	2.3
1989	2.7	5.5	4.2	7.2	3.7	9.3	7.3	19.6	. . .	. . .	4.3	2.2
1990	2.7	5.6	4.2	6.9	3.5	8.9	6.9	17.9	. . .	. . .	3.9	2.1
1991	2.8	5.5	4.3	6.6	4.1	8.5	6.4	14.6	. . .	. . .	3.8	2.3
1992	2.7	5.3	4.2	6.3	3.8	8.2	6.1	14.0	. . .	. . .	3.8	2.2
1993	2.6	5.3	4.3	6.0	3.5	6.4	5.7	13.5	. . .	. . .	3.9	2.0
1994	2.8	5.1	4.2	5.7	3.3	6.2	5.6	12.6	. . .	. . .	3.9	2.1
1995	2.8	4.9	4.0	5.5	3.1	5.9	5.5	11.8	. . .	. . .	3.5	2.1
1996	2.7	5.0	3.9	5.3	3.0	5.6	5.3	11.1	. . .	. . .	3.3	1.9
1997	2.6	5.1	3.8	5.2	2.9	5.4	5.1	10.8	. . .	. . .	3.1	1.5
1998	2.6	4.9	3.8	5.0	2.8	5.2	5.0	12.0	. . .	. . .	2.9	1.4
1999	2.5	4.9	3.5	4.9	2.8	4.9	4.9	11.3	. . .	. . .	3.1	1.2
2000	1.8	4.9	3.3	4.6	2.6	4.7	4.8	10.6	. . .	. . .	2.9	1.2
2001	1.7	4.8	2.8	4.5	2.6	4.6	4.7	10.0	. . .	. . .	2.6	1.1
2002	1.7	4.4	2.8	4.3	2.5	4.5	4.5	9.3	. . .	. . .	2.5	1.0
2003	1.7	3.9	2.7	4.2	2.5	4.4	4.4	8.8	. . .	. . .	2.5	1.0
2004	1.6	3.7	2.7	3.9	2.4	4.5	4.3	8.1	. . .	. . .	2.5	0.9
2005	1.6	3.6	2.7	3.7	2.4	4.2	4.2	7.9	. . .	. . .	2.3	1.0
2006	1.5	3.4	2.6	3.8	2.3	4.3	4.1	7.7	. . .	. . .	2.2	1.0
2007	1.4	3.3	2.5	3.5	2.3	4.0	4.1	7.4	. . .	. . .	2.2	1.0
2008	1.5	3.3	2.3	2.8	2.3	3.7	4.0	7.2	5.7	. . .	2.2	1.1
2009	1.5	3.3	2.3	3.0	1.7	3.7	4.0	7.0	5.1	. . .	2.2	1.1
2010	1.6	3.3	2.2	3.0	1.6	3.8	3.9	6.6	4.9	. . .	2.1	1.2
2011	1.6	2.9	2.1	3.0	1.6	3.7	3.8	6.4	4.6	. . .	2.0	1.2

Note: Agriculture includes agriculture, forestry, hunting, and fishing.

[1]Unified Germany from 1991 onward; data for previous years relate to the former West Germany.
[2]Sectoral employment is only partially adjusted to U.S. concepts prior to 1984.
. . . = Not available.

Table 10-7. Percent of Employment in Industry, Adjusted to U.S. Concepts, 12 Countries, 1970–2011

(Percent.)

Year	United States	Australia	Canada	France	Germany¹	Italy	Japan	Korea	South Africa	Spain	Sweden	United Kingdom²
1970	33.1	34.6	29.8	. . .	48.7	38.8	35.7	17.2	. . .	. . .	37.9	. . .
1971	31.7	34.3	29.4	39.3	47.7	39.0	35.9	17.7	. . .	. . .	37.1	42.0
1972	31.4	33.5	29.2	39.5	47.0	38.8	36.2	17.9	. . .	. . .	36.3	41.2
1973	32.0	33.4	29.5	39.6	46.8	38.4	37.0	19.6	. . .	. . .	36.3	40.9
1974	31.4	33.0	29.5	39.3	45.9	38.4	36.8	21.7	. . .	. . .	36.3	40.6
1975	29.5	31.5	28.1	38.8	44.5	38.3	35.6	23.5	. . .	. . .	35.8	39.0
1976	29.6	31.0	27.9	38.1	44.1	37.5	35.6	26.1	. . .	. . .	34.8	38.1
1977	29.7	30.4	27.5	37.7	43.8	37.6	35.1	27.2	. . .	. . .	33.7	38.0
1978	30.0	29.3	27.3	37.1	43.5	37.4	34.8	29.2	. . .	. . .	32.4	37.7
1979	30.2	29.0	27.5	36.5	43.3	37.0	34.7	29.7	. . .	. . .	31.9	37.3
1980	29.3	28.6	27.3	36.1	42.9	37.0	35.1	28.7	. . .	. . .	31.5	36.2
1981	28.9	28.3	26.9	35.5	42.2	36.5	35.1	27.5	. . .	. . .	30.6	34.3
1982	27.2	27.4	25.0	33.5	41.3	36.1	34.5	27.6	. . .	. . .	29.5	33.1
1983	25.7	25.9	24.2	32.8	40.6	35.1	34.4	28.9	. . .	. . .	29.1	32.0
1984	26.1	25.5	24.3	32.0	40.3	33.4	34.5	30.5	. . .	. . .	29.0	34.0
1985	25.8	24.8	24.3	31.0	40.1	32.6	34.6	30.5	. . .	. . .	29.0	33.6
1986	25.5	24.1	24.2	30.2	39.9	32.0	34.2	31.6	. . .	. . .	29.1	32.9
1987	25.0	23.9	24.1	29.8	39.5	31.5	33.5	33.8	. . .	. . .	28.7	31.7
1988	24.8	23.9	24.3	29.5	39.0	31.5	33.9	34.6	. . .	. . .	28.3	31.7
1989	24.7	24.2	24.3	29.4	38.9	31.5	34.1	34.8	. . .	. . .	28.4	31.6
1990	24.2	23.2	23.6	29.5	38.9	31.4	33.9	35.0	. . .	. . .	28.2	31.0
1991	23.4	22.0	22.0	29.2	39.8	31.4	34.2	36.5	. . .	. . .	27.2	31.3
1992	22.8	21.7	21.3	28.3	38.9	31.3	34.3	35.4	. . .	. . .	25.6	28.9
1993	22.3	21.8	20.7	27.2	37.8	32.5	34.0	33.7	. . .	. . .	24.5	28.3
1994	22.3	21.8	20.9	26.5	36.6	32.5	33.7	33.3	. . .	. . .	24.0	26.6
1995	22.4	21.4	21.2	26.1	35.3	32.2	33.1	33.1	. . .	. . .	25.0	26.4
1996	22.3	21.1	21.1	25.6	34.4	31.6	32.9	32.3	. . .	. . .	25.2	26.4
1997	22.4	20.8	21.5	25.4	33.9	31.4	32.8	31.1	. . .	. . .	25.0	24.3
1998	22.2	20.6	21.6	25.1	33.6	31.4	31.7	27.7	. . .	. . .	24.9	24.1
1999	21.7	20.2	21.7	24.9	33.2	31.1	31.3	27.2	. . .	. . .	24.2	23.4
2000	22.0	20.6	21.8	24.6	32.8	30.6	30.9	27.8	. . .	. . .	23.6	22.7
2001	21.3	19.8	21.7	24.6	32.3	30.4	30.1	27.2	. . .	. . .	23.1	22.3
2002	20.3	20.0	21.8	24.2	31.7	30.3	29.0	27.1	. . .	. . .	22.5	21.7
2003	20.0	19.9	21.6	23.8	31.0	30.3	28.5	27.3	. . .	. . .	21.9	20.9
2004	20.0	20.3	21.7	23.5	30.7	30.3	27.6	26.6	. . .	. . .	21.9	20.4
2005	19.8	20.1	21.4	23.2	29.2	30.4	27.1	26.1	. . .	. . .	21.1	20.2
2006	19.9	20.2	20.9	23.1	29.0	29.8	27.1	25.5	. . .	. . .	21.1	20.2
2007	19.8	20.2	20.5	22.8	29.2	29.9	27.0	25.1	. . .	. . .	20.8	20.2
2008	19.1	20.5	20.4	22.2	29.0	28.9	26.5	24.6	25.1	. . .	20.8	19.5
2009	17.6	19.9	19.1	21.4	27.5	28.3	25.5	23.7	23.6	. . .	19.3	18.2
2010	17.2	19.7	19.0	20.9	27.1	27.6	24.9	24.3	23.8	. . .	19.1	17.9
2011	17.3	19.5	19.1	20.9	27.0	27.3	24.9	24.2	23.6	. . .	19.1	17.7

Note: Industry includes manufacturing, mining, and construction.

¹Unified Germany from 1991 onward; data for previous years relate to the former West Germany.
²Sectoral employment is only partially adjusted to U.S. concepts prior to 1984.
. . . = Not available.

Table 10-8. Percent of Employment in Manufacturing, Adjusted to U.S. Concepts, 12 Countries, 1970–2011

(Percent.)

Year	United States	Australia	Canada	France	Germany[1]	Italy	Japan	Korea	South Africa	Spain	Sweden	United Kingdom[2]
1970	26.4	24.4	22.3	. . .	39.5	27.7	27.4	13.2	. . .	. . .	27.7	. . .
1971	24.7	24.1	21.8	28.5	37.4	28.0	27.4	13.4	. . .	. . .	27.4	33.9
1972	24.3	23.5	21.8	28.8	36.9	27.9	27.3	13.6	. . .	. . .	27.2	32.9
1973	24.8	23.3	22.0	28.9	36.7	27.9	27.8	15.8	. . .	. . .	27.6	32.3
1974	24.2	22.9	21.7	28.8	36.5	28.1	27.6	17.3	. . .	. . .	28.4	32.4
1975	22.7	21.3	20.2	28.5	35.7	28.0	26.1	18.6	. . .	. . .	28.1	31.0
1976	22.8	21.2	19.2	28.0	35.2	27.7	25.8	21.3	. . .	. . .	27.0	30.2
1977	22.7	20.9	18.8	27.7	35.1	27.6	25.3	21.6	. . .	. . .	26.0	30.4
1978	22.7	19.9	18.9	27.2	34.8	27.3	24.8	22.3	. . .	. . .	25.0	30.1
1979	22.7	19.6	19.2	26.7	34.5	26.9	24.6	22.8	. . .	. . .	24.7	29.5
1980	22.1	19.4	19.1	26.3	34.0	26.9	25.0	21.6	. . .	. . .	24.3	28.3
1981	21.7	19.2	18.5	25.8	33.4	26.3	25.1	20.4	. . .	. . .	23.4	26.5
1982	20.4	18.6	17.2	24.4	32.8	25.8	24.7	21.1	. . .	. . .	22.5	25.5
1983	18.4	17.8	16.8	24.1	32.2	25.0	24.8	22.5	. . .	. . .	22.4	24.3
1984	18.5	17.3	17.1	23.7	32.1	23.9	25.2	23.2	. . .	. . .	22.5	24.9
1985	18.1	16.1	17.0	23.0	32.3	23.2	25.3	23.4	. . .	. . .	22.6	24.8
1986	17.8	15.6	17.1	22.3	32.3	22.9	24.9	24.7	. . .	. . .	22.8	24.6
1987	17.3	15.4	16.7	21.8	32.0	22.5	24.4	27.0	. . .	. . .	22.0	23.2
1988	17.3	15.3	16.6	21.4	31.6	22.6	24.5	27.7	. . .	. . .	21.7	23.5
1989	17.2	15.1	16.5	21.2	31.6	22.8	24.5	27.8	. . .	. . .	21.7	22.7
1990	16.8	14.4	15.8	21.3	31.6	22.6	24.3	27.2	. . .	. . .	21.0	22.3
1991	16.3	13.8	14.8	21.1	30.7	22.1	24.6	27.6	. . .	. . .	19.9	22.8
1992	15.9	13.7	14.3	20.4	29.5	22.0	24.6	26.2	. . .	. . .	18.9	21.3
1993	15.4	13.5	14.0	19.7	28.1	24.1	23.9	24.5	. . .	. . .	18.3	21.1
1994	15.4	13.5	14.0	19.3	26.6	24.3	23.4	24.0	. . .	. . .	18.2	19.0
1995	15.5	13.1	14.4	19.0	25.2	24.2	22.7	23.6	. . .	. . .	19.0	19.0
1996	15.3	12.8	14.4	18.7	24.3	23.7	22.5	22.7	. . .	. . .	19.3	19.1
1997	15.2	12.9	14.8	18.6	24.0	23.5	22.2	21.4	. . .	. . .	19.3	16.6
1998	15.0	12.3	15.0	18.4	24.1	23.7	21.4	19.6	. . .	. . .	19.1	16.3
1999	14.3	11.8	15.3	18.2	23.8	23.4	21.0	19.8	. . .	. . .	18.5	15.6
2000	14.4	12.0	15.3	17.9	23.9	22.9	20.7	20.3	. . .	. . .	18.0	14.8
2001	13.5	11.6	15.0	17.8	23.7	22.4	20.2	19.8	. . .	. . .	17.5	14.2
2002	12.6	11.5	15.0	17.4	23.6	22.3	19.1	19.1	. . .	. . .	16.7	13.7
2003	12.3	11.0	14.6	17.0	23.3	22.1	18.8	19.0	. . .	. . .	16.2	12.6
2004	11.8	10.9	14.5	16.7	23.1	21.9	18.3	18.5	. . .	. . .	16.0	11.8
2005	11.5	10.4	13.8	16.4	22.2	21.6	18.1	18.1	. . .	. . .	15.0	11.5
2006	11.3	10.0	12.9	16.1	22.0	21.2	18.3	17.5	. . .	. . .	14.7	11.2
2007	11.2	9.9	12.1	15.7	22.2	21.2	18.3	17.1	. . .	. . .	14.3	11.1
2008	10.9	9.8	11.5	14.6	22.2	20.1	18.0	16.8	14.4	. . .	13.9	10.4
2009	10.2	9.3	10.6	13.9	20.5	19.5	17.2	16.3	13.4	. . .	12.5	9.7
2010	10.1	8.9	10.3	13.3	20.1	18.9	16.9	16.9	13.3	. . .	12.2	9.8
2011	10.2	8.5	10.2	13.4	20.0	19.0	16.8	16.9	13.3	. . .	12.2	9.8

[1]Unified Germany from 1991 onward; data for previous years relate to the former West Germany.
[2]Sectoral employment is only partially adjusted to U.S. concepts prior to 1984.
. . . = Not available.

Table 10-9. Percent of Employment in Services, Adjusted to U.S. Concepts, 12 Countries, 1970–2011

(Percent.)

Year	United States	Australia	Canada	France	Germany[1]	Italy	Japan	Korea	South Africa	Spain	Sweden	United Kingdom[2]
1970	62.5	57.3	62.6	. . .	42.8	41.1	47.4	32.4	. . .	. . .	53.9	. . .
1971	64.0	58.0	63.1	44.7	44.3	40.9	48.6	34.1	. . .	. . .	55.1	54.8
1972	64.4	58.6	63.9	45.5	45.4	42.2	49.3	31.6	. . .	. . .	56.2	55.8
1973	63.9	59.2	64.0	46.3	46.0	43.4	49.9	30.6	. . .	. . .	56.5	56.1
1974	64.6	60.0	64.2	47.4	47.2	44.2	50.6	30.3	. . .	. . .	57.0	56.6
1975	66.5	61.6	65.8	48.3	48.8	45.0	52.0	30.8	. . .	. . .	57.7	58.2
1976	66.6	62.4	66.5	49.6	49.7	46.1	52.5	29.5	. . .	. . .	59.0	59.1
1977	66.7	62.9	67.1	50.5	50.3	46.6	53.3	31.1	. . .	. . .	60.2	59.2
1978	66.5	64.3	67.5	51.5	50.8	47.2	53.8	32.4	. . .	. . .	61.5	59.5
1979	66.4	64.5	67.4	52.4	51.4	48.1	54.5	34.5	. . .	. . .	62.3	60.0
1980	67.3	64.9	67.8	53.2	51.9	48.8	54.8	37.3	. . .	. . .	62.9	61.2
1981	67.7	65.2	68.3	54.2	52.8	50.2	55.2	38.3	. . .	. . .	63.8	63.0
1982	69.4	66.1	70.1	56.9	53.8	51.5	56.1	40.3	. . .	. . .	64.9	64.2
1983	70.9	67.5	70.8	57.9	54.6	52.6	56.7	41.4	. . .	. . .	65.4	65.3
1984	70.7	68.3	70.9	58.9	55.0	54.9	57.0	42.4	. . .	. . .	65.8	63.4
1985	71.2	69.1	71.0	60.3	55.4	56.4	57.0	44.6	. . .	. . .	66.1	64.1
1986	71.6	69.8	71.1	61.4	55.8	57.3	57.7	44.8	. . .	. . .	66.2	64.9
1987	72.1	70.3	71.4	62.2	56.4	58.1	58.5	44.3	. . .	. . .	66.8	66.0
1988	72.4	70.3	71.3	62.8	57.1	58.7	58.5	44.8	. . .	. . .	67.3	66.0
1989	72.6	70.3	71.5	63.4	57.4	59.2	58.6	45.6	. . .	. . .	67.3	66.2
1990	73.1	71.2	72.2	63.6	57.6	59.7	59.2	47.1	. . .	. . .	67.9	66.9
1991	73.8	72.5	73.7	64.2	56.1	60.1	59.4	48.9	. . .	. . .	69.0	66.4
1992	74.5	73.0	74.5	65.4	57.3	60.5	59.6	50.6	. . .	. . .	70.6	68.9
1993	75.1	72.9	75.0	66.8	58.7	61.1	60.3	52.8	. . .	. . .	71.6	69.7
1994	74.9	73.1	74.9	67.8	60.1	61.3	60.7	54.1	. . .	. . .	72.1	71.3
1995	74.8	73.7	74.8	68.4	61.6	61.9	61.4	55.1	. . .	. . .	71.5	71.5
1996	75.0	73.9	75.0	69.1	62.6	62.8	61.8	56.6	. . .	. . .	71.5	71.7
1997	75.0	74.1	74.7	69.4	63.2	63.2	62.1	58.1	. . .	. . .	71.9	74.2
1998	75.2	74.5	74.6	69.9	63.6	63.4	63.3	60.3	. . .	. . .	72.2	74.5
1999	75.8	74.9	74.8	70.2	64.0	64.0	63.8	61.5	. . .	. . .	72.7	75.4
2000	76.2	74.5	74.9	70.8	64.6	64.7	64.3	61.6	. . .	. . .	73.5	76.1
2001	77.0	75.4	75.5	70.9	65.1	65.0	65.2	62.8	. . .	. . .	74.3	76.6
2002	78.0	75.6	75.4	71.5	65.8	65.2	66.5	63.6	. . .	. . .	75.0	77.3
2003	78.3	76.2	75.7	72.0	66.5	65.3	67.1	63.9	. . .	. . .	75.6	78.1
2004	78.4	76.0	75.6	72.6	66.9	65.2	68.1	65.3	. . .	. . .	75.6	78.7
2005	78.6	76.3	75.9	73.1	68.4	65.4	68.7	66.0	. . .	. . .	76.6	78.8
2006	78.6	76.4	76.5	73.1	68.7	65.9	68.8	66.8	. . .	. . .	76.7	78.8
2007	78.8	76.5	77.0	73.7	68.5	66.1	68.9	67.5	. . .	. . .	77.0	78.8
2008	79.4	76.2	77.3	75.0	68.7	67.4	69.5	68.2	69.2	. . .	77.0	79.4
2009	80.9	76.8	78.6	75.6	70.8	68.0	70.5	69.3	71.3	. . .	78.5	80.7
2010	81.2	77.0	78.8	76.1	71.3	68.6	71.2	69.1	71.3	. . .	78.8	80.9
2011	81.1	77.6	78.8	76.1	71.4	69.0	71.3	69.4	71.8	. . .	78.9	81.1

[1]Unified Germany from 1991 onward; data for previous years relate to the former West Germany.
[2]Sectoral employment is only partially adjusted to U.S. concepts prior to 1984.
. . . = Not available.

Table 10-10. Average Annual Hours Worked Per Employed Person, 16 Countries, 1970–2011

(Hours.)

Year	United States	Australia	Austria	Belgium	Canada	Denmark	France	Germany¹	Ireland	Italy	Japan	Netherlands	Norway	Spain	Sweden	United Kingdom
1970	1 911.8	...	...	1 875.1	1 930.5	1 901.6	1 970.1	1 966.4	...	...	2 033.0	1 844.7	1 834.9	...	...	...
1971	1 896.0	...	...	1 865.0	1 912.7	1 870.7	1 969.2	1 934.4	...	...	2 024.3	1 812.0	1 813.4	...	...	1 835.1
1972	1 892.6	...	...	1 839.1	1 901.9	1 813.5	1 918.2	1 911.3	...	...	2 040.2	1 812.6	1 780.5	...	...	1 856.5
1973	1 890.8	...	...	1 811.8	1 897.5	1 769.2	1 903.9	1 882.7	...	...	2 071.9	1 788.5	1 766.1	...	...	1 865.4
1974	1 862.9	...	...	1 783.9	1 883.1	1 757.7	1 873.2	1 843.2	...	...	2 022.8	1 736.1	1 744.9	...	...	1 850.4
1975	1 830.0	...	...	1 774.6	1 866.9	1 688.7	1 847.4	1 806.3	...	...	1 988.8	1 685.2	1 728.0	...	...	1 819.0
1976	1 823.6	...	...	1 777.5	1 838.1	1 697.6	1 874.4	1 818.8	...	...	2 023.1	1 672.0	1 674.4	...	...	1 811.9
1977	1 822.5	...	...	1 751.8	1 831.7	1 674.1	1 836.9	1 801.3	...	...	2 062.8	1 665.4	1 638.3	1 923.0	...	1 821.8
1978	1 830.2	1 840.0	...	1 735.2	1 837.6	1 655.0	1 806.5	1 782.3	...	...	2 095.1	1 634.0	1 601.9	1 899.8	...	1 823.1
1979	1 828.6	1 859.5	...	1 718.7	1 834.4	1 647.3	1 803.8	1 770.4	...	...	2 120.7	1 611.9	1 580.1	1 849.0	...	1 820.4
1980	1 814.6	1 834.3	...	1 698.8	1 808.9	1 670.0	1 795.3	1 751.0	...	1 858.8	2 137.1	1 601.6	1 579.7	1 835.1	1 531.0	1 790.3
1981	1 798.3	1 843.4	...	1 675.9	1 809.1	1 642.5	1 775.6	1 729.4	...	1 865.1	2 127.3	1 601.0	1 570.2	1 807.4	1 522.5	1 754.0
1982	1 786.0	1 794.2	...	1 661.4	1 788.2	1 652.2	1 703.3	1 718.2	...	1 876.5	2 122.1	1 586.5	1 558.9	1 807.4	1 536.7	1 750.1
1983	1 794.6	1 783.9	...	1 667.4	1 785.6	1 647.9	1 685.4	1 705.3	1 981.0	1 875.8	2 118.5	1 571.3	1 553.2	1 775.0	1 546.1	1 744.2
1984	1 811.5	1 806.6	...	1 691.4	1 789.7	1 642.2	1 679.3	1 693.7	1 964.0	1 865.4	2 131.2	1 562.9	1 548.3	1 738.1	1 548.3	1 750.5
1985	1 816.3	1 799.4	...	1 697.5	1 798.9	1 627.4	1 644.9	1 670.6	1 970.0	1 861.9	2 113.8	1 546.2	1 542.2	1 719.6	1 552.4	1 752.9
1986	1 797.2	1 806.1	...	1 677.5	1 797.3	1 630.3	1 640.1	1 651.6	2 003.0	1 870.4	2 111.7	1 531.2	1 538.2	1 719.6	1 550.4	1 747.6
1987	1 800.0	1 822.0	...	1 662.5	1 811.5	1 595.2	1 652.7	1 629.4	1 984.0	1 889.5	2 117.1	1 509.6	1 510.7	1 670.1	1 560.6	1 752.4
1988	1 814.2	1 812.0	...	1 650.4	1 830.4	1 577.0	1 662.5	1 624.2	1 991.0	1 893.2	2 119.3	1 506.3	1 513.3	1 674.6	1 580.4	1 759.5
1989	1 827.6	1 810.1	...	1 641.5	1 824.7	1 559.4	1 647.8	1 600.7	1 998.0	1 877.3	2 092.9	1 501.5	1 510.5	1 683.6	1 579.2	1 763.4
1990	1 809.4	1 792.3	...	1 655.4	1 806.8	1 545.8	1 644.0	1 577.6	1 988.0	1 866.6	2 065.1	1 495.5	1 502.6	1 683.6	1 575.5	1 750.7
1991	1 800.6	1 795.3	...	1 618.5	1 783.1	1 540.6	1 634.6	1 552.0	1 954.0	1 859.6	2 018.6	1 486.4	1 500.3	1 674.6	1 562.1	1 725.4
1992	1 792.7	1 809.0	...	1 595.5	1 781.7	1 561.1	1 637.0	1 564.4	1 908.0	1 862.8	1 975.6	1 492.9	1 510.1	1 671.0	1 579.9	1 718.6
1993	1 810.3	1 796.1	...	1 551.7	1 808.0	1 561.8	1 623.5	1 547.1	1 883.0	1 862.6	1 920.9	1 482.2	1 506.9	1 661.8	1 597.0	1 715.2
1994	1 826.6	1 807.0	...	1 551.6	1 824.6	1 553.8	1 613.9	1 544.8	1 883.0	1 856.5	1 911.8	1 490.1	1 505.0	1 658.7	1 635.0	1 725.4
1995	1 845.8	1 805.2	1 787.7	1 579.9	1 814.5	1 546.0	1 589.9	1 528.5	1 875.0	1 858.9	1 914.0	1 501.1	1 487.8	1 666.6	1 640.3	1 727.6
1996	1 843.4	1 775.0	1 819.2	1 554.0	1 831.2	1 535.9	1 591.9	1 511.0	1 882.0	1 873.1	1 915.4	1 505.5	1 482.6	1 662.2	1 652.8	1 727.0
1997	1 856.8	1 801.3	1 826.9	1 567.0	1 813.8	1 548.7	1 583.1	1 505.2	1 832.0	1 863.1	1 886.3	1 496.1	1 477.5	1 677.2	1 658.2	1 725.3
1998	1 869.9	1 801.9	1 805.0	1 577.9	1 809.5	1 563.7	1 570.4	1 499.1	1 754.0	1 879.7	1 863.9	1 484.7	1 475.6	1 689.6	1 656.5	1 721.8
1999	1 878.3	1 797.0	1 805.1	1 581.0	1 809.5	1 573.3	1 560.3	1 491.3	1 725.0	1 875.6	1 846.1	1 481.7	1 473.7	1 705.7	1 664.6	1 713.3
2000	1 856.9	1 799.1	1 799.5	1 545.0	1 802.5	1 585.5	1 523.0	1 470.8	1 719.0	1 861.4	1 860.3	1 479.6	1 455.2	1 730.6	1 641.7	1 697.6
2001	1 833.1	1 749.3	1 787.3	1 577.0	1 791.2	1 587.7	1 513.8	1 453.1	1 713.0	1 843.0	1 841.6	1 461.3	1 429.1	1 736.3	1 618.5	1 700.0
2002	1 814.0	1 754.9	1 784.8	1 580.0	1 771.0	1 578.8	1 475.7	1 441.4	1 698.0	1 830.9	1 829.0	1 435.2	1 414.0	1 734.0	1 595.0	1 682.5
2003	1 786.9	1 763.0	1 776.2	1 575.0	1 755.9	1 576.5	1 472.6	1 435.9	1 671.0	1 825.6	1 832.5	1 428.8	1 400.7	1 719.4	1 581.5	1 673.2
2004	1 787.4	1 743.7	1 781.9	1 549.0	1 773.7	1 579.4	1 500.6	1 436.2	1 668.0	1 826.1	1 839.8	1 417.4	1 420.5	1 704.5	1 605.9	1 670.5
2005	1 784.0	1 754.0	1 764.3	1 565.0	1 762.7	1 578.8	1 495.1	1 431.0	1 654.0	1 818.7	1 829.2	1 417.3	1 422.8	1 685.8	1 604.7	1 673.4
2006	1 783.8	1 727.2	1 740.8	1 566.1	1 759.5	1 585.6	1 472.8	1 424.0	1 645.0	1 814.8	1 838.5	1 413.8	1 419.9	1 672.9	1 599.3	1 667.7
2007	1 776.5	1 699.1	1 735.6	1 559.9	1 756.0	1 569.6	1 484.7	1 422.1	1 616.4	1 816.4	1 829.2	1 411.9	1 425.9	1 658.0	1 611.6	1 670.0
2008	1 765.4	1 749.7	1 718.5	1 567.9	1 746.2	1 572.5	1 491.6	1 421.9	1 601.0	1 802.8	1 810.6	1 414.6	1 429.4	1 662.7	1 616.9	1 664.9
2009	1 731.9	1 711.4	1 674.5	1 550.1	1 715.1	1 544.2	1 472.3	1 382.8	1 541.0	1 771.4	1 762.0	1 395.9	1 411.4	1 669.4	1 609.0	1 643.3
2010	1 742.0	1 707.2	1 663.5	1 551.1	1 724.5	1 546.2	1 477.7	1 407.7	1 545.0	1 775.1	1 782.3	1 425.1	1 423.8	1 674.2	1 642.9	1 647.2
2011	1 758.4	1 714.8	1 668.0	1 550.9	1 724.1	1 548.3	1 475.8	1 411.2	1 543.0	1 773.7	1 726.6	1 436.2	1 426.9	1 691.6	1 643.5	1 636.9

¹Unified Germany from 1991 onward; data for previous years relate to the former West Germany.
. . . = Not available.

Table 10-11. Percent Change in Average Annual Hours Worked Per Employed Person, 16 Countries, Selected Years, 1979–2011

(Percent.)

Country	1979–2011	1979–1990	1990–2000	2000–2007	2007–2011	2009–2010	2010–2011
United States	-0.1	-0.1	0.3	-0.6	-0.3	0.6	0.9
Australia	-0.3	-0.3	0.0	-0.8	0.2	-0.2	0.4
Austria	...	...	...	-0.5	-1.0	-0.7	0.3
Belgium	-0.3	-0.3	-0.7	0.1	-0.1	0.1	0.0
Canada	-0.2	-0.1	0.0	-0.4	-0.5	0.5	0.0
Denmark	-0.2	-0.6	0.3	-0.1	-0.3	0.1	0.1
France	-0.6	-0.8	-0.8	-0.4	-0.2	0.4	-0.1
Germany¹	...	-1.0	...	-0.5	-0.2	1.8	0.2
Ireland	...	...	-1.4	-0.7	-1.4	0.3	-0.1
Italy	...	...	0.0	-0.3	-0.6	0.2	-0.1
Japan	-0.6	-0.2	-1.0	-0.2	-1.4	1.2	-3.1
Netherlands	-0.4	-0.7	-0.1	-0.7	0.4	2.1	0.8
Norway	-0.3	-0.5	-0.3	-0.3	0.0	0.9	0.2
Spain	-0.3	-0.8	0.3	-0.6	0.5	0.3	1.0
Sweden	...	...	0.4	-0.3	0.5	2.1	0.0
United Kingdom	-0.3	-0.4	-0.3	-0.2	-0.5	0.2	-0.6

¹Data for Germany for years before 1991 pertain to the former West Germany.
. . . = Not available.

Table 10-12. Real Gross Domestic Product (GDP) Per Capita, 16 Countries, Selected Years, 1960–2011

(2011 U.S. dollars.)

Year	United States	Australia	Austria	Belgium	Canada	Denmark	France	Germany[1]	Ireland	Italy	Japan	Netherlands	Norway	Spain	Sweden	United Kingdom
1960	17 747	15 320	11 432	11 741	14 733	14 926	11 272	12 352	. . .	9 841	6 109	14 244	16 574	. . .	13 936	11 879
1961	17 862	14 849	11 974	12 285	14 894	15 697	11 688	12 753	. . .	10 577	6 772	14 463	17 452	. . .	14 659	12 107
1962	18 655	15 397	12 186	12 874	15 642	16 438	12 268	13 193	. . .	11 158	7 285	14 875	17 778	. . .	15 198	12 172
1963	19 192	16 018	12 602	13 335	16 168	16 383	12 805	13 433	. . .	11 698	7 846	15 157	18 312	. . .	15 920	12 662
1964	20 023	16 737	13 274	14 128	16 894	17 711	13 485	14 184	. . .	11 927	8 633	16 242	19 085	10 726	16 879	13 316
1965	21 044	17 200	13 565	14 498	17 647	18 416	14 000	14 779	. . .	12 213	9 022	16 869	19 938	11 275	17 359	13 571
1966	22 158	17 398	14 230	14 856	18 472	18 693	14 603	15 055	. . .	12 844	9 862	17 116	20 525	11 964	17 554	13 803
1967	22 472	18 268	14 549	15 346	18 672	19 580	15 195	14 974	. . .	13 667	10 840	17 820	21 623	12 334	18 553	14 110
1968	23 326	18 942	15 121	15 928	19 284	20 541	15 752	15 734	. . .	14 469	11 995	18 821	21 920	13 016	18 553	14 687
1969	23 816	19 847	16 015	16 938	19 966	21 764	16 736	16 748	. . .	15 265	13 274	19 871	22 718	14 010	19 345	14 972
1970	23 585	20 732	17 096	17 998	20 286	21 828	17 612	17 422	12 457	15 991	14 471	20 834	23 013	14 429	20 411	15 308
1971	24 071	20 571	17 890	18 625	20 507	22 367	18 376	17 777	12 886	16 206	14 909	21 466	24 146	14 901	20 463	15 582
1972	25 080	20 675	18 890	19 531	21 375	23 168	19 041	18 430	13 564	16 709	15 941	21 998	25 224	15 923	20 870	16 135
1973	26 281	21 305	19 704	20 620	22 585	23 894	20 138	19 216	14 101	17 779	16 983	23 009	26 169	16 974	21 658	17 298
1974	25 898	21 313	20 446	21 396	23 094	23 589	20 946	19 363	14 231	18 634	16 549	23 616	27 001	17 768	22 285	17 100
1975	25 590	21 509	20 426	21 017	23 175	23 234	20 615	19 265	14 188	18 136	16 848	23 414	28 201	17 703	22 765	17 016
1976	26 707	22 090	21 399	22 149	24 061	24 588	21 433	20 316	14 432	19 332	17 330	24 257	29 695	18 076	22 924	17 456
1977	27 656	22 226	22 462	22 227	24 603	24 993	22 099	21 041	15 134	19 743	17 918	24 719	30 794	18 333	22 476	17 886
1978	28 891	22 469	22 447	22 813	25 323	25 483	22 861	21 700	16 001	20 310	18 692	25 235	31 859	18 358	22 804	18 477
1979	29 467	23 085	23 713	23 279	26 027	26 423	23 547	22 589	16 433	21 458	19 551	25 569	33 135	18 231	23 628	18 981
1980	29 041	23 495	24 136	24 257	26 250	26 292	23 810	22 830	16 735	22 148	19 943	25 703	34 516	18 370	23 984	18 571
1981	29 488	24 096	24 039	24 189	26 836	26 073	23 909	22 907	16 952	22 308	20 625	25 325	34 930	18 241	23 906	18 328
1982	28 638	23 700	24 490	24 339	27 059	27 059	24 341	22 833	17 040	22 384	21 172	24 897	34 845	18 370	24 177	18 762
1983	29 662	23 295	25 254	24 418	26 200	27 799	24 511	23 273	16 799	22 638	21 672	25 313	36 073	18 607	24 603	19 472
1984	31 519	24 436	25 271	25 020	27 463	28 973	24 758	24 027	17 232	23 363	22 492	25 989	38 091	18 862	25 629	20 013
1985	32 531	25 448	25 879	25 426	28 514	30 129	25 033	24 648	17 525	24 009	23 768	26 540	40 011	19 229	26 149	20 733
1986	33 353	25 676	26 462	25 880	28 916	31 580	25 470	25 194	17 590	24 695	24 312	27 131	41 478	19 794	26 833	21 576
1987	34 114	26 529	26 801	26 454	29 751	31 623	25 941	25 543	18 228	25 480	25 188	27 472	42 019	20 841	27 668	22 640
1988	35 196	27 228	27 531	27 615	30 828	31 563	26 999	26 329	18 866	26 536	26 873	28 233	41 722	21 854	28 278	23 854
1989	36 111	27 965	28 472	28 470	31 073	31 731	27 966	27 085	20 021	27 415	28 208	29 310	41 964	22 865	28 869	24 405
1990	36 378	27 967	29 484	29 276	30 668	32 188	28 546	27 971	21 551	27 954	29 679	30 330	42 626	23 694	28 936	24 779
1991	35 812	27 373	30 196	29 702	29 655	32 568	28 700	30 761	21 767	28 355	30 549	30 820	43 741	24 241	28 419	24 253
1992	36 537	27 750	30 491	30 036	29 563	33 053	28 983	31 112	22 379	28 563	30 683	31 110	45 021	24 386	27 911	24 399
1993	37 094	28 593	30 400	29 630	29 923	32 907	28 668	30 579	22 784	28 399	30 638	31 279	46 001	24 060	27 179	25 097
1994	38 139	29 630	31 010	30 491	31 019	34 617	29 206	31 241	24 041	29 045	30 819	32 015	48 050	24 567	28 096	26 178
1995	38 640	30 264	31 789	31 122	31 562	35 509	29 699	31 672	26 218	29 885	31 340	32 844	49 803	25 185	29 052	26 935
1996	39 623	31 067	32 529	31 505	31 740	36 293	29 913	31 831	27 991	30 232	32 083	33 818	52 078	25 735	29 439	27 707
1997	40 897	32 025	33 243	32 603	32 754	37 295	30 461	32 322	30 723	30 706	32 518	35 082	54 589	26 660	30 248	28 703
1998	42 183	33 261	34 463	33 160	33 814	37 969	31 376	32 933	32 774	31 075	31 789	36 236	55 721	27 754	31 490	29 630
1999	43 716	34 255	35 614	34 255	35 396	38 814	32 246	33 526	35 632	31 432	31 669	37 679	56 462	28 922	32 918	30 459
2000	45 026	34 910	36 831	35 427	36 903	40 049	33 207	34 508	38 429	32 661	32 322	38 886	57 922	30 128	34 356	31 640
2001	45 046	35 303	37 005	35 590	37 157	40 190	33 574	34 966	39 638	33 257	32 346	39 336	58 776	30 883	34 694	32 428
2002	45 418	36 256	37 446	35 913	37 836	40 239	33 643	34 909	41 238	33 305	32 382	39 112	59 338	31 264	35 439	33 102
2003	46 137	36 963	37 603	36 053	38 199	40 289	33 709	35 174	42 273	32 979	32 876	39 059	59 572	31 700	36 123	34 230
2004	47 307	38 017	38 334	37 068	39 020	41 111	34 316	35 174	43 406	33 255	33 621	39 803	61 566	32 207	37 490	35 055
2005	48 312	38 677	38 988	37 513	39 818	41 996	34 683	35 431	44 720	33 351	34 056	40 515	62 731	32 818	38 535	35 792
2006	49 130	39 169	40 210	38 279	40 526	43 276	35 295	36 785	45 981	33 900	34 634	41 816	63 754	33 636	39 967	36 511
2007	49 571	40 357	41 534	39 108	40 973	43 774	35 882	38 036	47 250	34 261	35 392	43 360	64 772	34 182	41 003	37 588
2008	48 951	40 644	41 935	39 177	40 773	43 177	35 656	38 515	45 105	33 612	35 040	43 971	63 992	33 941	40 420	36 975
2009	47 041	40 447	40 209	37 775	39 161	40 441	34 351	36 649	41 661	31 543	33 144	42 143	62 137	32 432	38 057	35 279
2010	47 772	40 910	41 019	38 269	39 951	40 782	34 734	38 057	41 371	32 050	34 519	42 610	61 782	32 309	40 071	35 689
2011	48 282	41 340	42 066	38 767	40 489	40 930	35 133	39 186	41 537	32 100	34 294	42 824	61 869	32 501	41 316	35 688

[1]Unified Germany from 1991 onward; data for previous years relate to the former West Germany.

. . . = Not available.

Table 10-13. Real Gross Domestic Product (GDP) Per Employed Person, 16 Countries, 1960–2011

(2011 U.S. dollars.)

Year	United States	Australia	Austria	Bel-gium	Canada	Denmark	France	Ger-many[1]	Ireland	Italy	Japan	Nether-lands	Norway	Spain	Sweden	United Kingdom
1960	46 951	37 876	23 919	30 699	42 310	32 057	25 811	26 243	. . .	23 608	12 101	34 524	38 808	. . .	28 540	26 064
1961	48 026	37 578	25 052	31 988	42 986	33 454	27 057	27 081	. . .	25 384	13 348	35 015	40 630	. . .	29 919	26 476
1962	50 049	38 753	25 773	33 143	44 726	34 765	28 931	28 246	. . .	27 038	14 311	35 803	41 496	. . .	31 025	26 716
1963	51 519	39 954	27 010	34 343	46 032	34 501	30 486	28 971	. . .	29 036	15 437	36 487	42 892	. . .	32 515	27 894
1964	53 332	41 168	28 688	36 216	47 335	36 827	32 094	30 874	. . .	29 952	16 942	38 942	44 915	. . .	34 242	29 141
1965	55 397	41 799	29 708	37 361	48 569	37 901	33 541	32 344	. . .	31 705	17 619	40 660	46 870	. . .	35 306	29 597
1966	57 295	41 245	31 647	38 405	49 767	38 143	35 023	33 349	. . .	34 160	19 035	41 476	48 449	. . .	35 994	30 197
1967	57 383	43 014	33 139	40 069	49 664	40 293	36 640	34 366	. . .	36 162	20 745	43 809	51 176	. . .	37 607	31 412
1968	58 922	44 271	35 082	41 799	51 048	42 256	38 378	36 209	. . .	38 548	22 835	46 314	52 282	. . .	38 566	32 994
1969	59 294	46 210	37 352	43 827	51 982	44 140	40 489	38 314	. . .	41 195	25 372	48 654	54 160	. . .	39 750	33 771
1970	59 075	47 317	39 932	46 577	52 924	44 211	42 426	39 741	34 500	43 182	27 684	50 862	54 363	. . .	41 510	34 726
1971	60 822	48 001	41 518	47 950	53 779	45 606	44 478	40 800	35 673	43 953	28 696	52 517	56 941	36 966	41 984	35 561
1972	62 223	48 322	43 772	50 590	55 048	46 575	46 208	42 321	38 613	45 693	30 950	54 684	59 258	39 491	42 805	36 826
1973	63 727	49 132	45 279	53 108	56 030	47 730	48 583	43 815	40 220	48 266	32 697	57 271	61 472	41 506	44 337	38 957
1974	62 213	49 386	46 460	54 466	55 720	47 729	50 399	44 627	40 695	50 141	32 433	58 845	62 988	43 678	44 865	38 422
1975	62 785	50 564	46 636	54 443	55 708	47 775	50 236	45 379	41 576	49 056	33 518	58 887	65 071	44 802	45 120	38 372
1976	64 064	51 952	48 608	57 786	57 455	49 839	52 014	47 824	43 325	52 025	34 568	61 035	66 610	46 795	45 441	39 591
1977	64 693	52 009	50 428	58 295	58 433	50 953	53 407	49 313	44 629	53 194	35 657	62 511	67 496	48 436	44 625	40 510
1978	65 508	53 108	50 105	59 842	58 948	51 740	55 182	50 300	47 308	54 735	37 175	63 362	68 904	50 392	45 238	41 619
1979	65 717	54 218	52 614	60 565	58 643	53 274	56 735	51 395	46 902	57 359	38 814	63 295	70 918	51 579	46 301	42 368
1980	65 217	54 320	53 068	63 261	58 207	53 485	57 426	51 259	48 708	58 481	39 636	62 966	72 358	53 512	46 570	41 700
1981	66 133	55 430	53 202	64 268	58 541	53 893	58 087	51 469	50 079	59 023	40 980	62 753	72 549	54 753	46 402	42 281
1982	65 380	55 484	54 988	65 499	58 727	55 717	59 379	51 665	51 031	59 146	42 020	62 916	72 616	55 916	47 044	44 095
1983	67 453	56 282	56 991	66 577	59 893	57 189	60 175	52 959	51 108	59 645	42 660	64 792	75 578	57 104	47 786	46 125
1984	69 475	57 999	57 077	68 238	61 822	58 700	61 433	53 988	53 733	61 573	44 413	66 234	79 439	59 453	49 416	46 485
1985	70 921	59 379	58 308	69 040	62 800	59 652	62 583	54 480	55 021	62 702	46 972	66 694	81 430	61 463	49 983	47 681
1986	71 766	58 393	59 483	69 855	62 454	61 140	63 665	54 677	55 594	64 055	48 056	66 974	82 033	62 026	51 097	49 422
1987	72 217	59 953	60 319	70 941	63 398	61 044	64 643	54 680	57 276	65 949	49 832	66 837	81 831	62 474	52 445	50 956
1988	73 586	60 281	61 516	72 884	64 596	61 443	67 023	55 911	58 971	67 985	52 781	67 909	82 137	63 434	53 114	52 079
1989	74 712	60 370	63 141	74 262	64 830	62 069	68 650	57 020	62 355	69 812	54 808	69 057	85 387	64 171	53 805	52 074
1990	75 227	60 209	64 644	75 776	64 510	63 421	69 831	58 183	64 348	70 128	56 912	69 816	87 816	64 160	53 852	52 781
1991	75 754	61 099	66 042	76 905	64 284	64 625	70 461	63 557	65 617	69 895	57 632	70 172	91 448	65 013	54 058	53 248
1992	77 920	63 018	67 041	78 183	65 497	66 691	72 000	65 670	67 729	70 950	57 456	70 379	94 867	66 543	55 895	55 012
1993	79 081	65 245	67 708	77 937	66 712	67 687	72 358	65 853	68 268	72 534	57 337	70 966	96 828	67 780	57 766	57 244
1994	80 521	66 290	69 314	80 789	68 511	71 688	73 670	67 531	70 112	75 441	57 767	72 564	100 349	69 724	60 719	59 392
1995	81 408	65 954	71 294	81 457	69 203	72 756	74 480	68 418	73 596	77 779	58 701	73 178	102 420	70 309	62 108	60 535
1996	83 305	67 745	72 670	82 404	69 704	73 909	74 857	69 014	76 451	78 261	60 188	74 017	105 512	70 989	63 543	61 840
1997	85 154	69 881	73 781	84 892	71 145	75 006	75 978	70 317	80 313	79 278	60 726	74 865	108 034	71 645	66 183	63 099
1998	87 605	71 749	75 789	85 050	72 286	75 468	77 223	70 815	79 822	79 471	60 219	75 824	108 047	72 036	67 797	64 661
1999	90 477	73 540	77 109	86 860	74 412	76 665	77 975	71 073	82 405	79 532	60 937	77 388	109 227	72 816	69 459	65 793
2000	91 921	73 969	78 934	88 274	76 417	78 820	78 808	72 017	86 202	81 107	62 703	78 668	112 140	73 916	70 869	67 791
2001	92 858	75 003	79 085	87 792	76 837	78 508	79 072	72 917	87 607	80 999	63 406	78 211	113 969	74 227	70 289	69 178
2002	94 791	76 433	80 505	89 114	77 233	78 774	79 396	73 348	91 316	80 005	64 357	77 319	115 240	74 407	71 999	70 328
2003	96 243	77 125	80 685	89 920	76 858	80 021	80 010	73 709	93 381	78 664	65 422	78 023	117 754	74 324	74 084	72 332
2004	98 505	78 774	82 267	91 886	77 975	82 341	81 925	74 343	94 388	79 759	66 589	79 922	121 850	74 063	77 743	73 657
2005	99 803	78 498	83 259	92 187	79 318	83 449	82 873	74 963	94 773	80 122	66 983	81 506	123 404	73 663	80 008	74 937
2006	100 602	78 651	84 880	93 639	80 136	84 529	84 010	77 308	95 633	80 327	67 827	82 742	122 200	73 729	82 071	76 210
2007	101 409	79 803	86 467	94 811	79 976	83 547	84 746	78 504	97 050	80 764	69 007	83 928	120 490	74 052	82 913	78 430
2008	101 522	79 547	85 978	94 036	79 198	81 644	84 266	78 394	95 172	79 629	68 605	84 159	116 751	74 844	81 634	77 112
2009	102 185	80 038	83 369	91 566	78 242	78 597	82 695	74 344	96 352	76 438	65 844	81 039	115 316	77 209	79 432	75 275
2010	105 235	79 884	84 558	92 844	79 676	81 510	84 122	76 724	100 162	78 606	69 087	84 583	116 190	79 220	83 454	76 431
2011	106 541	80 330	85 816	93 317	80 357	82 378	85 152	77 978	102 983	78 813	68 537	85 437	116 251	81 417	84 816	76 638

[1]Unified Germany from 1991 onward; data for previous years relate to the former West Germany.
. . . = Not available.

Table 10-14. Real Gross Domestic Product (GDP) Per Hour Worked, 16 Countries, 1970–2011

(2011 U.S. dollars.)

Year	United States	Australia	Austria	Bel-gium	Canada	Den-mark	France	Ger-many[1]	Ireland	Italy	Japan	Nether-lands	Norway	Spain	Sweden	United Kingdom
1970	30.90	. . .	. . .	24.84	27.41	23.25	21.54	20.21	. . .	. . .	13.62	27.57	29.63	. . .	. . .	. . .
1971	32.08	. . .	. . .	25.71	28.12	24.38	22.59	21.09	. . .	. . .	14.18	28.98	31.40	. . .	. . .	19.38
1972	32.88	. . .	. . .	27.51	28.94	25.68	24.09	22.14	. . .	. . .	15.17	30.17	33.28	. . .	. . .	19.84
1973	33.70	. . .	. . .	29.31	29.53	26.98	25.52	23.27	. . .	. . .	15.78	32.02	34.81	. . .	. . .	20.88
1974	33.40	. . .	. . .	30.53	29.59	27.15	26.91	24.21	. . .	. . .	16.03	33.89	36.10	. . .	. . .	20.76
1975	34.31	. . .	. . .	30.68	29.84	28.29	27.19	25.12	. . .	. . .	16.85	34.94	37.66	. . .	. . .	21.10
1976	35.13	. . .	. . .	32.51	31.26	29.36	27.75	26.29	. . .	. . .	17.09	36.50	39.78	. . .	. . .	21.85
1977	35.50	. . .	. . .	33.28	31.90	30.44	29.07	27.38	. . .	. . .	17.29	37.54	41.20	25.19	. . .	22.24
1978	35.79	28.86	. . .	34.49	32.08	31.26	30.55	28.22	. . .	. . .	17.74	38.78	43.01	26.52	. . .	22.83
1979	35.94	29.16	. . .	35.24	31.97	32.34	31.45	29.03	. . .	. . .	18.30	39.27	44.88	27.90	. . .	23.27
1980	35.94	29.61	. . .	37.24	32.18	32.03	31.99	29.27	. . .	31.46	18.55	39.31	45.80	29.16	30.42	23.29
1981	36.78	30.07	. . .	38.35	32.36	32.81	32.71	29.76	. . .	31.65	19.26	39.20	46.20	30.29	30.48	24.11
1982	36.61	30.92	. . .	39.42	32.84	33.72	34.86	30.07	. . .	31.52	19.80	39.66	46.58	30.94	30.61	25.20
1983	37.59	31.55	. . .	39.93	33.54	34.70	35.70	31.06	25.80	31.80	20.14	41.24	48.66	32.17	30.91	26.44
1984	38.35	32.10	. . .	40.34	34.54	35.74	36.58	31.88	27.36	33.01	20.84	42.38	51.31	34.21	31.92	26.55
1985	39.05	33.00	. . .	40.67	34.91	36.65	38.05	32.61	27.93	33.68	22.22	43.13	52.80	35.74	32.20	27.20
1986	39.93	32.33	. . .	41.64	34.75	37.50	38.82	33.11	27.76	34.25	22.76	43.74	53.33	36.07	32.96	28.28
1987	40.12	32.90	. . .	42.67	35.00	38.27	39.11	33.56	28.87	34.90	23.54	44.27	54.17	37.41	33.61	29.08
1988	40.56	33.27	. . .	44.16	35.29	38.96	40.31	34.42	29.62	35.91	24.91	45.08	54.28	37.88	33.61	29.60
1989	40.88	33.35	. . .	45.24	35.53	39.80	41.66	35.62	31.21	37.19	26.19	45.99	56.53	38.12	34.07	29.53
1990	41.57	33.59	. . .	45.77	35.70	41.03	42.48	36.88	32.37	37.57	27.56	46.68	58.44	38.11	34.18	30.15
1991	42.07	34.03	. . .	47.51	36.05	41.95	43.11	40.95	33.58	37.59	28.55	47.21	60.95	38.82	34.61	30.86
1992	43.47	34.84	. . .	49.00	36.76	42.72	43.98	41.98	35.50	38.09	29.08	47.14	62.82	39.82	35.38	32.01
1993	43.68	36.33	. . .	50.23	36.90	43.34	44.57	42.57	36.25	38.94	29.85	47.88	64.26	40.79	36.17	33.38
1994	44.08	36.68	. . .	52.07	37.55	46.14	45.65	43.72	37.23	40.63	30.22	48.70	66.68	42.04	37.14	34.42
1995	44.10	36.53	39.88	51.56	38.14	47.06	46.85	44.76	39.25	41.84	30.67	48.75	68.84	42.19	37.86	35.04
1996	45.19	38.17	39.95	53.03	38.06	48.12	47.02	45.67	40.62	41.78	31.42	49.16	71.17	42.61	38.44	35.81
1997	45.86	38.79	40.39	54.17	39.23	48.43	47.99	46.72	43.84	42.55	32.19	50.04	73.12	42.72	39.91	36.57
1998	46.85	39.82	41.99	53.90	39.95	48.26	49.17	47.24	45.51	42.28	32.31	51.07	73.22	42.64	40.93	37.55
1999	48.17	40.92	42.72	54.94	41.12	48.73	49.97	47.66	47.77	42.40	33.01	52.23	74.12	42.69	41.73	38.40
2000	49.50	41.11	43.86	57.14	42.40	49.71	51.74	48.97	50.15	43.57	33.71	53.17	77.06	42.71	43.17	39.93
2001	50.66	42.88	44.25	55.67	42.90	49.45	52.24	50.18	51.14	43.95	34.43	53.52	79.75	42.75	43.43	40.69
2002	52.25	43.55	45.10	56.40	43.61	49.90	53.80	50.89	53.78	43.70	35.19	53.87	81.50	42.91	45.14	41.80
2003	53.86	43.75	45.42	57.09	43.77	50.76	54.33	51.33	55.88	43.09	35.70	54.61	84.06	43.23	46.84	43.23
2004	55.11	45.18	46.17	59.32	43.96	52.13	54.59	51.76	56.59	43.68	36.19	56.39	85.78	43.45	48.41	44.09
2005	55.94	44.75	47.19	58.91	45.00	52.86	55.43	52.38	57.30	44.05	36.62	57.51	86.74	43.70	49.86	44.78
2006	56.40	45.54	48.76	59.79	45.54	53.31	57.04	54.29	58.14	44.26	36.89	58.53	86.06	44.07	51.32	45.70
2007	57.08	46.97	49.82	60.78	45.54	53.23	57.08	55.20	59.39	44.46	37.73	59.44	84.50	44.66	51.45	46.96
2008	57.51	45.46	50.03	59.98	45.35	51.92	56.49	55.13	59.45	44.17	37.89	59.49	81.68	45.01	50.49	46.32
2009	59.00	46.77	49.79	59.07	45.62	50.90	56.17	53.76	62.53	43.15	37.37	58.06	81.70	46.25	49.37	45.81
2010	60.41	46.79	50.83	59.86	46.20	52.72	56.93	54.50	64.83	44.28	38.76	59.35	81.61	47.32	50.80	46.40
2011	60.59	46.84	51.45	60.17	46.61	53.20	57.70	55.26	66.74	44.43	39.70	59.49	81.47	48.13	51.61	46.82

[1]Unified Germany from 1991 onward; data for previous years relate to the former West Germany.
. . . = Not available.

Table 10-15. Real Gross Domestic Product (GDP) Per Capita and Per Employed Person, Average Annual Percent Change, 16 Countries, Selected Years, 1979–2011

(Percent.)

Category and country	1979–2011	1979–1990	1990–2000	2000–2007	2007–2011	2009–2010	2010–2011
Real GDP Per Capita							
United States	1.6	1.9	2.2	1.4	-0.7	1.6	1.1
Australia	1.8	1.8	2.2	2.1	0.6	1.1	1.1
Austria	1.8	2.0	2.2	1.7	0.3	2.0	2.6
Belgium	1.6	2.1	1.9	1.4	-0.2	1.3	1.3
Canada	1.4	1.5	1.9	1.5	-0.3	2.0	1.3
Denmark	1.4	1.8	2.2	1.3	-1.7	0.8	0.4
France	1.3	1.8	1.5	1.1	-0.5	1.1	1.1
Germany[1]	...	2.0	...	1.4	0.7	3.8	3.0
Ireland	2.9	2.5	6.0	3.0	-3.2	-0.7	0.4
Italy	1.3	2.4	1.6	0.7	-1.6	1.6	0.2
Japan	1.8	3.9	0.9	1.3	-0.8	4.1	-0.7
Netherlands	1.6	1.6	2.5	1.6	-0.3	1.1	0.5
Norway	2.0	2.3	3.1	1.6	-1.1	-0.6	0.1
Spain	1.8	2.4	2.4	1.8	-1.3	-0.4	0.6
Sweden	1.8	1.9	1.7	2.6	0.2	5.3	3.1
United Kingdom	2.0	2.5	2.5	2.5	-1.3	1.2	0.0
Real GDP Per Employed Person							
United States	1.5	1.2	2.0	1.4	1.2	3.0	1.2
Australia	1.2	1.0	2.1	1.1	0.2	-0.2	0.6
Austria	1.5	1.9	2.0	1.3	-0.2	1.4	1.5
Belgium	1.4	2.1	1.5	1.0	-0.4	1.4	0.5
Canada	1.0	0.9	1.7	0.7	0.1	1.8	0.9
Denmark	1.4	1.6	2.2	0.8	-0.4	3.7	1.1
France	1.3	1.9	1.2	1.0	0.1	1.7	1.2
Germany[1]	...	1.1	...	1.2	-0.2	3.2	1.6
Ireland	2.5	2.9	3.0	1.7	1.5	4.0	2.8
Italy	1.0	1.8	1.5	-0.1	-0.6	2.8	0.3
Japan	1.8	3.5	1.0	1.4	-0.2	4.9	-0.8
Netherlands	0.9	0.9	1.2	0.9	0.4	4.4	1.0
Norway	1.6	2.0	2.5	1.0	-0.9	0.8	0.1
Spain	1.4	2.0	1.4	0.0	2.4	2.6	2.8
Sweden	1.9	1.4	2.8	2.3	0.6	5.1	1.6
United Kingdom	1.9	2.0	2.5	2.1	-0.6	1.5	0.3

[1] Data for Germany for years before 1991 pertain to the former West Germany.
. . . = Not available.

Table 10-16. Real Gross Domestic Product (GDP) Per Hour Worked, Average Annual Percent Change, 16 Countries, Selected Years, 1979–2011

(Percent.)

Country	1979–2011	1979–1990	1990–2000	2000–2007	2007–2011	2009–2010	2010–2011
United States	1.6	1.3	1.8	2.1	1.5	2.4	0.3
Australia	1.5	1.3	2.0	1.9	-0.1	0.1	0.1
Austria	...	...	...	1.8	0.8	2.1	1.2
Belgium	1.7	2.4	2.2	0.9	-0.3	1.3	0.5
Canada	1.2	1.0	1.7	1.0	0.6	1.3	0.9
Denmark	1.6	2.2	1.9	1.0	0.0	3.6	0.9
France	1.9	2.8	2.0	1.4	0.3	1.4	1.4
Germany[1]	...	2.2	...	1.7	0.0	1.4	1.4
Ireland	...	...	4.5	2.4	3.0	3.7	2.9
Italy	...	...	1.5	0.3	0.0	2.6	0.3
Japan	2.4	3.8	2.0	1.6	1.3	3.7	2.4
Netherlands	1.3	1.6	1.3	1.6	0.0	2.2	0.2
Norway	1.9	2.4	2.8	1.3	-0.9	-0.1	-0.2
Spain	1.7	2.9	1.1	0.6	1.9	2.3	1.7
Sweden	...	...	2.4	2.5	0.1	2.9	1.6
United Kingdom	2.2	2.4	2.9	2.3	-0.1	1.3	0.9

[1] Data for Germany for years before 1991 pertain to the former West Germany.
. . . = Not available.

Chapter Eleven

CONSUMER EXPENDITURES

CONSUMER EXPENDITURES

HIGHLIGHTS

The principal objective of the Consumer Expenditure (CE) Survey is to collect information about the buying habits of American households. The survey breaks down expenditures for different demographic categories, such as income, age, family size, and geographic location. These data are used in a variety of government, business, and academic research projects and provide important weights for the periodic revisions of the Consumer Price Index (CPI).

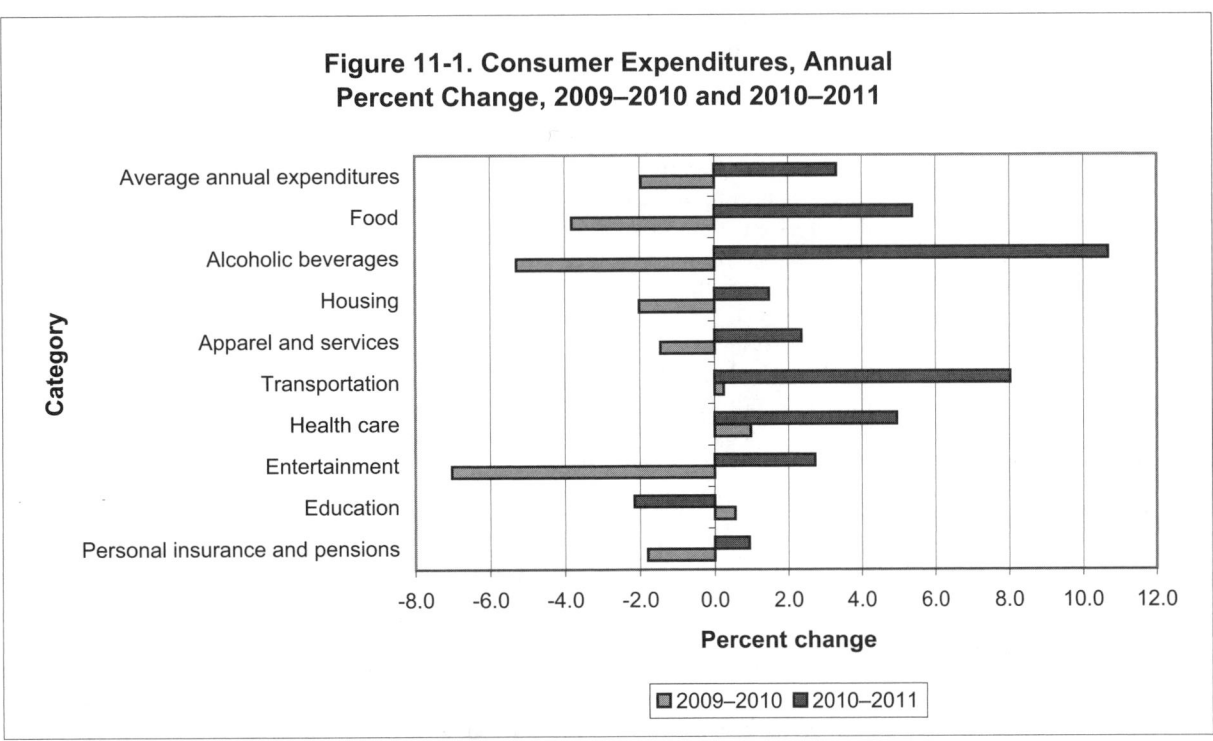

Figure 11-1. Consumer Expenditures, Annual Percent Change, 2009–2010 and 2010–2011

After declining from 2009 to 2010, average annual consumer expenditures increased in most categories from 2010 to 2011. In 2011, consumer expenditures increased 3.3 percent. Expenditures increased faster than average in alcoholic beverages (10.7 percent), transportation (8.0 percent), food (5.4 percent), and health care (4.9 percent). (See Table 11-1.)

OTHER HIGHLIGHTS

- While annual average expenditures increased for most categories, expenditures for education decreased 2.1 percent. (Table 11-1.)

- Average annual consumer expenditures varied substantially by age group. Those aged 45 to 54 years had the highest average expenditures at $58,050 followed by those 35 to 44 years at $57,271. Older age groups typically spent more in health care while those in younger age groups spent more on education. (See Table 11-10.)

- As educational attainment increased, so did average annual expenditures. Those with less than a high school diploma had average annual expenditures of $29,951 while those with a master's, professional, or doctoral degree had average annual expenditures of $75,731. (See Table 11-13.)

- Homeowners had far higher average annual expenditures than renters ($57,502 compared with $35,274). Meanwhile, those in urban areas had higher expenditures than those in rural areas ($50,348 compared with $42,540). (See Table 11-14.)

NOTES AND DEFINITIONS

Purpose, Collection, and Coverage

The buying habits of American consumers change over time because of changes in relative prices, real income, family size and composition, and other determinants of tastes and preferences. The introduction of new products into the marketplace and the emergence of new concepts in retailing also influence consumer buying habits. Data from the Consumer Expenditure Survey (CE), the only national survey that relates family expenditures to demographic characteristics, are of great importance to researchers. The survey data are also used to revise the Consumer Price Index market baskets and item samples.

Until the 1970s, the Bureau of Labor Statistics (BLS) conducted surveys of consumer expenditures approximately once every 10 years. The last such survey was conducted in 1972–1973. In late 1979, in a significant departure from previous methodology, BLS initiated a survey to be conducted on a continuous basis with rotating panels of respondents.

The current CE is similar to its 1972–1973 predecessor in that it consists of two separate components. Each component has its own questionnaire and sample: (1) the Interview Survey, in which an interviewer visits each consumer unit every three months for a twelve-month period; and (2) the Diary Survey, a record-keeping survey completed by other consumer units for two consecutive one-week periods. The Census Bureau, under contract to BLS, collects the data for both components of the survey. Beginning in 1999, the sample was increased from 5,000 to 7,500 households.

In 2003, the survey modified the questions on race and Hispanic origin to comply with the new standards for maintaining, collecting, and presenting federal data on race and ethnicity for federal statistical agencies. Beginning with the data collected in 2003, the CE tables use data collected from the new race and ethnicity questions. A number of new classifications were made with publication of the 2003 data.

Beginning with the publication of the 2004 tables, the CE has been implementing multiple imputations of income data. Prior to 2004, the CE only published income data collected from complete income reporters. The introduction of multiply imputed income data affects the published CE tables in several ways, because income data are now published for all consumer units (instead of for complete reporters only). The most obvious result of this change is seen on the tables showing expenditures categorized by income before taxes, including income by quintile. Starting with the 2004 data, columns describing income, expenditures, and characteristics for "total complete reporting" and "incomplete reporting of income" no longer appear in these tables, and the column entitled "all consumer units" appears

on all income tables. Due to the implementation of income imputation, data for 2004 are not strictly comparable to those of prior years, especially for the income tables. Averages for demographic characteristics and annual expenditures will change due to differences between the incomplete and complete income reporters in these categories. Furthermore, certain expenditures (such as personal insurance and pensions) are computed using income data. As a result of imputation, average annual values for these expenditures may be substantially different in the 2004 CE tables than in tables for previous years. The regular flow of data resulting from this design substantially enhances the usefulness of the survey by providing more timely information on consumption patterns within different kinds of consumer units.

The *Interview Survey* is designed to collect data on the types of expenditures that respondents can be expected to recall after a period of three months or longer. These include relatively large expenditures (such as those for property, travel, automobiles, and major appliances) and expenditures that occur on a regular basis (such as those for rent, utilities, insurance premiums, and clothing). The interview also obtains "global estimates" for food and other selected items. The survey collects data for approximately 95 percent of total expenditures. Each sample household is interviewed once per quarter, for five consecutive quarters.

The *Diary Survey* is designed to collect data on expenditures for frequently purchased items that are more difficult to recall over longer periods of time. Respondents complete a diary of expenses for two consecutive 1-week periods. Expenditures for tobacco, drugs (including nonprescription drugs), and personal care supplies and services are also collected in the Diary Survey.

Participants in both surveys record dollar amounts for goods and services purchased during the reporting period, regardless of whether payment was made at the time of purchase. Excluded from both surveys are business-related expenditures and expenditures for which the family is reimbursed. Information is collected on demographic and family characteristics at the initial interview for each survey.

The tables in this chapter present integrated data from the Diary Survey and the Interview Survey and provide a complete accounting of consumer expenditures and income, which neither survey component is designed to do alone. Data for some expenditure items are only collected in one of the surveys. For example, the Diary Survey does not collect data for expenditures on overnight travel or information on reimbursements, while the Interview Survey records these purchases. Examples of expenditures for which reimbursements are netted out include those for medical care, auto repair, and construction, repairs, alterations, and maintenance of property.

For items unique to one survey or the other, the choice of which survey to use as the source of data is obvious. However, there is considerable overlap in coverage between the two surveys. Integrating the data thus presents the problem of determining the appropriate survey component. When data are available from both survey sources, the more reliable of the two (as determined by statistical methods) is selected. As a result, some items are selected from the Interview Survey and others are selected from the Diary Survey.

Data Included in This Edition

Data for single characteristics are for calendar year 2011, and data for two cross-classified characteristics are for an average of calendar years 2010 and 2011. Income values from the survey are derived from "complete income reporters" only. Complete income reporters are defined as consumer units that provide values for at least one of the major sources of their income: wages and salaries, self-employment income, retirement income, dividends and interest, and welfare benefits. Some consumer units are defined as complete income reporters, even though they may not have provided a full accounting of all income from all sources.

Consumer units are classified by quintiles of income before taxes, age of reference person, size of consumer unit, region, composition of consumer unit, number of earners in consumer unit, housing tenure, race, type of area (urban or rural), and occupation.

Concepts and Definitions

A *consumer unit* comprises either (1) all members of a particular household related by blood, marriage, adoption, or other legal arrangements; (2) a person living alone, sharing a household with others, living as a roomer in a private home or lodging house or in permanent living quarters in a hotel or motel, but who is financially independent; or (3) two or more persons living together who pool their income to make joint expenditure decisions. Financial independence is determined by the three major expense categories: housing, food, and other living expenses. To be considered financially independent, at least two of the three major expense categories have to be provided by the respondent. The terms "family," "household," and "consumer unit" are used interchangeably in descriptions of the CE.

An *earner* is a consumer unit member, 14 years of age or older, who reported having worked at least 1 week during the 12 months prior to the interview date.

The *education of reference person* refers to the number of years of formal education of the reference person, on the basis of the highest grade completed. If enrolled at time of the interview, the interviewer records the grade currently attended. Persons not reporting the extent of their education are classified under no school or not reported.

The *householder* or *reference person* is the first member of the consumer unit mentioned by the respondent as owner or renter of the premises at the time of the initial interview.

Housing tenure refers to the family's principal place of residence during the survey. "Owner" includes families living in their own homes, cooperatives or condominium apartments, or townhouses. "Renter" includes families paying rent, as well as families living rent-free in lieu of wages.

Quintiles of income before taxes refers to the ranking of complete income reporters in ascending order, according to the level of total before-tax income reported by the consumer unit. The ranking is then divided into five equal groups. Incomplete income reporters are not ranked and are shown separately.

Total expenditures include the transaction costs, including excise and sales taxes of goods and services acquired during the interview period. Estimates include expenditures for gifts and contributions and payments for pensions and personal insurance.

Sources of Additional Information

More extensive descriptions and tables can be found in an updated version of Chapter 16 in the *BLS Handbook of Methods* and in an anthology of articles relating to consumer expenditures. These resources can be found on the BLS Web site at <http://www.bls.gov>.

Table 11-1. Consumer Expenditures, Annual Average of All Consumer Units, 2000–2011

(Number, dollar, percent.)

Item	2000	2001	2002	2003	2004	2005	2006	2007	2008	2009	2010	2011
NUMBER OF CONSUMER UNITS (THOUSANDS)	109 367	110 339	112 108	115 356	116 282	117 356	118 843	120 171	120 770	120 847	121 107	122 287
CONSUMER UNIT CHARACTERISTICS												
Income Before Taxes	44 649	47 507	49 430	51 128	54 453	58 712	60 533	63 091	63 563	62 857	62 481	63 685
Age of Reference Person	48.2	48.1	48.1	48.0	48.5	48.6	48.7	48.8	49.1	49.4	49.4	49.7
Average Number in Consumer Unit												
All persons	2.5	2.5	2.5	2.5	2.5	2.5	2.5	2.5	2.5	2.5	2.5	2.5
Children under 18 years	0.7	0.7	0.7	0.6	0.6	0.6	0.6	0.6	0.6	0.6	0.6	0.6
Persons 65 years and over	0.3	0.3	0.3	0.3	0.3	0.3	0.3	0.3	0.3	0.3	0.3	0.3
Earners	1.4	1.4	1.4	1.3	1.3	1.3	1.3	1.3	1.3	1.3	1.3	1.3
Vehicles	1.9	1.9	2.0	1.9	1.9	2.0	1.9	1.9	2.0	2.0	1.9	1.9
Percent Homeowner	66	66	66	67	68	67	67	67	66	66	66	65
With mortgage	39	40	41	41	42	43	43	43	42	41	41	40
Without mortgage	27	26	26	26	25	25	24	23	24	25	25	25
AVERAGE ANNUAL EXPENDITURES	38 045	39 518	40 677	40 817	43 395	46 409	48 398	49 638	50 486	49 067	48 109	49 705
Food	5 158	5 321	5 375	5 340	5 781	5 931	6 111	6 133	6 443	6 372	6 129	6 458
Food at home	3 021	3 086	3 099	3 129	3 347	3 297	3 417	3 465	3 744	3 753	3 624	3 838
Cereals and bakery products	453	452	450	442	461	445	446	460	507	506	502	531
Meats, poultry, fish, and eggs	453	452	798	825	880	764	797	777	846	841	784	832
Dairy products	325	332	328	328	371	378	368	387	430	406	380	407
Fruits and vegetables	521	522	552	535	561	552	592	600	657	656	679	715
Other food at home	927	952	970	999	1 075	1 158	1 212	1 241	1 305	1 343	1 278	1 353
Food away from home	2 137	2 235	2 276	2 211	2 434	2 634	2 694	2 668	2 698	2 619	2 505	2 620
Alcoholic Beverages	372	349	376	391	459	426	497	457	444	435	412	456
Housing	12 319	13 011	13 283	13 432	13 918	15 167	16 366	16 920	17 109	16 895	16 557	16 803
Shelter	7 114	7 602	7 829	7 887	7 998	8 805	9 673	10 023	10 183	10 075	9 812	9 825
Owned dwellings	4 602	4 979	5 165	5 263	5 324	5 958	6 516	6 730	6 760	6 543	6 277	6 148
Rented dwellings	2 034	2 134	2 160	2 179	2 201	2 345	2 590	2 602	2 724	2 860	2 900	3 029
Other lodging	478	489	505	445	473	502	567	691	698	672	635	648
Utilities, fuels, and public services	2 489	2 767	2 684	2 811	2 927	3 183	3 397	3 477	3 649	3 660	3 660	3 727
Household operations	684	676	706	707	753	801	948	984	998	1 011	1 007	1 122
Housekeeping supplies	482	509	545	529	594	611	640	639	654	659	612	615
Household furnishings and equipment	1 549	1 458	1 518	1 497	1 646	1 767	1 708	1 797	1 624	1 506	1 467	1 514
Apparel and Services	1 856	1 743	1 749	1 640	1 816	1 886	1 874	1 881	1 801	1 725	1 700	1 740
Transportation	7 417	7 633	7 759	7 781	7 801	8 344	8 508	8 758	8 604	7 658	7 677	8 293
Vehicle purchases (net outlay)	3 418	3 579	3 665	3 732	3 397	3 544	3 421	3 244	2 755	2 657	2 588	2 669
Gasoline and motor oil	1 291	1 279	1 235	1 333	1 598	2 013	2 227	2 384	2 715	1 986	2 132	2 655
Other vehicle expenses	2 281	2 375	2 471	2 331	2 365	2 339	2 355	2 592	2 621	2 536	2 464	2 454
Public transportation	427	400	389	385	441	448	505	538	513	479	493	516
Health Care	2 066	2 182	2 350	2 416	2 574	2 664	2 766	2 853	2 976	3 126	3 157	3 313
Health insurance	983	1 061	1 168	1 252	1 332	1 361	1 465	1 545	1 653	1 785	1 831	1 922
Medical services	568	573	590	591	648	677	670	709	727	736	722	768
Drugs	416	449	487	467	480	521	514	481	482	486	485	489
Medical supplies	99	100	105	107	114	105	117	118	114	119	119	134
Entertainment	1 863	1 953	2 079	2 060	2 218	2 388	2 376	2 698	2 835	2 693	2 504	2 572
Personal Care Products and Services	564	465	526	527	581	541	585	588	616	596	582	634
Reading	146	141	139	127	130	126	117	118	116	110	100	115
Education	632	648	752	783	905	940	888	945	1 046	1 068	1 074	1 051
Tobacco Products and Smoking Supplies	319	308	320	290	288	319	327	323	317	380	362	351
Miscellaneous	776	750	792	606	690	808	846	808	840	816	849	775
Cash Contributions	1 192	1 258	1 277	1 370	1 408	1 663	1 869	1 821	1 737	1 723	1 633	1 721
Personal Insurance and Pensions	3 365	3 737	3 899	4 055	4 823	5 204	5 270	5 336	5 605	5 471	5 373	5 424
Life and other personal insurance	399	410	406	397	390	381	322	309	317	309	318	317
Pensions and Social Security	2 966	3 326	3 493	3 658	4 433	4 823	4 948	5 027	5 288	5 162	5 054	5 106

Table 11-2. Shares of Annual Average Consumer Expenditures and Characteristics of All Consumer Units, 2000–2011

(Number, dollar, percent.)

Item	2000	2001	2002	2003	2004	2005	2006	2007	2008	2009	2010	2011
NUMBER OF CONSUMER UNITS (THOUSANDS)	109 367	110 339	112 108	115 356	116 282	117 356	118 843	120 171	120 770	120 847	121 107	122 287
CONSUMER UNIT CHARACTERISTICS												
Income Before Taxes	44 649	47 507	49 430	51 128	54 453	58 712	60 533	63 091	63 563	62 857	62 481	63 685
Age of Reference Person	48.2	48.1	48.1	48.4	48.5	48.6	48.7	48.8	49.1	49.4	49.4	49.7
Average Number in Consumer Unit												
All persons	2.5	2.5	2.5	2.5	2.5	2.5	2.5	2.5	2.5	2.5	2.5	2.5
Children under 18 years	0.7	0.7	0.7	0.6	0.6	0.6	0.6	0.6	0.6	0.6	0.6	0.6
Persons 65 years and over	0.3	0.3	0.3	0.3	0.3	0.3	0.3	0.3	0.3	0.3	0.3	0.3
Earners	1.4	1.4	1.4	1.3	1.3	1.3	1.3	1.3	1.3	1.3	1.3	1.3
Vehicles	1.9	1.9	2.0	1.9	1.9	2.0	1.9	1.9	2.0	2.0	1.9	1.9
Percent Homeowner	66	66	66	67	68	67	67	67	66	66	66	65
With mortgage	39	40	41	41	42	43	43	43	42	41	41	40
Without mortgage	27	26	26	26	25	25	24	23	24	25	25	25
AVERAGE ANNUAL EXPENDITURES	38 045	39 518	40 677	40 817	43 395	46 409	48 398	49 638	50 486	49 067	48 109	49 705
Food	13.6	13.5	13.2	13.1	13.3	12.8	12.6	12.4	12.8	13.0	12.7	13.0
Food at home	7.9	7.8	7.6	7.7	7.7	7.1	7.1	7.0	7.4	7.6	7.5	7.7
Cereals and bakery products	1.2	1.1	1.1	1.1	1.1	1.0	0.9	0.9	1.0	1.0	1.0	1.1
Meats, poultry, fish, and eggs	2.1	2.1	2.0	2.0	2.0	1.6	1.6	1.6	1.7	1.7	1.6	1.7
Dairy products	0.9	0.8	0.8	0.8	0.9	0.8	0.8	0.8	0.9	0.8	0.8	0.8
Fruits and vegetables	1.4	1.3	1.4	1.3	1.3	1.2	1.2	1.2	1.3	1.3	1.4	1.4
Other food at home	2.4	2.4	2.4	2.4	2.5	2.5	2.5	2.5	2.6	2.7	2.7	2.7
Food away from home	5.6	5.7	5.6	5.4	5.6	5.7	5.6	5.4	5.3	5.3	5.2	5.3
Alcoholic Beverages	1.0	0.9	0.9	1.0	1.1	0.9	1.0	0.9	0.9	0.9	0.9	0.9
Housing	32.4	32.9	32.7	32.9	32.1	32.7	33.8	34.1	33.9	34.4	34.4	33.8
Shelter	18.7	19.2	19.2	19.3	18.4	19.0	20.0	20.2	20.2	20.5	20.4	19.8
Owned dwellings	12.1	12.6	12.7	12.9	12.3	12.8	13.5	13.6	13.4	13.3	13.0	12.4
Rented dwellings	5.3	5.4	5.3	5.3	5.1	5.1	5.4	5.2	5.4	5.8	6.0	6.1
Other lodging	1.3	1.2	1.2	1.1	1.1	1.1	1.2	1.4	1.4	1.4	1.3	1.3
Utilities, fuels, and public services	6.5	7.0	6.6	6.9	6.7	6.9	7.0	7.0	7.2	7.4	7.6	7.5
Household operations	1.8	1.7	1.7	1.7	1.7	1.7	2.0	2.0	2.0	2.1	2.1	2.3
Housekeeping supplies	1.3	1.3	1.3	1.3	1.4	1.3	1.3	1.3	1.3	1.3	1.3	1.2
Household furnishings and equipment	4.1	3.7	3.7	3.7	3.8	3.8	3.5	3.6	3.2	3.1	3.0	3.0
Apparel and Services	4.9	4.4	4.3	4.0	4.2	4.1	3.9	3.8	3.6	3.5	3.5	3.5
Transportation	19.5	19.3	19.1	19.1	18.0	18.0	17.6	17.6	17.0	15.6	16.0	16.7
Vehicle purchases (net outlay)	9.0	9.1	9.0	9.1	7.8	7.6	7.1	6.5	5.5	5.4	5.4	5.4
Gasoline and motor oil	3.4	3.2	3.0	3.3	3.7	4.3	4.6	4.8	5.4	4.0	4.4	5.3
Other vehicle expenses	6.0	6.0	6.1	5.7	5.5	5.0	4.9	5.2	5.2	5.2	5.1	4.9
Public transportation	1.1	1.0	1.0	0.9	1.0	1.0	1.0	1.1	1.0	1.0	1.0	1.0
Health Care	5.4	5.5	5.8	5.9	5.9	5.7	5.7	5.7	5.9	6.4	6.6	6.7
Health insurance	2.6	2.7	2.9	3.1	3.1	2.9	3.0	3.1	3.3	3.6	3.8	3.9
Medical services	1.5	1.4	1.5	1.4	1.5	1.5	1.4	1.4	1.4	1.5	1.5	1.5
Drugs	1.1	1.1	1.2	1.1	1.1	1.1	1.1	1.0	1.0	1.0	1.0	1.0
Medical supplies	0.3	0.3	0.3	0.3	0.3	0.2	0.2	0.2	0.2	0.2	0.2	0.3
Entertainment	4.9	4.9	5.1	5.0	5.1	5.1	4.9	5.4	5.6	5.5	5.2	5.2
Personal Care Products and Services	1.5	1.2	1.3	1.3	1.3	1.2	1.2	1.2	1.2	1.2	1.2	1.3
Reading	0.4	0.4	0.3	0.3	0.3	0.3	0.2	0.2	0.2	0.2	0.2	0.2
Education	1.7	1.6	1.8	1.9	2.1	2.0	1.8	1.9	2.1	2.2	2.2	2.1
Tobacco Products and Smoking Supplies	0.8	0.8	0.8	0.7	0.7	0.7	0.7	0.7	0.6	0.8	0.8	0.7
Miscellaneous	2.0	1.9	1.9	1.5	1.6	1.7	1.7	1.6	1.7	1.7	1.8	1.6
Cash Contributions	3.1	3.2	3.1	3.4	3.2	3.6	3.9	3.7	3.4	3.5	3.4	3.5
Personal Insurance and Pensions	8.8	9.5	9.6	9.9	11.1	11.2	10.9	10.8	11.1	11.2	11.2	10.9
Life and other personal insurance	1.0	1.0	1.0	1.0	0.9	0.8	0.7	0.6	0.6	0.6	0.7	0.6
Pensions and Social Security	7.8	8.4	8.6	9.0	10.2	10.4	10.2	10.1	10.5	10.5	10.5	10.3

Table 11-3. Consumer Expenditures, Averages by Income Before Taxes, 2011

(Number, dollar, percent.)

Item	All consumer units	Less than $5,000	$5,000 to $9,999	$10,000 to $14,999	$15,000 to $19,999	$20,000 to $29,999	$30,000 to $39,999	$40,000 to $49,999	$50,000 to $69,999	$70,000 and over
NUMBER OF CONSUMER UNITS (THOUSANDS)	122 287	4 978	5 449	8 170	7 745	14 460	13 328	11 347	17 376	39 434
CONSUMER UNIT CHARACTERISTICS										
Income Before Taxes	63 685	-1 393	8 056	12 654	17 563	24 940	34 777	44 698	59 306	130 588
Income After Taxes	61 673	-995	8 155	12 803	17 955	25 136	34 750	44 196	58 070	124 804
Age of Reference Person	49.7	44.2	49.1	55.9	55.5	52.6	49.5	48.8	48.2	48.0
Average Number in Consumer Unit										
All persons	2.5	1.7	1.7	1.6	2.0	2.2	2.4	2.6	2.7	3.1
Children under 18 years	0.6	0.4	0.4	0.3	0.5	0.5	0.6	0.6	0.7	0.8
Persons 65 years and over	0.3	0.2	0.3	0.4	0.5	0.5	0.4	0.3	0.3	0.2
Earners	1.3	0.5	0.5	0.4	0.6	0.8	1.1	1.3	1.5	1.9
Vehicles	1.9	0.9	0.8	1.0	1.2	1.4	1.6	1.9	2.1	2.6
Percent Distribution										
Male	47	36	38	35	39	43	43	50	49	54
Female	53	64	62	65	61	57	57	50	51	46
Percent Homeowner	65	32	33	41	50	52	58	64	73	85
With mortgage	40	10	11	12	13	21	32	38	49	66
Without mortgage	25	22	22	29	37	31	26	26	24	19
AVERAGE ANNUAL EXPENDITURES	49 705	22 960	20 884	19 959	24 806	30 398	36 769	40 306	50 034	81 767
Food	6 458	3 452	3 595	3 272	3 748	4 278	5 326	5 154	6 546	9 775
Food at home	3 838	2 147	2 518	2 396	2 560	2 804	3 476	3 184	3 995	5 307
Cereals and bakery products	531	302	339	328	382	390	488	447	544	727
Meats, poultry, fish, and eggs	832	472	558	558	507	632	791	674	849	1 142
Dairy products	407	232	253	247	262	299	359	343	422	569
Fruits and vegetables	715	400	474	418	479	516	647	572	728	1 009
Other food at home	1 353	741	893	845	930	967	1 191	1 147	1 452	1 861
Food away from home	2 620	1 305	1 077	876	1 188	1 473	1 850	1 969	2 551	4 467
Alcoholic Beverages	456	223	222	149	145	212	315	309	384	844
Housing	16 803	8 578	8 134	8 481	9 852	11 721	13 425	14 562	16 888	25 689
Shelter	9 825	5 173	4 941	5 075	5 464	6 789	7 758	8 429	9 628	15 229
Owned dwellings	6 148	1 479	1 508	1 548	1 980	2 778	3 747	4 590	6 238	11 605
Rented dwellings	3 029	3 282	3 220	3 407	3 379	3 745	3 708	3 476	2 923	2 251
Other lodging	648	412	213	120	105	266	303	363	467	1 372
Utilities, fuels, and public services	3 727	2 079	2 075	2 271	2 739	2 989	3 338	3 666	4 000	4 958
Household operations	1 122	494	343	344	584	703	760	837	934	2 018
Housekeeping supplies	615	270	295	295	455	409	465	530	626	924
Household furnishings and equipment	1 514	562	480	496	611	832	1 104	1 100	1 701	2 560
Apparel and Services	1 740	1 126	938	740	819	942	1 468	1 175	1 767	2 821
Transportation	8 293	3 457	3 201	2 559	4 019	4 664	6 406	7 128	9 010	13 580
Vehicle purchases (net outlay)	2 669	1 122	1 090	283	1 106	1 035	1 988	1 957	2 879	4 824
Gasoline and motor oil	2 655	1 148	1 112	1 172	1 487	1 971	2 247	2 679	2 961	3 841
Other vehicle expenses	2 454	956	842	931	1 248	1 470	1 889	2 149	2 762	3 879
Public transportation	516	231	157	173	177	188	282	343	409	1 036
Health Care	3 313	1 235	1 098	1 578	2 024	2 646	2 751	3 317	3 722	4 742
Health insurance	1 922	703	649	913	1 238	1 625	1 703	1 963	2 189	2 649
Medical services	768	223	160	318	363	510	523	733	880	1 230
Drugs	489	240	239	269	366	427	426	493	535	643
Medical supplies	134	68	51	79	57	85	99	127	117	220
Entertainment	2 572	901	994	922	1 098	1 636	1 695	1 876	2 830	4 325
Personal Care Products and Services	634	256	287	249	305	367	479	519	620	1 053
Reading	115	48	48	44	60	72	76	89	132	188
Education	1 051	1 896	932	338	349	523	441	539	630	1 976
Tobacco Products and Smoking Supplies	351	299	305	332	328	361	379	416	392	321
Miscellaneous	775	538	376	329	343	599	551	656	682	1 246
Cash Contributions	1 721	639	468	540	1 049	885	1 104	1 269	1 561	3 123
Personal Insurance and Pensions	5 424	310	287	425	666	1 492	2 353	3 297	4 871	12 084
Life and other personal insurance	317	88	56	86	100	271	163	209	289	585
Pensions and Social Security	5 106	222	230	339	566	1 221	2 190	3 088	4 582	11 499

Table 11-4. Consumer Expenditures, Averages by Higher Income Before Taxes, 2011

(Number, dollar, percent.)

Item	All consumer units	Less than $70,000	$70,000 to $79,000	$80,000 to $99,999	$100,000 and over	$100,000 to $119,000	$120,000 to $149,999	$150,000 and over
NUMBER OF CONSUMER UNITS (THOUSANDS)	122 287	82 853	7 385	10 456	21 593	7 045	6 107	8 440
CONSUMER UNIT CHARACTERISTICS								
Income Before Taxes	63 685	31 842	74 742	89 108	169 776	108 549	133 318	247 261
Income After Taxes	61 673	31 626	72 895	86 417	161 148	105 125	127 734	232 086
Age of Reference Person	49.7	50.5	47.5	48.1	48.2	47.1	48.3	49.0
Average Number in Consumer Unit								
All persons	2.5	2.2	2.8	3.0	3.2	3.2	3.1	3.2
Children under 18 years	0.6	0.5	0.7	0.7	0.9	0.9	0.8	0.9
Persons 65 years and over	0.3	0.4	0.2	0.2	0.2	0.2	0.2	0.2
Earners	1.3	1.0	1.7	1.8	2.0	2.0	2.0	2.0
Vehicles	1.9	1.5	2.4	2.5	2.8	2.8	2.7	2.8
Percent Distribution								
Male	47	43	53	54	54	54	53	54
Female	53	57	47	46	46	46	47	46
Percent Homeowner	65	55	79	83	88	86	88	91
With mortgage	40	28	58	62	70	69	70	72
Without mortgage	25	27	20	21	18	17	18	19
AVERAGE ANNUAL EXPENDITURES	49 705	34 391	57 977	65 390	97 728	76 496	87 239	123 056
Food	6 458	4 854	7 679	8 139	11 233	9 569	10 674	13 055
Food at home	3 838	3 126	4 474	4 627	5 897	5 184	5 533	6 768
Cereals and bakery products	531	435	616	646	801	708	767	906
Meats, poultry, fish, and eggs	832	682	1 003	970	1 268	1 110	1 200	1 452
Dairy products	407	328	464	498	635	552	598	734
Fruits and vegetables	715	573	765	871	1 152	977	1 065	1 365
Other food at home	1 353	1 107	1 626	1 643	2 041	1 838	1 903	2 312
Food away from home	2 620	1 728	3 205	3 512	5 336	4 385	5 141	6 286
Alcoholic Beverages	456	269	563	670	1 018	745	934	1 311
Housing	16 803	12 568	19 178	20 926	30 212	23 660	27 420	37 700
Shelter	9 825	7 253	10 887	12 247	18 158	13 546	16 546	23 175
Owned dwellings	6 148	3 550	7 676	9 122	14 152	10 539	12 841	18 117
Rented dwellings	3 029	3 400	2 711	2 364	2 039	2 112	2 101	1 934
Other lodging	648	303	500	761	1 967	895	1 603	3 124
Utilities, fuels, and public services	3 727	3 141	4 273	4 537	5 395	4 903	5 126	6 001
Household operations	1 122	696	1 379	1 381	2 543	1 732	2 035	3 589
Housekeeping supplies	615	465	680	755	1 083	1 065	1 026	1 138
Household furnishings and equipment	1 514	1 013	1 959	2 005	3 032	2 414	2 688	3 797
Apparel and Services	1 740	1 218	1 984	2 220	3 380	2 833	2 779	4 272
Transportation	8 293	5 772	9 804	12 185	15 538	13 962	14 274	17 756
Vehicle purchases (net outlay)	2 669	1 642	3 095	4 455	5 595	4 966	4 878	6 639
Gasoline and motor oil	2 655	2 090	3 345	3 612	4 121	3 921	4 150	4 267
Other vehicle expenses	2 454	1 771	2 937	3 458	4 397	4 239	3 973	4 823
Public transportation	516	269	427	660	1 425	836	1 273	2 027
Health Care	3 313	2 632	4 130	4 106	5 258	4 590	5 038	5 976
Health insurance	1 922	1 576	2 392	2 388	2 864	2 562	2 813	3 151
Medical services	768	547	1 060	973	1 413	1 177	1 304	1 688
Drugs	489	415	467	579	733	652	657	855
Medical supplies	134	93	211	166	249	198	263	282
Entertainment	2 572	1 733	3 110	3 373	5 193	4 092	4 566	6 564
Personal Care Products and Services	634	433	829	828	1 236	997	1 054	1 567
Reading	115	81	123	151	228	169	214	289
Education	1 051	610	756	1 117	2 809	1 729	1 722	4 497
Tobacco Products and Smoking Supplies	351	365	402	401	255	356	249	173
Miscellaneous	775	550	951	898	1 517	1 081	1 240	2 079
Cash Contributions	1 721	1 054	2 019	2 099	3 996	2 178	3 242	6 059
Personal Insurance and Pensions	5 424	2 254	6 449	8 275	15 856	10 536	13 835	21 758
Life and other personal insurance	317	190	350	399	755	437	677	1 078
Pensions and Social Security	5 106	2 064	6 099	7 876	15 100	10 099	13 158	20 681

Table 11-5. Consumer Expenditures, Averages by Quintiles of Income Before Taxes, 2011

(Number, dollar, percent.)

Item	All consumer units	Lowest 20 percent	Second 20 percent	Third 20 percent	Fourth 20 percent	Highest 20 percent
NUMBER OF CONSUMER UNITS (THOUSANDS)	122 287	24 435	24 429	24 473	24 520	24 430
CONSUMER UNIT CHARACTERISTICS						
Income Before Taxes	63 685	9 805	27 117	46 190	74 019	161 292
Income After Taxes	61 673	10 074	27 230	45 563	72 169	153 326
Age of Reference Person	50.0	52.0	52.0	49.0	48.0	48.0
Average Number in Consumer Unit						
All persons	2.5	1.7	2.2	2.6	2.8	3.2
Children under 18 years	0.6	0.4	0.5	0.7	0.7	0.8
Persons 65 years and over	0.3	0.4	0.5	0.4	0.3	0.2
Earners	1.3	0.5	0.9	1.3	1.7	2.0
Vehicles	1.9	1.0	1.5	1.9	2.3	2.8
Percent Distribution						
Male	47	37	43	48	52	54
Female	53	63	57	52	48	46
Percent Homeowner	65	39	53	65	79	88
With mortgage	40	12	23	40	57	70
Without mortgage	25	28	30	26	22	18
AVERAGE ANNUAL EXPENDITURES	49 705	22 001	32 092	42 403	57 460	94 551
Food	6 458	3 547	4 659	5 620	7 466	10 991
Food at home	3 838	2 448	3 051	3 496	4 364	5 828
Cereals and bakery products	531	344	428	480	603	798
Meats, poultry, fish, and eggs	832	532	703	745	929	1 252
Dairy products	407	253	317	380	458	626
Fruits and vegetables	715	448	566	633	791	1 136
Other food at home	1 353	871	1 038	1 257	1 582	2 015
Food away from home	2 620	1 099	1 608	2 125	3 103	5 163
Alcoholic Beverages	456	170	265	324	528	994
Housing	16 803	8 771	12 136	14 944	18 840	29 321
Shelter	9 825	5 159	6 969	8 611	10 815	17 572
Owned dwellings	6 148	1 638	2 957	4 819	7 635	13 688
Rented dwellings	3 029	3 324	3 758	3 436	2 585	2 046
Other lodging	648	197	255	356	594	1 839
Utilities, fuels, and public services	3 727	2 284	3 072	3 687	4 280	5 309
Household operations	1 122	430	718	829	1 223	2 411
Housekeeping supplies	615	344	440	542	694	1 052
Household furnishings and equipment	1 514	553	936	1 275	1 828	2 976
Apparel and Services	1 740	850	1 140	1 453	1 988	3 266
Transportation	8 293	3 256	5 142	7 592	10 205	15 264
Vehicle purchases (net outlay)	2 669	827	1 358	2 208	3 392	5 557
Gasoline and motor oil	2 655	1 227	1 981	2 694	3 295	4 073
Other vehicle expenses	2 454	1 020	1 599	2 322	3 043	4 281
Public transportation	516	182	204	367	475	1 352
Health Care	3 313	1 489	2 611	3 319	3 994	5 149
Health insurance	1 922	875	1 613	1 951	2 360	2 811
Medical services	768	275	495	756	939	1 373
Drugs	489	278	418	496	532	722
Medical supplies	134	62	85	117	162	244
Entertainment	2 572	981	1 622	2 121	3 107	5 027
Personal Care Products and Services	634	270	408	549	742	1 202
Reading	115	50	72	101	135	219
Education	1 051	807	474	562	827	2 585
Tobacco Products and Smoking Supplies	351	316	359	409	403	266
Miscellaneous	775	385	579	593	883	1 434
Cash Contributions	1 721	687	931	1 311	1 910	3 766
Personal Insurance and Pensions	5 424	422	1 693	3 505	6 431	15 068
Life and other personal insurance	317	81	218	217	353	717
Pensions and Social Security	5 106	341	1 474	3 288	6 078	14 351

Table 11-6. Consumer Expenditures, Averages by Occupation of Reference Person, 2011

(Number, dollar, percent.)

Item	Self-employed workers	Wage and salary earners						Retired	All others, including those not reporting
		Total wage and salary earners	Managers and professional workers	Technical sales and clerical workers	Service workers	Construction workers and mechanics	Operators, fabricators, and laborers		
NUMBER OF CONSUMER UNITS (THOUSANDS)	5 288	76 476	30 520	20 233	13 165	3 852	8 706	21 891	18 631
CONSUMER UNIT CHARACTERISTICS									
Income Before Taxes	83 041	75 319	103 075	64 780	49 313	58 862	49 112	38 340	40 217
Income After Taxes	80 285	72 683	98 601	62 654	48 644	57 336	48 268	37 429	39 686
Age of Reference Person	49.1	43.7	44.8	42.8	42.8	43.2	43.3	73.9	46.2
Average Number in Consumer Unit									
All persons	2.7	2.6	2.6	2.6	2.7	2.9	2.8	1.7	2.8
Children under 18 years	0.8	0.7	0.7	0.7	0.7	0.9	0.8	0.1	0.9
Persons 65 years and over	0.2	0.1	0.1	0.1	0.2	0.1	0.1	1.2	0.2
Earners	1.7	1.7	1.7	1.7	1.7	1.7	1.7	0.2	0.6
Vehicles	2.3	2.0	2.2	1.9	1.7	2.3	2.0	1.6	1.5
Percent Distribution									
Male	59	52	48	41	49	91	74	41	30
Female	41	48	52	59	51	9	26	59	70
Percent Homeowner	71	63	74	58	50	62	57	81	50
With mortgage	46	47	58	43	34	46	40	22	30
Without mortgage	25	16	16	15	15	16	17	60	20
AVERAGE ANNUAL EXPENDITURES	60 041	54 885	69 177	50 000	40 955	46 197	40 722	38 302	38 932
Food	7 407	6 896	8 171	6 462	5 491	6 238	5 707	5 197	5 883
Food at home	4 395	3 893	4 442	3 593	3 209	3 929	3 638	3 378	3 975
Cereals and bakery products	623	533	609	508	435	535	466	481	549
Meats, poultry, fish, and eggs	900	839	905	768	719	929	919	710	925
Dairy products	513	409	481	378	315	368	382	368	410
Fruits and vegetables	816	725	871	646	586	673	607	658	710
Other food at home	1 543	1 387	1 575	1 292	1 155	1 423	1 263	1 162	1 381
Food away from home	3 012	3 003	3 730	2 869	2 281	2 309	2 069	1 819	1 908
Alcoholic Beverages	761	521	634	516	374	529	335	346	237
Housing	19 123	18 262	22 425	17 081	14 420	15 600	13 348	13 583	13 934
Shelter	11 313	10 933	13 547	10 228	8 643	8 919	7 758	7 064	8 102
Owned dwellings	7 430	6 934	9 548	6 012	4 383	5 436	4 433	4 843	4 091
Rented dwellings	2 950	3 336	2 887	3 778	3 943	3 078	3 082	1 510	3 578
Other lodging	933	663	1 113	437	317	405	244	712	432
Utilities, fuels, and public services	4 061	3 838	4 238	3 719	3 374	3 739	3 460	3 470	3 476
Household operations	1 265	1 225	1 707	1 099	754	974	653	1 056	737
Housekeeping supplies	699	618	753	566	476	550	492	666	518
Household furnishings and equipment	1 785	1 648	2 181	1 469	1 173	1 418	985	1 327	1 101
Apparel and Services	1 732	1 888	2 288	1 878	1 396	1 362	1 436	1 286	1 675
Transportation	9 244	9 491	11 212	8 938	7 409	8 848	8 187	5 745	6 111
Vehicle purchases (net outlay)	2 518	3 174	3 906	2 897	2 340	2 755	2 701	1 618	1 871
Gasoline and motor oil	3 022	3 001	3 245	2 853	2 616	3 393	2 896	1 751	2 192
Other vehicle expenses	2 875	2 744	3 170	2 754	2 091	2 471	2 344	1 950	1 747
Public transportation	829	572	892	434	362	230	246	426	302
Health Care	4 132	3 069	3 946	2 819	2 102	2 343	2 347	4 664	2 493
Health insurance	2 295	1 734	2 203	1 581	1 247	1 406	1 329	2 953	1 376
Medical services	1 077	780	1 032	736	465	504	595	833	551
Drugs	582	427	542	388	303	324	337	699	470
Medical supplies	177	128	168	114	86	109	86	178	96
Entertainment	3 379	2 772	3 721	2 367	1 937	2 085	1 913	2 116	2 059
Personal Care Products and Services	687	691	919	608	521	414	443	560	476
Reading	142	113	169	93	68	57	57	155	71
Education	1 079	1 242	1 872	878	877	600	712	208	1 247
Tobacco Products and Smoking Supplies	316	358	239	372	381	649	575	220	485
Miscellaneous	1 223	799	1 021	734	602	751	488	748	578
Cash Contributions	1 978	1 733	2 522	1 287	1 172	1 576	921	2 210	1 024
Personal Insurance and Pensions	8 840	7 052	10 038	5 966	4 205	5 145	4 252	1 263	2 660
Life and other personal insurance	477	339	499	281	188	198	207	267	239
Pensions and Social Security	8 363	6 712	9 539	5 685	4 017	4 947	4 045	996	2 420

Table 11-7. Consumer Expenditures, Averages by Number of Earners, 2011

(Number, dollar, percent.)

Item	All consumer units	Single consumer		Consumer units of two or more persons			
		No earner	One earner	No earner	One earner	Two earners	Three or more earners
NUMBER OF CONSUMER UNITS (THOUSANDS)	122 287	15 120	20 990	11 874	26 302	38 387	9 614
CONSUMER UNIT CHARACTERISTICS							
Income Before Taxes	63 685	18 804	45 875	31 943	60 959	92 683	104 027
Income After Taxes	61 673	18 654	43 613	31 889	59 273	89 449	101 208
Age of Reference Person	49.7	67.5	43.9	63.8	47.7	43.6	47.0
Average Number in Consumer Unit							
All persons	2.5	1.0	1.0	2.4	3.1	3.1	4.5
Children under 18 years	0.6	X	X	0.4	1.1	0.9	1.1
Persons 65 years and over	0.3	0.7	0.1	1.2	0.3	0.1	0.1
Earners	1.3	X	1.0	X	1.0	2.0	3.3
Vehicles	1.9	0.9	1.2	1.7	1.9	2.4	3.1
Percent Distribution							
Male	47	37	54	44	41	52	47
Female	53	63	46	56	59	48	53
Percent Homeowner	65	57	45	74	65	73	77
With mortgage	40	12	31	21	42	57	58
Without mortgage	25	45	14	53	24	16	18
AVERAGE ANNUAL EXPENDITURES	49 705	23 640	35 529	38 183	50 945	64 755	72 867
Food	6 458	2 950	4 083	5 876	6 891	8 082	10 416
Food at home	3 838	2 049	2 087	3 948	4 315	4 558	6 253
Cereals and bakery products	531	303	273	559	589	632	868
Meats, poultry, fish, and eggs	832	383	406	865	976	969	1 518
Dairy products	407	220	222	426	446	492	642
Fruits and vegetables	715	415	393	719	804	846	1 135
Other food at home	1 353	727	793	1 380	1 499	1 619	2 090
Food away from home	2 620	901	1 996	1 928	2 576	3 524	4 163
Alcoholic Beverages	456	144	514	340	365	594	700
Housing	16 803	9 913	12 565	13 673	17 743	21 058	21 164
Shelter	9 825	5 753	8 201	6 948	10 186	12 418	11 988
Owned dwellings	6 148	2 828	3 878	4 392	6 258	8 601	8 398
Rented dwellings	3 029	2 723	3 962	1 835	3 182	2 959	2 815
Other lodging	648	203	361	722	746	859	775
Utilities, fuels, and public services	3 727	2 313	2 429	3 765	4 105	4 314	5 354
Household operations	1 122	844	583	872	1 096	1 633	1 081
Housekeeping supplies	615	374	332	683	661	754	842
Household furnishings and equipment	1 514	629	1 020	1 404	1 694	1 939	1 898
Apparel and Services	1 740	810	1 160	1 367	1 902	2 146	2 976
Transportation	8 293	2 713	5 552	5 673	8 477	11 267	14 025
Vehicle purchases (net outlay)	2 669	585	1 703	1 482	2 687	3 864	4 696
Gasoline and motor oil	2 655	908	1 753	1 937	2 804	3 502	4 466
Other vehicle expenses	2 454	1 015	1 700	1 877	2 467	3 234	4 031
Public transportation	516	205	396	376	520	667	833
Health Care	3 313	2 522	1 817	4 662	3 584	3 688	3 910
Health insurance	1 922	1 514	1 030	2 976	2 059	2 091	2 161
Medical services	768	496	446	752	849	940	1 001
Drugs	489	396	255	766	539	507	594
Medical supplies	134	117	86	169	136	150	154
Entertainment	2 572	1 224	1 728	2 214	2 597	3 456	3 407
Personal Care Products and Services	634	346	416	533	665	798	979
Reading	115	97	86	133	115	131	129
Education	1 051	522	968	353	945	1 259	2 389
Tobacco Products and Smoking Supplies	351	218	282	332	384	376	539
Miscellaneous	775	524	613	807	718	979	806
Cash Contributions	1 721	1 372	1 499	1 876	1 744	1 901	1 783
Personal Insurance and Pensions	5 424	285	4 247	345	4 815	9 021	9 648
Life and other personal insurance	317	132	213	231	353	420	433
Pensions and Social Security	5 106	¹153	4 034	¹114	4 462	8 601	9 214

¹Data are likely to have large sampling errors.
X = Not applicable.

Table 11-8. Consumer Expenditures, Averages by Size of Consumer Unit, 2011

(Number, dollar, percent.)

Item	All consumer units	One person	Two or more persons	Two persons	Three persons	Four persons	Five or more persons
NUMBER OF CONSUMER UNITS (THOUSANDS)	122 287	36 110	86 177	38 445	18 886	16 245	12 601
CONSUMER UNIT CHARACTERISTICS							
Income Before Taxes	63 685	34 540	75 897	69 877	76 582	88 037	77 586
Income After Taxes	61 673	33 162	73 620	67 287	73 832	85 776	76 954
Age of Reference Person	49.7	53.8	48.0	54.2	44.9	41.7	42.0
Average Number in Consumer Unit							
All persons	2.5	1.0	3.1	2.0	3.0	4.0	5.7
Children under 18 years	0.6	X	0.9	0.1	0.7	1.6	2.7
Persons 65 years and over	0.3	0.3	0.3	0.5	0.2	0.1	0.2
Earners	1.3	0.6	1.6	1.2	1.7	1.9	2.1
Vehicles	1.9	1.1	2.2	2.1	2.2	2.4	2.4
Percent Distribution							
Male	47	46	47	49	43	46	46
Female	53	54	53	51	57	54	54
Percent Homeowner	65	50	71	75	68	70	66
With mortgage	40	23	47	40	48	58	54
Without mortgage	25	27	24	34	20	13	12
AVERAGE ANNUAL EXPENDITURES	49 705	30 613	57 614	52 385	58 388	65 597	62 429
Food	6 458	3 638	7 590	6 431	7 466	8 983	9 747
Food at home	3 838	2 072	4 545	3 691	4 410	5 411	6 400
Cereals and bakery products	531	285	629	502	596	782	893
Meats, poultry, fish, and eggs	832	397	1 007	776	984	1 224	1 510
Dairy products	407	221	481	393	464	567	682
Fruits and vegetables	715	402	840	703	804	980	1 159
Other food at home	1 353	767	1 588	1 318	1 563	1 858	2 156
Food away from home	2 620	1 567	3 045	2 740	3 056	3 571	3 347
Alcoholic Beverages	456	370	491	569	448	449	358
Housing	16 803	11 456	19 034	17 119	19 371	21 886	20 694
Shelter	9 825	7 176	10 935	9 851	11 026	12 750	11 769
Owned dwellings	6 148	3 438	7 283	6 483	7 194	8 949	7 709
Rented dwellings	3 029	3 443	2 856	2 367	3 154	3 117	3 565
Other lodging	648	295	796	1 000	678	684	495
Utilities, fuels, and public services	3 727	2 380	4 291	3 843	4 313	4 767	5 011
Household operations	1 122	692	1 302	979	1 559	1 780	1 287
Housekeeping supplies	615	348	721	702	675	751	811
Household furnishings and equipment	1 514	859	1 784	1 744	1 797	1 838	1 816
Apparel and Services	1 740	1 021	2 030	1 634	2 016	2 404	2 842
Transportation	8 293	4 367	9 929	8 637	10 321	11 682	11 042
Vehicle purchases (net outlay)	2 669	1 235	3 269	2 638	3 479	4 251	3 618
Gasoline and motor oil	2 655	1 399	3 181	2 708	3 255	3 675	3 875
Other vehicle expenses	2 454	1 418	2 879	2 678	3 020	3 061	3 067
Public transportation	516	316	600	614	567	696	481
Health Care	3 313	2 112	3 815	4 197	3 744	3 455	3 209
Health insurance	1 922	1 232	2 211	2 450	2 130	2 012	1 861
Medical services	768	467	894	903	992	869	749
Drugs	489	314	561	672	487	453	467
Medical supplies	134	99	148	172	134	121	133
Entertainment	2 572	1 522	3 005	2 915	2 876	3 416	2 957
Personal Care Products and Services	634	388	735	698	737	806	763
Reading	115	90	126	147	117	112	92
Education	1 051	782	1 163	746	1 400	1 764	1 310
Tobacco Products and Smoking Supplies	351	255	390	352	422	399	447
Miscellaneous	775	577	857	887	900	753	835
Cash Contributions	1 721	1 446	1 836	2 225	1 547	1 468	1 559
Personal Insurance and Pensions	5 424	2 588	6 612	5 827	7 023	8 019	6 576
Life and other personal insurance	317	179	375	366	431	387	302
Pensions and Social Security	5 106	2 409	6 237	5 461	6 592	7 632	6 274

X = Not applicable.

Table 11-9. Consumer Expenditures, Averages by Composition of Consumer Unit, 2011

(Number, dollar, percent.)

Item	Husband and wife consumer units						Other husband and wife consumer units	One parent, at least one child under 18 years	Single person and other consumer units
	Total	Husband and wife only	Husband and wife with children						
			Total	Oldest child under 6 years	Oldest child 6 to 17 years	Oldest child 18 years or over			
NUMBER OF CONSUMER UNITS (THOUSANDS)	60 144	25 270	29 097	5 825	14 661	8 612	5 777	6 956	55 187
CONSUMER UNIT CHARACTERISTICS									
Income Before Taxes	86 700	78 823	93 677	91 014	93 029	96 583	86 014	37 188	41 942
Income After Taxes	83 761	75 607	90 701	87 873	90 795	92 455	84 468	37 199	40 687
Age of Reference Person	49.8	58.1	42.6	32.0	40.9	52.5	50.2	37.7	51.1
Average Number in Consumer Unit									
All persons	3.2	2.0	4.0	3.5	4.2	3.9	5.0	2.9	1.7
Children under 18 years	0.9	X	1.6	1.5	2.2	0.6	1.5	1.7	0.2
Persons 65 years and over	0.4	0.7	0.1	(1)	(1)	0.2	0.6	(1)	0.3
Earners	1.6	1.2	1.9	1.7	1.7	2.3	2.2	0.9	0.9
Vehicles	2.5	2.4	2.6	2.1	2.5	3.0	2.7	1.1	1.3
Percent Distribution									
Male	53	55	51	54	51	48	50	16	44
Female	47	45	49	46	49	52	50	84	56
Percent Homeowner	80	85	76	66	76	84	78	37	52
With mortgage	54	44	61	61	64	58	60	26	27
Without mortgage	26	41	15	5	12	26	19	11	25
AVERAGE ANNUAL EXPENDITURES	63 972	57 658	69 724	65 948	70 709	70 412	63 925	37 553	35 709
Food	8 315	6 895	9 557	8 028	9 813	10 042	9 149	5 676	4 539
Food at home	4 944	3 935	5 785	5 010	5 877	6 080	5 792	3 526	2 674
Cereals and bakery products	687	535	820	673	864	832	771	519	362
Meats, poultry, fish, and eggs	1 084	820	1 275	921	1 276	1 480	1 492	790	564
Dairy products	533	420	636	597	650	635	576	355	276
Fruits and vegetables	926	761	1 067	996	1 059	1 122	1 041	600	500
Other food at home	1 714	1 400	1 987	1 824	2 030	2 011	1 912	1 262	972
Food away from home	3 370	2 960	3 772	3 018	3 936	3 962	3 357	2 150	1 865
Alcoholic Beverages	515	610	459	424	459	479	307	246	421
Housing	20 664	18 329	22 788	25 009	23 158	20 648	20 185	14 563	12 882
Shelter	11 780	10 404	13 122	14 571	13 609	11 311	11 040	8 426	7 872
Owned dwellings	8 620	7 622	9 646	10 295	9 974	8 649	7 821	3 405	3 799
Rented dwellings	2 145	1 471	2 649	3 608	2 792	1 758	2 550	4 851	3 764
Other lodging	1 015	1 312	826	668	843	905	669	170	308
Utilities, fuels, and public services	4 540	4 073	4 797	3 989	4 856	5 244	5 288	3 445	2 876
Household operations	1 451	1 021	1 891	3 679	1 660	1 074	1 127	1 185	756
Housekeeping supplies	826	800	860	834	851	890	762	392	415
Household furnishings and equipment	2 067	2 029	2 118	1 935	2 182	2 129	1 969	1 115	964
Apparel and Services	2 184	1 715	2 541	2 157	2 587	2 687	2 745	1 835	1 243
Transportation	10 972	9 474	12 182	10 698	12 218	13 120	11 466	5 471	5 732
Vehicle purchases (net outlay)	3 609	2 793	4 302	3 562	4 382	4 666	3 686	1 394	1 805
Gasoline and motor oil	3 472	2 923	3 852	3 205	3 921	4 173	3 955	2 119	1 832
Other vehicle expenses	3 204	3 056	3 319	3 297	3 168	3 588	3 311	1 636	1 742
Public transportation	687	702	709	633	747	693	514	323	354
Health Care	4 479	5 127	3 910	3 486	3 753	4 465	4 489	1 892	2 222
Health insurance	2 619	3 004	2 268	2 161	2 157	2 530	2 708	797	1 304
Medical services	1 026	1 089	990	883	960	1 111	924	821	480
Drugs	661	829	505	328	485	658	701	211	337
Medical supplies	173	205	148	113	151	166	156	63	101
Entertainment	3 418	3 286	3 591	2 956	4 086	3 161	3 220	1 821	1 747
Personal Care Products and Services	819	761	884	707	915	938	785	548	444
Reading	148	177	132	107	136	141	104	52	88
Education	1 340	716	1 904	729	1 739	2 978	1 246	553	798
Tobacco Products and Smoking Supplies	342	293	320	204	312	411	666	322	364
Miscellaneous	897	902	865	973	811	883	1 070	668	656
Cash Contributions	2 227	2 824	1 833	1 589	1 877	1 924	1 595	665	1 303
Personal Insurance and Pensions	7 652	6 549	8 759	8 882	8 843	8 533	6 899	3 241	3 270
Life and other personal insurance	463	473	473	509	443	501	368	135	181
Pensions and Social Security	7 189	6 077	8 286	8 373	8 400	8 032	6 531	3 107	3 089

[1]Value less than or equal to 0.05.
X = Not applicable.

Table 11-10. Consumer Expenditures, Averages by Age of Reference Person, 2011

(Number, dollar, percent.)

Item	All consumer units	Under 25 years	25 to 34 years	35 to 44 years	45 to 54 years	55 to 64 years	65 years and over	65 to 74 years	75 years and over
NUMBER OF CONSUMER UNITS (THOUSANDS)	122 287	7 743	20 463	21 699	24 821	21 688	25 873	14 079	11 794
CONSUMER UNIT CHARACTERISTICS									
Income Before Taxes	63 685	27 514	58 179	77 376	78 519	75 517	43 232	52 521	32 144
Income After Taxes	61 673	27 495	56 851	75 537	75 234	72 115	42 326	51 161	31 779
Age of Reference Person	49.7	21.7	29.5	39.6	49.6	59.2	74.8	68.9	81.8
Average Number in Consumer Unit									
All persons	2.5	2.1	2.9	3.3	2.8	2.1	1.7	1.9	1.6
Children under 18 years	0.6	0.5	1.1	1.4	0.7	0.2	0.1	0.1	(¹)
Persons 65 years and over	0.3	(¹)	(¹)	(¹)	0.1	0.1	1.4	1.4	1.3
Earners	1.3	1.3	1.5	1.6	1.7	1.3	0.5	0.6	0.3
Vehicles	1.9	1.1	1.7	2.0	2.3	2.1	1.6	1.9	1.3
Percent Distribution									
Male	47	47	48	48	46	49	43	46	39
Female	53	53	52	52	54	51	57	54	61
Percent Homeowner	65	15	43	62	72	79	81	83	79
With mortgage	40	10	38	53	54	46	22	31	12
Without mortgage	25	5	5	9	18	32	59	52	67
AVERAGE ANNUAL EXPENDITURES	49 705	29 912	48 097	57 271	58 050	53 616	39 173	44 646	32 688
Food	6 458	4 354	6 211	7 765	7 424	6 520	5 158	5 804	4 408
Food at home	3 838	2 382	3 447	4 594	4 421	3 908	3 309	3 594	2 980
Cereals and bakery products	531	336	479	644	610	515	469	479	458
Meats, poultry, fish, and eggs	832	527	733	1 006	965	894	671	759	569
Dairy products	407	244	379	481	475	394	359	387	326
Fruits and vegetables	715	424	627	841	803	734	663	713	605
Other food at home	1 353	850	1 230	1 622	1 567	1 372	1 147	1 255	1 021
Food away from home	2 620	1 973	2 764	3 171	3 003	2 611	1 849	2 210	1 429
Alcoholic Beverages	456	418	513	497	494	468	338	422	241
Housing	16 803	10 282	17 026	19 979	18 782	17 173	13 706	15 105	12 046
Shelter	9 825	6 732	10 480	12 068	11 111	9 755	7 178	7 966	6 237
Owned dwellings	6 148	1 277	4 826	7 844	7 774	7 002	4 953	5 802	3 939
Rented dwellings	3 029	5 111	5 338	3 714	2 582	1 784	1 480	1 234	1 772
Other lodging	648	345	316	510	756	969	745	929	525
Utilities, fuels, and public services	3 727	1 918	3 296	4 065	4 318	4 053	3 485	3 782	3 131
Household operations	1 122	505	1 359	1 494	969	958	1 093	952	1 261
Housekeeping supplies	615	268	420	702	691	722	636	695	568
Household furnishings and equipment	1 514	858	1 471	1 650	1 693	1 685	1 314	1 711	849
Apparel and Services	1 740	1 448	1 818	2 227	1 978	1 719	1 129	1 195	1 052
Transportation	8 293	5 474	8 860	9 700	9 505	8 991	5 751	6 962	4 309
Vehicle purchases (net outlay)	2 669	2 068	3 203	3 434	2 624	2 953	1 588	1 858	1 267
Gasoline and motor oil	2 655	1 840	2 726	3 188	3 270	2 713	1 755	2 218	1 201
Other vehicle expenses	2 454	1 265	2 402	2 565	2 985	2 746	1 994	2 343	1 581
Public transportation	516	300	529	513	626	579	414	543	260
Health Care	3 313	841	2 094	2 762	3 411	4 048	4 769	5 038	4 449
Health insurance	1 922	456	1 237	1 581	1 801	2 196	3 076	3 154	2 982
Medical services	768	254	546	694	942	1 013	786	894	656
Drugs	489	93	229	377	515	690	714	791	623
Medical supplies	134	38	82	110	153	149	193	199	188
Entertainment	2 572	1 345	2 423	2 926	3 169	2 769	2 009	2 493	1 437
Personal Care Products and Services	634	324	570	736	709	695	567	609	517
Reading	115	45	74	100	113	149	157	163	148
Education	1 051	2 253	1 049	818	1 879	866	247	262	229
Tobacco Products and Smoking Supplies	351	256	378	343	465	401	212	289	120
Miscellaneous	775	285	606	781	947	931	753	821	674
Cash Contributions	1 721	367	1 130	1 570	1 722	2 112	2 392	2 526	2 231
Personal Insurance and Pensions	5 424	2 220	5 346	7 068	7 453	6 775	1 985	2 957	825
Life and other personal insurance	317	67	138	308	401	534	280	361	183
Pensions and Social Security	5 106	2 154	5 207	6 760	7 052	6 242	1 706	2 596	643

¹Value less than or equal to 0.05.

Table 11-11. Consumer Expenditures, Averages by Race of Reference Person, 2011

(Number, dollar, percent.)

| Item | All consumer units | White, Asian, and other races | | | Black |
		Total	White and other races	Asian	
NUMBER OF CONSUMER UNITS (THOUSANDS)	122 287	107 168	102 121	5 048	15 118
CONSUMER UNIT CHARACTERISTICS					
Income Before Taxes	63 685	66 243	65 295	85 415	45 552
Income After Taxes	61 673	64 018	63 153	81 521	45 052
Age of Reference Person	49.7	50.0	50.3	45.1	47.4
Average Number in Consumer Unit					
All persons	2.5	2.5	2.5	2.7	2.6
Children under 18 years	0.6	0.6	0.6	0.6	0.7
Persons 65 years and over	0.3	0.3	0.3	0.3	0.2
Earners	1.3	1.3	1.3	1.4	1.1
Vehicles	1.9	2.0	2.0	1.6	1.3
Percent Distribution					
Male	47	48	47	58	38
Female	53	52	53	42	62
Percent Homeowner	65	68	68	54	45
With mortgage	40	42	42	38	31
Without mortgage	25	26	27	16	14
AVERAGE ANNUAL EXPENDITURES	49 705	51 538	51 113	60 136	36 644
Food	6 458	6 695	6 623	8 163	4 743
Food at home	3 838	3 955	3 931	4 439	2 989
Cereals and bakery products	531	548	545	618	405
Meats, poultry, fish, and eggs	832	834	821	1 094	822
Dairy products	407	429	434	337	246
Fruits and vegetables	715	741	725	1 059	527
Other food at home	1 353	1 403	1 407	1 332	988
Food away from home	2 620	2 740	2 692	3 724	1 754
Alcoholic Beverages	456	492	501	311	199
Housing	16 803	17 199	17 019	20 834	13 985
Shelter	9 825	10 067	9 859	14 269	8 111
Owned dwellings	6 148	6 500	6 416	8 209	3 651
Rented dwellings	3 029	2 855	2 756	4 843	4 268
Other lodging	648	712	687	1 217	192
Utilities, fuels, and public services	3 727	3 730	3 753	3 279	3 701
Household operations	1 122	1 166	1 145	1 593	810
Housekeeping supplies	615	641	653	393	426
Household furnishings and equipment	1 514	1 594	1 609	1 300	938
Apparel and Services	1 740	1 750	1 721	2 324	1 669
Transportation	8 293	8 623	8 542	10 281	5 944
Vehicle purchases (net outlay)	2 669	2 818	2 787	3 450	1 608
Gasoline and motor oil	2 655	2 716	2 737	2 283	2 221
Other vehicle expenses	2 454	2 540	2 514	3 075	1 833
Public transportation	516	549	503	1 473	283
Health Care	3 313	3 512	3 542	2 919	1 897
Health insurance	1 922	2 019	2 025	1 882	1 238
Medical services	768	834	842	667	300
Drugs	489	516	527	285	300
Medical supplies	134	145	148	84	59
Entertainment	2 572	2 731	2 753	2 301	1 432
Personal Care Products and Services	634	648	650	602	533
Reading	115	125	126	111	48
Education	1 051	1 131	1 075	2 267	479
Tobacco Products and Smoking Supplies	351	363	374	152	260
Miscellaneous	775	811	817	696	521
Cash Contributions	1 721	1 774	1 793	1 405	1 341
Personal Insurance and Pensions	5 424	5 682	5 579	7 771	3 593
Life and other personal insurance	317	327	326	337	250
Pensions and Social Security	5 106	5 355	5 252	7 434	3 344

Table 11-12. Consumer Expenditures, Averages by Hispanic Origin of Reference Person, 2011

(Number, dollar, percent.)

Item	All consumer units	Hispanic[1]	Not Hispanic		
			Total	White, Asian, and other races	Black
NUMBER OF CONSUMER UNITS (THOUSANDS)	122 287	15 222	107 065	92 163	14 901
CONSUMER UNIT CHARACTERISTICS					
Income Before Taxes	63 685	49 966	65 635	68 907	45 400
Income After Taxes	61 673	49 501	63 404	66 396	44 899
Age of Reference Person	49.7	42.9	50.7	51.2	47.5
Average Number in Consumer Unit					
All persons	2.5	3.4	2.4	2.4	2.6
Children under 18 years	0.6	1.1	0.6	0.5	0.7
Persons 65 years and over	0.3	0.2	0.3	0.4	0.2
Earners	1.3	1.6	1.2	1.3	1.1
Vehicles	1.9	1.6	1.9	2.0	1.3
Percent Distribution					
Male	47	49	46	48	37
Female	53	51	54	52	63
Percent Homeowner	65	46	68	71	45
With mortgage	40	32	41	43	31
Without mortgage	25	14	26	28	14
AVERAGE ANNUAL EXPENDITURES	49 705	42 086	50 782	53 056	36 573
Food	6 458	6 373	6 470	6 743	4 717
Food at home	3 838	3 849	3 836	3 970	2 971
Cereals and bakery products	531	493	536	556	402
Meats, poultry, fish, and eggs	832	968	814	813	825
Dairy products	407	388	409	435	243
Fruits and vegetables	715	778	707	735	521
Other food at home	1 353	1 221	1 371	1 431	979
Food away from home	2 620	2 524	2 634	2 773	1 746
Alcoholic Beverages	456	281	480	525	192
Housing	16 803	15 648	16 965	17 449	13 943
Shelter	9 825	9 766	9 834	10 122	8 053
Owned dwellings	6 148	4 713	6 352	6 791	3 638
Rented dwellings	3 029	4 806	2 777	2 543	4 222
Other lodging	648	248	705	788	193
Utilities, fuels, and public services	3 727	3 462	3 764	3 773	3 713
Household operations	1 122	755	1 174	1 233	812
Housekeeping supplies	615	536	625	656	425
Household furnishings and equipment	1 514	1 129	1 567	1 666	940
Apparel and Services	1 740	1 989	1 706	1 714	1 658
Transportation	8 293	7 520	8 402	8 798	5 938
Vehicle purchases (net outlay)	2 669	2 208	2 734	2 919	1 593
Gasoline and motor oil	2 655	2 721	2 645	2 714	2 220
Other vehicle expenses	2 454	2 174	2 493	2 596	1 844
Public transportation	516	417	530	570	280
Health Care	3 313	1 774	3 531	3 793	1 906
Health insurance	1 922	1 008	2 052	2 182	1 247
Medical services	768	453	812	896	296
Drugs	489	237	524	560	304
Medical supplies	134	75	142	155	59
Entertainment	2 572	1 738	2 688	2 888	1 431
Personal Care Products and Services	634	611	638	654	531
Reading	115	46	125	138	48
Education	1 051	624	1 111	1 212	485
Tobacco Products and Smoking Supplies	351	164	377	396	262
Miscellaneous	775	476	817	864	526
Cash Contributions	1 721	812	1 850	1 930	1 353
Personal Insurance and Pensions	5 424	4 030	5 622	5 951	3 583
Life and other personal insurance	317	115	346	361	251
Pensions and Social Security	5 106	3 915	5 276	5 590	3 332

[1]May be of any race.

Table 11-13. Consumer Expenditures, Averages by Education of Reference Person, 2011

(Number, dollar, percent.)

Item	All consumer units	Less than a college graduate					College graduate or more		
		Total	Less than a high school graduate	High school graduate	High school graduate with some college	Associate's degree	Total	Bachelor's degree	Master's, professional, or doctoral degree
NUMBER OF CONSUMER UNITS (THOUSANDS)	122 287	85 229	16 146	30 810	25 361	12 912	37 058	23 578	13 480
CONSUMER UNIT CHARACTERISTICS									
Income Before Taxes	63 685	48 337	32 564	46 370	52 965	63 664	98 983	90 962	113 013
Income After Taxes	61 673	47 482	32 502	45 664	51 734	62 203	94 311	87 120	106 888
Age of Reference Person	49.7	50.3	54.6	51.6	47.2	47.8	48.4	47.1	50.6
Average Number in Consumer Unit									
All persons	2.5	2.5	2.8	2.5	2.3	2.6	2.5	2.5	2.4
Children under 18 years	0.6	0.6	0.8	0.6	0.6	0.7	0.6	0.6	0.6
Persons 65 years and over	0.3	0.3	0.5	0.4	0.3	0.2	0.3	0.3	0.3
Earners	1.3	1.2	1.0	1.2	1.2	1.4	1.4	1.4	1.4
Vehicles	1.9	1.8	1.4	1.9	1.9	2.1	2.0	2.0	2.0
Percent Distribution									
Male	47	45	43	46	47	40	51	50	52
Female	53	55	57	54	53	60	49	50	48
Percent Homeowner	65	60	52	63	58	67	76	74	79
With mortgage	40	34	23	34	37	44	54	53	55
Without mortgage	25	26	29	29	21	23	22	21	24
AVERAGE ANNUAL EXPENDITURES	49 705	41 253	29 951	39 704	45 355	50 819	68 903	65 051	75 731
Food	6 458	5 732	4 971	5 648	5 907	6 486	8 026	7 615	8 807
Food at home	3 838	3 591	3 564	3 595	3 510	3 774	4 365	4 184	4 718
Cereals and bakery products	531	495	486	495	483	528	606	590	639
Meats, poultry, fish, and eggs	832	818	883	812	779	839	862	838	910
Dairy products	407	371	359	357	367	424	484	465	521
Fruits and vegetables	715	637	651	642	627	627	881	816	1 009
Other food at home	1 353	1 270	1 186	1 288	1 254	1 357	1 532	1 476	1 640
Food away from home	2 620	2 142	1 407	2 053	2 397	2 712	3 661	3 431	4 089
Alcoholic Beverages	456	333	155	287	427	465	722	689	785
Housing	16 803	14 042	10 843	13 571	15 259	16 744	23 123	21 702	25 621
Shelter	9 825	7 944	6 238	7 585	8 787	9 281	14 152	13 245	15 737
Owned dwellings	6 148	4 493	2 651	4 443	5 008	5 904	9 954	9 192	11 287
Rented dwellings	3 029	3 102	3 441	2 845	3 279	2 945	2 862	2 926	2 751
Other lodging	648	349	146	297	500	432	1 335	1 127	1 699
Utilities, fuels, and public services	3 727	3 530	3 074	3 622	3 484	3 968	4 180	4 091	4 337
Household operations	1 122	801	432	714	1 006	1 069	1 859	1 654	2 217
Housekeeping supplies	615	545	429	536	551	692	762	746	795
Household furnishings and equipment	1 514	1 222	669	1 114	1 431	1 734	2 169	1 966	2 535
Apparel and Services	1 740	1 462	1 274	1 385	1 552	1 686	2 343	2 232	2 554
Transportation	8 293	7 257	4 859	7 120	8 061	8 964	10 662	10 565	10 813
Vehicle purchases (net outlay)	2 669	2 286	1 231	2 258	2 564	3 123	3 549	3 613	3 437
Gasoline and motor oil	2 655	2 538	2 006	2 552	2 613	3 021	2 924	2 934	2 905
Other vehicle expenses	2 454	2 141	1 388	2 061	2 533	2 466	3 158	3 192	3 082
Public transportation	516	292	233	249	351	354	1 031	825	1 390
Health Care	3 313	2 929	2 257	2 986	3 020	3 449	4 192	4 022	4 490
Health insurance	1 922	1 705	1 325	1 803	1 743	1 874	2 421	2 334	2 573
Medical services	768	647	444	612	703	876	1 045	980	1 157
Drugs	489	465	403	458	456	575	541	546	536
Medical supplies	134	111	85	113	119	124	185	162	225
Entertainment	2 572	2 108	1 223	1 967	2 465	2 822	3 616	3 499	3 822
Personal Care Products and Services	634	514	367	479	573	662	901	851	992
Reading	115	78	40	70	95	116	200	172	251
Education	1 051	662	252	380	1 109	966	1 943	1 900	2 019
Tobacco Products and Smoking Supplies	351	437	400	521	384	386	152	183	97
Miscellaneous	775	659	392	615	715	987	1 040	907	1 269
Cash Contributions	1 721	1 218	769	1 144	1 376	1 648	2 878	2 580	3 398
Personal Insurance and Pensions	5 424	3 822	2 150	3 533	4 413	5 438	9 108	8 134	10 812
Life and other personal insurance	317	248	136	264	218	406	477	414	585
Pensions and Social Security	5 106	3 574	2 014	3 269	4 195	5 032	8 631	7 719	10 226

Table 11-14. Consumer Expenditures, Averages by Housing Tenure and Type of Area, 2011

(Number, dollar, percent.)

Item	All consumer units	Housing tenure				Type of area			
		Homeowner			Renter	Urban			Rural
		Total	Homeowner with mortgage	Homeowner without mortgage		Total	Central city	Other urban	
NUMBER OF CONSUMER UNITS (THOUSANDS)	122 287	79 353	49 120	30 233	42 934	112 203	35 763	76 440	10 084
CONSUMER UNIT CHARACTERISTICS									
Income Before Taxes	63 685	76 634	89 156	56 289	39 751	64 986	56 256	69 070	49 207
Income After Taxes	61 673	73 883	85 962	54 257	39 107	62 902	54 520	66 823	48 003
Age of Reference Person	49.7	54.1	48.3	63.5	41.6	49.3	46.9	50.5	53.9
Average Number in Consumer Unit									
All persons	2.5	2.6	2.9	2.1	2.3	2.5	2.4	2.6	2.5
Children under 18 years	0.6	0.6	0.8	0.3	0.7	0.6	0.6	0.6	0.6
Persons 65 years and over	0.3	0.4	0.2	0.8	0.1	0.3	0.3	0.3	0.4
Earners	1.3	1.3	1.6	0.9	1.1	1.3	1.2	1.3	1.2
Vehicles	1.9	2.3	2.4	2.1	1.2	1.8	1.5	2.0	2.4
Percent Distribution									
Male	47	47	50	44	45	47	46	47	44
Female	53	53	50	56	55	53	54	53	56
Percent Homeowner	65	100	100	100	X	63	48	70	83
With mortgage	40	62	100	X	X	40	31	44	41
Without mortgage	25	38	X	100	X	23	17	26	42
AVERAGE ANNUAL EXPENDITURES	49 705	57 502	64 852	45 300	35 274	50 348	45 147	52 773	42 540
Food	6 458	7 244	7 666	6 402	4 996	6 489	6 102	6 666	6 090
Food at home	3 838	4 286	4 440	3 963	3 005	3 824	3 517	3 964	4 013
Cereals and bakery products	531	593	616	546	414	528	467	556	565
Meats, poultry, fish, and eggs	832	921	953	853	668	830	781	852	866
Dairy products	407	461	471	441	306	402	356	423	465
Fruits and vegetables	715	800	827	744	556	721	679	740	639
Other food at home	1 353	1 511	1 574	1 380	1 060	1 343	1 234	1 393	1 478
Food away from home	2 620	2 958	3 227	2 439	1 991	2 665	2 585	2 702	2 077
Alcoholic Beverages	456	500	536	427	376	470	530	443	290
Housing	16 803	18 680	22 380	12 653	13 330	17 226	16 039	17 779	12 115
Shelter	9 825	10 315	13 462	5 202	8 920	10 211	9 877	10 368	5 529
Owned dwellings	6 148	9 399	12 506	4 352	139	6 308	4 773	7 027	4 362
Rented dwellings	3 029	44	46	40	8 548	3 228	4 523	2 622	824
Other lodging	648	873	910	811	233	675	582	719	343
Utilities, fuels, and public services	3 727	4 412	4 682	3 973	2 460	3 723	3 259	3 940	3 766
Household operations	1 122	1 366	1 497	1 153	671	1 164	1 054	1 215	660
Housekeeping supplies	615	745	752	729	373	609	487	665	685
Household furnishings and equipment	1 514	1 842	1 987	1 596	905	1 519	1 362	1 591	1 475
Apparel and Services	1 740	1 882	2 014	1 632	1 474	1 771	1 773	1 770	1 371
Transportation	8 293	9 766	11 039	7 690	5 567	8 266	6 906	8 900	8 606
Vehicle purchases (net outlay)	2 669	3 200	3 757	2 295	1 687	2 646	2 156	2 876	2 916
Gasoline and motor oil	2 655	3 072	3 439	2 474	1 884	2 613	2 080	2 863	3 115
Other vehicle expenses	2 454	2 915	3 206	2 433	1 599	2 462	2 030	2 662	2 370
Public transportation	516	580	637	489	398	544	640	499	205
Health Care	3 313	4 220	4 012	4 564	1 635	3 303	2 637	3 615	3 426
Health insurance	1 922	2 452	2 290	2 715	943	1 922	1 524	2 108	1 928
Medical services	768	974	986	954	386	771	621	842	727
Drugs	489	623	579	698	240	477	381	521	632
Medical supplies	134	171	157	198	66	134	111	144	139
Entertainment	2 572	3 133	3 390	2 691	1 533	2 566	2 136	2 766	2 652
Personal Care Products and Services	634	728	780	636	460	644	576	675	526
Reading	115	143	139	149	65	117	104	124	94
Education	1 051	1 103	1 376	656	954	1 107	1 112	1 105	425
Tobacco Products and Smoking Supplies	351	327	347	295	394	336	315	347	507
Miscellaneous	775	920	940	890	507	773	663	824	798
Cash Contributions	1 721	2 138	1 951	2 441	951	1 746	1 492	1 865	1 438
Personal Insurance and Pensions	5 424	6 717	8 281	4 174	3 034	5 533	4 761	5 895	4 201
Life and other personal insurance	317	437	517	307	95	300	223	337	504
Pensions and Social Security	5 106	6 280	7 764	3 867	2 938	5 233	4 538	5 558	3 697

X = Not applicable.

Table 11-15. Consumer Expenditures, Averages by Population Size of Area of Residence, 2011

(Number, dollar, percent.)

Item	All consumer units	Outside urban area	Urban consumer units						
			Total	Less than 100,000	100,000 to 249,999	250,000 to 999,999	1,000,000 to 2,499,999	2,500,000 to 4,999,999	5,000,000 and over
NUMBER OF CONSUMER UNITS (THOUSANDS)	122 287	24 284	98 002	18 380	9 654	20 541	15 673	17 413	16 341
CONSUMER UNIT CHARACTERISTICS									
Income Before Taxes	63 685	58 489	64 972	49 560	59 222	60 185	70 781	77 091	73 240
Income After Taxes	61 673	56 922	62 851	48 494	58 003	58 598	68 198	73 530	70 700
Age of Reference Person	49.7	53.7	48.7	49.1	48.4	48.2	48.9	47.9	50.0
Average Number in Consumer Unit									
All persons	2.5	2.6	2.5	2.4	2.4	2.4	2.5	2.6	2.7
Children under 18 years	0.6	0.6	0.6	0.6	0.6	0.6	0.6	0.7	0.6
Persons 65 years and over	0.3	0.4	0.3	0.3	0.3	0.3	0.3	0.3	0.3
Earners	1.3	1.2	1.3	1.2	1.3	1.3	1.3	1.4	1.3
Vehicles	1.9	2.5	1.7	1.8	2.0	1.8	1.8	1.7	1.4
Percent Distribution									
Male	47	46	47	44	46	48	49	49	46
Female	53	54	53	56	54	52	51	51	54
Percent Homeowner	65	84	60	61	61	61	62	61	56
With mortgage	40	44	39	33	40	40	44	43	36
Without mortgage	25	40	21	27	21	22	18	17	20
AVERAGE ANNUAL EXPENDITURES	49 705	47 786	50 182	39 926	46 947	48 528	52 049	58 241	55 203
Food	6 458	6 256	6 507	5 591	6 169	6 418	6 754	7 055	6 958
Food at home	3 838	3 966	3 806	3 447	3 877	3 838	3 773	3 985	3 949
Cereals and bakery products	531	561	523	473	505	536	512	546	555
Meats, poultry, fish, and eggs	832	848	829	749	825	813	799	856	929
Dairy products	407	448	397	374	406	406	395	401	401
Fruits and vegetables	715	658	729	630	686	731	679	797	824
Other food at home	1 353	1 452	1 329	1 220	1 456	1 352	1 386	1 384	1 238
Food away from home	2 620	2 290	2 701	2 144	2 292	2 581	2 981	3 070	3 010
Alcoholic Beverages	456	376	476	340	388	418	557	584	548
Housing	16 803	14 377	17 405	12 654	15 704	16 197	17 928	20 349	21 640
Shelter	9 825	7 128	10 494	6 649	8 935	9 357	10 777	12 722	14 523
Owned dwellings	6 148	5 638	6 274	3 874	5 505	5 673	6 740	7 679	8 241
Rented dwellings	3 029	1 001	3 532	2 314	2 876	3 073	3 312	4 124	5 446
Other lodging	648	489	687	460	555	611	724	918	837
Utilities, fuels, and public services	3 727	3 981	3 664	3 399	3 664	3 487	3 614	4 013	3 859
Household operations	1 122	854	1 189	834	1 005	1 087	1 321	1 428	1 441
Housekeeping supplies	615	761	579	506	618	566	634	590	589
Household furnishings and equipment	1 514	1 653	1 480	1 268	1 481	1 701	1 583	1 596	1 228
Apparel and Services	1 740	1 510	1 796	1 340	1 756	1 602	1 968	1 975	2 192
Transportation	8 293	9 517	7 990	7 030	8 082	7 924	8 061	9 125	7 806
Vehicle purchases (net outlay)	2 669	3 264	2 521	2 307	3 087	2 538	2 473	2 827	2 127
Gasoline and motor oil	2 655	3 316	2 491	2 427	2 526	2 506	2 465	2 734	2 287
Other vehicle expenses	2 454	2 648	2 406	2 051	2 132	2 377	2 555	2 777	2 451
Public transportation	516	289	572	246	337	503	568	786	940
Health Care	3 313	3 702	3 217	2 939	3 309	3 337	3 203	3 317	3 230
Health insurance	1 922	2 171	1 860	1 679	2 026	1 899	1 910	1 955	1 769
Medical services	768	771	767	661	729	823	646	793	925
Drugs	489	620	457	440	403	492	502	440	439
Medical supplies	134	140	133	158	151	123	146	130	97
Entertainment	2 572	2 887	2 495	2 126	2 388	2 514	2 672	2 920	2 333
Personal Care Products and Services	634	607	641	495	556	654	692	736	687
Reading	115	109	117	106	107	126	111	134	113
Education	1 051	526	1 181	822	1 071	1 117	1 202	1 374	1 502
Tobacco Products and Smoking Supplies	351	472	320	395	421	313	311	321	195
Miscellaneous	775	878	749	554	685	693	784	1 027	745
Cash Contributions	1 721	1 597	1 751	1 568	1 633	1 800	1 838	2 135	1 475
Personal Insurance and Pensions	5 424	4 972	5 535	3 966	4 678	5 418	5 969	7 189	5 778
Life and other personal insurance	317	425	290	236	309	294	323	320	274
Pensions and Social Security	5 106	4 547	5 245	3 730	4 369	5 123	5 646	6 870	5 504

Table 11-16. Consumer Expenditures, Averages by Region of Residence, 2011

(Number, dollar, percent.)

Item	All consumer units	Region[1]			
		Northeast	South	Midwest	West
NUMBER OF CONSUMER UNITS (THOUSANDS)	122 287	22 538	27 107	44 901	27 741
CONSUMER UNIT CHARACTERISTICS					
Income Before Taxes	63 685	71 733	60 897	58 780	67 810
Income After Taxes	61 673	69 334	59 394	57 205	64 909
Age of Reference Person	49.7	50.8	49.1	50.2	48.7
Average Number in Consumer Unit					
All persons	2.5	2.4	2.4	2.5	2.6
Children under 18 years	0.6	0.6	0.6	0.6	0.7
Persons 65 years and over	0.3	0.4	0.3	0.3	0.3
Earners	1.3	1.3	1.3	1.2	1.3
Vehicles	1.9	1.6	2.0	1.9	2.0
Percent Distribution					
Male	47	45	46	45	50
Female	53	55	54	55	50
Percent Homeowner	65	64	68	68	58
With mortgage	40	39	43	39	39
Without mortgage	25	24	25	28	19
AVERAGE ANNUAL EXPENDITURES	49 705	54 547	47 192	45 699	54 745
Food	6 458	6 799	6 236	5 980	7 188
Food at home	3 838	4 099	3 841	3 505	4 169
Cereals and bakery products	531	610	545	478	538
Meats, poultry, fish, and eggs	832	882	791	811	868
Dairy products	407	444	409	356	458
Fruits and vegetables	715	811	696	612	825
Other food at home	1 353	1 351	1 401	1 248	1 481
Food away from home	2 620	2 700	2 395	2 474	3 019
Alcoholic Beverages	456	491	387	386	614
Housing	16 803	19 557	14 926	14 968	19 373
Shelter	9 825	12 033	8 409	8 110	12 193
Owned dwellings	6 148	7 642	5 691	5 110	7 060
Rented dwellings	3 029	3 567	2 153	2 505	4 297
Other lodging	648	823	565	494	835
Utilities, fuels, and public services	3 727	4 096	3 486	3 898	3 385
Household operations	1 122	1 267	934	967	1 439
Housekeeping supplies	615	641	645	567	642
Household furnishings and equipment	1 514	1 520	1 451	1 427	1 714
Apparel and Services	1 740	1 905	1 624	1 615	1 926
Transportation	8 293	8 435	8 114	8 264	8 399
Vehicle purchases (net outlay)	2 669	2 675	2 805	2 736	2 420
Gasoline and motor oil	2 655	2 510	2 632	2 794	2 569
Other vehicle expenses	2 454	2 519	2 223	2 400	2 713
Public transportation	516	730	453	334	698
Health Care	3 313	3 368	3 620	3 160	3 216
Health insurance	1 922	2 023	2 029	1 846	1 859
Medical services	768	788	928	677	742
Drugs	489	425	508	507	495
Medical supplies	134	132	155	131	120
Entertainment	2 572	2 632	2 505	2 350	2 950
Personal Care Products and Services	634	627	582	606	739
Reading	115	130	123	88	140
Education	1 051	1 620	1 095	680	1 145
Tobacco Products and Smoking Supplies	351	356	364	391	268
Miscellaneous	775	858	764	661	903
Cash Contributions	1 721	1 809	1 675	1 613	1 869
Personal Insurance and Pensions	5 424	5 961	5 178	4 936	6 016
Life and other personal insurance	317	406	296	307	282
Pensions and Social Security	5 106	5 554	4 882	4 629	5 734

[1]The states that comprise the Census regions are: Northeast—Connecticut, Maine, Massachusetts, New Hampshire, New Jersey, New York, Pennsylvania, Rhode Island, and Vermont; South—Alabama, Arkansas, Delaware, District of Columbia, Florida, Georgia, Kentucky, Louisiana, Maryland, Mississippi, North Carolina, Oklahoma, South Carolina, Tennessee, Texas, Virginia, and West Virginia; Midwest—Illinois, Indiana, Iowa, Kansas, Michigan, Minnesota, Missouri, Nebraska, North Dakota, Ohio, South Dakota, and Wisconsin; and West—Alaska, Arizona, California, Colorado, Hawaii, Idaho, Montana, Nevada, New Mexico, Oregon, Utah, Washington, and Wyoming.

Table 11-17. Consumer Expenditures, Averages for Single Men by Income Before Taxes, 2010–2011

(Number, dollar, percent.)

Item	All single men	Complete reporting of income						
		Less than $5,000	$5,000 to $9,999	$10,000 to $14,999	$15,000 to $19,999	$20,000 to $29,999	$30,000 to $39,999	$40,000 and over
NUMBER OF CONSUMER UNITS (THOUSANDS)	16 630	1 430	1 470	2 049	1 582	2 532	2 047	5 521
CONSUMER UNIT CHARACTERISTICS								
Income Before Taxes	39 167	-3 803	7 894	12 546	17 306	24 635	34 462	83 178
Income After Taxes	37 601	-3 391	7 910	12 501	17 130	24 263	33 255	79 035
Age of Reference Person	48.2	40.0	43.7	51.5	55.4	50.1	47.7	47.6
Average Number in Consumer Unit								
All persons	1.0	1.0	1.0	1.0	1.0	1.0	1.0	1.0
Persons 65 years and over	0.2	0.1	0.2	0.3	0.4	0.3	0.2	0.1
Earners	0.7	0.4	0.5	0.4	0.4	0.7	0.8	0.9
Vehicles	1.3	0.7	0.8	0.9	1.3	1.3	1.4	1.6
Percent Homeowner	45	20	22	33	48	41	50	60
With mortgage	24	5	5	10	15	14	28	44
Without mortgage	21	15	17	23	33	26	22	16
AVERAGE ANNUAL EXPENDITURES	31 288	20 034	15 807	17 519	22 086	24 955	30 944	48 391
Food	3 916	2 669	2 855	2 502	2 929	2 991	3 817	5 448
Food at home	1 871	1 353	1 717	1 519	1 753	1 576	1 834	2 261
Cereals and bakery products	255	190	233	223	258	221	255	292
Meats, poultry, fish, and eggs	397	297	467	306	369	318	352	484
Dairy products	187	135	171	140	166	160	186	229
Fruits and vegetables	338	246	298	287	320	261	302	427
Other food at home	694	485	547	564	641	616	739	829
Food away from home	2 046	1 316	1 138	982	1 176	1 415	1 983	3 186
Alcoholic Beverages	507	326	395	234	200	286	494	823
Housing	11 203	6 768	5 924	7 216	8 297	9 800	11 422	16 570
Shelter	7 411	4 659	4 077	4 734	5 135	6 253	7 536	11 142
Owned dwellings	3 231	787	665	1 163	1 962	1 988	3 321	6 216
Rented dwellings	3 806	3 466	3 259	3 466	3 055	4 059	3 982	4 200
Other lodging	374	406	153	104	118	206	234	726
Utilities, fuels, and public services	2 232	1 269	1 250	1 723	2 131	2 240	2 432	2 882
Household operations	497	259	183	240	322	405	427	855
Housekeeping supplies	252	158	120	125	262	235	230	343
Household furnishings and equipment	811	424	294	395	447	667	797	1 348
Apparel and Services	746	461	354	259	655	452	895	1 127
Transportation	4 769	3 674	2 255	2 675	3 475	4 059	5 238	6 957
Vehicle purchases (net outlay)	1 364	1 390	663	683	798	972	1 646	2 034
Gasoline and motor oil	1 516	912	909	1 014	1 097	1 524	1 659	2 083
Other vehicle expenses	1 571	1 164	571	843	1 410	1 356	1 661	2 265
Public transportation	318	208	111	135	170	206	273	575
Health Care	1 654	949	581	1 265	1 568	1 653	1 868	2 208
Health insurance	980	374	380	689	975	1 060	1 240	1 274
Medical services	367	377	51	264	259	287	311	576
Drugs	239	161	128	274	299	244	243	251
Medical supplies	67	[1]37	[1]22	37	35	63	75	107
Entertainment	1 545	808	872	974	1 121	1 380	1 532	2 287
Personal Care Products and Services	194	123	107	99	135	149	188	298
Reading	76	76	46	47	56	62	80	108
Education	908	2 460	1 372	572	498	773	443	856
Tobacco Products and Smoking Supplies	364	328	280	389	400	455	388	327
Miscellaneous	690	685	152	293	319	440	499	1 232
Cash Contributions	1 629	542	353	557	1 743	975	1 350	3 020
Personal Insurance and Pensions	3 086	165	261	439	690	1 480	2 731	7 131
Life and other personal insurance	131	86	26	59	71	168	122	200
Pensions and Social Security	2 955	79	236	380	620	1 313	2 609	6 931

[1]Data are likely to have large sampling errors.
X = Not applicable.

Table 11-18. Consumer Expenditures, Averages for Single Women by Income Before Taxes, 2010–2011

(Number, dollar, percent.)

Item	All single women	Complete reporting of income						
		Less than $5,000	$5,000 to $9,999	$10,000 to $14,999	$15,000 to $19,999	$20,000 to $29,999	$30,000 to $39,999	$40,000 and over
NUMBER OF CONSUMER UNITS (THOUSANDS)	19 164	1 811	1 973	3 373	2 481	2 930	2 258	4 337
CONSUMER UNIT CHARACTERISTICS								
Income Before Taxes	29 080	2 136	8 064	12 603	17 329	24 466	34 383	69 792
Income After Taxes	28 107	2 215	8 132	12 540	17 146	24 224	33 760	66 068
Age of Reference Person	57.6	46.2	57.2	65.1	65.4	60.2	54.0	52.5
Average Number in Consumer Unit								
All persons	1.0	1.0	1.0	1.0	1.0	1.0	1.0	1.0
Persons 65 years and over	0.4	0.3	0.4	0.6	0.6	0.5	0.3	0.2
Earners	0.5	0.4	0.3	0.2	0.3	0.5	0.7	0.9
Vehicles	0.9	0.6	0.6	0.7	0.9	1.0	1.1	1.2
Percent Homeowner	55	27	36	50	57	58	62	73
With mortgage	23	8	9	9	13	22	32	47
Without mortgage	32	19	26	41	45	36	30	25
AVERAGE ANNUAL EXPENDITURES	28 688	17 462	15 718	17 424	22 417	26 696	32 485	50 285
Food	3 241	2 447	2 338	2 329	2 508	2 986	3 286	5 025
Food at home	2 057	1 472	1 746	1 753	1 742	1 961	1 989	2 824
Cereals and bakery products	284	220	266	252	262	280	279	346
Meats, poultry, fish, and eggs	383	304	335	358	320	361	357	503
Dairy products	223	152	198	196	186	207	253	288
Fruits and vegetables	419	291	354	345	357	416	385	583
Other food at home	748	505	593	602	617	698	715	1 102
Food away from home	1 184	975	591	576	766	1 025	1 297	2 201
Alcoholic Beverages	215	148	76	62	110	117	252	513
Housing	11 459	7 535	6 924	7 771	9 668	11 065	13 238	18 302
Shelter	7 037	4 894	4 152	4 572	5 567	6 593	8 222	11 688
Owned dwellings	3 654	1 631	1 255	1 756	2 507	3 204	4 463	7 604
Rented dwellings	3 093	3 045	2 734	2 711	2 941	3 193	3 344	3 460
Other lodging	291	219	163	104	119	195	415	624
Utilities, fuels, and public services	2 464	1 464	1 776	2 048	2 436	2 618	2 807	3 250
Household operations	713	557	226	383	677	830	817	1 141
Housekeeping supplies	426	257	335	315	378	342	386	695
Household furnishings and equipment	820	364	436	454	610	683	1 005	1 528
Apparel and Services	1 046	743	520	555	631	749	1 149	2 092
Transportation	3 690	1 813	1 711	1 846	2 948	3 629	4 608	6 676
Vehicle purchases (net outlay)	938	[1]501	[1]204	[1]166	771	819	1 364	2 012
Gasoline and motor oil	1 080	649	667	708	865	1 155	1 407	1 640
Other vehicle expenses	1 357	510	711	825	1 103	1 440	1 470	2 328
Public transportation	315	153	130	147	210	215	367	696
Health Care	2 429	1 162	1 315	1 934	2 756	2 718	2 789	3 266
Health insurance	1 399	654	761	1 228	1 668	1 594	1 600	1 742
Medical services	524	227	287	246	509	609	554	905
Drugs	402	206	208	356	480	420	515	477
Medical supplies	106	77	59	104	99	96	120	143
Entertainment	1 432	741	856	773	1 089	1 374	1 723	2 510
Personal Care Products and Services	524	249	333	270	364	428	600	1 009
Reading	93	44	42	49	81	87	107	174
Education	503	1 245	571	284	321	378	371	586
Tobacco Products and Smoking Supplies	172	211	206	209	124	180	143	150
Miscellaneous	645	287	220	514	409	607	680	1 201
Cash Contributions	1 098	505	400	532	877	957	1 316	2 212
Personal Insurance and Pensions	2 139	333	206	296	534	1 421	2 222	6 568
Life and other personal insurance	188	36	60	107	135	367	160	296
Pensions and Social Security	1 951	297	146	189	399	1 054	2 062	6 272

[1]Data are likely to have large sampling errors.

Table 11-19. Consumer Expenditures, Averages for Age Groups by Income Before Taxes: Reference Person Under 25 Years of Age, 2010–2011

(Number, dollar, percent.)

Item	Total	Complete reporting of income						
		Less than $5,000	$5,000 to $9,999	$10,000 to $14,999	$15,000 to $19,999	$20,000 to $29,999	$30,000 to $39,999	$40,000 and over
NUMBER OF CONSUMER UNITS (THOUSANDS)	7 888	1 469	1 090	892	726	1 062	810	1 840
CONSUMER UNIT CHARACTERISTICS								
Income Before Taxes	27 191	2 814	7 423	12 468	17 472	24 890	34 483	67 450
Income After Taxes	27 129	2 967	7 547	12 683	17 883	25 391	34 565	66 398
Age of Reference Person	21.6	20.6	20.9	21.4	21.6	21.9	22.3	22.3
Average Number in Consumer Unit								
All persons	2.1	1.3	1.5	1.6	2.0	2.3	2.5	3.0
Children under 18 years	0.5	0.2	0.3	0.4	0.5	0.6	0.6	0.6
Persons 65 years and over	([1])	([1])	([1])	([1])	([1])	([1])	([1])	([1])
Earners	1.3	0.7	0.9	0.8	1.1	1.3	1.5	2.1
Vehicles	1.1	0.4	0.6	0.7	1.0	1.1	1.4	1.9
Percent Distribution								
Male	46	42	49	45	37	43	46	53
Female	54	58	51	55	63	57	54	47
Percent Homeowner	14	2	2	4	10	10	18	38
With mortgage	10	1	1	1	2	6	12	29
Without mortgage	5	1	1	3	7	4	6	9
AVERAGE ANNUAL EXPENDITURES	28 684	14 845	16 497	18 445	22 870	28 075	32 753	50 876
Food	4 209	2 820	2 369	2 871	3 605	3 812	4 432	6 543
Food at home	2 286	1 147	1 191	1 600	2 168	2 140	2 704	3 481
Cereals and bakery products	324	169	173	201	386	308	365	475
Meats, poultry, fish, and eggs	485	201	173	354	420	434	583	807
Dairy products	231	127	141	130	195	256	264	343
Fruits and vegetables	409	205	208	265	388	366	500	636
Other food at home	837	446	496	650	780	776	991	1 219
Food away from home	1 923	1 672	1 179	1 271	1 437	1 672	1 728	3 062
Alcoholic Beverages	412	231	364	262	172	421	396	665
Housing	9 918	4 710	5 759	6 984	8 750	10 248	12 453	16 964
Shelter	6 444	3 339	4 036	4 743	5 369	6 480	7 876	10 946
Owned dwellings	1 198	[2]132	[2]75	[2]103	228	520	1 030	4 095
Rented dwellings	4 959	2 850	3 640	4 459	4 966	5 666	6 581	6 540
Other lodging	287	357	320	[2]180	[2]176	294	265	311
Utilities, fuels, and public services	1 867	712	889	1 240	1 773	2 012	2 501	3 348
Household operations	463	176	223	258	549	556	662	774
Housekeeping supplies	274	109	136	137	190	263	292	492
Household furnishings and equipment	870	374	475	606	868	937	1 122	1 403
Apparel and Services	1 503	951	680	650	1 112	1 456	1 443	2 730
Transportation	5 076	1 872	2 438	2 979	4 164	5 302	6 058	9 765
Vehicle purchases (net outlay)	1 826	[2]493	[2]835	[2]769	[2]1356	1 960	2 455	3 819
Gasoline and motor oil	1 663	797	981	1 153	1 482	1 788	2 020	2 850
Other vehicle expenses	1 299	400	471	860	1 093	1 269	1 226	2 620
Public transportation	287	182	151	197	232	286	357	477
Health Care	807	249	241	191	565	688	1 211	1 866
Health insurance	430	88	126	[2]83	207	338	691	1 078
Medical services	245	88	53	40	221	250	363	537
Drugs	97	63	44	35	109	73	106	189
Medical supplies	35	[2]11	[2]18	[2]32	[2]28	26	51	62
Entertainment	1 287	610	727	811	847	1 414	1 570	2 259
Personal Care Products and Services	336	196	168	177	271	410	376	542
Reading	42	26	37	40	49	39	36	61
Education	2 077	2 776	2 872	2 228	1 730	1 667	1 203	1 729
Tobacco Products and Smoking Supplies	270	150	212	226	196	329	349	385
Miscellaneous	281	47	171	242	103	274	280	588
Cash Contributions	340	83	100	152	212	277	325	870
Personal Insurance and Pensions	2 126	123	359	632	1 093	1 738	2 621	5 910
Life and other personal insurance	44	. . .	[2]3	[2]17	[2]22	[2]11	[2]37	148
Pensions and Social Security	2 082	123	356	615	1 071	1 727	2 585	5 763

[1]Value less than or equal to 0.05.
[2]Data are likely to have large sampling errors.
. . . = Not available.

Table 11-20. Consumer Expenditures, Averages for Age Groups by Income Before Taxes: Reference Person 25 to 34 Years of Age, 2010–2011

(Number, dollar, percent.)

Item		Complete reporting of income								
	Total	Less than $5,000	$5,000 to $9,999	$10,000 to $14,999	$15,000 to $19,999	$20,000 to $29,999	$30,000 to $39,999	$40,000 to $49,999	$50,000 to $69,999	$70,000 and over
NUMBER OF CONSUMER UNITS (THOUSANDS)	20 314	607	672	906	1 108	2 502	2 634	2 235	3 513	6 137
CONSUMER UNIT CHARACTERISTICS										
Income Before Taxes	58 891	1 087	8 075	12 689	17 632	25 224	34 636	44 677	59 012	113 689
Income After Taxes	57 698	1 511	8 588	13 326	18 712	25 792	35 094	44 916	58 031	109 401
Age of Reference Person	29.6	29.2	28.8	29.0	29.0	29.4	29.4	29.5	29.6	30.2
Average Number in Consumer Unit										
All persons	2.9	2.5	2.6	2.6	2.8	2.6	2.7	2.9	2.9	3.1
Children under 18 years	1.1	1.2	1.3	1.2	1.3	1.1	1.1	1.1	1.0	1.0
Persons 65 years and over	(1)	(1)	(1)	(1)	(1)	(1)	(1)	(1)	(1)	(1)
Earners	1.5	0.5	0.7	0.8	1.0	1.2	1.3	1.5	1.6	1.9
Vehicles	1.7	0.7	0.9	0.9	1.1	1.3	1.4	1.7	1.9	2.2
Percent Distribution										
Male	47	38	41	37	37	47	46	51	50	51
Female	53	62	59	63	63	53	54	49	50	49
Percent Homeowner	44	12	14	18	19	21	32	40	53	70
With mortgage	38	2	7	9	11	16	26	34	47	65
Without mortgage	6	10	7	9	8	5	6	6	6	4
AVERAGE ANNUAL EXPENDITURES	47 378	24 065	24 188	21 607	25 248	29 591	36 506	39 847	47 270	74 666
Food	6 153	3 516	4 832	3 918	3 997	4 108	5 340	5 377	6 119	8 730
Food at home	3 394	2 088	3 362	2 743	2 604	2 618	3 033	3 091	3 455	4 280
Cereals and bakery products	460	281	404	324	384	367	431	411	481	571
Meats, poultry, fish, and eggs	723	460	949	639	562	592	672	655	700	874
Dairy products	366	257	317	265	272	284	307	336	369	481
Fruits and vegetables	621	327	546	448	445	472	555	537	609	836
Other food at home	1 224	762	1 145	1 066	941	904	1 068	1 152	1 297	1 518
Food away from home	2 759	1 428	1 471	1 175	1 393	1 490	2 307	2 286	2 664	4 450
Alcoholic Beverages	493	326	133	173	197	193	386	342	511	866
Housing	16 931	9 516	9 710	9 368	10 720	11 644	13 533	14 865	16 895	25 058
Shelter	10 465	5 782	6 179	5 696	6 659	7 257	8 394	9 308	10 426	15 431
Owned dwellings	4 975	504	757	703	1 032	1 438	2 482	3 260	5 018	10 333
Rented dwellings	5 165	5 150	5 260	4 876	5 588	5 724	5 778	5 887	5 096	4 408
Other lodging	326	[2]128	[2]161	[2]117	[2]39	95	133	160	312	691
Utilities, fuels, and public services	3 262	2 387	2 076	2 294	2 579	2 582	2 869	3 283	3 450	4 075
Household operations	1 311	401	384	384	569	660	820	908	1 056	2 541
Housekeeping supplies	442	165	290	304	304	272	337	435	459	632
Household furnishings and equipment	1 451	781	782	690	608	873	1 112	931	1 502	2 378
Apparel and Services	1 949	1 336	1 517	984	1 054	1 204	1 713	1 482	1 787	3 038
Transportation	8 550	3 162	3 479	3 147	4 127	5 550	6 839	7 170	8 387	13 772
Vehicle purchases (net outlay)	3 308	[2]1 317	[2]1 016	[2]784	1 185	1 852	2 446	2 403	2 828	6 080
Gasoline and motor oil	2 469	1 008	1 309	1 373	1 743	1 851	2 181	2 469	2 669	3 294
Other vehicle expenses	2 291	597	912	829	1 026	1 663	1 903	1 961	2 459	3 483
Public transportation	482	240	242	161	173	184	309	337	432	915
Health Care	1 948	516	458	433	707	995	1 492	1 867	2 270	3 130
Health insurance	1 162	284	207	215	455	498	902	1 080	1 436	1 876
Medical services	495	156	135	102	128	336	343	530	539	784
Drugs	215	63	84	92	97	120	160	212	218	344
Medical supplies	77	[2]13	[2]32	[2]24	27	40	87	45	77	127
Entertainment	2 356	819	1 091	947	1 046	1 361	1 636	1 812	2 606	3 848
Personal Care Products and Services	544	214	352	282	280	345	428	438	549	845
Reading	68	27	57	26	24	36	48	60	66	113
Education	944	3 008	1 108	813	853	1 117	724	568	944	918
Tobacco Products and Smoking Supplies	370	477	457	332	387	340	437	489	381	287
Miscellaneous	637	191	356	174	235	260	416	618	616	1 119
Cash Contributions	1 102	674	295	346	499	595	691	927	1 009	1 954
Personal Insurance and Pensions	5 332	284	343	665	1 122	1 844	2 825	3 831	5 130	10 988
Life and other personal insurance	153	[2]99	[2]12	[2]22	29	43	72	94	139	323
Pensions and Social Security	5 180	186	331	643	1 093	1 801	2 753	3 737	4 990	10 665

[1]Value less than or equal to 0.05.
[2]Data are likely to have large sampling errors.

Table 11-21. Consumer Expenditures, Averages for Age Groups by Income Before Taxes: Reference Person 35 to 44 Years of Age, 2010–2011

(Number, dollar, percent.)

Item	Total	Complete reporting of income								
		Less than $5,000	$5,000 to $9,999	$10,000 to $14,999	$15,000 to $19,999	$20,000 to $29,999	$30,000 to $39,999	$40,000 to $49,999	$50,000 to $69,999	$70,000 and over
NUMBER OF CONSUMER UNITS (THOUSANDS)	21 805	479	577	780	944	1 978	2 179	2 099	3 456	9 313
CONSUMER UNIT CHARACTERISTICS										
Income Before Taxes	76 749	-84	8 020	12 684	17 564	24 980	34 726	44 571	59 394	130 852
Income After Taxes	74 833	231	8 544	13 276	18 453	26 011	34 997	44 426	58 712	126 180
Age of Reference Person	39.6	39.8	39.1	39.4	39.6	39.7	39.3	39.6	39.5	39.7
Average Number in Consumer Unit										
All persons	3.3	2.3	2.5	2.4	2.7	3.1	3.0	3.3	3.4	3.6
Children under 18 years	1.3	1.0	1.1	1.0	1.2	1.3	1.2	1.3	1.4	1.5
Persons 65 years and over	([1])	([1])	([1])	([1])	([1])	([1])	([1])	([1])	([1])	([1])
Earners	1.6	0.5	0.6	0.8	1.0	1.2	1.3	1.5	1.7	1.9
Vehicles	2.0	0.7	0.9	1.0	1.1	1.3	1.6	1.9	2.1	2.5
Percent Distribution										
Male	48	32	33	35	33	40	40	50	51	54
Female	52	68	67	65	67	60	60	50	49	46
Percent Homeowner	63	27	24	25	35	32	52	57	67	83
With mortgage	54	13	8	12	18	20	43	47	58	77
Without mortgage	9	14	16	13	17	12	9	10	10	7
AVERAGE ANNUAL EXPENDITURES	56 629	22 520	19 766	22 551	27 733	31 119	37 987	42 841	49 980	82 038
Food	7 624	3 710	3 567	4 101	5 151	5 167	6 173	6 302	7 186	10 038
Food at home	4 425	2 569	2 677	3 019	3 609	3 542	4 110	3 881	4 254	5 306
Cereals and bakery products	626	348	368	418	500	456	534	520	620	776
Meats, poultry, fish, and eggs	951	667	660	711	802	907	995	887	885	1 057
Dairy products	469	290	217	278	350	342	394	362	453	604
Fruits and vegetables	814	446	454	492	659	612	806	691	770	992
Other food at home	1 565	818	978	1 121	1 298	1 226	1 381	1 420	1 526	1 877
Food away from home	3 199	1 141	890	1 081	1 543	1 625	2 062	2 421	2 932	4 733
Alcoholic Beverages	497	[2]167	[2]87	192	173	220	339	382	391	771
Housing	20 021	10 209	8 331	9 637	11 032	12 326	13 709	15 264	18 098	27 970
Shelter	12 104	6 396	4 869	6 034	6 646	7 466	8 435	9 113	10 887	16 878
Owned dwellings	7 997	2 046	956	1 076	1 751	1 947	4 096	4 854	6 990	13 233
Rented dwellings	3 594	4 229	3 906	4 901	4 788	5 422	4 175	4 116	3 645	2 651
Other lodging	513	[2]122	[2]7	[2]58	[2]107	97	165	143	252	993
Utilities, fuels, and public services	4 071	2 342	2 473	2 562	2 976	3 027	3 442	3 760	4 146	4 908
Household operations	1 465	447	223	283	551	490	598	793	1 047	2 502
Housekeeping supplies	682	369	289	344	288	457	415	476	586	1 001
Household furnishings and equipment	1 699	655	477	414	570	885	819	1 122	1 432	2 682
Apparel and Services	2 134	967	1 405	1 178	1 288	1 356	1 609	1 603	1 816	2 963
Transportation	9 229	3 209	2 862	2 903	4 338	5 124	7 222	7 188	8 475	13 048
Vehicle purchases (net outlay)	3 168	[2]1 005	[2]912	[2]366	[2]630	1 669	2 399	1 890	2 799	4 835
Gasoline and motor oil	2 861	1 190	1 064	1 428	1 659	2 031	2 436	2 748	2 867	3 599
Other vehicle expenses	2 670	832	784	1 041	1 810	1 174	2 141	2 315	2 505	3 697
Public transportation	529	182	103	68	239	251	247	235	304	917
Health Care	2 672	1 120	652	819	1 074	1 267	1 725	2 238	2 692	3 809
Health insurance	1 517	[2]398	322	328	409	617	1 043	1 363	1 586	2 171
Medical services	687	424	111	227	374	406	398	467	649	998
Drugs	358	224	192	215	229	199	210	328	357	479
Medical supplies	110	[2]74	[2]27	50	62	46	74	80	99	160
Entertainment	3 004	1 068	764	1 158	1 251	1 468	1 723	2 000	2 569	4 616
Personal Care Products and Services	709	288	333	342	366	433	482	533	603	1 017
Reading	90	27	18	26	26	39	35	50	85	144
Education	891	[2]392	194	82	259	339	400	540	445	1 570
Tobacco Products and Smoking Supplies	350	372	515	570	419	422	387	462	360	261
Miscellaneous	851	172	307	597	677	432	340	1 287	635	1 153
Cash Contributions	1 551	457	408	387	637	707	928	1 253	1 197	2 392
Personal Insurance and Pensions	7 005	363	322	558	1 040	1 818	2 915	3 739	5 427	12 287
Life and other personal insurance	294	[2]54	[2]31	[2]25	76	83	156	137	241	499
Pensions and Social Security	6 711	309	291	533	964	1 735	2 758	3 601	5 186	11 788

[1]Value less than or equal to 0.05.
[2]Data are likely to have large sampling errors.

Table 11-22. Consumer Expenditures, Averages for Age Groups by Income Before Taxes: Reference Person 45 to 54 Years of Age, 2010–2011

(Number, dollar, percent.)

Item	Total	Less than $5,000	$5,000 to $9,999	$10,000 to $14,999	$15,000 to $19,999	$20,000 to $29,999	$30,000 to $39,999	$40,000 to $49,999	$50,000 to $69,999	$70,000 and over
						Complete reporting of income				
NUMBER OF CONSUMER UNITS (THOUSANDS)	24 938	749	811	1 163	991	2 133	2 236	2 188	3 764	10 902
CONSUMER UNIT CHARACTERISTICS										
Income Before Taxes	79 056	-16 012	8 014	12 586	17 691	24 950	34 728	44 814	59 678	136 781
Income After Taxes	75 753	-15 707	8 209	12 893	17 910	25 263	34 514	44 127	58 246	129 751
Age of Reference Person	50	50	50	50	50	49	50	50	50	50
Average Number in Consumer Unit										
All persons	2.8	1.9	1.7	1.8	2.3	2.5	2.5	2.5	2.8	3.2
Children under 18 years	0.6	0.4	0.3	0.3	0.5	0.6	0.5	0.5	0.6	0.8
Persons 65 years and over	0.1	(1)	(1)	(1)	0.1	0.1	0.1	0.1	0.1	0.1
Earners	1.6	0.6	0.6	0.5	0.9	1.1	1.4	1.5	1.8	2.1
Vehicles	2.3	1.3	1.0	1.1	1.3	1.5	1.7	2.1	2.3	3.0
Percent Distribution										
Male	47	44	48	44	39	43	40	46	42	53
Female	53	56	52	56	61	57	60	54	58	47
Percent Homeowner	72	41	37	35	43	50	60	68	77	90
With mortgage	54	25	18	15	22	30	42	49	60	73
Without mortgage	18	16	18	20	20	21	19	19	17	17
AVERAGE ANNUAL EXPENDITURES	57 919	28 186	20 316	20 366	24 735	28 940	34 913	41 163	49 364	86 670
Food	7 325	3 680	3 256	3 417	3 967	4 426	4 827	5 354	6 577	10 421
Food at home	4 395	2 518	2 450	2 575	2 777	3 050	3 218	3 274	4 010	5 922
Cereals and bakery products	605	356	389	319	370	423	457	462	525	820
Meats, poultry, fish, and eggs	966	535	498	669	626	672	727	780	896	1 271
Dairy products	464	287	253	282	276	323	337	329	420	630
Fruits and vegetables	811	508	466	449	473	562	599	548	708	1 118
Other food at home	1 549	832	845	856	1 032	1 071	1 098	1 155	1 461	2 083
Food away from home	2 931	1 162	806	842	1 190	1 375	1 609	2 080	2 568	4 499
Alcoholic Beverages	453	221	¹57	164	140	135	294	268	366	731
Housing	18 840	11 273	9 007	8 809	10 137	11 316	12 610	14 619	16 769	26 285
Shelter	11 315	7 653	5 594	5 384	5 625	6 700	7 447	8 624	9 934	15 855
Owned dwellings	7 969	3 584	2 077	1 652	1 817	2 781	3 945	5 182	7 005	12 675
Rented dwellings	2 537	3 650	3 251	3 705	3 704	3 751	3 378	3 134	2 505	1 658
Other lodging	809	²419	²265	²28	²103	168	124	308	424	1 522
Utilities, fuels, and public services	4 265	2 582	2 334	2 435	3 020	3 237	3 540	3 706	4 206	5 316
Household operations	964	348	313	249	340	369	468	621	689	1 570
Housekeeping supplies	670	273	332	312	567	436	362	450	552	969
Household furnishings and equipment	1 626	416	434	429	585	575	793	1 218	1 388	2 575
Apparel and Services	1 974	853	1 111	429	1 061	1 313	1 344	1 270	1 473	2 957
Transportation	9 379	4 273	3 218	2 775	3 969	4 431	6 170	7 553	8 530	13 687
Vehicle purchases (net outlay)	2 834	²977	²1 137	²374	1 019	525	2 119	2 232	2 517	4 343
Gasoline and motor oil	2 921	1 329	1 259	1 340	1 491	2 081	2 187	2 638	2 983	3 802
Other vehicle expenses	3 004	1 817	690	883	1 304	1 627	1 653	2 420	2 684	4 428
Public transportation	621	151	131	178	156	198	211	263	346	1 113
Health Care	3 336	1 397	658	1 449	1 439	1 979	2 327	2 601	3 310	4 673
Health insurance	1 774	822	406	618	700	957	1 257	1 423	1 746	2 508
Medical services	911	266	94	277	364	558	596	639	1 036	1 278
Drugs	506	263	141	530	343	371	371	438	434	657
Medical supplies	145	46	16	24	33	93	103	101	95	230
Entertainment	3 130	1 581	927	916	1 101	1 428	1 565	2 060	2 775	4 827
Personal Care Products and Services	691	252	234	224	284	319	387	475	567	1 070
Reading	108	90	23	25	40	39	55	64	79	175
Education	1 987	953	502	117	162	225	485	572	824	3 874
Tobacco Products and Smoking Supplies	457	480	450	547	578	535	530	521	515	372
Miscellaneous	942	1 443	245	396	411	366	640	639	827	1 345
Cash Contributions	1 734	951	269	617	416	683	929	1 148	1 218	2 804
Personal Insurance and Pensions	7 561	740	359	483	1 029	1 745	2 751	4 019	5 533	13 450
Life and other personal insurance	421	209	²64	83	126	109	186	246	297	712
Pensions and Social Security	7 140	530	295	401	903	1 637	2 565	3 772	5 235	12 738

¹Value less than or equal to 0.05.
²Data are likely to have large sampling errors.

Table 11-23. Consumer Expenditures, Averages for Age Groups by Income Before Taxes: Reference Person 55 to 64 Years of Age, 2010–2011

(Number, dollar, percent.)

Item	Total	Complete reporting of income								
		Less than $5,000	$5,000 to $9,999	$10,000 to $14,999	$15,000 to $19,999	$20,000 to $29,999	$30,000 to $39,999	$40,000 to $49,999	$50,000 to $69,999	$70,000 and over
NUMBER OF CONSUMER UNITS (THOUSANDS)	21 524	745	835	1 241	1 077	2 312	2 043	2 073	3 031	8 166
CONSUMER UNIT CHARACTERISTICS										
Income Before Taxes	72 237	1 228	8 340	12 597	17 577	24 923	35 126	44 569	59 542	135 941
Income After Taxes	69 384	1 309	8 434	12 645	17 605	24 783	34 744	43 753	57 824	129 373
Age of Reference Person	59.2	59.1	59.6	59.5	59.7	59.5	59.3	59.2	59.3	58.9
Average Number in Consumer Unit										
All persons	2.1	1.4	1.5	1.4	1.8	1.9	2.1	2.0	2.2	2.5
Children under 18 years	0.2	[1]0.1	0.2	[1]0.1	0.2	0.1	0.2	0.1	0.2	0.2
Persons 65 years and over	0.1	([2])	([2])	([2])	0.1	0.1	0.2	0.1	0.1	0.1
Earners	1.3	0.3	0.3	0.4	0.6	0.8	1.1	1.2	1.4	1.9
Vehicles	2.2	1.1	0.9	1.1	1.4	1.7	1.9	2.2	2.3	2.8
Percent Distribution										
Male	48	42	37	40	47	43	41	47	53	54
Female	52	58	63	60	53	57	59	53	47	46
Percent Homeowner	79	47	42	48	62	72	75	83	87	92
With mortgage	46	19	14	17	27	30	41	47	53	60
Without mortgage	34	29	27	31	35	41	34	36	33	32
AVERAGE ANNUAL EXPENDITURES	52 299	24 160	20 792	20 950	27 065	30 062	35 705	40 518	49 027	81 071
Food	6 298	3 854	3 999	3 143	3 678	3 794	4 733	4 796	5 819	9 372
Food at home	3 796	2 519	2 879	2 309	2 361	2 660	3 052	3 074	3 566	5 274
Cereals and bakery products	511	336	348	310	297	379	448	413	490	696
Meats, poultry, fish, and eggs	844	550	733	483	568	621	672	663	767	1 173
Dairy products	386	241	276	254	230	279	309	341	373	522
Fruits and vegetables	714	446	592	402	439	490	532	525	638	1 038
Other food at home	1 342	946	929	860	826	891	1 092	1 132	1 297	1 845
Food away from home	2 501	1 335	1 121	833	1 317	1 134	1 680	1 722	2 253	4 098
Alcoholic Beverages	436	263	298	143	159	152	189	290	349	780
Housing	16 938	9 948	8 027	8 797	10 519	11 507	12 677	13 759	15 992	24 361
Shelter	9 577	5 708	4 614	5 128	5 607	6 557	6 916	7 794	8 801	13 899
Owned dwellings	6 890	2 384	1 588	1 807	2 986	3 915	4 345	5 683	6 774	10 960
Rented dwellings	1 737	2 962	2 739	3 131	2 457	2 148	2 235	1 708	1 364	1 120
Other lodging	950	362	[1]286	191	163	494	336	403	663	1 819
Utilities, fuels, and public services	4 016	2 456	2 271	2 332	3 113	3 277	3 601	3 607	4 098	5 099
Household operations	928	388	309	434	394	425	578	620	892	1 509
Housekeeping supplies	719	529	357	400	564	430	554	615	616	1 051
Household furnishings and equipment	1 697	867	477	503	841	817	1 028	1 123	1 585	2 802
Apparel and Services	1 648	1 005	704	651	793	776	1 268	1 084	1 325	2 725
Transportation	8 554	3 122	2 875	2 923	5 174	4 807	6 472	8 142	8 823	12 506
Vehicle purchases (net outlay)	2 770	[1]841	[1]907	[1]361	1 702	1 271	2 058	2 918	2 817	4 191
Gasoline and motor oil	2 466	1 137	930	1 204	1 544	1 857	2 108	2 306	2 599	3 311
Other vehicle expenses	2 754	954	935	1 205	1 751	1 455	2 106	2 518	2 986	3 964
Public transportation	564	189	104	153	177	224	199	400	421	1 040
Health Care	3 954	1 790	1 262	1 804	2 037	3 027	3 158	3 545	4 172	5 500
Health insurance	2 154	1 018	634	1 018	979	1 756	1 669	2 058	2 463	2 883
Medical services	978	289	288	364	444	697	778	745	864	1 507
Drugs	677	379	308	340	570	501	626	643	731	863
Medical supplies	145	104	33	83	45	73	85	98	114	246
Entertainment	2 740	1 238	1 109	1 049	1 449	1 574	1 704	2 069	2 425	4 376
Personal Care Products and Services	648	261	298	252	266	313	460	480	559	1 058
Reading	137	67	28	49	59	66	79	103	145	219
Education	891	[1]92	[1]480	[1]219	137	222	246	574	411	1 818
Tobacco Products and Smoking Supplies	425	451	405	509	502	536	453	402	444	362
Miscellaneous	1 037	605	458	457	333	660	705	679	1 608	1 353
Cash Contributions	2 003	890	555	517	1 068	734	850	1 234	1 596	3 596
Personal Insurance and Pensions	6 591	573	293	438	892	1 898	2 711	3 361	5 359	13 047
Life and other personal insurance	503	138	105	106	162	512	264	268	442	821
Pensions and Social Security	6 088	435	188	332	729	1 385	2 447	3 093	4 917	12 226

[1]Data are likely to have large sampling errors.
[2]Value less than or equal to 0.05.

Table 11-24. Consumer Expenditures, Averages for Age Groups by Income Before Taxes: Reference Person 65 Years of Age and Over, 2010–2011

(Number, dollar, percent.)

Item		Complete reporting of income								
	Total	Less than $5,000	$5,000 to $9,999	$10,000 to $14,999	$15,000 to $19,999	$20,000 to $29,999	$30,000 to $39,999	$40,000 to $49,999	$50,000 to $69,999	$70,000 and over
NUMBER OF CONSUMER UNITS (THOUSANDS)	25 228	869	1 379	3 160	3 114	4 607	3 274	2 223	2 956	3 645
CONSUMER UNIT CHARACTERISTICS										
Income Before Taxes	42 284	203	8 464	12 674	17 408	24 881	34 783	44 975	59 058	125 519
Income After Taxes	41 498	-177	8 305	12 606	17 372	24 698	34 445	44 552	58 280	121 741
Age of Reference Person	74.8	76.1	76.6	77.1	76.7	75.8	74.6	73.8	72.9	71.6
Average Number in Consumer Unit										
All persons	1.7	1.3	1.2	1.2	1.4	1.7	1.8	2.0	2.1	2.3
Children under 18 years	0.1	([1])	([1])	([1])	([1])	([1])	0.1	0.1	0.1	0.1
Persons 65 years and over	1.4	1.2	1.1	1.1	1.2	1.4	1.5	1.5	1.5	1.5
Earners	0.5	0.1	0.1	0.1	0.1	0.3	0.4	0.6	0.8	1.2
Vehicles	1.6	1.0	0.8	0.9	1.2	1.5	1.7	1.9	2.2	2.5
Percent Distribution										
Male	43	36	28	26	33	41	47	53	54	60
Female	57	64	72	74	67	59	53	47	46	40
Percent Homeowner	81	66	60	64	74	80	88	90	91	95
With mortgage	22	7	12	12	12	18	22	26	30	43
Without mortgage	59	59	48	52	62	62	66	64	61	53
AVERAGE ANNUAL EXPENDITURES	38 027	23 291	18 615	18 570	23 480	29 935	36 667	38 782	50 015	77 801
Food	4 862	3 012	2 791	2 749	3 062	3 832	4 760	4 948	6 474	8 755
Food at home	3 131	2 256	2 189	2 102	2 232	2 670	3 119	3 207	4 182	4 684
Cereals and bakery products	443	343	323	324	339	401	449	443	549	620
Meats, poultry, fish, and eggs	666	455	470	463	447	530	639	644	961	1 036
Dairy products	338	226	257	216	241	292	339	366	447	491
Fruits and vegetables	620	478	407	421	441	546	623	616	808	927
Other food at home	1 065	754	732	678	765	902	1 069	1 138	1 416	1 609
Food away from home	1 730	757	602	647	829	1 162	1 641	1 741	2 293	4 071
Alcoholic Beverages	317	170	60	61	125	183	288	293	447	858
Housing	13 380	10 057	7 802	7 938	9 366	11 089	13 205	13 951	16 463	24 395
Shelter	7 104	5 642	4 120	4 413	4 972	5 780	6 822	7 351	8 423	13 444
Owned dwellings	4 918	2 982	2 000	2 342	2 876	3 628	5 114	5 504	6 373	10 378
Rented dwellings	1 496	2 256	1 960	1 953	1 972	1 824	1 133	1 188	1 049	801
Other lodging	690	404	[2]161	118	125	327	574	660	1 001	2 265
Utilities, fuels, and public services	3 445	2 583	2 279	2 340	2 779	3 232	3 518	3 795	4 139	5 043
Household operations	971	1 030	404	419	608	815	889	983	1 103	2 115
Housekeeping supplies	650	342	465	348	422	498	605	730	947	1 086
Household furnishings and equipment	1 210	460	534	419	584	764	1 370	1 092	1 850	2 708
Apparel and Services	1 047	188	758	536	515	715	945	974	1 428	2 316
Transportation	5 503	3 164	2 343	2 037	3 208	4 217	5 380	5 410	7 687	12 107
Vehicle purchases (net outlay)	1 543	[2]964	[2]262	[2]229	688	1 102	1 403	1 033	2 120	4 562
Gasoline and motor oil	1 580	893	768	735	1 017	1 391	1 625	1 880	2 354	2 652
Other vehicle expenses	1 977	1 101	1 143	928	1 338	1 553	2 008	2 159	2 618	3 700
Public transportation	403	206	171	145	165	172	345	338	594	1 193
Health Care	4 805	3 111	2 167	2 575	3 337	4 725	5 220	5 821	6 257	7 292
Health insurance	3 080	1 752	1 531	1 636	2 232	3 143	3 474	3 729	4 011	4 377
Medical services	790	855	170	366	409	670	713	916	1 045	1 637
Drugs	758	392	362	469	590	766	861	934	1 017	950
Medical supplies	176	113	103	103	106	146	173	241	184	329
Entertainment	1 956	811	999	908	1 148	1 633	1 862	1 723	2 992	3 856
Personal Care Products and Services	542	296	330	240	363	429	487	604	706	1 075
Reading	149	80	58	57	84	123	153	147	223	304
Education	220	[2]181	[2]40	35	48	99	159	112	262	840
Tobacco Products and Smoking Supplies	219	163	126	132	190	208	231	240	305	288
Miscellaneous	763	663	303	385	365	737	753	643	771	1 688
Cash Contributions	2 333	1 269	709	688	1 423	1 372	2 220	2 336	3 359	5 888
Personal Insurance and Pensions	1 930	126	130	227	245	573	1 004	1 580	2 641	8 139
Life and other personal insurance	297	104	91	129	164	255	267	321	411	649
Pensions and Social Security	1 633	[2]22	39	98	81	318	737	1 258	2 230	7 490

[1]Value less than or equal to 0.05.
[2]Data are likely to have large sampling errors.

Chapter Twelve

AMERICAN TIME USE SURVEY

AMERICAN TIME USE SURVEY

HIGHLIGHTS

This chapter presents data from the American Time Use Survey (ATUS). The survey was introduced in the sixth edition of the *Handbook of U.S. Labor Statistics*. Its purpose is to collect data on the activities people do during the day and the amount of time they spend on each one.

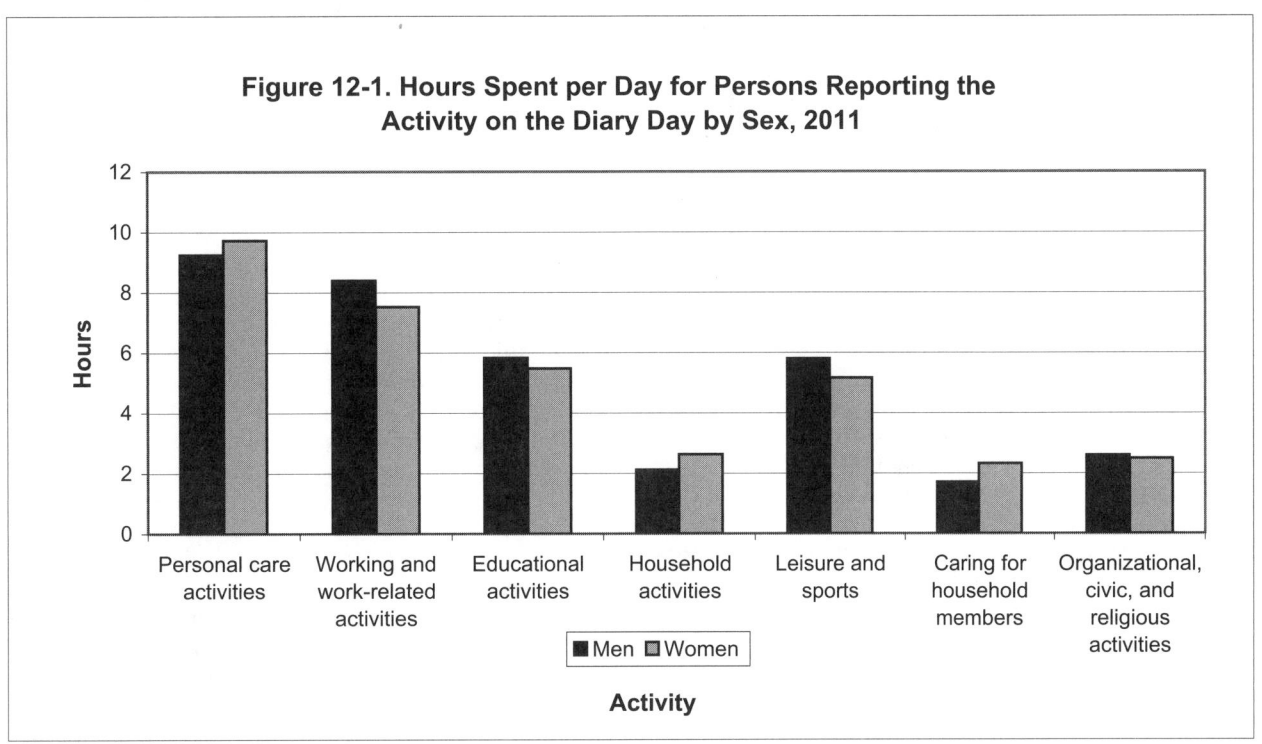

Figure 12-1. Hours Spent per Day for Persons Reporting the Activity on the Diary Day by Sex, 2011

On days that they worked, men worked 47 minutes more than women. This difference partly reflects women's greater likelihood of working part-time. However, even among full-time workers, men worked longer (8.3 hours compared with 7.8 hours). Meanwhile, women spent more time on household activities and caring for and helping household members. (See Table 12-3.)

OTHER HIGHLIGHTS

- Approximately 82 percent of employed persons worked on an average weekday while only 35.1 percent of employed persons worked on an average Saturday, Sunday, or holiday. (See Table 12-3.)

- Multiple jobholders were far more likely to work at home than single job holders (30.6 percent compared with 20.2 percent). (See Table 12-5.)

- The more education a person attained, the greater the likelihood they worked at home. On the days that they worked, 36 percent of employed persons age 25 years and over with a bachelor's degree or higher did some work at home, compared with only 11 percent of those with less than a high school diploma. (See Table 12-5.)

- Nearly 40 million people were eldercare providers in the United States in 2011. Those aged 45 to 54 years were most likely to provide eldercare while those 25 to 34 years were least likely to provide eldercare. (See Table 12-8.)

NOTES AND DEFINITIONS

Survey Methodology

While the Bureau of Labor Statistics (BLS) has long produced statistics about the labor market, including information about employment, hours, and earnings, the American Time Use Survey (ATUS) marks the first time that a federal statistical agency has produced estimates on how Americans spend another critical resource—their time. Data collection for the ATUS began in January 2003. Sample cases for the survey are selected monthly, and interviews are conducted continuously throughout the year. In 2011, approximately 12,500 individuals were interviewed.

ATUS sample households are chosen from the households that have completed their eighth (final) interview for the Current Population Survey (CPS), the nation's monthly household labor force survey. (See Chapter 1 of this *Handbook* for a description of the CPS.) ATUS sample households are selected to ensure that estimates will be representative of the nation.

An individual age 15 years or older is randomly chosen from each sample household. This "designated person" takes part in a one-time telephone interview about his or her activities on the previous day (the "diary day").

All ATUS interviews are conducted using Computer Assisted Telephone Interviewing. Procedures are in place to collect information from the small number of households that did not provide a telephone number during the CPS interview.

Concepts and Definitions

Average day reflects an average distribution across all persons in the reference population and all days of the week. Average day measures for the entire population provide a mechanism for seeing the overall distribution of time allocation for society as a whole. The ATUS collects data about daily activities from all segments of the population age 15 and over, including persons who are employed and not employed. Many activities are not typically done on a daily basis, and some activities are only done by a subset of the population.

Average hours per day refers to time spent in a 24-hour day (between 4 a.m. on the diary day and 4 a.m. on the interview day) doing a specified activity.

Average hours per day, persons reporting the activity on the diary day is computed using responses only from those engaged in the particular activity on the diary day.

Average hours per day, population is computed using all responses from the sample population, including those from respondents who did not do the particular activity on their diary day. These estimates reflect the total number of respondents engaged in an activity and the total amount of time they spent on the activity.

Diary day the day about which the designated person reports. For example, the diary day of a designated person interviewed on Tuesday would be Monday.

Household children refers to children under 18 years of age who reside in the household of the ATUS respondent. The children may be related to the respondent (such as their own children, grandchildren, nieces, nephews, brothers, or sisters) or not related (such as foster children or children of roommates). For secondary childcare calculations, respondents are asked about care of household children under 13 years of age.

Earnings

Usual weekly earnings represent the earnings of full-time wage and salary workers before taxes and other deductions and include any overtime pay, commissions, or tips usually received (at the main job in the case of multiple jobholders). Usual weekly earnings are only updated in ATUS for about a third of employed respondents—if the respondent changed jobs or employment status or if the CPS weekly earnings value was imputed. This means that the earnings information could be out of date because the CPS interview was done 2 to 5 months prior to the ATUS interview. Respondents are asked to identify the easiest way for them to report earnings (hourly, weekly, biweekly, twice monthly, annually, or other) and how much they usually earn in the reported time period. Earnings reported on a basis other than weekly are converted to a weekly equivalent. The term "usual" is as perceived by the respondent. If the respondent asks for a definition of usual, interviewers are instructed to define the term as more than half the weeks worked during the past 4 or 5 months.

Weekly earnings ranges refers to the ranges used to represent approximately 25 percent of full-time wage and salary workers. For example, 25 percent of full-time wage and salary workers with one job only had weekly earnings of $500 or less. These dollar values vary from year to year.

Employment Status

Employed persons are those who, at any time during the seven days prior to the interview: 1) did any work at all as paid employees, worked in their own business professions, or on their own farms, or usually worked 15 hours or more an unpaid workers in family-operated enterprises; and 2) all those who were not working but had jobs or businesses from which they were temporarily absent due to illness, bad weather, vacation, childcare problems, labor-management disputes, maternity or paternity leave, job training, or other family or personal reasons, whether or not they were paid for the time off or were seeking other jobs.

Employed full time workers are those who usually work 35 hours or more per week at all jobs combined.

Employed part time workers are those who usually work fewer than 35 hours per week at all jobs combined.

Not employed includes persons are not employed if they do not meet the conditions for employment. Not employed workers include those classified as unemployed as well as those classified as not in the labor force (using CPS definitions).

The numbers of employed and not employed persons in this report do not correspond to published totals from the CPS. While the information on employment from the ATUS is useful for assessing work in the context of other daily activities, the employment data are not intended for analysis of current employment trends. Compared to the CPS and other estimates of employment, the ATUS estimates are based on a much smaller sample and are only available with a substantial lag.

Major Activity Category Definitions

Caring for and helping household members refers to time spent doing activities to care for or help any child (under age 18) or adult in the household, regardless of relationship to the respondent or the physical or mental health status of the person being helped. Caring for and helping activities for household children and adults are coded separately in subcategories.

Caring for and helping non-household members includes time spent caring for and helping any child or adult who is not part of the respondent's household, regardless of the relationship to the respondent or the physical or mental health status of the person being helped.

Eating and drinking includes all time spent eating or drinking (except when identified by the respondent as part of a work or volunteer activity), whether alone, with others, at home, at a place of purchase, in transit, or somewhere else.

Educational activities include taking classes (including Internet and other distance-learning courses), doing research and homework, and taking care of administrative tasks, such as registering for classes or obtaining a school ID. For high school students, before- and after-school extracurricular activities (except sports) also are classified as educational activities.

Household activities are those done by respondents to maintain their households. These include housework, cooking, yard care, pet care, vehicle maintenance and repair, and home maintenance, repair, decoration, and renovation. Food preparation is always classified as a household activity.

Leisure and sports includes sports, exercise, and recreation; socializing and communicating; and other leisure activities, such as watching television, reading or attending entertainment events.

Organizational, civic, and religious activities captures time spent volunteering for or through an organization, performing civic obligations, and participating in religious and spiritual activities.

Other activities, not elsewhere classified includes security procedures related to traveling, traveling not associated with a specific activity category, ambiguous activities that could not be coded, or missing activities that were considered too private to report.

Personal care activities consist of sleeping, bathing, dressing, health-related self-care, and personal or private activities. Receiving unpaid personal care from others (for example, "my sister put polish on my nails") is also captured in this category.

Primary activity is the main activity of a respondent at a specified time.

Purchasing goods and service includes the purchase of consumer goods as well as the purchase or use of professional and personal care services, household services, and government services. Most purchases and rentals of consumer goods, regardless of mode or place of purchase or rental are classified in this category.

Secondary activity is an activity done at the same time as a primary activity. With the exception of the care of children under age 13, information on secondary activities is not systematically collected in the ATUS.

Telephone calls, mail, and email captures telephone communication and handling household or personal mail and email. Telephone and Internet purchases are classified in purchasing goods and services.

Working and work-related activities refers to time spent working, doing activities as part of one's job, engaging in income-generating activities (not as part of one's job), and job search activities. "Working" includes hours spent doing the specific tasks required of one's main or other job, regardless of location or time of day. Travel time related to working and work-related activities includes time spent commuting to and from one's job, as well as time spent traveling for work-related activities, generating income, and job searching.

Sources of Additional Information

Additional information, including expanded definitions and estimation methodology, is available from BLS news release USDL 12-1246, "American Time Use Survey—2011 Results," and the *ATUS User's Guide*, June 2008. All of these resources are available on the BLS Web site at <http://www.bls.gov/tus/>.

Table 12-1. Average Hours Per Day Spent in Primary Activities[1] for the Total Population and for Persons Reporting the Activity on the Diary Day, by Activity Category and Sex, 2010 and 2011 Annual Averages

(Hours, percent.)

Activity	Hours per day, total population			Percent of population reporting the activity on the diary day			Hours per day for persons reporting the activity on the diary day		
	Both sexes	Men	Women	Both sexes	Men	Women	Both sexes	Men	Women
2010									
All Activities[2]	24.00	24.00	24.00	X	X	X	X	X	X
Personal care activities	9.47	9.25	9.67	99.9	99.9	100.0	9.48	9.26	9.68
Sleeping	8.67	8.56	8.76	99.9	99.9	99.9	8.68	8.58	8.77
Eating and drinking	1.25	1.29	1.21	95.9	96.1	95.7	1.30	1.34	1.26
Household activities	1.79	1.42	2.14	75.5	66.8	83.7	2.38	2.13	2.56
Housework	0.57	0.26	0.87	34.7	20.0	48.5	1.65	1.30	1.79
Food preparation and cleanup	0.56	0.32	0.79	54.8	41.3	67.5	1.02	0.77	1.16
Lawn and garden care	0.21	0.31	0.12	9.9	12.3	7.6	2.14	2.51	1.57
Household management	0.12	0.10	0.15	17.7	14.0	21.3	0.70	0.71	0.69
Purchasing goods and services	0.75	0.62	0.86	43.9	40.2	47.4	1.70	1.55	1.81
Consumer goods purchases	0.37	0.30	0.44	39.8	36.6	42.9	0.94	0.83	1.03
Professional and personal care services	0.08	0.06	0.10	8.1	6.2	9.8	0.99	0.97	1.00
Caring for and helping household members	0.51	0.33	0.67	25.0	19.6	30.1	2.03	1.70	2.24
Caring for and helping household children	0.40	0.26	0.54	21.3	16.3	26.0	1.90	1.57	2.09
Caring for and helping non-household members	0.21	0.19	0.23	12.3	11.3	13.3	1.72	1.73	1.72
Caring for and helping non-household adults	0.08	0.08	0.08	8.0	7.7	8.3	1.01	1.08	0.95
Working and work-related activities	3.50	4.09	2.94	44.7	50.1	39.6	7.82	8.15	7.44
Working	3.14	3.65	2.66	42.0	46.8	37.4	7.48	7.79	7.11
Educational activities	0.47	0.47	0.48	8.4	7.8	9.0	5.61	5.96	5.32
Attending class	0.28	0.30	0.26	5.6	5.8	5.5	4.92	5.20	4.65
Homework and research	0.16	0.13	0.18	5.9	5.3	6.5	2.68	2.53	2.80
Organizational, civic, and religious activities	0.35	0.30	0.40	14.8	11.9	17.6	2.34	2.49	2.25
Religious and spiritual activities	0.16	0.13	0.18	9.2	7.3	11.0	1.69	1.84	1.59
Volunteering (organizational and civic activities)	0.15	0.13	0.18	7.0	5.7	8.2	2.19	2.23	2.16
Leisure and sports	5.18	5.57	4.82	95.8	96.1	95.4	5.41	5.79	5.05
Socializing and communicating	0.70	0.68	0.73	37.0	34.4	39.5	1.90	1.97	1.85
Watching television	2.73	2.94	2.53	79.4	80.4	78.4	3.44	3.66	3.22
Participating in sports, exercise, and recreation	0.31	0.42	0.20	18.5	21.5	15.6	1.66	1.93	1.30
Telephone calls, mail, and e-mail	0.18	0.13	0.21	23.0	18.0	27.8	0.76	0.75	0.77
Other activities n.e.c.	0.35	0.33	0.36	18.8	18.1	19.6	1.84	1.84	1.85
2011									
All Activities[2]	24.00	24.00	24.00	X	X	X	X	X	X
Personal care activities	9.49	9.25	9.72	100.0	100.0	100.0	9.49	9.25	9.73
Sleeping	8.71	8.62	8.80	99.9	99.9	99.9	8.72	8.63	8.81
Eating and drinking	1.24	1.27	1.21	95.9	96.5	95.3	1.29	1.32	1.27
Household activities	1.77	1.37	2.16	74.0	65.0	82.5	2.40	2.11	2.62
Housework	0.58	0.27	0.87	33.8	18.9	47.8	1.71	1.43	1.82
Food preparation and cleanup	0.56	0.31	0.79	53.4	40.1	66.0	1.04	0.76	1.20
Lawn and garden care	0.19	0.26	0.13	9.1	11.5	6.8	2.12	2.28	1.85
Household management	0.12	0.10	0.14	16.2	13.9	18.4	0.76	0.73	0.78
Purchasing goods and services	0.72	0.62	0.82	42.6	38.4	46.6	1.70	1.61	1.77
Consumer goods purchases	0.37	0.31	0.43	39.1	35.4	42.5	0.95	0.87	1.01
Professional and personal care services	0.07	0.05	0.10	7.2	5.3	9.0	1.02	0.85	1.11
Caring for and helping household members	0.51	0.33	0.67	24.4	19.5	29.1	2.08	1.70	2.31
Caring for and helping household children	0.39	0.24	0.54	20.8	15.7	25.6	1.90	1.54	2.10
Caring for and helping non-household members	0.21	0.19	0.22	11.7	10.9	12.5	1.77	1.75	1.80
Caring for and helping non-household adults	0.07	0.08	0.06	7.7	7.5	7.8	0.93	1.05	0.82
Working and work-related activities	3.57	4.23	2.95	44.6	50.4	39.2	7.99	8.39	7.52
Working	3.20	3.81	2.63	42.1	47.9	36.7	7.60	7.96	7.17
Educational activities	0.47	0.49	0.45	8.4	8.5	8.3	5.65	5.83	5.48
Attending class	0.28	0.30	0.25	5.4	5.7	5.1	5.12	5.31	4.93
Homework and research	0.15	0.14	0.16	5.7	5.7	5.7	2.65	2.55	2.74
Organizational, civic, and religious activities	0.35	0.30	0.40	14.0	11.7	16.2	2.53	2.59	2.49
Religious and spiritual activities	0.15	0.12	0.19	9.1	7.0	11.0	1.71	1.76	1.69
Volunteering (organizational and civic activities)	0.15	0.14	0.16	6.1	5.6	6.6	2.47	2.48	2.45
Leisure and sports	5.21	5.55	4.89	95.2	95.7	94.8	5.47	5.80	5.16
Socializing and communicating	0.70	0.63	0.77	35.6	32.3	38.8	1.97	1.95	1.98
Watching television	2.75	2.99	2.53	78.3	79.7	77.0	3.51	3.75	3.28
Participating in sports, exercise, and recreation	0.30	0.39	0.22	18.6	20.4	16.9	1.64	1.93	1.31
Telephone calls, mail, and e-mail	0.16	0.11	0.20	21.2	16.5	25.7	0.73	0.66	0.78
Other activities n.e.c.	0.29	0.29	0.30	16.5	15.4	17.6	1.78	1.88	1.69

Note: Data refer to respondents age 15 years and over, unless otherwise specified.

n.e.c. = Not elsewhere classified.

[1]A primary activity is designated by a respondent as his or her main activity. Other activities done simultaneously are not included.
[2]All major activity categories include related travel time.
X = Not applicable.

Table 12-2. Average Hours Per Day Spent in Primary Activities[1] for the Total Population, by Age, Sex, Race, Hispanic Origin, and Educational Attainment, 2011 Annual Averages

(Hours.)

Characteristic	Personal care activities	Eating and drinking	Household activities	Purchasing goods and services	Caring for and helping household members	Caring for and helping non-household members	Working and work-related activities	Educational activities	Organizational, civic, and religious activities	Leisure activities	Telephone calls, mail, and e-mail	Other activities n.e.c.
Both Sexes, 15 Years and Over	9.49	1.24	1.77	0.72	0.51	0.21	3.57	0.47	0.35	5.21	0.16	0.29
15 to 19 years	10.29	1.08	0.72	0.46	0.18	0.16	0.88	3.33	0.32	5.98	0.18	0.42
20 to 24 years	9.95	1.15	1.14	0.61	0.44	0.14	3.83	0.98	0.32	5.09	0.10	0.23
25 to 34 years	9.30	1.18	1.47	0.61	1.01	0.17	4.95	0.37	0.24	4.24	0.12	0.34
35 to 44 years	9.18	1.18	1.92	0.76	1.05	0.20	4.60	0.13	0.33	4.23	0.13	0.29
45 to 54 years	9.17	1.19	1.95	0.83	0.44	0.26	4.67	0.07	0.34	4.69	0.14	0.25
55 to 64 years	9.30	1.30	2.02	0.73	0.14	0.27	3.83	0.03	0.36	5.55	0.20	0.27
65 to 74 years	9.63	1.49	2.32	0.90	0.08	0.25	1.44	0.00	0.47	6.90	0.23	0.27
75 years and over	10.17	1.46	2.54	0.83	0.05	0.13	0.28	0.00	0.63	7.39	0.20	0.31
Men, 15 Years and Over	9.25	1.27	1.37	0.62	0.33	0.19	4.23	0.49	0.30	5.55	0.11	0.29
15 to 19 years	10.14	1.06	0.60	0.33	0.13	0.13	0.80	3.23	0.31	6.77	0.10	0.40
20 to 24 years	9.78	1.17	0.85	0.51	0.11	0.20	4.00	1.03	0.32	5.71	0.09	0.21
25 to 34 years	8.97	1.18	1.03	0.51	0.51	0.21	6.01	0.45	0.15	4.51	0.08	0.37
35 to 44 years	8.96	1.22	1.29	0.62	0.70	0.21	5.63	0.12	0.33	4.51	0.13	0.28
45 to 54 years	8.94	1.28	1.56	0.68	0.39	0.17	5.33	*	0.28	4.97	0.09	0.28
55 to 64 years	9.04	1.35	1.61	0.68	0.15	0.18	4.47	0.00	0.31	5.82	0.13	0.24
65 to 74 years	9.40	1.60	2.19	0.84	0.06	0.28	1.70	0.00	0.33	7.21	0.14	0.23
75 years and over	9.89	1.49	2.11	0.84	0.10	0.11	0.46	*	0.60	7.96	0.13	0.27
Women, 15 Years and Over	9.72	1.21	2.16	0.82	0.67	0.22	2.95	0.45	0.40	4.89	0.20	0.30
15 to 19 years	10.45	1.10	0.85	0.59	0.23	0.20	0.97	3.44	0.33	5.14	0.26	0.44
20 to 24 years	10.13	1.13	1.43	0.72	0.78	0.08	3.65	0.93	0.32	4.45	0.11	0.25
25 to 34 years	9.63	1.18	1.91	0.71	1.51	0.13	3.89	0.28	0.33	3.98	0.15	0.30
35 to 44 years	9.40	1.14	2.52	0.90	1.39	0.19	3.59	0.14	0.32	3.95	0.13	0.31
45 to 54 years	9.39	1.11	2.32	0.98	0.48	0.34	4.03	0.11	0.40	4.41	0.18	0.23
55 to 64 years	9.54	1.25	2.40	0.77	0.14	0.36	3.24	0.04	0.40	5.30	0.27	0.29
65 to 74 years	9.84	1.40	2.44	0.96	0.10	0.22	1.21	0.00	0.59	6.63	0.30	0.29
75 years and over	10.36	1.44	2.84	0.82	0.02	0.15	0.15	0.00	0.65	7.00	0.25	0.34
White, 15 Years and Over	9.45	1.28	1.85	0.73	0.52	0.21	3.63	0.43	0.33	5.14	0.15	0.29
Men	9.22	1.30	1.43	0.61	0.34	0.19	4.32	0.47	0.30	5.43	0.10	0.28
Women	9.66	1.25	2.25	0.84	0.70	0.22	2.96	0.39	0.35	4.86	0.19	0.31
Black, 15 Years and Over	9.84	0.91	1.36	0.71	0.39	0.23	3.12	0.64	0.52	5.77	0.20	0.30
Men	9.41	1.00	1.07	0.63	0.26	0.19	3.30	0.65	0.40	6.56	0.17	0.35
Women	10.18	0.84	1.60	0.78	0.49	0.27	2.97	0.64	0.61	5.13	0.22	0.26
Hispanic,[3] 15 Years and Over	9.90	1.19	1.83	0.74	0.68	0.14	3.39	0.71	0.27	4.79	0.10	0.27
Men	9.71	1.21	1.16	0.65	0.40	0.14	4.06	0.79	0.24	5.25	0.09	0.28
Women	10.10	1.17	2.53	0.83	0.98	0.14	2.68	0.62	0.29	4.29	0.11	0.26
Marital Status and Sex												
Married, spouse present	9.28	1.32	2.10	0.80	0.75	0.20	3.87	0.09	0.38	4.80	0.13	0.28
Men	9.07	1.35	1.61	0.71	0.53	0.17	4.70	0.05	0.34	5.10	0.09	0.29
Women	9.49	1.29	2.60	0.88	0.98	0.22	3.02	0.13	0.42	4.50	0.17	0.28
Other marital statuses	9.72	1.15	1.44	0.65	0.25	0.22	3.26	0.87	0.33	5.63	0.18	0.30
Men	9.45	1.18	1.09	0.51	0.11	0.21	3.71	0.99	0.26	6.05	0.13	0.29
Women	9.95	1.13	1.73	0.77	0.38	0.22	2.88	0.76	0.39	5.27	0.23	0.31
Educational Attainment, 25 Years and Over												
Less than a high school diploma	10.02	1.07	2.20	0.66	0.47	0.20	2.43	0.04	0.44	6.12	0.10	0.25
High school graduate, no college[4]	9.50	1.20	2.10	0.74	0.42	0.25	3.29	0.06	0.32	5.71	0.13	0.29
Some college or associate degree	9.34	1.24	1.97	0.74	0.55	0.25	4.04	0.20	0.32	4.93	0.15	0.27
Bachelor's degree and higher[5]	9.01	1.42	1.71	0.85	0.70	0.17	4.65	0.16	0.40	4.42	0.21	0.31

Note: 0.00 = Estimates are approximately zero.

* = Figure does not meet standards of reliability or quality.
[1]A primary activity is designated by a respondent as his or her main activity. Other activities done simultaneously are not included.
[2]All major activity categories include related travel time.
[3]May be of any race.
[4]Includes persons with a high school diploma or equivalent.
[5]Includes persons with bachelor's, master's, professional, and doctoral degrees.

Table 12-3. Average Hours Worked Per Day by Employed Persons on Weekdays and Weekends, by Selected Characteristics, 2011 Annual Averages

(Number, percent.)

Characteristic	Total employed (thousands)	Employed persons who worked on an average day			Employed persons who worked on an average weekday			Employed persons who worked on an average Saturday, Sunday, or holiday[1]		
		Number (thousands)	Percent of employed	Hours per day[2]	Number[3] (thousands)	Percent of employed	Hours per day[2]	Number[4] (thousands)	Percent of employed	Hours per day[2]
Both Sexes[5]	149 386	101 723	68.1	7.60	122 234	81.8	7.99	52 421	35.1	5.71
Full-time worker	115 758	83 389	72.0	8.10	101 936	88.1	8.46	39 288	33.9	5.87
Part-time worker	33 628	18 334	54.5	5.60	20 399	60.7	5.64	13 180	39.2	5.22
Men[5]	80 057	56 108	70.1	8.00	67 181	83.9	8.40	29 684	37.1	5.81
Full-time worker	67 465	49 523	73.4	8.30	60 067	89.0	8.70	24 735	36.7	6.00
Part-time worker	12 592	6 585	52.3	5.70	7 209	57.3	5.97	4 969	39.5	4.79
Women[5]	69 329	45 616	65.8	7.20	55 061	79.4	7.48	22 719	32.8	5.57
Full-time worker	48 292	33 866	70.1	7.80	41 874	86.7	8.13	14 517	30.1	5.63
Part-time worker	21 036	11 750	55.9	5.50	13 198	62.7	5.45	8 212	39.0	5.47
Multiple Job Holding Status										
Single job holder	135 219	90 504	66.9	7.60	109 619	81.1	7.92	44 000	32.5	5.61
Multiple job holder	14 167	11 219	79.2	8.10	12 654	89.3	8.61	8 135	57.4	6.20
Educational Attainment, 25 Years and Over										
Less than a high school diploma	9 665	6 104	63.2	7.70	7 506	77.7	7.79	2 627	27.2	7.19
High school graduate, no college[6]	35 501	23 603	66.5	8.00	29 206	82.3	8.24	9 866	27.8	5.98
Some college or associate degree	33 149	23 383	70.5	7.80	27 864	84.1	8.13	12 667	38.2	6.26
Bachelor's degree or higher[7]	49 050	35 610	72.6	7.60	43 384	88.4	8.09	17 323	35.3	4.62

Note: Data refer to persons age 15 years and over, unless otherwise specified.

[1]Holidays are New Year's Day, Easter, Memorial Day, Labor Day, Thanksgiving Day, the Fourth of July, and Christmas Day. In 2011, data were not collected for the day after Christmas.
[2]Includes work at main and other job(s) and excludes travel related to work.
[3]Number was derived by multiplying the "total employed" by the percentage of employed persons who worked on an average weekday.
[4]Number was derived by multiplying the "total employed" by the percentage of employed persons who worked on an average Saturday, Sunday, or holiday.
[5]Includes workers whose hours vary.
[6]Includes persons with a high school diploma or equivalent.
[7]Includes persons with bachelor's, master's, professional, and doctoral degrees.

Table 12-4. Average Hours Worked Per Day at Main Job Only by Employed Persons on Weekdays and Weekend Days, by Selected Characteristics, 2011 Annual Averages

(Number, percent.)

Characteristic	Total employed (thousands)	Worked on an average day			Worked on an average weekday			Worked on an average Saturday, Sunday, or holiday[1]		
		Number (thousands)	Percent	Hours per day[2]	Number[3] (thousands)	Percent	Hours per day[2]	Number[4] (thousands)	Percent	Hours per day[2]
Class of Worker										
Wage and salary workers	139 058	93 326	67.1	7.62	113 625	81.7	7.93	44 910	32.3	5.72
Self-employed workers[5]	9 965	6 352	63.7	6.54	7 212	72.4	7.02	4 151	41.7	4.39
Occupation										
Management, business, and financial operations	23 525	17 499	74.4	7.86	21 936	93.2	8.39	7 034	29.9	4.01
Professional and related	34 315	23 461	68.4	7.26	28 803	83.9	7.70	10 856	31.6	4.53
Services	27 015	16 484	61.0	7.14	18 467	68.4	7.28	11 621	43.0	6.57
Sales and related	15 467	11 052	71.5	7.21	12 344	79.8	7.45	7 655	49.5	6.19
Office and administrative support	18 628	12 247	65.7	7.48	15 416	82.8	7.67	5 004	26.9	6.16
Farming, fishing, and forestry	*	*	*	8.53	*	*	8.55	*	*	*
Construction and extraction	7 815	4 794	61.3	8.26	5 988	76.6	8.34	1 217	15.6	7.04
Installation, maintenance, and repair	5 349	3 690	69.0	8.21	4 811	89.9	8.48	1 342	25.1	6.20
Production	7 865	4 926	62.6	8.22	6 310	80.2	8.51	2 018	25.7	6.30
Transportation and material moving	8 399	5 219	62.1	8.13	6 399	76.2	8.42	2 342	27.9	6.21
Earnings of Full-Time Wage and Salary Earners[6]										
$0 to $540	24 083	16 346	67.9	7.92	20 003	83.1	8.12	7 747	32.2	6.70
$541 to $810	23 911	17 134	71.7	8.10	21 474	89.8	8.32	6 566	27.5	6.34
$811 to $1,230	23 882	16 508	69.1	8.17	20 659	86.5	8.44	5 954	24.9	5.73
$1,231 and higher	23 866	17 017	71.3	8.16	21 323	89.3	8.78	7 650	32.1	4.39

Note: Data refer to persons age 15 years and over, unless otherwise specified.

[1]Holidays are New Year's Day, Easter, Memorial Day, Labor Day, Thanksgiving Day, the Fourth of July, and Christmas Day. In 2011, data were not collected for the day after Christmas.
[2]Includes work at main job only and excludes travel related to work.
[3]Number was derived by multiplying the "total employed" by the percentage of employed persons who worked on an average weekday.
[4]Number was derived by multiplying the "total employed" by the percentage of employed persons who worked on an average Saturday, Sunday, or holiday.
[5]Includes self-employed workers whose businesses are unincorporated. Self-employed workers whose businesses are incorporated are classified as wage and salary workers.
[6]These values are based on usual weekly earnings. Each earnings range represents approximately 25 percent of full-time wage and salary workers who held only one job.
* = Figure does not meet standards for reliability or quality.

Table 12-5. Average Hours Worked Per Day at All Jobs by Employed Persons at Workplaces or at Home, by Selected Characteristics, 2011 Annual Averages

(Number, percent.)

Characteristic	Total employed (thousands)	Employed persons who reported working on an average day[1]								
		Number (thousands)	Percent	Average hours of work	Location of work[2]					
					Persons who reported working at their workplaces on an average day			Persons who reported working at home on an average day[3]		
					Number (thousands)	Percent	Average hours of work at workplace	Number (thousands)	Percent	Average hours of work at home
Full- and Part-Time Status and Sex										
Both sexes[4]	149 386	101 723	68.1	7.64	86 637	85.2	7.86	21 699	21.3	2.88
Full-time worker	115 758	83 389	72.0	8.10	72 057	86.4	8.27	17 276	20.7	3.00
Part-time worker	33 628	18 334	54.5	5.55	14 580	79.5	5.84	4 423	24.1	2.41
Men[4]	80 057	56 108	70.1	8.00	48 166	85.8	8.21	11 568	20.6	2.72
Full-time worker	67 465	49 523	73.4	8.30	42 976	86.8	8.47	10 150	20.5	2.75
Part-time worker	12 592	6 585	52.3	5.72	5 190	78.8	6.02	1 418	21.5	2.47
Women[4]	69 329	45 616	65.8	7.21	38 471	84.3	7.43	10 131	22.2	3.06
Full-time worker	48 292	33 866	70.1	7.81	29 081	85.9	7.97	7 126	21.0	3.34
Part-time worker	21 036	11 750	55.9	5.46	9 390	79.9	5.74	3 005	25.6	2.39
Multiple Job Holding Status										
Single job holder	135 219	90 504	66.9	7.59	77 549	85.7	7.82	18 268	20.2	2.82
Multiple job holder	14 167	11 219	79.2	8.05	9 088	81.0	8.19	3 431	30.6	3.20
Educational Attainment, 25 Years and Over										
Less than a high school diploma	9 665	6 104	63.2	7.72	5 645	92.5	7.49	669	11.0	4.10
High school graduate, no college[5]	35 501	23 603	66.5	7.96	21 327	90.4	8.14	2 640	11.2	3.48
Some college or associate degree	33 149	23 383	70.5	7.83	20 192	86.4	8.01	4 693	20.1	2.94
Bachelor's degree or higher[6]	49 050	35 610	72.6	7.59	27 754	77.9	7.99	12 662	35.6	2.71

Note: Data refer to persons age 15 years and over, unless otherwise specified.

[1] Includes work at main and other job(s) and excludes travel related to work.
[2] Respondents may have worked at more than one location.
[3] "Working at home" includes any time the respondent reported doing activities that were identified as "part of one's job"; this category is not restricted to persons whose usual workplace is their home.
[4] Includes workers whose hours vary.
[5] Includes persons with a high school diploma or equivalent.
[6] Includes persons with bachelor's, master's, professional, and doctoral degrees.

Table 12-6. Average Hours Worked Per Day at Main Job Only by Employed Persons at Workplaces or at Home, by Selected Characteristics, 2011 Annual Averages

(Number, percent.)

Characteristic	Total employed (thousands)	Employed persons who reported working on an average day[1]								
		Number (thousands)	Percent	Hours of work	Location of work[2]					
					Persons who reported working at their workplaces on an average day			Persons who reported working at home on an average day[3]		
					Number (thousands)	Percent	Hours of work at workplace	Number (thousands)	Percent	Hours of work at home
Class of Worker										
Wage and salary worker	139 058	93 326	67.1	7.62	81 347	87.2	7.83	17 012	18.2	2.62
Self-employed worker[4]	9 965	6 352	63.7	6.54	3 642	57.3	6.84	3 553	55.9	3.95
Occupation										
Management, business, and financial operations	23 525	17 499	74.4	7.86	13 803	78.9	8.24	5 981	34.2	3.16
Professional and related	34 315	23 461	68.4	7.26	18 393	78.4	7.84	7 855	33.5	2.34
Services	27 015	16 484	61.0	7.14	14 659	88.9	7.18	1 564	9.5	3.88
Sales and related	15 467	11 052	71.5	7.21	9 314	84.3	7.37	2 214	20.0	3.15
Office and administrative support	18 628	12 247	65.7	7.48	11 205	91.5	7.66	1 564	12.8	2.97
Farming, fishing, and forestry	*	*	*	8.53	*	*	8.63	*	*	*
Construction and extraction	7 815	4 794	61.3	8.26	4 535	94.6	8.37	486	10.1	*
Installation, maintenance, and repair	5 349	3 690	69.0	8.21	3 467	94.0	8.30	416	11.3	2.81
Production	7 865	4 926	62.6	8.22	4 743	96.3	8.21	254	5.2	*
Transportation and material moving	8 399	5 219	62.1	8.13	4 495	86.1	7.99	274	5.2	*
Earnings of Full-Time Wage and Salary Earners[5]										
$0 to $480	24 083	16 346	67.9	7.92	15 318	93.7	7.94	1 151	7.0	3.08
$481 to $730	23 911	17 134	71.7	8.10	15 859	92.6	8.17	1 928	11.3	2.05
$731 to $1,150	23 882	16 508	69.1	8.17	14 447	87.5	8.37	3 279	19.9	2.47
$1,151 and higher	23 866	17 017	71.3	8.16	14 083	82.8	8.52	5 069	29.8	2.68

Note: Data refer to persons age 15 years and over, unless otherwise specified.

[1]Includes work at main job only and excludes travel related to work.
[2]Respondents may have worked at more than one location.
[3]"Working at home" includes any time the respondent reported doing activities that were identified as "part of one's job"; this category is not restricted to persons whose usual workplace is their home.
[4]Includes self-employed workers whose businesses are unincorporated. Self-employed workers whose businesses are incorporated are classified as wage and salary workers.
[5]These values are based on usual weekly earnings. Each earnings range covers approximately 25 percent of full-time wage and salary workers.
* = Figure does not meet standards for reliability or quality.

Table 12-7. Average Hours Per Day Spent by Persons Age 18 Years and Over Caring for Household Children Under 18 Years, by Sex of Respondent, Age of Youngest Household Child, and Day, 2007–2011 Combined Annual Averages

(Number.)

Activity	Hours per day caring for household children								
	Total			Weekdays			Weekends and holidays[1]		
	Both sexes	Men	Women	Both sexes	Men	Women	Both sexes	Men	Women
Persons in Households with Children Under 18 Years									
Caring for household children as a primary activity	1.33	0.88	1.71	1.41	0.88	1.87	1.13	0.88	1.34
Physical care	0.44	0.24	0.62	0.47	0.24	0.66	0.39	0.22	0.52
Education-related activities	0.10	0.06	0.13	0.13	0.07	0.17	0.03	0.02	0.04
Reading to/with children	0.04	0.02	0.05	0.04	0.03	0.05	0.03	0.02	0.04
Talking to/with children	0.05	0.03	0.06	0.05	0.03	0.07	0.03	0.02	0.04
Playing/doing hobbies with children	0.29	0.26	0.32	0.27	0.23	0.31	0.34	0.33	0.34
Looking after children	0.08	0.05	0.09	0.07	0.04	0.09	0.09	0.08	0.10
Attending children's events	0.06	0.05	0.07	0.05	0.03	0.06	0.08	0.07	0.08
Travel related to care of household children	0.17	0.11	0.22	0.21	0.13	0.27	0.09	0.07	0.10
Other childcare activities	0.11	0.06	0.15	0.13	0.07	0.19	0.06	0.04	0.07
Persons in Households with Youngest Child 6 to 17 Years									
Caring for household children as a primary activity	0.78	0.53	1.01	0.86	0.54	1.15	0.60	0.49	0.69
Physical care	0.15	0.08	0.21	0.17	0.09	0.25	0.10	0.06	0.14
Education-related activities	0.11	0.07	0.16	0.15	0.08	0.20	0.04	0.03	0.05
Reading to/with children	0.02	0.01	0.02	0.02	0.01	0.02	0.02	0.01	0.02
Talking to/with children	0.06	0.03	0.08	0.06	0.03	0.09	0.04	0.02	0.05
Playing/doing hobbies with children	0.07	0.08	0.06	0.06	0.03	0.07	0.10	0.11	0.08
Looking after children	0.05	0.03	0.06	0.04	0.02	0.06	0.06	0.05	0.07
Attending children's events	0.07	0.06	0.09	0.06	0.05	0.07	0.10	0.09	0.12
Travel related to care of household children	0.16	0.11	0.20	0.19	0.12	0.25	0.09	0.08	0.09
Other childcare activities	0.09	0.05	0.13	0.11	0.05	0.15	0.05	0.04	0.07
Persons in Households with Youngest Child Under 6 Years									
Caring for household children as a primary activity	1.97	1.32	2.50	2.06	1.30	2.68	1.75	1.36	2.08
Physical care	0.78	0.43	1.07	0.81	0.43	1.11	0.72	0.42	0.97
Education-related activities	0.08	0.05	0.11	0.11	0.06	0.14	0.02	0.01	0.03
Reading to/with children	0.06	0.04	0.07	0.06	0.05	0.07	0.05	0.04	0.07
Talking to/with children	0.03	0.02	0.04	0.04	0.02	0.05	0.02	0.01	0.03
Playing/doing hobbies with children	0.55	0.48	0.61	0.52	0.43	0.59	0.62	0.59	0.64
Looking after children	0.11	0.08	0.13	0.10	0.06	0.13	0.13	0.13	0.13
Attending children's events	0.04	0.03	0.05	0.03	0.02	0.05	0.04	0.05	0.04
Travel related to care of household children	0.19	0.12	0.24	0.23	0.14	0.30	0.08	0.07	0.10
Other childcare activities	0.13	0.07	0.18	0.16	0.08	0.23	0.06	0.04	0.08

Note: Universe includes respondents age 18 years and over living in households with children under 18 years of age, whether or not they provided childcare.

Table 12-8. Number and Percent of U.S. Population and Various Subpopulations Who Were Eldercare Providers, by Sex, 2011 Annual Averages

(Number in thousands.)

Characteristic	Total			Men			Women		
	Total civilian noninstitu-tional population	Eldercare providers[1]		Total civilian noninstitu-tional population	Eldercare providers[1]		Total civilian noninstitu-tional population	Eldercare providers[1]	
		Number	Percent of population		Number	Percent of men		Number	Percent of women
Age									
Total, 15 years and over	243 651	39 794	16.3	118 356	17 652	14.9	125 296	22 142	17.7
15 to 24 years	42 225	5 418	12.8	21 512	2 961	13.8	20 713	2 457	11.9
25 to 34 years	41 365	4 185	10.1	20 712	2 076	10.0	20 654	2 109	10.2
35 to 44 years	39 498	5 223	13.2	19 446	2 293	11.8	20 052	2 931	14.6
45 to 54 years	43 850	10 198	23.3	21 455	4 117	19.2	22 395	6 080	27.2
55 to 64 years	36 991	8 303	22.4	17 802	3 527	19.8	19 189	4 776	24.9
65 years and over	39 721	6 468	16.3	17 430	2 679	15.4	22 292	3 789	17.0
Race and Hispanic or Latino Ethnicity[2]									
White	198 911	33 302	16.7	97 631	14 750	15.1	101 280	18 552	18.3
Black or African American	29 347	4 671	15.9	13 178	1 954	14.8	16 169	2 717	16.8
Hispanic or Latino ethnicity[3]	35 267	3 510	10.0	18 176	1 909	10.5	17 091	1 601	9.4
Employment Status									
Employed	149 386	25 334	17.0	80 057	12 084	15.1	69 329	13 250	19.1
Full-time workers	115 758	18 916	16.3	67 465	9 981	14.8	48 292	8 935	18.5
Part-time workers	33 628	6 418	19.1	12 592	2 103	16.7	21 036	4 314	20.5
Not employed	94 266	14 460	15.3	38 299	5 568	14.5	55 967	8 892	15.9
Educational Attainment, 25 Years and Over									
High school graduate or less	86 052	11 930	13.9	42 240	5 300	12.5	43 812	6 630	15.1
Some college or associate degree	50 397	9 808	19.5	22 741	3 840	16.9	27 656	5 968	21.6
Bachelor's degree and higher	64 977	12 639	19.5	31 863	5 551	17.4	33 115	7 088	21.4
Parent of Household Children Under 18 Years									
Parent of 1 or more household children	67 880	9 040	13.3	29 899	3 707	12.4	37 981	5 333	14.0
Not a parent of a household child	175 772	30 755	17.5	88 457	13 945	15.8	87 315	16 809	19.3

[1]Eldercare providers are those who in the previous 3 to 4 months cared for someone with a condition related to aging. Estimates were calculated for persons who cared for at least one person age 65 or over.
[2]Not all subcategories are shown.
[3]May be of any race.

Table 12-9. Number and Percent of Eldercare Providers by Sex and Selected Characteristics, 2011 Annual Averages

(Number.)

Characteristic	Eldercare providers[1]					
	Total		Men		Women	
	Number	Percent	Number	Percent	Number	Percent
Total, 15 years and over	39 794	100.0	17 652	100.0	22 142	100.0
Parent of Household Children Under 18 Years						
Parent of 1 or more household children	9 040	22.7	3 707	21.0	5 333	24.1
Not a parent of a household child	30 755	77.3	13 945	79.0	16 809	75.9
Number of Care Recipients						
Caring for 1 person	27 416	68.9	11 579	65.6	15 837	71.5
Caring for 2 persons	9 044	22.7	4 470	25.3	4 574	20.7
Caring for 3 or more persons	3 334	8.4	1 604	9.1	1 731	7.8
Relationship to Care Recipient						
Total, all eldercare providers[2]	39 794	100.0	17 652	100.0	22 142	100.0
Caring for a spouse or unmarried partner[3]	1 731	4.3	696	3.9	1 035	4.7
Caring for a parent	16 879	42.4	7 097	40.2	9 782	44.2
Caring for a grandparent[4]	7 605	19.1	3 376	19.1	4 228	19.1
Caring for another related person	8 253	20.7	4 281	24.3	3 971	17.9
Caring for someone else	10 095	25.4	4 499	25.5	5 596	25.3
Eldercare providers caring for 1 person only	27 416	100.0	11 579	100.0	15 837	100.0
Caring for a spouse or unmarried partner	1 516	5.5	622	5.4	894	5.6
Caring for a parent	11 436	41.7	4 627	40.0	6 809	43.0
Caring for a grandparent[4]	4 895	17.9	1 979	17.1	2 916	18.4
Caring for another related person	4 807	17.5	2 377	20.5	2 430	15.3
Caring for someone else	4 762	17.4	1 973	17.0	2 788	17.6
Care of Household Members						
Provided eldercare to household members only	5 200	13.1	2 618	14.8	2 583	11.7
Provided eldercare to nonhousehold members only	33 886	85.2	14 628	82.9	19 258	87.0
Provided eldercare to both household and nonhousehold persons	708	1.8	406	2.3	301	1.4
Frequency of Care[5]						
Provided care daily	8 076	20.3	3 403	19.3	4 674	21.1
Provided care several times a week	9 399	23.6	4 332	24.5	5 067	22.9
Provided care once a week	7 944	20.0	3 866	21.9	4 078	18.4
Provided care several times a month	8 069	20.3	3 458	19.6	4 610	20.8
Provided care once a month	4 513	11.3	1 881	10.7	2 632	11.9
Other	1 793	4.5	712	4.0	1 081	4.9
Duration of Care[6]						
Provided care less than 1 year	9 552	24.0	3 755	21.3	5 797	26.2
Provided care 1 to 2 years	10 417	26.2	4 645	26.3	5 772	26.1
Provided care 3 to 4 years	6 095	15.3	2 752	15.6	3 343	15.1
Provided care 5 years or more	13 730	34.5	6 501	36.8	7 230	32.7

Note: Data refer to persons 15 years and over.

[1]Eldercare providers are those who in the previous 3 to 4 months cared for someone with a condition related to aging. Estimates were calculated for persons who cared for at least one person age 65 or over.
[2]Estimates in relationship subcategories sum to more than 100 percent because some eldercare providers cared for more than one person.
[3]Care for a spouse or partner may be underreported.
[4]Persons caring for a grandparent with whom they lived are included in the category "Caring for another related person."
[5]Survey participants were asked how often they provided care in the past 3 to 4 months; this information was used to categorize them by frequency of care. Corresponding time and percent estimates were measured using information about care provided on the diary day.
[6]For persons who provided eldercare to more than 1 person, the duration of care is calculated based on the person for whom they had cared the longest.

Table 12-10. Percent of Eldercare Providers Who Provided Care and the Time They Provided This Care, by Day of Week and Selected Characteristics, 2011 Annual Averages

(Number.)

Characteristic	Number of eldercare providers	Percent of eldercare providers who provided care per day[1]			Average hours per day eldercare providers[1] spent providing care			Average hours per day eldercare providers[1] spent providing care on days they engaged in the activity		
		Total, all days	Weekdays	Weekends and holidays	Total, all days	Weekdays	Weekends and holidays	Total, all days	Weekdays	Weekends and holidays
Total, 15 years and over	39 794	23.6	22.2	26.7	0.74	0.69	0.84	3.12	3.09	3.16
Sex										
Men	17 652	22.2	21.2	24.3	0.57	0.54	0.65	2.58	2.53	2.67
Women	22 142	24.8	23.0	28.5	0.87	0.81	0.99	3.50	3.52	3.47
Age										
15 to 24 years	5 418	14.6	15.0	*	0.14	0.12	*	0.97	*	*
25 to 34 years	4 185	11.2	9.2	15.0	*	*	*	*	*	*
35 to 44 years	5 223	19.0	18.8	19.6	0.46	0.46	0.46	2.42	2.47	2.33
45 to 54 years	10 198	25.9	24.8	28.0	0.93	0.95	0.90	3.60	3.83	3.20
55 to 64 years	8 303	27.1	22.9	36.0	0.92	0.73	1.35	3.42	3.17	3.75
65 years and over	6 468	35.0	34.3	36.6	1.13	1.13	1.13	3.23	3.30	3.09
Race and Hispanic or Latino Ethnicity[2]										
White	33 302	23.7	22.2	26.8	0.71	0.65	0.84	3.02	2.95	3.13
Black or African American	4 671	24.8	23.6	27.7	0.81	0.81	0.82	3.27	3.41	2.96
Hispanic or Latino ethnicity[3]	3 510	29.3	*	21.2	0.73	*	0.55	2.51	2.49	2.57
Employment Status										
Employed	25 334	19.0	16.8	23.7	0.46	0.38	0.62	2.41	2.25	2.64
Full-time workers	18 916	17.7	15.8	21.6	0.47	0.38	0.63	2.63	2.42	2.94
Part-time workers	6 418	22.7	19.4	30.6	0.43	0.36	0.59	1.89	1.86	1.94
Not employed	14 460	31.8	31.5	32.3	1.23	1.22	1.24	3.86	3.87	3.85
Educational Attainment, 25 Years and Over										
High school graduate or less	11 930	28.2	27.2	30.2	0.89	0.89	0.88	3.14	3.26	2.93
Some college or associate degree	9 808	22.9	20.2	28.7	0.90	0.84	1.04	3.93	4.14	3.61
Bachelor's degree and higher	12 639	23.7	22.3	26.6	0.72	0.64	0.89	3.05	2.88	3.35
Parent of Household Children Under 18 Years										
Parent of 1 or more household children	9 040	18.0	17.1	19.8	0.61	0.65	0.53	3.39	3.81	2.67
Not a parent of a household child	30 755	25.3	23.6	28.9	0.77	0.70	0.94	3.06	2.95	3.26
Number of Care Recipients										
Caring for 1 person	27 416	25.2	24.5	26.8	0.84	0.80	0.93	3.32	3.25	3.45
Caring for 2 persons	9 044	20.0	16.1	27.4	0.51	0.41	0.71	2.56	2.52	2.60
Caring for 3 or more persons	3 334	20.2	18.6	23.7	0.52	*	*	2.56	2.65	*
Relationship to Care Recipient										
Eldercare providers caring for 1 person only	27 416	25.2	24.5	26.8	0.84	0.80	0.93	3.32	3.25	3.45
Caring for a spouse or unmarried partner[4]	1 516	*	*	*	3.65	3.90	3.11	5.54	5.77	4.99
Caring for a parent	11 436	31.1	29.5	35.0	1.04	0.95	1.24	3.34	3.24	3.54
Caring for a grandparent[5]	4 895	11.0	12.0	8.6	0.12	0.09	*	1.13	*	2.29
Caring for another related person	4 807	23.4	21.7	27.0	0.64	*	*	2.72	*	*
Caring for someone else	4 762	14.6	14.1	15.5	0.39	*	*	2.69	2.33	*
Care of Household or Nonhousehold Members[2]										
Providing eldercare to household members only	5 200	64.9	*	67.4	2.62	2.46	2.98	4.04	3.86	4.42
Providing eldercare to nonhousehold members only	33 886	17.1	15.9	19.7	0.44	0.42	0.50	2.59	2.64	2.51
Frequency of Care[6]										
Provided care daily	8 076	64.6	64.1	65.6	2.55	2.54	2.57	3.95	3.97	3.92
Provided care several times a week	9 399	27.4	27.2	28.1	0.60	0.54	0.72	2.17	2.00	2.57
Provided care once a week	7 944	11.7	6.9	21.3	0.22	0.09	0.47	1.85	1.32	2.20
Provided care several times a month	8 069	5.4	4.4	7.5	0.08	0.05	0.14	1.39	1.04	*
Provided care once a month	4 513	3.5	3.2	4.2	0.08	*	*	2.38	*	*
Duration of Care[7]										
Provided care less than 1 year	9 552	16.2	15.0	18.9	0.43	*	*	2.66	2.73	*
Provided care 1 to 2 years	10 417	22.9	22.7	23.5	0.71	0.69	0.75	3.08	3.03	3.19
Provided care 3 to 4 years	6 095	30.9	28.4	36.9	0.94	1.01	0.78	3.04	3.55	2.12
Provided care 5 years or more	13 730	26.0	24.1	30.2	0.88	0.74	1.19	3.38	3.06	3.93

* = Figure does not meet standards of reliability or quality.
[1]Eldercare providers are those who in the previous 3 to 4 months cared for someone with a condition related to aging. Estimates were calculated for persons who cared for at least one person age 65 or over.
[2]Not all subcategories are shown.
[3]May be of any race.
[4]Care for a spouse or partner may be underreported.
[5]Persons caring for a grandparent with whom they lived are included in the category "Caring for another related person."
[6]Survey participants were asked how often they provided care in the past 3 to 4 months; this information was used to categorize them by frequency of care. Corresponding time and percent estimates were measured using information about care provided on the diary day.
[7]For persons who provided eldercare to more than one person, the duration of care is calculated based on the person for whom they had cared the longest.

Table 12-11. Time Spent Providing Eldercare and Percent of the Eldercare Provider Population Engaging in Various Caregiving Activities, by Sex, 2011 Annual Averages

(Percent.)

Characteristic	Eldercare time spent in selected activities, percent distribution			On days they provided care					
				Percent[1] who engaged in the activity			Average hours spent providing care		
	Total	Men	Women	Total	Men	Women	Total	Men	Women
Total	100.0	100.0	100.0	100.0	100.0	100.0	3.12	2.58	3.50
Activities reported as care done for those 65 and over									
Eating and drinking	7.3	4.5	8.7	22.1	18.2	24.8	0.23	0.12	0.31
Household activities	22.6	23.5	22.0	40.2	33.0	45.3	0.70	0.61	0.77
Purchasing goods and services	4.6	4.7	4.5	16.2	15.3	16.9	0.14	0.12	0.16
Caring for and helping household members	6.3	4.2	7.5	16.6	14.1	18.4	0.20	0.11	0.26
Caring for and helping nonhousehold members	10.0	10.4	9.8	25.2	21.6	27.9	0.31	0.27	0.34
Working and work-related activities	6.5	*	*	4.8	5.6	4.2	0.20	*	*
Organizational, civic, and religious activities	2.5	*	2.6	4.5	2.7	5.8	0.08	*	0.09
Leisure and sports	31.9	32.8	31.5	36.5	32.9	39.0	1.00	0.84	1.10
Telephone calls, mail, and e-mail	1.0	0.8	1.1	6.4	5.5	7.1	0.03	0.02	0.04
Traveling	5.4	6.0	5.0	25.5	22.6	27.5	0.17	0.16	0.18
Other activities, not elsewhere classified	2.0	*	1.4	6.0	4.8	6.8	0.06	*	0.05

[1]Percents sum to more than 100 percent because some eldercare providers did more than one care activity on days they provided care.

* = Figure does not meet standards of reliability or quality.

Chapter Thirteen

INCOME IN THE UNITED STATES
(CENSUS BUREAU)

INCOME IN THE UNITED STATES (CENSUS BUREAU)

This chapter presents data on income and earnings in the United States collected by the Census Bureau. Income, as distinguished from earnings, includes income from pensions, investments, and other sources and is measured as real income in 2011 dollars.

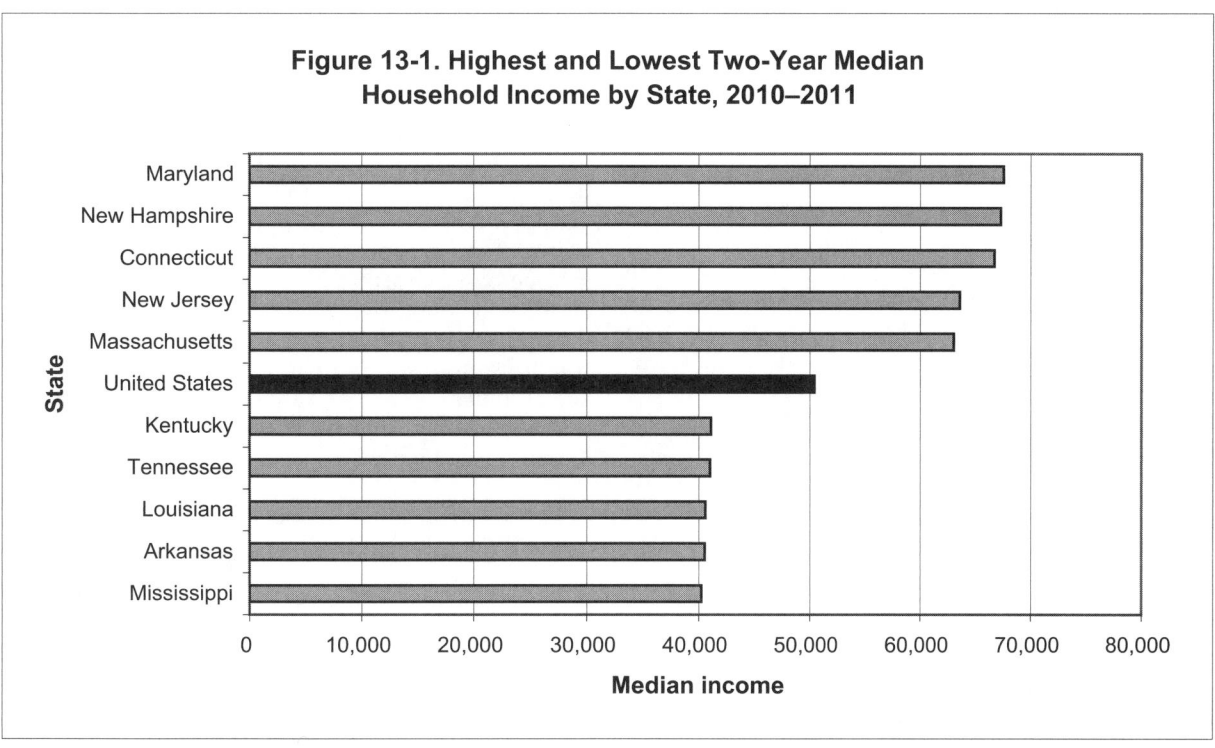

Figure 13-1. Highest and Lowest Two-Year Median Household Income by State, 2010–2011

In 2010–2011, the two-year average median income was $50,443, a slight decrease of $51,513 in 2009–2010. Median income was the highest in Maryland ($67,551) followed by New Hampshire ($67,307) and Connecticut ($66,748). (See Table 13-5.)

OTHER HIGHLIGHTS

- Median income also varied significantly by race and ethnic origin. In 2011, Asians had the highest median income at $65,129 followed non-Hispanic Whites ($55,412), Hispanics ($38,642) and Blacks ($32,229). (See Table 13-1.)

- In 2011, 21.0 percent of households had incomes of $100,000 or more. In 2006, before the recession, 23.1 percent of households had an income of $100,000 or more. (See Table 13-2.)

- Although median income was the lowest in the South, it was the only region that did not experienced a decline from 2010 to 2011. Median income fell 4.1 percent in the West, 2.1 percent in the Midwest, and 1.5 percent in the Northeast between 2010 and 2011. (See Table 13-1.)

- Median family income in the United States was $61,455 in 2011. Mississippi continued to have the lowest family income at ($46,304). Maryland had the highest median family income at $83,823 followed by Connecticut ($83,106) and New Jersey ($82,255). (See Table 13-6.)

NOTES AND DEFINITIONS

Collection and Coverage

The data in tables 13-1 through 13-5 are from the Annual Social and Economic Supplement (ASEC) to the 2012 Current Population Survey (CPS). The CPS ASEC provides timely estimates of household income and individual earnings, as well as the distribution of that income. The population represented is the civilian noninstitutionalized population living in the United States. Members of the Armed Forces living off post or with their families on post are included if at least one civilian adult lives in the household, hence, the CPS ASEC universe is slightly larger than the CPS universe which does not include persons who are on active duty in the armed forces.

The data in Tables 13-6 and 13-7 come from the American Community Survey (ACS). The ACS is an annual survey that covers the same type of information that had been collected every 10 years from the decennial census long form questionnaire. The ACS eliminated the need for a separate long form in the 2010 Census. The CPS ASEC and ACS surveys differ in the length and detail of its questionnaire, the number of households interviewed, the methodology used to collect and process the data, and, consequently, in the income and poverty estimates produced.

The sample size of the ACS is much larger (approximately 3.3 million in 2011) compared to the sample size of the CPS ASEC (100,000). Although it is smaller, the CPS ASEC is a high quality source of information due to its detailed questionnaire and experienced interviewing staff. Another notable difference between the two surveys is that the ACS is a mandatory whereas the CPS ASEC is voluntary.

Concepts and Definitions

The *Gini index of income inequality* (also known as the Gini ratio, Gini coefficient, or index of income concentration) is a statistical measure that summarizes the dispersion of income across an entire income distribution. Values range from 0 to 1. A Gini value of 1 indicates "perfect" inequality; that is, one household has all the income and the rest have none. A value of zero indicates "perfect" equality, a situation in which all households have equal income.

Equivalence-adjusted income inequality is another way to measure income inequality. Equivalence adjusted income takes into consideration the number of people living in the household and how these people share resources and take advantage of economies of scale. For example, the household-income-based distribution treats income of $30,000 for a single-person household and a family household similarly, while the equivalence-adjusted income of $30,000 for a single-person household would be more than twice the equivalence-adjusted income of $30,000 for a family household with two adults and two children. The equivalence adjustment used here is based on a three-parameter scale that reflects:

1. On average, children consume less than adults.
2. As family size increases, expenses do not increase at the same rate
3. The increase in expenses is larger for a first child of a single-parent family than the first child of a two-adult family.

Additional Information

Additional information is available in the Census publication "Income, Poverty, and Health Insurance Coverage in the United States: 2011," on the Census Bureau Web site at <http://www.census.gov/hhes/www/income/income.html>.

Table 13-1. Income and Earnings Summary Measures, by Selected Characteristics, 2010 and 2011

(Numbers in thousands, dollars, percent; income in 2011 dollars.)

Characteristic	2010			2011			Percent change in real median income (2011 less 2010)	
		Median income (dollars)			Median income (dollars)			
	Number	Estimate	90 percent confidence interval[1] (+/-)	Number	Estimate	90 percent confidence interval[1] (+/-)	Estimate	90 percent confidence interval[1] (+/-)
ALL HOUSEHOLDS	119 927	50 831	552	121 084	50 054	413	-1.5	1.00
Type of Households								
Family households	79 539	63 331	451	80 506	62 273	448	-1.7	0.80
Married-couple	58 656	74 782	739	58 949	74 130	945	-0.9	1.30
Female householder, no husband present	15 235	32 978	615	15 669	33 637	813	2.0	2.60
Male householder, no wife present	5 648	51 384	1 557	5 888	49 567	2 144	-3.5	5.00
Nonfamily households	40 388	30 511	597	40 578	30 221	420	-0.9	1.90
Female householder	21 420	26 165	641	21 383	25 492	517	-2.6	2.70
Male householder	18 968	36 605	814	19 195	35 482	797	-3.1	2.70
Race[2] and Hispanic Origin of Householder								
White	96 306	53 340	430	96 964	52 214	370	-2.1	0.70
White, not Hispanic	83 314	56 178	757	83 573	55 412	539	-1.4	1.20
Black	15 265	33 137	846	15 583	32 229	837	-2.7	2.60
Asian	5 212	66 286	2 673	5 374	65 129	2 577	-1.7	4.50
Hispanic[3]	14 435	38 818	988	14 939	38 624	900	-0.5	3.10
Age of Householder								
Under 65 years	94 190	56 850	589	94 241	55 640	476	-2.1	1.00
15 to 24 years	6 231	29 114	1 462	6 180	30 460	949	4.6	5.10
25 to 34 years	19 487	51 450	934	19 846	50 774	694	-1.3	1.80
35 to 44 years	21 458	63 355	842	21 241	61 916	693	-2.3	1.50
45 to 54 years	24 767	64 307	979	24 195	63 861	1 845	-0.7	2.80
55 to 64 years	22 246	58 256	1 133	22 779	55 937	1 162	-4.0	2.10
65 years and older	25 737	32 454	580	26 843	33 118	583	2.0	2.20
Nativity of Householder								
Native born	103 232	51 736	460	103 965	50 801	393	-1.8	0.80
Foreign born	16 695	45 354	1 781	17 119	44 431	1 244	-2.0	4.00
Naturalized citizen	8 568	54 616	1 649	8 874	51 926	1 159	-4.9	3.20
Not a citizen	8 127	37 561	949	8 246	37 894	1 261	0.9	3.80
Disability Status of Householder								
Households with householder aged 18 to 64	93 997	56 916	572	94 050	55 683	477	-2.2	1.00
With disability	8 951	26 300	1 176	8 793	25 420	1 128	-3.3	5.10
Without disability	84 632	60 378	743	84 787	59 411	734	-1.6	1.30
Region								
Northeast	21 721	54 667	1 739	21 774	53 864	1 467	-1.5	3.30
Midwest	26 772	49 762	913	26 865	48 722	1 138	-2.1	2.20
South	44 912	46 875	891	45 604	46 899	737	0.1	1.70
West	26 522	54 630	1 307	26 840	52 376	987	-4.1	2.10
Residence								
Inside metropolitan statistical areas	100 343	52 736	439	101 526	51 574	432	-2.2	0.80
Inside principal cities	39 956	45 258	1 261	40 616	43 571	1 087	-3.7	2.40
Outside principal cities	60 387	57 763	704	60 910	57 277	756	-0.8	1.20
Outside metropolitan statistical areas[4]	19 584	41 440	1 053	19 558	40 527	945	-2.2	2.30
Earnings of Year-Round Full-Time Workers								
Men with earnings	56 283	49 463	830	57 993	48 202	779	-2.5	1.90
Women with earnings	43 179	38 052	247	43 683	37 118	254	-2.5	0.80
Disability Status								
Workers without disability, age 15 and older								
Men with earnings	53 948	49 798	864	55 655	48 493	777	-2.6	2.00
Women with earnings	41 869	38 152	243	42 462	37 174	258	-2.6	0.80
Workers with disability, age 15 and older								
Men with earnings	1 655	42 868	1 062	1 622	42 211	2 700	-1.5	6.60
Women with earnings	1 229	32 873	996	1 152	34 168	2 635	3.9	8.80

[1] A 90-percent confidence interval is a measure of an estimate's variability. The larger the confidence interval in relation to the size of the estimate, the less reliable the estimate.
[2] Federal surveys now give respondents the option of reporting more than one race. Therefore, there are two basic ways of defining a race group. A group such as Asian may be defined as those who reported Asian and no other race (the race-alone or single-race concept) or as those who reported Asian regardless of whether they also reported another race (the race-alone-or-in-combination concept). This table shows data using the race-alone concept. The use of the single-race population does not imply that it is the preferred method of presenting or analyzing data; the Census Bureau uses a variety of approaches. Information on people who reported more than one race, such as White and American Indian and Alaska Native or Asian and Black or African American, is available from Census 2010 through American FactFinder. About 2.9 percent of respondents reported more than one race in Census 2010.
[3] May be of any race.
[4] The "outside metropolitan statistical areas" category includes both micropolitan statistical areas and territory outside of metropolitan and micropolitan statistical areas.

Table 13-2. Households, by Total Money Income, Race, and Hispanic Origin of Householder, 1967–2011

(Numbers in thousands, percent, dollars; income in 2011 CPI-U-RS adjusted dollars.)

Race and Hispanic origin of householder and year	Number	Total	Under $15,000	$15,000 to $24,999	$25,000 to $34,999	$35,000 to $49,999	$50,000 to $74,999	$75,000 to $99,999	$100,000 to $149,999	$150,000 to $199,000	$200,000 and over	Median income (dollars) Value	Median income (dollars) Standard error	Mean income (dollars) Value	Mean income (dollars) Standard error
All Races															
1967[1]	60 813	100.0	17.0	11.7	11.8	20.4	22.8	9.3	5.1	1.1	0.9	42 056	153	47 037	153
1968	62 214	100.0	15.5	11.5	12.2	19.1	23.9	10.4	5.6	1.1	0.7	43 868	159	49 630	159
1969	63 401	100.0	15.2	11.1	11.3	18.5	23.8	11.5	6.5	1.3	0.9	45 499	168	51 763	163
1970	64 778	100.0	15.3	11.2	11.5	18.0	23.5	11.4	6.7	1.4	0.9	45 146	165	51 695	165
1971[2]	66 676	100.0	15.6	11.9	11.5	17.8	23.1	11.3	6.7	1.3	0.9	44 707	173	51 417	163
1972[3]	68 251	100.0	14.8	11.5	11.2	16.7	23.0	12.2	7.8	1.8	1.1	46 622	178	54 262	168
1973	69 859	100.0	14.1	12.0	10.5	16.7	22.6	12.6	8.4	1.8	1.4	47 563	181	55 006	167
1974[4,5]	71 163	100.0	14.1	12.1	11.5	17.4	22.1	12.2	7.9	1.6	1.1	46 057	177	53 860	169
1975[5]	72 867	100.0	14.7	12.8	11.9	16.8	22.1	12.0	7.2	1.7	0.9	44 851	182	52 373	163
1976[6]	74 142	100.0	14.5	12.2	11.6	16.1	22.6	12.4	7.8	1.7	1.0	45 595	169	53 632	165
1977	76 030	100.0	14.3	12.5	11.6	15.7	22.2	12.4	8.2	1.8	1.2	45 884	172	54 430	166
1978	77 330	100.0	13.8	12.0	11.6	15.3	21.9	13.0	8.9	2.2	1.3	47 659	193	56 094	215
1979[7]	80 776	100.0	14.1	11.6	11.7	15.3	21.6	13.0	9.1	2.2	1.3	47 527	225	56 457	214
1980	82 368	100.0	14.4	12.1	11.8	15.8	21.5	12.5	8.8	2.0	1.2	46 024	236	54 737	200
1981	83 527	100.0	14.9	12.5	12.0	15.9	20.9	12.0	8.8	1.9	1.2	45 260	237	54 070	197
1982	83 918	100.0	15.2	12.5	11.7	16.2	20.7	11.6	8.7	2.1	1.3	45 139	204	54 399	201
1983	85 407	100.0	14.8	12.6	11.9	15.8	20.3	12.0	8.8	2.4	1.4	44 823	204	54 516	204
1984[8]	86 789	100.0	14.5	12.3	11.3	15.8	20.2	12.3	9.5	2.5	1.6	46 215	210	56 625	208
1985[9]	88 458	100.0	14.6	11.7	11.2	15.6	20.3	12.1	10.2	2.6	1.7	47 079	255	57 939	229
1986	89 479	100.0	14.2	11.2	11.0	15.0	20.2	12.8	10.5	3.1	2.0	48 746	253	60 223	245
1987[10]	91 124	100.0	13.9	11.3	10.6	15.0	19.7	12.9	11.1	3.2	2.1	49 358	233	61 382	252
1988	92 830	100.0	13.7	11.1	10.9	14.7	20.1	12.8	11.1	3.4	2.3	49 737	243	62 145	278
1989	93 347	100.0	13.0	11.2	10.4	15.0	19.9	13.0	11.5	3.5	2.6	50 624	278	63 958	278
1990	94 312	100.0	13.1	11.2	10.8	14.9	20.3	12.8	11.1	3.3	2.5	49 950	255	62 395	264
1991	95 669	100.0	13.7	11.8	10.8	15.5	19.4	12.4	10.9	3.3	2.2	48 516	234	61 071	251
1992[11]	96 426	100.0	14.0	12.1	10.9	14.8	19.1	12.7	10.7	3.2	2.3	48 117	228	61 003	256
1993[12]	97 107	100.0	14.0	12.2	10.8	15.2	18.4	12.5	10.9	3.5	2.7	47 884	224	63 497	343
1994[13]	98 990	100.0	13.5	12.4	10.8	14.9	18.2	12.6	11.0	3.7	2.9	48 418	221	64 729	348
1995[14]	99 627	100.0	12.9	11.8	10.4	15.0	19.2	12.4	11.5	3.6	3.0	49 935	289	65 852	360
1996	101 018	100.0	12.9	11.6	10.6	14.6	18.7	12.7	11.7	4.0	3.1	50 661	256	67 263	377
1997	102 528	100.0	12.4	11.2	10.9	14.1	18.6	12.8	12.2	4.2	3.6	51 704	239	69 430	388
1998	103 874	100.0	11.8	11.0	10.2	14.2	18.4	13.0	12.9	4.4	3.9	53 582	317	71 455	386
1999[15]	106 434	100.0	11.2	10.9	10.2	14.0	18.2	12.7	13.6	4.7	4.5	54 932	256	73 885	383
2000[16]	108 209	100.0	11.1	10.6	10.2	14.1	18.3	13.0	13.2	5.2	4.3	54 841	172	74 621	294
2001	109 297	100.0	11.5	10.9	10.4	13.9	18.1	12.8	13.2	4.8	4.4	53 646	164	73 947	295
2002	111 278	100.0	11.9	10.8	10.6	13.8	18.0	12.9	13.2	4.8	4.2	53 019	174	72 326	271
2003	112 000	100.0	12.4	11.2	10.0	14.1	17.7	12.3	13.2	4.9	4.3	52 973	230	72 232	264
2004[17]	113 343	100.0	12.4	11.1	10.5	13.9	17.9	12.4	12.8	5.0	4.1	52 788	233	71 997	271
2005	114 384	100.0	12.3	11.0	10.6	13.6	18.2	12.1	12.9	4.8	4.5	53 371	179	72 977	275
2006	116 011	100.0	11.9	10.7	10.7	13.6	18.1	11.9	13.3	5.2	4.6	53 768	231	74 259	287
2007	116 783	100.0	11.9	11.0	10.4	13.6	17.5	12.5	13.4	5.1	4.5	54 489	152	73 337	256
2008	117 181	100.0	12.4	11.1	10.8	13.7	17.7	12.3	12.7	4.9	4.2	52 546	143	71 475	253
2009[18]	117 538	100.0	12.4	11.3	11.0	13.8	18.0	11.9	12.5	4.9	4.3	52 195	223	71 278	255
2010[19]	119 927	100.0	13.4	11.8	10.6	13.7	17.6	11.5	12.5	4.7	4.2	50 831	335	69 518	371
2011	121 084	100.0	13.5	11.5	10.9	13.9	17.6	11.5	11.9	4.9	4.2	50 054	251	69 677	368
White[20]															
1967[1]	54 188	100.0	15.5	10.9	11.4	20.9	23.8	9.9	5.5	1.1	0.9	43 857	159	48 756	165
1968	55 394	100.0	14.2	10.7	11.8	19.5	25.0	11.0	5.9	1.1	0.8	45 675	170	51 415	170
1969	56 248	100.0	13.8	10.3	10.8	18.6	24.9	12.3	6.9	1.4	1.0	47 484	174	53 683	179
1970	57 575	100.0	14.0	10.6	11.1	18.2	24.5	12.0	7.1	1.5	1.0	47 023	181	53 504	176
1971[2]	59 463	100.0	14.2	11.2	11.2	18.0	24.0	11.9	7.2	1.4	1.0	46 762	178	53 279	173
1972[3]	60 618	100.0	13.3	10.8	10.9	16.8	23.9	12.9	8.4	1.9	1.2	48 910	188	56 372	183
1973	61 965	100.0	12.7	11.3	10.1	16.7	23.4	13.4	9.0	1.9	1.5	49 848	190	57 133	181
1974[4,5]	62 984	100.0	12.6	11.5	11.1	17.5	23.0	12.8	8.4	1.8	1.2	48 167	181	55 855	181
1975[5]	64 392	100.0	13.2	12.2	11.7	16.9	22.8	12.6	7.7	1.8	1.0	46 903	171	54 308	179
1976[6]	65 353	100.0	12.9	11.6	11.4	16.2	23.4	13.1	8.3	1.9	1.1	47 762	198	55 695	180
1977	66 934	100.0	12.8	11.8	11.4	15.8	23.0	13.2	8.8	2.0	1.3	48 250	203	56 557	183
1978	68 028	100.0	12.3	11.5	11.4	15.4	22.6	13.6	9.4	2.4	1.4	49 545	218	58 173	234
1979[7]	70 766	100.0	12.4	11.0	11.4	15.5	22.4	13.7	9.7	2.4	1.5	49 831	237	58 683	234

[1]Implementation of a new Curent Population Survey (CPS) Annual Social and Economic Supplements (ASEC) processing system.
[2]Introduction of 1970 census sample design and population controls.
[3]Full implementation of 1970 census–based sample design.
[4]Implementation of a new CPS ASEC processing system. Questionnaire expanded to ask 11 income questions.
[5]Some of these estimates were derived using Pareto interpolation and may differ from published data that were derived using linear interpolation.
[6]First-year medians were derived using both Pareto and linear interpolation. Before this year, all medians were derived using linear interpolation.
[7]Implementation of 1980 census population controls. Questionnaire expanded to show 27 possible values from a list of 51 possible sources of income.
[8]Implementation of Hispanic population weighting controls and introduction of 1980 census–based sample design.
[9]Recording of amounts for earnings from longest job increased to $299,999. Full implementation of 1980 census–based sample design.
[10]Implementation of a new CPS ASEC processing system.
[11]Implementation of 1990 census population controls.
[12]Data collection method changed from paper and pencil to computer-assisted interviewing. In addition, the 1994 ASEC was revised to allow for the coding of different income amounts on selected questionnaire items. Limits either increased or decreased in the following categories: earnings limits increased to $999,999, Social Security limits increased to $49,999, Supplemental Security Income and public assistance limits increased to $24,999, veterans' benefits limits increased to $99,999, and child support and alimony limits decreased to $49,999.
[13]Introduction of 1990 census sample design.
[14]Full implementation of 1990 census–based sample design and metropolitan definitions, 7,000 household sample reduction, and revised editing of responses on race.
[15]Implementation of the 2000 census–based population controls.
[16]Implementation of a 28,000 household sample expansion.
[17]Data revised to reflect a correction to the weights in the 2005 ASEC.
[18]Median income is calculated using $2,500 intervals. Beginning with 2009 income data, the Census Bureau expanded the upper income intervals used to calculate medians to $250,000 or more.
[19]Implementation of 2010 census-based population controls.
[20]For 2001 and earlier years, the CPS allowed respondents to report only one race group.

Table 13-2. Households, by Total Money Income, Race, and Hispanic Origin of Householder, 1967–2011
—*Continued*

(Numbers in thousands, percent, dollars; income in 2011 CPI-U-RS adjusted dollars.)

Race and Hispanic origin of householder and year	Number	Percent distribution										Median income (dollars)		Mean income (dollars)	
		Total	Under $15,000	$15,000 to $24,999	$25,000 to $34,999	$35,000 to $49,999	$50,000 to $74,999	$75,000 to $99,999	$100,000 to $149,999	$150,000 to $199,000	$200,000 and over	Value	Standard error	Value	Standard error
White[20]—Continued															
1980	71 872	100.0	12.7	11.5	11.6	16.0	22.3	13.1	9.4	2.1	1.3	48 555	249	56 946	218
1981	72 845	100.0	13.0	11.9	11.8	16.1	21.7	12.7	9.5	2.0	1.3	47 820	221	56 336	214
1982	73 182	100.0	13.4	11.8	11.6	16.4	21.4	12.2	9.4	2.3	1.5	47 256	215	56 641	222
1983	74 376	100.0	12.8	12.0	11.7	16.2	21.1	12.6	9.4	2.6	1.6	47 006	212	56 778	221
1984[8]	75 328	100.0	12.7	11.7	11.1	16.0	21.0	13.0	10.1	2.7	1.8	48 755	245	58 961	229
1985[9]	76 576	100.0	12.9	11.1	11.0	15.7	21.0	12.7	10.8	2.8	1.9	49 651	265	60 317	253
1986	77 284	100.0	12.4	10.7	10.8	15.0	20.9	13.4	11.2	3.3	2.2	51 248	249	62 732	268
1987[10]	78 519	100.0	11.9	10.8	10.5	15.1	20.5	13.6	11.9	3.4	2.3	52 003	261	64 005	277
1988	79 734	100.0	11.7	10.5	10.7	14.9	20.8	13.4	11.8	3.6	2.5	52 579	311	64 796	305
1989	80 163	100.0	11.1	10.8	10.3	15.1	20.5	13.6	12.2	3.7	2.8	53 251	259	66 622	308
1990	80 968	100.0	11.2	10.8	10.6	15.1	20.8	13.4	11.8	3.5	2.7	52 099	239	64 912	290
1991	81 675	100.0	11.7	11.4	10.7	15.6	20.0	13.0	11.6	3.5	2.4	50 840	246	63 649	277
1992[11]	81 795	100.0	11.9	11.7	10.8	15.0	19.7	13.5	11.4	3.4	2.6	50 588	245	63 757	284
1993[12]	82 387	100.0	12.0	11.7	10.7	15.3	19.1	13.2	11.5	3.7	2.9	50 518	294	66 344	383
1994[13]	83 737	100.0	11.7	11.8	10.8	15.0	18.7	13.2	11.6	4.0	3.2	51 065	287	67 582	393
1995[14]	84 511	100.0	11.2	11.4	10.3	15.1	19.6	13.0	12.2	3.9	3.2	52 411	274	68 476	397
1996	85 059	100.0	11.1	11.3	10.5	14.6	19.2	13.2	12.4	4.3	3.4	53 044	274	69 934	414
1997	86 106	100.0	10.8	10.9	10.6	14.1	18.9	13.3	12.9	4.5	3.9	54 452	345	72 518	442
1998	87 212	100.0	10.2	10.6	10.0	14.2	18.9	13.6	13.6	4.7	4.3	56 376	282	74 696	440
1999[15]	88 893	100.0	9.6	10.6	10.1	14.0	18.5	13.2	14.3	4.9	4.8	57 131	289	76 570	433
2000[16]	90 030	100.0	9.9	10.2	9.9	14.1	18.4	13.5	13.8	5.4	4.7	57 356	253	77 389	332
2001	90 682	100.0	10.0	10.6	10.1	13.8	18.4	13.2	13.9	5.1	4.8	56 554	266	76 874	330
White Alone[21]															
2002	91 645	100.0	10.4	10.4	10.3	13.5	18.4	13.5	14.0	5.0	4.5	56 366	229	75 219	306
2003	91 962	100.0	10.8	10.8	9.9	14.0	18.0	12.7	13.9	5.2	4.6	55 801	219	75 314	302
2004[17]	92 880	100.0	10.8	10.7	10.3	13.7	18.3	12.8	13.6	5.3	4.5	55 556	218	74 906	308
2005	93 588	100.0	10.7	10.6	10.4	13.6	18.5	12.8	13.6	5.1	4.8	55 938	244	75 993	315
2006	94 705	100.0	10.3	10.4	10.4	13.6	18.5	12.4	14.0	5.4	5.0	56 526	164	77 089	321
2007	95 112	100.0	10.3	10.7	10.2	13.5	17.9	13.0	14.1	5.4	4.9	56 531	167	76 290	291
2008	95 297	100.0	10.8	10.9	10.5	13.6	18.1	12.9	13.4	5.2	4.6	54 645	159	74 366	286
2009[18]	95 489	100.0	10.7	11.0	10.6	13.9	18.4	12.3	13.3	5.2	4.5	54 380	161	73 970	285
2010[19]	96 306	100.0	11.5	11.5	10.4	13.8	18.0	12.1	13.2	5.0	4.5	53 340	261	72 633	418
2011	96 964	100.0	11.6	11.1	10.8	14.1	18.0	12.0	12.5	5.3	4.5	52 214	225	72 812	422
White, Not Hispanic[20]															
1972[3]	58 005	100.0	13.2	10.5	10.6	16.6	24.1	13.1	8.6	2.0	1.3	49 608	236	57 026	255
1973	59 236	100.0	12.6	11.1	9.9	16.6	23.4	13.7	9.2	2.0	1.6	50 287	235	57 771	244
1974[4,5]	60 164	100.0	12.5	11.2	11.0	17.4	23.1	13.1	8.7	1.9	1.2	48 578	239	56 484	247
1975[5]	61 533	100.0	12.9	12.0	11.5	16.8	23.0	12.9	7.9	1.9	1.0	47 257	251	54 973	266
1976[6]	62 365	100.0	12.6	11.4	11.3	16.1	23.6	13.3	8.6	2.0	1.2	48 736	284	56 410	252
1977	63 721	100.0	12.5	11.6	11.1	15.7	23.2	13.5	9.0	2.0	1.4	49 207	277	57 257	270
1978	64 836	100.0	12.0	11.3	11.2	15.3	22.7	13.9	9.6	2.5	1.5	50 478	266	58 859	253
1979[7]	67 203	100.0	12.2	10.8	11.2	15.4	22.5	13.9	9.9	2.5	1.5	50 532	280	59 362	260
1980	68 106	100.0	12.4	11.2	11.4	15.9	22.6	13.4	9.7	2.2	1.3	49 415	108	57 695	260
1981	68 996	100.0	12.7	11.7	11.7	16.0	21.8	12.9	9.7	2.1	1.3	48 510	247	57 046	237
1982	69 214	100.0	13.0	11.5	11.5	16.4	21.6	12.4	9.7	2.4	1.5	48 048	242	57 474	246
1983	69 648	100.0	12.3	11.8	11.6	16.1	21.4	12.9	9.7	2.7	1.7	48 214	243	58 269	249
1984[8]	70 586	100.0	12.1	11.4	10.9	16.0	21.2	13.2	10.4	2.8	1.9	49 768	276	59 986	268
1985[9]	71 540	100.0	12.3	10.7	10.8	15.6	21.3	13.0	11.2	2.9	2.0	50 767	259	61 491	279
1986	72 067	100.0	11.9	10.3	10.6	15.0	21.1	13.8	11.5	3.5	2.3	52 413	270	63 977	294
1987[10]	73 120	100.0	11.3	10.4	10.3	15.0	20.8	13.9	12.3	3.5	2.4	53 433	297	65 257	303
1988	74 067	100.0	11.1	10.2	10.5	14.7	21.1	13.8	12.2	3.7	2.6	54 028	318	66 118	311
1989	74 495	100.0	10.5	10.5	10.1	15.0	20.6	13.9	12.6	3.9	2.9	54 396	266	67 957	333
1990	75 035	100.0	10.7	10.4	10.4	15.0	21.0	13.7	12.2	3.7	2.8	53 290	249	66 350	300
1991	75 625	100.0	11.1	11.1	10.5	15.5	20.2	13.4	12.1	3.7	2.5	52 054	256	65 015	290
1992[11]	75 107	100.0	11.3	11.3	10.6	14.8	19.9	13.9	11.9	3.6	2.7	52 286	324	65 377	302
1993[12]	75 697	100.0	11.3	11.3	10.4	15.1	19.4	13.6	12.0	3.9	3.1	52 377	307	68 092	406
1994[13]	77 004	100.0	11.0	11.4	10.6	14.9	18.9	13.6	12.1	4.2	3.4	52 713	279	69 303	411

[3]Full implementation of 1970 census–based sample design.
[4]Implementation of a new CPS ASEC processing system. Questionnaire expanded to ask 11 income questions.
[5]Some of these estimates were derived using Pareto interpolation and may differ from published data that were derived using linear interpolation.
[6]First-year medians were derived using both Pareto and linear interpolation. Before this year, all medians were derived using linear interpolation.
[7]Implementation of 1980 census population controls. Questionnaire expanded to show 27 possible values from a list of 51 possible sources of income.
[8]Implementation of Hispanic population weighting controls and introduction of 1980 census–based sample design.
[9]Recording of amounts for earnings from longest job increased to $299,999. Full implementation of 1980 census–based sample design.
[10]Implementation of a new CPS ASEC processing system.
[11]Implementation of 1990 census population controls.
[12]Data collection method changed from paper and pencil to computer-assisted interviewing. In addition, the 1994 ASEC was revised to allow for the coding of different income amounts on selected questionnaire items. Limits either increased or decreased in the following categories: earnings limits increased to $999,999, Social Security limits increased to $49,999, Supplemental Security Income and public assistance limits increased to $24,999, veterans' benefits limits increased to $99,999, and child support and alimony limits decreased to $49,999.
[13]Introduction of 1990 census sample design.
[14]Full implementation of 1990 census–based sample design and metropolitan definitions, 7,000 household sample reduction, and revised editing of responses on race.
[15]Implementation of the 2000 census–based population controls.
[16]Implementation of a 28,000 household sample expansion.
[17]Data revised to reflect a correction to the weights in the 2005 ASEC.
[18]Median income is calculated using $2,500 intervals. Beginning with 2009 income data, the Census Bureau expanded the upper income intervals used to calculate medians to $250,000 or more.
[19]Implementation of 2010 census-based population controls.
[20]For 2001 and earlier years, the CPS allowed respondents to report only one race group.
[21]Beginning with the 2003 CPS, respondents were allowed to choose one or more races. White alone refers to people who reported White and did not report any other race category. The use of this single-race population does not imply that it is the preferred method of presenting or analyzing the data; the Census Bureau uses a variety of approaches. Information on people who reported more than one race, such as White and American Indian and Alaska Native or Asian and Black or African American, is available from Census 2010 through American FactFinder. About 2.9 percent of respondents reported more than one race in Census 2010.

Table 13-2. Households, by Total Money Income, Race, and Hispanic Origin of Householder, 1967–2011
—Continued

(Numbers in thousands, percent, dollars; income in 2011 CPI-U-RS adjusted dollars.)

Race and Hispanic origin of householder and year	Number	Percent distribution											Median income (dollars)		Mean income (dollars)	
		Total	Under $15,000	$15,000 to $24,999	$25,000 to $34,999	$35,000 to $49,999	$50,000 to $74,999	$75,000 to $99,999	$100,000 to $149,999	$150,000 to $199,000	$200,000 and over	Value	Standard error	Value	Standard error
White, Not Hispanic[20]—Continued															
1995[14]	76 932	100.0	10.3	10.8	10.0	14.9	20.0	13.4	12.8	4.2	3.5	54 480	284	70 710	423
1996	77 240	100.0	10.3	10.7	10.1	14.5	19.4	13.7	13.0	4.6	3.6	55 365	380	72 049	. . .
1997	77 936	100.0	10.0	10.5	10.2	13.9	19.1	13.8	13.6	4.8	4.2	56 695	296	74 841	. . .
1998	78 577	100.0	9.5	10.1	9.6	13.8	19.1	14.0	14.3	5.0	4.6	58 480	336	77 088	471
1999[15]	79 819	100.0	9.1	10.1	9.7	13.6	18.5	13.6	15.0	5.2	5.2	59 604	377	79 080	468
2000[16]	80 527	100.0	9.6	9.7	9.6	13.7	18.3	13.8	14.5	5.8	5.0	59 586	239	79 743	358
2001	80 818	100.0	9.7	10.1	9.8	13.5	18.4	13.5	14.6	5.4	5.2	58 825	244	79 328	360
White Alone, Not Hispanic[21]															
2002	81 166	100.0	10.0	9.9	9.8	13.1	18.4	13.8	14.7	5.4	4.8	58 634	230	77 656	330
2003	81 148	100.0	10.3	10.3	9.5	13.5	18.1	13.1	14.6	5.6	5.0	58 426	282	78 126	331
2004[17]	81 628	100.0	10.3	10.3	9.9	13.3	18.2	13.2	14.3	5.7	4.8	58 237	267	77 703	338
2005	82 003	100.0	10.1	10.0	10.0	13.2	18.4	13.2	14.3	5.5	5.2	58 507	198	79 036	349
2006	82 675	100.0	9.7	9.8	10.0	13.2	18.4	12.8	14.7	5.8	5.4	58 478	210	80 032	354
2007	82 765	100.0	9.8	10.2	9.7	13.1	17.8	13.3	14.9	5.9	5.3	59 573	268	79 383	320
2008	82 884	100.0	10.1	10.4	10.0	13.1	18.3	13.4	14.2	5.6	5.0	58 006	235	77 406	317
2009[18]	83 158	100.0	10.0	10.5	10.1	13.7	18.5	12.7	14.0	5.6	4.9	57 106	293	76 797	314
2010[19]	83 314	100.0	10.7	11.0	9.9	13.4	18.1	12.5	14.1	5.3	5.0	56 178	460	75 646	475
2011	83 573	100.0	10.9	10.5	10.3	13.7	18.2	12.4	13.3	5.7	5.0	55 412	328	76 063	478
Black[20]															
1967[1]	5 728	100.0	30.9	19.0	15.5	15.9	12.7	3.5	2.0	0.3	0.2	25 464	424	30 598	341
1968	5 870	100.0	27.8	19.3	15.9	16.2	13.8	4.6	2.1	0.2	-	26 934	391	32 803	346
1969	6 053	100.0	26.9	18.1	15.6	17.3	14.6	5.0	2.2	0.2	0.1	28 702	423	34 169	363
1970	6 180	100.0	27.5	16.9	15.5	16.1	15.1	5.9	2.5	0.4	0.2	28 621	393	34 948	377
1971[2]	6 578	100.0	28.5	17.9	14.5	16.3	14.7	5.3	2.5	0.2	0.1	27 622	411	34 228	352
1972[3]	6 809	100.0	27.8	17.5	14.1	15.8	15.2	6.4	2.6	0.4	0.3	28 549	428	36 064	385
1973	7 040	100.0	25.9	18.0	13.4	16.6	16.4	5.8	3.1	0.5	0.2	29 342	457	36 437	362
1974[4,5]	7 263	100.0	26.7	17.4	15.0	16.4	14.9	6.7	2.6	0.2	0.1	28 645	346	35 626	317
1975[5]	7 489	100.0	27.9	18.2	13.2	16.4	15.1	6.3	2.7	0.4	-	28 157	414	35 147	312
1976[6]	7 776	100.0	27.2	17.6	13.5	15.4	16.4	6.4	3.1	0.3	0.1	28 401	352	36 286	323
1977	7 977	100.0	26.6	18.9	14.0	14.7	15.5	6.3	3.5	0.4	0.3	28 473	382	36 482	325
1978	8 066	100.0	27.3	16.4	13.5	14.8	15.7	7.4	4.3	0.6	0.1	29 774	630	38 051	497
1979[7]	8 586	100.0	27.5	16.8	14.0	14.3	15.5	7.5	3.9	0.4	0.2	29 256	534	37 540	462
1980	8 847	100.0	28.6	17.3	13.8	14.2	14.8	7.1	3.5	0.5	0.1	27 973	528	36 304	447
1981	8 961	100.0	30.2	17.5	13.5	14.1	14.5	6.4	3.5	0.3	0.1	26 835	451	35 251	427
1982	8 916	100.0	30.1	17.6	12.6	14.7	15.2	6.3	2.9	0.5	0.2	26 782	430	35 239	441
1983	9 236	100.0	30.2	16.8	13.7	14.1	14.1	6.7	3.9	0.5	0.1	26 675	500	35 479	438
1984[8]	9 480	100.0	29.2	17.3	12.8	14.7	13.7	7.1	4.2	0.8	0.2	27 774	534	37 042	456
1985[9]	9 797	100.0	28.4	16.0	13.1	14.5	14.9	7.4	4.6	0.8	0.3	29 540	574	38 542	500
1986	9 922	100.0	29.1	14.8	12.5	14.6	15.1	7.6	4.9	0.9	0.4	29 525	580	39 613	538
1987[10]	10 192	100.0	29.3	15.2	12.0	15.2	14.1	7.8	4.7	1.2	0.6	29 682	568	40 077	551
1988	10 561	100.0	28.9	15.3	12.0	14.0	14.4	7.8	5.8	1.3	0.5	29 974	625	41 063	599
1989	10 486	100.0	27.4	14.6	11.8	14.5	15.8	7.9	6.3	1.3	0.4	31 669	644	42 023	571
1990	10 671	100.0	27.7	14.7	12.2	13.9	16.1	8.2	5.5	1.2	0.6	31 155	711	41 394	559
1991	11 083	100.0	29.3	14.6	11.5	14.5	15.9	7.4	5.1	1.4	0.4	30 287	636	40 330	527
1992[11]	11 269	100.0	29.2	15.7	11.9	14.1	14.9	7.6	5.0	1.1	0.6	29 457	602	39 972	542
1993[12]	11 281	100.0	28.3	15.8	12.2	14.8	13.9	7.5	5.5	1.3	0.7	29 939	592	41 734	693
1994[13]	11 655	100.0	26.3	16.1	11.7	14.2	14.6	8.4	6.2	1.7	0.9	31 555	587	43 908	630
1995[14]	11 577	100.0	24.9	15.5	11.8	15.0	16.6	8.0	6.1	1.2	0.8	32 815	560	44 548	762
1996	12 109	100.0	24.9	14.8	12.1	14.8	15.5	9.5	6.2	1.4	0.9	33 518	659	46 333	905
1997	12 474	100.0	23.4	14.1	13.3	14.5	16.7	9.3	6.2	1.6	0.9	35 000	602	46 056	661
1998	12 579	100.0	23.4	14.7	12.5	14.6	15.5	8.9	7.2	2.0	1.1	34 933	547	47 043	628
1999[15]	12 838	100.0	21.1	13.7	12.1	14.5	16.4	9.3	8.5	3.1	1.3	37 673	702	51 917	745
2000[16]	13 174	100.0	19.7	13.8	12.9	14.8	17.7	9.4	8.0	2.4	1.3	38 747	513	51 168	519
2001	13 315	100.0	21.0	13.7	12.6	15.1	16.6	9.9	7.9	1.9	1.3	37 438	441	49 860	526

[1]Implementation of a new Curent Population Survey (CPS) Annual Social and Economic Supplements (ASEC) processing system.
[2]Introduction of 1970 census sample design and population controls.
[3]Full implementation of 1970 census–based sample design.
[4]Implementation of a new CPS ASEC processing system. Questionnaire expanded to ask 11 income questions.
[5]Some of these estimates were derived using Pareto interpolation and may differ from published data that were derived using linear interpolation.
[6]First-year medians were derived using both Pareto and linear interpolation. Before this year, all medians were derived using linear interpolation.
[7]Implementation of 1980 census population controls. Questionnaire expanded to show 27 possible values from a list of 51 possible sources of income.
[8]Implementation of Hispanic population weighting controls and introduction of 1980 census–based sample design.
[9]Recording of amounts for earnings from longest job increased to $299,999. Full implementation of 1980 census–based sample design.
[10]Implementation of a new CPS ASEC processing system.
[11]Implementation of 1990 census population controls.
[12]Data collection method changed from paper and pencil to computer-assisted interviewing. In addition, the 1994 ASEC was revised to allow for the coding of different income amounts on selected questionnaire items. Limits either increased or decreased in the following categories: earnings limits increased to $999,999, Social Security limits increased to $49,999, Supplemental Security Income and public assistance limits increased to $24,999, veterans' benefits limits increased to $99,999, and child support and alimony limits decreased to $49,999.
[13]Introduction of 1990 census sample design.
[14]Full implementation of 1990 census–based sample design and metropolitan definitions, 7,000 household sample reduction, and revised editing of responses on race.
[15]Implementation of the 2000 census–based population controls.
[16]Implementation of a 28,000 household sample expansion.
[17]Data revised to reflect a correction to the weights in the 2005 ASEC.
[18]Median income is calculated using $2,500 intervals. Beginning with 2009 income data, the Census Bureau expanded the upper income intervals used to calculate medians to $250,000 or more.
[19]Implementation of 2010 census-based population controls.
[20]For 2001 and earlier years, the CPS allowed respondents to report only one race group.
[21]Beginning with the 2003 CPS, respondents were allowed to choose one or more races. White alone refers to people who reported White and did not report any other race category. The use of this single-race population does not imply that it is the preferred method of presenting or analyzing the data; the Census Bureau uses a variety of approaches. Information on people who reported more than one race, such as White and American Indian and Alaska Native or Asian and Black or African American, is available from Census 2010 through American FactFinder. About 2.9 percent of respondents reported more than one race in Census 2010.
. . . = Not available.
- = Quantity zero.

Table 13-2. Households, by Total Money Income, Race, and Hispanic Origin of Householder, 1967–2011
—Continued

(Numbers in thousands, percent, dollars; income in 2011 CPI-U-RS adjusted dollars.)

Race and Hispanic origin of householder and year	Number	Percent distribution										Median income (dollars)		Mean income (dollars)	
		Total	Under $15,000	$15,000 to $24,999	$25,000 to $34,999	$35,000 to $49,999	$50,000 to $74,999	$75,000 to $99,999	$100,000 to $149,999	$150,000 to $199,000	$200,000 and over	Value	Standard error	Value	Standard error
Black Alone[22]															
2002	13 465	100.0	21.7	14.1	12.7	15.8	15.2	9.2	7.3	2.3	1.6	36 288	489	50 021	578
2003	13 629	100.0	22.4	14.5	12.0	15.1	15.9	8.8	7.8	2.0	1.3	36 252	472	49 075	526
2004[17]	13 809	100.0	23.2	13.9	12.3	15.6	15.3	9.4	6.9	2.0	1.4	35 834	373	48 382	524
2005	14 002	100.0	22.9	15.0	12.3	14.3	16.3	8.3	7.3	2.4	1.3	35 551	347	48 910	531
2006	14 354	100.0	22.4	14.1	12.9	14.5	16.1	8.5	7.5	2.2	1.7	35 661	269	50 339	622
2007	14 551	100.0	22.3	13.9	12.4	14.6	15.9	9.3	8.0	2.3	1.4	36 790	515	50 582	564
2008	14 595	100.0	22.5	13.5	13.3	15.4	15.9	8.5	7.4	2.2	1.3	35 744	461	48 608	520
2009[18]	14 730	100.0	22.5	14.6	13.8	14.3	15.5	9.2	6.8	2.0	1.3	34 167	413	48 283	551
2010[19]	15 265	100.0	25.2	14.6	12.4	14.4	15.1	8.2	6.9	2.0	1.3	33 137	515	46 375	646
2011	15 583	100.0	25.6	15.0	12.2	13.5	15.3	8.0	6.8	2.1	1.5	32 229	509	47 255	803
Black Alone or in Combination															
2002	13 778	100.0	21.6	14.1	12.7	15.8	15.3	9.2	7.4	2.3	1.7	36 477	480	50 425	588
2003	13 969	100.0	22.3	14.5	12.1	15.0	16.0	8.9	7.8	2.1	1.3	36 306	456	49 302	522
2004[17]	14 151	100.0	23.1	13.8	12.3	15.6	15.4	9.5	7.0	2.1	1.3	36 001	330	48 532	516
2005	14 399	100.0	22.8	15.0	12.2	14.2	16.4	8.3	7.4	2.4	1.3	35 661	340	49 225	536
2006	14 709	100.0	22.2	14.1	12.8	14.6	16.2	8.5	7.6	2.3	1.7	35 843	265	50 748	622
2007	14 976	100.0	22.2	13.9	12.3	14.6	15.8	9.3	8.1	2.3	1.4	36 979	504	50 799	555
2008	15 056	100.0	22.3	13.5	13.3	15.4	16.0	8.5	7.5	2.3	1.3	35 877	459	48 761	510
2009[18]	15 212	100.0	22.4	14.6	13.8	14.2	15.5	9.1	6.8	2.1	1.4	34 341	438	48 528	541
2010[19]	15 909	100.0	25.0	14.7	12.5	14.3	14.9	8.2	6.9	2.0	1.4	33 170	485	46 934	647
2011	16 165	100.0	25.4	14.9	12.1	13.5	15.3	8.0	6.9	2.1	1.6	32 366	553	47 506	773
Asian and Pacific Islander[20]															
1987[10]	. . .	100.0	11.2	11.4	9.0	11.1	18.3	13.6	16.5	5.9	3.0	61 034	2 269	. . .	. . .
1988	1 913	100.0	9.9	11.0	8.4	12.2	19.9	13.1	15.9	6.2	3.4	58 948	2 422	73 698	2 201
1989	1 988	100.0	9.3	8.6	7.9	13.1	20.3	14.7	15.8	4.8	5.4	63 226	1 709	78 599	2 287
1990	1 958	100.0	9.8	8.4	8.9	11.5	19.9	13.9	17.0	6.2	4.3	64 142	1 900	77 424	2 192
1991	2 094	100.0	11.1	8.8	9.7	13.4	17.8	14.4	14.4	6.3	4.0	58 699	1 894	74 528	2 197
1992[11]	2 262	100.0	11.4	10.1	8.5	12.0	20.0	12.8	15.9	5.3	3.7	59 371	1 714	73 583	2 023
1993[12]	2 233	100.0	13.5	9.6	9.1	13.1	14.5	14.2	16.8	5.5	3.8	58 775	2 891	77 010	3 101
1994[13]	2 040	100.0	11.0	10.2	8.1	13.4	16.8	14.9	14.6	5.8	5.2	60 751	2 302	78 879	2 811
1995[14]	2 777	100.0	12.2	9.4	6.6	13.1	20.3	13.8	14.2	5.7	4.7	59 516	1 493	80 931	3 265
1996	2 998	100.0	11.8	7.9	8.6	12.1	19.0	12.3	17.0	7.2	4.0	61 772	2 214	80 715	2 895
1997	3 125	100.0	10.9	8.1	8.1	11.9	18.8	14.2	16.6	6.5	4.8	63 222	1 758	82 282	2 550
1998	3 308	100.0	10.2	8.3	8.3	13.1	17.8	12.7	17.5	6.5	5.6	64 265	1 789	82 965	2 396
1999[15]	3 742	100.0	10.7	6.9	7.4	12.4	16.6	13.2	15.7	8.6	8.6	68 787	2 424	90 960	2 305
2000[16]	3 963	100.0	8.7	7.1	7.5	11.2	17.1	14.9	16.8	9.3	7.5	72 821	1 242	95 077	1 973
2001	4 071	100.0	9.6	7.4	8.4	12.1	17.1	13.3	16.8	7.8	7.5	68 137	1 626	92 940	2 194
Asian Alone[23]															
2002	3 917	100.0	9.4	7.9	8.3	12.4	17.2	13.0	17.5	7.5	6.8	65 792	1 151	87 572	1 708
2003	4 040	100.0	12.6	9.3	5.1	11.3	16.8	13.7	16.5	8.3	6.4	68 113	1 338	85 569	1 515
2004[17]	4 123	100.0	9.8	7.9	7.4	11.2	17.9	13.4	16.9	8.2	7.3	68 470	1 455	91 109	1 762
2005	4 273	100.0	10.8	7.6	7.1	9.5	18.5	12.5	17.9	7.4	8.8	70 385	820	92 277	1 628
2006	4 454	100.0	9.5	7.2	8.0	10.1	17.7	12.1	17.6	9.9	8.0	71 658	1 867	98 491	2 119
2007	4 494	100.0	9.7	7.9	7.5	10.8	16.0	13.5	18.2	8.9	7.6	71 704	1 502	92 221	1 627
2008	4 573	100.0	11.2	8.2	7.8	11.1	15.6	12.4	17.6	8.5	7.6	68 564	1 448	90 028	1 570
2009[18]	4 687	100.0	11.3	7.2	8.6	10.1	17.1	11.9	16.8	8.2	8.8	68 649	1 329	95 222	1 935
2010[19]	5 212	100.0	10.6	9.4	7.1	10.8	17.9	11.3	16.7	8.7	7.5	66 286	1 625	87 252	1 749
2011	5 374	100.0	10.6	8.8	8.3	11.3	17.4	12.8	17.4	6.6	6.8	65 129	1 567	85 644	2 073
Asian Alone or in Combination															
2002	4 079	100.0	9.6	7.8	8.4	12.3	17.5	13.0	17.5	7.4	6.6	65 366	989	86 858	1 651
2003	4 235	100.0	12.6	9.2	5.3	11.2	17.0	13.7	16.5	8.3	6.3	67 579	1 507	84 883	1 460
2004[17]	4 346	100.0	9.8	7.8	7.4	11.2	18.1	13.6	16.9	8.2	7.0	68 404	1 379	90 649	1 711
2005	4 500	100.0	10.7	7.5	7.0	9.9	18.3	12.6	17.9	7.4	8.7	70 332	840	92 163	1 608
2006	4 664	100.0	9.4	7.1	7.9	10.3	17.8	12.3	17.6	9.8	7.8	71 281	1 804	97 638	2 044
2007	4 715	100.0	9.7	7.8	7.5	11.0	16.0	13.7	17.8	9.0	7.5	71 458	1 503	91 726	1 569
2008	4 805	100.0	11.0	8.2	7.8	11.3	15.6	12.5	17.6	8.3	7.6	68 491	1 476	90 172	1 553
2009[18]	4 940	100.0	11.3	7.3	8.6	10.4	16.8	11.9	16.7	8.2	8.7	68 234	1 505	94 487	1 856
2010[19]	5 550	100.0	10.3	9.5	7.3	11.2	17.9	11.5	16.5	8.4	7.4	65 531	1 511	86 354	1 659
2011	5 705	100.0	10.7	8.9	8.2	11.2	17.3	12.8	17.3	6.5	7.1	64 995	1 564	85 785	2 053

[10]Implementation of a new CPS ASEC processing system.
[11]Implementation of 1990 census population controls.
[12]Data collection method changed from paper and pencil to computer-assisted interviewing. In addition, the 1994 ASEC was revised to allow for the coding of different income amounts on selected questionnaire items. Limits either increased or decreased in the following categories: earnings limits increased to $999,999, Social Security limits increased to $49,999, Supplemental Security Income and public assistance limits increased to $24,999, veterans' benefits limits increased to $99,999, and child support and alimony limits decreased to $49,999.
[13]Introduction of 1990 census sample design.
[14]Full implementation of 1990 census–based sample design and metropolitan definitions, 7,000 household sample reduction, and revised editing of responses on race.
[15]Implementation of the 2000 census–based population controls.
[16]Implementation of a 28,000 household sample expansion.
[17]Data revised to reflect a correction to the weights in the 2005 ASEC.
[18]Median income is calculated using $2,500 intervals. Beginning with 2009 income data, the Census Bureau expanded the upper income intervals used to calculate medians to $250,000 or more.
[19]Implementation of 2010 census-based population controls.
[20]For 2001 and earlier years, the CPS allowed respondents to report only one race group.
[22]Black alone refers to persons who reported Black and did not report any other race category.
[23]Asian alone refers to persons who reported Asian and did not report any other race category.
. . . = Not available.

Table 13-2. Households, by Total Money Income, Race, and Hispanic Origin of Householder, 1967–2011
—Continued

(Numbers in thousands, percent, dollars; income in 2011 CPI-U-RS adjusted dollars.)

Race and Hispanic origin of householder and year	Number	Percent distribution										Median income (dollars)		Mean income (dollars)	
		Total	Under $15,000	$15,000 to $24,999	$25,000 to $34,999	$35,000 to $49,999	$50,000 to $74,999	$75,000 to $99,999	$100,000 to $149,999	$150,000 to $199,999	$200,000 and over	Value	Standard error	Value	Standard error
Hispanic[24]															
1972[3]	2 655	100.0	15.5	16.9	15.7	21.9	18.9	6.8	3.3	0.4	0.5	36 910	721	42 425	721
1973	2 722	100.0	15.0	16.3	16.0	19.2	21.8	7.4	3.7	0.4	0.3	36 849	837	42 812	697
1974[4,5]	2 897	100.0	16.0	17.8	14.6	19.5	20.4	7.1	3.7	0.5	0.4	36 633	802	42 437	691
1975[5]	2 948	100.0	18.8	18.1	15.2	18.7	18.8	6.6	2.9	0.5	0.4	33 695	745	40 001	711
1976[6]	3 081	100.0	19.6	16.6	15.1	18.0	19.2	7.7	3.2	0.4	0.2	34 392	733	40 642	661
1977	3 304	100.0	17.4	16.0	15.7	18.6	19.9	7.2	4.3	0.7	0.3	35 995	632	42 479	656
1978	3 291	100.0	16.9	15.1	15.3	18.0	20.5	8.6	4.5	0.9	0.2	37 342	905	44 110	892
1979[7]	3 684	100.0	17.1	14.8	15.1	17.4	19.7	9.0	5.2	1.1	0.5	37 655	1 086	45 561	915
1980	3 906	100.0	18.5	16.5	14.5	17.6	18.4	8.6	4.6	0.9	0.5	35 475	962	43 331	863
1981	3 980	100.0	18.5	16.1	13.9	18.2	18.7	8.5	4.8	0.8	0.4	36 305	994	43 596	833
1982	4 085	100.0	20.8	17.2	14.1	17.0	17.4	7.9	4.3	0.9	0.5	33 965	897	41 919	850
1983	4 326	100.0	21.3	16.1	14.0	17.7	16.9	8.1	4.7	0.9	0.2	34 137	865	41 570	798
1984[8]	4 883	100.0	20.9	15.5	13.8	16.2	18.0	9.0	5.0	1.1	0.4	35 034	878	43 564	849
1985[9]	5 213	100.0	20.8	16.8	12.8	16.7	17.2	8.5	5.8	1.0	0.4	34 814	813	43 501	708
1986	5 418	100.0	19.5	16.2	13.5	15.8	17.9	8.8	6.5	1.3	0.5	35 932	936	45 371	746
1987[10]	5 642	100.0	20.1	15.3	12.8	16.9	16.9	9.5	5.8	1.5	1.1	36 621	795	46 943	869
1988	5 910	100.0	19.9	14.4	13.2	16.8	18.0	9.2	5.9	1.7	1.0	37 193	943	47 486	1 007
1989	5 933	100.0	18.5	14.0	13.1	16.4	18.2	10.4	6.6	1.8	1.0	38 391	744	49 023	842
1990	6 220	100.0	18.3	15.8	13.0	16.6	19.1	8.6	6.1	1.5	0.9	37 251	764	46 662	769
1991	6 379	100.0	18.9	15.9	13.2	17.0	17.5	8.9	6.0	1.8	0.9	36 496	760	46 496	744
1992[11]	7 153	100.0	19.9	16.0	13.6	17.0	16.8	8.6	5.9	1.4	0.8	35 491	733	45 268	711
1993[12]	7 362	100.0	19.8	16.5	13.4	17.8	15.8	8.5	5.8	1.4	1.1	35 078	705	46 427	976
1994[13]	7 735	100.0	20.5	16.4	12.9	16.0	16.5	8.5	6.3	1.8	1.0	35 147	653	47 395	1 183
1995[14]	7 939	100.0	21.0	16.9	13.8	16.5	15.3	8.5	5.7	1.3	0.9	33 499	730	45 722	1 026
1996	8 225	100.0	18.8	16.7	14.0	16.1	16.6	8.5	6.3	1.7	1.2	35 551	689	48 539	1 123
1997	8 590	100.0	19.0	14.5	14.1	16.1	17.7	8.4	6.9	1.9	1.5	37 205	664	50 136	1 012
1998	9 060	100.0	17.1	15.1	13.0	17.4	16.8	9.7	7.4	1.9	1.5	39 038	752	52 749	1 122
1999[15]	9 579	100.0	14.3	14.5	13.5	17.2	18.2	10.0	8.4	2.2	1.6	41 501	603	54 519	968
2000[16]	10 034	100.0	13.3	14.2	12.5	17.3	19.2	11.1	8.3	2.3	2.0	43 319	624	57 437	827
2001	10 499	100.0	13.5	14.5	13.1	16.6	18.5	11.0	8.5	2.7	1.6	42 640	541	56 383	713
2002	11 339	100.0	13.8	13.8	14.2	16.9	18.1	10.6	8.4	2.5	1.8	41 385	603	56 117	750
2003	11 693	100.0	15.0	14.6	13.2	17.7	17.4	9.8	8.1	2.3	1.8	40 351	561	54 379	602
2004[17]	12 178	100.0	15.0	14.2	13.9	16.7	18.7	9.5	7.9	2.5	1.7	40 806	572	54 626	668
2005	12 519	100.0	14.9	14.5	13.4	16.3	18.9	9.6	8.1	2.4	1.9	41 437	411	54 307	546
2006	12 973	100.0	14.7	13.9	13.1	16.3	18.9	9.6	8.9	2.9	1.7	42 145	563	56 416	647
2007	13 339	100.0	14.6	14.2	13.7	16.3	18.0	10.8	8.2	2.5	1.7	41 956	564	55 135	580
2008	13 425	100.0	16.0	14.0	14.4	16.5	16.9	9.6	8.3	2.9	1.6	39 604	508	53 872	558
2009[18]	13 298	100.0	15.8	14.4	14.4	15.2	17.8	9.7	8.4	2.5	1.9	39 887	526	54 766	601
2010[19]	14 435	100.0	17.1	14.7	13.5	15.5	17.4	9.8	8.0	2.5	1.6	38 818	600	53 015	681
2011	14 939	100.0	16.5	14.7	14.0	16.8	17.0	9.2	7.5	2.6	1.6	38 624	547	52 352	594

[3]Full implementation of 1970 census–based sample design.
[4]Implementation of a new CPS ASEC processing system. Questionnaire expanded to ask 11 income questions.
[5]Some of these estimates were derived using Pareto interpolation and may differ from published data that were derived using linear interpolation.
[6]First-year medians were derived using both Pareto and linear interpolation. Before this year, all medians were derived using linear interpolation.
[7]Implementation of 1980 census population controls. Questionnaire expanded to show 27 possible values from a list of 51 possible sources of income.
[8]Implementation of Hispanic population weighting controls and introduction of 1980 census–based sample design.
[9]Recording of amounts for earnings from longest job increased to $299,999. Full implementation of 1980 census–based sample design.
[10]Implementation of a new CPS ASEC processing system.
[11]Implementation of 1990 census population controls.
[12]Data collection method changed from paper and pencil to computer-assisted interviewing. In addition, the 1994 ASEC was revised to allow for the coding of different income amounts on selected questionnaire items. Limits either increased or decreased in the following categories: earnings limits increased to $999,999, Social Security limits increased to $49,999, Supplemental Security Income and public assistance limits increased to $24,999, veterans' benefits limits increased to $99,999, and child support and alimony limits decreased to $49,999.
[13]Introduction of 1990 census sample design.
[14]Full implementation of 1990 census–based sample design and metropolitan definitions, 7,000 household sample reduction, and revised editing of responses on race.
[15]Implementation of the 2000 census–based population controls.
[16]Implementation of a 28,000 household sample expansion.
[17]Data revised to reflect a correction to the weights in the 2005 ASEC.
[18]Median income is calculated using $2,500 intervals. Beginning with 2009 income data, the Census Bureau expanded the upper income intervals used to calculate medians to $250,000 or more.
[19]Implementation of 2010 census-based population controls.
[24]Because Hispanics may be of any race, data in this report for Hispanics overlap with data for racial groups. Hispanic origin was reported by 13.2 percent of White householders who reported only one race, 3.1 percent of Black householders who reported only one race, and 1.9 percent of Asian householders who reported only one race. Data users should exercise caution when interpreting aggregate results for the Hispanic population and for race groups, because these populations consist of many distinct groups that differ in socioeconomic characteristics, culture, and recentness of immigration. Data were first collected for Hispanics in 1972.

Table 13-3. Income Deficit or Surplus of Families and Unrelated Individuals by Poverty Status, 2011

(Numbers of families and unrelated individuals in thousands, deficits and surpluses in dollars.)

Characteristic	Total	Size of deficit or surplus								Average deficit or surplus (dollars)		Deficit or surplus per capita (dollars)	
		Under $1,000	$1,000 to $2,499	$2,500 to $4,999	$5,000 to $7,499	$7,500 to $9,999	$10,000 to $12,499	$12,500 to $14,499	$15,000 or more	Estimate	90 percent confidence interval[1] (+/-)	Estimate	90 percent confidence interval[1] (+/-)
Below Poverty Threshold, Deficit													
All families	9 497	659	925	1 497	1 215	1 040	957	914	2 289	9 576	175	2 745	55
Married-couple families	3 652	298	402	622	486	402	346	377	718	8 887	309	2 334	80
Families with a female householder, no husband present	4 894	270	417	692	614	538	539	467	1 355	10 317	218	3 069	74
Families with a male householder, no wife present	950	91	106	183	114	99	72	69	216	8 409	493	2 887	173
Unrelated individuals	12 416	1 095	2 137	2 508	1 363	1 212	4 101	–	–	6 401	109	6 401	109
Above Poverty Threshold, Surplus													
All families	71 033	543	1 061	1 769	1 975	2 002	2 037	2 025	59 620	71 714	763	23 240	272
Married-couple families	55 311	263	493	966	1 163	1 151	1 173	1 280	48 824	80 408	923	25 624	308
Families with a female householder, no husband present	10 783	216	439	604	624	632	654	533	7 081	37 611	1 293	12 814	475
Families with a male householder, no wife present	4 938	64	129	198	189	219	210	213	3 716	48 806	2 645	17 250	994
Unrelated individuals	42 101	1 439	2 073	3 081	2 829	2 700	2 268	2 377	25 335	32 440	757	32 440	757

[1]A 90 percent confidence interval is a measure of an estimate's variability. The larger the confidence interval in relation to the size of the estimate, the less reliable the estimate.
 – = Quantity represents or rounds to zero.

Table 13-4. Income Distribution Measures Using Money Income and Equivalence-Adjusted Income, 2010 and 2011

(Percent distribution.)

Measure	2010				2011				Percent change (2010–2011)			
	Money income		Equivalence-adjusted income		Money income		Equivalence-adjusted income		Money income		Equivalence-adjusted income	
	Estimate	90 percent confidence interval[1] (+/-)	Estimate	90 percent confidence interval[1] (+/-)	Estimate	90 percent confidence interval[1] (+/-)	Estimate	90 percent confidence interval[1] (+/-)	Estimate	90 percent confidence interval[1] (+/-)	Estimate	90 percent confidence interval[1] (+/-)
Shares of Aggregate Income by Percentile												
Lowest quintile	3.3	0.04	3.4	0.05	3.2	0.05	3.4	0.05	-1.2	1.79	0.1	2.04
Second quintile	8.5	0.08	9.2	0.08	8.4	0.07	9.0	0.07	-1.0	1.06	-1.6	1.03
Middle quintile	14.6	0.10	15.0	0.10	14.3	0.10	14.8	0.10	-1.9	0.84	-1.9	0.77
Fourth quintile	23.4	0.14	23.1	0.13	23.0	0.14	22.8	0.14	-1.8	0.77	-1.6	0.74
Highest quintile	50.3	0.30	49.2	0.29	51.1	0.28	50.0	0.30	1.6	0.73	1.6	0.71
Top 5 percent	21.3	0.38	21.0	0.36	22.3	0.38	22.1	0.38	4.9	2.28	5.3	2.28
Summary Measures												
Gini index of income inequality	0.470	0.003	0.456	0.003	0.477	0.003	0.463	0.003	1.60	0.80	1.70	0.81

[1]A 90-percent confidence interval is a measure of an estimate's variability. The larger the confidence interval in relation to the size of the estimate, the less reliable the estimate.

Table 13-5. Two-Year-Average[1] Median Household Income, by State, 2000 to 2011

(Income in 2011 CPI-U-RS adjusted dollars.)

State	2000–2001	2001–2002	2002–2003	2003–2004	2004–2005	2005–2006	2006–2007	2007–2008	2008–2009	2009–2010	2010–2011
UNITED STATES	54 244	53 333	52 996	52 881	53 080	53 570	54 129	53 518	52 371	51 513	50 443
Alabama	45 466	45 839	46 285	44 587	43 207	42 568	44 062	46 124	44 191	42 073	42 407
Alaska	70 947	69 425	64 684	64 477	64 977	63 663	65 633	67 587	65 720	62 134	58 552
Arizona	53 105	51 963	50 008	51 274	52 167	52 086	51 631	50 111	48 484	48 168	48 498
Arkansas	40 570	41 422	39 812	40 395	41 944	41 785	42 795	42 802	39 832	39 059	40 553
California	60 592	59 673	59 797	59 449	59 117	60 667	61 083	60 007	59 209	57 428	54 681
Colorado	62 879	61 565	60 724	60 831	59 356	60 126	64 226	64 991	61 154	60 390	60 381
Connecticut	66 649	67 258	66 980	66 412	65 543	67 545	69 594	68 571	67 784	68 041	66 748
Delaware	64 396	62 543	61 008	58 578	58 119	58 761	58 855	56 089	53 804	55 801	55 808
District of Columbia	53 069	50 573	51 964	53 411	51 786	52 956	54 581	56 578	56 896	57 223	56 988
Florida	48 508	46 903	47 598	47 962	48 897	50 240	50 313	48 266	47 353	46 652	45 281
Georgia	54 406	53 885	52 789	50 348	50 855	53 977	53 903	50 526	46 867	45 477	45 741
Hawaii	63 794	59 702	61 262	65 177	67 808	68 051	68 451	66 856	61 308	59 885	60 232
Idaho	48 851	47 866	49 484	52 317	51 856	51 223	52 451	51 443	49 293	48 793	47 997
Illinois	59 408	56 025	54 306	55 041	55 311	55 026	55 624	56 292	55 534	53 883	51 483
Indiana	52 334	51 307	51 599	51 141	49 646	49 771	51 063	50 034	47 526	47 026	46 020
Iowa	52 796	51 687	50 964	51 137	52 619	53 628	53 369	52 715	52 782	51 874	50 391
Kansas	53 119	52 947	53 686	51 494	48 658	49 616	51 710	51 309	48 451	47 198	46 827
Kentucky	48 097	47 395	45 564	43 785	42 341	43 163	43 420	42 889	43 860	43 569	41 129
Louisiana	41 225	42 424	41 746	42 176	43 138	41 801	42 758	43 071	44 484	44 090	40 599
Maine	47 592	46 293	45 729	47 298	49 907	50 758	51 433	50 643	49 572	49 626	49 568
Maryland	69 615	69 262	67 247	65 983	68 854	70 368	71 107	68 872	66 928	66 765	67 551
Massachusetts	63 722	64 355	62 320	62 126	63 238	63 129	62 569	63 213	62 634	62 557	63 085
Michigan	58 334	55 314	54 229	52 686	51 616	53 592	53 910	52 781	50 118	47 982	48 308
Minnesota	68 890	67 606	66 442	65 700	64 632	62 582	62 841	60 176	58 095	56 393	55 896
Mississippi	41 556	38 462	39 316	40 703	39 629	38 310	39 591	39 255	37 427	38 073	40 227
Missouri	55 708	52 997	53 497	51 844	49 848	49 626	49 816	48 997	49 615	49 200	46 518
Montana	41 810	42 181	42 630	41 071	41 710	44 420	46 604	46 084	43 607	42 492	41 430
Nebraska	54 965	54 453	53 639	52 956	53 674	54 459	53 523	53 166	52 497	53 082	54 888
Nevada	58 721	56 943	55 731	55 730	55 873	56 931	58 480	57 912	55 559	53 374	49 929
New Hampshire	65 861	67 186	68 557	67 801	66 650	67 389	71 215	71 215	68 187	67 991	67 308
New Jersey	65 800	66 995	68 379	67 176	69 411	74 463	70 778	66 927	68 071	66 439	63 646
New Mexico	43 957	43 204	43 629	45 018	45 988	44 761	46 383	46 047	44 818	46 108	44 270
New York	53 357	52 983	52 395	52 744	53 757	54 071	53 442	52 901	52 683	52 003	50 994
North Carolina	49 262	47 066	45 619	46 750	48 182	46 423	45 797	46 022	44 393	44 577	45 210
North Dakota	46 242	45 364	47 337	48 058	47 654	47 198	48 497	51 525	52 176	52 561	54 488
Ohio	54 597	53 223	53 292	52 243	51 096	51 064	52 231	51 143	48 567	47 720	45 991
Oklahoma	43 797	45 408	44 742	45 536	45 269	43 347	45 101	47 523	48 137	46 285	46 459
Oregon	53 969	52 346	51 590	49 865	49 843	51 703	53 512	54 263	52 758	51 841	51 862
Pennsylvania	55 172	54 196	52 816	52 510	52 929	53 709	53 309	53 118	52 103	50 175	49 874
Rhode Island	56 599	55 558	53 853	55 876	57 043	58 476	59 373	57 209	54 879	53 697	51 143
South Carolina	48 504	47 606	47 164	46 563	46 209	45 271	46 076	45 997	43 566	43 056	41 549
South Dakota	49 018	48 873	47 840	48 639	49 330	50 194	50 513	52 126	50 977	47 418	47 003
Tennessee	44 995	45 876	46 091	45 609	45 366	45 396	45 040	43 079	41 979	41 147	41 044
Texas	51 167	51 051	49 109	48 658	48 507	48 015	49 132	49 259	49 172	49 269	48 902
Utah	61 123	59 989	60 047	60 415	61 861	62 043	59 501	61 695	63 329	59 911	56 991
Vermont	51 768	52 790	53 330	54 629	57 385	58 200	54 695	52 186	53 913	56 276	54 777
Virginia	62 711	62 937	64 521	63 944	60 351	61 763	63 945	64 462	64 095	62 856	62 444
Washington	54 759	55 233	57 292	58 770	58 895	59 696	62 023	61 079	61 241	60 630	57 392
West Virginia	38 054	37 200	38 385	39 901	40 863	42 422	44 257	42 673	41 073	43 292	42 974
Wisconsin	58 247	57 497	56 985	55 518	52 947	54 552	56 642	54 553	53 605	52 833	51 999
Wyoming	51 108	50 085	50 876	53 047	52 787	51 997	52 674	54 295	55 367	54 433	54 178

[1]The 2-year-average median is the sum of two inflation-adjusted single-year medians divided by 2.

Table 13-6. Median Family Income in the Past Twelve Months, by the Number of Earners and State, 2011

(Income in 2011 inflation-adjusted dollars.)

State	Total	No earners	1 earner	2 earners	3 or more earners
UNITED STATES	61 455	29 761	43 942	81 462	98 820
Alabama	51 991	24 986	39 307	74 202	91 733
Alaska	75 786	33 575	52 713	93 263	118 569
Arizona	55 328	35 140	41 253	76 346	89 740
Arkansas	48 713	25 235	35 765	67 425	88 260
California	65 476	27 828	47 433	88 491	97 076
Colorado	69 110	35 281	48 544	86 101	107 174
Connecticut	83 106	33 814	57 154	104 800	124 209
Delaware	69 663	42 091	47 305	88 622	111 464
District of Columbia	75 603	14 761	49 168	133 109	125 897
Florida	53 958	33 377	41 065	73 419	88 908
Georgia	55 001	24 790	40 378	76 420	91 703
Hawaii	74 234	38 783	48 907	86 715	122 910
Idaho	52 814	33 320	40 938	65 218	82 914
Illinois	65 579	30 464	46 522	85 466	101 353
Indiana	57 148	29 689	41 236	75 101	93 697
Iowa	62 821	33 052	41 351	76 596	94 350
Kansas	61 947	34 596	41 714	76 307	94 618
Kentucky	51 917	24 184	39 209	72 753	92 411
Louisiana	53 601	22 366	37 197	79 571	100 225
Maine	58 375	29 390	40 647	76 276	95 960
Maryland	83 823	36 360	57 088	108 116	127 135
Massachusetts	80 425	29 189	54 475	101 596	119 757
Michigan	58 068	32 824	44 116	78 706	94 615
Minnesota	71 321	35 735	47 122	86 076	102 385
Mississippi	46 304	21 511	35 505	66 498	91 644
Missouri	56 616	30 201	40 259	74 976	94 532
Montana	56 217	35 170	41 443	67 331	87 236
Nebraska	63 491	33 194	41 012	75 770	94 252
Nevada	56 544	33 417	44 013	74 315	93 996
New Hampshire	76 609	34 353	51 522	91 527	112 697
New Jersey	82 255	34 136	59 906	107 472	124 517
New Mexico	51 744	27 808	37 571	73 947	85 071
New York	66 852	25 933	46 821	91 446	109 552
North Carolina	54 082	27 929	39 885	74 811	89 437
North Dakota	66 924	31 989	40 714	80 791	100 059
Ohio	58 565	29 416	41 946	78 189	95 251
Oklahoma	53 742	27 552	39 841	71 421	88 780
Oregon	58 356	33 925	42 285	74 880	87 928
Pennsylvania	63 283	29 738	46 477	81 744	100 441
Rhode Island	69 604	27 722	45 945	89 383	110 105
South Carolina	52 240	27 931	38 442	73 133	87 567
South Dakota	62 059	30 120	37 299	73 460	88 821
Tennessee	52 273	26 347	39 082	71 481	86 996
Texas	58 016	26 446	40 389	78 646	90 464
Utah	62 809	37 136	49 942	70 621	94 927
Vermont	66 190	30 273	45 086	81 488	100 396
Virginia	74 500	35 657	52 247	94 245	110 237
Washington	68 628	36 645	51 655	87 946	101 828
West Virginia	49 693	26 079	40 658	73 400	90 782
Wisconsin	63 732	33 597	42 776	78 599	96 656
Wyoming	68 629	32 633	44 417	85 721	107 165

Table 13-7. Median Family Income in the Past Twelve Months, by Size of Family and State, 2011

(Income in 2011 inflation-adjusted dollars.)

State	Total	2-person families	3-person families	4-person families	5-person families	6-person families	7-or-more-person families
UNITED STATES	61 455	55 396	62 485	74 563	68 855	63 489	62 993
Alabama	51 991	48 166	51 156	63 388	58 754	56 537	48 631
Alaska	75 786	70 172	80 531	86 581	84 215	77 481	68 993
Arizona	55 328	54 000	54 526	59 786	60 479	51 550	51 944
Arkansas	48 713	45 394	48 491	55 444	55 560	50 142	51 452
California	65 476	61 752	66 034	74 122	63 826	61 902	68 075
Colorado	69 110	64 300	70 794	85 027	70 878	61 642	56 825
Connecticut	83 106	71 400	84 638	100 451	103 090	101 232	89 887
Delaware	69 663	61 436	71 798	83 424	87 311	86 645	67 827
District of Columbia	75 603	80 298	68 072	76 230	58 969	99 137	69 727
Florida	53 958	50 711	53 820	63 937	60 572	52 411	56 546
Georgia	55 001	50 901	55 050	65 851	56 710	52 383	54 944
Hawaii	74 234	62 601	74 460	82 973	79 384	102 177	112 825
Idaho	52 814	48 884	49 482	61 058	58 363	59 205	67 105
Illinois	65 579	58 647	67 328	79 138	72 946	66 569	63 473
Indiana	57 148	51 551	57 721	69 328	69 189	61 868	58 805
Iowa	62 821	57 659	63 243	76 777	70 858	73 896	64 547
Kansas	61 947	55 698	64 571	74 853	67 628	66 436	67 617
Kentucky	51 917	45 866	54 485	66 409	59 389	63 647	52 419
Louisiana	53 601	46 763	54 730	68 921	64 795	58 025	61 003
Maine	58 375	52 148	59 200	78 310	66 662	60 275	59 395
Maryland	83 823	72 191	85 438	106 707	98 550	91 431	96 687
Massachusetts	80 425	66 076	80 822	101 523	103 741	92 244	91 184
Michigan	58 068	51 554	60 464	72 366	70 529	58 910	54 343
Minnesota	71 321	62 363	75 350	87 319	83 575	70 413	70 131
Mississippi	46 304	42 221	45 128	58 047	52 238	45 436	42 449
Missouri	56 616	50 734	58 342	70 687	70 049	64 053	57 683
Montana	56 217	53 260	55 822	65 695	61 785	63 825	53 951
Nebraska	63 491	58 336	65 872	75 495	71 280	63 420	58 686
Nevada	56 544	54 545	53 950	65 212	58 646	58 506	60 528
New Hampshire	76 609	64 495	81 243	97 441	90 037	102 628	115 636
New Jersey	82 255	68 284	83 292	101 682	100 740	99 974	83 034
New Mexico	51 744	50 911	47 732	60 368	52 650	49 228	52 517
New York	66 852	58 106	67 652	81 522	79 697	74 712	73 230
North Carolina	54 082	50 762	55 197	63 665	60 192	54 339	47 358
North Dakota	66 924	60 245	67 295	84 896	77 105	73 164	59 732
Ohio	58 565	52 139	59 724	72 764	69 138	66 644	57 300
Oklahoma	53 742	50 529	52 415	63 069	59 464	58 019	53 865
Oregon	58 356	53 941	60 941	65 950	63 691	56 913	59 977
Pennsylvania	63 283	54 091	67 452	80 414	78 381	69 333	62 812
Rhode Island	69 604	60 358	75 306	82 086	78 125	85 326	78 730
South Carolina	52 240	49 523	52 447	60 143	56 467	56 683	42 756
South Dakota	62 059	56 029	64 494	72 460	70 963	61 147	56 979
Tennessee	52 273	47 631	53 963	63 719	59 636	49 905	52 181
Texas	58 016	54 762	59 276	65 932	59 234	53 219	53 764
Utah	62 809	54 952	62 144	65 240	73 771	72 277	76 879
Vermont	66 190	60 451	66 400	84 011	71 665	72 520	77 222
Virginia	74 500	64 593	76 012	89 803	83 309	85 945	84 645
Washington	68 628	63 803	69 844	81 582	68 982	64 447	63 076
West Virginia	49 693	43 633	53 679	65 403	62 224	71 054	57 699
Wisconsin	63 732	57 479	64 441	79 648	74 227	69 323	65 710
Wyoming	68 629	61 912	72 194	77 137	86 951	63 953	86 123

Chapter Fourteen

OCCUPATIONAL SAFETY AND HEALTH

OCCUPATIONAL SAFETY AND HEALTH

HIGHLIGHTS

This chapter includes data on work-related illnesses and injuries and fatal work injuries from the Injuries, Illnesses, and Fatalities (IIF) program. Data are classified by industry and selected worker characteristics.

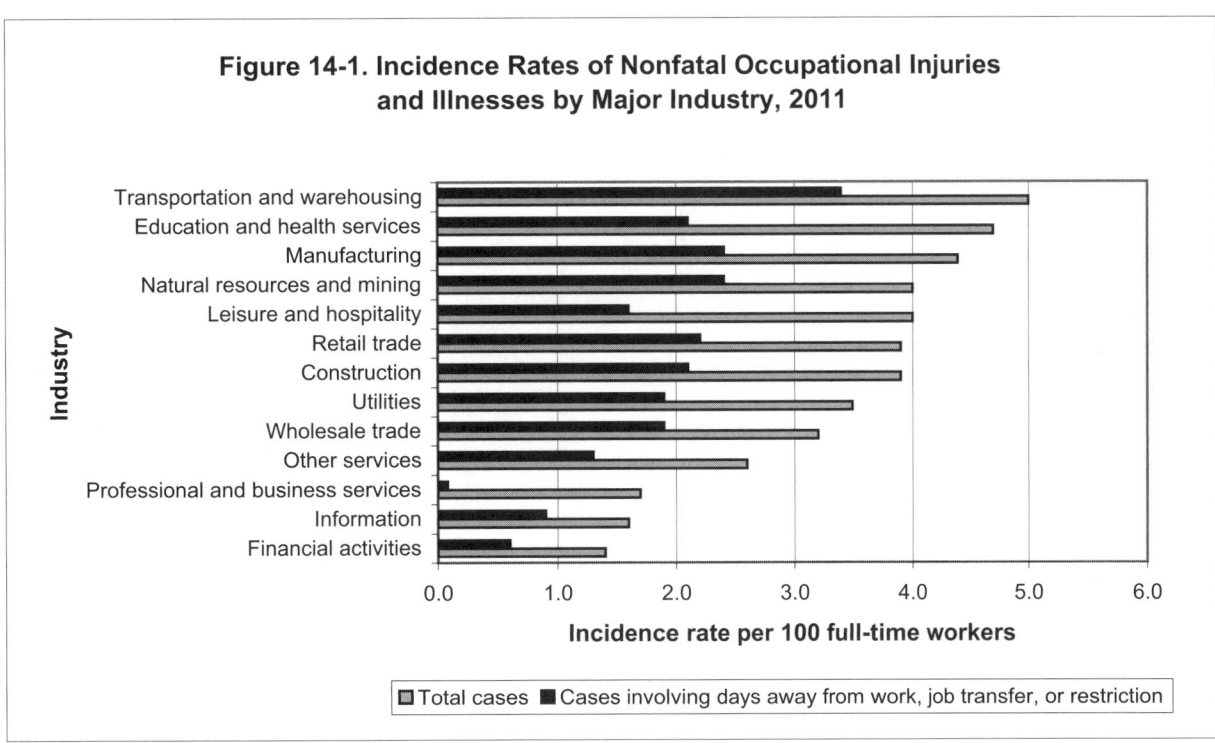

Figure 14-1. Incidence Rates of Nonfatal Occupational Injuries and Illnesses by Major Industry, 2011

In 2011, transportation and warehousing continued to have the highest incidence rate of non-fatal occupational injuries and illnesses among all major industries at 5.0 per 100 full-time workers. Rates for injuries and illness requiring days away from work were much lower, ranging from 0.4 per 100 full-time workers in financial activities to 3.4 per 100 full-time workers in transportation and warehousing. (See Table 14-1.)

OTHER HIGHLIGHTS

- After declining for several years, the rate of nonfatal occupational injuries and illnesses for all workers in the private industry remained steady at 3.5 cases per 100 full-time workers. (See Table 14-1.)

- Workers aged 45 to 54 years old had the highest number of nonfatal occupational injuries and illnesses followed by those aged 35 to 44 while those ages 16 to 19 years had the lowest number. (See Table 14-6.)

- According to preliminary data, 4,609 workplace fatalities occurred in 2011, a decline of 1.8 percent from 2010. Men were far more likely than women to be killed on the job, accounting for nearly 92 percent of all fatalities. (See Table 14-9.)

- Transportation and warehousing accounted for the highest number of workplace fatalities at 1,213. Within transportation and warehousing, motor vehicle operators accounted for the highest number of fatalities (851) while water transportation workers accounted for the least (14). (See Table 14-10.)

NOTES AND DEFINITIONS

Collection and Coverage

The Injuries, Illnesses, and Fatalities (IIF) program at the Bureau of Labor Statistics (BLS) provides annual reports on the number of workplace injuries, illnesses, and fatalities. BLS has reported annually on the number of work-related injuries, illnesses, and fatalities since 1972 after the Occupational Safety and Health Act of 1970 was passed.

Nonfatal Occupational Injuries and Illnesses

The Survey of Occupational Injuries and Illnesses is a federal-state program in which employer's reports are collected annually from over 230,000 private industry establishments and processed by state agencies cooperating with the BLS. Summary information on the number of injuries and illnesses is copied by these employers directly from their recordkeeping logs to the survey questionnaire. The questionnaire also asks for the number of employee hours worked (needed in the calculation of incidence rates) as well as its average employment (needed to verify the unit's employment-size class).

Occupational injury and illness data for coal, metal, and nonmetal mining and for railroad activities were provided by the Department of Labor's Mine Safety and Health Administration and the Department of Transportation's Federal Railroad Administration. The survey excludes all work-related fatalities as well as nonfatal work injuries and illnesses to the self employed; to workers on farms with 10 or fewer employees; to private household workers; and, nationally, to federal, state, and local government workers.

Injuries and illnesses logged by employers conform with definitions and recordkeeping guidelines set by the Occupational Safety and Health Administration, U.S. Department of Labor. Under those guidelines, nonfatal cases are recordable if they are occupational illnesses or if they are occupational injuries which involve lost worktime, medical treatment other than first aid, restriction of work or motion, loss of consciousness, or transfer to another job. Employers keep counts of injuries separate from illnesses and also identify for each whether a case involved any days away from work or days of restricted work activity, or both, beyond the day of injury or onset of illness.

Occupational injuries, such as sprains, cuts, and fractures, account for the vast majority of all cases that employers log and report to the BLS survey. Occupational illnesses are new cases recognized, diagnosed, and reported during the year. Overwhelmingly, those reported are easier to directly relate to workplace activity (e.g., contact dermatitis or carpal tunnel syndrome) than are long-term latent illnesses, such as cancers. The latter illnesses are believed to be under recorded and, thus, understated in the BLS survey.

Concepts and Definitions

Days away from work are cases that involve days away from work, days of restricted work activity, or both.

The data are presented in the form of *incidence rates*, defined as the number of injuries and illnesses or cases of days away from work per 100 full-time employees. The formula is (N/EH) x 200,000, where N = number of injuries and illnesses or days away from work, EH = total hours worked by all employees during the calendar year, and 200,000 represents the base for 100 full-time equivalent workers (working 40 hours per week, 50 weeks per year).

Median days away from work is a measure used to summarize the varying lengths of absences from work among the cases with days away from work. The median is the point at which half of the cases involved more days away from work and half involved less days away from work.

Occupational illness is an abnormal condition or disorder (other than one resulting from an occupational injury) caused by exposure to environmental factors associated with employment. It includes acute and chronic illnesses and diseases that may have been caused by inhalation, absorption, ingestion, or direct contact. Long-term latent illnesses can be difficult to relate to the workplace and are believed to be understated in this survey.

Occupational injury is any injury—such as a cut, fracture, sprain, or amputation—that results from a work accident or from exposure to an incident in the work environment.

Fatal Occupational Injuries

The Bureau of Labor Statistics (BLS) Census of Fatal Occupational Injuries (CFOI) produces comprehensive, accurate, and timely counts of fatal work injuries. CFOI is a federal-state cooperative program that has been implemented in all 50 states and the District of Columbia since 1992. To compile counts that are as complete as possible, the census uses multiple sources to identify, verify, and profile fatal worker injuries. Information about each workplace fatality—occupation and other worker characteristics, equipment involved, and circumstances of the event—is obtained by cross referencing the source records, such as death certificates, workers' compensation reports, and federal and state agency administrative reports. To ensure that fatalities are work-related, cases are substantiated with two or more independent source documents, or a source document and a follow-up questionnaire.

Data compiled by the CFOI program are issued annually for the preceding calendar year. These data are used by safety and health policy analysts and researchers to help prevent fatal work injuries by:

- Informing workers of life threatening hazards associated with various jobs;

- Promoting safer work practices through enhanced job safety training;

- Assessing and improving workplace safety standards; and

- Identifying new areas of safety research.

The National Safety Council has adopted the Census of Fatal Occupational Injuries figure, beginning with the 1992 data year, as the authoritative count for work related deaths in the United States.

Sources of Additional Information

For more extensive definitions and description of collection methods see Chapter 9 in the *BLS Handbook of Methods* and BLS news release USDL 12-2204, "Nonfatal Occupational Injuries and Illnesses Requiring Days Away from Work, 2011," USDL 12-2121, "Workplace Injuries and Illnesses–2011," and USDL 12-1888, "National Census of Fatal Occupational Injuries in 2011 (Preliminary Results)," available on the BLS Web site at <http://www.bls.gov/iif/>.

Table 14-1. Incidence Rates[1] of Nonfatal Occupational Injuries and Illnesses, by Selected Industries and Case Types, 2011

(Number, rate per 100 full-time workers.)

Industry[2]	NAICS code[3]	2011 average annual employment (thousands)[4]	Total recordable cases	Cases with days away from work, job transfer, or restriction			Other recordable cases
				Total	Cases with days away from work[5]	Cases with job transfer or restriction	
PRIVATE INDUSTRY[6]		107 654	3.5	1.8	1.1	0.7	1.7
Goods-Producing[6]		18 849	4.2	2.3	1.2	1.1	1.9
Natural resources and mining[6,7]		1 645	4.0	2.4	1.4	0.9	1.6
Agriculture, forestry, fishing and hunting[6]	11	975	5.5	3.2	1.8	1.4	2.3
Crop production[6,8]	111	414	5.5	3.2	1.7	1.5	2.2
Animal production[6,8]	112	164	6.7	4.1	2.3	1.8	2.6
Forestry and logging	113	57	5.0	3.3	2.9	0.3	1.8
Fishing, hunting and trapping	114	9	4.8	1.6	1.1	*	3.2
Support activities for agriculture and forestry	115	332	4.8	2.7	1.5	1.1	2.2
Mining[7]	21	670	2.2	1.4	0.9	0.5	0.9
Oil and gas extraction	211	149	0.9	0.5	0.4	0.1	0.4
Mining (except oil and gas)[9]	212	208	3.0	1.9	1.5	0.5	1.1
Support activities for mining	213	312	2.3	1.4	0.8	0.6	0.9
Construction	23	5 577	3.9	2.1	1.5	0.7	1.8
Construction of buildings	236	1 260	3.6	1.9	1.2	0.7	1.7
Heavy and civil engineering construction	237	826	3.5	2.0	1.2	0.7	1.5
Specialty trade contractors	31-33	3 491	4.1	2.2	1.6	0.6	1.9
Manufacturing	31	11 628	4.4	2.4	1.1	1.3	2.0
Food manufacturing	311	1 459	5.6	3.5	1.5	2.1	2.1
Beverage and tobacco product manufacturing	312	186	6.9	5.3	*	2.5	1.6
Textile mills	313	121	3.5	2.0	0.9	1.1	1.5
Textile product mills[8]	314	120	3.5	1.9	0.9	1.0	1.5
Apparel manufacturing[8]	315	163	2.5	1.1	0.6	0.6	1.4
Leather and allied product manufacturing	316	30	6.1	3.4	1.7	1.7	2.7
Wood product manufacturing	321	338	6.5	3.5	1.9	1.6	3.0
Paper manufacturing	322	386	3.4	1.9	1.0	0.9	1.5
Printing and related support activities	323	478	2.9	1.6	0.8	0.8	1.3
Petroleum and coal products manufacturing	324	110	2.0	1.0	0.5	0.6	0.9
Chemical manufacturing	325	808	2.4	1.4	0.7	0.7	1.0
Plastics and rubber products manufacturing[8]	326	632	4.9	2.8	1.3	1.5	2.1
Nonmetallic mineral product manufacturing	327	367	5.4	3.0	1.7	1.4	2.4
Primary metal manufacturing	331	376	6.1	3.5	1.8	1.7	2.7
Fabricated metal product manufacturing	332	1 312	5.6	2.6	1.3	1.3	3.0
Machinery manufacturing[8]	333	1 016	4.4	2.0	1.0	1.0	2.3
Computer and electronic product manufacturing	334	1 091	1.4	0.7	0.4	0.3	0.7
Electrical equipment, appliance, and component manufacturing	335	367	3.1	1.6	0.6	1.0	1.5
Transportation equipment manufacturing[8]	336	1 338	5.2	2.7	1.1	1.6	2.5
Furniture and related product manufacturing[8]	337	354	5.3	2.7	1.3	1.5	2.6
Miscellaneous manufacturing		576	3.3	1.7	0.8	0.9	1.5
Service-Providing		88 805	3.3	1.6	1.0	0.6	1.6
Trade, transportation, and utilities[10]		24 925	3.9	2.3	1.3	1.0	1.6
Wholesale trade	42	5 580	3.2	1.9	1.1	0.9	1.3
Merchant wholesalers, durable goods	423	2 763	2.8	1.5	0.9	0.7	1.3
Merchant wholesalers, nondurable goods	424	1 961	4.4	2.9	1.6	1.3	1.5
Wholesale electronic markets and agents and brokers	44-45	856	1.9	1.0	0.6	*	0.9
Retail trade	44	14 774	3.9	2.2	1.2	1.0	1.7
Motor vehicle and parts dealers	441	1 680	3.9	1.9	1.3	0.6	2.0
Furniture and home furnishings stores	442	443	4.0	2.4	1.5	0.9	1.5
Electronics and appliance stores	443	518	2.1	0.8	0.5	0.3	1.3
Building material and garden equipment and supplies dealers	444	1 157	5.4	3.5	1.7	1.8	1.9
Food and beverage stores	445	2 860	4.7	2.7	1.4	1.2	2.0
Health and personal care stores	446	999	2.2	0.9	0.6	0.3	1.3
Gasoline stations	447	833	2.5	1.1	0.7	0.4	1.4
Clothing and clothing accessories stores	448	1 424	2.6	0.9	0.7	0.3	1.6
Sporting goods, hobby, book, and music stores	451	595	2.6	1.2	0.6	0.6	1.3
General merchandise stores	452	3 050	4.6	3.0	1.3	1.7	1.7
Miscellaneous store retailers	453	795	4.0	1.6	0.9	0.7	2.4
Nonstore retailers	454	420	2.9	1.7	1.1	0.6	1.2

Note: Components may not sum to totals because of rounding.

[1]The incidence rates represent the number of injuries and illnesses per 100 full-time workers and were calculated as: (N/EH) x 200,000 (where N = number of injuries and illnesses; EH = total hours worked by all employees during the calendar year; 200,000 = base for 100 equivalent full-time workers working 40 hours per week, 50 weeks per year).
[2]Totals include data for industries not shown separately.
[3]North American Industry Classification System—United States, 2007.
[4]Employment is expressed as an average annual value and is derived primarily from the Bureau of Labor Statistics's (BLS) Quarterly Census of Employment and Wages (QCEW) program.
[5]Days away from work cases include those that result in days away from work with or without job transfer or restriction.
[6]Excludes farms with fewer than 11 employees.
[7]Data for mining include establishments not governed by the Department of Labor's Mine Safety and Health Administration (MSHA) rules and reporting, such as those in oil and gas extraction and related support activities. Data for mining operators in coal, metal, and nonmetal mining are provided to BLS by MSHA. Independent mining contractors are excluded from the coal, metal, and nonmetal mining industries. These data do not reflect the changes the Occupational Safety and Health Administration (OSHA) made to its record-keeping requirements effective January 1, 2002; thus, estimates for these industries are not comparable to estimates in other industries.
[8]Industry scope changed in 2009.
[9]Data for mining operators in this industry are provided to BLS by MSHA. Independent mining contractors are excluded. These data do not reflect the changes OSHA made to its record-keeping requirements effective January 1, 2002; thus, estimates for these industries are not comparable to estimates in other industries.
[10]Data for employers in rail transportation are provided to BLS by the Department of Transportation's Federal Railroad Administration (FRA).
* = Figure does not meet standards of reliability or quality.

Table 14-1.　Incidence Rates[1] of Nonfatal Occupational Injuries and Illnesses, by Selected Industries and Case Types, 2011—*Continued*

(Number, rate per 100 full-time workers.)

Industry[2]	NAICS code[3]	2011 average annual employment (thousands)[4]	Total recordable cases	Cases with days away from work, job transfer, or restriction			Other recordable cases
				Total	Cases with days away from work[5]	Cases with job transfer or restriction	
Service-Providing—*Continued*							
Transportation and warehousing[10]	48	4 018	5.0	3.4	2.3	1.1	1.6
Air transportation	481	450	7.3	5.5	4.3	1.2	1.8
Rail transportation[10]	482	*	1.9	1.4	1.3	0.1	0.5
Water transportation	483	62	2.0	1.6	1.2	0.3	0.4
Truck transportation	484	1 289	4.9	3.2	2.3	0.9	1.7
Transit and ground passenger transportation	485	426	4.7	2.9	2.1	0.8	1.8
Pipeline transportation	486	42	1.5	1.2	*	0.2	0.4
Scenic and sightseeing transportation	487	28	3.5	2.1	1.7	0.5	1.3
Support activities for transportation	488	560	3.8	2.5	1.6	0.8	1.3
Couriers and messengers	492	523	6.6	4.5	2.6	1.9	2.1
Warehousing and storage	493	637	5.5	3.8	1.8	1.9	1.7
Utilities	22	553	3.5	1.9	1.0	0.9	1.6
Information		2 693	1.6	0.9	0.6	0.3	0.7
Publishing industries (except Internet)	511	748	1.3	0.7	0.4	0.2	0.6
Motion picture and sound recording industries	512	356	2.1	0.6	0.3	0.2	1.5
Broadcasting (except Internet)	515	294	1.9	1.2	0.6	0.5	0.7
Telecommunications[8]	517	901	2.1	1.4	1.0	0.4	0.7
Data processing, hosting, and related services[8]	518	244	0.6	0.3	0.2	0.1	0.4
Other information services[8]	519	149	0.6	0.3	0.2	0.1	0.3
Financial activities		7 506	1.4	0.6	0.4	0.2	0.7
Finance and insurance	52	5 543	0.8	0.3	0.2	0.1	0.6
Monetary authorities–central bank	521	21	1.0	0.4	0.3	([11])	0.6
Credit intermediation and related activities	522	2 549	1.1	0.3	0.3	0.1	0.7
Securities, commodity contracts, and other financial investments and related activities	523	823	*	0.1	0.1	([11])	0.2
Insurance carriers and related activities	524	2 066	0.7	0.2	0.2	([11])	0.5
Funds, trusts, and other financial vehicles	525	85	0.6	0.2	0.1	0.1	0.4
Real estate and rental and leasing	53	1 962	3.0	1.7	1.1	0.6	1.3
Real estate	531	1 430	2.8	1.6	1.1	0.5	1.2
Rental and leasing services	532	506	3.7	2.2	1.1	1.1	1.5
Lessors of nonfinancial intangible assets (except copyrighted works)	533	25	0.6	0.2	0.2	*	0.4
Professional and business services		17 299	1.7	0.8	0.5	0.3	0.9
Professional, scientific, and technical services[8]	54	7 712	1.0	0.4	0.3	0.1	0.7
Management of companies and enterprises	55	1 920	1.4	0.6	0.4	0.2	0.8
Administrative and support and waste management and remediation services	56	7 668	2.7	1.5	1.0	0.5	1.2
Administrative and support services[8]	561	7 303	2.5	1.4	1.0	0.4	1.2
Waste management and remediation services	562	365	4.9	3.0	2.0	1.0	1.9
Education and health services		19 065	4.7	2.1	1.3	0.9	2.5
Educational services	61	2 580	2.1	0.9	0.6	0.3	1.2
Health care and social assistance	62	16 485	5.0	2.3	1.4	1.0	2.7
Ambulatory health care services	621	6 116	2.7	0.9	0.7	0.3	1.7
Hospitals	622	4 689	6.8	2.7	1.6	1.1	4.1
Nursing and residential care facilities	623	3 152	7.8	4.7	2.5	2.2	3.1
Social assistance	624	2 528	3.6	1.9	1.2	0.7	1.7
Leisure and hospitality		13 515	4.0	1.6	1.0	0.6	2.4
Arts, entertainment, and recreation	71	2 066	4.5	2.2	1.2	0.9	2.4
Performing arts, spectator sports, and related industries	711	408	6.0	2.4	1.4	0.9	3.7
Museums, historical sites, and similar institutions	712	130	4.5	2.3	1.5	0.8	2.3
Amusement, gambling, and recreation industries	713	1 527	4.1	2.1	1.2	0.9	2.1
Accommodation and food services	72	11 449	3.9	1.5	1.0	0.5	2.4
Accommodation	721	1 830	5.1	2.8	1.5	1.3	2.3
Food services and drinking places	722	9 619	3.6	1.2	0.8	0.3	2.4
Other services		3 803	2.6	1.3	0.9	0.4	1.2
Other services, except public administration	81	3 803	2.6	1.3	0.9	0.4	1.2
Repair and maintenance	811	1 174	3.2	1.7	1.3	0.4	1.5
Personal and laundry services	812	1 298	2.4	1.4	0.8	0.5	1.0
Religious, grantmaking, civic, professional, and similar organizations	813	1 330	2.0	0.8	0.5	0.3	1.2

Note: Components may not sum to totals because of rounding.

[1] The incidence rates represent the number of injuries and illnesses per 100 full-time workers and were calculated as: (N/EH) x 200,000 (where N = number of injuries and illnesses; EH = total hours worked by all employees during the calendar year; 200,000 = base for 100 equivalent full-time workers working 40 hours per week, 50 weeks per year).

[2] Totals include data for industries not shown separately.

[3] North American Industry Classification System—United States, 2007.

[4] Employment is expressed as an average annual value and is derived primarily from the Bureau of Labor Statistics's (BLS) Quarterly Census of Employment and Wages (QCEW) program.

[5] Days away from work cases include those that result in days away from work with or without job transfer or restriction.

[8] Industry scope changed in 2009.

[10] Data for employers in rail transportation are provided to BLS by the Department of Transportation's Federal Railroad Administration (FRA).

[11] Data too small to be displayed.

* = Figure does not meet standards of reliability or quality.

Table 14-2. Incidence Rates[1] of Nonfatal Occupational Injuries and Illnesses, by Major Industry Sector, Employment Size, and Ownership, 2011

(Rate per 100 full-time workers.)

Industry sector	All establishments	Establishment employment size (workers)				
		1 to 10	11 to 49	50 to 249	250 to 999	1,000 or more
ALL INDUSTRIES INCLUDING STATE AND LOCAL GOVERNMENT[2]	3.8	1.8	3.3	4.4	4.2	4.5
Private Industry[2]	3.5	1.8	3.2	4.2	3.7	3.8
Goods Producing[2]	4.2	3.0	4.8	4.9	3.7	3.3
Natural resources and mining[2,3]	4.0	*	4.2	4.7	3.3	3.0
Construction	3.9	3.3	4.6	4.2	2.6	1.2
Manufacturing	4.4	2.5	5.0	5.1	3.9	3.4
Service Providing	3.3	1.6	2.9	4.0	3.7	3.9
Trade, transportation, and utilities[4]	3.9	2.0	3.5	4.7	4.8	4.3
Information	1.6	*	1.6	2.3	1.3	1.2
Financial activities	1.4	1.4	1.4	1.7	1.2	0.7
Professional and business services	1.7	1.2	2.1	1.8	1.5	0.9
Education and health services	4.7	1.3	2.9	5.6	5.6	5.7
Leisure and hospitality	4.0	1.6	3.3	4.9	6.1	5.0
Other services, except public administration	2.6	1.8	2.6	4.0	2.9	2.0
State and Local Government[2]	5.7	*	4.7	5.5	6.4	5.8
State government[2]	4.6	*	*	3.9	6.6	4.1
Local government[2]	6.1	*	5.0	5.8	6.4	6.7

[1]The incidence rates represent the number of injuries and illnesses per 100 full-time workers and were calculated as: (N/EH) x 200,000 (where N = number of injuries and illnesses; EH = total hours worked by all employees during the calendar year; 200,000 = base for 100 equivalent full-time workers working 40 hours per week, 50 weeks per year).
[2]Excludes farms with fewer than 11 employees.
[3]Data for mining include establishments not goverened by the Mine and Safety and Health Administration rules and reporting such as those in oil and gas extraction and related support activities.
[4]Data for employers in railroad transportation are provided to the Bureau of Labor Statistics (BLS) by the Federal Reserve Administration, U.S. Department of Transportation.
* = Figure does not meet standards of reliability or quality.

Table 14-3. Number of Cases and Incidence Rate[1] of Nonfatal Occupational Injuries and Illnesses for Industries with 100,000 or More Cases, 2011

(Number, rate per 100 full-time workers.)

Industry sector	NAICS Code	2011 Annual average employment (thousands)	Total cases (thousands)	Incidence rate
ALL INDUSTRIES INCLUDING STATE AND LOCAL GOVERNMENT[2]		126 140.9	3 807.4	3.8
Elementary and secondary schools (local government)	6 111	7 126.5	249.3	5.0
General medical and surgical hospitals (private industry)	6 221	4 381.9	237.1	6.8
Food services and drinking places (private industry)	722	9 619.1	209.8	3.6
Specialty trade contractors (private industry)	238	3 490.6	123.5	4.1
Ambulatory health care services (private industry)	621	6 116.5	122.9	2.7
Administrative and support services (private industry)	6 231	1 662.5	104.7	8.2
Nursing care facilities (private industry)	561	7 303.0	104.3	2.5
General merchandise stores (private industry)	452	3 050.1	101.3	4.6

[1]The incidence rates represent the number of injuries and illnesses per 100 full-time workers and were calculated as: (N/EH) x 200,000 (where N = number of injuries and illnesses; EH = total hours worked by all employees during the calendar year; 200,000 = base for 100 equivalent full-time workers working 40 hours per week, 50 weeks per year).
[2]Excludes farms with fewer than 11 employees.

Table 14-4.   Incidence Rates[1] of Nonfatal Occupational Injuries and Illnesses, by Major Industry Sector, Category of Illness, and Ownership, 2011

(Rate per 100 full-time workers.)

Industry sector	Total cases	Skin diseases or disorders	Respiratory conditions	Poisonings	Hearing loss	All other illnesses
ALL INDUSTRIES INCLUDING STATE AND LOCAL GOVERNMENT[2]	20.6	3.3	1.8	0.3	2.1	13.2
Private Industry[2]	18.0	2.8	1.5	0.2	2.1	11.3
Goods Producing[2]	31.0	4.0	1.5	0.2	8.1	17.2
Natural resources and mining[2,3]	19.8	5.5	1.6	0.5	1.3	10.9
Construction	11.3	2.0	1.0	0.2	0.4	7.6
Manufacturing	40.8	4.6	1.7	0.1	12.3	22.1
Service Providing	14.6	2.5	1.5	0.2	0.5	9.8
Trade, transportation, and utilities[4]	12.7	1.8	0.9	0.3	1.3	8.4
Information	9.3	0.7	0.3	0.1	0.6	7.6
Financial activities	7.9	0.6	*	0.1	*	5.7
Professional and business services	8.4	1.8	0.9	0.2	0.3	5.1
Education and health services	28.0	4.6	2.8	0.2	0.1	20.3
Leisure and hospitality	14.5	4.2	1.5	0.5	0.1	8.2
Other services, except public administration	8.4	1.1	2.1	*	0.2	4.9
State and Local Government[2]	36.3	6.3	3.7	0.4	1.6	24.3
State government[2]	32.5	3.5	3.2	0.4	1.4	24.0
Local government[2]	37.7	7.3	3.8	0.4	1.7	24.4

[1]The incidence rates represent the number of injuries and illnesses per 100 full-time workers and were calculated as: (N/EH) x 200,000 (where N = number of injuries and illnesses; EH = total hours worked by all employees during the calendar year; 200,000 = base for 100 equivalent full-time workers working 40 hours per week, 50 weeks per year).
[2]Excludes farms with fewer than 11 employees.
[3]Data for mining include establishments not governed by the Mine and Safety and Health Administration rules and reporting such as those in oil and gas extraction and related support activities.
[4]Data for employers in railroad transportation are provided to the Bureau of Labor Statistics (BLS) by the Federal Reserve Administration, U.S. Department of Transportation.
* = Figure does not meet standards of reliability or quality.

Table 14-5.   Number of Cases of Nonfatal Occupational Injuries and Illnesses, by Major Industry Sector, Category of Illness, and Ownership, 2011

(Rate per 100 full-time workers.)

Industry sector	Total cases	Skin diseases or disorders	Respiratory conditions	Poisonings	Hearing loss	All other illnesses
ALL INDUSTRIES INCLUDING STATE AND LOCAL GOVERNMENT[1]	207.5	33.3	18.1	2.5	20.7	132.9
Private Industry[1]	155.4	24.3	12.8	1.9	18.4	98.0
Goods Producing[1]	55.9	7.2	2.7	0.4	14.7	31.0
Natural resources and mining[1,2]	3.3	0.9	0.3	0.1	0.2	1.8
Construction	5.5	1.0	0.5	0.1	0.2	3.7
Manufacturing	47.1	5.3	1.9	0.2	14.2	25.5
Service Providing	99.5	17.1	10.1	1.6	3.7	67.1
Trade, transportation, and utilities[3]	26.2	3.7	1.9	0.6	2.8	17.3
Information	2.2	0.2	0.1	([4])	0.1	1.8
Financial activities	5.3	0.4	*	0.1	*	3.8
Professional and business services	11.0	2.4	1.2	0.3	0.4	6.7
Education and health services	40.2	6.6	4.0	0.3	0.2	29.2
Leisure and hospitality	12.2	3.6	1.3	0.4	0.1	6.9
Other services, except public administration	2.4	0.3	0.6	*	0.1	1.4
State and Local Government[1]	52.1	9.0	5.3	0.6	2.4	34.9
State government[1]	12.9	1.4	1.3	0.2	0.6	9.5
Local government[1]	39.2	7.6	4.0	0.4	1.8	25.4

[1]Excludes farms with fewer than 11 employees.
[2]Data for mining include establishments not governed by the Mine and Safety and Health Administration rules and reporting such as those in oil and gas extraction and related support activities.
[3]Data for employers in railroad transportation are provided to the Bureau of Labor Statistics (BLS) by the Federal Reserve Administration, U.S. Department of Transportation.
[4]Data too small to be displayed.
* = Figure does not meet standards of reliability or quality.

Table 14-6. Number of Nonfatal Occupational Injuries and Illnesses Involving Days Away from Work,[1] by Selected Worker Characteristics and Private Industry, 2011

(Number.)

Characteristic	Total private[2,3,4]	Goods-producing			
		All goods-producing	Natural resources and mining[2,3]	Construction	Manufacturing
TOTAL CASES	908 310	223 920	23 280	71 600	129 030
Sex					
Men	559 740	191 790	20 290	69 650	101 840
Women	344 730	31 970	2 950	1 920	27 110
Age					
16 to 19 years	20 030	3 660	640	1 360	1 660
20 to 24 years	85 940	19 380	2 870	6 050	10 450
25 to 34 years	198 660	52 320	6 550	20 310	25 470
35 to 44 years	202 270	52 060	5 340	17 170	29 560
45 to 54 years	225 680	57 610	4 570	17 870	35 180
55 to 64 years	133 740	30 940	2 450	6 820	21 660
65 years and over	26 670	3 560	390	580	2 600
Length of Service with Employer					
Less than 3 months	88 540	28 520	4 830	10 530	13 160
3 to 11 months	163 570	42 020	4 640	14 570	22 810
1 to 5 years	315 900	68 040	7 490	24 530	36 020
More than 5 years	325 090	82 450	5 710	21 190	55 550
Race and Hispanic Origin					
White only	377 530	109 670	5 280	41 320	63 080
Black only	70 290	11 880	440	1 690	9 750
Hispanic only[5]	117 210	41 370	9 440	12 360	19 570
Asian only	12 070	2 580	100	320	2 160
Native Hawaiian or Pacific Islander only	2 880	470	20	170	280
American Indian or Alaskan Native only	4 350	790	40	230	510
Hispanic[5] and other race	500	70	*	*	50
Multiple races	660	130	*	20	110
Not reported	322 840	56 960	7 940	15 500	33 520

Characteristic	Service-providing							
	All service-providing	Trade, transportation, and utilities[4]	Information	Financial activities	Professional and business services	Education and health services	Leisure and hospitality	Other services
TOTAL CASES	684 390	277 490	14 030	27 360	71 240	182 270	85 330	26 680
Sex								
Men	367 950	194 120	10 520	16 100	46 510	37 260	43 950	19 480
Women	312 750	80 250	3 500	11 250	24 710	144 530	41 330	7 190
Age								
16 to 19 years	16 370	6 500	80	120	1 120	2 480	5 480	600
20 to 24 years	66 560	26 170	630	2 060	6 610	15 140	12 650	3 290
25 to 34 years	146 330	56 060	3 050	4 810	18 180	38 490	21 100	4 640
35 to 44 years	150 210	61 960	3 530	6 230	16 130	39 690	16 630	6 040
45 to 54 years	168 070	71 520	4 110	7 480	16 070	46 410	15 130	7 340
55 to 64 years	102 800	42 510	2 240	5 030	8 920	31 170	9 170	3 760
65 years and over	23 110	9 940	190	1 290	2 210	6 420	2 490	560
Length of Service with Employer								
Less than 3 months	60 020	24 510	370	1 210	8 290	11 270	11 310	3 070
3 to 11 months	121 550	45 850	1 330	5 620	14 430	31 050	18 500	4 770
1 to 5 years	247 860	94 100	4 160	9 870	28 460	70 470	31 520	9 270
More than 5 years	242 640	106 960	7 910	10 390	19 090	66 870	21 990	9 440
Race and Hispanic Origin								
White only	267 850	104 370	3 680	10 850	30 590	74 590	29 880	13 880
Black only	58 410	15 770	540	1 770	5 700	26 860	5 880	1 900
Hispanic only[5]	75 840	24 080	560	4 900	11 420	14 160	17 050	3 670
Asian only	9 490	2 350	70	430	740	3 260	2 110	530
Native Hawaiian or Pacific Islander only	2 410	680	20	110	250	620	390	340
American Indian or Alaskan Native only	3 560	1 520	20	70	260	940	580	170
Hispanic[5] and other race	430	150	*	*	60	130	80	*
Multiple races	530	200	*	*	20	180	100	*
Not reported	265 880	128 360	9 130	9 230	22 210	61 540	29 270	6 150

Note: Components may not sum to totals because of rounding.

[1] Days away from work cases include those that result in days away from work with or without restricted work activity.
[2] Excludes farms with fewer than 11 employees.
[3] Data for mining include establishments not governed by the Department of Labor's Mine Safety and Health Administration (MSHA) rules and reporting, such as those in oil and gas extraction and related support activities. Data for mining operators in coal, metal, and nonmetal mining are provided to the Bureau of Labor Statistics (BLS) by MSHA. Independent mining contractors are excluded from the coal, metal, and nonmetal mining industries. These data do not reflect the changes the Occupational Safety and Health Administration (OSHA) made to its record-keeping requirements effective January 1, 2002; thus, estimates for these industries are not comparable to estimates in other industries.
[4] Data for employers in rail transportation are provided to BLS by the Federal Railroad Administration, U.S. Department of Transportation.
[5] May be of any race.
* = Figure does not meet standards of reliability or quality.

Table 14-7. Number, Incidence Rate,[1] and Median Days Away from Work[2] for Nonfatal Occupational Injuries and Illnesses Involving Days Away from Work[3] for Gender and Age Groups in Private Industry, State Government, and Local Government, 2011

(Number, rate.)

Characteristic	Total private, state, and local governments			Private industry[4,5,6]			State government[4,5,6]			Local government[4,5,6]		
	Number	Incidence rate	Median days away from work	Number	Incidence rate	Median days away from work	Number	Incidence rate	Median days away from work	Number	Incidence rate	Median days away from work
TOTAL CASES	1 181 290	117.3	8	908 310	105.2	8	72 650	183.4	11	200 330	192.7	8
Gender												
Male	718 130	128.0	10	559 740	112.3	9	39 360	231.8	12	119 020	260.4	10
Female	458 250	103.7	7	344 730	95.3	7	33 150	147.0	10	80 370	139.1	7
Not reported	4 910	*	12	3 840	*	14	140	*	9	930	*	8
Age												
14–15	200	*	2	200	*	2	*	*	*	*	*	*
16–19	21 030	109.0	3	20 030	108.3	3	190	92.3	7	810	125.1	3
20–24	95 670	112.6	5	85 940	109.0	5	3 730	185.5	8	6 000	140.0	5
25–34	244 410	107.1	6	198 660	98.8	6	12 140	151.7	10	33 610	171.5	8
35–44	270 880	119.8	9	202 270	104.8	9	18 540	211.0	12	50 080	204.0	8
45–54	309 620	128.9	11	225 680	111.3	12	23 240	220.8	12	60 700	223.1	9
55–64	180 270	117.9	12	133 740	106.9	14	11 960	153.0	13	34 570	172.2	10
65 and over	35 210	99.9	14	26 670	88.7	14	1 390	94.7	18	7 140	189.7	11

[1]The incidence rates represent the number of injuries and illnesses per 100 full-time workers and were calculated as: (N/EH) x 200,000 (where N = number of injuries and illnesses; EH = total hours worked by all employees during the calendar year; 200,000 = base for 100 equivalent full-time workers working 40 hours per week, 50 weeks per year).

[2]Median days away from work is the measure used to summarize the varying lengths of absences from work among the cases with days away from work.

[3]Days away from work cases include those that result in days away from work with or without restricted work activity.

[4]Excludes farms with fewer than 11 employees.

[5]Data for mining include establishments not governed by the Mine Safety and Health Administration rules and reporting, such as those in Oil and Gas Extraction and related support activities.

[6]Data for employers in rail transportation are provided to BLS by the Federal Railroad Administration, U.S. Department of Transportation.

* = Figure does not meet standards of reliability or quality.

Table 14-8. Number, Percent Distribution, and Median Days Away from Work[1] for Nonfatal Occupational Injuries and Illnesses Involving Days Away from Work[2] for Race or Ethnic Origin and Length of Service in Private Industry, State Government, and Local Government, 2011

(Number, rate.)

Characteristic	Total private, state, and local governments			Private industry[3,4,5]			State government[3,4,5]			Local government[3,4,5]		
	Number	Percent	Median days away from work	Number	Percent	Median days away from work	Number	Percent	Median days away from work	Number	Percent	Median days away from work
TOTAL CASES	1 181 290	100.0	8	908 310	100.0	8	72 650	100.0	11	200 330	100.0	8
Race or Ethnic Origin												
White only	487 260	41.2	7	377 530	41.6	7	24 130	33.2	11	85 600	42.7	7
Black only	94 380	8.0	8	70 290	7.7	7	9 970	13.7	13	14 120	7.0	9
Hispanic or Latino only[6]	134 000	11.3	10	117 210	12.9	8	2 650	3.6	17	14 150	7.1	18
Asian only	14 020	1.2	7	12 070	1.3	7	460	0.6	14	1 490	0.7	8
Native Hawaiian or Pacific Islander only	3 480	0.3	12	2 880	0.3	11	230	0.3	28	370	0.2	14
American Indian or Alaskan Native only	5 230	0.4	5	4 350	0.5	5	200	0.3	5	680	0.3	4
Hispanic or Latino and other race[6]	590	. . .	16	500	0.1	14	*	*	*	90	. . .	22
Multi-race	760	0.1	8	660	0.1	7	*	*	*	90	. . .	11
Not reported	441 580	37.4	10	322 840	35.5	10	34 990	48.2	10	83 740	41.8	10
Length of Service with Employer												
Less than 3 months	93 460	7.9	6	88 540	9.7	6	1 510	2.1	7	3 410	1.7	5
3–11 months	178 370	15.1	7	163 570	18.0	6	5 120	7.0	9	9 680	4.8	7
1–5 years	388 320	32.9	7	315 900	34.8	7	21 020	28.9	10	51 400	25.7	7
More than 5 years	496 930	42.1	11	325 090	35.8	12	43 040	59.2	13	128 800	64.3	10

[1]Median days away from work is the measure used to summarize the varying lengths of absences from work among the cases with days away from work.
[2]Days away from work cases include those that result in days away from work with or without restricted work activity.
[3]Excludes farms with fewer than 11 employees.
[4]Data for mining include establishments not governed by the Mine Safety and Health Administration rules and reporting, such as those in Oil and Gas Extraction and related support activities.
[5]Data for employers in rail transportation are provided to BLS by the Federal Railroad Administration, U.S. Department of Transportation.
[6]May be of any race.
. . . = Not available.
* = Figure does not meet standards of reliability or quality.

Table 14-9. Fatal Occupational Injuries, by Selected Worker Characteristics and Selected Event or Exposure, Preliminary 2011

(Number, percent.)

Characteristic	Fatalities		Selected event or exposure[1] (percent of total for characteristic category)			
	Number	Percent	Homicides	Highway[2]	Falls	Struck by object
TOTAL	4 609	100	10	23	14	10
Employee Status						
Wage and salary workers[3]	3 594	78	9	26	15	10
Self-employed[4]	1 015	22	13	14	13	12
Sex						
Men	4 234	92	9	23	14	11
Women	375	8	21	27	14	4
Age[5]						
Under 16 years	10	([6])	10	. . .	. . .	. . .
16 to 17 years	14	([6])	14	. . .	7	. . .
18 to 19 years	58	1	14	16	5	12
20 to 24 years	288	6	9	28	8	9
25 to 34 years	704	15	13	19	10	10
35 to 44 years	858	19	12	25	12	8
45 to 54 years	1 207	26	10	23	16	11
55 to 64 years	911	20	8	26	17	11
65 years and over	558	12	6	21	22	12
Race and Hispanic Origin						
White	3 257	71	8	25	14	10
Black	433	9	21	29	8	9
Hispanic[7]	729	16	10	14	22	11
American Indian or Alaskan Native	29	1	. . .	. . .	14	14
Asian	113	2	35	24	8	4
Native Hawaiian or Pacific Islander	3	([6])	. . .	. . .	. . .	. . .
Multiple races	15	([6])	. . .	. . .	7	. . .
Other or not reported	30	1	13	40	. . .	. . .

Note: Totals for 2011 are preliminary. Totals for major categories may include subcategories not shown separately. Components may not sum to totals because of rounding.

[1]The figure shown is the percentage of the total fatalities for that demographic group.
[2]"Highway" includes deaths to vehicle occupants resulting from traffic incidents that occur on the public roadway, shoulder, or surrounding area. It excludes incidents occurring entirely off the roadway, such as in parking lots or on farms; incidents involving trains; and deaths of pedestrians or other non-passengers.
[3]May include volunteers and other workers receiving compensation.
[4]Includes self-employed workers, owners of unincorporated businesses and farms, paid and unpaid family workers, and members of partnerships; may also include owners of incorporated businesses.
[5]There were eight fatalities for which there was insufficient information to determine the age of the decedent.
[6]Less than or equal to 0.5 percent.
[7]May be of any race.
. . . = Not available.

Table 14-10. Fatal Occupational Injuries, by Occupation and Selected Event or Exposure, Preliminary 2011

(Number, percent.)

Occupation[1]	Fatalities		Selected event or exposure (percent of total for characteristic category)[2]			
	Number	Percent	Homicide	Highway[3]	Falls	Struck by object
TOTAL	4 609	100	10	23	14	10
Management	456	10	13	14	9	12
Top executives	34	1	21	18	18	. . .
Operations specialties managers	28	1	36	18	. . .	. . .
Other management	388	8	11	14	8	14
Business and financial operations	29	1	14	48	. . .	. . .
Computer and mathematical	5	(4)	. . .	. . .	. . .	. . .
Architecture and engineering	39	1	. . .	26	8	. . .
Engineers	26	1	. . .	31	. . .	. . .
Life, physical, and social science	22	(4)	. . .	18	23	. . .
Community and social services	22	(4)	27	41	. . .	. . .
Legal	13	(4)	. . .	. . .	. . .	. . .
Education, training, and library	34	1	. . .	12	24	. . .
Arts, design, entertainment, sports, and media	53	1	. . .	6	21	. . .
Entertainers and performers, sports and related workers	37	1	. . .	3	11	. . .
Health care practitioners and technical	54	1	17	20	7	. . .
Health diagnosing and treating practitioners ...	37	1	19	24	. . .	. . .
Health technologists and technicians	16	(4)	. . .	. . .	. . .	. . .
Health care support	20	(4)	15	25	. . .	. . .
Protective service	278	6	40	21	6	. . .
Fire fighting and prevention workers	31	1	. . .	16	13	. . .
Law enforcement workers	149	3	45	28	2	. . .
Other protective service workers	74	2	51	5	11	. . .
Food preparation and serving related	45	1	42	. . .	16	. . .
Supervisors, food preparation and serving workers	11	(4)	45	. . .	. . .	. . .
Building and grounds cleaning and maintenance ..	265	6	3	9	31	15
Building cleaning and pest control workers	52	1	10	12	40	. . .
Grounds maintenance workers	182	4	2	9	28	17
Personal care and service	72	2	28	6	12	. . .
Sales and related	228	5	45	14	7	4
Supervisors, sales workers	121	3	49	11	4	7
Retail sales workers	61	1	61	. . .	13	. . .
Sales representatives, services	9	(4)	11	. . .	. . .	. . .
Sales representatives, wholesale and manufacturing	14	(4)	. . .	50	. . .	. . .
Office and administrative support	92	2	15	33	18	3
Material recording, scheduling, dispatching, and distributing workers	54	1	15	43	11	. . .
Farming, fishing, and forestry	262	6	2	11	6	24
Agricultural workers	138	3	. . .	17	7	7
Fishing and hunting workers	40	1	2	. . .	. . .	. . .
Forest, conservation, and logging workers	67	1	. . .	. . .	. . .	75
Construction and extraction	770	17	1	12	32	12
Supervisors, construction and extraction workers	99	2	1	22	30	16
Construction trades workers	511	11	1	8	37	9
Extraction workers	92	2	1	20	14	24
Installation, maintenance, and repair	362	8	2	13	18	18
Vehicle and mobile equipment mechanics, installers, and repairers	115	2	2	13	3	38
Other installation, maintenance, and repair	203	4	2	13	26	7
Production	218	5	6	6	18	13
Supervisors, production workers	31	1	13	13	10	. . .
Metal workers and plastic workers	66	1	2	. . .	23	18
Transportation and material moving	1 213	26	5	50	5	9
Air transportation workers	72	2	. . .	. . .	. . .	. . .
Motor vehicle operators	851	18	6	67	3	7
Water transportation workers	14	(4)	. . .	. . .	. . .	. . .
Material moving workers	227	5	2	12	14	16
Military	54	1	9	19	6	. . .

Note: Totals for 2011 are preliminary. Totals for major categories may include subcategories not shown separately. Components may not sum to totals because of rounding. There were three fatalities for which there was insufficient information to determine a specific occupation classification.

[1]Based on the 2010 Standard Occupational Classification (SOC) system.
[2]The figure shown is the percentage of total fatalities for that occupation group.
[3]"Highway" includes deaths to vehicle occupants resulting from traffic incidents that occur on the public roadway, shoulder, or surrounding area. It excludes incidents occurring entirely off the roadway, such as in parking lots or on farms; incidents involving trains; and deaths of pedestrians or other non-passengers.
[4]Less than or equal to 0.5 percent.
. . . = Not available.

Chapter Fifteen

GREEN JOBS, TECHNOLOGIES, AND PRACTICES

GREEN JOBS, TECHNOLOGIES, AND PRACTICES

HIGHLIGHTS

This chapter includes data from the Green Technologies and Practices (GTP) survey and the Green Goods and Services (GGS) survey.

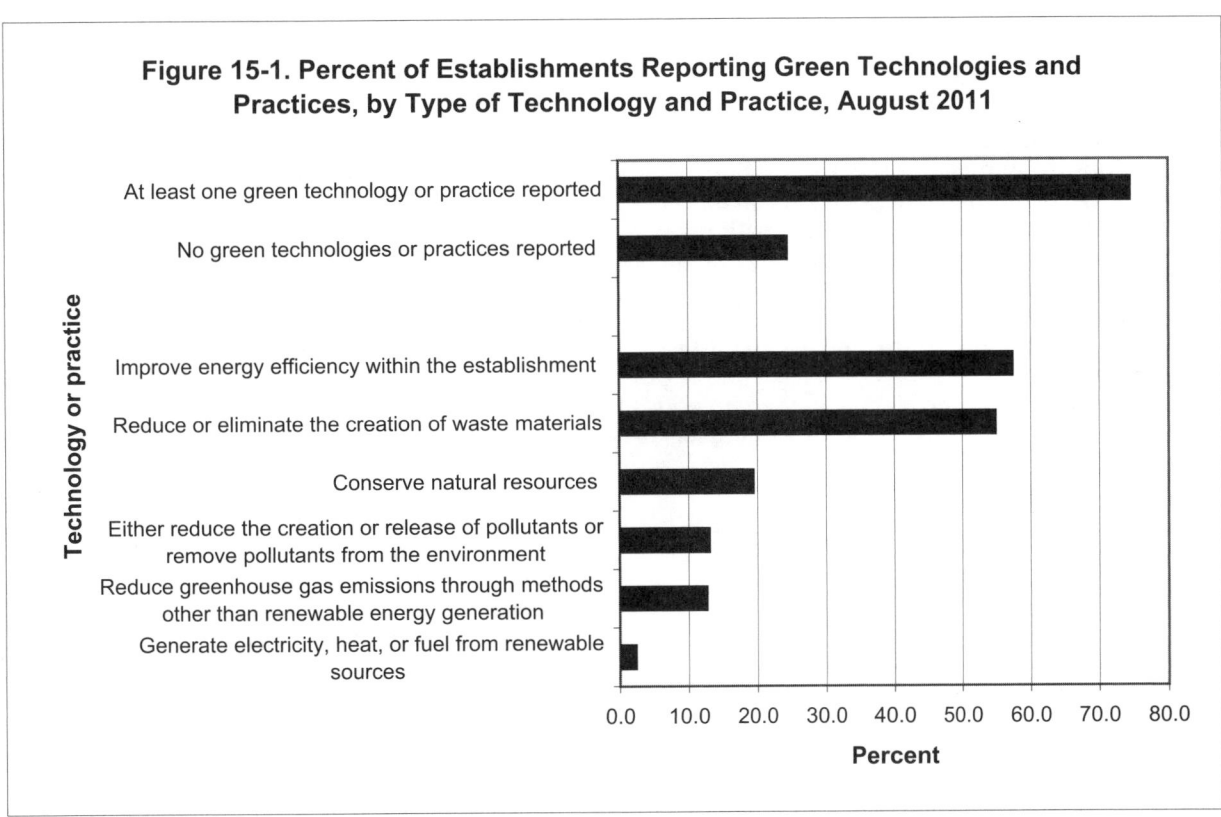

Figure 15-1. Percent of Establishments Reporting Green Technologies and Practices, by Type of Technology and Practice, August 2011

Nearly 75 percent of all establishments reported the use of at least one green technology or practice in August 2011. The most common practice involved improving energy efficiency within the establishment (57.4 percent), using technologies or practices to reduce or eliminate the creation of waste materials (54.9 percent), and conserving natural resources (19.4 percent). (See Table 15-1.)

OTHER HIGHLIGHTS

- In August 2011, 26.0 percent of establishments reported using two green technologies or practices while only 2.6 percent reported using five or more practices. (See Table 15-3.)

- Approximately 854,700 jobs were held by workers who spent more than half of their time in green technologies and practices. (See Table 15-4.)

- The South had the largest number of GTP jobs at 267,600 followed by the West (220,300), the Midwest (198,200) and the Northeast (168,500). (See Table 15-4.)

- Transportation and material moving accounted for 27.7 percent of total employment in establishments that received all of their revenue from green goods and services. Five of the six largest detailed occupations were in the transportation and moving occupations. (See Table 15-6.)

NOTES AND DEFINITIONS

GREEN JOBS

In 2010, the Bureau of Labor Statistics (BLS) first received funding to develop new data on green jobs. Green jobs are defined as jobs in businesses that produce goods or services that benefit the environment or conserve natural resources, or jobs in which workers' duties involve making their businesses production processes more environmentally friendly.

The BLS measures green jobs in two ways. The *process approach* identifies establishments that use environmentally friendly production processes and practices and counts the associated jobs. To implement the process approach, BLS created the Green Technologies and Practices (GTP) survey which collects data on jobs associated with the use of environmentally friendly production processes. The other approach currently being used by the BLS is the *output approach* which identifies establishments that produce green goods and services and counts the associated jobs. The Green Goods and Services (GGS) survey identifies whether the establishment is producing any green goods and services and, if so, to measure the number of associated jobs in the establishment.

GREEN TECHNOLOGIES AND PRACTICES

Collection and Coverage

The Green Technologies and Practices (GTP) survey is a survey of establishments designed to measure the use of technologies and practices that lessen the environmental impact of an establishment's production processes. The survey also collects occupational employment and wage data for wage and salary workers who spent more than half of their time involved in green technologies and practices during the survey reference period, the pay period including August 12, 2011. The GTP survey is based on a probability sample of about 35,000 business establishments.

Survey forms were mailed to sampled business establishments. Seventy percent of sampled establishments responded to the GTP survey. Respondents were asked whether or not they used each of the following six green technologies and practices listed earlier during the pay period that included August 12, 2011:

1. Generate electricity, heat, or fuel from renewable sources primarily for use within the establishment.

2. Use technologies or practices to improve energy efficiency within the establishment.

3. Use technologies or practices in operations to reduce greenhouse gas emissions through methods other than renewable energy generation and energy efficiency.

4. Use technologies or practices to either reduce the creation or release of pollutants or toxic compounds as a result of operations, or to remove pollutants or hazardous waste from the environment.

5. Use technologies or practices to reduce or eliminate the creation of waste materials as a result of operations.

6. Use technologies or practices in operations to conserve natural resources, excluding the use of recycled inputs in production processes.

They were also asked to provide the number of employees who spent more than half of their time involved in green technologies and practices during the reference period. For such workers, respondents were asked to provide job titles and brief job descriptions, as well as the number of workers, by occupation, in each of 12 specific wage intervals. Respondents were instructed to report part-time workers at their hourly rates. Full-time workers could be reported by either hourly rates or annual salaries, depending on how the worker was paid.

Concepts and Definitions

Establishments are typically a single physical location at which economic activity occurs (e.g., store, factory, restaurant, etc.). When a single physical location encompasses two or more distinct economic activities, it is treated as two or more separate establishments if separate payroll records are available and certain other criteria are met.

Green technologies and practices are defined as technologies and practices that lessen the environmental impact of an establishment's production processes. Employers were asked whether they had used each of the six green technologies and practices listed above during the reference period. Examples of the types of technologies and practices included in each of the six categories were provided.

GTP employment refers to the number of jobs in which workers spend more than half of their time involved in green technologies and practices.

Wages are money that is paid or received for work or services performed in a specified period. For the purposes of the GTP survey, wages are straight-time, gross pay, exclusive of premium pay. Base rate pay, cost-of-living allowances, guaranteed pay, hazardous duty pay, incentive pay such as commissions and production bonuses, and tips are included.

Sources of Additional Information

For more extensive definitions and description of collection methods see BLS news release USDL-12-1291, "Green Technologies and Practices—August 2011."

Table 15-1. Number and Percent of Establishments Reporting Green Technologies and Practices, by Type of Technology or Practice, by Census Region, August 2011

(Number, percent.)

Type of green technology or practice reported	United States		Northeast		Midwest		South		West	
	Number of establish-ments	Percent of establish-ments	Number of establish-ments	Percent of establish-ments	Number of establish-ments	Percent of establish-ments	Number of establish-ments	Percent of establish-ments	Number of establish-ments	Percent of establish-ments
Total, all establishments	6 624 600	100.0	1 309 100	100.0	1 419 400	100.0	2 369 600	100.0	1 526 500	100.0
No green technologies or practices reported	1 691 100	25.5	321 200	24.5	339 900	24.0	674 200	28.5	355 800	23.3
At least one green technology or practice reported	4 933 500	74.5	988 000	75.5	1 079 400	76.0	1 695 400	71.5	1 170 700	76.7
By Type of Technology or Practice										
Generate electricity, heat, or fuel from renewable sources primarily for use within the establishment	153 300	2.3	35 300	2.7	29 200	2.1	39 200	1.7	49 700	3.3
Use technologies or practices to improve energy efficiency within the establishment	3 799 400	57.4	775 400	59.2	858 700	60.5	1 271 100	53.6	894 200	58.6
Use technologies or practices in operations to reduce renewable energy generation and energy efficiency	835 000	12.6	173 900	13.3	163 400	11.5	267 600	11.3	230 100	15.1
Use practices to either reduce the creation or release of pollutants or toxic compounds as a result of operations, or to remove pollutants or hazardous waste from the environment	861 400	13.0	161 500	12.3	187 700	13.2	288 800	12.2	223 400	14.6
Use technologies or practices to reduce or eliminate the creation of waste materials as a result of operations	3 636 700	54.9	761 400	58.2	812 800	57.3	1 130 300	47.7	932 200	61.1
Use technologies or practices in operations to conserve natural resources (excluding use of recycled inputs in production process)	1 286 800	19.4	246 700	18.8	266 900	18.8	445 700	18.8	327 500	21.5

Table 15-2. Number and Percent of Establishments Reporting Green Technologies and Practices, by Industry, August 2011

(Number, percent.)

Industry	Number of establishments reporting at least one green technology or practice	Total number of establishments	Percent of establishments reporting at least one green technology or practice
Total, All Industries	4 933 500	6 624 600	74.5
Agriculture, forestry, fishing and hunting	64 600	81 900	78.9
Mining, quarrying, and oil and gas extraction	13 400	27 100	49.4
Utilities	16 900	23 800	71.1
Construction	403 200	570 200	70.7
Manufacturing	221 700	295 200	75.1
Wholesale trade	302 400	422 700	71.5
Retail trade	712 900	916 500	77.8
Transportation and warehousing	126 800	209 200	60.6
Information	94 600	112 800	83.9
Finance and insurance	294 700	389 300	75.7
Real estate and rental and leasing	206 700	281 500	73.4
Professional, scientific, and technical services	540 200	742 600	72.8
Management of companies and enterprises	29 500	41 500	71.1
Administrative and waste services	252 100	359 900	70.0
Educational services	114 300	142 100	80.5
Health care and social assistance	560 800	736 900	76.1
Arts, entertainment, and recreation	80 200	102 200	78.5
Accommodation and food services	439 900	564 100	78.0
Other services (except public administration)	360 200	480 400	75.0
Public administration	98 300	124 700	78.8

Table 15-3. Number and Percent of Establishments Reporting Green Technologies and Practices, by Number of Green Technologies or Practices Reported, August 2011

(Number, percent.)

Number of green technologies and practices reported	Number of establishments	Percent of establishments
Total, All Establishments	6 624 600	100.0
No green technologies or practices reported	1 691 100	25.5
At least one green technology or practice reported	4 933 500	74.5
By Number of Practices Reported		
One	1 646 700	24.9
Two	1 721 800	26.0
Three	976 100	14.7
Four	421 600	6.4
Five	136 400	2.1
Six	30 900	0.5

Table 15-4. Employment for Workers Spending More than Half of Their Time Involved in Green Technologies and Practices (GTP Employment), by Census Region, August 2011

(Number, percent.)

Region	GTP employment[1]	GTP employment in area as a percent of U.S. GTP employment	GTP employment as a percent of total area employment
United States[2]	854 700	100.0	0.7
Census Regions			
Northeast[3]	168 500	19.7	0.7
Midwest[4]	198 200	23.2	0.7
South[5]	267 600	31.3	0.6
West[6]	220 300	25.8	0.8

[1]Defined as employees who spend more than half of their time involved in green technologies and practices.
[2]Detail may not sum to total due to rounding.
[3]Includes Connecticut, Maine, Massachusetts, New Hampshire, New Jersey, New York, Pennsylvania, Rhode Island, and Vermont.
[4]Includes Indiana, Illinois, Iowa, Kansas, Michigan, Minnesota, Missouri, Nebraska, North Dakota, Ohio, South Dakota, and Wisconsin.
[5]Includes Alabama, Arkansas, Delaware, District of Columbia, Florida, Georgia, Kentucky, Louisiana, Maryland, Mississippi, North Carolina, Oklahoma, South Carolina, Tennessee, Texas, Virginia, and West Virginia.
[6]Includes Alaska, Arizona, California, Colorado, Hawaii, Idaho, Montana, Nevada, New Mexico, Oregon, Utah, Washington, and Wyoming.

Table 15-5. Employment for Workers Spending More than Half of Their Time Involved in Green Technologies and Practices (GTP Employment), by Industry, August 2011

(Number, percent.)

Industry	Industry GTP employment[1]	Industry GTP employment as a percent of total GTP employment	Industry GTP employment as a percent of total industry employment
Total GTP Employment, All Industries[2]	854 700	100.0	0.7
Agriculture, forestry, fishing and hunting	18 900	2.2	1.5
Mining, quarrying, and oil and gas extraction	3 100	0.4	0.4
Utilities	16 800	2.0	2.1
Construction	134 100	15.7	2.3
Manufacturing	57 600	6.7	0.5
Wholesale trade	22 900	2.7	0.4
Retail trade	39 700	4.6	0.3
Transportation and warehousing	35 100	4.1	0.7
Information	3 600	0.4	0.1
Finance and insurance	4 700	0.6	0.1
Real estate and rental and leasing	10 500	1.2	0.5
Professional, scientific, and technical services	99 800	11.7	1.3
Management of companies and enterprises	3 900	0.5	0.2
Administrative and waste services	151 900	17.8	2.0
Educational services	30 800	3.6	0.3
Health care and social assistance	63 900	7.5	0.4
Arts, entertainment, and recreation	12 900	1.5	0.5
Accommodation and food services	58 800	6.9	0.5
Other services (except public administration)	27 800	3.2	0.7
Public administration	57 800	6.8	0.8

[1]Defined as employees who spend more than half of their time involved in green technologies and practices.
[2]Detail may not sum to total due to rounding.

NOTES AND DEFINITIONS

OCCUPATIONAL EMPLOYMENT AND WAGES IN GREEN GOODS AND SERVICES

Collection and Coverage

The Occupational Employment and Wages in Green Goods and Services (GGS-OCC) program provides occupational employment and wage information for businesses that produce green goods or provide green services. Green goods and services fall into one or more of the following categories:

1. *Energy from renewable sources.* Electricity, heat, or fuel generated from renewable sources. These energy sources include wind, biomass, geothermal, solar, ocean, hydropower, and landfill gas and municipal solid waste.

2. *Energy efficiency.* Products and services that improve energy efficiency. Included in this group are energy efficient equipment, appliances, buildings, and vehicles, as well as products and services that improve the energy efficiency of buildings and the efficiency of energy storage and distribution, such as Smart Grid technologies.

3. *Pollution reduction and removal, greenhouse gas reduction, and recycling and reuse.* These are products and services that either reduce or eliminate the creation or release of pollutants or toxic compounds, reduce greenhouse gas emissions through methods other than renewable energy generation and energy efficiency, or reduce or eliminate the creation of waste materials.

4. *Natural resources conservation.* Products and services that conserve natural resources. Included in this group are products and services related to organic agriculture and sustainable forestry; land management; soil, water, or wildlife conservation; and storm water management.

5. *Environmental compliance, education and training, and public awareness.* These are products and services that enforce environmental regulations, provide education and training related to green technologies and practices, and increase public awareness of environmental issues.

The GGS-OCC estimates are based on data for 333 of the nearly 1,200 detailed (6-digit) 2007 NAICS industries. BLS identified these 333 industries as those in which businesses potentially produced green goods or provided green services as their primary activity.

Establishments in the GGS-OCC sample received two mail survey forms, one for the Green Goods and Services (GGS) survey and one for the Occupational Employment Statistics (OES) survey. Among GGS-OCC sample units, the overall national response rates for the GGS survey were 66.4 percent based on establishments and 59.9 percent based on weighted employment. Response rates for the OES survey were 66.7 percent based on establishments and 65.3 percent based on weighted employment. About 48.6 percent of sampled establishments, representing 42.6 percent of weighted sample employment, responded to both surveys.

Concepts and Definitions

Employees are all part-time and full-time workers who are paid a wage or salary. The estimates do not cover the self employed, owners and partners in unincorporated firms, household workers, or unpaid family workers.

Industries are a group of establishments that produce similar products or provide similar services. For example, all establishments that manufacture automobiles are in the same industry.

Occupations are a set of activities or tasks that employees are paid to perform. Workers are classified into occupations based on their job duties and, in some cases, on the skills, education, and/or training required. Workers with similar job duties are classified in the same occupation, regardless of the industry in which they are employed.

Sources of Additional Information

For more extensive definitions and description of collection methods see BLS news release USDL-12-1941, "Occupational Employment and Wages in Green Goods and Services—November 2011."

Table 15-6. Employment, Percent of Employment, and Annual Mean Wages for All-Green Establishments, by Occupational Group, November 2011

Occupation	Employment	Percent of employment in all green establishments	Annual mean wage[1]
All Occupations	1 949 520	100.0	48 210
Management	95 360	4.9	110 220
Business and financial operations	83 740	4.3	71 250
Computer and mathematical	25 540	1.3	77 270
Architecture and engineering	105 670	5.4	77 130
Life, physical, and social science	174 930	9.0	57 660
Community and social service	3 030	0.2	47 170
Legal	6 670	0.3	115 150
Education, training, and library	13 090	0.7	53 440
Arts, design, entertainment, sports, and media	22 200	1.1	50 750
Healthcare practitioners and technical	7 900	0.4	66 640
Healthcare support	70	([2])	35 260
Protective service	26 320	1.4	44 090
Food preparation and serving related	2 160	0.1	27 190
Building and grounds cleaning and maintenance	35 620	1.8	29 080
Personal care and service	18 780	1.0	24 320
Sales and related	84 560	4.3	38 020
Office and administrative support	194 440	10.0	37 260
Farming, fishing, and forestry	29 260	1.5	25 670
Construction and extraction	137 060	7.0	44 910
Installation, maintenance, and repair	135 470	6.9	49 140
Production	208 180	10.7	39 240
Transportation and material moving	539 470	27.7	35 390

Note: Data represent occupational employment and wages for establishments that received all of their revenue from green goods and services. Establishments that did not generate revenue, such as government establishments, nonprofits, or startups without positive revenue, reported all of their employment associated with the production of green goods or provision of green services.

[1]Annual wages have been calculated by multiplying the hourly mean wage by a "year-round, full-time" hours figure of 2,080 hours; for those occupations where an hourly mean wage is not published, the annual wage has been directly calculated from the reported survey data.
[2]Less than 0.05 percent.

Table 15-7. Employment in All-Green Establishments, by Occupational Group and Industry, November 2011

Occupation	Industry[1]							
	All in-scope industries[2]	Agriculture, forestry, fishing, and hunting	Utilities	Construction	Manufacturing	Wholesale trade	Retail trade	Transportation and warehousing
All Occupations[3]	1 949 520	41 840	142 030	92 130	266 510	80 640	66 570	454 710
Management	95 360	1 200	7 760	5 450	13 470	3 740	780	9 010
Business and financial operations	83 740	650	6 980	3 270	8 340	2 350	550	6 740
Computer and mathematical	25 540	120	2 150	380	3 810	...	...	1 190
Architecture and engineering	105 670	260	18 810	2 000	19 110	...	...	1 970
Life, physical, and social science	174 930	5 000	7 620	50	1 580	...	...	210
Community and social service	3 030	100	...	...	...	...	80	40
Legal	6 670	...	160	30	40	...	...	240
Education, training, and library	13 090	...	40	...	...	...	120	290
Arts, design, entertainment, sports, and media	22 200	100	610	...	...	...	...	230
Healthcare practitioners and technical	7 900	50	1 140	140	470	...	...	290
Healthcare support	70	...	...	...	...	...	...	...
Protective service	26 320	990	6 300	...	460	180	550	5 260
Food preparation and serving related	2 160	40	...	...	...	...	...	1 070
Building and grounds cleaning and maintenance	35 620	180	1 180	40	920	360	400	2 740
Personal care and service	18 780	...	...	...	...	...	...	12 250
Sales and related	84 560	450	440	2 770	7 440	5 550	47 040	4 840
Office and administrative support	194 440	2 340	17 530	8 650	23 500	11 060	10 350	28 310
Farming, fishing, and forestry	29 260	26 770	...	...	110	...	...	...
Construction and extraction	137 060	70	12 260	53 100	5 990	960	...	8 150
Installation, maintenance, and repair	135 470	800	20 930	10 650	23 190	4 140	...	38 260
Production	208 180	300	35 890	1 510	135 510	12 110	1 600	1 380
Transportation and material moving	539 470	2 360	2 120	3 830	21 340	39 360	4 820	332 250

Occupation	Industry[1]					
	Information	Professional and technical services	Management of companies and enterprises	Administrative and waste services	Other services, except public administration	Public administration
All Occupations[3]	25 460	138 360	7 870	274 700	36 190	276 020
Management	1 320	11 610	1 240	12 800	3 880	20 200
Business and financial operations	330	10 630	1 560	5 340	3 040	31 840
Computer and mathematical	930	7 930	...	1 260	420	6 140
Architecture and engineering	...	34 400	730	4 820	160	23 110
Life, physical, and social science	...	38 790	...	2 920	3 070	112 530
Community and social service	...	...	...	...	1 590	500
Legal	...	510	...	70	330	5 270
Education, training, and library	1 790	160	...	...	760	860
Arts, design, entertainment, sports, and media	8 970	3 670	...	210	2 350	3 560
Healthcare practitioners and technical	...	420	...	1 760	...	1 840
Healthcare support	...	...	...	...	...	...
Protective service	...	200	...	180	...	8 280
Food preparation and serving related	...	...	...	...	310	...
Building and grounds cleaning and maintenance	210	820	...	21 390	620	3 510
Personal care and service	...	...	...	40	870	...
Sales and related	3 120	3 010	70	6 480	1 230	830
Office and administrative support	4 750	15 980	2 270	32 670	5 350	25 320
Farming, fishing, and forestry	...	...	...	30	120	1 890
Construction and extraction	...	3 060	...	43 910	800	8 200
Installation, maintenance, and repair	250	1 800	810	15 340	9 480	6 910
Production	1 260	4 440	...	10 950	670	2 400
Transportation and material moving	2 460	930	4	114 540	980	12 140

Note: Data represent occupational employment and wages for establishments that received all of their revenue from green goods and services. Establishments that did not generate revenue, such as government establishments, nonprofits, or startups without positive revenue, reported all of their employment associated with the production of green goods or provision of green services.

[1] Includes only industries that are in scope for GGS within each sector. For more information, see the notes at the beginning of the chapter.
[2] Data represent occupational employment and wages for establishments that received all of their revenue from green goods and services. Establishments that did not generate revenue, such as government establishments, nonprofits, or startups without positive revenue, reported all of their employment associated with the production of green goods or provision of green services.
[3] Occupations listed will not sum to all-occupations totals because the totals include occupational groups for which data are not shown.
. . . = Not available.

Table 15-8. All-Green Utilities Establishments: Employment, Percent of Total Employment, and Annual Mean Wages for the Largest Occupations, November 2011

Occupation	Employment	Percent of employment	Annual mean wage[1]
All Occupations[2]	142 030	100.0	62 500
Water and wastewater treatment plant and system operators	20 200	14.2	44 560
Nuclear engineers	8 170	5.8	96 270
Security guards	5 270	3.7	43 580
Industrial machinery mechanics	5 100	3.6	61 830
Power plant operators	4 530	3.2	57 620
Nuclear power reactor operators	4 380	3.1	77 660
First-line supervisors of production and operating workers	4 020	2.8	69 930
Maintenance and repair workers, general	3 880	2.7	47 180
Nuclear technicians	3 630	2.6	75 370
Office clerks, general	3 520	2.5	37 640

Note: Data represent occupational employment and wages for establishments that received all of their revenue from green goods and services. Establishments that did not generate revenue, such as government establishments, nonprofits, or startups without positive revenue, reported all of their employment associated with the production of green goods or provision of green services.

[1]Annual wages have been calculated by multiplying the hourly mean wage by a "year-round, full-time" hours figure of 2,080 hours; for those occupations where an hourly mean wage is not published, the annual wage has been directly calculated from the reported survey data.
[2]Occupations listed will not sum to all-occupations total because the total includes occupations for which data are not shown.

Table 15-9. All-Green Construction Establishments: Employment, Percent of Total Employment, and Annual Mean Wages for the Largest Occupations, November 2011

Occupation	Employment	Percent of employment	Annual mean wage[1]
All Occupations[2]	92 130	100.0	47 850
Insulation workers, floor, ceiling, and wall	8 210	8.9	30 390
Carpenters	7 860	8.5	39 900
Construction laborers	7 680	8.3	38 020
First-line supervisors of construction trades and extraction workers	5 830	6.3	62 870
Electricians	5 390	5.9	54 230
Heating, air conditioning, and refrigeration mechanics and installers	5 190	5.6	43 010
Plumbers, pipefitters, and steamfitters	4 730	5.1	41 330
Secretaries and administrative assistants, except legal, medical, and executive	2 810	3.1	35 200
Construction managers	2 610	2.8	86 130
Operating engineers and other construction equipment operators	2 440	2.6	53 510

Note: Data represent occupational employment and wages for establishments that received all of their revenue from green goods and services. Establishments that did not generate revenue, such as government establishments, nonprofits, or startups without positive revenue, reported all of their employment associated with the production of green goods or provision of green services.

[1]Annual wages have been calculated by multiplying the hourly mean wage by a "year-round, full-time" hours figure of 2,080 hours; for those occupations where an hourly mean wage is not published, the annual wage has been directly calculated from the reported survey data.
[2]Occupations listed will not sum to all-occupations total because the total includes occupations for which data are not shown.

Table 15-10. All-Green Professional, Scientific, and Technical Services Establishments: Employment, Percent of Total Employment, and Annual Mean Wages for the Largest Occupations, November 2011

Occupation	Employment	Percent of employment	Annual mean wage[1]
All Occupations[2]	138 360	100.0	68 350
Environmental scientists and specialists, including health	12 130	8.8	67 700
Environmental engineers	7 990	5.8	82 060
Environmental science and protection technicians, including health	7 250	5.2	43 150
Architects, except landscape and naval	5 770	4.2	83 560
Chemists	4 710	3.4	55 660
General and operations managers	4 650	3.4	132 580
Geoscientists, except hydrologists and geographers	4 280	3.1	66 700
Secretaries and administrative assistants, except legal, medical, and executive ..	3 980	2.9	36 210
Mechanical engineers	3 970	2.9	88 750
Chemical technicians	3 310	2.4	38 600

Note: Data represent occupational employment and wages for establishments that received all of their revenue from green goods and services. Establishments that did not generate revenue, such as government establishments, nonprofits, or startups without positive revenue, reported all of their employment associated with the production of green goods or provision of green services.

[1]Annual wages have been calculated by multiplying the hourly mean wage by a "year-round, full-time" hours figure of 2,080 hours; for those occupations where an hourly mean wage is not published, the annual wage has been directly calculated from the reported survey data.
[2]Occupations listed will not sum to all-occupations total because the total includes occupations for which data are not shown.

INDEX